ry

ury

Editor in Chief: Dawn P. Dawson

Editorial Director: Christina J. Moose
Project Editor: Desirée Dreeuws
Manuscript Editors: Rowena Wildin Dehanke
Rebecca Kuzins
Acquisitions Editor: Mark Rehn
Editorial Assistant: Dana Garey

Research Supervisor: Jeffry Jensen
Research Assistant: Keli Trousdale
Photo Editor: Cynthia Breslin Beres
Production Editor: Andrea E. Miller
Graphics and Design: James Hutson
Layout: William Zimmerman

Cover photos (pictured left to right, top to bottom): Nelson Mandela (Ullstein Bild/The Granger Collection, New York); Frida Kahlo (Susana Gonzalez/Bloomberg News/Landov); Luciano Pavarotti (Ullstein Bild/The Granger Collection, New York); Benazir Bhutto (Stephen Hird/Reuters/Landov); Stephen Hawking (AP/Wide World Photos); Bill Gates (Ullstein Bild/The Granger Collection, New York); Dalai Lama (Maurizio Gambarini/DPA/Landov); Mikhail Gorbachev (Hulton Archive/Getty Images); Marilyn Monroe (Hulton Archive/Getty Images)

Some of the essays in this work originally appeared in the following Salem Press sets: *Dictionary of World Biography* (© 1998-1999, edited by Frank N. Magill) and *Great Lives from History* (© 1987-1995, edited by Frank N. Magill). New material has been added.

Library of Congress Cataloging-in-Publication Data

Great lives from history. The 20th century, 1901-2000 / editor, Robert F. Gorman.
p. cm.
Expanded rev. ed. of: Dictionary of world biography / Frank N. Magill, editor. 1998-c2000.
Includes bibliographical references and indexes.
ISBN 978-1-58765-345-2 (set : alk. paper) — ISBN 978-1-58765-346-9 (v. 1 : alk. paper) — ISBN 978-1-58765-347-6 (v. 2 : alk. paper) — ISBN 978-1-58765-348-3 (v. 3 : alk. paper) — ISBN 978-1-58765-349-0 (v. 4 : alk. paper) — ISBN 978-1-58765-350-6 (v. 5 : alk. paper) — ISBN 978-1-58765-351-3 (v. 6 : alk. paper) — ISBN 978-1-58765-352-0 (v. 7 : alk. paper) — ISBN 978-1-58765-353-7 (v. 8 : alk. paper) — ISBN 978-1-58765-354-4 (v. 9 : alk. paper) — ISBN 978-1-58765-355-1 (v. 10 : alk. paper)
1. Biography—20th century. I. Gorman, Robert F. II. Dictionary of world biography. III. Title: 20th century, 1901-2000. IV. Title: Twentieth century, 1901-2000.
CT120.G687 2008
920.02—dc22
2008017125

First Printing

CONTENTS

Publisher's Note

Great Lives from History: The Twentieth Century, 1901-2000 (10 vols.) is the eighth installment in the revised and expanded *Great Lives* series, which provides in-depth critical essays on important men and women in all areas of achievement, from around the world and throughout history. The series was initiated in 2004 with *The Ancient World, Prehistory-476 C.E.* (2 vols.) and followed in 2005 by *The Middle Ages, 477-1453* (2 vols.) and *The Renaissance & Early Modern Era, 1454-1600* (2 vols.); in 2006 by *The Seventeenth Century, 1601-1700* (2 vols.) and *The Eighteenth Century, 1701-1800* (2 vols.); and in 2007 by *The Nineteenth Century, 1801-1900* (4 vols.) and *Notorious Lives* (3 vols.). The entire series covers more than 4,400 lives in essays ranging from 3 to 5 pages in length.

Scope of Coverage

Great Lives from History: The Twentieth Century, 1901-2000 is broad in scope and features 1,334 essays covering 1,348 individuals. The editors have included in this set those persons recognized for shaping world history, coverage that is essential in any liberal arts curriculum. Major world leaders and other figures—philosophers, scientists, inventors, educators, theologians, novelists, critics, social reformers, business leaders—are covered here, but this set also has an extra concentration of new or updated material on women and ethnic and racial minorities. This set also includes coverage of personages who have identified as lesbian, gay, or bisexual.

This set covers a wide range of subjects and topics, many that are particular to the twentieth century. Areas of coverage include film, television, and radio; the nuclear age; the space race; computers and the World Wide Web; genetics; environmental and peace movements; team sports; decolonization; inventions and technological advances; science, health, medicine; astrophysics and nuclear physics; the League of Nations, United Nations, European Community, Arab nationalism, Organization of American States, African nationalism, OPEC; two World Wars and the Cold War; global terrorism; global capitalism; and consumerism.

By category, the contents include persons whose achievements fall into one or more of the following areas: agriculture (7), anthropology (13), archaeology (5), architecture (19), art (81), astronomy (26), aviation and space exploration (35), banking and finance (3), biochemistry (19), biology (35), botany (1), business and industry (59), cartography (2), chemistry (32), church government (10), church reform (6), civil rights (42), colonial administration (3), communications (15), computer science (7), conservation and environmentalism (9), crime (12), dance (28), diplomacy (124), economics (27), education (63), engineering (27), exploration and colonization (11), fashion (3), film (92), genetics (17), geography (6), geology (7), government and politics (387), historiography (17), horticulture (4), invention and technology (62), journalism (59), labor movement (14), landscape architecture (2), language and linguistics (7), law (45), literature (221), mathematics (29), medicine (49), metallurgy (1), meteorology (3), military affairs (69), monarchy (16), music (98), Native American affairs (1), natural history (5), naval service (2), oceanography (3), oratory (3), patronage of the arts (6), peace advocacy (31), philanthropy (29), philology (1), philosophy (71), photography (14), physics (84), physiology (19), political science (21), psychiatry and psychology (29), public administration (4), public health (11), publishing (7), radio (11), religion and theology (65), scholarship (40), science (29), sex research (3), social reform (134), social sciences (19), sociology (13), sports (48), television (30), theater and entertainment (105), urban development (4), warfare and conquest (45), women's rights (54), and zoology (4). The set also features coverage of 245 women from around the world.

The persons covered in these volumes are identified with one or more of the following countries or regions: Algeria (1), Argentina (5), Armenia (1), Australia (15), Austria (30), Azerbaijan (1), Belarus (11), Biafra (1), Bolivia (2), Brazil (5), Burma (2), Cambodia (3), Canada (37), Chad (1), Chile (24), Colombia (1), Congo, Democratic Republic of the (3), Costa Rica (1), Croatia (1), Cuba (3), Czech Republic (13), Czechoslovakia (7), Denmark (5), Dominican Republic (1), Dutch East Indies (2), Egypt (6), El Salvador (2), England (132), Estonia (2), Ethiopia (2), Finland (3), France (100), Georgia, Republic of (3), Germany (118), Ghana (3), Greece (6), Guatemala (1), Guinea (1), Haiti (2), Hungary (8), Iceland (1), India (17), Indonesia (3), Iran (4), Iraq (2), Ireland (14), Israel (9), Italy (34), Ivory Coast (1), Jamaica (1), Japan (18), Jordan (2), Kenya (3), Korea (North or South, 6), Latvia (5), Lebanon (1), Liberia (1), Libya (1), Lithuania (3), Macedonia (1), Malawi (1), Malaysia (1), Martinique (2), Mexico (12), Morocco (1), Mozambique (1), Netherlands (9), New Zealand (3), Nicaragua (1), Nigeria (5), Northern Ireland (1), Norway (9), Pakistan (4), Palestine (1), Panama (1), Peru (3), Philippines (2), Poland (21), Portugal (2), Prussia (11), Romania (8), Russia (66), Saudi Arabia (5), Scotland (8), Senegal (1), Serbia and Montenegro (2), Singapore (1), Slovakia (2), Slovenia (1), Somalia (1), South Africa (11), Soviet Union (38), Spain (16), Sri Lanka (1), Sweden (13), Switzerland (14), Syria (1), Taiwan (1), Tanzania (2), Thailand (1), Tibet (1), Trinidad and Tobago (2), Tunisia (1), Turkey (4), Uganda (4), Ukraine (11), United States (579), Vatican City (6), Vietnam (6), Wales (5), Yugoslavia (3), Zambia (1), and Zimbabwe (2).

EXPANDED COVERAGE

This series is a revision and major expansion of the 10-volume *Dictionary of World Biography* (*DWB*) series (1998-1999), which in turn was a revision and reordering of Salem's 30-volume *Great Lives from History* series (1987-1995). The expanded *Great Lives* differs in substantial ways from *DWB*:

- The coverage of each *Great Lives* set has been increased significantly. In the 10-volume *Twentieth Century, 1901-2000* set, 1,033 of 1,334 essays are from *DWB/20th Century* and *Great Lives: American Women*, 288 are new, and 166 have been heavily or completely updated. The bibliographies of the original 1,033 essays have been updated.

- Quotations from primary-source documents as well as informative lists, such as filmographies, have been added as sidebars to enhance and supplement the text throughout.

- A section of world maps has been added to the front matter of each volume to allow students to locate personages and place them in geographical context.

- All essays from the original *DWB* on twentieth century personages are reprinted in this new series with updated and annotated bibliographies; librarians may confidently weed their shelves of *DWB/20th Century*.

ESSAY LENGTH AND FORMAT

Each essay ranges from 1,500 to 3,000 words in length (roughly 3 to 5 pages) and displays standard ready-reference top matter offering easy access to biographical information:

- The essay title is the name of the individual; editors have chosen the name as it is most commonly found in Western English-language sources.

- The individual's nationality and occupation or historical role follow on the second line, including reign dates and terms of office for rulers and heads of state.

- A summary paragraph highlighting the individual's historical importance indicates why the person is studied today.

- The *Born* and *Died* lines list the most complete dates of birth and death available, followed by the most precise locations available, as well as an indication of when these are unknown, only probable, or only approximate; both contemporary and modern place-names (where different) are listed. A question mark (?) is appended to a date or place if the information is considered likely to be the precise date or place but remains in question. A "c." denotes circa and indicates that historians have only enough information to place the date of birth or death near the year listed. When a range of dates is provided for birth or death, historians are relatively certain that the birth or death year could not have occurred outside the date range.

- *Also known as* lists other versions of the individual's name, including full names, given names, alternative spellings, pseudonyms, and nicknames.

- *Area(s) of achievement* lists all categories of contribution, from Agriculture, Architecture, and Art through Social Reform, Theater and Entertainment, and Women's Rights.

The body of each essay, which also includes a byline for the contributing writer-scholar, is divided into the following three parts:

- *Early Life* provides facts about the individual's upbringing and the environment in which he or she was reared, as well as the pronunciation of his or her name, if unfamiliar to English speakers. Pronunciation guidelines are provided for those individuals whose names could be difficult to pronounce for English speakers. Where little is known about the person's early life, historical context is provided.

- *Life's Work*, the heart of the essay, consists of a straightforward, generally chronological, account of the period during which the individual's most significant achievements were accomplished.

- *Significance* is an overview of the individual's place in history.

The end matter of each essay includes the following resources:

- *Further Reading*—annotated bibliography, a starting point for further research.

- *See also*—lists cross-references to essays in the set covering related personages.

- *Related articles*—lists essays of interest in Salem's companion *Great Events from History* series: *The Twentieth Century, 1901-1940* (6 vols., 2007); *The Twentieth Century, 1941-1970* (6 vols., 2008); and *The Twentieth Century, 1971-2000* (6 vols., 2008).

SPECIAL FEATURES

Several features distinguish this series as a whole from other biographical reference works. The front matter includes the following aids:

- *Complete List of Contents:* This alphabetical list of contents appears in all ten volumes.

- *Key to Pronunciation:* A key to in-text pronunciation of unfamiliar names appears in all volumes. Pronunciation guidelines for difficult-to-pronounce names are provided in the first paragraph of the essay's "Early Life" section.

- *List of Maps and Sidebars:* An alphabetical list, permuted by keywords in the sidebars' or maps' titles, included in each volume.

- *Maps:* The front matter of each volume contains a section of maps displaying major regions of the world during the twentieth century.

The back matter to Volume 10 includes several appendixes and indexes:

- *Rulers and Heads of State*, a geographically arranged set of tables listing major world rulers and leaders, from ancient times through the twentieth century, including their regnal dates or terms of office. Surprisingly few biographical references offer vetted, editorially researched data on world leaders of this scope in one location.

- *Chronological List of Entries:* individuals covered, arranged by birth year.

- *Category Index:* entries by area of achievement, from Agriculture to Zoology.

- *Geographical Index:* entries by country or region.

- *Personages Index:* an index of all persons, including those discussed within the text.

- *Subject Index:* a comprehensive index including personages, concepts, books, artworks, terms, battles, civilizations, and other topics of discussion, with full cross-references from alternative spellings and to the category and geographical indexes.

USAGE NOTES

The worldwide scope of *Great Lives from History* resulted in the inclusion of names and words transliterated from languages that do not use the Roman alphabet. In some cases, there is more than one transliterated form in use. In many cases, transliterated words in this set follow the American Library Association and Library of Congress (ALA-LC) transliteration format for that language. However, if another form of a name or word has been judged to be more familiar to general readers, it is used instead. The variants for names of essay subjects are listed in ready-reference top matter and are cross-referenced in the subject and personages indexes. The Pinyin transliteration was used for Chinese topics, with Wade-Giles variants provided for major names and dynasties. In a few cases, a common name that is not Pinyin has been used. Sanskrit and other South Asian names generally follow the ALA-LC transliteration rules, although again, the more familiar form of a word is used when deemed appropriate for general readers.

Titles of books and other literature appear, upon first mention in the essay, with their full publication and translation data as known: an indication of the first date of publication or appearance, followed by the English title in translation and its first date of appearance in English.

Throughout the set, readers will find a limited number of abbreviations used in both top matter and text, including "r." (reigned), "b." (born), "d." (died), and "fl." (flourished).

CONTRIBUTORS

Salem Press would like to extend its appreciation to all involved in the development and production of this work. Special thanks go to Robert F. Gorman, Associate Professor at Texas State, who developed the contents list and coverage notes for contributing writers to ensure the set's relevance to high school and undergraduate curricula. The essays were written and signed by scholars of history, political science, regional studies, and literature, as well as by independent scholars. Without their expert contributions, a project of this nature would not be possible. A full list of their names and affiliations appears in the front matter of this volume.

CONTRIBUTORS

Douglas Carl Abrams
Bob Jones University

Michael Adams
*City University of New York,
Graduate Center*

Patrick Adcock
Henderson State University

Bland Addison, Jr.
*Worcester Polytechnic
Institute*

Stephen R. Addison
University of Central Arkansas

Linda Adkins
University of Northern Iowa

Richard Adler
*University of Michigan—
Dearborn*

John Aiken
*State University of New York,
Buffalo*

C. D. Alexander
University of Minnesota

John M. Allswang
*California State University,
Los Angeles*

Arthur L. Alt
College of Great Falls

Thomas L. Altherr
*Metropolitan State College of
Denver*

J. Stewart Alverson
*University of Tennessee,
Chattanooga*

Emily Alward
*Henderson, Nevada, District
Libraries*

Michael S. Ameigh
St. Bonaventure University

Eleanor B. Amico
University of Wisconsin—Oshkosh

Richard J. Amundson
Columbus College

Peggy J. Anderson
Wichita State University

Stanley Archer
Texas A&M University

Deborah Elwell Arfken
*University of Tennessee,
Chattanooga*

Andy Argyrakis
Tribune Media Services

Christopher Armitage
*University of North Carolina,
Chapel Hill*

James R. Arnold
*University of California,
San Diego*

Dorothy B. Aspinwall
University of Hawaii

William Aspray
Charles Babbage Institute

Mary Welek Atwell
Radford University

Bryan Aubrey
*Maharishi International
University*

Theodore P. Aufdemberge
Concordia College

Tom L. Auffenberg
Ouachita Baptist University

Mario Azevedo
University of North Carolina

Abdulla K. Badsha
University of Wisconsin—Madison

Ann Marie B. Bahr
South Dakota State University

Brian S. Baigrie
University of Calgary

William J. Baker
University of Maine

Ann Stewart Balakier
University of South Dakota

Betty Balanoff
Roosevelt University

Jane L. Ball
Wilberforce University

Rikard Bandebo
*University of London, Birkbeck
College*

Carl L. Bankston III
Tulane University

John W. Barker
University of Wisconsin—Madison

Dan Barnett
California State University, Chico

Xavier Baron
*University of Wisconsin—
Milwaukee*

David Barratt
Asheville, North Carolina

Thomas F. Barry
Himeji Dokkyo University

Maryanne Barsotti
Warren, Michigan

Melissa A. Barton
*University of Colorado,
Boulder*

Iraj Bashiri
University of Minnesota

Dorathea K. Beard
Northern Illinois University

Erving E. Beauregard
University of Dayton

Graydon Beeks
Pomona College

Peter K. Benbow
University of Oxford

Raymond D. Benge, Jr.
*Tarrant County College,
Northeast*

Alvin K. Benson
Utah Valley State College

Ronald M. Benson
Millersville University

Charles Merrell Berg
University of Kansas

S. Carol Berg
College of St. Benedict

Summer Chick Bergen
NASA Johnson Space Center

Gordon Bergquist
Creighton University

Milton Berman
University of Rochester

Robert L. Berner
*University of Wisconsin—
Oshkosh*

Massimo D. Bezoari
Coker College

Terry D. Bilhartz
Sam Houston State University

Roger E. Bilstein
*University of Houston—
Clear Lake*

Cynthia A. Bily
Adrian College

Donald S. Birn
*State University of New York,
Albany*

Margaret Boe Birns
New York University

Nicholas Birns
Eugene Lang College

Louis R. Bisceglia
San Jose State University

Brian L. Blakeley
Texas Tech University

George P. Blum
University of the Pacific

Steve D. Boilard
*California Legislative Analyst's
Office*

Scott Bouvier
*California State University,
Los Angeles*

David Warren Bowen
Livingston University

Newell D. Boyd
Houston Baptist University

John H. Boyle
California State University, Chico

Michael R. Bradley
Motlow State Community College

John Braeman
University of Nebraska

Harold Branam
University of Pennsylvania

Gerhard Brand
*California State University,
Los Angeles*

Rennie W. Brantz
Appalachian State University

Robert Briggs
Madison High School

Jeanie R. Brink
Arizona State University

John A. Britton
Francis Marion College

Wesley Britton
*Harrisburg Area Community
College*

J. R. Broadus
University of North Carolina

William S. Brockington, Jr.
*University of South Carolina—
Aiken*

Howard Bromberg
University of Michigan

Terrill Brooks
Baker College

Jerry H. Brookshire
Middle Tennessee State University

Alan Brown
Livingston University

Kendall W. Brown
Brigham Young University

Kenneth H. Brown
*Northwestern Oklahoma State
University*

Robert W. Brown
Pembroke State University

Dallas L. Browne
*York College, City University of
New York*

Mary Hanford Bruce
Monmouth College

Thomas W. Buchanan
Ancilla Domini College

David D. Buck
*University of Wisconsin—
Milwaukee*

Jeffrey L. Buller
Georgia Southern University

Michael A. Buratovich
Spring Arbor University

Michael H. Burchett
Limestone College

William H. Burnside
John Brown University

Donald Burrill
*California State University,
Los Angeles*

Stephen Burwood
*State University of New York,
Binghamton*

Joanne E. Butcher
University of Miami

Richard Butts
University of Toronto

Joseph P. Byrne
Belmont University

John A. Calabrese
Texas Woman's University

Charles Cameron
Los Angeles, California

Edmund J. Campion
University of Tennessee

Pamela Canal
Independent Scholar

Byron D. Cannon
University of Utah

Elof Axel Carlson
*State University of New York,
Stony Brook*

Russell N. Carney
Missouri State University

David A. Carpenter
Eastern Illinois University

John M. Carroll
Lamar University

Allison Carter
Rowan College of New Jersey

Diane S. Carter
Macomb Township, Michigan

P. John Carter
St. Cloud State University

Gilbert T. Cave
Lakeland Community College

Fran E. Chalfont
State University of West Georgia

Dennis Chamberland
Independent Scholar

Deborah Charlie
*California State University,
Northridge*

Frederick B. Chary
Indiana University Northwest

Dennis W. Cheek
*Ewing Marion Kauffman
Foundation*

Michael W. Cheek
American University

Victor W. Chen
Chabot College

Peng-Khuan Chong
Plymouth State College

Eric Christensen
Independent Scholar

Sandra Christenson
*California State University,
Northridge*

Julia A. Clancy-Smith
University of Virginia

Donald N. Clark
Trinity University

Ellen Clark
Independent Scholar

Michael J. Clark
*California State University,
Hayward*

Thomas Clarkin
University of Texas, San Antonio

Bonnidell Clouse
Indiana State University

Robert G. Clouse
Indiana State University

Paul M. Cohen
Lawrence University

Robert Cole
Utah State University

John J. Conlon
University of South Florida, St. Petersburg

Thomas H. Conner
Hillsdale College

Maureen Connolly
Duarte, California

Bernard A. Cook
Loyola University

James J. Cooke
University of Mississippi

Richard A. Cosgrove
University of Arizona

Albert B. Costa
Duquesne University

Frances A. Coulter
Oachita Baptist University

James A. Cowan
East Tennessee State University

Loren W. Crabtree
Colorado State University

David Crain
South Dakota State University

Frederic M. Crawford
Middle Tennessee State University

Lee B. Croft
Arizona State University

Lesley Hoyt Croft
Arizona State University

Carol I. Croxton
University of Southern Colorado

LouAnn Faris Culley
Kansas State University

Victoria Hennessey Cummins
Austin College

John C. K. Daly
Illinois State University

Carol Damian
Florida International University

Annette Daniel
Arkansas College

J. D. Daubs
University of Illinois, Urbana-Champaign

Anita Price Davis
Converse College

Donald E. Davis
Illinois State University

Nathaniel Davis
Harvey Mudd College

Robert R. Davis, Jr.
Ohio Northern University

Ronald W. Davis
Western Michigan University

Kwame Dawes
University of South Carolina, Sumter

Frank Day
Clemson University

Mary Jo Deegan
University of Nebraska, Lincoln

Rowena Wildin Dehanke
Altadena, California

Bill Delaney
San Diego, California

Margaret B. Denning
Sioux Falls College

Charles A. Desnoyers
La Salle University

James I. Deutsch
George Washington University

James E. Devlin
State University of New York, Oneonta

Joseph Dewey
University of Pittsburgh, Johnstown

Tom Dewey II
University of Mississippi, Oxford

Robert E. Dewhirst
Northwest Missouri State University

John E. DiMeglio
Mankato State University

Cecilia Donohue
Madonna University

David R. Dorondo
Western Carolina University

Paul E. Doutrich
York College of Pennsylvania

Charles A. Dranguet, Jr.
Southeastern Louisiana University

Desirée Dreeuws
Claremont Graduate University

Thomas Drucker
University of Wisconsin—
Whitewater

Frederick Dumin
Washington State University

David Allen Duncan
Tennessee Wesleyan College

Joyce Duncan
East Tennessee State University

Kathleen E. Dunlop
East Carolina University

John P. Dunn
Valdosta State University

William V. Dunning
Central Washington University

Bruce L. Edwards
Bowling Green State University

David G. Egler
Western Illinois University

Harry J. Eisenman
University of Missouri, Rolla

Robert P. Ellis
Worcester State College

Nancy L. Erickson
Erskine College

Thomas L. Erskine
Salisbury University

Paul F. Erwin
University of Cincinnati

Kevin Eyster
Madonna University

Julia S. Falk
Michigan State University

Stephen C. Feinstein
University of Wisconsin—River
Falls

Thomas R. Feller
Nashville, Tennessee

Donald M. Fiene
University of Tennessee, Knoxville

Paul Finkelman
State University of New York,
Binghamton

K. Thomas Finley
State University of New York,
Brockport

Richard B. Finnegan
Stonehill College

Edward Fiorelli
Saint John's University

David Marc Fischer
New York, New York

David G. Fisher
Lycoming College

Robert K. Flatley
Kutztown University

George J. Flynn
State University of New York,
Plattsburgh

Kirk Ford, Jr.
Mississippi College, Clinton

Robert J. Forman
Saint John's University

Lydia Forssander-Song
Trinity Western University

Douglas A. Foster
David Lipscomb College

Robert J. Frail
Centenary College

Donald R. Franceschetti
University of Memphis

Catherine Francis
Towson State University

Linda Fraser
Independent Scholar

Timothy C. Frazer
Western Illinois University

Thomas B. Frazier
Cumberland College

Richard G. Frederick
University of Pittsburgh

John C. Fredriksen
Salem State College

Leslie Friedman
Lively Foundation

Peter K. Frost
Williams College

C. George Fry
Saint Francis College

Daniel J. Fuller
Kent State University—
Tuscarawas

Jean C. Fulton
Landmark College

Cecilia M. Garcia
Washington, D.C.

Gilbert Geis
University of California, Irvine

Jeffery L. Geller
Pembroke State University

Dana Gerhardt
Valencia, California

Corinne Lathrop Gilb
Wayne State University

K. Fred Gillum
Colby College

Kristin L. Gleeson
Landsale, Pennsylvania

Sheldon Goldfarb
University of British Columbia

Robert M. Goldman
Virginia Union University

Marvin Goldwert
New York Institute of Technology

Douglas Gomery
University of Maryland

Margaret C. Gonzalez
Southeastern Louisiana University

Nancy M. Gordon
Amherst, Massachusetts

Robert F. Gorman
Texas State

Norbert J. Gossman
University of Detroit

Sidney Gottlieb
Sacred Heart University

Clinton A. Gould
University of Pennsylvania

Karen Gould
Austin, Texas

Lewis L. Gould
University of Texas, Austin

Daniel G. Graetzer
Seattle, Washington

Lloyd J. Graybar
Eastern Kentucky University

Reva Greenburg
Rhode Island College

Johnpeter Horst Grill
Mississippi State University

Marlene San Miguel Groner
*State University of New York,
Farmingdale*

Christopher E. Guthrie
Tarleton State University

Myra G. Gutin
Rider University

Michael Haas
College of the Canyons

William I. Hair
Georgia College

Irwin Halfond
McKendree College

Gavin R. G. Hambly
University of Texas, Dallas

Maureen A. Harp
Regis High School, New York

E. Lynn Harris
University of Illinois, Chicago

Robert Harrison
*University of Arkansas Community
College*

Fred R. van Hartesveldt
Fort Valley State College

John Harty
University of Florida

Paul B. Harvey, Jr.
Pennsylvania State University

Julia B. Boken Hasan
New York, New York

David Haugen
Western Illinois University

Margaret Hawthorne
South Hadley High School

Robert M. Hawthorne, Jr.
Unity College

Karen L. Hayslett-McCall
University of Texas, Dallas

Sidney Heitman
Colorado State University

Peter B. Heller
Manhattan College

Jonathan E. Helmreich
Allegheny College

Michael F. Hembree
Florida State University

Carlanna L. Hendrick
Francis Marion College

Michael Hennessy
Texas State University

Diane Andrews Henningfeld
Adrian College

Michael Hernon
University of Tennessee, Martin

Julius M. Herz
Temple University

Sally Hibbin
Parallax Pictures Ltd.

Fred W. Hicks
University of South Carolina

Richard L. Hillard
University of Arkansas, Pine Bluff

Michael Craig Hillman
University of Texas

Shawn Hirabayashi
New Haven, Connecticut

Samuel B. Hoff
Delaware State University

James R. Hofmann
*California State University,
    Fullerton*

Neil W. Hogan
East Stroudsburg University

Kimberley M. Holloway
King College

John R. Holmes
*Franciscan University of
    Steubenville*

Roberta M. Hooks
Potsdam College

Gregory D. Horn
*Southwest Virginia Community
    College*

Pierre L. Horn
Wright State University

William L. Howard
Chicago State University

Ron Huch
Dickinson State University

Tom A. Hull
Marshfield High School

Patrick Norman Hunt
Stanford University

E. D. Huntley
Appalachian State University

Mary Hurd
East Tennessee State University

Raymond Pierre Hylton
Virginia Union University

Earl G. Ingersoll
*State University of New York,
    Brockport*

Teresa Iodice-Dadin
Canadian College of Osteopathy

Robert Jacobs
Central Washington University

Jennifer Raye James
Tulsa, Oklahoma

Duncan R. Jamieson
Ashland University

Willoughby G. Jarrell
Kennesaw State College

Shakuntala Jayaswal
University of New Haven

Alphine W. Jefferson
College of Wooster

Reese V. Jenkins
Rutgers University

Robert L. Jenkins
Mississippi State University

Maude M. Jennings
Ball State University

Albert C. Jensen
*Central Florida Community
    College*

Jeffry Jensen
Pasadena, California

Charles T. Johnson
Valdosta State University

D. Barton Johnson
*University of California, Santa
    Barbara*

Edward Johnson
University of New Orleans

Judith R. Johnson
Wichita State University

Lloyd Johnson
Campbell University

Loretta Turner Johnson
Mankato State University

Sheila Golburgh Johnson
Santa Barbara, California

Yvonne Johnson
*St. Louis Community College,
    Meramec*

David M. Jones
University of Wisconsin—Oshkosh

Philip Dwight Jones
Bradley University

Morgane Jourdren
University of Angers

J. A. Jungerman
University of California, Davis

David Kasserman
Independent Scholar

Cynthia Lee Katona
Ohlone College

Robert B. Kebric
University of Louisville

Susan E. Keegan
Mendocino College

Jacquelyn Kegley
*California State University,
    Bakersfield*

Jeanette Keith
Vanderbilt University

Nannette Fabré Kelly
Imperial Valley College

Nancy D. Kersell
Northern Kentucky University

John C. Kilburn, Jr.
*Texas A&M International
    University*

Karen A. Kildahl
South Dakota State University

Leigh Husband Kimmel
Indianapolis, Indiana

Richard D. King
Ursinus College

Roy Henry Kirby III
*Virginia Polytechnic Institute and
    State University*

Wm. Laird Kleine-Ahlbrandt
Purdue University

Anne Klejment
University of St. Thomas

Paul M. Klenowski
Thiel College

James Kline
Santa Barbara, California

Christopher S. W. Koehler
Davis, California

Phillip E. Koerper
Jacksonville State University

Grove Koger
Boise State University

Christian Koontz
University of Detroit Mercy

Eve Kornfeld
San Diego State University

Lillian D. Kozloski
*Smithsonian, National Air &
    Space Museum*

Beth Kraig
Pacific Lutheran University

Arnold Krammer
Texas A&M University

Lynn C. Kronzek
University of Judaism

Paul E. Kuhl
Winston-Salem State University

Kathryn Kulpa
University of Rhode Island

Mildred C. Kuner
*Hunter College, City University
    of New York*

David Z. Kushner
University of Florida

Shlomo Lambroza
St. Mary's College of Maryland

Philip E. Lampe
University of the Incarnate Word

Pavlin Lange
Los Angeles, California

P. R. Lannert
Austin, Texas

Tom Lansford
University of Southern Mississippi

Karl G. Larew
Towson State University

Bruce L. Larson
Mankato State University

Eugene S. Larson
Los Angeles Pierce College

Jack M. Lauber
*University of Wisconsin—
    Eau Claire*

William T. Lawlor
*University of Wisconsin—
    Stevens Point*

Harry Lawton
*University of California,
    Santa Barbara*

Richard M. Leeson
Fort Hays State University

Ann M. Legreid
University of Central Missouri

Denyse Lemaire
Rowan University

Virginia W. Leonard
Western Illinois University

Van Michael Leslie
Union College

David Lester
Richard Stockton College

Gregory A. Levitt
University of New Orleans

Leon Lewis
Appalachian State University

Scott Lewis
Chicago, Illinois

Terrance L. Lewis
Clarion University

Thomas Tandy Lewis
St. Cloud State University

Kriste Lindenmeyer
*Tennessee Technological
University*

Ellen B. Lindsay
Las Cruces, New Mexico

Michael Linton
Northwestern College

Thomas Lisk
North Carolina State University

Monroe H. Little, Jr.
Indiana University

James Livingston
Northern Michigan University

Janet Alice Long
Acton, California

John W. Long
Rider College

Roger D. Long
Eastern Michigan University

Rita E. Loos
Framingham State College

Raymond M. Lorantas
Drexel University

Janet Lorenz
Los Angeles, California

Donald W. Lovejoy
Palm Beach Atlantic University

Adele Lubell
Bronx, New York

Al Ludwick
Augusta Chronicle-Herald

David C. Lukowitz
Hamline University

R. C. Lutz
Madison Advisors

Garrett L. McAinsh
Hendrix College

Joanne McCarthy
Tacoma, Washington

Sandra C. McClain
James Madison University

Arthur F. McClure
Central Missouri State University

Robert McColley
University of Illinois

C. Thomas McCollough
Centre College

C. S. McConnell
University of Calgary

Jean McConnell
*Eastern New Mexico State
University*

Mark R. McCulloh
Davidson College

Irene E. McDermott
Pasadena, California

Roxanne McDonald
New London, New Hampshire

Mary McElroy
Kansas State University

Margaret McFadden
Appalachian State University

Susan MacFarland
Gainesville State College

George McJimsey
Iowa State University

Timothy J. McMillan
Humboldt State University

Patricia McNeal
Indiana University

David W. Madden
*California State University,
Sacramento*

Paul Madden
Hardin-Simmons University

Paul D. Mageli
Kenmore, New York

Sally Ward Maggard
West Virginia University

Yale R. Magrass
*University of Massachusetts—
Dartmouth*

Bill Manikas
Gaston College

Barry Stewart Mann
Alliance Theatre

Carl Henry Marcoux
University of California, Riverside

Henry S. Marks
Independent Scholar

Annette Marks-Ellis
Antelope Valley College

Lyndon Marshall
College of Great Falls

Elaine Mathiasen
Gaston, Oregon

Katherine Kearney Maynard
Rider College

Norbert Mazari
Sonoma State University

Laurence W. Mazzeno
Alvernia College

Patrick Meanor
State University of New York,
Oneonta

Jonathan Mendilow
Rider University

Bernard Mergen
George Washington University

Michael W. Messmer
Virginia Commonwealth
University

Eric Metchik
Salem State College

Nancy Meyer
Academy of Television Arts &
Sciences

Julia M. Meyers
Duquesne University

Michael R. Meyers
Pfeiffer University

L. Craig Michel
Independent Scholar

Ken Millen-Penn
Fairmont State University

Edmund Miller
Long Island University, C. W. Post
Campus

Gordon L. Miller
Mercer Island, Washington

Jane Ann Miller
Dartmouth College

Timothy C. Miller
Millersville University

Dennis J. Mitchell
Jackson State University

Christian H. Moe
Southern Illinois University,
Carbondale

Eric Wm. Mogren
Ann Arbor, Michigan

Peter Monaghan
Seattle, Washington

David W. Moore
Loyola University

Ronald O. Moore
University of Tennessee,
Chattanooga

William Howard Moore
University of Wyoming

William V. Moore
College of Charleston

Gordon R. Mork
Purdue University

Robert E. Morsberger
California State Polytechnic
University, Pomona

Jay Mullin
Queensborough Community
College, City University of
New York

Raymond Lee Muncy
Harding University

Donna Mungen
Los Angeles Times

Daniel P. Murphy
Hanover College

David Murphy
Kentucky State University

Alice Myers
Bard College at Simon's Rock

Wayne Narey
Arkansas State University

Pellegrino Nazzaro
Rochester Institute of Technology

Jerome L. Neapolitan
Tennessee Technological
University

Nancy J. Nersessian
Princeton University

Brian J. Nichelson
United States Air Force Academy

Michael R. Nichols
Texas Christian University

Augustine Nigro
Atlantic Cape Community
College

Richard L. Niswonger
John Brown University

John Nizalowski
Mesa State College

Norma C. Noonan
Augsburg College

James G. Nutsch
North Carolina A&T State
University

Nkeonye Nwankwo
California State University,
Long Beach

Elvy Setterqvist O'Brien
Williamstown, Massachusetts

James H. O'Donnell, III
Marietta College

Keith W. Olson
University of Maryland, College Park

Kathleen O'Mara
State University of New York, Oneonta

Arsenio Orteza
St. Thomas More High School

Paul Michael O'Shea
University of Oregon

Gary B. Ostrower
Alfred University

James Owen
Purdue University

Lisa Paddock
Cape May Court House, New Jersey

William A. Paquette
Tidewater Community College

Robert J. Paradowski
Rochester Institute of Technology

Joyce M. Parks
Satellite Beach, Florida

Judith A. Parsons
Sul Ross State University

Robert L. Patterson
Armstrong State College

James Pauff
Tarleton State University

Thomas R. Peake
King College

David Peck
Laguna Beach, California

Karen Resnick Pellón
Independent Scholar

William E. Pemberton
University of Wisconsin—La Crosse

Betsey Pender
University of North Florida

Matthew Penney
Concordia University

James Persoon
Grand Valley State University

Nis Petersen
New Jersey City University

Robert C. Petersen
Middle Tennessee State University

Barbara Bennett Peterson
California State University, San Bernardino

John R. Phillips
Purdue University Calumet

Lela Phillips
Andrew College

Michael Phillips
University of Texas, Austin

Rebecca Phillips
West Virginia University, Parkersburg

Allene Phy-Olsen
Austin Peay State University

Donald K. Pickens
North Texas State University

H. Alan Pickrell
Emory & Henry College

Richard V. Pierard
Gordon College

Adrienne Pilon
North Carolina School of the Arts

Louis Pinkett
Minsk State Linguistics University

Julio César Pino
Kent State University

J. P. Piskulich
Oakland University

A. J. Plotke
Cornell University

Marilyn Plotkins
Suffolk University

Marguerite R. Plummer
Louisiana State University, Shreveport

Marjorie J. Podolsky
Penn State Erie—Behrend College

Ronald L. Pollitt
University of Cincinnati

Clifton W. Potter, Jr.
Lynchburg College

Dorothy Potter
Lynchburg College

Annette Potts
Monash University

Janet M. Powers
Gettysburg College

Luke A. Powers
Tennessee State University

Richard Gid Powers
College of Staten Island, City University of New York

Norma Fain Pratt
University of California, Los Angeles

Verbie Lovorn Prevost
*University of Tennessee,
Chattanooga*

Charles Pullen
Queens University

Diane Quinn
Seattle, Washington

Edna Quinn
Salisbury State University

Sanford Radner
Montclair State College

Steven J. Ramold
Eastern Michigan University

Colin Ramsey
*University of Arkansas,
Little Rock*

Thomas Rankin
Concord, California

R. Kent Rasmussen
Thousand Oaks, California

Eugene L. Rasor
Emory & Henry College

John David Rausch, Jr.
West Texas A&M University

James A. Rawley
University of Nebraska, Lincoln

John D. Raymer
Holy Cross College

Dennis Reinhartz
University of Texas, Arlington

Rosemary M. Canfield Reisman
Charleston Southern University

Peter P. Remaley
Eastern Kentucky University

Walter F. Renn
Middle Tennessee State University

Clark G. Reynolds
College of Charleston

Leo P. Ribuffo
George Washington University

Richard E. Rice
James Madison University

Betty Richardson
*Southern Illinois University,
Edwardsville*

Edward A. Riedinger
Ohio State University

Edward J. Rielly
Saint Joseph's College of Maine

John Neil Ries
Cincinnati, Ohio

John S. Rigden
University of Missouri, St. Louis

Joseph F. Rishel
Duquesne University

S. Fred Roach
Kennesaw College

Craig H. Roell
University of Texas, Austin

Charles W. Rogers
*Southwestern Oklahoma State
University*

Mary Rohrberger
Oklahoma State University

Fred S. Rolater
Middle Tennessee State University

Carl Rollyson
*Baruch College, City University
of New York*

Hari S. Rorlich
University of Southern California

Paul Rosefeldt
Delgado Community College

Joseph Rosenblum
*University of North Carolina,
Greensboro*

Helaine Ross
*Northwestern State University of
Louisiana*

John Alan Ross
Eastern Washington University

Robert Ross
Southern Methodist University

Joseph R. Rudolph, Jr.
Towson University

Victor Anthony Rudowski
Clemson University

Nancy Ellen Rupprecht
*Middle Tennessee State
University*

Irene Struthers Rush
Boise, Idaho

J. Edmund Rush
Boise, Idaho

Constance B. Rynder
University of Tampa

Concepcion Saenz-Cambra
*University of London, Birkbeck
College*

Allen Safianow
Indiana University, Kokomo

Dorothy C. Salem
Cuyahoga Community College

Virginia L. Salmon
*Northeast State Community
College*

John Santore
Pratt Institute

Stephen Satris
Clemson University

Richard Sax
Lake Erie College

Stephen P. Sayles
University of La Verne

Daniel C. Scavone
University of Southern Indiana

Jean Owens Schaefer
University of Wyoming

Elizabeth D. Schafer
Loachapoka, Alabama

John Scheckter
Long Island University

Nancy Schiller
*State University of New York,
Buffalo*

Helmut J. Schmeller
Fort Hays State University

J. Christopher Schnell
*Southeast Missouri State
University*

Maxwell P. Schoenfeld
*University of Wisconsin—
Eau Claire*

John Richard Schrock
Emporia State University

Thomas C. Schunk
Quincy College, Illinois

Rose Secrest
Independent Scholar

Elizabeth A. Segal
Ohio State University

Robert W. Seidel
Los Alamos National Laboratory

Robert W. Sellen
Georgia State University

Brion Sever
Monmouth University

Heather L. Shaffer
Temple University

Francis Michael Sharp
University of the Pacific

Melvin Shefftz
*State University of New York,
Binghamton*

John C. Sherwood
University of Oregon

Martha A. Sherwood
Kent Anderson Law Associates

T. A. Shippey
St. Louis University

William I. Shorrock
Cleveland State University

R. Baird Shuman
*University of Illinois, Urbana-
Champaign*

Anne W. Sienkewicz
Monmouth, Illinois

Narasingha P. Sil
Western Oregon University

Charles L. P. Silet
Iowa State University

Donald C. Simmons, Jr.
South Dakota Humanities Council

L. Moody Simms, Jr.
Illinois State University

Jules Simon
University of Texas, El Paso

Sanford S. Singer
University of Dayton

Carl Singleton
Fort Hays State University

Kyle S. Sinisi
Kansas State University

Shumet Sishagne
Christopher Newport University

Paul A. Siskind
University of Minnesota

Amy Sisson
*University of Houston—
Clear Lake*

Andrew C. Skinner
Brigham Young University

Douglas D. Skinner
*Texas State University,
San Marcos*

Jane A. Slezak
*Fulton Montgomery Community
College*

Genevieve Slomski
New Britain, Connecticut

Caroline M. Small
Burtonsville, Maryland

Robert W. Small
Massasoit Community College

Marjorie Smelstor
Ball State University

Christopher E. Smith
Michigan State University

Clyde Curry Smith
*University of Wisconsin—
River Falls*

Harold L. Smith
University of Houston—Victoria

Stefan Halikowski Smith
University of Wales, Swansea

James Smythe
Pepperdine University

Mortimer Snell
Independent Scholar

Christy J. Snider
Berry College

A. J. Sobczak
Santa Barbara, California

Katherine Socha
St. Mary's College of Maryland

Norbert C. Soldon
West Chester University

Katherine R. Sopka
Four Corners Analytic Sciences

George Soule
Carleton College

Sherry G. Southard
Oklahoma State University

Zia Southard
Independent Scholar

James E. Southerland
Brenau University

Kenneth S. Spector
University of Massachusetts

Joseph L. Spradley
Wheaton College

C. Fitzhugh Spragins
Arkansas College

Brian Stableford
Reading, United Kingdom

August W. Staub
University of Georgia

S. J. Stearns
*College of Staten Island, City
University of New York*

Paul D. Steeves
Stetson University

David Stefancic
Saint Mary's College

Stanley R. Stembridge
Northeastern University

David L. Sterling
University of Cincinnati

Glenn Ellen Starr Stilling
Appalachian State University

Jean Thorleifsson Strandness
North Dakota State University

Anthony N. Stranges
Texas A & M University

Marlene Bradford Stranges
Independent Scholar

Leslie Stricker
Park University

Fred Strickert
Wartburg College

Paul Stuewe
Green Mountain College

Roger H. Stuewer
University of Minnesota

Taylor Stults
Muskingum College

David C. Stuntz
*Pennsylvania State University—
Behrend College*

Susan A. Stussy
Kansas City, Kansas

Darlene Mary Suarez
San Diego State University

Joyce Suellentrop
Kansas Newman College

Donald Sullivan
University of New Mexico

James Sullivan
*California State University,
Los Angeles*

J. K. Sweeney
South Dakota State University

Patricia E. Sweeney
Derby Neck Library

Glenn L. Swygart
Tennessee Temple University

James Tackach
Roger Williams University

Robert D. Talbott
University of Northern Iowa

Teresa Neva Tate
National Geographic Society

Alice F. Taylor
Shorter College

Thomas J. Taylor
University of Akron

Emily Teipe
Fullerton College

Terry Theodore
University of North Carolina,
Wilmington

J. A. Thompson
University of Kentucky

Thomas C. Thompson
University of California, Riverside

Thomas John Thomson
Limestone College

H. Christian Thorup
Cuesta College

Anthony Tinsley
Appalachian State University

Brian G. Tobin
Lassen College

Rebecca Tolley-Stokes
East Tennessee State University

James H. Toner
Norwich University

Kenneth W. Townsend
Coastal Carolina University

David Travis
New York University in Florence

Paul B. Trescott
Southern Illinois University

David Trevino
Donna Klein Jewish Academy

Judith Ann Trolander
University of Minnesota, Duluth

Lois M. Trostle
California State University,
Fresno

Spencer C. Tucker
Texas Christian University

Catherine Udall Turley
Arizona State University

David Underdown
Yale University

Jiu-Hwa Lo Upshur
Eastern Michigan University

Jeffrey A. VanDenBerg
Drury University

George W. Van Devender
Hardin-Simmons University

Abraham Verghese
East Tennessee State University

Sara Vidar
Los Angeles, California

Charles L. Vigue
University of New Haven

K. Steven Vincent
North Carolina State University

Mary E. Virginia
Venice, Florida

Paul R. Waibel
Liberty University

William T. Walker
Chestnut Hill College

Zuoyue Wang
University of California,
Santa Barbara

Carol M. Ward
Clemson University

Mary C. Ware
State University of New York,
Cortland

Duncan Waterson
Macquarie University

William E. Watson
Immaculata University

Donald A. Watt
Dakota Wesleyan University

Linda S. Watts
Drake University

Jane Carter Webb
Christopher Newport University

Shawncey Webb
Taylor University

Marcia J. Weiss
Point Park College

William M. Welch, Jr.
Troy State University

James Michael Welsh
Salisbury State University

Michael J. Welsh
Illinois State University

Craig Werner
University of Wisconsin—Madison

Derrick Harper West
Davis, California

Winifred Whelan
St. Bonaventure University

Orren P. Whiddon
Independent Scholar

Robert E. Whipple
Fullerton College

Richard Whitworth
Ball State University

Sherrill Whyte
University of California, Berkeley

Kenneth Wilburn
East Carolina University

John D. Wild
Independent Scholar

Thomas Willard
University of Arizona

Abiodun Williams
Georgetown University

Cynthia J. Williams
*Hobart and William Smith
Colleges*

Donna Glee Williams
*North Carolina Advance Center of
Teaching*

Lance Williams
University of Missouri—Rolla

Michael W. Williams
*University of North Carolina,
Charlotte*

Sue Williams
Yavapai College

Judith Barton Williamson
Sauk Valley Community College

William Van Willis
*California State University,
Fullerton*

Harold A. Wilson
University of Florida

Raymond Wilson
Fort Hays State University

Richard L. Wilson
*University of Tennessee,
Chattanooga*

Sharon K. Wilson
Fort Hays State University

John D. Windhausen
Saint Anselm College

Mary A. Wischusen
Wayne State University

Michael Witkoski
University of South Carolina

Susan Wladaver-Morgan
Portland, Oregon

Thomas P. Wolf
Indiana University Southeast

Sheri P. Woodburn
Cupertino, California

Scott Wright
University of St. Thomas

Lisa A. Wroble
*Collier County Schools and
Edison College*

Susan J. Wurtzburg
University of Utah

Malcolm M. Wynn
Stetson University

Lamont H. Yeakey
*California State University,
Los Angeles*

Clifton K. Yearley
*State University of New York,
Buffalo*

Won Z. Yoon
Siena College

Ivan L. Zabilka
*Lexington Kentucky Public
Schools*

James Edward Zacchini
Marquette University

Kristen L. Zacharias
Albright College

Robert Zaller
Drexel University

Philip R. Zampini
Westfield State College

Robert F. Zeidel
University of Nebraska, Lincoln

KEY TO PRONUNCIATION

Many of the names of personages covered in *Great Lives from History: The 20th Century, 1901-2000* may be unfamiliar to students and general readers. For these unfamiliar names, guides to pronunciation have been provided upon first mention of the names in the text. These guidelines do not purport to achieve the subtleties of the languages in question but will offer readers a rough equivalent of how English speakers may approximate the proper pronunciation.

Vowel Sounds

Symbol	Spelled (Pronounced)
a	answer (AN-suhr), laugh (laf), sample (SAM-puhl), that (that)
ah	father (FAH-thur), hospital (HAHS-pih-tuhl)
aw	awful (AW-fuhl), caught (kawt)
ay	blaze (blayz), fade (fayd), waiter (WAYT-ur), weigh (way)
eh	bed (behd), head (hehd), said (sehd)
ee	believe (bee-LEEV), cedar (SEE-dur), leader (LEED-ur), liter (LEE-tur)
ew	boot (bewt), lose (lewz)
i	buy (bi), height (hit), lie (li), surprise (sur-PRIZ)
ih	bitter (BIH-tur), pill (pihl)
o	cotton (KO-tuhn), hot (hot)
oh	below (bee-LOH), coat (koht), note (noht), wholesome (HOHL-suhm)
oo	good (good), look (look)
ow	couch (kowch), how (how)
oy	boy (boy), coin (koyn)
uh	about (uh-BOWT), butter (BUH-tuhr), enough (ee-NUHF), other (UH-thur)

Consonant Sounds

Symbol	Spelled (Pronounced)
ch	beach (beech), chimp (chihmp)
g	beg (behg), disguise (dihs-GIZ), get (geht)
j	digit (DIH-juht), edge (ehj), jet (jeht)
k	cat (kat), kitten (KIH-tuhn), hex (hehks)
s	cellar (SEHL-ur), save (sayv), scent (sehnt)
sh	champagne (sham-PAYN), issue (IH-shew), shop (shop)
ur	birth (burth), disturb (dihs-TURB), earth (urth), letter (LEH-tur)
y	useful (YEWS-fuhl), young (yuhng)
z	business (BIHZ-nehs), zest (zehst)
zh	vision (VIH-zhuhn)

COMPLETE LIST OF CONTENTS

VOLUME 1

VOLUME 2

VOLUME 3

VOLUME 4

VOLUME 5

VOLUME 6

VOLUME 7

VOLUME 8

VOLUME 9

VOLUME 10

LIST OF MAPS AND SIDEBARS

VOLUME 1

VOLUME 2

VOLUME 3

VOLUME 4

VOLUME 5

Volume 8

VOLUME 9

VOLUME 10

Great Lives from History

Maps

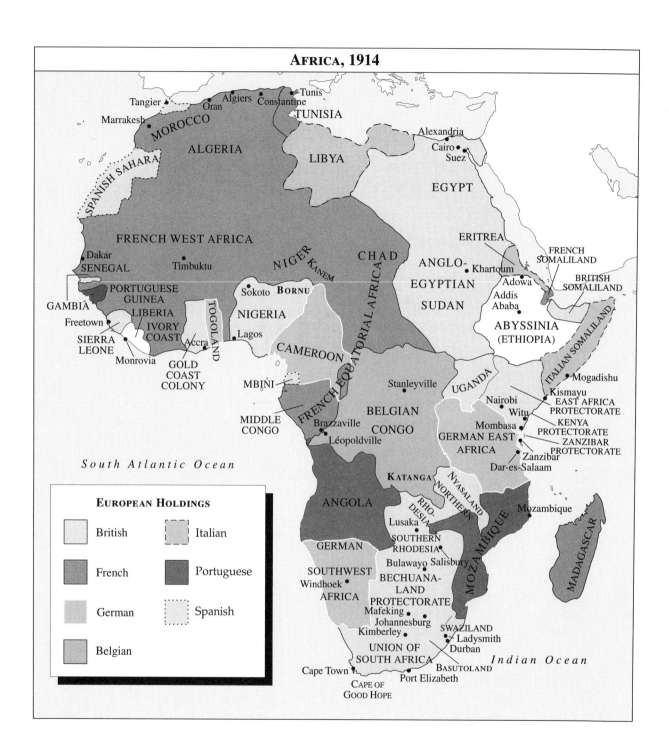

Africa, 1914

European Holdings

- British
- French
- German
- Belgian
- Italian
- Portuguese
- Spanish

South Atlantic Ocean

Indian Ocean

MOROCCO
Tangier
Marrakesh
Algiers · Oran · Constantine
Tunis
TUNISIA
ALGERIA
LIBYA
SPANISH SAHARA
Alexandria
Cairo · Suez
EGYPT
FRENCH WEST AFRICA
Dakar
SENEGAL
Timbuktu
NIGER
KANEM
CHAD
ERITREA
ANGLO-EGYPTIAN SUDAN
Khartoum
FRENCH SOMALILAND
BRITISH SOMALILAND
Adowa
Addis Ababa
ABYSSINIA (ETHIOPIA)
GAMBIA
PORTUGUESE GUINEA
LIBERIA
Freetown
SIERRA LEONE
IVORY COAST
Monrovia
Accra
TOGOLAND
GOLD COAST COLONY
Sokoto
BORNU
NIGERIA
Lagos
CAMEROON
MBINI
MIDDLE CONGO
FRENCH EQUATORIAL AFRICA
Brazzaville
Léopoldville
BELGIAN CONGO
Stanleyville
UGANDA
Nairobi
Witu
Mombasa
GERMAN EAST AFRICA
Dar-es-Salaam
Zanzibar
ITALIAN SOMALILAND
Mogadishu
Kismayu
EAST AFRICA PROTECTORATE
KENYA PROTECTORATE
ZANZIBAR PROTECTORATE
KATANGA
NYASALAND
NORTHERN RHODESIA
ANGOLA
Lusaka
RHODESIA
Mozambique
MOZAMBIQUE
MADAGASCAR
GERMAN SOUTHWEST AFRICA
Windhoek
SOUTHERN RHODESIA
Bulawayo · Salisbury
BECHUANALAND PROTECTORATE
Mafeking
Johannesburg
Kimberley
UNION OF SOUTH AFRICA
SWAZILAND
Ladysmith
Durban
BASUTOLAND
Cape Town
Port Elizabeth
CAPE OF GOOD HOPE

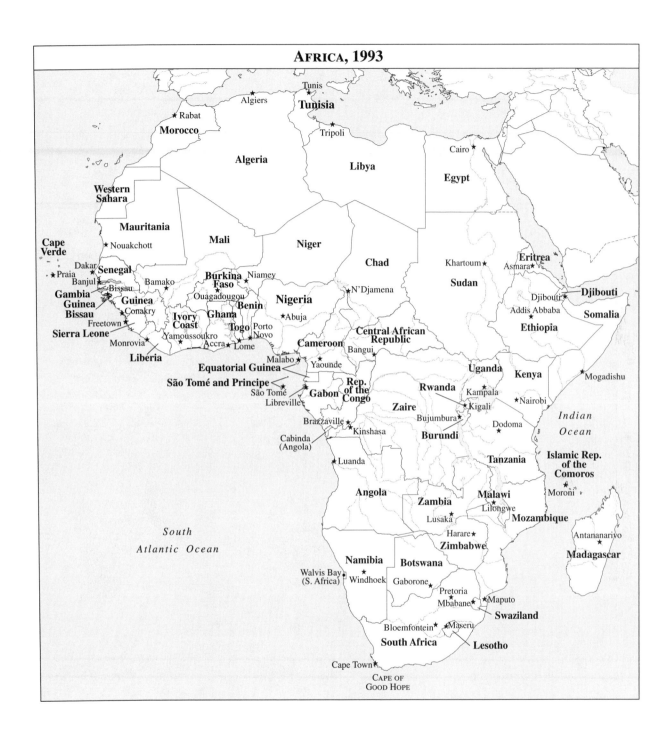

AFRICA, 1993

Tunis★
Tunisia
Algiers ★
★ Rabat
Morocco
Tripoli ★
Cairo ★
Algeria
Libya
Egypt
Western
Sahara
Mauritania
★ Nouakchott
Mali
Niger
Chad
Khartoum ★
Eritrea
Asmara ★
Cape
Verde
★ Praia
Dakar ★
Senegal
Banjul ★
Niamey ★
Bamako
Burkina
Faso
Djibouti ★
Djibouti
Gambia
Guinea
Bissau
Bissau ★
Guinea
Ouagadougou ★
N'Djamena ★
Sudan
Addis Abbaba ★
Somalia
Conakry ★
Nigeria
Benin
Abuja ★
Ethiopia
Freetown ★
Ivory
Coast
Ghana
Togo
Porto
Novo
Sierra Leone
Yamoussoukro ★
Accra ★
Lome ★
Cameroon
Central African
Republic
Monrovia ★
Liberia
Malabo ★
Yaounde ★
Bangui ★
Uganda
Kenya
Mogadishu ★
Equatorial Guinea
São Tomé and Principe
Gabon
Rep.
of the
Congo
Rwanda
Kampala ★
São Tomé ★
Libreville ★
Zaire
Kigali ★
Nairobi ★
Indian
Ocean
Brazzaville ★
Kinshasa ★
Bujumbura ★
Dodoma ★
Cabinda
(Angola)
Burundi
★ Luanda
Tanzania
Islamic Rep.
of the
Comoros
South
Atlantic Ocean
Angola
Zambia
Malawi
Lilongwe ★
Moroni ★
Lusaka ★
Mozambique
Harare ★
Antananarivo ★
Zimbabwe
Madagascar
Namibia
Botswana
Walvis Bay
(S. Africa) ★
Windhoek ★
Gaborone ★
Pretoria ★
Mbabane ★ ★ Maputo
Swaziland
Bloemfontein ★ ★ Maseru
South Africa
Lesotho
Cape Town ★
CAPE OF
GOOD HOPE

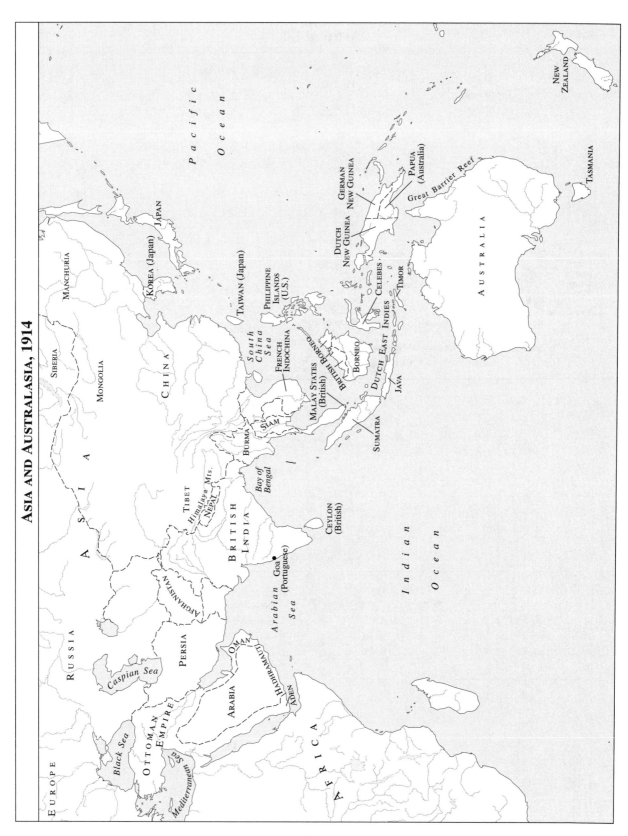

ASIA AND AUSTRALASIA, 1914

EUROPE

RUSSIA

SIBERIA

MONGOLIA

MANCHURIA

A S I A

CHINA

JAPAN

KOREA (Japan)

TIBET

Himalaya Mts.

NEPAL

TAIWAN (Japan)

Pacific Ocean

South China Sea

PHILIPPINE ISLANDS (U.S.)

BURMA

SIAM

FRENCH INDOCHINA

MALAY STATES (British)

BRITISH BORNEO

BORNEO

CELEBES

DUTCH EAST INDIES

TIMOR

German New Guinea

Dutch New Guinea

PAPUA (Australia)

Great Barrier Reef

SUMATRA

JAVA

AUSTRALIA

NEW ZEALAND

TASMANIA

BRITISH INDIA

Bay of Bengal

CEYLON (British)

Indian Ocean

AFGHANISTAN

PERSIA

Caspian Sea

Black Sea

OTTOMAN EMPIRE

Mediterranean Sea

ARABIA

OMAN

HADHRAMAUT

ADEN

Arabian Sea

Goa (Portuguese)

AFRICA

ASIA AND AUSTRALASIA, 1993

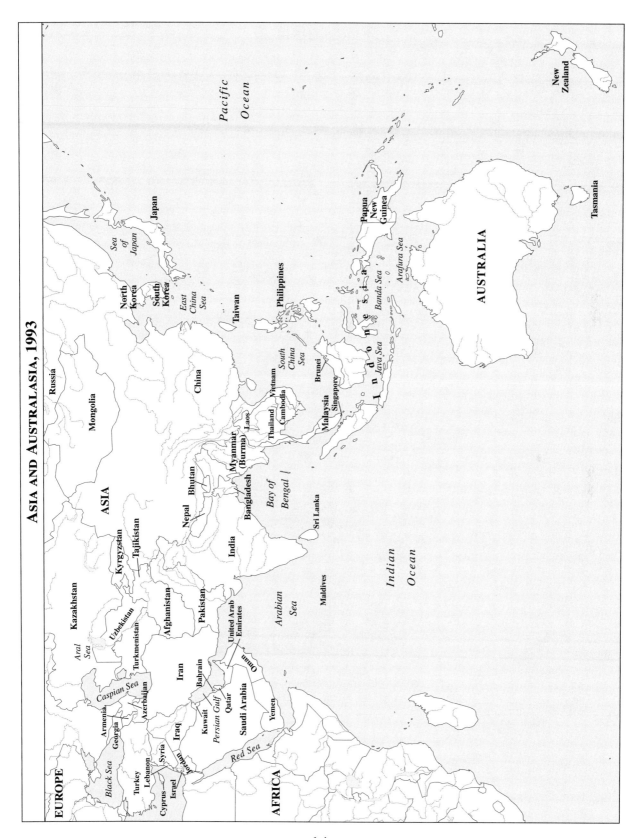

EUROPE

ASIA

Russia

Mongolia

Kazakhstan

Aral Sea

Uzbekistan

Turkmenistan

Kyrgyzstan

Tajikistan

Caspian Sea

Armenia

Georgia

Black Sea

Turkey

Lebanon

Cyprus

Israel

Syria

Jordan

Iraq

Iran

Afghanistan

Pakistan

Kuwait

Bahrain

Qatar

United Arab Emirates

Saudi Arabia

Oman

Yemen

Persian Gulf

Red Sea

AFRICA

Arabian Sea

Maldives

Indian Ocean

India

Nepal

Bhutan

Bangladesh

Bay of Bengal

Sri Lanka

Myanmar (Burma)

Laos

Thailand

Cambodia

Vietnam

China

South China Sea

North Korea

South Korea

East China Sea

Sea of Japan

Japan

Taiwan

Philippines

Brunei

Malaysia

Singapore

I n d o n e s i a

Java Sea

Banda Sea

Arafura Sea

Papua New Guinea

AUSTRALIA

Tasmania

New Zealand

Pacific Ocean

EUROPE, 1914

Arctic Ocean

Iceland

NORWAY

SWEDEN

*Atlantic
Ocean*

IRELAND

GREAT BRITAIN

North Sea

Baltic Sea

DENMARK

NETHERLANDS

BELGIUM

GERMAN
EMPIRE

RUSSIA

FRANCE

SWITZER-
LAND

AUSTRO-HUNGARIAN
EMPIRE

ROMANIA

Black Sea

PORTUGAL

SPAIN

Corsica

ITALY

Adriatic Sea

MONTE-
NEGRO

SERBIA

ALBANIA

BULGARIA

Thrace

Sardinia

GREECE

OTTOMAN
EMPIRE

Sicily

MOROCCO

ALGERIA

TUNISIA

*Mediterranean
Sea*

Crete

Cyprus

AFRICA

LIBYA

EGYPT

EUROPE, 1993

NORTH AND CENTRAL AMERICA, 1914

Bering
Sea

Bering Strait

Arctic
Ocean

GREENLAND
(Denmark)

TERRITORY
OF ALASKA

Baffin Bay

KLONDIKE

Northwest
Territories

Hudson
Bay

DOMINION

British
Columbia

Alberta

Saskatchewan

Manitoba

Ontario

OF   CANADA

Quebec

NEWFOUNDLAND

Washington

Montana

North
Dakota

Minnesota

Great Lakes

St. Lawrence River

Maine
Vermont
New Hampshire
Massachusetts

Oregon

Idaho

South
Dakota

Wisconsin

Michigan

New
York

Rhode Island
Connecticut

Nevada

Wyoming

Nebraska

Iowa

Penn-
sylvania

New Jersey

California

Utah

Colorado

Kansas

Missouri

Illinois

Indiana

Ohio

Ohio River

Delaware
Maryland
Virginia

Colorado River

Arizona

New
Mexico

Oklahoma

Kentucky

Tennessee

West Virginia
North Carolina
South Carolina

Rio Grande

Arkansas

Mississippi River

Texas

Louisiana

Mississippi

Alabama

Georgia

Florida

Pacific

Ocean

M E X I C O

Gulf of
Mexico

Atlantic   Ocean

CUBA

HAITI

PUERTO
RICO

JAMAICA

DOMINICAN
REPUBLIC

BELIZE

Caribbean

Sea

CENTRAL   AMERICA

HONDURAS

GUATEMALA

EL
SALVADOR

COSTA RICA

PANAMA

NICARAGUA

SOUTH   AMERICA

NORTH AND CENTRAL AMERICA, 1993

Bering Sea

Bering Strait

Arctic Ocean

Beaufort Sea

GREENLAND
(Denmark)

Baffin Bay

Alaska

Gulf of Alaska

Yukon

Nuuk ★

Labrador Sea

Northwest Territories

Hudson Bay

C A N A D A

British Columbia

Alberta

Saskatchewan

Manitoba

Ontario

Quebec

Newfoundland

Ottawa ●

St. Lawrence River

New Brunswick

Prince Edward Island

Nova Scotia

Maine

Vermont

New Hampshire

Massachusetts

Rhode Island

Connecticut

New Jersey

Delaware

Maryland

Pacific Ocean

Washington

Montana

North Dakota

Oregon

Idaho

Wyoming

South Dakota

Minnesota

Wisconsin

Michigan

Great Lakes

New York

Penn-sylvania

U N I T E D   S T A T E S

Nevada

Utah

Nebraska

Iowa

Illinois

Indiana   Ohio

Ohio River

California

Colorado River

Colorado

Kansas

Missouri River

Kentucky

Tennessee

Washington, D.C.

Virginia

West Virginia

North Carolina

South Carolina

Arizona

New Mexico

Oklahoma

Arkansas

Mississippi River

Mississippi

Alabama

Georgia

Rio Grande

Texas

Louisiana

Florida

M E X I C O

Gulf of Mexico

Hawaii

Havana ★

THE BAHAMAS

Puerto Rico

San Juan

Atlantic Ocean

CUBA

JAMAICA

Kingston ★

HAITI

Port-au-Prince

Santo Domingo

DOMINICAN REPUBLIC

Key to Caribbean countries (shown by number on map):

1. British Virgin Islands
2. United States Virgin Islands
3. St. Martin
4. St. Kitts and Nevis
5. Antigua and Barbuda
6. Montserrat
7. Guadeloupe
8. Dominica
9. Martinique
10. St. Lucia
11. St. Vincent and the Grenadines
12. Grenada
13. Barbados
14. Trinidad and Tobago

Mexico City ★

BELIZE

Belmopan ★

GUATEMALA

Guatemala City ★

EL SALVADOR

San Salvador ★

NICARAGUA

Managua ★

COSTA RICA

San José ★

C E N T R A L   A M E R I C A

Tegucigalpa ★

HONDURAS

PANAMA

Panama City ★

Caribbean Sea

1
2
3
4
5
6
7
8
9
10
11
12
13
14

SOUTH AMERICA

SOUTH AMERICA, 1914

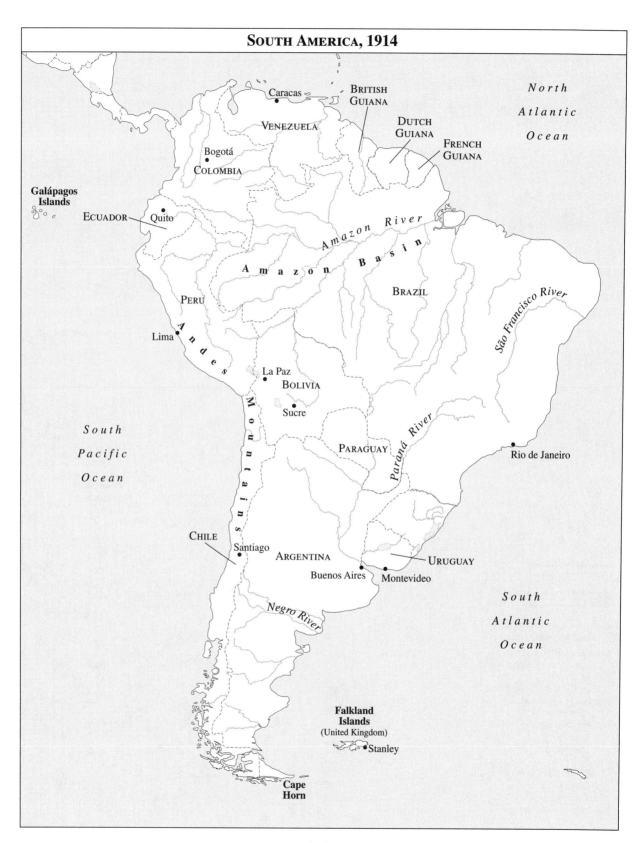

North
Atlantic
Ocean

Caracas

BRITISH
GUIANA

VENEZUELA

DUTCH
GUIANA

FRENCH
GUIANA

Bogotá

COLOMBIA

**Galápagos
Islands**

ECUADOR   Quito

Amazon River

Amazon Basin

BRAZIL

São Francisco River

PERU

Lima

Andes

La Paz

BOLIVIA

Sucre

South
Pacific
Ocean

PARAGUAY

Paraná River

Rio de Janeiro

CHILE

Santiago

ARGENTINA

Buenos Aires   Montevideo   URUGUAY

South
Atlantic
Ocean

Negro River

**Falkland
Islands**
(United Kingdom)
Stanley

**Cape
Horn**

SOUTH AMERICA, 1993

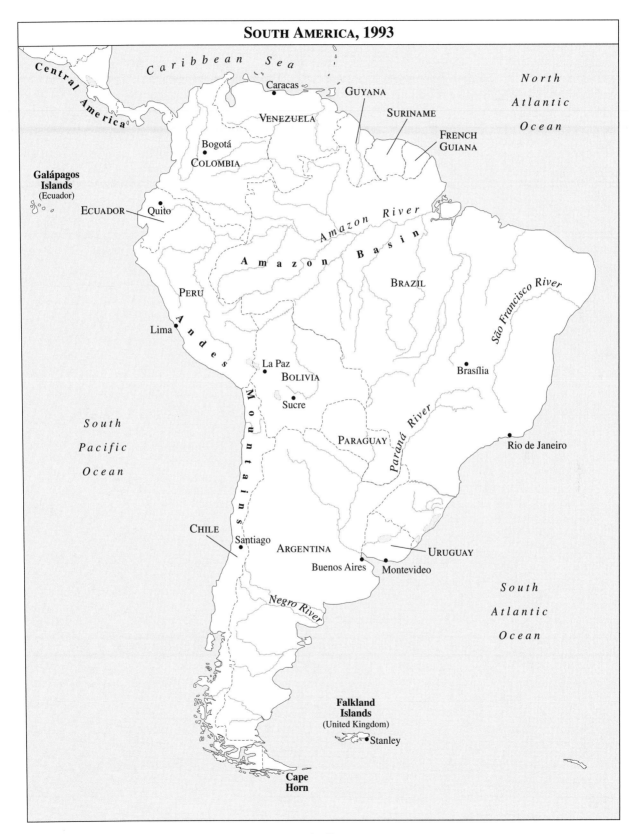

Central America

Caribbean Sea

Caracas

VENEZUELA

GUYANA

SURINAME

FRENCH GUIANA

North Atlantic Ocean

Bogotá

COLOMBIA

Galápagos Islands
(Ecuador)

ECUADOR

Quito

Amazon River

Amazon Basin

BRAZIL

São Francisco River

PERU

Lima

Andes Mountains

La Paz

BOLIVIA

Sucre

Brasília

South Pacific Ocean

PARAGUAY

Paraná River

Rio de Janeiro

CHILE

Santiago

ARGENTINA

URUGUAY

Buenos Aires

Montevideo

South Atlantic Ocean

Negro River

Falkland Islands
(United Kingdom)

Stanley

Cape Horn

The 20th Century

1901-2000

ALVAR AALTO
Finnish architect

Aalto was one of the founders of the International Style in architecture, but he went beyond the geometrical cubism that was the hallmark of this style by incorporating into his mature work classical and Romantic elements. In the process, Aalto became not only Finland's most famous architect but also a national hero, a symbol of the Finnish ideal of sisu, *or fortitude.*

BORN: February 3, 1898; Kurotane, Finland
DIED: May 11, 1976; Helsinki, Finland
ALSO KNOWN AS: Hugo Alvar Henrik Aalto (full name)
AREA OF ACHIEVEMENT: Architecture

EARLY LIFE

Alvar Aalto (AHL-vahr AHL-toh) was born in the small village of Kurotane in west-central Finland, where his father was a land surveyor. Sometime before 1907, the family moved to Jyväskylä, the administrative and trading center for the densely forested lake region of central Finland. Aalto went through secondary school there, graduating in 1916; he served on the so-called White side in the civil war that followed the declaration of Finnish independence in the wake of the Russian Revolution. He first showed his interest in and bent for architecture by his involvement in the design and construction of his parents' summer home in Alajärvi (1918). He studied architecture at the Helsinki Polytechnic Institute, graduating in 1921. There were two major influences from those years that would play a significant role in shaping his future career. One influence was Armas Lindgren, a former partner of Eliel Saarinen and, with Saarinen, a leader of the Finnish National Romantic movement. Inspired by Finland's medieval stone churches and Karelian loghouses, that movement expressed itself architecturally in a monumental rough-hewn stone style. The other influence on Aalto was the architectural historian Gustaf Nyström, Finland's leading exponent of Greek architecture and champion of the classical model as the appropriate style for the newly independent nation.

Aalto's early practice consisted primarily of designing buildings and facilities for exhibitions and fairs. His first independent architectural work was a complex of exhibition pavilions at the Tempere (Finland) Industrial Exposition in 1922. The following year, Aalto opened his own office in Jyväskylä. Probably the most important turning point in his career was his partnership with and marriage to Aino Marsio in the spring of 1924. Their honeymoon trip to Greece and Italy reinforced the attraction that classical models had for him. By the later 1920's, Aalto had achieved a growing local reputation. His projects included the railway employees' housing project (1923-1924) and Workers Club (1923-1924) in Jyväskylä; the Civil Guards' House (1925) in Seinäjoki; the Villa Väinölä (1925-1926) and Municipal Hospital (1927) in Alajärvi; the Civil Guards' House (1926-1929) in Jyväskylä; and the Muuarame Parish Church (1927-1929).

LIFE'S WORK

The beginning of Aalto's meteoric rise from a local to an international figure dates from his winning in 1927 first place in the competition for design of the headquarters of the Southwestern Agricultural Cooperative in Turku; his accompanying relocation of his office to that city, Finland's oldest and its former capital; and his friendship (later partnership) with Erik Bryggman, one of Finland's most respected and sophisticated architects. A multipurpose structure housing a theater, offices, a hotel, restaurants, and shops whose sharp and bold exterior lines appear to have reflected the influence of the so-called *Wagnerschule* (the disciples of the Viennese architect Otto Wagner), the Southwestern Agricultural Cooperative building (1927-1928) established Aalto as an architect of the first rank. That reputation was further solidified by two follow-up Turku projects. The first was an apartment block utilizing a system of precast concrete devised by its developer, Juho Tapani. Aalto's major contribution was the facade, where broad steel window sashes provide a strong feeling of horizontality and give the appearance of a continuous glass band. Even more significant was the *Turan Sanomat* newspaper plant and offices (1928-1929), a reinforced concrete structure with a white facade marked by long strips of steel window sash, plate glass display windows, and geometrical regularity. The work was widely hailed as Finland's first International Style building and established Aalto as a leading figure in the Congrès Internationaux d'Architecture Moderne.

The most important single commission of Aalto's career was the tuberculosis sanatorium at Paimio, near Turku. The distinction of the Paimio sanatorium (1930-1933) lay not so much in its individual details—striking

Alvar Aalto. (Hulton Archive/Getty Images)

vanced fusion of aesthetic and technological considerations of any example of modern architecture of its time."

From the first days of their practice, Aalto and his wife-partner Aino were involved in the design of furniture. Aalto's first major success in this area was his folding chair; there followed his development of bent plywood chairs, culminating in the cantilevered spring leaf supported chair of 1935. From 1933 on, Aalto's furniture sold widely throughout the world. The expansion of his involvement beyond furniture to include the design of fabrics, glassware, and lighting fixtures led to the formation of the Artek Company, a partnership with Maire Gullichsen to produce and distribute Finnish-designed household furnishings.

Many of Aalto's architectural commissions in the 1930's grew out of his association with Maire Gullichsen and her husband, Harry, the heads of one of Finland's largest industrial combines. One of the most famous of those projects was the Sunila Pulp Mill (1934-1935). Aalto not only dealt brilliantly with the difficult technical problems involved—such as smokestacks, conveyors, ventilators, processing facilities, and the like—but also achieved an aesthetic quality rarely found in industrial plants. Along with exploiting the visual contrast between the brick cubic form of the manufacturing plant and the white concrete storage sheds, Aalto successfully adapted the complex to the rough Baltic granite outcropping of the site. Further evidence of Aalto's movement from the pared-down functionalism of the pure International Style to the more Romantic use of natural materials was shown by his own home and studio in Helsinki (1935-1936) and his all-wood Finnish Pavilion for the Paris World's Fair of 1937. The masterpiece of his mature architecture, however, was the summer house he designed for the Gullichsens near Noormarkuu, approximately one hundred miles northwest of Helsinki, called the Villa Mairea (1937-1938). The L-shaped, two-story house consisted of a series of articulated rectangular volumes, accented and augmented by the free-form shape of the entrance shed, the irregular volume of Maire Gullichsen's painting studio, and the kidney-shaped swimming pool. To provide privacy, the interior was partitioned into living and service areas. Its most striking feature was Aalto's use of wood and natural stone to harmonize the structure with the surrounding fir forest. The house—given wide publicity by the exhibition of Aalto's architecture and

as each was—but rather in Aalto's success in creating a unified and integrated total environment for the comfort and convenience of the patients, including furniture, beds, lavatories, window arrangements, ventilating systems, room color schemes, and even washbasins designed to be splash proof. The international acclaim that the sanatorium attracted was reinforced by another masterpiece—Aalto's 1933 design for the Municipal Library at Viipuri (now Vyborg). The library (1933-1935, destroyed when the city and the entire province of Karelia was ceded to the Soviet Union after the Russian-Finnish Winter War of 1939-1940) strikingly demonstrated Aalto's technical virtuosity in its concealed natural-gravity ventilation, circular lightwells piercing the ceiling, and the superb acoustics of the auditorium with its wavelike wood ceiling. At the same time, the work revealed Aalto's shift from the rigid and spartan geometrical forms of the International Style to use curvilinear forms, exposed wood textures, and irregular spatial arrangements. The building represented "the most ad-

furniture put on by New York City's Museum of Modern Art in 1938—became the model (lamentably watered down in practice in most instances) for post-World War II domestic architecture throughout the world and nowhere more so than in the United States.

Aalto's first project done in the United States was the Finnish Pavilion for the New York World's Fair of 1939-1940. He was sufficiently attracted by the possibility of relocating to the United States that in 1940 he accepted a position at the Massachusetts Institute of Technology (MIT). As a Finnish patriot, however, he returned to his homeland that fall because of the threat of renewed war between Finland and the Soviet Union. At the war's end, he taught part-time at MIT until 1951. His Baker House dormitory (1946-1949) for that institution—a Z-shaped structure to maximize the number of rooms with windows facing on the Charles River, with undulating walls, dark, rough, brick facades, and cantilevered, twin, straight-run stairways stretching the length of its main entrance (rear) facade—is the foremost example of Aalto's work in the United States.

Aalto was hit hard by the death of his wife Aino in January, 1949. In 1952, however, he married Elissa Mäkiniemi, a member of his office staff, and, like Aino, she became his partner in his architectural practice. Aalto's international reputation brought him in the 1950's and 1960's a series of major Finnish commissions, including the National Pension Bank (1952-1956), the "Ratatalo" office building (1953-1955), and Finlandia Hall (1962-1965), a concert hall and conference center complex (all in Helsinki); the main building of the Helsinki Technical University at Otaniemi (1955-1964); the Vuoksenniska Church in Imatra (1956-1958); and the Seinäjoki Civic Center (1952-1965). The masterwork of the last phase of his career was the Cultural Center (1958-1962) at Wolfsburg, West Germany. The building combines virtually every feature that had become identified as Aalto hallmarks; the fanlike arrangement of the main auditorium and meeting rooms; sunken forms or double-height spaces open to the sky or skylighted, irregular shaped volumes, undulating ceilings, and richly textured wood surfaces.

Aalto was awarded in 1957 the Royal Gold Medal of Architecture in Great Britain and in 1963 the Gold Medal of the American Institute of Architects. As he grew older, however, he became increasingly reclusive until he was inaccessible to all except a handful of longtime friends. The physical and mental impairments of age aggravated by a lifetime of heavy drinking sapped his creative energies during the last decade of his life. Aalto died May 11, 1976, in Helsinki. His death at the age of seventy-eight marked the departure of the last of the twentieth century's architectural giants.

SIGNIFICANCE

Over the course of Aalto's fifty-four years of practice, he produced, exclusive of single-family dwellings, more than two hundred finished buildings plus the plans for scores more projects that were never built. He thus ranks second only to Frank Lloyd Wright as the most productive major architect of the twentieth century. In addition, he was highly successful aesthetically and financially in the design of furniture, home furnishings, and textiles. Until the post-World War II period, Aalto was probably more appreciated abroad than in his homeland. By the time of his death, however, his name was regarded as synonymous with Finnish architecture.

Aalto's stature as a giant of modern architecture rests on three major achievements. The first is his technical virtuosity. Perhaps the outstanding example—one reflecting the influence of the Finnish environment with its months of limited sunlight—was his handling of site, building layout, and window and skylight arrangements to maximize the amount of natural light available. The second was his interest in, and concern for, the total environment of each building. Every detail was planned and coordinated to promote the comfort, convenience, and well-being of his buildings' users or residents. The third was his success in transcending the limitations of the International Style in which he had first made his reputation. He did so by alternating rectangular volumes with more irregular forms; by brilliantly exploiting the textural possibilities of wood, natural stone, and, in the last phase of his career, thanks to the influence of Frank Lloyd Wright, red brick; and by his talent for harmonizing his structures with the natural environment of the site.

—John Braeman

FURTHER READING

Dunster, David, ed. *Alvar Aalto.* New York: Rizzoli, 1979. Includes an informative essay by Raji-Liisa Heinonen, "Some Aspects of 1920's Classicism and the Emergence of Functionalism in Finland." The other two main essays—Demetri Porphyrios's "Heterotopia: A Study in the Ordering Sensibility of the Work of Alvar Aalto," and Steven Groak's "Notes on Responding to Aalto's Buildings"—are murky exercises in architectural criticism. The rest of the volume consists of brief written descriptions with accompanying lavish illustrations—many in full color—

of twenty Aalto buildings dating over the full span of his career.

Gutheim, Frederick. *Alvar Aalto*. New York: George Braziller, 1960. Gutheim's brief biographical sketch in this volume for the Braziller Masters of World Architecture Series, written at the height of Aalto's reputation, is adulatory, is not wholly reliable, and devotes disproportionately too much space to Aalto's experiments in large-scale town planning (none of which fully materialized) and his post-World War II Finnish commissions. The work is still a useful introduction. There are approximately eighty pages of black-and-white photographs and floor or site plans.

Loftin, Laurence Keith, III. *An Analysis of the Work of Finnish Architect Alvar Aalto*. Lewiston, N.Y.: Edwin Mellon Press, 2005. Loftin, a professor of architecture, examines the nuances of Aalto's work, including the architect's designs for his own house, offices, and summer home. Includes sketches, plans, and photographs.

Pearson, Paul David. "Alvar Aalto." In *Macmillan Encyclopedia of Architects*, edited by Adolf K. Placzek. 4 vols. New York: Macmillan and Free Press, 1982. A brief but comprehensive, balanced, and judicious survey of Aalto's career and work that should be the starting point for all interested students. The major weakness—apart from the inevitable scanting on details—is that the format allows only a handful of small-sized black-and-white photographs for illustrations.

_____. *Alvar Aalto and the International Style*. New York: Whitney Library of Design, 1978. This thoroughly researched and documented account of the first half of Aalto's career, up to the death of his first wife in January, 1949, is regarded as the authoritative treatment of that phase of Aalto's life. Pearson not only analyzes in his text all of Aalto's projects, built and unbuilt, from the period, but illustrates most with reproductions of sketches/plans and photographs.

Quantrill, Malcolm. *Alvar Aalto: A Critical Study*. New York: Schocken Books, 1983. A full one-volume account of Aalto's long, productive career. The first chapter examines Aalto's pronouncements on the nature of architecture; the second looks at "Modern Finnish Architecture—Background and Evolution." The remainder of the text traces the evolution of Aalto's work, with extended analyses of the more important projects and extensive photographs and copies of plans to illustrate the points made. There is, in addition, an invaluable sixteen-page bibliography of books, exhibition catalogs, and articles.

Ray, Nicholas. *Alvar Aalto*. New Haven, Conn.: Yale University Press, 2005. A brief but comprehensive look at Aalto's life, work, theories, and relevance for the twenty-first century. Ray, an architect and professor, argues that Aalto's theories were in opposition to those of other architects of his day.

Schildt, Göran. *Alvar Aalto*. 2 vols. Translated by Timothy Binham. New York: Rizzoli, 1984-1987. The first volume, covering up to 1927, should be regarded as the official biography. Schildt—who was Aalto's favorite architectural critic—tends to worship Aalto, but he utilizes previously untapped archival materials to shed light on the development of Aalto's art, work style, and personality. Contains 278 color and black-and-white illustrations. The second volume of this biography covers the years from the late 1920's until 1939. This volume has the virtues and weaknesses of its predecessor but is must reading not only for serious students of Aalto but also for those interested in the development of modern architecture, at least as viewed through the eyes of one of its major shapers. Like the first volume, this one is generously illustrated.

SEE ALSO: Eugène Freyssinet; Tony Garnier; Antonio Gaudí; Frank Gehry; Walter Gropius; Le Corbusier; Erich Mendelsohn; Ludwig Mies van der Rohe; Piet Mondrian; J. J. P. Oud; Frank Lloyd Wright.

RELATED ARTICLES in *Great Events from History: The Twentieth Century:*

1901-1940: 1937: Prouvé Pioneers Architectural Prefabrication; 1937-1938: Aalto Designs Villa Mairea.

1941-1970: September 28, 1966: Breuer Designs a Building for the Whitney Museum.

HANK AARON
American baseball player

Aaron, a perennial star of Major League Baseball, set several all-time records. His most famous record was surpassing Babe Ruth's career home run mark of 714. Aaron also was well known for his tenacity in the face of racism both on and off the field.

BORN: February 5, 1934; Mobile, Alabama
ALSO KNOWN AS: Henry Louis Aaron (full name); Henry Aaron; Hammerin' Hank; the Hammer
AREA OF ACHIEVEMENT: Sports

EARLY LIFE

Hank Aaron (EHR-uhn) was born to a large and loving family during the middle of the Great Depression. With his laborer father continually battling unemployment, and the family victimized by the odious Jim Crow laws of the time, the Aarons were facing challenging circumstances. Aaron grew up in the economically depressed area called Down the Bay, but, despite his introverted demeanor, he had many friends and enjoyed the company of his siblings. He was very athletic and enjoyed playing several sports, but he particularly excelled at football and baseball. The shy but fun-loving Aaron played baseball at two high schools, winning championships and gaining the interest of professional scouts. Even at this early age, Aaron showed a real talent for hitting hard line drives to all parts of the ball park. With keen vision, strong wrists, and a beautiful swing, he was clearly an outstanding batter, but he also excelled at base running and had a strong and accurate throwing arm. Aaron was such an outstanding player that he usually competed against players several years older. His mother worried about the potentially harmful influences Aaron was encountering and tried vainly to keep him near home, but she was fighting a losing battle.

Aaron's adult career began with the local semiprofessional team, the Pritchett Athletics. Mobile, Alabama, had much baseball talent at the time and, in addition to Aaron, had produced or would produce major league Hall of Fame players Satchel Paige, Willie McCovey, and Billy Williams. Aaron's next team was the Mobile Black Bears, but he clearly outclassed that level of competition quickly. Playing for the Bears was not a high-paying proposition, but it did lead him to meeting an agent who managed to land the young slugger a contract with a well-known and prestigious Negro League team, the Indianapolis Clowns.

After leading the Clowns to victory in the 1952 Negro League World Series, Aaron secured a tryout with one of the most successful and revered teams in Major League Baseball, the Brooklyn Dodgers. Incredibly, the Dodgers, who had brought integration to the major leagues in 1947 with Jackie Robinson and who now employed several outstanding African American players, chose not to offer Aaron a contract. At this point, his meteoric rise in baseball appeared stalled, perhaps hopelessly so.

LIFE'S WORK

By 1952, only six of the eighteen major-league teams had African American players, and the Dodgers, the team with the strongest record in that area, had just rejected Aaron. Other teams, however, were interested, and he signed with another National League team, the Boston Braves. The team paid $10,000 for Aaron's contract, a fortune in the eyes of the young Alabaman, and he began preparing for his minor-league career. The Braves were about to abandon Boston, a city that for decades had been more enamored with the Braves' hometown rival, the Red Sox. By 1953, the team would be in Milwaukee.

Aaron spent the rest of the 1952 season playing for the Braves' farm, or minor-league, team in Eau Claire, Wisconsin, where he again outperformed his teammates and the competition and won an award for the best rookie in the league. At Eau Claire he encountered few examples of overt racism, but there were only three African Americans on the roster and Eau Claire was a nearly all-white city. At Jacksonville, Florida, in 1953, the situation was substantially worse. This was the infamous Southern League, which had maintained the prohibition of black players long after the major leagues had integrated. African American players were refused at hotels and restaurants that welcomed their white teammates, and the crowd routinely hurled vile and hateful names at the black players from the stands. Nevertheless, Aaron had another outstanding season, and by 1954, the Milwaukee Braves could no longer deny him a space on its big-league team.

After Braves left fielder Bobby Thomson broke his ankle in a game, Aaron's place on the team was secured. Aaron's first major-league game was April 13, 1954, and the debut was inauspicious at best. Battling against Joe Nuxhall, the left-hander of the Cincinnati Reds, Aaron went without a hit in five at bats. The rookie remained

Hank Aaron. (AP/Wide World Photos)

them the following year). In 1959, the Braves and Dodgers ended the season in a tie, but the Dodgers won the play-off series.

In 1966, after years of falling attendance, the Braves left Milwaukee for Atlanta, but Aaron's slugging continued. Babe Ruth's long-held career home run mark of 714, which had stood since 1935, seemed in range for Aaron. After hitting 47 home runs in 1971, 34 in 1972, and 40 in 1973, Aaron trailed Ruth's mark by only one home run entering the 1974 season. The pressure of the pursuit wore Aaron down physically and emotionally, and he received a barrage of hate mail and death threats. The Braves opened the season in Cincinnati on April 4, and with his first swing of the year Aaron hit a three-run home run, tying Ruth's mark. By the time the Braves played their first home game against the Dodgers on April 8, the hype and media attention was overwhelming, yet Aaron connected for a home run off left-hander Al Downing. Finally, Aaron received the honors and recognition he had for so long deserved.

confident and two days later achieved his first hit in the majors, a single against the St. Louis Cardinals and pitcher Vic Raschi. Later that month, Aaron connected for the first of his 755 career home runs, also against Raschi. Over the course of the 1954 season, he batted a very respectable .280 with thirteen home runs before also suffering a broken ankle, which ended his year prematurely.

In the team's clubhouse, Aaron's reception was somewhat less than welcoming. Rookies usually were treated with an indifference bordering on hostility, but Aaron's treatment included comments made to him personally and to the press. Statements made by some of his veteran teammates showed they believed him to be lazy and not very bright. His manager, Charlie Grimm, was quoted as calling him "Stepanfetchit" and first baseman Joe Adcock questioned his work ethic. Aaron moved with a languid but athletic grace that seemed effortless to less-gifted players. Even at the major-league level, his graceful movement was interpreted as dilatory loping.

Nevertheless, through the 1950's and into the 1960's, Milwaukee embraced its slugging outfielder. Year after year, Aaron excelled. He led the league four times in home runs and twice in batting average. He won the award for National League Most Valuable Player in 1957. Aaron twice led the Braves to the World Series, helping them defeat the Yankees in 1957 (they lost to

SIGNIFICANCE

Aaron played through 1976, spending his last two years in baseball as a player with the Milwaukee Brewers of the American League. He finished his career with 755 home runs, an elusive mark not matched until August 7, 2007, by Barry Bonds of the San Francisco Giants.

Both as a player and in retirement, Aaron never hesitated to speak out against any form of injustice. Through most of his career, he toiled in the shadows of flashier contemporaries such as Willie Mays and Mickey Mantle, but in the end his achievements outdistanced both of them. As great as that career was, however, it was dwarfed by his admirable personal traits such as concern for others, honesty, and diligence.

—*Thomas W. Buchanan*

FURTHER READING

Aaron, Hank, and Lonnie Wheeler. *I Had a Hammer: The Hank Aaron Story.* New York: HarperCollins, 1991. This illustrated autobiographical work excels particularly in covering Aaron's early years and provides a forum for his personal opinions.

Gutman, Bill. *It's Outta Here!* Lanham, Md.: Taylor Trade, 2005. This book consists of chapters dealing with various sluggers and home run chases. The section on Aaron is clear, succinct, and interesting.

Tolan, Sandy. *Me and Hank: A Boy and His Hero, Twenty-five Years Later.* New York: Free Press, 2000. This source offers a perspective from a longtime Aaron fan and admirer and relates well the impact Aaron's career had on fans of baseball.

SEE ALSO: Wilt Chamberlain; Ty Cobb; Joe DiMaggio; Lou Gehrig; Michael Jordan; Sadaharu Oh; Frank Robinson; Jackie Robinson; Bill Russell; Babe Ruth; Billy Sunday; Tiger Woods.

RELATED ARTICLES in *Great Events from History: The Twentieth Century:*
1901-1940: January 3, 1920: New York Yankees Acquire Babe Ruth.
1941-1970: April 15, 1947: Robinson Breaks the Color Line in Major-League Baseball.
1971-2000: April 8, 1974: Aaron Breaks Ruth's Home Run Record; October 2, 1974: Robinson Becomes Baseball's First African American Manager.

FERHAT ABBAS
Premier of the Provisional Government of Algeria (1958-1961)

Abbas, regarded as the "grand old man of Algerian politics," was an assimilationist in the 1930's and nonviolent radical nationalist in the 1940's. His Manifesto of the Algerian People marked a turning point in the development of an Algerian national independence movement. Realizing that peaceful means would not bring an end to colonialism, Abbas became a revolutionary nationalist, joined the National Liberation Front in 1956, and quickly became its international spokesperson.

BORN: October 24, 1899; Tahar, Algeria
DIED: December 24, 1985; Algiers, Algeria
AREAS OF ACHIEVEMENT: Government and politics, diplomacy

EARLY LIFE

Ferhat Abbas (fehr-HAT ahb-BAHS) was the seventh of thirteen children born to Abbas Sáid and Achoura (Maza) Abbas. His father, a rather prosperous *cáid* (local administrative chief) in the northern Constantine village of Chahna, who possessed clear ties to the French government, had received the rosette and silver braid of a commander of the Legion of Honor for his service to France. Abbas received a typical French education, attending primary school in Djidjelli and the *lycée* at Phillippeville. After obtaining his *baccalauréat*, he did three years of compulsory military service in a medical corps at Bône. Discharged in 1923 with the rank of sergeant, he then entered the College of Pharmacy at the University of Algiers.

Spending eight years rather than the usual six pursuing his diploma in pharmacy, Abbas was more interested in politics and literature than in chemistry and biology.

His years at the university were an apprenticeship for his future public life. He avidly read the works of Victor Hugo and Sophocles as well as the Declaration of the Rights of Man and of the Citizen and began publishing articles in *At-Takaddoun* (progress) and *Le Trait d'Union* (connecting link) that were highly critical of French colonialism. Writing under the pseudonym Kémal Abencérages, the young Abbas argued against the regime's systematic humiliation imposed on the Arabo-Berber Algerian population.

Elected president of the Association of Muslim Students at the University of Algiers in 1926, Abbas appealed in his writings to young educated Algerian men like himself, but he also wrote about the discrimination endured by Muslim soldiers in the French army, Algerian workers in France, and the Algerian intelligentsia. His ideology at that point was assimilationist; he argued for Algerian Muslims to be granted French citizenship with full equality and an end to discrimination. In 1933, he opened a pharmacy in Sétif, which would be his political base for many years. The following year, he married the daughter of a wealthy landowner from Djidjelli, but the marriage, an unhappy union, did not last. With his first book, *Le Jeune Algérien* (1930; the young Algerian), a series of articles on colonial injustices, he began a career in literature and politics that would last thirty-five years.

LIFE'S WORK

The struggle for political and economic emancipation of Algerians was the major work of Abbas's life. His plans for realizing that goal and its final form were not always the same, for his ideas and strategies changed over time. In the February 23, 1936, issue of *L'Entente*, a weekly

that he founded in 1933, Abbas asserted in an article entitled "Je suis la France" (I am France) that the Algerian
nation had never existed, a statement that was used
against him by his rivals for years to come. He also argued at that time that there could be no French Algeria
without the emancipation of the indigenous people. In
the 1930's, Abbas was willing to criticize the colonial
system and work to dismantle it from within. He argued
for assimilation, the full integration of Algerians as citizens of France. His position differed from that of the
Muslim modernists such as Shaikh Abdulhamid ben
Badis of the Association of Ulama (Muslim scholars),
who popularized the idea of the Algerian nation, and secular nationalists such as Messali Hadj of L'Étoile Nord-
Africaine (North African star), who identified with European socialists. Between 1933 and 1936 he was a town
councillor from Sétif, a district representative for Constantine, and a fiscal delegate to Algiers. Early in 1938,
he founded the Algerian People's Union, a party in-

Ferhat Abbas. (Hulton Archive/Getty Images)

tended to mobilize the masses around a program of Algerian integration into France but with full recognition of
Muslim Algerian customs, tradition, and language.

As World War II began, Abbas volunteered to serve in
the French forces. Captured by the Germans after a brief
period in the medical corps, he was discharged in August, 1940, and returned to political journalism and his
pharmacy in Sétif. After French general Hari-Honoré
Giraud rejected his appeal to enlist Muslims in the war of
liberation (from German occupation), Abbas turned
away from the path of assimilation. On February 10,
1943, he published his Manifesto of the Algerian People,
a document submitted two days later to the French administration and signed by twenty-two elected representatives of Muslim Algerians. The manifesto called for the
abolition of colonialism, an Algerian constitution that
would guarantee freedom and equality to all, the redistri-
bution of settler land to Algerian peasants, the recognition of Arabic and French as official languages, the release of political prisoners, and the separation of church
and state. It was an Algerian "declaration of the rights of
man," a call for an autonomous Algerian state within a
French Union. Several months later, Abbas was interned
for nationalist agitation but then released in December
prior to the governor's promulgation of a new ordinance
(of March 7, 1944) granting French citizenship to an elite
group of Muslims.

Opposition to the ordinance and its denial of Algerian
nationhood crystallized around Abbas, who founded a
new party, the Friends of the Manifesto and of Liberty, in
Sétif on March 14, 1944. The party initially secured the
support of Hadj's followers and the *ulama* (Muslim intelligentsia). In September, a party journal, *Égalité* (equality), was launched to promote the party's three-point program; the nonviolent struggle against colonialism, the
creation of a self-governing Algerian republic in federation with France, and the elimination of special privilege.
Militant nationalism, however, was developing rapidly.
By March, 1945, delegates at the Congress of the Friends
of the Manifesto rejected the idea of federation with
France and endorsed an independent Algerian government free to choose its own alliances. Then in May, 1945,
an uprising developed that permanently changed the
character of the Algerian nationalist movement. It began
in Sétif on May 8, 1945, with a demonstration at which
police fired on placard-carrying demonstrators and
quickly spread countrywide with Algerians attacking
Europeans and vice versa. Algerian anticolonial protest
met with fierce repression by police forces and armed
settler vigilante groups. Estimates of Algerians killed

during the following six weeks ranged from eight to twenty thousand.

In early 1946, Abbas formed a new party, the Democratic Union of the Algerian Manifesto (UDMA), a party of middle-class moderates and not a coalition that included Muslim factions and secular radicals. His party won eleven of the thirteen seats in the Second Constituent Assembly (an all-Muslim body) with a program calling for a secular Algerian republic secured through nonviolent means. Hadj, who had been jailed, was released in the summer of 1946 and established another party, the Movement for the Triumph of Democratic Liberties (MTLD), which won more seats in 1947 than Abbas's party. The following year, unity talks between all the nationalist groups commenced. A secret organization (OS) to prepare for armed resistance also formed and came into public view in 1950 with a series of robberies that were carried out to finance the resistance.

Abbas, who on September 17, 1945, married an Algerian-born French woman, Marcelle Stoetzel (with whom he had a son, Halim) maintained his middle-of-the-road position within the nationalist movement. His political preoccupations—equality, secularism, social justice, Algerian autonomy, and federalism—were reiterated in the pages of *La République algérienne* (formerly *Égalité*), which he edited. From 1947 to 1955, he served as a member of the Algerian Assembly, and for a time he served in the intercolonial assembly, the French Union. Although labeled a moderate nationalist, on two occasions he was jailed by the French. The atmosphere in Algeria at the time was extremely tense, for there were trials of OS members and continued arrests of suspected militants. In 1953, the Revolutionary Committee for Unity and Action (CRUA) was formed by younger nationalists attached to the OS (Ben Bella, Muhammad Boudiaf Larbi Ben M'Hidi, Mourad Didouche) who were frustrated by Hadj's control of the Algerian Progressive Party (PPA) and MTLD. The following year, CRUA created two interlocking revolutionary organizations, the National Liberation Front (FLN) and the National Liberation Army (ALN); the latter was the military wing and the former the political wing of a national independence movement. The FLN war for national liberation began on November 1, 1954.

Abbas, essentially opposed to violence, remained aloof and even tried to act as an intermediary between the French and the FLN. French repression of the struggle and their brutal counterinsurgency strategies drew indigenous support to the FLN, including that of Abbas. He apparently joined the FLN in May, 1955, but did not publicly announce it until April 26, 1956, in Cairo. There he proclaimed that UDMA no longer existed, that the FLN represented the force for liberation, and that there would be no peace until the French were out of Algeria. With his entrance into the FLN, the party gained increased respectability, for the "grand old man of Algerian politics" had abandoned "moderation" for revolutionary violence, having lost all faith in French goodwill.

Abbas traveled often through Europe, Latin America, and the Middle East to secure support for Algerian independence. In 1957, he was appointed FLN delegate to the United Nations. The following year, he made a special appeal to the Vatican to intervene on behalf of a just peace. Shortly after the French Fourth Republic collapsed in May, 1958, and General Charles de Gaulle assumed power, the FLN based in Cairo announced on September 19, 1958, the formation of the Provisional Government of the Republic of Algeria (GPRA) with the dual purpose of intensifying the war for independence and extending the diplomatic offensive. As the most respected figure in Algerian politics, Abbas was unanimously regarded as the best choice for premier, a position he held until August, 1961, but which involved more prestige than power.

In September, 1959, Abbas responded to de Gaulle's first offer of Algerian self-determination by means of a referendum to be held four years after a cease-fire. While agreeing with de Gaulle in principle, Abbas declared that the general had to deal directly with the GPRA to obtain a cease-fire and that a free referendum was impossible with the French army in control and thousands of Algerians in prison. De Gaulle's partition plan to protect the rights of settlers, and French intentions to retain ownership of Saharan natural resources (such as oil) were rejected. Abbas issued his own appeal to European Algerians to cooperate in bringing about self-determination; the appeal met with great bitterness.

Amid continuing hostilities in 1960, preliminary negotiations for a cease-fire began in Melun, France, but quickly broke down. Later that year, Abbas visited both the Soviet Union, which granted de facto recognition to the FLN, and the People's Republic of China, which offered military aid. Following de Gaulle's referendum of January 8, 1961, in which (despite the FLN's boycott) French voters supported Algerian self-determination, talks between France and the FLN began in earnest. These resulted within a year in the Evian Accords, arranging for Algerian independence on July 7, 1962. Abbas, though, was replaced as premier in August, 1961, by Benyoussef Ben Khedda, who was considered to be more sympathetic to the left wing in the FLN. With independence in 1962, Abbas became president of the National Assembly, serving one year. His commitment to liberal parliamentary politics led him to resist efforts by Ahmed Ben Bella, the first president, to have the FLN control the assembly, and in 1964 he was placed under house arrest. Released in 1965 after Ben Bella was deposed and also placed under house arrest, the "grand old man of Algerian politics" remained in retirement one of the honored leaders of Algerian independence.

SIGNIFICANCE

The life of Ferhat Abbas, like that of his beloved nation, was a struggle for equality and dignity. His life manifested the search for identity prevalent in the politics and literature of Algeria. With his clipped mustache, avuncular features, and neatly sober dress, he epitomized the Westernized, middle-class Algerian *évolué*. His public career is key to understanding the story of Algerian nationalism and the revolution, for it was symptomatic of how the liberal moderate—through repeated disillusionment—became transformed into a revolutionary nationalist.

Abbas's life, like his father's, exemplified the way the French colonial system could work for a few. He rose successfully through the ranks of the legislative posts open to Muslims. Everything about him was oriented toward the West, France, and indeed, middle-class France. More comfortable with French than Arabic, educated and cultured, he still was not an equal citizen in his homeland. Hence, he sought equality his entire life, abandoning his integrationist views in the 1940's, endorsing nonfederalist independence and eventually armed struggle. Equality and social justice remained his goals.

—*Kathleen O'Mara*

FURTHER READING

Abun-Nasr, Jamil M. *A History of the Maghrib*. 2d ed. New York: Cambridge University Press, 1975. A multicentury survey of the region that contains an excellent description and analysis of French colonialism and Algerian national resistance.

Clark, Michael K. *Algeria in Turmoil*. New York: Praeger, 1959. This work includes extensive coverage of Abbas and the nationalist factions in the 1930's and 1940's. It is decidedly biased in favor of the French colonial administration.

Horne, Alistair. *A Savage War of Peace: Algeria, 1954-1962*. London: Macmillan, 1977. Reprint. New York: New York Review of Books, 2006. The story of the Algerian war and its main players. This is probably the most readable and dramatic account of Algerian nationalism. Contains a succinct account of Abbas and his middle-class followers.

Ottaway, David, and Marina Ottaway. *Algeria: The Politics of a Socialist Revolution*. Berkeley: University of California Press, 1970. This work focuses on the final years of the liberation war and the first six years of independence. Sympathetic to the FLN, it contains valuable descriptions of the major figures, including Abbas.

Quandt, William B. *Revolution and Political Leadership: Algeria, 1954-1968*. Cambridge, Mass.: MIT Press, 1969. With a focus on political leadership in the national movement, especially the FLN, Abbas is one of the more sympathetic individuals here. He was interviewed extensively by the author.

SEE ALSO: Nnamdi Azikiwe; Félix Éboué; Charles de Gaulle; Haile Selassie I; Félix Houphouët-Boigny; Jomo Kenyatta; Lord Lugard; Mobutu Sese Seko; Kwame Nkrumah; Julius Nyerere; Ahmed Sékou Touré; Moïse Tshombe; William V. S. Tubman.

RELATED ARTICLES in *Great Events from History: The Twentieth Century:*

1941-1970: May 8, 1945: Algerian Nationalists Riot at Sétif; July 5, 1962: Algeria Gains Independence from France; June 19, 1965: Boumédienne Seizes Power from Dictator in Algeria.

RALPH ABERNATHY
American civil rights leader

Abernathy, one of the greatest African American civil rights leaders of the twentieth century, led the Montgomery bus boycott with Martin Luther King, Jr., helped found the Southern Christian Leadership Conference (SCLC), and organized the Poor People's Campaign after King's assassination.

BORN: March 11, 1926; near Linden, Marengo County, Alabama

DIED: April 17, 1990; Atlanta, Georgia

ALSO KNOWN AS: Ralph David Abernathy (full name)

AREAS OF ACHIEVEMENT: Civil rights, religion and theology

EARLY LIFE

Ralph Abernathy (AB-ur-na-thee) was the son of William L. Abernathy and Louivery (Bell) Abernathy. He was one of twelve children in the Abernathy family and the grandson of a slave. Abernathy's early years were spent on the family farm, where he learned hard work and dedication from his father. William was an influential figure in his son's life. As the leader in the rural community of Linden, William served on the school board and was the first African American to serve on a jury in the county, according to later interviews given by his son. Abernathy recalled that his father was a tall, handsome man. Abernathy himself grew into a stocky man of five feet eight inches, weighing about 185 pounds.

Abernathy served overseas in the U.S. Army during World War II. This experience provided him with firsthand knowledge of segregation, since black soldiers were routinely treated as second-class citizens. However, his time in the Army also gave him access to the G.I. Bill. Through the money provided for education by the government, Abernathy was able to earn a bachelor of science degree in mathematics from Alabama State College in 1950. He had already achieved his first goal in 1948 when he was ordained a Baptist minister. By 1951 Abernathy had completed a master's degree in sociology from Atlanta University. In the same year, he became the pastor of the First Baptist Church in Montgomery, Alabama.

While he was a graduate student in Atlanta, Georgia, Abernathy made the acquaintance of Martin Luther King, Jr., at a service at Ebenezer Baptist Church, where King's father served as pastor. The friendship grew when King was appointed pastor of the Dexter Avenue Church in Montgomery in 1954. The bond between King and Abernathy remained strong for the remainder of King's life.

LIFE'S WORK

Abernathy first rose to prominence for his role in the 1955-1956 Montgomery, Alabama, bus boycott. At the time, all buses in Montgomery had segregated seating: All African Americans were expected to sit at the rear of the bus. Whites and blacks were forbidden by law to sit next to each other or in the same parallel row. In addition, if there were no seats when a white person got on the bus, African Americans had to give up their seats for the white person.

On December 1, 1955, Rosa Parks, a seamstress, was on her way home from work. She was tired, and her shoulders and neck hurt from working all day. When a

Ralph Abernathy. (Library of Congress)

white man got on the full bus, she refused to give up her seat. She was immediately arrested. The arrest mobilized the Montgomery African American leaders. Abernathy, a young but widely known minister, joined forces with the leaders the day after Parks's arrest. He immediately began planning a bus boycott as a nonviolent way of protesting the arrest. The reasoning behind the boycott was clear: The Montgomery bus company depended on its riders for income, and the vast majority of riders were African American. Therefore, if African Americans refused to ride the buses, they would hurt the company that enforced the laws of segregation.

At the same time, Abernathy suggested to fellow strategist Edward Nixon that King be included in their group. King's Dexter Avenue Baptist Church served as the headquarters and meeting place for the organizers. Abernathy, King, and Nixon, with other African American leaders, formed a group called the Montgomery Improvement Association to oversee the boycott. Plans for the boycott were finalized, and the protest was scheduled to begin on Monday, December 5, 1955, the day of Parks's trial. The organizers had hoped that most African Americans would not ride the buses, but they could not have predicted that the buses would remain 90 percent empty throughout the day.

What started as a one-day protest grew into a year-long struggle. Abernathy and King emphasized the nonviolent nature of the protests. For one year, black citizens shared rides, walked to work, and found alternative means of transportation, shunning the city's nearly empty buses. During this time, black drivers and pedestrians were constantly harassed by police for real or imagined infractions; King himself went to jail when charged with driving thirty miles per hour in a twenty-five-mile-per-hour zone. Further, many African American leaders were arrested under an old antiboycott law. However, King was the only one who was brought to trial.

On November 13, 1956, at King's trial, word came from Washington, D.C., that the U.S. Supreme Court had decided that Alabama's bus segregation laws were unconstitutional. Finally, on December 21, 1956, more than one year after Parks's arrest, Abernathy and King rode on the first integrated bus in Montgomery.

In January, 1957, Abernathy, King, and African American leaders from other southern states met at Ebenezer Baptist Church in Atlanta to form a group that would coordinate existing protest groups and spread bus actions throughout the South. Known initially as the Southern Negro Leaders Conference on Transportation, this group soon took the name Southern Christian Lead-

ership Conference (SCLC) and became one of the most important civil rights organizations in the country.

The Supreme Court's decision and the formation of the SCLC, however, led to violence in Montgomery. Abernathy's home and church, along with King's home and four additional homes, were bombed. The violence did not deter Abernathy and King from pursuing their goal of nonviolent protest. They organized sit-ins, marches, and voter-registration drives in cities such Selma and Birmingham, Alabama; St. Augustine, Florida; and Albany, Georgia, in their quest to desegregate the South. They were thrown in jail at least seventeen different times. Abernathy eventually gave up his church in Montgomery so that he could move to Atlanta to be closer to the SCLC headquarters. His ties to King became increasingly tight, and most acknowledge that Abernathy was King's closest friend and adviser. In 1965 Abernathy became the vice president of the SCLC at King's request.

In 1967 Abernathy and King turned their attention to the economic condition of most African Americans. In spite of great gains in legal rights, a disproportionate number of African Americans still lived in poverty. Even worse, as industry turned increasingly toward automation, many workers were being put out of their jobs. In response, King and Abernathy began planning the Poor People's Campaign, which they envisioned as a large-scale demonstration to be held in Washington, D.C. Although the campaign was scheduled to begin in March, 1968, King instead went to Memphis, Tennessee, in support of garbagemen on strike for higher wages. While there, he was assassinated on April 4, 1968, just outside the motel room he and Abernathy shared.

Abernathy became the new president of the SCLC on April 5, 1968, a role he fulfilled until 1977. As leader of the SCLC, he continued King's plans for the Poor People's Campaign and a march on Washington. King's death spurred many to volunteer for the march. Beginning in May, 1968, hundreds of protestors arrived in Washington and built a town of huts and shacks on federal land near the Lincoln Memorial. Dubbed Resurrection City, the shantytown finally housed about 2,500 people. During the weeks of the campaign, Abernathy met with legislators and detailed the protestors' demands. On June 19, a large rally was held in support of legislation to end poverty. Some estimates put the total crowd at fifty thousand people. On June 24, 1968, when their permit expired, the demonstrators were forcibly evicted by the National Guard. Abernathy resisted the eviction and was put in jail.

Abernathy continued to lead the SCLC until 1977,

when he resigned under pressure from other leaders. He decided to run for Congress but was unsuccessful in his bid. During the following years, he worked on his autobiography, *And the Walls Came Tumbling Down*, published in 1989. While the book offered readers an inside look at the Civil Rights movement, many were puzzled by Abernathy's allegations that King had engaged in extramarital affairs. The charges cast a pall over the book and Abernathy's last years. After a long career as a minister and fighter for civil rights, Abernathy died in Atlanta on April 17, 1990.

SIGNIFICANCE

Abernathy was at the heart of the Civil Rights movement, which lasted from 1954 to 1968. He was instrumental in assembling the talent needed for leadership in the Montgomery bus boycott and may have been partially responsible for bringing his friend, Martin Luther King, Jr., into the struggle. Perhaps Abernathy's greatest contribution to the movement was the counsel, advice, and friendship he gave King during the years when they led the SCLC together.

By all accounts, Abernathy did not have the poise or charisma that King had, and he remained overshadowed by King throughout his life. Even after King's death, he was subjected to comparisons with the fallen leader. Nevertheless, Abernathy's role at a crucial time in race relations in the United States was an important one, for even from the shadows, he worked to effect permanent change.

—*Diane Andrews Henningfeld*

FURTHER READING

Abernathy, Donzaleigh. *Partners to History: Martin Luther King, Jr., Ralph David Abernathy, and the Civil Rights Movement*. New York: Crown, 2003. Abernathy's youngest daughter recounts how her father and King worked together in the Civil Rights movement, chronicling the Montgomery bus boycott, March on Washington, and other movement activities.

Abernathy, Ralph David. *And the Walls Came Tumbling Down*. New York: Harper & Row, 1989. Abernathy's autobiography is an important book that offers readers insight into Abernathy's understanding of his own position within the King circle. Unfortunately, Abernathy's decision to include material concerning King's alleged extramarital affairs overshadowed the rest of the book for most reviewers.

Garrow, David J. *Bearing the Cross: Martin Luther King, Jr., and the Southern Christian Leadership Conference*. New York: William Morrow, 1986. In this exhaustively researched 1987 Pulitzer Prize-winning autobiography, Garrow provides the benchmark biography of King. At the same time, he provides a close look at the founding and growth of the Southern Christian Leadership Conference, an important topic for any Abernathy student.

Kasher, Steven. *The Civil Rights Movement: A Photographic History, 1954-68*. New York: Abbeville, 1996. As the title suggests, this book is filled with stunning photographs of the Civil Rights movement. However, the book is also rich with well-documented text and a selected bibliography that will be invaluable to any student of the movement or Abernathy's life.

Murray, Paul T. *The Civil Rights Movement: References and Resources*. New York: G. K. Hall, 1993. An extremely useful book for any student who wants to know more about the movement and Abernathy. Contains bibliographic information for further study.

Robinson, Jo Ann Gibson. *The Montgomery Bus Boycott and the Women Who Started It*. Knoxville: University of Tennessee Press, 1987. The memoir of the founder of the Women's Political Council, one of the leading civil rights organizations in Montgomery at the time of the boycott.

Williams, Juan. *Eyes on the Prize: America's Civil Rights Years, 1954-1965*. New York: Viking, 1987. Journalist Juan Williams offers a highly readable account of the Civil Rights movement. The book ends before the death of King and the ascendancy of Abernathy to the head of SCLC.

Young, Andrew. *An Easy Burden: The Civil Rights Movement and the Transformation of America*. New York: HarperCollins, 1996. Young, a close associate of King and Abernathy and an early leader of the SCLC, provides another insight into the Civil Rights movement and its leaders.

SEE ALSO: Ralph Bunche; W. E. B. Du Bois; Marcus Garvey; Barbara Jordan; Martin Luther King, Jr.; Malcolm X; Thurgood Marshall; A. Philip Randolph; Paul Robeson; Ida B. Wells-Barnett; Walter White.

RELATED ARTICLES in *Great Events from History: The Twentieth Century*:

1941-1970: December 5, 1955-December 21, 1956: Montgomery Bus Boycott; January 10, 1957: SCLC Forms to Link Civil Rights Groups; March 21-25, 1965: Selma-Montgomery March; April 4, 1968: Assassination of Martin Luther King, Jr.

CHINUA ACHEBE
Nigerian novelist and poet

Achebe's first and best-known novel, Things Fall Apart, *is a founding text of postcolonial African literature and has become a central work of world literature. His use of a mixture of simple English and Ibo phrases in his works, which include poetry and short stories as well as novels, reflects a uniquely African heritage.*

BORN: November 16, 1930; Ogidi, Nigeria
ALSO KNOWN AS: Albert Chinualumogu Achebe (birth name)
AREAS OF ACHIEVEMENT: Literature, government and politics

EARLY LIFE

Chinua Achebe (CHIHN-wah ah-CHAY-bay) was born in Ogidi, Nigeria, a large Ibo village in the rainforest lands not far from the banks of the Niger River. He was the second youngest of six children born to Janet Iloegbunam Achebe and Isaiah Achebe, a teacher-catechist for the Church Missionary Society and one of the first people of his region to convert to Christianity. Achebe's family was distinguished, as his grandfather had acquired three of the four possible titles in the village. Although as a boy he was educated as a Christian, learning to admire all things European and to reject things that were African, Achebe still was able to find beauty in traditional African culture. Since his father did not sever connections with his non-Christian relatives, Achebe established a relationship with his people's traditional world.

Achebe began his education in the Christian mission school of his birthplace, first studying English when he was eight years old. At age fourteen, he won a scholarship to Government College Umahia and in 1948 was chosen to be one of the first students to study at University College, Ibadan (later the University of Ibadan). While attending Ibadan, Achebe rejected his given English name (Albert) and began to use the African Chinualumogu (shortened to Chinua), which implies the meaning "God will fight for me." He also dropped his planned study of medicine and instead chose to pursue a degree in literature, receiving his B.A. in 1953.

At this time, Achebe began to write short stories and essays, some of which centered on the conflict between Christianity and traditional African cultures, a subject that later would become the focal point for much of his

works. After graduation, Achebe taught secondary school for less than a year before joining the Nigerian Broadcasting Service (NBS) as "talks producer" in 1954. He traveled to London in 1957 to study at the British Broadcasting Corporation Staff School and there encountered novelist Gilbert Phelps, who admired Achebe's manuscript of his first novel, *Things Fall Apart*, and helped him find a publisher for the novel.

LIFE'S WORK

In *Things Fall Apart* (1958), Achebe focused on the Nigerian experience of European colonialism and dominance, developing his major themes from an African viewpoint and portraying the many aspects of the communal life of the Ibo people of Umuafia in the late nineteenth century at both the societal and individual levels. He wrote the book in part to correct the sympathetic but wrong-headed interpretations of Nigerian culture published by white novelists and amateur anthropologists. The novel is short, utilizing a close-knit style that creates an effective picture of the clash between the Ibo and European cultures at a time when white missionaries and officials were first penetrating eastern Nigeria.

The story focuses on two closely intertwined tragedies—the public tragedy of the Ibo culture as it is eclipsed by the European culture and the individual tragedy of Okonkwo, an important resident of Umuafia who sees his traditional world changing and collapsing and is powerless to stop it. *Things Fall Apart* was met with wide critical acclaim and has been translated into forty-five languages. Moreover, published just two years before Nigeria won independence from Great Britain, the novel portrayed the vitality of indigenous culture before colonial rule and helped fuel the nation's optimism for its future.

Achebe's second novel, *No Longer at Ease*, was published in 1960. As in his first novel, Achebe took the novel's title from a poem by T. S. Eliot. This work examines African society in the era of independence and continues the saga of the Okonkwo family with Ox's grandson Obi, an educated Christian who has left his village for a position as a civil servant in urban Lagos, Nigeria. The story deals with the tragedy of a new generation of Nigerians who, although educated and Westernized, are nevertheless caught between the opposing cultures of traditional Africa and urban Lagos.

In 1961, Achebe was appointed director of external broadcasting for Nigeria. This position required that

Achebe travel to Britain as well as other parts of the world. That same year he married Christie Chinwe Okoli, with whom he would have four children. During this time, Achebe's short-story collection *The Sacrificial Egg, and Other Short Stories* (1962) was published. Two years later he completed *Arrow of God* (1964). In this, his third novel, Achebe once again painted a picture of cultures in collision, and once again his novel attracted much attention, which added to the high esteem in which he was already held. The novel tells the tragedy of Ezeulu, a spiritual and political leader in a village during the 1920's who must contend not only with the developing English colonial administration but also with Christianity. His attempts to honor his god, Ulu, and protect his village from famine backfire. As one who assumes responsibility for his culture and people, he nevertheless cannot adapt to changing circumstances and, eventually offending the British authorities, winds up in jail.

A Man of the People, which would be Achebe's last novel for more than two decades, was published in 1966. With this novel, Achebe continued to develop the urban themes that he had presented in *No Longer at Ease*, but this time with a satirical edge. Set in the early days of a newly independent African nation, the novel centers on a teacher who joins a political party intent on reform and reveals how corrupt politicians used to their own advantage the political system that they had inherited from the departed imperial power. The novel culminates in scandal, a rigged election, and a military coup—a stark picture of Africans, now distanced from their original culture, struggling to convert from colonialism to self-government. (The novel was published just as a real military coup occurred in Nigeria.)

After a massacre of Ibos in Northern Nigeria in 1966, Achebe resigned his position with NBS and moved to the Eastern Region of Nigeria, where he intended to go into publishing. When the region declared its independence as the separate state of Biafra, however, Achebe became personally involved with the ensuing civil war, serving the short-lived Biafran government from 1967 to 1970. During this period of his life, Achebe produced only one piece of work, the children's book *Chike and the River* (1966).

In the years following the war, Achebe produced three collections of poetry: *Beware, Soul-Brother, and Other Poems* (1971, 1972), *Christmas in Biafra, and Other Poems* (1973), and *Don't Let Him Die: An Anthology of Memorial Poems for Christopher Okigbo* (1978). In addition, Achebe was a coeditor of *Aka Weta: An Anthology of Igbo Poetry* (1982). With this turn to poetry as a medium for his creative talents, Achebe was able to dis-

tinguish himself as both a great novelist and a fine poet. During this period, Achebe also wrote a collection of short stories entitled *Girls at War* (1983), most of them first published twenty years earlier during his student days; like his novels the stories reflect conflicts between traditional and modern values. He also coedited another collection, *African Short Stories* (1984). In addition, he produced three works of juvenile literature as well as a number of essays. In the 1980's, Achebe's *Things Fall Apart* was adapted for stage, radio, and television.

In 1971, Achebe had accepted a post at the University of Nigeria in Nsukka. The following year, Achebe and his family moved temporarily to the United States, where he took a position with the University of Massachusetts as a professor in the Department of Afro-American Studies. In addition, during this period, he taught at several American institutions as a visiting professor. While in the United States, he was awarded an honorary doctor of letters degree from Dartmouth College. Additionally, Achebe shared, with a Canadian, the 1972 Commonwealth Prize for the best book of poetry in his *Beware, Soul-Brother, and Other Poems*. In 1976, he returned to Nsukka, where he held the rank of professor and edited *Okike*, a literary journal. In the 1980's he was involved in politics, supporting a presidential candidate and briefly serving in the honorary role of deputy national president.

Chinua Achebe. (Rocon/Engu, Nigeria)

15

The year 1987 saw Achebe return to the novel as an expression of his now world-renowned talents. His work *Anthills of the Savannah* was well received and earned a nomination for the Man Booker Prize. According to Charles R. Larson, writing for the *Chicago Tribune*, "no other novel in many years has bitten to the core, swallowed and regurgitated contemporary Africa's miseries and expectations as profoundly as *Anthills of the Savannah*." The story is set in the fictional West African nation of Kangan and follows the careers of three childhood friends who enter politics. The ambition of one to become permanent president of the country eventually brings them all into conflict, and they all die in political violence, an indictment of the exploitation of power and use of violence for political ends.

Achebe wrote four collections of essays of political and literary subjects: *Morning Yet on Creation Day* (1975), *The Trouble with Nigeria* (1983), and *Hopes and Impediments: Selected Essays* (1988). In the last is a controversial essay that criticizes Joseph Conrad's famous novella *Heart of Darkness* (1902) for its racist, dehumanizing portrayal of Africans. He reemphasized this theme of Western intellectual condescension toward Africa in *Home and Exile* (2001).

In 1990, just after Achebe had been chosen to be chair of the village council of Ogidi, where he lived, he was involved in a serious car accident. He subsequently had to use a wheelchair after a six-month recuperation in a London hospital. Shortly thereafter he accepted a teaching position as Charles P. Stevenson Professor of Languages and Literature at Bard College in Annandale-on-Hudson, New York.

Achebe's literary works have been widely honored. He received the Nigerian National Trophy, Nigerian National Merit Award (twice), and Peace Prize of the German Book Trade. In 2007 he was awarded a Man Booker Prize, England's most prestigious literary honor, for his career. In 2004 he refused to accept the title Commander of the Federal Republic, Nigeria's second-highest honor, to protest government policies. Recipient of some thirty honorary doctorates, Achebe is also a member of the American Academy of Arts and Letters.

SIGNIFICANCE

Achebe is among the founders of the new literature of Nigeria, which has flourished since the 1950's. It is a literature that draws on traditional oral history as well as a modern, rapidly changing African society. As a founder of this movement, Achebe paved the way for other notable African writers such as Elechie Amadie and Cyprian

Ekwensi. In addition, he influenced an entire second generation of African writers. Achebe also helped shape and set into place the now characteristic features of the African novel, especially the effective use of very simple language, peppered with African words and proverbs highly reminiscent of traditional African speech patterns. As Bruce King commented in *Introduction to Nigerian Literature*, "Achebe was the first Nigerian writer to successfully transmute the conventions of the novel, a European art form, into African literature."

Achebe's novels, which comment strongly on the stages of change that have affected the entire African continent in the past one hundred years, are not only chronicles of events and trends in African history but also extremely artistic expressions that contain a definite purpose. Unlike many novelists, Achebe rejects the notion that the writer is an individual who writes for his or her own personal pleasure or merely for the purpose of artistic expression. Instead, Achebe considers the novelist an educator. For example, in an interview with Bernth Lindfors, Achebe stated,

> One big message of the many that I try to put across, is that Africa was not a vacuum, before the coming of Europe, that culture was not unknown in Africa, that culture was not brought to Africa by the white world.

Through his novels, his poetry, his short stories, his career as an educator, and his editing of the African Writers series for Heinemann Educational Books, Achebe succeeded in founding and nurturing a major literary movement of the twentieth century. Indeed, in 2007, African writer Nadine Gordimer, a Nobel laureate, hailed Achebe as "the father of modern African literature."

—Norbert Mazari

FURTHER READING

Booker, M. Keith, ed. *The Chinua Achebe Encyclopedia*. Westport, Conn.: Greenwood Press, 2003. An excellent source both for scholars of African literature and for those new to Achebe and the literature of Africa. Includes hundreds of alphabetically arranged entries covering Achebe's life and writings.

Cartney, Wilfred. *Whispers from a Continent: The Literature of Contemporary Black Africa*. New York: Random House, 1969. A survey of black African writers. Contains critical analyses of *Arrow of God*, *A Man of the People*, and *No Longer at Ease* as well as a discussion of how each ties into a relationship with African culture and European colonialism. Includes discussion of other writers of the Nigerian literature movement.

Emenyonu, Ernest N., and Iniobong I. Uko, eds. *Emerging Perspectives on Chinua Achebe.* 2 vols. Trenton, N.J.: Africa World Press, 2003-2004. A collection of essays by literary scholars examining Achebe's work. The first volume provides critical discussion of *Things Fall Apart* and other novels, as well as Achebe's short stories and children's stories. The second volume explores Achebe's literary theories and how he applied these theories in his fiction.

Githae-Mugo, Micere. *Visions of Africa.* Nairobi: Kenya Literature Bureau, 1978. Provides original interpretations of the works of Achebe as well as four other writers and examines their works of fiction against a sociopolitical background. Also examines Achebe's personal experiences and how they affected his writings.

Heywood, Christopher. *A Critical View on Chinua Achebe's "Things Fall Apart."* London: British Council, 1985. A critical analysis of Achebe's first novel. Discusses Achebe's life and work as well as his personal experiences and views on books and writing in general. Also includes selected writings from some of Achebe's critics.

Owomoyela, Oyekan. *African Literatures: An Introduction.* Waltham, Mass.: Crossroads Press, 1979. A survey of African novels, short stories, poetry, and drama. Introduces major works and their authors. Contains critical and biographical information on Achebe and his first four novels. Written for general readers interested in African literature.

Ravenscroft, Arthur. *Chinua Achebe.* New York: Longmans, Green, 1969. A full discussion of Achebe's first four novels, including critical and literary analysis and a brief summary of each of the four novels. Also contains biographical information on the author.

Sallah, Tijan M., and Ngozi Okonjo-Iweala. *Chinua Achebe, Teacher of Light: A Biography.* Trenton, N.J.: Africa World Press, 2003. A brief but updated biography of Achebe intended for students and general readers. Includes maps, a bibliography, and an index.

Wren, Robert M. *Chinua Achebe, "Things Fall Apart."* New York: Longman, 1980. A guide to Achebe's first novel. Each chapter in *Things Fall Apart* is summarized with questions at the end of each section. Provides a brief introduction to Achebe's life. Contains background information on the novel, the characters, and the time period covered.

SEE ALSO: Aimé Césaire; Joseph Conrad; Frantz Fanon; Nadine Gordimer; Jomo Kenyatta; Sir V. S. Naipaul; Alan Paton; Léopold Senghor; Wole Soyinka.

DEAN ACHESON
American secretary of state (1949-1953)

As secretary of state, Acheson conducted negotiations leading to the establishment of the North Atlantic Treaty Organization and dealt with crises involving the victory of communism in China and American participation in the Korean War. His policies determined the basic framework of U.S. security commitments in Europe and Asia during the Cold War.

BORN: April 11, 1893; Middletown, Connecticut
DIED: October 12, 1971; Sandy Spring, Maryland
ALSO KNOWN AS: Dean Gooderham Acheson (full name)
AREAS OF ACHIEVEMENT: Government and politics, diplomacy, law

EARLY LIFE
Dean Acheson (ACH-a-suhn) was the son of a Canadian couple who moved to the United States. His father, Edward Acheson, had served with a Canadian militia regiment before settling on a career as an Episcopalian minister. Eleanor Gooderham Acheson, the boy's mother, was from a prosperous and socially prominent family in Toronto. Margot and Edward, Jr., a sister and a younger brother, were born during the next ten years. Acheson recalled that his childhood was unusually happy, a golden age of games, pony riding, and Fourth of July celebrations. He never quarreled with his father until he was in college; he had a particularly fond and close relationship with his mother. During his adolescent years, Acheson was educated at the Groton School in southeastern Connecticut. After six languid years there, he spent the summer of 1911 in Canada, working on the Temiscaming and Northern Ontario Railroad; the experience of unrelenting physical labor among rough-hewn railway men left enduring memories of life in the wild that Acheson cherished in later life. That autumn, he enrolled at Yale University, and with only a modicum of effort he received passing grades and was graduated in 1915.

Dean Acheson. (Library of Congress)

Acheson then entered the law school of Harvard University; he found academic demands there far more rigorous but also more challenging and stimulating. Particularly rewarding was his relationship with Professor Felix Frankfurter, who encouraged him in the study of constitutional law. For some time Acheson had seen his sister's roommate at Wellesley College, Alice Stanley, the daughter of a Michigan lawyer; in 1917 he married her. The following year, after he had earned his law degree, Acheson enlisted in the Naval Auxiliary Reserve, and for several months, until World War I ended, he served as an ensign at the Brooklyn Navy Yard. He then intended to pursue graduate studies in law, but after six months at Harvard, Professor Frankfurter obtained a position for him as secretary to Supreme Court Justice Louis D. Brandeis. In 1919, Acheson moved to Washington, D.C.; as he attended to the myriad details of cases brought before the high court, he received lasting impressions of Brandeis's unstinting standards of excellence. Devoted to the justice's work, Acheson provided needed assistance and support when Brandeis's wife suffered a nervous breakdown. In appreciation, Brandeis

made an unusual offer, extending Acheson's appointment as his secretary for a second year.

LIFE'S WORK

At about this time, Acheson's life became more settled. A daughter, Jane Acheson, was born in 1919, followed by a son, David, and a younger daughter, Mary. In 1920, the family moved into a small house in Washington; later they acquired a quaint old farmhouse in Sandy Spring, Maryland, which Acheson regarded as a welcome refuge from legal and political cares. By his own account, Acheson was a liberal in politics, and the Republican ascendancy of the 1920's evidently deepened these convictions. In 1921, he joined Covington and Burling, a promising new law firm in the nation's capital. Although often aroused by political issues, he spent the next twelve years handling cases at law, some of which had international implications. In 1922, he represented Norway in proceedings arising from wartime shipping contracts; with others in the firm, Acheson argued this case before the Court of International Justice in the Hague. Other legal work concerned corporations or involved claims of water rights in the United States.

Acheson was six feet three inches tall, with a spare but powerful build. He had brown hair, which he combed back in spite of its tendency to recede in later years. He had thick, bushy eyebrows that seemingly were underscored by the mustache he had cultivated since early adulthood; to the delight of cartoonists, he often combed the ends upward, producing a curiously flamboyant effect. His manner perplexed many of those around him. He could be supercilious to the point of overt arrogance, but he could also act with a distinct stoicism, which possibly arose from his father's religious calling. He was able to endure direct affronts with quiet dignity. His style of speaking and writing, which was urbane and refined, bore the hallmarks of careful and discriminating reading; at times he would invoke great American or British thinkers or quote aphorisms in Latin.

In 1933, Franklin D. Roosevelt's Democratic administration assumed power, and Felix Frankfurter's intercession with the new president secured for Acheson an appointment as undersecretary of the treasury. Major disagreements ensued, however, over the government's policy of manipulating the price of gold in an effort to stimulate economic growth. Acheson had misgivings about the legal basis for such action and believed that it was improper in view of existing gold contracts. After six months in office, he resigned and returned to his law practice. In 1939, Frankfurter was nominated as a Supreme Court justice; Acheson served as adviser and representative to his old mentor during the Senate confirmation hearings. Acheson then became chair of a committee advising the attorney general. During the next year, President Roosevelt considered means by which American destroyers might be sent to Britain, to aid in its war with Nazi Germany; Acheson assisted in legal work facilitating this transfer of military vessels. In 1941, Acheson was appointed assistant secretary of state for economic affairs. He played an important part in financial planning during World War II and aided in the establishment of such organizations as the World Bank and the International Monetary Fund. As undersecretary of state from 1945 to 1947, he participated in deliberations leading to the European Recovery Program, or Marshall Plan. He was also the chair of a special committee that considered problems surrounding proposals for the international control of atomic energy.

Although Acheson had often expressed his wishes for a return to private life, and indeed left the State Department in 1947, President Harry S. Truman appreciated his experience and his skill in coordinating administrative work. Accordingly, Acheson accepted his appointment to the nation's highest diplomatic post, in January, 1949. He had first to deal with proposals for mutual security arrangements, which had been considered among Western nations as a means to deal with Soviet expansionism. Enlarging on projects that had already been advanced, involving Great Britain and several European states, Acheson carried out negotiations for a formal defense alliance. By reassuring hesitant states, such as Norway and Denmark, and encouraging those eager to join, such as Italy, the particular concerns of various governments were reconciled. In all, twelve original members joined the Atlantic alliance, which, while committed to maintaining peace, affirmed that an armed attack on any signatory would be regarded as an attack on all. Acheson also appeared before the United States Senate and adroitly dispelled the doubts of those who were wary of overseas commitments. In July, 1949, the Senate ratified the North Atlantic Treaty, and thus the nation embarked on a military alliance in peacetime.

More intractable were problems in China, where for several years Communist insurgents steadily had won control of major provinces; in October, 1949, they entered the capital, whereupon their Nationalist opponents fled to the island of Formosa. The State Department and the administration at large had come under criticism for their seeming inaction. Acheson, called on to answer for the United States' China policy, firmly insisted that no

reasonable measures could have prevented a Communist victory; he held to this position both in the State Department's official publications and in his testimony before the Senate.

Anxiety also had arisen about communist influence in the United States. An alleged Communist, Alger Hiss, was a former State Department officer who at one time had worked under Acheson. When he was convicted of perjury, Acheson expressed his personal compassion for Hiss. The secretary of state's critics charged that he was doing little to oppose communist inroads. Senator Joseph McCarthy later insinuated that Acheson was somehow subservient to international communism.

In Korea, communist forces launched a direct attack from across the demarcation line dividing the peninsula, in June, 1950; President Truman, on consultation with Acheson and other members of his cabinet, authorized the use of American troops to drive back the invaders. During the crisis, Acheson coordinated efforts to obtain support from America's allies and the United Nations. By November, North Korean troops had been compelled to retreat, but Chinese Communist armies then entered the war and threatened the wholesale rout of United Nations forces. While insisting on the stalwart defense of positions in Korea, Acheson resisted demands for direct action against China itself. Nevertheless, General Douglas MacArthur, the U.S. and U.N. commander in Korea, called for expanded action and, in defiance of a standing directive from Washington, issued his own version of possible peace terms in a virtual ultimatum to the other side. President Truman consulted with other military leaders and members of his cabinet; they concluded that MacArthur had exceeded his authority and, in April, 1951, he was removed from his command. Acheson supported this measure; in June, 1951, he testified before the Senate for eight days in justification of Truman's decision. Throughout the Korean War, Acheson maintained that the peninsula had to be defended, but in a limited war that would avoid the risk of major confrontations elsewhere. Thus he supported the defense of Formosa but rejected proposals for involving Nationalist China in action against the Communists.

Diplomatic activity affecting other parts of the world was guided by Acheson's concerns for European security and the defense of Asia. He authorized American aid to support French forces fighting communist guerrillas in Indochina; Middle Eastern concerns, such as a major government crisis in Iran in March, 1951, and the Egyptian revolution of July, 1952, he handled guardedly. In September, 1951, the United States concluded negotia-

tions for a peace treaty with Japan, which Acheson endorsed as a means of strengthening U.S. security arrangements in the Far East.

When Republican Dwight D. Eisenhower became
president in January, 1953, Acheson left the State Department. During the last eighteen years of his life he took on
the role of elder statesman. He published seven books;
two collections of essays and an anthology of his letters
appeared posthumously. He did perform some legal work,
and once again he was involved in international litigation
at the Hague. Widely respected for his deftly conjoined
views of politics and diplomacy, he was in some demand
as a public speaker. Although he did not seek any permanent appointments, he was called back to Washington as
an adviser during the Cuban Missile Crisis of 1962; Presidents Lyndon B. Johnson and Richard M. Nixon also
consulted with him on means by which a resolution
might be found for the Vietnam War. Late in life he was
increasingly affected by physical ailments, which he
bore with some fortitude. Finally, on October 12, 1971,
Acheson died of a heart attack and was found slumped
over his desk at his home in Sandy Spring, Maryland.

SIGNIFICANCE

Having witnessed political upheaval on the international
stage during the first half of the twentieth century, Acheson became secretary of state during a critical period,
when the United States' role in world politics awaited
clear definition. After World War II, various responses
were considered to meet challenges from the Soviet
Union and its allies. Profoundly distrustful of the coun-
sels of isolationism, which still appeared in certain
guises, Acheson also was skeptical that international organizations such as the United Nations in and of themselves would ensure peace and security. His approach
was to underscore the commitment of the United States
to international order, first and foremost by organizing
the Atlantic alliance and involving the United States directly in the defense of Europe. Communist advances in
Asia he took to be manifestations of Soviet ambitions in
the Far East; nevertheless, he recognized the limitations
of the United States' ability to act. It could not reverse the
course of events in China, where massive political turmoil had engulfed the world's most populous nation;
even while at war in Korea, the United States could not
court wider and more dangerous confrontations. The
course Acheson charted established commitments for
the defense of Korea and Japan but left the United States
with somewhat broader concerns about Communist penetration in other regions of the world as well.

Acheson's views of foreign policy were distinctively
shaped by the temper of his times; he had seen the rise of
dictators preceding World War II, and his dealings with
the Soviet Union came during the most intransigent period of Stalinist diplomacy, when most other Communist
parties monotonously echoed the Soviet line. Thus the
measures Acheson took reflected certain assumptions
about the postwar world; during his later years, he steadfastly maintained that the Soviet Union benefited from
the efforts of Chinese and Vietnamese communism. For
a time he defended American involvement in Vietnam;
only after several years of war did he conclude that victory there was not possible. Much in the world changed
after he left the State Department, and many new concerns arose, but the basic structure of U.S. foreign policy
continued to rest on security alliances Acheson negotiated for the common defense of Western Europe and of
major Asian nations in the Pacific region.

—*J. R. Broadus*

FURTHER READING

Acheson, Dean. *Among Friends*. Edited by David S.
    McLellan and David C. Acheson. New York: Dodd,
    Mead, 1980. A group of letters selected from among
    those written between 1918 and the last month of his
    life, this collection often shows Acheson in various
    offhand moods, commenting on issues of the day to
    his family, friends, and public officials. Useful as a
    guide to his way of thinking over the years.

_____. *Morning and Noon*. Boston: Houghton Miff-
    lin, 1965. Whimsical sketches of Acheson's first
    forty-eight years, which recapture childhood joys, as-
    sess his education, and point to the influence of great
    jurists, such as Felix Frankfurter and Louis D. Bran-
    deis, in the development of his legal career. The for-
    mation of his political outlook and his brief but stormy
    period of service in the Treasury Department are also
    discussed.

_____. *Present at the Creation: My Years in the State
    Department*. New York: W. W. Norton, 1969. Sweep-
    ing panoramic memoirs that trace the entire ambit
    of Acheson's formal diplomatic career, written with
    some regrets but no apologies. Acheson was forth-
    right in his judgments of men and events, and his dry,
    mordant wit is often in evidence; particularly vivid
    and illuminating are his reflections on the Atlantic
    alliance, the Korean War, and Senator Joseph Mc-
    Carthy's anticommunist campaign. For this work,
    Acheson was awarded the Pulitzer Prize.

_____. *This Vast External Realm*. New York: W. W.

Norton, 1973. Acheson's unsentimental views of international power politics, and his unshaken conviction that Soviet influence must be kept in check, are set forth in this collection of articles and speeches. Also noteworthy are his piquant suggestions for instilling a greater sense of realism in American diplomacy.

Beisner, Robert L. *Dean Acheson: A Life in the Cold War*. New York: Oxford University Press, 2006. An exhaustive eight-hundred-page biography of Acheson's long and influential career.

Brinkley, Douglas. *Dean Acheson: The Cold War Years, 1953-1971*. New Haven, Conn.: Yale University Press, 1992. Portrait of Acheson's life after he retired as secretary of state, recounting how he became an elder statesman and adviser to Presidents John F. Kennedy and Lyndon B. Johnson and reconciled with his former nemesis, Richard M. Nixon.

McLellan, David S. *Dean Acheson: The State Department Years*. New York: Dodd, Mead, 1976. A careful scholarly examination of Acheson's diplomatic practice, this work delineates his approach to foreign policy from among the divergent standpoints that existed at the time in the State Department and in other branches of government. Due balance is assigned to the demands of Cold War crises abroad and domestic political pressures that affected Acheson's positions on issues that shaped the postwar world.

McNay, John T. *Acheson and Empire: The British Accent in American Foreign Policy*. Columbia: University of Missouri Press, 2001. Revisionist history, in which the author argues that Acheson's consistent vision of empire influenced his foreign policy initiatives.

Smith, Gaddis. *Dean Acheson*. New York: Cooper Square, 1972. This thoroughgoing and thoughtful exposition of Acheson's work as secretary of state, volume sixteen of the series The American Secretaries of State and Their Diplomacy, sets forth the particular means by which his handling of European and Asian crises defined America's foreign policy objectives. Sympathetic though not uncritical, the author is incisive in conveying the historical context against which American diplomacy under Acheson was carried out.

Stupak, Ronald J. *The Shaping of Foreign Policy: The Role of the Secretary of State as Seen by Dean Acheson*. New York: Odyssey Press, 1969. A brief study of problems of organization and bureaucracy in the State Department, this work is studded with the terminology of political science and reaches no larger conclusions about the direction of American foreign policy under Acheson's stewardship.

SEE ALSO: Louis D. Brandeis; John Foster Dulles; Felix Frankfurter; Alger Hiss; Ho Chi Minh; Charles Evans Hughes; Cordell Hull; John F. Kennedy; Henry Kissinger; Douglas MacArthur; Joseph McCarthy; Franklin D. Roosevelt; Harry S. Truman.

RELATED ARTICLES in *Great Events from History: The Twentieth Century*:

1941-1970: March 8, 1949: Vietnam Is Named a State; April 4, 1949: North Atlantic Treaty Organization Is Formed; June 25, 1950-July 27, 1953: Korean War; November 3, 1950: United Nations General Assembly Passes the Uniting for Peace Resolution; September 1, 1951: Security Pact Is Signed by Three Pacific Nations Against Communist Encroachment.

JANE ADDAMS
American social reformer and educator

Addams, a writer of hundreds of books and articles and a cofounder and director of the Hull House settlement in Chicago, promoted a variety of social reforms designed to facilitate the adjustment to urban, industrial America from 1890 to 1935.

BORN: September 6, 1860; Cedarville, Illinois
DIED: May 21, 1935; Chicago, Illinois
AREAS OF ACHIEVEMENT: Social reform, education, women's rights

EARLY LIFE

Jane Addams (AD-amz) was born in the village of Cedarville in northern Illinois. Her father, John Huy Addams, owned a local mill and had investments in land and other enterprises in several states; his belief in civic responsibility led him to represent his district in the Illinois senate from 1854 to 1870. Her mother, Sarah, died when Jane was barely two years old, and an older sister supervised the Addams household until John Addams remarried in 1868. Anna Haldeman Addams, the widow of a Freeport merchant, was a self-educated woman with a high regard for social position, travel, dress—in general, the cultural aspects of life. Jane received tutelage from her stepmother in these areas, which supplemented the information she gleaned from books in the local subscription library, conveniently located in John Addams's house. Her formal education began in the village school in Cedarville; in 1877, she entered nearby Rockford Female Seminary (of which her father was a trustee), an institution dedicated to instilling in young women religious piety, cultural awareness, and domesticity. That Jane became president of her class, valedictorian, and editor of the class magazine attests her popularity and intellectual qualities.

Shortly after Jane's graduation from the seminary, in 1881, John Addams died. This shock combined with Jane's indecision about a career to produce several years of irresolution and depression. She began medical study at the Woman's Medical College in Philadelphia, but poor health forced her to leave after a few months. She was then bedridden for six months following an operation on her spine to correct the slight curvature caused by childhood spinal tuberculosis. At the urging of her stepmother, she toured Europe for twenty-seven months from 1883 to 1885, absorbing Old World culture with Anna and a few college classmates. Her purposelessness

persisted after her return. She accompanied her stepmother to Baltimore for two winters and engaged in some charity work there, but her nervous depression continued. It was not until her second trip to Europe, in 1887-1888, in the company of her former teacher, Sarah Anderson, and college friend, Ellen Gates Starr, that she perceived a means to reconcile her intellectual and cultural interests with a useful career. In London she visited Toynbee Hall, a social settlement in the city's East End, and discussed the institution's social and cultural activities with its founder, Canon Samuel A. Barnett. She also toured the People's Palace, an institute for the working class. These experiences acquainted her with the attempts of other educated men and women to deal with the problems of modern society by living and working in a poor neighborhood. Before leaving Europe she discussed her plan for founding a Chicago settlement with Starr; a few months after arriving home, the two women opened Hull House, on September 18, 1889.

LIFE'S WORK

While the model of Toynbee Hall initially influenced Addams's establishment of Hull House, the ethnically mixed population around the Halsted Street settlement had a greater impact on its development in the 1890's. When the two women residents moved into the old Hull mansion, they had no formal program of activities and sought to establish contact with their neighbors by sharing their literary enthusiasms in a series of "reading parties." Soon, however, the needs of area residents dictated programs. A wide variety of activities evolved in the first decade, including classes, clubs, social and cultural events, and a day nursery. Many of these activities drew on the cultural backgrounds of immigrants; Greeks staged classical Greek dramas at the Hull House Theater, and Italian and German immigrants discussed Dante and Johann Wolfgang von Goethe. As the functions of the settlement multiplied and Hull House added new buildings, Addams stood as the central figure—still a young woman, her brown hair drawn back into a bun, her pleasant face distinguished by pensive dark eyes—radiating goodwill and competence.

Her changed awareness of the nature of urban problems began to emerge in the 1890's. While her original impulse in establishing Hull House had reflected the religious and humanitarian principles of her early years, a combination of circumstances now led her to consider the causes of poverty and maladjustment to industrial society. Florence Kelley, who came to Hull House as a resident in the early 1890's, contributed her infectious interest in scientific investigations of the neighborhood as a basis for reform proposals. Her work culminated in the 1895 publication of *Hull-House Maps and Papers: A Presentation of Nationalities and Wages in a Congested District of Chicago, Together with Comments and Essays on Problems Growing Out of the Social Conditions*, a series of essays by Hull House residents, including "The Settlement as a Factor in the Labor Movement," by Addams. Addams was critical of current labor practices, an outgrowth of her involvement in the unsuccessful mediation of the Pullman strike in 1894. She also criticized the response to the depression of 1893-1894 by existing charitable organizations, which too often stressed laziness and other individual vices as the determinants of poverty. Her developing view was to consider the underlying causes of labor problems and social ills: the dislocation caused by modern industrial organization. Her promotion of scientific inquiry was abetted by members of the new Department of Sociology at the University of Chicago, particularly Albion Small, who encouraged her to publish in the *American Journal of Sociology*, which he began editing in 1896.

Addams's far-flung activities of the early 1900's aimed at achieving harmony between industrialism, on the one hand, and traditional ideas of morality and culture, on the other. She was particularly interested in children and their development through educational and social activities. She promoted public parks and playgrounds in Chicago, established a kindergarten at Hull House, and set up a Hull House camp for neighborhood children outside the city. She promoted reform in education, believing that traditional educational methods and subjects insufficiently prepared children for modern life. She served on the Chicago Board of Education from 1905 to 1908 and was a founder of the National Society for the Promotion of Industrial Education. (Founded in 1906, the Society's efforts culminated in the 1917 Smith-Hughes Act, which provided federal support for vocational education in high schools.) She was also a founding member of the National Child Labor Committee, which supported compulsory education laws as well as restrictive legislation for child labor in factories.

By the time she published her autobiographical masterpiece, *Twenty Years at Hull House* (1910), Addams was widely recognized as an expert in social problems and a spokesperson for major programs for progressive reform. A leading suffragist (and officer of the National

American Woman Suffrage Association from 1911 to 1914), she was attracted to the woman's suffrage and industrial justice planks of the Progressive Party in 1912. She delivered a stirring speech seconding Theodore Roosevelt's nomination at the party's convention in Chicago and subsequently traveled more than seven thousand miles campaigning for the party. When Woodrow Wilson won the election, she opined that he would pursue a program of Progressive democracy. The war in Europe in 1914 impaired Progressive aspirations for reform, however, and directed Addams's attention to the cause she would pursue for the rest of her life: world peace.

During the period of American neutrality, until April, 1917, Addams worked for international arbitration, believing that neutral nations could resolve the war's causes and mediate with the belligerents. With Carrie Chapman Catt, she issued a call to women to attend a conference in Washington in January, 1915, resulting in the formation of the Woman's Peace Party, with Addams as its chair. Later in the year, she was elected president of the International Conference of Women at the Hague. (When the group reorganized after the war as the Women's Interna-

Jane Addams. (Library of Congress)

tional League for Peace and Freedom, she was elected president and retained the post until 1929.) When mediation did not materialize and the United States entered the war, she did not support the war effort, although in 1918 she worked for Herbert Hoover's Department of Food Administration, which she viewed as a humanitarian response to the upheaval of war. Her patriotism came under attack, and the Daughters of the American Revolution withdrew her lifetime honorary membership. In the years following the war, she continued to search for ways to ensure lasting peace; her efforts were recognized by the award of the Nobel Peace Prize in 1931, which she shared with Nicholas Murray Butler.

Her final years were marked by tributes and honors from organizations throughout the world. Her activities were hampered, however, by failing health. She underwent major surgical operations and suffered a heart attack in the early 1930's; she died on May 21, 1935. Following services at Hull House, she was buried in the cemetery at Cedarville.

SIGNIFICANCE

Jane Addams was in the vanguard of Progressive reformers. Rather than exhibiting a populist-type aversion to modern industrial conditions, she shared with other urban reformers a belief that social, political, and economic relationships could be modified in a democratic fashion to deal with changed conditions. The belief in evolutionary change toward a new "social morality" was the theme of her first book, *Democracy and Social Ethics* (1902), a collection of essays on such diverse topics as charity organizations, family relationships, women in domestic employment, labor-management relations in industry, education, and the roles of bosses and reformers in politics.

Her experiences at Hull House provided her with a vantage point that few other reformers enjoyed. Observations of the ordinary led her to formulate social theories. For example, her reflections on the activities of neighborhood children led to a remarkable book, *The Spirit of Youth and the City Streets* (1909), in which she discussed the importance of the natural instinct toward play among children and the "urban democracy" exhibited on the playground.

The neighborhood was also a place where social experimentation could occur, where ideas could be translated to practice, for Addams was a rare combination of social theorist and pragmatic reformer. As such, she attracted other educated and talented people to join the settlement, many of whom were young women who faced

the same career quandary with which she had dealt in the 1880's. She was willing to draw on the observations and ideas of this group in formulating her own programs. This open-minded deference to ideas, including those of William James and John Dewey, may have been her greatest strength in attempting to apply democratic idealism to an urban industrial setting in new ways that represented a profound break from the genteel tradition in which she was reared and educated.

Her attitude toward war rested on the same ideal of Progressive democracy as her social theories. Like other Progressives, she believed that war destroyed social progress and moral civilization. Unlike most other Progressives, however, she could not support U.S. involvement in the war, citing as her reasons the sanctity of human life and the irrationality of war as an instrument of change. As a practical idealist, she supported such postwar initiatives as the League of Nations, the World Court, and the Kellogg-Briand Pact, hoping that they would serve as instruments to direct world public opinion against war. In international affairs, as well as in industrial relations, Addams was always willing to pursue numerous programs, never losing her faith in achieving human progress through social change.

—*Richard G. Frederick*

FURTHER READING

Addams, Jane. *Democracy and Social Ethics*. Edited by Anne Firor Scott. New York: Macmillan, 1902. Reprint. Cambridge, Mass.: Belknap Press, 1964. Originally published in 1902, this book was a compilation of earlier magazine articles (revised for the book), which addressed the problem of applying ethics to an evolving democratic system. This edition includes an excellent introduction to the life and thought of Addams by the editor.

_____. *The Social Thought of Jane Addams*. Edited by Christopher Lasch. Indianapolis, Ind.: Bobbs-Merrill, 1965. An excellent introduction to Addams through her published and unpublished writings. Following a biographical introduction by Lasch, the material is organized under five subject headings, which reflect Addams's diverse interests.

_____. *Twenty Years at Hull House with Autobiographical Notes*. New York: Macmillan, 1910. A good source for understanding Addams and the Progressive reform movement, as the book is at once autobiography, publicity for Hull House, and a consideration of reform ideas in the twenty years preceding its publication.

Davis, Allen F. *American Heroine: The Life and Legend of Jane Addams*. New York: Oxford University Press, 1973. A balanced biography that establishes Addams's writing and other activities in a broader cultural context. The most realistic appraisal of her accomplishments.

Farrell, John C. *Beloved Lady: A History of Jane Addams' Ideas on Reform and Peace*. Baltimore: Johns Hopkins University Press, 1967. The first study to analyze the thought of Addams, rather than concentrate on her humanitarian sentiments or involvement in settlement activity. Particularly good in demonstrating that her ideas often conflicted with later historical accounts of the "average" Progressive reformer.

Joslin, Katherine. *Jane Addams: A Writer's Life*. Urbana: University of Illinois Press, 2004. Joslin argues that Addams's emergence as a public figure stemmed from her books and essays. She describes how Addams rejected scholarly writing in favor of a combination of fictional and analytical prose that appealed to a wide readership.

Knight, Louise W. *Citizen: Jane Addams and the Struggle for Democracy*. Chicago: University of Chicago Press, 2005. An insightful account of the early years of Addams's life, from 1860 through 1899, which depicts her personality flaws as well as her compassion.

Lasch, Christopher. *The New Radicalism in America, 1889-1963: The Intellectual as a Social Type*. New York: Alfred A. Knopf, 1965. In a perceptive essay on Addams, Lasch examines her early life and motivation for reform; he finds that her gradual emergence as an adherent to the "new radicalism" (marked by interest in educational, cultural, and sexual reform) was based on the conflict between the genteel values of her parents' generation and her own perceptions of life and society.

Levine, Daniel. *Jane Addams and the Liberal Tradition*. Madison: State Historical Society of Wisconsin, 1971. An intellectual biography of Addams, which asserts that she was a radical in urging rapid change. The book deals with three facets of her life: Hull House, her publicizing of social problems, and activism in national affairs.

Linn, James Weber. *Jane Addams: A Biography*. New York: D. Appleton-Century, 1935. An admiring but thorough biography by Addams's nephew. Not interpretive, but valuable for detail, as the author had access to all of Addams's manuscripts and files prior to her death, and discussed with her the proposed biography.

SEE ALSO: Emily Greene Balch; Nicholas Murray Butler; Carrie Chapman Catt; Dorothy Day; Julia C. Lathrop; Frances Perkins; Margaret Sanger; Lillian D. Wald; Ida B. Wells-Barnett.

RELATED ARTICLES in *Great Events from History: The Twentieth Century*:

1901-1940: February 23, 1905: First American Service Organization Is Founded; 1910: *Euthenics* Calls for Pollution Control; April 9, 1912: Children's Bureau Is Founded; April 28-May 1, 1915: International Congress of Women; June 15, 1917, and May 16, 1918: Espionage and Sedition Acts; 1925: Hamilton Publishes *Industrial Poisons in the United States*.

KONRAD ADENAUER
Chancellor of the Federal Republic of Germany (1949-1963)

Between 1917 and 1933, Adenauer served as lord mayor of Cologne, becoming, after 1945, founder of the Federal Republic of Germany and its first chancellor. He proved decisively that civilian rule could lead effectively and provide economic success and societal well-being.

BORN: January 5, 1876; Cologne, Germany
DIED: April 19, 1967; Rhöndorf, West Germany
AREAS OF ACHIEVEMENT: Government and politics, diplomacy

EARLY LIFE

Konrad Adenauer (KAWN-rad AD-a-now-ur) was born into a devoutly Roman Catholic family of modest means that had produced bakers, bricklayers, reserve army officers, and local officials. In short, he was imbued with the ideals of hard work, self-sacrifice, and persistence. Above all, his home was steeped in the Rhenish tradition of Roman Catholicism and moderately liberal social values. These characteristics informed Adenauer's entire life, and, like his lifelong affection for the Rhineland's hills and rivers, they never left him.

After receiving a classical Catholic education, Adenauer took a bank clerk's job while preparing for university studies. These studies eventually took him to universities in Freiburg im Breisgau, Munich, and Bonn. Passing the bar in 1899, Adenauer entered civil service in the state prosecutor's office in Cologne.

As a Catholic Rhinelander, Adenauer lived figuratively and literally on the periphery of the German Empire created in 1871 and was inherently suspicious of an imperial system dominated by Prussia's Protestant elite. He treasured his region's specific cultural identity and socioeconomic evolution, neither readily compatible with Prussia's oftentimes autocratic and militarist virtues. While Adenauer's Rhenish homeland was an integral part of Prussia, the Catholic western provinces had long resented distant Berlin's domination.

LIFE'S WORK

As with most politicians of stature, Adenauer's career began locally. Establishing himself in Cologne, he joined the Center Party, a minority political party representing German Roman Catholics. Subsequently, Adenauer became administrative assistant to Cologne's lord mayor in 1906. Hardworking and politically loyal, he became

mayoral candidate in his own right in 1917, even as Germany collapsed at the end of World War I.

Adenauer's steady pragmatism and determination to succeed allowed him not only to become lord mayor but also to execute numerous major civic improvements in the face of Germany's defeat. In the process, Cologne became a European center of social and political progressivism. Adenauer soon built a solid base of political support, using his genuine gifts of persuasion—"oversimplification," his detractors said—to help keep the Rhineland part of Germany at a time of rumored annexation by France or a separate Rhenish state. Expediently, Adenauer too flirted with separatism, but his political acumen cautioned that Rhenish independence was chimerical.

By 1919, Adenauer valued such caution. No longer merely lord mayor of Cologne, he had become a skilled and tenacious regional politician. Eliciting strong support from his followers and outwitting his less skilled opponents, he quickly established a reputation as an effective civilian leader in a country traditionally respecting only those in uniform. His reputation would carry him far in the post-1945 era.

During the interwar period, Adenauer devoted his energies to his beloved Cologne. One of Adenauer's most important early tasks was the refounding of the city's university. Utterly determined, Adenauer convinced the Prussian state government—despite budgetary difficulties and strident opposition from the neighboring University of Bonn—to reestablish the University of Cologne in 1919-1920. More immediately beneficial were Adenauer's efforts to improve Cologne's appearance and commercial accessibility. Between 1919 and 1929, he directed the razing of Cologne's outmoded fortifications. He replaced them with an extensive ring of parks around the growing metropolis. Additionally, Adenauer greatly expanded Cologne's commercial importance by modernizing the riverine harbor facilities in the city's heart. Improving and rationalizing the living conditions of the metropolitan area's population, he also directed the annexation of neighboring townships and oversaw the construction of numerous apartment projects. Adenauer greatly eased Cologne's transition from large provincial city to conurbation. More important, the office of lord mayor sharply honed his administrative and political skills, which would serve him well after the war.

With the coming of the Nazi horror in 1933, Adenauer

found himself, like so many others, unable to prevent the impending catastrophe. Depression-era economic chaos had vastly exacerbated the still-nagging shock of Germany's loss of World War I and the revolution of 1918. Consequent political radicalization benefited extremists such as the Nazis and the communists. Feeding voraciously on the country's discontent and privation, these groups completely paralyzed Germany's democracy. The ultimate results were dictatorship and war.

On March 13, 1933, Adenauer was forced from his office as lord mayor. Failing to convince Berlin's Nazi overlords to spare him and his family from persecution, Adenauer went into secret, self-imposed internal exile in the Catholic monastery of Maria Laach in northwestern Germany. Between 1934 and 1937, fearful sojourns followed in Berlin and at Rhöndorf on the Rhine near Bonn. In Rhöndorf, Adenauer eventually built a new home for his family; the Nazis had banned him from his native Cologne.

From 1937 to 1944, Adenauer and his family lived as normal an existence as the travail of dictatorship and war would allow. A devoted father and husband, Adenauer held such normality to be critically important. In 1944, however, this normality was shattered by his imprisonment following the failed attempt by German army officers to kill Adolf Hitler. Escaping with the help of a friend, Adenauer was later recaptured and sent to a Gestapo prison. By the end of 1944, however, he had been reunited with his family, surviving both the Nazi terror and the total defeat of Hitler's Germany.

Liberating Cologne, United States forces immediately reinstated Adenauer as lord mayor. He was summarily dismissed, however, as British units assumed control of the city. Ironically, this dismissal freed Adenauer for a major role in the larger, tortured process of Germany's reconstruction. A new political party, Christian Democratic Union (CDU), served as Adenauer's vehicle. Absorbing the old Catholic Center Party, it united the middle class, a German tradition of social progressivism, and moderate political values. Skillfully outmaneuvering his Berlin rivals, Adenauer became the dominant personality of the new party by 1947. Artfully exploiting the simultaneous rift between the superpowers, he also helped to convince the United States, Great Britain, and France by 1948 that an entirely new, democratic German state should be created: the Federal Republic of Germany.

Adenauer was absolutely convinced that a Western-oriented, federated republic was Germany's sole hope for the postwar world. As head of one of the two strongest West German political parties, Adenauer assumed that he should play a leading role in that republic's formation. Throughout the difficult formative process in 1948-1949, Adenauer pursued a dual objective: to make the state-in-being acceptable to the Western allies and simultaneously to foil proposals from his domestic opposition, principally in the Social Democratic Party.

Born in May, 1949, the new German republic possessed an unmistakable Western alignment, enjoyed genuine democratic government, and operated, in nascent form, the socially responsive free-market system, which helped make the Federal Republic of Germany the economic miracle of the 1950's. As the republic's first chancellor, Adenauer would hold the office until his retirement in 1963.

Almost alone among German statesmen to 1949, Adenauer held that any new Germany must renounce nationalism for Europe's sake. Underlying the foreign policy he directed in his dual role as chancellor and foreign minister, this idea earned for Adenauer the sharp domestic criticism that such policies doomed Germany's reunification. Adenauer countered that only a federal republic, firmly anchored in a united, militarily strong Western

Konrad Adenauer. (Library of Congress)

ADENAUER PROMISES RESTITUTION

In a speech before the Bundestag on September 27, 1951, Federal Republic of Germany chancellor Konrad Adenauer, on behalf of his nation, assumed responsibility for making reparations to the Jewish people for the horrors of the Holocaust.

The federal government and the great majority of the German people are deeply aware of the immeasurable suffering endured by the Jews of Germany and by the Jews of the occupied territories during the period of National Socialism. The great majority of the German people did not participate in the crimes committed against the Jews, and wish constantly to express their abhorrence of these crimes. While the Nazis were in power, there were many among the German people who attempted to aid their Jewish fellow-citizens in spite of the personal danger involved. They were motivated by religious conviction, the urgings of conscience, and shame at the base acts perpetrated in the name of the whole German people. In our name, unspeakable crimes have been committed and they demand restitution, both moral and material, for the persons and properties of the Jews who have been so seriously harmed. . . .

Europe, could compel the Soviet Union to surrender its European satellites. In any case, Adenauer's anti-Prussian sentiments made accepting a supposedly temporary German division all the easier. Though this division has proven much longer-lived than Adenauer ever anticipated, his policies eliminated Germany's ancient enmity toward France and incorporated the federal republic's enormous economic potential into the growing European community. In the process, Adenauer oversaw the transformation of his country from ruined enemy of the Western world to self-assertive ally and valued friend.

SIGNIFICANCE

Throughout his long and remarkably productive career, Adenauer maintained that the Western world is a cultural and historical community possessing fundamental and unique values not common to the East. No great theorist, he nevertheless consistently attempted, as lord mayor of Cologne and as chancellor and foreign minister of the Federal Republic of Germany, to realize these values daily for his countryfolk. Though often haughty and imperious, he possessed the unique ability to transform himself from local politician to international statesman. In doing so, he steadfastly opposed all tyrannies, even at the cost of his personal safety. Intolerant of incompetence, he earned the respect of both supporters and opponents and led much of Germany through one of its most trying periods.

While absorbed in his beloved Cologne before 1933, Adenauer transferred his public devotion to a larger cause after 1945: that of helping Germany recover from the Nazi era's shame and criminality. Shepherding the young Federal Republic of Germany through the pain of occupation and reconstruction, Adenauer saw his country reacquire full sovereignty in 1955. Furthermore, he demonstrated that the German people could successfully overcome past mistakes to become respected and valued allies. Though never mastering Germany's division, Adenauer's reconciliation of the federal republic with the West must be recognized as a historic achievement.

Less tangible but equally important, Adenauer represented an often overlooked German tradition of social responsibility and middle-class, liberal democracy. He guided this tradition to an unparalleled degree of popular acceptance in Germany. In a society traditionally too ready to glorify things martial, Adenauer proved decisively that civilian rule could lead effectively and provide economic success and societal well-being. In the final analysis, that accomplishment stands as his enduring legacy.

—*David R. Dorondo*

FURTHER READING

Alexander, Edgar. *Adenauer and the New Germany: The Chancellor of the Vanquished.* Translated by Thomas E. Goldstein. New York: Farrar, Straus, and Cudahy, 1957. In this early and enthusiastic biography, Alexander attempts to show, on two levels, Germany's objective achievements under Adenauer and Adenauer's personal development. Alexander presents an extensive section on German reunification and an epilogue by Adenauer himself.

Augstein, Rudolf. *Konrad Adenauer.* Translated by Walter Wallich. London: Secker & Warburg, 1964. Augstein presents a sometimes unflattering picture of Adenauer, and he faults particularly Adenauer's acceptance of Germany's postwar division.

Craig, Gordon. *From Bismarck to Adenauer: Aspects of German Statecraft.* Rev. ed. New York: Harper & Row, 1965. A great American historian of Germany depicts Adenauer's statecraft in the diplomatic context, reaching back to Otto von Bismarck. In a brief, excellent account, Craig stresses the role played by Adenauer's personal characteristics in policy formulation.

Granieri, Ronald J. *The Ambivalent Alliance: Konrad Adenauer, the CDU/CSU, and the West, 1949-1966.* New York: Berghahn Books, 2002. Recounts how Adenauer worked to solidly integrate the newly created Federal Republic of Germany with Western nations.

Hiscocks, Richard. *The Adenauer Era.* Philadelphia: J. B. Lippincott, 1966. Hiscocks presents a rather straightforward biography of Adenauer. The work is fairly evenly divided between treatments of Adenauer's accomplishments after 1945 and a general examination of postwar Western German society and politics. Hiscocks includes a short introduction on the historical setting surrounding Adenauer's post-1945 achievements.

Prittie, Terence. *Konrad Adenauer, 1876-1967.* Chicago: Cowles, 1971. Prittie's work provides a well-written, balanced, and thorough examination of Adenauer's life and work. Adenauer's early life and services to Cologne receive fair treatment as do Adenauer's experiences during the Nazi period. A solid investigation of Adenauer's postwar career follows. Includes numerous representative illustrations.

Williams, Charles. *Adenauer: The Father of the New Germany.* New York: Wiley, 2000. In this readable, intelligent biography, Williams describes how Adenauer's chancellorship laid the foundations for a new Germany and Europe by creating economic prosperity, political democracy, and improved relations with France.

SEE ALSO: David Ben-Gurion; Dietrich Bonhoeffer; Willy Brandt; Bernhard von Bülow; Alcide De Gasperi; Ludwig Erhard; Adolf Hitler; Martin Niemöller; Franz von Papen; Walter Ulbricht; Chaim Weizmann.

RELATED ARTICLES in *Great Events from History: The Twentieth Century:*

1941-1970: 1949-1961: East Germans Flee to West to Escape Communist Regime; September 21-October 7, 1949: Germany Splits into Two Republics; July 1, 1950: European Payments Union Is Formed; April 10, 1951: Bundestag Passes Legislation on Codetermination; September 10, 1952: Germany Agrees to Pay Reparations to Israel; October 23, 1954: Western European Union Is Established; August 13, 1961: Communists Raise the Berlin Wall; September 30, 1961: Organization for Economic Cooperation and Development Forms.

HALIDE EDIB ADIVAR
Turkish writer and social reformer

Adıvar, a leading Turkish nationalist as well as writer and social reformer, played a prominent role in the Young Turks Revolution of 1908-1909 and an even more critical part in the Nationalist Revolution, led by Atatürk between 1919 and 1924. As such she was one of the first Turkish women to take an active, indeed militant, interest in national politics. She was the first Turkish graduate of the American College for Girls in Istanbul, and she is credited with writing the first novel in Turkish.

BORN: 1884; Istanbul, Ottoman Empire (now in Turkey)

DIED: January 9, 1964; Istanbul, Turkey

ALSO KNOWN AS: Halide Edib (birth name)

AREAS OF ACHIEVEMENT: Literature, social reform, government and politics, women's rights

EARLY LIFE

Halide Edib Adıvar (hah-lee-DAY ehd-EEB ahd-ih-VAHR) lived during a critical period in the history of modern Turkey—from the twilight of the Ottoman Empire under Sultan Abdülhamid II until the aftermath of the first military coup in the early 1960's. These eighty years brought momentous changes and upheavals to Turkish society; Adıvar participated actively in those changes, influencing the course of her country's social and political evolution. She was born in the ancient, imperial capital of Istanbul, then the center of the Ottoman Empire. Her family lived in the neighborhood of Beshik-tash, on a hill overlooking the Sea of Marmara, not far from the Yildiz Palace, which served as the residence of the Ottoman ruler. Adıvar's father, Mehmed Edib Bey, enjoyed an important government office, the position of first secretary to the sultan's privy purse, which made the family part of the inner circle of the ruling elite. Her mother, Bedrfem Hanim, died of tuberculosis when Adıvar was quite young, and her father remarried sometime before her fourth birthday.

Because of her father's admiration for the English and for British ways of bringing up children, Adıvar's early childhood was quite different from that normally accorded upper-class Turkish Muslim girls. She was dressed, reared, and even fed in the English manner and sent to a nearby kindergarten run by Greek Christians. A childhood illness ended her first experience with modern, Western-type education, and Adıvar was sent to live with her grandmother. In her grandmother's more traditional household, the young girl was introduced to popular lore, folk medicine, and literature, as well as the milieu of conservative Turkish Muslim women. Later she would draw on this fund of popular beliefs and lore in her writings. A local Islamic teacher—the imam of the nearby mosque-school—taught her to read and write as well as instructing her in the Qur'ān. All of this changed when Adıvar was eleven, for her father enrolled her for a year in the American College for Girls in Istanbul, where she studied English, eventually becoming remarkably fluent in the language. Until 1899, she continued her studies under an English governess as well as several well-known Turkish tutors, then reentered the American College for Girls, where she was the only Turkish student. In 1901, she was graduated and married her former tutor, a mathematician named Salih Dheki Bey, with whom she had two sons.

LIFE'S WORK

The first decade of the twentieth century was a tumultuous era in Turkish history, and, during this time, Adıvar read widely not only in classical Ottoman literature but also in European classics such as those of William Shakespeare and Émile Zola. In 1908 came the Young Turks Revolution, which represented a turning point in the centuries-old Ottoman system of rule, because the autocratic power of the sultan was limited, the constitution of 1876 was restored, and a new political elite eventually came to power. It was during the events of 1908 that Adıvar became a political essayist and writer, publishing articles in the daily newspaper *Tanin* that pressed for social and educational reforms along Western lines. Among the things that she advocated were gradual educational changes and the emancipation of women. Her writings brought her instant literary fame as well as arousing the opprobrium of more reactionary elements in society.

Less than a year later, a counterrevolutionary attempt by those supporting the ancien régime occurred in Istanbul during the spring of 1909. Fearing repression, Adıvar traveled in disguise with her two young sons to Egypt and then went to England for several months. While in England, she experienced two things that she later regarded as instrumental in the formation of her own Turkish nationalism—a stay in Cambridge, where she heard a debate on the matter of Irish home rule, and a visit to Parliament, which she says "inspired me almost with pious emotion." In addition, she met with prominent woman suffragists, then campaigning for expanded political and legal rights.

In October of 1909, Adıvar returned to Turkey, since the counterrevolutionary movement had been suppressed. Caring for her son during his bout with typhoid, Adıvar composed her first novel during nighttime vigils. *Seviye Talip*, published in 1910, "exposed social shams and conventions," and, while immensely popular, it also encountered severe criticism. At that time, Adıvar was invited to join the teaching staff of the Women Teachers' Training College, where she collaborated with another leading educational reformer, Nakiye Elgün, in modernizing the institution's curriculum and administration. The year 1910 also brought personal distress to Adıvar, as her husband married a second wife—polygamy not yet being outlawed in Turkey—and thus she divorced him. At this time, Adıvar became involved in a new cultural ideology, known as Turkism, and she wrote a second novel, *Yeni Turan* (1912; the new Turan), which was influenced by this movement.

Resigning her post at the Women Teachers' Training College, Adıvar next accepted a position as inspector general of the Ewkaf (religious) schools, then in the process of being modernized. In addition, she was active in a new women's association, The Women's Club, which was involved in various community services. Both of these activities exposed her to popular social classes very different from her own background; later these experiences would furnish material for her novels as well as heighten her social consciousness.

Late in 1914, the Ottoman Empire entered World War I on the side of Germany and Austria, a decision that ultimately resulted in the empire's demise. During the difficult war years, Adıvar pursued her work of educational reform, organizing orphanages and the Red Crescent (Turkish Red Cross) not only in Turkey but also in Syria. In 1917, she was married a second time to Adnan Adıvar, a doctor who was also a prominent member of the ruling Committee of Union and Progress. The Ottoman defeat by the Allies in 1918 brought political chaos to Turkey as well as foreign occupation and the Greek invasion of 1919. While the victorious powers met in Versailles throughout 1919 to decide Turkey's fate, armed resistance to the Greek army erupted in Anatolia, as did mass protests against the partition of the country by the Allies. In these expressions of popular opposition to European imperialism, Adıvar played once again a leading role, even addressing a huge crowd in Istanbul's great Sultan Ahmed Square on May 23, 1919. By then, public speaking was not new to Adıvar. A decade earlier she had given the commencement speech at the American College, the first time ever that a Turkish woman had formally addressed a mixed audience of men and women in public.

While an ardent nationalist, Adıvar was opposed to violence to achieve Turkish independence, and she even attempted to arrange for an American mandate in Turkey between 1919 and 1920 to avoid further clashes between the European forces and the Turkish army, then under the command of Mustafa Kemal (Atatürk). In 1920, she and her husband were forced to flee Istanbul to avoid arrest by the Allied powers. They took refuge in the Anatolian countryside and, after a journey full of hardships, reached Ankara, where the provisional Turkish government had been established to fight for the country's independence. The difficulties of escape and the couple's desperate flight across rural Anatolia formed the core of her 1923 novel, *Ateştan gömlek* (*The Shirt of Flame*, 1924), which was later made into a Turkish film by the same title. As was true earlier when she worked among the poor classes of Istanbul, her experiences among the peasantry made Adıvar painfully aware of the unfavorable conditions suffered by rural peoples.

Once in Ankara, where she and her family resided in a mud hut, Adıvar devoted her energies fully to the nationalist cause. She worked for the Agricultural School and for the Anatolian news agency and contributed articles to the daily newspaper. Her pivotal importance as a nationalist figure is attested by the fact that she was admitted to Atatürk's circle of political intimates and also was condemned to death in absentia by the sultan's government in Istanbul. During the Turkish-Greek wars, Adıvar was instrumental once again in organizing women, relief works, and the Turkish Red Crescent, even laboring as a nurse in a provincial hospital. While moving in the highest male-dominated nationalist organizations—Adıvar was even made a sergeant major in the army—she did not abandon her feminist concerns and goals.

With the nationalist victory in November of 1922, the Adıvars returned to Istanbul, because Adnan had been named as the representative of the ministry of foreign affairs to the former capital, Ankara now being the seat of government. The next few years witnessed deep divisions within the ranks of the nationalists. Because the Adıvars held firm to their liberal ideological stance, as opposed to the more radical position of the Turkish Republic's first president, Atatürk, they were unjustly accused of plotting against the increasingly authoritarian president. Finally, Adıvar and her husband left Turkey in 1924 for Europe, where they spent the next fourteen years in exile.

During those years, the couple resided first in England and then in France for nearly a decade since Adnan was appointed to a teaching position at the École des Langues Orientales Vivantes in Paris. While in England between 1924 and 1928, Adıvar wrote her memoirs; she remains one of the few Middle Eastern women ever to write an autobiography, another genre borrowed from the West. Published in two volumes, her memoirs appeared in 1926 and 1928 under the titles of *Memoirs of Halide Edib* and *The Turkish Ordeal*. In 1929, she traveled to the United States to give a series of lectures at various American universities and returned for the 1931-1932 academic year to teach at Columbia University as a visiting professor. Adıvar later toured the Indian subcontinent to give lectures devoted to political and cultural/religious changes in the Turkish Republic, which greatly interested Muslims all over the world. At the same time, she continued to produce novels, composing her only work of fiction in English, *The Clown and His Daughter*, which appeared in 1935.

Atatürk's death in 1938 meant that the Adıvars could return to Turkey for good the next year. There Adıvar was made the chair of the newly created Department of English at the University of Istanbul. Between 1950 and 1954, she served as a member of Parliament. Because of her husband's death in 1955 and her increasingly delicate state of health, she retired from public life. Adıvar died on January 9, 1964, at the age of eighty, in a suburb of Istanbul and was greatly mourned by her countryfolk.

SIGNIFICANCE

Although her style has often been criticized by the literary establishment, Adıvar remains one of the most widely read authors of her generation. Her creative output is staggering. In addition to twenty novels, she published short stories, essays, literary criticism, plays, memoirs, articles pressing for a wide range of social reforms, and translations from European languages into Turkish. Not content with the pen as an instrument for needed social changes, Adıvar lived passionately what she advocated in her writings. It is difficult to find among her feminist peers, whether in the Middle East or in Western Europe, a woman or man who matches Adıvar in terms of courage, vitality, and devotion to national as well as internationalist causes. She merits well the sobriquet Joan of Arc of Turkey.

—*Julia A. Clancy-Smith*

FURTHER READING

Adıvar, Halide. *Memoirs of Halide Edib*. 1926. Reprint. Piscataway, N.J.: Gorgias Press, 2004. This is an absolutely indispensable as well as fascinating account of the author's life from early childhood until the end of her educational mission in Syria in 1917. It represents a precious source of information for historians of this period in Turkish history.

_____. *The Turkish Ordeal*. 1928. Reprint. Westport, Conn.: Hyperion, 1981. This is the subsequent volume of Adıvar's memoirs dealing with the nationalist era from 1918 to 1922. It provides insights not only into her own activities but also into those of an entire generation of Turkish nationalists.

_____. *The Shirt of Flame*. New York: Duffield, 1924. One of her novels that belongs to her second phase of writing devoted to the Turkish war of liberation. It draws on her personal experiences and was regarded as a pioneering work in the period.

Iz, Fahir. "Khālide Edīb." In *The Encyclopedia of Islam*, edited by H. A. R. Gibb et al. New. ed. Leiden, the Netherlands: Brill, 1954-2002. Volume 4 includes the fullest English-language treatment of Adıvar's life and work. It synthesizes much research in Turkish on Adıvar that is otherwise inaccessible to English-speaking audiences.

Kinross, Lord. *Atatürk: A Biography of Mustafa Kemal*. New York: William Morrow, 1965. Kinross's biography of the founder of modern Turkey is the definitive work in English. Essential to an understanding of the nationalist and early Republican periods, the work also contains information regarding Adıvar's contribution to the Turkish independence movement.

Lewis, Bernard. *The Emergence of Modern Turkey*. 3d ed. New York: Oxford University Press, 2002. While Lewis only mentions Adıvar in passing, this is the essential background text for understanding the culture and society in which she lived and the historical changes she not only experienced but also helped to shape.

Mango, Andrew. *Atatürk: The Biography of the Founder of Modern Turkey*. Woodstock, N.Y.: Overlook Press, 2000. Exhaustively researched, balanced, and comprehensive biography of Atatürk that includes discussion of Adıvar.

SEE ALSO: Atatürk; Enver Paşa; Indira Gandhi; İsmet Paşa; Golda Meir; Sarojini Naidu; Vijaya Lakshmi Pandit; Eleuthérios Venizélos.

RELATED ARTICLES in *Great Events from History: The Twentieth Century:*

1901-1940: July 24, 1908: Young Turks Stage a Coup in the Ottoman Empire; May 19, 1919-September 11, 1922: Greco-Turkish War.

ALFRED ADLER
Austrian psychiatrist

Adler, the founder of individual psychology, introduced such fundamental mental-health concepts as "inferiority feeling," "lifestyle," "striving for superiority," and "social interest." The first to occupy a chair of medical psychology in the United States, Adler pioneered the use of psychiatry in both social work and early childhood education.

BORN: February 7, 1870; Penzing, Austria
DIED: May 28, 1937; Aberdeen, Scotland
AREAS OF ACHIEVEMENT: Psychiatry and psychology, medicine

EARLY LIFE

Alfred Adler (AD-lur) was the second of seven children of Leopold Adler, a Jewish Hungarian grain merchant from the Burgenland, and his wife, a native of Moravia. Though reared on a farm, Adler was exposed to the rich cultural life of Vienna's golden age. The death of a younger brother and his own bout with pneumonia at the age of five caused Adler to resolve to study medicine. He received his medical degree in 1895 from the University of Vienna. Much later, Adler would be awarded his Ph.D. from the Long Island College of Medicine in New York. In 1895, Adler married Raissa Timofejewna Epstein, a Moscow-born student. Together they had three daughters and a son. Two of his children, Kurt and Alexandra, later took up the practice of psychiatry. By 1897, Adler was practicing general medicine in Vienna, specializing in ophthalmology. His zeal for reform was indicated in articles in various socialist newspapers.

Though Adler's first professional monograph had been a study of the health of tailors, by 1900 he had become interested in neurology and in psychopathological symptoms. His review in 1902 of Sigmund Freud's book on dream interpretation led to an invitation to join the Vienna Psychoanalytic Society. Though closely associated with Freud (they attended the first International Congress on Psychoanalysis together in 1908), Adler insisted that he was neither Freud's disciple nor his student. This fact was revealed in 1907 in his *Studie über Minderwertigkeit von Organen* (*Study of Organ Inferiority and Its Psychical Compensation*, 1917). In 1911, Adler and nine others resigned from Freud's circle to found the Society for Free Psychoanalysis. Freud then launched what has been called an "almost scurrilous attack" on Adler. For his part, Adler acknowledged his respect for Freud but explained his major intellectual disagreements with him. Adler denied the dominance of the biological over the psychological in human behavior, refusing to see sex as the primary determinant of personality. Adler stressed freedom, not determinism, in conduct, believing that Freud compared humans to animals or machines, forgetting to emphasize what makes them unique, namely, concepts and values. Adler resolved to champion a holistic, humanistic psychology. By 1912, his *Über den nervösen Charakter* (*The Neurotic Constitution*, 1917) indicated the directions being taken by Adlerian or individual psychology.

During World War I, Adler served in the Austro-Hungarian army as a military doctor on the Russian front at Kraków and Brunn. Returning from three years in the war, Adler established what was probably the world's first child-guidance clinic in Vienna in 1919. Soon thirty such centers were operating in Vienna, Munich, and Berlin. Adler emerged as the first psychiatrist to apply mental hygiene in the schools, lecturing meanwhile at the Pedagogical Institute. A pathfinder of family therapy or community psychiatry, Adler involved students, teachers, and parents in treatment. Innovative counseling was done before a restricted audience as a teaching device. By 1926, Adler was much in demand as a lecturer in Europe and North America, and his work was commanding wide recognition.

LIFE'S WORK

Adler's life's work was focused on four areas. Adler was preeminently an educator. In 1926, he became a visiting professor at Columbia University, and in 1932 he became the first professor of medical psychology in the United States, teaching at the Long Island College of Medicine in New York. By then his visits to Vienna were seasonal and occasional, terminating after the rise of fascism in Austria and Germany and the Nazi suppression of his clinics. Adler's lectures were copied and published as *Menschenkenntnis* (1927; *Understanding Human Nature*, 1918), a text that is still a classic.

Second, Adler was widely read as an author. Increasingly his works were directed toward the general public, such as *What Life Should Mean to You* (1931) and *Der Sinn des Lebens* (1933; *Social Interest: A Challenge to Mankind*, 1939). Other volumes included *The Case of Miss R* (1929), *Problems of Neurosis* (1929), *The Case of Miss A* (1931), and *The Pattern of Life* (1930). After

Alfred Adler. (Library of Congress)

first psychiatrists to apply his therapeutic techniques to the treatment of criminals, to the practice of social work, and to the education of American children.

Finally, Adler was in demand as a lecturer. The disarming gentleness that won for him acceptance from patients made him a winsome communicator to audiences. Soon as facile in English as his native German, Adler, a tenor, spoke slowly with occasional silences, pauses that were said to add to the profundity of his remarks. His was a soft voice, but one that was conciliatory and persuading in tone. His piercing eyes and friendly manner evoked a warm response. Though described as stocky and pudgy, Adler conveyed a feeling of intensity and energy with his swift movements and quickness of thought. His broad interests, cinema, cafés, music (he had a fine singing voice), drama, and hiking, established many points of contact with his auditors. It was while on a lecture tour that Adler died at age sixty-seven of a heart attack on Union Street, Aberdeen, Scotland, on May 28, 1937. His daughter, Alexandra, then a research fellow in neurology, completed the tour. Adler's teaching was institutionalized by a series of five international congresses he directed between 1922 and 1930 and since his death by the International Association of Individual Psychology.

Adler believed that the principal human motive was a striving for perfection. He argued in 1907 in *Study of Organ Inferiority and Its Psychical Compensation* that physical disability or inadequacy in the child may result in psychical compensation. Overcompensation can occur. Ludwig van Beethoven, who was losing his hearing, became a master musician. Demosthenes, a stutterer, became a compelling orator. Compensation, however, can produce not only genius but also neurotic and psychotic adaptations to life. In *The Neurotic Constitution*, Adler admitted that inferiority feeling was a condition common to all children. Children respond with an aggression drive (or, later, a striving for superiority). Adler spoke of a masculine protest (found in both males and females), which is any "attempt to overcome socially conditioned feelings of weakness" (such weaknesses being perceived as feminine).

Behavior, Adler taught, is goal oriented. For that reason, his individual psychology is teleological, not causal, as was Freud's. Adler concentrated on the consequences as much as the antecedents of actions. By the age of four or five, Adler insisted, the child has set goals for himself. These goals grow out of the self-image the child has evolved, as well as his or her opinion of the world. The self is a product not only of objective or external factors, such as birth order, but also of subjective or internal fac-

his death, Adler's papers were edited by Heinz L. and Rowena R. Ansbacher as *Superiority and Social Interest* (1964) and *The Individual Psychology of Alfred Adler* (1956).

Third, Adler was much sought as a therapist. For Adler, the psychiatrist did not treat mental disease. Rather, he discovered the error in the patient's way of life and then led him or her toward greater maturity. Therapy was a kind of teaching, with the emphasis on health, not sickness, and on the client's total network of relationships. Adler wanted to know the patient not simply "in depth but in context." The therapist was to be an enabler, helping the patient "see the power of self-determination" and "command the courage" to alter his or her entire world and his or her interpretation of it. In analysis, Adler relied on such diagnostic tools as dream interpretation, the meaning of early childhood recollections, and the role of birth order. Not only was therapy social as well as personal, but also it was to be preventive as well as restorative. Adler established clinics to help avoid such life failures as neurosis and psychosis. Adler was one of the

tors, such as interpretation and opinion. A person's creative power resides in "the ability to choose between various ways of reacting to a situation." As a person seeks maturity and wholeness, he or she selects goals that promise fulfillment and the means by which to attain them. A lifestyle becomes apparent.

Life, for Adler, consisted in meeting three main problems or fulfilling three main tasks that are "inseparably tied up with the logic of man's communal life." These tasks are occupational, associational, and sexual. A choice of work or vocation reveals the primary influences present in the child before the age of thirteen. Association with others, the development of a significant and healthy system of interpersonal relationships, is crucial. Love and marriage, or sex, is the most important of those associations, for from this relationship comes the next generation.

Failures in life, that is, neurotics (mildly dysfunctional) and psychotics (severely dysfunctional), are those who do not develop social interest. Self-bound, they are crippled with intense inferiority feelings and become obsessed with themselves. Withdrawal from life may result because of a belief that one is unable to compete. Another unhealthy adaptation is the evolving of a superiority that is useful only to themselves. Normality or health for Adler meant moving toward constructive social interest, where the person functions creatively for the welfare of all.

Adler's wide range of activities and his inclusive and practical teachings caused him to become a major new influence in psychiatry in the years following World War I. That impact has been a constant through the subsequent decades.

Significance

Through a creative career on two continents as an educator, author, therapist, and lecturer, Adler indicated new directions for the infant science of psychiatry. A contemporary of such physicians of the mind as Sigmund Freud and Carl Jung in Europe and William James in the United States, Adler became one of the founders of the science of mental health. A persuasive and popular communicator, Adler was able to involve the general public in the application of the findings of psychiatry. As a result, what once had been seen as an arcane field provided conversation for cocktail parties. Capitalizing on this widespread public interest, Adler pioneered the application of mental-health techniques to pedagogy, child psychology, school reform, and the teaching and training of an entire generation of educators.

Social work in the United States is also greatly indebted to the insights of Adler, yet it is in the field of psychotherapy that he has had his most lasting influence. Subsequent practitioners of the art of healing the mind, as diverse as Karen Horney, Harry Stack Sullivan, Franz Alexander, and Ian Suttie, have been assisted by the teachings of Adler. Adler remains one of the giants of medicine and psychiatry and of twentieth century creative thought.

—C. George Fry

Further Reading

Adler, Alfred. *The Individual Psychology of Alfred Adler*. Edited by Heinz L. Ansbacher and Rowena R. Ansbacher. New York: Grove Press, 1956. An excellent anthology of materials by Adler, culled from lectures by two of his disciples. The extracts are accompanied by a complete bibliography and critical annotations of the essays.

Bottome, Phyllis. *Alfred Adler: Apostle of Freedom*. New York: G. P. Putnam's Sons, 1939. 3d ed. London: Faber & Faber, 1957. The author's husband was Adler's secretary. For that reason, the information offered in this 315-page biography rests on eyewitness observation and access to primary papers. Bottome believed Adler to be "at once the easiest of men to know and the most difficult, the frankest and the most subtle, the most conciliatory and the most ruthless."

Dreikurs, Rudolf. *Fundamentals of Adlerian Psychology*. New York: Greenberg, 1950. This concise study initially appeared in 1933. Originally written in German, it dates from the decade of Adler's death and reflects his later thinking. It should be supplemented by more recent works.

Grey, Loren. *Alfred Adler, the Forgotten Prophet: A Vision for the Twenty-first Century*. Westport, Conn.: Praeger, 1998. A relatively brief overview of Adler's life and his ideas about psychotheraphy.

Orgler, Hertha. *Alfred Adler, the Man and His Work: Triumph Over the Inferiority Complex*. 3d rev. ed. London: G. W. Daniel, 1963. This classic study, first published in 1939, is a must for beginning research. Drawing on both contemporary and second-generation opinion of Adler and individual psychology, Orgler's book attempts to view the subject in the light of his own growth toward wholeness.

Rallner, Joseph. *Alfred Adler*. Translated by Harry Zohn. New York: Frederick Ungar, 1983. This work by a German scholar is concise yet comprehensive in its treatment.

SEE ALSO: Sigmund Freud; Karen Horney; Helen Keller; Maria Montessori; Harry Stack Sullivan.
RELATED ARTICLES in *Great Events from History: The Twentieth Century:*

1901-1940: 1904: Freud Advances the Psychoanalytic Method; 1930's: Jung Develops Analytical Psychology.

ALVIN AILEY
American dancer and choreographer

Ailey was the first African American to create a multicultural concert dance company. His Alvin Ailey American Dance Theater became internationally renowned for its creative fusion of traditional ballet and modern dance. Ailey not only addressed the racism and injustice faced by blacks in the United States and around the world but also choreographed for performances of white composers.

BORN: January 5, 1931; Rogers, Texas
DIED: December 1, 1989; New York, New York
ALSO KNOWN AS: Alvin Ailey, Jr. (full name)
AREAS OF ACHIEVEMENT: Dance, education

EARLY LIFE

Alvin Ailey (AY-lee) was born in rural Texas to Lula Elizabeth Cliff and Alvin Ailey, Sr. Alvin was a large baby, intensely curious and alert, who "got busy," according to his mother, "as soon as he was born." Abandoned by her husband shortly after Alvin's birth, his mother earned her living picking cotton and cleaning houses for white people.

In his autobiography Ailey recalled the vicious racism of his Texas childhood, but remembered, too, the warm support of the relatives with whom he and his mother lived. Young Ailey absorbed the music and rituals of the African American church but was also exposed to the rough, honky-tonk life of a local saloon and the blues played by traveling musicians. These contrasting experiences would influence his best work.

Ailey attributes his lifelong sense of inferiority that made him undervalue his work to the absence of his father. His mother was often a harsh disciplinarian; nevertheless, their loving relationship sustained him throughout his life. When Ailey was six years old, his mother began living with Amos Alexander, whom Ailey remembered with kindness.

When Ailey was twelve, he and his mother moved to Los Angeles. In a crucial decision, he abandoned his friends who were heading toward a life of crime and chose instead to pursue his artistic interests. At multicultural Jefferson High School, Ailey developed his talent for languages and became a voracious reader. A failure at most sports, he nonetheless excelled at gymnastics, especially floor exercises.

Ailey's teachers took their students to theater and musical performances, inspiring Ailey to haunt the matinees and vaudeville houses in the Los Angeles theater district. He was electrified by a performance of Katherine Dunham's black dance troupe and imagined new possibilities for himself. Encouraged by high school classmates Carmen and Yvonne de Lavallade, Ailey began dance classes with Lester Horton, a white teacher who welcomed black students. After high school, Ailey moved to San Francisco to take college courses, planning to be a teacher. However, at the age of twenty-two, lured by the dance world, he returned to the Horton school to begin his career as a dancer.

LIFE'S WORK

When Horton died of a heart attack in 1953, Ailey began creating original dances for the company. Horton believed that a dance company was a family that collaborated to create their performances, a philosophy Ailey later continued with his own dancers.

Ailey began the practice of keeping notebooks with his choreography directions, poetry, and creative ideas, a practice that would continue for the rest of his life. In 1954 the Horton company performed Ailey's first works, *According to St. Francis* and *Mourning Morning*.

After a brief return to California, Ailey and Carmen de Lavallade went to New York City, performing as lead dancers in the Broadway musical *House of Flowers* (written by Truman Capote). Ailey followed this with a role in the musical *Jamaica*. Although Ailey's technical skills were never highly developed, he was strikingly handsome and commanded the stage with his athletic ability and sensuality. After a brief stage career, he decided to make dance his career.

In 1958, Ailey and his dancers began what Ailey

called "the station wagon tours," driving cross-country in a station wagon packed with stage scenery. One stop was the Jacob's Pillow Dance Festival in Massachusetts. The performance, however, met with a disappointing review. Also in 1958, Ailey choreographed *Blues Suite*, which was performed by a pick-up company of dancers at the Young Men's Hebrew Association (YMHA) at 92nd Street in New York City, a venue for the performing arts. This dance, rooted in his memories of the rough life at the Texas saloon of his childhood, marked the beginning of what would become the Alvin Ailey American Dance Theater.

In 1960, *Revelations*, which was based on the gospel hymns and spirituals from his early church experience, opened at the YMHA. *Revelations* was a highly emotional and spiritual history of black people in America, from the times of slavery to the performance's finale in contemporary times, depicting a rousing portrayal of a church revival meeting, "Rocka My Soul." Both *Blues Suite* and *Revelations* are considered masterpieces of dance theater, and they have been revised and are still performed by the company.

Although funding his young dance company was always a problem, Ailey's work was recognized as breaking new ground in modern dance. He admired the work of George Balanchine, who dominated the field of classical ballet, but disliked the style of Balanchine's dancers, who displayed blank expressions and danced with precise movements. In contrast, Ailey envisioned dance as a performance art, one that was often improvised and expressive of strong personalities. His male dancers were noted for their sensuality and athletic ability. Lighting, costumes, and theatricality distinguished Ailey's work from that of other concert dance companies.

Some criticized Ailey for creating not "serious art" but "entertainment." He also faced the contemporary racism that limited African Americans to the role of a "Negro" dance style. Ailey believed passionately that African American music, art, and dance belonged in the mainstream of American culture. His company was multicultural and included African Americans, Asians, whites, and Latinos.

The company, supported by U.S. government grants and the National Endowment for the Arts, gained an international reputation; it performed in Africa, Asia, and Europe. Ailey loved surprise and often unnerved his dancers by assigning them different roles just before performance time. Despite his frequent temperamental tirades, his dancers remained fiercely loyal to him, and they believed deeply in the mission of the company.

In 1965, Ailey withdrew from the stage to become artistic director of the company. Joining the company that year was Judith Jamison, the statuesque, ballet-trained dancer who would perform lead roles for fifteen years. For Jamison, Ailey created *Cry*, "dedicated to all black women everywhere—especially our mothers." The 1970's and early 1980's were prolific years for Ailey. His dances included *Masekela Language* (1969), *Cry* (1971), *Night Creature* (1975; with the music of Duke Ellington), *Memoria* (1979; in memory of dancer Joyce Trisler), and *For Bird—with Love* (1984; a tribute to Charlie Parker). However, Ailey, feeling intense pressure as someone who was black, gay, and an artist,

Alvin Ailey. (Library of Congress)

was increasingly troubled by personal insecurities. Outwardly charming, he was lonely and had difficulty trusting even those closest to him.

During these years Ailey spent money wildly, abused cocaine and alcohol, and had sexual encounters with men from the street. In 1979 he suffered an emotional breakdown, leading to a public scandal. He was diagnosed as having manic depression (now called bipolar disorder) and spent several months in a mental hospital. Stabilized by the drug lithium, he returned to his creative intensity, although with occasional lapses into his former excesses.

Recognized for his groundbreaking work in modern dance, Ailey received numerous awards, among them the United Nations Peace Medal, the Scripps American Dance Festival Award, and the Kennedy Center Honor for lifetime contribution to American culture through the performing arts.

Ailey died in 1989 from AIDS-related complications. He was buried at Rose Hills Park in Whittier, California.

SIGNIFICANCE

In his brief career, Ailey created seventy-nine original dances that changed the face of modern dance in America and earned him an international reputation. His work continues to be performed by the Alvin Ailey Dance Theater and other dance companies. Under his innovative leadership, African American culture came into the mainstream of American arts. Largely through his efforts, American dance has become multicultural with the racial stereotyping of the past diminished, if not eliminated.

With Jamison as artistic director of the company, Ailey's legacy continued. The company regularly performs throughout the world. The company's smaller repertory ensemble, Ailey II, trains young dancers and performs in schools, hospitals, and prisons. Ailey Camp and the Ailey Dance School provide outreach programs for urban youth in several cities. In 2004 the company established a permanent home at 55th Street and 9th Avenue in Manhattan.

—Marjorie J. Podolsky

FURTHER READING

Ailey, Alvin, with A. Peter Bailey. *Revelations: The Autobiography of Alvin Ailey*. New York: Carol, 1995. A fragmentary autobiography, with the collaboration of A. Peter Bailey, who completed the text after Ailey's death. A frank revelation of Ailey's insecurities, emotional issues, and drug use.

DeFrantz, Thomas. *Dancing Revelations*. New York: Oxford University Press, 2004. An academic treatment of race, gender, and sexuality implicit in Ailey's work. Includes detailed descriptions of his major works.

Dunning, Jennifer. *Alvin Ailey: A Life in Dance*. New York: Da Capo Press, 1998. An acclaimed biography, revealing both Ailey's creative genius and his personal difficulties. Especially valuable are the insights from Ailey's notebooks and Dunning's extensive interviews with those closest to him.

Foulkes, Julia L. *Modern Bodies: Dance and American Modernism from Martha Graham to Alvin Ailey*. Chapel Hill: University of North Carolina Press, 2002. The history and social significance of the American modern dance movement, highlighting Ailey's contribution to modern dance.

Tracy, Robert. *Ailey Spirit: The Journey of an American Dance Company*. New York: Stewart, Tabori & Chang, 2004. A collection of superb color photographs of individuals and groups of dancers in performance, with the history of the company and quotations from dancers. Essential for those who have not seen the company perform.

SEE ALSO: George Balanchine; Mikhail Baryshnikov; Isadora Duncan; Katherine Dunham; Martha Graham; Rudolf Laban; Serge Lifar; Léonide Massine; Vaslav Nijinsky; Rudolf Nureyev; Ruth St. Denis.

RELATED ARTICLES in *Great Events from History: The Twentieth Century*:
1941-1970: October, 1956: Joffrey Founds His Ballet Company; March 30, 1958: Ailey Founds His Dance Company.
1971-2000: 1983-1984: Festivals Mark a Peak in the Dance Created by Black Artists.

JoAnne Akalaitis
American theater director and playwright

Akalaitis was one of the preeminent American theatrical directors of the late twentieth century. Unlike most directors on the commercial stage, she developed her productions using a collaborative method. Her work as a playwright and a director is considered eclectic and avant-garde.

BORN: June 29, 1937; Cicero, Illinois
AREA OF ACHIEVEMENT: Theater and entertainment

EARLY LIFE

JoAnne Akalaitis (ak-a-LI-tihs) was born and reared in a blue-collar suburb of Chicago. Her parents, Clement Akalaitis, a supervisor at General Electric, and Estelle, née Mattis, were of Lithuanian Roman Catholic ancestry. As a child, JoAnne Akalaitis attended Lithuanian school, where she appeared in many plays. Still, she did not pursue her interest in drama when she reached college, preferring instead to take a bachelor's degree in philosophy from the University of Chicago in 1960. Akalaitis won a fellowship to pursue graduate studies in philosophy at Stanford University, but she eventually dropped out of that program and instead used the money to study at the Actor's Workshop in San Francisco. She met her future collaborators there and in workshops with the San Francisco Mime Troupe.

Eager to expand her theatrical experience, Akalaitis moved to New York in 1963 and to Paris in late 1964. In Paris, she collaborated with Lee Breuer and Ruth Maleczech, friends from San Francisco, on a production of *Play by Samuel Beckett* and met other experimental artists, such as composer Nadia Boulanger and director Jerzy Grotowsky. Another participant in the project was American composer Philip Glass, whom Akalaitis married on July 15, 1965.

In 1968, when her first child, Juliet, was six months old, Akalaitis joined Maleczech in studying for a month with Grotowski, the leader of the movement of the "poor," or actor-centered, theater. This experience shaped the rest of Akalaitis's career. She came to the realization that the psychological motivation of a character must have a physical dimension or manifestation. Also, she came to believe that the actor was not just an interpreter of other people's art, but an artist in his or her own right, just as much as the playwright. She said, "I saw a whole development of Stanislavsky that involved the body, that involved my own personal history, and involved my value as an artist."

When she returned to New York, in late 1969, Akalaitis formed a theater collective with Maleczech, Breuer, Glass, and David Warrilow. During the troupe's rehearsals in 1970, which were held in Glass's beach house in Nova Scotia, Canada, Akalaitis was pregnant with her second child. At first, the men in the group expected her and Ruth Maleczech, who was also pregnant, to cook, clean, and care for the babies, in addition to rehearsing all day. She said, "We decided that the men had to wash the dishes and the company had to pay for the babysitter. And at that time, there was resistance to it.... [N]ow it's different, it's accepted."

Akalaitis's desire for the equitable distribution of housekeeping responsibilities continued to manifest itself as her career progressed. Though she and Glass divorced in 1974, they continued to share the upbringing of their children. "He does it three days and I do it three, then we alternate every other Saturday. Because he's involved in performing, I take care of the children when he's on tour, and he takes them when I'm on tour," she said in a 1976 interview.

It was Akalaitis who suggested that the new theater company take the name of a nearby Nova Scotian mining town, Mabou Mines. The troupe debuted its first play, Lee Breuer's *The Red Horse Animation*, at the Guggenheim Museum in New York City in November, 1970.

LIFE'S WORK

"I think all the people involved in the group really started their artistic lives—in a sense we were reborn—when Mabou Mines began," Akalaitis later said about her work with the theatrical group. The group staged several "animations," works that could be considered performance art, under Breuer's direction in the early 1970's. When the Mabou Mines performed three plays by Samuel Beckett at the Theater for the New City Festival, their work caught the attention of New York's theater "establishment," and they were invited to play at Joseph Papp's Public Theater in 1976.

For her direction of her first production, *Cascando*, by Samuel Beckett, with the Mabou Mines company, Akalaitis won her first Obie Award for excellence in an off-Broadway production. From this point on, Akalaitis changed her focus from acting to directing. She went on to stage her own script, *Dressed Like an Egg*, based on the writings of the French novelist Colette, with Mabou

Mines at the Public Theater in 1977. Akalaitis won her second Obie Award for this production.

In 1978, Akalaitis won a Guggenheim Fellowship and used it to cowrite, design, and direct a play about Antarctica, called *Southern Exposure*, with Mabou Mines in 1979. This effort brought her a third Obie Award.

Her 1980 collaboration with Mabou Mines was called *Dead End Kids: A History of Nuclear Power*, about the dangers of atomic energy and weapons. It played at the Public Theater for more than two hundred performances and also found success on tour at regional theaters around the country. The script was made into a film in 1986, which Akalaitis also directed.

Akalaitis won the Rosamond Gilder Award from the New Drama Forum and a Drama Desk Award for her 1981 direction of Franz Xaver Kroetz's *Request Concert*. Also in 1981, Akalaitis acted the role of Mrs. Lammle in the play *Dark Ride* by Len Jenkins. The following year, she directed a piece called *Red and Blue* by Michael Hurson. In 1983, she staged a multimedia production called *The Photographer* with music by her former husband, Philip Glass, at the Next Wave Festival at the Brooklyn Academy of Music.

Akalaitis staged two notable works in 1984. The first was *Through the Leaves* by Franz Xaver Kroetz. Ruth Maleczech and Frederick Neumann, her colleagues from Mabou Mines, won Obie Awards for their acting in this production. Akalaitis went on to direct an unconventional staging of Samuel Beckett's *Endgame* in Cambridge, Massachusetts, at the American Repertory Theater. Beckett became so upset when he learned that she had wavered from his exact stage directions that he threatened to go to court to stop the production. He finally allowed the show to go on, with the provision that his caveat denouncing the production be attached to every play program.

Akalaitis directed another iconoclastic production at the American Repertory Theater late in 1985, a new translation of Jean Genet's *The Balcony*. In 1986, she directed herself and Ruth Maleczech in *Help Wanted* by Franz Xaver Kroetz. In the same year, she traveled to the Mark Taper Forum in Los Angeles to create a work entitled *Green Card*, about the American immigrant experience—a play considered by many to contain the hallmarks of her work as a playwright. In 1987, Akalaitis staged Georg Büchner's play *Leon and Lena* at the Guthrie Theatre in Minneapolis. She returned to that theater in 1989 to direct *The Screens* by Jean Genet.

She finally came to national prominence, however, when she was asked to direct William Shakespeare's *Cymbeline* at the New York Shakespeare Festival in the summer of 1989. In May of 1990, Joseph Papp invited her to become one of his four artistic associates. She accepted, resigning from Mabou Mines, and in 1991 directed Shakespeare's two-part historical drama *Henry IV*.

In August of that year, Joseph Papp, who was suffering from cancer, resigned his post as artistic director of the New York Shakespeare Festival and named Akalaitis as his successor. Her tenure was brief and bitter. That fall, she conducted a town meeting of playwrights to discuss their concerns. She wanted to promote the works of new playwrights in spite of the severe budget cuts that wracked her organization. In the spring of 1992, Akalaitis staged *'Tis Pity She's a Whore* by John Ford. In December, she mounted Georg Büchner's *Woyzeck*. On March 13, 1993, the board of directors of the New York Shakespeare Festival suddenly fired Akalaitis and named African American playwright George C. Wolfe as her replacement. Akalaitis was given scarcely a week to clean out her desk. She had planned to stage Shakespeare's *Henry VIII* that summer for the New York Shakespeare Festival. Instead she directed a Lincoln Center Theater Company production of a play by Jane Bowles called *In the Summer House*, which opened in August.

Apparently, Akalaitis's sudden dismissal was influenced by the savage reviews of her work written by *New York Times* theater critic Frank Rich. Robert Brustein warned, in a 1993 article in *The New Republic*, that Rich and the festival board of directors were, "still in the grip of Reagan-Bush conservatism, despite the recent change in administration, and a bottom-line mentality continues to rule our art." He called this movement New Aesthetic Populism, a "war on the arts" from the center. Brustein stated that Rich exposed his "continuing indifference to art with any depth or daring. . . . It is bad enough for one newspaper to control the destiny of commercial production, but when a powerful critic begins to arbitrate the conduct of non-profit institutions, then a shudder passes through the entire theater community."

Akalaitis concurred with this opinion, saying, "The center of this story is an agenda on the part of *The New York Times*. . . . In this case, it's not that the board [of directors] has a strong opinion—it has no opinion. It's waiting to be told what to think by the newspapers."

Brustein predicted that Akalaitis would continue to be a strong artist who might be better suited to independence than the administrative duties inherent in running a large theater. However, he worried that there might not be any place left that she will want to work, given the conservative nature of the present climate of the cultural world. His prediction proved correct, but his worries were unfounded.

Akalaitis soon found a long-term venue that allows her to practice and teach her style. She became an artist in residence at the Court Theatre in Chicago, cochair of the Direction Program at the Juilliard School, and, beginning in 1998, Wallace Benjamin Flint and L. May Hawver Flint Professor of Theater at Bard College in Annandale-on-Hudson, New York. Her seminars in acting and classes on theater have gained her a reputation for being a quirky, informal, and inspiring professor. She frequently teaches students her famous exercises to prepare actors for their roles during rehearsals. For example, each actor writes the story of the character's life, even for unnamed chorus characters; there are also group physical exercises designed to accustom actors to moving and speaking together. Akalaitis holds classes for her Bard College students in her house, often cooking for them, and she invites philosophers, curators, and actors to be guest speakers.

After her dismissal from the Shakespeare Festival, Akalaitis continued to direct classic plays, investing them with a novel spirit. In 1997 she staged a version of Euripides' Iphigenia Cycle at the Court Theatre. Her version, which combined *Iphigenia at Aulis* and *Iphigenia in Tauris*, contained contemporary flourishes in costuming, scenery, and music (rap music, for example) and won appreciative reviews. Chris Jones, reviewing the tragedy in *American Theatre*, called it one of Akalaitis's finest achievements.

In 2001 she directed a operatic treatment of Franz Kafka's short story "In the Penal Colony" (1914), a horrific tale of a prison dominated by an enigmatic machine that executes prisoners. The music was provided by Glass and the libretto by Rudolph Wurlitzer, and although Akalaitis employed the thoroughgoing collaborativeness for which she is renowned, the spirit of the piece was hers. In one key innovation, she has Kafka appear in the story and uses material from his diaries in the dialogue. She denied that the opera was overtly political (although the opening coincided with the execution of Oklahoma City bomber Timothy McVeigh); instead, she said, the play is about the horror of being an artist.

Among her other projects were *Phèdre* (2003, New York; written 1677), a tragedy by Jean Racine; *The Birthday Party* (2004) by Harold Pinter, a play about psychological torture; *Quartet* (2005, Court Theatre) by Heiner Müller, a play about seduction and murder; and a sequence of four one-act plays by Samuel Beckett in

2007, *Act Without Words* I and II, *Eh Joe,* and *Rough for Theatre*, starring ballet star Mikhail Baryshnikov.

In addition to her five Obie Awards, Akalaitis has received National Endowment for the Arts grants, an Edwin Booth Award, a Rosamund Gilder Award for Outstanding Achievement in Theatre, and a Pew Charitable Trusts National Theatre Artistry Residency Program grant.

SIGNIFICANCE

Frank Rich, the theater critic whose brutal assaults on Akalaitis may have resulted in her downfall, admitted in 1981, "Almost single-handedly she is giving new life to the whole notion of political theater." Her power grew with the nascent women's movement in the late 1960's and early 1970's. She began as a pregnant actor, demanding equality in housekeeping chores with her male counterparts. Even though she was a single mother, she continued in her career, growing more experienced and skilled as a theatrical director. Akalaitis remained true to her artistic vision, even when that meant she had to stand up to Samuel Beckett or to suffer a dismissal from the Shakespeare Festival that Robert Brustein described as "unusually brusque and humiliating."

Akalaitis faced the practical problems of raising a family while working in the theater. She struggled against sexism, anti-intellectualism, and political conservatism. However, she has persisted, providing leadership in the theater world and maintaining integrity in both her personal and professional life.

—*Irene E. McDermott*

FURTHER READING

Brustein, Robert. "Akalaitis Axed." *New Republic*, April 26, 1993. Brustein writes a sympathetic interpretation of the events that led up to Akalaitis's dismissal from her post as artistic director of the New York Shakespeare Festival. He includes a review of the last production there under her tenure, a musical version of the play *Wings* by Arthur Kopit.

Kafka, Alexander C. "A Maverick Theater Director Finds an Appreciative Audience." *Chronicle of Higher Education* 51, no. 4 (September, 17, 2004): A48. Focuses on Akalaitis's work as director of the theater department at Bard College, including her efforts to find an appreciative audience, career background, and influence on her students.

Kalb, Jonathan. "JoAnne Akalaitis." *Theater* 15 (Spring, 1984): 6-13. Kalb interviews Akalaitis on her directing theories. She discusses the projects she was involved in then, such as *Dead End Kids* and *Green Card*. She talks about the importance of her children to her work and the practical problems of being a working single mother.

Kenvin, Roger. "JoAnne Akalaitis." In *Notable Women in the American Theatre: A Biographical Dictionary*. Edited by Alice M. Robinson, Vera Mowry Roberts, and Milly S. Barranger. New York: Greenwood Press, 1989. This is the most scholarly biographical article on Akalaitis available. Covers her career up to her directing debut at the New York Shakespeare Festival.

O'Quinn, Jim. "Change of Will." *American Theatre* 10 (May-June, 1993): 43. O'Quinn gives a factual interpretation of the events that led up to the firing of Akalaitis from the Shakespeare Festival. He summarizes Akalaitis's reaction to the event and the reactions of the American theater world.

Saivetz, Deborah. *An Event in Space: JoAnne Akalaitis in Rehearsal*. Hanover, N.H.: Smith and Kraus, 2000.

Saivetz examines Akalaitis's origins as a cofounder of Mabou Mines and explains how she was influenced by playwrights Jean Genet and Samuel Beckett and other members of the avant-garde. The author also reviews Akalaitis's rehersal exercises and describes her working methods on two major productions.

Sommer, Sally R. "JoAnne Akalaitis." *Drama Review* 20 (September, 1976): 3-16. Sommer interviewed Akalaitis for a special magazine issue subtitled "Actors and Acting." Akalaitis talks about her life as an actress in the collaborative environment of the Mabou Mines and addresses the problems of being a single mother working in the professional theater.

SEE ALSO: Samuel Beckett; Nadia Boulanger; Cheryl Crawford; Jean Genet; Konstantin Stanislavsky.

RELATED ARTICLE in *Great Events from History: The Twentieth Century:*

1971-2000: June, 1986: Akalaitis's *Green Card* Confronts Audiences with Harsh Realities.

ANNA AKHMATOVA
Russian poet

Akhmatova was one of the most acclaimed and revered poets of twentieth century Russia, struggling throughout her life to express with intimacy and insight the plight of women in an adverse society. For long periods she was forbidden to publish her works, but by the end of her life her poetic inspiration of others had earned for her the International Taormina Poetry Prize (Italy, 1964) and an honorary degree from the University of Oxford in England in 1965.

BORN: June 23, 1889; Bol'shoy Fontan, near Odessa, Ukraine, Russian Empire (now in Ukraine)

DIED: March 5, 1966; Domodedovo, near Moscow, Soviet Union (now in Russia)

ALSO KNOWN AS: Anna Andreyevna Gorenko (birth name)

AREA OF ACHIEVEMENT: Literature

EARLY LIFE

Anna Akhmatova (awk-MAH-toh-vah) was born Anna Andreyevna Gorenko, the daughter of Andrei Gorenko, a naval officer who left the military soon after her birth to take a position as maritime engineer with the government. This position required him to move to Tsarskoe

Selo (now Pushkin), a town near the capital city of St. Petersburg (now Leningrad) in which one of the czar's palaces was located together with the residences of many of the nobles and highly placed government functionaries. This move well suited Anna's mother, the aristocratic Inna Erazmovna (née Stogova), since her family, the Stogovs, claimed a noble heritage. She liked to socialize with the nobility, yet she took pride in her early associations with members of the "People's Will" Party of radicals who had assassinated Czar Alexander II in 1881. This ambiguity of sympathies had the effect on young Anna and her four siblings, Inna, Andrei, Iya, and Victor, of restraining them from political alignments throughout their lives.

Anna grew up in the privileged atmosphere of Tsarskoe Selo, attending school in the same town where the great poet Alexander Pushkin had once been a student. She was attracted to poetry and could recite both French and Russian verse from memory. She attended poetry readings at the home of Innokenty Annensky, an influential Symbolist poet, and began to write verse of her own in about 1904. Through her elder brother, she met the talented young poet Nikolai Gumilyov, who was immediately attracted to her. Anna's slim figure and distinctive

Anna Akhmatova (front row center) receives an honorary degree, Oxford, 1965. (Hulton Archive/Getty Images)

face, with its slightly humped Roman nose, gave her a prepossessive presence that later attracted the attention of artists. Gumilyov courted her persistently, sponsoring her into participation in the "Guild of Poets," an organization seminal to the development of "Acmeism," a philosophy of poetry that demanded communicative clarity and a sense of connection with the poetic heritage of Western Europe. In 1907, Gumilyov was the first to publish one of Anna's poems in his journal *Sirius*. It was in this year also that Anna's father's extravagant lifestyle and his constant womanizing caused a separation in the Gorenko family. Anna went to Kiev with her mother, finishing her studies at the Fundukleevskaya Gymnaziya there and enrolling in the faculty of law at the Kiev College for Women. She soon withdrew from the study of law and moved back to St. Petersburg to study literature. It was at this time that she chose the pseudonym "Akhmatova," the name of her maternal great-grandmother, a Tatar princess. She took a pseudonym at the request of her father that the Gorenko family not be embarrassed by her publication of poetry.

LIFE'S WORK

In 1910, Akhmatova married Gumilyov. For the next two years they traveled abroad, spending much of the time in Paris, where Akhmatova became friendly with the still unknown artist Amadeo Modigliani, who sketched her as a dancer and as an Egyptian queen. The marriage, however, soon foundered, with both Akhmatova and Gumilyov chafing under its traditional confinements. Gumilyov traveled on his own to Abyssinia to collect African folk songs, and Akhmatova returned to stay with her mother at a cousin's estate to give birth to her son, Lev Nikolayevich Gumilyov, in October of 1912. In 1912 also, Akhmatova's first collection of verse, *Vecher* (evening), appeared. The collection's lyrics on a young woman's realization of love and her expectation of grief brought Akhmatova both acclaim and popularity in a degree only to be envied by Gumilyov. The subsequent successes of Akhmatova's collections—*Chetki* (1914; rosary) and *Belaia staia* (1917; white flock)—and her long poem, "U samogo morya" (1914; "By the Seashore," 1969), only served to increase their estrangement. In

1914, Gumilyov joined the cavalry and went off to fight in World War I, where he was decorated for bravery. Akhmatova stayed with a succession of friends, leaving her son to be reared by Gumilyov's widowed mother.

The social turmoil associated with the end of the war, the Russian Revolution of 1917, and the subsequent civil war effectively beheaded the country, with a great many intellectuals and people of established artistic reputations leaving to live and work elsewhere. Akhmatova, however, would not leave, even though her life became more difficult. In 1918, she divorced Gumilyov to marry Vladimir Shileiko, a scholar of Assyrian antiquity who opposed his wife's poetic activities. Nevertheless, Akhmatova managed to publish the collection *Podorozhnik* (1921; plantain), giving therein her poetic refusal to emigrate. She visited frequently with other poets, including Osip Mandelstam, and she attended the funeral of Aleksandr Blok. In 1921 she grieved over the death of Gumilyov, who was executed by the Soviet Cheka for his alleged involvement in a counterrevolutionary plot. In the 1922 collection *Anno Domini MCMXXI*, a distinctly religious dimension is evident in Akhmatova's lyric ponderings on love and human travail.

From 1922 until 1940, Akhmatova was unable to publish any new works of poetry. She was considered an "internal émigré" whose apolitical works were incompatible with the new criterion of social utility. She continued work on a collection she called *Trostnik* (1926-1940; the reed), dedicating poems to Mandelstam and to Boris Pasternak, and she wrote some scholarly articles on the life and works of Pushkin. The mass arrests of the 1930's included many people close to Akhmatova. Mandelstam was arrested, released, and arrested again, finally to perish in the labor camps. Marina Tsvetayeva, another major poetess of modern Russia and a poetic admirer of Akhmatova, was arrested soon after returning from emigration and shortly after an emotional meeting with Akhmatova in Moscow. Akhmatova's son Lev was arrested twice, the second time being released only to fight in World War II. Her companion since 1926 (she divorced Shileiko in 1928), art critic Nikolai Punin, was also arrested. Akhmatova's response to all this suffering is contained in the monumental poetic dirge *Rekviem* (1963; *Requiem*, 1964), which was finished in 1940 but remained unpublished in the Soviet Union. In 1940 also, Akhmatova was allowed to prepare an edition of her early works entitled *Iz shesti knig* (from six books), but this edition was quickly withdrawn from publication. That same year she began work on her beautiful poetic opus *Poema bez geroa* (1960; *A Poem Without a*

Hero, 1973), which she continued to perfect until her death.

World War II occasioned a relaxation of the governmental strictures on poetry, and Akhmatova, who was living in Leningrad during the early days of the terrible Nazi siege, was allowed to speak to her fellow Leningraders by radio, inspiring them with her poetry and her words of encouragement. In October of 1941, however, Akhmatova was evacuated, first to Moscow, and then to Tashkent, from which a collection of selected early verse was published in 1943. The publication of her poem "Muzhestvo" ("Courage," 1976) in the Communist Party newspaper *Pravda* in 1942 had signaled her temporary return to governmental grace, and her poems were subsequently published in several journals. After the war, however, the Communist Party decided to reimpose the former controls on literature, choosing specifically to reorganize two journals, *Zvezda* and *Leningrad*, and to denounce Akhmatova and the humorist Mikhail Zoshchenko, who had been published in them. Akhmatova, termed "half-nun, half-harlot" by Stalinist stalwart Andrei Zhdanov, was subsequently expelled from the Soviet Writers Union. Akhmatova's son Lev was arrested once more, only to be released in 1956 after Nikita S. Khrushchev's denunciation of Joseph Stalin's "cult of personality" and the associated "thaw" in the Soviet social and artistic climate. Akhmatova survived this period on a meager pension by selling translations of verse from several languages to others. Several volumes of these translations have since been published as separate imprints. One cycle of poems, *V khvale mira* (1950; in praise of peace), was ostensibly written in conformance to governmental canon to ease the plight of her son.

After 1958, Akhmatova was officially "rehabilitated." An edition of her earlier poetry, supplemented by more recent works, was published under the title *Beg vremeni* (1965; the flight of time). A large new collection, *Sed'maya kniga* (1965; partial translation as *The Seventh Book*, 1976), containing poetic musings on poetry itself, on symbolism, and on death, as well as parts of *A Poem Without a Hero*, was also published. Approaching her seventies and ailing from a weakened heart, Akhmatova was recognized as the "grande dame" of Russian letters. She began to act as a mentor to others, protesting, for example, the internal exile of the young Joseph Brodsky, a future Nobel laureate. She met the famed American poet Robert Frost. In 1964, she traveled abroad to receive the Taormina Poetry Prize in Italy, and in 1965 she was awarded an honorary doctorate at the University of Oxford in England. Her death in March of 1966 deprived

Russian literature of a great poet. Her body was flown from Moscow to Leningrad, where it lay in state, visited by hundreds, in the Nikolsky Cathedral. She is buried in the town of Komarovo.

SIGNIFICANCE

Millions of Russians know at least one Akhmatova poem by heart, many of them committing their individual favorite to memory at a time when the poem's publication was banned. Many Russian poets have imitated Akhmatova's dirgelike recitation style. They admire her not only for the quality of her poetry but also for her lifelong advocacy of poetry as an enrichment of life, as a catalyst to sharing life's most profound values with others. Her poetry was mature from its very beginnings and is often praised for its intimacy of expression and for its touching insights into the human condition. She was especially sensitive to the problems faced by women in society, and she consciously served as a role model for later numbers of feminist poets.

Akhmatova was clearly apolitical in her achievements, appealing instead to the emotional bases of human existence, yet she remained loyal to her beloved Russian people through the sternest of its governmental trials of her. Recognizing her genius for expression of the deepest emotions and the loftiest thoughts, Akhmatova was ever true to her talent, persevering to transmit her gift to others despite the most constant and daunting of hardships. Her love lyrics and her poetic explorations of grief are regarded to be among the finest in any language. Translations of her verse and international scholarship concerning her verse and her life have ensured for her a prominent place in world literature.

—Lee B. Croft

FURTHER READING

Akhmatova, Anna A. *Poems*. Translated by Lyn Coffin, with an introduction by Joseph Brodsky. New York: W. W. Norton, 1983. Selected, high-quality verse translations of Akhmatova's poems, including several not found elsewhere. The insightful introduction by Brodsky lends the book biographical and critical significance.

_____. *Poems of Akhmatova*. Translated by Stanley Kunitz, with an introduction by Kunitz and Max Hayward. Boston: Little, Brown, 1973. A concise biographical sketch by Max Hayward, together with verse translations by Kunitz. A nice feature of this collection is that it pairs Akhmatova's Russian versions with Kunitz's translations on opposing pages.

_____. *Selected Poems*. Edited by Walter Arndt. Translated by Arndt, Robin Kemball, and Carl R. Proffer. Ann Arbor, Mich.: Ardis, 1976. This collection includes a fine article entitled "The Akhmatova Phenomenon" and a chronicle of Akhmatova's life. The translations are especially well done and well explained by notes.

Driver, Sam N. *Anna Akhmatova*. New York: Twayne, 1972. This is the first English biography, written six years after Akhmatova's death. The first third of the book deals with biographical facts and the remainder with a thematic explanation of the poetry. It is a concise yet scholarly work, and perhaps the best primary introduction to Akhmatova's life.

Feinstein, Elaine. *Anna of All the Russias: The Life of Anna Akhmatova*. New York: Knopf, 2006. A comprehensive biography based on newly acquired material, including memoirs, letters, journals, and interviews. Feinstein outlines the price Akhmatova paid for her political and personal passions.

Gerstein, Emma. *Moscow Memoirs: Memories of Anna Akhmatova, Osip Mandelstam, and Literary Russia Under Stalin*. Edited and translated by John Crowfoot. Woodstock, N.Y.: Overlook Press, 2004. Gerstein, a literary scholar in the Soviet Union, recounts her friendships with Akhmatova and other prominent writers, describing how they coped with and suffered from the political repression of their era.

Haight, Amanda. *Anna Akhmatova: A Poetic Pilgrimage*. New York: Oxford University Press, 1976. A substantially more detailed biographical treatment of Akhmatova's life by a Western scholar personally acquainted with Akhmatova. This work is a valuable resource for specialists as well as general readers.

Ketchian, Sonia. *The Poetry of Anna Akhmatova: A Conquest of Time and Space*. Munich: Otto Sagner Verlag, 1986. A brilliant scholarly study of themes and method in Akhmatova's poetry. Here, too, is a complete inclusion and recapitulation of recent Akhmatova scholarship, both Soviet and Western. The work, however, would appeal primarily to literary scholars.

Mandelstam, Nadezhda. *Hope Against Hope: A Memoir*. Translated by Max Hayward, with an introduction by Clarence Brown. New York: Atheneum, 1976. This memoir by Mandelstam's widow includes many glimpses into Akhmatova's life as well and is especially valuable to those wishing to understand what a poet's life was like in the Soviet Union of the Stalin era.

Rosslyn, Wendy. *The Prince, the Fool, and the Nunnery: The Religious Theme in the Early Poetry of Anna Akhmatova.* Amersham, England: Avebury, 1984. An examination of the interplay of religion and love in Akhmatova's early collections, this book also contains considerable biographical detail. Poems are included in both Russian and English translation.

SEE ALSO: Aleksandr Blok; Vladimir Mayakovsky; Boris Pasternak; Marina Tsvetayeva.
RELATED ARTICLE in *Great Events from History: The Twentieth Century:*
   1941-1970: November, 1962: Solzhenitsyn Depicts Life in a Soviet Labor Camp in *One Day in the Life of Ivan Denisovich.*

AKIHITO
Emperor of Japan (r. 1989-   )

By linking the ancient traditions of Japan to the modern age, Emperor Akihito, Japan's nonpolitical head of state, came to symbolize his nation's commitment to democracy in the face of its militaristic past.

BORN: December 23, 1933; Tokyo, Japan
ALSO KNOWN AS: Akihito Tsugu-no-miya
AREAS OF ACHIEVEMENT: Government and politics, monarchy

EARLY LIFE

The news of the birth of Akihito (ah-kee-hee-toh) was the cause of great celebration among the Japanese people. Within court circles, there was considerable pressure on Emperor Hirohito to take a concubine because his wife, the former Princess Nagako Kuni, had provided only four daughters. Had a son not been born, the military might have made the lack of a male heir the official excuse to depose Hirohito, who was opposed to Japan's increasing militarism at home and abroad. Japanese tradition demanded a continuous, unbroken line of male heirs succeeding the founder of Japan's imperial dynasty, the Sun Goddess, Amaterasu.

Named Akihito (shining pinnacle of virtue) Tsugu-no-miya (prince of the august succession and enlightened benevolence) during a name-bestowing ceremony (*gomeimei shiki*) on December 29, 1933, Japan's crown prince was bathed in sanctified water in a bathtub hewn from rare and costly woods. Akihito's naming document was placed in a lacquered casket wrapped in cloth of gold and presented at the Imperial Shrine on the grounds of Tokyo's Imperial Palace to bestow the blessings of the gods on the new prince.

For his third birthday, the crown prince was dressed in a red suit to celebrate the end of his babyhood and his wearing of white clothes. By tradition, Akihito was taken from his parents at age three and given his own separate residence in a wing of Omiya Villa, the home of his paternal grandmother, the Dowager Empress Sadako. There he was raised by court chamberlains, visiting his parents on weekends, when they shared dinners together. In 1940, Crown Prince Akihito entered Gakushuin, or Peers School, continuing the educational tradition of previous Japanese emperors. During the Allied bombings of Japan, Akihito was taken to the mountains for safety. When the war was over, Akihito witnessed the devastation of war firsthand when he returned to Tokyo and saw his former residence reduced to ashes on the Imperial Palace grounds.

The 1945 Japanese surrender and Hirohito's renunciation of his divinity coincided with a proposal by Prince Higashikuni, Hirohito's cousin, that the emperor abdicate in favor of the twelve-year-old crown prince with Hirohito's oldest brother, Prince Chichibu, as regent. The proposal did not gain widespread support, largely because General Douglas MacArthur respected the emperor and preferred keeping him on the throne.

Akihito's education continued after the war in the reorganized Gakushuin Junior High and Senior High Schools at Koganei Palace. In a letter written by Empress Nagako to her son dated August 30, 1945, the empress urged Akihito to study hard and endure the unendurable without making mistakes to establish a great nation and to turn bad luck into good. During the Allied occupation, Akihito was reportedly rebuked by his father, the emperor, because he had developed a fondness for Spam and Hershey Bars. Hirohito admonished his son to live like his people and share their privations, which included a diet of plain brown rice and an occasional sweet potato.

The decision to hire Elizabeth Gray Vining, an American Quaker, to teach Akihito English, was entirely the emperor's. Akihito's young life was frequently characterized as lonely. He was expected to keep his grief, anguish, and fears to himself. Opportunities to speak out and show his feelings were always denied him. Vining's task was to expand the crown prince's contacts with other boys his age, which she did by including in the tutoring sessions the sons of selected officials or former nobles, and Akihito's younger brother Prince Masahito. In addition to teaching Akihito English, Vining also helped Akihito understand Western culture and democracy. In 1951, Crown Prince Akihito finished his high school curriculum and entered the political and economics department at Gakushuin University. On November 10, 1952, Akihito was formally declared of age and *kotaishi*, imperial heir. He received the crown of adulthood and promised the emperor to be ever conscious of his station, cultivate virtue, and carry knowledge into new fields. Akihito was also ready to begin the search for a wife.

LIFE'S WORK

After World War II and the imposition on Japan of an American-style constitution, members of the imperial family were no longer required to select spouses from among the old aristocracy, whose titles and positions had been abolished. The Imperial Household Agency, which regulates the daily lives of the emperor and his family, began a search, determined that Japan's future empress should come from one of the old families or a family of good name and have been educated at the Gakushuin School for women. Akihito's choice was Michiko Shoda, the daughter of a prominent industrialist who had been educated at a Roman Catholic school. The crown prince had met her on the tennis courts at Kuruizawa, an exclusive resort in the Japanese mountains. Shoda's family discouraged her from accepting the proposal, fearful of the burdens that membership in the imperial family would impose on their daughter. However, Akihito's persistence won over Shoda, and they were married April 10, 1959.

Akihito's marriage to a commoner marked the first time the son of an emperor had married outside the aristocracy. Crown Princess Michiko met with opposition from among the old court and the Empress Nagako. Reputedly, the stress created by the imperial court's "old guard" forced Crown Princess Michiko into a period of seclusion for four months. Nevertheless, within the first decade of their marriage, three children were born to Akihito and Michiko, sons Naruhito and Akishino, and a daughter, Sayako.

Crown Prince Akihito frequently traveled overseas on behalf of Emperor Hirohito and has visited thirty-seven nations. In 1953, Akihito represented Japan at the coronation of Queen Elizabeth II. The United States was the first nation that the crown prince and his wife visited together after their marriage. As members of the imperial family, the crown prince and princess annually participated in the New Year's reception, New Year's lectures, New Year's poetry readings, and imperial garden parties. Akihito and Michiko's travels within Japan focus on educational, cultural, and social welfare projects. The crown prince was the honorary president or patron of the Third Asian Games (1958), the International Sports Games for the Disabled (1964), the Pacific Science Congress (1966), the Universiade in Tokyo (1967), the Japan World Exposition in Osaka (1970), and the International Skill Contest for the Disabled (1981).

Crown Prince Akihito and Princess Michiko in 1976. (Hulton Archive/Getty Images)

Akihito is a noted ichthyologist and for more than twenty-five years has made a taxonomic study of gobiid fish. A member of the Ichthyological Society of Japan, Akihito has published twenty-six papers in the society's journal, and in 1985 he was selected the society's honorary president at the Second International Conference on Indo-Pacific Fishes. Akihito has written entries on the species of gobiid fishes that were published in 1984 in *The Fishes of the Japanese Archipelago* as well as the introduction to a special issue of *Science* devoted to "Science in Japan." He is both an elected and honorary member of the Linnaean Society of London. As crown prince, Akihito developed a great interest in natural life, conservation, and history. He is also an avid tennis player, swimmer, skier, and horseback rider. He is fond of both classical music and jazz and plays chamber music on the cello accompanied by his wife on the harp or piano and his eldest son on viola.

Because of Hirohito's extended battle with cancer, starting in 1987, Akihito assumed more of the emperor's duties, including the opening of the Diet, placing the imperial seal on state documents, and receiving foreign ambassadors. On the death of Hirohito on January 7, 1989, Akihito became emperor, receiving the sacred sword, necklace, and mirror, the symbols of the imperial authority. Emperor Akihito adopted the reign name of Heisei, meaning "peace fulfilled" or "achieving peace." Court astrologers designated November 12, 1990, for Akihito's accession to the Chrysanthemum Throne. The date corresponded to the *daijosai*, or great food-offering ritual, during which Akihito would commune with the sun goddess and emerge transformed into a *kami*, or godlike being. The ceremony was not without controversy because the rituals involved ancient Shinto rites that were associated with Japan's pre-World War II militaristic past. Several of Japan's political parties boycotted the enthronement ceremonies.

As emperor, Akihito has traveled to Korea, China, Thailand, Malaysia, and Indonesia, countries previously occupied by Japan during World War II. In each nation, Akihito delivered a strongly worded apology for Japan's wartime behavior. Akihito emphasizes that Japan is now a nation of peace. In 1994, a planned visit to and expression of regret at Pearl Harbor by Akihito was postponed because of opposition from Japanese rightists. Emperor Akihito's visit to Great Britain in 1998 was strongly opposed by British survivors of Japanese concentration camps, who turned their backs on the royal coach carrying Queen Elizabeth and Emperor Akihito to Buckingham Palace. Akihito expressed sorrow for the wartime

suffering of British former prisoners of war, but the emperor's purely symbolic role prevented him from expressing a stronger statement or offering financial compensation. That remains the responsibility of the elected Japanese government.

Akihito has been mandated to perform his duties as sanctioned by Japan's postwar constitution. He must remain above politics and refrain from any political commentary. He signs political documents, greets foreign dignitaries, opens the Diet, and presides over state banquets. Akihito is responsible for the maintenance of Shinto shrines and performing more than forty religious events each year. Each event is officially commemorated by the emperor's writing a poem.

In the twenty-first century, Japan's imperial family presents to the nation the image of a popular nuclear family. Additional media coverage is given to the activities of Empress Michiko and the wives of the emperor's two sons. The Heisei court is more open, and many barriers between the imperial family and the people have been removed. The imperial family speaks directly to ordinary citizens and visits the elderly, handicapped, orphans, and others in need. The emperor and empress visit the sites of major natural disasters and personally comfort victims. They attend concerts and exhibitions, and have even been seen dancing in public. The emperor's official car stops for red lights as required of any Japanese citizen. Nevertheless, although the imperial court is more accessible to the media, Japan still maintains strong censorship laws that prevent direct comment or criticism about the emperor and his family.

In the two decades since Akihito's ascension, the emperor and the imperial family are more visible to the Japanese people but still isolated behind the walls of the Imperial Palace under the protection of the Imperial Household Agency. Carefully scripted press conferences allow the emperor and empress to answer only previously submitted questions from the press corps. The emperor and empress have traveled to each of Japan's forty-seven prefectures, putting a more human face on the imperial institution, and at the discretion of the government, they represent Japan at major international events. Controversy surrounding the emperor comes from the militaristic legacy of Japan during the emperor's childhood and World War II. Asian and European nations are still seeking apologies for Japanese occupation of their lands and other grievances. Such apologies can come from the emperor only with governmental approval. When Emperor Akihito visited the former Japanese island of Saipan in 2005 to honor Japan's war dead with Shinto ceremonies, there was some international unease about whether Japan was reviving its prewar militaristic stance.

Although the emperor remains above criticism, the empress has had several bouts of a loss of voice and stress-related illnesses that seem to come from subtle attacks on her role as an overbearing presence on the emperor. The 2005 wedding of the imperial couple's only daughter, Princess Sayako, to a commoner generated public discussion of the inequities facing women born into the imperial family: They lose their titles, incomes, and residences by marriage to outsiders while the emperor's sons retain all rights and see their wives raised from commoners to members of the imperial family. The attendance of the emperor and empress at the wedding of their daughter at the Imperial Hotel in Tokyo was a major break with tradition.

The daughters of the imperial family became a topic of discussion in the 1990's and early twenty-first century when the emperor and empress's two sons, Naruhito and Akishino, had married but neither had produced a male heir. Crown Prince Naruhito, the heir apparent, married Masako Owada in 1993, but the marriage had produced only a daugher, Aiko, in 2001. Prince Akishino, the second son, had married Kiko Kawashima in 1990, but his marriage had resulted in only daughters Mako (1991) and Kako (1994). The Japanese government considered revising the laws of succession to allow Crown Prince Naruhito's only child, a daughter, to succeed. The discussion of female succession led to a great national debate, giving the emperor and the imperial family more visibility than normally allowed. Historically, before the adoption in 1868 of a Western-style constitution, Japan had been governed at different times by regent empresses. Rumors circulated that Crown Princess Masako had suffered a nervous breakdown over her inability to produce a male heir and the severity of court protocol that restricted her relationships and personal and professional contacts. The announcement in January, 2006, that Prince Akishino's wife was pregnant persuaded the government to temporarily shelve any succession law changes. The birth of Prince Hisahito in late 2006 has apparently ended the current debate on allowing female succession, although the issue has created more attention to the rights of full equality for Japanese women.

SIGNIFICANCE

Although the role of the emperor of Japan is not what it was in the years before World War II, to some people and nations, the emperor remains a symbol of nationalism and militarism. The Japanese diet's decision to restore the pre-World War II national anthem and officially adopt the Rising Sun flag generated concern about an increase in Japanese nationalism. Although the Japanese constitution renounces war and forbids the maintenance of a military force, Japan's parliament is reviewing major changes to the constitution that would allow the conversion of its police forces into regular armed forces.

The perception of the role of the emperor and the imperial family, however, has changed with the ascension of the first emperor to never claim divinity. The public criticism of the movement to allow female succession revealed a generational divide between younger and female Japanese and older, more patriarchal citizens. As emperor, Akihito is the historical, ceremonial, and cultural symbol of a Japanese nation in transition that remains committed to democracy as it restores selected imperial traditions. Emperor Akihito is the mortal, not divine, link between the Japanese people, their past, and future.

—William A. Paquette

FURTHER READING

Behr, Edward. *Hirohito, Behind the Myth*. New York: Villard Books, 1989. A detailed analysis of the controversial reign of Hirohito and a discussion about the role of the new emperor, Akihito, in modern Japan.

Bix, Herbert P. *Hirohito and the Making of Modern Japan*. New York: HarperCollins, 2000. A controversial study using previously unpublished primary sources to reveal Hirohito's intimate involvement in the events leading to and including World War II and his acceptance of General MacArthur's conditions to enable the monarchy to survive.

Fujitani, T. *Splendid Monarchy and Pageantry in Modern Japan*. San Diego: University of California Press, 1998. A study of the Japanese monarchy in the twentieth century chronicling the institution's adaptations in order to survive.

Lebra, Takie Sugiyama. "Self and Other in Esteemed Status: The Changing Culture of Japanese Royalty from Showa and Heisei." *Journal of Japanese Studies* 23, no. 2 (Summer, 1997): 257-289. A comparative study of the changing role accorded Japan's imperial family during the reigns of Hirohito and Akihito.

Packard, Jerrold M. *Sons of Heaven: A Portrait of the Japanese Monarchy*. New York: Charles Scribner's Sons, 1987. Provides a well-written history of the culture and traditions surrounding Japan's imperial family, the world's oldest.

Philomene, Marie, and Masako Saito, eds. *Tomoshibi Light*. New York: Weatherhill, 1991. A collection of poetry written by Emperor Akihito and Empress Michiko during their travels that continues the imperial family's tradition of composing poems in the form known as *waka*.

Seagrave, Sterling, and Peggy Seagrave. *The Yamato Dynasty*. New York: Broadway Books, 1999. The authors challenge the traditional view of the imperial family's neutral and uninvolved status in the events leading to World War II and Japan's defeat.

Simon, Charlie May. *The Sun and the Birch: The Story of Crown Prince Akihito and Crown Princess Michiko*. New York: E. P. Dutton, 1960. Biographical sketches of Japan's future emperor and empress obtained from press reports and palace communications at the time of their 1959 wedding.

Vining, Elizabeth Gray. *Windows for the Crown Prince*. Philadelphia: J. B. Lippincott, 1952. A biography of Crown Prince Akihito, written by his Quaker American teacher. Covers Akihito's life from 1946 to 1950.

SEE ALSO: Elizabeth II; Ichirō Hatoyama; Hirohito; Hayato Ikeda; Douglas MacArthur.

RELATED ARTICLES in *Great Events from History: The Twentieth Century:*
> **1941-1970:** May 3, 1947: Japan Becomes a Constitutional Democracy; May 3, 1947: Japanese Constitution Grants New Rights to Women.

FIRST VISCOUNT ALANBROOKE
British military leader

Brooke became the chief spokesman for British strategic priorities during World War II. More than any other English military leader, he helped to shape the strategy that brought victory to the Western Allies in the war.

BORN: July 23, 1883; Bagnères de Bigorre, France
DIED: June 17, 1963; Hartley Wintney, Hampshire, England
ALSO KNOWN AS: Alan Francis Brooke (birth name); Baron Alanbrooke of Brookeborough; Sir Alan Francis Brooke
AREAS OF ACHIEVEMENT: Military affairs, diplomacy

EARLY LIFE

First Viscount Alanbrooke was born Alan Francis Brooke, the sixth son of Sir Victor Brooke and Alice Bellingham Brooke. Both of his parents belonged to the Protestant Ascendancy class in Ireland. This class, and his family, the fighting Brookes of Colebrooke, County Fermanagh, had a long tradition of military service to the British crown. That Brooke was born and grew up in France was a consequence of his mother's preference for the sun of southern France over the Irish climate. Privately educated, young Brooke spoke fluent French and German, while his English matured more slowly.

At age eighteen, Brooke entered the Royal Military Academy, Woolwich, to prepare for the traditional family vocation. With a fine mind for mathematics, he was well suited for the Royal Field Artillery, into which he was commissioned in 1902. In 1909, he was accepted into the prestigious Royal Horse Artillery.

In 1914, Brooke married Jane Richardson, daughter of Colonel John Richardson, and the marriage produced a son and a daughter. Jane Richardson Brooke died following an auto accident in 1925. Four years later, Brooke married Benita Lees, daughter of Sir Harold Pelly and widow of Sir Thomas Lees, who had died of wounds in World War I. The second marriage also produced one son and one daughter. Brooke had his full share of personal tragedy, his younger daughter dying from a riding accident in 1961 when he was in old age. Brooke's second wife brought a calming influence to his finely strung temperament, however, and the marriage was a constant, vital source of strength to him throughout his most strenuous years of service.

During World War I, Brooke served on the main front in France. His work in handling artillery was rated outstanding, and when war ended in 1918 he was a brevet lieutenant colonel and had been awarded the Distinguished Service Order and bar. His interwar appointments testified to his growing reputation as a thoughtful professional soldier. He was selected for the first postwar Army Staff College course in 1919, and he returned as an instructor in 1923. He was also an early student at the new Imperial Defense College, which stressed interservice and political-military relationships in wartime. There, too, he later returned as an instructor. He was appointed Commandant of the School of Artillery in 1929. In the 1930's, Brooke commanded an infantry brigade and later Great Britain's only mobile division, forerunner of the armored divisions of World War II. In August, 1939, he was appointed commander in chief, Southern Command. His command was transformed on the outbreak of war into the Second Army Corps of the British Expeditionary Force (BEF), which was sent to the Continent to stand beside the French army, as in 1914.

In September, 1939, Brooke was a fifty-six-year-old corps commander who had added to his expertise as a gunner the experience of commanding infantry and armored units. His staff and defense college studies had allowed him to examine closely, and to think carefully about, the business of war. Brooke was a man of medium build, with dark features; his eyes, set off by his prominent nose, had a quizzical look and gave to his face an owl-like appearance that was not misleading, for the owl is a traditional symbol of wisdom. Many found Brooke's austere professionalism somewhat forbidding. In fact, he was a rather shy, private man of highly strung temperament. The discipline of military command did not allow him the luxury of easy comradeship. He was, and all who knew him sensed that he was, a master of his chosen craft.

LIFE'S WORK

The main German offensive in the west came in May, 1940, and it quickly isolated the Allied forces in northern France and Belgium from the bulk of the Allied armies to the south of the Somme River. These northern forces, including the bulk of the BEF, fell back toward the sea around the port of Dunkirk. Brooke commanded the Second Army Corps with distinction during the difficult withdrawal into the Dunkirk perimeter, successfully coping with the crisis on the BEF's northern flank created by the Belgian army's surrender. Only when he was ordered back to England did Brooke's composure momentarily fail him: He turned over command of his corps on the beach at La Panne with tears streaming down his cheeks.

On his return to England, Brooke was asked to build up a new BEF south of the Somme in France. This was the desire of the United Kingdom's new prime minister, Winston Churchill, who saw it as necessary to bolster the French will to resist. Brooke, on return to France, quickly saw that the French will to go on was itself gone. He urged withdrawal of what British troops remained in France before it was too late. Churchill, with his indomitable will and perseverance, was reluctant to accept

First Viscount Alanbrooke. (Library of Congress)

Brooke's advice. The first encounter of the two men was thus a telephone conversation between Le Mans and London, and it set the tone for their future relationship. The prime minister's inspired leadership at times ran beyond what it was possible to accomplish, and Brooke's professional judgment and powers of lucid argument would be required to save Churchill from himself. The prime minister yielded to Brooke's persuasion, and nearly 140,000 British troops got back home in this second evacuation.

In July, 1940, Brooke was appointed commander in chief of the home forces and was thus entrusted with the task of defeating the anticipated German invasion of England. It never came, but Brooke's appointment signified the confidence placed in him. In late 1941, Churchill asked Brooke to become Chief of the Imperial General Staff (CIGS) in succession to his close friend, Field Marshal Sir John Dill. The latter had found the task of working with the prime minister an exhausting chore that disintegrated too often into unproductive argument. The heart of the problem was that in Churchill's strength there lay potential weaknesses. His great courage, formidable willpower, and inexhaustible energy inspired Great Britain's whole war effort but also tended to outrun military resources; the soldiers could not do the impossible. The prime minister took all restraint badly. He expected the military to turn every post into a winning post and was upset when they did not. He could not resist poking and prodding field commanders to act, even against their better judgment. Sometimes the prime minister was right to do so, but as a rule it was asking for trouble. One task of the CIGS was to stand between the prime minister and field commanders and interpret each to the other. Brooke took up the post understanding what lay ahead for him in working with Churchill: "I have the greatest respect for him and a real affection for him so that I hope I may be able to stand the storms of abuse which I may well have to bear frequently!" When the United States entered the war in December, 1941, Brooke persuaded Churchill to take Field Marshal Dill with him to Washington, where the prime minister sought to forge a common strategy with the Americans and to leave Dill there as head of the British Military Mission. This was inspired advice, for Dill quickly gained the trust and respect of the Americans and helped smooth out many Allied difficulties.

In March, 1942, Brooke became chair of the Chiefs of Staff Committee, where he sat with his navy and air force colleagues to formulate British military strategy in conjunction with the prime minister, who was also minister of defense. In effect, Brooke became Great Britain's leading military spokesperson, both to his own government and to Great Britain's allies. Neither of these relationships was an easy one. Brooke and Churchill at times each found the other hard to work with, but in combination they produced a strategy that was equally inspired by the prime minister's vision and grasp of the largest issues and disciplined by the CIGS's professional realism.

With his American allies, Brooke could agree on the goal of bringing the German army to battle on a large scale as necessary for victory in Europe. The Allies differed, however, on the issues of time and place. The Americans wanted to attack directly from Great Britain onto the Continent as early as the autumn of 1942 and no later than the summer of 1943. Brooke believed that before such an invasion could succeed, the German army would have to be weakened and the Anglo-American armies strengthened. The British wanted a campaign in the Mediterranean to clear Africa of enemy forces and to drive Italy out of the war, thus stretching and wearing down German resources, even while the Allies were gaining in strength. The Americans feared that a Mediterranean campaign would funnel off Allied resources on such a scale that an invasion of northwest Europe would be postponed until 1944. This was what happened: Anglo-American forces entered northwest Africa in late 1942, invaded Sicily and then Italy in 1943, and landed in northwest Europe only in June, 1944. As the German army proved hard enough to defeat in the campaign of 1944-1945, Brooke's strategic judgment must be respected.

The success of Brooke's strategy was at a personal cost. Churchill in early 1943 had promised him command of the invasion of northwest Europe, but as it became clear over time that the American contribution to that campaign would be preponderant, so inevitably there would have to be an American commander. Brooke took this hard when the prime minister broke it to him. With military victory came promotion and honors. Brooke was raised to the rank of field marshal in 1944 and was created Baron Alanbrooke in 1945 and Viscount Alanbrooke in 1946. The same year, he was created a Knight of the Garter and admitted to the Order of Merit. The most distinguished member of the Royal Regiment of Artillery, Alanbrooke became Master Gunner of St. James's Park in 1946. A dedicated and skilled ornithologist, he served as president of the London Zoological Society from 1950 to 1954. He died at his home in Hartley Wintney, Hampshire, on June 17, 1963.

SIGNIFICANCE

Most military men are remembered for the great battles they won or for the extraordinary feats of heroism they performed. Alanbrooke falls into neither category. His service was unique because he was called on to work with a statesman of unique genius who did not conform to the normal rules of military-political relationships in wartime. Churchill was the driving dynamo that energized Great Britain's entire war effort. His great energy, however, needed to be kept flowing along productive lines. His most inspired conceptions needed sound professional execution, and his less inspired ideas required reasoned resistance. This last was not achieved without some sparks flying. Churchill found in Alanbrooke the completely professional soldier. Indeed, Churchill's chief staff officer, General Sir Hastings Ismay, who spent nearly two decades in close contact with soldiers and statesmen at the highest levels and observed the work of eight Chiefs of the Imperial General Staff, concluded that Brooke was the best of them all.

—Maxwell P. Schoenfeld

FURTHER READING

Alanbrooke, First Viscount. *War Diaries, 1939-1945: Field Marshal Lord Alanbrooke*. Edited by Alex Danchev and Daniel Todman. Berkeley: University of California Press, 2001. The publication of Alanbrooke's entire wartime diaries, which he began keeping in September, 1939, amplifies the information contained in the two books by Arthur Bryant, which were based on diary excerpts. The complete diary provides an added view of Alanbrooke's frustration in trying to carry out the Allied war strategy and his despair over what he believed was Winston Churchill's failure to understand that strategy.

Bryant, Arthur. *The Turn of the Tide, 1939-1943: A Study Based on the Diaries and Autobiographical Notes of Field Marshal the Viscount Alanbrooke, K.G., O.M.* London: Collins, 1957. Throughout World War II, Alanbrooke kept a diary (intended for his wife's eyes), into which he wrote about his feelings and reactions to the events of each day. An outlet for the stress of his exacting duties, the diary entries give readers a false view of Alanbrooke, for it is only the inner strains that are recorded and not the professional skill he displayed in coping with his arduous duties.

_____. *Triumph in the West, 1943-1946: A Study Based on the Diaries and Autobiographical Notes of Field Marshal the Viscount Alanbrooke, K.G., O.M.* London: Collins, 1959. The material quoted by Bryant from the diaries made graphically clear how difficult a master Winston Churchill could be at times. Churchill himself was deeply upset by their publication, which in turn distressed Alanbrooke. It is their successful partnership, to which these two volumes also testify, that needs to be remembered amid all the controversy.

Butler, J. R. M., ed. *Grand Strategy*. 6 vols. London: Her Majesty's Stationery Office, 1956-1972. Volumes 3-6 in this official series give a clear picture of the strategic options, discussions, and decisions that occurred from the invasion of the Soviet Union in June, 1941, to V-J Day in August, 1945. While the emphasis is British, the views of the United States and the Soviet Union are also covered.

Calvocoressi, Peter, and Guy Wint. *Total War*. New York: Penguin Books, 1972. This volume gives a good overview of the course of World War II and provides a context in which to place the strategic debates that took up so much of Brooke's time and energy.

Fraser, David. *Alanbrooke*. New York: Atheneum, 1982. A biography that is outstanding in its portrait of Alanbrooke. General Sir David Fraser, a distinguished soldier and former Vice Chief of the General Staff, was ideally equipped to understand his subject and the milieu in which he worked.

Pogue, Forrest C. *George C. Marshall*. 3 vols. New York: Viking Press, 1963-1973. Marshall was Brooke's opposite on the American Joint Chiefs of Staff, and the chief American strategic spokesman. Volumes 2 and 3 give the U.S. perspective on the issues that sometimes separated the two allies in what remains the outstanding example of two sovereign nations working effectively together in wartime.

SEE ALSO: Lord Allenby; Sir Winston Churchill; T. E. Lawrence; George C. Marshall; Bernard Law Montgomery; First Viscount Slim.

RELATED ARTICLES in *Great Events from History: The Twentieth Century:*

MADELEINE ALBRIGHT
American secretary of state (1997-2001)

As ambassador to the United Nations and as the first woman to hold the office of U.S. secretary of state, Albright helped shape a foreign policy emphasizing an activist but not unilateral role for the United States.

BORN: May 15, 1937; Prague, Czechoslovakia (now in Czech Republic)
ALSO KNOWN AS: Marie Jana Korbel (birth name)
AREAS OF ACHIEVEMENT: Government and politics, diplomacy

EARLY LIFE

Madeleine Albright was born Marie Jana Korbel in Prague, Czechoslovakia, shortly before Nazi Germany took control of the country. Her father, Josef Korbel, was an intellectual and a member of the Czech diplomatic corps. Her mother, Anna Speeglova Korbel, was the daughter of a prosperous family. Albright had two siblings: Katherine Korbel Silva and John Joseph Korbel. Albright's grandparents were Jewish, and three of them died in the Holocaust—a fact Albright revealed only after her appointment as secretary of state. Her parents converted to Roman Catholicism, apparently to escape persecution, and Albright grew up celebrating Christian rituals such as Christmas and Easter.

Albright's earliest experiences were shaped by World War II. When German agents took power in Czechoslovakia in 1938, her father, an outspoken opponent of the Nazis, was targeted for execution. While Josef Korbel tried to get false diplomatic papers that would get his family out of the country, he and his wife walked the streets of Prague with the infant Albright, making sure they stayed in public places where the Nazis would not assault him. They were able to escape to England. Albright later recalled staying in London air-raid shelters and sleeping under a steel table during bombing raids. During her stay, she became fluent in English. After the war, the Korbel family returned briefly to Prague. Josef soon resumed his diplomatic career, which took him to Belgrade, Yugoslavia, and then to New York, where he was assigned a position at the United Nations.

While the Korbels were in New York, Czechoslovakia experienced another coup; the communists took charge and Josef Korbel was once again a wanted man. The family was granted political asylum in the United States, and in 1949 they moved to Colorado, where Josef became a professor of international relations at the Uni-

versity of Denver. A respected scholar and the author of many books on diplomacy, Josef Korbel was Albright's first major intellectual authority. She has attributed many of her views to her father's influence.

In Colorado, Albright attended a small private high school. She won a scholarship to Wellesley College in Massachusetts, where she majored in political science, edited the college newspaper for a year, and campaigned for Democratic presidential candidate Adlai Stevenson. In 1959, she graduated with honors.

Only three days after graduation, Albright married Joseph Medill Patterson Albright, the heir of a prominent newspaper family. They moved to Chicago, where he was employed with the *Chicago Sun-Times*. Albright, however, was told that as a journalist's spouse, she would never be hired by a newspaper. Instead, she worked briefly in public relations for the *Encyclopedia Britannica* before the family moved to New York City in 1961. During the next six years, Albright gave birth to three daughters: twins, named Alice and Anne, and Katherine. She also enrolled in the graduate program in public law and government at Columbia University.

LIFE'S WORK

Albright has credited her success to her willingness to work hard. While she pursued graduate study and raised a family, she typically awoke at 4:30 A.M. and worked late into the night. She earned a master's degree, a certificate in Russian studies, and, in 1976, a doctorate. Her dissertation concerned the role of the press in the 1968 crisis in Czechoslovakia, during which dissidents tried to end Soviet control of the country. The dissertation, like much of her later career and writing, would combine her fascinations with journalism and foreign policy. At Columbia, Albright studied with Professor Zbigniew Brzezinski, who directed the Institute on Communist Affairs. Along with her father, Brzezinski would be one of Albright's most important intellectual mentors.

In 1968, Albright's husband was transferred to Washington, D.C., where he became the bureau chief of *Newsday*. Albright became involved with her daughters' private school, for which she organized several successful fund-raising projects. As a result, a friend recommended her as a fund-raiser for Senator Edmund Muskie's campaign for the 1972 Democratic presidential nomination. Although Muskie did not win the nomination, he hired Albright to serve as the chief legislative assistant in his Senate office. She was especially involved in assisting Muskie with his duties as a member of the Senate Foreign Relations Committee.

When Jimmy Carter was elected president in 1976, he appointed Brzezinski to be his national security adviser. Brzezinski brought Albright onto the staff of the National Security Council, where she worked as congressional liaison. When Ronald Reagan became president in 1981, Albright moved from governmental service to a position as senior fellow in Soviet and Eastern European Affairs at the Center for Strategic and International Studies. In 1982, Albright and her husband separated, and she began to devote herself wholeheartedly to her career as a foreign policy analyst and advocate. With the support of a fellowship from the Smithsonian Institution's Woodrow Wilson Center for Scholars, she published *Poland: The Role of the Press in Political Change* (1983).

In 1982 Albright joined the faculty of Georgetown University, where she remained until 1993 and where she returned after her service as secretary of state. Her experience as a faculty member was a decided success. She served as a professor of international affairs and directed the school's Women in Foreign Service program. She was named teacher of the year on four occasions. While on the Georgetown faculty, Albright began inviting a variety of guests from academia, the diplomatic service, journalism, and politics to her home for discussions of international issues. Among those who attended Albright's "salons" was the governor of Arkansas, Bill Clinton; among the topics was the shape that U.S. foreign policy might take when the Democrats regained the White House.

Albright coordinated foreign policy for Democratic presidential nominee Walter Mondale and vice presidential nominee Geraldine Ferraro during the 1984 campaign. Four years later, she was senior foreign policy adviser and a major speechwriter for Democratic candidate Michael Dukakis. During the next four years, Albright served as president of the Center for National Policy, a Democratic think tank and a resource for members of Congress, where she dealt principally with Eastern European affairs. She was also involved with the Georgetown Leadership Seminar, an annual session for government officials, bankers, journalists, and military officers. Albright was a frequent guest on the public television program *Great Decisions*, which provided a chance to reach a larger audience with her views on international affairs.

When Bill Clinton ran for president in 1992, Albright helped to write the foreign policy sections of the Democratic party platform as well as position papers for the nominee. She was, therefore, an obvious choice for a diplomatic post in the Clinton administration. In December, 1992, the president-elect named her U.S. Ambassador to the United Nations and made her a member of his cabinet.

Albright brought great energy to her role at the United Nations. She traveled to the capital of every member nation of the Security Council, visited Somalia when U.S. troops were stationed there, and went to Bosnia, where she strongly advocated greater American involvement in the conflict with Serbia. In 1995, she attended the U.N. Conference on Women, held in China, where she spent a day escorting First Lady Hillary Clinton. She also led the First Lady on a tour of Prague in 1996.

Albright increased the visibility of the seven women ambassadors to the United Nations by organizing lunches for them. She also led the effort to oust Secretary-General

Madeleine Albright. (Hulton Archive/Getty Images)

Boutros Boutros-Ghali from his leadership post. Boutros-Ghali was intensely unpopular with conservatives in the U.S. Congress, and her opposition to him later helped to win Senate approval for her appointment as secretary of state. While serving in the United Nations, Albright remained closely tied to the decision-making process in Washington, D.C., where she attended cabinet meetings and sessions of the National Security Council's principals' group.

After Clinton was reelected in 1996, it soon became apparent that Secretary of State Warren Christopher would step down from his post. The president considered several former senators and career diplomats to fill the position, but he eventually chose to nominate Albright. She was easily confirmed by the Senate, which supported her nomination by a vote of 99-0.

As secretary of state, Albright faced instability in many areas of the world, financial crises that had diplomatic repercussions, and a reconsideration of relations with some of the United States' friends and adversaries. For example, in the Middle East, hostile relations with Iraq continued as Saddam Hussein apparently persisted in threatening his neighbors and in resisting United Nations inspections of his country's weapons capabilities. The United States maintained a hard line against the Iraqi leader while trying to ease the hardships endured by the people of that country. On the other hand, a dialogue emerged between the United States and Iran, with Secretary Albright suggesting that the two former adversaries might look for common ground. She encouraged the Israelis and Palestinians to continue their peace process and negotiate the future of the disputed territories.

With respect to Europe, Albright was an enthusiastic supporter of an expansion of the North Atlantic Treaty Organization (NATO) to include Poland and the Czech Republic and of the Good Friday agreement to resolve the political and religious conflicts in Northern Ireland. She advocated a strong multilateral response to the crisis in Bosnia, including a U.S. "police" presence, economic assistance, and punishment of war criminals. Albright also encouraged economic assistance to Russia to avert a political and economic emergency there. The secretary of state visited a number of African nations, as well as important Asian countries such as Korea, Japan, and China. In addition to reaffirming support for the United States' traditional allies, she explicated President Clinton's policy that promoted expanded trade with China while keeping the issue of human rights on the diplomatic agenda. In light of the nuclear tests conducted by India and Pakistan, Albright called for both countries to

sign the Comprehensive Test Ban Treaty and reaffirmed the administration's desire that the U.S. Senate ratify the treaty. She also urged Congress to provide assistance through the International Monetary Fund to Indonesia and other countries experiencing economic crises and to appropriate funds to pay the United States' obligations to the United Nations.

Unlike some of her predecessors who saw foreign policy as a very personal achievement, Albright believed in developing a highly competent team to carry out the U.S. diplomatic agenda. For example, during Albright's term in the Department of State, Richard Holbrooke, who had negotiated the Dayton Agreement to resolve the Bosnian crisis, became ambassador to the United Nations. Albright described Holbrooke's appointment as part of her program to surround herself with strong people. Albright was also involved in promoting the humanitarian element in international development efforts, focusing on the connections between economic investments and everyday family life in less-developed countries.

Albright was particularly aware of the connection between the status of women around the world and its implications for U.S. foreign policy. She pressed for Senate ratification of the Convention on the Elimination of All Forms of Discrimination Against Women (CEDAW) and emphasized the need to stabilize birth rates, educate women, and involve them in international development efforts. She used her office to promote the empowerment of women as an integral element in achieving peace and prosperity and to attempt to increase the representation of women in diplomatic service. Albright saw herself as part of a network of female foreign ministers, many of whom became acquainted through their service in the United Nations. In response to questions about how she was viewed by leaders of countries whose cultures did not recognize the equality of women, Albright stated that she was always viewed with the highest respect. She noted that having a woman represent the most powerful country in the world was a message in itself.

Albright left the State Department in 2001 when Republican president George W. Bush took office. Since leaving her cabinet post, Albright has written two books, a memoir called *Madame Secretary* (2003) and *The Mighty and the Almighty: Reflections on America, God, and World Affairs* (2006), which considers the role of religion in world affairs. She also formed a strategic consulting firm, the Albright Group, resumed her faculty position as a professor at the Georgetown School of Foreign Service, held an appointment as distinguished scholar at the University of Michigan, and served on the board of directors of the New York Stock Exchange. She has traveled abroad widely with organizations promoting human rights. In the latter role, Albright led a 2006 delegation to Africa as part of the Commission on Legal Empowerment of the Poor. She also served as a foreign observer of the 2007 Nigerian elections in conjunction with her involvement with the National Endowment for Democracy.

Albright has strongly criticized the conduct of the Bush administration for its arrogance and unilateralism. She has argued that the war in Iraq is the worst disaster in American foreign policy and that its unintended consequences undermine the future security of the Middle East. Albright contends that the United States, rather than operating independently, must form partnerships with other nations to address vital issues of energy, environmental conditions, and terrorism. In Albright's view, terrorism is a method used by diverse groups to achieve their political goals. Unless Americans learn what terrorism is intended to accomplish, fighting a "war" on the method will be futile. She has said that to regain the trust of other nations, the United States must display not only its military power but also its power to do good. In her view, because the biggest problem in the world is the gap between the rich and the poor, addressing that gap should be an American priority.

As a political scientist, Albright has described the world as being in the process of a systemic change, whereby the old dominance of nation-states is challenged by larger forces such as globalization and by fragmentation through ethnic separatism and the power of actors who are not nations, such as the leaders of militant religious movements. Thus the system is far more chaotic than it was during the relative stability of the Cold War. Such a time of change requires a moral and multilateral foreign policy. Albright has expressed the hope that future presidential administrations will follow such an approach.

SIGNIFICANCE

Prior to Albright's appointment as secretary of state, no woman had held such a high position in the U.S. diplomatic service. Only one woman, Jeane Kirkpatrick, had preceded Albright as ambassador to the United Nations. Albright assumed the secretary of state's post with a reputation for being candid, and she was also outspoken about affirming her identity as a woman. Immediately after assuming her post, she noted that the secretary of state's office had been designed with a male occupant in

mind: It was equipped with conveniences such as racks for men's suits and drawers for socks. Albright noted that apparently, she did not fit the traditional image of the secretary of state.

With respect to foreign policy, Albright was an enthusiastic advocate of the assertive use of U.S. power and influence if not military engagement. She stated that her "mind-set is Munich"; in other words, her view was formed by the experience of Czechoslovakia. At Munich in 1938, diplomats from Great Britain and France effectively handed control of her native country over to Adolf Hitler in return for his promise to cease aggression. Hitler then promptly took over Czechoslovakia, continued his conquests, and provoked World War II. In Albright's view, the lesson of Munich was that nations should not compromise with aggression; however, she always held that diplomacy must precede and would often avert conflict.

As secretary of state, Albright was a severe critic of nations charged with violations of human rights, including Cuba, Iraq, and Iran. On the other hand, she had to find ways to balance disapproval of China's internal repression with efforts to promote trade with the world's most populous country. During her tenure, the Department of State faced instability in Russia, conflicts in the Middle East, and tensions caused by the expansion of NATO, but the United States was able to avoid military involvement in any major foreign conflicts. She has been a severe critic of the Bush administration's unilateral approach to international affairs and especially to its conduct in the war in Iraq.

Albright had an important influence in two areas of public life: as a model of a woman who achieved success in a nontraditional role and as a major architect of American foreign policy at the end of the twentieth century.

—*Mary Welek Atwell*

FURTHER READING

Albright, Madeleine. *Madame Secretary: A Memoir.* New York: Miramax Books, 2003. Albright relates the story of her private life and career, focusing on her time as ambassador to the United Nations and as the first female secretary of state. She integrates her theoretical approach to international affairs with anecdotes and descriptions of world figures.

_____. *The Mighty and the Almighty: Reflections on America, God, and World Affairs.* New York: Harper-Collins, 2006. Albright argues that effective foreign policy requires a recognition and an understanding of the importance of religion in international politics.

She asserts the importance of finding common ground among religious traditions as an important tool in building peaceful relations.

Dobbs, Michael. *Madeleine Albright: A Twentieth-Century Odyssey*. New York: Henry Holt, 1999. Written by a reporter for *The Washington Post*, this journalistic biography emphasizes Albright's European background and her life experiences as well as her career in public service.

Gibbs, Nancy. "The Many Lives of Madeleine." *Time*, February 17, 1997. Gibbs writes that Albright's rise to the highest governmental position of any woman in U.S. history resulted from her political strategy, determination, diplomatic prowess, and perfectionism.

Lippman, Thomas. *Madeleine Albright and the New American Diplomacy*. Boulder, Colo.: Westview Press, 2000. Lippman, a reporter for *The Washington Post* who traveled with Secretary of State Albright for more than two years, focuses on her role in that office. He describes Albright's campaign for the position, her frustrations with the Middle East peace process, and her efforts to ensure a democratic government in the Russian Federation.

Sciolino, Elaine. "Madeleine Albright's Audition." *The New York Times Magazine*, September 22, 1996. Sciolino evaluates Albright's career as a key member of Clinton's foreign policy team and discusses her chances of becoming secretary of state.

SEE ALSO: Boutros Boutros-Ghali; Jimmy Carter; Bill Clinton; Hillary Rodham Clinton; Elizabeth Dole; Oveta Culp Hobby; Saddam Hussein; Frances Perkins; Shirley Temple.

RELATED ARTICLES in *Great Events from History: The Twentieth Century:*

1941-1970: December 13, 1968: Hardin Argues for Population Control.

1971-2000: August 7, 1998: Terrorists Bomb U.S. Embassies in East Africa; October 15-23, 1998: Wye River Accords.

HANNES ALFVÉN
Swedish physicist

Alfvén developed magnetohydrodynamics, a branch of physics that studies the propagation of currents and electromagnetic waves through fluids, and studied its applications to plasmas, leading to his description of the physics of the aurora, radiation belts around planets having magnetic fields, and other astrophysical phenomena.

BORN: May 30, 1908; Norrköping, Sweden
DIED: April 2, 1995; Djursholm, Sweden
ALSO KNOWN AS: Hannes Olof Gösta Alfvén (full name); Hannes O. G. Alfven; Olof Johannesson
AREAS OF ACHIEVEMENT: Physics, astronomy

EARLY LIFE

Hannes Alfvén (HAHN-nehs ahl-VAYN) was born in Norrköping, Sweden. His parents, Johannes Alfvén and Anna-Clara Romanus, were both medical doctors. His mother was one of the first female doctors in Sweden, and his father showed an interest in science beyond medicine. Hugo Alfvén, one of his uncles, was a well-known musical composer. Another uncle was an inventor, and a third uncle was interested in astronomy. As a child, Alfvén was given a book on astronomy, which sparked his lifelong interest. He was a member of the radio club in high school, and he built a radio receiver. However, his hometown had no radio station. Stockholm, which did have a radio station, was too far away from Norrköping for its signal to be heard. With much effort, Alfvén was able to hear a station located in Aberdeen, Scotland. With this success, he became interested in electrical engineering.

In 1926, Alfvén entered Uppsala University, where he studied electrical engineering and physics. He was awarded a doctorate in 1934 after submitting his doctoral thesis, "Investigations of the Ultra-short Electromagnetic Waves." Alfvén later said that his doctoral research was a continuation of the activities he participated in with the radio club in high school.

LIFE'S WORK

Alfvén was appointed a lecturer in physics at Uppsala University in 1934, where he combined his interests in electricity and astronomy. The high energies achieved by "cosmic rays," ions that move through space at speeds close to that of light and that continuously hit the earth's atmosphere, puzzled astrophysicists. Alfvén became interested in the physical mechanisms that could accelerate charged particles in space to such high energies. He was particularly critical of earlier work on this topic, believing that researchers presented ideas that were not constrained by the results of the most recent experiments.

Alfvén was convinced that the origin of the cosmic rays could be explained simply by applying "kinetic gas theory," an approach that was successfully applied to explain the macroscopic properties of gases, such as pressure, temperature, or volume, by considering their microscopic properties of composition and motion, to the conditions that are found in space. Alfvén proposed a mechanism for the acceleration of cosmic rays based on the presence of electromagnetic fields in space. A version of that mechanism, expanded upon by Enrico Fermi and now known as the Fermi mechanism, remains the favored mechanism to explain cosmic ray acceleration.

In 1937, Alfvén was appointed a research physicist at the prestigious Nobel Institute for Physics in Stockholm. He devoted much of his career to making scientists aware of the importance of electric fields and electric currents in space. His work on cosmic ray acceleration led him to propose the existence of a galactic magnetic field. At that time, interstellar space was believed to be a vacuum, so the accepted view was that there could be no significant magnetic field in space because the magnetic fields of the stars were too weak to reach that far. Alfvén suggested that "plasma," a gas of positively charged ions, could, in interstellar space, conduct electric currents strong enough to produce a significant magnetic field. This galactic magnetic field was finally discovered many years after Alfvén first proposed it.

In 1940, Alfvén was appointed professor in the theory of electricity at the Royal Institute of Technology, also in Stockholm. It was here that he did the research that brought him the most recognition. Electromagnetic waves were known not to penetrate more than a few wavelengths into solid conductors. However, in 1942, Alfvén published calculations showing that low-frequency electromagnetic waves, now called Alfvén waves, should propagate through the interior of fluids, such as plasmas.

Alfvén frequently set out to solve a particular problem but was able to generalize the results to be more broadly applicable. He was investigating the mechanism for the production of "sunspots," magnetic disturbances on the sun that appear darker than the surrounding area, when he discovered what came to be called Alfvén waves. While trying to model magnetic disturbances of the sun, Alfvén recognized that electric currents in the solar plasma would result in wave motion. At that time elec-

tromagnetic theory and fluid motion theory were separate fields of physics, but Alfvén's work combined them into a new field called "magnetohydrodynamics." It was not until 1949 that Alfvén waves were first detected. Stig Lundquist, a physicist working in Alfvén's laboratory, produced them in liquid mercury.

The importance of Alfvén's work was not immediately recognized by the scientific community. It was difficult to test Alfvén's theories because plasmas were thought to occur only rarely under natural conditions, typically in lightning strikes. With the development of nuclear weapons and efforts to develop nuclear fusion as an energy source, plasmas were routinely being generated by the 1950's, and magnetohydrodynamics became an important field of study. In addition, Alfvén proposed that plasmas should occur in the atmosphere of the earth and in a variety of locations in space. He spent much of his professional career investigating the occurrence of plasmas in space, and discussing their significance. Alfvén was awarded the 1970 Nobel Prize in Physics for his work on magnetohydrodynamics.

Two decades before the Explorer I satellite discovered Earth's Van Allen radiation belt, a ring of charged particles that surrounds the earth, Alfvén gave an intuitive explanation of how energetic charged particles can orbit around a magnetized planet. Before Alfvén developed his method of calculating the path a charged particle follows in a magnetic field, particle paths had to be calculated by a tedious and time-consuming numerical integration technique. Alfvén separated the motion into two components, one describing the gyration of the particle perpendicular to the local magnetic field and the second describing the drift of the center of motion. Using this technique, Alfvén noted that a ring of charged particles would be stable around a planet with a magnetic field. However, he failed to take the next step of recognizing that such a ring of charged particles could exist around the earth. That step was taken by Fred Singer, in 1956, after hearing a lecture by Alfvén.

Alfvén regarded himself as a generalist, who investigated a variety of phenomena that involved plasmas and their effects in a variety of contexts, while many other physicists concentrated their efforts on one field of research. Thus, he was sometimes regarded as an interloper, trying to explain a phenomenon that other researchers thought to be outside his area of expertise. When he developed his model of "aurora," a luminous atmospheric phenomenon appearing as bands of light in the night sky, the model was initially rejected by the leading atmospheric physicists, and Alfvén could not publish his results in any of the leading scientific journals. Finally, he published his model, now the accepted explanation for aurora, in an obscure journal.

In 1950 Alfvén, working with Nicolai Herlofson, proposed the mechanism for emission of "synchrotron radiation"—light emitted when high-speed electrons spiral through magnetic fields—by astronomical objects. This radiation was discovered in 1956 by Geoffrey Burbidge.

As Alfvén's research interests evolved, his title at the Royal Institute of Technology was changed to professor of electronics in 1945 and to professor of plasma physics in 1963. In 1967, Alfvén was appointed a professor of physics at the University of California, San Diego. He divided his time between California, where he worked from fall until spring, and Sweden, where he worked from spring until fall.

Later in life, Alfvén became interested in humankind's ultimate fate, and he explored issues such as population growth, the environment, and disarmament. He and his wife, Kerstin, cowrote *Living on the Third Planet* (1972), which explored their views on these issues. Alfvén retired in 1991 and lived in Sweden until his death, at the age of eighty-six, in 1995.

SIGNIFICANCE

Alfvén made significant contributions to understanding the physics of plasmas, including theories describing the behavior of aurora in Earth's atmosphere, Van Allen radiation belts, the effect of solar magnetic storms on the earth's magnetic field, the earth's magnetosphere, and the dynamics of plasmas in the Milky Way galaxy. Many of Alfvén's ideas were ahead of their time. He predicted phenomena well before they were discovered, leading, oftentimes, to his work being forgotten by the time the phenomenon he predicted was observed.

Later in his life, Alfvén used the prestige he gained from the Nobel Prize to influence national and international policy. He joined the Pugwash movement, a group of influential scholars who sought to reduce the danger of armed confrontation in the nuclear era. He also became concerned with the lack of planning for the disposal of radioactive waste from nuclear power reactors, and he was influential in the debate that resulted in restrictions on the use of nuclear power in Sweden.

—George J. Flynn

FURTHER READING

Alfvén, Hannes. "Memoirs of a Dissident Scientist." *American Scientist*, May-June 1988, 249-251. A firsthand account of Alfvén's scientific achievements and his efforts to have his ideas accepted by the scientific community.

Dardo, Mauro. *Nobel Laureates and Twentieth-Century Physics*. New York: Cambridge University Press, 2004. Chronicles major developments in physics since 1901, the year the first Nobel Prize in Physics was awarded. Includes discussion of the work of prize winners.

Falthammar, Carl-Gunne, and Alexander J. Dessler. "Hannes Alfvén." *Proceedings of the American Philosophical Society* 150, no. 4 (2006): 649-662. An extensive biography of Alfvén, explaining how he developed interests in physics and astronomy, describing his successes, failures, and his difficulty in getting his revolutionary ideas accepted by the scientific community.

_____. "The Life and Times of a Premier Space Physicist." *Earth in Space* 9, no. 5 (January, 1996). An account of Alfvén's scientific accomplishments, focusing on his achievements in atmospheric and space science.

SEE ALSO: Svante August Arrhenius; Niels Bohr; Louis de Broglie; Enrico Fermi; Werner Heisenberg; Pyotr Leonidovich Kapitsa; Georges Lemaître; Hendrik Antoon Lorentz; Jan Hendrik Oort; Linus Pauling; Max Planck; Johannes Stark; James Van Allen; Steven Weinberg; Hideki Yukawa.

RELATED ARTICLE in *Great Events from History: The Twentieth Century:*

MUHAMMAD ALI
American boxer

Ali was probably the greatest as well as the best-recognized sports personality of the twentieth century. He brought heavyweight boxing matches to areas of the world never before regarded as important in boxing circles.

BORN: January 17, 1942; Louisville, Kentucky
ALSO KNOWN AS: Cassius Marcellus Clay, Jr. (birth name); Cassius Clay; The Greatest
AREA OF ACHIEVEMENT: Sports

EARLY LIFE

Muhammad Ali (ah-LEE) was born Cassius Marcellus Clay, Jr., in Louisville, Kentucky, to Cassius Marcellus Clay, Sr., and Odessa Lee Grady Clay. His father was a commercial artist specializing in sign painting; he also painted murals for churches and taverns. His mother sometimes worked as a domestic for four dollars a day to help support the family. Some of the Clays trace their name to Ali's great-great-grandfather, who was a slave of Cassius Marcellus Clay, a relative of Henry Clay and ambassador to Russia in the 1860's.

Known during boyhood as a mischievous child and lover of practical jokes, Ali was considered indolent by his father. He often remarked that eating and sleeping were Ali's two most strenuous activities. That changed when Ali became involved in boxing at the age of twelve. Unlike most boxers, however, he was reared in a lower-middle-class environment. When, at age twelve, Ali's bicycle was stolen, he reported the theft to a Louisville police officer who gave boxing lessons in a gymnasium operated in Ali's neighborhood. This white police officer, Joe Elsby Martin, was to guide Ali through most of his amateur boxing career. After six weeks of boxing lessons, Ali had his first fight, weighing in at eighty-nine pounds. He won a split decision and was regarded as an average boxer at that time. Yet two characteristics had already manifested themselves in Ali, his dedication to his newfound interest, a dedication to make himself into "the greatest" (a slogan he adopted relatively early in his career), and his propensity to talk back to people, particularly his detractors. He was known as a smart aleck, a sassy person.

Ali attended Du Valle Junior High School and was graduated from Central High School in Louisville, 376th in his class of 391. He was known more for his marble-shooting and rock-throwing prowess than for any inter-est in academics. Ali's first public exposure came in Louisville, when he was booked for fights on *Tomorrow's Champions*, a local weekly television boxing show. By this time, he was also training four hours a day under Fred Stoner, a black trainer at the Grace Community Center, a gymnasium in the all-black section of Louisville. Ali later said that Stoner molded his style, his stamina, and his system.

During his illustrious amateur career, Ali won 100 of 108 fights, six Kentucky Golden Gloves championships, and two national Amateur Athletic Union championships. During his last two years as an amateur, he lost only once, to Amos Johnson in the 1959 Pan-American Games trials. By this time, he wanted to box professionally, but Martin convinced him to remain an amateur and enter the 1960 Olympics, as this would give him national recognition and ensure his professional success. Ali, who was already advertising himself as the next heavyweight champion of the world, stopped off in New York City on the way to the Olympic Games in Rome and visited Madison Square Garden, then the Mecca of professional boxing. He won the light-heavyweight title at the Olympics and returned to the United States in triumph. Soon afterward, however, he was refused service in a restaurant in his hometown and had to fight a white motorcycle gang leader to escape from the restaurant. This incident so embittered him that he threw his Olympic Gold Medal into the Ohio River.

When Ali turned to professional boxing in 1960, he was already six feet three inches tall. In his heyday, he weighed more than 200 pounds, usually weighing in at around 220 pounds. Ali did not look like a boxer. His rather large, round face was unmarked, and he was not muscle-bound. Bodybuilding has long been an anathema to boxers; heavy surface muscles restrict the movement of hands and arms, and Ali's forte already was speed and defense in the ring. Indeed, one of his most celebrated slogans was "Float like a butterfly, sting like a bee."

Three days before his first professional fight, on October 29, 1960, Ali signed a contract with eleven white businessmen from Louisville and New York City. These men were willing to invest in a potential heavyweight champion. Known as the Louisville Sponsoring Group, it was headed by William Faversham, Jr., vice president of the Brown-Forman Distillers Corporation. Ali received a ten-thousand-dollar bonus for signing, a salary of four thousand dollars annually for the first two years

Muhammad Ali. (AP/Wide World Photos)

and six thousand dollars annually for the following four years, as well as having all of his expenses paid. He was also to receive 50 percent of all of his earnings.

Ali began his professional training under former light-heavyweight champion Archie Moore. Angelo Dundee soon supplanted Moore, also becoming Ali's de facto manager during Ali's early professional career. Angelo was calm under fire and saved Ali's championship at least twice. He was an excellent cornerman who had come up through the ranks. His brother, Chris Dundee, was at the time promoting a weekly fight card in Miami Beach. Angelo joined Chris, and they established their training headquarters on the second floor of a two-story building on the corner of Fifth Street and Washington Avenue, in Miami Beach. This gymnasium later became known as the Fifth Street Gym and was probably the best-known and most respected training center in the United States.

Ali won his first seven fights as a professional, beginning with the defeating of Tunney Hunsaker. Some of his early fights were held in Louisville, and his first national television exposure was against Alonzo Johnson. Johnson was then twenty-seven years old and an experienced boxer. The bout, televised by the National Broadcasting Company (NBC) on the Gillette Cavalcade of Sports,

was a difficult one for Ali, but he won and was on his way.

Ali was soon showing all the braggadocio for which he became noted: talking constantly to confuse his opponents, writing short ditties deriding them, and predicting the round in which he would stop them. There was, however, a method to his madness. His behavior increased the spectators' enthusiasm for his fights and brought him fame and fortune, along with derision. It is said that Ali had watched the antics of Gorgeous George, one of the first truly flamboyant wrestlers to appear on television, noting his ability to enrage most of the spectators at his matches. Yet these same spectators paid as much money for tickets to see George lose as his fans paid to see him win. Fifty percent of all revenue from fights was still coming to Ali. More than twelve thousand people came to see him knock out Alejandro Lavorante in California in five rounds, and his fight with Archie Moore in California in November, 1962, drew more than sixteen thousand people. In March, 1963, he fought Doug Jones in Madison Square Garden, filling it for the first time in more than a decade; more than eighteen thousand people came to see him fight, paying $105,000 for this privilege. Ali then went to England to box British heavyweight champion Henry Cooper. Ali predicted a victory by a fifth-round knockout of Cooper, but late in the third round, Cooper knocked Ali down and stunned him. Dundee, however, noticed that one of Ali's gloves was split, and the extra minutes needed to fix it enabled Ali to clear his head. Cooper's propensity to be cut easily allowed Ali to win by a technical knockout in the fifth round, as he had predicted.

LIFE'S WORK

Ali finally had the opportunity to fight for the heavyweight championship of the world. Sonny Liston was then regarded as the quintessential champion and was a prohibitive favorite to retain his crown. Yet at the weigh-in before the fight in Miami Beach on February 25, 1964, Ali distracted Liston with a carefully rehearsed display of hysteria and paranoia. During the fight, he taunted Liston and, using his superior speed and longer reach, peppered Liston with long-range jabs and right-hand punches. He so wore down his opponent that Liston was unable to answer the bell for the seventh round. Ali was declared the heavyweight champion of the world. In a return match with Liston, held in Lewiston, Maine, on May 25, 1965, Ali knocked him out with a very quick right-hand punch in the first round. He next defeated the former champion, Floyd Patterson, winning a technical knockout in the twelfth round, in Las Vegas, Nevada. Many believed that Ali could have ended the fight earlier but instead chose to bait and mock Patterson unmercifully. In 1966, he stopped all five of his challengers. Only one, George Chavallo, went the distance. Early in 1967, he defeated Ernie Terrell and was recognized as the undisputed heavyweight champion. Only one month later, he knocked out Zora Folley.

By this time, Ali's activities beyond the ring were receiving more notoriety than were his successful title defenses. Immediately after he won the championship from Liston, he announced that he had joined the black nationalist Nation of Islam and changed his name from Cassius Clay to Muhammad Ali. Popularly known as the Black Muslims, the sect was then regarded by white America as a dangerous and subversive antiwhite group. (Ali converted to mainstream Sunni Islam in 1975.) Also, Ali had been married twice by this time. His first marriage to Sonje Roi was dissolved in 1966. His second marriage was to Belinda Boyd (Khalilah Toloria), producing four children. He wooed Belinda when she was seventeen years old and working in a Chicago Nation of Islam bakery. They were divorced in 1977. He was married a third time, to Veronica Porsche, in 1977. This third marriage produced two children.

Many whites began to compare Ali to the former champion Jack Johnson, a black boxer who had defied the stereotypes of his time by living a fast and integrated life. This comparison was odd, in a way, for Ali was probably the best-trained heavyweight champion of all time, and he neither smoked nor drank. In 1966, the Selective Service Board reclassified him as 1-A, thus removing his deferred status of 1-Y. Ali then appealed, citing conscientious-objector status on religious grounds. He formally refused induction into the Army on April 18, 1967. The World Boxing Association then stripped him of his championship, as did the New York Athletic Commission. Therefore, for three years, during what was the prime of his athletic life, Ali was unable to fight. In 1970, however, a federal court ruled that the revocation of his license was arbitrary and unreasonable, and Ali was able to resume his career.

In 1971 Ali lost his bid to regain the title when Joe Frazier knocked him down in the fifteenth round of a fight in Madison Square Garden; the decision went unan-imously to Frazier in what was dubbed as the fight of the century. Against all odds, on October 30, 1974, Ali again won the heavyweight crown. After two losses and fifteen wins, he faced George Foreman (who in the meantime had won the title from Frazier) in Kinshasa, Zaire (now Democratic Republic of the Congo), Africa, on October 30, 1974, in what became known as the Rumble in the Jungle. Here he used his "rope-a-dope" tactics, lying back on the ring ropes and letting Foreman tire himself out. Only his superior hand speed and movement enabled him to do this. Foreman was knocked out in the eighth round. During this period, Ali lived very well, with Belinda, his second wife, on what was described as a baronial, four-and-a-half-acre estate, with a three-car garage containing his-and-hers Rolls Royces. During this period, Ali successfully defended his title against Frazier in the Philippines, in what became known as the Thrilla in Manila. However, Ali's skills were waning; after barely defeating two mediocre boxers, he lost his crown to Leon Spinks in Las Vegas, Nevada, on February 15, 1978. Summoning all of his strength, Ali trained hard for a rematch, winning the title for an unprecedented third time on September 15, 1978. He lost his last major fight to Larry Holmes in October, 1980, but his final match was against twenty-seven-year-old Trevor Berbick in the Bahamas, which he lost in a unanimous decision.

During his career, Ali earned more than fifty million dollars. Much of this money went for taxes, an expensive lifestyle, and divorces; a third of it went to Herbert Muhammad, who became Ali's manager of record in 1966. By the 1980's Ali was showing signs of mental and physical decay, the result of Parkinson's disease, not, as some conjectured, from brain damage resulting from his fights. Ali retired permanently in 1981 with a career record of fifty-six wins (thirty-seven of them by knockouts) and five losses. The formal diagnosis of Parkinson's disease came in 1982. At the time Ali could claim, with justice, that he was the most famous man in the world.

In retirement Ali became an iconic sports figure, receiving recognition in many forms. *Forbes* magazine placed him thirteenth on its Celebrity One Hundred list, the Kentucky Athletic Hall of Fame picked him as Kentucky Athlete of the Century, and both *Sports Illustrated* and the British Boxing Association selected him as sportsman of the twentieth century. He was inducted into the International Hall of Fame and the Olympic Hall of Fame. He received the Spirit of America Award, the Otto Hahn Peace Medal in Gold from the United Nations Association of Germany, and the Presidential Medal of Freedom. In 1996 he was accorded the honor of lighting the Olympic flame at the Summer Games in Atlanta, Georgia, where he was presented a gold medal to replace the one that he had lost. In 2007 Princeton University awarded him an honorary doctorate of humanities.

In retirement Ali involved himself in humanitarian programs. The Muhammad Ali Center in Louisville, which opened in 2005, not only preserves the boxing memorabilia of Ali but also his ideals: peace, social responsibility, and personal growth. The Muhammad Ali Parkinson Center at the Barrow Neurological Institute in Phoenix, Arizona, provides treatment, research, and education for patients and families. Ali has supported delivery of food and medical services to places such as the Ivory Coast, Indonesia, Mexico, and Morocco, often traveling to these countries to promote the humanitarian effort, and he has lobbied before state legislatures and Congress for laws to protect children and to regulate professional boxing. In *The Soul of a Butterfly: Reflections on Life's Journey* (2004), Ali discusses the meaning of religion and forgiveness as he reflects on turning points in his life.

Ali lives in Scottsdale, Arizona, with his fourth wife, Yolanda, whom he married following his divorce from Porsche in 1986. He has nine children. Despite the slurring of speech, tremors, and muscular stiffness from Parkinson's disease, he travels frequently.

SIGNIFICANCE

Ali is considered the premier heavyweight champion of all time. He is credited with reviving interest in boxing and helping promote international acceptance of the sport. His fights in the Congo and Manila made him history's most recognized boxer, and in 1998 a documentary film about the African bout, *When We Were Kings*, won an Academy Award; in 2001 actor Will Smith recreated Ali's youthful exuberance in the biographical film *Ali*. Nevertheless, Ali's stand for the principles in which he believes cost him dearly. Most Americans came to admire him for his courage if not for his beliefs. George Plimpton captured Ali's standing in writing of his appearance during the 1996 Olympic Games opening ceremony: "It was a kind of epiphany that those who watched realized how much they missed him and how much he had contributed to the world of sport."

—*Henry S. Marks*

FURTHER READING

Ali, Muhammad, with Hana Yasmeen Ali. *The Soul of a Butterfly: Reflections on Life's Journey*. New York: Simon & Schuster, 2004. Ali's memoir focuses on his spiritual evolution, recounting his life from his childhood to his eventual role as an activist for peace and for wider understanding of Parkinson's disease.

Brenner, Teddy, and Barney Nagler. *Only the Ring Was Square*. Englewood Cliffs, N.J.: Prentice-Hall, 1981. Typical breezy sports biography, but with interesting sidelights into Ali's career.

Brunt, Stephen. *Ali: The Opposition Weighs In*. Guilford, Conn.: Lyons Press, 2002. Brunt tells of Ali's fights from the perspective of fifteen of his opponents, including Joe Frazier, Ken Norton, George Foreman, and Larry Holmes. Provides many insights into Ali's style and character. Includes photographs.

Greene, Bob. "Muhammad Ali Is the Most Famous Man in the World." *Esquire*, December, 1983. Tidbits of Ali's later life and a synopsis of Ali's career in an appendix labeled "Dossier."

Marqusee, Mike. *Redemption Song: Muhammad Ali and the Spirit of the Sixties*. 2d ed. New York: Verso, 2005. Marqusee describes Ali's conversion from a prizefighter to a cultural icon and how this transformation was influenced by the rebellious decade of the 1960's.

Massaquoi, Hans J. "The Private World of Muhammad Ali." *Ebony*, September, 1972. Depicts the opulent lifestyle of Ali when he was still fighting. Provides many examples of Ali's personal beliefs, especially on women's rights.

Muhammad Ali. New York: Harry N. Abrams, 2004. There is little text in this coffee-table book, but its dozens of black-and-white and color photographs by Magnum photographers testify wonderfully to the spirit and skill of Ali during his heyday as a boxer.

Pacheco, Freddy. *Fight Doctor*. New York: Simon & Schuster, 1983. Pacheco was Ali's physician until splitting with him shortly before Ali's first fight with Leon Spinks. He was the first to notice deterioration in Ali's physical and mental well-being and the first to advise Ali to quit fighting.

Remnick, David. *King of the World: Muhammad Ali and the Rise of an American Hero*. New York: Random House, 1998. Remnick's biography focuses on Ali's character, describing how Ali created himself as a new type of boxing champion who defied the traditional stereotypes of his profession.

SEE ALSO: Jack Dempsey; Rocky Marciano.

RELATED ARTICLES in *Great Events from History: The Twentieth Century:*

1941-1970: September 23, 1952: Marciano Wins His

First Heavyweight Boxing Championship; February 25, 1964: Clay Defeats Liston to Gain World Heavyweight Boxing Title; November, 1965: *The Autobiography of Malcolm X Is Published.*

1971-2000: October 30, 1974: Ali and Foreman Rumble in the Jungle; November 22, 1986: Tyson Becomes Youngest World Heavyweight Boxing Champion.

LORD ALLENBY
British military leader

After a career of some note that involved him in the Boer War and the western front of World War I, Allenby achieved signal successes for Allied arms by commanding the military forces that captured Jerusalem, Damascus, and Aleppo during the Middle Eastern campaigns of 1917 and 1918.

BORN: April 23, 1861; Brackenhurst, near Southwell, Nottinghamshire, England
DIED: May 14, 1936; London, England
ALSO KNOWN AS: Edmund Henry Hynman Allenby
AREAS OF ACHIEVEMENT: Military affairs, warfare and conquest

EARLY LIFE
There was little in his family background to suggest that Lord Allenby (AL-lehn-bee), born Edmund Henry Hynman Allenby, would achieve lasting renown as a military commander. Although one of his paternal forebears of the eighteenth century was a direct descendant of Oliver Cromwell, for the most part his ancestors had been given to other pursuits. Hynman Allenby, his father, was known as a country gentleman without much aptitude for business or professional callings; his marriage to Catherine Anne Cane, the daughter of a minister, produced three daughters and three sons, of whom Edmund was the second child, the first son. He was born on April 23, 1861, at Brackenhurst, a family estate near Southwell in Nottinghamshire. As a boy, Edmund was educated at a local vicarage and at a nearby school in Haileybury. In 1878, it was decided that he should take the entrance examinations for the Indian Civil Service; during each of the next two years, however, he failed in the competitive tests that admitted only about one out of every seven candidates. At this stage, then, a military career seemed appropriate as a second choice; after a brief period of preparation, Allenby entered the Royal Military College at Sandhurst as a cadet in 1881. He was graduated from his course with honors, and in 1882, several weeks after his twenty-first birthday, he was granted a commission in the Sixth Inniskilling Dragoons and went on to join British forces in South Africa.

Although during his first assignments Allenby, and other British officers and men, had little more to deal with than minor expeditions into Bechuanaland and Zululand, his initial period of service did acquaint him with imperial military problems in a way that could not be imparted on English parade grounds. He was promoted to captain and then to adjutant. In 1890, his first term of service was completed, and his unit returned home; he subsequently sought entrance to the British Staff College. Allenby failed narrowly the first year he took the examination; on his second attempt, in 1895, he was admitted. He became the first officer from his regiment to enter that institution. Among others who joined the college when he did was Douglas Haig, captain of the Seventh Hussars, with whom he worked during World War I. During this time, Allenby also spent some time in Scotland, where he met Adelaide Mabel Chapman, the third daughter of a landowner from Wiltshire. After about a year's courtship, during which he had to persuade her father that as a cavalry officer he could support a household, they were married during the college's winter vacation, on the next to last day of 1896. Theirs was an enduring and happy union, which provided solace from the cares and anxieties of military work; they shared a common love of the outdoors, and both had a passion for travel. In 1897, Allenby was promoted to major, and also qualified as an army interpreter in French. During the first month of 1898, his son and only child, Michael, was born at the home of his wife's family in Wiltshire.

Allenby cast an imposing figure. He was fairly tall and heavyset; as a young man he weighed at least 185 pounds, though throughout his later life he successfully resisted any tendency to further bulkiness. He had broad squarish regular features with a long straight nose; his eyes, which others regarded as direct and penetrating, were gray-blue. He was clean-shaven, with the exception of a thick bushy mustache he had cultivated since his early days of military work. Photographs from his first assignments show incipient recession of his hairline, which expanded into large-scale baldness during his later years. Allenby was characterized by direct, forceful movements; he had a deep stentorian voice, which when challenging subordinates frequently became a bellow. He was curt, brusque, and regarded as a man of few words. Some considered him shy or lonely, while others were astonished on those occasions when he displayed the breadth of his interests.

LIFE'S WORK

Allenby was assigned to the Third Cavalry Brigade in Ireland and became a brigade major. He then rejoined his original regiment during the Boer War of 1899-1902. He demonstrated himself capable of taking calculated risks without unduly placing his forces in jeopardy. Some of his men testified to the calm lucidity with which he met unexpected threats. His troops took part in the advance to

Lord Allenby. (Library of Congress)

Bloemfrontein early in the conflict and were widely called on to combat guerrilla actions across a wide front. Allenby acquired a high reputation for his skill in protecting convoys, as his men did not suffer defeat in this series of engagements that was undertaken to protect British positions throughout the region.

During routine peacetime preparations in England, Allenby took part in cavalry exercises designed to anticipate possible contingencies in Europe. Although some of the plans devised by the British general staff took into account the actual needs that subsequently arose in Belgium and France, such measures were later criticized for lack of thoroughness. This failing was traced in part to financial limitations imposed on such maneuvers. For his part, Allenby's insistence on strict adherence to discipline and dress regulations was unpopular with some subordinates and enlisted men. On the other hand, his human concerns were demonstrated when, in the summer of 1905, he supported another man and a woman in the water after a yachting accident, and kept them afloat for twenty minutes until help came. For this action, he received a formal testimonial from the Royal Humane Society.

In August, 1914, when Great Britain entered World War I, Allenby commanded the cavalry division of the British Expeditionary Force; his first efforts on the western front required providing cover for retreating infantry on the routes from Mons to the Marne. Although he and other British commanders eventually were able to establish a stable front, some criticism was directed at Allenby's handling of his part of this difficult operation: For a period of five days, communications had broken off among units under his command. In September, Allied forces began to counterattack; there was later some speculation whether British cavalry could have accomplished more at this time. In 1915, Allenby became commander of the Fifth Corps, on the Ypres salient in Flanders, and then of the Third Army in France. During a difficult period of warfare from fixed positions, relatively little could be accomplished against determined German resistance; moreover, relations between Allenby and Sir Douglas Haig, the British commander in chief, became markedly strained. Offensive operations were commenced at Arras in April, 1917, but gradually ground to a halt, in part owing to lack of support from French forces in the area. Although early in this engagement his men had scored some gains against the Germans, Allenby was notably displeased with the outcome of action in this sector, and there was continuing friction with Haig over the appointment of subordinate officers and various tactical matters.

After some pronounced misgivings (he believed, for a time, that he was being shuffled away from the main front) in June Allenby accepted an assignment in an entirely different theater.

When the Ottoman Empire had entered the war on the side of the Central Powers, defense of the Suez Canal had become a pressing concern for the British Empire. Moreover, it was thought subsequently in some quarters that resolute action in the western Arab lands, or in the Balkans, might assist in bringing the war as a whole to a more rapid, and victorious, conclusion. Previous ventures, however, from the Allies' standpoint had proved disappointing or of limited utility: In 1915, a landing alongside the Dardanelles failed ignominiously, and some headway, but decidedly mixed results had been gained in Iraq. The Russian Revolutions of 1917 called into question the gains czarist forces had achieved in eastern Anatolia. Sir Archibald Murray, Allenby's predecessor, had led forces across the Sinai peninsula, but they had been halted before the fortifications about Gaza. On this front, each side had drawn on other national armies. German commanders, as well as troops, formed a particularly prominent contingent fighting alongside the Ottoman army; the most important contributions to British forces in the area had come from Australia and New Zealand.

Soon after he arrived in Egypt, Allenby learned that his son, Michael, who had earned the Military Cross after entering the armed forces, had been killed by a shell splinter during the action in France. This great shock was suffered with much quiet courage; plans went forward for an assault on the inland city of Beersheba, in Palestine. At the end of October, a partial success was achieved: Imperial cavalry rolled up opposing forces without enveloping them. On the left flank, however, Allenby's men broke through to Gaza. He immediately shifted many of his forces to this sector, and they advanced beyond Jaffa. It then became possible to menace Ottoman positions from the west and the south. Although for a time progress was blocked on both fronts, and it was necessary to contend with a bitter and bloody counterattack around Nablus, men and supplies were moved up the plains in sufficient numbers to invest Jerusalem; unharmed and intact, the holy city was surrendered on December 9, 1917. As one of the few positive accomplishments achieved by that time, this striking achievement was received with great acclamation in Allied countries. On the other hand, as additional plans were considered, storms and unusually inclement weather complicated further preparations in Palestine. Furthermore, as Ger-

man forces on the western front began to take the offensive, in March and April, 1918, two full divisions and some other units were transferred from Allenby's army to the European theater. Indian troops that were sent out to replace them in many cases were inexperienced and took some time to adjust to desert warfare.

During the spring and summer, Allenby was concerned largely with the training and reorganization of his forces. On another level, he allowed full scope for British officers to direct irregular operations against the Hijaz Railway and other lines of communications within the Ottoman lands. Curiously enough, for all of his rigidity where matters of ceremony, dress, and discipline were concerned, a bemused Allenby was entirely willing to authorize Colonel T. E. Lawrence's efforts among Arab guerrillas who steadily harassed their opponents. Indeed, after the war Allenby was unsparing in his tribute to the other man's courage and resourcefulness. After some small-scale engagements on the part of the regular army, by September a vast cavalry and infantry offensive, supported by the Royal Air Force, was launched on the Plain of Megiddo. At Nazareth, British forces came close to capturing the opposing commander in chief. Control of the entire area west of the Jordan River was assured; to the east, major thrusts were launched as well, notably against Amman. By the end of September, Damascus, which had no fortifications of consequence, lay open, and Arab nationalist factions began to take control of the city. By October 1, a brigade of Australian Light Horse and other elements of the Desert Mounted Corps had arrived. Homs and Tripoli, cities farther north in Syria, were captured during the next week. Allenby then accepted one of his general's proposals for an advance to Aleppo; this objective was realized in a bold stroke on October 26, 1918. Four days later, after further inconclusive action in this area, the Ottoman government bowed to Allied pressure in Macedonia and in the Arab provinces and requested an armistice. According to official British records, during the last six weeks of the campaign Allenby's men had taken seventy-five thousand prisoners and had suffered 5,666 casualties in battle. During this time, the Fifth Cavalry Division, in the vanguard, had traversed about 550 miles.

Allenby had been knighted during the middle of the war and thereafter received other awards for his accomplishments in the Middle East. During the first year of peace, he was made a viscount. He also received honorary degrees from Oxford, Cambridge, and other universities. His achievements were further recognized by his appointment in March, 1919, as special High Commissioner for Egypt; his exercise of this office, however, involved administrative and diplomatic functions with which he was distinctly ill at ease. Nevertheless, his work in that country did much to assist in the development of Egypt's political institutions. He arrived in the middle of a short-lived revolution that had broken out following protests at the exile of prominent national leaders; Allenby insisted that they be allowed to return. Negotiations over Egypt's political relationship with Great Britain were a difficult, protracted affair. In his impatience with what he regarded as London's delaying tactics, Allenby issued a virtual ultimatum to Prime Minister David Lloyd George and threatened to resign if his terms were not met. The conditions, which were granted in February, 1922, included the termination of Great Britain's protectorate and its unilateral recognition of Egypt as an independent and sovereign state. Great Britain did retain particular rights where imperial communications and defense, as well as other matters of mutual interest, were concerned. Allenby also encouraged the promulgation of Egypt's constitution of 1923, which was important for the development of parliamentary politics in that country. However progressive and forward-looking he may have been in dealing with political concerns in Egypt, the severity of his reaction to a single incident brought about the termination of Allenby's administrative career. In November, 1924, one of Allenby's personal friends, Sir Lee Stack, the governor-general of the Sudan and commander of the Egyptian army, was murdered in Cairo. Without waiting for instructions from his government, Allenby imposed an indemnity on the Egyptian treasury at large and ordered other punitive measures. In the wake of widespread protests against his high-handedness, he summarily resigned his position in Egypt and left the country in June, 1925.

Allenby in effect retired from active service. While he established a home in the British capital, during his later years he and his wife traveled widely. They visited Australia, New Zealand, Canada, the United States, and also many parts of Asia and Africa. Allenby also found ample time to pursue fishing and ornithology. He also sought to promote public consciousness of military concerns and acted as president of organizations to assist cadets and to provide for the needs of older veterans. On certain occasions he delivered public lectures. He died rather suddenly, and evidently rather peacefully, on May 14, 1936: He had suffered a fatal brain hemorrhage and was found lying across his desk in his study at his home in London.

SIGNIFICANCE

The great renown that Lord Allenby received was largely a result of a single series of campaigns in the western Arab lands. His previous career had been distinguished but not extraordinary. His actions during the Boer War and on the western front brought him to the forefront of British commanders, but in and of themselves they would not have assured him such a notable place in modern history. He neither sought nor shunned fame or advancement; his efforts in the Middle Eastern theater represented the use of forces at his disposal to maximum advantage. In 1917 and 1918, he took some risks in difficult terrain and under demanding climatic conditions. Nevertheless, he acted when he was assured that his forces had a clear superiority over their opponents. It has sometimes been maintained that his victories were achieved against uninspired leadership on the other side, and it probably was so that the Ottoman general staff was riven by rivalries and disagreements between Turkish and German commanders.

On the other hand, the German commanders in chief, Erich von Falkenhayn and Otto Liman von Sanders, were serious and determined warriors; the former was one of the war's most highly regarded generals. Some Turkish leaders of note were also posted on this front. Two of them later won recognition as Atatürk and İsmet Paşa. The Turkish War of Independence (1919-1922) in particular demonstrated their capacities for leadership. Allenby's efforts have been considered as among the last major cavalry actions in modern warfare. The scope and extent of advances in this theater compared favorably with other epic operations of past wars, and on a tactical level, there was a curious juxtaposition of the old to the modern. During the desert campaigns, Allenby's forces employed one of the earlier uses of airpower, and with nearly complete command of the skies, Allenby's troops were able to pursue their opponents more readily.

Because of the evolution of military technology, this peculiar combination of mounted and mechanized operations could not easily be emulated by subsequent tacticians in the area. On the political level, the Arab campaigns opened the way for a new and turbulent era in Middle Eastern politics. Allenby had little to do with the division of much of the area into British and French mandatory states; while he attempted to remain evenhanded when conflicting claims of Arab nationalists and Zionists arose, his mission in the Levant did not much involve him in this controversy. Although it ended badly, his work in Egypt did much to advance the political development of that country. Moreover, in a much wider gyre, the consequences of war and upheaval in the Middle East were to change permanently the political landscape of the region; while he certainly could not have anticipated many of the results, Allenby's mark in history will invariably be associated with the passing of Ottoman rule during new phases in the historical destinies of the Arab lands.

—J. R. Broadus

FURTHER READING

Falls, Cyril. *Armageddon: 1918*. Philadelphia: J. B. Lippincott, 1964. A brisk, concise account of the Arab campaigns that also assesses the relative importance of these operations in the larger context of World War I. The author concludes with some reflections on the subsequent course of events in the Middle East.

Gardner, Brian. *Allenby of Arabia, Lawrence's General.* New York: Coward-McCann, 1966. This crisp popular narrative, which seeks to reclaim a place of honor for Allenby alongside T. E. Lawrence, is rather objective and has some convincing passages about the commander's development as a tactician. In many places, the author has drawn on the vast corpus of manuscript letters, mainly to his mother and wife, that Allenby left behind him. A British version, under the title *Allenby*, was published one year before the American edition.

Hughes, Matthew. *Allenby and British Strategy in the Middle East, 1917-1919.* Portland, Oreg.: F. Cass, 1999. An account of the Palestinian campaign fought by the British-led Egyptian Expeditionary Force from 1917 until its withdrawal from Syria in 1919, including a reassessment of Allenby's role as campaign commander.

Long, C. W. R. *British Pro-Consuls in Egypt, 1914-1929: The Challenge of Nationalism.* New York: RoutledgeCurzon, 2005. Describes the activities of Allenby and three other pro-consuls in Egypt and their major opponent, Sa'ad Zaghul, leader of the nationalist WAFD party who fought for Egyptian independence.

MacMunn, George Fletcher, and Cyril Falls. *Military Operations, Egypt and Palestine.* 2 vols. London: H. M. Stationery Office, 1928-1930. Vast comprehensive official history; indispensable source for the operations discussed here. Numerous materials con-

cerning the Arab campaigns were consulted during the preparation of this work.

Massey, William Thomas. *Allenby's Final Triumph.* London: Constable, 1920. The last of several works on the Middle Eastern theater by an accredited correspondent from London newspapers. The author's observations of desert fighting up to the armistice with the Ottoman Empire are recorded in vivid terms.

Savage, Raymond. *Allenby of Armageddon: A Record of the Career and Campaigns of Field-Marshall Viscount Allenby.* Indianapolis, Ind.: Bobbs-Merrill, 1926. A favorable early account written by a member of Allenby's campaign staff, this work has some interesting impressions of its subject's character. Savage at one time was also a literary agent for T. E. Lawrence.

Wavell, Archibald Percival. *Allenby—A Study in Greatness: The Biography of Field-Marshal Viscount Allenby of Megiddo and Felixstowe.* 2 vols. London: George G. Harrap, 1940-1943. A wide-ranging and sympathetic portrait of Allenby as a soldier and statesman. In addition to considering previous military work outside the Middle East, the author in his second volume discusses at length the positive aspects of his subject's administrative work in Egypt. To substantiate certain points, some of Allenby's letters are quoted in places.

_____. *The Palestine Campaigns.* 1928. 3d ed. London: Constable, 1941. Systematic, officially sponsored history dealing with the operations of 1917 and 1918 from a tactical point of view; the author abundantly acknowledges Allenby's inspired judgment in this theater. Wavell served on this front, rising to the rank of brigadier general in 1918. Later, during World War II, he had a checkered career as a commander in his own right.

SEE ALSO: First Viscount Alanbrooke; Atatürk; T. E. Lawrence; Bernard Law Montgomery; First Viscount Slim.

SALVADOR ALLENDE
President of Chile (1970-1973)

Allende, the first socialist president of Chile, was one of the most important political figures in twentieth century Latin America. Elected in 1970 in his fourth bid for Chile's highest office, he inaugurated a controversial program of reform that, opposed both by Chilean elite interests and the United States, culminated in his overthrow and assassination in 1973.

BORN: June 26, 1908; Valparaíso, Chile
DIED: September 11, 1973; Santiago, Chile
ALSO KNOWN AS: Salvador Allende Gossens (full name)
AREA OF ACHIEVEMENT: Government and politics

EARLY LIFE

Salvador Allende (SAHL-vah-dohr ah-YEHN-day) was born in Valparaíso, Chile, the last of four brothers and one of the eight children of Salvador Allende Castro and Laura Gossens Uribe. Allende's father was a public defender with a strong interest in social justice, whose own father, Ramon Allende Padin, had been a prominent politician and a Chilean freemason. Laura Gossens, in contrast, was a devout Roman Catholic from a well-to-do family. Allende, a religious agnostic, was himself to be a lifelong freemason.

Allende spent the first eight years of his life in the northern rural town of Tacna, which had once been part of Peru and was returned to it in 1931. Returning to Valparaíso, he was educated at the Liceo Eduardo de la Barra and took an M.D. from the University of Chile in 1933. Already an activist, he supported the short-lived Socialist Republic of Chile proclaimed in 1932 by Marmaduke Groves, a friend of the Allende family. The republic was overthrown in a military coup sponsored by landed interests and British and American industrialists—a coalition similar to the one that would overthrow Allende four decades later.

Allende was arrested for his support of the republic and was put through five trials before being released. Unable to secure a hospital staff appointment as a doctor, he worked in clinics for the poor, performed autopsies in a morgue, and was exiled for a time to the desolate northern port city of Caldera. A cofounder of the Chilean Socialist Party, he became its leader in Valparaíso and was elected to the Chilean National Congress in 1937. During the earthquake of January 25, 1939, in Santiago, he met his future wife, Hortensia Bussi Soto, whom he married

later that year and with whom he had three daughters: Carmen, Beatriz, and Isabel. He also joined the staff of Pedro Aguirre Cerda, and in September, 1939, became minister of public health in Aguirre Cerda's Popular Front government. Allende served in this capacity until 1942, working to reform what he described in his book *La Realidad Médico Social de Chile* (1939; Chile's social and medical reality) as the "invisible tragedy" of the country's unequal health system.

LIFE'S WORK

After Cerda's death in November, 1941, Allende resigned his position in protest at the rightward drift of Cerda's successor, Juan Antonio Ríos. In 1943, Allende was elected secretary-general of the Socialist Party, which promptly split over his insistence that Communists remain part of the left coalition. Allende continued to defend the civil rights of Communists, including their participation in public life, in the Cold War atmosphere of the late 1940's. Elected to the Chilean senate in 1945

Salvador Allende. (AP/Wide World Photos)

(and a continuous member until 1970), he had emerged as the most prominent political figure of the country's left by the late 1940's.

In 1952, Allende made the first of four consecutive bids for the presidency of the republic. The left split again on the Communist question, with most members of the Popular Socialist Party supporting a former dictator, Carlos Ibáñez, who campaigned on a populist platform. Running on the Socialist Party ticket, Allende won only 5.5 percent of the vote, but he was vindicated when Ibáñez soon shed his electoral persona as the General of Hope and turned to the right. With broad left-wing support, including that of the newly legalized Communist Party, Allende was narrowly defeated in his second presidential run in 1958, getting 28.5 percent of the vote to 31.6 percent for the victorious Jorge Alessandri, son of a popular former president (and mistaken by some voters for his father).

Allende actually received his highest share of the popular vote—38.6 percent—in his 1964 campaign against Eduardo Frei, but the latter was elected when the right abandoned its own preferred candidate, Julio Durán, and threw its support behind the moderately reformist Frei to block a socialist victory. Allende was elected speaker of the senate in 1966, despite his embrace of the regime of Fidel Castro in Cuba. In 1967 he met with the survivors of Che Guevara's guerrilla band after Guevara's death.

Chile fielded three major presidential candidates again in 1970. Allende, running on the coalition ticket of the Popular Unity Party, won a plurality with 36.2 percent of

---

THE U.S. CONNECTION TO THE CHILEAN COUP

In a telephone conversation at 11:50 A.M. on September 16, 1973, just five days following the overthrow of Salvador Allende, U.S. secretary of state Henry Kissinger and President Richard M. Nixon discussed the implications of the coup and the role played by the United States. (Editor's note: [?] indicates unintelligible parts of the conversation.)

KISSINGER: Hello.

NIXON: Hi, Henry.

KISSINGER: Mr. President.

NIXON: Where are you. In New York?

KISSINGER: No, I am in Washington. I am working. I may go to the football game this afternoon if I get through.

NIXON: Good. Good. Well it is the opener. It is better than television. Nothing new of any importance, or is there?

KISSINGER: Nothing of great consequence. The Chilean thing is getting consolidated and of course the newspapers are bleeding because a pro-Communist government has been overthrown.

NIXON: Isn't that something. Isn't that something.

KISSINGER: I mean instead of celebrating—in the Eisenhower period we would be heroes.

NIXON: Well we didn't—as you know—our hand doesn't show on this one though.

KISSINGER: We didn't do it. I mean we helped them . . . created the conditions as great as possible [?]

NIXON: That is right. And that is the way it is going to be played. But listen, as far as people are concerned let me say they aren't going to buy this crap from the liberals on this one.

KISSINGER: Absolutely not.

NIXON: They know it is a pro-Communist government and that is the way it is.

KISSINGER: Exactly. And pro-Castro.

NIXON: Well the main thing was. Let's forget the pro-Communist. It was an anti-American government all the . . . way.

KISSINGER: Oh, wildly.

NIXON: And your expropriating. I notice the memorandum you sent up of the confidential conversation . . . set up a policy for reimbursement on expropriations and cooperation with the United States for breaking relations with Castro. Well what the hell that is a great treat [?] if they think that. No don't let the columns and the bleeding on that . . .

KISSINGER: Oh, oh it doesn't bother me. I am just reporting it to you.

NIXON: Yes, you are reporting it because it is just typical of the crap we are up against.

KISSINGER: And the unbelievable filthy hypocrisy.

NIXON: We know that.

KISSINGER: Of these people. When it is South Africa, if we don't overthrow them there they are raising hell.

NIXON: Yes, that is right.

---

some 3 million votes cast, with Alessandri polling 34.9 percent and Radomiro Tomic, the new leader of Frei's Christian Democratic Party, a relatively distant third at 27.8 percent. Lacking a majority, Allende was elected, according to constitutional provision, by congress on October 24, and he assumed office on November 3.

The failure of Frei's administration, which had stemmed neither rising inflation nor unemployment, had created an opening on the left, and many in Chile and the United States looked on Allende's prospective election with foreboding. A visit to North Vietnam in 1969 by the socialist leader did little to allay fears. Washington had a long tradition of manipulating Latin American elections, with the support of American business and banking interests and the cooperation of the AFL-CIO. It had heavily funded Frei's campaign, and U.S. national security adviser Henry Kissinger ominously declared in June, 1970, "I don't see why we need to stand by and watch a country go communist due to the irresponsibility of its own people." On October 22, seven weeks after the election, General René Schneider, head of Chile's armed forces, was killed during an apparent kidnapping attempt. Schneider had been a principled opponent of military interference in civilian affairs, and his murder was widely interpreted as an attempt to clear the way for a coup.

For the moment, the strategy backfired, and Allende's election by the congress two days later was an affirmation of civilian rule. Nonetheless, Allende was obliged to accept restrictions on his power to appoint commanding officers and to remove civilian bureaucrats before assuming office. He controlled only a weakened executive, with a suspicious congress, a hostile army, and a supreme court determined to thwart him.

Despite these concessions, Allende pressed what he took to be a popular mandate. "I am *not* the President of all the Chilean people," he declared, signaling his intention to pursue reform in the teeth of whatever opposition it might arouse. In truth, Allende had a strong base of working-class support and a degree of consensus from centrist constituencies on critical aspects of his program, particularly the nationalization of Chile's copper industry. Idealistic *allendistas* fanned out into Chile's shantytowns to bring social services to the poor, giving many people economic dignity for the first time. Wages were raised while prices and rents were frozen. To pay for this, Allende called on workers to voluntarily increase productivity, which rose 14 percent in the first year of his administration. Furthermore, Allende remembered his early commitment to health care. The government instituted children's nutritional programs, and hospitals were ordered to accept all patients regardless of their ability or inability to pay. Mass cultural events were organized, and developing world delegations arrived to offer congratulations, topped by a visit from Castro. On July 11, 1971, the so-called Day of National Dignity, the copper, iron ore, steel, and nitrate industries were nationalized.

The United Popular Party increased its share of the vote in municipal and congressional elections over that of the presidential election itself through 1973. Nonetheless, the center-right electorate was increasingly alienated, while the United States pursued an active program of economic and political sabotage. Workers and peasants, responding to the challenge, began to seize factories and farms. Militant leftists within Allende's coalition urged him to cultivate radical elements within the military to forestall a coup. While Allende resisted this, right-wing officers carried out their own purge of loyalist elements. On June 29, 1973, a military coup against the government was narrowly averted; on August 23, the constitutionalist general Carlos Prats, head of the armed forces, was compelled to resign in favor of General Augusto Pinochet Ugarte, who was actively plotting Allende's overthrow.

As tensions mounted, more than 750,000 Chileans demonstrated in Santiago on Allende's behalf on September 4. Allende himself offered to conduct a popular referendum on his presidency. Within days, on September 11, a well-organized military coup toppled Allende's government in a day of brutal and methodical bloodshed. Allende, barricaded in the presidential residence La Moneda but deserted by his guard and attended only by a few followers, announced by radio that he was about to "pay with my life defending the principles so dear to this homeland." La Moneda was bombed to rubble, and the sixty-five-year-old Allende, machine-gun in hand, met death in a hail of bullets.

SIGNIFICANCE

Allende was the first socialist leader democratically elected to power in the Western Hemisphere. As resolutely committed to democracy as he was to socialism, he was in life and even more in death a beacon for those who believed that social justice was compatible with a respect for constitutional norms, and that one could not be meaningfully exercised without the other. His brief experiment, against insurmountable odds, left a permanent legacy, but also deep divisions within Chilean society.

A long period of political repression followed under the regime of General Pinochet (1973-1990), and democratic normalization returned only gradually thereafter as Pinochet continued to hold the reins of military power. The political left remained effectively marginalized even under the nominally "socialist" administrations of Ricardo Lagos and Michelle Bachelet (the first female president of Chile). Pinochet himself was apprehended while traveling in London on a Spanish government warrant, and judicial proceedings against him were finally begun. He died under house arrest in Chile in December, 2006.

Allende's example did inspire Latin populist leaders early in the twenty-first century, notably the government of Hugo Chavez in Venezuela, but the dilemma of achieving a fully socialist and democratic revolution against entrenched elites remains unresolved. In the United States itself, revelations of the Central Intelligence Agency's complicity in Allende's overthrow were to shine a harsh light on the limits of America's toleration of any challenge to its power and interests, whether democratically constituted or not.

—Robert Zaller

FURTHER READING

Cockcroft, James D., ed. *Salvador Allende Reader: Chile's Voice of Democracy.* New York: Ocean Press, 2000. Excerpts and addresses by Allende, with an introduction.

Collier, Simon, and William F. Stater. *A History of Chile, 1808-2002.* 2d ed. New York: Cambridge University Press, 2004. A standard history of Chile, from independence to the post-Pinochet years.

Falcoff, Mark. *Modern Chile, 1970-1989: A Critical History.* New Brunswick, N.J.: Transaction Books, 1991. A close socioeconomic analysis of the Allende years, with a brief postscript on the Pinochet era.

Sigmund, Paul E. *The Overthrow of Allende and the Politics of Chile, 1964-1976.* Pittsburgh, Pa.: University of Pittsburgh Press, 1977. An account of the Allende years from the perspective of the failed "revolution in liberty" program of his predecessor, Eduardo Frei.

Veneros, Diana. *Allende: Un Ensayo Psicobiografica.* Santiago, Chile: Random House Mondadori, 2003. A portrait of Allende that draws on interviews with colleagues, family members, and others who knew him.

SEE ALSO: Oscar Arias Sánchez; Jean-Bertrand Aristide; Plutarco Elías Calles; Lázaro Cárdenas; Fernando Henrique Cardoso; Fidel Castro; Che Guevara; Víctor Raúl Haya de la Torre; Henry Kissinger; Francisco Madero; Pablo Neruda; Álvaro Obregón; Eva Perón; Juan Perón; Augusto Pinochet.

RELATED ARTICLES in *Great Events from History: The Twentieth Century:*

1941-1970: 1964-1970: Frei "Chileanizes" Chile's Copper Industry; September 4, 1970: Allende Wins a Close Election in Chile.

1971-2000: 1973: ITT Actions Cause Suspicion of Involvement in a Chilean Coup; September 11, 1973: Chilean Military Overthrows Allende; 1974: Medical Group Exposes Torture in Greece and Chile; January, 1983: National Commission Against Torture Studies Human Rights Abuses; December 14, 1989: Chilean Voters End Pinochet's Military Rule.

LUIS W. ALVAREZ
American physicist

A Nobel Prize-winning physicist with diverse interests, Alvarez discovered the radioactive isotope tritium and worked on the atomic bomb. He was aboard the plane that dropped the bomb on Hiroshima, Japan, during World War II. Like many atomic scientists, he believed nuclear weapons would discourage war. After his retirement, he and his son theorized that a meteor impact caused the extinction of the dinosaurs, a theory that has since become widely accepted.

BORN: June 13, 1911; San Francisco, California
DIED: September 1, 1988; Berkeley, California
ALSO KNOWN AS: Luis Walter Alvarez (full name)
AREAS OF ACHIEVEMENT: Physics, invention and technology, geology, military affairs

EARLY LIFE

Luis Walter Alvarez (AHL-vah-rehz) was born in San Francisco to physician and medical researcher Walter Alvarez and Harriet Smyth Alvarez. Walter Alvarez was a respected researcher and internist who strongly encouraged young Luis's interest in mechanics and electronics. Harriet Alvarez, trained as a school teacher, taught her son through the second grade, which allowed him to skip part of third grade and stay a year ahead in school.

The young Alvarez often accompanied his father to the lab where he conducted physiological research. Although Alvarez did not find the medical research very interesting, he was, however, fascinated by the electrical equipment. He learned to construct circuits by age ten.

In 1926, Walter Alvarez was offered a job at the Mayo

Clinic, so the family moved to Rochester, Minnesota. The young Alvarez's high school science courses were not special to him, but after he attended his first physics lecture, on the electromagnetic spectrum, his interest was caught. Alvarez left for college at the University of Chicago, where he spent his first two years as an unexceptional chemistry major. After taking the course Advanced Experimental Physics: Light as a junior, he switched to studying physics and finished the curriculum to graduate three months early in 1932 with a bachelor of science degree. His enthusiasm and aptitude impressed his professors. The same year he began graduate school, also at Chicago, and proceeded to earn his master's degree in 1934 and his Ph.D. in 1936.

A few days after his exams, he married Geraldine "Gerry" Smithwick. The couple moved to California for Alvarez to begin working at Berkeley's Radiation Laboratory under Ernest Lawrence, who won a Nobel Prize in physics in 1939 for inventing the cyclotron. Lawrence

Luis W. Alvarez. (© The Nobel Foundation)

became a mentor and friend to Alvarez, whose impressive career was just beginning.

LIFE'S WORK

Alvarez began work in Lawrence's laboratory as a cyclotron operator in 1936. The cyclotron was used primarily for producing artificial radiation for the study of radioactive half-lives and newly discovered radioisotopes. Alvarez began reading everything he could obtain on nuclear physics. During his first year at Berkeley, he discovered the process of K-electron capture, whereby an atomic nucleus absorbs an electron from its innermost shell of its orbital electrons and becomes a different nuclide.

Although he received many job offers from other institutions in 1937, Alvarez stayed at the Radiation Laboratory, with the promise of becoming an instructor at Berkeley the following summer. In 1939, Alvarez and graduate student Bob Cornog found that helium 3 was stable and nonradioactive, while hydrogen 3 (tritium) was unstable and radioactive, contrary to the prevailing hypothesis. The discovery of tritium proved vital to the atomic bomb program. Shortly after tritium's discovery, German scientists discovered nuclear fission.

In 1940, Alvarez left Berkeley for the Massachusetts Institute of Technology (MIT) in Cambridge, to work on the development of radar for World War II efforts. The same year, his son Walter was born. Alvarez developed several important radar technologies, including a narrow beam for directing airplane landing in poor weather, a method for locating and bombing targets on the ground that the pilot could not see, and an early-warning system for tracking aircraft movement in overcast skies.

Alvarez joined the staff of physicist Enrico Fermi at Argonne National Laboratories outside Chicago in 1943. At Argonne, Alvarez was able to again focus on research rather than administration. One of his first projects there was to develop a radiation detector for airplanes, which proved very important for gathering intelligence during and after the war. After six months at Argonne, Alvarez was assigned to the top-secret Manhattan Project in Los Alamos, New Mexico, where he worked on developing the atomic bomb.

The Alvarezes' daughter, Jean, was born four years to the day after Walter, in 1944, during Alvarez's first year at Los Alamos. His primary project there was to work on a detonator for the atomic bomb. He also developed a way of measuring the energy of the bomb from the air, and was present in a plane at the Trinity test on July 16, 1945. After Trinity, Alvarez was assigned to measure the energy of the atomic bomb that would be dropped on Hiroshima in 1945. Little Boy, as this bomb was known, had not been previously tested because of its high cost. Alvarez was on the *Great Artiste* with the measurement equipment. On his way back from Japan, he wrote a letter for his four-year-old son Walter to read when he was older, musing on the effects of the bomb. Like many atomic scientists, he believed that the bomb was terrible enough that it might lead to the end of war.

Alvarez's postwar basic research focused on particle accelerators for studying high-energy physics, although he continued to be sporadically involved in military research and affairs, including testifying at the hearing to determine the matter of J. Robert Oppenheimer, whose government security clearance had been revoked because of his left-wing ties at the heart of the Cold War. Alvarez was elected to the National Academy of Sciences in 1946.

In 1950, Alvarez became interested in the so-called bubble chamber for particle detection, which was invented by Donald A. Glaser. Alvarez proceeded to improve on Glaser's invention, and he was awarded the Nobel Prize in Physics in 1968 for his bubble chamber work. By this time, Alvarez had divorced, remarrying in 1958 to Janet Landis. They had two more children, Donald and Helen. Landis, who had an interest in physics and who worked at the Radiation Laboratory as well, shared a great deal of her husband's professional life.

Alvarez's oldest son Walter, a geologist, brought him a piece of Italian limestone that originated during the Cretaceous-Tertiary (K/T) boundary, the time when the dinosaurs became extinct. Alvarez, retired from Berkeley in 1978, set out to determine how long it took for the clay layer at the K/T boundary to form using radioactive iridium isotopes. While this attempt was unsuccessful, the two found that the iridium level in the clay was unusually high, and its composition was very different from the limestone above and below it, perhaps extraterrestrial in nature. The boundary clay has since been found all over the world.

DID AN ASTEROID KILL THE DINOSAURS?

In 1978, Luis W. Alvarez and his son Walter began an investigation of a single-centimeter layer of clay that was sandwiched between two limestone strata containing large deposits of Cretaceous-Tertiary fossils. Such fossils were significantly absent elsewhere in the sample. The clay deposit dated from the boundary between the Cretaceous and Tertiary periods, referred to as the K/T boundary, roughly 65 million years ago, when the dinosaurs disappeared and modern flora, apes, and large mammals appeared.

Alvarez and his son used a trace of iridium in the composition of the clay sample to determine how long it had taken for the clay to be deposited and so to calculate the time that had elapsed during the Cretaceous-Tertiary transition. Iridium is basically an extraterrestrial substance. All the iridium in Earth's crust is only one ten-thousandth of the iridium abundant in meteorites. Alvarez selected iridium because it was the best material to use in determining the amount of debris that fell on Earth during this crucial period. Iridium is deposited uniformly around Earth, and Alvarez wanted to account for these uniform deposits. He began with the theories of Sir George Stokes, who formulated the viscosity law, a calculation of the rate at which small particles fall in the air. Stokes had based this law on his observations of the fallout of ash from the huge volcanic eruption of Krakatoa near Java, Indonesia, in the 1880's. After discounting many possible hypotheses, such as a gigantic volcanic eruption, a supernova, or Earth's passing through a cosmic cloud of molecular hydrogen, Alvarez developed the hypothesis that an asteroid had collided with Earth.

According to his calculations, the asteroid had to be 10 kilometers in diameter. Its impact would have been catastrophic. As Alvarez said,

The worst nuclear scenario yet proposed considers all fifty thousand nuclear warheads in U.S. and Russian hands going off more or less at once. That would be a disaster four orders of magnitude less violent than the K/T asteroid impact.

Alvarez knew that the margin for error in discoveries was exponential, because of the possibility of mistakes in the data. As more data were collected from other sources, however, the argument became stronger. Although the asteroid hypothesis was not fully accepted by the scientific community, a number of predictions based on the theory have been verified experimentally and by computer simulation.

Alvarez considered various possible explanations for both the iridium-rich clay layer and the mass extinction, finally agreeing with the suggestion of astronomer Chris McKee that a ten-kilometer meteor striking the earth sixty-five million years ago would throw up enough dust, creating a dark, cold global climate for several years (later revised to months). In the K/T extinction, all land animals weighing more than fifty pounds disappeared from the fossil record. While Luis and Walter Alvarez and their colleagues initially met with some resistance from geoscientists, their theory is now widely accepted.

In his autobiography *Alvarez: Adventures of a Physicist*, he wrote that he believed the work on nuclear energy at Los Alamos had ended the cycle of European wars and that he hoped to see the elimination of all weapons, both conventional and nuclear. Alvarez died of cancer in his Berkeley home on September 1, 1988, only a year after publishing his autobiography.

SIGNIFICANCE

Alvarez was a brilliant physicist with unusually diverse research interests for a modern scientist. His contributions as a scientist and a teacher were extensive. The world has yet to achieve Alvarez's dream of an end to warfare. Indeed, nuclear technology continues to play a key role in global politics.

Alvarez's asteroid-extinction theory changed the field of geology. Most geologists now accept his theory for the K/T extinction, and research now focuses on the Permian mass extinction. The possibility of impact-extinction contributed to the theory of punctuated equilibrium proposed by paleontologists Niles Eldrege and Stephen Jay Gould. As a professor, Alvarez inspired several generations of physicists, many of whom have worked into the twenty-first century.

—*Melissa A. Barton*

FURTHER READING

Alvarez, Luis W. *Alvarez: Adventures of a Physicist*. New York: Basic Books, 1987. Alvarez's autobiography presents a strong picture of both his life and his personality, covering his childhood and academic influences as well as his professional career. Includes index.

Alvarez, Walter. *T. Rex and the Crater of Doom*. Princeton, N.J.: Princeton University Press, 1997. An informal, personal account by Walter Alvarez of how he and his father developed their impact-extinction theory. Includes notes and index.

Dardo, Mauro. *Nobel Laureates and Twentieth-Century Physics*. New York: Cambridge University Press, 2004. Chronicles major developments in physics since 1901, the year the first Nobel Prize in Physics was awarded. Discusses the work of the prizewinners.

Olesky, Walter. *Hispanic-American Scientists*. New York: Facts On File, 1998. Aimed at middle- and high-school students, this collection of profiles includes a short biography of Luis Alvarez. Includes further reading and index. Illustrated.

Powell, James Lawrence. *Night Comes to the Cretaceous: Comets, Craters, Controversy, and the Last Days of the Dinosaurs*. San Diego, Calif.: Harvest Books, 1998. An elegant treatment of the story of the development and testing of Walter and Luis Alvarez's asteroid-impact theory, now widely accepted by paleontologists. Includes figures, references, and index.

Rhodes, Richard. *The Making of the Atomic Bomb*. New York: Simon & Schuster, 1995. A Pulitzer Prize-winning account of the men and women who pioneered atomic physics and ultimately developed the atomic bomb. Includes bibliography and index.

Trower, Peter, ed. *Discovering Alvarez: Selected Works of Luis W. Alvarez with Commentary by His Students and Colleagues*. Chicago: University of Chicago Press, 1987. A collection of Alvarez's most influential articles, with commentary by the students and colleagues who worked closely with him. Includes publication and patent lists and photographs.

SEE ALSO: Percy Williams Bridgman; Sir James Chadwick; Arthur Holly Compton; Enrico Fermi; Stephen Jay Gould; Edwin Mattison McMillan; J. Robert Oppenheimer; Ernest Rutherford; Glenn Theodore Seaborg; Edward Teller.

RELATED ARTICLES in *Great Events from History: The Twentieth Century:*

VIKTOR A. AMBARTSUMIAN
Russian astrophysicist

Ambartsumian developed the astrophysics of stars and stellar origins and was instrumental in the theory of gigantic catastrophe formation in galaxies related to the evolution of stars and galaxies. He was the founder of the major school of theoretical astrophysics in the Soviet Union.

BORN: September 18, 1908; Tiflis, Georgia, Russian Empire (now Tbilisi, Georgia)
DIED: August 12, 1996; Byurakan Observatory, near Yerevan, Armenia
ALSO KNOWN AS: Viktor Amazaspovich Ambartsumian (full name)
AREAS OF ACHIEVEMENT: Astronomy, physics, mathematics

EARLY LIFE

Viktor A. Ambartsumian (ahm-bahrt-SEW-mee-uhn) was the son of a local teacher of literature. Early in school, he developed a passion for mathematics and physics and became extremely interested in the formation, evolution, and energy generation of stars and other heavenly bodies. Already at age eleven, he wrote two scientific papers: "The New Sixteen-Year Period for Sunspots" and "Description of Nebulae in Connection with the Hypothesis on the Origin of the Universe." Following his passion for science, he went to the University of Leningrad, from which he was graduated in 1928 with high honors. He performed so well and so amazed his instructors that he was offered a position at the university, where he stayed to teach until 1944. In that year, he went to Yerevan, Soviet Armenia, to become the founder and director of the Byurakan Observatory and its subsequent permanent director.

LIFE'S WORK

Very early in his career at the Byurakan Observatory, Ambartsumian became interested in the physics of stars and nebulas, combined with a general regard for astronomical topics of all characteristics. As a by-product of his work, he became the founder of the school for theoretical astrophysics in the Soviet Union, concentrating much of his time and effort on the cosmogony of stars and galaxies. It was his detailed work on the theory of stellar origins that brought him early recognition, particularly his explanation, derived by both reasoning and mathematics, of how gigantic catastrophic explosions had taken place elsewhere in the universe and how such explosions could take place in, or even be required for, the evolution of stars and galaxies. The idea originated from the work of Walter Baade and Hermann Minkowski, who first identified a radio source of extraordinary violence in the constellation of Cygnus. Baade had first announced that the radio source was associated with what appeared to be a closely connected pair of distant galaxies. In the photographs, it appeared that a gigantic collision was occurring, a supremely colossal event that could account for the extensive radio spectrum being emitted from that particular region of extragalactic space. Baade believed that events such as this catastrophe might even be common enough in the universe to account for the numerous extragalactic radio sources already identified by that time. Ambartsumian, however, in 1955 was able to gather enough evidence, both observational and theoretical, to show that the collision view was undoubtedly wrong. As an alternative, he proposed that vast explosions could occur within the core of a galaxy, creating a tremendous release of energy, somewhat analogous to supernova explosions, only on a galactic, rather than a stellar, scale. Mechanisms for such titanic explosions include chain-reaction supernovas erupting in the densely packed galactic core, interactions of normal matter and antimatter, the possible interactions of stars and interstellar materials with a superheavy black hole, or the total destruction of a galaxy's nucleus through some other mechanism involving fantastic releases of energy, much more than could ever be derived from simple atomic bomb explosions. The discovery of other galaxies (particularly that by Allan Sandage, who worked with M-82) in the process of definitely exploding has led to Ambartsumian's hypotheses becoming well established in current astrophysical thought.

In his role as founder of the Soviet school of combined theoretical physics and astronomy, Ambartsumian initiated the study of numerous topics, in some areas virtually inventing, redefining, and mathematically settling the field. He founded the quantitative theory for emissions of light energy from gaseous nebulas, a precursor to his ideas on how stars formed. As a method for forming such gaseous nebulas, he established a detailed synthesis for calculating the masses ejected by stars in their normal, nonstationary state, now called solar wind, and for those far enough along in their life history to become novas or exploding stars. To handle large groups of stars, such as

research as well. He unraveled the channels and produced a trustworthy chart of the Northwest Passage, the Arctic Ocean, and the Antarctic region, discovering islands beneath the Antarctic ice. His observations on terrestrial magnetism changed the minds of scientists everywhere. Amundsen's research, which included assessing the thickness of the ice caps, led to advances in oceanography, climatology, navigation, and the study of geomagnetism. His determination to be first in polar exploration and discovery drove him to turn apparent defeat into new opportunities. Twice he had dreamed of being first at the North Pole, once by sea and ice, once by airplane. Both times, however, even as he was preparing his own expeditions, someone else claimed those prizes.

Humans have only recently entered the polar regions, and Amundsen took part in the transition from sailing vessels to gasoline-powered ships. He was the first to sail the Arctic waters with an auxiliary motor. He saw the transition from dog sledges to mechanized sledges, and his race to the South Pole was followed by his use of both airships (dirigibles) and airplanes as the polar regions entered the air age. Unlike most explorers, Amundsen had been certain of what he wanted to do from early youth. He pursued the business of exploring in the polar regions with a single-minded concentration, undeterred by any other influence or suggestion.

—H. Christian Thorup

FURTHER READING

Amundsen, Roald Engelbregt Gravning. *Roald Amundsen: My Life as an Explorer*. Garden City, N.Y.: Doubleday, Page, 1927. A firsthand account of the explorations of Amundsen in his own words. Surprisingly, only a few vital statistics are presented. He details the flight of the *Norge* and his quarrel with Nobile, who claimed the honor for that flight. Published only months before the tragic death of Amundsen while seeking to rescue Nobile, it is an excellent source for the causes of their quarrel.

Bomann-Larsen, Tor. *Roald Amundsen*. Translated by Ingrid Christophersen. Stroud, England: Sutton, 2006. At the time of its publication, this translation from a book originally published in Norwegian was the only English-language biography of Amudsen. It is based on firsthand accounts and newly discovered documents.

Bowman, Gerald. *Men of Antarctica*. New York: Fleet, 1959. The story of Antarctic exploration based on the most significant expeditions. Bowman classifies Amundsen as one of the greatest explorers. This is an excellent source on Amundsen's race to the South Pole.

Fiennes, Sir Ranulph. *Race to the Pole: Tragedy, Heroism, and Scott's Antarctic Quest*. New York: Hyperion, 2004. Fiennes, also an explorer and the only person to reach both the North and South Poles by land, presents a revisionist view of Amundsen and Robert Falcon Scott's polar expeditions. In Fiennes's opinion, Scott was a hero, not an incompetent explorer who lost the race to the South Pole.

Hoyt, Edwin P. *The Last Explorer: The Adventures of Admiral Byrd*. New York: John Day, 1968. While this book centers on the explorations of Byrd, it presents the competitive and cooperative relations between polar explorers such as Amundsen and Byrd. It is a good source for the cooperative spirit that allowed sharing techniques, routes, and equipment for the icelands.

Kirwan, Laurence Patrick. *A History of Polar Explorations*. New York: W. W. Norton, 1960. A comprehensive look at the history and discovery of the polar regions, from the Greeks and the Norsemen to modern times. A good exposition on Amundsen's role in the heroic age of explorers.

Neatby, L. H. *Conquest of the Last Frontier*. Athens: Ohio University Press, 1966. The "last frontier" is identified as the American Arctic, which includes the Canadian Islands and the North Pole. The book is an excellent source for Amundsen's Northwest Passage, although Neatby ranks Amundsen's efforts below those of the American explorers.

Victor, Paul-Émile. *Man and the Conquest of the Poles*. Translated by Scott Sullivan. London: Hamish Hamilton, 1963. In terms of comprehension and detail, Victor's is an excellent source for understanding the interest in and knowledge of polar lands from the earliest times. An excellent source for Amundsen's Northwest Passage, Antarctic achievements, and first airship flight over the Arctic Ocean.

SEE ALSO: Richard Byrd; Fridtjof Nansen; Robert Edwin Peary; Knud Johan Victor Rasmussen; Alfred Wegener; Sir George Hubert Wilkins.

RELATED ARTICLES in *Great Events from History: The Twentieth Century*:

1901-1940: December 2, 1911: Australasian Antarctic Expedition Commences; December 14, 1911: Amundsen Reaches the South Pole.

1941-1970: June 23, 1961: Antarctic Treaty Goes into Force.

MARIAN ANDERSON
American opera singer

Anderson was a world-renowned contralto who was described as having a voice that came along only once in a hundred years. Anderson's career would come to have symbolic meaning in the battle against racial prejudice in the United States, as she became the first black soloist at New York's Metropolitan Opera when she sang there in 1955.

BORN: February 27, 1897; Philadelphia, Pennsylvania
DIED: April 8, 1993; Portland, Oregon
AREA OF ACHIEVEMENT: Music

EARLY LIFE
Marian Anderson was born in a black residential section of Philadelphia, Pennsylvania. Her father, John, sold ice and coal, and her mother, Anna, supplemented the modest family income by doing laundry. The family was active in the Union Baptist Church in Philadelphia, and Marian, at age six, was enrolled in its junior choir. She later joined the senior choir, demonstrating the range of her voice by singing all vocal parts. The church afforded many singing opportunities for Anderson, including travel with its choir.

While a student at South Philadelphia High School, she began to accompany herself on piano and appeared at various black college and church functions. Anderson's first voice lessons were with Mary S. Patterson. Through Patterson she was introduced to the music of Franz Schubert and began work with her first accompanist. Monies raised by the Philadelphia Choral Society enabled Anderson to continue study with contralto Agnes Reifsnyder. Prior to her high school graduation, she was accepted as a pupil with Giuseppe Boghetti. She began a wide range of music studies, including French and Italian arias.

Anderson and her accompanist expanded their touring after she was graduated. Practice was difficult on these early tours, as she was obliged to stay in private homes. She was very sensitive about disturbing her hosts; much of her time was spent with the host's neighbors and friends. At this early age, she was developing the regal, commanding physical presence that later reviewers would note.

At age twenty, Anderson considered giving up her career after a debut at New York Town Hall. The reviews were unfavorable and she did not yet have sufficient command of German to sing lieder. With her mother's encouragement, she overcame her despair, resuming the touring and lessons.

Two triumphs came in 1923 and 1925. The first was winning a contest sponsored by the Philharmonic Society; the second was winning first prize in a contest held at Lewisohn Stadium. She was chosen, out of three hundred competitors, to appear with the New York Philharmonic.

Anderson had a new tutor, Frank LaForge, and was under the management of Arthur Judson. She now had many engagements and received higher fees; she also, however, had to compete with well-established singers. Acknowledging that she was accepting the same engagements each year and that her command of German needed improvement, she decided to go abroad. She won a scholarship from the National Association of Negro Musicians and in 1926 sailed to England aboard the *Île de France*.

LIFE'S WORK
Anderson made many trips abroad, interspersed with American concert commitments, during her career. In 1929, she returned to New York for an engagement at Carnegie Hall. In 1930, she appeared at London's Wigmore Hall. She won a Julius Rosenwald scholarship, which enabled her to study abroad through 1933. She toured the Continent, spending considerable time in the Scandinavian countries, giving more than one hundred concerts in those countries. These tours were a great success; the Finnish composer Jean Sibelius dedicated his song "Solitude" to her. She gathered further esteem at the 1935 Mozarteum in Salzburg, Austria, receiving praises from Arturo Toscanini, who found her voice to be remarkable and rare.

The year 1935 also marked the beginning of Anderson's association with impresario Solomon Hurok and her second debut at New York Town Hall. Hurok, on the spur of the moment, had attended her Paris recital at the Salle Gaveayu. He signed her to an exclusive contract and was her manager for the remainder of her career. The second Town Hall appearance, December 31, 1935, revealed the progress Anderson had made. In this concert, the full range of her voice was presented, and the reviews were superb. The drama of the recital was heightened because Anderson sang with a cast around her ankle, which she had broken on the journey back to the United States. Later concerts at Carnegie Hall were equally successful.

Anderson's perseverance as a student and public performer in Europe had proved its worth.

Her reputation assured, Anderson began, in 1936, touring Europe, Africa, South America, Russia, and the United States. In that year, she also made an appearance before President Franklin D. Roosevelt and First Lady Eleanor Roosevelt. She began an intensive concert tour in the 1937-1938 season, giving seventy concerts in the United States, including the southern states. The following season, she gave seventy-five concerts in sixty cities.

Anderson was catapulted to national attention in 1939. The Daughters of the American Revolution refused to allow her to sing in its headquarters, Constitution Hall in Washington, D.C. Protests came from many leading figures, including Eleanor Roosevelt, who resigned from the organization. The United States government offered the Lincoln Memorial as an alternate site. There, on Easter Sunday, April 9, 1939, Marian Anderson sang before a crowd of seventy-five thousand people. The concert, an emotional and significant event, included Schubert's *Ave Maria* (1825) and a selection of black spirituals.

Marian Anderson. (Library of Congress)

Anderson was awarded the Spingarn Medal in 1939; the Bok Award followed in 1940, allowing her to establish the Marian Anderson Award for talented singers. In 1943, she married Orpheus K. Fisher, an architect. In 1955, at the age of fifty-three, she became the first black soloist at New York's Metropolitan Opera. The 1955 debut cast her in the role of Ulrica from Giuseppe Verdi's *A Masked Ball* (1857-1858). When she appeared on stage, she received a standing ovation.

Anderson became an emissary of the State Department in 1957 and made a concert tour of India and the Far East. In 1958, she was a delegate to the Thirteenth General Assembly of the United Nations. She sang at President John F. Kennedy's inaugural ball in 1963 and was awarded the Presidential Medal of Freedom by Lyndon B. Johnson. She made farewell tours in the United States and abroad in 1964-1965, retiring in 1965.

Anderson was awarded numerous honorary degrees and decorations from foreign governments. A tribute to her seventy-fifth birthday was held at Carnegie Hall; singers included Leontyne Price, who ended the program with Anderson's favorite, "He's Got the Whole World in His Hands." She said that the happiest day of her life was August 22, 1979, Marian Anderson Day in Philadelphia. In 1982, black singers Grace Bumbry and Shirley Verrett gave a joint recital at Carnegie Hall to honor her. She was chosen in 1986 by President Ronald Reagan to receive the National Medal of Arts.

Millions of listeners heard Anderson's voice; it was estimated in 1950 that she had performed before four million people. Her voice, compared to velvet, had a range of more than three octaves. Her repertoire included the song literature of Johann Sebastian Bach, Johannes Brahms, Ludwig van Beethoven, George Frideric Handel, Schubert, Gustav Mahler, and, always, black spirituals.

SIGNIFICANCE

Despite the success of black concert singer Roland Hayes, America of the 1920's and 1930's did not readily embrace black classical musicians. Anderson dealt with formidable racial barriers: She was turned away by a music school, had to travel in the Jim Crow train car, and faced the reluctance of concert managers to book her on tours. However, her church supported her career with funds and opportunities to sing. Her mother had instilled in her a deep faith that she could succeed. This she did in an era in the United States when vigorous protest against racism was unknown. The seriousness of her desire to sing, to achieve impeccable linguistic skills in her songs, and to broaden her repertoire strengthened her resolve to succeed. Anderson's long struggle to perfect her voice revealed her fortitude and inner strength.

—Sue Williams

FURTHER READING

Anderson, Marian. *My Lord, What a Morning*. New York: Viking Press, 1956. An endearing autobiography; reveals the determination of the author to become a serious classical singer. Balances the personal toll taken by her career with frank self-criticism and acknowledgment of support received from family, church, and coworkers. The author's even-tempered, philosophical personality in dealing with racism and balancing her career and home life shines through.

Hurok, Solomon, with Ruth Goode. *Impresario: A Memoir*. New York: Random House, 1946. Hurok, manager of opera, ballet, and theater stars, recounts his thirty-year career with clients such as Anna Pavlova, Isadora Duncan, and Marian Anderson. More than a manager, he shows himself a friend and champion of Anderson, smoothing her path in the era of segregation and plotting her career to her best advantage.

Keller, Allan. *Marian Anderson: A Singer's Journey*. New York: Scribner, 2000. Keller, a music professor, recounts Anderson's life, focusing on her career and musicianship. He describes her musical training, repertoire, touring schedule, and the vocal qualities that made her singing uniquely beautiful.

Klan, Barbara. "An Interview with Marian Anderson." *American Heritage* 27 (February, 1977): 51-57. Anderson's responses in this interview reflect little change in her overall philosophy since the 1956 autobiography. Answering standard questions about her career, she reveals that racist encounters, especially being turned away by a Philadelphia music school, made a permanent impression on her. Her relationship with Solomon Hurok is further explored here as well.

Lovell, John, Jr. *Black Song: The Forge and the Flame*. New York: Macmillan, 1972. This comprehensive study of the evolution of spirituals discusses their meaning and social impact and presents hundreds of examples of this distinctively American art form. Anderson is cited among artists who exposed audiences to spirituals on a national and international level. Includes the author's evaluation of Anderson's approach to this musical tradition.

Pleasants, Henry. *The Great Singers from the Dawn of Opera to Caruso*. New York: Simon & Schuster, 1966. Asserts that Anderson's slowness in achieving artistic maturity was the result of an inferior education. Comparing her early career to that of the sophisticated black tenor Roland Hayes, Pleasants shows the tremendous influence of the European tours. Offers a critical evaluation of Anderson's voice and its appeal in the course of this opinionated account of opera over three centuries.

Schonberg, Harold C. "A Bravo for Opera's Black Voices." *The New York Times Magazine*, January 17, 1982. A review of the 1982 joint concert of black stars Grace Bumbry and Shirley Verrett in honor of Anderson. (It was Bumbry's 1961 role as Venus in *Tannhäuser* that again stirred racial prejudices in the opera world.)

Truman, Margaret. *Women of Courage*. New York: William Morrow, 1976. Anderson is given as an example of one possessing fortitude in her career despite the hurdles of racial prejudice. A behind-the-scenes account of the rebuff by the Daughters of the American Revolution and Solomon Hurok's role in staging the appearance at Lincoln Memorial. A study of the evolution of women of courage in America, from frontier days to the twentieth century.

Vehanen, Kosti. *Marian Anderson: A Portrait*. New York: McGraw-Hill, 1941. Written by Anderson's accompanist from the start of her second Scandinavian tour until 1939. He urged her study of Scandinavian songs and arranged the meeting with Sibelius in Finland. Although disjointed, provides both a serious and whimsical account of their touring life and his contributions in perfecting her repertoire.

SEE ALSO: Louis Armstrong; Maria Callas; Enrico Caruso; John Coltrane; Duke Ellington; Ella Fitzgerald; Dizzy Gillespie; Billie Holiday; Jessye Norman; Charlie Parker; Leontyne Price; Beverly Sills; Bessie Smith.

RELATED ARTICLES in *Great Events from History: The Twentieth Century:*

MOTHER ANGELICA
American nun and television broadcaster

A cloistered, contemplative nun, Mother Angelica founded the Eternal Word Television Network (EWTN), the largest religious cable broadcasting network in the world. Traditional, earthy, and charismatic, she was abbess of a monastery, founder of two other religious communities, builder of the imposing Shrine of the Most Blessed Sacrament, and daily inspiration for millions of television viewers. Angelica is one of the most recognized Roman Catholic figures of the late twentieth century.

BORN: April 28, 1923; Canton, Ohio
ALSO KNOWN AS: Rita Antoinette Rizzo (birth name);
    Mother Mary Angelica
AREAS OF ACHIEVEMENT: Religion and theology,
    television, communications

EARLY LIFE
Mother Angelica (an-JEHL-ih-kah) was born Rita Antoinette Rizzo in the industrial town of Canton, Ohio, the only child of John and Mae Rizzo. When Angelica was six years old, her father deserted his family and left Mae to raise her in straitened circumstances. They alternated living with Mae's parents, the Gianfrancescos, and in shabby apartments. In 1931, Mae's divorce from John was finalized, which made Angelica the target of shame in the Roman Catholic schools she was attending. Although Mae resumed her family name of Francis, she had difficulty finding employment and was subject to bouts of suicidal depression.

When she was eighteen years old, Angelica had stomach spasms that made eating difficult. Nevertheless, she graduated from high school and gained employment; her abdomen was found to be distended. On January 8, 1943, Mae brought Angelica to see Rhoda Wise, a local Catholic mystic and purported healer and stigmatist. After Angelica prayed a nine-day novena prescribed by Wise, she claimed that her stomach ailment was cured. Angelica became devoted to the mystic, believing that through Wise's efforts she had not only become healed but, as Angelica wrote in a letter, she had been converted from "a lukewarm Catholic" to one so in love with Jesus "that there are times when I think I will die." She embarked on an intense program of devotions and began discerning a religious vocation. On August 15, 1944, without her mother's knowledge, Angelica joined the contemplative Franciscan order, the Poor Clares of Perpetual Adora-

tion, in an enclosed monastery in Cleveland. (Mae would eventually join the Franciscan Poor Clares herself, and become a nun in her daughter's monastery.)

LIFE'S WORK
Angelica had found her life's work as a cloistered nun, but her influence would extend far beyond the walls of the enclosed community. Initially, her vocation to religious life as a nun was questioned, as she was querulous, strong-minded, and sickly in body. Her perseverance impressed the sisters, however, and on November 8, 1945, she became a novice, taking the name Mary Angelica of the Annunciation. In 1950, Sister Angelica became one of the first nuns in the new Sancta Clara monastery established in Canton, Ohio, which pioneered outreach to the black community. Inspired by this work, Sister Angelica began dreaming of a new monastery to be located in the Deep South.

Despite back pain that necessitated surgery and wearing a brace, Angelica was appointed novice mistress, received the official title of "Mother," and began leading the effort to start a monastery in Birmingham, Alabama. As she raised money, Mother Angelica's entrepreneurial skills emerged, launching the sisters into business selling homemade fishing lures and home-roasted peanuts. On May 20, 1962, the new Our Lady of the Angels Monastery was dedicated with Mother Angelica as abbess and four sisters in cloister. Almost immediately, the sisters began selling recordings of Angelica's inspiring talks to the public. Over the next decade, Angelica's talks, both live and recorded, increased in popularity. In 1971, she began offering her talks on a weekly radio station. She also became a prolific author of booklets. By 1976, the monastery had installed a print shop to publish Angelica's fifty-seven spiritual booklets. Her compendium, *Mother Angelica's Answers, Not Promises*, would become a religious best seller when published in 1987. Even the onset of heart problems did not slow her pace.

On March 9, 1978, Angelica announced to her startled sisters that the monastery would establish a satellite studio in its garage to branch into television. This was the beginning of EWTN, or the Eternal Word Television Network, which was formally launched on August 15, 1981. Featuring Angelica's earthy, homespun talks and spirituality, EWTN produced a range of programs that appealed to both an intensely Catholic and a widespread ecumenical audience. EWTN's mission was to "communicate the teachings and the beauty of the Catholic Church and to help people grow in their love and understanding of God and His infinite mercy." Constantly one step ahead of mounting bills and debts, Angelica steadily expanded her studio, her programming, and her outreach.

In 1985, EWTN was carried on 220 cable systems and reached up to 2 million homes; by 1988, EWTN was reaching 12 million homes and was the fastest growing religious cable network in the nation. EWTN's growth brought it into apparent competition with the Catholic Telecommunications Network (CTNA) sponsored by the Conference of United States Bishops. In 1995, CTNA was liquidated after losing $14 million; that year, EWTN broadcasted to an international audience, and it reached forty million households. Further antagonizing several bishops, Angelica made charges of doctrinal deviation, liturgical abuse, and moral laxity. Her most notorious dispute was with Cardinal Roger Mahony (of the Los Angeles archdiocese) in 1997, when Angelica called his pastoral letter on the Eucharist insufficiently reverent. These tensions were of such concern to Angelica that in 2000 she resigned as chair of EWTN, transferring the network entirely to a lay board beyond direct episcopal control. Meanwhile, Angelica was overseeing completion of the $50 million Shrine of the Most Blessed Sacrament, the impressive new home for her religious community outside Birmingham. In the middle of these efforts, Angelica publicly prayed for healing with the Italian mystic, Paola Albertini; moments later she walked without the crutches and braces that she had been using since 1946. Angelica claimed this as another miraculous healing.

In the early years of the twenty-first century, EWTN would continue to grow, becoming the largest religious media organization in the world, transmitting twenty-four hours a day to more than 123 million homes in 140 countries on more than 4,800 cable systems, with an equally global outreach through radio, publishing, and the World Wide Web. Angelica remained the star of the network, preaching an intense and old-fashioned spirituality, criticizing liberalism, and displaying her own infirmities to console and encourage her audience.

SIGNIFICANCE

Angelica is the most visible Catholic television personality since Bishop Fulton J. Sheen of the 1950's and one of the most recognizable religious figures in the world. A disabled, cloistered nun, with no college degree and a vow to poverty, she built a billion-dollar media network that influences the spiritual life of hundreds of millions of Catholics and other Christians.

Angelica is known as much for her individual persona as for the size of her broadcasting network. As Cardinal J. Francis Stafford observed, "Mother Angelica represented the plain Catholic, who is 90 percent of the Church." A charismatic nun in classical religious habit, Angelica speaks simply of faith, chastity, obedience to the pope, and devotion to the observances and beliefs of historic Catholicism.

Anecdotal, combative, humorous—although some have labeled her cranky and cantankerous—Angelica became a unique television personality. Like Pope John Paul II before her, she used modern technology and media to preach a confident and traditional Catholic message. While denouncing secularism and feminism, she is herself an immensely powerful and successful woman who refused to show obeisance to bishops of the United States when she doubted their fidelity to Church teaching or the papacy. Like John Paul II, she embodies the message her global network was spreading, making use of her own infirmities and frailty to reinforce and emphasize Christian preaching.

—Howard Bromberg

FURTHER READING

Angelica, Mother. *Mother Angelica's Little Book of Life Lessons and Everyday Spirituality*. Edited by Raymond Arroyo. New York: Doubleday, 2007. A collection of Angelica's sayings and meditations.

Angelica, Mother M., and Christine Allison. *Mother Angelica's Answers, Not Promises*. San Francisco, Calif.: Ignatius Press, 1996. A compendium of Angelica's best-known talks, addressing issues of prayer, faith, chastity, guilt, forgiveness, and the final judgment.

Arroyo, Raymond. *Mother Angelica: The Remarkable Story of a Nun, Her Nerve, and a Network of Miracles*. New York: Doubleday, 2007. A sympathetic but not authorized biography by a long-time EWTN employee and co-host, based on three years of interviews with Mother Angelica and unrestricted access to her personal papers and her monastery archives.

Carroll, Colleen. *The New Faithful: Why Young Adults are Embracing Christian Orthodoxy*. Chicago: Loyola Press, 2004. Cites Angelica as one of the inspirations for the revival of Catholic orthodoxy.

Ferrara, Christopher A. *EWTN: A Network Gone Wrong*. Pound Ridge, N.Y.: Good Counsel, 2006. A harsh critique of the "heterodox" errors that the author, a Catholic traditionalist, finds rife in EWTN since the resignation of Angelica as the network's chair in 2000.

O'Neill, Dan. *Mother Angelica: Her Life Story*. New

York: Crossroad, 1986. An anecdotal biography that relies heavily on stories related by Angelica's sister nuns.

Raphael, Sister M. *My Life With Angelica.* Birmingham, Ala.: Our Lady of the Angels Monastery, 1982. An early publication from the sisters' first print shop, containing loving reminiscences of Angelica by Sister Mary Raphael, her closest associate. Includes rare photographs of the monastery and of community life.

SEE ALSO: Dorothy Day; Jerry Falwell; Indira Gandhi; Mahatma Gandhi; Billy Graham; Le Ly Hayslip;

L. Ron Hubbard; Sun Myung Moon; John R. Mott; Gunnar Myrdal; Fulton J. Sheen; Nathan Söderblom; Edith Stein; Billy Sunday; Mother Teresa.

RELATED ARTICLES in *Great Events from History: The Twentieth Century:*

1941-1970: 1945: Billy Graham Becomes a Traveling Evangelist; February 12, 1952-1957, and 1961-1968: Sheen Entertains and Instructs on American Television.

1971-2000: August 15, 1981: EWTN Begins Religious Broadcasting.

SIR NORMAN ANGELL
British journalist and editor

Angell fashioned complex ideas of international relations into simple, catchy depictions that enabled him to lead British peace movements before and after World War I. He was awarded the Nobel Peace Prize in 1933.

BORN: December 26, 1872; Holbeach, Lincolnshire, England

DIED: October 7, 1967; Croydon, Surrey, England

ALSO KNOWN AS: Sir Ralph Norman Angell Lane (full name)

AREAS OF ACHIEVEMENT: Peace advocacy, social reform, diplomacy, journalism, government and politics

EARLY LIFE

Norman Angell (AYN-jehl) was born into a middle-class Victorian family. Later, his mother's family name, Angell, was added to his own. He was the last of six children, and his precocious eccentricities were indulged by his parents. He was sent to a *lycée* in St. Omer, France, for his basic schooling (1884-1887), where he began the habit of independent thinking that characterized his entire career.

Unlike his peers, Angell chose not to continue his education at one of the English universities. Instead, he attended business school in London, becoming accomplished in shorthand. He went to Geneva for two more years of schooling at the university there (1888-1889). While in Geneva, he engaged in debates with revolutionaries over the great issues of the day. He earned his living as an editor of the *Geneva Telegraph*—a small English-

language newspaper. He was quite in the forefront of advanced European opinion, although the vacationers' newspaper that he edited was hardly a suitable forum. He returned to England an even greater iconoclast, especially with respect to religion. Before long, in 1890, Angell resumed his newspaper work as a reporter for a provincial publication in Ipswich. The radical contentiousness with which he put forward his arguments in print, however, was not conducive to increasing the newspaper's circulation. He was shortly relieved of his responsibilities and was without a job.

Angell was nineteen when he decided to emigrate to the United States. He headed for the Far West. He put his roots down as a homesteader and wrangler near Bakersfield, California. While he adapted to the rude surroundings, he had difficulties with the strident American jingoism of the 1890's. The form that American chauvinism took was doubly obnoxious because it was frequently anti-British. The status of his U.S. citizenship, which he claimed, remains unclear, but ultimately, Angell lost his property in Southern California because of the anti-British bias there.

Angell went north to San Francisco to find work as a reporter on the *San Francisco Chronicle.* Finding other newspaper opportunities more attractive, he worked his way across the United States. After working on newspapers in Chicago, St. Louis, and New Orleans, Angell left the United States in the late fall of 1897 to return to England.

His next job, however, turned up in France. In Paris, in 1898, he landed a job as editor of a failing English-language newspaper, the *Daily Messenger.* He kept the publication afloat for seven years. On the demise of the *Daily Messenger*, its place among the Paris dailies was quickly filled by an experiment of London newspaper baron Lord Northcliffe (Alfred Harmsworth). Angell was asked by Northcliffe to head the operation of his new English-language daily called the *Continental Daily Mail*. Immediately the paper was an enormous success, and Angell was well paid and well within the good graces of Northcliffe.

Two years earlier, in 1903, Angell had written and published his first book, titled *Patriotism Under Three Flags*. The book lambasted the type of narrowminded nationalism that he had encountered in England, France, and especially the United States. His future boss in England, Northcliffe, was, in fact, among the chief offending jingoists he cited. Yet the decisively different nationalist views of Northcliffe and the emerging internationalist views of Angell did not impair their relationship. Angell carved a considerable niche in Northcliffe's publishing empire. He was not satisfied, however, with being a "kept" editor. What he wanted to say could not be expressed within the confines of a newspaper column.

LIFE'S WORK

Using his two middle names "Norman Angell" for the first time, Angell consolidated his views on European international relations in a small pamphlet titled *Europe's Optical Illusion* (1909), in which he expressed the ideas that he would then expand into his seminal work the next year as *The Great Illusion* (1910, revised 1933)—the new title suggested by Northcliffe. *The Great Illusion* became a huge hit with Edwardian England and with the leading opinion-makers on the Continent as well. In his work, Angell drew heavily on his contemporary Jacques Novicow, and on the nineteenth century liberal internationalism of Richard Cobden, to show that war between industrialized nations would yield no permanent advantage. Nations were too greatly interdependent to reap any real lasting benefit from war. To think an advantage could be gained from war was the "Great Illusion."

Angell's was an argument made amid the naval and weapons races between England, Germany, and the other great powers. Consequently, it was one very ripe for its time. Even Conservative British leaders with ties to the Crown and imperial defense circles embraced Angell's thesis. Under the aegis of Lord Esher and former prime minister Lord Balfour, a Norman Angell peace movement was instituted in 1912. Angell quit his position with Northcliffe and took to the lecture circuit. He converted people to his cause everywhere. He was

Sir Norman Angell. (© The Nobel Foundation)

especially successful gathering young recruits from study groups held at Cambridge and Oxford; scores of Englishmen, such as future Nobel laureate Philip John Noel-Baker, testified to the almost evangelical impact of Angell's message at this time.

Angell's physical appearance was deceptive. He was well below average height; his slight physique, encased in a frail frame, was topped by an enormous head. He was mild-mannered almost to the point of shyness, and genuinely modest in personal conversation. Once behind the podium, however, he continually astonished listeners by booming forth in a forceful, deep voice that was bolstered by a spirited assertiveness. A Scottish observer characterized Angell as having a teacher's face with a voice that left little doubt as to the presiding genius of the classroom. Others testified to his pedagogical qualities as well. Further testimony to his effectiveness as a speaker is seen in the vast amount of correspondence that he received from the public, especially students and schoolteachers who had heard him lecture and wanted to know more about his writings.

Norman Angellism took two continents by storm.

Within a matter of months groups banded together at meeting halls and schools in England, France, Germany, and the United States with *The Great Illusion* as the basis for discussion and affiliation. For two years the scurry continued, and Angell's word reached high into the middle-class and ruling-class circles of England and other countries. In the summer of 1914, however, with the crisis leading to World War I, Angell's movement collapsed as quickly as it had risen. Angell tried to isolate and cauterize the damage by creating a Neutrality League to pledge nonparticipation in the war, but his efforts were useless. With the declaration of war by Great Britain, Angell's support evaporated. The "Great Illusion" became itself an illusion of human rationalism in August, 1914.

Angell searched for an alternative to the war hysteria. Early into the war, he began a radical association with E. D. Morel, Bertrand Russell, future Labour prime minister Ramsay MacDonald, and others. They formed the Union of Democratic Control (UDC). The group was quickly ostracized for allegedly unpatriotic, seditious, pro-German activities. Although Angell's role with the UDC was actually very limited, he was tarred with the same brush, despite his efforts (in conjunction with the American publication *The New Republic* and Walter Lippmann) to bring the United States into the war on Great Britain's side. Angell's passport was revoked; he was further attacked in print as a pacifist fool, as the one who said that war could not occur, as the one who said that war could not pay. These were charges that he spent his life fruitlessly trying to rebut.

During the war, Angell also shifted politically to the left with an overt attachment to the young Labour Party. At war's end, he was sent as an observer to Paris to monitor the negotiations at Versailles. He emerged from France very critical of the Versailles settlement and wrote about it widely. The subsequent debts debacle emanating from the Versailles peace treaty tended to underscore Angell's ideas about the interconnectedness of national economies, although the lesson was apparently lost on the English at the time. Angell was voted down badly in two attempts at Parliament on a Labour ticket in 1922 and 1923. He became increasingly disillusioned with the possibilities of changing ideas and reordering society and bought an island off the Essex coast and retired to rustic simplicity.

After several years of inertia, Angell had had enough of rusticity. In 1928, he was offered the editorship of *Foreign Affairs*—the journal of his old associate, Morel, of the UDC. Angell used this forum to push the Labour Party leadership toward adopting a pro-League of Nations foreign policy.

Angell returned more directly to the center of politics in 1929 when he won a Labour seat in Parliament for the Yorkshire working-class constituency of North Bradford. While engaged in many nuts-and-bolts issues of economic dislocation, Angell's chief influence remained in foreign affairs. He was involved with several policy formulation committees of the parliamentary Labour Party. Prime Minister MacDonald retained him as a confidant through two years of the Labour government.

When the political crisis of 1931 caused a break between MacDonald and his Labour Party council, Angell chose to retire from Parliament to pursue work on behalf of the peace movement in England. He had earlier in the year accepted a knighthood

---

A PSYCHOLOGICAL CASE FOR PEACE

In The Great Illusion (1910), *Norman Angell argued that peace was not only a viable alternative to war but also inevitable. Both the public and Great Britain's leading politicians were fascinated by Angell's arguments. This excerpt is from the chapter "The Psychological Case for Peace."*

National entities, in their birth, activities, and death, are controlled by the same laws that govern all life—plant, animal, or national—the law of struggle, the law of work; to show, among other things, that in the changing character of men's ideals there is a distinct narrowing of the gulf which is supposed to separate ideal and material aims. Early ideals, whether in the field of politics or religion, are generally dissociated from any aim of general well-being. In early politics, ideals are concerned simply with personal allegiance to some dynastic chief, a feudal lord, or a monarch; the well-being of a community does not enter into the matter at all. Later the chief must embody in his person that well-being, or he does not obtain the allegiance of a community of any enlightenment; later, the well-being of the community becomes the end in itself, without being embodied in the person of an hereditary chief, so that the people realize their efforts, instead of being directed to the protection of the personal interests of some chief, are as a matter of fact directed to the protection of their own interests, and their altruism has become communal self-interest, since the self-sacrifice of the community for the sake of the community is a contradiction in terms.

from MacDonald and was now styled on his speaker notices as Sir Norman Angell. The title lent him a degree of respectability that put more people in his audiences, more money in his pocket, and more confidence in his achievement within the measure of English society.

In September of 1931, however, at the very time that Angell chose to work for peace, the British peace movement began to unravel. The question of the use of sanctions against Japan for its invasion of Manchuria caused a split between the essentially internationalist supporters of a strong League of Nations backed by force, and the basically absolutist pacifists who decried the use of sanctions as simply a disguised instrument of war.

Angell was caught in the middle with ties to both groups. In the beginning, he tried to harmonize the pacifists and internationalists of the National Peace Council, the No More War movement, the War Resisters' International, and the League of Nations Union. Yet at heart, Angell was a fervent internationalist, very much in favor of a strong League of Nations. Consequently, throughout much of the mid-1930's he was engaged in a Sisyphean campaign in print and on the podium to bring pacifists around to accepting the collective security principles of the League of Nations. He worked diligently on behalf of the Peace Ballot campaign of 1934-1935, which reflected his conception of a buoyed League of Nations.

In reality, Angell conducted a two-front war during these years. He was officially the principal publicity adviser for the League of Nations Union in Great Britain. When he was not trying to achieve harmony in the peace movement, he was defending the League of Nations against the clever nationalist press attack against it by Lord Beaverbrook and Lord Rothermere. Sometimes, this defense involved personal confrontations between Angell and Beaverbrook. The fact that Angell was chosen as the journalist best qualified for this task (because of his work experience with Northcliffe) reveals the great weight attached to his opinions.

Angell was not alone in his efforts on behalf of the League of Nations Union. He was joined by Lord Cecil, Oxford classicist Gilbert Murray, Arthur Henderson, Noel-Baker, and others. Ultimately, all except Murray would receive the Nobel Peace Prize for their work during these years; Angell was awarded his Nobel Peace Prize in 1933.

The controversy over sanctions reached a climax with the invasion of Ethiopia by Benito Mussolini in 1935. The failure of Great Britain and France to support effective sanctions by the League of Nations spelled death for that institution as an alternative source of deterrence.

With it went the collective security principle for which Angell had so long argued. Angell and his colleagues of the League of Nations Union had to face the reality of the demise of internationalism. In the last half of the 1930's, Angell moved over to a more conventional view of international relations.

As appeasement began to emerge as the policy of the British government, Angell moved toward a balance-of-power position. In this, he was very close to Winston Churchill's stance, and Angell and his colleagues met with Churchill to seek points of cooperation. In the ensuing swing of opinion against Prime Minister Neville Chamberlain, Angell became an ardent critic of appeasement.

With the coming of World War II, Angell spent his time in the same fashion he had spent the previous war. He came to the United States in 1940 and wrote and spoke in an effort to gain the United States' entry into the war. After the United States became involved in the war, Angell remained to lecture on behalf of Anglo-American unity. Much of his time was occupied with speeches explaining Labour socialism and Great Britain's role in India and the Empire in general. Toward the end of the war, he became a strong exponent of an Anglo-American special relationship as a bulwark against Soviet aggression.

After the war, Angell remained in the United States, mainly in New York City, for six more years. He was an early supporter of the United Nations, although he never saw the United Nations in the same way that he had viewed the League of Nations. Actually, Angell had abandoned most of his internationalist ideas in the middle of the 1930's. Ironically, he became very chauvinistic, even racist, very defensive of Anglo-Saxon achievement, and very much a defender of British imperialism. All these aspects can be found in his writings, including the early ones. Yet they can just as easily be ignored because he had the noble goal of international harmony as his object.

Angell returned to England for good in 1951 after more than eleven years in the United States. He wrote and published his autobiography, *After All*, the same year. His general sense of failure pervaded the entire set of recollections. He took up residence in a spartan cottage in Haslemere, Surrey. When he ran out of money in 1960, he sold his books and papers to Ball State University in Muncie, Indiana. In 1966, he visited Ball State to receive an honorary doctorate degree. Although nearly ninety-four years old, Angell remained a formidable lecturer. He died in Croydon, on October 7, 1967.

SIGNIFICANCE

Angell struck a chord for peace that existed deeply within Edwardian society. The widespread desire for peace was manifest in the universality of enthusiasm with which his book and his movement were greeted in the five years before World War I. The horrors of World War I made Angell's proposed alternative to war that much more appealing.

Much of Angell and his work was ephemeral and elusive. He wrote haphazardly and expediently, occasionally merely for pelf. As someone uncharitably said, he wrote the same book forty-four times. Yet despite the truth of these charges, Angell clearly played a significant role in the international peace movement. Whenever liberal internationalism is studied, whenever the League of Nations is studied, whenever popular peace movements are studied, whenever peace leaders are studied, and whenever lists of the most influential books are compiled, then Angell and *The Great Illusion* have to be considered as an enduring reality of history.

—*Louis R. Bisceglia*

FURTHER READING

Angell, Norman. *After All: The Autobiography of Norman Angell.* New York: Farrar, Straus and Young, 1951. Angell's very impressionistic autobiography. At times misleading.

Ashworth, Lucian M. *Creating International Studies: Angell, Mitrany, and the Liberal Tradition.* Brookfield, Vt.: Ashgate, 1999. Examines the writings of Angell and David Mitrany to describe how liberal internationalism laid the foundation for the study of international relations as an academic discipline.

Birn, Donald. *The League of Nations Union, 1918-1945.* Oxford, England: Clarendon Press, 1981. A thorough look at the organization to which Angell devoted so much time during the 1930's.

Bisceglia, Louis. *Norman Angell and Liberal Interna-tionalism in Britain, 1931-35.* New York: Garland, 1982. Multifaceted study of Angell as a lecturer, journalist, author, politician, economist, disarmament campaigner, peace advocate, and internationalist.

_____. "Norman Angell and the 'Pacifist' Muddle." *Bulletin of the Institute of Historical Research* 45 (May, 1972): 104-121. Shows the weakness of Angell's internationalist reason when placed against a religious belief of pacifism.

Ceadel, Martin. *Pacifism in Britain, 1914-1945.* Oxford, England: Clarendon Press, 1980. Places "Angellism" within the overall peace movement in Great Britain.

Marrin, Albert. *Sir Norman Angell.* Boston: Twayne, 1979. A biographical study of Angell. A good place to start research.

Miller, J. D. B. *Norman Angell and the Futility of War.* New York: St. Martin's Press, 1986. A detailed study of the international relations theory of the interwar era.

Swartz, Marvin. *The Union of Democratic Control in British Politics During the First World War.* Oxford, England: Clarendon Press, 1971. A critical assessment of Angell and his colleagues.

Weinroth, Howard. "Norman Angell and *The Great Illusion:* An Episode in Pre-1914 Pacifism." *Historical Journal* 17 (September, 1974): 551-574. The author relates Angell to the intricacies of pacifist ideology in the Edwardian era.

SEE ALSO: Lord Beaverbrook; Neville Chamberlain; Sir Winston Churchill; Alfred and Harold Harmsworth.

RELATED ARTICLES in *Great Events from History: The Twentieth Century:*

1901-1940: 1910: Angell Advances Pacifism; November 25, 1910: Carnegie Establishes the Endowment for International Peace; November 7, 1914: Lippmann Helps to Establish *The New Republic.*

MAYA ANGELOU
American poet and writer

Angelou, best known for her rhythmic, gospel-inspired poetry and candid autobiographical works, namely I Know Why the Caged Bird Sings, *professed a philosophy that spoke to women, especially black women, facing seemingly insurmountable obstacles and challenges in life: "You may encounter many defeats but you must not be defeated."*

BORN: April 4, 1928; St. Louis, Missouri
ALSO KNOWN AS: Marguerite Annie Johnson (birth name)
AREAS OF ACHIEVEMENT: Literature, dance, television, film, education, women's rights, civil rights

EARLY LIFE

Maya Angelou (MI-ah AN-jeh-lew) was born Marguerite Annie Johnson in St. Louis, Missouri, to Vivian Baxter and Bailey Johnson. Following her parents' divorce when she was three years old, Angelou and her brother were sent to live with their paternal grandmother, Annie Henderson, in Stamps, a poor rural section of Arkansas. Angelou's grandmother, whom she called Momma, was the stable force in Angelou's early life. Annie was a strong, religious woman who made sure that the family went to church regularly. Religion and spiritual music were important factors in the Johnson family life. Angelou also enjoyed a close relationship with her brother, Bailey, who gave her the name Maya.

Angelou and her brother lived with their grandmother and Uncle Willie in the rear of the Johnson store, which Annie had owned for twenty-five years. Because the store was the center of activity for the local black community, Angelou saw at first hand the indignities that black residents suffered as a result of the prejudices of whites in Stamps.

Angelou faced a severely traumatic experience when she was just seven and a half years old. During one of her visits to her mother in St. Louis, a friend of Angelou's mother raped her. When her mother's brothers found out about the rape, they killed the man responsible. Believing that she had caused the man's death by speaking his name, Angelou refused to speak for five years following these traumatic events. With the encouragement of Mrs. Flowers, an educated black woman from Stamps, Angelou regained her speech. Under Mrs. Flowers's further guidance, Angelou began to read the works of William Shakespeare, Edgar Allan Poe, Langston Hughes, and Paul Laurence Dunbar.

After graduating at the top of her eighth grade class in Stamps, she went to Los Angeles to pass the summer with her father, but after being attacked by his girlfriend, she lived for a month in a junk yard with runaways from many races. The experience, she later wrote, deeply affected her views of race. Angelou and her brother continued their education in San Francisco, living with their mother. While still in high school, she worked as the first black woman streetcar conductor in San Francisco.

At the age of seventeen, having just graduated from George Washington High School and unmarried, Angelou gave birth to her son, Guy Johnson. To support herself and Guy, she took jobs as a waitress, cook, and nightclub singer. In 1950, she married Tosh Angelos, a former sailor of Greek ancestry, but they were divorced after a few years. (Angelou's surname was derived from that of her former husband.)

Angelou continued her early interest in music and

Maya Angelou. (Courtesy, Central Arkansas Library)

dance by studying with Martha Graham. She went on to tour twenty-two countries during 1954 and 1955 as the premier dancer in Porgy and Bess. Her travels with the cast took her to Italy, France, Greece, Yugoslavia, and Egypt. During the late 1950's, Angelou and Guy lived in a houseboat commune in California, where they went barefoot, wore jeans, and let their hair grow long. These experiences brought Angelou into contact with a variety of people from different countries and of different races.

As Angelou became interested in a writing career, she moved to New York in 1958 and joined the Harlem Writers Guild. In addition to working on her writing, she starred in the New York production of Jean Genet's *The Blacks* (1960) with Godfrey Cambridge and collaborated with Cambridge to produce, direct, and star in *Cabaret for Freedom* (1960).

In 1960, Angelou and Guy moved to Cairo, Egypt, with a South African freedom fighter, Vusumzi Make. In Egypt, she served as an editor for *Arab Observer*, an English-language newspaper. Two years later, she and Guy moved to the West African nation of Ghana, where she worked for three years as a writer, as an assistant administrator for the University of Ghana, and as a feature editor for *African Review*.

LIFE'S WORK

Angelou's firsthand knowledge of the harmful effects of racism led her to political activism in the 1960's, working for civil rights and for a wider understanding of African American culture. In the 1960's, at the request of Martin Luther King, Jr., Angelou served as the northern coordinator of the Southern Christian Leadership Conference. Her knowledge of black traditions and cultures went beyond political activism as well. She produced *Blacks, Blues, Black* (1968) for National Educational Television, a ten-part series that explores African traditions in American life. Other television credits include *Assignment America* (1975), *The Legacy* (1976), *The Inheritors* (1976), and *Trying to Make It Home* (1988).

In the first volume of her now-classic autobiographical novel, *I Know Why the Caged Bird Sings* (1970), Angelou shares her experience of growing up as a poor black female in the segregated rural South. The book is candid about issues of racism, sexism, child rape, sexuality, and other topics, and it remains a target of censors opposed to its explicitness and seeking to ban it from public schools and libraries. The book has been one of the most frequently challenged books in the United States, according to the American Library Association. Throughout her career, however, and despite these challenges,

Angelou continued to draw on her own experiences as the subject matter for her work. She published five more volumes of her personal narrative showing how she was able to overcome obstacles such as racism and sexism to achieve personal success.

In *Gather Together in My Name* (1974), Angelou writes about a difficult period in her life, a time when she was forced to work at menial jobs to support herself and her son. In *Singin' and Swingin' and Gettin' Merry Like Christmas* (1976), Angelou describes her life as a dancer and actor, including her travels with the cast of *Porgy and Bess*. The next two volumes, *The Heart of a Woman* (1981) and *All God's Children Need Traveling Shoes* (1986), describe the rise of her career. *A Song Flung Up to Heaven* (2002) concerns her return to the United States and involvement in the Civil Rights movement. Angelou told George Plimpton in an interview for the *Paris Review* that the prevailing theme running through all the autobiographies was her love for her son; she also placed these works in the tradition of the slave narrative that extends back into the early nineteenth century.

An early exposure to spirituals and gospel music deeply influenced Angelou's poetry, which displays a clear rhythm of gospel music and which reveals a woman whose faith sustained her in difficult times. She published several volumes of poetry: *Just Give Me a Cool Drink of Water 'fore I Diiie* (1971), which earned a Pulitzer Prize nomination; *Oh Pray My Wings Are Gonna Fit Me Well* (1975), whose title came from a nineteenth century spiritual; *And Still I Rise* (1978); *Shaker, Why Don't You Sing?* (1983); *Now Sheba Sings the Song* (1987); *I Shall Not Be Moved* (1990); *A Brave and Startling Truth* (1995); *Amazing Peace* (2005); *Mother: A Cradle to Hold Me* (2006); and *Celebrations: Rituals of Peace and Prayer* (2006).

Angelou began publishing books for children in 1986 with *Mrs. Flowers: A Moment of Friendship*, which is a selection from *I Know Why the Caged Bird Sings*. Nine more followed, illustrated with drawings or photographs: *Life Doesn't Frighten Me* (1993, an extended poem), *Soul Looks Back in Wonder* (1993, with others), *My Painted House, My Friendly Chicken, and Me* (1994), and *Kobe and His Magic* (1996). In 2004 she published *Angelina of Italy*, *Isaac of Lapland*, *Renee Marie of France*, and *Michael of Hawaii*.

The diversity of Angelou's experiences and considerable talents led her into dance, theater, and film as well. As an actor, she is probably best known for her portrayal of Kunta Kinte's grandmother in the television production of Alex Haley's *Roots* (1977). She played the role of the grandmother in the 1993 television film *There Are No Children Here*. In addition to her acting career, she produced and directed for the stage and screen. She also wrote the screenplays for *Georgia, Georgia* (1972) and *All Day Long* (1974), and collaborated on the teleplay for *Sister, Sister* (1982). In 1995 she had a cameo role in *How to Make an American Quilt*, and in 1998 she directed her first film, *Down in the Delta*, making her the first African American woman to be a Hollywood director. She also appeared in the television version of *Down in the Delta* (1999), *The Amen Corner* (1999), and *The Runaway* (2000), and served as a host for the show *Oprah & Friends* on the AM Satellite Radio in 2006.

In 2005, Angelou published a cookbook, *Hallelujah: The Welcome Table*. Two volumes of essays appeared in the 1990's: *Wouldn't Take Nothing for My Journey Now* (1993) and *Even the Stars Look Lonesome* (1997). According to *The New Yorker* writer Hilton Als, these works are collections of "homilies strung together with autobiographical texts" that stress Angelou's inner journey.

Angelou received many honors. *Ladies' Home Journal* named her Woman of the Year in Communications in 1976. She received honorary doctorates from the University of Arkansas, Claremont Graduate University, Ohio State University, Atlanta University, Wheaton College, Occidental College, Columbia College, Kean College, Smith College, Mills College, Lawrence University, and Wake Forest University, and others. At the request of U.S. president Bill Clinton, Angelou wrote and delivered the commemorative poem at his inauguration on January 20, 1993. This poem, "On the Pulse of Morning," was later published by Random House and is perhaps her best-known work among American readers.

Angelou won a Grammy Award for Best Spoken Word or Non-Musical Album (1995), North Carolina's Woman of the Year Award from the Black Publishers Association (1997), the Humanitarian Contribution Award (1997), the Alston/Jones International Civil and Human Rights Award (1998), the Christopher Award (1998), and the National Medal of Arts (2000). In 2001, *Ladies' Home Journal* named her among the thirty most powerful women in the nation.

Angelou also spent much of her career as a teacher, beginning with a lectureship at the University of California, Los Angeles, in 1966. She was writer-in-residence at the University of Kansas in 1970, and distinguished visiting professor at Wake Forest University, Wichita State University, and California State University, Sacramento. Since 1981, Angelou has held a lifetime appointment as Reynolds Professor of American Studies at Wake Forest.

During her travels abroad, and through much study, Angelou became fluent in French, Spanish, Italian, Arabic, and Fante, a West African language.

SIGNIFICANCE

In *I Know Why the Caged Bird Sings*, Angelou evokes an authentic portrait of what it was like to be black, poor, and female in the segregated South during the 1930's. In the autobiographical novel she reveals herself as a strong, determined black woman who overcomes adversities and emerges triumphant. These personal evocations, with their candor and sincerity, are Angelou's legacy.

Angelou was consistent in producing a literature that spoke to other black women who struggled to live their lives and to support their families, all while trying to maintain a positive outlook on life. As she matured as a writer, Angelou extended her message of hope and possibility to include all persons, regardless of race or color.

—Judith Barton Williamson

FURTHER READING

Angelou, Maya. *I Know Why the Caged Bird Sings: The Collected Autobiographies of Maya Angelou*. New York: Modern Library, 2004. A hefty but handy collection of all six of Angelou's memoirs, the central source for any study of her life and milieu.

Bloom, Harold, ed. *Maya Angelou*. Philadelphia: Chelsea House, 2001. A collection of essays about Angelou, including analyses of her poetry and the autobiographical content of her work. Includes an introduction by Bloom, a noted literary critic.

Braxton, Joanne M. *Black Women Writing Autobiography: A Tradition Within a Tradition*. Philadelphia: Temple University Press, 1989. Discusses how Angelou employs the image of the protecting mother as a primary archetype within her work. Traces Angelou's development of themes common to black female autobiography: the centrality of the family, the challenges of child rearing and single parenthood, and the burden of overcoming negative stereotypes of African American women.

Cud Joe, Selwyn. "Maya Angelou and the Autobiographical Statement." In *Black Women Writers (1950-1980)*, edited by Mari Evans. Garden City, N.Y.: Anchor Press, 1983. Cud Joe discusses the importance of Angelou's biographical work, arguing that she represents "the condition of Afro-American womanhood in her quest for understanding and love rather than for bitterness and despair." Cud Joe stresses that by telling the story of her own life in *I Know Why the Caged Bird Sings*, Angelou has shown readers what it means to be a black woman or girl in the United States.

Elliott, Jeffrey M., ed. *Conversations with Maya Angelou.* Jackson: University Press of Mississippi, 1989. A collection of more than thirty interviews with Angelou that originally appeared in various magazines and newspapers, accompanied by a chronology of her life. Provides a multifaceted perspective on the creative issues that have informed Angelou's work as an autobiographer and a poet.

Hilton, Als. "Songbird." *The New Yorker*, August 5, 2002. Written soon after the publication of Angelou's last volume of autobiography, *A Song Flung Up to Heaven*, this well-written, substantial article discusses, sometimes critically, her early life and the literary value, inspiration, and social impact of each autobiography.

Lupton, Mary Jane. "Singing the Black Mother: Maya Angelou and Autobiographical Continuity." *Black American Literature Forum* 24 (Summer, 1990): 257-275. A scholarly assessment of Angelou's literary contributions to the genre of autobiography, placing her within the rich context of African American narratives.

O'Neal, Sondra. "Reconstruction of the Composite Self: New Images of Black Women in Maya Angelou's Continuing Autobiography." In *Black Women Writers (1950-1980)*, edited by Mari Evans. Garden City, N.Y.: Anchor Press, 1983. O'Neal argues that Angelou's primary contribution to the canon of African American literature lies in her realistic portrayal of the lives of black people, especially black women. O'Neal goes on to demonstrate the ways in which Angelou successfully destroys many of the stereotypes of black women.

Tate, Claudia, ed. *Black Women Writers at Work.* New ed. New York: Continuum, 1989. In this collection of interviews, Tate explores the personal lives and works of such contemporary African American writers as Gwendolyn Brooks, Alice Walker, and Toni Morrison. In the interview, Angelou discusses the importance of black role models.

SEE ALSO: Margaret Atwood; James Baldwin; Gwendolyn Brooks; Louise Erdrich; Frantz Fanon; Martha Graham; Lorraine Hansberry; Zora Neale Hurston; Kate Millett; Toni Morrison; Alice Walker; Oprah Winfrey.

RELATED ARTICLES in *Great Events from History: The Twentieth Century:*

1971-2000: April-June, 1976: Shange's *for colored girls . . .* Presents the Black Female Psyche; 1980's-1990's: Innovative Black Filmmakers Achieve Success; November 3, 1992: Clinton Wins the U.S. Presidency; October 16, 1995: Farrakhan Leads the Million Man March.

VIRGINIA APGAR
American physician

Noted for contributions in anesthesiology, public health, genetics, and basic research, Apgar is best remembered for the Apgar Newborn Scoring System, a system of health evaluation that has saved the lives of countless infants worldwide.

BORN: June 7, 1909; Westfield, New Jersey
DIED: August 7, 1974; New York, New York
AREAS OF ACHIEVEMENT: Medicine, physiology, public health, genetics

EARLY LIFE

Virginia Apgar (AP-gahr) was born in Westfield, New Jersey. She may have become interested in science through the influence of her father, who built a telescope and experimented with radio waves and electricity in his basement laboratory. She never knew what caused her to go into medicine, but by the time she went to college, Apgar knew she wanted to be a doctor. At Mount Holyoke College, she relied on scholarships and several jobs, including one in the zoology laboratory, to support herself. After she completed her bachelor's degree in 1929, Apgar entered the College of Physicians and Surgeons at Columbia University in September. The stock market crashed that October, and Apgar had to borrow money during the Great Depression to continue her education. She owed nearly $4,000 (a considerable sum in those days) when she graduated in 1933, but finished fourth in her class.

Columbia awarded her a coveted surgical internship,

but she was advised not to continue in surgery, since she had to support herself at a time when even male surgeons were having difficulty establishing themselves in New York City. Apgar decided to enter anesthesia, which was considered a more suitable field for a woman at the time. Although anesthesia was considered a nurse's job, surgeons were beginning to acknowledge that surgical advances were dependent on advances in anesthesia. Many of these same medical professionals believed that women physicians were ideally suited to develop the field of medical anesthesiology. Apgar completed her surgical internship in 1935 and spent the next two years in an anesthesiology residency program at Columbia, at the University of Wisconsin in Madison, and at Bellevue Hospital in New York.

LIFE'S WORK

In 1938, Apgar was named as director of the division of anesthesia at Columbia. She worked hard to overcome formidable problems in staff recruitment, an overwhelming workload, resistance from surgeons who refused to accept anesthesiologists as their equals, and an inadequate salary. (Physician anesthetists were not permitted to charge professional fees.) She was the only staff member in the division until 1940. By 1945, however, more anesthetics were administered by physicians than by nurses, and by 1948, there were eighteen residents in the program. (The number of nurse anesthetists on staff decreased from fourteen in 1937 to four in 1948.) Apgar's workload improved when many physicians returned from World War II to enter anesthesiology. Apgar often came into conflict with older surgeons who were accustomed to giving nurse anesthetists orders, but eventually she was able to win over the younger surgeons. The problem with getting satisfactory financial compensation was resolved only after Apgar threatened to resign in 1940 and a separate budget for the anesthesia division was funded in 1941.

By 1946, anesthesia was becoming recognized as a specialty on a national level. There was a move at Columbia to establish a physician-only department, separate from surgery, with a strong research program. Apgar expected to be made chair of this new department. In 1949, however, a Bellevue anesthesiologist with a research background replaced her as head of the division. Six months later, when the division was made a department, Apgar was appointed professor, making her the first female full professor at Columbia University.

Freed from administration of the department, Apgar moved on to obstetric anesthesia, where she made her

Virginia Apgar. (Library of Congress)

greatest contribution. Before her development of the Apgar score, there was no standard evaluation of the transition of the newborn to life outside the uterus. The initial examination of the infant at birth was often haphazard and disorganized, since obstetricians often devoted most of their attention to mothers. In response to a medical student's question about evaluating the newborn at the time of delivery, Apgar developed her scoring system in 1949. She listed five categories—heart rate, respiratory effort, muscle tone, reflex irritability, and color—that should be assessed at one minute after birth to indicate the need for resuscitation. (Eventually, the score would be repeated at five and ten minutes after birth to evaluate the baby's response to resuscitation.) Each category was to be scored as 0, 1, or 2 points and then added for a total score for the baby. A score between 7 and 10 indicated that the newborn was in satisfactory condition; a score between 4 and 7 indicated the need for further observation and possible intervention; and a score of less than 4 alerted the staff to the need for immediate intervention, with concerns about the survival of the infant. The score was first published in 1953 and was eventually adopted throughout the world.

Apgar had always appreciated the need for research, but her heavy clinical workload and administrative duties had left her little time to pursue her interest in this area. With the development of new technology to measure blood gases, pH levels, and blood levels, she was able to collaborate with Duncan Holaday, an anesthesiologist-researcher, and L. Stanley James, a pediatrician, to study the effects of labor and delivery and maternal anesthetics on the baby's condition, using the Apgar score as a standard evaluation. Low Apgar scores noted in babies with poorly oxygenated blood (hypoxia) or pH imbalanced blood (acidosis) could alert attending physicians that these conditions should be promptly treated. During her studies, Apgar was the first person to catheterize the umbilical artery of the newborn, a procedure that became an essential component of neonatal care. In their studies of the effects on the newborn of anesthetics given to the mother during labor, Apgar and her coworkers discovered that cyclopropane gas, which had been considered a harmless anesthetic, markedly depressed the newborn. After reviewing the data, Apgar is said to have remarked, "There goes my favorite gas." The obstetrical use of cyclopropane declined dramatically after the research was published. Another Apgar study with significant implications for neonatal care was a collaborative research project, involving twelve institutions and 17,221 infants. It determined, unequivocally, that the Apgar score, especially as assessed at five minutes after birth, was a good predictor of neonatal survival and neurologic development.

Apgar assisted in the education of more than 250 physicians in anesthesiology, and her ideas inspired both practice and research. Her motto was "Do what is right and do it now." She always admitted her mistakes—at a time when errors were usually denied—and her constant encouragement, her honesty, and her humility enabled students to accept criticism without being offended.

After a distinguished career of thirty years at Columbia-Presbyterian Medical Center, Apgar decided to improve her knowledge of statistics related to research, and she left anesthesiology to earn a master of public health degree from Johns Hopkins University School of Hygiene and Public Health. She considered her pursuit of this degree at the age of fifty to be her most significant decision. It changed her whole life, and she never regretted it.

In 1959, Apgar was persuaded to join the National Foundation-March of Dimes, where she headed the division on congenital malformations from 1959 to 1967 and directed the foundation's basic research program from 1969 to 1972. This period was a critical time in the foundation's history, when the focus of its mission was being diverted from preventing poliomyelitis to the prevention of all birth disorders. From 1973 until the time of her death, Apgar served as the foundation's vice president for medical affairs. As principal fund-raiser, she increased the foundation's annual income from $19 million in 1959 to $46 million in 1974, helping to fund research into the many causes of birth disorders as well as their prevention and treatment. As comfortable with the public as she was with her medical colleagues, Apgar made frequent public talks and coauthored a book for parents about birth disorders, *Is My Baby All Right?* (1972). During this time, she also served as a research fellow in medicine at Johns Hopkins University and a clinical professor of pediatrics at Cornell University Medical College, where she was the first physician in North America to have an appointment that included teratology (birth disorders) as a subspecialty.

In recognition of her important scientific contributions, Apgar received many honors. The American Academy of Pediatrics named a prestigious award for her and the American Society of Anesthesiologists presented her with the Ralph Waters Medal. In 1973, she was awarded the Gold Medal of Columbia University for special service to medicine. Her undergraduate alma mater, Mount Holyoke College, named an academic chair in her honor. In addition, Apgar received four honorary degrees and was honored by *Ladies' Home Journal* as Woman of the Year in 1973.

Apgar's private life was full and rewarding—she was a gifted musician, an avid gardener, an aviator, a photographer, and a philatelist. She was also an untiring student: When she died in 1974 at age sixty-five, she was commuting from her March of Dimes work in New York to Johns Hopkins University in Baltimore to study genetics.

SIGNIFICANCE

During her career, Apgar received international recognition for her pioneering work in anesthesiology, neonatology, and teratology. She probably did more to improve the health of mothers and infants than anyone during the twentieth century. Modern obstetricians, pediatricians, and nurses include the Apgar score—a scientifically validated standard for evaluating the newborn—in their vocabulary as a result of her concern for babies during the critical first few moments after birth. As a professor of anesthesiology at the Columbia-Presbyterian Medical Center for more than twenty years, Apgar assisted in the delivery of more than seventeen thousand babies. Apgar's research laid the foundation for the development of perinatology, and countless infant deaths have been prevented because of her work. She was a wonderful teacher, and her ideas inspired much productive research.

When she could not become a surgeon because she was a woman, Apgar became an anesthesiologist. When she could not become department chair, Apgar entered obstetrical anesthesia. When she believed there was no room for her to advance at Columbia-Presbyterian Medical Center, Apgar became enormously successful in preventing birth disorders and developing the field of teratology. While not publicly supportive of feminism, Apgar was outraged at the restrictions facing women. Nevertheless, she believed there were ample opportunities, particularly within various medical fields, for both men and women who were willing to overcome their limitations. She considered women more competitive, more rational, more sincere, and stronger than men. She took advantage of every available opportunity, made an incalculable contribution to society, created a marvelous career, and served as a role model for women, and men, everywhere.

—Edna B. Quinn

FURTHER READING

Apgar, Virginia, and Joan Beck. *Is My Baby All Right? A Guide to Birth Defects*. New York: Trident Press, 1972. A book written to answer the questions of parents and general readers, in nontechnical terms, about birth disorders. There are interesting details of Apgar's life in the preface and "About the Authors" section.

"Baby Monitor." *Science*, August 4, 2006. Explains the Apgar score as well as the course of its development by Apgar.

Calmes, Selma. "Virginia Apgar: A Woman Physician's Career in a Developing Specialty." *Journal of the American Medical Women's Association* 39 (November-December, 1984): 184-188. The best source of information about Apgar's early life and career at Columbia University. The article's wealth of detail comes from its author's skillful use of such primary sources as Apgar's diary, letters, and reports.

Diamonstein, Barbaralee. *Open Secrets: Ninety-four Women in Touch with Our Time*. New York: Viking Press, 1972. An entertaining interview with Apgar that reveals her delightful sense of humor and opinions on many topics.

Kass-Simon, G., and Patricia Farnes, eds. *Women of Science: Righting the Record*. Bloomington: Indiana University Press, 1990. Contains only a brief paragraph about Apgar, but the preface and introduction give valuable feminist insights into the context in which women scientists have worked and the obstacles they have had to overcome.

Mitford, Jessica. *The American Way of Birth*. New York: E. P. Dutton, 1992. Mitford's work provides little direct coverage of Apgar's life, yet it does give a historical overview of the changing attitudes toward childbirth that have prevailed from medieval times through the twentieth century and their impact on American obstetrical medicine. Although her acerbic comments fall short of a purely objective history, Mitford does provide a context for understanding modern obstetrical practices as well as childbirth alternatives, such as delivery by licensed nurse midwives and lay midwives.

Vare, Ethlie Ann, and Greg Ptacek. *Mothers of Invention: From the Bra to the Bomb—Forgotten Women and Their Unforgettable Ideas*. New York: William Morrow, 1988. Although this work is primarily devoted to women inventors in fields outside medicine, it does include a sketch on Apgar that provides details of her research as well as her fund-raising efforts on behalf of the National Foundation-March of Dimes.

SEE ALSO: Albert Calmette; Harvey Williams Cushing; Marian Wright Edelman; William Crawford Gorgas; Julia C. Lathrop; William J. and Charles H. Mayo; Dorothy Reed Mendenhall; Susan La Flesche Picotte; Jonas Salk; Benjamin Spock; Helen Brooke Taussig; Lillian D. Wald.

RELATED ARTICLE in *Great Events from History: The Twentieth Century*:

1971-2000: May 21, 1981: World Health Organization Adopts a Code on Breast-Milk Substitutes.

GUILLAUME APOLLINAIRE
Italian poet and critic

Apollinaire left an enduring mark on the poetry and painting of the twentieth century. He was a spokesperson for the Symbolists and an exponent of Surrealism. Indeed, the word "Surrealist" appeared for the first time in his writing. His poem "La Jolie Rousse" (the pretty redhead) became and has remained the charter of free verse.

BORN: August 26, 1880; Rome, Italy
DIED: November 9, 1918; Paris, France
ALSO KNOWN AS: Guillaume Albert Wladimir
　　Alexandre Apollinaire de Kostrowitzky (birth
　　name); Wilhelm Apollinaris
AREAS OF ACHIEVEMENT: Literature, art

EARLY LIFE

The person known since his twentieth year as Guillaume Apollinaire (gee-yohm ah-paw-lee-nehr) was the illegitimate son of Angélique Alexandrine de Kostrowitzky, a member of the Polish nobility whose family had taken refuge at the papal court. She first registered her son under a false name but a month later had him baptized as Guillaume Albert Wladimir Alexandre Apollinaire de Kostrowitzky. The mystery of his father's identity lasted for seventy years; he has since been identified as Francesco Flugi d'Aspermont of a family originally from Switzerland. Wilhelm, or "Kostro," as he was called at different times, had a younger brother, Albert, before his mother's liaison ended a few years later. For a time, the father's brother, a member of the Benedictine Order, helped with the expenses of the boys' education. They were sent to Roman Catholic schools in Monaco, Cannes, and Nice, where they were exceedingly devout and diligent.

In 1897 and 1898, Wilhelm became fascinated by ancient history, by magic, and by erotic literature. By that time he was apparently a militant atheist, treating religion satirically and grossly, although at times nostalgically, and steeping himself in exoticism and obscene writings. The knowledge thus gained served as material for his poetry and stories.

By 1900, Wilhelm was living with his mother in Paris and making a precarious living in minor secretarial jobs. The following year, he went, as a tutor to the young daughter of the viscountess of Milhau, to Germany, where he fell hopelessly in love with Annie Playden, a blond, English governess who shared his duties. Her parents refused to allow her to marry Wilhelm, but this attachment, along with some extensive traveling in Europe, resulted in a series of stories collected in *L'Hérésiarque et Cie* (1910; *The Heresiarch and Co.*, 1965). It contained the first tale, written in 1902, that he had signed with the name Guillaume Apollinaire. His love for Annie Playden also inspired his most famous poem, "La Chanson du mal-aimé" ("The Song of the Poorly Loved"). All of his life, his love affairs were to provide inspiration for his best poetry.

LIFE'S WORK

By 1903, Apollinaire had become friends with André Salmon and Alfred Jarry. The three men founded a small review, *Le Festin d'ésope*, which lasted for nine issues. About the same time, Apollinaire met Max Jacob and Pablo Picasso, who was to be his friend for many years. The result was a significant artistic and literary collaboration. Now too Apollinaire made the acquaintance of

Guillaume Apollinaire.

Maurice de Vlaminck and André Derain, with whom he drank, played cards, and visited hashish dens and brothels. He became increasingly well known in Paris cafés as a friendly and ebullient talker. The usual subjects of conversation were aesthetics and painting, and everyone was feverishly preoccupied with innovation. In 1905, Apollinaire's first writing on art appeared: two articles on Picasso.

In 1909, after a long delay, *Mercure de France* published the fifty-nine stanzas of "La Chanson du mal-aimé." Apollinaire's place in the literary world was now secure. From 1911 on, he wrote a regular column for *Mercure de France*, usually championing new painters. In addition, he had been since 1910 the regular art critic for *L'Intransigeant*. In his articles, he sought to establish his authority by discovering, explaining, and promoting the newest movements in literature and painting: He campaigned for the Fauves, the Unanimists, Henri Matisse, Picasso, Georges Braque, and Alfred Jarry. He became the principal spokesperson for cubism.

CUBISM

Guillaume Apollinaire describes the nature of what was then a new form of art called cubism in this translation from his 1913 work Les Peintres cubistes *(the cubist painters).*

Verisimilitude is no longer of any importance, since the artist sacrifices everything to truths inherent in a higher form of Nature, which he divines although he has not yet discovered it. The subject is hardly, or not at all, taken into account.

Generally speaking, modern art rejects most of the ways in which the great artists of the past have sought to please.

Though the aim of painting is now, as ever, to please the eye, the art-lover is invited to take in it a pleasure different from that which he takes in the sight of natural objects.

Thus we are progressing in the direction of an entirely new form of art, which will have the same relationship to painting as the term has been understood till now, that music has to literature.

It will be pure painting, just as music is pure literature.

The pleasure a music lover takes in a concert is quite different from that which he feels when listening to natural sounds such as the murmuring of a stream, the crashing of a torrent, the whistling of the wind in a forest or the harmonies, founded on reason rather than aesthetics, of human language....

The social function of great poets and great artists is constantly to renew the manner in which nature appears to the eyes of Mankind.

Source: Les Peintres cubistes: Méditations esthétiques. In *Guillaume Apollinaire and the Cubist Life,* translated by Cecily Mackworth (New York: Horizon Press, 1963).

In 1911, Apollinaire had the harrowing experience of being imprisoned for five days on the strength of a false accusation that he had received and hidden objects stolen from the Louvre. He was desolated. Despite his acquittal, newspapers continued to attack him; his position as leader of the avant-garde was threatened, as was his legal right to stay in France. Added to these worries was his lack of funds. His spirits revived with the invitation to become associate editor of a new review, *Soirées de Paris.* His first article advised the abandonment of "likeness" and of subject matter in painting. He could not be cowed.

In the summer of 1912, Apollinaire read a nearly finished version of "Zone" to the Spanish painter Francis Picabia and his wife. This date is important because of the resemblance of "Zone" to Blaise Cendrars's "Pâques à New York" (Easter in New York), published in 1912. Since Apollinaire regularly published Cendrars's work in *Les Soirées,* the influence may well have been mutual.

Apollinaire had for some time wanted to marry the painter Marie Laurencin, but his mother opposed the

marriage on the grounds of an insufficient dowry. The liaison lasted until the fall of 1912; the breakup inspired one of the poet's best-known lyrics, "Le Pont Mirabeau" ("Mirabeau Bridge"). The climax of Apollinaire's career came in 1913: His two most important volumes appeared, *Alcools,* translated into English in 1964, and *Les Peintres cubistes: Méditations esthétiques* (*The Cubist Painters: Aesthetic Meditations,* 1944). The complete lack of punctuation in *Alcools,* insisted on by the author, profoundly shocked the public.

In the spring of 1914, Apollinaire was asked to write art reviews for the *Paris-Journal.* He wrote a review daily, with three exceptions, between May and the outbreak of war, including the first calligramme—a poem whose words form a design. He considered the calligramme his most important innovation.

When Apollinaire applied for French citizenship, he was refused. He fled to Nice, where he met the aristocratic madcap Louise Coligny-Châtillon (called "Lou"), with whom he fell in love. For a brief period he gave himself up to an orgy of opium smoking and general debauchery; then suddenly he left for Nîmes and joined the artillery. Lou followed, and, although their violent love affair soon ended, it inspired many of Apollinaire's best poems in *Calligrammes* (1918; English translation, 1980).

In January, 1915, he wrote that he found the soldier's life ideal for him. He left for the front on Easter Sunday. Even from the trenches, he continued his voluminous correspondence. He wrote letters and poems to Lou and to all of his old friends and to a new love, Madeleine Pagès, to whom he became engaged. Under fire in the front line, he printed on gelatin plates twenty-five copies of *Case d'armons* (1915; a bunker), a collection of verse and drawings.

In November, he was transferred to an infantry company in the Champagne offensive, where, despite real hardship, he wrote frequently to Pagès. On March 17, he was reading *Mercure de France* in a trench, when he found that his blood was dripping onto the paper. Shrapnel had wounded his head more seriously than he at first had realized; he was moved back to Paris, where he was trepanned on May 11. While in the hospital, Apollinaire put together some unpublished stories in a volume that he entitled *Le Poète assassiné* (*The Poet Assassinated*, 1923), which was published in 1916. At the end of this year, he renewed acquaintance with Jacqueline Kolb, a redhead whom he called Ruby, and moved back to his sixth floor apartment on the Boulevard Saint-Germain, where he found the domestic tranquillity that he had never before known.

Apollinaire's friends organized a banquet on December 31, 1916, to welcome him home and to celebrate the publication of *The Poet Assassinated*. The ninety guests included practically all the famous writers and painters of the period. One of the guests, Pierre Reverdy, founded the following March the review *Nord-Sud*, in which Apollinaire's contributions helped to open the way for Dada and Surrealism. In June, 1917, Apollinaire personally oversaw the production of his first play: *Les Mamelles de Tirésias* (*The Breasts of Tiresias*, 1961). Its buffoonery and vulgarity excited immense interest.

With the continuing deterioration of Apollinaire's health, he relied increasingly on Kolb; they were married quietly in May, 1918. She had inspired his only important poem since his release from the hospital, "La Jolie Rousse," a summary of his attitude toward conventional and the new experimental poetry. He went on working despite depression and nagging health problems. Then, only two days before the Armistice, he died of Spanish influenza.

SIGNIFICANCE

It would be difficult to overestimate the impact of Apollinaire on the art and poetry of the twentieth century. Perhaps, as one of his biographers, Francis Steegmuller, claims and some of Apollinaire's painter friends hinted, the poet had no real knowledge of art, or perhaps, as Professor Leroy Breunig and numerous artists and historians have proclaimed, he was one of the greatest art critics of the century. At any rate, his vigorous and ceaseless championship of the struggling innovators of his time led to the serious acceptance of Fauvism, cubism, primitive art, abstract art, and eventually Dada and Surrealism.

Apollinaire's stories and his one play pale into insignificance by the side of his critical writings and poetry. In one article written shortly before his death, he explains that the new spirit consists largely of surprise and that poets should not abandon the traditional elements but should try to capture contemporary life. He foresaw a synthesis of the arts, aided by films and photography. In his autobiographical ars poetica, "La Jolie Rousse," he does not advocate the overthrow of the old "Order" but advises the acceptance of "Adventure" and leads the way. Apollinaire's numerous volumes of verse, especially *Alcools* and *Calligrammes*, place him among the masters of French lyric and elegiac poetry. His vision of poetic and artistic freedom is an enduring legacy.

—*Dorothy B. Aspinwall*

FURTHER READING

Adéma, Marcel. *Apollinaire*. Translated by Denise Folliot. New York: Grove Press, 1955. A prime source of biographical material, the bible of scholars researching the poet and his epoch.

Bates, Scott. *Guillaume Apollinaire*. Rev. ed. Boston: Twayne, 1989. This book offers detailed erudite analyses of Apollinaire's major works and informed judgments on his place in French literature and in the development of art criticism. It emphasizes the importance to the entire world of Apollinaire's vision of a cultural millennium propelled by science and democracy and implemented by poetry. Included are a chronology, a twenty-six-page glossary of references, notes, and selected bibliographies of both primary and secondary sources.

Couffignal, Robert. *Apollinaire*. Translated by Eda Mezer Levitine. Tuscaloosa: University of Alabama Press, 1975. This is a searching analysis of some of Apollinaire's best-known works, including "Zone," strictly from the Catholic point of view. It traces his attitude toward religion from his childhood to his death. The book contains a chronology, translations of ten texts, both poems and prose with the author's comments, a bibliographical note, and an index.

Hicken, Adrian. *Apollinaire, Cubism, and Orphism.* Burlington, Vt.: Ashgate, 2002. Describes how Apollinaire's poetic imagery influenced the painting of Pablo Picasso, Raoul Dufy, and the other artists with whom Apollinaire was acquainted.

Shattuck, Roger. *The Banquet Years.* Rev. ed. New York: Vintage Books, 1968. In the two long chapters devoted to Apollinaire, "The Impresario of the Avant-garde" and "Painter-Poet," the author gives a year-by-year and at times even a month-by-month account of Apollinaire's life, loves, friends, employment, writings, and speeches. The tone is judicial, the critical judgments fair and balanced. Includes a bibliography and an index.

Steegmuller, Francis. *Apollinaire: Poet Among the Painters.* New York: Farrar, Straus, 1963. This is an exhaustive, extremely well-documented, unbiased, and highly readable biography. Contains a preface, translations, numerous photographs and illustrations, two appendixes, notes, and an index.

SEE ALSO: André Breton; Marc Chagall; Robert Delaunay; Marcel Duchamp; Paul Éluard; Max Ernst; Roger Fry; Eugenio Montale.

RELATED ARTICLES in *Great Events from History: The Twentieth Century:*

1901-1940: January 21, 1908: *The Ghost Sonata* Influences Modern Theater and Drama; May 19, 1909: Diaghilev's Ballets Russes Astounds Paris; 1913: Apollinaire Defines Cubism; October, 1924: Surrealism Is Born.

1941-1970: October 31, 1959: Ionesco's *Rhinoceros* Receives a Resounding Worldwide Reception; 1961: Esslin Publishes *The Theatre of the Absurd.*

CORAZON AQUINO
President of the Philippines (1986-1992)

Aquino succeeded Philippine president Ferdinand Marcos to become Asia's first female president. The widow of Benigno Aquino, Jr., a senator assassinated under orders of the despotic Marcos, Aquino chose government reform as the primary thrust of her political platform.

BORN: January 25, 1933; Tarlac province, the Philippines

ALSO KNOWN AS: María Corazon Cojuangco (birth name); Cory Aquino

AREAS OF ACHIEVEMENT: Government and politics, social reform

EARLY LIFE

Corazon Aquino (KOHR-ah-zohn ah-KEE-noh) was born María Corazon Cojuangco, the daughter of Don Jose Cojuangco and Doña Demetria Sumulong, in Paniqui in the Tarlac district of the Philippines. The sixth of eight children, Aquino was always intelligent, and her wealthy family educated her at the best schools. She graduated first in her class at St. Scholastica's College in Manila (a prominent girl's school with classes ranging from grade school to junior college level) and then studied at a number of exclusive prep schools in the United States: Ravenhill Academy (Philadelphia), the Notre Dame Convent School (New York), and the College of Mount Saint Vincent (also in New York). In college, Aquino gravitated to liberal arts, acquiring a bachelor of arts degree in French.

After completing her undergraduate degree, Aquino returned to the Philippines. Rather than beginning her teaching career as planned, however, she found herself drawn toward the study of law and politics. With the blessing of her parents, she attended Far Eastern University and, in 1955, fell in love with the young, charismatic Benigno "Ninoy" Aquino, Jr., who at the tender age of twenty-two had already served as a war correspondent for *The Manila Times*, been awarded a Philippine Legion of Honor Award from President Elpidio Quirino, and was a key adviser to President Ramon Magsaysay. A personable and magnetic man, Ninoy had just been elected mayor of Concepción in Tarlac province when he met Corazon Cojuangco, and the young couple found that they had much in common. Both were members of the Philippines' Liberal Party, both were idealistic, and both wanted their country to be more progressive politically and socially. They married, and subsequently had five children: Maria Elena Aquino, Aurora Corazon Aquino, Benigno Aquino III, Victoria Eliza Aquino, and Kristina Bernadette Cojuangco.

LIFE'S WORK

Ninoy Aquino became a governor and, later, a senator, but his political speeches frequently questioned the policies of President Ferdinand Marcos. As the only Liberal Party member to have succeeded in being elected to the Senate, Aquino was politically unpopular among his colleagues. His speeches targeted not only the military excesses of President Marcos, but also the fiscal excesses of Marcos's wife, Imelda. He became the most popular choice to become the next president, which, ironically, sealed his political fate. A short time after President Marcos declared martial law on September 21, 1971, Aquino was arrested and charged with murder, illegal possession of firearms, and subversion. He was sentenced to death by firing squad; however, his political power proved too intimidating to the politically weakened President Marcos. Bowing to public pressure for

Corazon Aquino, Time's *Woman of the Year, 1987.* (Hulton Archive/Getty Images)

Aquino's release, Marcos allowed Corazon Aquino to secretly take her ailing husband into exile in the United States, unaware that she had promised her husband that they would eventually return. In 1983, having heard that Marcos's health was failing due to lupus, the Aquinos decided that the time was right to return to the Philippines. It was a decision that would dramatically change the young woman's expectations for the future. Stepping down onto the tarmac at the Manila International Airport on August 21, 1983, Corazon Aquino witnessed the brutal assassination of her beloved husband. In horror, she vowed to continue Ninoy's political fight, and she became an influential leader within the Lakas ng Bayan, or Laban Party (the People's Power Party).

Because his health was so fragile, President Marcos shocked the nation with his sudden call for a presidential election to take place during February of 1986. Although originally slated to act as running mate to opposition favorite Senator Salvador Laurel of Batangas, Corazon Aquino had greater political sway than Laurel did, and public opinion favored her. Her supporters gathered one million signatures in one week to ensure that Aquino, rather than Laurel, would be the coalition's representative.

After a tumultuous campaign, the February elections were held to great public fanfare. Although the media initially reported that Aquino had lost the election to President Marcos, too many people believed the outcome was fraudulent. Aquino herself expressed doubt that the votes had been properly tabulated. Consequently, she refused to admit defeat, and both Marcos and Aquino held rival inaugurations on February 25. President Marcos tried to use his remaining political power to stay in power but found the pressure of public demonstrations, the threat of a military revolt, and the censure of foreign governments such as the United States to be too great to overcome, and he voluntarily left the country.

With her main political rival disgraced and exiled, Corazon Aquino took up the challenge of repairing the damage that twenty years of autocratic rule had done to her country. She conceived of a federal government realigned and reorganized under a Freedom Constitution, a constitution that would be democratically established and subject to both internal and external public review. The new constitution's official acceptance (it was ratified February 7, 1987) made Aquino's vision real and permanent, as the constitution became the basis by which congressional and local elections could take place in the Philippines.

Like her late husband, Aquino was widely praised

both inside and outside the Philippines. Her previous schooling and residency in the United States made her particularly appealing to mainstream Americans. Not surprisingly, she was selected as *Time* magazine's Woman of the Year for 1986 because of her progressive political stance and her dogged determination to persevere in the face of not only intense political upheaval but also a slew of natural disasters that ripped apart her country. Besides being repeatedly attacked by Marcos loyalists and having to defend her fledgling government against numerous coup attempts, Aquino had to lead recovery efforts following an eruption of Mount Pinatubo in 1991, a 7.7 magnitude earthquake, and a category five typhoon that collectively devastated the countryside.

Exhausted by her tenure as president, Aquino chose not to run again for office. Instead, she supported Defense Secretary Fidel V. Ramos as her candidate of choice for the 1992 Philippine elections. Many Filipinos were unhappy with Aquino's choice of successor, especially because he was not as personally charismatic and lacked the support of the Catholic Church. Although he did manage to win office, his victory was hard-won and lacked a clear mandate from the Filipino public.

SIGNIFICANCE

Aquino was renowned not only for being one of the first female leaders of an Asian country but also for her many humanitarian activities and awards: In 1996 she received the J. William Fulbright Prize for International Understanding; in 1998 she received the Ramon Magsaysay Award for International Understanding, an award created in honor of the former president and friend of her late husband; in 2001 she was awarded a World Citizenship Award; in 2002 she became chair for the Board of Trustees of the Asian Institute of Management; and in November, 2006, *Time* magazine published an extensive article detailing Aquino's work as a political reformer and naming her an Asian Hero. She received many honorary doctorates, including degrees in humanities from the University of Oregon (1995), San Beda College (2000), and Seattle University (2002); in humane letters from her alma mater, the College of Mount Saint Vincent in New York; and in international relations from Boston University. Aquino also has been involved with microfinance projects for beginning entrepreneurs and social welfare and scholarship assistance through the Benigno Aquino Memorial Foundation, a fund established in honor of her beloved husband.

—*Julia M. Meyers*

FURTHER READING

Burton, Sandra. *Impossible Dream: The Marcoses, the Aquinos, and the Unfinished Revolution*. New York: Warner Books, 1988. One of the most interesting aspects of the Marcos/Aquino election scandal is just how polarized the two candidates became in the court of public opinion. Burton explains the basis of the adulation of Ninoy and Corazon Aquino, the hatred of Ferdinand Marcos, and the impetus for the 1986 revolt.

D'Amico, Francine, and Peter R. Beckman, eds. *Women in World Politics: An Introduction*. Westport, Conn.: Bergin & Garvey, 1995. This scholarly collection of essays studies the impact of female leadership on world politics. Includes biographies of Violeta Barrios de Chamorro, Indira Ghandi, and Margaret Thatcher as well as excerpts from the published memoirs of other female political figures.

Komisar, Lucy. *Corazon Aquino: The Story of a Revolution*. New York: G. Braziller, 1987. Komisar treats readers to a lively and highly readable biography of Corazon Aquino, detailing her transformation from the reclusive wealthy wife of a political firebrand to the role as social reformer and noted humanitarian.

Ohrn, Deborah Gore, ed. *Herstory: Women Who Changed the World*. New York: Viking, 1995. Ohrn outlines the increasing influence of women in a variety of social spheres, including that of international politics. She presents life stories of women in the arts, the sciences, and the political forum, finding common threads between the disparate fields.

Reid, Robert H. *Corazon Aquino and the Brushfire Revolution*. Baton Rouge: Louisiana State University Press, 1995. This is a fairly dense scholarly history of Corazon Aquino's rise to power from her husband's assassination through her election to the Philippine presidency. It also provides a look at her role within the Laban party.

SEE ALSO: William F. Halsey; Douglas MacArthur; Ferdinand Marcos; William Howard Taft.

YASIR ARAFAT

President of the Palestinian Authority (1996-2004)

Arafat was the founder of Fatah, a Palestinian revolutionary and sometimes terrorist organization that became the founding block of the Palestine Liberation Organization. A controversial figure who was a freedom fighter to his own people and a terrorist to Israelis and others, he moved the Palestinians from near obscurity in the 1960's to the forefront of the world's attention.

BORN: August 24, 1929; Cairo, Egypt
DIED: November 11, 2004; Paris, France
ALSO KNOWN AS: Mohammed Abd al-Rauf Arafat al-Qudwa al-Husseini (birth name); Moḥammad ʿAbdar-Raʿūf al-Qudwah al-ḥusaynī; Yāsir ʿArafāt
AREAS OF ACHIEVEMENT: Diplomacy, government and politics, warfare and conquest

EARLY LIFE

Yasir Arafat (YA-sur A-rah-faht) was born Mohammed Abd al-Rauf Arafat al-Qudwa al-Husseini in Cairo. His mother, Hamida, was a cousin of Hajj Amin al Husseini, the mufti of Jerusalem and Palestinian leader during the British mandate over Palestine. Arafat was one of seven children from his father's first marriage. His father, Abd al-Rauf Arafat al-Qudwa, was from the Qudwa family of Gaza and the Khan Yunis, and a member of the Muslim Brotherhood. Arafat's family moved back to Gaza from Cairo in 1939, and he was reared by an uncle after the death of his parents.

After World War II, when Arafat was in his teens, he became active in Palestinian student causes. He belonged to the group Futuwah, a youth organization affiliated with the Husseini clan that feuded with the rival Nashashibis. In 1946 he was active in smuggling arms into Palestine from Egypt. He fought in the 1948 Arab-Israeli War in battles south of Jerusalem. From 1951 to 1956, Arafat attended Fuʾād I University (now Cairo University) as a civil engineering student. He underwent commando training with a Gaza brigade in the Egyptian army in 1951 and later became involved in groups that staged hit-and-run operations against the British around the Suez Canal. In 1952, Arafat was elected president of the Union of Palestinian Students.

In August, 1956, Arafat attended the International Student Congress in Prague and then became chairman of the Union of Palestinian Graduates. This position allowed him to establish contacts with Palestinians in other countries. He began work as a construction engineer. In the October, 1956, Suez War, Arafat fought in the Egyptian army as a bomb disposal expert.

LIFE'S WORK

In 1956, Arafat, along with Khalil al-Wazir (also known as Abu Jihad), formed Fatah (victory) and became its spokesperson. The principle of the new organization was that its members should not belong to any Arab political party or other movement. This, he believed, was a way to demonstrate that Palestinians did not want to interfere in Arab internal politics. During 1957, Arafat moved to Kuwait and worked for the Kuwaiti government's department of water supply as a civil engineer; he also established a construction company that hired Palestinians. Many important Fatah contacts were made in this period. He established the first of Fatah's underground cells. In July, 1962, President Ahmed Ben Bella of Algeria became the first Arab head of state to recognize Fatah. Arafat met Ben Bella in December, 1962, and opened a Fatah office in Algiers under the name Bureau de la Palestine. Fatah subsequently developed along collective leadership lines. Arafat believed that Arab unity was key to liberating Palestine and that unity had to come from the people. His idea was to capture the imagination of the Palestinian people.

In 1964, the Palestine Liberation Organization (PLO) was formed by the Arab States in Cairo, led by Ahmed Shukairy but in essence controlled by Egypt. Arafat, trying to assert Palestinian independence, had many difficulties with Arab regimes that wanted to control Palestinian resistance. In May, 1966, Arafat, Abu Jihad, and twenty other Fatah members were arrested by the Syrian government on specious murder charges after a Syrian plot backfired, leading to the deaths of two Fatah members.

During the June, 1967, Six-Day War, Arafat and Abu Jihad fought on the Syrian front as irregulars. Arafat's reaction to Arab defeat was despair but was also to begin a popular war of liberation. Arafat was in favor of immediate resumption of guerrilla warfare as a way to avert the psychological burden of Arab defeat. On June 23, 1967, the Fatah Central Committee confirmed the idea of returning to military confrontation, and Arafat was appointed military commander. Some small operations began in August, but Israeli security forces had uncovered most of the cells by the end of the year. Arafat believed that irregular fighting allowed the Palestinians to fix their identity. Arafat stayed in the West Bank until the end of the year and then escaped to Jordan. The years 1968 to 1970 saw Jordan used as a base for attacks against Israel.

On March 21, 1968, the Battle of Karameh occurred between Israelis and Palestinian-Jordanian forces, marking the first Palestinian military victory over Israel since 1948. Karameh was viewed as "resurrection of the Palestinian people." Many volunteers came to PLO circles. In addition, a Palestinian bureaucracy was established and intellectuals became involved in the revival of Palestinian culture. The relationship between Arafat and President Gamal Abdel Nasser of Egypt blossomed after Karameh, and Arafat became the chief spokesperson for the PLO. Arafat's solution to the Palestine problem in 1968 was to espouse the idea of forming a Democratic State of Palestine. From Fatah's perspective, this meant dismantling Israel by politics and nonviolence, but from Israel's view, the dismantling appeared to be based on violence. The nonviolent solution was ultimately rejected by the PLO, which sought the extinction of Israel through violent means according to its 1964 covenant.

In early 1969, Arafat took over the PLO and made it into an umbrella organization, independent of the Arab regimes. Arafat himself became a symbol of resistance, more than a freedom fighter, to some. The PLO covenant bound all to "armed struggle." Arafat was elected chairman of the PLO executive committee. On November 3, 1969, the Cairo Agreement, which allowed the PLO to base itself in Lebanon, bear arms, use Lebanese territory to attack Israel, and have direct rule over the Palestinian refugee camps, was concluded. Arafat became supreme commander of the Palestine Armed Struggle Command (PASC).

During September, 1970, however, Arafat lost control of the extremists, particularly the Popular Front for the Liberation of Palestine (PFLP). Although the PFLP was suspended from the Central Committee of the Palestine Resistance, a civil war broke out in Jordan, and the PLO, including Arafat's forces, was defeated by the Jordanian army. There is some opinion that the PLO disaster in Jordan could have been averted if Arafat had used force to control the radicals. Arafat, however, seemed unwilling to restrain the leftists out of respect for the principle of national unity. Arafat also believed that use of violence against the Left would have destroyed "democracy" within the PLO.

The result was the rise of terror as a tactic by Palestinian groups after 1970. Black September, led by the PFLP, was the most violent early group. It was responsible for the 1971 assassination of the Jordanian prime minister

Wasfi Tal; the May, 1972, Lod Airport massacre; and the August, 1972, massacre of Israeli Olympic athletes in Munich. Arafat subsequently made a tactical alliance with the PLO Left and committed himself to armed struggle.

The first change toward moderation came in February, 1974, with a PLO working paper that indicated a willingness to accept a political settlement in exchange for a mini-state on the West Bank and in Gaza. Unofficial contacts were established with Israelis by the end of 1973, but it was not until 1977 that the Palestine National Council supported the idea of negotiations on the mini-state idea. At the Rabat Conference in 1974, the PLO was recognized as the sole legitimate representative of the Palestinian people.

On November 13, 1974, Arafat was invited to address the United Nations (U.N.) General Assembly, and he called for establishment of national authority on any land in the West Bank and Gaza. Arafat was treated as head of state. He asserted that, "Today, I have come bearing an olive branch and a freedom-fighter's gun. Do not let the olive branch fall from my hand." To critics, the gesture

Yasir Arafat. (AP/Wide World Photos)

seemed hypocritical, while his appearance in traditional Arab dress appeared as an example of political transformation in a changing world: yesterday a terrorist, today a diplomat. U.N. General Assembly Resolution 3236 of November 14, 1974, recognized the PLO as a representative of the Palestinian people and the right of the Palestinians to self-determination, national independence, and sovereignty. The PLO achieved diplomatic recognition from more than eighty states by the 1980's as well as observer status at the United Nations.

Arafat's 1974 successes, however, were short-lived. In 1975, the PLO became involved in the Lebanon Civil War, bringing the PLO into conflict with Syria, which did not want an independent Palestinian movement. Arafat moved in and out of Lebanon during the late 1970's, trying to position PLO forces and arrange ceasefires. The November, 1977, Sadat Peace Initiative with Israel and Anwar el-Sadat's historic visit to Jerusalem soured the relationship between Arafat and Sadat, as the Egyptian president appeared to usurp a role specifically delegated to the PLO.

In January, 1978, the PLO appeared to splinter further over the issue of legitimate leadership and the issue of armed struggle. Abu Nidal established a faction (Black June) and insisted that he, not Arafat, was the real representative of Fatah. Several Palestinian supporters of Arafat were assassinated by Abu Nidal's group, and he, in turn, was sentenced in absentia to death by Fatah leadership. In April, 1978, a mutiny within Fatah was led by Abu Daoud. Arafat tried to heal the rift by integrating all militias under Fatah. Arafat, in his attempt to maintain Palestinian unity, often gave contradictory statements about what exactly was the ultimate desire of the Palestinians. In 1978, for example, in a discussion with U.S. congressman Paul Findley, he indicated that he would accept a Palestinian state in the West Bank and Gaza but "would reserve the right, of course, to use non-violent means to bring about the eventual unification of all of Palestine."

In 1982, U.S. president Ronald Reagan proposed a peace plan that Arafat considered but that the Palestine National Council (PNC) ultimately rejected. This plan would have required Arafat to work jointly with King Hussein I of Jordan on Palestinian rights, which was something that President Hafez al-Assad of Syria did not want. Hussein desired a Palestinian state in confederation with Jordan, a situation that would narrow the independence of a PLO state. Arafat later accepted the idea of a joint Palestinian-Jordanian delegation, but Hussein insisted on including West Bank representatives in the del-

egation as well. Assad, in response, planned a Fatah rebellion. By 1985, Hussein indicated that the PLO would have to accept U.N. Resolution 242 of 1967, and an agreement was made between Arafat and Hussein accepting the land-for-peace principle. Yet PLO terrorist actions continued, undercutting Arafat's desire for moderation.

PLO leadership was caught short by the Intifada, the Palestinian uprising on the West Bank and Gaza that began on December 8, 1987. That uprising was begun largely because Arab states had become more interested in the Iraq-Iran War that was drawing to a close than the Palestine question. While the Intifada was spontaneous in its origins, PLO leadership moved in to control much of the activity and strikes and to provide financial support for those under Israeli occupation.

On November 15, 1988, the PNC declared an independent Palestinian state without specific borders and conditionally accepted U.N. Resolutions 242 and 338 and the 1947 Partition Plan. There was no straight answer from Arafat as to whether this meant recognition of Israel. During December, 1988, there were many clarifications, which finally led to American recognition of the PLO. In early December in Stockholm, Arafat indicated that he had accepted the existence of Israel. On December 13, he addressed a special session of the U.N. General Assembly in Geneva after having been refused a visa by the U.S. Department of State. In his address he fell short of a full renunciation of terrorism but called for peace talks. A day later, on December 14, another statement by Arafat provided another clarification on "the right of all parties concerned in the Middle East conflict to exist in peace and security . . . including the state of Palestine, Israel, and other neighbors." He also renounced all forms of terrorism. These statements satisfied the United States government and ended the diplomatic isolation of the PLO from Washington, D.C. At the same time, Arafat was critical of what appeared to be unconditional support of Israel by the United States because it encouraged hardline positions within Israel.

Despite the recognition of Israel and renunciation of terrorism, questions still existed regarding Arafat's attitudes toward Palestinian moderates and the wishes of Palestinians under occupation. During January, 1989, moderates who suggested ending the Intifada made threats against Arafat. Arafat's general position by the end of the 1980's was to support the creation of a Palestinian state on the West Bank, in Gaza, and in East Jerusalem, with support from an international conference involving all parties of the Arab-Israeli conflict.

By 1993 a significant shift had taken place in Palestinian-Israeli relations. After intensive negotiations and under pressure from the United States to come to an agreement, Arafat and Israeli prime minister Yitzhak Rabin signed the Oslo Peace Accords, in which Israel agreed to give up some of the occupied territories to autonomous Palestinian control. Rabin, however, was soon assassinated by a zealot opposed to the peace process. The promise of these accords and Arafat's role in negotiating them led the Nobel Institute to award its 1994 Peace Prize to Arafat, Rabin, and Israeli foreign minister Shimon Peres. On January 20, 1996, Arafat was elected president (or "head," *ra'is* in Arabic) of the newly established Palestinian Authority, an interim governing organization established during the negotiations in Oslo. However, because Hamas (an Arabic acronym for "Islamic resistance movement") and other hard-line anti-Israeli organizations boycotted the elections, Arafat's victory was problematic. Moreover, his relations with the new conservative prime minister, Benjamin Netanyahu, were difficult. Again under international pressure, the two leaders signed the Wye River Agreement in 1998. Netanyahu's pledged concession of West Bank land cost him the support of his party. Arafat in turn struggled to maintain the support of the more militant Palestinian factions, while pledging to suppress terrorism against Israeli targets. As a condition of the peace process, the Palestinian Authority expunged from its constitution its commitment to destroy Israel, but Arafat sought to appease his political opponents by declaring his intention to form the long-awaited Palestinian state.

At the U.S.-sponsored 2000 Camp David summit to negotiate a final settlement to the Palestinian-Israeli conflict, Netanyahu's successor, leftist Ehud Barak, offered Arafat what looked to be the long-sought deal: a Palestinian state in the West Bank and Gaza strip, the dismantling of some Israeli settlements, and a capital in a Jerusalem suburb. However, Arafat rejected the offer and refused to make a counteroffer, to the fury of President Bill Clinton, who was pressuring both sides to come to an agreement. Although negotiations continued, Prime Minister Barak withdrew from them. Two months later, the Second Intifada began and grew steadily in intensity. Israel elected conservative Ariel Sharon to deal with it. Meanwhile, George W. Bush was elected president of the United States. Both proclaimed Arafat to be an obstacle to peace and sought to isolate him. As Hamas and the Al-Aqsa Martyrs' Brigade launched suicide attacks on Israel, Arafat appeared either to tacitly approve of or to be unable to stop the violence. Additionally, these groups sometimes fought with Arafat's Fatah organization.

In 2002, shortly after a suicide bomb killed 135 Israelis, Sharon lost all patience with Arafat. Israeli forces invaded the West Bank and trapped Arafat in his command. He was allowed to leave only after extensive negotiations, whereupon the command post was destroyed, greatly reducing Arafat's active control of events in the West Bank. At the same time there were increasing complaints within the Palestinian population over corruption in the PLO and about Arafat's style of rule, which was autocratic and often severe. Arafat, his wife, Suha, and their daughter lived modestly, but when *Forbes* magazine reported that Arafat had some $300 million in personal wealth, the revelation fueled the corruption controversy. Arafat was widely thought to use the money to maintain a network of supporters, while winking at corruption among his lieutenants to keep them loyal. At the same time social work performed by Hamas, as well as its military ventures, won supporters away from the PLO.

Arafat's physical isolation prevented him from receiving proper medical care for his deteriorating health. His condition rapidly worsened in 2004. On October 29, he flew to France for treatment at a military hospital near Paris. The origin and nature of his illness were mysterious, although one doctor diagnosed idiopathic thrombocytopenic purpura, a sustained low platelet count in the blood from an unknown cause and typically manifesting in bruising and bleeding from soft tissues, such as the gums. On November 3, he fell into a coma, which steadily deepened. He died eight days later. Controversy immediately erupted. That cirrhosis of the liver was a prime factor in his death led to several rumors, most prominently that he had been poisoned. An autopsy might have settled the matter, but Arafat's wife forbade it. He was buried in Ramallah in the West Bank on November 12 after Israel, because of security concerns, refused to honor his wish to be laid to rest in East Jerusalem's Al-Aqsa Mosque.

SIGNIFICANCE

Although Arafat did not succeed in creating a fully independent Palestinian state, he was ultimately the symbol of the Palestinian revolution. As a world traveler and charismatic leader, he appeared to be wedded to the Palestinian revolution and was able to be all things to all people. Part of his leadership success was his ability to keep the PLO's ideology simple, especially in rejecting extraneous issues and refusing to make his organization a tool of any specific Arab regime. Ideologically, Arafat's bottom line was that Palestine was Arab land and hence Israel would never be formally recognized. Arafat was also able to obtain large financial subsidies for the Palestinian cause from oil-producing Arab regimes, which in turn increased the financial power of the PLO in Lebanon through the summer of 1982.

Arafat, however, was often said to equivocate. Indeed, *Time* magazine began his obituary, "Arafat was a grand obfuscator." His obscure statements about renunciation of terrorism and recognition of Israel did not allow him to win full support of the United States or Western European powers for the Palestinian cause. During his tenure as PLO leader, Arafat was also criticized for his individualism—his insistence that he be free to take personal initiatives, which often led to broad promises without the support of all PLO groups. He was also criticized by other Palestinian groups for enriching himself and the leadership at the expense of those in the camps. The strategy of delaying peace until the Arabs were strong enough to dictate terms was criticized by peace advocates outside the Middle East. It also backfired: Although Mahmoud Abbas (also known as Abu Mazen) won the January, 2005, election to succeed Arafat, the PLO lost control of the Palestinian Authority to Hamas in January, 2006, elections. As a result, the European Union and United States withdrew financial support, and the Palestinians had to deal with greater poverty and renewed cycles of fighting and uneasy truces, not only with Israel but also among Palestinian parties. Arafat's life is a testimony to the complexity of the Palestinian question and the fact that it is interwoven into Arab politics.

—*Stephen C. Feinstein*

FURTHER READING

Becker, Jillian. *The PLO*. London: Weidenfeld & Nicolson, 1984. A history of the PLO that defines the organization as a terrorist group and takes a negative view toward Arafat as a leader.

Friedman, Thomas. *From Beirut to Jerusalem*. New York: Farrar, Straus and Giroux, 1989. This is an exceptionally interesting examination of Israeli, Palestinian, and Lebanese politics by a Pulitzer Prize-winning bureau chief of *The New York Times* in Beirut and Jerusalem.

Karsh, Efraim. *Arafat's War: The Man and His Struggle for Israeli Conquest*. New York: Grove Press, 2003. Karsh argues that the collapse of the peace process, begun after the Oslo Accords, came about because Arafat was more interested in destroying Israel than in establishing a Palestinian state.

Mishal, Shaul. *The PLO Under Arafat: Between Gun and Olive Branch*. New Haven, Conn.: Yale University Press, 1986. A structural examination of the PLO that in a scholarly way distinguishes Arafat from other Palestinian leaders and examines the mechanics of the PLO.

Rubenstein, Richard. *Alchemists of Revolution*. New York: Basic Books, 1987. A critical examination of the structure of terrorism as it developed during the 1970's and 1980's. Special attention is paid to Arafat as representative of a figure who is a freedom fighter to his own people and a terrorist to outsiders.

Rubin, Barry, and Judith Colp Rubin. *Yasir Arafat: A Political Biography*. New York: Oxford University Press, 2003. The authors document Arafat's career, from his days as a student to his eventual leadership of the Palestinian people, pointing out his errors of judgment and history of duplicity. Includes a useful chronology and glossary of names and political movements.

Samuels, David. "In a Ruined Country." *The Atlantic*, September, 2005. A brief biography of Arafat, analyzing how his failure to achieve a lasting peace with Israel led to the destruction of Palestine.

Walker, Tony, and Andrew Gowers. *Arafat: The Biography*. Rev. ed. London: Virgin, 2003. The authors interviewed Arafat himself and hundreds of senior Palestinian and Israeli officials to provide this account of Arafat's transition from terrorist to statesman to failed Palestinian leader.

SEE ALSO: Hafez al-Assad; George H. W. Bush; Bill Clinton; Hussein I; Gamal Abdel Nasser; Yitzhak Rabin; Ronald Reagan.

RELATED ARTICLES in *Great Events from History: The Twentieth Century:*

DIANE ARBUS
American photographer

A pivotal figure in contemporary documentary photography, Arbus created startling images of people dismissed by society and often forgotten by artists—little people, twins, transvestites, and physically disabled individuals—that were always controversial and often misunderstood.

BORN: March 14, 1923; New York, New York
DIED: July 26, 1971; New York, New York
ALSO KNOWN AS: Diane Nemerov (birth name)
AREA OF ACHIEVEMENT: Photography

EARLY LIFE

Diane Arbus (AHR-buhs) was born to a wealthy family in New York City. Her father, David Nemerov, owned a fashionable Fifth Avenue department store called Russeks, which his wife's family had founded. Arbus attended Ethical Culture and Fieldston schools, which were considered to be progressive institutions. At school, Arbus exhibited much creativity, particularly in art class, where she sketched, painted in oils, sculpted, and made collages.

When she was thirteen she met Allan Arbus, a copy boy in her father's department store and an aspiring actor. They fell madly in love, and for the next four years carried on a passionate courtship with clandestine meetings, secret phone calls, rendezvous in Central Park, and hand-delivered letters. Aside from her brother, Howard, with whom Diane always shared a close relationship, Allan became the most important person in Diane's life.

Under Allan's influence, Diane began creating her own style and look. In her parents' home she had been taught, like many children, that hairiness, menstruation, and body odors made one "impure." Rebelling against her parents' preoccupation with cleanliness, Diane always believed in female naturalness. She could understand neither why women were kept in a state of innocence about their bodies nor why they were denied their sensuality. In time Diane chose to wear no deodorant. As she grew older, people—particularly men—would comment in embarrassed tones about her body odor. Nevertheless, she always carried herself proudly, ignoring their comments.

In 1941, when Diane was eighteen, she and Allan were married. Three years later she bore a daughter, whom she named Doon. It was during this period that she began to express an interest in photography. When her husband returned from the Army, where he was trained as a photographer, he decided to go into fashion photography, with Diane as his partner. The couple had dabbled in this work briefly in 1941 and had been rather successful, although neither had any interest in fashion. Diane's father asked the couple to take advertising photographs for his store, and in the beginning of their career, Diane and Allan worked only inside the photography studio at Russeks. The couple collaborated as photographers for almost twenty years, eventually producing fashion photographs for *Harper's Bazaar*. Despite her early efforts, Diane once said that she did not begin photographing seriously until she was thirty-eight years old. Before that she had spent her time as a wife and mother.

LIFE'S WORK

Between 1955 and 1957, Diane Arbus studied photography under Lisette Model, the most famous teacher of photography in the country at the time. Model taught Arbus everything she knew and encouraged her pupil to concentrate on personal photographs and to develop further what Model recognized as a uniquely incisive documentary eye. Soon after Arbus began her studies with Model, she began to devote herself fully to documenting transvestites, twins, midgets, and asylum inmates, as well as various other people on the streets and in their homes. Model knew that Arbus was fragile as a person but strong as an artist. She also understood that Arbus needed to shoot photographs to relieve her mind of the faces and specters that were haunting it. Through some mysterious, unconscious force, Arbus was beginning to create in her photographs a kind of art that would be both a release and a vindication of her life, and Model more than anyone understood this.

Arbus later commented to friends that her desire to be daring originated in an overly protective, overly organized childhood in which she broke the monotony and defied the security of home by being naughty. What she rebelled against in her childhood was not the restrictions, however, but the loss of reality imposed by her sheltered life. She was determined to reveal what others had been taught to turn their backs on. As she had rejected her family values, she rejected fashion and went on to look for experiences less fictitious, more factual, and also to respond to a growing sense of self-awareness.

In 1965, three of Arbus's earliest photographs were included in a show at the Museum of Modern Art called

"Recent Acquisitions," along with the work of two other influential new photographers, Garry Winogrand and Lee Friedlander. Her images, which stripped away all artiness and evoked powerful emotions, were described as direct and primitive. These were photographs to which the public was not accustomed. Arbus's focus had sharpened and her vision and her discomfort had become more pronounced. The electronic flash and the square format she was using gave her more control and outlined her subjects in nightmarish detail. Her camera was described as an x-ray machine that in an uncanny way could capture what her subject was feeling.

Arbus questioned why ugliness, deviations, and flaws were so unacceptable. She depicted her subjects with a stark directness beyond value judgments. For her, existence was amoral. Later in her career, still pursuing what was specifically different, she began to photograph ordinary people out of an awareness of the gap between intention and effect. She believed that because people are not content with the exterior they are given, they create an entirely new set of peculiarities in an effort to project a different image. Thus, while each person is unique, most want to be unique in another way. Arbus photographed the resulting collision of interests. Some efforts to change were more obvious than others: men dressing as women, and women dressing as men. Others were less drastic, such as middle-aged women dressing like teenagers. There were also the costumes that identified one person with another, as in the case of twins, or with a cause, as in the case of protesters, or those who disguise identity with masks.

In not attaching values, in not seeking out people for their physical distinctions alone, but for their uniqueness in the context of their whole being, Arbus was not exploitative. She had a tremendous ability to empathize, which allowed her subjects to trust her. Despite her empathy, she realized that "It's impossible to get out of your skin into somebody else's. . . . That somebody else's tragedy is not the same as your own." Her empathy was always balanced by her sense of herself as a photographer, her desire not to avoid the facts. She was simultaneously detached and intimate. While she was empathetic, she realized that the camera would be clinical. The resulting photograph would combine her ideas, the subjects' responses to her, and the camera's indiscriminate record.

Arbus's approach to photography was as radical as her subject matter. Her sources were not confined to the conventional history of photography. She was influenced in part by the snapshot and news photography and

detested the photographs of those she believed were too self-consciously aware of themselves as artists, such as Edward Weston, Ansel Adams, and Harry Callahan. The photographers she most respected were those who understood darkness, particularly Weegee (Arthur Fellig), Gyula Halasz Brassai, and William Brandt.

"New Documents," the photography exhibit at the Museum of Modern Art that opened March 6, 1967, was probably the high point of Arbus's life. It introduced Arbus's work to the world. Although the show received mixed reviews from critics, the photographic community's response was notably silent. When her portrait of identical twins appeared in the exhibit, the twins' parents protested that the image was a distortion and tried to stop the picture from being reproduced elsewhere because they thought their daughters would be exploited. Eventually "The Twins" became Arbus's most famous photograph—her trademark—and was reproduced on posters, her book cover, and even inspired Stanley Kubrick in his making of the1980 horror film, *The Shining*.

Arbus rarely exhibited or published her noncommercial photographs. She was so secretive about her work that even her closest friends and her children were unfamiliar with the entire body of her work. In 1970, Arbus made a limited portfolio containing ten photographs, but by then she had established an international reputation as one of the pioneers of the "new" documentary style. Her work was often compared with that of August Sander, whose "Men Without Muscles" expressed similar concerns, although in a seemingly less unmerciful manner.

In July of 1971, Arbus took her own life in Greenwich Village, New York. Her brother, poet Howard Nemerov, gave the eulogy at her funeral and later wrote a poem for his sister entitled "To D—Dead by Her Own Hand," which has since been reprinted extensively.

SIGNIFICANCE

Toward the end of her short but intense career (ten productive years as a photographer), Arbus was regarded as a consummate professional. Her images, mainly of people, appeared to many as metaphors for the uneasy dislocations of a society at war with itself and others. Since her suicide in 1971, her life and work have undergone increased scrutiny. To some extent this increased interest is attributable to the upsurge of interest that often occurs after an artist's death and also to society's tendency to assume that a woman artist's suicide vindicates the assumption that women are too delicate for the demands of artistic creation. Her death brought even more attention to her name and photographs. In the following year,

Arbus became the first American photographer to be represented at the Venice Biennale. A major retrospective at the Museum of Modern Art, New York, in 1972, which traveled throughout the United States and Canada, was viewed by more than 7.25 million people. The next year, a Japanese retrospective traveled through Western Europe and the Western Pacific.

Arbus was very proud of her work. In her short span of years as a photographer, she changed the way photographers saw the world. She knew that she had succeeded at carving out territory of her own, and no one could enter without reckoning with what she had done. She believed that there were things that nobody would photograph unless she photographed them.

—Genevieve Slomski

FURTHER READING

Arbus, Diane. *Diane Arbus: Magazine Work.* Edited by Doon Arbus and Marvin Israel. Millerton, N.Y.: Aperture, 1984. In the years since its publication, this monograph has remained the foundation for all critical assessments of Arbus's life and work. As a collection of some of her best work and a clue to her intentions, the book is a roughly chronological record of her magazine work. Numerous reproductions and bibliography.

_____. *Revelations.* New York: Random House, 2003. Published in conjunction with a traveling exhibition of Arbus's photographs that premiered at the San Francisco Museum of Art in 2003. Includes information about the works in the exhibition, essays about Arbus's life and work, and a chronology of key events in her life.

_____. "The Vertical Journey: Six Movements of a Moment Within the Heart of the City." *Esquire,* July, 1960. The photographs in this piece, accompanied by terse captions by Arbus herself, established her both as a professional photographer and also a talented writer.

Bosworth, Patricia. *Diane Arbus: A Biography.* New York: Alfred A. Knopf, 1984. In this insightful book, the author follows Arbus's progress as a photographer and discusses her influences. Through the voices of her friends and colleagues, her mother, sister, and brother, Bosworth charts the dangerous and ultimately fatal course of Arbus's struggle to confront the fears and anguish that pursued her throughout her life. Notes and sources included.

Rubinfien, Leo. "Where Diane Arbus Went." *Art in America* 93, no. 9 (October, 2005): 65. Assessment of Arbus's photographs, including a discussion of her interest in eccentricity and masquerade and her influence on other photographers.

Tucker, Anne. *The Woman's Eye.* New York: Alfred A. Knopf, 1973. In this work devoted to the most prominent female photographers of the time, the author discusses Arbus's early years of rebellion through her mature work, stressing her radical approach to documentary photography. Contains numerous reproductions.

Walsh, George, Colin Naylor, and Michael Held, eds. *Contemporary Photographers.* New York: St. Martin's Press, 1982. A biographical collection of essays on photographers. The section devoted to Arbus discusses the photographer's major preoccupations, her early career, and her contributions to the field of documentary photography. Includes list of individual and group exhibitions and a bibliography of primary and secondary material.

SEE ALSO: Margaret Bourke-White; Imogen Cunningham; George Eastman; Dorothea Lange; Leni Riefenstahl; Susan Sontag; Edward Steichen; Alfred Stieglitz.

RELATED ARTICLES in *Great Events from History: The Twentieth Century:*

1901-1940: 1907: Lumières Develop Color Photography.

1971-2000: June 14, 1989: Mapplethorpe's Photographs Provoke Controversy.

HANNAH ARENDT
German-born American philosopher and critic

One of the most challenging political philosophers of the twentieth century, Arendt adopted an Aristotelian approach to explore the origins of totalitarianism, the structure of human consciousness, and the nature of violence and evil.

BORN: October 14, 1906; Hannover, Germany
DIED: December 4, 1975; New York, New York
AREAS OF ACHIEVEMENT: Philosophy, political science, social sciences, scholarship

EARLY LIFE

Hannah Arendt (eh-REHNT) was the only child of Paul and Martha (Cohn) Arendt, a German-Jewish couple who lived in Hannover. Arendt's father was an engineer and the family moved to the town of Königsberg, the former capital of East Prussia, where the young Hannah grew up. She attended the University of Königsberg shortly after World War I, receiving a bachelor's degree

Hannah Arendt. (Library of Congress)

from that institution in 1924. Later that same year, she began postgraduate study with the existentialist philosopher Martin Heidegger at the University of Marburg. Arendt met Hans Jonas (her future colleague at the New School for Social Research in New York City) when she and Jonas were the only two Jewish students to enroll in a New Testament seminar offered at Marburg by the biblical scholar Rudolf Bultmann.

Arendt's education continued at the University of Heidelberg, where she studied philosophy with Karl Jaspers. During her years at Heidelberg, Arendt began to be influenced by Jasper's Christian existential philosophy and his view that each individual is ultimately responsible for his or her own actions. In 1928, when Arendt was only twenty-two years old, the University of Heidelberg granted Arendt a doctorate. In the following year, her dissertation was published as *Der Liebesbegriff bei Augustin* (1929; *The Idea of Love in St. Augustine*). In September of 1929, Arendt married the young Jewish philosopher Günther Stern, whom she had met in 1925 during her postgraduate training in Marburg.

As the National Socialist movement (the Nazis) began to gain power in Germany, Arendt felt that her Jewish heritage was placing her in increasing danger. She fled to Paris in 1933, and began to work for Youth Aliyah, a relief organization that attempted to find homes in Palestine for Jewish orphans. Her relationship with Stern began to deteriorate during the 1930's, and the couple obtained a divorce in France in 1937. Arendt's activity in relief work continued, however, until 1940, when she married Heinrich Blücher, a professor of philosophy. Blücher was to remain one of Arendt's most important mentors during the course of their thirty-year marriage.

In 1941, France was invaded by the Nazis, forcing Arendt and Blücher to move to the United States. From 1944 until 1946, Arendt performed humanitarian work for the Conference on Jewish Relations in New York City. At the same time, she worked to preserve the writings of several Jewish authors, many of whose works had been suppressed by the Nazis during World War II. In 1946, Arendt assumed the position of chief editor for Schocken Books, remaining at that post until 1948. She applied for American citizenship in 1950, and was granted full citizenship during the following year.

LIFE'S WORK

Arendt began to draw the attention of international scholars in 1951 with the publication of her first major book, *The Origins of Totalitarianism*. In this work, she suggested that the roots of both communism and National Socialism could be traced not only to the imperialism of the nineteenth century but also to the anti-Semitism rampant throughout Europe at that time. Arendt's thesis initially met with mixed reviews. Many scholars praised the extensive research that was reflected in *The Origins of Totalitarianism* and concurred with its view that the rise of modern dictatorships resulted from the collapse of the nation-state. Nevertheless, many critics also rejected Arendt's view that anti-Semitism had been a decisive factor in shaping all forms of totalitarianism in the twentieth century. Arendt was criticized for taking too personal a view of modern history and for failing to be objective in her interpretation of events. Since the original publication of *The Origins of Totalitarianism*, however, Arendt's central thesis has gained considerable academic support.

In 1958, Arendt's Walgreen lectures delivered at the University of Chicago were published as *The Human Condition*. With its groundbreaking distinction between work, labor, and activity, and its optimistic view that political activity can enhance civilization, this book improved Arendt's reputation as a scholar. One of Arendt's most influential works, *The Human Condition* uses an Aristotelian approach to address issues of concern in modern society. Nevertheless, several critics found the book's prose style to be extremely dense, even awkward. Arendt's literary style continued to be criticized following the publication of several of her later works.

Arendt became the first woman to hold the rank of full professor at Princeton University when she accepted the position of visiting professor of politics in 1959. Soon after, her major study of modern society and its values, *Between Past and Future* (1961), was published. In this work, Arendt argued that by rejecting both tradition and authority modern society had deprived itself of the basis for establishing generally approved standards of behavior. Her view that moral relativism had left the twentieth century without a shared system of values was to be echoed repeatedly in the decades that followed.

In 1963, Arendt completed the work that was to reach her largest general audience.

Eichmann in Jerusalem: A Report on the Banality of Evil began as a series of articles for *The New Yorker* magazine. Adolf Eichmann, a leading official of the Nazis, had been captured in Argentina by agents of the Israeli intelligence service in May of 1960. His war crimes trial in Israel attracted international attention and inspired *The New Yorker* to send Arendt to Jerusalem for her perspectives on the trial.

Coining the phrase "the banality of evil," Arendt characterized Eichmann not as a Nazi fanatic but merely as an officious bureaucrat whose personal ambition had caused him to be responsible for horrific actions. Unlike the prison guards and the executioners who took an active role in exterminating the Jews, Eichmann was (in Arendt's view) little more than a "paper shuffler" whose duties had resulted in unimaginable suffering. The Nazi regime, Arendt continued, did not arise because of the fanaticism of a few of its leaders but because of a collapse of conscience throughout Europe. Jewish leaders themselves, Arendt contended, were not wholly guiltless in permitting the Holocaust to occur. To imply that one person was single-handedly responsible for the murder of millions was to attribute more power to him than any individual can possibly have. Finally, Arendt's book criticized the Israeli government for its conduct of the trial.

With the publication of *Eichmann in Jerusalem*, Arendt found herself once again on the defensive for her views. While many scholars had regarded her interpretation of history as excessively Zionist in *The Origins of Totalitarianism*, there were some critics who now accused her of being anti-Semitic for criticizing the Israeli

---

ON THE BANALITY OF EVIL

Hannah Arendt defined "banality of evil" in the final pages of her controversial book on Adolf Eichmann, Eichmann in Jerusalem, *first published as a series of articles in* The New Yorker *magazine in 1963.*

[W]hen I speak of the banality of evil, I do so only on the strictly factual level, pointing to a phenomenon which stared one in the face at the Eichmann trial. . . . Except for an ordinary diligence in looking out for his personal advancement, he had no motives at all. And this diligence in itself was in no way criminal. . . . He merely, to put the matter colloquially, never realized what he was doing. . . . It was sheer thoughtlessness—something by no means identical with stupidity—that predisposed him to become one of the greatest criminals of that period. And if this is "banal" and even funny, if with the best will in the world one cannot extract any diabolical or demonic profundity from Eichmann, that is still far from calling it commonplace.

court in *Eichmann in Jerusalem*. Despite years of service to Jewish relief organizations, Arendt found her book condemned by the Jewish humanitarian league B'nai B'rith ("Sons of the Covenant") as a "distortion" of history.

Despite this criticism, Arendt's academic career continued to prosper. In the same year that *Eichmann in Jerusalem* was published, Arendt accepted a professorship from the highly prestigious Committee on Social Thought at the University of Chicago. *On Revolution* (1963), a philosophical and political comparison of the French and American revolutions, was also released at this time. In 1967, Arendt left Chicago to begin teaching at the New School for Social Research in New York City. During that same year, Arendt was the only nonspecialist invited to speak at Harvard University at a conference commemorating the fiftieth anniversary of the Russian Revolution.

Arendt's collection of intellectual profiles, *Men in Dark Times*, appeared in 1968. Despite the title of that work, its most influential essays were those that dealt with women, including the German socialist leader Rosa Luxemburg and the Danish author Isak Dinesen. *On Violence*, Arendt's philosophical essay dealing with the use of force in society, was published in 1970.

That same year Arendt's second husband, Heinrich Blücher, died. Although Arendt mentioned to friends at the time that she would not be able to continue her work without Blücher, she soon occupied herself with several major projects. *The Jew as Pariah: Jewish Identity and Politics in the Modern Age* (1978) helped to restore Arendt's tarnished reputation in the Jewish community. *The Life of the Mind* (1978) was envisioned as a three-volume work, only about half of which was ever completed. In this massive study Arendt attempted to explore what she regarded as the three major activities of human consciousness: thought, will, and judgment. Both *The Jew as Pariah* and the completed portions of *The Life of the Mind* were published posthumously.

Arendt died suddenly in New York on December 4, 1975, the victim of an apparent heart attack. Four days later, Arendt was eulogized at Riverside Memorial Chapel in New York City by Hans Jonas, her longtime friend and colleague at the New School for Social Research, and the novelist and essayist Mary McCarthy, who served as Arendt's literary executor.

SIGNIFICANCE

Hannah Arendt's political philosophy resulted from the union of three independent strands in her intellectual training: Her Jewish heritage led her to seek philosophical explanations for human suffering and exposed her to the threat of anti-Semitic totalitarianism; her familiarity with the existential philosophy of Heidegger, Jaspers, and Bultmann encouraged her to develop an emphasis on individual responsibility; and her study of the Greek and Roman classics led her to adopt the methods of classical philosophy in her study of the problems afflicting modern society.

Criticized both for excessive Zionism and anti-Semitism in her writing, Arendt was, in the end, an original thinker who resisted all categorization. Her rigorous philosophical analysis of political issues and, in the last decade of her life, of human consciousness itself made her works among the most influential texts in political philosophy to be written since World War II. Running counter to the pessimistic tone found in a great deal of modern scholarship, Arendt viewed political life as a potentially heroic activity that is fully in keeping with the highest values of Western culture.

—*Jeffrey L. Buller*

FURTHER READING

Canovan, Margaret. *The Political Thought of Hannah Arendt*. New York: Harcourt Brace Jovanovich, 1974. Arguing that Arendt's works are more useful for their general interpretation than their specific solutions to problems, Canovan sees Arendt as challenging the basic assumptions of modern thought. Canovan also concludes that Arendt's view of politics was "romantic."

Glazer, Nathan. "Hannah Arendt's America." *Commentary* 60 (September, 1975): 61-67. This article, written for general readers, argues that Arendt's interpretation of European fascism is correct but that her attempts to see parallels between prewar Germany and postwar America are generally misleading.

Jonas, Hans. "Hannah Arendt." *Social Research* 43 (Spring, 1976): 3-5. A reprint of the eulogy delivered by Jonas at Riverside Memorial Chapel in New York City on December 8, 1975. It provides a fascinating personal assessment of Arendt's importance by a colleague who knew her well.

Parekh, Bhikhu C. *Hannah Arendt and the Search for a New Political Philosophy*. London: Macmillan, 1981. This challenging analysis of Arendt's philosophy explores how she sought to reconcile an Aristotelian world view with the existentialism of Jaspers and others. Parekh argues that Arendt's most original contribution to modern thought was her integration of politics into the general conception of "culture."

Social Research 44 (Spring, 1977). This entire issue is devoted to articles dealing with various aspects of Arendt's thought and its impact. Twelve scholars contributed to this special issue, including Robert Nisbet on Arendt and the American Revolution, Elisabeth Young-Bruehl on Arendt's story-telling, Erich Heller on Arendt as a critic of literature, and Hans Morgenthau on Arendt and totalitarianism.

Villa, Dana, ed. *The Cambridge Companion to Hannah Arendt.* New York: Cambridge University Press, 2000. Collection of essays examining the primary themes of Arendt's work, including totalitarianism, nationalism, evil, the Holocaust, freedom, and political action.

Whitfield, Stephen J. *Into the Dark: Hannah Arendt and Totalitarianism.* Philadelphia: Temple University Press, 1980. The most thorough analysis of the issues raised by Arendt's *The Origins of Totalitarianism,* this book also contains extensive notes and an excellent bibliography.

Young-Bruehl, Elisabeth. *Hannah Arendt, for Love of the World.* 1982. 2d ed. New Haven, Conn.: Yale University Press, 2004. An excellent work detailing Arendt's intellectual and personal life. Highly readable, it also contains a useful analysis of Arendt's

philosophical works and a few rarely available examples of poetry by Arendt.

_____. *Why Arendt Matters.* New Haven, Conn.: Yale University Press, 2006. Young-Bruehl reassesses Arendt's major works and ideas, placing them in the context of twenty-first century politics.

SEE ALSO: Rudolf Bultmann; Martin Heidegger; Edmund Husserl; Karl Jaspers; Max Nordau; Edith Stein; Simon Wiesenthal.

RELATED ARTICLES in *Great Events from History: The Twentieth Century:*

1901-1940: 1927: Heidegger Publishes *Being and Time.*

1941-1970: January 20, 1942: Wannsee Conference and the "Final Solution"; February, 1942: Lewis Explores the Mind of Evil in *The Screwtape Letters*; November 20, 1945-October 1, 1946: Nazi War Criminals Are Tried at Nuremberg; 1946: Jaspers Examines Germany's Collective Responsibility for War Crimes; April 11-August 14, 1961: Eichmann Is Tried for War Crimes; 1963: Arendt Speculates on the Banality of Evil.

1971-2000: May 11, 1987: Barbie Is Tried for Nazi War Crimes; April 18, 1988: Israel Convicts Demjanjuk of Nazi War Crimes.

OSCAR ARIAS SÁNCHEZ
President of Costa Rica (1986-1990, 2006-   )

As president of Costa Rica, Arias drafted the Esquipulas II peace accord, signed by Arias and the presidents of Nicaragua, Honduras, El Salvador, and Guatemala. This accord, for which Arias received the 1987 Nobel Peace Prize, became the impetus for democracy and peace in war-torn Central America.

BORN: September 13, 1941; Heredia, Costa Rica
ALSO KNOWN AS: Oscar Arias
AREAS OF ACHIEVEMENT: Government and politics, diplomacy, peace advocacy

EARLY LIFE

Oscar Arias Sánchez (AHR-ee-ahs SAHN-chays) was born into one of the leading families of Costa Rica. His father, Juan Rafael Arias Trejos, was descended from a line of legislators and government ministers and was head of the Costa Rican Central Bank. Oscar's mother,

Lillian Arias Sánchez, was the daughter of one of the wealthiest coffee plantation owners in the nation.

Arias was raised in the town of Heredia, near the capital city of San José in Costa Rica's central plateau. Sick with asthma as a child, Arias was a voracious reader who aspired to political office. After attending Catholic schools, Arias enrolled in Boston University in 1959 and attended Harvard University during one summer. After describing his views on Central America in a letter to president-elect John F. Kennedy, Arias was invited to meet with Kennedy in Hyannis Port, Massachusetts. The Kennedy administration would become a model for Arias's vision in politics.

Deciding on a political career, Arias left Boston after two years and enrolled in the University of Costa Rica. Graduating in 1967, he studied political science at the University of Essex and the London School of Economics in England for two years before returning to Costa

Rica in 1969 as a professor of political science (he would be awarded a Ph.D. in 1974). President José Figueres appointed Arias as an economic adviser in 1970 and to a cabinet position as minister of planning and political economy in 1972. That year Arias published his book *Pressure Groups in Costa Rica*, in which he argued that the central government must resist the pressure that interest groups can apply to a small democracy. In 1973, Arias married Margarita Penón Góngora, also from a wealthy family. They would have two children before eventually divorcing.

LIFE'S WORK

Beginning a steady rise through politics, Arias was appointed international secretary for Costa Rica's leading party, the Partido Liberación Nacional (PLN) in 1975. In 1978, he was elected to the National Assembly of Costa Rica as a deputy from Heredia. In 1979, he was elected general-secretary of the PLN, its leading post, positioning himself to achieve his dream of the presidency. In 1986, Arias secured the PLN candidacy after a contested primary. After winning a hard-fought election, Arias was sworn in as president on May 6, 1986.

Oscar Arias Sánchez. (© The Nobel Foundation)

President Arias set about fulfilling an ambitious domestic agenda promised in his campaign. Sixteen thousand homes were constructed in 1986, and the number of farming cooperatives expanded to five hundred fifty. Even more ambitiously, Arias tied Costa Rica's domestic problems to its foreign policy and, in particular, to the violence afflicting Costa Rica's Central American neighbors. Although Costa Rica had been a peaceful democracy since former president Figueres's constitutional revolution of 1948 (Costa Rica also abolished its army in 1949), the same could not be said for its neighbors. The government of the Frente Sandinista de Liberación Nacional (Sandinista National Liberation Front), better known as the Sandinistas, was fighting a vicious civil war against the counterrevolutionary Contras in Nicaragua. The Frente Farabundo Martí para la Liberación Nacional (Farabundo Martí National Liberation Front, or FMLN) rebels were fighting the government in El Salvador. Guatemala and Honduras were marked by chaos, poverty, and murderous death squads. Arias took the position that the regional conflicts threatened both Costa Rica's democracy—its northern border overrun by Contra forces—and its debt-laden economy, heavily dependent on aid from the United States and the earnings from tourist revenue.

There had been earlier ventures at peacemaking, such as those of the Contadora group of Latin America foreign ministers (which began in the early 1980's), Arias's own San José peace ideas launched at his presidential inauguration, and a 1986 summit meeting in Esquipulas, Guatemala. On February 17, 1987, Arias invited the presidents of Nicaragua, Honduras, Guatemala, and El Salvador to finalize a concrete treaty with him in a joint meeting in Guatemala City. At 4:00 A.M. on August 7, the five presidents emerged from their hotel room with the Arias peace plan, called the Procedure to Establish a Firm and Lasting Peace in Central America, or the Esquipulas II accord. The accord required each country to take specific steps to implement democracy by such measures as freeing political prisoners; instituting a National Reconciliation Commission to oversee amnesty; negotiating with political groups willing to abide by peaceful measures; and guaranteeing freedom of the press, a pluralist party system, and fair elections to be monitored by international observers. As an essential condition, all five nations had to commit to ending the arming and funding of foreign insurgencies. Also, the nations would meet in regional conferences to negotiate arms reduction, discuss the refugee crisis, and monitor progress.

Progress in implementing Esquipulas II was difficult but steady. Honduras and Guatemala stopped supplying arms to the Nicaraguan conflict. The governments and rebels in El Salvador, Guatemala, and Nicaragua agreed to cease-fires, peacekeepers, and internationally monitored elections. In 1990, National Opposition Union candidate Violetta Chamorro defeated Sandinista president Daniel Ortega, dramatic proof of progress toward peace.

In 1987, Arias was awarded the Nobel Peace Prize for proposing and for encouraging the signing of the peace accord. After leaving the presidency in 1990, as mandated by the Costa Rican constitution, Arias traveled around the world speaking on demilitarization, securing peace by ending poverty, and ending global arms trafficking. Arias used his Nobel Prize money to set up the Arias Foundation for Peace and Human Progress to secure "just and peaceful" societies in Central America. He also received numerous other awards for his peace initiative, awards including the Martin Luther King Peace Prize in 1987 and the Albert Schweitzer Prize for Humanitarianism in 1988.

Building on Costa Rica's pacifist tradition, Arias set out to persuade war-torn nations to abolish their armies. Panama abolished its army in 1994; Haiti in 2000; the island nations of Dominica and of Saint Kitts and Nevis thereafter. In 1995, Arias, with other Nobel Peace laureates, drafted the Arms Trade Treaty to limit the export of arms, which led both the European Union and the United Nations to curb sales of arms to small nations. In 2006, Arias, widely regarded as the most significant figure in Costa Rican history, was elected to a second term as president of Costa Rica.

SIGNIFICANCE

Arias's greatest achievement as a politician is the Esquipulas II accord, which proposed concrete objectives for achieving peace and democracy in one of the most war-torn and unstable regions of the world—Central America. Despite nearly universal skepticism toward Arias's efforts, Esquipulas II proved a strong impetus in the movement toward peace in Central America, as Nicaragua, El Salvador, Honduras, and Guatemala began to institute safeguards for human rights and heal conflicts that had persisted for decades. Arias's efforts helped Central America become a safer, more democratic, and more peaceful region.

Arias's success was rooted in the history and experi-

CENTRAL AMERICAN DEMOCRACY

The Arias peace plan, excerpted below, was signed by the five Central American presidents on August 7, 1987.

The Governments [of Costa Rica, Nicaragua, Honduras, El Salvador, and Guatemala] commit themselves to promote an authentic democratic, pluralist and participatory process that includes the promotion of social justice; respect for human rights, [state] sovereignty, the territorial integrity of states and the right of all nations to freely determine, without outside interference of any kind, its economic, political, and social model; and to carry out in a verifiable manner those measures leading to the establishment, or in their instances, the improvement of representative and pluralist democratic systems which would provide guarantees for the organization of political parties, effective popular participation in the decision making process, and to ensure free access to different currents of opinion, to honest electoral processes and newspapers based on the full exercise of citizens' rights.

For the purpose of verifying the good faith in the development of this democratization process, it will be understood that there shall exist complete freedom of press, television and radio. . . .

---

ences of Costa Rica. In that sense, Arias can be seen as insistently recommending the Costa Rican experience as the model for all Central America: free elections, an end to exporting arms to foreign insurgents, and a free press. Similarly, Arias was able to export Costa Rica's example of abolishing its own military to Panama, Haiti, and other island nations of the Caribbean.

Arias carried out his Central American initiatives as a relatively young man; as a former president, he continued his peace efforts with the United Nations, the Carter Foundation, and his own Arias Foundation. His greatest legacy remains a future prospect: If the pacific and democratic initiatives he promoted in Central America and the Caribbean can inspire cessation of violence in other war-torn parts of the globe, his legacy is assured.

—*Howard Bromberg*

FURTHER READING

Booth, John. *Costa Rica: Quest for Democracy.* Boulder, Colo.: Westview Press, 1999. Part of the Nations of the Modern World series, this work analyzes Costa Rica's successful democracy in terms of its history, social structure, political culture, and economy, noting Arias's democratizing and peacemaking role throughout.

Cox, Vicki. *Oscar Arias Sanchez: Bringing Peace to Central America.* New York: Chelsea House, 2007. Part of the Modern Peacemakers series of biographies intended for high school students, this book focuses on Arias's efforts to end warfare in Central America. An appendix includes Arias's Nobel Prize acceptance speech and a helpful chronology.

Peduzzi, Kelli. *Oscar Arias, Peacemaker and Leader Among Nations*. Milwaukee, Wis.: Gareth Stevens Children's Books, 1991. Part of the People Who Have Helped the World biographical series for younger readers, this book centers on Arias's work to bring peace to Nicaragua in 1987.

Rojas Gomez, Claudia Fiorella. "Spiritualizing the Political: A Rhetorical Analysis of Oscar Arias's Discourse on Peace." Ann Arbor, Mich.: UMI, 1992. A doctoral dissertation analyzing the rhetoric of Arias's speeches according to the so-called cluster-agon critical method. Appendix includes English versions of Arias's three major addresses on peace.

Rolbein, Seth. *Nobel Costa Rica: A Timely Report on*

Our Peaceful Pro-Yankee, Central America Neighbor. New York: St. Martin's Press, 1989. A journalistic account both of Figuere's constitutional revolution, of Arias's presidency, and the years leading up to Arias's Nobel Peace Prize.

SEE ALSO: Salvador Allende; Fernando Henrique Cardoso; Víctor Raúl Haya de la Torre; John F. Kennedy; Rigoberta Menchú; Daniel Ortega.

RELATED ARTICLES in *Great Events from History: The Twentieth Century:*

1941-1970: November 22, 1969: Inter-American Court of Human Rights Is Established.

1971-2000: 1978-1985: Guatemalan Death Squads Target Indigenous Indians; December 10, 1987: Arias Sánchez Receives the Nobel Peace Prize; February 25, 1990: Sandinistas Are Defeated in Nicaraguan Elections.

JEAN-BERTRAND ARISTIDE
President of Haiti (1991, 1994-1996, 2001-2004)

After years of autocratic rule under the Duvaliers, populist priest Aristide won the Haitian presidency by a democratic vote. A major goal as president was to aid the poor. His tenure in office included being overthrown in a coup in 1991. He returned in 1994 to resume office after U.S. military intervention, won a second term in 2000, but was ousted in yet another coup in 2004.

BORN: July 15, 1953; Port Salut, Haiti
AREA OF ACHIEVEMENT: Government and politics

EARLY LIFE

Orphaned as an infant, Jean-Bertrand Aristide (zhahn-behr-trahn ay-ree-steed) was raised by the Salesian order of the Roman Catholic Church, whose mission was to minister to the general needs of the poor, especially orphaned children. He was educated in parochial schools and a seminary before attending the University of Haiti to earn a degree in psychology.

Aristide was four years old when Haiti came under the dictatorial and corrupt rule of François (Papa Doc) Duvalier. Duvalier repressed opposition with a reign of physical terror: the Tonton Macoutes, his paramilitary force. Leading Voodoo cultists were used to exert psychological terror on dissidents. Duvalier's nineteen-

year-old son, Jean-Claude Duvalier (Baby Doc) continued the presidential dynasty after his father's death in 1971. Under the Duvaliers, Haiti became the poorest nation in the Western Hemisphere, while a small number of leading families and the Duvaliers amassed great wealth. Demonstrations against Duvalier began in earnest in October, 1985, and they did not stop until February, 1986, when Duvalier fled to exile in Paris.

As a program director at the Catholic radio station (Radio Cacique) and as a newspaper editorialist, Aristide established a reputation as a critic of Baby Doc's government and an advocate of changes to benefit Haiti's poor. His powerful oratory in sermons urged the poor to take responsibility for instituting needed changes. His words also earned Aristide death threats from the Tonton Macoutes. For Aristide to continue to live in Haiti would mean not living at all.

From 1979 to 1985, Aristide studied theology abroad in Israel, Egypt, and Great Britain, ultimately earning a master of theology degree from the University of Montreal in Canada. During this period he returned to Haiti (1982) only to receive his ordination as a priest of the Salesian order. In Haiti in 1985, he became the parish priest at St. Jean Bosco, one of the poorest parishes in Port-au-Prince. He used his polished oratory to help drive Baby Doc from power in 1986.

Jean-Bertrand Aristide. (AP/Wide World Photos)

LIFE'S WORK

Aristide's continued emphasis that liberation theology priests work with the poor to correct continuing abuses and inequalities angered the military caretaker regimes of generals Prosper Avril and Henri Namphy, who succeeded Baby Doc. Aristide survived several assassination attempts, the worst being an attack in 1988 by about one hundred armed Tonton Macoutes, who attacked the congregation at St. Jean Bosco Church during Mass. Aristide barely escaped with his life, but thirteen of the congregation lay dead and seventy were badly wounded. The church itself was burned to the ground. To prevent further attacks, Aristide was expelled from the Salesian order and sent to Rome. Mass demonstrations at Port-au-Prince, however, blocked any means of sending Aristide abroad. He remained at Port-au-Prince ministering to the needs of street children and opening medical clinics and trade schools.

For the next four years Haiti was ruled by a number of ineffective provisional governments, mostly as regimes by military "caretakers." During this period a constitution for a democratic parliamentary government was drafted. To prevent a recurrence of the Duvalier lifetime presidency, the Haitian constitution barred any president from serving two consecutive terms in office. That this provision was adopted in 1987 by referendum, abolished in 1988 following a military coup, and readopted in 1990 when civilian governance was restored, underlined the precarious nature of the transition into a democratic government. Finally, in December, 1990, following concerted pressure by the United Nations, the Organization of American States, and the United States, Haiti's first real democratic election was held under the watchful eyes of many international observers.

A few months before the elections a mass popular movement taking the name of the Lavalas (which means "flood" in Creole) convinced Aristide to run for president against the frontrunner, a respected career diplomat named Marc Bazin, several other candidates supported by leading families, and the head of the Tonton Macoutes. Having Aristide on the presidential ticket would send a message about the needs of the poor. Indeed, Aristide's six weeks of campaign oratory was permeated with this theme. Few understood that because the poor would be voting in this free and monitored election, all bets should have been on an Aristide victory. The hastily formed Lavalas Party did not realize, however, that Aristide's popularity would not translate into a sweep of their party's candidates for seats in the newly formed parliament. Aristide won more than two-thirds of the vote for president, promising major reforms to uplift the poor people of Haiti. Few could doubt his integrity and sincerity, but many could doubt his ability to survive for long.

Upon taking office, Aristide pledged that he would cleanse the civil service of corrupt officials and Duvalier loyalists, fight against drug trafficking, and demolish all remaining vestiges of the Tonton Macoutes. His dedication was underscored when he pledged to give his entire presidential salary to charity. Clearly such a person could not be trusted by the former power structure. On September 30, 1991, with Aristide in New York attending a meeting of the United Nations (U.N.), a military coup led by General Raoul Cédras took control of the country. Hundreds of Aristide's supporters were killed in the streets while protesting the military's actions, and several thousand more would be killed in the subsequent two years of military rule. More than forty thousand Haitians would become the new "boat people," refugees fleeing oppression in their native land to seek asylum. Most would be returned by the United States to an uncertain fate in Haiti.

In spite of embargos on Haitian exports and on key imports such as oil, the military regime remained in power. As repression accelerated, a resolution was passed by the U.N. Security Council to restore the constitutionally elected government. After talks between Cédras and Aristide, brokered by the United Nations and the administration of U.S. president Bill Clinton, failed to produce results, it was obvious that decisive action needed to be taken. Under U.N. mandate in mid-September, 1994, more than twenty thousand U.S. troops prepared to launch Operation Restore Democracy. At the same time, former U.S. president Jimmy Carter was dispatched to Haiti with a small group of negotiators to offer the military junta a last-minute deal. With U.S. troops airborne, the Cédras military regime agreed to step down and permit Aristide to serve the remaining twenty-seven months of his presidential term.

SIGNIFICANCE

Aristide returned to Haiti on October 15, 1994, to finish his term, which ended in February, 1996. One of his first acts was to dismantle the troublesome Haitian military and replace it with a civilian police force. As promised

during his exile, nine state-owned enterprises were privatized and controls over customs duties and interest rates were lifted, all to ease concerns of affluent Haitians. To please his mass support base, the minimum wage was doubled. When parliamentary elections were held in June, 1995, Aristide's Lavalas Party won a sweeping victory. When presidential elections were held on December 17, 1995, Aristide's vice president, René Préval, won 88 percent of the vote. Thus, Haiti's first democratic transition took place.

On November 26, 2000, with his Fanmi Lavalas, or Lavalas Family Party (formed in 1996 after Aristide broke his relationship with then-vice president, Préval) firmly in control of parliament, Aristide registered as a candidate for Haiti's next presidential election. However, claiming major irregularities in the unmonitored parliamentary elections, opposition parties boycotted the presidential elections. Although receiving more than 90 percent of the vote, voter turnout was low. For the next four years both the parliament and the president were viewed by a significant number of Haitians as illegitimate.

Although a coup against Aristide failed in July, 2001, opposition to his rule mounted and violence once again became a daily part of Haitian political life. Aristide's own supporters used violence against opponents, including students at the state university (December 5, 2003). By the spring of 2004, with a large rebel force moving toward Port-au-Prince, Aristide and his wife left Haiti for South Africa in an American plane escorted by U.S. military and diplomatic personnel. An international peacekeeping force headed to Haiti to try to maintain order. Democracy, stability, and sustained reform to alleviate poverty continued to be elusive in Haiti. The lifelong populist, advocate for the poor, and crusading priest had shown that democratic elections in Haiti, on occasion, could take place.

—Irwin Halfond

FURTHER READING

Aristide, Jean-Bertrand. *Eyes of the Heart: Seeking a Path for the Poor in the Age of Globalization.* Edited by Laura Flynn. Monroe, Maine: Common Courage Press, 2000. Aristide writes of the negative effects of globalization on the poor people of Haiti. At eighty-nine pages, a brief, accessible work. Includes an index.

Dupuy, Alex. *Prophet and Power: Jean-Bertrand Aristide, the International Community, and Haiti.* Lanham, Md.: Rowman & Littlefield, 2006. An analysis of the struggle for democracy in Haiti by a leading scholar on Haiti. Includes bibliographic references and index.

Griffiths, Leslie. *Aristide Factor*. New York: Oxford University Press, 1997. A major study and analysis of Aristide's role in Haitian politics. Includes bibliographic references and index.

Pezzullo, Ralph. *Plunging into Haiti: Clinton, Aristide, and the Defeat of Diplomacy*. Jackson: University of Mississippi Press, 2007. An insider's view of Haitian political struggles and U.S. diplomatic efforts at policy resolution. Includes bibliographic references and index.

SEE ALSO: Oscar Arias Sánchez; Aung San Suu Kyi; Benazir Bhutto; Fernando Henrique Cardoso; Jimmy Carter; Fidel Castro; Bill Clinton; François Duvalier; Víctor Raúl Haya de la Torre.

RELATED ARTICLES in *Great Events from History: The Twentieth Century*:

1971-2000: December 16, 1990: Aristide Wins First Democratic Election in Haiti; July 31, 1994: United Nations Authorizes the Use of Force in Haiti.

EDWIN H. ARMSTRONG
American electrical engineer and inventor

From the infancy of radio, Armstrong was the leading edge of its technical development, inventing the basic circuitry of modern AM-FM broadcasting. His finest invention, however, was the wideband frequency modulation (FM) system of broadcasting, which provided a static and distortion-free technique that was far superior to AM.

BORN: December 18, 1890; New York, New York
DIED: January 31, 1954; New York, New York
AREAS OF ACHIEVEMENT: Engineering, invention and technology, radio

EARLY LIFE

Edwin H. Armstrong was born to a middle-class New York City family. His youth was a reflection of America's fascination with the revolutionary technical innovations then transforming the nation. As a boy, Armstrong displayed a markedly precocious ability with things mechanical and developed a strong interest in trains and locomotives. He read voraciously of the then-popular Horatio Alger "Rags to Riches" adventure books for boys as well as the new science-fiction stories. He declared in later life that his career in science began at fourteen, when, after reading about the exploits of inventor Guglielmo Marconi, he decided to become an inventor himself. Fabricating his own coherers, detectors, and hand-wound coils, he had, by his midteens, built his own spark-based station for listening to wireless broadcasts. Radio had become his consuming interest by the time he entered Columbia University to study electrical engineering. While working there in the graduate radio laboratory, he was exposed to Lee de Forest's then-recent invention of the Audion, or three-element vacuum tube.

Although de Forest had at that time used the tube only for the amplification of audio signals, Armstrong immediately saw the possibility of using the tube to generate radio frequency signals, and in a short time he developed the regenerative or feedback amplification circuit. Because he was unable to persuade his father to fund a prompt patent application, his claim for the invention was delayed until January, 1913, when a drawing of the regenerative circuit was notarized. By this time, de Forest had realized this important application of the Audion tube and filed his own patent, followed by Alexander Meissner in Germany and C. S. Franklin in England.

Thus, when Armstrong was graduated from Columbia University in May, 1913, he found himself embroiled in an international dispute over patent rights to a major invention, defending his position against some of the greatest names in radio. This legal dispute over patent rights was the beginning of a pattern that would follow him for the remainder of his life.

LIFE'S WORK

Armstrong's time during his twenties was spent in bitter litigation with de Forest. Although de Forest eventually won the patent, de Forest continued the deep animosity between the two by maintaining interference proceedings for the next ten years.

During World War I, Armstrong served in Paris as a U.S. Signal Corps officer attached to the radio laboratory of the École Militaire. By his later account, he was there struck by the difficulty of building triode amplifiers capable of intercepting the extremely weak, shortwave signals then used by the Germans in their field communications. The amplifiers in use could not sustain the power levels required without breaking into self-driven oscillation from unwanted feedback.

Armstrong's solution was to convert the incoming signal to a fixed frequency by heterodyning it to a local oscillator in the receiver and obtaining the needed sensitivity by processing the signal at the lower imposed frequency, where stability was more readily secured. It was an elegant design and has proved basic to all later receiver circuitry. In the summer of 1920, after additional research at Columbia University, he was awarded the United States patent for the superheterodyne receiver circuit.

Although he possessed the most fundamental receiver and transmitter patents, Armstrong's position was by no means secure. His patent for the regenerative circuit was under attack by de Forest in the U.S. Patent Office, incurring heavy legal expenses. In the fall of 1920, he sold the superheterodyne receiver patent to Westinghouse for $335,000 in cash, with an additional $200,000 to be paid if he won the interference proceedings against de Forest.

While setting up a courtroom demonstration in 1921,

Edwin H. Armstrong. (AP/Wide World Photos)

he noticed an unusual mode of radio detection and, following experimental development, filed patent application for the superregenerative detector, which was awarded in 1922. In 1924, his patent for the superheterodyne circuit was challenged by the American Telephone and Telegraph Company (AT&T), which possessed the American rights to the patent of Lucien Levy, a French radio engineer. Levy claimed to have invented the superheterodyne receiver during the war while stationed at the École Militaire and that Armstrong had stolen the invention while serving there in the signal corps. Armstrong spent his energy and personal financial resources defending the patent position in the courts against bitter professional and sometimes personal attacks. Although he retained rights to the regenerative circuits, he ultimately lost all the claims for the superheterodyne circuit to Levy, backed by AT&T.

During these legal battles, from 1928 to 1933, he developed, with little assistance, his most critical invention, the wideband frequency modulation (FM) system of broadcasting, which provided a static and distortion-free technique that was far superior to AM. In the winter of 1933, he was awarded four patents that completely covered the FM system and which established him as its sole inventor. As the newly appointed professor of electrical engineering at Columbia University, he announced his invention to the world by reading a paper before the Institute of Radio Engineers and surprising his audience with a demonstration broadcast from an experimental station he operated with the help of a friend. His system was obviously superior to any AM system in use, yet its introduction was met with the skepticism of industry, which had invested heavily in AM broadcasting. Much of the remainder of his life was spent in trying to have FM adopted as the prime radio broadcasting system. He refined the techniques, set up stations, and traveled extensively, but with little result.

During World War II, he developed FM units for military communications, demonstrated long-range FM signaling, and worked on continuous-wave FM radar. Harassed by seemingly never-ending patent litigation and frustrated by the slow adoption of his FM broadcasting system, Armstrong committed suicide in New York on January 31, 1954.

SIGNIFICANCE

Armstrong's career spanned the golden age of radio development and broadcasting and reflected the spirit of the individual scientific pioneer that was typical of the early twentieth century. His work, from his undergraduate days, was always on the very basic phenomena of radio operations, his early contributions making possible the dream of voice radio transmission.

Much of his energy in the later years of his life was spent fighting challenges to his patents. If this time could have been devoted to invention and research, his scientific output could have been much higher. Despite this drain on him, he invented some of the most important circuits of modern radio, his creative output spanning the whole of his career.

Although he died feeling frustrated and unrecognized, the world has since seen the adoption of his systems as the standard of broadcasting and his ranking as one of the great scientists of modern electronics. His awards include the First Medal of Honor from the Society of Radio Engineers, the Franklin Medal, and the United States Medal of Merit. He is one of twenty world scientists honored in the Pantheon of the Union Internationale des Télécommunications in Geneva.

—*Orren P. Whiddon*

FURTHER READING

Aitken, Hugh G. J. *The Continuous Wave: Technology and American Radio, 1900-1932.* Princeton, N.J.: Princeton University Press, 1985. The best history of the development of radio available. Covers Armstrong's patent and business dealings in depth as well as his impact on the development of the Radio Corporation of America (RCA) and Westinghouse as the dominant companies of early radio. Very well researched and documented, both historically and technically.

_____. *Syntony and Spark: The Origins of Radio.* Reprint. Princeton, N.J.: Princeton University Press, 1985. An excellent chronological history of the technical evolution of radio. Gives a broad picture of Armstrong's technical innovations and how they affected the rapid pace of radio's development at the time.

Evans, Harold, with Gail Buckland and David Lefer. *They Made America: From the Steam Engine to the Search Engine, Two Centuries of Innovators.* New York: Little, Brown, 2004. Armstrong is one of seventy American inventors and entrepreneurs who are profiled in this book.

Hamilton, Neil A. *Lifetimes: The Great War to the Stock Market Crash, American History Through Biography and Primary Documents.* Westport, Conn.: Greenwood Press, 2002. A biographical encyclopedia for high school students that includes essays about significant Americans. Contains an essay about Armstrong.

Lessing, Lawrence. *Man of High Fidelity: Edwin Howard Armstrong.* Philadelphia: J. B. Lippincott, 1956. The only biography yet written on the life of Armstrong, and the only source for information on his private life. Well written but sympathetic toward Armstrong's difficulties. Provides a more personable view of the legal charges and accusations against Armstrong.

Lewis, Tom. *Empire of the Air: The Men Who Made Radio.* New York: Edward Burlingame Books, 1991. This companion volume to a television documentary of the same name focuses on the role played by Armstrong, Lee de Forest, and David Sarnoff in the creation of radio in the United States.

_____. "Radio Revolutionary." *American Heritage of Invention and Technology* 1 (Fall, 1985): 34-41. A sympathetic but accurate brief account contrasting his tragic life with his triumphant inventions, especially FM.

SEE ALSO: Lee de Forest; Auguste and Louis Lumière; Vladimir Zworykin.

RELATED ARTICLES in *Great Events from History: The Twentieth Century:*

LOUIS ARMSTRONG
American musician

Armstrong's importance to the development of jazz is inestimable. Whether played or sung, almost all aspects of jazz style and technique were influenced directly by his innovations of the 1920's. His concepts of range, tone, phrasing, and rhythm, along with his sophisticated choice of pitch, were widely imitated.

BORN: August 4, 1901; New Orleans, Louisiana
DIED: July 6, 1971; New York, New York
ALSO KNOWN AS: Satchmo; Ambassador Satch (nickname)
AREA OF ACHIEVEMENT: Music

EARLY LIFE

The son of Willie Armstrong, a turpentine worker, and Mary Ann (or Mayann) Armstrong, the granddaughter of slaves, Louis (LEW-ee) Armstrong was born in a district of New Orleans, Louisiana, called, according to Armstrong, the Battlefield. Armstrong himself said that "Daniel" (given in many sources) was never part of his name, and that he was not even sure how he acquired it. Prostitution, shootings, knifings, drunkenness, and gambling were common in the area where Armstrong spent the first years of his life. His parents separated when he was five. He and his sister lived in poverty with his mother and grandmother near the dance halls and saloons, whose music, along with what he sang and heard in church, was his initial influence. As a boy, Armstrong worked at odd jobs, sang for pennies, and formed part of a strolling vocal quartet. After firing a pistol into the air on New Year's Eve of 1913, he was arrested, taken to jail, and then sent to the Colored Waifs' Home, generally known as the Jones Home, in New Orleans. There he received his first formal musical training from Peter Davis, the home's bandmaster and drill instructor. Within the year, Armstrong was playing the cornet and leading the home's brass band.

When he was finally released to his mother, who was ill, in 1914, Armstrong supported both of them by working at various day-jobs, including delivering coal and selling newspapers. He also began taking cornet lessons from his lifelong idol, jazz cornetist Joe "King" Oliver. Armstrong quickly undertook the development of those jazz skills that he had, until then, been able to admire only at a distance. Slowly, he became one of the most sought-after musicians in New Orleans, one of the few who was good enough to earn his living by playing. In

1918, he married Daisy Parker; they would be divorced in 1923.

After King Oliver left for an engagement in Chicago in 1919, Armstrong replaced him in Kid Ory's Brownskin Band. Given his improvising abilities, clarity of tone, formidable technique, and rhythmic freedom, Armstrong soon became a drawing card in his own right. Joining Fate Marable's band on various Mississippi excursion boats, he played up and down the river in the summers of 1920 and 1921. Around this time, Armstrong wrote one of his first songs, "Get Off Katie's Head" (published as "I Wish I Could Shimmy Like My Sister Kate"); he received from the publishers neither the fifty dollars they had promised for the song nor credit as the composer. In New Orleans, he continued to play at various clubs and also did street parade work, appearing regularly with Pap Celestin's Tuxedo Band.

LIFE'S WORK

As Armstrong's reputation spread, Fletcher Henderson, a rising bandleader in New York, offered him a job. Armstrong was timid and agreed to the move only if his friend, drummer Zutty Singleton, was hired too. Since Henderson already had a drummer, Armstrong remained in New Orleans until King Oliver summoned him to Chicago in the summer of 1922. Oliver's Original Creole Jazz Band was unusually disciplined, and the demands of his second cornetist's role further improved Armstrong's musicianship. The sensitivity and discipline of his second cornet parts to Oliver's lead are especially apparent on a recording of "Mabel's Dream." While his first recorded solo with the band, "Chimes Blues," is undistinguished, it was toward individual, not collective, playing that Armstrong moved—steadily and surely. Nevertheless, it took Lillian (Lil) Hardin, the band's pianist, whom he married in 1924, to persuade him to leave an environment that had begun to restrict him. Armstrong's sense of obligation ran deep.

In 1924, Armstrong reluctantly accepted Fletcher Henderson's invitation to join his big band in New York. As a section player, Armstrong conformed in his ensemble playing to the stiff rhythms then favored by Henderson, but his sophisticated solos brought a novel style to the city's dance and jazz music. He exerted a broad influence on New York musicians, among them Henderson's arranger, Don Redman, who soon developed orchestral counterparts to Armstrong's devices. While in New York,

Armstrong made a memorable series of recordings with Perry Bradford's Jazz Phools, with Clarence Williams's groups, and as an accompanist to Bessie Smith and other blues singers.

Generally known as Satchmo (an abbreviation for "Satchel-mouth"), Armstrong acquired early a basic strength and beauty of sound that is apparent in his work with Oliver and Henderson. To the melodic richness, emotional depth, and rhythmic variety of the blues, he added an already exceptional technique allowing every note to be full and every phrase to be perfectly shaped. No matter what the tempo, his playing sounded unhurried: such relaxation led to a deep and consistent swing. All these abilities combined with a vein of melodic invention so rich that it did not falter for many years.

An essential part of his style once he left Oliver's band, Armstrong's singing was inimitable. He sang like he played, or vice versa, which is not surprising given the important connection in the African heritage between speech and music. His scat singing (using nonsense syllables) was clearly a vocalization of his instrumental inflection and phrasing. Armstrong once made the unlikely claim that he invented scat singing, but he was the first to use it on records. His voice had a buoyancy and roughness that quickly became legendary.

A more accomplished musician for his big band schooling and brimming with energy and inventiveness, Armstrong returned to Chicago in 1925. There, he played with his wife's group and with bands headed by Erskine Tate and Carroll Dickerson. For most of 1927, he led his own group. Armstrong had also begun making a series of recordings under his own name in 1925. He established an international reputation with these records, revealing the power of his musical ideas and his range and originality as an improviser. These recordings also show Armstrong looking for an appropriate accompaniment for his increasingly virtuosic solo style.

The earliest of these accompanying groups—those of the Hot Five and Hot Seven recordings with Hardin, the Dodds brothers, Kid Ory, and Johnny St. Cyr— were modeled on New Orleans ensembles. Masterpieces of the later New Orleans style such as "Butter and Egg Man," "Struttin' with Some Barbeque," and "Potato Head Blues" come from this 1926-1927 period. Then in 1928, Armstrong turned to a more modern small band, collaborating with Earl Hines and Zutty Singleton. Trumpet, piano, and drums dominated, there being no further pretense of New Orleans equality. Armstrong now appeared at his most modernistic; the music is characterized by virtuosity, double-time spurts, complex ensembles, rhythmic juggling, and unpredictable harmonic alterations. From this period come "West End Blues," "Beau Koo Jack," and "Weatherbird Rag," the latter a remarkable duet with Hines.

It is difficult to see how Armstrong's intense musical conversation with Hines could have been maintained longer than it was. Consequently, in mid-1929, Armstrong adopted the format he was to use until 1947, a big band providing a neutral accompaniment to his now large-scale, virtuoso conceptions of his playing and singing. Perhaps his further development was possible only against a purely subsidiary background. Initial results were excellent, with 1933 marking the peak of this period. Having done everything then possible with traditional jazz material, he began to concentrate on a popular repertory. While his technical innovations ceased, he still performed with great artistic merit, demonstrating his power and maturity on such classics as "Body and Soul," "Star Dust," "Sweethearts on Parade," and "I Gotta Right to Sing the Blues."

After 1933, Armstrong embarked increasingly on an all-too-thorough commercialization of his talent under the guidance of his longtime manager, Joe Glaser. His

Louis Armstrong. (Library of Congress)

popular hits began with Fats Waller's "Ain't Misbehavin'," which he debuted in the *Hot Chocolates* revue of 1930, and culminated in the hit song from the Broadway show *Hello, Dolly!* in the 1960's. There was a strong streak of ham in Armstrong, and his comic posing and patter, which endeared him to many, embarrassed others, such as Benny Goodman, who thought his music excellent and his vaudevillian antics corny and unworthy of him.

Over the years, Armstrong seemed to become more and more indifferent to what he played and with whom he played. A meaningful context was lacking, given the gap between his own majestic playing and his often abysmal accompaniment. Even his magic was unable to transform the increasing amount of novelty material he recorded. Nevertheless, Armstrong also used his craft and experience to distill and simplify his playing. In place of virtuoso performance, every note was made to count.

During the 1930's, Armstrong toured and recorded with large groups, both in the United States and in Europe. He worked off and on with such bandleaders and musical directors as Luis Russell, Chick Webb, and Les Hite. Throughout the late 1930's, he played residencies and toured with his own orchestra. Armstrong also began to make film appearances, the first in *Pennies from Heaven* with Bing Crosby in 1936. Hundreds of records of his own and other groups made him influential as a player and singer of popular music and brought him an ever wider audience. His best recordings of the 1930's are nearly all remakes of old successes, including "Save It, Pretty Mama," "Mahogany Hall Stomp," and "Monday Date." Obtaining a divorce from Lil, Armstrong married Alpha Smith in 1938. The marriage was not built on a very sound foundation, and no one was surprised when it did not last. In 1942, Armstrong married Lucille Wilson, the woman who was to be his wife for the rest of his life.

Eventually, Armstrong returned to playing with small groups; there were still some great records to come, as well as many pleasant ones. Following successful appearances with small groups in 1947, including one in the film *New Orleans*, he formed his All-Stars, with which he worked until his death. A sextet based on the New Orleans model, its instrumentation remained the same, though the personnel varied. Among those associated with the All-Stars over the years were pianist Earl Hines, trombonists Trummy Young and Jack Teagarden, clarinetists Ed Hall and Barney Bigard, and drummers Cozy Cole and Sid Catlett. Armstrong was frequently able to demonstrate with the All-Stars his superb quality as a jazz musician.

During the 1950's, besides working in the United States and Canada, the All-Stars toured in Europe, South America, Africa, Australia, and the Far East. Exasperated by the Eisenhower administration's do-nothing policy toward black civil rights in the South, Armstrong, in protest, once canceled his Department of State-backed tour of the Soviet Union. This was not the Armstrong of records or stage; regardless of such social activism, Armstrong always seemed the wellspring of goodness, which was very advantageous to the image of jazz, both at home and abroad.

Throughout the 1960's, the All-Stars did even more international touring, earning for Armstrong the nickname Ambassador Satch. He had come to symbolize jazz to the world. During the late 1960's, illness incapacitated Armstrong several times, taking its toll on his playing. For more than a year, in 1969 and 1970, he was only able to sing in public appearances. He resumed playing but suffered a heart attack in March of 1971. Armstrong died in New York City on July 6 of that year.

SIGNIFICANCE

Louis Armstrong's contribution to the development of jazz was partly that of innovator and stylist, partly one of pure virtuosity, both imaginatively and technically, and partly one of showmanship. He was responsible, more than anyone else, for the fact that jazz became not so much a collective ensemble style as a soloist's art. Moreover, he was the bridge between Dixieland and swing, the next important development in jazz. By the time of his death, he had exerted a profound influence on his fellow jazz musicians—such as trumpeters Roy Eldridge, Dizzy Gillespie, and Miles Davis—to whom Armstrong is "Pops," the patriarch of their own stylistic development.

The influence of Armstrong on the history of jazz—dubbed by some as "America's classical music"—is so pervasive that it has on occasion been blithely dismissed by those who fault him for not having kept up with the changes in the music. It is clear, however, that Armstrong's continued success as player and singer helped make jazz a vital force in the general culture of the United States and, to some degree, of the rest of the world. His radiant optimism, his virtuosity, and his indefatigable sense of fun played an important role in promoting jazz everywhere.

—L. Moody Simms, Jr.

FURTHER READING

Armstrong, Louis. *Swing That Music*. New York: Longmans, Green, 1936. An autobiography by the musician that provides a personal perspective on his life.

_____. *Satchmo: My Life in New Orleans*. Englewood Cliffs, N.J.: Prentice-Hall, 1955. A later autobiography; like his earlier work, it should be read in conjunction with a well-researched biographical treatment.

Brothers, Thomas. *Louis Armstrong's New Orleans*. New York: W. W. Norton, 2006. A chronicle of Armstrong's early life, describing how his years in New Orleans, a hotbed of musical activity in the early twentieth century, nurtured both jazz and Armstrong's musicianship.

Chilton, John, and Max Jones. *Louis: The Louis Armstrong Story, 1900-1971*. Boston: Little, Brown, 1971. A reasonably good biography of Armstrong.

Collier, James Lincoln. *Louis Armstrong: An American Genius*. New York: Oxford University Press, 1983. The definitive biography. Factually reliable, and good in dealing with the myths and sheer fiction that have become part of the Armstrong story. (Collier points up, for example, the inaccuracy behind the commonly listed birth date for Armstrong, July 4, 1900.) Contains a brief discography.

_____. *The Making of Jazz: A Comprehensive History*. Boston: Houghton Mifflin, 1978. An excellent history of jazz, including a chapter devoted to Armstrong, "The First Genius."

Giddins, Gary. *Satchmo: The Genius of Louis Armstrong*. 2d rev. ed. New York: DaCapo Press, 2001. Comprehensive biography by a prominent jazz writer and historian. Includes photographs and discography.

Schuller, Gunther. *Early Jazz: Its Roots and Musical Development*. Vol. 1, *The History of Jazz*. New York: Oxford University Press, 1986. The definitive study of the development of jazz prior to the early 1930's. Armstrong's significance is emphasized. Uses an ethnomusicological approach to the African elements in jazz.

Tirro, Frank. *Jazz: A History*. 2d ed. New York: W. W. Norton, 1993. A solid jazz history, good on detail.

Williams, Martin. *Jazz Masters of New Orleans*. New York: Macmillan, 1967. A collection of essays on New Orleans jazz musicians, including Armstrong.

SEE ALSO: Ray Charles; John Coltrane; Duke Ellington; Ella Fitzgerald; Dizzy Gillespie; Benny Goodman; Billie Holiday; Charlie Parker; Oscar Peterson; Bessie Smith.

RELATED ARTICLES in *Great Events from History: The Twentieth Century:*

1901-1940: 1920's: Harlem Renaissance; February 15, 1923: Bessie Smith Records "Downhearted Blues"; November, 1925: Armstrong Records with the Hot Five; December 4, 1927: Ellington Begins Performing at the Cotton Club; 1933: Billie Holiday Begins Her Recording Career.

1941-1970: March 28, 1946: Parker's Playing Epitomizes Bebop; January 21, 1949-March 9, 1950: Davis Develops 1950's Cool Jazz; July 17-18, 1954: First Newport Jazz Festival Is Held.

NEIL ARMSTRONG
American astronaut and aviator

Armstrong was the first person to walk on the Moon. He was commander of the Apollo 11 spacecraft, which made the first piloted lunar landing mission in history, and he had an early career as a test pilot.

BORN: August 5, 1930; Wapakoneta, Ohio
ALSO KNOWN AS: Neil Alden Armstrong (full name)
AREAS OF ACHIEVEMENT: Aviation and space exploration, science, invention and technology

EARLY LIFE

Neil Armstrong, the first person to set foot on the Moon, was born on a farm in Auglaize County near Wapakoneta, Ohio. He was the elder son of Stephen Armstrong and Viola Armstrong; his younger brother, Dean Alan, was born in Jefferson, Ohio, and had a long career with the Delco Division of General Motors Corporation at Anderson, Indiana; Neil also had a sister, June Louise. Stephen Armstrong was an auditor for the state of Ohio, and his work took the family across the state to many towns. The Armstrongs moved from Warren to Jefferson, to Ravenna, to St. Mary's, Upper Sandusky, and finally to a more permanent home in Wapakoneta. The Armstrongs were descendants of Scotch-Irish immigrants, while the mother's ancestors were of German background. Neil's father eventually was made the assistant director of mental hygiene and corrections of the state of Ohio.

Armstrong began his formal education in the public schools of Warren, Ohio, where he attended Champion Heights Elementary School. His advanced reading ability (he had read ninety books in the first grade) permitted him to skip the second grade. Known as a shy and modest boy, he played baseball and football with friends and enjoyed school activities.

Influenced by his father, Armstrong had an early interest in aviation. His family attended the National Air Races at the Cleveland airport, and as a six-year-old boy, he accompanied his father in a plane called a Tin Goose (Ford TriMotor) that provided air rides near their home in Warren. During the Great Depression, Armstrong developed a deep interest in building model airplanes, a hobby that soon filled his room with the smell of glue and balsa wood. He quickly advanced from hobby kits to creating bigger and more powerful models of his own, which he tested at the town park. During his high school years, to improve his homemade planes, Armstrong built

a seven-foot-long wind tunnel in the basement of his family's house. He was also an enthusiastic fan of science fiction, especially that of H. G. Wells.

One neighbor, Jacob Zint, owned a powerful telescope and often invited youngsters to look at the Moon, stars, and planets. Armstrong remembered these stargazing experiences as awe inspiring and began more study of the universe. He loved to learn; his schoolbooks, which his parents saved, reflect his thorough study and wide reading in the fields of science and mathematics. With his collection of the popular *Air Trails* magazine, he kept pace with aviation advancements. As a high school student, at the age of fifteen, he worked in stores to earn enough money to take flying lessons. On his sixteenth birthday, even before he had a driver's license, he was granted a student pilot's license. He later said that he had decided to become an aircraft designer and thought that a good designer needed to know how to fly.

Armstrong rode his bicycle day after day in 1946 to the Auglaize Flying Field at Wapakoneta, where flight instructor Aubrey Knudegard trained him to fly in an Aeronca 7AC Champion, built in Middletown, Ohio. The Aeronca Airplane Company had been a pioneer in the production of light, single-wing aircraft for private flying, and Armstrong learned to fly the plane with skill. Since the initial flights in 1903 of the Wright brothers at Kitty Hawk, North Carolina, the growth of aerospace research had been concentrated at the Wright-Patterson Air Force Base in Dayton, Ohio, and the Miami Valley had become a center of postwar aviation development and testing. Armstrong was flying from a local airfield not far from this national air base. He also became an Eagle Scout in the Boy Scouts of America.

In the fall of 1947, following his graduation from Wapakoneta High School, Armstrong entered Purdue University at Lafayette, Indiana, on a United States Navy scholarship. Enrolled in the College of Engineering, he had completed about two years of study when the navy ordered him to report to Pensacola, Florida, for special flight training. After the outbreak of the Korean War in July, 1950, Armstrong was the youngest member of his unit, Fighter Squadron 51, when it was sent overseas for active duty. He flew seventy-eight combat missions from the flight deck of the aircraft carrier the USS *Essex*. One mission nearly cost him his life: His Panther jet, damaged by antiaircraft fire, nicked a cable stretched across a North Korean valley; with grim determination and skill, he guided the plane back into South Korea before parachuting to safety. Armstrong won three Air Medals for his combat duty. (Author James Michener modeled his classic 1953 novel *The Bridges of Toko-Ri* after Armstrong and some other fliers in the squadron.)

On completion of his navy service in 1952, Armstrong returned to Purdue to finish his bachelor of science degree in aeronautical engineering and was graduated in 1955. On campus, he met Janet Shearon of Evanston, Illinois, who shared his love for flying; their college courtship led to marriage on January 28, 1956. Three children were born to the Armstrongs: Eric, born in 1957, Karen, born in 1959 (she died near the age of three), and Mark, born in 1963.

Armstrong had by then matured into a handsome aviator with a strong physical stature, standing nearly six feet tall. Reserved in speech but quite able to express himself, Armstrong had keen blue eyes that reflected the intensity of concentration and the good judgment of his mind. Always a good listener, he had absorbed a remarkable amount of information about airborne flight and often drew vital information from that reservoir.

LIFE'S WORK

Armstrong went to work at the Lewis Flight Propulsion Laboratory in Cleveland, serving as a research pilot. After six months at Lewis, he transferred to the High Speed Flight Station at Edwards Air Force Base in California, where he served as an aeronautical research pilot testing many pioneering aircraft, including the X-15 rocket airplane (he took it to more than 200,000 feet above Earth's surface and flew at speeds of nearly four thousand miles per hour), the X-1, F-100, F-101, F-102, F-104, F5D, B-47, and the paraglider. In all, he flew more than two hundred different kinds of aircraft. While in California, he began his master of science degree in aerospace engineering at the University of Southern California, completing it in 1969.

Spurred by the Soviet Union's successful launching of the first Earth-orbiting satellite, Sputnik 1, on October 4, 1957, the United States in 1958 established the National Aeronautics and Space Administration (NASA) to coordinate all space research projects sponsored by the federal government. Soon the United States was sending its satellites skyward, and NASA began training spacecraft pilots called "astronauts" for orbital flights. Explorer 1 became the first successful American data-gathering space satellite, launched in January, 1958. It was Soviet cosmonaut Yuri Gagarin, however, who became the first human in space orbit, in April, 1961,

aboard the Vostok 1; the United States sent its first piloted capsule into suborbital flight in May, 1961, with Alan B. Shepard, Jr., flying in *Freedom 7*. That month, President John F. Kennedy, in an address to Congress, called for the nation to land the first person on the Moon by the end of the decade, a goal that was achieved.

While still working at NASA's facility at Edwards Air Force Base (consolidated into NASA), Armstrong applied to be one of the United States' astronauts. The requirements favored men from military units, but Armstrong was accepted in 1962; he was the first civilian admitted to the astronaut program by NASA. The Armstrongs moved to El Lago, Texas, and Armstrong joined the nation's second recruit class of astronauts in training at the new NASA Manned Spacecraft Center in Houston for a two-year intensive program of classroom study and training for space travel.

NASA developed three space programs while Armstrong worked as an astronaut. The first, designated Project Mercury, was to develop the technology and experience to send a person into Earth orbit. On February 20, 1962, the first piloted orbital flight launched by the United States carried John Glenn as pilot of a three-orbit

Neil Armstrong. (Library of Congress)

ENGINEERING THE POSSIBLE

Intensely private and unassuming, Neil Armstrong avoided public appearances after his days as an astronaut, but on July 20, 1999, the thirtieth anniversary of the first lunar landing, he gave a lighthearted speech before the National Press Club in Washington, D.C., on behalf of the National Academy of Engineering. Describing the mission as one of humanity's greatest engineering achievements, he observed that while "science is about what is, engineering is about what can be."

space trip. The Gemini program, created in 1962, launched a series of two-person spacecraft in Earth orbit during 1965 and 1966, including two unpiloted and ten piloted ventures. Project Apollo, created in 1960, was redirected in 1962 to land on the Moon by 1970, using a three-person crew. Nine crewed Apollo missions of lunar orbit or landings were made by the end of that program in 1972.

Armstrong was assigned as a command pilot for the Gemini 8 mission launched on March 16, 1966. He successfully performed the first docking of two vehicles (one piloted, the other unpiloted) in space. He and David R. Scott found the two crafts pitching and spinning out of control; Armstrong detached their Gemini capsule, and then, as it began to roll even faster, brought it back under control and made an emergency landing in the Pacific Ocean. He also served as commander of the backup crew for Gemini 11 and late in 1966, at the request of President Lyndon B. Johnson, went on a twenty-four-day goodwill tour of South America with other astronauts.

It was as spacecraft commander of Apollo 11, the first piloted lunar landing mission in history, that Armstrong gained the distinction of being the first to land a craft on the Moon and the first to step on its surface, an event that was achieved on July 20, 1969, four days after the craft's launch. Michael Collins served as command module pilot of the *Columbia*, which orbited the Moon while Armstrong and Colonel Edwin E. Aldrin, Jr., aboard the four-legged lunar module called the *Eagle*, landed near the Sea of Tranquillity (at about 4:18 P.M., eastern daylight time) and explored the surface before the rendezvous with the *Columbia* for the return trip.

The next day, *The New York Times* ran the headline, "Men Walk on Moon: Astronauts Land on Plain; Collect Rocks, Plant Flag." Relating one of humanity's most historic moments, a journalist recounted,

About six and a half hours [following the lunar landing], Mr. Armstrong opened the landing craft's hatch, stepped slowly down the ladder and declared as he planted the first human footprint on the lunar crust:

"That's one small step for man, one giant leap for mankind."

His first step on the moon came at 10:56:20 P.M., as a television camera outside the craft transmitted his every move to an awed and excited audience of hundreds of millions of people on Earth.

Colonel Aldrin soon joined Armstrong and, in a two-and-a-half-hour stay outside the *Eagle*, the two set up a camera for live television transmission, conducted seismographic and laser experiments, planted a United States flag, and collected samples of Moon soil and rocks. After twenty-two hours, they blasted off to rejoin the *Columbia*, climbed back into the command module, jettisoned the lunar *Eagle*, and returned to earth to splash down southeast of Hawaii and were personally welcomed by President Richard M. Nixon aboard the USS *Hornet*. Nixon said: "You have taught man how to reach for the stars."

For eighteen days after the splashdown, the three lunar astronauts were kept in isolation to avoid any contamination from the Moon's environment. New York City welcomed them with the greatest ticker-tape parade since Charles A. Lindbergh's solo flight to Paris in 1927. At the White House, they received the nation's highest civilian honor: The Medal of Freedom was given to each of them. In the next months, they visited twenty-two nations and were awarded medals and citations from governments and scientific organizations around the world.

Armstrong was reassigned to the position of deputy associate administrator for aeronautics, Office of Advanced Research and Technology, NASA Headquarters, Washington, D.C. He was responsible for the coordination and management of NASA research and technology work related to aeronautics. Warned in his correspondence with Charles A. Lindbergh of the dangers of fame, he resolutely shunned the limelight and evaded reporters and photographers. From then on his name was among the best known on the planet, but he could travel anywhere without being recognized.

In the fall of 1971, at the urging of his friend, Paul Herget, astronomer and professor of space science, whose work in the field of minor planets and in satellite orbits had won world recognition, Armstrong accepted an appointment as professor of engineering at the University of Cincinnati, an interdisciplinary post he retained until 1980. After their return to Ohio, the Armstrongs lived on a farm near Lebanon, Warren County, where their sons were graduated from high school.

Between 1979 and 1981, Armstrong worked part-time for the Chrysler Corporation and appeared in a national advertising campaign for the Detroit car manufacturer. For a short time, he and his brother Dean owned and operated the Cardwell International Corporation, a producer and exporter of oil field equipment. He later headed CTA, an aviation company based in Charlottesville, Virginia. Sought by many major corporations, Armstrong accepted positions on the board of directors of several companies, including Gates Learjet and United Airlines. In the 1980's, although carefully guarding his schedule, he became a popular speaker at national conventions and trade associations as well as a commencement speaker for many universities, some of which awarded him honorary degrees. He turned down offers from both major political parties to run for office.

Following the explosion of the *Challenger* space shuttle on January 28, 1986, in which seven astronauts lost their lives, President Ronald Reagan named William Rogers chair and Neil Armstrong vice chair of a presidential commission to investigate the causes of the *Challenger*'s failure. For the next six months, Armstrong served as an active member of that commission, appearing on television and before Congress with the chair to report on the findings of the body. After the Rogers Commission disbanded, Armstrong served on the board of directors of Thiokol, the corporation that had manufactured the rocket booster that caused the disaster.

In 1989 he was divorced from Janet. During a golf tournament in 1992, Armstrong met Carol Held Knight; they married two years later. In addition to creating difficulties in his first marriage, his fame sometimes caused him embarrassment and problems. He stopped signing autographs in 1994 after learning that the autographed items were being sold for thousands of dollars on such venues as the Internet company eBay, and he twice initiated lawsuits against those who used his name, words, or—in one case—hair without his permission or knowledge. He donated the settlements to charities.

Armstrong retired from business on May 7, 2002, resigning as chair of the board of EDO Corporation, an advanced technology firm serving defense, intelligence, and commercial markets in New York. He had become chair in 2000.

In 2005 a long-standing controversy was revived over what exactly Armstrong had said when he first stepped onto the Moon's surface. He always maintained that he had said "That's one small step for a man, one giant leap for mankind"; however, the "a" went unheard and the resulting statement, seemingly a mere redundancy, was sometimes ridiculed. A computer programmer in Australia, Peter Shann Ford, reprocessed the audio recording with advanced computer equipment and discovered that Armstrong was correct; an "a," only 35 milliseconds long, emerged from the reprocessing. Hidden in the static of the original transmission, the correct version reflected Armstrong's modest attempt to deflect attention from himself and include all humanity in the event.

Honors came early to Armstrong for his moon landing and continued throughout his life. The Boy Scouts gave him the Distinguished Eagle Scout Award and Silver Buffalo Award. He also received the Congressional Space Medal of Honor, Robert H. Goddard Memorial Trophy, and the National Aeronautics Association's Collier Trophy. Many places have been named after him, including a moon crater near his landing site, schools, streets, and, in 2004, the new engineering building at his alma mater.

SIGNIFICANCE

When the three astronauts of Apollo 11 addressed a joint session of the United States Congress on September 16, 1969, Armstrong recalled how they had left a bronze plaque on the *Eagle*'s remnants. It declared: "Here men from the planet Earth first set foot upon the Moon. July 1969, A.D. We came in peace for all mankind." Such sentiments reflect the noble convictions of Armstrong: He saw his individual role in the gigantic space exploration mission as that of only one member of the nation's great team; his accomplishment as a victory for the whole of human endeavor: "a giant leap for mankind," "in peace for all mankind." Hence, he was able to return quietly to university and business activities after becoming the world's greatest explorer of all time.

Governor James A. Rhodes led a drive for the erection of a globelike museum honoring Armstrong on the edge of his hometown at Wapakoneta, which houses a vast collection of the awards, citations, gifts, and honors given the Ohio native. As a new American hero, a skillful and courageous commander in the tradition of Christopher Columbus, Ferdinand Magellan, and others, Armstrong confidently walked on the Moon first and confidently returned to work among his fellows. Through it all he remained unassuming about his achievement. He said in 2005, "I was elated, ecstatic and extremely surprised that we were successful."

—Paul F. Erwin

FURTHER READING

Brinkley, Douglas. "The Man and the Moon." *American History* 39 (August, 2004): 26-78. A substantial, enjoyable article that discusses Armstrong's famous reticence and shyness, reluctant participation in the Johnson Space Center Oral History Project, ferocious ability to concentrate on whatever he is doing, and role in U.S. aerospace programs.

Crouch, Tom D. *The Giant Leap: A Chronology of Ohio Aerospace Events and Personalities, 1815-1969*. Columbus: Ohio Historical Society, 1971. A graphic story of human flight from the time of early balloons, aircraft, and dirigibles through to Apollo 11's splashdown in 1969.

Hansen, James R. *First Man: The Life of Neil A. Armstrong*. New York: Simon & Schuster, 2005. Highly acclaimed biography that recounts Armstrong's career in flying, portraying him as a great but reluctant hero.

Mallon, Thomas. "Moon Walker." *The New Yorker*, October 3, 2005. A shrewd, provocative review of Armstrong's career and examination of his character that came out, in part, as a review of James R. Hansen's biography.

Wagener, Leon. *One Giant Leap: Neil Armstrong's Stellar American Journey*. New York: Forge, 2004. A well-researched, balanced, and updated biography of Armstrong.

Westman, Paul. *Neil Armstrong: Space Pioneer*. Minneapolis, Minn.: Lerner, 1980. A preliminary biography of Armstrong in conversational style packed into sixty-four pages with fine black-and-white photographs largely supplied by NASA. Contains an appendix of all United States piloted space flights from Mercury 3 through Project Apollo.

SEE ALSO: Yuri Gagarin; John Glenn; John F. Kennedy; Sergei Korolev; Shannon W. Lucid; Sally Ride; Alan Shepard; Valentina Tereshkova; Konstantin Tsiolkovsky.

RELATED ARTICLES in *Great Events from History: The Twentieth Century:*

1941-1970: April, 1959-November 15, 1966: NASA Launches Project Gemini; June 8, 1959-December 31, 1968: X-15 Rocket Aircraft Program; July 20, 1969: First Humans Land on the Moon.

1971-2000: January 28, 1986: *Challenger* Accident.

SVANTE AUGUST ARRHENIUS
Swedish physicist and chemist

Arrhenius was a pioneer in the interdisciplinary science of physical chemistry. He also helped establish the international reputation of the Nobel Prizes, clarified the physical effects of light pressure from the sun, and developed the conception, called "panspermia," that life was introduced on Earth by spores from space.

BORN: February 19, 1859; Castle of Vik, near Uppsala, Sweden
DIED: October 2, 1927; Stockholm, Sweden
AREAS OF ACHIEVEMENT: Chemistry, physics, astronomy

EARLY LIFE

Svante August Arrhenius (SVAWN-teh OW-gehst ahr-RAY-nee-uhs) was born at the castle of Vik, near Uppsala, Sweden. His family had engaged in farming for several generations and had also produced some members of at least modest accomplishment. One relative had written published hymns, an uncle was a scholar, and Arrhenius's own father had attended the University of Uppsala

briefly and held a responsible position as superintendent of grounds for the university.

From an early age, Arrhenius showed skill in calculating, and at the Cathedral School in Uppsala he displayed some ability in mathematics and physics. In 1876, at the age of seventeen, Arrhenius enrolled at the University of Uppsala, the oldest and best-known Swedish institution. There to study physics, he ultimately discovered that his instructors were overly committed to experimental topics and were either unaware of or opposed to the rapid developments in theoretical physics. Thus, in 1881 he moved to Stockholm to study with Erik Edlund. By 1884, Arrhenius submitted his doctoral dissertation to the University of Uppsala, but his talent was largely unrecognized and he was granted the lowest possible honor above an outright rejection.

Arrhenius's thesis, built on the work of Michael Faraday and Sir Humphry Davy, described an effective experimental method for determining the electrical conductivity of compounds in extremely dilute solutions. The thesis also included a preliminary outline of a theory of electrolytic conductivity, in which Arrhenius claimed that the salt was dissociated into two ions in the solution. This ionization increased the number of particles in a given volume, allowing Arrhenius to explain the high osmotic pressures found by Jacobus Henricus van't Hoff as well as the decreased freezing points and increased boiling points of solutions.

Professor Per Teodor Cleve established the initial response toward Arrhenius's work by ignoring it, presuming that it was no more significant than other student theories. Fortunately, Wilhelm Ostwald recognized the significance of the work and its foundational nature for subsequent developments in the theory of electrolysis.

LIFE'S WORK

Arrhenius, disappointed by the reception of his work, began a campaign to win acceptance by sending copies of his dissertation to several scholars throughout Europe. His work was favorably received by Sir William Ramsay in England and Ostwald in Russia. When Ostwald came to Sweden to visit, his influence secured a lectureship for Arrhenius at Uppsala in 1884 and a travel grant from the Swedish Academy of Sciences in 1886 so that Arrhenius could study further in Europe.

From 1886 to 1891, Arrhenius worked with some of the finest physicists of Europe, including Ostwald in Riga and later in Leipzig, Friedrich Kohlrausch in Würzburg, Ludwig Boltzmann in Graz, and van't Hoff in Amsterdam. During this time, the ionization theory met with extensive resistance. Incomplete atomic theory contributed to the difficulty of accounting for the formation and stable existence of the ions, and certain strong solutions remained anomalous, but Ostwald advocated the fruitfulness of the new theory, demonstrating that it could account for a wide variety of chemical phenomena. When Ostwald joined with van't Hoff to found *Zeitschrift für physikalische Chemie*, Arrhenius took advantage of the opportunity to publish a revised version of his theory of electrolytic dissociation in the first issue. The three close friends thus formed a formidable association promoting the theory.

In 1891, Arrhenius refused a professorship at Giessen, Germany, to become a lecturer at the Högskola, the technical high school in Stockholm, an institution devoted to teaching research methodology in a free form without degrees. Although an outstanding faculty did genuinely creative work, the school was always underequipped. Despite opposition, Arrhenius became a professor in 1895 and later a rector. He and other leaders sought to surpass Uppsala and in the process transformed

Svante August Arrhenius. (© The Nobel Foundation)

the Högskola into the University of Stockholm. Beginning in 1898, he was active in formulating the procedures governing the Nobel Prizes and served on the physics committee from 1900 to 1927.

During these years, Arrhenius continued research in electrolytic conductivity, the viscosity of solutions, the effects of temperature on reaction velocity, and atmospheric conductivity. The results of his research appeared in *Lärobok I teoretisk elektrokemi* (1900; *Textbook of Electrochemistry*, 1902); in 1903, he published *Lehrbuch der kosmischen Physik* (treatise on cosmic physics). Also during this period, Arrhenius's interdisciplinary interests continued to expand. In 1902 and 1903, he studied in Denmark and Germany, working on physiological problems in serum therapy. In 1904, he delivered lectures at the University of California on principles of physical chemistry applied to toxins and antitoxins. In 1905, he refused the offer of a professorship and a private laboratory in Berlin to become the director of the Nobel Institute for Physical Chemistry, near Stockholm, a post he held until his death twenty-two years later.

Settling in Stockholm, Arrhenius began an intense period of writing. In 1906, his California lectures appeared as *Theorien der Chemie* (*Theories of Chemistry*,

1907) and as *Immunochemistry* (1907). That year, cosmologists also became aware of him through *Das Werden der Welten*, a German translation of *Världarnas utveckling* (1906; *Worlds in the Making*, 1908). The second law of thermodynamics seemed to many physicists and astronomers to point to the heat death of the universe. Arrhenius sought to discount heat exhaustion with a self-renewing model of the universe in which burned-out solar objects were replaced by new stars arising from nebulas that were increasing in temperature.

In this intense period of labor, Arrhenius also published *Människan inför världsgåtan* (1907; *The Life of the Universe as Conceived by Man from Earliest Ages to the Present Time*, 1909), which represented a different approach to the older plurality of worlds (life on other planets) debate. Arrhenius supported other scientists who argued that life was universally diffused throughout the universe from already inhabited planets that gave out spores that were spread through space and reached planets that had evolved to a habitable state. Arrhenius intended this as an alternative to William Thomson's claim that meteorites were the means of seeding the planets with life. These proposals have since been given the descriptive name panspermia, and while they were high in explanatory value they have held little interest since the discovery of intense ultraviolet radiation in space.

Honors came to Arrhenius as the quality of his research was recognized. He was finally elected to the Swedish Academy of Sciences in 1901, and the widespread acceptance of his theory was recognized in 1903, when he was awarded the Nobel Prize in Chemistry. In 1902, he received the Davy Medal of the Royal Society of London and became an associate of the German Chemical Society. On a visit to the United States in 1911, he received the first Willard Gibbs Medal and became an associate of the American Academy of Sciences. In addition, he became a foreign member of the Royal Society in 1911, received the Faraday Medal of the Chemical Society in 1914, and was awarded numerous honorary doctorates.

Throughout his career, Arrhenius continued to conduct research and write. He delivered the 1911 Silliman Lectures at Yale, which were published as *Theories of Solutions* (1912). In 1915, he made a second contribution to biochemistry with *Quantitative Laws in Biological Chemistry*, and in 1918 *The Destinies of the Stars* appeared in English. Despite Arrhenius's confidence in the existence of life throughout the universe, he refrained from excesses and took Percival Lowell to task for imagining more than could be proved. In 1926, Arrhenius

published his last major effort, *Erde und Weltall*, a revision and combination of his earlier books on cosmology. He died on October 2, 1927.

SIGNIFICANCE

Ironically, Arrhenius is now most frequently cited for one of his least enduring ideas, that of life originating on planets as the result of panspermia. He is less well known for his more significant accomplishments as a founder of physical chemistry. His reach across disciplinary lines contributed to a fruitful period of research in both physics and chemistry. He strongly wished to internationalize Swedish scientific activity and saw the Nobel Prizes as a means of accomplishing this goal. His role in writing the regulations governing the administration and awarding of these prizes contributed greatly to establishing them as the most significant international scientific award. Offering a satisfactory explanation of the aurora borealis and establishing the existence of light pressure from the sun were his enduring contributions to atmospheric physics and astronomy. His good humor and command of languages (German, French, and English) made him popular wherever scholars gathered and won for him an enduring place in the memories of those with whom he worked.

—Ivan L. Zabilka

FURTHER READING

Cowen, Robert C. "Yes, It's Hotter. But Why?" *Christian Science Monitor*, August 24, 2000. Examines the causes of global warming and describes how Arrhenius's work predicted this disturbing environmental development.

Crawford, Elisabeth. *The Beginnings of the Nobel Institution: The Science Prizes, 1901-1915*. New York: Cambridge University Press, 1984. This significant scholarly work presents a comprehensive and detailed account of the early history of the science prizes. It also gives extensive detail of Arrhenius's involvement in the organizing of the prizes and his actions in promoting and blocking particular recipients.

Dardo, Mauro. *Nobel Laureates and Twentieth-Century Physics*. New York: Cambridge University Press, 2004. Chronicles major developments in physics since 1901, the year the first Nobel Prize in Physics was awarded. Includes information about the work of Arrhenius and other prize winners.

Farber, Eduard. *The Evolution of Chemistry*. New York: Ronald Press, 1952. Although providing minimal biographical information, this book contains a brief but clear explanation of Arrhenius's theory of dissociation. This theory was Arrhenius's most original work and the foundation of his receiving the Nobel Prize. A useful source.

_____, ed. *Great Chemists*. New York: Interscience, 1961. This work contains an abridgment and translation of an earlier work on Arrhenius. It is thorough, accurate, and one of the more authoritative English sources. As with most of the available biographical material concerning Arrhenius, there is very little about his private life in the English abridgment, a shortcoming of the book since it tends to decontextualize Arrhenius's place in the science of the day.

Jaffe, Bernard. *Crucibles: The Story of Chemistry*. New York: Simon & Schuster, 1948. One chapter of this book contains a popular and dramatic account of Arrhenius's career, depicting him as a hero who overcame great opposition from entrenched science to receive the recognition that he deserved.

Larson, Cedric A. "Svante August Arrhenius." *Science Digest* 46 (August, 1959): 83-89. This is a readily available, brief, and accurate biography. Since this is a popular account of his life, the explanations of the science with which Arrhenius was involved are simple. The account of his life is somewhat more personal than the other available sources.

SEE ALSO: Viktor A. Ambartsumian; André-Louis Danjon; Edwin Powell Hubble; Jan Hendrik Oort; F. Sherwood Rowland; Carl Sagan; Karl Schwarzschild.

RELATED ARTICLE in *Great Events from History: The Twentieth Century:*
1901-1940: 1938: Callendar Connects Industry with Increased Atmospheric Carbon Dioxide.

DOROTHY ARZNER
American film director

An exception within the Hollywood film industry, Arzner was a major film director in the Hollywood studio system from the late 1920's through the early 1940's.

BORN: January 3, 1897; San Francisco, California
DIED: October 1, 1979; La Quinta, California
AREA OF ACHIEVEMENT: Film

EARLY LIFE

Although she was born in San Francisco, Dorothy Arzner (AHRZ-nur) grew up around the film stars, directors, and stage personalities who gathered at her father's well-known Hollywood restaurant, the Hoffman Café. D. W. Griffith, Charles Chaplin, Eric von Stroheim, Hal Roach, and Mack Sennett among others met at the round table Louis Arzner's café featured for its show business guests. When asked later in life about her early years in Hollywood's film colony, Arzner remarked that it was a wonder that she went into films at all since she spent her youth being terrified by actors who were always tossing her up into the air.

After graduating from the Westlake School, Dorothy entered the University of Southern California, where she planned to study medicine. During World War I, she volunteered as an ambulance driver, an experience, among others, that deterred her from further medical studies.

The Hollywood studios expanded after the war and demand for workers rose dramatically as a result of the devastating flu epidemic of 1918. In 1919, Dorothy Arzner, who had never expected to work in the motion picture business, went to Famous Players-Lasky (later Paramount Studios) looking for a job, and she was hired as a $15-per-week script typist. Shortly after her arrival, she was made script supervisor. Arzner later confided that her work in the script department taught her the basics of film structure.

Soon Arzner began training as an assistant cutter responsible for splicing and assembling motion picture film negatives into a unified work. By 1921, she had moved to a Paramount subsidiary, Realart Studios, as chief editor. During the next year she cut more than fifty films and trained other editors. In 1922, she went back to Paramount to work on Fred Niblo's *Blood and Sand*, a vehicle starring Rudolph Valentino for which she earned her first credit. Next, James Cruze took her on location as the editor for his epic western, *The Covered Wagon*. By the mid-1920's, Arzner had a reputation as one of the best cutters in the business. She also began to write scenarios, some of which were filmed by Paramount's best directors. Impatient to begin her own career as a director, Arzner threatened to leave Paramount, but she was placated when the studio gave her her first directing assignment. She brought *Fashions for Women* (1927) in under budget and ahead of deadline, completing her apprenticeship and opening a position for herself as a director within the Hollywood studio system.

LIFE'S WORK

Capitalizing on the success of her first film, Arzner secured her place at Paramount by making two more silent comedies in 1927. *Ten Modern Commandments* starred Esther Ralston, who had been acclaimed for her role in *Fashions for Women*, and *Get Your Man* featured the "it" girl, Clara Bow. Next she was asked to direct Paramount's first sound film, *Manhattan Cocktail* (1928). That she was chosen suggests that either Arzner was highly regarded as a professional and therefore capable of tackling the new technology or that she was expendable and could be blamed if the film failed. She made her first talking picture in 1929, a remake of *The Wild Party*, a silent film she had edited in 1923. Again, the

film starred Clara Bow and launched the career of Fredric March, who had appeared in the stage version from which the film was adapted. Through the years, Arzner became known as something of a career maker and was responsible for directing films that established a number of actors who later became major Hollywood stars.

Arzner was very busy during the early 1930's. In 1930, three of her films were released by Paramount: *Sarah and Son*, *Anybody's Woman*, and an episode for a compilation film *Paramount on Parade*. In addition, Arzner worked on two more films: *Behind the Makeup*, which she codirected with Robert Milton, and *Charming Sinners*, which she completed for the same director. *Sarah and Son* was the first film that was scripted by playwright and screenwriter Zoë Akins—with whom Arzner was to work later—and it made Ruth Chatterton into an international star. A smash hit at the box office, *Sarah and Son* established Arzner as one of Paramount's most sought-after directors. When *Anybody's Woman* also became a hit, Arzner remarked that the studio would give her anything she wanted. She next directed *Honor Among Lovers* (1931), which featured Ginger Rogers in one of her earliest roles and advanced the rising careers of Fredric March and Claudette Colbert. In a somewhat daring move, Arzner ended the film with Colbert's heroine running off to take a world cruise with her boss (March) before she had divorced her first husband. It is a mark of Arzner's success that the studio did not interfere with the film's ending. Her next film was a far more typical "woman's picture." Despite its script by Akins, Arzner's *Working Girls* (1931) did not do well at the box office and became her least successful film of the 1930's. In 1932, she made *Merrily We Go to Hell*, her last film for Paramount. A bittersweet comedy, the film has received critical attention, especially for the ingenuity and courage of its central female character as played by Sylvia Sidney. In spite of the film's success, Arzner left Paramount to work as an independent director and moved from studio to studio for the rest of her professional career.

The first film that Arzner made as a freelance director was *Christopher Strong*

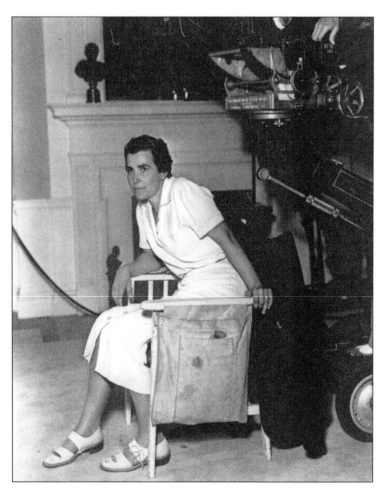

Dorothy Arzner. (Library of Congress)

(1933), which was scripted by Akins and shot at RKO for producer David O. Selznick. The story goes that Arzner rescued her leading lady, Katharine Hepburn, from a jungle picture by literally bringing her down out of a tree. *Christopher Strong* became one of Arzner's most famous films, and Hepburn's performance as a headstrong woman aviator helped boost her fledgling career. The critics were largely complimentary, and studio executive Samuel Goldwyn admired the film so much that he hired Arzner to make an adaptation of Émile Zola's novel *Nana*, which was released in 1934. The film was designed to launch the career of the Russian actor Anna Sten, who Goldwyn hoped would rival Greta Garbo. Moving over to Columbia Pictures, Arzner made *Craig's Wife* (1936), a film based on the well-known play by George Kelly, whose niece Grace eventually became a film star herself. *Craig's Wife* starred Rosalind Russell, who received an Oscar nomination for her portrayal of an obsessive housewife. Joan Crawford was sufficiently impressed by the film, or at least by Russell's Oscar nomination, that she took the lead in Arzner's next film, *The Bride Wore Red* (1937), which was shot at Metro-Goldwyn-Mayer (MGM) with a screenplay by Tess Slesinger from a Ferenc Molnár play. Arzner disliked the superficiality of the film's plot, but she became a lifelong friend of Crawford.

Although she did not know it at the time, Arzner was to direct only two more pictures. The first, *Dance, Girl, Dance* (1940), adapted from a Vicki Baum story by Tess Slesinger, once again helped to advance the careers of its principal actors: Maureen O'Hara and Lucille Ball. Subsequently, it also generated a sizable body of critical commentary, particularly for its feminist perspectives. During the early part of World War II, Arzner made some training films for the Women's Army Corps (WAC). In 1943, however, she returned to Columbia to make her final film, a war picture starring Merle Oberon as a member of the Norwegian underground entitled *First Comes Courage*.

At this time a serious illness forced Arzner to take a temporary leave from directing; eventually, her retirement became permanent. Nevertheless, Arzner did not entirely leave filmmaking. She established the first filmmaking course at the Pasadena Playhouse and taught film at the University of California, Los Angeles, for four years during the 1960's. She also shot some fifty Pepsi commercials for television during Crawford's association with that company. Arzner was the first woman member of the Directors Guild of America (DGA); at a Guild tribute in 1975, her former student Francis Ford

---

FILMS OF DOROTHY ARZNER

Dorothy Arzner was the only major woman director during the golden age of Hollywood. Between 1927 and 1943, she directed the following films.

1922 *Blood and Sand* (additional footage; uncredited)
1927 *Fashions for Women*
1927 *Ten Modern Commandments*
1927 *Get Your Man*
1928 *Manhattan Cocktail*
1929 *The Wild Party*
1930 *Behind the Make-Up* (uncredited)
1930 *Sarah and Son*
1930 *Paramount on Parade*
1930 *Anybody's Woman*
1931 *Honor Among Lovers*
1931 *Working Girls*
1932 *Merrily We Go to Hell*
1933 *Christopher Strong*
1934 *Nana*
1936 *Craig's Wife*
1937 *The Last of Mrs. Cheyney* (uncredited)
1937 *The Bride Wore Red*
1940 *Dance, Girl, Dance*
1943 *First Comes Courage*

Coppola attested to her influence on his directing career. In 1979, Arzner died at the age of eighty-two at La Quinta, near Palm Springs, California, where she had spent the last years of her life.

SIGNIFICANCE

Arzner was the only major woman director during the Golden Age of Hollywood and as such occupies a unique position in film studies and a central one for feminist film criticism. Although Arzner denied any overtly feminist intentions in her cinema and often talked of herself as just one of the "boys" who made motion pictures at the studios, her films are increasingly read as promoting opposition to the dominant male-centered, or patriarchal, ideology of American studio films. As interest in gender studies has grown, increasingly Arzner's work has been examined as well for its possible lesbian content. There is still controversy over whether her films developed a fuller expression of same-gender sexuality than was otherwise occasionally available in other films of the period.

Regardless of Arzner's own sexual orientation, her films are receiving increasing attention from both film scholars and the general public alike. She has become recognized as one of the best American directors of the 1930's, and her films have been revived around the world. It is a recognition that might have come sooner had she not cut short her career in the mid-1940's. Not only are her films praised for their overall quality, but Arzner herself is being acknowledged for the careers she helped to launch or further. Not just another marginal Hollywood professional, Arzner is considered a major directing talent, one significant enough to rank with her male counterparts as a cocreator of the classic Hollywood cinema of the interwar years.

—*Charles L. P. Silet*

FURTHER READING

Doty, Alexander. "Whose Text Is It Anyway? Queer Cultures, Queer Auteurs, and Queer Authorship." *Quarterly Review of Film and Video* 15 (November, 1993): 41-54. Doty examines Arzner's films along with those of her contemporary, director George Cukor. Doty attempts to demonstrate that these works, although made for heterosexual audiences, were subtly influenced by the directors' being lesbian (Arzner) and gay (Cukor).

Fuller, Graham. "The Caring, and Ambiguous, Arzner Touch." *The New York Times*, February 6, 2000. Profile of Arzner with opinions on the films she directed, including the 1933 film *Christopher Strong*, starring Katharine Hepburn.

Heck-Rabi, Louise. "Dorothy Arzner: An Image of Independence." In *Women Filmmakers: A Critical Reception*. Metuchen, N.J.: Scarecrow Press, 1984. Heck-Rabi's chapter on Arzner places her within the context of Hollywood's "boom" years. Surveys film critics' assessments of Arzner's career, discusses the revival of interest in her work during the 1970's, and includes a filmography of motion pictures directed by Arzner.

Houston, Beverle. "Missing in Action: Notes on Dorothy Arzner." *Wide Angle* 6, no. 3 (1984): 24-31. This essay introduces Arzner's work and examines four of her films to judge how effectively they violate the specular practices of classic Hollywood films.

Johnston, Claire, ed. *The Work of Dorothy Arzner: Towards a Feminist Cinema*. London: British Film Institute, 1975. This first short monograph on Arzner contains critical essays, an interview with Arzner, and a comprehensive filmography.

Kort, Melissa Sue. "'Spectacular Spinelessness': The Men in Dorothy Arzner's Films." In *Men by Women*, edited by Janet Todd. New York: Holmes & Meier, 1981. The author argues that it is not the weakness of the men but the strength of the women in her films that marginalizes males in her narratives.

Lesage, Julia. "The Hegemonic Female Fantasy in *An Unknown Woman* and *Craig's Wife*." *Film Reader* 5 (1982): 83-94. According to Lesage, the countervailing tendencies in Arzner's *Craig's Wife* attack the hegemonic female fantasies promoted by Hollywood—fantasies that flattened out contradictions in women's lives and promoted conventional solutions to women's issues.

Mayne, Judith. *Directed by Dorothy Arzner*. Bloomington: Indiana University Press, 1994. Based on research in archival collections at the University of California, Los Angeles, this book-length work is more properly a critical study of Arzner's career than a definitive biography. Mayne explores the connections between Arzner's provocative depiction of women in her films and her identity as a lesbian at a time when such an identity was commonly repressed and ignored.

_____. "Female Authorship Reconsidered." In *The Woman at the Keyhole: Feminism and Women's Cinema*. Bloomington: Indiana University Press, 1990. Mayne raises questions about how clearly Arzner's life and films can be read as raising lesbian issues. Considers whether her films present anything more sustained or developed than the occasional lesbian images that have routinely appeared in other Hollywood films.

SEE ALSO: Lucille Ball; Charles Chaplin; Cecil B. DeMille; Federico Fellini; Samuel Goldwyn; D. W. Griffith; Katharine Hepburn; Alfred Hitchcock; Fritz Lang; Anita Loos; Steven Spielberg; François Truffaut.

RELATED ARTICLES in *Great Events from History: The Twentieth Century:*

MARY KAY ASH
American businesswoman

Ash founded Mary Kay Cosmetics, a Fortune 500 company based on direct sales by women who demonstrate beauty products in homes. She is best known for not only her business acumen but also her motivational techniques, including awarding pink Cadillacs as prizes to her sales force.

BORN: May 12, 1918; Hot Wells, Texas
DIED: November 22, 2001; Dallas, Texas
ALSO KNOWN AS: Mary Kathlyn Wagner (birth name)
AREAS OF ACHIEVEMENT: Business and industry, fashion

EARLY LIFE

Born Mary Kathlyn Wagner in Hot Wells, Texas, a small town twenty-five miles from Houston, Mary Kay Ash was the youngest of four children of Edward Alexander and Lula Vember (Hastings) Wagner. The family owned a hotel where Lula Wagner's good cooking attracted customers. Edward Wagner fell ill with tuberculosis, spent three years in a sanitarium, and returned home an invalid. The Wagners sold the hotel and moved to Houston, where Lula leased and managed a café on Washington Avenue. Lula put in fourteen-hour days as cook and manager, so it became seven-year-old Mary Kay's job to clean, cook, and care for her dad. Mary Kay also learned to take the streetcar downtown to shop for her own clothes. Her persuasive powers as a business executive grew out of her youthful experiences trying to convince salespeople that she had the money and authorization from her mother.

Lula Wagner's loving encouragement and her exemplary work ethic inspired Ash to excel. In addition to achieving excellent grades in school, Ash sold the most tickets for her school's May Fete. She learned to type fast enough to win a class trophy, won honors on the debate team, and gave speeches that earned recognition for her as the second best speaker in Texas. Ash applied her sales skills to her extracurricular activities as well, earning distinction as a top seller of Girl Scout cookies.

One of Ash's closest competitors was her friend Dorothy Zapp, who was rich, smart, and capable. Ash continually aspired to outdo Zapp when it came to selling school tickets or achieving high grades. The Zapp family appreciated Ash for her persistence and intelligence and included her in their family vacations and Christmas parties. Zapp and Ash shared joys, sorrows, and secrets.

Eventually, their lives began to follow separate paths when Dorothy went off to college, a luxury that Ash's family could not afford during the Depression.

After condensing four years of studies into three, Ash was graduated from Reagan High School at the age of seventeen. After graduation, she was married to Ben Rogers. Rogers was a musician who played guitar with the Hawaiian Strummers, a band that was featured on a local radio program. With the arrival of the couple's three children, he took a day job at a gas station and played music at night.

Pressured by the tough economic times and her compulsion to work, Ash began to sell children's books for the Child Psychology Bookshelf. Ida Blake, a company saleswoman, encouraged Ash and taught her to drive a car, enabling her to sell books throughout Houston. When Ben lost his job at the gas station, the couple began

Mary Kay Ash. (AP/Wide World Photos)

to work together selling cookware, but were forced to abandon the venture because of poor sales during the continuing economic depression. In 1939, Ash began to work part-time for Stanley Home Products.

Like her own future company, Stanley Home Products conducted direct sales parties at people's homes. Ash was not successful at first. Realizing she had a lot to learn, she borrowed twelve dollars to attend the company's annual convention in Dallas. Motivated by the recognition given to the company's leading salesperson—in this case, a crown and alligator handbag awarded to a woman—Ash resolved to be next year's winner, a resolve she announced to the president of the company. Taking steps to ensure her success, Ash attended a demonstration conducted by the current winner, took nineteen pages of notes, and memorized the woman's sales pitch. Ash's determination and hard work put her at the top of sales the next year. Instead of winning the coveted alligator purse, however, she was given a flounder light, a light used by fishermen.

Such lack of consideration embittered Ash as she labored to succeed in the male-dominated world of sales. Nevertheless, she managed to rise above these slights to pursue her career goals while still caring for her family. During World War II, her husband joined the Army and was sent abroad. Fortunately, Ash's sales career as a Stanley dealer was flourishing and provided the family with a steady income.

In 1942, she decided to pursue her dream to become a medical doctor. Since married women were not supposed to take places from men, Ash posed as an unmarried student and enrolled in premedical courses at the University of Houston. A woman dean called her in to discuss the results of a three-day aptitude test and informed her that she had tested higher in marketing and sales than in science. That news plus the prospect of making a ten-year commitment to become a doctor on top of her heavy workload as wife, mother, and saleswoman persuaded Ash to drop out of college and work full-time for Stanley instead. Shortly thereafter, her husband was mustered out of the Army and informed Ash that he had met another woman and wanted a divorce after eleven years of marriage.

LIFE'S WORK

The postwar years marked a new chapter in Ash's life. As a young career woman and a divorced parent, she had little time to wallow in pity since her children depended on her for their emotional and financial support. She joined what her mother described as the "Five O'Clock Club,"

rising at 5:00 A.M. to plan her household chores and the day's three sales parties. Her children were also involved and learned to package her products, keep accounts, and do household chores. As her income rose, Ash hired a housekeeper. After being named a manager at Stanley and moving to Dallas, Ash thought she would continue to progress within the company hierarchy. Instead, she encountered a glass ceiling—a variety of gender-based barriers that hindered her advancement at Stanley.

In 1952, she transferred to World Gift Company in Houston, where she became a top saleswoman, then an area manager, and finally a training director. In this capacity, she visited forty-three states and traveled three weeks out of every month. As she rose through the ranks, she faced discrimination. A male assistant, whom she had trained, was named as her boss and given twice her salary. Another incident involved an efficiency expert who told Ash she had too much power. Eventually, the company decided to transfer her every six months. In 1963, she voluntarily retired from the company.

After leaving World Gift Company, Ash decided to write her memoirs. While reviewing her business experiences, she wrote down her ideas for a dream company. In her ideal company, the Golden Rule would be practiced. Above all, the company would be sympathetic to the concerns of working women and especially to those of working mothers. All she needed was a product, and she remembered an invention she had been introduced to by the daughter of a deceased tanner of hides—homemade cosmetics. She had been using these cosmetics, in spite of their smell, since 1952, and she bought the formulas for them in 1963.

Ash began preparations to launch her new company. A month before Mary Kay Cosmetics was scheduled to open, her second husband of several years died of a heart attack. An executive in the vitamin industry, he was to be in charge of the new company's finances and administration. The crisis caused by his death was overcome when her youngest son Richard agreed to take over the financial end of the company. Against the advice of her lawyer and accountant, Ash opened her company on September 13, 1963, backed by her life savings of $5,000.

The first year of retail sales, amounting to nearly $200,000, were encouraging to the beginning staff of nine sales representatives. Eventually, the company established certain guidelines for sales. Independent salespeople, known as beauty consultants, were encouraged to purchase a makeup case containing the company's products, to make extensive telephone contacts among their friends and neighbors, to organize intimate home-based parties demonstrating the products, and to sell the makeup for twice what they paid for it. Each time a consultant recruited additional sales representatives, she was awarded a percentage of their sales forever. No cap was placed on the consultants' earnings. As their sales increased, consultants advanced through the ranks to sales director and eventually to national sales director. The company placed particular emphasis on individual recognition, providing bonuses and prizes in the form of jewelry, fur coats, and complimentary Cadillacs and sponsoring annual sales conventions to highlight the success of each sales representative.

The business skyrocketed and the company went public in 1968. From 1973 to 1983, the company's stock price rose by 670 percent. Between 1984 and 1985, however, the company's growth slowed, and Mary Kay and Richard decided to buy back publicly held stock and become a family-owned business again. Initially, all three of Ash's children worked for her company, although her oldest daughter Marilyn left after four years because of an injured back.

Ash married businessman Melville Jerome Ash in 1966. Their marriage was happy, and they built a large $4 million circular house in Dallas. Mel was popular with the staff at Mary Kay Cosmetics, even though he tried to get Mary to spend less time at the office. He died of cancer in 1980.

By the early 1990's, Mary Kay Cosmetics was operating in nineteen countries and was included on the *Fortune* 500 list of the largest industrial companies in America. Of its estimated 350,000 beauty consultants, some 15 percent work abroad. Four subsidiaries were established in Australia, Canada, Argentina, and Germany, and the company's worldwide wholesale sales were estimated at $609 million in 1992.

In 1993, Ash dedicated the Mary Kay Museum, which exhibits thirty years of the company's history. In that year she received the Dallas Mother of the Year Award and the Outstanding Texas Citizen Award from the Exchange Clubs. In 1990 she won the Woman of Achievement Award from the General Federation of Women's Clubs. She appeared on most of the prominent television talk shows and *Sixty Minutes*. In 1987, she received the Churchwoman of the Year Award from Religious Heritage of America. She was especially proud of the Horatio Alger Distinguished American Citizen Award she received from Norman Vincent Peale, and she served on

---

MAKING THINGS HAPPEN

In her 1981 autobiography Mary Kay: The Story of America's Most Dynamic Businesswoman, *Mary Kay Ash explained the sort of person she was determined to become.*

There are four kinds of people in this world:

- those who make things happen
- those who watch things happen
- those who wonder what happened
- those who don't know that anything happened!

I knew from a very early age that I wanted to be first on that list. And in the years since, I have learned that people who do succeed are set apart by their personalities, objectives, and abilities. Specifically, this means that they have:

- enthusiasm (with purpose)
- discipline
- willingness (to work, to serve, to learn)
- determination
- appreciation of others

---

the Horatio Alger Association Board of Directors. A major philanthropist, she supported many causes such as the Prestonwood Baptist Church and cancer research. She was the author of three books: her autobiography, a best-selling book containing her management philosophy, and another book about her life and business principles.

SIGNIFICANCE

Despite criticism of her emphasis on a rather traditional image of women, Ash considered herself a feminist with a difference. She built her dream company by offering women opportunities for financial independence, career advancement, and personal fulfillment. On the way up, employees could gain recognition and were feted at an annual seminar. By the 1990's, there were four separate seminars held consecutively to accommodate thirty-five thousand consultants over a two-week period each July in Dallas. Ash focused her efforts on motivating her salespeople, building up their self-confidence by recognizing their improved personal appearance and sales. In addition to providing financial incentives, Ash praised and applauded them and gave them personal notes and calls. Her consultants idolized her.

Ash created an egalitarian culture as she promised. In 1993, Mary Kay Cosmetics was listed for the second time among *The 100 Best Companies to Work for in America*. It boasted more than one thousand male sales representatives and a line of men's skin care products.

The company existed without a glass ceiling. It refused to take away commissions from sales representatives who moved. There was no favoritism, ageism, racism, or sexism. Personal testimonies from those who had gained riches beyond their dreams come from all walks of life, including African Americans, farm wives, and the elderly. Most employees worked part-time, and they set their own work hours.

—Virginia W. Leonard

FURTHER READING

Ash, Mary Kay. *Mary Kay.* New York: Harper & Row, 1981. An autobiography that is the basis for secondary works on Ash and Mary Kay Cosmetics. The book reveals her analytical mind, which was able to work out principles for personal and corporate success in the middle of setbacks, frustrations, discrimination against women, divorce, child-rearing, and housework.

_____. *Mary Kay on People Management.* New York: Warner Books, 1984. This *New York Times* best seller emphasizes recognition as the most powerful of all motivators. Ash underscores the importance of the Golden Rule and that businesses should be more like families and "praise people to success."

_____. *Miracles Happen: The Life and Timeless Principles of the Founder of Mary Kay, Inc.* New York: Quill, 2003. Ash recounts her business philosophy and the principles on which she built her cosmetics empire.

Brands, H. W. *Masters of Enterprise: Giants of American Business from John Jacob Astor and J. P. Morgan to Bill Gates and Oprah Winfrey.* New York: Free Press, 1999. Brands examines the lives and careers of Ash and twenty-four other entrepreneurs to discover the common elements to their success.

Cohen, Sherry Suib. *Tender Power.* Reading, Mass.: Addison-Wesley, 1989. The author believes that women can revolutionize corporate structure through "tender power" by creating a nurturing, cooperative business environment emphasizing peer recognition. As the president and chief operating officer of Mary Kay Cosmetics, Dick Bartlett championed the concept of tender power, and Ash is cited as an example of the concept in action.

Farnham, Alan. "Mary Kay's Lessons in Leadership." *Fortune*, September 20, 1993, 68-77. An article that focuses on the power of recognition and other motivational techniques as displayed at the company's annual seminar in Dallas. Provides a snapshot overview of the corporate structure and describes the support role assigned to husbands whose wives work for the company. Illustrated.

Rosenfield, Paul. "The Beautiful Make-Up of Mary Kay." *Saturday Evening Post*, October, 1981, 58-63, 106-107. A cheerful, upbeat review that provides a summary of Ash's achievements and a snapshot overview of her company and its corporate structure.

Rozakis, Laurie. *Mary Kay.* Vero Beach, Fla.: Rourke Enterprises, 1993. An entry in the publisher's Made in America series, this biography is directed at juvenile readers and provides a concise introduction to Ash's life and career, highlighting her struggle to achieve.

SEE ALSO: Coco Chanel; Estée Lauder; Madam C. J. Walker; Oprah Winfrey.

RELATED ARTICLES in *Great Events from History: The Twentieth Century:*

1901-1940: 1920's: Chanel Defines Modern Women's Fashion; November, 1936: Carnegie Redefines Self-Help Literature; June 25, 1938: Federal Food, Drug, and Cosmetic Act.

1941-1970: Spring, 1947: Dior's "New Look" Sweeps Europe and America; March 19, 1954: Laura Ashley Fashion Company Is Founded; October 18, 1968: Lauren Creates the Polo Clothing Line.

1971-2000: July 1, 1985: Home Shopping Service Is Offered on Cable Television; 1990: Avon Begins Operations in China.

H. H. ASQUITH
Prime minister of the United Kingdom (1908-1916)

As prime minister, Asquith steered the British government through a period of acute crisis that saw passage of major social reform legislation, legal alteration of the constitutional relationship between the two houses of Parliament, severe differences between parties regarding the future position of Ireland within the United Kingdom, and British entry into World War I.

BORN: September 12, 1852; Morley, Yorkshire, England

DIED: February 15, 1928; The Wharf, Sutton Courtney, Berkshire, England

ALSO KNOWN AS: Herbert Henry Asquith (full name); Viscount Asquith of Morley; first earl of Oxford and Asquith

AREAS OF ACHIEVEMENT: Government and politics, diplomacy

EARLY LIFE

H. H. Asquith (AS-kwihth) was the second son of Joseph Dixon Asquith and Emily Willans Asquith. The security of Asquith's middle-class youth was affected by his father's death when he was eight and by his mother's always precarious health. Sent with his elder brother to live in London, he was educated at the City of London School. Having gained a classical scholarship, he entered Balliol College, Oxford, in 1870. He obtained first-class degrees in both Classical Mods (1872) and Greats (1874) and was awarded the Craven Scholarship. He became president of the Oxford Union during his last term. He was elected a fellow of Balliol in 1874. In 1876, he was called to the bar, but his interest in the law was always to be secondary to his commitment to politics. Asquith's success at the bar was not assured until 1888, when he served with distinction as junior counsel for Charles Stuart Parnell in clearing his name of charges that were brought in *The Times* of London. Asquith became a Queen's Counsel in 1890.

In 1877, Asquith and Helen Melland, the daughter of a Manchester physician, were married. The union produced four sons and a daughter. Asquith's first wife died in 1891, leaving him with five children to rear. In 1894, he was married to Emma Alice Margaret "Margot" Tennant, the daughter of a wealthy Liberal businessman. They had five children, but only one son and one daughter survived infancy. Margot Asquith was a nota-ble figure in her own right; her notorious outspokenness was not always helpful to her husband's political career, but her numerous connections and lavish hospitality were.

LIFE'S WORK

In 1886, Asquith was elected to Parliament for the Scottish seat of East Fife as a supporter of William Ewart Gladstone's policy of granting home rule to Ireland. In the 1893 general election, Asquith was returned for East Fife, and Gladstone invited him to enter the cabinet as Home Secretary. Asquith was just short of his fortieth birthday. It was a brilliant start, and Gladstone's confidence was sustained by Asquith's solid record in office. The prime minister, however, continued to pursue Irish home rule as his main, and ultimately unachieved, goal. Asquith's early enthusiasm for this cause dimmed as he perceived that the issue was too narrow to garner the support of the whole Liberal Party, and he regretted the opportunities lost for constructive legislation as home rule consumed parliamentary time and the government's energies. When Gladstone resigned in 1894 and was succeeded by Lord Rosebery, Asquith was not unhappy, but Rosebery's imperialist policies further divided the Liberal Party, which gave up office in 1895.

Asquith had made his mark in the brief Liberal government. His ease in debate, the clarity of his presentations, and his fine speaking voice all were assets. Of medium height, he was solidly built, and in his later years was somewhat overweight. His fine forehead, prominent nose, and even features were in time crowned by white hair that gave him a dignified appearance appropriate to the high station he would achieve. A decade would pass, however, before the Liberals and Asquith would return to political office.

In 1899, the Liberal members of Parliament chose Sir Henry Campbell-Bannerman as party leader. The Boer War (1899-1902) worked to exacerbate divisions in the Liberal Party and to separate its new leader from Asquith, who publicly objected to Campbell-Bannerman's description of British actions in South Africa as "methods of barbarism." When it became likely in 1905 that the Conservatives would soon surrender office, Asquith was among those "Liberal Imperialists" who were reluctant to see Campbell-Bannerman become prime minister without first reaching terms with him. Yet when Campbell-Bannerman offered Asquith the chancellorship of

H. H. Asquith. (Library of Congress)

Campbell-Bannerman, whose health was failing rapidly, tendered his resignation in early April, 1908, to the king, who sent for Asquith to form a new government as prime minister. At age fifty-five, at the peak of his powers and generally regarded as the best and obvious choice for the premiership, Asquith took up the position he would hold for eight years and eight months of almost uninterrupted crisis. He made relatively few changes in the cabinet he inherited. Notably, David Lloyd George became Chancellor of the Exchequer and Winston Churchill entered the cabinet as president of the Board of Trade in succession to Lloyd George.

The general election of 1906 had given the Liberal Party, with its Labour and Irish Nationalist allies, a huge majority in the House of Commons. The hereditary House of Lords, however, remained overwhelmingly Conservative in composition, and regularly rejected important Liberal bills that had passed the representative house by large majorities. Constitutional crisis between the two houses finally came over the 1909 budget, which sought new revenues for naval armaments and social programs by levying new taxes, notably on land values. The Lords summarily rejected the budget, thus challenging the Commons' traditional power of the purse.

The government went to the people in January, 1910, in what was essentially a referendum on which house would have the last word on finance. The voters returned 275 Liberals, along with forty Labour and eighty-two Irish, to give the government a good working majority over the 273 Conservatives elected. While this decided the matter of the budget, which now went through the Lords without a division, it left the Liberals dependent on their allies for their majority. Both Labour and Irish had a price for their support, with the latter calling on the government to redeem the standing Liberal pledge to give Ireland home rule.

The immediate issue, however, was constitutional: Would the government insist on legislation limiting the veto power of the House of Lords? Asquith was determined that the power of the Lords should be legally circumscribed, and that if the House of Lords refused to accept this, the king would have to solve the constitutional impasse by creating enough new peers to carry such legislation through the upper house. The king consented to do so, subject to the voters' sustaining the government and its policy in another election, held in December, 1910, and slightly increased the government's majority.

The bill the Lords were now asked to accept denied them any veto over financial legislation and left them a two-year suspensory veto on all other legislation. In re-

the Exchequer and thus the virtual succession to the premiership, Asquith quickly accepted.

Asquith soon achieved recognition as the new government's most effective speaker. In cabinet, Asquith's judicious turn of mind and shrewd political judgment reinforced his claims as Campbell-Bannerman's heir apparent. He also proved to be a highly capable Chancellor of the Exchequer, who in his 1907 budget distinguished for the first time between rates of taxation on earned and unearned incomes, a feature that has remained a part of the British tax system. Asquith's 1908 budget was the first to make provision for old-age pensions. Both budgets give grounds for viewing Asquith as one of the founders of the modern British welfare state.

turn for an increase in its powers, the House of Commons was made more representative of the will of the people by shortening the statutory length of a parliament from seven to five years. If the House of Lords refused these proposals, it would face a flood tide of new peers. The Lords escaped this fate by passing the Parliament Act in August, 1911. Asquith's determination had given the cause of representative democracy its most important victory in twentieth century Great Britain over the dead hand of the past and the power of the privileged few. The price, however, had been high: Party disputes had acquired a rancorous edge, the Liberals had lost their independent majority in the Commons, and the government now had to bring in an Irish home rule bill.

Although the Lords used their suspensory veto to delay its passage from 1912 to 1914, a home rule bill became law in the latter year. Home rule had aroused determined opposition in Protestant Ulster, which did not wish to be subordinated to a Roman Catholic Dublin parliament. When Ulsterites threatened armed resistance, it appeared to some army officers stationed at the Curragh camp in Ireland that they might be called on to impose home rule on a resisting Ulster. They indicated in March, 1914, that they would rather leave the service than do that. When an improper reassurance was given them by the war secretary, Asquith himself took over the office, which he still occupied when war broke out in July. On Great Britain's entry into World War I, Asquith appointed the nonpolitical soldier Lord Kitchener to the post.

Asquith's government was strained to its capacity to cope with a conflict whose scope and duration appeared open-ended. Crisis came in May, 1915, when the government was accused of inadequate provision of artillery shells to the army, and when the First Sea Lord, Admiral Sir John Fisher, resigned because of differences with his political chief, the First Lord of the Admiralty, over naval resources for the campaign at the Dardanelles. Churchill, who had been First Lord since 1911, was deeply committed to this campaign to gain the straits and Gallipoli Peninsula as steps to securing Constantinople and driving Turkey out of the war.

The Conservative leadership, who had observed a party truce since the outbreak of war, informed Asquith that they must share responsibility for war policy or be free to criticize that policy. Accordingly, Asquith formed a coalition government, bringing in the Tories and excluding Churchill and Richard B. Haldane, both strongly disliked by the Conservatives. A Labour Party representative was also included in the government, while Lloyd George became head of a new ministry of munitions. When Lord Kitchener died in the summer of 1916, Lloyd George became the new secretary of state for war.

Asquith's coalition government was never a happy one, and Lloyd George, supported by many Tories, believed that Asquith himself was insufficiently vigorous to lead Great Britain to victory. After some bitter infighting, in December, 1916, Asquith resigned and Lloyd George succeeded him as prime minister. The price of an activist prime minister was conflict between the premier and military leadership. This led to General Sir Frederick Maurice charging in May, 1918, that the government had incorrectly stated the number of troops it had furnished to the army in France in early 1918, prior to the German spring offensive. When Asquith called for a select committee to investigate the general's charges, the government treated the issue as a vote of confidence, which it won handily, although about a hundred Liberals voted with Asquith.

When victory came in November, 1918, the Lloyd George coalition government went to the people for a renewed mandate. The prime minister and the Tory Party leader, Bonar Law, issued a letter of endorsement to their supporters, which did not include most of those Liberals who had voted with Asquith in the Maurice debate. Asquith disdainfully called the coalition leaders' letter of endorsement a "coupon," a name that has stuck to the 1918 election. The voters, however, overwhelmingly supported the government, and only about twenty-five independent or Asquithian Liberals were returned to the new parliament. Asquith was not among them, having been defeated in East Fife after thirty-two years. He reentered the Commons for Paisley, Scotland, early in 1920.

Asquith's last significant action in the House of Commons came after the 1923 general election, in which the voters rejected a Conservative Party platform that included tariffs and made the Labour Party second in representation, with 191 seats to the Tories' 258 seats. The 158 Liberals, led by Asquith, gave their support to Labour, which thus formed a government for the first time in British history. This did not benefit the Liberals, who were reduced to forty seats following the 1924 general election, and Asquith was defeated at Paisley. He accepted a peerage as earl of Oxford and Asquith in 1925; the same year he was made a Knight of the Garter. He resigned as leader of the Liberal Party in October, 1926, after prolonged disagreements with Lloyd George over party matters. Asquith died on February 15, 1928, and was buried in Sutton Courtney, Berkshire.

SIGNIFICANCE

Asquith's finest achievement was the Parliament Act of 1911, which remains a landmark on Great Britain's path to full representative democracy. Although Asquith's liberalism was broad enough to encompass a considerable role for state action, he was sensitive to the rank-and-file Liberal conviction that the state should intrude minimally on the individual. This principle was sorely tested in World War I, and once a coalition government was formed in May, 1915, the key issue facing Asquith was that of conscription. As military service, with its risk of death or maiming, is the ultimate requirement the state can demand of the citizen, many Liberals deeply opposed it, while Tories increasingly demanded it. For too long, Asquith juggled the issues; to many observers, it seemed that he was seeking more to preserve balance within the government than to win the war.

Asquith's penchant for trying to finesse divisive issues was fortified by a growing self-indulgence. At one stage in the war, a sympathetic but acute observer commented,

> It was very typical of him that in the middle of this tremendous crisis he should go away for the week-end. Typical both of his qualities and of his defects; of his extraordinary composure and of his easy going habits.

When he had exhausted all expedients, Asquith carried through conscription in May, 1916, but he had forfeited the sympathy of the Liberal faithful without appeasing his critics, who believed that winning the war required decisive people and stern measures. The test of total war thus damaged the high reputation that Asquith had won in peace.

—Maxwell P. Schoenfeld

FURTHER READING

Asquith, Emma Alice Margaret. *Autobiography.* 2 vols. London: Thornton Butterworth, 1920, 1922. An entertaining autobiography, although lacking in dispassionate judgment and objectivity.

Asquith, Herbert Henry. *Letters to Venetia Stanley.* Selected and edited by Michael Brock and Eleanor Brock. New York: Oxford University Press, 1982. Between January, 1912, and May, 1915, Asquith wrote some 560 letters to a woman thirty years his junior; the correspondence ended abruptly when she informed him that she intended to marry a man who was one of his own government ministers. In these letters, the prime minister generously revealed both his feelings and state secrets, thus providing a remarkable insight into his life during its most strenuous years.

_____. *Memories and Reflections, 1852-1927.* 2 vols. London: Cassell, 1928. While Asquith disclaimed that he was writing autobiography, these volumes were surely intended to leave to posterity his view of events and his image of himself.

Clifford, Colin. *The Asquiths.* London: John Murray, 2002. Recounts the lives of Asquith and his four children, describing how the family was adversely affected by World War I. While Asquith struggled to direct the conflict, his three sons bravely fought in the trenches.

Jenkins, Roy. *Asquith, Portrait of a Man and an Era.* London: Collins, 1978. Himself a distinguished Chancellor of the Exchequer, Jenkins brings to his account the insights of a practicing politician. The 1978 edition contains passages suppressed in the original 1964 edition in deference to the feelings of Lady Violet Bonham Carter, daughter of Asquith, guardian of his memory, and herself an active politician and member of Parliament.

Koss, Stephen. *Asquith.* London: A. Lane, 1976. Generally regarded as the best biography of Asquith, it is critical without being unfair, and assesses his strengths and weaknesses with sensitivity and thoughtfulness.

Lloyd, Trevor Owen. *Empire to Welfare State: English History, 1906-1976.* New York: Oxford University Press, 1979. The early chapters of this distinguished survey present a good picture of the course of English history during Asquith's most active years and provide the context for his life's work.

Packer, Ian. *Liberal Government and Politics, 1905-1915.* New York: Palgrave Macmillan, 2006. An analysis of British Liberalism during the early years of the twentieth century, describing the major concerns of Liberals and how the party fashioned its domestic and foreign policies. Concludes with a section on Asquith's government and World War I.

Spender, John A., and Cyril Asquith. *The Life of Herbert Henry Asquith, Lord Oxford and Asquith.* 2 vols. London: Hutchinson, 1932. Written by a distinguished Liberal publicist and one of Asquith's sons, these volumes present the official view of Asquith as one of the presiding deities within the shrine of political Liberalism.

SEE ALSO: Sir Winston Churchill; George Nathaniel Curzon; Edward VII; George V; Lord Kitchener; Lord Lansdowne; Bonar Law; David Lloyd George.

RELATED ARTICLES in *Great Events from History: The Twentieth Century:*
  1901-1940: April, 1909-August, 1911: Parliament Act Redefines British Democracy; May 31, 1910: Formation of the Union of South Africa; 1911- 1920: Borden Leads Canada Through World War I; September 15, 1914: Irish Home Rule Bill; November 5, 1914: British Mount a Second Front Against the Ottomans.

HAFEZ AL-ASSAD
President of Syria (1971-2000)

Assad ruled Syria autocratically for nearly thirty years, bringing stability and modernization to a country plagued by political turmoil and economic underdevelopment. During his presidency, Syria became a powerful regional actor, a central player in the Arab-Israeli conflict, and the dominant force in neighboring Lebanon.

BORN: October 6, 1930; Qardāha, Latakia Province, Syria
DIED: June 10, 2000; Damascus, Syria
AREA OF ACHIEVEMENT: Government and politics

EARLY LIFE

Hafez al-Assad (hah-FEHZ ahl-ah-SAHD) was born in the remote village of Qardāha in the Ansariya Mountains of Syria, near the Mediterranean coast. His father, Ali Suleiman, was noted for his physical strength and sense of fairness, bringing the family considerable respect in the tight-knit communities of the Ansariya. Ali Suleiman's reputation resulted in a change in the family name just before the birth of Hafez, from Wahhish (meaning savage) to Assad (meaning lion).

Like others in the Ansariya region, the Assads were members of the Alawite sect, a small heterodox branch of Shia Islam. The blending of some Christian beliefs, nature worship, and reverence for Ali (cousin of the Prophet Muhammad and the fourth caliph), placed Alawites outside the mainstream of Islamic beliefs, explaining in part their long-standing social, economic, and geographic isolation from the Sunni Islam majority in Syria. Until at least the 1950's, most Alawites lived either as subsistence farmers and herders in the mountains or worked as domestic servants for Sunni families in the cities.

Assad was the first member of his family to attend secondary school, finishing in 1951 in the coastal town of Latakia. He was a bright, hardworking, and highly ambitious student. It was in high school that Assad became politically active. He was elected to student government and became embroiled in the ideological debates between Arab nationalists, communists, and Islamists that permeated postindependence Syria (Syria gained independence from France in 1946). Assad joined the new Baʿth (meaning rebirth) Party in high school, attracted by its calls for pan-Arabism, anticolonialism, socialism, and secularism.

In 1952, Assad entered the Air Force College in Aleppo. The military was one of the few avenues for advancement for poor, marginalized Alawites, and Assad used this education to become a top-class pilot and to further his political ambitions. The years after his graduation in 1955 were tumultuous ones in Syria and the broader Middle East. The rise of Gamal Abdel Nasser of Egypt and the ongoing Arab-Israeli conflict, including the 1956 Suez Canal crisis, dominated regional affairs. Domestically, Syria endured numerous military coups d'état and political instability, including an ill-fated union between Syria and Egypt from 1958 to 1961, which Assad opposed because of Syria's subservience to Egypt in the newly merged country.

LIFE'S WORK

After rising up the ranks of the military, Assad became defense minister in 1966, after fellow Baʿthist officers overthrew the government. From this post he oversaw the disastrous defeat of Syria and its Arab allies by Israel in the June, 1967, Arab-Israeli war. Among other humiliations, this war led to the Israeli occupation of Syria's Golan Heights, a strategic region just 40 miles from Syria's capital city of Damascus. Assad would spend the rest of his life unsuccessfully trying to win back the Golan.

In September, 1970, another military misadventure brought Assad to power in Syria. That month Jordan's King Hussein launched an attack on guerrilla fighters of the Palestine Liberation Organization (PLO) who were establishing a virtual state within a state in Jordan and seeking the overthrow of Hussein. The Syrian government, led by Nureddin al-Atassi and Salah Jadid, sent ground troops into northern Jordan to intervene on behalf of the Palestinians. The Jordanian air force, backed by veiled threats from Israel, attacked the Syrian troops and forced their retreat. Assad refused to send air support to the Syrian troops and used the chaos to stage a bloodless coup. The party was purged in a so-called corrective revolution, Assad loyalists were placed in key positions, and Assad officially became president by a March, 1971, referendum.

Assad's consolidation of power in 1970-1971 quickly cemented into a repressive authoritarian regime based on single-party rule, a cult of personality, and a wide-ranging internal security and intelligence system called Mukhabarat. Although Alawites constituted less than 12 percent of the population, they filled most of the top political and security positions. This, along with the socialist and secular ideology of the Baʿth Party, alienated the organization the Muslim Brotherhood (Sunni), which several times attempted to assassinate the president. The Islamist insurgency culminated in an uprising in Hama in February, 1982. In response, Assad unleashed Mukhabarat forces under the command of his brother, Rifaat al-Assad, against the city, killing at least ten thousand residents before finally quelling the uprising.

Although brutally intolerant of political opposition, Assad is credited with bringing stability and development to Syria. During his long presidency Syria made significant strides in public education, social reforms, industrialization, and modernization of the state's infrastructure. With the exception of ensuring the internal security of his regime, however, Assad was far more engaged in foreign affairs than with domestic policy.

In October, 1973, Assad and Egyptian president Anwar el-Sadat launched a surprise attack against Israel to regain territory lost in the 1967 war. After initial gains Egypt's troops stopped and dug into their positions. Assad felt betrayed by Sadat, and Israel quickly turned the tide of the battle to its advantage. Israeli troops retook Golan and threatened to continue on to Damascus before the United States and the Soviet Union intervened to establish a cease-fire. Assad was further outraged when Sadat broke with his Arab allies to negotiate a separate peace treaty with Israel at Camp David in Maryland in 1978.

The 1970's also witnessed Syria's intervention in Lebanon. In 1976 the Lebanese government, dominated by a Christian minority, requested Syrian military assistance during the Lebanese civil war. With the agreement of the Arab League, President Assad sent in his army to bolster the government and to attempt to restore order. This may have been prompted in part by Assad's sense that Lebanon was historically connected to Syria. It was also a way to assert control over the PLO, which had set up operations in Lebanon following its expulsion from Jordan. Whatever the initial motivations, tens of thousands of Syrian troops would remain in Lebanon for the next three decades.

Syria's presence in Lebanon inevitably brought it into conflict with Israel, which invaded Lebanon in 1982 in an attempt to destroy the PLO. The fighting during this period also gave rise to a Shia resistance movement in Lebanon called Hezbollah, or Party of God. Inspired by the Islamic revolution in Iran in 1979, Hezbollah wanted to assert the demographic weight of Shia Muslims in Lebanon and was virulently opposed to Israel. The party became a powerful force in regional politics. Assad, along with Iran, supported Hezbollah as a way to indirectly combat Israel.

For the first twenty years of Assad's presidency Syria was closely aligned with the Soviet Union. The collapse of communism was a devastating blow to Syria's economy and military. The loss of Soviet support was thus the key factor in Assad's decision to side with the United States-led coalition in the 1991 Persian Gulf War to oust Iraq from Kuwait. Syria sought better relations with the Arab oil kingdoms and a thawing of tensions with the United States, the sole remaining superpower. This policy shift led to numerous, ultimately unsuccessful, attempts throughout the 1990's to negotiate a peace settlement between Syria and Israel.

SIGNIFICANCE

During the 1990's, Assad worked to secure a final legacy of his long rule: the succession of his son as president. Originally this was to be his eldest son Basil, but he died in a car crash in 1994. Bashar al-Assad, an ophthalmologist by training and the next son in line, was then groomed and successfully assumed power following his father's death in June, 2000.

After a brief initial period of liberalization under Bashar, Syria began to function in much the same authoritarian manner as it did under Assad. Assad's legacy also remains strong in regional politics, with most of the key issues of Lebanon, the Arab-Israeli conflict, sponsorship of terrorism, and the rise of Islamism dominating Syrian policy into the twenty-first century.

—Jeffrey A. VanDenBerg

FURTHER READING

Hinnebusch, Raymond. *Syria: Revolution from Above*. New York: Routledge, 2002. Examines the development of the Syrian state under Assad, with a focus on the Ba'th Party's consolidation of power, economic development, and state-society relations.

Lesch, David W. *The New Lion of Damascus: Bashar al-Asad and Modern Syria*. New Haven, Conn.: Yale University Press, 2005. Chapters 2-4 offer analyses of the Assad family, Hafez al-Assad's rule, and Syria's role in the Middle East. Informed by personal interviews with Bashar al-Assad, Hafez's son and successor to the presidency.

Ma'oz, Moshe. *Asad: The Sphinx of Damascus*. New York: Weidenfeld and Nicholson, 1988. A political biography written by a leading Israeli scholar of modern Syria.

Perthes, Volker. *The Political Economy of Syria Under Asad*. New York: St. Martin's Press, 1997. A detailed study of Syrian economic development and the interplay between the state, the economy, and society since 1970. Emphasizes the role of economic factors in explaining the policy decisions of President Assad.

Ryan, Curtis R. "Syrian Arab Republic." In *The Government and Politics of the Middle East and North Africa*, edited by David E. Long and Bernard Reich. 4th ed. Boulder, Colo.: Westview Press, 2002. An informative introduction to Syrian government and political history.

Seale, Patrick. *Asad of Syria: The Struggle for the Middle East*. Berkeley: University of California Press, 1995. The classic biography of Hafez al-Assad, by a leading British writer on the Middle East. Research for the biography included interviews with Assad, his family, and many top Syrian officials.

SEE ALSO: Yasir Arafat; Menachem Begin; David Ben-Gurion; Moshe Dayan; Abba Eban; Faisal; Hussein I; Golda Meir; Gamal Abdel Nasser; Anwar el-Sadat.

RELATED ARTICLES in *Great Events from History: The Twentieth Century*:

1941-1970: March 2-October 20, 1969: Sino-Soviet Tensions Mount Along the Ussuri River Border.

1971-2000: October 6-26, 1973: Yom Kippur War; 1978-1980: Syrian Bar Association Demands Political Reform in Syria; March 17, 1992, and July 18, 1994: Terrorists Attack Israeli Embassy and Jewish Center in Argentina.

FRED ASTAIRE
American dancer

Astaire was one of the greatest popular dancers of the twentieth century. His films with Ginger Rogers and other partners defined the essence of the American motion picture musical.

BORN: May 10, 1899; Omaha, Nebraska
DIED: June 22, 1987; Los Angeles, California
ALSO KNOWN AS: Frederick Austerlitz (birth name)
AREAS OF ACHIEVEMENT: Dance, theater and entertainment, film

EARLY LIFE

Fred Astaire (eh-STEHR) was born Frederick Austerlitz, the son of Frederic and Ann Austerlitz, in Omaha, Nebraska. The elder Austerlitz worked in the brewing business. Frederick's ambitious and stage-struck mother soon mapped out a show-business career for her son and her daughter Adele, who was eighteen months older than Frederick. Realizing that her children had talent as singers and dancers, Ann relocated her children to New York City, where Adele and Frederick studied at the Ned Wayburn school in Manhattan. Frederick soon displayed a gift for dancing, including the new style of tap-dancing. By the time Frederick was eight, he and his sister were already onstage in the entertainment medium known as vaudeville.

Over the next decade, the siblings changed their name to Astaire and began gaining the attention of theatrical producers. In 1917 they appeared in Sigmund Romberg's *Over the Top*. The show flopped, but the Astaires received good critical notices. Throughout the 1920's the Astaires were a smash success on Broadway and in London. They sang and danced in George Gershwin's *Lady Be Good* (1924) and in *The Band Wagon* (1931), a hit revue that featured songs by Howard Dietz and Arthur Schwartz. By this time, however, Adele had decided to marry an English nobleman and leave show business. It was time for Fred Astaire to go out on his own.

LIFE'S WORK

In the early 1930's, Astaire went to Hollywood, California, to begin a career in motion pictures. According to motion picture legend, one insider's reaction to Astaire was, "Can't sing. Balding. Can dance a little." The story is probably a fable, but it did suggest the problems that Astaire faced in making the shift from the stage to the motion picture studio. In fact, success came relatively quickly. He soon signed a contract to appear in *Dancing Lady* (1933) with Joan Crawford and was also committed to team with newcomer Ginger Rogers in *Flying Down to Rio* (1933). With his film career now well under way, Astaire married Phyllis Livingston Potter in New York City on July 12, 1933. The Astaires had a son, Fred, Jr., and a daughter, Ava. Phyllis would die of lung cancer in 1955. It was a devastating personal loss for Astaire.

Astaire's first motion picture with Rogers, *Flying Down to Rio*, was not a starring vehicle for either of the performers. Amid the rather confused plot, it became apparent that Astaire was an adroit comic actor and that he had a pleasant way with a song on the screen. When Astaire and Rogers danced, however, the screen came alive with the indefinable chemistry that became a key to their enduring popularity. *Flying Down to Rio* was a surprise hit, largely because of the Astaire-Rogers magic. Happy executives at Radio-Keith-Orpheum (RKO) Pictures Corporation at once began planning a full-fledged starring performance for the hot new team.

Their next motion picture, *The Gay Divorcee* (1934), established the format that would dominate the Fred and Ginger series throughout the 1930's. The dance numbers rather than the thin and silly plot kept the story moving. The high points of the film were two songs: Cole Porter's "Night and Day," which depicted Astaire and Rogers in a musical seduction, and the elaborately staged "The Continental," which ran for sixteen minutes. Audiences again responded by flocking to the theaters, and the box office receipts helped keep RKO going throughout the 1930's. The Astaire-Rogers combination became one of the big attractions of the decade.

Of the eight films that Astaire and Rogers did as costars in the 1930's, the standouts were Irving Berlin's *Top Hat* (1935), which included such outstanding songs as "Cheek to Cheek" and "Isn't It a Lovely Day?"; *Swing Time* (1936), directed by George Stevens, with a dazzling score by Jerome Kern and Dorothy Fields that included "A Fine Romance" and "The Way You Look Tonight"; and *Shall We Dance* (1937), which included songs by George and Ira Gershwin such as "Let's Call the Whole Thing Off" and "They Can't Take That Away

from Me." Lesser works, which nonetheless contained many pleasant moments and good dances, were *Roberta* (1935), *Follow the Fleet* (1936), and *The Story of Vernon and Irene Castle* (1939).

A primary factor that made the motion pictures succeed at the box office, with the critics, and with moviegoers for several generations was Astaire's insistence that the dances be filmed with the fewest interruptions possible. He devised innovative camera techniques to make such shots possible, and the result was the flowing, graceful duets that came to be the trademarks of such films as *Top Hat* and *Swing Time*. Astaire and Rogers were a creative partnership, and the key to their success was hard work, imagination, and good taste. They were able to convey the essence of romance on-screen even though they were never romantically involved in person. Without an indecent word or an erotic gesture, the couple danced in a manner that exuded sex appeal.

Astaire created an indelible image of sophistication and elegance in these films. Tall, thin, and graceful, he

Fred Astaire. (Library of Congress)

epitomized style and charm. At a time when upper-class Americans wore top hats, white ties, and tails for an evening out, Astaire could dress in a more fashionable way than the average man. He moved with ease on the dance floor and made his carefully rehearsed numbers seem spontaneous and fresh. Because of his experience with his sister, he knew how to make his partners stand out. Of all the women he danced with, Rogers blended with him the best, and her skill brought out the excellence in his craft.

Although he was not a technically gifted singer, Astaire had a pleasing, lilting voice that had a dancer's sense of the rhythm and the lyrics of a tune. Songwriters such as Berlin, the Gershwins, and Jerome Kern enjoyed composing for Astaire because they knew he would showcase their words and music in the most effective manner. Astaire introduced such standards as "Cheek to Cheek," "A Fine Romance," "They Can't Take That Away from Me," and "One for my Baby and One More for the Road." As Mel Torme and other gifted popular singers have remarked, Astaire was an influential vocalist whose style impressed many song stylists in the 1930's and 1940's.

At the end of the 1930's, Astaire and Rogers went their separate ways. The parting was amicable, but their films had begun to lose money, and Rogers wanted to try her abilities as a serious actor. They would be reunited once in *The Barkleys of Broadway* (1949), in which some of their old magic was evident in their dance numbers.

As a dancer, Astaire remained a star attraction throughout the 1940's. Some of his most exciting work included his "Begin the Beguine" duet with Eleanor Powell in *Broadway Melody of 1940* (1940). Their tapping talents made this an electric example of popular dance at its finest. Other excellent achievements from this period of Astaire's work included his teaming with Bing Crosby in *Holiday Inn* (1942), his pairing with Judy Garland in *Easter Parade* (1948), and *The Band Wagon* (1953), which many of his admirers consider his best motion picture from the post-Rogers era. In the film *Royal Wedding* (1951), Astaire used camera artistry and imagination to create a rotating room so he could show himself dancing on walls and the ceiling in the number "You're All the World to Me."

Astaire continued to make motion pictures into the 1950's, including *Daddy Long Legs* (1955) and *Funny Face* (1957). In 1958 he turned to television, and his program *An Evening with Fred Astaire* garnered nine Emmy Awards for him and his partner Barry Chase. He won additional Emmy Awards for similar programs in 1959 and 1960. As his dancing career wound down, Astaire turned to acting in a more sustained manner. Some of his better performances included his role as a scientist in the antinuclear film *On the Beach* (1959) by Stanley Kramer and the light comedy *The Notorious Landlady* (1962). He recalled some of his best work during his brief appearance in *That's Entertainment* (1974), where he even performed briefly with his old friend and fellow dancer Gene Kelly. On June 24, 1980, Astaire married Robyn Smith, a former jockey. In 1981 he received the Life Achievement Award of the American Film Institute. At that occasion, he said, "All the dances in the film clips shown tonight look good to me." He died of the effects of pneumonia and old age on June 22, 1987.

SIGNIFICANCE

Astaire created a personal style of dance and song that came to symbolize the era of the 1930's in American entertainment. In the middle of the Great Depression, he took audiences away from their troubles and into a world of romance and gaiety. In his clothes, walk, song style, and dancing moments, Astaire embodied elegance and sophistication. His achievement was the product of hard work. He was a perfectionist who insisted on take after take until he had just the images he desired on the screen. The audiences saw only the spontaneity and the fun in the final product.

In the process, Astaire was responsible for some of the great moments in the history of American film. Several of the motion pictures that he and Rogers made are among the best musicals ever done. His dancing in other films such as *The Band Wagon* and *Royal Wedding* are masterpieces of imagination and artistry. Throughout his long and distinguished career, Fred Astaire gave amusement and pleasure to millions of people. His style of dancing transcended national boundaries and became universal in its appeal. Actor James Cagney once said, "Fred Astaire is the greatest dancer I've ever seen in my life." Generations of moviegoers would agree.

—Lewis L. Gould

FURTHER READING

Adler, Bill. *Fred Astaire: A Wonderful Life*. New York: Carroll & Graf, 1987. An admiring biography with many fascinating quotations from people who knew Astaire.

Astaire, Fred. *Steps in Time*. New York: Harper & Bros., 1959. Astaire's autobiography is interesting for his insights into his career, but it is not very revealing for personal details of his life.

Croce, Arlene. *The Fred Astaire and Ginger Rogers Book*. New York: E. P. Dutton, 1972. An eminent film critic examines the films of Astaire and Rogers in a perceptive and analytic manner. An indispensable source for Astaire's artistry.

Gallafent, Edward. *Astaire and Rogers*. New York: Columbia University Press, 2002. Gallafent, a film studies scholar, analyzes the nine RKO Studios' films in which the two appeared in the 1930's and the subsequent films they made after they separated.

Hackl, Alfons. *Fred Astaire and His Work*. Vienna: Josef Schwarz Erbin, 1970. A valuable source book that lists all of Astaire's theater, film, television, and singing appearances to 1970.

Henderson, Amy, and Dwight Blocker Bowers. *Red Hot and Blue: A Smithsonian Salute to the American Musical*. Washington, D.C.: National Portrait Gallery and the National Museum of American History, 1996. This superb overview of the musical and its heritage has some incisive remarks about the impact of Astaire and Rogers on the evolution of an American art form.

Rogers, Ginger. *Ginger: My Story*. New York: HarperCollins, 1991. The autobiography of Astaire's most famous dancing partner includes insights about their on-screen partnership and the films they made together.

Thomas, Bob. *Astaire: The Man, the Dancer*. New York: St. Martin's Press, 1984. The best biography written while Astaire was still alive to cooperate with the author.

Torme, Mel. *My Singing Teachers: Reflections on Singing Popular Music*. New York: Oxford University Press, 1994. Torme's book has a brief but significant chapter on Astaire's singing style that indicates the esteem in which other singers held him.

SEE ALSO: Irving Berlin; Bing Crosby; Judy Garland; George Gershwin; Ira Gershwin; Cole Porter; Frank Sinatra.

RELATED ARTICLES in *Great Events from History: The Twentieth Century*:

1901-1940: 1933: *Forty-Second Street* Defines 1930's Film Musicals; September 6, 1935: *Top Hat* Establishes the Astaire-Rogers Dance Team.

1941-1970: 1944-1957: Kelly Forges New Directions in Cinematic Dance.

NANCY ASTOR
American-born British politician

Born a Virginian, Astor was the first woman to sit in the British House of Commons. Always a controversial figure because of her direct views on almost every subject, from temperance to race relations, she was a zealous campaigner, especially for the rights of women and children.

BORN: May 19, 1879; Danville, Virginia
DIED: May 2, 1964; Grimsthorpe Castle, Lincolnshire, England
ALSO KNOWN AS: Nancy Witcher Langhorne (birth name); Nancy Witcher Astor; Viscountess Astor of Hever Castle
AREAS OF ACHIEVEMENT: Government and politics, social reform, women's rights

EARLY LIFE

Nancy Astor (AS-tohr) was born Nancy Witcher Langhorne in Danville, Virginia. Her mother, Nannie Witcher Keene, was of Irish descent; her father, Chiswell "Chillie" Dabney Langhorne, had been a soldier in the Confederate army. Ten of their eleven children were born in Danville, a moderate-sized southern city notable for its tobacco markets and cotton mills. Nancy was the third of five surviving daughters.

Although various members of the Langhorne family had distinguished themselves in Virginia politics since the eighteenth century, the Civil War and Reconstruction had devastated the southern aristocracy. Chillie (pronounced "Shillie") Langhorne was forced to take a number of menial jobs and eventually decided, when Nancy was six years old, to move to Richmond, the state capital, to better his situation.

It was several years before his luck turned, but Chillie was eventually able to make a fortune contracting laborers for the railroad. In 1892, he bought a country house, Mirador, and settled down to lead the life of a Virginia gentleman. Hunting, riding, and gracious hospitality were considered more important than a formal education, especially for a young girl. Nancy attended several schools and loved to read, and though she was no scholar, she was no mere social butterfly. She had strong religious

Nancy Astor. (Library of Congress)

feelings and briefly considered becoming a missionary. A searching for spiritual values and concern for the poor were to be important aspects of her personality throughout her life.

All the Langhorne women were attractive. Irene, Nancy's elder sister, received more than sixty proposals of marriage before she accepted that of Charles Dana Gibson and became the model for the Gibson Girl. Nancy was not as conventionally beautiful as her sister, but she was a striking woman, small and athletic, with sparkling blue eyes.

In 1897, Nancy married Robert Gould Shaw II of Boston. The marriage was not a success. Shaw was a heavy drinker, and Nancy, only eighteen and homesick for Mirador, refused to play the role of a submissive wife. Soon they were separated, and they were divorced in 1903 so that Shaw could marry another woman. From this unpleasant experience, Nancy bore her first son and also conceived a lifelong aversion to drunkenness.

After the divorce, Nancy, her mother, and a friend visited Europe to lift her spirits. A few months later, Nannie

Langhorne died unexpectedly, and Nancy stayed at Mirador to keep house for her father. Chillie soon saw that this arrangement was not satisfactory; his daughter was miserable, and he and Nancy were temperamentally too alike. In 1904, he sent her and her sister Phyllis to England, where they visited friends and moved freely in society. The following year, accompanied by her father, Nancy met Waldorf Astor, son of William Waldorf Astor, one of the world's wealthiest men. The attraction was mutual, and they were married in May, 1906. The senior Mr. Astor gave the young couple his magnificent country house Cliveden as a wedding present.

Like many wealthy and well-educated men of his day, Waldorf decided to enter politics. In 1910, he was elected Conservative member for Plymouth, beginning an association with that city that would be a part of his and Nancy's political lives for thirty-five years.

In 1914, Nancy reached a spiritual crisis. She had had an extended period of illnesses and found no comfort in either conventional medicine or conventional religion. Her sister Phyllis introduced her to Christian Science. Nancy embraced its tenets with enthusiasm and attempted to convert her family and friends. Her missionary efforts were not entirely successful, but they, along with a military hospital set up at Cliveden during World War I, provided an outlet for her boundless energies.

LIFE'S WORK
In the general election of 1918, women in Great Britain were allowed for the first time to vote and to be elected to Parliament. A number of women stood for election, but all were defeated except a Sinn Féin candidate who refused to take the oath of allegiance.

Death, not the rising feminist movement, decided who would be the first woman in Parliament. In 1916, William Waldorf Astor had been given a peerage, which meant that the younger Waldorf could stay in the House of Commons only as long as his father lived. In October, 1919, First Viscount Astor died. Shortly thereafter, the Plymouth Conservatives approached Nancy Astor, who agreed to stand. She won her first election against two men, with a majority of more than five thousand votes.

Astor's resounding success was not based solely on her husband's reputation and support, although both were important. She was a natural politician, full of confidence. She knew the people of Plymouth, especially the poor among whom she had worked as the wife of a member of Parliament, and they supported her. She had a lively wit and loved to confront hecklers. She was never shy.

On December 1, 1919, Astor was officially introduced to the House of Commons by David Lloyd George and Arthur Balfour. Most of Astor's new colleagues were polite, although some, like Winston Churchill, disapproved of women politicians on principle and Astor in particular. Her bold, direct manners did not change; she was always ready to interrupt or even make personal remarks about another member. Members who took themselves too seriously found this disconcerting.

For two years, Astor was the only woman member, and so it was natural that she pursued women's issues, though not to the exclusion of others. Her first speech was on controlling the sales of drink. In 1923, she was able to put through an act that limited the sale of drink to minors. Particularly prior to the 1930's, she concerned herself with such social issues as widows' pensions, equal guardianship of children, nursery schools, the raising of the school age, naval and dockyard conditions—an interest particularly important to Plymouth—and slum clearances. Nor was her influence limited to Parliament and the various women's groups of which she was a member. As mistress of Cliveden, where she held court not unlike a modern Elizabeth I, Astor was the center of an ever-changing galaxy of European, English, and American politicians, literary figures such as Henry James, T. E. Lawrence, and George Bernard Shaw, family and friends, Christian Scientists, and anyone to whom she happened to take a fancy, particularly Virginians abroad.

Astor had very definite ideas on almost every subject, both foreign and domestic. She believed in an Anglo-American alliance for the improvement of the rest of the world. She inclined to pacifism, believing that one had to accept the existence of dictators, however personally unpleasant they might be. In 1931, she, Waldorf, Shaw, and others visited the Soviet Union, which at the time was a very unusual thing for a Western politician to do. Shaw was sympathetic to the communist system, but Astor terrified the interpreters by boldly asking Joseph Stalin why he had killed so many of his own people. (Stalin's answer, after he ordered a translation of her question, was that many deaths were necessary to establish the communist state.)

Although neither of the Astors came home converted to communism, this trip created bad publicity in Great Britain, particularly for Nancy Astor. Her greatest political mistake, however, was in not recognizing the cruel insanity of Adolf Hitler, whom she never met, before World War II began. Like Neville Chamberlain, she learned too late the impossibility of dealing with a tyran-

nical madman. Her support of appeasement led to numerous accusations that the Astors and their friends, the so-called Cliveden set, were forming a pro-Nazi secret government. Once the conflict began, she would throw herself into war work with her usual energy, but Astor's political star was fading, even as that of her rival, Churchill, was beginning rapidly to rise.

Plymouth was hit by the Blitz in March, 1941, and again in 1943 and 1944, suffering some of the worst air raids of any British city during the war. Waldorf was lord mayor of Plymouth from 1939 to 1944, and much of the time he and Nancy stayed in the city, doing what they could.

Both Nancy and Waldorf were sixty-five in 1944, and the strains of war had affected them deeply, though in different ways. With the war's ending, the British people wanted new leaders and new ideas. The "Cliveden set" myth had never been entirely forgotten. Waldorf was ill with asthma and a heart condition. Nancy's tactlessness had increased, making her enemies both within and without her party. She was becoming a political liability.

Nancy seemed unaware of any difficulties, but Waldorf feared she would lose the next election. He and their children persuaded her not to stand again, but she accepted retirement with obvious reluctance. After twenty-six years, her remarkable political career had come to an abrupt end, and not by her own choice. She blamed Waldorf, and for several years they drifted apart, but they grew closer again as his health declined. He died in September, 1952. Nancy lived another twelve years but without ever finding another vocation. She traveled widely. She attempted an autobiography but abandoned it. Gradually her health failed, and she died peacefully on May 2, 1964, at the age of eighty-four.

SIGNIFICANCE

Astor was a pioneer in British politics and a great host; she was also a phenomenon, an atypical woman who inspired affection or hatred but almost never indifference. Yet she had many of the virtues and faults of her social class: She was honest, determined, and a loyal friend, but also tyrannical, rude, and unrealistic. She was a mass of contradictions. A wealthy woman, she was a spokesperson for the poor; a society figure, she crusaded for temperance; a combative individual, she tried to work for world peace. History has not passed its final judgment on Nancy Astor—perhaps it never will.

—Dorothy Potter

FURTHER READING

Astor, Michael. *Tribal Feeling*. London: John Murray, 1963. Nancy Astor attempted an autobiography in the 1940's but for various reasons abandoned it. Her son Michael remedied this loss in his book of personal recollections, on which later biographers have heavily relied.

Collis, Maurice. *Nancy Astor: An Informal Biography*. New York: E. P. Dutton, 1960. Conceived and written in the late 1950's, this biography has the distinction of being the first written about Astor and also the only one published while she was still alive. There are both advantages and disadvantages in dealing with a living subject. Compared to later works, which have the benefit of time and more material available, it is more flattering and less detailed.

Grigg, John. *Nancy Astor: A Lady Unshamed*. Boston: Little, Brown, 1981. A short, concise, and generally favorable account of Astor's colorful career. Numerous pictures and good documentation of sources.

Harrison, Rosina. *Rose: My Life in Service*. New York: Viking Press, 1975. Harrison was a lady's maid to Astor for thirty-five years, and so her view is unique, though limited. Her account of this mistress-servant relationship adds depth and enlightenment to the often contradictory personality of Astor.

Langhorne, Elizabeth. *Nancy Astor and Her Friends*. New York: Praeger, 1974. The author, who is related to Astor by marriage, concentrates in this work on the Astors' circle of friends, with an emphasis on British politics. Especially useful in describing events leading up to World War II.

Musolf, Karen J. *From Plymouth to Parliament: A Rhetorical History of Nancy Astor's 1919 Campaign.* New York: St. Martin's Press, 1999. A thorough account of Astor's first parliamentary campaign, describing the obstacles she had to overcome, including creating an acceptable persona, attracting women voters, confronting her opponents, and handling hecklers and the press.

Rose, Norman. *The Cliveden Set: Portrait of an Exclusive Fraternity*. London: Jonathan Cape, 2000. An account of the activities of Astor, her husband, and their friends, who exerted considerable influence on British foreign policy. Includes information about the group's alleged pro-Nazism.

Sykes, Christopher. *Nancy: The Life of Lady Astor*. New York: Harper & Row, 1972. Generally acknowledged to be the standard biography of Astor, this comprehensive study deals with an abundance of accounts, letters, and events in a clear and objective style. Covers the subject admirably and with restraint.

Winn, Alice. *Always a Virginian*. Lynchburg, Va.: J. P. Bell, 1975. A series of family reminiscences. Winn's accounts are detailed but episodic, and readers, who unlike the author is not a Langhorne, have to search for dates. Like many family memoirs, however, it is lively and has many vivid descriptions of even small events.

SEE ALSO: Arthur Balfour; Margaret Bondfield; David Lloyd George; Dame Enid Muriel Lyons; Frances Perkins; Jeannette Rankin; Eleanor Roosevelt; Nellie Tayloe Ross; Jeanne Sauvé.

RELATED ARTICLE in *Great Events from History: The Twentieth Century:*

1901-1940: July 2, 1928: Great Britain Lowers the Voting Age for Women.

ATATÜRK
President of Turkey (1923-1938)

Through his skills as a politician, general, and statesman, Atatürk founded the modern state of Turkey in 1923 out of the ashes of the old Ottoman Empire.

BORN: May 19, 1881; Salonika, Ottoman Empire (now Thessaloníki, Greece)
DIED: November 10, 1938; Istanbul, Turkey
ALSO KNOWN AS: Mustafa (birth name); Mustafa Kemal; Mustafa Kemal Atatürk
AREAS OF ACHIEVEMENT: Government and politics, diplomacy, military affairs

EARLY LIFE

Atatürk (AT-a-turk), the founder of Turkey who selected the name Atatürk in 1934, was born in Salonika, a major port in what was then the Ottoman Empire's province of Macedonia (now part of Greece). His parents, Ali Rīza and Zubeyde, had given him the name Mustafa in honor of an older brother who had died in infancy. As Mustafa, Atatürk's early years were marked by his family's declining fortunes. His father lost all his money in a salt venture. When his application for readmission to the civil service was rejected, he took to drinking heavily and died of tuberculosis, leaving behind nothing for Zubeyde and her family. She was forced to sell the house and move to her brother's farm outside Salonika. During his years in the country, Mustafa developed into a strong and muscular young man. Later in life he would suffer from a variety of illnesses, some, in part, brought about by his own problems with alcohol.

By age twelve Mustafa had decided on his future career. Without telling his mother, he convinced a friend's father who was a major in the army to allow him to sit for the entrance exam to the Military Secondary School in Salonika. Even when Mustafa passed the exam, he still needed his mother's written consent, which he received after she had a dream in which she envisioned a brilliant military career for her son. Mustafa proved to be an excellent student. He was so good in mathematics that his instructor began to call him Kemal ("perfection"). During his student days, he realized the importance of understanding cultures other than his own. To that extent he read extensively in European political thought while simultaneously learning French. By the end of his time at the academy, he had started to learn German. Thus Atatürk's intellectual foundation was laid at a time of growing change within the Ottoman Empire.

This intellectual growth also fostered a strong sense of nationalism and a belief that for his nation to survive, it needed to be modernized along European lines. In 1906 (he was now a captain in the army), while stationed in Damascus, Atatürk joined a secret society known as the Fatherland Movement. Two years later, this organization, of which Atatürk was a recognized leader, merged with another nationalistic group called the Young Turks. In 1908 a rebellion broke out against the sultan's rule. The end result was the election of a parliamentary government and the establishment of a constitution. Shortly after the revolt, Atatürk broke with the leadership of the Young Turks, citing that a serving army officer should resign if he wished to participate in politics.

In 1912, Atatürk was sent to Libya during the war between the Ottoman Empire and Italy. The defeat of the Ottoman army, coupled with other military defeats in the Balkans during that same year, caused Atatürk to become highly critical of the government's handling of the conflicts. Despite his comments, Atatürk's growing popularity prevented any public rebuke. In 1913 he was transferred to Sofia, Bulgaria, where he began to see the increasing German influence within the Ottoman state—something that Atatürk feared would draw the nation into a European conflict. In late 1914 this fear became a reality when the Ottoman Empire entered World War I on the side of Germany.

Atatürk's service in the war made him a hero. During the Gallipoli campaign, units under his command helped to repel an Allied attack that threatened to cut the Turkish army in two. From 1916 until the end of the war, he served in a variety of capacities, including commander of a Turkish army in Syria. With the end of the conflict in November, 1918, he returned to Constantinople in time to see the Allied navy arriving—a sign that the fate of his country was now in enemy hands.

LIFE'S WORK

The defeat of the Ottoman Empire in 1918 set the stage for Atatürk's greatest achievement—the creation of the modern Turkish state. While the sultan and his ministers acquiesced to the Allied demands laid out in the armistice, Atatürk remained defiant. As with his earlier attacks against the sultanate, Atatürk's popularity with the people and influence within the army prevented the government from undertaking any retribution. In an attempt to reduce his growing influence, Atatürk was sent to

Anatolia in May, 1919, to supervise the disbanding of the army in that region. Despite attempts to remove him from the center of events in Constantinople, Atatürk used his new assignment to position himself as the de facto leader of the Turkish National Movement emerging in that area. In July the organization met at Erzurum, where they drafted the National Pact. This document called for the right of self-determination for the Turkish people and a pledge to defend the nation's natural boundaries at all costs.

In September a larger meeting was convened at Sivas. The sultan responded to the demands of the Nationalists by allowing a parliamentary election, in which they emerged victorious. Before the newly elected parliament could accomplish anything, however, British forces occupying Constantinople dissolved the body. Under Atatürk's leadership, the Nationalists responded by convening their own Turkish Grand National Assembly in Ankara—the embryonic capital of the new Turkish republic—beginning in April, 1920.

The work of the assembly and the cause of Turkish nationalism were given a further boost by two events in June of 1920. The Treaty of Sevres, which formally ended the conflict between the Ottoman Empire and the Allies, became public knowledge. The document called for a drastic reduction in the size of the Turkish state, placed its finances under foreign control, and proposed that the Bosporus and Dardanelles straits be placed under international control. It was also in June that the Greeks, encouraged by their British allies, launched an invasion of Anatolia. For the next two years, the Turkish armies, under the leadership of Atatürk, fought to free Anatolia from Greek occupation. By August, 1922, the Greeks had been defeated. As Atatürk's armies approached the Dardanelles, Great Britain called for an Allied effort to prevent their reoccupation by the Nationalists. When no other nation voiced its support, the British were forced to enter into negotiations with the victorious Nationalists.

In November the sultan fled, and the sultanate was abolished. In the same month, negotiations for a new peace treaty with the Allies began in Lausanne, Switzerland. In the final document, signed in July, 1923, the Nationalists—now the only political party in Turkey—achieved virtually all their demands as outlined in the National Pact. On October 29, 1923, the Turkish Republic was proclaimed and the capital officially moved to Ankara. Atatürk, now president and head of the nation's only political party, was in the position to focus on his ultimate goal: modernizing Turkey along Western lines.

For Atatürk, Westernization could not occur without first secularizing many traditional Turkish institutions. In early 1924 the caliphate (the religious equivalent of the sultanate) was abolished. Theological schools and the religious courts were also closed. Two years later the Islamic legal system was replaced by a civil code. The traditional fez was outlawed and replaced by Western-style hats. The Gregorian calendar was adopted. In 1928 the Latin alphabet replaced Arabic characters. Six years later Atatürk announced one of his most significant reforms when he granted voting rights to women and allowed them to run for seats in parliament. It was also in 1934 that all Turks were compelled to adopt surnames. Atatürk himself had selected Atatürk (father of the Turks).

The modernization of Turkey extended beyond social and cultural institutions. Economic reforms were adopted. The government invested heavily in industrialization. In 1934 a five-year plan, modeled along Soviet lines, was implemented. Western farming methods and machinery

Atatürk. (Hulton Archive/Getty Images)

were adopted to make crop production more efficient. The government even subsidized certain crops by guaranteeing their prices. In the international field, Atatürk negotiated a series of economic and defensive treaties with neighboring nations—most notably, the Treaty of Angora with Great Britain and Iraq (signed in 1926) and the Balkan Defense Pact with Greece, Romania, and Yugoslavia (signed in 1934)—that assisted in promoting regional security and stability. In 1932 Turkey further committed itself to internationalism by joining the League of Nations.

Atatürk's reforms did not go unopposed. Religious conservatives resisted—without success—attacks against the traditional influence of Islam in society. In 1925 a revolt began in Kurdistan. One year later, members of the Young Turk movement attempted to assassinate Atatürk. The Turkish president used many methods—some quite ruthless—to combat this opposition. To curb any public protests over his policies, Atatürk utilized the Republican People's Party (RPP; founded in 1923) to foster nationalism and a sense of unity. As the only legally recognized party, the RPP also helped suppress all political opposition. The Kurdish revolt was brutally suppressed in April, 1925. The conspirators in the assassination attempt were publicly tried and executed.

The last months of Atatürk's life were dominated by health problems. In March, 1938, a public announcement regarding his illness (cirrhosis of the liver) was made. On the same day that Adolf Hitler and Benito Mussolini met with the prime ministers of France and Great Britain to decide the fate of Czechoslovakia, Atatürk fell into a coma. He recovered for a short time, but on November 10, 1938, he died, ironically, in the sultan's palace in Istanbul. A nation deeply mourned the man known to them as Father Turk.

SIGNIFICANCE

Atatürk's greatest achievement and lasting legacy is the modern Turkish state. His exploits, however, go beyond building a new nation. At a time when Turkey faced invasion and occupation, it was Atatürk who provided the iron-willed leadership to rally the Turkish people at what can arguably be considered their darkest hour. His policies, while challenged by some, not only stabilized the country but also enabled it to begin to compete with Western nations on a more even level. As a man, Atatürk was somewhat of a contradiction. His scandalous private behavior and his seeming disregard for the Islamic faith offended and alienated the conservative religious element. However, the vast majority of his people over-

looked this side, choosing instead to focus on his achievements in the areas of social, economic, and political reform to define a man that to this very day serves as an inspiration for many in Turkey.

—*Charles T. Johnson*

FURTHER READING

Kazancigil, Ali, and Ergun Ozbudun. *Ataturk: Founder of a Modern State*. 1981. Reprint. London: Hurst, 1997. A series of articles by scholars in the field that focus on Atatürk's influence on Turkey's cultural, political, and economic structure. Includes biographical notes on the various authors.

Kinross, Lord Patrick Balfour. *Ataturk: A Biography of Mustafa Kemal, Father of Modern Turkey*. New York: William Morrow, 1964. Provides a detailed discussion of Atatürk's work before the end of World War I, his influence during the Turkish war of independence, and his work as the founder of modern Turkey. Includes maps, pictures, and bibliography.

Mango, Andrew. *Atatürk: The Biography of the Founder of Modern Turkey*. Woodstock, N.Y.: Overlook Press, 2000. Exhaustively researched, balanced, and comprehensive biography, detailing Atatürk's life before the establishment of the Turkish republic. Includes discussion of his efforts to modernize the country.

Palmer, Alan. *Kemal Ataturk*. London: Sphere Books, 1991. A concise and highly readable narrative designed to appeal to general readers. Includes a chronology, maps, and a brief bibliography.

Pettifer, James. *The Turkish Labyrinth: Ataturk and the New Islam*. London: Viking-Penguin, 1997. A detailed study of the influence of Atatürk's reforms on the shaping of the modern Turkish state after his death. Also discusses how these reforms influenced Turkey's relations with its immediate neighbors in Europe and Central Asia. Includes chronology and bibliography.

Sheldon, Garrett War. *Jefferson and Ataturk: Political Philosophies*. New York: P. Lang, 2000. Compares the political theories of the two leaders, pointing out similarities in their ideas and the political climates in which they came to power.

Volkan, Vamik D., and Norman Itzkowitz. *The Immortal Ataturk: A Psychobiography*. 1984. Reprint. Chicago: University of Chicago Press, 1986. Those skeptical of any work subtitled a "psychobiography" should not let that prevent them from reading this insightful and thought-provoking work. This book is unique in that Volkan and Itzkowitz utilize little-known material from the memoirs of many people who worked with and served under Atatürk.

SEE ALSO: Halide Edib Adıvar; Lord Allenby; Enver Paşa; İsmet Paşa; T. E. Lawrence; Eleuthérios Venizélos.

RELATED ARTICLES in *Great Events from History: The Twentieth Century:*
1901-1940: 1911-1912: Italy Annexes Libya; February 19, 1915-January 9, 1916: Gallipoli Campaign Falters; May 19, 1919-September 11, 1922: Greco-Turkish War.

CLEMENT ATTLEE
Prime minister of the United Kingdom (1945-1951)

As prime minister, Attlee led his Labour government as it became a close ally with the United States, granted Indian independence, nationalized major sectors of the economy, established a welfare state, and restructured the postwar economy. With his decisiveness, sound judgment, and managerial abilities, Attlee himself contributed significantly to that success.

BORN: January 3, 1883; London, England
DIED: October 8, 1967; London, England
ALSO KNOWN AS: Clement Richard Attlee (full name)
AREAS OF ACHIEVEMENT: Government and politics, diplomacy, economics

EARLY LIFE

Clement Attlee (AT-lee) was born in Putney, near London. He was reared in a large, late-Victorian, Christian, upper-middle-class family by his father, Henry, an eminent solicitor, and his mother, née Ellen Watson, a sensitive and affectionate woman. Small and ill as a child, Attlee was shy and loved reading. His conventional upper-middle-class education was at public school (Haileybury) and at University College, Oxford, where he took second class honors in modern history. Influenced by his older brother Tom and by the works of Thomas Carlyle, John Ruskin, and William Morris, Attlee developed a social consciousness while working at the Haileybury Club, a boys' club in Stepney, in London's East End slums, and he chose to live nearby. Attlee became its manager from 1907 to 1909 and then served a year as secretary at the famous settlement house Toynbee Hall. His education and personal experience helped him become a tutor and lecturer in the Social Services Department of the new, pioneering London School of Economics from 1913 to 1923. With great empathy and respect for the poor, Attlee decided that self-help projects were not sufficient; society itself must be changed. Attlee thus became a socialist, not from a Marxist or any other

theoretical position, but because of his concern for social justice and social efficiency. A volunteer in World War I, he reached the rank of major and served in Gallipoli, Mesopotamia, and France.

LIFE'S WORK

Returning from the war, Attlee immersed himself in local London Labour Party politics. Already balding at age thirty-six, with a mustache, of medium height and build, his voice weak though crisp, Attlee was physically unimpressive. Yet he was effective because he was trusted. He was experienced in leadership, articulate though not effusive in speech, knowledgeable of local problems, decisive in action, and a conciliator not linked to any personal or policy factions. These characteristics would later propel him to high national office.

An effective manager of the Labour Party's borough elections in Stepney, Attlee became its mayor (1919-1920) and then an alderman (1920-1927). The well-respected, young, and enthusiastic Attlee was soon elected to Parliament in 1922. Even though he moved from Stepney following his marriage to Violet Millar in 1922, his long personal ties to his constituency allowed him to be continually reelected to Parliament, even in 1931, when most other Labour MPs were defeated, thus catapulting him to deputy leader of the party in Parliament. Meanwhile, he had served as parliamentary private secretary (1922-1924) to the party leader, Ramsay MacDonald, and then as a junior minister in the first Labour government (1924) as undersecretary in the War Office. Attlee's appointment to the Simon Commission on India (1927-1930) sparked his interest in India. The commission's work, though, prevented his obtaining office initially in the second Labour government (1929-1931), though he eventually held minor positions including that of postmaster general.

Faced with an international financial crisis and projected escalating governmental deficits, the Labour gov-

Clement Attlee. (Library of Congress)

ernment collapsed in August, 1931. When MacDonald remained as prime minister of the new coalition cabinet, the bitter Labour Party expelled him from membership. Following the sudden October election that decimated Labour's ranks, Attlee emerged as deputy leader. Now considered on the party's left, he worked tirelessly and effectively so that the small Labour contingent in Parliament fulfilled the traditional role of the opposition party, himself having to speak often in Parliament on wide-ranging subjects. Attlee also prevented the parliamentary Labour Party from being dominated by the party's national executive committee or by the Trades Union Congress. While seldom original in his thoughts, he supported currents within Labour advocating that the party never take office again unless it had majority support in Parliament and that in office the party implement socialism: nationalization of some major enterprises, economic planning, and expanded social services.

Chosen leader of the small party in Parliament on the eve of the 1935 general election, Attlee was, surprisingly, reelected leader even after all the other major Labourites returned to Parliament. World War II greatly enhanced his position. He led criticism of Prime Minister

Neville Chamberlain's ineffectiveness in war, decided on the Commons censure debate that toppled Chamberlain, and brought his party into a coalition government under the new prime minister, Winston Churchill. Attlee immediately persuaded Churchill to restructure and improve the governmental machinery and to establish only a small war cabinet, on which Attlee served for its entirety (1940-1945) as lord privy seal (1940-1942) and officially as deputy prime minister (1942-1945). Attlee was a superb team player—and often leader. Besides serving as acting leader of the House of Commons and chairing cabinet meetings during Churchill's absences, Attlee presided over the major domestic policies committee (as lord president of the council, 1943-1945), was responsible for colonial and Pacific theater issues (as dominions secretary, 1942-1943), and influenced planning for postwar Germany. This wide experience as well as his control over Labour Party personnel in the coalition enhanced his status, even though several other Labourites were much better known to the public.

Following Germany's defeat, Labour resigned from the coalition government and new elections were held. Labour won a surprising and massive victory, with 393 seats to the Conservatives' 220 and others' 18. As prime minister, Attlee presided over one of the strongest and most active governments in British history. A financially exhausted Great Britain was faced with major new postwar military obligations in Germany, Greece, southeast Asia, and elsewhere; continuing worldwide colonial concerns; a need for postwar economic recovery; and a commitment to expanded social services, now expected by both the party and the electorate. Attlee's great contribution was to direct his ministry to tackle all those issues almost simultaneously, and many of them successfully.

On international matters, Attlee worked closely with Ernest Bevin, his foreign secretary and now closest political ally. Because they agreed in principle, Attlee usually allowed Bevin great latitude. While anticommunist, they initially expected Great Britain to work with both the United States and the Soviet Union; as the Cold War evolved, they then led Great Britain into a close relationship with the United States and encouraged it to play an active role in Western Europe. Great Britain also received significant American support through an early loan and then Marshall Plan aid. Attlee himself worked well with President Harry S. Truman, whom he met twice in 1945 and again in December, 1950, concerning the Korean War. Attlee also launched Great Britain (without the cabinet's knowledge) into its own nuclear program for civilian and military use when the United

States in 1945 reneged on its wartime agreement of mutual sharing of atomic developments with Great Britain and Canada.

On colonial matters, Attlee allowed a muddled British policy on Palestine, resulting in a United Nations' solution and an Arab-Israeli War that discredited Great Britain in both camps. Attlee personally guided British action on independence for India and Pakistan, however, and he boldly appointed Lord Mountbatten as viceroy to produce the settlement there.

Attlee was strongest in 1945-1946 as his government implemented massive new programs concerning nationalization (of coal, transportation, gas, and electricity), a national health service, a coherent national insurance system of social services, and postwar economic recovery. After Great Britain's difficult year of 1947, Attlee was never quite as effective. The 1950 general election reduced the party's parliamentary majority to five, and Attlee and some other key leaders appeared old, weary, and ill. Attlee did reassert himself in foreign affairs to support the United States in the Korean War and also, on behalf of Western Europe, to temper American actions in Asia while ensuring a strong and mutual Western commitment in Europe.

Attlee called a new election in 1951 and resigned as prime minister following the narrow Conservative victory. He remained as party leader until 1955 (having served twenty years, the longest in Labour history), and he was created Earl Attlee (1955) and made a Knight of the Garter (1956). An elder statesman, he occasionally made reasoned public appeals to the American government during the Cold War era. He lived very modestly in retirement, survived his wife, and died on October 8, 1967.

SIGNIFICANCE

In a 1984 poll of members of the British Politics Group, Attlee was ranked as the fourth most successful British prime minister since 1830 (behind Churchill, William Ewart Gladstone, and Benjamin Disraeli). Attlee's gift was the ability to manage a very talented but often discordant group of Labourites, ensuring that they worked in concert and took action on multifarious pressing issues. Remarkably he led a united party into and out of a war coalition and then into Great Britain's most active peacetime government; this lasted with only brief interruption for twelve years. Moreover, he made a long-term impact on Great Britain's policy-making process through improved cabinet procedures and the restructuring and expanding of the cabinet committee system.

Many other actions of Attlee and his government have had a long-lasting effect on Great Britain, both internally and internationally. The successful transfer of power to India and Pakistan and the creation of a multiracial Commonwealth set a tone for further British decolonization, which, despite some tension and violence, was more successful than for most other European colonial empires.

As the Cold War developed, the Attlee government recognized Great Britain's's inability to pursue its traditional balance-of-power policies and perceived a need for major American commitments to Europe and for significant West European cooperation, as reflected in the Marshall Plan and the North Atlantic Treaty Organization (NATO), which Great Britain helped mold. Favoring European cooperation over integration, however, Attlee and his government steered Great Britain away from the negotiations that led France, West Germany, Italy, and three others eventually to form the European Economic Community, which Great Britain only joined in 1973.

Attlee's initiation of Great Britain as a nuclear power was begun before the United States asserted its strong commitment to Europe in alliance with Great Britain. Since the 1950's, both Great Britain's nuclear arms and its American alliance have become controversial issues within Great Britain, especially within the Labour Party, and have affected Attlee's reputation. After all, Attlee himself helped gain the American public's and congressional support of Great Britain—a socialist Great Britain, at that.

Great Britain also retains the postwar Labour government's domestic pattern of a mixed economy, a welfare state, and modest planning agencies. In the public mind, this is Attlee's greatest legacy. Its supporters praise Attlee for successfully presiding over its establishment, while latter-day Labour advocates of much more extensive socialist programs acclaim his achievement of (for what is to them) a successful first-stage peaceful revolution. It was significant that the prime minister of Labour's first government with a majority in Parliament and with major programs to implement was not a demagogue who polarized Great Britain politically but was the sensible, modest, taciturn, and eminently respectable Clement Attlee.

—Jerry H. Brookshire

FURTHER READING

Attlee, C. R. *As It Happened.* Melbourne, Vic.: William Heinemann, 1954. Drafted while he was prime minister and published while he was still party leader, this autobiography is brief, restrained, and noncontroversial. As such, the book has been much criticized, but it is vintage Attlee.

_____. *The Labour Party in Perspective.* London: Victor Gollancz, 1937. Later republished with a new introduction while prime minister, this general analysis of the party and its programs by its new leader reflects his efforts to unite the party and to demonstrate both its respectability and convictions to Labour supporters and to the entire electorate.

Burridge, Trevor. *Clement Attlee: A Political Biography.* London: Jonathan Cape, 1985. This fine, modest-sized biography is well written and thoroughly researched. It admirably develops Attlee's role in relationship to others within the Labour Party, Parliament, and the war and postwar governments.

Harris, Kenneth. *Attlee.* New York: W. W. Norton, 1983. This very readable biography designed for a knowledgeable public is by an experienced political journalist who incorporated into his sources extensive interviews, including several with the retired Attlee. This official and highly favorable work treats both the public and private Attlee.

Moore, R. J. *Escape from Empire: The Attlee Government and the Indian Problem.* Oxford, England: Clarendon Press, 1983. This is a detailed scholarly reexamination, from the Labour government's perspective, of the transfer of power to India. In this third work of Moore's trilogy on India, Attlee's contribution is discussed throughout, although it is well balanced by an effective recognition of others, most notably Stafford Cripps.

Morgan, Kenneth O. *Labour in Power, 1945-1951.* Oxford, England: Clarendon Press, 1984. A profound and sustained treatment, this work is favorable to Attlee and his governments. It admirably relates the actions of the Attlee governments to the wider British twentieth century political experience.

Pelling, Henry. *The Labour Governments, 1945-51.* New York: St. Martin's Press, 1984. One of the most respected historians of British Labour history here presents a short and forceful work with a sobering reassessment of Attlee's governments—their problems and their achievements. Attlee's positive role is seldom stressed, except for his handling of the cabinet and of India.

Reid, Alastair J., and Henry Pelling. *A Short History of the Labour Party.* New ed. New York: Palgrave Macmillan, 2005. A concise, fluent, and updated survey, this book is often recommended for first reading when beginning a study of the British Labour Party.

Swift, John. *Labour in Crisis: Clement Attlee and the Labour Party in Opposition, 1931-40.* New York: Palgrave, 2001. Outlines the development of Attlee and his Labour Party from the collapse of the second Labour government in 1931 to their entrance into a coalition with Winston Churchill in 1940. Describes how the Labour Party helped win World War I and how Attlee rose from obscurity to become a major figure in Churchill's wartime cabinet.

Williams, Francis. *A Prime Minister Remembers: The War and Post-War Memoirs of the Rt. Hon. Earl Attlee.* London: Heinemann, 1961. Based on extensive recorded interviews with the retired Attlee and on some of his private papers, these reminiscences are more personal, lively, and penetrating than his earlier autobiography. Williams was an experienced Labour journalist and press officer to Attlee while he was prime minister.

SEE ALSO: H. H. Asquith; Stanley Baldwin; Lord Beaverbrook; Ernest Bevin; Louis Botha; Neville Chamberlain; Sir Winston Churchill; Sir Anthony Eden; Charles de Gaulle; Louis Mountbatten; Franklin D. Roosevelt; Joseph Stalin; Harry S. Truman.

RELATED ARTICLES in *Great Events from History: The Twentieth Century:*

1941-1970: July 17-August 2, 1945: Potsdam Conference; July 26, 1945: Labour Party Forms Britain's Majority Government.

MARGARET ATWOOD
Canadian novelist and literary critic

Atwood has become the most prominent Canadian writer of the past several decades. Her novels, beginning with The Handmaid's Tale, *have become international best sellers, and her work as a writer of poetry, fiction, and critical essays is highly regarded by academics. In addition, she has become a strong voice for women, the environment, and for human rights in general.*

BORN: November 18, 1939; Ottawa, Ontario, Canada
ALSO KNOWN AS: Margaret Eleanor Atwood (full name)
AREAS OF ACHIEVEMENT: Literature, women's rights

EARLY LIFE

Margaret Atwood (AT-wood) was born in Ottawa, Ontario, to Carl Edmund Atwood, a zoology professor, and Margaret Dorothy Killam, a dietician and nutritionist. She had a sister, Ruth, who was twelve years younger than her, and a brother, Harold, who was two years older than Margaret; he was for Margaret the more important sibling. As young children, Margaret and Harold spent half of each year in the woods of northern Ontario and Quebec, helping their father collect insects, whose damage to Canadian forests he reported to the government. The remote, primitive living quarters—tents and later a rustic cabin, without electricity, running water, or other amenities—had a profoundly formative effect on Margaret's life, especially in developing a strong voice as an environmentalist. Much of the year Atwood and her brother were home-schooled by their mother, and because the forest camp had no playmates for them, the two children became best friends. They read and played children's games together, regardless of gender differences. Atwood had unconventional role models in a father who shared domestic chores and in a mother who adapted easily to the exigencies of living in the woods, replacing skirts with slacks and acting out her conviction that women could do what men did.

In her later childhood, after her father became a university professor and the family spent more of the year in "civilization," Atwood had to adjust to "socialization." The experience in "the bush," however, had long-term benefits. Until adolescence, Atwood and her brother continued to be best friends and playmates. As she herself claims, both were talented in science and literature, and it might have been she who became the scientist and

her brother the literature professor or writer. When at age sixteen she informed her parents that she wanted to become a writer, they hesitated, not so much because writers generally were men, but because few writers of either gender could support themselves on writing alone. Atwood developed a feminist sensibility, not by reading one of the early writers of the twentieth century women's movement, such as Simone de Beauvoir, but by measuring the constraints on women's aspirations in her society against the model of a mother who was comfortable as a woman doing things outside and beyond what was socially acceptable for a woman to do.

LIFE'S WORK

Although Atwood began to write by the time she was sixteen years old, she became serious about writing while a student at the University of Toronto in the late 1950's. In 1961 she published her first book, *Double Persephone*, for which she received the E. J. Pratt Medal for Poetry. That year she also received a Woodrow Wilson Fellow-

Margaret Atwood. (Courtesy, Vancouver International Writers Festival)

ship and began graduate work at Radcliffe College, where she completed an M.A. in 1962 and continued to work toward a Ph.D. in literature. From 1963 to 1965 she was on leave from Harvard (with which Radcliffe had merged), working in market research in Toronto, teaching at the University of British Columbia, and drafting her first novel, *The Edible Woman* (1969). In 1966 she published her next book, *The Circle Game*, which received the 1967 Governor-General's Award for Poetry. In 1967 her book *The Animals in That Country* won first prize in the Centennial Commission Poetry Competition. Also in 1967, she married James Polk, an American, whom she had met at Harvard. In the next years she continued to teach, first at Sir George Williams University in Montreal and then at the University of Alberta. *The Edible Woman* and two more poetry collections—*The Journals of Susanna Moodie* and *Procedures for Underground*, published by Oxford University Press in 1970—signaled the clear beginning for Atwood of a successful career as a writer.

During the late 1970's and early 1980's Atwood continued to establish herself as a leading Canadian writer, and her success in publishing her writing made it possible for her to discontinue teaching and working for pay altogether. In 1976 another index of her success as a poet was the publication of her *Selected Poems* by Oxford and Simon & Schuster. In 1978, *Two-Headed Poems* and in 1984, *Interlunar* appeared, along with collections of shorter fiction—*Dancing Girls* in 1977, *True Stories* in 1981, and *Bluebeard's Egg* in 1983—but her reputation was most substantially grounded in her novels—*Surfacing* (1972), *Lady Oracle* (1976), *Life Before Man* (1979), and *Bodily Harm* (1981).

Atwood's dystopian and feminist novel *The Handmaid's Tale* (1985) proved to be a quantum leap in her career. In addition to winning the Governor General's Award in 1986, the book, about—among other topics—Christian fundamentalism, fascism, women's subjugation, and women's empowerment, all under a totalitarian state, was the first novel through which much of her later audience came to know her work. In 1990, *The Handmaid's Tale* was adapted for film, with a screenplay by Harold Pinter, and in 2000 the novel was adapted for op-

---

IRIS'S DAYDREAM

The Blind Assassin (2000), Margaret Atwood's Booker Prize-winning novel, is a complex story of two sisters: the reserved Iris and the more emotional Laura. Part of the story is told in the form of a journal, which the eighty-three-year-old Iris writes for her granddaughter, Sabrina, whom Iris has not seen since Sabrina was a child. Iris concludes her journal by describing her dream of seeing Sabrina again.

One evening there will be a knock at the door and it will be you....

You'll knock. I'll hear you, I'll shuffle down the hallway, I'll open the door. My heart will jump and flutter; I'll peer at you, then recognize you: my cherished, my last remaining wish. I'll think to myself that I've never seen anyone so beautiful, but I won't say so; I wouldn't want you to think I've gone scatty....

I'll invite you in. You'll enter. I wouldn't recommend it to a young girl, crossing the threshold of a place like mine, with a person like me inside it—an old woman, an older woman, living alone in a fossilized cottage, with hair like burning spiderwebs and a weedy garden full of God knows what. There's a whiff of brimstone about such creatures: you may even be a little frightened of me. But you'll also be a little reckless, like all the women in our family, and so you will come in anyway. Grandmother, you will say; and through that one word I will no longer be disowned....

What is it that I'll want from you? Not love: that would be too much to ask. Not forgiveness, which isn't yours to bestow. Only a listener, perhaps; only someone who will see me. Don't prettify me though, whatever else you do: I have no wish to be a decorated skull.

But I leave myself in your hands. What choice do I have? By the time you read this last page, that—if anywhere—is the only place I will be.

---

era. When her next novel, *Cat's Eye*, appeared in 1989, its success was significantly enhanced by the large readership Atwood had first gained through the critical and popular success of *The Handmaid's Tale*. Perhaps because the judges regretted having overlooked *The Handmaid's Tale*, *Cat's Eye* was short-listed for the Booker Prize, awarded annually to the best novel published in the United Kingdom and British Commonwealth, which includes Canada.

The Man Booker Prize (as it has been called since 2002 when the Man Group, an investments firm, began to sponsor the award) stands as a monument to Atwood's burgeoning reputation. *The Robber Bride* (1993), the novel that followed *Cat's Eye*, was not short-listed for the prize, but what was listed was Atwood's next novel, *Alias Grace* (1996). Finally she received the prize for *The Blind Assassin* (2000), and some in the Margaret Atwood Society began to anticipate that some October she might receive a telephone call from Stockholm informing her she had won the Nobel Prize for Literature. Although that so-called Crown Jewel has yet to arrive, Atwood has received many prizes too numerous to list, as well as dozens of honorary degrees, notably from Oxford (1998), Cambridge (2001), Harvard (2004), and the Sorbonne (2005). It is worth noting that *Oryx and Crake* (2003), paired by Atwood with *The Handmaid's Tale* as speculative fiction, was short-listed for the Man Booker Prize, recognition perhaps better deserved by the earlier novel in that "pair," and yet a clear indication of international respect for her writing.

In recent years she has published collections of her poetry, such as *Morning in the Burned House* (1995), and books of short fiction, such as *Wilderness Tips* (1991) and *Moral Disorder* (2006), along with books for children, such as *Rude Ramsay and the Roaring Radishes* (2003) and *Bashful Bob and Doleful Dorinda* (2004). In 2005 she published the novel *The Penelopiad: The Myth of Penelope and Odysseus*. She has also published several collections of her essays, ranging from the quirky *Good Bones and Simple Murders* (1994) and *The Tent* (2006) to *Negotiating with the Dead: A Writer on Writing* (2002), based on the Clarendon lectures she gave at Oxford in 1991. Through her public performances in interviews, readings from her work, academic lectures, and talks, Atwood became a leading spokesperson for Canadian culture.

SIGNIFICANCE

When Atwood graduated with a bachelor's degree in English in 1961 from Victoria College, University of Toronto, there was very little Canadian literature. She jokes that she knew virtually all the aspiring young poets in Canada because they could easily fit into a small room. When she began writing, many Canadians who aspired to become writers assumed that the "great, good place" to write was Paris or New York, and certainly not in Canada. Few Canadian presses even published Canadian writing. Atwood and her American husband Polk became deeply involved in a new Canadian press, House of Anansi, established by friend Dennis Lee.

In the 1970's, Atwood was a leader in the nationalist movement to establish a Canadian culture, distinct from the culture of Canada's giant neighbor to the south, whose residents usually thought of Canada as the place "where the cold weather comes from." Through her novels, poetry, short stories, essays, and children's books, Atwood has become one of the best-known and most highly regarded Canadian writers, one who inspired a movement to develop a truly Canadian literature.

—*Earl G. Ingersoll*

FURTHER READING

Cooke, Nathalie. *Margaret Atwood: A Biography*. Toronto, Ont.: ECW Press, 1998. Although, as Cooke indicates, this is not an authorized biography, she had access to Atwood's papers at the University of Toronto, exchanged correspondence with the author over a period of three years, and interviewed family and friends of Atwood.

Howells, Coral Ann, ed. *The Cambridge Companion to Margaret Atwood*. New York: Cambridge University Press, 2006. A selection of essays that examine Atwood's writings on a variety of topics, including female bodies, history, power politics, and home and nation. Looks, also, at Atwood as a Canadian.

Ingersoll, Earl G., ed. *Margaret Atwood: Conversations*. Princeton, N.J.: Ontario Review Press, 1990. These twenty-one interviews were selected from more than one hundred in which Atwood participated from the early 1970's to the late 1980's. Generally, they are literary interviews whose interviewers are academics well-versed in her writing.

_____. *Waltzing Again: New and Selected Conversations with Margaret Atwood*. Princeton, N.J.: Ontario Review Press, 2006. This collection comprises eight conversations from the earlier volume and thirteen more recent interviews. Like the earlier collection, it offers Atwood's views on her life, work, and the contemporary literary scene.

Sullivan, Rosemary. *The Red Shoes: Margaret Atwood Starting Out*. Toronto, Ont.: HarperFlamingo Canada, 1998. As Sullivan herself asserts, this is not a biography in the conventional sense, in part because it focuses on Atwood's early life. Some readers have been disappointed by its reported lack of accuracy.

SEE ALSO: Halide Edib Adıvar; Mavis Gallant; Charlotte Perkins Gilman; Selma Lagerlöf; Halldór Laxness; Kate Millett; Toni Morrison; Alice Munro; Nathalie Sarraute; Alice Walker; Virginia Woolf.

W. H. AUDEN
British poet

During a career that spanned nearly fifty years, Auden produced a vast and varied body of poetry ranging from comic songs and memorable love lyrics to longer poems and poetic sequences that reflected his deep concern for the social, political, and religious conditions of twentieth century life. He also wrote libretti for opera, much of it with his life partner Chester Kallman.

BORN: February 21, 1907; York, England
DIED: September 29, 1973; Vienna, Austria
ALSO KNOWN AS: Wystan Hugh Auden (full name)
AREAS OF ACHIEVEMENT: Literature, music

EARLY LIFE

W. H. Auden (AW-duhn) was born in York, England. His father, George Auden, was a medical doctor whose scholarly interests included psychology, geology, and archaeology. His mother, Constance Bicknell Auden, earned a degree in French and trained as a nurse prior to marriage. Both parents, especially his mother, were devout Anglicans, and Auden grew up in a house where intellectual pursuits and religious devotion were highly prized. As a boy, he developed a fascination for the ruined industrial landscapes and mining machinery that sometimes figure in his work. He imagined growing up to be a mining engineer.

Auden was educated at St. Edmund's School in Surrey (1915-1920) and Gresham's School in Holt (1920-1925). Though interested in science at St. Edmund's, Auden nevertheless became head of the literary society. By the time he left the school, he was fully aware that he was gay, having developed an intense attraction to a member of the school staff. In March, 1922, prompted by a question from a school friend at Gresham's, Auden realized suddenly that his true vocation was to be a poet. At around this time, he began to lose his Christian faith.

During his remaining time at Gresham's, Auden wrote poems modeled on the work of various poetic mentors, ranging from William Wordsworth to Thomas Hardy. At Christ Church, Oxford, where he enrolled initially as a science student, Auden ended up studying English and continued to write poetry, much of it influenced by T. S. Eliot. At Oxford (1925-1928), he published poems in magazines, and in 1928, his friend Stephen Spender privately printed *Poems*, a pamphlet of Auden's early work.

LIFE'S WORK

After taking his degree, Auden lived for a time in Berlin (1929) and then taught at two preparatory schools, Larchfield Academy (1930-1932) and Downs School (1932-1935). The 1930's constitute what some have called the English phase of his career, a time of intense productivity and intellectual experimentation that made him a literary celebrity. He published two influential collections of verse, *Poems* (1930) and *Look Stranger!* (1936) (American edition, *On This Island*, 1937). He also collaborated with his friend Christopher Isherwood on three experimental plays for the Group Theatre, including *The Dog Beneath the Skin* (1935). Auden traveled extensively during this time. A visit to Iceland with poet Louis MacNeice resulted in their joint travel book *Letters from Iceland* (1937). That same year, Auden traveled to Spain to work for the republican cause in the Spanish Civil War, publishing *Spain* (1937), a propaganda poem in pamphlet form. Near the end of the decade, a visit to war-torn China with Isherwood resulted in another collaboration, *Journey to a War* (1939), which includes Auden's highly regarded sonnet sequence, "In Time of War."

W. H. Auden. (© Jill Krementz)

In 1939, Auden moved to the United States to escape the social and artistic confinement he felt in England. He made his living as a freelance writer and as a teacher, taking temporary appointments at various colleges, including Michigan, Swarthmore, Bryn Mawr, Bennington, Barnard, and Mount Holyoke. Most of the time, however, Auden lived and wrote in New York and came to consider himself a New Yorker. Shortly after arriving in the United States, Auden met and fell in love with Chester Kallman, an eighteen-year-old college student from Brooklyn. Though their sexual relationship was short lived, the two remained companions for the rest of their lives, and Auden regarded their relationship as a marriage.

Another major shift at the beginning of the 1940's was Auden's return to Christianity, which transformed his writing. The main poetic work of the ensuing decade was a series of long poems informed by Auden's renewed Christianity and his reading of Protestant theology. These poems appeared in *The Double Man* (1941) (British title, *New Year Letter*), *For the Time Being* (1944), and *The Age of Anxiety* (1947), which won a Pulitzer Prize. Auden's other volumes during the 1940's include *Another Time* (1940) and *The Collected Poetry* (1945).

In 1948, Auden moved again, renting a house on the island of Ischia off the Italian coast. He spent summers on Ischia for nearly a decade, writing poetry there and returning to New York each winter, where he wrote prose as a means of supporting himself. In Italy he began to write a less cerebral, more earthbound poetry, joyously celebrating the here-and-now, as he does in the first poem he wrote in Italy, "In Praise of Limestone." During this period, Auden also began to collaborate with Kallman on opera libretti, the most enduring of which is *The Rake's Progress*, with music by Igor Stravinsky. *The Rake's Progress* was first performed in Venice in 1951. Auden and Kallman later collaborated with the composers Hans Werner Henze and Nicholas Nabokov.

In the middle of his Italian decade, Auden was elected Professor of Poetry at Oxford University, an honor that required him to deliver a series of lectures, which later were published in his prose volume *The Dyer's Hand* (1962). Important new books of poetry during this decade were *Nones* (1951) and *The Shield of Achilles* (1955), which contains the major poetic sequence "Horae Canonicae."

Auden left Italy in 1958 and moved to Kirchstetten, an Austrian village, where he purchased a modest farmhouse. For the rest of his life, Auden summered in Aus-

tria, settling into a domestic routine as a citizen of the village and traveling to nearby Vienna with Kallman to attend operas. During this phase of his life, Auden continued to write prolifically, producing poetry, prose, and (with Kallman) libretti. His best collections from the Austrian years are generally thought to be *About the House* (1965), which includes a series of poems about his beloved farmhouse, and *City Without Walls* (1969).

In 1972, increasingly ill and lonely, Auden decided to leave New York for good and spend winters at Christ Church, Oxford, which had offered him a residence. His return to England was disappointing, for he found Oxford changed, the atmosphere no longer congenial. He spent the next summer in Austria, as usual. On the way back to England in the autumn, he stopped overnight in Vienna to give a poetry reading. He died of a heart attack in his hotel bed early the next morning, September 29, 1973, and was buried five days later in Kirchstetten. A memorial stone was installed in London's Westminster Abbey the following year.

SIGNIFICANCE

Auden is generally recognized as one of the most important poets of the twentieth century. Unlike many poets of the time, he addressed public, civic concerns. In the 1930's many regarded him as a spokesperson for a new generation, a diagnostician of social and political ills. In the 1940's, he continued to speak, sometimes as a critic, sometimes as a healer, in an era that he himself famously dubbed "the age of anxiety." In the last twenty years of his life, he became in some sense a Cold War poet, his work addressing the challenges of living a humane, ethical life in an increasingly hostile world.

While notably a public poet, Auden also wrote intensely personal lyrics and songs, which transcend the time in which they were written. He wrote movingly about love, death, friendship, and other great themes of lyric poetry, often using traditional verse forms. In 1994, *Tell Me the Truth About Love*, a pamphlet containing several of his love poems from the 1930's, became a surprise best seller, confirming his stature as a poet whose work is both timely and timeless.

—*Michael Hennessy*

FURTHER READING

Auden, W. H. *Collected Poems*. Edited by Edward Mendelson. New York: Modern Library, 2007. Contains authorized versions of all the poems Auden wished to preserve. Useful appendixes give variant titles and titles of poems excluded from this edition.

_____. *The Dyer's Hand*. New York: Vintage, 1990. Selected prose writings about art, literature, music, and contemporary life, including the lectures Auden delivered as Oxford professor of poetry.

_____. *The English Auden: Poems, Essays, and Dramatic Writings, 1927-1939*. Edited by Edward Mendelson. New York: Random House, 1977. Selection of early work, most of it first published prior to Auden's departure for the United States.

_____. *Selected Poems*. Edited by Edward Mendelson. Expanded ed. New York: Vintage, 2007. Poems from every phase of Auden's career, including work omitted from *Collected Poems*. Reprints original versions of poems later revised by Auden.

Carpenter, Humphrey. *W. H. Auden: A Biography*. Boston: Houghton Mifflin, 1981. Detailed biography that draws on recollections of those who knew Auden personally and on letters and manuscripts previously unavailable to the reading public.

Davenport-Hines, Richard. *Auden*. New York: Pantheon, 1995. Comprehensive biography that gives greater attention to Auden's poetry than does Carpenter.

Fuller, John. *W. H. Auden: A Commentary*. Princeton, N.J.: Princeton University Press, 1998. Detailed annotations and interpretations of Auden's poems, plays, and libretti. Organized chronologically, with a comprehensive general index and index of titles and first lines.

Mendelson, Edward. *Early Auden*. New York: Viking, 1981. History and interpretation of Auden's work from 1927 to his departure for the United States in 1939.

_____. *Later Auden*. New York: Farrar, Straus and Giroux, 1999. Continuation of *Early Auden*, tracing Auden's development as a thinker and poet from 1939 to his death in 1973.

SEE ALSO: Benjamin Britten; Jean Cocteau; Hart Crane; E. E. Cummings; T. S. Eliot; Langston Hughes; Igor Stravinsky.

RELATED ARTICLES in *Great Events from History: The Twentieth Century:*

1901-1940: 1911-1923: Rilke's *Duino Elegies* Redefines Poetics; September, 1930: Auden's Poems Speak for a Generation.

1941-1970: February 20, 1949: Pound Wins the Bollingen Prize; September 11, 1951: Stravinsky's *The Rake's Progress* Premieres in Venice.

AUNG SAN SUU KYI
Burmese political activist

Suu Kyi, through nonviolent activism and peaceful resistance, advocated on behalf of the Burmese people against military rule in Burma, called Myanmar by the regime. She endured house arrest—a form of imprisonment—and separation from her family. She earned the Nobel Peace Prize in 1991, one of many awards recognizing her passion for and commitment to human rights.

BORN: June 19, 1945; Rangoon, Burma (now Yangon, Myanmar)

AREAS OF ACHIEVEMENT: Government and politics, social reform, civil rights, peace advocacy

EARLY LIFE

Aung San Suu Kyi (awng san soo chee) was two years old when her father, General Aung San, died at the hands of assassins. He had led the Anti-Fascist People's Freedom League, supported democracy, and helped Burma (now Myanmar) struggle against those illegally in power.

Suu Kyi's mother, Khin Kyi, arranged monthly memorial services to keep Aung San's memory alive. Khin served Burma by assuming her late husband's seat in parliament, pursuing nursing, and opening her home to nursing students of all nationalities. When Suu Kyi's nine-year-old brother Aung San Lin drowned in a local pond in 1953, Suu Kyi's grief-stricken mother finished her workday before returning home to join family and to view his dead body. Suu Kyi learned that duty and others come first.

Suu Kyi accompanied her mother to New Delhi, where she served as ambassador to India (1960). After attending high school at the Convent of Jesus and Mary, Suu Kyi entered Delhi University. She studied the teachings of Mahatma Gandhi, a martyr who often used voluntary starvation—a peaceful practice that affected only himself directly—to show determination and conviction.

While attending St. Hugh's College in Oxford (1964-1967), Suu Kyi met British student Michael Aris, a Tibetan studies major. Suu Kyi traveled in the summers to Africa, Spain, and Algiers, where she helped build homes for widows of Algerian soldiers. After graduation, she worked as assistant secretariat to the Advisory Committee on Administration and Budgetary Questions at the United Nations (1969-1971) and volunteered at Bellevue Hospital.

Suu Kyi corresponded with Aris in Bhutan, explained her obligations to the Burmese people, and asked that he help her fulfill these obligations, if necessary. They married in London on January 1, 1972, and traveled to Japan and India. While Aris tutored the royal family in Bhutan and headed the government's translation department, Suu Kyi was the research officer on United Nations Affairs for the Bhutan foreign ministry.

Suu Kyi and Aris had two children, Alexander, born in 1973, and Kim, born in 1977, both in England, where Michael was working on Tibetan and Himalayan studies at Oxford University. Suu Kyi cataloged Burmese books in the Bodleian Library at Oxford and cared for the family.

LIFE'S WORK

By 1985, Suu Kyi was a researcher in Japan, bringing her son Kim with her. Her husband and son Alexander went to the Indian Institute of Advanced Studies in Simla for Michael's fellowship. The four reunited after Suu Kyi completed her research, which was published as *Aung San* (1984), *Let's Visit Burma* (1985), *Let's Visit Nepal* (1985), and *Let's Visit Bhutan* (1985). Michael, still an Oxford scholar, wrote on the Himalayas and Tibet.

A graduate student at London University's School of Oriental and Asian Studies, Suu Kyi returned to Burma when her mother suffered a stroke (March 31, 1988). In Burma she found violence and death and the Burma Socialist Programme Party (BSPP) in power. Suu Kyi wrote to the BSPP and urged peace, delivering her first political speech on August 26, with her sons and husband in attendance. Later that year, Suu Kyi became secretary of the newly formed National League for Democracy (NLD). She counseled, advised, urged nonviolence, and publicized Burma's concerns.

The State Law and Order Restoration Council (SLORC), now called the State Peace and Development Council, or SPDC, soon assumed power, opposing the NLD and changing Burma's official name to "Myanmar." The Burmese people were powerless, even when the SLORC agreed to a 1989 election. Suu Kyi organized her opposition to the SLORC with secret videotapes and short-wave broadcasts. She wore a jacket and hat combination that was to become a fashion statement and a sym-

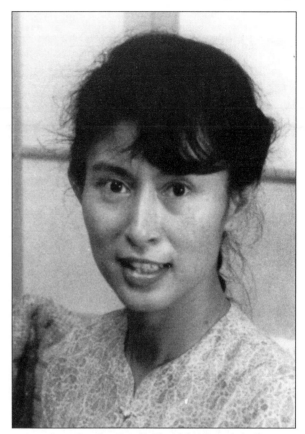

Aung San Suu Kyi. (© The Nobel Foundation)

bol for the NLD. On April 5, 1989, Suu Kyi led a group of NLD members on a march down a city street; six soldiers kneeled and aimed rifles at her, yet she continued to walk calmly. It did not take long for her legend to spread.

Results of the May, 1989, election showed that the NLD had won most of the open government seats, but the SLORC ignored the returns. They made illegal all newspapers—except one—permitted the detention of "criminals" up to three years without trial or charges, and placed Suu Kyi under house arrest on July 20. Suu Kyi's sons were with her. Her calmness and imprisonment became world news. Her husband, in Scotland for his father's funeral, found her in the third day of her hunger strike to demand humane treatment for NLD members.

When the SLORC promised fair treatment for the NLD, Suu Kyi stopped fasting. She had lost twelve pounds in twelve days and had to receive nourishment intravenously. She remained a political prisoner, but the SLORC allowed her to correspond with her family, which at this time was in England. The SLORC finally

A DATED BURMESE PROVERB

In 1995, the Burmese government released Aung San Suu Kyi, human rights activist and recipient of the 1991 Nobel Peace Prize, after almost six years of house arrest. On August 31, 1995, she delivered a videotaped address to the NGO Forum on Women in Beijing, China.

There is an outmoded Burmese proverb still recited by men who wish to deny that women too can play a part in bringing necessary change and progress to their society: "The dawn rises only when the rooster crows." But Burmese people today are well aware of the scientific reasons behind the rising of dawn and the falling of dusk. And the intelligent rooster surely realizes that it is because dawn comes that it crows and not the other way round. It crows to welcome the light that has come to relieve the darkness of night. It is not the prerogative of men alone to bring light to this world: women with their capacity for compassion and self-sacrifice, their courage and perseverance, have done much to dissipate the darkness of intolerance and hate, suffering and despair. . . .

The last six years afforded me much time and food for thought. I came to the conclusion that the human race is not divided into two opposing camps of good and evil. It is made up of those who are capable of learning and those who are incapable of doing so. Here I am not talking of learning in the narrow sense of acquiring an academic education, but of learning as the process of absorbing those lessons of life that enable us to increase peace and happiness in our world. Women in their role as mothers have traditionally assumed the responsibility of teaching children values that will guide them throughout their lives. It is time we were given the full opportunity to use our natural teaching skills to contribute towards building a modern world that can withstand the tremendous challenges of the technological revolution which has in turn brought revolutionary changes in social values.

come is the money she has in a bank account from publishing *Freedom from Fear* (1995).

The SLORC had denied Suu Kyi most visitors. It refused Michael's visits even after he developed prostate cancer. (Michael died on March 27, 1999.) He had last seen Suu Kyi in 1995. After her husband's death, Suu Kyi continued to urge help not for herself but for her people, who continued to suffer under the SLORC. Global attention to Suu Kyi's cause has included that of musicians such as Eric Clapton, Paul McCartney, U2, the Indigo Girls, R.E.M., and Pearl Jam, who launched the album *For the Lady* on October 26, 2004. Profits from the sale of the album go to the United States Campaign for Burma (USCB). Predictably, Myanmar banned the album and even established a law against singing "freedom songs." Those found in violation of this law received a seven-year prison term.

Suu Kyi's imprisonment began in 1989. Although she was offered her freedom if she left Myanmar, she chose to remain in her country and has endured—with dignity—house arrest as a symbol of peace and determination to her people. The world has recognized her sacrifices for peace, awarding her more than twenty-five peace and humanitarian prizes, including the Nobel Peace Prize. She remains true to her priorities of nonviolence, democracy, and freedom.

—Anita Price Davis

allowed her husband—but not her boys—to visit; his luggage was full of food for Suu Kyi. Malnourished, Suu Kyi had thin hair, poor vision, spinal degeneration, a weight sometimes below 100 pounds, and heart and breathing problems. When he left, Michael took with him Suu Kyi's writings, composed during her captivity.

SIGNIFICANCE

The world has recognized Suu Kyi's sacrifices. By 1991, she had earned the Rafto Prize (for her work promoting human rights), the European parliament's Sakharov Prize for Freedom of Thought, seventeen other humanitarian awards, and the Nobel Peace Prize. The Nobel committee acknowledged Suu Kyi as a model of human determination and bravery. Her family continues to accept her awards because Suu Kyi fears that the SLORC would deny her return if she left Myanmar. All prize money goes to the people of Myanmar, and Suu Kyi's only in-

FURTHER READING

Abrams, Irwin. *Nobel Lectures, Peace 1991-1995*. Singapore: World Scientific, 1999. This volume contains Alexander Aris's acceptance speech on behalf of his mother, who received the Nobel Peace Prize in 1991. He spoke of his mother's dedication, sacrifice, and plight, and reminded the audience that his mother's quest is spiritual.

Aung San Suu Kyi. *Freedom from Fear, and Other Writings*. New York: Penguin Books, 1995. In 1995 the Myanmar government allowed Suu Kyi to leave her home temporarily. Includes a foreword by Anglican archbishop Desmond Tutu.

Davis, Anita Price, and Marla Selvidge. *Women Nobel Peace Prize Winners*. Jefferson, N.C.: McFarland, 2006. Main features of the essay on Suu Kyi include her portrait, quotations from Michael Aris, an overview of politics in Myanmar, and a complete biography of Suu Kyi. This volume also features a biography of every female Nobel Peace Prize recipient, through 2005.

Ling, Bettina. *Aung San Suu Kyi: Standing for Democracy in Burma*. New York: Feminist Press at the City University of New York, 1999. A biography of Suu Kyi that traces her political activism in the face of adversity and antidemocracy in Myanmar/Burma. Written especially for younger readers.

Wintle, Justin. *The Perfect Hostage: A Life of Aung San Suu Kyi*. London: Hutchinson, 2007. An academic biography of Suu Kyi, for advanced readers. Recom-

mended for its accuracy but, as one reviewer noted, short on accurate details.

SEE ALSO: Jean-Bertrand Aristide; Benazir Bhutto; Indira Gandhi; Mahatma Gandhi; Le Ly Hayslip; Martin Luther King, Jr.; Albert Lutuli; Nelson Mandela; Andrei Sakharov; Mother Teresa; U Thant.

RELATED ARTICLES in *Great Events from History: The Twentieth Century:*

1901-1940: April 1, 1937: Britain Separates Burma from India.

1971-2000: August 8, 1988: Auspicious Day of 8/8/88 Turns Deadly in Rangoon.

SRI AUROBINDO
Indian religious leader and philosopher

Aurobindo was one of the leading politicians and great religious thinkers in twentieth century India. He was a leader of the first national political party with a platform demanding the independence of India from British rule. His writings and actions helped to revitalize India politically and spiritually.

BORN: August 15, 1872; Calcutta, India
DIED: December 5, 1950; Pondicherry, India
ALSO KNOWN AS: Aurobindo Ghose (birth name)
AREAS OF ACHIEVEMENT: Government and politics, religion and theology, philosophy

EARLY LIFE

Sri Aurobindo (shree ar-oh-BIHN-doh) was the son of Krishna Dhan Ghose, a respected physician who, after his preliminary degree, went to England for further study. Ghose returned the year before Aurobindo was born with not only a secondary degree but also a love of England and an atheistic bent. In 1879, Aurobindo was taken with his two elder brothers to be educated in England. Ghose arranged for them to board with the Drewetts, cousins of an English friend. He asked that the boys be given an English education without any contact with Indian or Eastern culture. Mrs. Drewett, a devout Christian, went a step further and did her best to convert them. Aurobindo remained in England for fourteen years, supported at first by Ghose, then through scholarships.

Aurobindo was first taught by the Drewetts. In 1884, he was able to be enrolled in St. Paul's School in London.

A prize student, Aurobindo in 1890 went to King's College at the University of Cambridge with a senior classical scholarship. In the same year, he passed the open competition for preparation for the Indian Civil Service. He scored record marks in Greek and Latin. Praised for his scholarship in those languages, Aurobindo was also fluent in French. In addition, he taught himself enough German and Italian that he could study Goethe and Dante in their native tongues. He also wrote poetry, an avocation that would lead to some published work. Other than poetry, Aurobindo's only extracurricular activities were general reading and membership in the Indian Majlis, an association of Indian students at Cambridge. It was in this association that Aurobindo first expressed his desire for Indian independence.

In 1892, Aurobindo passed the classical tripos examination in the first division. He did not, though, apply for his B.A. degree. He also completed the required studies for the Indian Civil Service but failed to pass the riding exam. It was suggested that his failure was the result of his inability to stay on the horse, but Aurobindo claimed to have failed expressly by not presenting himself at the test. His reason for doing so was his distaste for an administrative career. It happened that a representative of the Maharaja of Baroda was visiting London. He was petitioned by friends of Aurobindo, and Aurobindo was offered an appointment in the Baroda service. He left for India in 1893.

Aurobindo began with secretariat work for the maharaja, moved on to a professorship in English, and culminated his career in the service as vice principal of the Baroda College. By the time he had left Baroda, Aurobindo had learned Sanskrit and several modern Indian languages, and he had begun to practice yoga.

LIFE'S WORK

At the time of Aurobindo's return to India, the Indian Congress, presided over by moderates, was satisfied with the current state of affairs. At best they would petition the colonial government with suggestions. Dissatisfied with the effect they were having conditions in India, Aurobindo began political activities in 1902. Prevented from public activity while in the Baroda service, he established contacts during his leaves. His original intent was to establish an armed revolutionary movement that would, if necessary, oust the English. Toward this end he helped organize groups of young men who would acquire military training.

In 1905, with the unrest caused by the Bengal partition, Aurobindo participated openly in the political scene. He took a year's leave without pay and then, at the end of the year, resigned from the Baroda service. In his politi-

Sri Aurobindo. (Library of Congress)

cal work he met other Indians desiring Indian independence. Most notable among these was Bal Gangadhar Tilak. Eventually, with Tilak and others, Aurobindo formed the Nationalist Party. With Tilak as their leader, they overtook the congress with their demand for *swadeshi*, or India's liberty. Content to remain behind the scenes, Aurobindo concentrated on propaganda. He helped edit the revolutionary paper *Bande Matarum*, which called for a general boycott of English products, an educational system by and for Indians, noncooperation with the English government, and establishment of a parallel Indian government.

Aurobindo eventually moved into the limelight, which resulted in several arrests. Finally, in 1908, he was imprisoned for a year while on trial for sedition. Though acquitted, his and the other leaders' arrests effectively disrupted their movement. On his release, Aurobindo found the party organization in disarray. He tried to reorganize but had limited success. In 1910, responding to a spiritual call, Aurobindo retired from political life and went to the French Indian enclave, Pondicherry.

Aurobindo's spiritual life had a gradual growth that was marked by a few specific events. Contrary to the usual method of following a guru, Aurobindo practiced by himself, calling on masters only when he believed that he needed help. He began his practice in 1904. In 1908, feeling stifled, he consulted the guru Vishnu Lele. Following Lele's instructions, after three days of meditation Aurobindo achieved complete silence of the mind, or Nirvana.

The next event that marked Aurobindo's development occurred when he was incarcerated. He spent most of his time reading the *Bhagavad Gita* and the *Upanishads*, and meditating. The realization came to him of spiritual planes above the conscious mind and of the divinity in all levels of existence. It was at this time that the germ for the work that would consume the rest of his life took seed. It was not until 1910 that Aurobindo was told by an inner voice that he was to go to Pondicherry. In Pondicherry, Aurobindo began his work in earnest. His purpose was to cause the manifestation of the divine, via the supermind, into the lower levels of existence, and thus move humankind toward its ultimate evolutionary goal. Aurobindo did not, though, remove himself from the world. He received visitors, continued his reading, and corresponded with disciples and friends.

In 1914, Aurobindo met Paul Richard and Mira Richard. Paul persuaded Aurobindo to write a monthly periodical that would put forth his thinking. This became the *Arya* (1916-1921). In it, some of Aurobindo's major works, *The Life Divine* (1914-1919), *The Synthesis of Yoga* (1915), and *The Human Cycle* (1916-1918), appeared serially. They were later published in book form. Mira Richard came to be Aurobindo's main disciple, then his spiritual partner. She left Pondicherry with Paul in 1915 but returned to stay in 1920. When Aurobindo and Mira met, Mira found the spiritual leader to whom she had been introduced psychically as a youth. She came to be known as the "Mother" and eventually took over the management of Aurobindo's household.

With more time to concentrate on his spiritual task, Aurobindo succeeded in penetrating the veil between the upper and lower planes of consciousness. On November 24, 1926, he accomplished the descent of what he termed the "Overmind." All that remained was for him to bring the final plane via the "Supermind" into the physical, and thus divinize, or transform, life on this plane. That India's independence came on his birthday was significant to Aurobindo: He saw it as an affirmation of his efforts.

Aurobindo, with his task not yet complete, died on December 5, 1950, in Pondicherry. His passing, though, was not like that of the average person; witnessed by outside observers, among whom were doctors, his body remained without decomposition for five days. The Mother announced that Aurobindo had come to her and explained his *mahasamadhi*, or the leaving of his body. Humanity was not ready for the descent of the Supermind because Aurobindo had found too much resistance on this plane. He explained that he would return by manifesting himself in the first person who achieved the Supermind in the physical.

SIGNIFICANCE

Aurobindo was a spiritual man driven to serve others. His success in education was largely for the satisfaction of his father. Involvement in politics was his attempt to serve his fellow Indian. He saw that for India to thrive spiritually and physically, Indians would have to throw off the yoke of the English. Aurobindo's retirement was in part the effect of a shift of focus. He no longer saw life in national terms, but universal. The development of what he saw was needed by India for true change was needed by all humankind.

Aurobindo helped organize a movement that ignited a fire in Indians and that led eventually to their independence. His spiritualism has been the subject of many religious and philosophical writings and a few international symposiums. His ashram, or commune, continued to grow after his death, and in 1968 Auroville was founded.

—*Shawn Hirabayashi*

FURTHER READING

Bolle, Kees W. *The Persistence of Religion*. Leiden, the Netherlands: E. J. Brill, 1965. A study of Tantrism as a vehicle to examine India's religious history, with a chapter of its manifestation in Aurobindo's philosophy. It offers a different perspective of Aurobindo's work in an objective style.

Bruteau, Beatrice. *Worthy Is the World: The Hindu Philosophy of Sri Aurobindo*. Rutherford, N.J.: Fairleigh Dickinson University Press, 1971. A good introduction to Aurobindo's philosophy. Contains an interesting biography of Aurobindo's spiritual life and a good bibliography.

Ghose, Sri Aurobindo. *The Future Evolution of Man*. Compiled by P. B. Saint-Hilaire. Wheaton, Ill.: Theosophical Publishing House, 1974. A compilation of quotations from Aurobindo's three major works, *The Life Divine*, *The Human Cycle*, and *The Synthesis of Yoga*. A good introduction to and summary of his works. Includes a bibliography of other Aurobindo works, with explanatory notes.

_____. *Sri Aurobindo: A Life Sketch*. Calcutta: Arya, 1937. Aurobindo's biography told in his own words in the third person. A brief overview of his life up to his days in Pondicherry.

Kluback, William. *Sri Aurobindo Ghose: The Dweller in the Lands of Silence*. Edited by Michael Finkentahl. New York: P. Lang, 2001. An overview of Aurobindo's ideas, focusing on the universality of his thinking.

Purani, A. B. *The Life of Sri Aurobindo*. 3d ed. Pondicherry, India: Sri Aurobindo Ashram, 1964. Despite its complicated organization and a devoted view, this work is perhaps the most authoritative biography of Aurobindo. It has excellent documentation of Aurobindo's early life and is filled with quotations from Aurobindo.

Radhakrishnan, Sarvepalli, and Charles Moore, eds. *A Sourcebook in Indian Philosophy*. Princeton, N.J.: Princeton University Press, 1957. A good introduction to Indian philosophy, including Aurobindo's contemporaries. It offers insight into Aurobindo's philosophy by way of contrast.

Sethna, K. D. *The Vision and Work of Sri Aurobindo*. Pondicherry, India: Sri Aurobindo Ashram, 1968. The first three chapters, in which Sethna debates with a Western philosopher via correspondence, offer a good, clear explication of Aurobindo's philosophy. In later chapters there is a tendency toward proselytism.

Zaehner, R. C. *Evolution in Religion*. Oxford, England:

Clarendon Press, 1971. An interesting study comparing Aurobindo and Pierre Teilhard de Chardin, a Jesuit monk. Both of the twentieth century, although they did not know of each other and had little respect for each other's religion, they are nevertheless interestingly compared. Offers a different perspective on Aurobindo's philosophy.

SEE ALSO: Indira Gandhi; Mahatma Gandhi; Mohammed Ali Jinnah; Sarojini Naidu; Jawaharlal Nehru;

Vijaya Lakshmi Pandit; Pierre Teilhard de Chardin; Mother Teresa; Bal Gangadhar Tilak.

RELATED ARTICLES in *Great Events from History: The Twentieth Century:*
1901-1940: March 12-April 5, 1930: Gandhi Leads the Salt March; March 5, 1931: India Signs the Delhi Pact.
1941-1970: August 15, 1947: India Gains Independence from the United Kingdom; January 30, 1948: Gandhi Is Assassinated.

NNAMDI AZIKIWE
President of Nigeria (1963-1966)

Azikiwe founded modern Nigerian nationalism and was the leader of Nigeria's independence struggle. He became the first president of the Republic of Nigeria in 1963 and retained that position until ousted during a 1966 coup. He also founded the University of Nigeria at Nsukka and was its first chancellor.

BORN: November 16, 1904; Zungeru, Nigeria
DIED: May 11, 1996; Enugu, Nigeria
ALSO KNOWN AS: Benjamin Azikiwe (birth name); Zik (nickname)
AREAS OF ACHIEVEMENT: Government and politics, education

EARLY LIFE

Nnamdi Azikiwe (n-DAH-may ah-zee-KEE-way) was an Ibo who was born in Northern Nigeria and spoke fluent Hausa, the Northern trade language. Fluency in Hausa helped him become a national leader later in life. Azikiwe was educated at the Church Missionary Society's Central School at Onitsha, the Hope Waddell Training Institute in Calabar, and the Methodist Boys' High School in Lagos. While in high school, he read the work of Marcus Garvey. At age sixteen he vowed to redeem Africa. That same year, Kwegyir Aggrey spoke at his school and told the students. "Nothing but the best is good enough for Africa." Since both of Azikiwe's heroes, Garvey and Aggrey, were based in the United States, Azikiwe was determined to go there, acquire an education, and return to uplift Nigeria.

Zik, as he was known to his classmates, was graduated at the head of his high school class in 1925. Without money or backers, he decided to stow away on a ship to get to the United States. He reached Ghana before this

plan collapsed. He trained for the police force in Ghana, but his parents asked that he return to Nigeria, and he obeyed. Azikiwe's father opposed his plan to study in the United States but changed his mind when he himself was insulted by a young white clerk who called Azikiwe's father an "uneducated black ape." Azikiwe's father decided that only education would ensure respect for Africans, so he decided to help his son further his education by giving him six hundred dollars.

Once in the United States, Azikiwe was helped by sympathetic Americans. He also earned money from menial jobs to help pay for his education. He remembered reading about Abraham Lincoln and James Garfield working their way up from log cabins to the White House through sacrifice, hard work, and determination. He spent every spare hour reading or playing sports. Azikiwe's first two years of study at Howard University were under American diplomat and future Nobel Peace Prize winner Ralph Bunche. Bunche said that Azikiwe had remarkable mental ability, integrity, courage, industry, and promise. In 1929, Azikiwe attended Lincoln University in Pennsylvania, earning his B.A. by 1930. Azikiwe served as a graduate instructor at Lincoln for two years while enrolled in Columbia University's School of Journalism. Within two years, he had earned an M.A. in political science from Lincoln University, a certificate in journalism from Columbia University, and an M.A. in anthropology from the University of Pennsylvania.

While in the United States, Azikiwe gained journalistic experience writing for the *Baltimore Afro-American*, the *Philadelphia Tribune*, and the *Associated Negro Press* in Chicago. He was awarded two honorary doctorates, a doctorate of literature from Lincoln and an L.L.D. from Howard University.

LIFE'S WORK

In 1934, Azikiwe returned to Africa and became the editor in chief of a Ghanian newspaper, the *African Morning Post*. Colonial authorities found one of his articles seditious, and he was charged, convicted, then later acquitted on appeal. In 1937, he returned to Nigeria. He fought against colonial rule and founded the *West African Pilot* and four other newspapers in a chain controlled by Zik Enterprises Limited. His businesses were soon worth more than two million dollars. He used this network of newspapers to agitate for change. In his editorials he argued for one-person, one-vote, direct elections, African control of the civil service, and the Nigerianization of the armed forces. With Herbert Macaulay, he founded the National Convention of Nigeria and the Cameroons, or NCNC, in 1942. His papers spread his radical political ideals to every corner of Nigeria and helped increase the membership of the NCNC. The NCNC embraced all Nigerian tribes and was national in scope. It fought for the working class and for self-rule. Azikiwe by this time was the undisputed leader of the Ibo and a prominent national leader.

In the teeth of sustained agitation spearheaded by Azikiwe as president of the NCNC, Great Britain decided to grant Nigeria self-rule in 1951. In the subsequent elections, Azikiwe was elected to represent Lagos. The Yoruba-dominated Action Group, under Chief Obafemi Awolowo, won control of the legislature in the Western Region, where Lagos was located. Azikiwe became leader of the opposition, but the Action Group blocked his election to the federal assembly. Bitter rivalry began between the Ibo-controlled NCNC and the Yoruba-controlled Action Group Party. Ethnic conflicts ultimately led to bloody civil war and caused the deaths of more than one and a half million people, many of whom were children.

The NCNC controlled the Eastern Region. The British accused Azikiwe of withdrawing $5.6 million in government funds and putting this money in his own African Continental Bank to save it from collapse. He was tried and found guilty of improper conduct. Azikiwe argued that this was merely a trick to postpone independence. Nigeria's rank and file, as well as the masses, viewed Azikiwe as their redeemer. Thus, he was able to survive the crisis and disband the Regional Legislature without difficulty. He called elections, and he and the NCNC were swept into power. He resigned from the Western Legislature and became the premier of Eastern Nigeria until the 1959 preindependence elections for the federal government were called. None of the major parties contesting this election won a decisive majority. Three parties contested the 1959 elections—the Northern Peoples Congress, the NCNC, and the Action Group. The Northern Peoples Congress won more seats than any other party, followed by the NCNC. These two parties decided to form a coalition government. The Action Group formed the opposition.

Azikiwe was appointed governor-general of Nigeria and Deputy Leader of the National Peoples Congress. Abubakar Tafawa Balewa became the prime minister. Although Azikiwe often used the threat of communism to speed up independence, his vast business holdings made him favor capitalist development. This was also true of Tafawa Balewa. The fact that both men spoke Hausa drew them close together and strengthened the bond of trust between them. In October, 1963, Nigeria became a republic. It now had both internal self-government and control over its foreign affairs. Azikiwe was appointed president of the Federal Parliament because of his leading role in the independence struggle and his great popularity.

Azikiwe founded the University of Nigeria at Nsukka. This school helped unify Nigeria by expanding a common pattern of education and high levels of literacy in English, which facilitated interethnic movement and understanding. As a result, a homogeneous class of educated Africans would begin to exert considerable influence on the process of modernization and the development of a national identity.

As president, Azikiwe helped write a federal constitution that was the supreme law of the land. He fought against all forms of corruption, favoritism, tribalism, and discrimination. He stated that he wanted to build on the American model, wherein "each one cares enough to share enough so that everyone has enough." In line with this thought, he encouraged the modernization of farming, but here he encountered a serious problem that led to suffering and despair. In 1961, Nigeria's leading earner of foreign exchange was cocoa. Yoruba farmers excelled in cocoa production and were among the most efficient and prosperous cocoa producers on earth. Azikiwe asked them to pay federal taxes on the cocoa that they sold. Many balked at this request and refused to comply. Discontent mounted, and soon the federal government uncovered a plot to overthrow the government. Awolowo of the Action Group was arrested on charges of instigating the coup attempt. He was tried, found guilty, and sentenced to ten years in prison. The Yoruba were incensed that their leader had been jailed. Rioting broke out, and a state of emergency was declared in the Western Region. The Western Region became an area of chronic unrest.

To implement his plan for sharing Nigeria's resources fairly, Azikiwe called for a census. This created problems, as regions padded figures to secure more than their share of the federal budget, so a recount was mandated. Again the same problem arose. The census demonstrated that the North had an absolute majority by itself. Both Southern regions feared that this meant their eternal domination by the North. Most people in the North were Muslim and most Southerners were Christian, so this census created unmanageable tensions. Western missionaries had located most of their schools in the South. This meant that the best-educated people and those most fluent in English were mainly Southerners. Civil service examinations were written in English. Northerners went to Qur'ān school, which emphasized Arabic, which handicapped their students in competitive national exams. The North felt discriminated against and wanted jobs assigned by quotas. Southerners wanted jobs allocated based on competition. If the census was correct, the North would win the argument based on its numerical strength. Southerners wanted a merit system. Inability to agree on how to conduct a decisive census made sharing Nigeria's wealth problematic and inflamed passions.

The army feared general civil disorder as these problems lingered inconclusively. In 1966, the government was overthrown, and Prime Minister Abubakar Tafawa Balewa and several other prominent officials were assassinated. Azikiwe was out of the country and thus was spared. An Ibo, General Ironsi, led the coup. Since Azikiwe, who was also an Ibo, was the only major political leader spared death, Northerners concluded that the coup was part of an Ibo conspiracy to take over Nigeria and control its wealth for themselves. A general massacre of Ibos living in the North followed. Ibos who could escape streamed home to the Eastern Region of the South.

Azikiwe had long encouraged mineral exploration, and oil was discovered, by coincidence, at this time in the East. Azikiwe asked Ibo leaders to share this wealth with the nation. Ibo leaders such as Colonel Ojukwu were so distressed by the massive killing of Ibo in the North and the inability of the federal government to protect Ibo that they refused to agree to share oil revenue. They seceded instead and formed the state of Biafra. Azikiwe's counsel of calm and reason was ignored, leading to the tragedy of Nigeria's civil war.

Azikiwe isolated himself in his home at Nsukka for part of the war and devoted himself to journalism and writing. His best-known books include *My Odyssey* (1970) and *Liberia in World Politics* (1934). The burning and destruction of the library at the University of Nigeria at Nsukka was a great loss to Azikiwe.

Azikiwe joined the Biafran government in 1967 and worked abroad to win recognition for it. After several years of carnage, it became clear that secession had failed. From this point on, Azikiwe worked for national reunification and reconciliation. He stayed overseas until 1972, when he returned to assume chancellorship of Lagos University. In 1979, civilian rule was restored and Azikiwe entered the political arena as a presidential candidate. Shehu Shagari won the election and defeated Azikiwe a second time in 1983. The military regime planned to restore civilian rule in 1991 but banned all former officeholders from actively seeking election.

SIGNIFICANCE

The spirit behind the nationalist mass movement that led to independence, Azikiwe was the major actor in the struggle to gain independence. He embodies the bold, aggressive style of southern Nigerian leadership. It is said that, as founder of the NCNC, he forged one of the most efficient and effective political machines in Africa. Azikiwe became the first president of the Republic of Nigeria and invited steel and oil companies to help Nigeria develop its resources. Nigeria's oil industry is one enduring monument to his enterprise and foresight.

Expansion of educational opportunities was one of his major goals. He founded the University of Nigeria at Nsukka, extended primary and secondary education, and encouraged Nigerians to seek opportunities abroad. Nigeria has more students studying in the United States than the rest of Africa combined. More than a simple story of rags to riches, Azikiwe's life story embodies the ambitions and ideals of modern Africa. His inspiring rise from dusty army barracks to state house has motivated millions to improve their lives.

—*Dallas L. Browne*

FURTHER READING

Azikiwe, Nnamdi. *My Odyssey.* New York: Praeger, 1970. A very detailed account of Azikiwe's genealogy, his quest for education, and his trials and successes. This book provides excellent insights into the creation of his business empire and of the preindependence struggle.

Candee, Marjorie Dent, ed. *Current Biography Yearbook, 1957.* New York: H. W. Wilson, 1957. Discusses the machinations of the preindependence struggle. It explains the intrigue and tensions that almost sabotaged Nigeria, as well as Azikiwe's role in cementing unity.

Jones-Quartey, K. A. B. *A Life of Azikiwe*. Baltimore: Penguin Books, 1965. Written by a former student of Azikiwe, this book explains Azikiwe's fascination with Garvey and Aggrey and their significance for Nigeria. Provides a great history of the formation of the NCNC but, being written before 1966, has nothing on either of the coups that have rocked Nigeria or on the civil war.

Lipschutz, Mark, and R. Kent Rasmussen, eds. *Dictionary of African Historical Biography*. 2d ed. Berkeley: University of California Press, 1986. A brief biographical sketch. This work contains a discussion of Azikiwe's relationship with Herbert Macaulay and a discussion of the origins of the NCNC. Briefly describes Azikiwe's role as founder of the struggle for independence.

Lynch, Hollis R. "Azikiwe." In *The McGraw-Hill Encyclopedia of World Biography*, vol. 1. New York: McGraw-Hill, 1973. A brief look at Azikiwe's life up to the date of publication. Includes a bibliography and a photograph of Azikiwe.

Taylor, Sidney, ed. *The New Africans*. New York: G. P. Putnam's Sons, 1967. Excellent discussion of the tension and animosity between Awolowo and Azikiwe. This work suggests that, when one ethnic group dominates control of valued resources in a multiethnic state, the result can be extreme imbalance, exaggerated competition, conflict, and violence.

Tijani, Hakeem Ibikunle. *Britain, Leftist Nationalists, and the Transfer of Power in Nigeria, 1945-1965*. New York: Routledge, 2006. This examination of leftist ideology and political movements in colonial and postcolonial Nigeria includes a chapter about Azikiwe's ideas, "Reconstructing the Zikist Movement, 1945-1950."

Zachernuk, Philip S. *Colonial Subjects: An African Intelligentsia and Atlantic Ideas*. Charlottesville: University Press of Virginia, 2000. An intellectual history of Africa from precolonial times in 1840 to the earliest years of independence in 1960. Focuses on how southern Nigerian intellectuals, including Azikiwe, conceived of Africa's place in the world.

SEE ALSO: Ferhat Abbas; Félix Éboué; Haile Selassie I; Félix Houphouët-Boigny; Jomo Kenyatta; Mobutu Sese Seko; Kwame Nkrumah; Julius Nyerere; Ahmed Sékou Touré; Moïse Tshombe; William V. S. Tubman.

RELATED ARTICLES in *Great Events from History: The Twentieth Century*:

1941-1970: 1960: Africa's Year of Independence.

1971-2000: January, 1983: Nigeria Expels West African Migrant Workers; December 31, 1983: Nigerian Military Topples President Shagari.

WALTER BAADE
German astronomer

Baade was one of the most influential astronomers of the twentieth century. He made major discoveries that led to greater scientific understanding of stellar and galactic evolution, was instrumental in the discovery of the supernova phenomenon, and introduced the concept of stellar populations.

BORN: March 24, 1893; Schröttinghausen, Westphalia, Germany
DIED: June 25, 1960; Bad Salzuflen, Westphalia, Germany
ALSO KNOWN AS: Wilhelm Heinrich Walter Baade (full name)
AREA OF ACHIEVEMENT: Astronomy

EARLY LIFE

Walter Baade (BAH-duh), christened Wilhelm Heinrich Walter Baade, was the oldest son of Konrad Baade and Charlotte Baade. Walter suffered a hip disorder from birth that plagued him his entire life. Konrad was a schoolmaster, and had hopes of his son studying theology and entering the clergy. From 1903 to 1912, the young Baade studied at Friedrichs Gymnasium (a German secondary school), where he showed a strong aptitude for science. He then spent a year at the University of Münster before transferring to the University of Göttingen in 1913.

Baade continued studies at Göttingen until 1919, when he received his Ph.D., with his doctoral thesis looking at the eclipsing binary star Beta Lyrae. His hip injury exempted Baade from military service in World War I, though he was pressed into service from 1916 to 1918 performing aerodynamics weapons research. The Göttingen Observatory was poorly equipped, and Baade did not get much observing experience. After receiving his Ph.D., Baade took a position at the Hamburg Observatory in Bergedorf, operated by the University of Hamburg, where he became an expert in observational astronomy. Baade married Johanna "Muschi" Bohlmann, a computational assistant at the University of Hamburg, in 1929. Asteroid 966 Muschi was named for her.

LIFE'S WORK

Baade became a well-known astronomer because of his work at Bergedorf, where he discovered Comet Baade (C/1922 U1) and the asteroid 944 Hidalgo. For many years 944 Hidalgo was the most distant asteroid discovered; it had an orbit that ranged nearly as far as Saturn. Baade secured a Rockefeller Fellowship to travel to Harvard, Yerkes Observatory in Wisconsin, and Mount Wilson Observatory in Southern California for a year beginning in 1926. Then, in 1929, Baade traveled together with famed optician Bernhard Voldemar Schmidt to the Philippines to observe a solar eclipse. In 1931, Walter Adams of Mount Wilson Observatory, greatly impressed with Baade from his earlier work there, offered him a permanent staff position. Baade quickly accepted, and he and his wife moved to California, where he would remain for most of his life.

At Mount Wilson, Baade began work with Fritz Zwicky studying a certain type of nova that he had referred to as a *hauptnova* (chief nova) in a lecture that Baade had given at Hamburg a few years earlier. The two astronomers realized that novae of this type were far too luminous to be anything other than an exploding star. Together, they worked out the physics of stellar explosions and the phenomenon that is now called a "supernova," a term Baade and Zwicky coined to replace Baade's earlier *hauptnova* designation.

By the late 1930's, the Nazis had secured much power in Germany. Baade worked very hard to help a Jewish friend and colleague, Rudolph Minkowski from the University of Hamburg, escape from Germany and the Nazis. Disgusted with what was happening in Germany, Baade reportedly initiated an application for U.S. citizenship, but the paperwork was lost. Scornful of the bureaucracy that had lost his paperwork, Baade never reapplied. Thus, when the United States entered World War II, Baade, still a German citizen living in California, was declared an enemy alien. However, his colleagues at Mount Wilson managed to keep him from being sent to an internment camp by ensuring the U.S. government that he would remain in the immediate vicinity of Mount Wilson for the duration of the war.

With most of the observatory's scientists performing research elsewhere in support of the war effort, Baade had the place to himself. Adding to this ideal situation for Baade was that the greater Los Angeles area, which Mount Wilson overlooks, was under blackout conditions early in the war because of fears of a possible Japanese invasion along the West Coast. The night skies at Mount Wilson were the darkest they had been since the observatory was built. Under such dark skies, Baade began studies of the Andromeda galaxy. He found that there were two distinct types of stars in the galaxy. One type, which he called Population I, was found in the spiral arms of the galaxy and was bluer than the other type. The second type, which he called Population II, was found in the central regions of the galaxy, in its globular clusters, and in its elliptical satellite galaxies. Population II stars were much redder and dimmer on average than the Population I stars. More research showed that Population I stars are far richer in metals than are Population II stars. (Astronomers call anything other than hydrogen and helium a "metal.") Theoretical studies later showed that this implies that Population I stars formed more recently and Population II stars formed earlier in the history of the galaxy. Researchers can make this implication because metals are produced in the fusion reactions in the cores of stars and are seeded into space when stars die, which allows them to become constituents of the next generation of stars.

Baade next turned his attention to Cepheid variable stars. Cepheid variables are pulsating stars whose pulsation period is related to their luminosity. The brighter Cepheids pulsate slower than the dimmer ones. This relationship can be used to determine distances to star clusters and nearby galaxies. Baade's studies showed that Cepheids fall into two categories, based upon their stellar population. By placing them into their separate types, Baade was able to improve the period-luminosity relationship and thus also provide for improved distance determinations. He found that nearly all distances to galaxies had been underestimated by a factor of at least two. The universe was, therefore, far larger, and far older, than had been thought. This was great news for geologists, for they had been coming up with ages for the earth that were billions of years older than cosmologists were computing for the universe. After Baade's correction, the two ages were closer in agreement. This also provided an age for the universe more consistent with that needed for George Gamow's big bang cosmology.

Baade finally retired in 1958. However, retirement did not stop him from working. In 1959, Baade taught a graduate class at Harvard on stellar and galactic evolution and how those topics can be better understood using stellar populations. Later, Cecilia Payne-Gaposchkin edited transcripts of his lectures and they were published as *Evolution of Star and Galaxies* (1963). Baade then flew to Australia, where he traveled and repeated his Harvard lectures.

Finally, in late 1959, Baade returned to his beloved boyhood home of the Westphalia region of Germany. He had plans to write some much delayed papers and to teach at the University of Göttingen. He also was considering doing more work at Hamburg's Bergedorf Observatory. However, his congenital hip disorder had become far worse, and he was in constant pain. By early 1960, the condition had progressed to where he was beginning to suffer paralysis of his legs. He underwent major surgery to correct some of the problems. He was instructed to remain in bed for five months after the surgery, a "confinement," as he called it, that was very difficult for him. Finally, he was allowed to sit up in a wheelchair, but he died days later, on June 25, in Bad Salzuflen. It has been speculated that perhaps a blood clot may have formed as a complication of his surgery and the five-month convalescence. Sitting up may have dislodged the clot.

SIGNIFICANCE

Baade published less than many other astronomers. However, nearly every paper that he did publish had a major impact on astronomy and astrophysics, helping to shape twentieth century astronomy. Often regarded by some as "just" an observational astronomer, Baade's grasp of astrophysics was extraordinary.

Walter Baade. (California Institute of Technology)

Baade's discovery of Population I and Population II stars was one of the most important discoveries in stellar astronomy. It set the stage for astrophysicists to understand stellar and galactic evolution. Modern astronomical thought no longer groups stars into only two distinct populations. Rather, stars are now thought to lie along a continuum of metallicities, that is, the constitution of a star varies in its amount of matter beyond the chemical elements helium and hydrogen. Nonetheless, the terms "Population I" and "Population II" are still used by astronomers, and the metallicity of a star is considered an important measurement.

Baade's, and Zwicky's, research on supernovae was a major step forward in understanding the evolution of high-mass stars, and his work with distance scales also was instrumental in supporting the big bang cosmology and putting the steady state model to rest.

—*Raymond D. Benge, Jr.*

FURTHER READING

Baade, Walter. *Evolution of Stars and Galaxies.* Cambridge, Mass.: Harvard University Press, 1963. A transcript of a series of lectures given by Baade, edited by Cecilia Payne-Gaposchkin, that clearly explain Baade's work in stellar evolution and galactic astronomy.

Osterbrock, Donald E. *Walter Baade: A Life in Astrophysics.* Princeton, N.J.: Princeton University Press, 2001. A well-researched, recommended biography of Baade by a historian of astronomy. Includes a bibliography.

_____. "Walter Baade, Master Observer." *Mercury* 31, no. 4 (July/August, 2002): 32-41. A brief biography of Baade, focusing mostly on the highlights of his life.

SEE ALSO: Viktor A. Ambartsumian; André-Louis Danjon; George Gamow; George Ellery Hale; Sir Fred Hoyle; Henrietta Swan Leavitt; Georges Lemaître; Jan Hendrik Oort; Henry Norris Russell; Bernhard Voldemar Schmidt; Karl Schwarzschild; Max Wolf.

RELATED ARTICLES in *Great Events from History: The Twentieth Century:*

1901-1940: 1929: Hubble Confirms the Expanding Universe; Winter, 1929-1930: Schmidt Invents the Corrector for the Schmidt Camera and Telescope; 1934: Zwicky and Baade Propose a Theory of Neutron Stars.

1941-1970: 1948-1951: Ryle's Radio Telescope Locates the First Known Radio Galaxy; August, 1952: Baade Corrects an Error in the Cepheid Luminosity Scale.

LEO BAECK
German-born British rabbi and scholar

Teacher, author, historian of religion, philosophical-theological thinker, and outstanding articulator of modern Judaism, Baeck was the leading rabbi in Germany before World War II and one of the foremost rabbinical scholars of the twentieth century.

BORN: May 23, 1873; Lissa, Prussia (now Leszno, Poland)
DIED: November 2, 1956; London, England
AREAS OF ACHIEVEMENT: Religion and theology, scholarship, philosophy

EARLY LIFE

One of the most important rabbinical scholars of the twentieth century, Leo Baeck (behk) was descended from a well-established rabbinical family. He was born in the Prussian town of Lissa (now Leszno, Poland) to Rabbi Samuel Baeck. Educated during the German-

Jewish renaissance that produced such outstanding Jewish thinkers as Sigmund Freud, Albert Einstein, Franz Kafka, and Martin Buber, Baeck studied for the rabbinate at the conservative Jewish Theological Seminary of Breslau and the University of Breslau, where he read religion, philosophy, and languages. In 1895, he completed the Ph.D. in philosophy at the University of Berlin, where he was a student of Wilhelm Dilthey and Ernst Troeltsch. A Reform Jew, Baeck was ordained at the progressive Academy for the Study of Judaism in Berlin in 1897, where he also studied. A rabbi of the Reform wing of Judaism, he began his ministry in the Silesian town of Opole. In 1907, he moved to Düsseldorf, where his preeminence as a Jewish scholar had already brought him acclaim. In 1912, he was appointed to Oranienburger, the most prominent synagogue in Berlin, where he become the leading rabbi of the capital of Germany.

His scholarship won for him an invitation to teach

homiletics and Midrash (interpretative rabbinical literature) at his alma mater, the Academy for the Study of Judaism. Though teaching was a favorite occupation, he declined the title of professor, preferring to be known as rabbi. An assimilated German Jew, he nevertheless remained fully identified with all aspects of Jewish life. His sermons were solemn explorations, painstaking "Dialogues with God," as they have been called. As an army chaplain on the eastern and western fronts in the 1914-1918 war, he became a pacifist. He was married and became the father of a daughter who emigrated to England before the war.

LIFE'S WORK

Baeck's first major publication was a review article responding to a provocative work by Protestant theologian Adolf von Harnack, *Das Wesen des Christentums* (1900; *What Is Christianity?*, 1901), which depicted Jesus and early Christianity as unrelated to Jewish religious and cultural tradition and Judaic thought as inferior to Christian belief. Rejecting Harnack's conclusions and scholarship, Baeck stressed Jesus' importance as a profoundly Jewish teacher who revered the traditions of the Prophets. In his magnum opus, *Das Wesen des Judentums* (1905; *The Essence of Judaism*, 1936), Baeck defended the Jewish faith against overt or implied attacks. Basing his work on a profound knowledge of Jewish sources, deep historical knowledge, and neo-Kantian rationalism, Baeck traced the development of Judaism's central concepts—Torah, Talmud, and Halacha—from the Exodus to modern times. Interpreting Judaism as revolutionary and dynamic ethical monotheism, he stressed its development as a response to ethical demands, the categorical "ought" of the divine imperative, on generations of Jews, making Jewish history an ongoing vehicle of continuing revelation. In Judaism, he saw the highest expression of morality with a universal message. While Jewry, he argued, is unique, every people is a mystery, each "a question posed by God."

During the 1920's, Baeck expanded his studies, which led him to greater appreciation of the mystical aspects of Judaism, to which he gave place in a much-revised edition (1922) of his great work. Also in 1922, Baeck published a remarkable essay, *Romantische Religion* (romantic religion), a bold critique of the differences between Christianity and Judaism, which brought the dialogue between the two faiths to greater clarity and intensity. Baeck contrasted Christianity with Judaism, the former characterized as an emotional, sentimental, and "romantic" religion longing for redemption in the next

Leo Baeck. (Library of Congress)

world, the latter as a "classical," rational faith, commanded to work for the improvement of life in this world. Baeck's scholarship brought him to international prominence. During the interwar years, he became head of numerous German-Jewish organizations and was honored by many national German-Jewish groups.

Baeck's most outstanding service was rendered as the leader of German Jewry after the National Socialists came to power in 1933. So great was international respect for Baeck that the Nazis hesitated to destroy him. They offered him emigration, but, though he received attractive offers from England and the United States to take a position, he remained with his stricken community.

During the Nazi persecutions, he became the chief spokesperson for Jews in Germany. He was appointed president of the National Agency of German Jews and head of the Jewish Central Committee for Aid and Improvement. In these positions, he faced the arduous task of negotiating with the Nazi government, trying to mitigate the persecution of his people. He presided over efforts at emigration, economic assistance, charity, education, and culture with annual budgets running into millions of dollars. By prudent diplomacy he helped arrange the emigration of more than forty thousand Jews, many of them young people. He devoted his influence and diplomatic skills to defending whatever rights were left to Jews in Nazi Germany, to lessening or delaying Nazi persecution, and to upholding the morale of the beleaguered German-Jewish community. Despite the hostile environment and his many responsibilities, he continued a prodigious scholarship.

On the eve of World War II, Baeck accepted the presidency of the World Union for Progressive Judaism and was appointed as the leader of the newly formed National Organization of the Jews of Germany. Baeck was continuously endangered, arrested and released four times, and repeatedly interrogated by the Gestapo. A week before World War II began, he led a last trainload of children to safety in England, then returned. With the outbreak of the war, he was not heard from and widely feared dead, but the rabbi continued his work. His synagogue had been burned in the 1938 national pogrom, but he continued to hold services, denouncing from the pulpit the modern paganism and idolatry of the state. On one occasion, the police raided his service and sent all congregants less than sixty years of age to work as forced laborers. On the next Sabbath, he continued his services and others came.

In January, 1943, at sixty-nine, Baeck was arrested and sent to the Theresienstadt (Terezin) concentration camp in Czechoslovakia. Although millions died in the Nazi camps, including most of Baeck's family, Baeck miraculously survived. His discipline, inner strength, and vitality came to his rescue. He inspired a certain respect even among his captors, who sometimes acquiesced in his refusal to yield to their demands. In 1944, he was made head of the Council of Elders and became the center of a spiritual resistance against the Nazis. He held illegal services, led secret prayer meetings, and ran extensive educational programs in philosophy and religion, despite a Schutzstaffel (SS) ban punishable by death.

As rabbi, Baeck strengthened thousands of his people and served as pastor to many Christians, interned because of mixed heritage. He became a distributor of food to the sick and dying and ministered to those in despair. He encouraged his people to take consolation in their goodness. When all other rights were taken, he said, some yet remained: the right to be decent, self-respecting, spiritual, cultivated, and Jewish. He encouraged his people not to fear death. Reliably informed of the gassing at Auschwitz, Baeck decided not to tell his fellow inmates. Paul Tillich and others who praised Baeck have criticized him for this silence.

Despite raging typhus and starvation in the camp, Baeck remained sound. His survival seems also the result of providential mistake: In the spring of 1945, a Rabbi Beck of Moravia died, and the SS mistakenly reported Baeck's death to Gestapo headquarters. Shortly before liberation, Adolf Eichmann discovered the error and told Baeck that it would be rectified. Before that threat was fulfilled, however, the Russians liberated the camp. Baeck was one of fewer than 17,000 survivors of nearly 140,000 Jews sent to Theresienstadt. After two months, he was flown to London, where he settled with his daughter and son-in-law. At the age of seventy-two, the resilient rabbi took up his work again. A hero in the postwar world, he was elected founding president of the Society for Jewish Study, president of the Association of Synagogues in Great Britain, and chair of the World Union for Progressive Judaism.

In 1950, Baeck became a British citizen. He sought to be a voice of reconciliation with Germany, but he thought it no longer possible for Jews to live there and urged them to leave. He became president of the Council for the Protection of the Rights and Interests of Jews from Germany. At the same time, Baeck made it clear that he considered the Nazi government, and not the collective German people, responsible for the destruction of the European Jews, citing numerous acts of German-Christian assistance to Jews under the Nazis. A magnanimous man, Baeck harbored no visible bitterness toward the Germans.

Despite the loss of his personal manuscripts and library of fifteen thousand books, Baeck continued to write and publish. Some of his best works are among his final writings, notably *Die Pharisäer: Ein Kapitel judischer Geschichte* (1934; *The Pharisees, and Other Essays*, 1947), which includes writings suppressed by the Nazis. His final work, the end of forty years of adult experience, is his classic *Dieses Volk: Jüdische Existenz* (two volumes, 1955-1957; *This People Israel: The Meaning of Jewish Existence*, 1964), much of which was written on scraps of paper at Theresienstadt. Monumental in scope, it covers three thousand years of Jewish history. In *This People Israel*, he emphasized the essence of Judaism as a dialectical polarity between "mystery" and "command," an eternal "thou shalt," in the form of divine instructions or commands of love and justice emanating from the divine "mystery." He interpreted "commandment" as a discipline that the Jew willingly accepts and that does not permit him to utilize emotion as the chief means of attaining grace. Piety, Baeck believed, is achieved by upholding the obligations that exist between humans, and even ritual observance is directed toward this end.

Baeck regarded the reawakening of national Jewish consciousness as one of the great signs of Jewish renaissance. Though not a Zionist, he was an early supporter of Zionist activities. With Einstein, he wrote a plea in 1948 urging Palestinian Jews and their Arab neighbors to disown the terrorists of both sides and for Jews to focus on a peaceful and democratic basis for Jewish settlement in Palestine.

In the course of his public work, he traveled throughout Europe, the United States, and Israel. He lectured at the new Hebrew University of Jerusalem, and from 1948 to 1953 was a visiting professor of the history of religion at Hebrew Union College in Cincinnati, Ohio. He lectured to audiences across the United States in behalf of Reform Judaism. He had a particular sympathy for the United States and looked there rather than to Israel for the center of Jewish religious vitality. He was received by President Harry S. Truman and, on the anniversary of Abraham Lincoln's birthday, said the prayer before the United States House of Representatives.

The Holocaust did not shake Baeck's conviction that the Jewish encounter with European culture had yielded inestimable Jewish values. He mourned the German-Jewish world that had perished and was particularly anxious that the history of German Jewry and its achievements in Jewish and general cultural life and thought should not be forgotten or falsified. In 1954, when the Council of Jews from Germany established an institute devoted to researching and writing the history of the Jews of German-speaking countries, and especially of the "Jewish renaissance," with offices in London, Jerusalem, and later in New York, it would be named the Leo Baeck Institute, and Baeck became its first president. Though he could not participate fully in its activities, Baeck expressed his full support. Also bearing his name is Leo Baeck College in London, which annually ordains rabbis who serve around the world.

Baeck died in London on November 2, 1956, after a brief illness. His death caused bereavement of Jews around the world, who counted him among their greatest figures. German Jews especially regarded him as a source of profound inspiration and their political leader during the final dark days in Germany.

SIGNIFICANCE

Baeck was one of Germany's great articulators of Reform Judaism and equal to the most sophisticated of his contemporaries on the highest level of cultural and philo-

sophical thought. In a climate unfavorable to spiritual values and speculation about the relationship of God, man, and the world, he expounded one of the clearest expositions of liberal Jewish religious thought in the twentieth century. He raised the consciousness of modern Jewry, inspired pride in Jewish heritage, and was a strong voice against the secularizing tendencies among emancipated Jews of the twentieth century. He was the spiritual leader of German Jewry during the Nazi era and a paradigm for German-Jewish courage during the Holocaust. The last representative of a once-great community in the hour of destiny, Baeck embodied the best and perhaps some of the flaws of German Jewry, which placed its hope in German culture and civilization. Now almost a legendary figure, a saint of modern Judaism and the symbol of German Jewry, Baeck lived through the worst epoch in Jewish history with wisdom, magnanimity, and a vibrant soul.

—Walter F. Renn

FURTHER READING

Altman, Alexander. *Leo Baeck and the Jewish Mystical Tradition.* New York: Leo Baeck Institute, 1973. A careful analysis of Baeck's growing appreciation for the role of mysticism in the Jewish religion and his reconciliation of it with Judaism as a classic, rational faith. Includes bibliographical references.

Baeck, Leo. "A People Stands Before Its God." In *We Survived: Fourteen Histories of the Hidden and Hunted in Nazi Germany*, edited by Eric H. Boehm. 1949. Updated ed. Boulder, Colo.: Westview Press, 2003. An important personal memoir of the Nazi years by Baeck. A major source for some aspects of these years.

Baker, Leonard. *Days of Sorrow and Pain: Leo Baeck and the Berlin Jews.* New York: Macmillan, 1978. A well-written full-scale biography of Baeck that won a 1979 Pulitzer Prize. Illustrated, with an extensive bibliography.

Bamberger, Fritz. *Leo Baeck: The Man and the Idea.* New York: Leo Baeck Institute, 1958. An insightful assessment of Baeck's contributions as teacher, thinker, and scholar.

Cohen, Arthur A. *The Natural and the Supernatural Jew: An Historical and Theological Introduction.* New York: Pantheon Books, 1962. A trenchant interpretation of Baeck's *The Essence of Judaism* and *Romantische Religion*.

Friedlander, Albert H. *Leo Baeck: Teacher of Theresienstadt.* New York: Holt, Rinehart and Winston, 1968. An intellectual biography by Baeck's student and disciple in Cincinnati. Treats Baeck's theology and development as a religious thinker from his early life to his relationship with the Nazis. Includes a critical analysis of *The Essence of Judaism* and *This People Israel*, an extensive bibliography, and an index.

_____. "Leo Baeck: The Teacher." *European Judaism* 34, no. 1 (Spring, 2001): 40. Profile of Baeck's life and work, including a discussion of his book *Essence of Judaism* and his interpretation of the Bible.

Leschnitzer, Adolf. "The Unknown Leo Baeck: 'Teacher of the Congregation.'" *Commentary* 23 (May, 1957): 419-421. A valuable essay on Baeck's character and personal manner by one who worked with him from 1933 to 1939 as chief of the education division of the National Agency of German Jews.

Liebschutz, Hans. "Between Past and Future: Leo Baeck's Historical Position." In *Yearbook: Leo Baeck Institute*. New York: Leo Baeck Institute, 1966. An interpretive essay on Baeck's philosophy and theology by one of the most revered founders of the Leo Baeck Institute.

SEE ALSO: Hannah Arendt; Martin Buber; Lucy S. Dawidowicz; Anne Frank; Adolf von Harnack; Franz Kafka; Edith Stein.

RELATED ARTICLE in *Great Events from History: The Twentieth Century:*
1901-1940: 1923: Buber Breaks New Ground in Religious Philosophy.

MIKHAIL BAKHTIN
Russian scholar

Bakhtin had a major impact on literary theory, especially on point of view in the novel, on the philosophy and interrelatedness of language and society, on the extension of areas of linguistics and schools of literary theory, and on modern philosophy, presenting an alternative to systems based on Greek philosophers.

BORN: November 17, 1895; Orel, Russia
DIED: March 7, 1975; Moscow, Soviet Union (now in Russia)
ALSO KNOWN AS: Mikhail Mikhailovich Bakhtin (full name); P. N. Medvedev (pseudonym); V. N. Voloshinov (pseudonym)
AREAS OF ACHIEVEMENT: Language and linguistics, literature, philosophy, scholarship

EARLY LIFE

Mikhail Bakhtin (mee-KIL bahk-TEEN) was born in the provincial capital of Orel, Russia. Untitled and unpropertied, he came from a noble family who, like their city, dated back to the late Middle Ages. His father and grandfather were owner and manager, respectively, of state banks. The third of five children, Mikhail was closer to his elder brother Nikolai than to his three sisters or his parents. A German governess taught the boys Greek poetry in German translation.

When Bakhtin was nine years old, the family moved to Vilnius, the Russian-ruled capital of Lithuania. In this multiethnic center, his outlook was broadened even

though the schools and church that he attended were Russian. He was influenced by new movements such as Symbolism and by the spirit of revolutionary change. A lifelong process of debate and dialogue was begun between Bakhtin and his brother and with others. Bakhtin's extensive reading included, among others, Friedrich Nietzsche and Georg Wilhelm Friedrich Hegel. Six years later, Bakhtin's family moved to Odessa, a major city of the Ukraine. Bakhtin attended and finished the school known as the first gymnasium; he then attended the University of Odessa for one year, studying with the philological faculty. At sixteen, he contracted osteomyelitis.

From 1914 to 1918, Bakhtin attended the University of St. Petersburg, rooming with his brother Nikolai. Of several professors, the most influential was Faddei F. Zelinsky, credited with laying the foundation for Bakhtin's knowledge of philosophy and literature. Bakhtin's graduation in 1918, following Nikolai's departure for the White Army in 1917 and eventual self-exile to England, marked the end of the preparatory stage of his life.

LIFE'S WORK

During the years 1918 through 1929, Bakhtin established lifelong friendships with artistic and intellectual people, developed and expressed his own ideas, did extensive work on his own writings, married, and saw his first works published. He became the center of a series of informal groups comprising people from a wide variety of backgrounds, areas of achievement, and political and ideological persuasions. At Nevel, where he and his family moved in 1918, members of the Bakhtin circle included Lev Vasilyevich Pumpiansky, Valentin Nikolayevich Voloshinov, and the musician Maria Veniaminova Yudina. Bakhtin maintained his personal and philosophical commitment to Christianity at a time when all religions were suppressed in the Soviet Union. His first known publication was a two-page article in a local periodical in 1919 entitled *Iskusstvo I otvetstvennost* (art and responsibility). The ideas he expressed in this article were later developed into those of his mature works.

In 1920, Bakhtin moved to nearby Vitebsk, where the circle re-formed and expanded to include new members such as Ivan Ivanovich Sollertinsky and Pavel Nikolayevich Medvedev. In addition to writing and keeping notebooks, Bakhtin taught at Vitebsk Higher Institute of Education and held several other positions. The worsening of his osteomyelitis was complicated by typhoid in 1921, and he was nursed by Elena Aleksandrovna Okolovich; their fifty-year marriage began later that year and ended with her death in 1971.

Bakhtin spent the years 1924 through 1929 in Leningrad, where he lived on a progressively reduced medical pension. His health prohibited public activity, but he was able to meet with members of his circle and to lecture in private apartments. Works published by his friends contained his ideas but their Marxist ideology, thus making them politically acceptable for publication. Opinion varies as to authorship of these collaborative works. Some scholars believe that Bakhtin wrote them in their entirety; some believe that he composed the bulk of these texts, with his friends adding the requisite ideology; others are convinced that the works were actually written by those under whose names they were published, and merely reflect the influence of Bakhtin. One work signed by the scientist Ivan Ivanovich Kanaev questions the claims of vitalism. Of the four works attributed to Medvedev, the best known is *Formal' nyi metod v literaturovedenii: Kriticheskoe vvedenie v sotsiologicheskuyu poetiku* (1928; *The Formal Method in Literary Scholarship*, 1978). One of Voloshinov's seven titles is *Marksizm I filosofiya yazyka* (1929; *Marxism and the Philosophy of Language*, 1973). Only these twelve works are questioned; other books signed by these men are accepted as theirs, thus providing scholars with a basis for comparison.

The year 1929 was a turning point in Bakhtin's life. He was arrested and sentenced to exile in Siberia for ten years for political and religious reasons (he was never tried). Also he published his first major work under his own name (and the first since 1919): *Problemy tvorchestva Dostoevskogo* (expanded to *Problemy poetiki Dostoevskogo*, 1963; *Problems of Dostoevsky's Poetics*, 1973, 1984). Bakhtin's sentence in Siberia was reduced for reasons of health; a good review of his book by the minister of education and the fact that the questioners believed him to be the author of the disputed texts probably also helped his case.

He was allowed to go to Kustanai from 1930 to 1934, traveling without guard and choosing his own work. After a year of unemployment he was employed as an accountant for the local government, later teaching local workers his clerical skills. Here as elsewhere he was well liked. In 1934, he chose to remain for two more years; that same year he published an article based on his observations there.

In 1936, Bakhtin ended his self-exile by moving to Saransk and teaching in the Mordovian Pedagogical Institute. The next year, for political reasons, he moved to Savelovo, about one hundred kilometers from Moscow. In 1938, the first of a series of misfortunes overtook him: His right leg was amputated. An article on satire he was asked to contribute to a literary encyclopedia never appeared because the volume was canceled. As a result of the vicissitudes of wartime, several works by Bakhtin that had been accepted and were awaiting publication did not appear. In 1940, he lectured on the novel at the Gorky Institute in Moscow, writing a dissertation for that institution on François Rabelais, which was published in an expanded version as *Tvorchestvo Fransua Rable I narodnaya kul'tura srednevekov'ya I Renessansa* (1965; *Rabelais and His World*, 1968), a work rivaling *Problems of Dostoevsky's Poetics* in importance. In 1941, he began teaching German in the Savelovo schools while working on yet another important endeavor: articles about the novel, collected and translated in *Voprosy literatury I estetiki* (1975; *The Dialogic Imagination*, 1981), in which he expanded his ideas on polyphonic communication to dialogic communication, which included the self and others or the author, characters, and reader. From 1942 to 1945, he taught Russian in Savelovo.

In 1945, Bakhtin returned to Saransk, where he was promoted to the rank of docent and made department chair. In 1946, he submitted his dissertation, defending it the following year. The committee compromised and granted him the lesser degree of candidate in 1951, precluding publication at that time. In 1957, he saw his institute become a university. The next year, he was promoted to chair of the Department of Russian and Foreign Literature at this newly formed institution.

Recognition came slowly. With few publications in his own name, Bakhtin was little known beyond his own circle of friends. Attention to the book on Fyodor Dostoevski marked a change: Vladimir Seduro, an American, mentioned the book in a published work in 1955; the next year, his old antagonist, the Formalist critic Viktor Shklovsky, treated the Dostoevski book in a Soviet work; in 1958, the influential Slavicist Roman Jakobson, a pioneering figure in the application of linguistics to literary study, having mentioned Bakhtin to members of the International Conference of Slavists in 1956, shared preview copies of his review of Shklovsky's book, publishing his review in 1959. Young intellectuals led by Vadim Valerianovich paid Bakhtin homage and pressed for publication of his works. The revised Dostoevski book and the revised dissertation, 1963 and 1965, established his reputation. Other works followed, some posthumously.

Poor health forced both of the Bakhtins to move to Moscow in 1969 and to nearby Grivno in 1970. Bakhtin's wife died of a heart condition in 1971. Bakhtin then moved first to a hotel for writers and in 1972 to his own apartment at 21 Krasnoarmeyskaya Street in Moscow, where he lived and, in spite of osteomyelitis and emphysema, wrote until his death on March 7, 1975. His funeral ceremonies were both civil and religious.

SIGNIFICANCE

For much of his life, Bakhtin was a relatively obscure figure, though in his last years he attained a measure of fame among literary specialists in the Soviet Union and saw his work begin to appear in the West. In the decade following his death, as previously unpublished works became available and early works were reissued, there was an explosion of interest in Bakhtin, to the extent that he has become one of the most influential literary theorists of the twentieth century.

In part, Bakhtin's influence can be attributed to his appeal to critics and readers who value pluralism and cultural diversity. Most of the now widely used terms and concepts that Bakhtin introduced to critical discourse directly reflect his sense of literature as an interplay of voices, of meanings, of languages. "Dialogic" thinking recognizes this multiplicity (or "heteroglossia," as Bakhtin termed it); "monologic" thinking attempts to suppress it. Bakhtin's pluralism and his emphasis on the social context of meaning have made an impact not only on literary studies but also on linguistics, philosophy, theology, and the social sciences.

—*George W. Van Devender*

FURTHER READING

Berrong, Richard M. *Rabelais and Bakhtin: Popular Culture in "Gargantua and Pantagruel."* Lincoln: University of Nebraska Press, 1986. Reexamines Bakhtin's treatment against the backdrop of Soviet history.

Bonetskaia, N. K. "Mikhail Bakhtin's Life and Philosophical Ideas." *Russian Studies in Philosophy* 43, no. 1 (Summer, 2004): 5-34. An overview of Bakhtin's life, career, achievements, and philosophical ideas.

Clark, Katerina, and Michael Holquist. *Mikhail Bakhtin.* Cambridge, Mass.: Belknap Press, 1984. The standard biography and more, this work traces the intellectual/political history of Russia and the Soviet Union, discusses primary works, and shares opinions about ideology and authorship. A valuable resource. The bibliography of primary works is helpful.

Emerson, Caryl. "Bakhtin After the Boom: Pro and Con." *Journal of European Studies* 32, no. 1 (March, 2002): 3. An overview of Bakhtin's life and work, including a discussion about the translations of his books and the inclusion of his work in graduate seminars.

Kershner, R. B. *Joyce, Bakhtin, and Popular Culture: Chronicles of Disorder.* Chapel Hill: University of North Carolina Press, 1989. Applies Bakhtin's literary theories to the works of James Joyce. Discusses Bakhtin's "dialogism" in a subchapter.

Lachmann, Renate. *Bakhtin and Carnival: Culture as Counter-Culture.* CHS Occasional Papers 14. Minneapolis: University of Minnesota Press, 1987. Treats the idea of carnival in *Rabelais and His World* against the unfolding of Russian history before, during, and since the revolution.

Morson, Gary Saul, and Caryl Emerson, eds. *Rethinking Bakhtin: Extensions and Challenges.* Evanston, Ill.: Northwestern University Press, 1989. This introduction to Bakhtin treats his life situation, the publishing and republishing of his works, and the disputed texts, arriving at conclusions different from those of Clark and Holquist. Essays by the editors and others develop ideas set forth in the introduction. Translations of Bakhtin's two prefaces to Tolstoy's works are included. A valuable counterpart to Clark and Holquist.

Nordquist, Joan, comp. *Mikhail Bakhtin.* Social Theory: A Bibliographic Series 12. Santa Cruz, Calif.: Reference and Research Services, 1988. An excellent bibliographic tool, more recent and fuller than the bibliography in the book by Clark and Holquist. Includes both primary and secondary works.

Patterson, David. *Literature and Spirit: Essays on Bakhtin and His Contemporaries.* Lexington: University of Kentucky Press, 1988. Essays, all by the author, relate Bakhtin to figures as diverse as Michel Foucault, André Gide, and Martin Heidegger. Patterson agrees with Clark and Holquist on Bakhtin's Christianity.

Tikhanov, Galin. *The Master and the Slave: Lukács, Bakhtin, and the Ideas of Their Time.* New York: Oxford University Press, 2000. A comparative study of the ideas of Bakhtin and György Lukács concerning aesthetics, cultural theory, literary history, and philosophy.

SEE ALSO: Roland Barthes; Walter Benjamin; Noam Chomsky; Jacques Derrida; Émile Durkheim; Martin Heidegger; Jacques Lacan; Claude Lévi-Strauss; Jean-Paul Sartre; Ferdinand de Saussure.

GEORGE BALANCHINE
Russian-born American choreographer

Balanchine, considered the greatest choreographer of the twentieth century, transformed ballet into a diverse, vibrantly contemporary, American medium. He established a training tradition and brought ballet to the forefront of the performing arts in the United States.

BORN: January 22, 1904; St. Petersburg, Russia
DIED: April 30, 1983; New York, New York
ALSO KNOWN AS: Georgi Melitonovitch Balanchivadze (birth name)
AREA OF ACHIEVEMENT: Dance

EARLY LIFE

George Balanchine (bal-ehn-SHEEN) was born in St. Petersburg, Russia, a city more European than Russian in its culture. His father, Meliton Balanchivadze, was a composer of modest means best known for his arrangements of folk songs from his native Georgia in the Caucasus. As a child, Balanchine studied the piano and considered careers in the military or the church. These early plans foretold his future work, which was to combine extraordinary physical discipline with spiritual expression inspired by music.

Balanchine entered the world of ballet by accident. Unable to enroll in the Imperial Naval Academy in August, 1914, he accompanied his sister to an audition at the Imperial School of Ballet and was invited to audition as well. He passed (she failed), and, because of the family's financial difficulties, he was enrolled and left there the same day. A reluctant student (he immediately ran away from school), Balanchine nevertheless passed the probationary first year. The turnaround in his attitude toward the profession chosen for him occurred during his second year, when he appeared in a performance of Peter Ilich Tchaikovsky's ballet *The Sleeping Beauty* (1890), performed by the Imperial Ballet Company at the Maryinsky Theatre. The experience dazzled him, and performing became the motivation for undergoing the rigorous training at the school.

Meanwhile, political events were affecting the cloistered, tradition-bound existence of his world. Balanchine entered the Imperial School of Ballet the month in which World War I was declared, and in 1917, the Bolshevik Revolution closed the school until the following year, during which time Balanchine scrounged the city for food and took menial jobs to survive. The commissar for education, Anatole Lunarcharsky, convinced Vladimir Ilyich Lenin, chair of the Soviet government, that the performing arts should be considered a valuable heritage of the working class rather than a decadent practice of the aristocracy. While the argument saved the school, this same viewpoint would eventually threaten Balanchine's early choreographic career.

Reminiscences of fellow students from this period refer to Balanchine's modest, untemperamental, yet authoritative manner and his great capacity for gaiety and wit. He was a slender, dark-haired man with brooding eyes reflecting an intense concentration.

The groundwork for Balanchine's unique contributions to choreography was laid as he explored his varied artistic interests. While still a student, he distinguished himself by his unusual musical ability and by choreographing small works for student concerts. On graduation in 1921, he entered the Imperial Ballet Company as a member of the corps de ballet and at the same time became a student at the Petrograd (Leningrad) Conservatory of Music for three years to study piano and composition. At the end of his studies, deciding that he could not become a significant composer, he directed his life totally to the world of ballet.

In the early days of the revolution, there were no consistent policies to inhibit a young choreographer such as Balanchine in his experimentation. Influenced by aspects of the choreography of Marius Petipa (1822-1910), the established Michel Fokine, and his contemporary Kasyan Goleizovsky, Balanchine was drawn to develop a new dance vocabulary that would interpret music and evoke moods, unfettered by the constraints of presenting an actual story and undistracted by complicated costumes and scenery.

In 1923, after the second of his controversial special performances, "Evenings of the Young Ballet," the directors of the Maryinsky Theatre announced that any dancers taking part in such programs without special permission would be fired. This decree effectively ended Balanchine's endeavors in the Soviet Union. The following year, he joined a small performing group that had received permission to tour in Germany, and with the first of his four dancer wives, Tamara Gevergeyeva (later Geva), Balanchine left the Soviet Union for the West.

Balanchine saw his education as having two phases: his training in Russia and his five years as choreographer with Sergei Diaghilev's Ballets Russes, a post he obtained shortly after he left the Soviet Union in 1924. Diaghilev was an impresario of remarkable vision and taste, who employed the most notable artists of the early twentieth century, including painters Pablo Picasso and Henri Matisse, composers Igor Stravinsky and Erik Satie, and dancers Anna Pavlova and Vaslav Nijinsky, to create and perform ballets throughout Europe. Both the intellectual elite and the fashionable society of Europe were fascinated by Diaghilev's experimentation and achievements. Balanchine's lifelong collaboration and friendship with Stravinsky date from these years.

LIFE'S WORK

Two of Balanchine's highly acclaimed works of the 1920's were considered to be turning points in choreographic development: *Apollo* (1928), for its contemporary interpretation of classical ballet style, which closely reflected Stravinsky's score; and *The Prodigal Son* (1929), a biblical theme to music by Sergei Prokofiev, danced expressionistically with a vocabulary inspired by circus movements. After Diaghilev's death in 1929, Balanchine choreographed for several companies including the newly formed Ballet Russe de Monte Carlo and his own struggling group Les Ballets 1933, in Paris.

At this point, Lincoln Kirstein, a wealthy, cultivated young American, who sought to establish ballet as a permanent art form in the United States, approached Bal-

anchine and convinced him to embark on this endeavor, assisted by several benefactors, notably Nelson Rockefeller and Edward Warburg. The School of American Ballet opened in New York City in January, 1934, followed a year later by the American Ballet company. Its first performance included *Serenade* (1935; music by Tchaikovsky), considered by many to be Balanchine's signature work. During this early period, Balanchine was considered by some critics to be too international and decadent in flavor and therefore not "American" enough to develop an American style and a school of ballet. His experiences in the following dozen years gave him the broadest possible scope of American theatrical enterprises and at the same time enriched them with his own innovations.

The precarious financial position of his company caused Balanchine to affiliate it with the Metropolitan Opera Company. He presented his first Stravinsky Festival in 1937 with *Apollo*, *The Card Game*, and *The Fairy's Kiss*. He then worked for the Ringling Brothers Circus (he and Stravinsky created a ballet for elephants), Broadway (eighteen musicals and revues), and Hollywood (four films). In the cinema and musical comedy he introduced diversified choreography integrated into the plot, a dream ballet sequence that was a favorite of Broadway choreographers for thirty years, and innovations in filming dance utilizing the advantages of camera effects.

Balanchine's American Ballet company was summoned back into temporary existence by the State Department in 1941, for a goodwill tour of Latin America. This tour marked the first performing arts sponsorship by the United States government and the beginning of cultural exchange programs. The School of American Ballet became a permanent institution, producing young American dancers of the highest caliber under Balanchine's exacting standards.

Balanchine and Kirstein founded the Ballet Society in 1946. The premiere included one of his most unusual works, *The Four Temperaments*, to music by Paul Hindemith, a forceful yet impersonal and technically difficult ballet. In 1948 came *Orpheus* (with music by Stravinsky), in which the choreography interpreted the Greek legend with great poignancy and dramatic style.

In 1948, the Ballet Society became the New York City Ballet, the resident company of the New York City Center for Music and Drama (owned by the City of New York), the first American ballet company to become a public institution. By this time, Balanchine had choreographed more than fifty ballets and was nurturing a nucleus of dancers, trained at his school, who would develop into the ideal Balanchine dancer: slim, elongated, with impeccable technique and a highly developed sense of musical phrasing that would combine to respond to Balanchine's complex interpretation of music.

Frequent European tours beginning in 1950 established the company as one of the most important in the world, with a unique repertory and style that would nevertheless continue to be controversial. Important ballets followed, including *La Valse* (music by Maurice Ravel), *Metamorphoses* (Hindemith), *Opus 34* (Arnold Schoenberg), *Ivesiana* (Charles Ives), and *Western Symphony* (Hershy Kay), the last of which reflected Balanchine's enthusiasm for the Wild West. He was also a guest choreographer for leading European ballet and opera companies.

Balanchine was fascinated by female dancers and often said that "ballet is woman." His second marriage was to Vera Zorina, his third to Maria Tallchief. His fourth wife, the brilliant young dancer Tanaquil LeClercq, contracted polio in 1956. Although it was feared that Balanchine would retire after this tragedy, he returned to the company the following year and continued to develop his repertory for the next twenty-five years. *Agon* (1937; music by Stravinsky) completed his Greek mythology trilogy. A contest of technique between dancers, it presented seventeenth century dance forms updated by contemporary rhythms. *The Nutcracker* (1954; music by Tchaikovsky) his first evening-length ballet, became an annual, sold-out Christmas season presentation.

In 1962, the New York City Ballet made a State Department-sponsored tour of the Soviet Union. While acclaimed for the quality of the dancers and for his choreographic abilities, Balanchine was sharply criticized in the Moscow press for his plotless ballets. Yet the Moscow audience, reticent at first, became highly enthusiastic. Leningrad, more cultivated and Europeanized, was captivated by the performances, which coincided with the beginning of a reaction against Soviet realism in the arts. Throughout the tour, the Soviets attempted to point out Balanchine's ties to Russian culture. Diplomatically,

George Balanchine. (Hulton Archive/Getty Images)

Balanchine would accept the honors bestowed on him on behalf of the United States and the New York City Ballet and then assert that he was an American.

Tangible successes followed in the 1960's. The Ford Foundation made an unprecedented grant in 1963 of more than $7.75 million, almost all of which was awarded to Balanchine's organizations. In 1964, the New York City Ballet became the resident company of the New York State Theatre at Lincoln Center, which was probably the first theater to be designed according to the specifications of a choreographer. In 1967, the company established a yearly summer residency at the Saratoga Performing Arts Center in New York. Balanchine choreographed four full-length ballets during this decade: William Shakespeare's *A Midsummer Night's Dream* (music by Felix Mendelssohn), *Harlequinade* (Ricardo Drigo), *Don Quixote* (Nicholas Nabokov), and *Jewels*, the first full-length plotless ballet, with music by Gabriel-Urbain Fauré, Stravinsky, and Tchaikovsky.

Notable achievements in the 1970's were festivals for Stravinsky and Ravel (the latter included *Le Tombeau de Couperin*, choreographed entirely for sixteen members of the corps de ballet, with no soloists), a full-length *Coppelia* (music by Leo Delibes), the highly popular *Vienna Waltzes*, and the first of a series of ballet telecasts for *Dance in America* on National Educational Television. In the 1980's, despite failing health, Balanchine presented a Tchaikovsky Festival and a retrospective Stravinsky Festival. He died in 1983 in New York City.

SIGNIFICANCE

Balanchine brought the Old World art of ballet to the United States, blended its traditions into a contemporary, diversified language, and established his version of it around the country and the world as a uniquely American product. His school became the first institution in the United States to establish permanent, high-quality standards of dance training. He choreographed children's roles into many of his ballets to give children the same opportunity he had had to experience the joys and wonder of the theater. He organized lecture-demonstration tours for schools, free ballet performances for underprivileged children, free annual seminars for dance teachers, and gave free advice and use of his ballets to other ballet companies. The landmark grant from the Ford Foundation was the signal for other philanthropic foundations to contribute to performing arts organizations in the United States.

In evolving a contemporary choreography, Balanchine was influenced primarily by music, and as such exposed his audience to a vast range of modern as well as earlier composers, including the Americans George Gershwin, John Philip Sousa, and Richard Rodgers. He brought a tradition-bound art form into the twentieth century, freeing it from the excesses of stylization that had obscured the beauty and expressiveness of dance. When presenting a story, a subtly portrayed emotion or outlook, he produced mime and nonballetic aspects that were easily recognizable from everyday gestures. Balanchine's ballets explored different cultures, human relationships, and theatrical forms, and integrated them into his unique interpretation of the music. He emphasized what has

been called an American energy in his dancers. He developed their technical range at all levels and for both sexes, achieving more harmonious dance compositions by greater participation of all the dancers on the stage.

Balanchine's fifty years of work in the United States brought to millions a highly developed art form that was respectful of its traditions yet forged ahead in innovations and integrated various cultures and fields.

—*Karen Resnick Pellón*

FURTHER READING

Ashley, Merrill. *Dancing for Balanchine*. New York: E. P. Dutton, 1984. Autobiography of a Balanchine dancer with Balanchine as special focus. Gives a fascinating account of Balanchine's methods as teacher, choreographer, and mentor.

Balanchine, George, and Francis Mason. *Balanchine's Complete Stories of the Great Ballets*. Garden City, N.Y.: Doubleday, 1977. Plot summaries and historical data on four hundred important ballets. Includes valuable articles by Balanchine of his life and views of ballet.

Duberman, Martin B. *The Worlds of Lincoln Kirstein*. New York: Alfred A. Knopf, 2007. This biography of Kirstein, the driving force behind the New York City Ballet, describes how he brought Balanchine to the United States and how the two worked together to create a premier American ballet company.

Fisher, Barbara Milberg. *In Balanchine's Company: A Dancer's Memoir*. Middletown, Conn.: Wesleyan University Press, 2006. Fisher, a dancer with the New York City Ballet from 1946 through 1958, recalls her experiences working with Balanchine. An articulate and perceptive memoir that describes Balanchine's choreographic methods and the evolution of some of his best-known ballets.

Gottlieb, Robert. *George Balanchine: The Ballet Maker*. New York: HarperCollins/Atlas Books, 2004. Gottlieb, a former board member of the New York City Ballet, provides a brief but complete biography.

Katz, Leslie George, and Harvey Simmonds, comp. *Choreography by George Balanchine: A Catalogue of Works*. New York: Eakins Press Foundation, 1983. Complete chronological list of Balanchine's 425 works with opening-night casts and notes, and extensive bibliography. Indispensable catalog of Balanchine's work.

Kirstein, Lincoln. *Thirty Years: The New York City Ballet*. New York: Alfred A. Knopf, 1978. Interesting, though chatty and somewhat rambling, selective memoirs. Worthwhile secondary text by Balanchine's patron and adviser.

McDonagh, Don. *George Balanchine*. Boston: Twayne, 1983. Concise, well-rounded biography combined with analytical discussion of selected ballets and Balanchine's development. An invaluable study.

Reynolds, Nancy. *Repertory in Review: Forty Years of the New York City Ballet*. New York: Dial Press, 1977. Excellent historical perspective on the company's repertory and periods, including informative article on the school and Balanchine.

Teachout, Terry. *All in the Dances: A Brief Life of George Balanchine*. Orlando, Fla.: Harcourt, 2004. Solid introduction to Balanchine's life and art for students and general readers, written in a style one critic described as "pithy, conversational, and vivid."

SEE ALSO: Alexandra Danilova; Agnes de Mille; Sergei Diaghilev; Dame Margot Fonteyn; Paul Hindemith; Serge Lifar; Léonide Massine; Vaslav Nijinsky; Rudolf Nureyev; Anna Pavlova.

RELATED ARTICLES in *Great Events from History: The Twentieth Century:*

1901-1940: December 6, 1934: Balanchine's *Serenade* Inaugurates American Ballet; April 5, 1938: Ballet Russe de Monte Carlo Debuts.

1941-1970: November 20, 1946: First Performance by Balanchine and Kirstein's Ballet Society; March 12, 1963: Nureyev and Fonteyn Debut Ashton's *Marguerite and Armand*; 1968: Mitchell and Shook Found the Dance Theatre of Harlem.

1971-2000: Fall, 1980: Baryshnikov Becomes Artistic Director of American Ballet Theatre.

EMILY GREENE BALCH
American social reformer and economist

Among the first generation of women to graduate from college in large numbers, Balch authored the frequently cited Our Slavic Fellow Citizens, *cofounded the Women's International League for Peace and Freedom in 1915, and, as a reward for her peace activism, won the Nobel Peace Prize in 1946.*

BORN: January 8, 1867; Jamaica Plain (now Boston), Massachusetts

DIED: January 9, 1961; Cambridge, Massachusetts

AREAS OF ACHIEVEMENT: Social reform, peace advocacy, economics, education

EARLY LIFE

Emily Greene Balch (bawlch) was born in Jamaica Plain, Massachusetts. Her parents were Unitarians of English descent who could trace their ancestors to the early seventeenth century American colonies. Her father, Francis Vergnies Balch, was a lawyer. Her mother, Ellen Maria (Noyes) Balch, was a housewife who had six children and died at the age of forty-seven, when Emily was seventeen.

Balch received an unusually good education for her time. While attending private schools, she lived with her family in suburban Boston. At a time when women college graduates were regarded as social oddities and were less likely to marry, her father encouraged her to go to college. She chose the new school of Bryn Mawr because

that was where her best friend was going. Bryn Mawr was founded by members of the Quaker religion, a religion that Balch eventually adopted. She was graduated in three years with a major in classics and won Bryn Mawr's European fellowship as the outstanding senior. After privately studying sociology with Franklin H. Giddings, she used the fellowship to spend a year in Paris researching the public relief system there. The result was her book, *Public Assistance of the Poor in France*, published by the American Economic Association in 1893.

LIFE'S WORK

Balch's career can be divided into several phases, the first of which centered on social work. She became an expert on agencies and laws dealing with juvenile delinquency, and, in 1895, published the seventy-two-page *Manual for Use in Cases of Juvenile Offenders and Other Minors in Massachusetts*. Four years later, concerned women in Chicago brought about the first juvenile court. Subsequently, Balch revised her manual twice, in 1903 and 1908. Meanwhile, she met Jane Addams and others involved in the settlement house movement. In 1892, Balch joined a group of female college graduates in founding Denison House in Boston and headed that settlement during its first year. Through her continued involvement in Denison House, Balch came into direct contact with the poor, learning at first hand about working conditions and obstacles to labor organizing. After

Emily Greene Balch. (© The Nobel Foundation)

several years of charitable volunteering, however, she decided that she would have more impact as a teacher of social and economic subjects, inspiring her students to work for reform and guiding them in the best ways to achieve it.

To prepare for teaching, the second phase of Balch's career, she studied briefly at Radcliffe (then called Harvard Annex), the University of Chicago, and the University of Berlin. At the last institution, she became especially familiar with socialism. Attending with her was another woman from Boston, Mary Kingsbury, who was later married to a student from Russia, Vladimir Simkhovitch, and who founded Greenwich House, a settlement in New York City. Balch and Kingsbury became lifelong friends and were also part of a national network of settlement leaders and reformers, many of them women, that provided support for one another's goals and causes. On Balch's return to Boston in 1896, she accepted a half-time position teaching economics at Wellesley College. The following year, she became a full-time instructor, in 1903, an associate professor, and in 1913, a professor.

At Wellesley, she taught courses on socialism with Karl Marx's *Das Kapital* (1867) as the text, as well as courses on the labor movement, urban problems, economic history, and immigration. Balch was the kind of teacher who was actively involved in what she taught and who sought to stimulate a similar involvement on the part of her students. After 1913, Balch headed Wellesley's Department of Economics and Sociology. She also continued her social activism. At one point, the president of Wellesley told Balch that she was not given the normal promotion because she had loaned two hundred dollars to a union whose bitter strike she had supported. If such a warning had any effect on Balch, it was to deepen her commitment to social activism. Balch was among the founders, in 1903, of the Women's Trade Union League, serving for a time as its president. She also served on a variety of boards and commissions, including Boston's City Planning Board (1914-1917), two state commissions—one on industrial education (1908-1909) and another on immigration (1913-1914)—and the committee on immigration of the Progressive Party (1912).

Balch's landmark accomplishment as a professor was her definitive study of Slavic immigration, published as *Our Slavic Fellow Citizens* in 1910. When Balch began this project on a sabbatical leave in 1904, the systematic study of a particular immigrant group was largely untried. Balch did her research on both sides of the Atlantic—traveling to Austria-Hungary to investigate the conditions that caused immigrants to leave their homeland and then traveling around the United States to visit Slavic communities. To facilitate her research, she acquired a rudimentary knowledge of the Czech language. In addition to her sabbatical year, she took a second year off without pay and met all of her own research expenses. She described how the Slavs, by migrating, had gained in both self-respect and freedom, and she predicted that they would add richness and vitality to American culture. *Our Slavic Fellow Citizens* dispelled many misconceptions and prejudices directed against immigrants and provided ammunition for those fighting against a restrictive immigrant policy. The work is still frequently cited and excerpted in books about immigration.

When World War I broke out, Balch began her involvement in peace activities, which constituted the third and best-known phase of her career. A number of women connected with the settlement-house movement, Balch among them, followed Jane Addams's lead and, in 1915, went to The Hague in the Netherlands for the International Women's Congress for Peace and Freedom. The

U.S. Congress moved to send representatives to meet with heads of state to urge them to back a plan for neutral mediation of the war. Out of more than eleven hundred voting members, Balch was chosen as one of the seven official representatives. She visited with top officials in half a dozen countries, including President Woodrow Wilson. The scheme came to nothing, but Balch helped edit the proceedings of the peace congress and also joined Alice Hamilton and Jane Addams in writing *Women at The Hague* (1915). The peace congress was significant in that it was the initial gathering of women from many countries to work for peace. As such, it laid the foundation for the Women's International League for Peace and Freedom, formed first as the Woman's Peace Party in 1915.

Balch thought that Henry Ford's ideas on how peace could be obtained were crude, but with no overtly positive government response to the mediation efforts of the Women's Congress, Balch, in 1916, participated in the Ford-sponsored Neutral Conference for continuous mediation in Stockholm. Again, she met with President Wilson to push for a plan for mediation. During this period, the United States was moving toward war.

As peace work continued to occupy Balch, her ties to Wellesley loosened. She took a sabbatical leave during 1916-1917 to take courses at Columbia University and to work for various peace organizations. She was active in the Women's Peace Party, the Fellowship of Reconciliation, the Collegiate Anti-Militarism League, and the Committee Against Militarism. Once the United States declared war, pacifism became decidedly unpatriotic. Balch, however, did not swerve from her beliefs. At a time when faculty were not protected by tenure, she thought it prudent to extend her leave from Wellesley. In 1918, she published her thoughts on the impending peace settlement, *Approaches to the Great Settlement*. Also, about that time, her Wellesley appointment expired, and the college declined to reappoint her, the final decision coming in 1919. That decision ended Balch's academic career of more than twenty years and left her professionally stranded without a pension at the age of fifty-two. Faculty protests were ineffective. While Balch's pacifist activities were the main reason for Wellesley's action, her liberal social views on other issues played a role. Balch refused to press her case further. As time passed, Wellesley's position softened. The college invited her back to speak in 1935, and, in 1946, Wellesley's president helped Balch secure the Nobel Peace Prize.

During this time, Balch found a job on the editorial staff of *The Nation*. Then, with the establishment of the League of Nations, the Women's International League for Peace and Freedom decided to open an office in Geneva. Balch was the group's secretary-treasurer and had the task of finding suitable quarters and developing the organization's work with the League of Nations. She oversaw publication of a newsletter, entertained visitors from around the world, made the headquarters a quiet retreat from the bustle going on in the League of Nations, and organized the group's Third International Congress in 1921. In 1922, she went to Varese, Italy, to organize a summer school, but at the last minute switched the location of the school to Lugano, Switzerland, because fascist bands had invaded Varese. Exhausted, she resigned from her official duties with the Women's International League in the fall of 1922 but continued her involvement with that organization. A special league project in 1927 was an investigation of social, economic, and political conditions in Haiti, which the U.S. Marines had occupied since 1915. Balch accompanied five others to Haiti, then edited and wrote most of their report, which was published as *Occupied Haiti* (1927). Subsequently, Balch met with President Coolidge. Several years later, Herbert Hoover's policy of restoring self-government was reminiscent of the recommendations made by the Women's International League.

During the early 1930's, Balch was president of the American section of the Women's International League for Peace and Freedom. She continued to maintain a lively interest in a variety of international issues, ranging from disarmament to the Spanish Civil War. In the mid-1930's, she was once again elected secretary-treasurer of the Women's International League, and then, later, honorary president.

Balch believed that pacifists needed to confront the moral issues that arose as a result of World War II. Two of Balch's concerns were the treatment of Japanese Americans and refuge for Jews from Nazi Germany. Her international outlook was vindicated: In 1946, she was a corecipient of the Nobel Peace Prize with John R. Mott, the international Young Men's Christian Association leader. She gave the seventeen-thousand-dollar award to the Women's League.

Balch never married and refused the offers of women friends to live with them permanently, preferring to live her life in her own way. She eschewed fashionable dress, but she enjoyed sketching with pastels and, in 1941, published a book of poetry, *The Miracle of Living*. Her disciplined intelligence, varied interests, and public experiences were the expressions of a rich inner life. Active in League affairs into her nineties, she died in a nursing home in Cambridge, Massachusetts, at the age of ninety-four.

SIGNIFICANCE

Balch represents the best of the first generation of women to be graduated from college in significant numbers. These women believed themselves to be special, and they felt an obligation to do something useful with their college education. Initially, Balch was attracted to social work, a profession unique in that women not only dominated it numerically but also in terms of leadership. Balch became part of a lifelong network of women reformers, even though she soon left social work for college teaching. As a professor, her greatest accomplishment was the highly regarded *Our Slavic Fellow Citizens*. A woman of firm convictions, she persisted in pacifist activities even though they cost her her college career. Much of her peace efforts went into the Women's International League for Peace and Freedom, an organization that is also part of her legacy as idealistic, determined, and with high intellectual standards.

—*Judith Ann Trolander*

FURTHER READING

Balch, Emily Greene. "Women for Peace and Freedom." *Survey Graphic* 35 (October, 1946): 358-360. Balch's World War II observations on Europe and on the Women's International League for Peace and Freedom.

Bussey, Gertrude, and Margaret Tims. *Women's International League for Peace and Freedom, 1915-1965: A Record of Fifty Years' Work*. London: George Allen and Unwin, 1965. Balch is frequently mentioned in this historical account of the organization, which absorbed so much of her peace efforts.

Davis, Allen F. *American Heroine: The Life and Legend of Jane Addams*. New York: Oxford University Press, 1973. A biographical account of Jane Addams that is also a good source for her relationship to Balch.

"Plain People: 'A' for Effort." *Time*, November, 1946, 33. A brief account of the circumstances surrounding Balch's receipt of the Nobel Peace Prize.

Randall, John Herman, Jr. "Emily Greene Balch." *The Nation*, January, 1947, 14-15. Recalls Balch's work on the editorial staff of *The Nation*.

_____. *Emily Greene Balch of New England: Citizen of the World*. Washington, D.C.: Women's International League for Peace and Freedom, 1946. A twelve-page summary of Balch's career.

Randall, Mercedes M. *Improper Bostonian: Emily Greene Balch*. New York: Twayne, 1964. A charming, insightful, and carefully crafted biography. The author was an associate of Balch in the Women's International League for Peace and Freedom.

Whipps, Judy D. "The Feminist Pacifism of Emily Greene Balch." *NWSA Journal* 18, no. 3 (Fall, 2006): 122-132. Discusses Balch's pacifist activities within the context of contemporary politics, pointing out the similarities between the work of twentieth and twenty-first century peace activists.

SEE ALSO: Jane Addams; Carrie Chapman Catt; Dorothy Day; Emma Goldman; Mother Jones; Julia C. Lathrop; Frances Perkins; Margaret Sanger; Lillian D. Wald; Ida B. Wells-Barnett.

RELATED ARTICLE in *Great Events from History: The Twentieth Century:*

1901-1940: April 28-May 1, 1915: International Congress of Women.

JAMES BALDWIN
American novelist and essayist

During the racial unrest in the United States in the 1960's, Baldwin was the most visible and respected literary figure of the Civil Rights movement. His best work focused on racial concerns and homosexuality.

BORN: August 2, 1924; New York, New York
DIED: December 1, 1987; St. Paul de Vence, France
ALSO KNOWN AS: James Arthur Baldwin (full name)
AREAS OF ACHIEVEMENT: Literature, civil rights

EARLY LIFE
James Baldwin, the son of Berdis Jones Baldwin and the stepson of David Baldwin, a Baptist preacher, was born and grew up in New York City's black ghetto, Harlem; he was the oldest of nine children. By the time he was fourteen years old, Baldwin, then a student in New York's De Witt Clinton High School, was preaching in Harlem's Fireside Pentecostal Church. His earliest writing appeared in *The Magpie*, his high school's student newspaper, to which he contributed three stories before becoming editor in chief, a job he shared with fellow student Richard Avedon.

On graduation from high school in 1942, Baldwin, rejected for military service, took a job working for a railroad in New Jersey. He had just renounced the church and, although he never went back to it and scorned Christianity for what he perceived as its racism, much of the rhythm of black preaching and much of the drama of evangelical church services are found in most of his work. Baldwin sought refuge in the church during an uncertain period in his adolescence, but as he analyzed seriously his position as both a member of a racial minority and gay, he found in literature more helpful solutions to the problems that plagued him than he had found in religion.

Between 1942 and 1944, Baldwin held menial jobs, some of them in the thriving wartime defense industries. A turning point came for him in 1944, when, having moved to New York City's Greenwich Village, he met Richard Wright, one of the leading black writers in the United States. Baldwin was working on his first novel, "In My Father's House," at that time. Although the novel remained unpublished, Wright arranged for Baldwin to receive the Eugene F. Saxton Memorial Trust so that he could concentrate on his writing. Baldwin first appeared in print in 1946 in *The Nation*, where he published a book review. He also wrote book reviews for *The New Leader* during the same year.

In 1948, Baldwin, slight of stature and with a countenance that reflected both intensity and anguish, received the Rosenwald Fellowship. This award enabled him to move to Paris. That year, he also published an essay, "The Harlem Ghetto," and a short story, "Previous Condition," in *Commentary*. Baldwin was to live abroad for the next decade, in the middle of which his first novel, *Go Tell It on the Mountain* (1953), was published.

LIFE'S WORK
Baldwin's first two novels, *Go Tell It on the Mountain* and *Giovanni's Room* (1956), are autobiographical. The former concentrates on the problems of growing up black in a predominantly white United States. The book explores the impact that religion has had on the black experience in the United States and accurately depicts the

James Baldwin. (© John Hoppy Hopkins)

economic and social struggles with which black families coped on a regular basis. The book is also concerned with the sexual tensions that existed for blacks coming of age and beset by deep-seated interracial conflicts.

Giovanni's Room, set in France, was one of many novels on homosexuality to appear between 1948 and 1956. The protagonist's lover, Giovanni, kills an older man who forces him into a sexual encounter and is duly tried, found guilty, and executed for this crime. David, the protagonist, has to cope not only with feeling guilty about his homosexuality but also with feelings of not having been the loyal friend that Giovanni needed.

When *Go Tell It on the Mountain* appeared, Baldwin was working on a play, *The Amen Corner*, which was performed at Howard University in 1954 but that took nearly a decade to reach Broadway (where it was produced in 1964 largely because of the New York success of Baldwin's *Blues for Mister Charlie*, which the American National Theater Association brought to Broadway in the spring of 1964).

The publication of *Go Tell It on the Mountain* led to Baldwin's being awarded a Guggenheim Fellowship in 1954, which afforded him the opportunity to do extensive revisions on *The Amen Corner* and to complete his much-acclaimed *Notes of a Native Son* (1955), a fierce, well-written book that articulates the outrage that Baldwin, as a sensitive black American, felt because of the social inequities that face blacks. Perhaps this book makes its greatest impact with its contention that racial hatred destroys not only the objects of that hatred but also the people who are possessed by it. *Notes of a Native Son* was to become one of the most influential statements about racial inequality during the Civil Rights movement that was beginning to gain momentum in the late 1950's and that emerged full-blown in the 1960's.

Giovanni's Room brought Baldwin increased recognition in the form of a *Partisan Review* fellowship and an award from the National Institute of Arts and Letters. He returned to the United States from France in 1957 and made his first visit to the South. He wrote about this trip in both *Harper's Magazine* and *Partisan Review*. A Ford Foundation grant-in-aid enabled him in November,

---

SELF-IDENTITY THROUGH STRUGGLE

In this passage from The Fire Next Time *(1963), James Baldwin discusses the ultimate good that can be realized from living a life of "endless struggle": autonomy, certainty, and a knowingness "that is unshakable."*

It is entirely unacceptable that I should have no voice in the political affairs of my own country, for I am not a ward of America; I am one of the first Americans to arrive on these shores.

This past, the Negro's past, of rope, fire, torture, castration, infanticide, rape; death and humiliation; fear by day and night, fear as deep as the marrow of the bone; doubt that he was worthy of life, since everyone around him denied it; sorrow for his women, for his kinfolk, for his children, who needed his protection, and whom he could not protect; rage, hatred, and murder, hatred for white men so deep that it often turned against him and his own, and made all love, all trust, all joy impossible—this past, this endless struggle to achieve and reveal and confirm a human identity, human authority, yet contains, for all its horror, something very beautiful. I do not mean to be sentimental about suffering—enough is certainly as good as a feast—but people who cannot suffer can never grow up, can never discover who they are. That man who is forced each day to snatch his manhood, his identity, out of the fire of human cruelty that rages to destroy it knows, if he survives his effort, and even if he does not survive it, something about himself and human life that no school on earth—and, indeed, no church—can teach. He achieves his own authority, and that is unshakable.

1959, to return to Paris, where he spent the winter. On returning to the United States in the spring of 1960, Baldwin wrote articles for *Esquire* and *Mademoiselle*. In the late summer, he went to Tallahassee, Florida, as a participant in strategy sessions held by the newly formed Congress of Racial Equality (CORE), and in so doing he cast his lot with the activists in the Civil Rights movement.

In 1961, Baldwin published another collection of essays, *Nobody Knows My Name: More Notes of a Native Son*. This collection, vivid and subtle, emphasizes that blacks are simultaneously like and unlike other people. Baldwin depicts the black quest as a quest for love and for acceptance at the personal and interpersonal levels as well as at the broader social level.

Baldwin held that humankind's only possible salvation is love, although as time passed, Baldwin became increasingly pessimistic about the possibility of the human race approaching the idyllic state that (as he cautioned in his two earliest collections of essays) must be achieved if the race is to survive. Baldwin accused Americans of not judging individuals by their work but rather of leaping to conclusions about them based on preexisting stereotypes.

In his next novel, *Another Country* (1962), Baldwin dealt with love between a black woman and a white man who defy the conventions of their society and whose quest is to discover their own and each other's real identities. Again, Baldwin emphasizes that people are individuals. It does not matter with whom or how they pursue love. Society and its mores should have nothing to do with such matters because it is the individuals and their love that are all-important. In the year in which *Another Country* was published, Baldwin traveled to Africa in an attempt to find a closer identity with his heritage.

Baldwin's collection of essays issued under the title *The Fire Next Time* (1963) focuses on the mental and spiritual turmoil of American blacks. Enthusiastically received by Civil Rights activists of the time, the book won for Baldwin the George Polk Memorial Award. Though he lived largely outside the United States, Baldwin had become the undisputed literary leader of the Civil Rights movement.

Going to Meet the Man (1965) appeared shortly after *Blues for Mister Charlie* and *The Amen Corner* were presented on Broadway. Interest in Baldwin was high. His next novel, however, *Tell Me How Long the Train's Been Gone* (1968), was badly misfocused and did not have the impact of much of his earlier work. Some critics thought that Baldwin was on a downhill course after the publication of this book. *No Name in the Street* (1972), *One Day, When I Was Lost* (1972), and *If Beale Street Could Talk* (1974) did little to recapture his fading reputation. His collaborations, *Nothing Personal* (1964) with Richard Avedon, *A Rap on Race* (1971) with Margaret Mead, and *A Dialogue* (1975) with Nikki Giovanni, were not taken as seriously as his earlier works had been. He redeemed himself, however, in the eyes of many readers with *Just Above My Head* (1979), a novel about a child evangelist that reiterates much that Baldwin had previously written about the need for love and for judging people as individuals.

The Devil Finds Work (1976) was received with some critical indifference, but *The Evidence of Things Not Seen* (1985), on the Atlanta child murders and the trial of the alleged killer, has had a significant impact and was considered of sufficient importance to be reprinted by the American Bar Association. Baldwin's nonfiction writing has been collected in *The Price of the Ticket: Collected Nonfiction, 1948-1985* (1985).

SIGNIFICANCE

Baldwin served as the conscience of the Civil Rights movement and as the conscience of liberal whites, to whom he pointed out that the destructive force of racial intolerance and bigotry is felt not only by those at whom it is aimed but also by those within the dominant society. Baldwin's voice was anguished, but he was a well-informed spokesperson for the cause of racial equality, having been brought up in a society from which he continually felt alienated. Not only was Baldwin able to identify the problems caused by racial strife, but, more important, he was able to propose an overall solution based on love and acceptance.

Baldwin usually communicated more persuasively in his essays than he did in his novels, where he sometimes fell victim to the problem that he warned others against, that of dealing with stereotypes rather than with well-defined individuals.

—*R. Baird Shuman*

FURTHER READING

Balfour, Katharine Lawrence. *The Evidence of Things Not Said: James Baldwin and the Promise of American Democracy*. Ithaca, N.Y.: Cornell University Press, 2000. Balfour argues that Baldwin was a "democratic thinker" concerned about the promise and failure of American democracy, and she reexamines his work from that perspective.

Bloom, Harold, ed. *James Baldwin*. Philadelphia: Chelsea House, 2006. Collection of essays, including a biography, with an introduction by Bloom.

Clark, Kenneth B. *The Negro Protest: James Baldwin, Malcolm X, Martin Luther King Talk with Kenneth B. Clark*. Boston: Beacon Press, 1963. Clark's interview with Baldwin focuses more on the writer's political stance than on him as a literary figure. The portion of the book devoted to Baldwin provides strong insights into his moral philosophy and into his hopes for the human race, which he was later to moderate.

Eckman, Fern Marja. *The Furious Passage of James Baldwin*. New York: M. Evans, 1966. Eckman's critical biography depicts the inner tumult that was the driving force behind Baldwin's most forceful writing. Shows the effect that Baldwin's religious upbringing and that his own early religious involvement had in shaping his thinking.

Kinnamon, Keneth, ed. *James Baldwin: A Collection of Critical Essays*. Englewood Cliffs, N.J.: Prentice-Hall, 1973. These thirteen well-chosen and representative essays deal with Baldwin from a variety of critical standpoints. They range from critical biography to essays on Baldwin's ontology. The editor provides a penetrating, short introduction.

Macebuh, Stanley. *James Baldwin: A Critical Study.* New York: Third Press, 1973. This study focuses on Baldwin's inner torment and relates it directly to the religious influences of his early youth. Claims that much of his best writing is an attempt to exorcise his personal dread of hell.

O'Daniel, Therman B., ed. *James Baldwin: A Critical Evaluation.* Washington, D.C.: Howard University Press, 1977. Contains one of the best considerations of Baldwin's prose style as well as insights into his Americanness and his ability to focus on his alienation particularly when he was living abroad. The twenty-two essays in the book are enhanced by a comprehensive bibliography, which, although dated, provides a good starting point for researchers.

Pratt, Louis H. *James Baldwin.* New York: Twayne, 1978. An excellent overview with a well-selected bibliography and a succinct but useful chronological table. The book is sometimes more event-oriented than idea-oriented. It will, however, be serviceable to readers lacking familiarity with Baldwin and his work.

Sylvander, Carolyn Wedin. *James Baldwin.* New York: Frederick Ungar, 1980. A brief but valuable study, balancing Baldwin, the political activist, and Baldwin, the writer. The book is carefully thought out and objective. The bibliography is also useful.

SEE ALSO: Lorraine Hansberry; Langston Hughes; Zora Neale Hurston; Jack Kerouac; Toni Morrison; Paul Robeson; Alice Walker.

RELATED ARTICLES in *Great Events from History: The Twentieth Century:*

1901-1940: 1940: Wright's *Native Son* Depicts Racism in America.

1941-1970: 1963: Baldwin Voices Black Rage in *The Fire Next Time.*

STANLEY BALDWIN
Prime minister of the United Kingdom (1923-1924, 1924-1929, 1935-1937)

Baldwin was the dominant political figure in British politics during the 1920's and 1930's and was prime minister on three separate occasions. He personified both the attempt to narrow class differences during that era and the unsuccessful policies to avoid a second world war.

BORN: August 3, 1867; Bewdley, Worcestershire, England

DIED: December 14, 1947; Astley Hall, Worcestershire, England

ALSO KNOWN AS: First Earl Baldwin of Bewdley; Viscount Corvedale of Corvedale

AREA OF ACHIEVEMENT: Government and politics

EARLY LIFE

Stanley Baldwin was born in Bewdley, Worcestershire, England, four miles from his father's iron mill. His father, Alfred Baldwin, had reinvigorated the family firm, and he was also successful in politics. Even though Baldwin came to represent the typical Englishman, his mother, Louisa MacDonald, was Scottish and Irish. She was the daughter of a Methodist minister and became a minor novelist and poet. One of her sisters married the Pre-Raphaelite painter Sir Edward Burne-Jones, and another became the mother of the writer Rudyard Kipling, who was one of Baldwin's closest friends. Stanley was an only child and often lonely because of his father's business and political interests and his mother's uncertain health. He early came to love the English countryside and as a young boy was an avid reader of novels and history. As expected of one of his social class, he entered the exclusive public school of Harrow in 1881 and Trinity College, Cambridge, in 1885, where he studied history. He was an indifferent student and left the university in 1888 to join the family firm. He had earlier, however, considered becoming a clergyman in the Church of England: His later political career at times reflected his spiritual concerns.

The Baldwin firm had a history of excellent labor relations. Strikes and lockouts were unknown, and the managers knew the names and family background of all of the employees. This was influential in the formation of Baldwin's attitudes toward the working class: Conflict was to be avoided in the search for a unified community. Yet life was not all work, for Baldwin loved long walks, tennis, village cricket, and the locale where he first met his future wife, Lucy Ridsdale. They were married in 1892 and eventually had seven children. Lucy was more extroverted than Baldwin, and they complemented each other well. It was an ideal relationship that endured more than fifty years.

Baldwin's father died in 1908, and Baldwin replaced him as a Conservative member of the House of Commons. He spoke seldom and remained an obscure backbencher until the fall of H. H. Asquith in late 1916. In David Lloyd George's coalition government, Baldwin became the parliamentary private secretary to Bonar Law, the head of the Conservative Party. The many sacrifices made in World War I affected Baldwin deeply. His cousin, Kipling, lost a son, and his mentor, Law, lost two. After the war ended, Baldwin sent an anonymous letter to *The Times* of London, stating that he had personally given one-fifth of his estate, £120,000, to the government to help defray the enormous cost of the war. He hoped that others would follow his example, but few did. During the war, he had become joint financial secretary to the Treasury. In early 1921, he joined the cabinet as president of the Board of Trade but was overshadowed by such figures as Lloyd George, Law, Winston Churchill, Austen Chamberlain, and the first earl of Birkenhead.

LIFE'S WORK

The attitudes and atmosphere of the postwar world offended Baldwin's traditionalism. He was particularly disturbed by the cynicism and opportunism of many of his fellow members of the government, not least by Lloyd George himself. It appeared to Baldwin that the leaders of the coalition were interested only in maintaining themselves in power at whatever cost. When it was proposed that the coalition continue, Baldwin, though a member of the government, opposed it, and in October, 1922, Lloyd George resigned, never to hold office again. Law became prime minister, and because several leading Conservatives refused to abandon the idea of a new coalition, Baldwin, a less prominent figure, became Chancellor of the Exchequer.

In May, 1923, Law was forced to resign as prime minister as a result of ill health. The two leading candidates to replace him were Foreign Secretary Lord Curzon and Baldwin. Curzon expected to be appointed, but his abrasive personality and his membership in the House of Lords were handicaps too great to overcome, and at the age of fifty-five, Baldwin became prime minister. It was a meteoric rise from the obscurity of a few years before.

Baldwin faced several handicaps. His party was still divided. In addition, the British economy was suffering from the effects of the war. For both political and economic reasons, Baldwin, to the shocked surprise of many, argued that the solution to Great Britain's economic problems was to adopt tariffs to protect domestic indus-

Stanley Baldwin. (Library of Congress)

try. Free trade had been an article of faith for most since the mid-nineteenth century, and it had served Great Britain well, but Baldwin believed that it was no longer adequate in the competitive modern world. The result, however, was political defeat, and in January, 1924, the Labour Party, under Ramsay MacDonald, took power. Although Baldwin was harshly criticized, he remained the leader of the Conservatives.

The Labour Party did not have a majority in the House of Commons, and in October the government was defeated. For the second time, Baldwin became prime minister. By then, he had established his personal ascendancy over the House of Commons. During his long career he spent many hours in the House, developing a sensitive feeling for its various moods. He cultivated members of the Labour Party in the attempt to incorporate that party into the polity of the nation and to eliminate its potentially revolutionary aims. Baldwin's oratory was not spectacular, but he was one of the most compelling speakers in the Commons, with his appeal to traditional, moral, and national values. Physically he was of average height and gave the impression of a man comfortably at ease in the English countryside, broad-shouldered, his hair parted down the middle, and often with pipe in hand.

Baldwin's second government lasted from 1924 until 1929. He was able to reunify the Conservative Party by bringing into the cabinet Austen Chamberlain and Birkenhead. More controversially, he appointed Churchill as Chancellor of the Exchequer. Churchill, a Liberal for many years and a close associate of Lloyd George, had only recently rejoined the Conservatives. It was brilliant politics by Baldwin: He brought a potentially formidable opponent into his government and at the same time detached Churchill from Lloyd George's orbit. Yet Baldwin's political success was purchased at some cost. Baldwin's solution to the economic woes of the 1920's was tariffs, but Churchill was a free trader, and during those five years the policy of protection was abandoned.

Economic problems were at the root of the greatest crisis of those years. Even before World War I, Great Britain had begun to lose its industrial advantage to Germany and the United States; the war accelerated that process. During the immediate postwar years, the coal industry had done well, but by the early 1920's the coal mines on the Continent had recovered. The result was conflict between the British coal-mine owners and the working miners. The former wished to reduce wages and lengthen the hours of work; the latter resisted both. Finally, in May, 1926, the miners' union, supported by most other Labour organizations, called a general strike. Much of the ordinary business of Great Britain came to a halt. Baldwin, who was sympathetic to the plight of the miners, nevertheless saw the strike as a challenge to constitutional government, and he refused to negotiate until the strike was called off. Baldwin, a master of the new medium, radio, appealed to the nation for an end to the strike, promising all parties that they could trust him to be fair. After several days, the general strike collapsed. Baldwin, however, failed to follow through on his promise, and although he won a political victory, the chance to reorganize the coal industry was lost.

His administration had successes. At the ministry of health, Neville Chamberlain proved to be an able domestic reformer, and at the Foreign Office, his brother, Austen, negotiated the Treaty of Locarno (1925), which seemed to establish permanently and peacefully the national borders of Western Europe. By 1929, however, the government had lost its momentum. Whatever Baldwin's merits, he was not a forceful or dynamic leader. During the election, the Conservatives campaigned on the uninspiring slogan, "Safety First." The result was

the return of the Labour Party to power. Some blamed Baldwin for the defeat, but his popularity remained high among the voters.

There were two challenges to his leadership during the next few years. Newspaper proprietors Lord Beaverbrook and Lord Rothermere launched a campaign through their papers in favor of free trade within the British Empire and the adoption of tariffs toward the rest of the world. Baldwin was in favor of tariffs but doubted the practicality of such a program at that time. In addition, Baldwin saw this move as a political attack on himself and his party, and he successfully forced Beaverbrook and Rothermere to retreat. Baldwin's other challenge came from Churchill over the future of India. Baldwin supported greater self-government for India, but Churchill disagreed, romantically looking to the past glories of the British Raj and warning of violence between Hindus and Muslims if the British yoke were removed. Churchill had considerable support, but again Baldwin triumphed.

By mid-1931, the worldwide economic depression had seriously affected Great Britain. Unemployment reached three million, and the Labour government was unable either to reduce it or to raise sufficient funds to maintain the welfare and other government programs. The result was a split in the cabinet over MacDonald's decision to reduce benefits. MacDonald wanted to resign as prime minister, but King George V urged him to form a new coalition to solve the crisis. Baldwin somewhat reluctantly agreed to join the new national government. Although the Conservatives were by far the largest component, Baldwin became Lord President of the Council instead of prime minister, but during the next several years it was he rather than MacDonald who was the real leader of the government.

While the domestic economy improved during the 1930's as the Depression waned, foreign affairs deepened into crisis. The Japanese invasion of Manchuria in 1931, the coming to power of Adolf Hitler in 1933, Benito Mussolini's assault on Ethiopia, and other developments abroad forced difficult decisions on the government. As a result of the casualties in World War I, pacifism was widespread in Great Britain during the interwar years, and faith was placed, too optimistically, in the League of Nations. No one wanted war. The question was how to avoid it: by pacifism or by a strong defense. Baldwin himself had an abhorrence of war and was more concerned with domestic matters than foreign policy; reluctantly, however, and perhaps too slowly, he did lead the government toward rearmament.

In 1935, after George V's Silver Jubilee, MacDonald stepped down, and for the third time Baldwin became prime minister. He continued to face difficult foreign policy decisions: to oppose Italy's invasion of Ethiopia at the risk of having Mussolini turn to Hitler for support, or to attempt to come to terms with Hitler and risk alienating France. Baldwin's last accomplishment, however, concerned the throne. In January, 1936, George V died and was succeeded by his son, Edward VIII, a popular figure among all classes in Great Britain. He had never married, and at the time he became king he was romantically attached to an American, Wallis Simpson, a divorcé who had remarried. In the fall of 1936, Mrs. Simpson filed for a divorce. Edward hoped that he could marry Simpson even though she might not officially become queen, but neither Baldwin, the opposition Labour Party, nor the overseas Dominions would accept such a solution. Edward's choices were limited either to marriage or to the kingship, but he could not have both. He chose the former and abdicated the throne in favor of his younger brother, who became George VI.

SIGNIFICANCE

Baldwin resigned in May, 1937, the recipient of praise and honors. He accepted an earldom and a seat in the House of Lords. Neville Chamberlain, the new prime minister, more actively pursued a policy of appeasement toward Hitler. He failed, and in September, 1939, World War II began. With the outbreak of war, Baldwin's reputation declined. The fall of France and other defeats called into question the British policies of the 1930's, and Baldwin bore the brunt of the criticism, much of which was unfair. Many who had opposed any rearmament during the 1930's now criticized Baldwin for not rearming faster. Some, like Churchill, failed to give Baldwin credit for what had been accomplished in spite of adverse public opinion. Others failed to differentiate between Baldwin's policies and those of Chamberlain. During Baldwin's last years, he spent most of his time at his country home, and as his health declined, his long walks ended. He was aware of his great unpopularity but understood the reasons. His wife died in 1945, and Baldwin followed in December, 1947. His ashes were placed in Worcester Cathedral.

Baldwin was so influential during the interwar years that the era is often referred to as the Age of Baldwin. He was consciously a unifying figure, seeking a societal consensus, wishing to bring the Labour Party into the political arena as reformers rather than as revolutionaries. He appeared to be, and in many ways was, the archetypal Englishman. He was more successful in politics than in economics, more comfortable in domestic matters than in foreign affairs, which made him more suited to the 1920's than to the troubled 1930's.

—Eugene S. Larson

FURTHER READING

Churchill, Winston S. *The Gathering Storm*. Vol. 1 in *The Second World War*. London: Cassell, 1948. This volume of Churchill's account of World War II has continued to influence both the scholarly and popular perception of the 1930's. As such, Baldwin plays a major, but not heroic role. The theme set down by the author reveals his interpretation: "How the English-speaking peoples through their unwisdom, carelessness and good nature allowed the wicked to rearm."

Gilbert, Martin. *Winston S. Churchill: The Prophet of Truth, 1922-1939*. Vol. 5. London: Heinemann, 1976. Gilbert's exhaustive biography of Churchill is one of the scholarly landmarks of the twentieth century. Baldwin is one of the leading characters as Gilbert follows Churchill through the interwar years.

Graves, Robert, and Alan Hodge. *The Long Week End*. New York: Macmillan, 1941. Graves, one of Great Britain's premier men of letters, and Hodge have collaborated in creating a readable social history of the years between the world wars. Inasmuch as the volume only incidentally concerns politics, Baldwin appears infrequently, but the authors brilliantly capture the social milieu of the Age of Baldwin.

Middlemas, Keith, and John Barnes. *Baldwin: A Biography*. London: Weidenfeld and Nicolson, 1969. This long study was the first major reinterpretation of Baldwin's life and career, and as such, it deliberately takes issue with the earlier assessments by Churchill and G. M. Young. The authors are not uncritical of Baldwin but make every effort to understand his actions and motivations in sympathetic terms.

Perkins, Anne. *Baldwin*. London: Haus, 2006. Perkins, a British journalist, provides this brief overview of Baldwin's life and political career, including the significant events during his three terms as prime minister. One of the entries in the British Prime Ministers of the Twentieth Century series.

Ramsden, John. *The Age of Balfour and Baldwin*. London: Longmans, Green, 1978. This volume continues the current scholarship regarding Baldwin and his career. It stresses the moral basis of Baldwin's leadership, his attempt to affect others outside the Conservative Party, his Englishness, and his position on the moderate Left of the political spectrum.

Taylor, A. J. P. *English History, 1914-1945*. New York: Oxford University Press, 1965. The Oxford History of England is, overall, the most satisfactory series of volumes on the history of England, and Taylor's volume is among the most provocative. Taylor is not an admirer of Baldwin, but his work is well worth reading and a good place to begin in the study of Great Britain in the twentieth century.

Williamson, Philip, and Edward Baldwin, eds. *Baldwin Papers: A Conservative Statesman, 1908-1947*. New York: Cambridge University Press, 2004. Contains Baldwin's letters, reports of his conversations, rele-

vant documents, and illustrations. Arranged chronologically and augmented with extensive commentary.

SEE ALSO: H. H. Asquith; Lord Beaverbrook; Sir Winston Churchill; George V; George VI; Adolf Hitler; Bonar Law; David Lloyd George.

RELATED ARTICLES in *Great Events from History: The Twentieth Century:*

1901-1940: 1920-1925: Great Britain Establishes Unemployment Benefits; May 3-12, 1926: British Workers Launch General Strike; June 17, 1930: Hoover Signs the Hawley-Smoot Tariff Act; December 10, 1936: Edward VIII Abdicates the British Throne.

ARTHUR BALFOUR
Prime minister of the United Kingdom (1902-1905)

As prime minister, and in many other high government offices, Balfour not only provided leadership to his country but also made noteworthy contributions to world peace and diplomacy. He sponsored the idea of a League of Nations and sponsored the Balfour Declaration, which, by endorsing Palestine as a national home for the Jewish people, sought Jewish support for the Allied cause during World War I.

BORN: July 25, 1848; Whittingehame, East Lothian, Scotland
DIED: March 19, 1930; Woking, Surrey, England
ALSO KNOWN AS: Arthur James Balfour (full name); Arthur James, first earl of Balfour; Arthur James Balfour of Whittingehame
AREAS OF ACHIEVEMENT: Government and politics, diplomacy, peace advocacy

EARLY LIFE

Arthur Balfour (BAHL-fuhr) was born to Lady Blanche Balfour, the daughter of the second marquess of Salisbury, and James Balfour, the descendant of an old Scottish family that had grown very wealthy from trade with India. Named Arthur, after his godfather, the duke of Wellington, Balfour could take wealth and contacts with influential people for granted as he grew up. His father, who died in 1856 of tuberculosis, was a member of Parliament. His mother's brother, Robert Cecil, third marquess of Salisbury and later prime minister, became an important figure in Balfour's early career.

Lady Blanche had given birth to nine children when she was widowed at the age of thirty-one. She never remarried, and she provided close and rigorous supervision to her children. Arthur, the oldest son, was to win the greatest renown, although several of the other children who survived to adulthood also had distinguished careers: Gerald was a member of Parliament for twenty years, Frank was an authority on genetics and held a chair at Cambridge University, Eleanor became the principal of Newnham College, and Eustace was a successful architect. The family was very close-knit; one sister, Alice, who like Balfour never married, devoted her later life to supervising his household. The Balfours were also devout, with a commitment to both the Church of England and the Presbyterian Church of Scotland.

When he was ten, Balfour was sent away from home to attend a private boarding school at Hoddeston in Hertfordshire. In 1861, he went on to study at Eton, where he was an indifferent student and not robust enough to take an active part in sports. Five years later, Balfour began his studies at Trinity College, Cambridge. There he developed an interest in the study of philosophy, a subject to which he considered devoting his career. He enjoyed Cambridge much more than Eton, although he was not a diligent scholar. He now began to take part in sports and games, an interest that continued to the end of his life.

In 1869, when he came of age, Balfour inherited the family estates. With wealth came responsibility, and he was often occupied with family and business affairs. His mother's death in 1872 increased this burden. He turned to his uncle, Lord Salisbury, for guidance in these years and under his patronage began a career in politics by standing for Parliament in January, 1874. He was returned unopposed as the Conservative member for Hertford.

LIFE'S WORK

At first, Balfour appeared no more promising in politics than he had as a student. He hesitated to speak or play an active role in the House of Commons and occupied himself with foreign travel and work on a book of philosophy. Published in 1879 as *A Defence of Philosophic Doubt*, the treatise was the first of several books that marked him as a shrewd but rather conventional intellectual talent.

When Salisbury became foreign secretary in 1878, he asked Balfour to become his parliamentary private secretary. This gave the young politician contacts and first-hand experience in diplomacy as he attended the Congress of Berlin. By 1880, when the Liberals under William Ewart Gladstone swept into office and forced Balfour into opposition, he was emerging as an articulate rising member of the Conservative Party. He soon became identified, along with Randolph Churchill, with an outspoken faction of Conservatives known as the "Fourth Party," raising objections to their own party leadership as well as Gladstone's government. When the Conservatives returned to office under Salisbury in 1885, Balfour became president of the Local Government Board. The following year he was made a member of the cabinet.

In 1887, Salisbury made his nephew chief secretary for Ireland, a challenging assignment in this period of unrest in Ireland. Balfour succeeded in removing some economic grievances in that troubled colony and had the good fortune to face an increasingly divided nationalist opposition. Nationalists distressed at his hard-line policies dubbed him "Bloody Balfour." At home, among his fellow Conservatives, he was lauded for his vigor and skills as an administrator.

In 1891, Balfour was promoted to First Lord of the Treasury and became his party's leader in the House of Commons. He acted as a deputy to his uncle, the prime minister, in formulating policy and was the chief Conservative legislative strategist and spokesperson. His achievements in this role were mixed; he had success with the Irish Local Government Act and some other pieces of legislation. Not a reformer, Balfour still showed foresight in such areas as transportation and urban housing, and he was ready to undertake constructive change.

Balfour was the logical choice to succeed his uncle as prime minister in 1902. The party over which he presided

Arthur Balfour. (NARA)

made his tenure in that office a rather difficult one. It was divided over such contentious issues as free trade and tariff reform, and Balfour had to work hard to keep it united. Moreover, he had no great popular following in the country at large. Nonconformists were especially upset by his Education Act of 1902, which retained government support for denominational schools operated by the Church of England. Faced with this opposition, Balfour resigned in 1905 and was defeated by the Liberals in the ensuing elections.

Balfour's greatest contributions as prime minister

THE BALFOUR DECLARATION

Foreign Office
November 2nd, 1917
Dear Lord Rothschild,

I have much pleasure in conveying to you, on behalf of His Majesty's Government, the following declaration of sympathy with Jewish Zionist aspirations which has been submitted to, and approved by, the Cabinet.

"His Majesty's Government view with favour the establishment in Palestine of a national home for the Jewish people, and will use their best endeavours to facilitate the achievement of this object, it being clearly understood that nothing shall be done which may prejudice the civil and religious rights of existing non-Jewish communities in Palestine, or the rights and political status enjoyed by Jews in any other country."

I should be grateful if you would bring this declaration to the knowledge of the Zionist Federation.

Yours sincerely,

Arthur James Balfour

came in the field of foreign policy. Coming into office in the aftermath of the Boer War (1899-1902), which had shown Great Britain to be dangerously isolated, he strengthened ties with other nations. This important reversal of British policy was marked by the Entente Cordiale with France in 1904. Moreover, he established the Committee of Imperial Defense to provide expert advice on military preparedness and responded forcefully to the German challenge in building warships. These accomplishments may not have helped him with the electorate, but they did secure his reputation in the area of foreign and defense policy and led to many future opportunities to serve his country.

Balfour's dismay at being thrown out of office was compounded when he lost his own seat in Parliament in 1906. A safer seat was soon found for him in the City of London, and he took up the position of leader of his party in opposition. These were difficult years for Balfour, as Joseph Chamberlain and other tariff reformers often railed against his leadership. Weakened in health and spirit, he became increasingly distrustful of the burgeoning democratic currents of the age. He resigned his leadership position in 1911, although remaining as a member of Parliament.

Troubled by the dangerous drift in international affairs, Balfour helped found the Garton Foundation in

1912 to work for world peace. When World War I erupted in 1914, he became an unhesitating supporter of the government's position. He was asked to resume membership on the Committee of Imperial Defense and in November, 1914, joined an inner cabinet known as the War Council. The following year he was made First Lord of the Admiralty in the Asquith coalition government. When David Lloyd George ousted H. H. Asquith from the new coalition in 1916, he made Balfour, by now a trusted almost nonpartisan elder statesman, his foreign secretary.

Balfour made many important contributions as minister for foreign affairs, although it is difficult to disentangle his policies from those of the very assertive prime minister whom he served. Perhaps the two contributions for which Balfour would be most remembered were his sponsorship of the idea of a League of Nations and the Balfour Declaration. This document, issued in November, 1917, sought Jewish support for the Allied cause by endorsing the idea that Palestine should become a national home for the Jewish people. It was endorsed by the Allied powers in 1920 and was later interpreted by Zionists as a commitment to make Palestine a Jewish state.

With the war over, Balfour left the Foreign Office in 1919. He remained a member of the cabinet, however, until 1922 as Lord President of the Council. He headed the British delegation to the Washington Naval Conference of 1921-1922, and enhanced his reputation as an astute diplomat and peacemaker there. At this conference, which achieved a substantial measure of naval disarmament, Balfour was able to cement good relations between Great Britain and the United States. He also was able to contribute to the work of the League of Nations organization in its early years, regularly representing his country there and chairing the first meeting of the League Council.

In 1922, Balfour was elevated to a peerage as the first earl of Balfour. Yet his political career did not end when he left the House of Commons. He was Lord President of the Council from 1925 until 1929, the year before his death. He was also president of the British Academy and a leader in other voluntary groups, such as the League of Nations Union.

SIGNIFICANCE

To the British public, the tall, graceful figure of Balfour came to symbolize the aristocrat in politics. His languid manner, taking for granted that his wealth and connections should bring him to the top, fitted this image. Yet much of Balfour is difficult to typecast. His intellectual interests, for example, were serious, as the four books he wrote on philosophy attest. If he was an athlete, he did not participate in the usual aristocratic sports, but, rather, was interested in bicycling and tennis. A respected but not outstanding prime minister, Balfour had a career that was in some ways more noteworthy after he left 10, Downing Street. The Balfour Declaration and his encouragement of the League of Nations and the cause of internationalism are the monuments to this second phase of his career.

—Donald S. Birn

FURTHER READING

Dugdale, Blanche E. C. *Arthur James Balfour, First Earl of Balfour*. 2 vols. New York: G. P. Putnam's Sons, 1937. Written by his niece, this popular work glosses over many aspects of Balfour's career.

Egremont, Max. *Balfour: A Life of Arthur James Balfour*. London: Collins, 1980. Based on manuscript sources but colorfully written, this is a good introduction to Balfour's career for general readers.

Green, E. H. H. *Balfour*. London: Haus, 2006. Brief overview of Balfour's life and diplomatic and political career. One of the volumes in the British Prime Ministers of the Twentieth Century series.

Hudson, David R. C. *The Ireland That We Made: Arthur and Gerald Balfour's Contribution to the Origins of Modern Ireland*. Akron, Ohio: University of Akron Press, 2003. Describes Britain's policy of constructive unionism in Ireland, a reform program instituted from 1887 through 1905 that was designed to reduce Irish support for home rule. As chief secretary for Ireland from 1887 through 1891, Balfour was one of those responsible for administering this policy.

Judd, Denis. *Balfour and the British Empire*. London: Macmillan, 1968. This scholarly work examines Balfour's attitude toward the Empire and places it in the context of a broader examination of "imperial evolution" from 1874 to 1932.

Mackay, Ruddock F. *Balfour: Intellectual Statesman*. New York: Oxford University Press, 1985. A scholarly reexamination of Balfour's career that concentrates on certain subjects on which the author has found new evidence.

Zebel, Sydney H. *Balfour: A Political Biography*. New York: Cambridge University Press, 1973. An account of Balfour's political career, this work is addressed to scholars and is well documented.

SEE ALSO: H. H. Asquith; George Nathaniel Curzon; Edward VII; George V; Lord Kitchener; Lord Lansdowne; Bonar Law; David Lloyd George.

RELATED ARTICLES in *Great Events from History: The Twentieth Century*:

1901-1940: April, 1909-August, 1911: Parliament Act Redefines British Democracy; November 2, 1917: Balfour Declaration Supports a Jewish Homeland in Palestine; September 10, 1919: Saint-Germain-en-Laye Convention Attempts to Curtail Slavery; April 26, 1920: Great Britain and France Sign the San Remo Agreement; November 12, 1921-February 6, 1922: Washington Disarmament Conference; July 24, 1922: League of Nations Establishes Mandate for Palestine; December 11, 1931: Formation of the British Commonwealth of Nations.

1941-1970: November 29, 1947-July, 1949: Arab-Israeli War Creates Refugee Crisis; May 14, 1948: Israel Is Created as a Homeland for Jews; December 9, 1949: United Nations Creates an Agency to Aid Palestinian Refugees.

LUCILLE BALL
American actor-entertainer

Starring in the television series I Love Lucy *during the 1950's, Ball established herself as that medium's most popular comedic actress. After the series ended, Ball purchased outright the show's production company, Desilu Productions, and became its president, the first woman to head a Hollywood studio since Mary Pickford in the 1920's and later.*

BORN: August 6, 1911; Jamestown, New York
DIED: April 26, 1989; Los Angeles, California
ALSO KNOWN AS: Lucille Désirée Ball (full name)
AREAS OF ACHIEVEMENT: Television, film, theater and entertainment, business and industry

EARLY LIFE

Lucille Ball was born in the small town of Celoron, New York, a suburb of Jamestown. Her father, Henry Durrell Ball, was a telephone lineman for the Bell Company, while her mother, Désirée "DeDe" Hunt, was often described as a lively and energetic young woman. Henry Ball's job required frequent transfers, and within three years after her birth, Lucille had moved from Jamestown to Anaconda, Montana, and then to Wyandotte, Michigan. While DeDe Ball was pregnant with her second child, Frederick, Henry Ball contracted typhoid fever and died in February, 1915.

At least one biographer has suggested that the grief associated with the loss of her father drove Lucille into playacting. Whether true or not, Ball's recollections of early childhood were, for the most part, happy. She and her brother lived with doting grandparents and a strong, independent mother. Her grandfather, Fred Hunt, was an eccentric socialist who enjoyed the theater. He frequently took the family to local vaudeville shows and encouraged young Lucy to take part in both her own and school plays.

At the age of fifteen, Ball dropped out of high school, and with her mother's approval, enrolled in the John Murray Anderson/Robert Milton School of the Theater in New York City. Among her fellow students was Bette Davis. At this stage in Ball's life, she was hopelessly beyond her element. Nervous and shy in a large city she hated, Ball lasted only six weeks at the school and returned to Celoron.

Ball later returned to New York and, despite a bout with potentially crippling rheumatoid arthritis, worked as a model with dress designer Hattie Carnegie. Her only significant success came when she was chosen by Liggett and Myers to promote cigarettes as "the Chesterfield Girl." Ball's entrance into the film industry came about fortuitously, when she accidentally ran into Sylvia Hahlo, a local theatrical agent, while walking up Broadway one day. Hahlo informed Ball of an opportunity to appear in the new Eddie Cantor film, *Roman Scandals* (1933), produced by Samuel Goldwyn. Ball auditioned and was hired as one of the twelve "Goldwyn Girls." It was a small part, that of a slave girl, and it would be many years after her work in B-pictures before she would achieve celebrity status, but Ball had found Hollywood.

LIFE'S WORK

During Ball's first years in Hollywood, she progressed from bit parts to featured roles, though rarely in major films. Indeed, over time Ball became known as a "Queen of the B's." Despite her talent, it was quite possible that she might never have progressed beyond that level had she not met Cuban vocalist and bandleader Desi Arnaz.

Arnaz was born in 1917, in Cuba, where his father was mayor of Santiago, an important seaport city. The Arnaz family was wealthy, and Desi was reared in relative luxury until the political revolution of 1933. Following his father's imprisonment, Desi Arnaz and his family fled to the United States. Desi worked his way through numerous menial jobs (including one in which he cleaned bird cages) before joining bandleader Xavier Cugat as a vocalist. In 1939, he came to Hollywood. It was on the set of RKO Studios, during the filming of *Too Many Girls* (1940), that Ball and Arnaz met; they were married on November 30, 1940.

The Ball-Arnaz marriage was tempestuous, to say the least. The two were from vastly different cultures and backgrounds. Unlike her television personality, Ball was conservative in nature and uncomfortable when not among friends. Arnaz had a more outgoing personality, with a fondness for both liquor and women.

Following Arnaz's Army service, Arnaz and Ball established their home on a five-acre site in Chatsworth, California (in Los Angeles County), which they called Desilu. The same appellation would later be applied to the studio they established. The early years of their marriage were marked by long periods of separation as their careers progressed in different directions. By the late 1940's, Ball had become established as a bona fide star, but she rarely appeared in roles that showcased the full range of her comedic talents. As an "aging" star in her thirties, she was constantly in danger of early replacement by up-and-coming younger actresses. Arnaz, meanwhile, was frequently on the road with his band, only rarely seeing Ball. Both wanted children and a stable family life but found this goal impossible to achieve while they were apart.

In 1948, the Columbia Broadcasting System (CBS) decided to produce a situation comedy on radio called *My Favorite Husband*. The premise of the show was that the housewife would be a scatterbrained, clumsy type who constantly would find herself in trouble. Ball was signed for the part and immediately established herself in the role. The series ran until March, 1951, by which time Ball was recognized as an astute, if sometimes abrasive, actress in the area of physical comedy. By that time, Ball and Arnaz had made the jump into television.

In 1950, CBS decided to develop a television series based on Ball's radio performance. Ball pressured the studio to cast Arnaz in the role of husband, a suggestion that met with strong opposition. Though Ball and Arnaz had appeared together on the Ed Wynn show in December, 1949, the network's major objection was the belief the public would not accept a Latin bandleader as her husband. Ball's answer was direct: "We ARE married!" To overcome the network's reservations, Ball suggested that she and Arnaz embark on a personal summer tour to highlight their act. In June, 1950, they premiered successfully in Chicago, proving their point. To compound their happiness, it became apparent Ball was pregnant. It was also during this period that the couple formed Desilu Productions, parent company for their studios.

With success came tragedy. In July, Ball suffered a miscarriage. After a period of recuperation, she and Arnaz returned to the stage with their act. The success of the tour finally convinced CBS to go ahead with a series, and in early 1951, preparations began. Ironically, Ball again became pregnant, delivering a healthy girl, Lucie Arnaz, in July.

Disagreements over the nature of the filming convinced Ball and Arnaz to purchase and develop their own studios. One of the most significant changes was their decision to use 35mm film, rather than the lesser quality kinescope medium, to record the show. In addition to providing working conditions more familiar to Ball and Arnaz and allowing them to work in Hollywood instead of producing live shows in New York, the use of 35mm film enabled the preservation of the earliest shows for posterity. William Frawley and Vivian Vance were added

to the cast, and the first filming of the *I Love Lucy* series took place on September 8, 1951.

I Love Lucy ran from October 15, 1951, the first televised show, to September 24, 1961. The original first-run episodes lasted for six years, with primetime reruns and numerous "specials" aired through 1961. At its peak, it was the highest rated show on television. One of the best-known episodes involved the birth of Little Ricky Ricardo—an episode that aired on the same night that Ball gave birth to her real son. Sadly, the marriage between Ball and Arnaz barely survived the end of the series. The day after the final show was filmed in March of 1960, Ball filed for divorce. Despite the end of their marriage, Ball and Arnaz never lost their love and respect for each other.

Following the demise of their series, Ball purchased Arnaz's shares of Desilu Productions in 1962, becoming the first woman to head a Hollywood studio since Mary Pickford many years before. After her subsequent marriage to comedian Gary Morton, Ball named him vice president of the studios. Although Arnaz possessed a wealth of business acumen and made most of the finan-

Lucille Ball. (Library of Congress)

cial and production decisions connected with founding and expanding the Desilu studios—facts rarely recognized by those familiar only with his typecast acting role on *I Love Lucy*—Ball continued to maintain the quality of programming associated with the studio. Although high-budget shows such as *Mission: Impossible* and *Star Trek* escalated costs to the studio, the quality of the studio's output remained high throughout the years of Ball's tenure as president.

Ball began a role on her own television series in 1962, *The Lucy Show*. The premise of the show, which also included Vance, was Ball as a widow with two children. Rather than Arnaz as the foil, Gale Gordon played the long-suffering male. Despite what eventually became a tiring plot, the show remained popular for much of its twelve-year run (including title and character changes), at one point being the highest rated show on television.

Desilu Productions was sold to the large Gulf + Western Industries in 1967, severing Ball's connection with the company. Despite her wealth, Ball was uncomfortable with the idea of retiring from show business. The film production of *Mame* (1974) was designed as a starring vehicle to revive Ball's film career, but it was a critical and financial disappointment. Ball continued to work sporadically on television, appearing in specials and even making an attempt at a new series in 1986. Sadly, an aging Ball found it difficult to attempt the kind of "serious" physical comedy at which she had once excelled, and she recognized that to do so would result in a caricature of herself. The sitcom, *Life with Lucy*, was canceled soon after its debut.

In December of 1986, Arnaz died after a lengthy battle against cancer; Ball was one of the last people to speak with him. In May, 1988, Ball suffered a stroke, becoming partially paralyzed. Continuing her recuperation, she developed heart problems. After undergoing heart surgery, she died suddenly on April 26, 1989.

SIGNIFICANCE

When *I Love Lucy* premiered during the 1951-1952 television season, only fifteen million television sets were to be found in American homes. Three years later, that number had doubled. In that time, Ball had become established as the most popular female comedian on television, and arguably the most popular female practitioner of physical comedy in the first half-century of prime-time television. Ball was not herself an inherently funny person; she looked at acting as a serious profession and "worked" at physical comedy. However, Ball had an inherent ability to observe a situation and, by exaggeration

of normal behavior, could present a routine that struck an observer with comedic overtones. It was a rare performer who could do so, while at the same time retaining the situation as one that was within the realm of possibility.

There is no question Ball had her faults and her detractors. At times, she exhibited anger and pettiness. Nevertheless, Ball could also recognize ability in those with whom she worked, and she felt secure enough in her position to allow her staff to do the jobs for which they were hired. Despite her well-publicized battles with Arnaz, she always recognized his importance to their careers, and Arnaz in turn never failed to give Ball credit where deserved. Most important perhaps, Ball recognized the importance of hard work in attaining success in one's career, and she was always willing to give help to aspiring performers who were dedicated to working hard as well.

—*Richard Adler*

FURTHER READING

Andrews, Bart. *Lucy & Ricky & Fred & Ethel*. Rev. ed. New York: E. P. Dutton, 1985. An outstanding biography of the characters from *I Love Lucy*. Includes a description of each individual show and special from the series. The volume provides a concise description of the lives and careers of both Frawley and Vance.

Arnaz, Desi. *A Book*. New York: William Morrow, 1976. In his autobiography, Arnaz provides an interesting inside look at Lucille Ball and their lives together. Despite their tumultuous marriage, the couple remained on cordial terms after their divorce.

Ball, Lucille, with Betty Hannah Hoffman. *Love, Lucy*. Foreword by Lucie Arnaz. New York: G. P. Putnam's Sons, 1996. A posthumously published memoir, written as a biography after Ball's death.

Davis, Madelyn Pugh, and Bob Carroll, Jr. *Laughing with Lucy: My Life with America's Leading Lady of Comedy*. Cincinnati, Ohio: Emmis Books, 2005. Davis wrote almost all of the episodes of *I Love Lucy* with Carroll, and the two also wrote for Ball's subsequent television series. Davis recounts Ball's television career and her personal experiences working with both Ball and Desi Arnaz.

Higham, Charles. *Lucy: The Life of Lucille Ball*. New York: St. Martin's Press, 1986. A well-written biography of Ball with strong emphasis on her early life prior to breaking into film. Contains good description of the first years of the *I Love Lucy* series.

Kanfer, Stefan. *Ball of Fire: The Tumultuous Life and Comic Art of Lucille Ball*. New York: Alfred A. Knopf, 2003. Recounts Ball's life and career, tracing her transformation from an unsophisticated young woman to a brilliant comedian.

Morella, Joe, and Edward Epstein. *Forever Lucy: The Life of Lucille Ball*. Secaucus, N.J.: Lyle Stuart, 1986. Not as detailed as some other biographies, but still an excellent study of Ball and Arnaz. Portions of the book cover the lives of their children and how they were affected by their parents' celebrity status.

Sanders, Covne Steven, and Tom Gilbert. *Desilu*. New York: William Morrow, 1993. Perhaps the most complete of the Arnaz-Ball biographies. A well-written, detailed study of Arnaz's and Ball's lives and careers until their deaths in 1986 and 1989, respectively. Some illustrations, and numerous quotations from contemporaries are included.

SEE ALSO: Dorothy Arzner; Bill Cosby; Samuel Goldwyn; Jerry Lewis; Mary Pickford.

RELATED ARTICLES in *Great Events from History: The Twentieth Century:*

1941-1970: June, 1948-1964: Variety Shows Dominate Television Programming; October 15, 1951-September 24, 1961: *I Love Lucy* Dominates Television Comedy; October 1, 1955-September, 1956: *The Honeymooners* Defines Situation Comedy; 1960's: Situation Comedies Dominate Television Programming.

1971-2000: January 12, 1971: Relevance Programs Change Entertainment Standards.

ROBERT D. BALLARD
American undersea explorer

As a pioneering undersea explorer, Ballard made several remarkable discoveries, including the resting place of the Titanic *and other ships, new life-forms along hot spots in the undersea Earth crust, and evidence supporting the theory of plate tectonics.*

BORN: June 30, 1942; Wichita, Kansas
ALSO KNOWN AS: Robert Duane Ballard (full name)
AREAS OF ACHIEVEMENT: Exploration and colonization, science, invention and technology, geology

EARLY LIFE
Robert D. Ballard was born in Wichita, Kansas, a distant relative of the gunslinger William "Bat" Masterson, who was for a time in the nineteenth century the sheriff of Wichita. When Ballard was still a young boy, his family resettled to Pacific Beach, a suburb of San Diego, California, where his father worked developing the Minuteman missile. Ballard began what would become a lifelong fascination with the world under the sea. He spent countless hours exploring along the shore, dreaming of submarines, and poring over the illustrations in an edition of his favorite book, Jules Verne's science-fiction novel *Vingt mille lieues sous les mers* (1869-1870; *Twenty Thousand Leagues Under the Sea*, 1873). When he was a senior in high school, he won a competition that enabled him to spend a summer training at the Scripps Institute of Oceanography in La Jolla, California.

Ballard's parents taught him to work hard to set and achieve his goals, and that lesson served him well while he was still a college student. At the University of California, Santa Barbara, he earned a degree in both chemistry and geology and completed the university's Reserve Officers' Training Corps (ROTC) program, earning a commission as an Army lieutenant doing intelligence work.

After graduation, Ballard began graduate study in oceanography in Hawaii, where he also took a part-time job as a dolphin trainer at Sealife Park. This job helped him develop his skills as a writer and public speaker. In 1966 he transferred to the Navy and took a job helping to design and develop missions for submersibles for the Ocean Systems Group of his father's employer, North American Aviation. Ballard liked this work because it combined his passions for applied science, or technology, and pure science. The next year the Navy sent him to Boston to serve as an oceanographic liaison officer in the Office of Naval Research. His duties included serving as the Navy's liaison to the Woods Hole Oceanographic Institution on Cape Cod, Massachusetts.

LIFE'S WORK
On his first tour of Woods Hole, Ballard was attracted to *Alvin*, an experimental miniature research submarine capable of taking three divers to a depth of 6,000 feet, where the water pressure exceeds one ton per square inch. Ballard spent as much time as his position allowed

Robert D. Ballard. (AP/Wide World Photos)

at Woods Hole, helping map the geology of the ocean floor in the Gulf of Maine. In September, 1969, he left the Navy and joined the staff at Woods Hole; three months later he descended in a submersible for the first time as part of a team studying the continental shelf off the coast of Florida.

During these years, Ballard was also a student in the Ph.D. program in marine geology and geophysics at the University of Rhode Island. For his doctoral dissertation research, Ballard attempted to advance the plate tectonics theories of Professor Patrick Hurley of the Massachusetts Institute of Technology. He used *Alvin* to make some forty dives in the Gulf of Maine and surrounding areas, helping develop the techniques that made it possible to use the vessel's remote manipulator arm to drill for and collect samples of bedrock. With data taken from these samples and the results of his earlier mapping work, he provided hard evidence that the continents sit on movable tectonic plates and that the American, European, and African continents were once connected. At the same time, his work helped the *Alvin* team demonstrate and expand the capabilities of the submersible, attracting much-needed interest and funding from both government and private agencies.

By the fall of 1971, *Alvin* had been rebuilt with a titanium pressure sphere, making it capable of descending to 12,000 feet, the average depth of the seafloor. This improvement made it possible for Ballard and others to explore the undersea mountain range known as the Mid-Atlantic Ridge in 1973 and 1974, in a project called the French American Mid-Ocean Undersea Study, or Project FAMOUS. With the French scientist Jean Francheteau, Ballard posited a new theory about the composition and activity of the Mid-Atlantic Ridge. By this time the capabilities of both Ballard and the submersibles were drawing scientific and popular attention, and Ballard found himself something of a celebrity. He was now chief scientist on many expeditions and was able to obtain the funding he needed for further exploration.

In 1977 Ballard led a team from Woods Hole in an exploration of the Galapagos Rift area of the Pacific Ocean near Ecuador. The team intended to study the vents that expelled warm water from beneath the ocean floor. These vents were so far beneath the ocean's surface that no sunlight could penetrate to them, and it was supposed that no living things would be found there. Surprisingly, the researchers discovered various forms of life, including clams, crabs, bacteria, and giant tube worms, many more than eight feet long, living near underwater geysers. Oceanographers were excited by the discovery, which spurred extensive research to learn more about the chemical and biological processes that make life possible in this unlikely environment.

Ballard's next major expedition took him to the ocean floor off the coast of Baja California, Mexico. There, in 1979, he was part of a research team that discovered "black smokers," underwater volcanoes spewing black fluids reaching temperatures of 350 degrees Celsius through chimneys made of sulfide mineral deposits.

With improvements to *Alvin* continually being made, Ballard began to think that an old dream of his might become a reality: He might be able to locate the giant ship *Titanic* on the ocean floor. *Titanic*, which had sunk in 1912 on its first voyage from England to New York City, was thought to lie some 13,000 feet below the surface— too far for divers or previous submersibles to go. Government and industry figures were eager to find the sunken ship, knowing the publicity would provide a tremendous public relations boost to the finders. The military hoped that technology developed for undersea exploration could also be used for submarine warfare. Private adventurers had been searching for the ship for years. Ballard was able to gather funding and the support of the Navy, and in 1982 he established the Woods Hole

Deep Submergence Laboratory (DSL). The lab team developed *Argo*, a sophisticated video sled about the size of a car, with floodlights and three cameras, and *Jason*, a smaller tethered robot vehicle that could be sent into tighter spaces than *Argo* could enter. The *Argo-Jason* system enabled a research crew onboard a ship to send and steer cameras out into the dark depths, and receive and interpret video pictures.

When testing of the *Argo-Jason* system was completed, Ballard and a team of French scientists launched a joint effort to locate the *Titanic*. The French, who had sophisticated sonar technology, would map the ocean floor in the area where the *Titanic* was thought to lie, and determine a smaller area for *Argo* to search. For five frustrating weeks, the French covered a 100-mile target area but did not locate the ship. A few days before the French left the area, Ballard and his team arrived. Drawing on the French data, the Americans limited their search to a narrower area and located the *Titanic* late in the night of August 31, 1985. A year later, Ballard returned to *Titanic*, and this time he sent the smaller *Jason* robot into the ship itself to photograph the interior. The pictures of the ship, with its recognizable central staircase and unopened bottles of wine, captured the imaginations of viewers around the world.

Ballard continued his exciting work, in 1989 establishing the JASON Project, a program that sent live images from *Jason* video robots to students at museums and science centers so that they could experience through "telepresence" some of the wonders of the undersea world. Greatly expanding the possibilities of distance learning, Ballard made it possible for more than a million students each year in thousands of classrooms around the world to work interactively with underwater cameras and other equipment far below the surface of the ocean. Ballard also pursued the interest in undersea archaeology he had demonstrated in his search for the *Titanic*: In the 1990's he located and photographed the German battleship *Bismarck*, American and Japanese warships sunk during World War II at Guadalcanal, the luxury ship *Lusitania*, and several trading ships from the Roman Empire, some as old as two thousand years.

Ballard retired from Woods Hole in 1997 and founded the Institute for Exploration, dedicated to expanding the fields of underwater archaeology and deep-sea geology. Two years later, the institute merged with the Mystic Aquarium in Connecticut to form the Sea Research Foundation's Institute for Exploration, with Ballard as president. The institute developed underwater vehicles that carry sensing and imaging equipment to depths far beyond where humans could safely go and that send data back to researchers at the surface.

In 1998, Ballard again set out to locate sunken ships, this time in the Pacific Ocean near the island of Midway, where an important battle was fought between the Japanese and the Allies during World War II. Using the latest technology for undersea exploration, Ballard and his crew found and photographed four Japanese carriers and the American aircraft carrier the USS *Yorktown* more than three miles below the surface.

Ballard's explorations continued into the twenty-first century. In 2002, working with the National Geographic Society, he located wreckage from John F. Kennedy's PT-109, which was sunk off the Solomon Islands during World War II. Ballard also managed to find and interview the two Solomon Island natives who rescued Kennedy and his crew after they had been shipwrecked. He and archaeologist George Bass led a group of marine archaeologists to explore ancient artifacts and mollusk remains 7,000 feet down in the Black Sea, using *Argus*, a remotely operated tethered underwater vehicle with optical cameras. The presence of shells from freshwater species identified during this expedition lent support to a much-debated theory that the Black Sea was settled by human beings before a large-scale flood devastated the area. In 2003 he returned to the wreck of the *Titanic* to document the decay that had befallen the ship in the eighteen years since Ballard had found it on the ocean floor.

Ballard's twin passions for exploration and for teaching led him to an active parallel career as a public speaker, television host, and teacher. He was awarded the Cairn Medal of the National Maritime Museum in 2002 and was invited to speak at the John F. Kennedy Presidential Library in 2005. In 2004, he became a professor of oceanography and director of the Institute for Archaelogical Oceanography at the University of Rhode Island.

SIGNIFICANCE

Throughout a career of more than thirty years, Ballard participated in more than one hundred dives and ventured out in more deep-diving submersibles than anyone else in the world. His explorations contributed greatly to knowledge of what lies beneath the surface of the oceans. Some discoveries, such as evidence in support of plate tectonic theory or the finding of life near hot vents on the ocean floor, were primarily of interest to other scientists and were presented in dozens of articles Ballard contributed to scientific journals. Ballard's discovery of the *Titanic* and the other lost ships thrilled people all over the world—both scientists and nonspecialists alike—in part because of his talent for making science and technology accessible to general audiences. Ballard wrote or cowrote more than a dozen books (including a juvenile biography and a children's pop-up book), as well as magazine articles and television programs.

Ballard also made great technological contributions, helping develop and refine submersibles, underwater video cameras, and robots to hold and move the cameras. Through his writing, speaking, and photography, and through the "telepresence" of the JASON Project, Ballard shared his discoveries with the world.

—*Cynthia A. Bily*

FURTHER READING

Allen, Christina G., Pat Cummings, and Linda C. Cummings, eds. *Talking with Adventurers: Conversations with Christina Allen, Robert Ballard, Michael Blakey, Ann Bowles, David Doubilet, Jane Goodall, Dereck and Beverly Joubert, Michael Novacek, Johan Reinhard, Rick West, and Juris Zarins*. Washington, D.C.: National Geographic Society, 1998. Ballard and the other scientists explain their jobs, including a typical working day and their most frightening experiences. This volume is intended for younger readers; the information it contains is useful and accessible.

Ballard, Robert D., and Rick Archbold. *The Lost Ships of Robert Ballard*. San Diego, Calif.: Thunder Bay Press, 2005. A large coffee-table book that celebrates several glorious sunken ocean liners and warships, including the *Titanic, Bismarck, Lusitania,* and *Andrea Doria,* that Ballard located on the ocean floor. Includes high-tech underwater photographs, as well as paintings and historical images.

_____. *Return to Midway*. Washington, D.C.: National Geographic Society, 1999. Ballard's exploration of ships sunk during the World War II battle at Midway, including the aircraft carrier USS *Yorktown,* which was found more than three miles below the surface of the ocean. Richly illustrated with photographs and paintings.

Ballard, Robert D., with Will Hively. *The Eternal Darkness: A Personal History of Deep-Sea Exploration*. Princeton, N.J.: Princeton University Press, 2000. Ballard provides an account of his own explorations and the efforts of other twentieth century explorers to investigate the ocean depths. Includes photographs, charts, and maps.

Ballard, Robert D., with Malcolm McConnell. *Explorations: My Quest for Adventure and Discovery Under the Sea*. New York: Hyperion, 1995. A complete account of Ballard's entire career in marine geology, this best-selling autobiography offers accessible explanations of his scientific achievements. This volume is more memoir than science and is thought by many to exaggerate Ballard's contributions to some projects, but it is lively reading, telling its story with dialogue and beautiful descriptive passages.

Hecht, Jeff. "20,000 Tasks Under the Sea." *New Scientist* 147 (September 30, 1995): 40-45. A description of Ballard's post-*Titanic* explorations of the Mediterranean Sea, looking for more than two-thousand-year-old sunken ships from the Roman Empire. For this feat of underwater archaeology, Ballard had the use of a U.S. Navy nuclear submarine, the NR-1, designed originally for deep-sea military surveillance and able to withstand high pressure and stay underwater for up to one month.

SEE ALSO: Jacques Cousteau; Harry Hammond Hess; Auguste and Jean-Felix Piccard; Alfred Wegener; Sir George Hubert Wilkins.

RELATED ARTICLES in *Great Events from History: The Twentieth Century:*

1901-1940: April 14-15, 1912: Sinking of the *Titanic.*

1941-1970: Spring, 1943: Cousteau and Gagnan Develop the Aqualung; July 20, 1964-October, 1965: Navy Conducts *Sealab* Expeditions.

1971-2000: 1977: Deep-Sea Hydrothermal Vents and New Life-Forms Are Discovered; September 1, 1985: Ballard Discovers the Lost Ship *Titanic.*

HASTINGS KAMUZU BANDA
President of Malawi (1966-1994)

Banda was the first prime minister and then president of the Central African country of Malawi after its independence in 1964. He developed the country as a one-party state and ruled it autocratically until a more democratic system replaced his administration.

BORN: c. 1898; near Kasungu, British Central Africa Protectorate (now Malawi)

DIED: November 25, 1997; Johannesburg, South Africa

AREA OF ACHIEVEMENT: Government and politics

EARLY LIFE

Hastings Kamuzu Banda (ka-MEWTZ-ew BAHN-dah) was born to Mphongo and Akupingamnyama Banda, farmers of the Chichewa tribe of Nyasaland, around 1898. The young Banda took the name Hastings when he was baptized by the Church of Scotland Mission, a Presbyterian group that had been associated with Nyasaland since its formation as a British colony in the late nineteenth century. Banda later became an elder in the church, and he would adopt many of its moral codes when president of Malawi.

Around 1915, Banda enrolled in Livingstonia Mission School in Southern Rhodesia for several years, then moved to South Africa to find work in Johannesburg. He worked as a clerk in the gold mines until 1925. He had come to the notice of Bishop Vernon of the African Methodist Church, who sponsored him so that he could continue his high school education in the United States. He enrolled at the Wilberforce Institute in Ohio, graduating in 1929. He wanted to become a medical doctor and briefly enrolled as a premedical student at Indiana University. He finally became a student at Meharry Medical College in Tennessee, graduating in 1937.

Banda wanted to return to Africa, but because his qualifications would not be recognized in the British colonies, he left for the United Kingdom to study at the Royal College of Physicians and Surgeons at the University of Edinburgh, Scotland. After qualification in 1941, he practiced in northern England from 1942 to 1945.

LIFE'S WORK

While in the United Kingdom, Banda began to meet politically active Africans from Nyasaland and the other countries of Central Africa. In 1946, after moving to London, he represented the Nyasaland African Congress at the fifth Pan African Congress in Manchester, England. Although he was now much more politically active in the movement for African independence, he decided not to return to Central Africa, as many urged, but to go to the Gold Coast (later Ghana) in West Africa, where he worked from 1954 to 1958.

Finally, fellow Nyasas Henry Chipembere and Kanyama Chiumi persuaded him to return to Nyasaland to fight the newly formed Central African Federation (CAF), which the Nyasas felt was dominated by white Southern Rhodesians. On July 6, 1958, Banda returned to Nyasaland after an absence of some forty-two years. The next month he became leader of the Nyasaland African Congress (NAC). By his speeches, he rapidly radicalized the Nyasas, and a state of emergency was declared in the ensuing confrontations with authorities. In March, 1959, Banda was imprisoned and the NAC banned. A substitute party, the Malawi Congress Party (MCP), was formed immediately ("Malawi" was Banda's coinage).

By 1960, Great Britain had accepted the dissolution of the CAF, and officials freed Banda. Elections were held in 1961 prior to independence, and Banda's MCP swept to victory. Self-government followed in 1962 and full independence in 1964. Banda was the first prime minister, serving from 1964 to 1966, during which time the country declared itself a republic with Banda as its first president (1966). He immediately made Malawi a one-party state, as several other African countries had done. In 1971 he became a life-president and was awarded the title of Ngwazi, which means "great lion" in Chichewa.

However, Banda's politics, unlike most of his contemporary African leaders, were conservative and pro-Western. He welcomed Western expertise and kept open diplomatic ties with South Africa, despite its apartheid policy. This made relationships with his neighbors difficult, but with Western capital he laid a solid infrastructure to the country and made it almost self-sufficient financially with major exports of tobacco, tea, and sugar. He even constructed a new capital, Lilongwe, improved education, and built a prestigious boarding school based on the British public-school concept. He also sought to improve the status of women.

To the outside world, Banda gave the impression of being a "civilized," pro-Western, benevolent autocrat, but at home, progress came at a high price in terms of personal freedoms. All citizens had to be a member of the

MCP, and police checks on membership cards were not uncommon. The Malawi Youth Pioneers, whose allegiance was to Banda, often acted as a branch of the police in selling and checking these cards. When Jehovah's Witnesses missionaries refused to become MCP members in the 1970's, they faced extreme harassment and were forced into exile.

The country also saw strict censorship and a dress code. Television was forbidden, and books, videos, and films had to pass through a censorship board. Churches had to be registered. Offenses to public decency, such as kissing in public or in cinemas, were rigorously enforced. A personality cult was fostered, and Banda's portrait appeared everywhere. He would be greeted in public by dancing women and waves of people wearing clothing that displayed his image. For some people, he became an idol.

Banda also mistreated those who were, or who were accused of being, opposed to him politically. Chiume was exiled, as was Chipembere when he demanded greater Africanization of Malawi in 1965. One year before, an equally patriotic Malawian, Orton Chirwa, who was a founding member of the MCP, had escaped the country. Banda had Chirwa and his wife, Vera, kidnapped from Zambia (a neighboring country), tried them for treason, and condemned to death. Only an international outcry made Banda commute the sentence to life imprisonment. Albert Nqumayo, secretary-general of the MCP, was hanged for treason, and a possible successor to Banda, Dick Matenje, was killed, reportedly in a car accident.

Finally, more democratic forces brought about a referendum on the one-party system in 1993. The system was overturned, and in fresh elections in 1994, Banda was defeated by Elson Bakili Muluzi, though the MCP remained a powerful force in Malawian politics. Banda's health finally failed. He went to South Africa for medical treatment, where he died in 1997.

SIGNIFICANCE

Banda made efforts to lessen his isolation from other African neighbors in the 1980's, but it was the end of apartheid in 1994, which coincided with the end of his personal rule, that brought Malawi back into the mainstream of African politics. This, and the peaceful transition to multiparty politics, unfortunately did not help the country's prosperity. A combination of events, including the drop in price of export crops, growing corruption, and financial mismanagement, left Malawi heavily indebted. More recently, drought and a huge HIV-AIDS epidemic

have undone much of the work of the Banda era. However, the new constitution, limiting the power of the MCP, brought the peaceful transition of government and the growth of democracy into local as well as national elections. Banda is still greatly revered, and a mausoleum dedicated to him was opened May 14, 2006, in Lilongwe.

—*David Barratt*

FURTHER READING

Arnold, Guy. *Africa: A Modern History*. London: Atlantic Books, 2005. An updated, definitive work that covers the whole of African history through the early years of the twenty-first century, putting the politics of Malawi in the wider context of the politics of Central Africa.

Baker, Colin. *Revolt of the Ministers: The Malawi Cabinet Crisis, 1964-1965*. New York: I. B. Tauris, 2001. Looks in detail at Banda's dismissal of almost his entire cabinet, as he moved toward the one-party system and the leadership cult.

Lwanda, John Lloyd. *Kamuzu Banda of Malawi*. Glasgow: Dudu Nsamba, 1993. The most positive of the biographies, written on the eve of Banda's departure from Malawian politics.

Short, Phillip. *Banda*. London: Routledge & Kegan Paul, 1974. The first official biography of Banda, when he was less than halfway through his term of office.

Virmani, K. K. *Dr. Banda in the Making of Malawi*. Delhi, India: Kalinga, 1992. An Asian writer considers Banda's role in the formation of Malawi. One of the few political studies available.

Williams, David T. *Malawi: The Politics of Despair*. Ithaca, N.Y.: Cornell University Press, 1979. A critical look at the one-party system as it was operated by Banda.

SEE ALSO: Nnamdi Azikiwe; Félix Éboué; Haile Selassie I; Félix Houphouët-Boigny; Jomo Kenyatta; Samora Machel; Mobutu Sese Seko; Robert Mugabe; Kwame Nkrumah; Ahmed Sékou Touré; Moïse Tshombe; William V. S. Tubman.

RELATED ARTICLES in *Great Events from History: The Twentieth Century:*

1941-1970: August 1, 1953-December 31, 1963: Formation of the Federation of Rhodesia and Nyasaland; March 3, 1959: Nyasaland Independence Leader Banda Is Arrested by British Colonials.

1971-2000: August, 1991: African Countries Begin to Revive Democratization.

SIR SURENDRANATH BANERJEA
Indian politician

Banerjea's dedication to moderation in the Indian struggle for liberation from Great Britain served as a political focus during some of the most dangerous times of modern Indian history. His position as one of the most respected Bengali leaders helped to stabilize and concentrate Indian protest into the channel of the Congress Party, which was to inherit Indian government after independence.

BORN: November 10, 1848; Calcutta (now Kolkata), India

DIED: August 6, 1925; Barrackpore, near Calcutta (now Kolkata), India

AREAS OF ACHIEVEMENT: Government and politics, journalism

EARLY LIFE

Surendranath Banerjea (soo-RAYN-draw-nawt BAH-nawr-jee) was born in Calcutta, a member of a respected Brahman family that supported and believed in the British presence in India. He was educated in local schools until about the age of ten, when he was sent to English-language schools, including Doveton College. His education was that of the English middle class, and, by the time he completed his bachelor of arts degree, Banerjea was fully Westernized. He was allowed to travel to England to study for admission to the Indian Civil Service, although at that time, such travel was costly to the Brahman caste. Nevertheless, in March, 1868, Banerjea left for London, where, in 1869, he passed the competitive examination for entry into the civil service. He was one of the very first Indians to do so. Before he could be assigned, however, his name was removed from consideration on the grounds that he was too old. This action on the part of the British commissioners was viewed by interested Indians as clearly biased, and, as a result of the uproar, Banerjea sued the commission. He won his suit and was reinstated, passing the final examinations for appointment in 1871.

Banerjea returned to India in August of that year to take up his post in the Bengal presidency at Calcutta. In 1873, he passed the departmental examination to become a first class magistrate, but, as a result of a clerical error, his conduct was judged inadequate, and he was summarily dismissed. In 1874, Banerjea returned to England to pursue legal study at the Middle Temple, but after satisfying the requirements, he was refused entry to the bar.

These two episodes in Banerjea's life were both, in the main, the result of British reluctance to allow Indians to participate in the governance of their own country. Other Indians of Banerjea's generation faced the same kind of obstacles with the same results. In Banerjea's case, the obstacles turned his attention toward public service of another kind. In 1876, he began a career of public speaking among Bengali students, calling for the unification of all Indians, appealing for Indian patriotism unrestricted by religion or local loyalty, and urging that Indians continue to give Great Britain their loyalty and gratitude. As part of his activities he was a founding member of the Indian Association and traveled throughout India speaking on the need for greater Indian self-government within a British context.

In 1877, the Indian Civil Service renewed its attempts to stop Indians from entering the organization, and between May and November of that year Banerjea was especially active. As a result of the many political meetings that Banerjea conducted, a formal Indian protest was issued, and directed, for the first time, to the London government rather than to the government of India. This decisive move placed Banerjea in the center of the growing political activity in India.

LIFE'S WORK

In January, 1879, Banerjea became the owner and editor of the weekly journal *Bengalee*, which he developed into the semiofficial publication of the Indian Association. He used its influence to comment on current events that affected relations between the British and Indians. His editorials and reporting increasingly discomfited the British authorities, and the voice of *Bengalee* was only one of many other similarly critical journals.

It was not until the issue of April 28, 1883, that the British took decisive action against Banerjea. *Bengalee* published on that date an article that was very critical of the actions of a justice in the Calcutta High Court; as a result, Banerjea was charged with contempt of court. He was found guilty and sentenced to two months' imprisonment. Immediately, the political activists throughout India rallied in protest, culminating in an open-air meeting of more than twenty thousand held in Calcutta. The money raised for his defense later served as the genesis for the Indian "National Fund," which was used throughout India to address, through rallies and publications, urgent Indian nationalist ideas and issues. This surge in unified political action led directly to the formation of the National Conference, which was the precursor of the National Congress.

The National Congress's second annual meeting in 1885 was the first that Banerjea attended. By the Fifth Congress, he, along with two others, was selected to go to England and speak about the situation in India. The emissaries met with most of the British luminaries of the day, including William Ewart Gladstone, and continued the theme of demanding rights for Indians within the British Empire. The mission was generally regarded as successful, and when the group returned in July, 1890, it was to the acclaim of the Indian nationalists.

Still, the British continued to make political errors of governance within India, and, given the temper of the times, each was more bitterly resented than the last. The partition of Bengal Province in 1905 was perhaps the final straw. The British planned to separate the administrative and political functions of the province into those of Eastern Bengal and Assam, which was to be composed of Assam, Dacca, Chittagong, Rajshahi (without Darjeeling), and Malda. The proposal made by then-viceroy George Nathaniel Curzon was vigorously opposed by Banerjea and the Congress Party, and the discontent it provoked led directly to the Swadeshi and boycott movements. Thus, Banerjea found himself a proponent, not of freedom within the Empire but of true nationalism and the abolition of British influence entirely. He consistently recommended restraint, and *Bengalee* urged restraint from any kind of lawlessness, but it was becoming obvious that matters within India had passed the point of peaceful coexistence within the imperial structure.

As Indian politics grew more radical, Banerjea found his influence waning. In an attempt to regain his position, he participated in the Bengal Provincial Conference of 1906, at Barisal. Banerjea at that time spoke out in support of the patriotic Indian nationalism that had come to be represented by the shouts of "Bande Mataram," or "The Mother," which swept over the convention. This combination, not unreasonably, alarmed the British government even further.

Still, by 1907 Banerjea was no longer at the forefront of Indian politics. The struggles between "extremists," who saw India's future as one outside Britain entirely, and "moderates" such as Banerjea, who still believed that India could flourish within a modified form of British government, could no longer be papered over. In that year, Banerjea and the moderates formally split from the extremists and, with Banerjea as chair, held a separate convention.

This All-India Conference codified everything in which Banerjea had believed since his first return from England. It drew up a completely new constitution for the Indian National Congress that rested firmly on the ideas of gradual reform and evolution of Indian political affairs to the point where the majority of positions would be held by Indians and yet insisted that all such change would remain within the framework of the British Empire. To the degree that the formal split between the two groups was confined by the formalities of the two conferences, it may be said with reason that Banerjea and his moderates defused an increasingly dangerous political situation for a time. The moderates were never in the position of representing the majority of Indian opinion, and Banerjea himself had come to represent retrograde political beliefs.

British political attitudes toward the government of India had also been changing during the early 1900's. The adoption of the "Minto Reforms" in 1909 seemed to represent a compromise between the imperialists, who believed India should always be governed as it had been governed, and the liberals, who with some foresight believed that concessions toward participation by Indians within government were necessary. The reforms were embraced with enthusiasm by Banerjea and his wing of Indian political activists. As part of his appreciation for them, during his speech at the Imperial Press Conference, which he attended in 1909 on behalf of the Indian press, he publicly thanked Lord Gilbert Minto. This loyalty did not go unremarked in England, nor in India.

In 1913, Banerjea was elected to the Bengal Legislative Council and to the Imperial Legislative Council. These bodies were, however, the type of bodies that the advocates of complete Indian self-government most deplored. His tenure lasted until 1916, and it was during this period that he was at his most outspoken in opposition to the home rule advocates who were attempting to form their own association through congress. He was successful in resisting the formal association, but it was to be the last success of that nature in excluding the self-government representatives from positions within the party. By 1916, these representatives, including Mahatma Gandhi, Chandra Pal, and Annie Besant, had effectively taken control of the party that Banerjea had been instrumental in creating.

Still, the British were appreciative of Banerjea's efforts to maintain a balance for India within the Empire. In 1921, he was knighted and appointed minister of local self-government—unfortunately for his position within Indian politics, the appointment came at the very time that the "non-Cooperators," or self-rule proponents, were personally renouncing such honorifics and resigning from such legislative councils as a mark of their dissatisfaction. In accepting the honors, Banerjea received an enormous amount of opprobrium, and his reputation did not recover. The final humiliation came in November of 1923, when Banerjea was defeated for the Bengal Legislature by Bidhan Chandra Roy, a "Swarajist" (self-government) candidate, little known by the populace.

SIGNIFICANCE

Banerjea had both the fortune and the misfortune to live through the most volatile period of modern Indian politics without ever changing the political opinions he had formed as a young man. His admiration for the British Liberal tradition remained firm throughout his life, and he acted on it in the best way he could. During his youth, he had the audacity to demand full privileges with the Empire as a citizen of the Empire, and he continued to believe that that position was a profoundly important one. He was unable, however, to recognize that the mood of India and of the Empire itself had altered dramatically, nor was he able to work effectively with representatives who more fully understood that change.

When Banerjea was elected unopposed in 1920 from the Barrackpore subdivision, he believed it was a tribute to his political position—indeed, such a triumph was almost unprecedented. By subsequently accepting the ministry from Bengal's governor lord Ronaldshay, he placed himself firmly on the losing side of Indian political life and, thus placed, was unable to reassume his former position.

Banerjea is best viewed as a "bridge" between the traditional roles that Indians had accepted under the British and the "Non-Cooperatives," who came to be accepted as the future of India. In that sense, his early political and personal bravery in opposing British bigotry was remarkable. If, in later years, he made errors of judgment, he did so only because he refused to change the commitments to moderation and belief in the system he had made as a young man.

—*A. J. Plotke*

FURTHER READING

Argov, Daniel. *Moderates and Extremists in the Indian Nationalist Movement, 1883-1920, with Special Reference to Surendranath Banerjea and Lajpat Rai.* New York: Asia Publishing, 1967. One of the very few scholarly examinations of Banerjea's life, although Argov draws very heavily on Banerjea's autobiography. Its meticulous detail and analysis make it ideal for more thorough investigation of Banerjea's life in comparison to his opponents.

Banerjea, Sir Surendranath. *A Nation in the Making: Being the Reminiscences of Fifty Years of Public Life.* London: Oxford University Press, 1925. Banerjea's calm self-appraisal of his own life, detailing the turning points and mistakes as he saw them. The old-fashioned presentation is balanced by the extreme precision and detail about virtually every incident that occurred and every individual whom he met.

Chintamani, Sir C. Yajneswara. *Indian Politics Since the Mutiny.* Allahabad, India: Kitabistan Press, 1937. A clear presentation by this leading Indian political philosopher of the development of the Congress Party, antipartition and Non-Cooperation during 1919-1935. Chintamani devotes considerable attention to Banerjea and his pivotal role within the party.

Desai, A. R. *The Social Background of Indian Nationalism.* London: Oxford University Press, 1948. Discusses the economic importance of Banerjea to modern India, while examining the role of the Indian press in the nationalist movement. Desai particularly emphasizes Banerjea's influence on the propagation of "moral values" as part of the movement.

Masselos, Jim. *Indian Nationalism: A History.* New Delhi: New Dawn Press, 2005. Masselos's account of Hindu nationalism includes information about Banerjea.

Philips, C. H., and Mary Doreen Wainwright, eds. *Indian Society and the Beginnings of Modernization, Circa 1830-1850.* London: School of Oriental and African Studies, 1976. A collection of articles that provide a useful background to understanding Banerjea's early influences and surroundings. J. F. Hilliker's "The Creation of a Middle Class as a Goal of Educational Policy in Bengal, 1833-1854," while very scholarly, is extremely helpful in seeing how the Indian middle class embraced Anglophilia in their lives and education.

Wolpert, Stanley. *A New History of India.* 6th ed. New York: Oxford University Press, 2000. This comprehensive one-volume history includes information about Banerjea and his significance to Indian history.

SEE ALSO: George Nathaniel Curzon; Indira Gandhi; Mahatma Gandhi.

RELATED ARTICLES in *Great Events from History: The Twentieth Century:*

1901-1940: June 6, 1903: Founding of the Weekly *Indian Opinion*; March, 1915: Defense of India Act Impedes the Freedom Struggle; 1920-1922: Gandhi Leads a Noncooperation Movement.

SIR FREDERICK G. BANTING
Canadian physician

Along with Charles Herbert Best, Banting is credited with having discovered insulin, one of the great scientific and humanitarian achievements of the twentieth century.

BORN: November 14, 1891; Alliston, Ontario, Canada
DIED: February 21, 1941; near Musgrave Harbor, Newfoundland, Canada
ALSO KNOWN AS: Sir Frederick Grant Banting (full name)
AREAS OF ACHIEVEMENT: Medicine, biology

EARLY LIFE
Frederick G. Banting was born on his parents' farm in Alliston, Ontario, and was of Irish-Scottish extraction. The youngest of five children, Frederick enjoyed the advantages of a boyhood in the country and developed an affection for animals and close ties to nature. At local schools he was considered to be a serious but otherwise undistinguished student, although his hardy upbringing did result in his excelling at sports and his tendency toward pugnacity was a particular asset on the athletic field. An important event in his early childhood was seeing Jane, a childhood friend, die of uncontrolled diabetes mellitus. Although, largely because of his father's encouragement, he had considered becoming a minister, he quickly realized that medicine was his true calling, and he entered the University of Toronto Medical School in 1912.

Banting was about six feet tall and somewhat shy. He had a particularly winning smile and a twinkle in his eye, and although some would characterize his features as "horsey," he was, when dressed up, a handsome man. Banting's five-year medical course at Toronto was shortened because of the war, and he recalled in his writings that he had "a very deficient medical training." Immediately after his graduation, Banting was sent to England. Before he left, he became engaged to his longtime girlfriend, Edith Roach. While serving in England he developed extensive surgical experience dealing with wounds. Six weeks before the end of the war, on learning that the medical officer of the Forty-sixth Battalion had been wounded, he went immediately to take the wounded doctor's place. Despite receiving a shrapnel wound in his right forearm and orders to return, he went on to the front line and continued serving the wounded until he collapsed from blood loss. The wound in the arm became in-

fected and amputation was threatened. Banting took over the care of his own wound, and with a meticulous program of dressing changes and many, many months of persistence, the wound finally healed. For his courage under fire, he received the Military Cross.

When Banting returned to Canada, he decided to enter practice in London, Ontario, because Edith was teaching in a nearby school. On July 1, 1920, Banting opened an office in the house that he bought in the residential area of London. His practice was slow at the outset; his first patient came in on July 29. One of his good friends at this time was William Tew, with whom he spent many evenings in the study of medicine. Studying was something that Banting enjoyed: It was a way to pass the time in his quiet practice. He resumed preparation for the difficult exam of Fellowship in the British Royal College of Surgeons. He also began assisting Dr. F. R. Miller of London's Western University, who was a well-known professor of physiology.

LIFE'S WORK
On Sunday, October 30, 1920, Banting, in preparing a lecture on the pancreas and on carbohydrate metabolism for physiology students, became aware of how little was known about the pancreas or diabetes. His copy of the November issue of the journal *Surgery, Gynecology, and Obstetrics* had just arrived, and he began to read an article titled "The Relation of the Islets of Langerhans to Diabetes with Special Reference to Cases of Pancreatic Lithiasis," by Moses Barron. Barron, while performing routine autopsies, had come on cases in which the pancreatic duct had been obstructed by a stone and had found that most of the pancreas had atrophied except for the islet cells. Previous evidence, as well as this new piece of pathological evidence, seemed to suggest that the islet cells were important in secreting directly into the bloodstream something that prevented diabetes. Banting ruminated over these findings through much of the night. Finally, at two o'clock in the morning, it suddenly occurred to him that the experimental ligation of the pancreatic duct and the subsequent degeneration of those parts of the pancreas responsible for external secretion into the duodenum might then result in one's being left with only that part of the pancreas important in the secretion of the internal factor thought to be important in diabetes. That would allow this factor to be isolated without being contaminated by the powerful enzymes, such as

trypsin, that the pancreas normally secretes into the duodenum. This thought made Banting tremendously excited, and he discussed his theory with Miller, at Western University, who encouraged him to consult John J. R. Macleod, a professor of physiology at the University of Toronto. The interview with Macleod was brief and, as far as Banting was concerned, unsatisfactory. It appeared that Macleod thought him ill-trained for the task he had outlined, and Banting thought that Macleod's scorn was thinly veiled. Macleod did not dismiss Banting outright, however, and left him the option of pursuing his hypothesis at Toronto. Banting returned to London and discussed his options at length with Miller.

At this point, Banting was considering a number of different routes he might take in his life. His practice was picking up and his income was rising, and he was constantly being encouraged by his fiancé to settle down into full-time practice. Sometime during the winter or spring, while Banting continued to debate over the wisdom of moving to Toronto, Edith apparently broke off the engagement with him. This apparently was the turning point in his decision to go to Toronto, where he again met with Macleod to plan the work. It appeared that Macleod was no more impressed than he had been earlier with Banting's knowledge of research, but he consented to Banting's use of the lab. Macleod assigned Charles Herbert Best, a young physiology student, to help Banting in his endeavor. Having given up his instructorship at Western University, sold his house and furnishings in London, and closed his office, Banting had burned his bridges behind him.

For more than a quarter century before Banting undertook his experiments, there was general agreement that the cause of diabetes was the failure of the pancreas to secrete enough of a certain mysterious substance necessary for the proper utilization of carbohydrates as a body fuel. As a result of this failure, the unassimilated sugar was constantly being secreted in the urine, drawing with it tremendous quantities of water and thereby leaving the victim with the triad of tremendous thirst, large volumes of urine, and increasing waste. The problem that had faced physiologists for years, and that had stumped them, was where this mysterious pancreatic secretion resided, as it apparently was not secreted into pancreatic ducts and must therefore be released into the bloodstream directly. Banting and Best began their experiments by ligating the pancreatic ducts of dogs with cat gut. They waited

almost seven weeks, which must have been a very nerve-racking period, at which time they opened the dog's abdomen, only to find, to their bitter disappointment, that the pancreas was not atrophied. The cat gut that had been used for ligatures had disintegrated, so that the gland, no longer blocked, did not degenerate. The experiment was repeated, and on July 30, Banting and Best again operated on the dogs and found the pancreases notably shriveled. They then cut the atrophied organ into small pieces, ground it up, and obtained a crude extract that they then injected into the same dog. By this time the dog had all the symptoms of diabetes, with tremendous sugar in his urine and weight loss. Within a few hours of injecting the substance into the dog, Banting and Best began to see increasing signs of returning strength in the dog, as well as a fall in the blood and urine sugar to normal levels.

This was a very solemn moment. Banting and Best, though quite thrilled with their discovery, were also worried, because it hardly seemed possible that they had achieved, in such a short time and with such crude extracts, what famous scientists had been unable to

Sir Frederick G. Banting. (National Institute of Health)

achieve. Over the next few weeks, Banting and Best refined the techniques both of producing the pancreatic lesion that would allow them to extract this new substance and of improving the method of extraction. They had read that the islets of Langerhans in the fetus were much larger than those in children after birth, and therefore they obtained fetuses from pregnant slaughtered cows and found that the fetal pancreas had oversize islets with a generous supply of this new substance that they termed isletin. When Macleod returned from a long sabbatical in Scotland and was presented with their experimental data, his initial reaction was one of caution. He seems also to have questioned the accuracy of some of the data, and engendered quite a bit of resentment and anger. The memorable part of the interview came when Banting, after relating the problems he had encountered in terms of working conditions, demanded from Macleod a salary, a room in which to work, help in looking after the dogs, and a new floor for the operating room—failing which he would leave. Macleod agreed to Banting's conditions, and Banting was to stay at Toronto. Banting and Best were eager to play the roles of the first human guinea pigs and injected ten units of insulin into each other's arms and suffered no ill effects. The first chance to test this substance on a human patient came on January 11, 1922, on a fourteen-year-old boy, who had almost reached the end of the life expectancy of a diabetic child. He had high levels of blood sugar and was expected to go into a coma and die within a few days. He was given a small quantity of insulin, injected under the skin, and within a few hours his blood sugar had dropped about 25 percent and the sugar in his urine decreased. After ten days of receiving insulin, the boy looked and felt better. When the insulin was stopped, the boy's condition deteriorated.

At Banting's request, James Bertram Collip, an expert in biochemistry, was invited to join the investigation. Things progressed quickly thereafter, and Banting and Best were able to present a paper at the American Physiological Society meeting in New Haven, Connecticut, on December 28, 1921. The world had become aware of their remarkable findings, but unfortunately, as word of their discovery grew, Banting had become increasingly dissatisfied with the state of affairs in the lab and suspicious that Macleod was trying to steal his results. To compound the problem, Collip walked into the lab one day and announced to Banting and Best that he had discovered the active principal in the pancreatic islets, but declined to tell them how he had come to his discovery. The only surviving artifact of this crisis in the lab is an agreement signed by Banting, Best, Collip, and Macleod,

dated January 25, 1922, in which all agreed not to take a step that would result in the process of obtaining a pancreatic extract being patented by a commercial firm. Banting became increasingly concerned that he and Best were being treated as technicians while the bulk of the work had been passed on to experts.

In April of 1922, the Toronto group prepared a paper summarizing the entire work to that point. The paper, "The Effect Produced on Diabetes by Extracts of Pancreas," was presented by Macleod at the meeting of the Association of American Physicians. On May 22, the Toronto group agreed to collaborate with Eli Lilly and Company, which turned all of its huge resources toward the production of this compound.

Much controversy still exists concerning who should actually receive the credit for discovering insulin. The Nobel assembly, on October 25, voted by secret ballot to award the 1923 Nobel Prize in Physiology or Medicine to Banting and Macleod. As soon as Banting heard that, he became angry at the thought of Macleod being given credit for the discovery. He immediately announced that he would share his prize with Best. Macleod, in turn, after some reflection, elected to share his portion with Collip. Numerous letters were written to the Nobel Committee by various persons, protesting the decision. Nicolas Paulesco in Bucharest had done preliminary experiments with pancreatic extract; had he proceeded more quickly, he might well have received the credit for discovering insulin.

Banting became an important public figure and was much sought-after as a speaker and teacher. The Banting and Best Department of Medical Research at the University of Toronto was separate from the rest of the university; it was Banting's own domain, populated by colorful, reportedly hard-drinking students and cronies, some of whom were also good scientists.

Banting became more interested in things other than medicine, including the arts, and took up painting. In 1924, Canada's most eligible bachelor was swept off his feet and was married to Marion Robertson, a doctor's daughter from Ontario. The marriage was short-lived and produced one child. In 1934, Banting was honored with a knighthood, becoming Sir Frederick G. Banting, K.B.E. When the war resumed in 1939, Banting had just been married again, to a technician in his department, and was pressed to serve as coordinating chair of Canada's medical research wartime effort. While in London in the winter of 1939-1940, he began to write a long account of the discovery of insulin. He returned to Canada in the spring of 1940. On February 21, 1941, he took off from Gander, Newfoundland, on board a Hudson bomber en route to England for a second time. The plane crashed in Newfoundland and Banting died in the wreck. There was much speculation as to the cause of his death and the nature of his mission.

SIGNIFICANCE

Banting's contribution is fundamental to the present era of medicine inasmuch as the understanding of proteins as molecules with a chemical structure that carries information between cells utilizing specific receptors all came about with the availability of insulin. The discovery of insulin has not by any means eliminated all the morbidity of diabetes, but it certainly has extended the lives of millions of diabetics, in many cases allowing them to live nearly normal lives.

—Abraham Verghese

FURTHER READING

Banting, Frederick G., and C. H. Best. "The Discovery and Preparation of Insulin." *University of Toronto Medical Journal* 1 (1923): 94-98. This account is a matter-of-fact report on the sequence of experiments leading to the discovery of insulin. The report avoids controversy, and the conflicts between Banting and Macleod are not discussed.

Bayliss, W. M. "Insulin, Diabetes, and Rewards for Discoveries." *Nature* 3, no. 2780 (February 10, 1923): 188-191. An excellent account of the discovery of insulin by another distinguished scientist. Bayliss did some preliminary experiments that, had he pursued them, could have led to his discovering insulin.

Bliss, Michael. *The Discovery of Insulin.* 3d pbk. ed. Toronto, Ont.: University of Toronto Press, 2000. A detailed account of the personalities and events leading to the discovery of insulin, with a short biography of Banting. Macleod is portrayed in a more favorable light than in other books. This book is perhaps the best researched and referenced book on the subject.

Burtness, H. I., and E. F. Cain. "A Thirty-fifth Anniversary of Insulin Therapy." *Diabetes* 7 (January/February, 1958): 59-61. A general overview of the impact of insulin on the therapy of diabetes. The almost normal lifestyle and longevity of patients with diabetes in the present day and age is in striking contrast to the days before insulin.

Harris, Seale. *Banting's Miracle: The Story of the Discoverer of Insulin.* Philadelphia: J. B. Lippincott,
1946. A biography of Banting that is biased in favor of Banting and against Macleod. It presents a good picture of Banting's personal life.

Howard, John M., and Walter Hess. *History of the Pancreas: Mysteries of the Hidden Organ.* New York: Kluwer Academic, 2002. Written by two academic pancreatic surgeons, this history of studies of the pancreas from antiquity to contemporary times includes information about Banting and the discovery of insulin.

Macleod, John James Rickard. "History of the Researches Leading to the Discovery of Insulin." *Bulletin of the History of Medicine* 52 (Fall, 1978): 295-312. This is Macleod's own account of the events leading to the discovery of insulin. A dry, factual account that avoids the controversy between Macleod and Banting.

Pratt, Joseph H. "A Reappraisal of Researches Leading to the Discovery of Insulin." *Journal of the History of Medicine* 9 (1954): 281-289. Another viewpoint on the controversy surrounding the discovery of insulin. Clearly, the researchers into the history of the discovery of insulin have all come away with different conclusions—this one portrays Macleod as less of a villain than other reports.

Wrenshall, G. A., G. Hetenyi, and W. R. Feasby. *The Story of Insulin: Forty Years of Success Against Diabetes.* London: Bodley Head, 1962. An account of insulin, its discovery and production, that is well written and highly readable. A fair and objective review of the events at Toronto.

SEE ALSO: Sir William Maddock Bayliss; Bernardo Alberto Houssay; August Krogh; John J. R. Macleod; Theobald Smith; George Hoyt Whipple; Rosalyn Yalow.

RELATED ARTICLES in *Great Events from History: The Twentieth Century:*

1901-1940: April-June, 1902: Bayliss and Starling Establish the Role of Hormones; 1921-1922: Banting and Best Isolate the Hormone Insulin.

1941-1970: October 21, 1969: Artificial Sweetener Cyclamate Is Banned from U.S. Consumer Markets.

1971-2000: May 14, 1982: Eli Lilly Releases the First Commercial Genetically Engineered Medication; November, 1983: Aspartame Is Approved for Use in Carbonated Beverages.

BAO DAI
Emperor of Vietnam (r. 1925-1945, 1954-1955)

Vietnam's last emperor, Bao was a tragic figure who initially sought more freedom and independence for his people but ended up collaborating with their foreign rulers before and during World War II. Furthermore, Bao could not lead Vietnam against Communist aggression and was ultimately deposed through constitutional change in 1955.

BORN: October 22, 1913; Hue, Vietnam
DIED: July 30, 1997; Paris, France
ALSO KNOWN AS: Nguyen Vinh Thuy (birth name);
    Vinh Thuy; Jean-Robert (baptismal name)
AREA OF ACHIEVEMENT: Government and politics

EARLY LIFE

Bao Dai (bah-oh di) was born in the Vietnamese imperial city of Hue. He was the only child of Emperor Khai Dinh, born by his second wife, Doan-Huy. Bao's birth name was Nguyen Vinh Thuy, and he had a personal name of Vinh Thuy. At this time, France ruled Vietnam as Indochina, a French colonial possession, and Vietnam's emperor served at the leisure of French authority. On March 10, 1922, Bao was named heir apparent, given a suitable palace as official residence on May 15, and then, at age nine, sent to Paris for schooling. He first attended Lycée Condorcet, then the Institute of Political Studies.

Bao's father died on November 6, 1925, requiring that the twelve-year-old Bao return to Vietnam. He was crowned at Hue as Emperor Bao Dai (Keeper of Greatness) on January 8, 1926. He quickly returned to school in Paris, while a regent discharged his imperial duties as directed by the French.

On September 6, 1932, Bao returned to Vietnam. Considered of age, he assumed imperial powers at Hue on September 10.

LIFE'S WORK

Initially, Emperor Bao was full of reformist energy. He immediately abolished the law that his subjects fill his every need. On May 2, 1933, with French approval, he dismissed his old ruling council, seeking to fill imperial positions with young men of promise. Among these men was Ngo Dinh Diem, minister of the interior.

Ardent reformers like Diem quickly clashed with the French who rejected any infringement upon their colonial prerogatives. Bao advised Diem to acquiesce or

leave office, and Diem departed. Bao's new prime minister, Pham Quynh, worked with the French, alienating Bao's regime from nationalist Vietnamese.

Having probed the narrow limits of French tolerance for Vietnamese freedom, Bao resigned himself to the role of a playboy. On March 20, 1934, he married the beautiful Catholic, French-educated billionaire's daughter Marie-Thérèse Thi Lan Nguyen Huu-Hao, who took the name of Nam Phuong (Southern Perfume Empress). As was possible in Vietnam, Bao married a second wife, his cousin, Phu Anh, in 1934. Even before the birth on January 4, 1936, of their son, Crown Prince Bao Long, Bao had a daughter, Princess Phuong Mai, with a Chinese lover, Hoang, whom he would marry in Hong Kong in 1946. Empress Nam Phuong had three girls and one more boy with her husband. Their new Bauhaus-style villa in Dalat was the place of frequent matrimonial strife, and at one time Nam Phuong tried to shoot Bao because of the strife.

After the outbreak of World War II on September 13, 1939, Bao suggested a four-point reform program to the French. Cynically, the French rejected the request, giving Bao a private plane as consolation for his acquiescence.

With the fall of France to Germany in 1940, Axis power Japan was able to occupy Vietnam in July, 1941. To support Japan efficiently, the Japanese left intact both French colonial administration and Bao's imperial government. Like the French, Bao served the Japanese, who used Vietnam as a military base at great cost to the Vietnamese population.

France was liberated several years later and rejoined the Allied war effort. However, on March 9, 1945, the Japanese succeeded in dismantling French rule in Indochina. Bao, prodded by Japan, declared the independence of the northern and central part of Vietnam on March 11. One day before surrendering to the Allies on August 15, Japan transferred southern Vietnam to Bao's empire, reuniting Vietnam for the first time since 1862.

Bao became the independent emperor of Vietnam, yet he was opposed by the fiercely nationalist Communist Viet Minh, led by Ho Chi Minh. Bao felt he lacked the military power to engage in a life-or-death struggle with the Communists. He agreed to abdicate on August 25, 1945, and was made a supreme adviser to Ho's Democratic Republic of Viet Nam (or North Vietnam, a republic proclaimed on September 2).

With the French returning to Vietnam in late 1945, Ho Chi Minh sent Bao to China to keep him from French contact. Bao agreed, and from China he flew to voluntary exile in Hong Kong on March 16, 1946. He assumed another name, married Hoang, and believed his political career had ended. In 1947, his first wife, Nam Phuong, took her and Bao's children with her to France.

Faced with serious Communist armed resistance, the French decided on the Bao solution in 1947. France tried to persuade Bao to lead a non-Communist state of Vietnam that was to remain dependent on the French. Bao forced the French to include all Vietnam into this new state. After signing a preliminary agreement on June 5, 1948, Bao flew to France. There, the Elysée Agreement between himself and French Fourth Republic president Vincent Auriol of March 8, 1949, laid the foundation for the State of Vietnam, created on June 4. On July 1, Bao was installed as head of the State of Vietnam. Even though he was not officially called emperor, virtually all Vietnamese considered him such.

Bao quickly became disillusioned with the lack of power for himself and for the Vietnamese people. As the war against the Viet Minh raged on, he returned to France, declining to lead the anti-Communist efforts. To the contrary, he let the gangster sect Binh Xuyen control the Saigon police, allegedly for $1.25 million.

After the Viet Minh victory over the French at Dien Bien Phu, and following the conclusion of the Geneva Accords of July 21, 1954, Bao remained head of the State of Vietnam. The state governed South Vietnam, with North Vietnam awarded to Ho Chi Minh's forces. Sensing that French power in Vietnam was replaced by the Americans, Bao accepted Diem, whom the United States favored, as his prime minister.

Residing in France, Bao left Diem in charge in South Vietnam. When Diem moved against the Binh Xuyen and defeated them on March 30, 1955, Bao called for Diem's ouster. Diem refused, and on July 7 announced that on October 23 there would be a referendum on turning South Vietnam into a republic without a head of state. As Bao left France only briefly to marry a fourth woman, Bui Mong Diep, in Saigon in 1955, Diem's victory in the referendum was assured. Diem, however, yielded to cheating and obtained an improbable 98.2 percent of the vote for the measure, winning an impossible 133 percent in Saigon. On October 26, the Republic of Vietnam was established and Bao lost his position as head of state.

In France, Bao lived privately. After the death of Nam Phuong in 1963, he married in 1972 his fifth wife, the French woman Monique Baudot, who became Imperial Princess Monique Vinh Thuy. That year Bao also permitted Communist North Vietnam to use him briefly in a denunciation of U.S. troops in South Vietnam, modeled on the Khmer Rouge's use of deposed Cambodian king Norodom Sihanouk. After the fall of Saigon in 1975, Bao visited exiled Vietnamese in the United States in 1982. In 1988, Bao converted from Buddhism to Catholicism and was baptized as Jean-Robert. He died in Paris on July 30, 1997.

SIGNIFICANCE

Bao's historical role was a tragic one. As a nineteen-year-old emperor, he idealistically sought freedom from France and independence for his country. Once rebuked, he settled on a course of accommodating those who would offer him physical safety and material comfort. He allowed the French to use him as a figurehead, indulging in pleasures granted in return for collaboration. When Japan occupied his country, he accommodated the new rulers as well.

Bao had two historical chances to assert himself. First, Japan's surrender on August 15, 1945, nominally left him in charge of all Vietnam, notwithstanding his tainted reputation because of his earlier collaboration. However, Bao declined to fight the Viet Minh and then develop an effective, popular imperial government as a genuine nationalist alternative to Communist rule.

Second, Bao became head of state in South Vietnam after the Geneva Conference of 1954 partitioned Vietnam into North and South. The Vietnamese people still considered him their emperor. He lost their affection and the affection of the best of the young, dynamic, anti-Communist Vietnamese looking for a leader to ensure the freedom of their truncated country when he stayed in France instead of joining his people in their struggles against the Communists.

—*R. C. Lutz*

FURTHER READING

Chapuis, Oscar. *The Last Emperors of Vietnam.* Westport, Conn.: Greenwood Press, 2000. Pages 27-30 and 152-175 provide useful and detailed discussion, but some facts and dates quoted do not always conform to historical consensus. Best used with other secondary sources.

Jacobs, Seth. *America's Miracle Man in Vietnam.* Durham, N.C.: Duke University Press, 2004. Hostile review of Bao's final nemesis, Ngo Dinh Diem. Chapters 1 and 5 deal with Bao, focusing on his deals with gangsters and his fights with Diem. Illustrated.

Karnow, Stanley. *Vietnam: A History*. 2d ed. New York: Viking Press, 1997. Remains the most widely available source in English. Presents mainstream U.S. historical assessments of Bao.

Lam, Quang Thi. *The Twenty-Five-Year Century*. Denton: University of North Texas Press, 2001. Autobiography of a South Vietnamese general illustrating young nationalist, anti-Communist Vietnam's disenchantment with Bao's remote rule as head of state from 1949 to 1955.

SEE ALSO: Ho Chi Minh; Ngo Dinh Diem; Nguyen Van Thieu; Vo Nguyen Giap.

RELATED ARTICLES in *Great Events from History: The Twentieth Century:*

1941-1970: November, 1946-July, 1954: Nationalist Vietnamese Fight French Control of Indochina; March 8, 1949: Vietnam Is Named a State; August, 1954-May, 1955: Operation Passage to Freedom Evacuates Refugees from North Vietnam; November 1-2, 1963: Vietnamese Generals Overthrow Diem Regime.

SAMUEL BARBER
American composer

Barber developed a style of musical composition that bridged the gap between nineteenth century Romanticism and twentieth century modernism.

BORN: March 9, 1910; West Chester, Pennsylvania
DIED: January 23, 1981; New York, New York
AREA OF ACHIEVEMENT: Music

EARLY LIFE

Samuel Barber was the son of a physician and a pianist; his maternal aunt was the famed contralto Louise Homer. Barber's family did not, however, particularly encourage his natural inclination toward music studies. They wanted him to be "an average American boy," and for them this meant active participation in athletics, particularly football. Barber, however, was in no way average. In a letter he wrote as a schoolboy, Barber expressed to his mother his determination to become a composer, and begged to be allowed to pursue music studies.

Clearly, Barber's family always recognized his talent, even though they did not want their son to subject himself to the uncertainties inherent in a career in music. Still, there was no way to hold back a prodigy, and the six-year-old Barber began piano studies with William Hatton Green, himself a former student of the Polish pianist and composer Theodor Leschetizky. These early studies firmly linked Barber to European Romanticism and would leave an indelible influence on his own distinctive style. By age ten, Barber had written the first act of an opera entitled "The Rose Tree." No doubt it would have been completed had the family cook, who was also the librettist, not left the Barber household for another position. Several songs dating from the early 1920's still

survive, however, in the archives of the Chester County Historical Society, West Chester, Pennsylvania.

Obviously, there was potential even in his youthful works, for with the sponsorship of Harold Randolph, then director of the Peabody Conservatory in Baltimore, Maryland, Barber was accepted as a charter student at the then recently founded Curtis Institute of Music in Philadelphia in 1924. He attended Curtis for eight years, during the first two of which he remained as well in his local high school to complete graduation requirements in 1926. His diversified studies at Curtis were in themselves remarkable and included composition with Rosario Scalero, piano with Isabella Vengerova, and voice with Emilio deGogorza. (A recording of his early song based on Matthew Arnold's poem "Dover Beach" was made with the Curtis String Quartet, Barber singing the tenor solo, on May 13, 1935. It was issued as a Victor 78 rpm, and is a collector's item since it represents the only example of Barber as vocalist.)

Photographs of Barber, most taken from the mid-1930's once his career had begun, show a young man who is at once patrician, elegant, and conservative, more like a prosperous businessman than a bohemian artist. His intelligent, piercing eyes and slightly aquiline nose remained his best features throughout his life and make the adjective "distinguished" entirely appropriate to describe Barber's appearance, even as a very young man. Except for white hair, slightly receding in his later years, Barber kept this youthful appearance to the last years of his life. His diction was similarly impeccable, perhaps in part from his vocal training, with only a trace of English accent behind otherwise uninflected speech. Unlike many composers, Barber had the ability to discuss his own compositions with great critical insight. Several radio interviews survive as transcriptions from the original broadcasts, the majority from the mid-1960's, the period following composition of his opera *Antony and Cleopatra* (1966).

LIFE'S WORK

Major recognition of Barber's talent came in 1928 when his Sonata for Violin and Piano won the Bearns Prize. This twelve-hundred-dollar award, substantial for the 1920's, encouraged the young composer. Barber would win the Bearns Prize a second time in 1935, for his overture and incidental music for Richard Brinsley Sheridan's play *The School for Scandal* (1777), by far a better-known composition, which has been recorded several times.

Barber's friendship with fellow composer Gian Carlo Menotti began during their years as fellow students at Curtis. Though an unlikely musical association given the style of Menotti, which follows in the wake of Italian *verismo*, the two collaborated on several important projects. Menotti, for example, staged the revised version of *Antony and Cleopatra* in 1975, for the Juilliard Opera in New York, and again in 1983, at his Spoleto Festival in Italy and his Festival of Two Worlds in Charleston, South Carolina. These productions were a critical success and largely responsible for the opera's increased acceptance. Barber and Menotti also shared a warm personal friendship as well as a home, Capricorn, at Mount Kisco, New York.

A European tour Barber took in 1932 was important for shaping his style as a composer. It was in the summer of that year that he completed the first movement and part of the scherzo of his Sonata for Violoncello and Piano, which won for him the American Academy's Prix de Rome in 1935, as well as a Pulitzer Traveling Scholarship, also in 1935. These grants allowed Barber an academic year in residence at the American Academy in Rome (1935-1936) and provided a setting for the world premiere of his Symphony no. 1 (In One Movement), which was given by the Augusteo Orchestra, Bernardino Molinari conducting. Famed conductor Artur Rodzinski, leading the Cleveland Orchestra, gave the American premiere later in 1936 (it was revised in 1942).

Barber's career was well under way by the mid-1930's, fostered as well by Arturo Toscanini's sponsorship. Barber had met Toscanini during the American Academy year. The maestro recalled his having conducted Barber's aunt, Louise Homer, in Christoph Gluck's *Orfeo ed Eurydice* (1762), and asked to see the

Samuel Barber. (Library of Congress)

young composer's work. What Toscanini saw were drafts of his Essay no. 1, the first of his Essays for Orchestra, and the Adagio for Strings. He would conduct these celebrated pieces with the National Broadcasting Company (NBC) Symphony Orchestra on November 5, 1938. Both works have since become standards of the symphonic literature. Though the Essays for Orchestra received mixed critical response at the time of its premiere, the Adagio for Strings gained immediate public acceptance. Its affecting lyricism makes it appreciable on first hearing. This was the music that the NBC radio network chose to play immediately after its announcement of President Franklin D. Roosevelt's death on April 12, 1945, and later it was adapted as part of the score for the motion picture *The Elephant Man* (1980). Barber would increasingly employ what he considered "literary" techniques in his compositions, and in his last years he would write other "essays," so called because they developed architechtonically from an orchestral thesis.

Barber's career continued to gain momentum in early 1941, when Eugene Ormandy and the Philadelphia Orchestra gave the premiere of his Violin Concerto, op. 14, with Albert Spalding as soloist. Though when first composed Iso Briselli, for whom it was intended, called its final movement "unplayable" and refused to accept the piece, it has come to be highly regarded by musicians as a virtuoso work; indeed, the Philadelphia Orchestra singled it out for a cash award during its 1957-1958 season.

As was the case for many artists, World War II imposed severe limitations on Barber's composing activities. He entered the Army in 1943 and served in a clerical position, though he did write his Commando March at this time. Though his name never publicly appeared as part of the controversy, it is generally known that the Army refused him permission to write a piece in honor of the Russian people. Protests on his behalf by his fellow artists, the best known of whom was the Metropolitan Opera's Lawrence Tibbett, probably were responsible for Barber's quiet transfer to the Air Force. It was at this time that Barber composed his first version of Symphony no. 2, a programmatic work that contained attempts to reproduce electronically the sounds and machinery of flight. Barber was never pleased with the work, and after several attempts to revise it by eliminating all programmatic material, he saw to the destruction of all remaining undistributed published copies and withdrew the title from his catalog of works.

Barber, unlike many composers, rarely conducted or taught. He had studied conducting in the 1930's under Fritz Reiner, but Reiner considered Barber mediocre, and this opinion seems to have discouraged the young composer. Barber did conduct in later life, but only when his reputation was needed to publicize one of his compositions. For example, his Cello Concerto (1945), though critically acclaimed, was recorded in 1950 only because Barber himself agreed to conduct the orchestra. Barber's teaching was limited to a brief period at Curtis immediately after graduation from that institution. He never gave master classes.

The years following the war were especially productive. On a commission from the American soprano Eleanor Steber, Barber wrote his immensely popular *Knoxville: Summer of 1915*, op. 24, based on the autobiographical memoir by James Agee. This work premiered April 9, 1948, with Serge Koussevitzky conducting Steber and the Boston Symphony. Here again, as he had in the Adagio for Strings and the first Essays for Orchestra, Barber showed his gift for lyricism and his affinity for literature. Indeed, the works of Barber that have these qualities are inevitably those that have remained audience favorites. *The Hermit Songs* (1952-1953), based on medieval Irish texts, are similarly popular. They premiered on October 30, 1953, at the Library of Congress, sung by Leontyne Price, who was just beginning her career, with Barber playing the piano accompaniment.

His success in vocal writing led to the opera *Vanessa*. This work, with libretto by Menotti, was given to popular acclaim but mixed critical reaction at the Metropolitan Opera Company with Steber in the title role on January 15, 1958. It did, however, win a Pulitzer Prize, and its audience popularity in several revivals led the Metropolitan Opera Company to commission *Antony and Cleopatra* for the September 16, 1966, inauguration of its new house at Lincoln Center. One problem with this work in its original form is that it was written as much to illustrate the new theater's performance capabilities as to present the composer's music. The Franco Zeffirelli production was especially lavish, and the difficult music, combined with what Barber himself believed was an inappropriate production, resulted in what is generally considered a failure, though Price, the Cleopatra of the premiere, always defended the music and kept Cleopatra's death music in her concert programs. It remains a bitter irony that the costumes for *Vanessa*, *Antony and Cleopatra*, and thirty-nine other Metropolitan Opera Company productions were destroyed in a warehouse fire on November 7, 1974.

Depression set in for Barber after the failure of *Antony and Cleopatra*. He sold his Mount Kisco home and set about revising the opera. Its revised version runs almost a full hour less than the original, and it was given with some success by the Juilliard School in 1975, with still more subsequently by Menotti at Charleston and Spoleto.

Barber's last years were plagued by hospitalization and treatment for cancer, and this affected his work. An eight-minute piece for oboe and string orchestra, written in 1978, is his last known composition. Though originally designed as part of an oboe concerto, it was given in late 1981 as *Canzonetta* by the New York Philharmonic, Zubin Mehta conducting, with Harold Gomberg as soloist.

SIGNIFICANCE

It is difficult to say exactly what legacy Barber has left American music. What is clear is that he was an immensely gifted composer whose gentle, lyrical style and precision allowed many members of the general audience an introduction to modern music that they would not otherwise have had. Barber could have used his gifts to pander to audience tastes. Though this would have assured him at least short-term popularity, he refused to do so.

His greatest accomplishment was his ability to use familiar nineteenth century Romantic musical forms in undeniably modern ways. To his last days, he rejected both extreme dissonance and stripped-down minimalism. His music was almost never "American-sounding" in the manner of George Gershwin or Aaron Copland, yet he ranks with them as one of the most often performed and recorded American composers of the twentieth century.

—Robert J. Forman

FURTHER READING

Ardoin, John. "Samuel Barber at Capricorn." *Musical America* 80 (March, 1960): 4-5. An intimate portrait of the composer's private life at the house in Mount Kisco, New York, which he shared with Menotti until 1974. Barber found inspiration in the landscape and through his association with his fellow composer and longtime friend.

Broder, Nathan. "The Music of Samuel Barber." *Musical Quarterly* 34 (July, 1948): 325-335. Though Barber based many orchestral compositions on the classical sonata form, he managed to do so without slavish adherence to the past. This article illustrates Barber's ability to introduce new techniques within more traditional structures.

Demuth, Norman. *Musical Trends in the Twentieth Century.* London: Rockliff, 1952. Compares Barber's virtuosity to that of Richard Strauss; even so, Barber's music is not neoclassical but represents a Romanticism appropriate to the twentieth century.

Dexter, Harry. "Samuel Barber and His Music." Parts 1, 2. *Musical Opinion* 72 (March/April, 1949): 285-286, 343-344. A two-part article that provides good criticism of Barber's style: his emotional control and the depth of feeling that he produces in spite of this control.

Felsenfeld, David. *Britten and Barber: Their Lives and Their Music.* Pompton Plains, N.J.: Amadeus Press, 2005. Includes a brief biography, essays about Barber and composer Benjamin Britten, and analyses of four of Barber's compositions recorded on an accompanying compact disc.

Friedewald, Russell Edward. *A Formal and Stylistic Analysis of the Published Music of Samuel Barber.* Ames: Iowa State University Press, 1957. A dissertation that distinguishes between Barber's music composed before and after 1939, noting the technical enrichment of the later work and Barber's adaptations of the classical sonata form.

Hennessee, Don A. *Samuel Barber: A Bio-Bibliography.* Westport, Conn.: Greenwood Press, 1985. Contains a brief biographical essay as well as a catalog of Barber's works and critical works available on them.

"Obituary: Mr. Samuel Barber." *The Times* (London), January 26, 1981: 14. A lengthy obituary that discusses Barber's career and sees him in the tradition of Romanticism as lyrical rather than neoclassical or experimental, generally rejecting many of the trends of modern music.

Simmons, Walter. *Voices in the Wilderness: Six American Neo-Romantic Composers.* Lanham, Md.: Scarecrow Press, 2004. Provides a biographical overview and analysis of Barber's compositions, including an assessment of his strengths and weaknesses and affinities with other composers.

SEE ALSO: Irving Berlin; Leonard Bernstein; Benjamin Britten; Aaron Copland; Claude Debussy; George Gershwin; Gustav Mahler; Gian Carlo Menotti; Leontyne Price; Richard Strauss; Arturo Toscanini; Kurt Weill.

RELATED ARTICLE in *Great Events from History: The Twentieth Century:*

1941-1970: December 24, 1951: *Amahl and the Night Visitors* Premieres on American Television.

JOHN BARDEEN
American physicist

Bardeen is one of the twentieth century's great solid-state theorists. His co-invention, with Walter Brattain, of the transistor began the revolution in electronics and computer technology. His superconductivity theory, or BCS-theory, had major implications in most areas of physics.

BORN: May 23, 1908; Madison, Wisconsin
DIED: January 30, 1991; Boston, Massachusetts
AREAS OF ACHIEVEMENT: Physics, engineering, invention and technology

EARLY LIFE

John Bardeen (bahr-DEEN), the second of five children, was born in Madison, Wisconsin, to Althea Harmer and Charles R. Bardeen. Charles was an anatomy professor and dean of the University of Wisconsin Medical School, and Althea was an interior decorator. Bardeen was a child prodigy who, at age nine, skipped from third grade in elementary school to seventh grade at the University of Wisconsin's high school in Madison. At the start of twelfth grade, he transferred to the public high school for its better laboratory facilities. After taking a few extra courses, Bardeen graduated from high school at age fifteen, the same year as his older brother William. Though he was studying with much older children, Bardeen thoroughly enjoyed playing games and sports with his peers and with his older brother. He played golf from a young age, and the sport turned into a lifelong passion. He was also a three-year varsity swimmer and water polo player at the University of Wisconsin. By all accounts reserved, Bardeen enjoyed his days with a college fraternity and maintained friendships with many types of people throughout his life. His other nonacademic pursuits included billiards, bowling, and playing cards.

Bardeen earned bachelor's (1928) and master's (1929) degrees in electrical engineering from Wisconsin. In his first year as a graduate student, he also studied quantum mechanics with American physicist John H. van Vleck (a 1977 Nobel laureate) and British theoretical physicist Paul A. M. Dirac (a 1933 Nobel laureate). In 1930, Bardeen took time away from his studies to work in Pittsburgh, Pennsylvania, as a geophysicist for Gulf Research and Development Corporation, where he invented a new form of electromagnetic oil prospecting. It was in Pittsburgh that he met his future wife, Jane Maxwell (they married in 1938).

In 1933, Bardeen began his doctoral studies in mathematical physics at Princeton University, where he had hoped to study under Albert Einstein. Einstein was not accepting graduate students, however, so Bardeen became the second research student for Hungarian physicist Eugene Wigner (a 1963 Nobel laureate) in Princeton's Mathematics Department. Before Bardeen completed his Ph.D. in 1936, he studied at Harvard University, working as a junior fellow of the Society of Fellows (1935-1938), under the guidance of van Vleck and American physicist Percy Williams Bridgman (a 1946 Nobel laureate).

LIFE'S WORK

Surrounded as a graduate student by many of the world's most brilliant scientists, Bardeen's interests were broad: mathematics, electrical engineering, solid-state and nuclear physics, and superconductivity. It did not take him long to make significant contributions to industry and society. During his time as an assistant professor at the University of Minnesota (1938-1941), the scientific requirements of World War II took him to the Naval Ordnance Laboratory in Washington, D.C. (1941-1945). Following the war, American Telephone & Telegraph's (AT&T) Bell Telephone Laboratories recruited Bardeen to work on solid-state devices. The Bardeens moved with their three children (James, William, and Elizabeth) to New Jersey.

Bardeen, a solid-state theorist, shared an office with experimentalists Walter Brattain and Gerald Pearson, a circumstance that turned fortuitous. As members of a team headed by William Shockley, Bardeen, and Brattain were tasked with finding a solid-state device that could replace the bulky, unreliable, and expensive vacuum tube and electromechanical switches used in AT&T's telephone network. During the war, Bell Labs worked with the semiconductor elements germanium and silicon, and its scientists thought that semiconductors could make reliable solid-state amplifiers. After two years of intense research, Bardeen and Brattain observed and effectively modeled the phenomenon of carrier injection and invented the point-contact transistor using the semiconductor germanium (December, 1947). With that transistor, they demonstrated an amplification of a spoken audio signal. Bell Labs announced the transistor in June, 1948.

In 1956, a surprised Bardeen received his first Nobel Prize in Physics for research on semiconductors and discovery of the transistor effect, an honor he shared with Brattain and Shockley. Transistors amplify or switch electrical signals and are the building blocks of modern solid-state electronic devices. Hearing-aid manufacturers were among the first to market commercial transistor products, and Jane Bardeen was given one of the first transistorized hearing aids.

To pursue his broader interests (in particular, superconductivity theory) Bardeen left Bell Labs in 1951 and became a professor of electrical engineering and of physics at the University of Illinois in Urbana. He held this post until his retirement in 1975, and stayed on as professor emeritus for the remainder of his life. Although a theorist, Bardeen preferred working with experimentalists so that he could analyze the data and base his theories on experimental clues.

Bardeen had long been intrigued by the process of superconductivity. In the 1950's, the only known superconductors were certain metals. Superconductors have no electrical resistance at very low temperatures. With no electrical resistance, superconductors efficiently carry a high-current density for long periods of time without heat loss. One highly successful application of superconductivity is magnetic resonance imaging (MRI) scanners, which use liquid helium-cooled superconducting magnets.

From the time of its discovery in 1911 to the mid-1950's, scientists had observed superconductivity but could not explain the physical mechanism responsible for the phenomenon. In 1957, Bardeen, his graduate student Bob Schrieffer, and postdoctoral student Leon Cooper developed the first successful theory of the superconductivity of metals, known as the Bardeen, Cooper, and Schrieffer (or BCS) theory. The team's seminal work on superconductivity was one of the major achievements in physics of the twentieth century and for which Bardeen won, in 1972, his second Nobel Prize in physics (which he shared with Cooper and Schrieffer). Bardeen kept abreast of scientific advancements after he became professor emeritus. He was thrilled about the 1986 discovery of high-temperature superconductors.

Bardeen's contributions to government and industry were significant. He served on the Science Advisory Committee (1959-1962) under Presidents Dwight D. Eisenhower and John F. Kennedy and on President Ronald Reagan's White House Science Council (1982-1983). Among his numerous awards, Bardeen was a 1977 Presidential Medal of Freedom recipient. He held a long relationship with Haloid Company (renamed Xerox Corporation), where he consulted between 1952 and 1982 and

was a member of its board of directors from 1961 to 1974. His advice was crucial for the research and development behind the first xerographic processes and materials and later for laser xerographic printing.

General Electric hired Bardeen as a consultant, and he had lifelong friendships with the directors of Sony Corporation's research laboratories in Japan. Indeed, Sony established the John Bardeen Chair in Physics and Electrical and Computer Engineering at the University of Illinois in 1989. The first recipient of the Sony professorship was Nick Holonyak, Jr., Bardeen's first graduate student, inventor of the first practical light-emitting diode (LED), and solid-state laser technology pioneer. In his tribute to Bardeen for the National Academy of Engineering (*Memorial Tributes* 6 [1993]: 2-11), Holonyak stated that Bardeen, "more than anyone else, can be said to be the 'godfather' of modern electronics." Bardeen's final scientific article appeared in the December, 1990, issue of *Physics Today*, just a month before his death. Bardeen learned he had lung cancer just one day before he died, on January 30, 1991, of cardiac arrest.

SIGNIFICANCE

The first person to win two Nobel Prizes in the same field, Bardeen's discoveries about the conductivity of solids form the basis for much of modern electronics. He was modest, had integrity, and was generous, never taking center stage and giving his colleagues and students their due credit.

Bardeen had incredible analytical skills and was able to solve problems in a way no other scientist had before him. He was revered by colleagues around the world, many of whom gathered in March of 1992 for the Bardeen Memorial Symposium at the meeting of the American Physical Society in Indianapolis, Indiana. In 1990, *Life* magazine named Bardeen one of the hundred most influential Americans of the twentieth century. Bardeen's influence stretched into the twenty-first century as companies founded by his students continued to thrive.

—*Sheri P. Woodburn*

FURTHER READING

Gonzalo, Julio A., and Carmen Aragó López, eds. *Great Solid State Physicists of the Twentieth Century*. River Edge, N.J.: World Scientific, 2003. Based on a plenary session at the Tenth International Meeting on Ferroelectricity in Madrid, Spain, in 2001, the editors focus on the achievements of John Bardeen, William H. Bragg, William L. Bragg, Peter Debye, and Lev Landau. Includes full transcripts of Bardeen's Nobel lectures and speeches given by Bardeen's Nobel Prize presenters.

Hoddeson, Lillian, and Vicki Daitch. *True Genius: The Life and Science of John Bardeen—The Only Winner of Two Nobel Prizes in Physics.* Washington, D.C.: Joseph Henry Press, 2002. Fascinating biography, in which the authors conducted many oral history interviews with Bardeen's family and colleagues.

Matricon, Jean, and Georges Waysand, eds. *The Cold Wars: A History of Superconductivity.* Translated by Charles Glashausser. New Brunswick, N.J.: Rutgers University Press, 2003. Assumes reader has basic knowledge of physics. Provides a comprehensive history of superconductivity, including the science behind it, discoveries, and how scientists dealt with social and political issues.

Riordan, Michael, and Lillian Hoddeson. *Crystal Fire: The Invention of the Transistor and the Birth of the In-formation Age.* New York: W. W. Norton, 1997. Compelling histories of the transistor and semiconductor, and their inventors.

SEE ALSO: Edwin H. Armstrong; Percy Williams Bridgman; Chester F. Carlson; Lee de Forest; Paul A. M. Dirac; Grace Murray Hopper; Konosuke Matsushita; Akio Morita; Vladimir Zworykin.

RELATED ARTICLES in *Great Events from History: The Twentieth Century:*

1901-1940: January 1, 1925: Bell Labs Is Formed.

1941-1970: December 23, 1947: Invention of the Transistor; 1957: Sony Develops the Pocket-Sized Transistor Radio; February-August, 1957: Bardeen, Cooper, and Schrieffer Explain Superconductivity.

1971-2000: September, 1972: Gell-Mann Formulates the Theory of Quantum Chromodynamics.

CHRISTIAAN BARNARD
South African surgeon

Barnard performed the first successful human heart transplantation on December 3, 1967, followed by his second successful heart transplantation on January 2, 1968. His success offered renewed and prolonged lives for many with heart disease.

BORN: November 8, 1922; Beaufort West, South Africa
DIED: September 2, 2001; Paphos, Cyprus
ALSO KNOWN AS: Christiaan Neethling Barnard (full name)
AREAS OF ACHIEVEMENT: Medicine, philanthropy

EARLY LIFE

Christiaan Barnard (BAHR-nahrd) was born in Beaufort West, South Africa. His family was of Afrikaner descent. Christiaan's father, a minister, earned little money, and the family lived on the edge of poverty. Christiaan, however, enjoyed a carefree childhood and a happy family life. He often went on nature hikes with his father, who taught him the names of the trees, the wildflowers, and the plants. His mother was a very determined woman, who insisted that her sons be first in school and never admit defeat. During his high school years, Barnard was usually first in his class. By the end of his senior year in high school, still first in his studies, he was chosen by his class to give the farewell address and, as a cadet, held the highest student rank of sergeant-major. Outside school, he formed a popular musical trio. Upon graduation Barnard left for Cape Town to study at the university there, hoping to enter the field of medicine. In Cape Town, he stayed with his brother and his wife.

LIFE'S WORK

Barnard was graduated with honors from the university and then earned two higher degrees at the University of Minnesota. Between 1953 and 1955, he studied under Owen H. Wangensteen, who described Barnard as a man with a singleness of purpose. Barnard demonstrated this when he operated on forty-nine dogs before he achieved success in an attempt to learn about an intestinal abnormality in the newborn. In three years, he completed the master of science and Ph.D. degrees in surgery.

Upon returning to Cape Town, Barnard continued his transplantation research while he practiced heart surgery and supported a family. Having read about the Soviet experimentation with transplantation of a dog's head, he performed two such operations himself. He filmed the operations and took the films to Moscow, where he hoped to learn more about transplantation. He later spent time at the Medical College of Virginia. Afterward he lectured at the University of Cape Town, where he was named head of cardiothoracic surgery in 1962 and was promoted to associate professor a year later.

Before his first successful orthotopic human-heart transplant, in which a recipient's heart is replaced by a donor's heart, Barnard and another brother, Marius, had performed some fifty unsuccessful experimental heart transplantations in dogs in their attempt to develop a successful technique. This search for a successful heart-transplantation technique was part of a worldwide ten-year study of heart transplantations. The groundbreaking experimentation that led to Barnard's successful operation was performed in 1960 by Norman E. Shumway of Stanford Medical Center in Palo Alto, California. James D. Hardy of the University of Mississippi Medical Center attempted a heart transplantation from a chimpanzee to a man dying of heart failure in 1964. After these early efforts, several researchers, including Richard Laver of the Medical College of Virginia, David Blumanstock of the Mary Imogene Bassett Hospital in Cooperstown, New York, and William Likoff of Philadelphia's Hahnemann Medical College and Hospital, were ready to perform human-heart transplantations at the first opportunity. Louis Washkansky was a fifty-five-year-old wholesale grocer who had suffered two heart attacks in a seven-year period. His diseased heart was twice the normal size and was not getting enough blood through clogged and closed coronary arteries. He also had diabetes, for which he had been taking insulin. His liver was enlarged, and increasingly his body was becoming edematous. Washkansky's doctor believed that his patient had only weeks to live.

On November 10, 1967, Barnard consulted with Washkansky and told him about the heart-transplantation technique. Washkansky agreed to the operation and signed the consent form. Barnard called in his team of thirty women and men, and they remained on a twenty-four-hour alert until a suitable donor was found.

In December, Barnard received notification of a donor, Denise Darvall, a woman who was mortally injured when she was hit by a speeding car. The donor's father gave his consent, and Barnard's team went to work. A team of doctors matched the blood types of Washkansky and Darvall and found them to be compatible. The transplantation proceeded before the pathologist could match the white cells of the two patients to estimate how strong a rejection reaction Washkansky's system would mount against the foreign protein of the transplanted heart. Barnard cut eight blood vessels and several ligaments to free the donor heart. He then moved to an adjacent operating room to continue with the surgery. The procedure

Christiaan Barnard. (Library of Congress)

took five hours. An hour later, Washkansky regained consciousness and attempted to speak. Thirty-six hours after he awakened, he ate a typical hospital meal and soon showed improvement. He was given antibiotics to guard against infection. His heart rate soon slowed to one hundred beats per minute and his liver shrank to near-normal size. His kidneys worked so well that he lost twenty pounds of edema fluid. Washkansky died eighteen days later as a result of double pneumonia, contracted because his immune system was weakened by drugs administered to suppress rejection of his heart. By this time, Barnard had already chosen Philip Blaiberg to receive the second transplanted heart. This transplantation took place on January 2, 1968, on the fifty-eight-year-old dentist. Blaiberg survived for nineteen and one-half months.

While Barnard was on a triumphal tour of the United States between the two operations, ethical questions were raised. How can one be certain that doctors will do everything to save a person's life after an accident or disease if they are considering the possible donation of organs? Marius Barnard noted that his brother had insisted

TAKING RISKS

Christiaan Barnard, in his youth, was more interested in mechanical engineering than medicine, but his interests took a turn and he became a general practitioner, later studying surgery in the United States. One day he was asked to work on a heart-lung machine and became fascinated by open-heart surgery. He returned to South Africa to open his own cardiac surgery unit. He recalled that his father had once shown him a cookie with the marks of a boy's teeth; the marks were those of one of Barnard's brothers, who died when only a few years old: "I realized that he died of a heart problem and that had he lived in my time as a cardiac surgeon I probably could have cured him."

Barnard maintained that his transplanting of a human heart in 1967 "wasn't such a big thing surgically. The technique was a basic one. The point is that I was prepared to take the risk. . . . My philosophy is that the biggest risk in life is not to take a risk."

Source: Quotations from an interview with Peter Hawthorne published in *Time* magazine (2005).

"heterotopic" heart transplantation, performing forty-nine of them between 1974 and 1983. In this procedure, also known as a "piggyback" transplantation, the donor's heart is placed alongside the patient's heart so that the original heart can act as a standby in case the donor's heart should undergo severe tissue rejection. The advent of advanced immunosuppressant drugs in the 1980's largely ended the need for this procedure. Barnard also led research that extended the time that donor hearts can be stored outside the body before surgery.

Barnard retired in 1983 at the age of sixty-one, primarily because rheumatoid arthritis made surgery painful and difficult. He diverted his interest to business, including a controversial connection with the rejuvenation therapy offered at the Clinique La Prairie in Switzerland. He acted as an adviser as the Oklahoma Transplantation Institute in Oklahoma City was established, and he wrote nine books on health and medicine in addition to a sequel, *The Second Life: Memoirs* (1993), to his autobiography, *Christiaan Barnard: One Life* (1969). Additionally, he traveled extensively, lecturing to both medical professionals and to the public. He launched the Christiaan Barnard Foundation to further his interest in charity to the poor and other humanitarian efforts, such as helping the victims of the 1986 Chernobyl nuclear disaster in the Soviet Union. Barnard died of complications from an acute asthma attack on September 2, 2001, while on vacation in Paphos, Cyprus. He left behind five children from three marriages.

that they wait to see if Darvall would survive; in fact they waited until the local medical examiner had declared her dead. On his second tour of the United States, Christiaan Barnard said that he followed the Hippocratic oath— "that the physician must do everything in his power to save life, to restore health, and at the very least to alleviate suffering." In the case of Washkansky, he said, life was not saved; in the case of Blaiberg, however, suffering was alleviated. Marius Barnard claimed that three criteria were used to determine death. A patient is considered dead, he said, "when the heart is no longer working, the lungs are no longer working and there are no longer any complexes" on the EEG (electroencephalogram). Another ethical question raised regarding heart transplantations was who should decide which person was to receive the donor heart if there was more than one candidate. Christiaan Barnard saw no problem with this issue: The person with the most urgent need for the heart should receive it.

Barnard led his team in performing ten more orthotopic transplantations. Six of the patients survived for about a year or longer, a remarkable achievement considering that methods to prevent the body from rejecting the transplanted heart were inchoate. His program in Cape Town emerged as one of the four centers worldwide for transplantation. The University of Cape Town promoted him to professor of surgical science in 1972, yet he was unhappy that he never received the title that he wanted: professor of cardiac surgery. His team pioneered the

SIGNIFICANCE

Barnard's accomplishments marked a milestone in medical science and in the organ-transplantation field. His success was part of the ongoing process in renewing and prolonging life. The first successful organ transplantation, involving the cornea, took place in 1905. By the 1950's, doctors at Boston's Peter Bent Brigham Hospital were successfully transplanting kidneys between identical twins. By the middle of the 1960's, doctors in Colorado and Minnesota were transplanting, with success, human livers and the pancreas with duodenum attached.

In the 1960's, at least 500,000 Americans needed heart transplantations, but there were not 500,000 heart donors. Michael E. DeBakey insisted that the ultimate solution was a completely artificial heart. Indeed, he and C. Walton Lillehei were already experimenting with artificial hearts. The National Institute of Health decided in 1963 that the eventual remedy for incurable heart disease would be a complete artificial heart. Since that achievement was years away, however, human-heart transplantations would be a valuable intermediate stage. Barnard predicted that the supply of heart donors would increase once the public was sufficiently educated on the subject. He was soon proven correct.

While world famous and friends with many political leaders of his times, such as French president Jacque Chirac and former Soviet general-secretary Mikhail Gorbachev, Barnard was a controversial figure within his profession. His mercurial temperament and outspokenness sometimes disaffected other physicians and medical personnel. As the American Heart Association concluded in its memorial to him, "Chris Barnard exhibited an unforgettable blend of vision, intelligence, action, kindness, charm, warmth, and humor, tempered by human frailties. Despite these frailties, he made the world a better place for his many patients, colleagues, and friends."

—*Bill Manikas*

FURTHER READING

Barnard, Christiaan. "A Human Cardiac Transplant: An Interim Report of a Successful Operation Performed at Groote Shuur Hospital." *South African Medical Journal* 41 (1967): 1271. Gives a description of the heart-transplantation procedure. Discusses the circumstances of the donor and recipient of the first successful heart transplantation. Lessons learned from the transplantation on Washkansky are discussed.

Barnard, Christiaan, and Curtis Bill Pepper. *Christiaan Barnard: One Life*. Toronto, Ont.: Collier-Macmillan Canada, 1969. Contains early accounts of Barnard's childhood years through his university studies. Con-

veys the drama of his first heart transplantation and ends with Washkansky's death.

Beck, W., Christiaan Barnard, and V. Schrvie. "Hemodynamic Studies in Two Long-term Survivors of Heart Transplants." *Journal of Thoracic and Cardiovascular Surgery* 62 (1971): 315-320. Provides a detailed comparative study of survivors of the procedure. Cardiovascular measurements are reported to demonstrate that the transplanted heart can function at a level necessary to sustain life and can withstand various stresses.

McRae, Donald. *Every Second Counts: The Race to Transplant the First Human Heart*. New York: G. P. Putnam's Sons, 2006. Recounts how Barnard and three American surgeons perfected techniques for human heart transplantation, each hoping to receive credit for performing the first operation. McRae presents a negative portrayal of Barnard, depicting him as a man with an inferiority complex, a troubled personal life, and an intense desire for publicity.

Miller, G. Wayne. *King of Hearts: The True Story of the Maverick Who Pioneered Open Heart Surgery*. New York: Times Books, 2000. Miller explains the cardiac surgery advances of C. Walton Lillehei, Barnard's mentor. The book supplies the context for Barnard's own advances, which are discussed.

SEE ALSO: Sir Frederick G. Banting; Sir William Maddock Bayliss; Harvey Williams Cushing; Willem Einthoven; August Krogh; William J. and Charles H. Mayo; Ernest Henry Starling; Helen Brooke Taussig.

RELATED ARTICLES in *Great Events from History: The Twentieth Century:*

1941-1970: 1967: Favaloro Develops the Artery Bypass Surgery; December 2, 1967: Barnard Performs the First Human Heart Transplant.

1971-2000: December 2, 1982: DeVries Implants the First Jarvik-7 Artificial Heart.

DJUNA BARNES
American novelist

A noted member of the American expatriate community in Paris, Djuna Barnes wrote a highly influential experimental novel and was a pioneer in developing lesbian literature.

BORN: June 12, 1892; Cornwall-on-Hudson, New York
DIED: June 18, 1982; New York, New York
ALSO KNOWN AS: Djuna Chappell Barnes (full name)
AREA OF ACHIEVEMENT: Literature

EARLY LIFE

Djuna Barnes (JEW-nah bahrnz) was born to an eccentric, bohemian family in the New York community of Cornwall-on-Hudson. Her mother, Elizabeth Chappell Barnes, was English and her father, Wald Barnes, American. Wald Barnes (a name he adopted in preference over his birth name, Henry Budington) pursued many cultural interests but does not seem to have been successful in any of them. He does, however, seem to have had an overwhelming and largely negative influence on his daughter. There is indirect but compelling evidence of incest. Djuna Barnes takes up the theme of father-daughter incest repeatedly in her work, although usually obliquely. Whatever the physical or psychological reality of what took place, Djuna was evidently presented by her father in 1910 to a man far older than she was—Percy Faulkner, the brother of the woman destined to become Wald Barnes's second wife. Djuna's relationship with Faulkner seems to have been both informal and brief.

Barnes had been educated at home. Some time after 1910 she moved to New York City, where she studied art at the Pratt Institute and the Art Students' League. Barnes showed promise as both writer and artist: By the time she was twenty-one, she was producing articles and illustrations for New York City newspapers. Within a few years, she was able to earn a good living writing for these papers and for such magazines as Harper's. Besides reporting on local events, she interviewed a number of personalities, many of them long since forgotten, and turned out stylized, satirical sketches reminiscent of English artist Aubrey Beardsley.

In 1915, Barnes moved to Greenwich Village, a bohemian section of New York City synonymous with the newest ideas and trends in society and the arts. Her first "book," a pamphlet entitled *The Book of Repulsive Women*, also appeared in 1915. It consisted of a handful of poems and drawings and announced another theme that was to dominate her work, lesbian sexuality.

Although she began to have many women lovers during this period, Barnes's sexual allegiance had not shifted entirely to women. About 1916, she was married to fellow writer Courtenay Lemon. This marriage may have been as informal as her first relationship with Faulkner; in any case, she and Lemon had separated by 1919. Sometime that year or the next she left for Europe and, except for brief trips home, remained there until 1940. During those twenty years she produced a number of works, including a novel that would come to be regarded as one of the most important American literary works of the century.

LIFE'S WORK

Once in Europe, Barnes was commissioned to write various celebrity profiles and subsequently lived in both Paris and Berlin. Among the figures she interviewed was Irish writer James Joyce, author of the novel *Ulysses* (1922), considered one of the most influential English-language works of the century. Barnes admired Joyce immensely, and declared after reading *Ulysses* that she would never write again. Nevertheless, she soon published her first substantial work, entitled simply *A Book* (1923). *A Book* consisted of stories, plays, poems, and drawings. The stories were the most important components of the work; many subsequently appeared—usually in reworked versions—in the collections *A Night Among the Horses* (1929) and *Spillwax* (1962). In style they are unexceptional, but in their subject matter—individuals cast adrift from ties of class or country—they are very much products of their time.

Barnes's next two works exhibited greater innovation: *A Ladies' Almanack* (1928, identified only as being "Written & Illustrated by a Lady of Fashion") and the novel *Ryder* (also 1928). *A Ladies' Almanack* is a short, mock-Elizabethan work that defies easy classification. Arranged in twelve sections, one for each month of the year, it is actually a gentle satire on the lesbian community of Paris. Those who were familiar with the community would be expected to recognize the real figures behind such characters as Evangeline Musset and Daisy Downpour.

Because of its sexual and scatological content, *A Ladies' Almanack* was privately printed in Dijon, France. *Ryder* was published openly in New York, but in a censored version that omitted several passages and drawings. *Ryder* is far longer and more stylistically complex than anything else Barnes had previously written. It draws on her painful and convoluted family history and clearly illustrates Barnes's interest in the intense literary experimentation that was going on around her.

The novel's central character, Wendell Ryder, has a wife and a mistress and children by each. The two families live an unconventional life together in one house, with the children being kept from school and Ryder finding himself chronically unable to choose between the two women who share his household. *Ryder* is an amalgam of styles and influences, ranging from the King James Version of the Bible to such English writers as Geoffrey Chaucer and Laurence Sterne. Despite its dark undercurrents, *Ryder* is light and airy in tone, if perhaps forbidding in its display of archaic language. Its risqué reputation made it a best seller for a short time, although in later years it has been read mainly as a precursor to Barnes's greater and more accessible novel, *Nightwood* (1936). *Ryder* was dedicated to "T. W." The initials belonged to Thelma Wood, Barnes's lover for a number of years and, next to her father, the most influential person in her life. Wood had been born in Missouri and was a gifted artist and sculptor. She and Barnes had met early in the 1920's and became a familiar, strikingly elegant couple in the expatriate community. They maintained an often-strained relationship for about a decade.

If in one sense *Ryder* is "about" Barnes's family, then *Nightwood* is "about" her relationship with Wood. *Nightwood* is set for the most part in Paris. Its eight sections revolve around the tangled lives of a group of expatriates, chief among them Robin Vote, a young American woman who seems to live beyond the categories—right, wrong, waking, sleeping, animal, human, and so on—that rule the others' existence. Another American, Nora Flood, has an intense affair with Robin, but loses her to Jenny Petherbridge. In her distress, Nora seeks out the bizarre Dr. Matthew O'Connor, an unlicensed physician whose long, drunken soliloquies on love and the night form the heart of the novel. O'Connor, who made his first appearance in *Ryder*, is Barnes's most brilliantly conceived character. Gay and a transvestite, he is able, like the mythological Greek character Tiresias, to experience both the male and female sides of existence.

Barnes's British editor, poet T. S. Eliot, thought very highly of *Nightwood* and wrote an introduction comparing its mood to that of Elizabethan tragedy. The novel was published in London in 1936 and in New York City in 1937. The reviews were mixed, but sophisticated readers and other writers were as enthusiastic as Eliot, and the book has remained in print ever since.

Barnes had worked on the manuscript of *Nightwood* on a visit to Morocco in 1933 and had finished it in England. She returned to France in 1939, only to flee to the United States in 1940 with the approach of war. She eventually took an apartment in her old haunt of Greenwich Village—an apartment she would keep for more than four decades, gaining the reputation of a recluse. She had complained of exhaustion after completing *Nightwood*, and it is hard to escape the conclusion that she had put a lifetime of painful experience into its composition.

Barnes did have in her a third major work: *The Antiphon* (1958), a play on which she labored for years. It treats a family strikingly similar to the one in *Ryder*, but from a tragic point of view. Its three acts take place on the same day in ruined Burley Hall, in which the aged Augusta and her daughter and three sons reenact the disintegration of their family. *The Antiphon* is a dense and stylistically forbidding work. Part of its difficulty stems

Djuna Barnes. (New Directions Publishing)

from the fact that Eliot insisted on extensive cuts before its publication. The result was tighter but more obscure. It received its world premiere in Stockholm, Sweden, in 1961 (where one of its translators was United Nations secretary-general Dag Hammarskjöld) but has rarely been performed since.

Barnes's last years were often difficult. She had no regular income and subsisted for the most part on gifts from a small band of friends and admirers, including Irish-born author and Nobel laureate Samuel Beckett. She rarely left her apartment and seems to have gone for months at a time without speaking to anyone.

Barnes continued to write but published very little. She resisted efforts to collect her early journalism, declaring it undeserving, and scorned those of her contemporaries who produced their memoirs. Almost everything she wished to be remembered for—*Spillway*, *Nightwood*, and *The Antiphon*—appeared in her *Selected Writings* in 1962, to respectful reviews. A small renewal of interest came with the publication of two late poems, "Quarry" and "The Walking Mort," in *The New Yorker* in 1969 and 1971 respectively. In their brief compass, these dense, dark poems are among her very best works. Barnes died a few days past her ninetieth birthday in 1982 after a short stay in a nursing home.

SIGNIFICANCE

Barnes's novel *Nightwood* has come to be regarded as one of the most important American novels of the twentieth century. Its highly poetic yet precise language, its rejection of realism, and its darkly comic vision rank it with such masterpieces as William Faulkner's *The Sound and the Fury* (1929) and Vladimir Nabokov's *Lolita* (1955). Although it has never achieved great popularity, it has had a continuing impact on Barnes's colleagues, influencing such American writers as Faulkner, Anaïs Nin, John Hawkes, and Thomas Pynchon, and such British novelists as Lawrence Durrell.

Barnes's body of work is also important as a pioneering, if highly ambivalent, depiction of lesbian sexuality in literature. As announced in *The Book of Repulsive Women* and *A Ladies' Almanack* and developed most fully in *Nightwood*, Barnes's treatment of lesbian sexuality is far from being a didactic endorsement of a particular way of life. *Nightwood* is not a celebration of lesbian love per se, but a monument to the anguish of all love. Barnes herself stood aside from all movements, holding out little hope for the improvement of man's or woman's lot. She scoffed at the idea of "women's liberation," and declared, in reference to a key relationship in her life,

that she was not a lesbian but had simply loved Thelma Wood.

—*Grove Koger*

FURTHER READING

Barnes, Djuna. *Interviews*. Edited by Alyce Barry. Washington, D.C.: Sun & Moon Press, 1985. A collection of forty-one interviews conducted between 1913 and 1931, accompanied by Barnes's original illustrations. Subjects range from Diamond Jim Brady to James Joyce. Taken in total, a useful memoir of the period in which Barnes developed as a writer.

Bombaci, Nancy. *Freaks in Late Modernist American Culture: Nathanael West, Djuna Barnes, Todd Browning, and Carson McCullers*. New York: Peter Lang, 2006. Bombaci analyzes the work of Barnes and others to examine what she calls "late modernist freakish aesthetics," or the use of distorted body images to reinvent modern progress narratives and challenge social assumptions.

Broe, Mary Lynn, ed. *Silence and Power: A Reevaluation of Djuna Barnes*. Carbondale: Southern Illinois University Press, 1991. An invaluable compilation of essays about Barnes's work, supplemented with photographs and drawings, many of the latter by Barnes herself. Some strictly biographical material appears in a series of "Reminiscences."

Field, Andrew. *Djuna: The Formidable Miss Barnes*. Austin: University of Texas Press, 1985. A revised and corrected version of the biography that first appeared in 1983. Criticized for its idiosyncratic arrangement and lack of notes, it is still a lively and admiring work. Photographs, extensive bibliography.

Martin, Ann. *Red Riding Hood and the Wolf in Bed: Modernism's Fairy Tales*. Toronto, Ont.: University of Toronto Press, 2006. Examines how Barnes, Virginia Woolf, and James Joyce used representations of fairy tales in their writing.

O'Neal, Hank. *"Life Is Painful, Nasty & Short... In My Case It Has Only Been Painful & Nasty": Djuna Barnes, 1978-1981: An Informal Memoir*. New York: Paragon House, 1990. Memoir by an admirer who handled many of Barnes's literary and financial affairs near the end of her life. A series of portraits from the 1950's by Barnes's friend, photographer Berenice Abbott, appears in an appendix.

Scott, James B. *Djuna Barnes*. Boston: Twayne, 1976. Thorough study of Barnes's work in an accessible format. Most biographical material appears in the opening chapter, "Early Life." Written before Andrew

Field revealed the more controversial aspects of Barnes's life. Chronology, bibliography.

SEE ALSO: Samuel Beckett; Colette; T. S. Eliot; James Joyce; Gertrude Stein.

RELATED ARTICLES in *Great Events from History: The Twentieth Century:*
1901-1940: Fall, 1905: Stein Holds Her First Paris Salons; 1925: Woolf's *Mrs. Dalloway* Explores Women's Consciousness.

KARL BARTH
Swiss theologian

Acclaimed by many as the dominant theologian of the twentieth century, Barth was a Swiss Reformed pastor, professor, and writer best known for his critique of nineteenth century Protestant liberal theology.

BORN: May 10, 1886; Basel, Switzerland
DIED: December 10, 1968; Basel, Switzerland
AREAS OF ACHIEVEMENT: Religion and theology, literature, scholarship, education

EARLY LIFE

Karl Barth (bahrt) was the eldest son of Johann Friedrich "Fritz" Barth and Anna Katharina Barth. Both of Barth's grandfathers were ministers within the Swiss Reformed Church. His father, also an ordained minister, was at the time of Karl's birth a teacher in the Evangelical School of Preachers in Basel. This conservative seminary had been founded about ten years earlier to counter the influence of Protestant liberal theology that was predominant in most of the larger European universities.

When Karl was three years old, his father accepted a position as a lecturer and subsequently as a professor of church history and the New Testament at the University of Bern. The academic environment of Bern, coupled with the conservative religious training within the Barth household, exerted considerable influence on Karl and his siblings. From his father, Karl acquired a love for history and politics, a seriousness about study, and an appreciation for the arts, especially music. On the eve of his confirmation, Karl "boldly resolved to become a theologian." Two of his younger brothers also followed their father into academic pursuits—Peter, as an editor of a critical edition of the works of John Calvin, and Heinrich, as a philosopher who many years later taught with his brother Karl on the faculty of the University of Basel.

Young Barth began his university studies at Bern. While receiving a solid grounding in Reformed theology, he also became intrigued with the theoretical and practical philosophy of Immanuel Kant and the liberal theology of Friedrich Schleiermacher. His enthusiasm for learning made Barth eager to continue his studies with Wilhelm Herrmann of Marburg, the leading neo-Kantian theologian of the day. In deference to his father's wish for him to remain within a more conservative academic environment, Barth postponed his matriculation at Marburg. Barth spent the following year at the University of Berlin, where he studied with the renowned church historian Adolf von Harnack; the next summer at school back in Bern; and a second year at the University of Tübingen under the tutelage of the conservative New Testament theologian Adolf Schlatter. Finally, in 1908 Barth was enrolled as a student of Herrmann at Marburg. From Herrmann, Barth learned to define faith in terms of "inner experience" that has its "ground" in the "inner life of Jesus" and is awakened in human consciousness by the influence of the Jesus of history. Three semesters later, Barth completed his formal course work, passed the theological examinations set by the church at Bern, and was ordained. Barth never pursued doctoral studies in theology.

LIFE'S WORK

On ordination in 1909, Barth returned to Marburg to become an assistant editor of *Die christliche Welt* (the Christian world), a liberal periodical that concentrated on the church's responsibility in the world. Later that year, Barth accepted a call as an apprentice pastor of a Reformed church in Geneva. At this time, Barth published an article in which he noted that theological graduates of liberal seminaries such as Marburg and Heidelberg were more reluctant to enter into practical pastoral work than were graduates of the more orthodox and pietistic institutions. Barth attributed this to the two central emphases of liberal theology: "religious individualism," which concentrated on the subjective and personal experience of the individual Christian, and "historical relativism," which postulated that there were no absolutes in history or religion. Although still a devotee of the

Karl Barth. (Library of Congress)

Protestant liberalism into which he was trained, Barth, even at this young age, was voicing a concern that contemporary Christian thought was in danger of becoming more anthropology than theology and was more a product of modern individualistic bourgeois idealism than of sound New Testament scholarship.

Between 1911 and 1921, Barth served as a pastor in Safenwil, Switzerland. It was during this pastorate that his theology underwent a gradual reorientation. The practical tasks of preparing sermons that integrated the content of the Bible with human concerns; the renewal of a friendship with Eduard Thurneysen, a neighboring pastor who seemed to have discovered the eschatologism of Christianity; and a growing appreciation for the existentialism of Søren Kierkegaard together contributed to Barth's intellectual metamorphosis. World events of the decade also influenced his theological persuasions. Following the outbreak of World War I, for example, Barth was dismayed when ninety-three scholars and artists—including his own teachers Harnack and Herrmann—signed a manifesto that supported the war policy of Kaiser Wilhelm. To Barth, this action called into question

his mentors' understanding of the Bible, history, and dogmatics. Furthermore, when workers in his local parish were involved in a struggle to achieve a just wage, Barth was compelled to turn his attention to social issues. Newly sensitized to the misery and exploitative conditions of his parishioners, Barth declared himself a Christian socialist and in 1915 joined the Social Democratic Party—an extraordinary action for a minister in that day. During this decade of disillusionment, Barth came to doubt the progressive notions of human grandeur and inevitable progress.

The work that catapulted Barth into the limelight of theological controversy was *Der Römerbrief* (*The Epistle to the Romans*, 1933), originally written in 1918, published in 1919, then radically revised and reissued in 1922. Barth's aim differed from that of other scholars of his day. While Barth did not reject the methods of biblical criticism (as conservative scholars did), he did denounce the value of commentaries that had no higher goal than to reconstruct the history of the biblical period. Barth's object, in contrast, was to let the Apostolic message of Paul's letter to the Romans break with full force on the present age. This message, according to Barth, was in violent contradiction to the optimistic spirit of nineteenth century liberalism, which presupposed an inner continuity between the divine and the "best" of human culture. The theme of Romans, Barth insisted, is "the infinite qualitative distinction" between time and eternity, or between human and God. Thus, against liberalism's willingness to allow God and humankind to coalesce, Barth injected the demand: "Let God be God!" Although this work was more critical than constructive, Barth's concept that religion itself is under divine judgment and is a human rather than strictly a divine phenomenon had a great impact on the future direction of Protestant thought.

On the basis of *The Epistle to the Romans*, Barth was invited to teach Reformed theology at the University of Göttingen. Leaving the pastorate for the teaching profession, Barth launched his academic career. In 1925, Barth left Göttingen to become a professor of dogmatics and New Testament exegesis at the University of Münster in Westphalia, a position he held until 1930. His publications during this period included *Die christliche Dogmatik im Entwurf* (1927; *Dogmatics in Outline*, 1949), a historically significant work because it revealed the early shape of Barth's systematic theological thinking. In this work, Barth rejected both anthropocentric and natural theology in favor of a theology grounded solely in the Word of God. For Barth, the proper subject of Christian theology is the Word of God, not the faith experience of the individual believer.

In 1930, Barth accepted a professorship at the University of Bonn. While at Bonn, Barth and his lifelong friend Thurneysen established a theological journal entitled *Theologische Existenz heute* (theological existence today). In this periodical, Barth and his associates expressed their vehement opposition to Adolf Hitler and the "German Christians" who advocated a synthesis of German National Socialism and the Gospel. Barth attracted the attention of the Nazi authorities in 1934 when he wrote the famous Barmen Confession, which called Christians to obedience to Jesus Christ alone "in life and death." Later, after he refused to begin his classes in Bonn with the customary "Heil Hitler!" and to take an unconditional oath of loyalty to the Führer, he was dismissed from his teaching post and expelled from Germany. Fleeing to his original home in Basel, Barth joined the faculty at the University of Basel in 1935 and remained there until his retirement in 1962. Barth continued lecturing and writing until his death in 1968.

An indefatigable worker and prolific writer, Barth produced more than five hundred books, articles, sermons, and papers during the course of his long and illustrious career. His magnum opus, *Die kirchliche Dogmatik* (*Church Dogmatics*, 1936-1969, 1975), the first volume of which appeared in 1932, grew to thirteen large books totaling more than nine thousand pages in German. Barth originally designed the mammoth project as a five-volume work, although the sheer length of his study necessitated subdividing each of the sections into part-volumes. It is impossible to reduce the breadth of his theology to a few meager structural principles. It is sufficient to say that Barth's emphasis remained singularly Christocentric. His system rested on the principle that theological understanding of any subject is fully dependent on the relationship of that subject with the Word as revealed solely in Jesus Christ.

SIGNIFICANCE

Barth's bold commentary on Paul's letter to the Romans was, in the words of a noted Roman Catholic divine, "a bombshell in the playground of the theologians." This critique of the "subjectivism" within Protestant theology was Barth's first of many statements that pointed to the dangers of allowing theology to become an ideology—that is, a creation of human culture. To Barth, liberal attempts to formulate a "reasonable Christianity" destroyed the validity of the concept of divine revelation (which, Barth insisted, was God-manifested and owed

nothing to human initiatives) and weakened the prophetic function of the church by allowing it simply to reflect rather than to critique human culture. Barth later said that in writing this book he was like the man in a dark church tower who accidentally tripped and caught hold of the bell rope to steady himself and, in doing so, alarmed the whole community. Indeed, this commentary—written to help the author clarify his own thinking—ignited a debate that significantly altered the course of twentieth century theology.

From this first book to the Theological Declaration of Barmen to his massive *Church Dogmatics*, Barth wrote with boldness and theological insight, perpetually calling the Christian Church back to the Bible and to its foundation in Jesus Christ. His impact has been great, in part because he provided an outline for a theology that was thoroughly biblical, without being fundamentalist. Described by Pope Pius XII as the greatest theologian since Thomas Aquinas, Barth has been acclaimed by Catholics and Protestants alike as a modern church father who stands prominently with Saint Athanasius, Saint Augustine, and John Calvin as a defender of the transcendence and sovereignty of God.

—*Terry D. Bilhartz*

FURTHER READING

Balthasar, Hans Urs von. *The Theology of Karl Barth*. Translated by John Drury. New York: Holt, Rinehart and Winston, 1971. An excellent single-volume interpretation and critique of Barth's method and theology by a Roman Catholic scholar.

Barth, Karl. *Church Dogmatics: A Selection*. Introduction by Helmut Gollwitzer. Edited and translated by G. W. Bromiley. New York: Harper & Row, 1962. Selections from the thirteen part-volumes of Barth's *Church Dogmatics*. A useful introduction to the writings of Barth.

Busch, Eberhard. *The Great Passion: An Introduction to Karl Barth's Theology*. Translated by Geoffrey W. Bromiley. Edited and annotated by Darrell L. Guder and Judith J. Guder. Grand Rapids, Mich.: William B. Eerdmans, 2004. Busch, Barth's biographer, friend, and assistant, explains Barth's theology.

_____. *Karl Barth: His Life from Letters and Autobiographical Texts*. Translated by John Bowden. Philadelphia: Fortress Press, 1976. Likely the best and most authoritative biography of Barth. Highly recommended.

Franke, John R. *Barth for Armchair Theologians*. Louisville, Ky.: Westminster John Knox Press, 2006. An introduction to Barth's life and ideas, tracing the evolution of his theology and its relevance to the twenty-first century.

Hunsinger, George, ed. *Karl Barth and Radical Politics.* Philadelphia: Westminster Press, 1976. A collection of essays that assess Barth's relationship with radical politics. Of particular interest is Friedrich-Wilhelm Marquardt's article "Socialism in the Theology of Karl Barth," which argues that the *initium* of Barth's theology was his encounter with social struggle and socialist praxis while he was a pastor in Safenwil.

Jüngel, Eberhard. *Karl Barth: A Theological Legacy.* Translated by Garrett E. Paul. Philadelphia: Westminster Press, 1986. A lucid and readable English translation of essays by Jüngel, a scholar who served as an assistant for one of the volumes of *Church Dogmatics.* This is a sympathetic yet scholarly introduction to the major themes in Barth's theology: the otherness of God, the humanity of God, Gospel, and law. Includes endnotes and a selected bibliography of the works of Barth.

Mueller, David L. *Karl Barth.* Waco, Tex.: Word Books, 1975. In Word Books' Makers of the Modern Theological Mind series. A useful introduction to the life and thought of Barth, written by a professor of theology.

Torrance, Thomas F. *Karl Barth: An Introduction to His Early Theology, 1910-1931.* London: SCM Press, 1962. An excellent discussion of Barth's controversial *The Epistle to the Romans* by one of the leading Barthian scholars. Includes a useful bibliography of Barth's works.

SEE ALSO: Dietrich Bonhoeffer; Emil Brunner; Rudolf Bultmann; Adolf von Harnack; Martin Heidegger; John XXIII; Jacques Maritain; Martin Niemöller; Pius X; Pius XI; Pius XII.

RELATED ARTICLES in *Great Events from History: The Twentieth Century:*

1941-1970: 1941: Bultmann Offers a Controversial Interpretation of the Christian Scriptures; March, 1941-January, 1943: Niebuhr Extols a Theory of Christian Realism.

ROLAND BARTHES
French literary critic

Barthes was one of the most important literary and cultural critics of the twentieth century. He made significant contributions to semiology and exemplified the ideal interdisciplinary scholar and writer, embracing and employing a wide range of studies and perspectives in his critical work.

BORN: November 12, 1915; Cherbourg, France
DIED: March 26, 1980; Paris, France
ALSO KNOWN AS: Roland Gérard Barthes (full name)
AREAS OF ACHIEVEMENT: Literature, language and linguistics, philosophy, scholarship

EARLY LIFE

Roland Barthes (roh-lahn bahrt) was born into the heart of the French bourgeoisie of Cherbourg. His father died in a World War I battle in 1916, leaving the family in reduced circumstances, although his mother learned the trade of bookbinding and kept the household together for the family. Roland's early brilliance at the *lycée* pointed to a career in the high academic circles reserved for graduates of the École Normale Supérieure; however, he contracted tuberculosis in 1941 and was forced to attend an-

other institution, the Sorbonne. In 1937, he was declared unfit for military service because of his illness, and he taught from 1939 to 1941 in *lycées* in Biarritz and Paris. He was, however, forced to abandon teaching when the tuberculosis flared up again, and he spent the war years in a Swiss sanatorium. After the war, he taught in Romania and Egypt before returning to France. During this period, he became further acquainted with literary criticism and linguistics and produced his first important book, *Le Degré zéro de l'écriture* (1953; *Writing Degree Zero,* 1967).

LIFE'S WORK

The distinguishing mark of Barthes's career was his refusal to be confined to one field of study, one critical position, or one group. He continually sought new areas to investigate after having made significant contributions to areas such as linguistics or semiology. Some have accused him of not developing or testing insights or breakthroughs he made; he has left it to others to complete systems in which he made seminal contributions. This refusal to be restricted to one position in a period of ideological rigidity is very attractive. A new work from

Barthes was always a new starting point for fresh investigations and never a mere recovering of old ground.

Through the 1940's and 1950's, Barthes worked in a branch of the French cultural service dealing with teaching abroad, and he was given a scholarship to study lexicology in 1950; however, he used that time to write his first books in the field of literary criticism. *Writing Degree Zero* is a Marxist rewriting of French literary history that was influenced by Jean-Paul Sartre and is, in part, an answer to Sartre's *Qu'est-ce que la littérature?* (1947; *What Is Literature?*, 1949). Barthes was associated until the late 1970's with the journal *Tel Quel*, which stood for a more formal approach to literary works.

In his first book, Barthes identifies two distinct periods of French literature. The first (or classical) runs from 1650, when the writers of that time began to see the "literariness" of language, to 1848, the year of revolution in all of Europe. The second (or modern) period began in the revolution and continues to the present; it is marked not by the representational mode of the early period but by a questioning and experimental type of literature. Later, in *S/Z* (1970; English translation, 1974), Barthes defined two types of literary writing: the readerly (or the representational) and the writerly (the experimental). In this respect, he was the champion of avant-garde literature. He was a supporter of the experiments of Alain Robbe-Grillet in the novel and defended him against received critical opinion. In *S/Z*, Barthes created a critical context in which these new writers could be discussed and understood.

Michelet par lui-meme (1954; *Michelet*, 1986) and *Sur Racine* (1963; *On Racine*, 1964) show Barthes moving away from the Marxism of Sartre to seeing a literary work as a system with codes or rules for functioning. In the book on Michelet, Barthes used many of the concepts of phenomenology in which the writer's ideology is ignored, and instead Barthes discovered in Michelet the use of opposing substances, such as warm and dry. These substances show the "existential thematics" of Michelet; Michelet's thought is dismissed as of no interest. *On Racine* is more consciously structuralist and psychoanalytic, as Barthes examines the conflict between authority and the "primal horde." Barthes ignored the usual academic and historical view of the work to reveal its structure as composed of interior and exterior "spaces." His irreverent treatment of the most sacred of French classics engendered a challenge from the academic world. Raymond Picard accused Barthes and his criticism of being a fraud, and Barthes replied with a defense of the new criticism that won the day. Barthes has consistently opposed

Roland Barthes. (Sygma)

a merely academic view of literature. Ironically, as a result of the notoriety of the Racine book and his innovative work, Barthes was appointed to teach at an academic institution, although it was not one of the first rank. He became a full-time teacher at the École Pratique des Hautes Études in 1962.

Mythologies (1957; English translation, 1972) shows another side of Barthes; he is in this book a semiologist examining the signs and signifiers found in popular culture as well as in literature. For example, Barthes examines wrestling as a system in which spectacle outweighs sport. In a similar fashion, striptease is seen as a sport that is "nationalized" and expresses the essence of the French. The aim of the book is demystification, to show that assumptions about a practice or institution as being natural are false; they are instead strictly structured codes of culture. The book also tends to treat serious subjects in a playful way and trivial ones with great seriousness in an amusing and enlightening manner.

Mythologies was very popular, but once more Barthes

refused to repeat or develop a successful mode. Next Barthes was to be a structuralist, and it is in this capacity that his greatest works were written. In *Essais critiques* (1964; *Critical Essays*, 1972), he defined structuralism as an "activity," not as a system. Its primary tools were the binary oppositions of Ferdinand de Saussure's linguistics, especially the opposition of the diachronic and synchronic and of *langue* (the language as a whole) and *parole* (the individual utterance). Perhaps the most thoroughgoing structuralist work Barthes produced is *S/Z*, in which he analyzed a story by Honoré de Balzac, "Sarrasine," in exhaustive detail. Barthes divides the analysis into codes: There is the proairetic code, which deals with plot; the hermeneutic code, which deals with suspense and enigmas; the semic code, which deals with character and other stereotypes; the symbolic code, which takes readers from literal details to the level of symbolism; and the referential code, which deals with social and cultural aspects of the work. It is a monumental dissection of one short story, and the commentary tends to swamp the text. It does show how various types of critical apparatus can be applied to a specific literary work, but they remain fragments, as Barthes refused to combine the codes into a unified system. Some critics have seen in this refusal the seeds of poststructuralism or deconstruction. The book takes structuralism as far as it can go in revealing the "system" of a work, but it remains tantalizingly incomplete.

Barthes turned from structuralism to what is the key element of his later work, feeling. *Le Plaisir du texte* (1973; *The Pleasure of the Text*, 1975) is a discussion and description of the many ways in which readers derive pleasure from a literary work. One of the most important ways that readers gain pleasure is not, for Barthes, from aesthetic contemplation of the whole but by ignoring the "whole" and "drifting" to passages that catch their interest and attention. For Barthes, the pleasure of the text is equated with the body, and the pleasure derived from the text is compared to sexual bliss. It is a more personal way of looking at literature than the systems Barthes discovered earlier using linguistics as a tool.

Barthes had become an eminent figure in French intellectual life by this time, and he was appointed to a chair at the prestigious Collège de France in 1976. Barthes refused to be a traditional academic as he continued to emphasize pleasure and feeling in his critical work. In *Fragments d'un discours amoureux* (1977; *A Lover's Discourse: Fragments*, 1978), he attempts to codify the language of love by using such texts as Johann Wolfgang von Goethe's *Die Leiden des jungen Werthers*

(1774; *The Sorrows of Werther*, 1779; better known as *The Sorrows of Young Werther*, 1902), and he traces the typical gestures and maneuvers of love. Each aspect of the language of love is illustrated and discussed. In "Making Scenes," for example, Barthes traces the etymology of words used in such scenes and finds that they take the rhetorical form of stichomythia. Love may have had a very defined code for Barthes, but his analysis was not merely intellectual, and it did not become more important than the object it described. *A Lover's Discourse* became Barthes's most popular book, testifying to the accuracy of his analysis and observations.

One of the last works by Barthes was *Roland Barthes par Roland Barthes* (1975; *Roland Barthes by Roland Barthes*, 1977), an autobiography done in fragments and memories. There are lists of such things as "I Like" and "I Don't Like." There are a few revealing sections in the book; Barthes includes a fragment on the "Goddess H" that speaks of the pleasures of homosexuality and hashish. There are also photographs of the young Barthes and his bourgeois environment at the beginning, but the rest of the book is arranged in alphabetical order for each topic he discusses. There is no narrative in this "autobiography," but a picture of the essential Barthes does emerge. One aspect of Barthes that is revealed in the book is his opposition to "doxa," or received opinion. He was always opposed to the rigidity of received authority.

Barthes's fertile mind continued to produce new and challenging works, such as his study of Japan, *L'Empire des signes* (1970; *Empire of Signs*, 1982), and a book on photography, *La Chambre claire: Note sur la photographie* (1980; *Camera Lucida: Reflections on Photography*, 1981). His reputation as an intellectual was not limited to France but was international. In early 1980, Barthes was tragically killed after a laundry truck struck him as he attempted to cross a Paris street near the Collège de France.

SIGNIFICANCE

Barthes was one of those rare individuals who made significant contributions to many fields. He was one of the first to see the applicability of semiology to a wide range of topics. He was not the first to discover how the structures of linguistics could be applied to all of the human sciences, but he was one of its most elegant practitioners. *S/Z* is one of the finest and fullest structuralist analyses extant. Furthermore, Barthes pointed the way for poststructuralism and showed how literary criticism could reveal not unity but fragmentation. He also never lost sight of the importance of emotion in literature and life and of the dangers of completing and fixing any system of thought. He freed criticism from a narrow academic view and led it to the multiplicity of voices it currently enjoys.

—*James Sullivan*

FURTHER READING

Allen, Graham. *Roland Barthes*. New York: Routledge, 2003. An introduction to Barthes's writings on numerous subjects, including existentialism, Marxism, semiotics, structuralism, and poststructuralism. Includes a guide to readily available translations of his work.

Barthes, Roland. *Roland Barthes by Roland Barthes*. Translated by Richard Howard. New York: Hill & Wang, 1977. A meditation by Barthes on some of the significant events and influences on his life. It is not the usual autobiography, but it is an excellent introduction to the delights and style of Barthes.

Brottman, Mikita. "Rumor, Gossip, and Scandal: Barthes and Tabloid Rhetoric." In *High Theory/Low Culture*. New York: Palgrave Macmillan, 2005. Brottman's analysis of popular culture includes this chapter on Barthes's theories.

Culler, Jonathan. *Roland Barthes*. New York: Oxford University Press, 1983. The best short study of Barthes's works. Culler divides the protean Barthes into such areas as "Mythologist" and "Hedonist," which enables readers to see the range of Barthes's mind. Contains clear, direct, and insightful discussions.

Gane, Mike, and Nicholas Gane, eds. *Roland Barthes*. 3 vols. Thousand Oaks, Calif.: Sage, 2004. An exhaustive overview of Barthes's theories, including critical assessments of his work in structuralism, poststructuralism, and semiotics.

Lavers, Annette. *Roland Barthes: Structuralism and After*. Cambridge, Mass.: Harvard University Press, 1982. A detailed, scholarly study of Barthes's literary criticism. Lavers discusses not only Barthes's thought but also critics who influenced and were influenced by him.

Sontag, Susan. "Writing Itself: On Roland Barthes." In *A Barthes Reader*. New York: Hill & Wang, 1982. Sontag provides a sympathetic and revealing introduction to Barthes's thought and an excellent selection of Barthes's writing. Students who wish to read Barthes should begin here.

Thody, Philip. *Roland Barthes: A Conservative Estimate*. Atlantic Highlands, N.J.: Humanities Press, 1977. A detailed analysis of the major works and positions of Barthes. It is not as scholarly or difficult as Lavers's book, but it is a good overall discussion.

Wasserman, George. *Roland Barthes*. Boston: Twayne, 1981. Part of Twayne's World Authors series. Begins with a brief biographical section followed by a critical overview of Barthes's works. Includes a bibliography, a chronology, and an index.

SEE ALSO: Walter Benjamin; Noam Chomsky; Jacques Derrida; Émile Durkheim; Roman Jakobson; Jacques Lacan; Claude Lévi-Strauss; Jean-Paul Sartre; Ferdinand de Saussure; Susan Sontag.

RELATED ARTICLES in *Great Events from History: The Twentieth Century:*

1941-1970: 1961: Foucault's *Madness and Civilization* Is Published; 1964-1972: Marcuse Publishes Foundational New Left Works; 1967: Derrida Enunciates the Principles of Deconstruction.

BÉLA BARTÓK
Hungarian composer and pianist

Bartók was one of the great champions of Hungarian music. He dispelled the misconceptions about Hungarian folk music that prior to his own work had been commonly associated with Roma, or Gypsy, music alone.

BORN: March 25, 1881; Nagyszentmiklós, Austro-
   Hungarian Empire (now Sînnicolau Mare, Romania)
DIED: September 26, 1945; New York, New York
AREAS OF ACHIEVEMENT: Music, scholarship

EARLY LIFE

Béla Bartók (BAY-lah BAHR-tohk) was born in Nagyszentmiklós (now Sînnicolau Mare) in the Austro-Hungarian Empire, in an area that is now part of Romania. Béla was the elder of two children born to Béla Bartók and Paula Yoit. He was named for his father, who was director of a government agricultural school in Nagyszentmiklós. The son suffered various illnesses throughout his growth years. He was later to suffer periodic bouts with bronchial infection and pneumonia that occasionally interfered with his musical career. Young Bartók's natural talent and interest for music were encouraged from the earliest age. His father, active in the musical life of the community, was an amateur musician who played the piano and the cello. His mother was a teacher and a talented amateur pianist. His mother gave him his first piano lesson when he was five years old.

Bartók's father died in 1888 when the boy was only seven years old, leaving Paula Bartók to support their two children through her teaching. The family moved several times during the next few years as Paula tried to provide the best educational and musical opportunities for her son. The family first moved to Nagyszőllős, which later became part of the Soviet Union, in 1889. It was there that Bartók composed his first pieces, several short compositions for the piano. In 1892, he gave his first public performance for a charity benefit. In 1894, the family finally settled in Pozsony, which is now Bratislava, Slovakia.

There, Bartók pursued his education at the gymnasium and began his study of the piano with various pianists. In Pozsony, Bartók was able to attend concerts and operas and participate in public performances himself. Bartók's years at Pozsony were productive ones that saw him complete a number of works for piano and also works in the category of chamber music. During this time, Bartók fell under the influence of Ernó Dohnányi, a composer/pianist, several years his senior, who had preceded him at the gymnasium and who had gone on to study at the Royal Academy of Music at Budapest.

Shortly before completing his studies at the gymnasium in Pozsony, Bartók, with his mother, traveled in December of 1898 to Vienna, where he auditioned for admission to the Vienna Conservatory. Full admission and scholarship notwithstanding, Bartók elected to follow in the footsteps of his friend and role model, Dohnányi, and attend the Royal Academy of Music at Budapest. There, he studied piano with István Thomán, a former pupil of Franz Liszt, and composition with Janos Koessler. Bartók, who passed through the program with relative ease and was graduated in 1903, was viewed by the faculty as a virtuoso pianist more than as a talented and promising young composer.

Bartók became interested in the music of Liszt and Richard Wagner while he was a student at the academy, eventually turning to the music of Richard Strauss for inspiration. His interest in Strauss was the result of having heard Strauss's tone poem *Thus Spake Zarathustra* (1896) performed in Budapest in 1902. He subsequently arranged a piano transcription of Strauss's *Ein Heldenleben* (1898), which he performed for the academy faculty, and went on to compose a symphonic poem, the *Kossuth Symphony* (1903). The symphony, which is divided into ten sections, was a patriotic composition that caused quite a controversy over the composer's deliberate distortion of the Austrian national anthem found in the work. The work was first performed in Budapest in 1904.

LIFE'S WORK

Central to the development of Bartók's mature style was his study of the Hungarian folk song. He first became interested after having heard a peasant song sung by a young woman in 1904. His early study soon revealed to him a significant difference between the Hungarian folk music and the Roma (Gypsy) music often mistaken as such by well-intentioned composers like Liszt and Johannes Brahms. The collection and study of Hungarian folk songs reflected, in part, Bartók's strong sense of patriotism, even as the *Kossuth Symphony* earlier had celebrated the Hungarian uprising against Austrian oppression in 1848. His research quickly led him into contact with Zoltán Kodály in 1905, a fellow Hungarian composer who was also doing research on Hungarian folk music. In 1906, the two traveled separately to remote regions of Hungary, taking down and recording folk songs, the final result being a collaboration and publication of twenty folk songs with piano accompaniment that was entitled *Hungarian Folksongs* (1907). For the next several years, Bartók continued his research of Hungarian folk songs, expanding the scope of his research to include folk songs of neighboring regions in Central Europe, including Romania and Czechoslovakia, among others. He ultimately collected thousands of songs from that general region.

His study and analysis of Hungarian folk songs led to the development of a highly personal style as he attempted to merge elements of folk music and art music together. Characteristic of his style are melodies based on modes or unusual scale structures and irregular rhythm patterns and measure groupings such as are often found in folk music. While his style is often diverse and complex, frequently utilizing much dissonance, some element of folk music is usually to be found in his works.

In 1907, Bartók's former professor, Thomán, retired, and Bartók was appointed to the faculty. The appointment provided Bartók with the financial stability necessary to pursue a career of research, performance, and composition. One of the first works to reveal Bartók's individual style was the opera *Duke Bluebeard's Castle*, which was composed in 1911 for a competition but which was not performed until 1918. The work is generally seen as the first of a trilogy, the other two works being the ballet *The Wooden Prince* (1917) and the pantomime *The Miraculous Mandarin* (1926). The first performance of *The Wooden Prince* marked Bartók's first public success, with the first performance of *Duke Bluebeard's Castle* the following year firmly establishing him as an international figure.

Included among the major works that Bartók composed are his six string quartets, which place him as the major composer in this genre in the twentieth century. He wrote extensively for the piano, frequently treating it more as a percussive instrument than a melodic one. This technique, developed by Bartók, marked a dramatic break with the way the piano had been used. The scope of his piano pieces varies from large extended works, such as the three piano concertos, to miniatures, such as the *Bagatelles* (1908). His most important work for piano is *Mikrokosmos*, which consists of 153 piano pieces in six volumes that were composed between the years 1926 and 1939. The level of difficulty ranges from the simplest pieces for beginners to works for the accomplished virtuoso.

Bartók was quite active as a concert artist and composer during the 1920's and 1930's, also continuing his work with folk-song research. In 1934, he left the teaching studio when the Hungarian Academy of Sciences commissioned him to prepare his collection of Hungarian folk songs for publication. In 1936, he composed *Music for Strings, Percussion, and Celesta*, regarded by many as his finest work. As the decade wore on Bartók became increasingly concerned as Hungary moved closer to Nazi Germany, and, when his mother died in December of 1939, he immediately began to make plans to leave the country.

He went to the United States in 1940 and settled in New York City. He was awarded an honorary doctorate in November of 1940 by Columbia University, from which he later received an appointment to continue his research in folk music. The appointment was short-lived, however, and in 1942 he found himself without a steady source of income and in poor health. His health had been steadily deteriorating for several months, and a medical examination in 1943 incorrectly diagnosed him with

Béla Bartók. (Library of Congress)

polycythemia, a condition characterized by an excess of red blood cells. Later, he was diagnosed as having leukemia.

As Bartók's health worsened and his financial problems increased because of the illness, the American Society of Composers, Authors, and Publishers came to his assistance and provided funds for his medical care. Two of his finest works date from this period when he was fighting the disease. The *Concerto for Orchestra* was commissioned in 1943 by Serge Koussevitzky, conductor of the Boston Symphony Orchestra. Koussevitzky conducted its premiere performance in 1944 with Bartók present. The other work, Piano Concerto no. 3, was completed shortly before his death in 1945, after Bartók had realized that his disease was terminal. Bartók died on September 26, 1945, in West Side Hospital in New York City. He was survived by his second wife, Ditta Pásztory Bartók, a former student who concertized in duo piano works with her husband; their only child, Peter Bartók; and a son, Béla Bartók, by his first wife, Marta Ziegler.

SIGNIFICANCE

Bartók's importance to the twentieth century is fourfold. He was a great virtuoso pianist who concertized throughout Europe and the United States. His former teacher, Thomán, compared him to Liszt, perhaps the greatest pianist of the nineteenth century. Early in Bartók's career, his great talent and skill as a performer placed him in the teaching studio at the Royal Academy. There he was a great influence to many aspiring young pianists, among them Fritz Reiner, who later became a world-famous conductor. Bartók became an ethnomusicologist through his study of the folk song. He collected folk songs over the years, studied and analyzed them, published them in collections, and wrote and published articles about his research in folk music. His research in this area redefined Hungarian folk music and preserved a great body of it that probably would have been lost except for his efforts in this field. Finally, through the study of folk music, Bartók developed a highly personal and original compositional style that reflected a fusion of folk music characteristics with certain characteristics of Western art music. His music has continued to increase in popularity since his death.

—Michael Hernon

FURTHER READING

Bartók, Béla. "Autobiography." In *Béla Bartók Essays*, edited by Benjamin Suchoff. New York: St. Martin's Press, 1976. This brief essay is by Bartók on Bartók. It provides readers with an invaluable opportunity to see what the composer has to say about his life and works.

Bayley, Amanda, ed. *The Cambridge Companion to Bartók*. New York: Columbia University Press, 2001. Collection of essays examining Bartók's life and music within the context of early twentieth century Hungarian history and nationalism, as well as analyzing Bartók's interest in folk music and his musical compositions.

Griffiths, Paul. *Bartók*. London: J. M. Dent & Sons, 1984. An excellent biography. There is some technical discussion of selected works, but the book is accessible to the general reader. Appendixes contain a calendar of events in Bartók's life, linking them with contemporary events and musicians. Includes a listing of his works by genre that offers such information as dates of composition, dates of revisions, a who, when, and where of first performances, and publishers. Contains a short selected bibliography.

Lampert, Vera, and László Somfai. "Béla Bartók." In *New Grove Dictionary of Music and Musicians*, edited by Stanley Sadie. 6th ed., vol. 2. New York: Macmillan, 1980. This is the best article in English about Bartók, his works, and his musical style. A listing of his works and an excellent bibliography are provided.

Lesznai, Lajos. *Bartók*. Translated by Percy M. Young. London: J. M. Dent & Sons, 1973. The author has attempted to establish a factually accurate biography through inquiry of people who knew Bartók personally. There is little technical treatment of selected works, making it accessible to the general public. Includes some photographs and a short selected bibliography.

Milne, Hamish. *Bartók: His Life and Times*. New York: Hippocrene Books, 1982. This biography, though short, provides interesting insights into Bartók's private and professional life and attempts to put his life into perspective with the times in which he lived. Highly recommended to the general reader.

Schneider, David E. *Bartók, Hungary, and the Renewal of Tradition: Case Studies in the Intersection of Modernity and Nationality*. Berkeley: University of California Press, 2006. Describes how Bartók was influenced by Hungarian art music as well as folk music, and how he incorporated these influences into his compositions.

Stevens, Halsey. *The Life and Music of Béla Bartók*. Rev. ed. New York: Oxford University Press, 1964. Although dated, this biography remains one of the best.

The book is divided into two major sections. The first section divides Bartók's life into three periods. The second section discusses Bartók's music by genre. The appendix contains a chronological list of works that includes the date of first performance when possible. Contains a good but dated bibliography. Recommended to the general reader.

SEE ALSO: Manuel de Falla; Vladimir Horowitz; Leoš Janáček; Herbert von Karajan; Jean Sibelius; Richard Strauss; Ralph Vaughan Williams.
RELATED ARTICLE in *Great Events from History: The Twentieth Century:*
1901-1940: 1904-1905: Bartók and Kodály Collect Hungarian Folk Songs.

MIKHAIL BARYSHNIKOV
Latvian-born American dancer and choreographer

The range and drive of dancer and choreographer Baryshnikov led him to develop new forms of expression in all kinds of dance. His art has been documented in film and television, leaving a lasting legacy to dance and the arts.

BORN: January 28, 1948; Riga, Latvia, Soviet Union (now in Latvia)
ALSO KNOWN AS: Mikhail Nikolaevitch Baryshnikov (full name)
AREAS OF ACHIEVEMENT: Dance, film, television

EARLY LIFE

Mikhail Baryshnikov (mee-KIL bah-RIHSH-nih-kohf), born in Riga, Latvia, was encouraged by his mother to explore athletics, but because his small stature precluded aggressive team sports, she encouraged him to pursue art. He studied the art of dance, beginning his ballet studies at age twelve. Theater became an escape after he lost his mother.

At age fifteen, Baryshnikov joined a Riga dance troupe, which gave him the opportunity to travel. During a tour of Leningrad he was invited to join the Vaganova Ballet Academy, the finest ballet school in the city. Baryshnikov demonstrated early that he had unique abilities, and was taken under the wing of Alexander Pushkin, the Vaganova's best-known teacher. Like his predecessor, ballet legend Rudolf Nureyev, Baryshnikov became Pushkin's prodigy. Pushkin became a surrogate father to the teenager, instilling in him a love of theater and literature.

In the stratified world of Soviet ballet there were two types of male dancers: the *danseur noble*, or romantic lead, and the *demi charactère*, or character dancer. Pushkin identified and encouraged Baryshnikov's versatility, range, and his eagerness to play all roles. In 1966 the Vaganova staged a student production of *Le Corsair* at the Kirov Ballet's Maryinsky Theatre. Baryshnikov's

performance, his gravity defying leaps, and his grand jeté, made him the talk of the ballet world.

LIFE'S WORK

After three years of study at the Vaganova school, Baryshnikov was invited to join the Kirov Ballet at the unprecedented level of solo artist. In 1967 he debuted in the *Peasant pas de deux* (a dance suite) in *Giselle* and partnered with prima ballerina Natalia Makarova in the Soviet-approved classics *The Nutcracker*, *Swan Lake*, and *Giselle*. The best choreographers of the day collaborated with the rising star of the Kirov. These choreographers included Leonid Yakobson, who choreographed *Vestris* for Baryshnikov.

Baryshnikov's virtuosity in the lead role for *Vestris* won him the gold medal in the Moscow International Ballet Competition in 1969. Acclaim afforded the Kirov dancers opportunities, and Baryshnikov, Makarova, and other members of the company toured London in 1970. For the first time, Baryshnikov was exposed to Western culture. He met secretly with Nureyev, who had defected in 1961. During the London tour Makarova defected to the West as well.

Baryshnikov returned to Leningrad and the Kirov. In 1970, Pushkin died of a heart attack. The ballet company suffered from bureaucratic pressures, and Baryshnikov grew frustrated with the company's artistic limitations. In 1974, Baryshnikov and members of the Kirov toured in Toronto, Canada. On June 29, after a matinee performance, Baryshnikov walked across a busy street to a waiting car and to freedom.

About one month later, Baryshnikov made his debut with the American Ballet Theatre (ABT), with Makarova, in *Giselle*. During the next four years with the ABT he added twenty-six roles to his repertoire, establishing a new standard for male dancers. His dance style changed as he pursued a more expressive and psychological ap-

Mikhail Baryshnikov. (AP/Wide World Photos)

proach to roles. Baryshnikov pushed the company to adapt new works and ballets they had never performed. He collaborated with modern dance choreographer Twyla Tharp, dancing to music by Frank Sinatra and the Beach Boys.

In 1977 he acted in the film *The Turning Point*, in a part written for him by the film's director, Herbert Ross. Ross's wife, Nora Kaye, was a former ballerina in the ABT and knew the dance world intimately. Baryshnikov was nominated for an Academy Award for Best Supporting Actor for his role as a seductive and brilliant dancer.

The ABT gave Baryshnikov the opportunity to stage and choreograph his own versions of classics. He reenvisioned *The Nutcracker* with Russian themes and a more complex role for the Nutcracker prince. He won praise for his performance in *Don Quixote* but mixed reviews for his unorthodox staging. In 1978, Baryshnikov left the ABT to join the New York City Ballet under George Balanchine. Balanchine's origins were in Russian ballet, but his dance style and choreography were completely different from those of Baryshnikov. In eigh-

teen months, Baryshnikov performed twenty-two new roles, working with both Balanchine and, as Balanchine weakened from a terminal illness, with Jerome Robbins. Baryshnikov left the New York City Ballet in 1979.

In 1980, Baryshnikov filmed a television special *Baryshnikov on Broadway*, for which he won an Emmy Award. The ABT offered Baryshnikov the position of artistic director and principal dancer. He accepted with the understanding that he could bring in new choreographers, premiere new productions, and do away with the old ABT star system.

Baryshnikov sought out other forms of expression during the 1980's. He filmed a second television special, *Baryshnikov in Hollywood*, as a tribute to Hollywood films. He starred in *White Nights* with actor-tap dancer Gregory Hines for director Taylor Hackford. In 1986 he worked with Ross on their second film, *Dancers*. He brought ballet performances of Balanchine's *Apollo* and *Who Cares?* and the fantasy ballet *Murder* to the American television audience through Public Broadcasting Service (PBS) productions of *Great Performances* and *Dance in America*.

At the ABT, Baryshnikov's personal projects were met with mixed success. His *Cinderella* received lukewarm reviews, while a staging of Kenneth McMillan's *Romeo and Juliet* was a financial and critical success. In 1988 he staged a production of *Swan Lake*, a project he had dreamed about doing since coming to the ABT. A few critics appreciated his dark, psychological approach, but many did not. In 1989, Baryshnikov announced his resignation from ABT. During the same period the dancer rehearsed the lead role in a Broadway production of Franz Kafka's *Metamorphosis* by avant-garde theater director Steven Berkoff.

In the 1990's, Baryshnikov partnered with friend and dancer Mark Morris in the White Oak Dance Project to showcase innovative contemporary dance in lean and mobile productions which could tour easily. He created a licensing and marketing company for clothing and perfume. Also, he spent more time with his longtime companion, former ballerina Lisa Rinehart, and their three children. In 1997 at the age of forty-nine, Baryshnikov visited Riga for the first time since his defection and danced at the Riga Opera House, dedicating his performance to the memory of his mother. In the same year he toured with the White Oak Dance Project, making new demands of his art and introducing new choreography to dance lovers. In 2000, he was awarded the American National Medal of Art at the Kennedy Center in Washington, D.C.

SIGNIFICANCE

Baryshnikov is considered one of the finest ballet dancers in history and achieved recognition as an international cultural icon. While his early success came from his many talents, it was his charisma and masculinity—not always associated with male dancers—that most likely contributed to his celebrity status and won him legions of fans.

His dance style, athletic abilities, artistry, and personality awakened public interest in classical dance in the 1970's and 1980's and sustained that interest as he made the transition from ballet to modern dance and from dancer to choreographer and artistic director. He is unique in the dance world for his wide-ranging repertoire. He embraced all forms of dance from the classics to jazz to modern to Broadway and shared his passion for dance with audiences around the world.

—Nancy Meyer

FURTHER READING

Aria, Barbara. *Misha: The Mikhail Baryshnikov Story.* New York: St. Martin's Press, 1989. Full biography of Baryshnikov's life, with photos. A vivid rendering of his life in the Soviet Union that also includes a look at his personal and professional relationships.

Baryshnikov, Mikhail. *Baryshnikov at Work: Mikhail Baryshnikov Discusses His Roles.* New York: Alfred P. Knopf, 1978. Text edited by Charles Engell France. Photographs by Martha Swope. Baryshnikov describes his working relationships with dancers and choreographers. Photographs provide visuals of the dancer in rehearsal and on stage in ballets.

Fraser, John. *Private View: Inside Baryshnikov's American Ballet Theatre.* New York: Bantam Books, 1988.

Details of Baryshnikov's tenure as artistic director at the ABT, relationships with dancers and staff, and the pressures of running a ballet company.

Glassman, Bruce S. *Mikhail Baryshnikov: Dance Genius.* Rev. ed. Woodbridge, Conn.: Blackbirch Press, 2001. A biography with photos, a time line of events in Baryshnikov's life, and a glossary of ballet terms.

Le Mond, Alan. *Bravo Baryshnikov.* New York: Grosset & Dunlap, 1978. Photos and text detailing Baryshnikov's performances.

Rose, Brian Jeffrey. *Television and the Performing Arts: A Handbook and Reference Guide to American Cultural Programming.* New York: Greenwood Press, 1986. Specific references about Baryshnikov's performances that were broadcast on television.

Townsend, Alecia Gael. *Mikhail Baryshnikov.* Vero Beach, Fla.: Rourke, 1993. A biography of the dancer written especially for young adults.

SEE ALSO: Alvin Ailey; George Balanchine; Sergei Diaghilev; Isadora Duncan; Michel Fokine; Serge Lifar; Léonide Massine; Vaslav Nijinsky; Rudolf Nureyev; Anna Pavlova; Jerome Robbins; Twyla Tharp.

RELATED ARTICLES in *Great Events from History: The Twentieth Century:*

1941-1970: March 12, 1963: Nureyev and Fonteyn Debut Ashton's *Marguerite and Armand.*

1971-2000: March 1, 1973: Tharp Stages *Deuce Coupe* for the Joffrey Ballet; Fall, 1980: Baryshnikov Becomes Artistic Director of American Ballet Theatre; October 24, 1990: Debut of Baryshnikov's White Oak Dance Project.

NIKOLAY GENNADIYEVICH BASOV
Russian physicist

Basov played a key role in the invention of quantum microwave amplification devices (masers) and light amplifiers that operate on the principle of stimulated emission of radiation (lasers). He collaborated with Aleksandr Prokhorov, with whom he shared the 1964 Nobel Prize in Physics, to produce the first Soviet maser and did pioneering work on the use of semiconductors in lasers.

BORN: December 14, 1922; Usman, Soviet Union (now in Russia)
DIED: July 1, 2001; Moscow, Russia
AREAS OF ACHIEVEMENT: Physics, science, invention and technology

EARLY LIFE

Nikolay Gennadiyevich Basov (NEE-koh-li gehn-nah-DEE-yeh-veech BAH-sohf) was the son of Gennadiy Fedorovich Basov, a professor, and Zinaida Adreevna Basova. Russian biographical sources, which are typically reticent about the personal lives of public figures, state only that he attended primary and secondary school in Voronezh. Completing secondary school in the early days of World War II, he enlisted in the army, enrolled in the Kiev school of military medicine, and afterward served as a lieutenant in the medical corps on the Ukrainian front.

Following the war, he enrolled in the Moscow Institute of Mechanics, from which he received *Kandidat Nauka* (roughly equivalent to an American doctoral degree) in 1950, only five years after beginning undergraduate study. Such rapid progress on the educational ladder was not unusual at the time. Soviet science was in the process of extremely rapid expansion in response to the demands of postwar reconstruction and an effort to achieve scientific and technological parity with the West, now perceived as a threat as Cold War tensions deepened. Thinning of the ranks of older scientists by the purges of the 1930's, wartime mortality, and the diversion of scientific effort toward immediate military concerns left the Soviet Union with an acute shortage of trained scientists. Consequently, there was great pressure to rush people through the educational system and to put them to work as soon as possible. Although the educational climate of postwar Russia has been much criticized for producing mediocrity, it did enable gifted individuals to exercise their abilities at an early age.

In 1948, while still a student, Basov joined the staff of the oscillation laboratory of the Lebedev Physics Institute in Moscow, first as a laboratory technician and later as a senior scientist. It was there that he began the fruitful collaboration with Aleksandr Prokhorov that led to their receiving the 1964 Nobel Prize in Physics for research on masers and lasers. He married Kseniya Tikhonova Nazarova in 1950, and together they had two sons, Gennadiy and Dmitri.

LIFE'S WORK

Basov's name is inextricably linked with laser research in the Soviet Union. Quantum amplification devices (masers and lasers) have been the focus of nearly all of his scientific endeavors during a long and fruitful career that began in the late 1940's with investigations on the use of microwave absorption spectra to study the structure of molecules. Absorption spectra are produced when electromagnetic radiation interacts with a substance in a low (ground) energy state. The substance absorbs certain frequencies of energy, becomes excited, and the pattern of frequencies absorbed gives important clues about the structure of the substance. To improve the sensitivity of their instruments, Basov and Prokhorov turned their efforts toward building a device, which they termed a molecular beam generator, that would produce a population of molecules all in the ground state. The design also produced a population of molecules in the excited state that could be used to amplify selected wavelengths by stimulated emission, a result that was to have far-reaching implications. A theoretical paper outlining such a device appeared in *Zhurnal eksperimentalnogo i teoreticheskogo fiziki* (journal of experimental and theoretical physics) in 1954. In the following year, Basov demonstrated the first Soviet maser (as microwave quantum amplifiers were dubbed by American workers). He received his Russian doctorate (a more advanced degree than the American doctorate) for this work in 1956.

This Russian maser research paralleled work being done by Charles Hard Townes and others in the United States but was completely independent of it, a fact that has been well documented and was recognized by the Nobel Committee. Scientists in the Soviet Union in the 1940's and early 1950's were effectively isolated from their Western counterparts. Much of the research on masers came under the heading of classified information on both sides of the Iron Curtain, and the Soviets in particular regarded even routine requests for scientific information from the West as subversive. Informal exchanges at scientific meetings, an important medium of exchange between scientists, did not occur, because Soviet scientists did not travel to the West.

After the discovery of masers, Basov turned toward devising a system based on the principle of stimulated emission of visible light. The maser demonstrated that this was theoretically possible, but there were practical difficulties in producing a population of predominantly excited molecules in the optical range. The story of the invention of the laser is one of a race between several Americans, working semi-independently of one another, and the entirely separate Russian group at the Lebedev Physics Institute. The distinction of producing the first working laser belongs to an American, but the Russians were not far behind and were noteworthy in their pioneering work with semiconductor lasers. In the following years, Basov, Prokhorov, and numerous coworkers

and subordinates conducted investigations into the design of a semiconductor, gas and chemical lasers, the use of lasers in controlled thermonuclear reactions, and a wide variety of practical applications of lasers in science and technology. An extensive bibliography of scientific publications from the 1970's and 1980's is testimony both to Basov's continuing activity in the field and to his prestige and influence as an academician and Nobel laureate.

In 1959, Basov and Prokhorov were awarded the Lenin Prize, the highest honor for individual achievement in the Soviet Union, for their work with masers and lasers, and in 1964 they shared the Nobel Prize in Physics with Townes, the leading American laser researcher. In 1966, Basov was elected full member of the Soviet Academy of Sciences and in 1967 was elected a member of its Presidium. The Academy of Sciences was the most prestigious scientific body in the Soviet Union, and membership in it carries with it both personal financial rewards and substantial political influence in matters such as funding of laboratories. Basov was active in establishing and advising laser research laboratories throughout the Soviet Union and abroad.

Politically as well as scientifically active and ambitious, Basov joined the Communist Party in 1951 and became a deputy to the Supreme Soviet in 1974 and a member of the Presidium of the Supreme Soviet in 1982. Such active involvement in party politics was unusual for a distinguished scientist in the Soviet Union.

SIGNIFICANCE

In his 1964 Nobel Prize lecture, Basov characterized himself as a scientist who combined the theoretical elucidation of physical principles with their practical applications, with emphasis on the practical. This is a reasonable description of his scientific approach, but more than that it is an affirmation of his orthodoxy and adherence to the Marxist philosophy of science, which emphasizes the concrete and service aspects of science over the theoretical—sometimes to the detriment of both, particularly when the decisions as to what is practical and what is mere "bourgeois theory" are made by those ignorant of scientific methodology.

The elaboration of the theory of stimulated emission of radiation (which had been predicted by Albert Einstein on a general basis in 1917) and the development of experimental quantum amplifiers were major developments in theoretical physics; the laser itself has, in the years since its invention, become one of the most important tools of science and industry.

Nikolay Gennadiyevich Basov. (© The Nobel Foundation)

A brilliant and productive scientist who devoted his career to a branch of physics with broad practical applications, Basov was patriotic, politically orthodox, politically adept, and close to being a model Soviet/Marxist scientist. Although the model may not be as appealing to Westerners as that of dissident scientists, it is an effective one, and Basov's scientific and administrative efforts on behalf of laser research made this branch of physics one of the showpieces of Soviet science.

—Martha A. Sherwood

FURTHER READING

Bertolotti, Mario. *The History of the Laser*. Bristol, England: Institute of Physics, 2005. Traces the history of the laser and those responsible for its discovery. Although Basov is not a principle character in the book, his work is mentioned and is placed within the context of other scientific developments.

_____. *Masers and Lasers: An Historical Approach*. Bristol, England: Adam Hilger, 1983. A technical account of the reasoning behind the development of the maser and laser. The narrative is likely to be difficult for nonspecialists. The contributions made by Prokhorov and Basov are discussed in some detail and placed in the context of research that was underway at the same time in the United States.

Brophy, James J. *Semiconductor Devices*. New York: McGraw-Hill, 1964. A useful background reference for understanding how semiconductor lasers function. Terminology is defined and explained in nonmathematical terms; the book is aimed at the nonspecialist using semiconductor devices who wants a basic understanding of how they function. There is a brief discussion of semiconductor lasers themselves.

Dardo, Mauro. *Nobel Laureates and Twentieth-Century Physics*. New York: Cambridge University Press, 2004. Chronicles major developments in physics since 1901, the year the first Nobel Prize in Physics was awarded. Includes information about the work of Basov and other prize winners.

Hecht, Jeff, and Dick Teresi. *Laser: Supertool of the Eighties*. New York: Ticknor & Fields, 1982. The bulk of this book (nine of fourteen chapters) is devoted to uses and potential uses of lasers in medicine, communications, warfare, manufacturing, energy production, publishing, holography, and the arts. There are good nontechnical descriptions of the general principle of laser action and the design and func-

tion of various masers and lasers. The section devoted to the history of the laser concentrates on the American contribution but does include some information on Basov and Prokhorov.

Isakov, A. I., O. N. Krokhin, D. V. Sobeltsyn, and I. I. Sobelman. "Nikolay Gennadiyevich Basov, on His Fiftieth Birthday." *Soviet Physics-Uspekhi* 16, no. 1 (1973): 165-166. This testimonial, written by a number of fellow physicists, gives a chronological account of Basov's life and research. Tends to present a one-sided view of the person portrayed. Provides a good review of Basov's scientific career but contains little personal data. The Soviet view of individual effort as a part of a master plan is also evident.

Parry, Albert. *The Russian Scientist*. New York: Macmillan, 1973. This book is a good, relatively neutral account of science in the Soviet Union, beginning in czarist times. Biographies of representative eminent Russian physical and natural scientists and mathematicians are given. A useful reference for a perspective on science administration in the Soviet Union and the importance of the Soviet Academy of Sciences.

Popovsky, Mark. *Manipulated Science: The Crisis of Science and Scientists in the Soviet Union Today*. Garden City, N.Y.: Doubleday, 1979. A Russian specialist in scientific journalism who emigrated to the United States, Popovsky presents a historical overview of the practice of science in the Soviet Union. The emphasis is on failures and weaknesses of the system and the dismal record of natural sciences under Joseph Stalin.

Weber, Robert L. *Pioneers of Science: Nobel Prize Winners in Physics*. Edited by J. M. A. Lenihan. Bristol, England: Adam Hilger, 1980. Consists of brief sketches of the lives of Nobel Prize-winning physicists to 1980. Its chief use is as a source of biographical data, and it includes personal data on Soviet scientists that Soviet sources do not include.

SEE ALSO: Albert Einstein; Pyotr Leonidovich Kapitsa; Igor Vasilyevich Kurchatov; Guglielmo Marconi; Max Planck; Sir Chandrasekhara Venkata Raman; Andrei Sakharov; Johannes Stark; Charles Hard Townes.

RELATED ARTICLE in *Great Events from History: The Twentieth Century:*
1941-1970: July, 1960: Invention of the Laser.

SIR WILLIAM MADDOCK BAYLISS
English physiologist

Bayliss made major discoveries in what was then the early science of physiology, especially of the heart, and in biochemistry relating to lymph flow, hormones and their actions, principles of enzyme action, and properties of colloidal biological systems.

BORN: May 2, 1860; Wolverhampton, Staffordshire, England
DIED: August 27, 1924; London, England
AREAS OF ACHIEVEMENT: Physiology, biochemistry, medicine, biology

EARLY LIFE

William Maddock Bayliss (BAY-lihs) was born to Moses Bayliss and Jane Maddock in the industrial town of Wolverhampton in the English Midlands. His father was a blacksmith who became a successful manufacturer of screws, nuts and bolts, and wrought-iron gates. William, the couple's only child to live to adult life, attended a small private school in Wolverhampton. He showed an early interest in natural science but later joined his father's business. His father was more interested in the technical aspects of the manufacturing process than in the commercial side, and William inherited his father's inclination to do things with his own hands. The boy soon tired of manufacturing and decided to study medicine, the only type of scientific education available to him at that time. He began his studies as an apprentice to a local medical practitioner and learned wound dressing and dispensing at the local hospital.

In 1880, Moses Bayliss retired, and the family moved to a newly built house in Hampstead, a London suburb. William had entered University College in London the preceding year and was following the medical curriculum. After an auspicious beginning in the preclinical sciences, he failed the anatomy examination and found that research, under Burdon Sanderson, a professor of physiology, was more to his liking.

In 1883, Sanderson became the Waynflete Chair of Physiology at Oxford, and in 1885, Bayliss followed him to Oxford, entering Wadham College as an undergraduate. At twenty-three, he was older than the other undergraduates, who jokingly called him "father Bayliss." He earned the name partly because of his age and partly because of his beard; he never shaved in his life. He enjoyed undergraduate life and made many lifelong friends at Oxford. In 1888, Bayliss returned to University College with a first-class honors degree in natural science and was appointed assistant in physiology.

His father's house in Hampstead was in the outermost suburbs of London, and Bayliss had to walk a mile and a half over Hampstead Hill to catch a horse-drawn bus to University College. The journey was tiring, and he set up a study and private laboratory at the house in Hampstead. This study and the house's four acres of grounds provided opportunity for recreation and social events. In later years, many young research workers from England and abroad were to enjoy Bayliss's diffident and kind manner as he hosted tennis parties, garden parties, "at home" days, and more formal dinner parties.

The manual skills that Bayliss inherited or learned from his father helped him master difficult electrical and physicochemical techniques not widely used by physiologists at that time, but his interests were more wide-ranging than physiology. Even on vacation he was a student of geology and fossils, of Roman and medieval antiquities, and of wildflowers and the plant and animal life of the seashore. Bayliss was an avid photographer, taking a heavy-plate camera and tripod on vacation. He took all the photographs that illustrated his books.

The single most significant event in Bayliss's life was Ernest Henry Starling's arrival at University College in 1890. Apart from marking the beginning of an extraordinarily fruitful research collaboration, their acquaintance led to the marriage of Bayliss and Gertrude Starling, his colleague's sister, in 1893.

LIFE'S WORK

Bayliss spent his entire career at University College, where he taught and performed research in physiology and related subjects. In 1892, he and Starling published a report of the electrical activity in the mammalian heart and recorded the first human electrocardiograms; part of the work was done at Oxford, where better equipment was available. After some work on vasomotor control that has not stood the test of time, he published two papers in 1894, again with Starling, which foreshadowed Starling's later work on the formation of lymph and autoregulation of the heart.

In the last years of the nineteenth century, Bayliss and Starling turned their attention to secretion in the small intestine. That work led to the discovery of the gastrointestinal hormone secretin in 1902. Secretin, which is secreted by the mucosa of the small intestine when exposed

Sir William Maddock Bayliss. (Library of Congress)

to acid material from the stomach, is a potent stimulus for pancreatic secretion. It was the first hormone to be identified.

Bayliss's important work was clouded by the accusation that he failed to anesthetize a dog during a demonstration as part of a public lecture on secretion in 1903. Stephen Coleridge, secretary of the National Vivisection Society, stated that the dog was not anesthetized, had struggled forcibly during the experiment, and had seemed to suffer extremely while in a fully conscious state. The accusation was reported fully in several London papers.

Such treatment of an animal would have meant the loss of Bayliss's license under the Vivisection Act, criminal charges, and the probable loss of his position at University College. Bayliss was persuaded to seek redress in the courts, probably at the urging of Starling and others, who saw this false accusation as a chance to blunt antivivisectionist sentiment. The antivivisectionists made an unfortunate choice of victim in Bayliss, who had the financial means to risk the hazards of a court action and whose gentle manner in the witness box was a great help to his case. In addition, while in the witness box, Coleridge did as much damage to his own case as time would allow. The jury trial, before the lord chief justice, lasted four days and ended in an award of two thousand pounds to Bayliss. Long lines waited to get into the court

each day, and the proceedings and verdict were reported in the London, provincial British, and French newspapers. Bayliss used the award to establish a research fund in physiology at University College; a wag suggested that it should be called the "Stephen Coleridge Vivisection Fund." That same year, Bayliss was promoted to assistant professor at University College. He was also elected to membership in the Royal Society.

After the work on secretin, Bayliss turned his attention to enzyme action and adsorption phenomenon. This work would occupy him for the rest of his life. He determined that enzymes act as catalysts and that their properties are in large part a result of their being in the colloidal state. Bayliss's findings were published in the monograph *The Nature of Enzyme Action* in 1908. He completed some preliminary work on the kinetics of enzyme action and in 1912 showed that enzymes are capable of synthesizing large molecules from smaller subunits.

Bayliss's interest in colloids led to investigations of the behavior of electrolytically dissociated colloids when they are enclosed in a nonpermeable membrane. He confirmed experimentally the theoretical basis for the physicochemical equilibrium and the electrical potential difference across biological membranes and laid the basis for understanding the electrical activity of nerve, muscle, and other cells.

In 1911, Bayliss was awarded a Royal Medal, and in 1912 he was appointed Professor of General Physiology, a chair specially created for him at University College. These honors did not detract from his accessibility and easy manner with students and less well-known colleagues. In his laboratory, he was always available to undergraduate as well as research students, and to visitors from other laboratories. He was often sympathetic to minorities when their views were attacked as a result of emotional prejudice and found time to support woman suffrage and birth control publicly.

From 1912 to 1914, Bayliss devoted most of his time to preparing his *Principles of General Physiology* (1915). He was best known for this book, which has been described as an apology for his life. The success of the book can be attributed not only to its wide range of topics but also to the style of the author, for it is a history of his mind and its achievements and of the accomplishments of the physiologists of the later nineteenth and the early twentieth century.

During World War I, Bayliss turned his attention to practical problems. After severe battlefield injury, it was common for a soldier initially to show signs of recovery, only to die a few hours later from circulatory collapse with a very low blood pressure. To prevent this secondary wound shock, Bayliss reported in 1916 that intravenous infusion of a solution of 6 percent gum acacia in saline, which had a viscosity and colloid osmotic pressure similar to blood, would raise and maintain the blood pressure. During the next two years, he showed that damaged tissues release vasodilators into circulation. The massive dilation of blood vessels that resulted, often coupled with blood loss from the wound, caused a profound and usually fatal fall in blood pressure. These changes could be reversed by an intravenous infusion of colloidal material. His observations are fundamental to modern methods of treating shock.

As a result of his work, many thousands of soldiers' lives were saved by intravenous infusions of gum acacia and saline. The gum acacia and saline solution was not ideal, but the success of this technique led to the availability of adequate supplies of blood on the battlefield in World War II.

Another practical problem that concerned Bayliss during the war was the nutritional health of the British population; submarine attacks on British shipping threatened the supply of food to the island. As chair of the Food (War) Committee, he published *The Physiology of Food and Economy of Diet* (1917), advocating an adequate intake of calories with the addition of fresh foodstuffs to supply necessary vitamins and minerals. The committee advised the government on the distribution and rationing of food based on scientific principles. As a result of these activities, the British diet was on the whole adequate if not always palatable.

Bayliss produced little original research in the last few years of his life but continued to work on lectures, reviews, and monographs relating to his earlier work, and to revise later editions of *Principles of General Physiology* and *The Nature of Enzyme Action*. Bayliss died in London in 1924.

SIGNIFICANCE

Bayliss lived and worked during the birth of modern physiology and contributed greatly to this science. He was one of the founders of the younger science of biochemistry. He made major contributions to the modern understanding of the physiology of the heart and the lymphatics, to the physiology and biochemistry of hormones, and to the biochemistry of enzyme action. This knowledge of hormones and enzymes is fundamental to understanding living systems; thus, his discoveries lie at the heart of the diagnostic and therapeutic methods of modern medicine. Bayliss also showed a desire for fair treatment for those less favored than himself, a desire for generosity to those whose scientific views differed from his, and a desire to help those who sought his help.

—*James A. Cowan*

FURTHER READING

Barcroft, H. "Lymph Formation by Secretion or Filtration." *Journal of Physiology* 260 (1976): 1-20. Detailed account of the experiments that led to Starling's explanation of the formation of lymph, including Bayliss's crucial contribution.

Bayliss, L. E. "William Maddock Bayliss, 1860-1924: Life and Scientific Work." *Perspectives in Biology and Medicine* 4 (Summer, 1961): 460-479. An account of Bayliss's life and work written by his son, also a physiologist. Includes a complete bibliography of Bayliss's scientific publications.

Hill, A. V. "Bayliss and Starling and the Happy Fellowship of Physiologists." *Journal of Physiology* 204 (1969): 1-13. An account of early twentieth century physiology and physiologists by a physiologist who trained under and worked with both Starling and Bayliss.

Howard, John M., and Walter Hess. *History of the Pancreas: Mysteries of the Hidden Organ*. New York: Kluwer Academic, 2002. Written by two academic pancreatic surgeons, this history of the pancreas from antiquity to contemporary times includes information about Bayliss and his work.

SEE ALSO: Sir Frederick G. Banting; Harvey Williams Cushing; Willem Einthoven; Bernardo Alberto Houssay; August Krogh; John J. R. Macleod; Ernest Henry Starling; George Hoyt Whipple.

RELATED ARTICLE in *Great Events from History: The Twentieth Century:*

1901-1940: April-June, 1902: Bayliss and Starling Establish the Role of Hormones.

CHARLES A. BEARD
American historian

More than any other twentieth century scholar, Beard shaped how Americans viewed their past. His attention to social, economic, and intellectual developments contrasted strikingly with the narrowly political, dynastic, and military focus of most competing texts of the time. His approach to history was present-minded, aimed at using the past to illuminate contemporary problems.

BORN: November 27, 1874; near Knightstown, Indiana
DIED: September 1, 1948; New Haven, Connecticut
ALSO KNOWN AS: Charles Austin Beard (full name)
AREAS OF ACHIEVEMENT: Historiography, political science, scholarship

EARLY LIFE

Charles A. Beard (beerd) was the younger of two sons of William Henry Harrison and Mary J. (Payne) Beard. His Beard forebears were Quakers who had settled in Guilford County, North Carolina. His father, at the start of the Civil War, had moved to Indiana, where he became a successful farmer, building contractor, and land speculator. Although his father was a self-proclaimed religious skeptic, Charles attended Quaker services as a boy and began his formal education in a local Quaker-run school.

After he was graduated from Knightstown High School in 1891, his father bought for him and his older brother a local newspaper. In 1895, however, Charles gave up journalism to attend DePauw University. Majoring in history, he finished his undergraduate studies in three years with an impressive academic record, culminating in his election to Phi Beta Kappa. He then went to Oxford University for further study in history. While at DePauw, he had begun to shift from his father's loyalty to the Republican Party to a sympathy for reform. His awakening sense of social consciousness was reinforced by his experiences in England. In response, Beard played a leading role in establishing at Oxford, in early 1899, a workingmen's college—named Ruskin Hall after the English artist-reformer John Ruskin—for the training of future working-class leaders.

Except for a brief return trip to the United States to marry his college sweetheart, Mary Ritter (also a noted historian), Beard stayed in England until the spring of 1902. From his base in Manchester, he traveled all over the country, promoting the Ruskin Hall movement in talks before workingmen's and cooperative society groups.

The major thrust of those talks—and the theme of his first book, *The Industrial Revolution* (1901)—was how advancing technology, if properly utilized for public benefit rather than private profit, had the potential for improving the human lot.

In 1902, after returning to the United States, he began graduate work at Columbia University. For his Ph.D. dissertation, he completed a study begun while he was at Oxford, on the evolution of the office of justice of the peace in England. He received his degree in 1904 and was kept on as a lecturer in the history department to teach the Western European survey and English history. Three years later, he was appointed an adjunct professor in the Department of Public Law, with the responsibility of inaugurating a new undergraduate program in politics. In 1910, he was promoted to associate professor; five years later, he was awarded a full professorship. With prodigious energy, he taught a broad range of different courses, trained a group of Ph.D. students who would go on to make reputations of their own in political science and history, and turned out almost a book a year along with an imposing roster of articles and reviews.

LIFE'S WORK

Beard first attracted attention in academic circles when he collaborated with his older colleague James Harvey Robinson in writing a two-volume text, *The Development of Modern Europe: An Introduction to the Study of Current History* (1907-1908). The authors focused on social, economic, and intellectual developments, a method that contrasted with the narrowly political, dynastic, and military focus of most of their contemporaries. Also, Beard and Robinson took a present-minded approach to history, aimed at using the past to illuminate contemporary problems. Beard's 1910 *American Government and Politics* made a similarly innovative contribution to the teaching of political science by looking beyond the formal institutional structure of the American system to how things actually worked. Repeatedly updated and revised, the work remained for years the standard text for college-level introductory American government courses.

Beard's dual concern with making government more responsive to the popular will and more efficient in its operations led him into involvement with the New York Bureau of Municipal Research, the United States' first research organization for the improvement of public administration. He served as supervisor of the bureau's Training School for Public Service (1915-1919) and as bureau director (1919-1920); he was instrumental in the expansion of its activities beyond the municipal level and its resulting reorganization into the National Institute of Public Administration; and he was the primary author of a set of recommendations for a far-reaching reorganization of New York state government that was carried out during the 1920's.

The debate during the Progressive Era over the legitimacy of judicial review led Beard to undertake a reexamination of the intentions of the framers of the U.S. Constitution. In his 1912 book *The Supreme Court and the Constitution*, he concluded that the framers had intended to give the U.S. Supreme Court power to declare acts of Congress unconstitutional because of their eagerness "to safeguard the rights of private property against any levelling tendencies on the part of the propertyless masses." He amplified this theme in his highly controversial *An Economic Interpretation of the Constitution of the United States*, published the following year. The crux of his ar-

Charles A. Beard. (Library of Congress)

gument was that the Constitution was "an economic document" aimed at protecting the interests of the monied class in the face of threats from the largely debt-ridden small farmers that constituted local popular majorities. He went on to conclude that the Constitution was pushed through by undemocratic, even "irregular," means. For supporting evidence, Beard relied heavily on long-forgotten Treasury Department records for the public securities holdings of those involved in the adoption of the Constitution. The prominence given this data fostered the impression that the framers were primarily motivated by the quest for personal financial gain. There is no question that Beard's purpose in emphasizing the economic motivation of the framers was to demythologize the Constitution as a bulwark for the defense of the political status quo against reform.

An Economic Interpretation of the Constitution of the United States has been sharply attacked by many later historians as simplistic or even simply wrong. Yet the work remains a landmark in the development of American historical scholarship. The volume was the first attempt to apply the prosopographical—or collective biography—approach to a major historical problem. Beard envisaged the book as the first in a series of studies that would apply the economic interpretation to the full span of American history. His 1914 survey *Contemporary American History, 1877-1913* traced the political, legal, social, and intellectual changes resulting from the triumph of industrial capitalism in the years after the Civil War.

In the following year's *Economic Origins of Jeffersonian Democracy*, Beard pictured the party battles of the 1790's between the Federalists and their Republican opponents as a continuation of the struggle over the Constitution between "capitalistic and agrarian interests." The climax of his attempt to apply an overarching economic interpretation to the study of the American past was the two-volume *The Rise of American Civilization* (1927), coauthored with Mary Beard. The aspect of this work that most impressed professional historians was his treatment of the Civil War as a "second American Revolution," responsible for the triumph of Northern capitalism over its agrarian rival. Its portrayal of the clash of rival economic interests as the real root of historical change would exercise a pervasive influence on the generation that came to intellectual maturity in the 1930's. At the same time, its wide popular appeal owed much to the breadth of the canvas on which the Beards sketched their story. Going beyond politics, the work aspired to treat the full range and variety of the American national experience: political, social, and economic thought, religion, literature, education, science, art and architecture, and even music.

Although Beard was personally a supporter of American involvement in World War I, he resigned his Columbia professorship in October, 1917, in protest at the firing of antiwar faculty members. He was one of the founders of the New School for Social Research in 1919, but he soon dropped out of active involvement to devote himself to freelance writing. His 1922 book *Cross Currents in Europe To-day* was a pioneering challenge to the widely held notion that World War I was caused solely by German aggression. That same year, he visited Japan, at the invitation of the Tokyo Institute for Municipal Research, to study and report on Japanese municipal government; he so impressed his hosts that he was brought back after the devastating Tokyo earthquake of 1923 to advise on rebuilding the city. In 1926, he was elected president of the American Political Science Association. An investigatory trip to Yugoslavia resulted in his writing, in collaboration with George Radin, *The Balkan Pivot: Yugoslavia, a Study in Government and Administration* (1929). Despite his lack of sympathy for the complacent politics of normalcy that dominated the United States in the 1920's, Beard remained optimistic about the possibilities of a future of "unlimited progress." He continued to see in the advance of technology the potential for bringing about "an ever wider distribution of the blessings of civilization—health, security, material goods, knowledge, leisure, and aesthetic appreciation."

Beard put forth this gospel of technological utopianism in magazine articles, in symposia that he edited such as *Whither Mankind: A Panorama of Modern Civilization* (1928), *Toward Civilization* (1930), and, most fully, in a 1930 book coauthored with his son William, *The American Leviathan: The Republic in the Machine Age.* Yet his confident assumption of inevitable, even automatic, progress was dealt shattering blows by the Great Depression, the emergence of totalitarian regimes in Europe, and, as the 1930's went on, the darkening threat of another major war. Beard still retained his hope for a better world; the difference was that he now emphasized that its achievement would require purposeful and intelligent direction. To provide a guide for what policies should be adopted was the purpose of two works—written with the research assistance of George H. E. Smith— that appeared in 1934: *The Idea of National Interest: An Analytical Study in American Foreign Policy* and *The Open Door at Home: A Trial Philosophy of National Interest.* On one hand, he called for national economic

planning—or what he termed "applied engineering rationality"—to restore prosperity. On the other, he pleaded for insulation of the United States from international-trade conflicts and power rivalries through policies aimed at achieving national economic self-sufficiency.

At a more philosophical level, Beard centered his attack on any deterministic system—including by implication his own earlier economic determinism—that denied the role of "ethical and esthetic values" in shaping history. This new approach was inextricably intertwined with his championship of historical relativism. Starting with his December, 1933, presidential address to the American Historical Association, "Written History as an Act of Faith," Beard sharply attacked the assumption of so-called scientific history in which the historian could "describe the past as it actually was." While acknowledging the existence of verifiable facts, he argued that the historian's selection and arrangement of those facts was a matter of choice that reflected his (or her) frame of reference: his values and interests; his political, social, and economic beliefs; his conception of "things deemed necessary, things deemed possible, and things deemed desirable." Beard's major platform for pushing the message of historical relativism was the Committee on Historiography of the Social Science Research Council. The committee's influential 1946 report, *Theory and Practice in Historical Study,* affirmed that all written history "is ordered or organized under the influence of some scheme of reference, interest, or emphasis—avowed or unavowed—in the thought of the author."

At the level of practical politics, Beard started out as an enthusiastic supporter of President Franklin D. Roosevelt's New Deal as marking a break with the rudderless laissez-faire of the past. As the dominating member of the American Historical Association's Commission on the Social Studies, he was the moving spirit behind its call for a major revision of the curriculum and teaching methods in the public schools to prepare students for the coming new age of democratic "collectivism." By the late 1930's, however, he had grown disillusioned with Roosevelt's failure to adopt meaningful national economic planning. More upsetting still, he had come to suspect that Roosevelt's foreign policies were leading the United States into war. He was convinced that whatever happened in Europe and Asia could not endanger United States security given this country's high degree of economic self-sufficiency and its geographical position behind the buffer of two oceans. He even accused Roosevelt of looking for foreign adventures to divert public attention from the administration's failure to restore domestic prosperity. He accordingly became a vocal spokesperson for maintaining American isolationism—or, to use his preferred term, for pursuing a "continental" policy.

The outcome of the war confirmed Beard's worst forebodings. American involvement had disrupted further reform at home, accelerated the centralization of power in the presidency and bureaucracy, and dangerously increased the influence of the military. Nor was the country's physical security safeguarded. On the contrary, the United States now faced a more dangerous enemy, the Soviet Union. The result was to strengthen Beard in his hostility toward more overseas commitments. Once again, he turned to history to supply a guide to the path his fellow countryfolk should take. In a series of works—most notably *The American Spirit: A Study of the Idea of Civilization in the United States* (1942), *The Republic: Conversations on Fundamentals* (1943), and *A Basic History of the United States* (1944)—he set forth what he saw as the essential elements that had combined to create in the United States a unique civilization. His theme was an exaltation of the American system of "constitutional government"—with its balance between majority rule and the protection of "fundamental rights," between centralization of power and local autonomy—as "an eternal contradiction to the principle of authoritarian, totalitarian, dictatorial government."

The reverse side of his praise for the realism, practical wisdom, and farsighted genius of the Founding Fathers was his obsession with demolishing what he saw as the Roosevelt myth. In the first two volumes of a planned trilogy on Roosevelt's foreign policies—*American Foreign Policy in the Making, 1932-1940: A Study in Responsibilities* (1946) and *President Roosevelt and the Coming of the War 1941: A Study in Appearances and Realities* (1948)—he accused Roosevelt of deceiving and misleading the American people by talking peace while secretly plotting war. He went so far as to suggest that Roosevelt "was not surprised by the Japanese attack [on Pearl Harbor] when it came on December 7." The volumes sparked angry, often personally vitriolic, attacks from Roosevelt's admirers—including many of Beard's former friends—that deeply pained him. He had suffered a serious illness in 1945, and his labors on the Roosevelt volumes further sapped his formerly robust constitution. He died on September 1, 1948, before finishing the research for the planned third volume on wartime diplomacy—"a victim," a former student eulogized, "of hard work induced by a passionate drive to tell the truth as he saw it."

SIGNIFICANCE

Beard was a major figure in the development of political science in the United States: He played a leading role in reorienting the study of American government from the description of formal institutional structures to a realistic analysis of how things actually operated; he was one of the Progressive Era's foremost experts on municipal government; and he was a pioneer in placing the study of public administration on a scientific, empirical basis. He looms even larger in the development of American historical scholarship. His application of the economic interpretation to American history was at the time an immensely liberating intellectual force; he was the leading spokesman for—and outstanding practitioner of—a "new history" that would broaden the scope of study of the past beyond politics to include the full range of human experience; and he did much to sensitize historians to the role played by their personal values and biases in shaping their interpretations.

Nor was Beard's influence limited to the academy. He reached, through his books and articles, a larger popular audience than probably any other American scholar of his time. As an activist in support of a wide range of causes, he achieved near-celebrity status. A 1938 survey taken by *The New Republic* of liberal-left-wing intellectuals ranked Beard second only to the economist and social philosopher Thorstein Veblen among those whose work had most influenced their own thinking. Shortly after Beard's death, a poll of educators, editors, and public figures gave first place to *The Rise of American Civilization* as the book that best explained American democracy. Even hostile critics acknowledged that Beard had been the twentieth century's "most powerful single figure in the teaching of American history."

—*John Braeman*

FURTHER READING

Barrow, Clyde W. *More Than a Historian: The Political and Economic Thought of Charles A. Beard.* New Brunswick, N.J.: Transaction, 2000. Barrow argues that Beard's ideas have new relevance in light of contemporary debates about U.S. foreign and domestic policies. His book reconstructs the sources of Beard's thinking and explores Beard's theory of American political development.

Beale, Howard K. *Charles A. Beard: An Appraisal.* Lexington: University Press of Kentucky, 1954. A collection of sympathetic—and at times overly eulogistic—appraisals of Beard as teacher, scholar, and public affairs activist by friends and admirers.

Benson, Lee. *Turner and Beard: American Historical Writing Reconsidered*. Glencoe, Ill.: Free Press, 1960. A sympathetic but not uncritical examination of Beard's application of the economic interpretation to the study of American history.

Higham, John, Leonard Krieger, and Felix Gilbert. *History*. Englewood Cliffs, N.J.: Prentice-Hall, 1965. An excellent and insightful survey of changing fashions in American historiography that illuminates Beard's place in that larger context.

Hofstadter, Richard. *The Progressive Historians: Turner, Beard, Parrington*. New York: Alfred A. Knopf, 1968. A lucidly written and penetrating analysis of the forces shaping the so-called Progressive school of American historiography and its influence by a distinguished historian who also had been strongly influenced by Beard's work.

Kennedy, Thomas C. *Charles A. Beard and American Foreign Policy*. Gainesville: University of Florida Press, 1975. A detailed tracing of Beard's view on foreign policy issues, with major focus on his 1930's isolationism.

Marcell, David W. *Progress and Pragmatism: James, Dewey, Beard, and the American Idea of Progress*. Westport, Conn.: Greenwood Press, 1974. Shows how Beard fit into the larger American tradition of pragmatic philosophy.

Nore, Ellen. *Charles A. Beard: An Intellectual Biography*. Carbondale: Southern Illinois University Press, 1983. A thoroughly researched and detailed account of Beard's intellectual development, but somewhat lifeless on the personal side.

Strout, Cushing. *The Pragmatic Revolt in American History: Carl Becker and Charles Beard*. New Haven, Conn.: Yale University Press, 1958. A still-useful introduction to the thought of two leading American exponents of historical relativism.

White, Morton G. *Social Thought in America: The Revolt Against Formalism*. New York: Viking Press, 1949. An influential, if too abstrusely written, account of the role played by Beard, along with such other figures as John Dewey and Thorstein Veblen, in reorienting American scholarship from formalistic description to realistic analysis.

SEE ALSO: Fernand Braudel; Nicholas Murray Butler; Lucy S. Dawidowicz; John Dewey; Leonard T. Hobhouse; Robert M. Hutchins; Vernon Louis Parrington; Henri Pirenne; Arnold Toynbee; Barbara W. Tuchman; Frederick Jackson Turner; Thorstein Veblen.

RELATED ARTICLES in *Great Events from History: The Twentieth Century:*

1901-1940: 1907: Meinecke Advances the Analytic Method in History; November 7, 1914: Lippmann Helps to Establish *The New Republic*; Summer, 1918: Rise of Cultural Relativism Revises Historiography; 1934: Toynbee's Metahistorical Approach Sparks Debate.

THE BEATLES
British singers-musicians

The Beatles popularized American rock and roll and became not only the major exponent of British rock around the world but also the greatest British, if not the Western world's, popular band ever.

ALSO KNOWN AS: The Fab Four
AREAS OF ACHIEVEMENT: Music, film

RINGO STARR

BORN: July 7, 1940; Liverpool, England
ALSO KNOWN AS: Richard Starkey (birth name)

JOHN LENNON

BORN: October 9, 1940; Liverpool, England
DIED: December 8, 1980; New York, New York

PAUL McCARTNEY

BORN: June 18, 1942; Liverpool, England
ALSO KNOWN AS: James Paul McCartney (full name)

GEORGE HARRISON

BORN: February 25, 1943; Liverpool, England
DIED: November 29, 2001; Los Angeles, California

EARLY LIVES
John Lennon was born the only son of Freddie and Julia (Stanley) Lennon, in Liverpool, England. After being deserted by his father and having a mother who could not properly care for him, Lennon was reared by his maternal aunt, Mimi. He was a bright, precocious boy who was

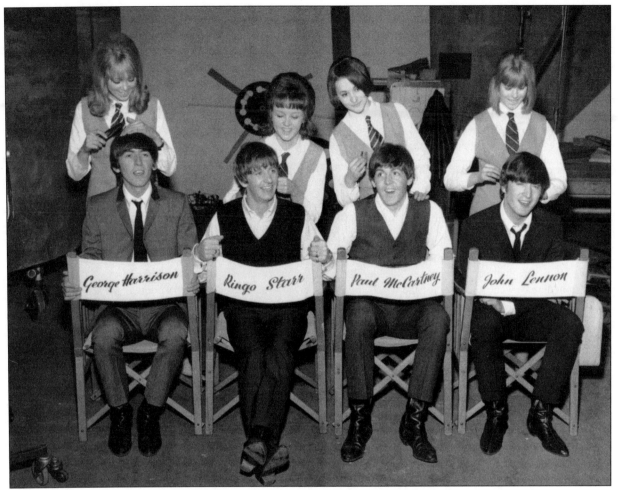

The Beatles in 1964. (AP/Wide World Photos)

given to countless acts of rebellion. As a teenager he found an outlet for his high spirits by forming a musical group called the Quarreymen.

While playing at a garden festival in 1955, Lennon met and befriended another teenager, Paul McCartney, who soon joined his band. McCartney, born to James and Mary (Mohin) McCartney in Liverpool, could not have been more different from Lennon: McCartney was quiet and obedient and gave his widowed father little trouble. In the next year, George Harrison, born to Harry and Louise Harrison, also in Liverpool, became the band's guitarist, thus inaugurating what would become the world's most celebrated rock and pop band.

In the group's early years, Stuart Sutcliffe, a gifted college friend of Lennon, tried to play bass, and a series of drummers came and went until Peter Best joined on the eve of their departure to play in Hamburg, West Ger-

many, in 1960. Through a series of four trips extending over two years, the Beatles (as they now called themselves) would play a grueling schedule in various Hamburg clubs and developed into a cohesive unit with a large repertoire of songs, many of which they would record later, on consecutive albums.

While in Hamburg, the group was recorded as a backup band to singer Tony Sheridan, and the single "My Bonnie" became a cult favorite among Liverpool teenagers. After a number of fans requested copies of the song from a local record store, the manager, Brian Epstein, was surprised to learn that members of the band lived and played nearby. A curious Epstein attended one of the band's concerts and impulsively asked to act as their manager. He then began a systematic campaign to polish their scruffy appearance and secure a recording contract.

Consistently rebuffed, the Beatles auditioned in 1962 for George Martin, a classically trained musician who had recorded comedy acts for a small record label. Martin was impressed with the group's musicianship and voices, but he was especially taken because they already had a considerable catalogue of original songs. Martin told Epstein that Best, however, was inadequate as a drummer and could not appear on recordings. Armed with the excuse for which they had been searching, the band replaced him with another Liverpool acquaintance, Ringo Starr (born Richard Starkey to Richard and Elsie Starkey), and the group was now solidified as a quartet.

LIVES' WORK

In October, 1962, the Beatles released their first single record, "Love Me Do," which was only moderately successful. However, their second release, "Please, Please Me," immediately went to the top of the charts, beginning a string of Beatles hits and a rise in national popularity. In April, 1963, they recorded their first album, *Please, Please Me*, a combination of original material and songs from their stage shows. They continued playing concerts throughout England. By August, the Beatles were so popular that they were invited to appear at the Royal Command Performance, a variety show given in honor of the royal family and broadcast over national television in the United Kingdom.

While the band had captivated England, its record company could not persuade its American subsidiary to release any records. *With the Beatles* appeared in England in November and was immediately popular, and the success of "I Want to Hold Your Hand" convinced the American subsidiary to release the song in January, 1964. A massive advertising campaign helped the song become an instant success—and for an English act that success was unprecedented. The group soon was invited to appear on *The Ed Sullivan Show*, a Sunday-night institution on American television. The small live audience at their performance was so frenzied that the term "Beatlemania" was coined to describe the hysteria that accompanied the group's appearance. Beatlemania would become the group's legacy.

For the next three years, the band toured almost nonstop, crossing the globe numerous times as it kept to a mind-numbing, wearying schedule. Remarkably, the band not only continued to record, but Lennon and McCartney also developed into an extraordinarily talented and prolific song-writing team. In June, 1964, England's queen Elizabeth II named the Beatles members of the Order of the British Empire.

In July, *A Hard Day's Night* was released as a film and album and was an international success. The fictional film attempted to chronicle the chaos that surrounded the lives of the otherwise patient and accepting musicians. The plot was episodic, but the heart of the film was the personalities of the Beatles themselves, and it was their wit and charm—the qualities that drew Epstein, Martin, the press, and countless others to them—that captivated audiences.

With their fourth album, *Beatles for Sale*, the band, exhausted from touring and the demands of popularity, revealed an especially somber mood. In fact, with the next album, *Help!*, the band continued a pattern begun with *Beatles for Sale*. Increasingly, and especially with the songs of Lennon, Beatles songs became not only reflections of an emotional state but also comments about the travails of success and popularity. The film of the same name, though also a popular success, is vastly inferior to the first Beatles film. In *Help!*, commercial exploitation overwhelms everything except the band's musical contributions.

Rubber Soul appeared in December, 1965, and like each previous album was an instant success. However, *Rubber Soul* was anything but another Beatles album, as the band explored new territory. Everything from the jacket cover to the songs' lyrics and the musical compositions suggests a new sophistication and a rising maturity. Quite simply, the Beatles were now making music unlike anything heard before, and it was a music they were finding increasingly difficult to duplicate on stage. "Norwegian Wood," for example, epitomizes some of the changes. For the first time, a Western pop record included the music of an Indian sitar (similar to a guitar). The album's foggy, obscure lyrics by Lennon were intentionally evasive in describing an extramarital affair he did not want discovered by his wife, Cynthia.

The departure signaled by *Rubber Soul* continued with the release of *Revolver* in 1966. Here, the group's use of mind-expanding drugs becomes far more pronounced, the melodies are more densely textured, and the lyrics are controlled and evocative. Lennon's songs, especially "She Said She Said" and "Tomorrow Never Knows," are particularly experimental in their exotic lyrics and unique use of tape loops.

As these albums reveal, the Beatles, by the end of 1966, had become a studio band. They had performed their last concert that year in San Francisco, California. For their next album, they planned an aural scrapbook of their lives in Liverpool and recorded three songs. When their record company insisted on a single, they released

"Penny Lane" and "Strawberry Fields Forever" and gradually changed the conception of the album to one of a song cycle performed by a fictional band.

With the release in June, 1967, of *Sgt. Pepper's Lonely Hearts Club Band*, the Beatles took their most daringly experimental step. Although working with the still-primitive recording equipment of the late 1960's, the band managed to produce an intricate aural paean to psychedelia. Songs were no longer three-minute ditties (in fact, the longest, "A Day in the Life," stands as a definite masterpiece), and the album sleeve featured song lyrics and an elaborate cover photograph that commented on the change in direction the group was taking.

Two months later, Epstein died of a drug overdose, the band temporarily focused themselves on an Indian mystic, and they emerged to produce their own television film, *Magical Mystery Tour*. While the record was popular, the film was a disaster, and for the first time critics panned the Beatles. Early in 1968, Lennon and McCartney announced the formation of Apple, their own record company and business enterprise, and a period of general artistic malaise ensued.

Finally, November, 1968, saw the release of *The Beatles* (popularly known as the White Album for its plain white jacket), a two-record album of thirty diverse songs featuring each member of the band. By now the songwriting team of Lennon and McCartney had effectively dissolved, and each member contributed his own distinctive pieces to the production. Though uneven in spots, the album stands as a wild burst of creative energy from a band suffering from much dissension and confusion. During this period Lennon's experiments with drugs developed into an addiction to heroin, which led to paranoia and lethargy. As he retreated into his relationship with Yoko Ono, the band foundered and tensions were further exacerbated. In December, *Yellow Submarine*, a cartoon film with four new Beatles songs, was released to laudatory reviews.

Sensing their dissolution, the Beatles decided to return to their musical roots and record their next album as a film crew recorded the event. The result was an acrimonious session that produced thirty hours of tape that no one could face editing. Producer Phil Spector was hired by the group, and *Let It Be* was released a year later; it was the band's final album.

The actual swan song for the Beatles came in the fall of 1969, however, with the release of *Abbey Road*, a gorgeous collection of disparate pieces of magically blending harmony. With *Abbey Road* the Beatles returned to the high production values that had been associated with

BEATLES DISCOGRAPHY	
1963	*Please Please Me*
1963	*With the Beatles*
1964	*Introducing . . . the Beatles*
1964	*Meet the Beatles!*
1964	*The Beatles' Second Album*
1964	*A Hard Day's Night*
1964	*Something New*
1964	*Beatles for Sale*
1964	*Beatles '65*
1965	*Beatles VI*
1965	*Help!*
1965	*Rubber Soul*
1966	*Yesterday . . . and Today*
1966	*Revolver*
1967	*Sgt. Pepper's Lonely Hearts Club Band*
1967	*Magical Mystery Tour*
1968	*The Beatles (White Album)*
1969	*Yellow Submarine*
1969	*Abbey Road*
1970	*Let It Be*
1970	*In the Beginning: The Early Tapes*
1977	*Live at the Hollywood Bowl*
1977	*Live at the Star Club (2 vols.)*
1988	*The Beatles Box Set*
1995	*Anthology 1*
1996	*Anthology 2*
1996	*Anthology 3*
2006	*Love*

their best work, and one side of the record is a collage of fragments that emerge as nothing short of an artistic triumph. Finally, in April, 1970, the group disbanded in anger, frustration, and financial chaos, and individual members pursued solo careers that sporadically produced even more brilliant music.

The Beatles' legacy continued, following Lennon's death in 1980, with a series of releases that revealed not only their astounding creativity but the range of their accomplishments. In 1995 the three surviving Beatles and producer George Martin collaborated on a television special, *The Beatles Anthology*, in which they reminisced about their years together and returned to the studio to complete two scraps of songs Lennon had composed years earlier. The film and ensuing DVD were supported by a collection of three CDs presenting alternate takes, a few new songs, and demos of Beatles standards. Arguably the highlight of the anthology is the two early versions of "Strawberry Fields Forever," which were blended and reconfigured into the widely recognized version of the song. In 2000, Capitol Records released *Beatles 1*, a collection of the band's number one hits, which reminded audiences how remarkable the group had been over a mere seven-year period in the 1960's.

Live at the BBC was released in 2001, featuring live studio performances from the early 1960's and Beatles originals as well as cover versions of previously unreleased songs. The year 2001 also saw the death of a second of the Fab Four: Harrison died on November 29 in Los Angeles, California.

Perhaps the most inventive and unexpected release came in 2006 with *Love*, an astounding remixed and reordered collection of at least twenty Beatles songs into aural collage. Martin and his son, Giles, produced the collection as a soundtrack for shows by the entertainment giant Cirque de Soleil, but the collection is so stunning and polished that it stands on its own.

SIGNIFICANCE

To understand the Beatles and their work, one must consider them as a 1960's phenomenon, for they mirrored and epitomized so much that has come to be associated with that dramatic decade. It was, therefore, oddly appropriate that as a new decade dawned, the leading musical group of the 1960's dissolved.

The Beatles were unique in many ways but no more so than in their legacy and collective influence. For British audiences, they represented something largely unprecedented in the twentieth century. When these northern boys, speaking in their distinctive accents, emerged from the backwaters of Liverpool, they demonstrated that English culture was not confined to London's boundaries. They furthermore revealed, to a rigidly class-conscious society, that anyone with talent could command national attention and succeed professionally.

For the world, the Beatles came to represent England after the war, an idealized England that knew how to have a good time and share it. Soon, anything British became the rage; a host of British bands, many quite talented and others only mediocre, dominated radio airwaves. World music changed dramatically as songs grew longer and more reflective, as production experiments and new recording technology proliferated, and as record packaging suddenly became an art form of its own.

For audiences everywhere, the Beatles suggested that change, in almost every conceivable form, was a necessary, even desirable circumstance. Thus, unintentionally, they popularized new fashions, verbal extravagance, and psychedelic drugs. For a generation weary of the promises of its parents, the Beatles, again unintentionally, acted as a social and personal conscience in the search for freedom and selfhood. With Lennon's murder on December 8, 1980, an era finally ended; there could be no return to the past. The Beatles were now ineradicably destroyed, and their generation had to give way for others to follow, though the band's legacy continues in numerous subtle and obvious ways.

—David W. Madden

FURTHER READING

The Beatles Anthology. San Francisco, Calif.: Chronicle Books, 2000. A comprehensive oral history of the Beatles, derived from recorded conversations with group members and others that allows the group to tell its own story. Features more than thirteen hundred photos, posters, and other documents.

Carr, Roy, and Tony Tyler. *The Beatles: An Illustrated Record*. New York: Harmony Books, 1981. Well written and carefully documented, this work gives a chronology of all British releases of Beatles records along with extraordinarily well-informed and illuminating descriptions and evaluations of the recordings.

Emerick, Geoff, and Howard Massey. *Here, There, and Everywhere: My Life Recording the Music of the Beatles*. New York: Gotham, 2006. A fascinating look at the Beatles in the studio by an insider. Emerick was the Beatles' principal engineer after 1966. His focus is on recording sessions, while giving profiles of each of the musicians, favoring McCartney for his affability and professionalism.

Friede, Goldie, Robin Titone, and Sue Weiner. *The Beatles A to Z: John Lennon, Paul McCartney, George Harrison, and Ringo Starr*. New York: Methuen, 1980. As the title suggests, this encyclopedic work is dedicated to all manner of trivia concerning the band. It is filled with informative notes and many little-known facts.

McKinney, Devin. *Magic Circles: The Beatles in Dream and History*. Cambridge, Mass.: Harvard University Press, 2003. Unlike any other study or memoir of the Beatles, this book not only traces the band's unlikely rise to international stardom but provides both a musical critique and a penetrating cultural examination of the dreams and aspirations of an entire generation. The Beatles are the nominal subjects of a study in history, sociology, aesthetics, and mythology.

Norman, Philip. *Shout! The Beatles in Their Generation*. 1981. Rev. and updated ed. New York: Simon &

Schuster, 2005. Possibly the single best book on the band. Norman culls thousands of pieces of obscure and critical facts to chronicle not only the history of the band but also the incalculable importance it had for a generation of listeners. An indispensable work.

Schaffner, Nicholas. *The Beatles Forever*. Harrisburg, Pa.: Cameron House, 1977. Schaffner approaches his subject as a highly informed (perhaps the most informed) and literate fan. The book abounds in revealing anecdotes. Another indispensable source.

Spitz, Bob. *The Beatles: The Biography*. New York: Little, Brown, 2005. Exhaustive biography tracing group members' from their family origins in Liverpool to their final days together. Spitz presents a balanced portrait of the Fab Four, documenting their musical genius as well as their rock-star excesses.

Unterberger, Richie. *The Unreleased Beatles: Music and Film*. Milwaukee, Wis.: Backbeat Books, 2006. This work provides a look at the astounding amount of material, musical and cinematic, that the Beatles completed but never released. It gives further testimony to the band's staggering creativity.

Wenner, Jann. *Lennon Remembers*. 1971. New ed. New York: Verso, 2000. The interview that appeared in *Rolling Stone* magazine in 1970, which dispelled notions of the Beatles as cute, innocuous boys. In all of his pain, Lennon reveals his and the band's frustrations and shortcomings.

SEE ALSO: Bob Dylan; Janis Joplin; Elvis Presley; Muddy Waters.

RELATED ARTICLES in *Great Events from History: The Twentieth Century:*

1941-1970: June, 1948-1964: Variety Shows Dominate Television Programming; January, 1963-1965: Beatles Revolutionize Popular Music; July 25, 1965: Dylan Performs with Electric Instruments; July 26 and September 24, 1965: Rolling Stones Release *Out of Our Heads*; June, 1967: Beatles Release *Sgt. Pepper's Lonely Hearts Club Band*.

1971-2000: November 8, 1971: Led Zeppelin Merges Hard Rock and Folk Music; December 8, 1980: Assassination of John Lennon; August 1, 1981: MTV Revolutionizes American Popular Culture.

SIMONE DE BEAUVOIR
French philosopher and novelist

Beauvoir cut across traditional academic fields to produce major works of literature, criticism, and philosophy, while her political activism anticipated the late twentieth century women's movement and made her a leading figure in the human rights, peace, and social reform movements.

BORN: January 9, 1908; Paris, France
DIED: April 14, 1986; Paris, France
ALSO KNOWN AS: Simone Lucie-Ernestine-Marie-Bertrand de Beauvoir (full name)
AREAS OF ACHIEVEMENT: Philosophy, women's rights, literature, social reform, peace advocacy

EARLY LIFE

Simone de Beauvoir (see-mohn duh boh-vwahr) was the eldest of two daughters born to Georges Bertrand and Françoise Brasseur de Beauvoir. Although her family was descended from the aristocracy, it teetered precariously on the brink of financial solvency, maintaining the status of upper-middle-class gentility with difficulty.

Beauvoir had a relatively happy childhood, which she described graphically in the first volume of her autobiography, *Mémoires d'une jeune fille rangée* (1958; *Memoirs of a Dutiful Daughter*, 1959). She especially treasured the summers that she spent at her grandfather's rambling estate at Meyrignac in Limousin, where she developed what would become lifelong passions for reading and hiking. In 1913, Beauvoir was enrolled at the private school Cours Désir.

In her autobiography, Beauvoir depicted herself as a precocious young girl chafing at the restraints placed on her both by society and by other persons' wills. The personal and ideological problems in her parents' marriage, created primarily by tension between her mother's religious piety and her father's cynical agnosticism, led Beauvoir to conclude that intellectual and spiritual life were mutually exclusive. This enabled her to reject both Roman Catholicism and the social role of "dutiful daughter" imposed on her by her parents. As Beauvoir entered her second decade, she developed an attraction for her cousin Jacques Laiguillon. Although she had strong feelings for him, she was afraid that their love would trap her into becoming a bourgeois wife, a role that she rejected as completely as she had the life of a "dutiful daughter."

In 1928, after completing her undergraduate education, she began working at the École Normale Supérieure on her *agrégation de philosophie*, a difficult postgraduate examination for teaching positions at *lycées* and universities in France. The next year, she met Jean-Paul Sartre, a fellow philosophy student. For the first time in her life Beauvoir found a soul mate who was her intellectual equal, a man with whom she knew she always would be compatible. In 1929, they passed the *agrégation* and began a liaison that would last a lifetime. During the same year, however, her happiness was marred by the death of her closest childhood friend, Elizabeth "Zaza" Mabille; this event marked both the end of the first volume of Beauvoir's memoirs and her childhood.

Simone de Beauvoir. (Hulton Archive/Getty Images)

LIFE'S WORK

Except for her work, the most important thing in Beauvoir's life was her relationship with Sartre. Because neither of them wanted children, they rejected the notion of traditional marriage in favor of a bond that they called an "essential" love, which was to be permanent but which would not exclude what they deemed "contingent" love affairs. In 1931, Sartre did suggest that they marry, but Beauvoir refused this proposal, arguing that they were not being true to their own principles.

In 1931, Beauvoir was appointed to teach in a *lycée* in Marseilles. The next year she transferred to Rouen, where she was reprimanded by *lycée* authorities for questioning women's traditional role in society. Sartre, also in Rouen, met Olga Kosakievicz, a former pupil of Beauvoir, with whom he fell in love. They experimented with a trio, which failed primarily because of Beauvoir's jealousy; the incident furnished her with the plot for her first novel, *L'Invitée* (1943; *She Came to Stay*, 1949). In 1936, Beauvoir was transferred to Paris, where Sartre was able to join her the following year.

Despite ominous clouds on the French political scene, in the prewar era Beauvoir and Sartre remained oblivious to the world around them, burying themselves in their work, their friends, and each other. The outbreak of World War II in 1939, however, marks a watershed in Beauvoir's life. Sartre's induction into the army brought Beauvoir face to face with social and political reality. They jointly adopted the philosophy of personal commitment, realizing that they had a responsibility to humanity as well as to themselves. During the German invasion of France in June, 1940, Sartre was taken prisoner, and Beauvoir, like many other Parisians, fled the capital only to return when the reality of defeat and German occupation became obvious. On April 1, 1941, Sartre was released and returned to Paris. Although Beauvoir and Sartre worked on the fringes of the French Resistance, they were not active participants in it.

During the war, both Beauvoir and Sartre abandoned their teaching careers to concentrate on writing. Her first novel, *She Came to Stay*, was an immediate success, and from 1943 on both she and Sartre were established as major new talents on the French intellectual horizon. In 1945, Beauvoir, Sartre, and others founded the journal *Les Temps modernes* as a vehicle for independent left-wing intellectual viewpoints. The same year, the novel that she had written during the war, *Le Sang des autres* (1945; *The Blood of Others*, 1948), was published to almost universal critical acclaim as the quintessential existentialist novel of the Resistance.

Her philosophical treatise, *Pour une morale de l'ambiguïté* (*The Ethics of Ambiguity*, 1948), a secular breviary of existentialist ethics, was published in 1947, the year Beauvoir first journeyed to the United States. There she met novelist Nelson Algren and began her first serious "contingent" love affair. Her four-year relationship with Algren resulted in a proposal of marriage, which she rejected both because of her commitment to Sartre and because of her disinclination to leave France. After several transatlantic visits, the affair ended in bitterness when Beauvoir used their relationship as a basis for her novel *Les Mandarins* (1954; *The Mandarins*, 1956), which won the prestigious Prix de Goncourt for literature in 1954.

Throughout her life, Beauvoir, an avid traveler, visited most of the world's exciting venues, recording her thoughts and storing her memories for use in her writing. In the fall of 1949, her most famous book, *Le Deuxième Sexe* (*The Second Sex*, 1953), was published. This massive work discusses the role and condition of women throughout history from biological, psychological, historical, sociological, and philosophical perspectives. Two of its most important tenets—the concept that man has defined himself as the essential being, the subject, who has consigned woman to the subordinate position of object or "Other," and the idea that there is no such thing as "feminine nature," that one is not born a woman but becomes one through social conditioning—served as an important basis for the resurrection of the women's liberation movement in the mid-twentieth century.

In 1952, Beauvoir began her second "contingent" liaison, this time with Claude Lanzmann, an able filmmaker and journalist seventeen years her junior. This affair, which ended in 1958, was to be the last important romantic interlude in her "essential" love relationship with Sartre.

Two important changes occurred in Beauvoir's life during the last half of the 1950's. First, her political views hardened and grew stronger as the culpability of the French army in the torture of Algerians became increasingly obvious and the world moved closer to the brink of nuclear war. Beauvoir's commitment to political activism intensified at this time, and she embarked on a series of public demonstrations against Charles de Gaulle, French torture in Algeria, nuclear war, and social

---

"ONE IS NOT BORN . . . A WOMAN"

Simone de Beauvoir's answer to her own blunt question "Woman?" has become a philosophical and political classic. The following is taken from her infamous and much-debated work The Second Sex, *first published in 1949 in France.*

Woman? Very simple, say the fanciers of simple formulas: she is a womb, an ovary; she is a female—this word is sufficient to define her. . . .

One is not born, but rather becomes, a woman. No biological, psychological, or economic fate determines the figure that the human female presents in society; it is civilization as a whole that produces this creature, intermediate between male and eunuch, which is described as feminine. Only the intervention of someone else can establish an individual as an Other. . . .

---

injustice. The second major change was in Beauvoir's writing. She all but abandoned fiction for several years to begin the first of what would become a four-volume autobiography and a variety of other nonfiction works. She would not return to the novel form until the publication of *Les Belles Images* (1966; English translation, 1969), which was followed in 1968 by her last major work of fiction, *La Femme rompue* (1967; *The Woman Destroyed*, 1968). These two volumes are shorter than her four earlier novels but, like them, follow in a long tradition of French women writers who have focused their work on women's lives and ambitions.

In 1967, Beauvoir again increased her commitment to political activism, raising the issue of women's rights in Israel and taking part in Bertrand Russell's Tribunal of War Crimes, which met in Copenhagen to investigate U.S. involvement in the Vietnam War. The following May, she and Sartre became active supporters of the revolutionary students at the Sorbonne. During this phase of her politically active life, Beauvoir was preparing *La Viellese* (1970; *The Coming of Age*, 1972), a lengthy but critically acclaimed study of aging that attacked modern society's indifference to the problems of the elderly.

In 1969, Beauvoir was elected to the consultative committee of the Bibliothèque Nationale (national library) as a "man of letters." Soon thereafter she became actively involved in the women's movement, joining a series of demonstrations led by the Mouvement de la Libération des Femmes in 1970. The next year she signed the Manifesto of 343, signed by French women who publicly admitted to having had illegal abortions. Soon after the publication of the manifesto, Beauvoir publicly declared herself to be a radical feminist, explaining that she had eschewed the reformist, legalistic feminism of the past but eagerly embraced the radical movement of the 1970's. In 1972, she joined street demonstrations protesting crimes against women and the next year began a feminist column in *Les Temps modernes*. She renewed this feminist commitment by becoming president of the Ligue des Droits des Femmes (French league of the rights of women) in 1974, the same year in which she was selected to receive the Jerusalem Prize for writers who have promoted the freedom of the individual.

On April 15, 1980, the lifelong "essential" love of Beauvoir and Jean-Paul Sartre ended with Sartre's death. The following year, Beauvoir published *La Cérémonie des adieux* (1981; *Adieux: A Farewell to Sartre*, 1984), a sober narrative that recorded Sartre's mental and physical decline with a brutal honesty that seemed to her to be the final tribute she could pay to him. Although Beauvoir wrote no major literary works after Sartre's death, she remained politically active. She died of pneumonia in a Paris hospital on April 14, 1986, and was entombed with Sartre's ashes in the Montparnasse Cemetery. More than five thousand people attended the funeral to which women's organizations throughout the world sent floral tributes.

Significance

Beauvoir lived her adult life in such a way that it illustrated the most important tenets of existentialist ethics, especially the concepts of social responsibility and commitment. Her development from a politically indifferent young woman to a socially committed adult and, finally, to a mature woman radical in the causes of women's rights (and human rights) is chronicled in the four volumes of her autobiography. While Beauvoir's existentialist views are presented somewhat didactically in her nonfiction and philosophical essays, in her novels they are infused with nuances of ambiguity and expressed in less strident prose. She used literature to present the real world to her readers by stripping away the insulating layers of hypocrisy that she believed bourgeois society installs to obscure truth. In this way, she believed, words could be enlisted as a weapon to help obliterate selfishness and indifference in the modern world.

In the post-World War II era, Beauvoir became one of the most visible and influential left-wing advocates of social justice, peaceful coexistence, and women's rights. Because her life and work supported her belief in sexual and social equality, Beauvoir contributed immeasurably by word and by example to elevating the consciousness of men and women as well as improving the quality of their lives. She is one of the most important writers of the twentieth century because of both the literature that she created and the legacy of social and political commitment that she provided.

—Nancy Ellen Rupprecht

Further Reading

Beauvoir, Simone de. *The Second Sex*. Translated and edited by H. M. Parshley. New York: Vintage Books, 1989. Beauvoir's classic, philosophical work on the position of women in society.

Bieber, Konrad. *Simone de Beauvoir*. Boston: Twayne, 1979. Combines a lengthy analysis of Beauvoir's autobiography with studies of her literary works and a short biography of her life. Bieber's work is well balanced, thoughtful, and impartial. Contains a short annotated bibliography.

Card, Claudia, ed. *The Cambridge Companion to Simone de Beauvoir*. New York: Cambridge University Press, 2003. Collection of essays examining Beauvoir's life and work, including her place in philosophical thought, her feminism, her thoughts on aging, and the influence of Martin Heidegger and Henri Bergson on her philosophy.

Marks, Elaine. *Simone de Beauvoir: Encounters with Death*. New Brunswick, N.J.: Rutgers University Press, 1973. Perhaps the best single work on Beauvoir's literary contribution. In addition to a brilliant and perceptive study of death in Beauvoir's literary and autobiographical works, Marks analyzes the themes and philosophy that permeate her literary canon.

Marso, Lori Jo, and Patricia Moynagh, eds. *Simone de Beauvoir's Political Thinking*. Urbana: University of Illinois Press, 2006. An examination of Beauvoir's political thought, with chapters on her "unsettling of the universal," her ethics, her work set against and also in comparison to that of philosopher Michel Foucault, and more. Bibliography and index.

Okely, Judith. *Simone de Beauvoir*. New York: Pantheon Books, 1986. A somewhat partisan treatment of Beauvoir that concentrates heavily on *The Second Sex* and Beauvoir's feminism. Contains an excellent chronology.

Rowley, Hazel. *Tête-à-Tête: Simone de Beauvoir and Jean-Paul Sartre*. New York: HarperCollins, 2005. A story of the couple's relationship to each other and with many other people as well. Rowley details the couple's many lovers, friendships, and affairs, demonstrating how their most significant commitments were not to each other but to their politics, writing, and philosophies.

Tidd, Ursula. *Simone de Beauvoir*. New York: Routledge, 2004. Part of the Routledge Critical Thinkers series, this brief but important work discusses Beauvoir's existentialism, ethics, her ideas on "becoming woman," feminism, literature, and aging. Includes an extensive bibliography and an index.

Whitmarsh, Anne. *Simone de Beauvoir and the Limits of Commitment*. New York: Cambridge University Press, 1981. Studies the life and works of Beauvoir in the light of her political convictions and her relationship with Sartre.

SEE ALSO: Henri Bergson; Charlotte Perkins Gilman; Martin Heidegger; Edmund Husserl; Gabriel Marcel; Muriel Rukeyser; Bertrand Russell; Jean-Paul Sartre; Edith Stein; Simone Weil; Virginia Woolf; Clara Zetkin.

RELATED ARTICLES in *Great Events from History: The Twentieth Century:*

1941-1970: June 25, 1943: Sartre's *Being and Nothingness* Expresses Existential Philosophy; 1949: Beauvoir's *The Second Sex* Anticipates the Women's Movement.

1971-2000: 1974: D'Eaubonne Coins the Term "Ecofeminism."

LORD BEAVERBROOK
Canadian businessman and politician

Beaverbrook created the most successful newspaper empire of his day and, in World War II, as minister of aircraft production, was greatly responsible for the victory in the Battle of Britain. After the war, Beaverbrook was one of Prime Minister Winston Churchill's chief advisers.

BORN: May 25, 1879; Maple, Ontario, Canada
DIED: June 9, 1964; Cherkley, Surrey, England
ALSO KNOWN AS: William Maxwell Aitken (birth name); Sir Maxwell Aitken; First Baron Beaverbrook
AREAS OF ACHIEVEMENT: Business and industry, military affairs, government and politics, journalism

EARLY LIFE

William Maxwell Aitken, best known as Lord Beaverbrook, was born in Maple, Ontario, Canada, where his father was a Presbyterian minister. The family soon moved to Newcastle, New Brunswick, where young Max grew up. His father, William Cuthbert Aitken, had emigrated from Scotland to pursue a ministerial career, and his mother, Jane Noble, Canadian by birth but also of Scottish ancestry, was the daughter of a storekeeper. Although later in life Beaverbrook referred to his relatively poor background, in fact it was comfortably middle-class. He was the third of ten children. His was a happy childhood and Beaverbrook early developed a reputation for mischief, something he kept throughout his life. He attended a local school but failed the Latin portion of his

college entrance examinations and instead chose the law for a career.

It was business and finance, however, which brought Beaverbrook his fortune. The early twentieth century was a period of economic expansion in Canada, and Beaverbrook became successful in taking over companies, combining them with others, and using the profits to invest again and again. He soon had economic interests not only in Canada but also in the West Indies and was a millionaire before his thirtieth birthday. Beaverbrook rarely became involved in the day-to-day operation of his companies. For him, the thrill and the reward of business were in the act of creation itself, with its challenge and excitement. He had little patience, became bored easily, and preferred the new to the old. Nevertheless, from a distance he watched his investments and rarely lost money.

In 1906, Beaverbrook married Gladys Henderson, the nineteen-year-old daughter of a Canadian military officer. Beaverbrook loved his wife, but not exclusively; he often left her alone, surrounded by luxury, as he pursued his business and other interests. They had three children, two boys and a girl. By 1910, Beaverbrook had also acquired financial interests in Great Britain, and in that year the family moved to London. He returned to Canada, but never for any length of time.

LIFE'S WORK

For most individuals, Beaverbrook's financial and business successes would have been sufficient accomplishments, but not for him. In London, he became acquainted with a leading Conservative politician, Bonar Law, also a

Beaverbrook, Lord

Lord Beaverbrook. (Library of Congress)

Canadian whose father had been a Presbyterian minister. Their relationship was initially financial but soon became political and personal; Law became Beaverbrook's hero. In December, 1910, with Law's support, Beaverbrook was elected to the House of Commons as a Conservative; the following year, Beaverbrook was granted a knighthood. Undoubtedly, his political successes were the result of his acquaintanceships and his money. In some circles, he had the reputation of being merely a Canadian adventurer and thus not quite proper, but he was generous to his friends and had a captivating personality that impressed not only Law but also such Liberal politicians as David Lloyd George and Winston Churchill. Beaverbrook was of average height, five feet nine inches, but because of his quickness, he often appeared smaller; when his eyes flashed and his smile spread all across his face, he seemed still a mischievous boy yet to grow up. He was always an apt subject for political cartoons.

Unlike Churchill, Beaverbrook found the day-to-day political world boring, and he cared little about the political issues that divided the various parties. Beaverbrook was more radical and less class-conscious than most British politicians of the day, but he opposed socialism and was very much the individualist who believed in capitalism. When World War I began, Beaverbrook joined the Canadian army. He still retained his interest in making new mergers out of old firms, however, and thus became intimately involved in the political revolution of December, 1916, which saw Lloyd George replace H. H. Asquith as prime minister of the coalition government in England. In 1917, Beaverbrook accepted a seat in the British House of Lords (obtaining the name Lord Beaverbrook, for a small river that flowed near his childhood home in New Brunswick). Later in the war, he became minister of information in Lloyd George's government.

Although he had helped Lloyd George become prime minister, Beaverbrook had doubts about the continuation of the coalition into peacetime. In 1921 and 1922, many political discussions were held at Cherkley, Beaverbrook's country home near London. Finally, in late 1922, Lloyd George fell, and Law became prime minister. Unfortunately for Beaverbrook, Law died of cancer within a year, and the new Conservative leader, Stanley Baldwin, distrusted Beaverbrook, who returned his sentiments.

During most of the 1920's and 1930's, Beaverbrook observed politics from the outside. Lloyd George's political influence was over, and although Churchill served in the Baldwin government during the 1920's, his relations with Beaverbrook lessened. Beaverbrook's great energies, however, found new outlets. During the war, he had purchased, primarily for political reasons, the London *Daily Express*, a successful newspaper in financial difficulty. In 1919, Beaverbrook began the *Sunday Express*, and a few years later he acquired the London *Evening Standard*. He had become one of the leading newspaper barons on Fleet Street. In the late nineteenth century, Alfred Harmsworth, later Lord Northcliffe, had founded, in his *Daily Mail*, a new style of journalism, addressed to the middle and lower classes rather than the traditional establishment, and whose function was to entertain rather than simply inform; the *Daily Mail* was exciting and it was cheap and had many readers. Beaverbrook followed the path earlier trod by Northcliffe but with a difference. The *Daily Express* was not directed to any particular portion of the British population but was rather Britain's first classless newspaper. Possibly it could have been created only by an outsider, a Canadian such as Beaverbrook who himself was not a product of the British social system.

Beaverbrook rarely entered the offices of his newspapers, but he was intimately involved in their operation. He would telephone several times a day, and, if abroad, he sent and received correspondence on a daily basis. Although he was nominally a member of the Conservative Party, Beaverbrook was not necessarily committed to many of the policies of that party, and after Law's death he was out of sympathy with the leadership as long as Baldwin was in power. His papers thus were not automatically supportive of any particular party position, and he had as writers and cartoonists individuals who reflected various views. On certain issues, however, Beaverbrook would allow little dissent. Possibly because he was Canadian by birth, he was committed to the preservation of the British Empire, although in reality he knew little about it, other than Canada. To maintain the Empire, Beaverbrook waged a campaign for what he called Empire Free Trade, or the concept that there should be some type of free trade within the Empire and tariffs erected against nonimperial countries. In the early 1930's, Beaverbrook pushed imperial goals and used his newspapers in doing so, but most politicians, particularly Baldwin, were opposed to his campaign, and his dream died. Still, his papers prospered, and eventually the *Daily Express* became the largest newspaper in the world, with a daily circulation of more than four million copies.

Given his belief in the British Empire, it is not surprising that Beaverbrook took an isolationist position toward Europe. After the no-man's-land of World War I, no one wished for another war, even with the rise of Adolf Hitler. Many in Britain tended toward pacifism in the 1930's or at most preferred to rely on the League of Nations. Beaverbrook had no faith in the league, wishing to rely on the British Empire; he was also no pacifist. He agreed with Churchill on the need for Britain to rearm but disagreed with Churchill's attempt to rally France and other continental nations against Germany. In the late 1930's, he supported Neville Chamberlain's policy of appeasement and approved of the Munich settlement that led to the dismemberment of Czechoslovakia. His newspapers stated, year after year, that there would be no war that year. In 1939, they were wrong, and World War II began.

In May, 1940, as Germany turned west against France, Chamberlain was replaced as prime minister by Churchill, and Beaverbrook once again returned to influence. Churchill was in his mid-sixties, and most of his peers from the Great War were either dead or retired. Beaverbrook was the exception. He gave Churchill a link to the past, but more important, Beaverbrook's energy and enthusiasm gave support to Churchill during the dark days of World War II. Beaverbrook's significance, however, transcended the personal. Churchill appointed him minister of aircraft production, a controversial move that was popular among neither the military nor the civil servants. It was an inspired appointment, however, and Beaverbrook was a brilliant minister, mobilizing resources, disbursing factories, and creating the fighter de-

fense that was able to resist Hitler's assaults during the Battle of Britain. His methods were unorthodox, and many thought that he was shortsighted in his concentration on fighter aircraft rather than bombers, but Beaverbrook was interested only in the day-to-day need of his nation to survive.

In 1941, Beaverbrook left the ministry of aircraft production and became minister of state, then minister of supply, and finally minister of production. In none of those positions, however, was he successful. He did not work well in committees and did not get along with other members of the cabinet. At most, Beaverbrook was willing to work under someone whom he greatly admired, such as Law or Churchill. In late 1941, Beaverbrook journeyed to Moscow and became a major supporter of military supplies for the Soviet Union and one of the major advocates for the opening of a second front in Europe against Germany. Churchill was less committed to an early cross-channel invasion, but after the decision had been made to invade Normandy in 1944, the two reconciled and Beaverbrook returned to the government. After victory in Europe, the wartime coalition disbanded and elections were held. Beaverbrook was one of Churchill's chief advisers, and when Churchill and the Conservatives were surprisingly defeated by the Labour Party, Beaverbrook was blamed, unfairly, for the debacle. It was the end of his political career; after 1945, he only watched from the sidelines.

SIGNIFICANCE

During the last twenty years of his life, Beaverbrook continued his active involvement in his newspapers, although he often denied that he was really in control. Before World War II, he had bought a villa in southern France, which he visited each year during his retirement. He became chancellor of the University of New Brunswick, gave much financial support to the university, and spent part of each fall in Canada. He never gave up his English country home, but now it was only a part-time residence. He became a collector of manuscripts, acquiring those of Lloyd George and Law, among others. He eventually returned to the writing of history; in the 1920's, he had written the story of the political crisis of 1916 (*Politicians and the War*, 1928-1932), and in his last decade he wrote two other major works on the period up to the fall of Lloyd George in 1922 (*Men and Power*, 1956; *The Decline and Fall of Lloyd George*, 1963). He also had been involved in the abdication crisis of 1936 and wrote a brief study of that episode (*The Abdication of Edward VIII*, 1966).

Beaverbrook opposed the onset of the Cold War, optimistically hoping that the wartime alliance with the Soviet Union could be continued. His last political crusade was against the proposal to have Britain join the Common Market in the early 1960's. He still believed that, for Britain, isolation from Europe and partnership with the Commonwealth nations was the proper course. His wife, Gladys, had died in 1927, but it was not until 1963 that Beaverbrook married again; the bride was Lady Christofor Dunn, widow of a wealthy Canadian friend. Beaverbrook often suffered from asthma, particularly in times of stress, but his general health remained good until well into his eighties. He died at Cherkley in June, 1964, and his ashes were returned to Newcastle, New Brunswick, the land of his birth.

Beaverbrook's Canadian background gave him a dimension that most of his British colleagues lacked. He was something of an outsider in England, but an influential outsider. He became Britain's most successful newspaper publisher, he was one of the foremost spokespeople for the concept of the British Empire, and finally, in World War II, he was among those most responsible for winning the Battle of Britain.

—Eugene S. Larson

FURTHER READING

Allen, Robert. *Voice of Britain: The Inside Story of the Daily Express*. Cambridge, England: P. Stephens, 1983. This somewhat brief and slight book is valuable as a short history of Beaverbrook's most successful newspaper and as a compendium of many illustrations of actual front pages, cartoons, and other material from the paper.

Busch, Briton C., ed. *Canada and the Great War: Western Front Association Papers*. Montreal: McGill-Queen's University Press, 2003. Includes the essay by Canadian national archivist Tim Cook, "Lord Beaverbrook and the Canadian War Records Office in the First World War."

Cannadine, David. *History in Our Time*. New Haven, Conn.: Yale University Press, 1998. Collection of essays about British history, including a profile of Lord Beaverbrook.

Churchill, Winston S. *The Second World War*. 6 vols. London: Cassell, 1948-1954. Churchill's personal account of World War II is one of the historical classics of the twentieth century. Beaverbrook plays an important part in the work, and Churchill praised him particularly for his contribution to victory in the Battle of Britain.

Cudlipp, Hugh. *The Prerogative of the Harlot: Press Barons and Power*. London: Bodley Head, 1980. Cudlipp, a journalist, worked for Beaverbrook and includes a long essay on Beaverbrook in his discussion of several twentieth century newspaper publishers, including William Randolph Hearst, Henry R. Luce, and Lord Northcliffe. The title refers to Stanley Baldwin's statement against Beaverbrook during the Empire Free Trade campaign.

Pound, Reginald, and Geoffrey Harmsworth. *Northcliffe*. London: Cassell, 1959. An extensive account of Beaverbrook's predecessor in the establishment of the popular press in Great Britain. Northcliffe had died in the early 1920's, but his brother, Lord Rothermere, was Beaverbrook's major newspaper rival during the interwar years.

Taylor, A. J. P. *Beaverbrook*. New York: Simon & Schuster, 1972. Taylor's biography is the major work on Beaverbrook. The author, one of Great Britain's most respected historians, was a personal friend during the last several years of Beaverbrook's life, and the portrait painted by Taylor is both admiring and sympathetic but is not entirely uncritical.

_____. *English History: 1914-1945*. New York: Oxford University Press, 1965. Beaverbrook's biographer has here written the volume in the Oxford History of England series that covers both a crucial period in the history of Great Britain and the primary portion of Beaverbrook's public life. Taylor's interpretations are not entirely unbiased, but those biases were often those of Beaverbrook himself.

Young, Kenneth. *Churchill and Beaverbrook: A Study in Friendship and Politics*. London: Eyre and Spottiswoode, 1966. An excellent and well-written account of the two larger-than-life figures. Young details not only their political relationship but also their long personal friendship, and it is the latter that particularly remains with readers.

SEE ALSO: Sir Norman Angell; Stanley Baldwin; Horatio W. Bottomley; Neville Chamberlain; Sir Winston Churchill; Alfred and Harold Harmsworth; William Randolph Hearst; Bonar Law; David Lloyd George; Clare Boothe Luce; Henry R. Luce; Duke of Windsor.

RELATED ARTICLES in *Great Events from History: The Twentieth Century:*

1901-1940: October, 1909: Canada Cement Affair Prompts Legislative Reform; August, 1930-1935: Bennett Era in Canada; July 10-October 31, 1940: Battle of Britain.

SAMUEL BECKETT
Irish poet, playwright, and novelist

Beckett created a corpus of drama and fiction that established him as one of the greatest writers of the twentieth century. He helped to inspire the New Novel movement, and his existentialist focus detailed the absurdities of human life.

BORN: April 13, 1906; Foxrock, near Dublin, Ireland
DIED: December 22, 1989; Paris, France
ALSO KNOWN AS: Samuel Barclay Beckett (full name)
AREAS OF ACHIEVEMENT: Literature, theater and entertainment

EARLY LIFE

Samuel Beckett (BEH-keht) was the second of two sons born to wealthy, Anglo-Irish, Protestant parents, William and Mary Beckett. William Frank Beckett, Jr., was a self-made businessman who amassed a considerable fortune as a quantity surveyor for builders. He was bluff, robust, and coarse, with a streak of stubborn cruelty that insisted his sons strain their bodies performing demanding athletic feats. Beckett's mother, Mary Roe (called "May"), came from a moneyed, leisured background that she defied by working as a nurse in the Dublin hospital where she met her husband-to-be. She was even more forceful and demanding than her husband, with a biting wit, imperious manner, and autocratic temperament. While William often laughed and sported with his boys, May grew increasingly stern, formal, and censorious. She may well have been the model for the troubled, embittered mothers in Beckett's works.

"I had little talent for happiness," Beckett recalled of his childhood. "I was often lonely." True, young Beckett excelled in athletics at the Portora Royal School in Northern Ireland, starring on the cricket and rugby teams, while also playing tennis, swimming, and boxing, but he puzzled his classmates with his aloofness, melancholy, reserve, and sullen rebelliousness; his teasing was often vicious. He followed his brother to Trinity College, Dublin, in 1923, spending his first two years there dabbling at his studies. In his third year, he discovered the charm of modern languages, improved his grades impressively, and took a cycling trip through France, in the summer of 1926, which instilled in him a growing fondness for that nation. In December, 1927, he received his B.A. degree from Trinity with first rank in modern languages. His reward was a two-year exchange lectureship at the distinguished École Normale Supérieure. The École's ex-change scholar at Trinity, Alfred Péron, became his lifelong friend and thawed some of Beckett's social shyness with his congeniality and popularity.

In Paris, Beckett was introduced to the great Irish expatriate author James Joyce. For years, Joyce served as both a surrogate father to Beckett and his standard for artistic integrity and commitment. Joyce welcomed Beckett into the coterie of willing young men who hunted down obscure references and took direction for their master's *Work in Progress*, which was to be published as *Finnegans Wake* (1939). At Joyce's urging, Beckett contributed an essay, "Dante . . . Bruno. Vico . . . Joyce," to a 1929 volume devoted to criticism of the novel that would consume sixteen years of Joyce's life. In 1930, Beckett translated, with Péron, the "Anna Livia Plurabelle" section of *Work in Progress*.

Concurrently, Beckett was seriously studying philosophy, particularly René Descartes. When the Parisian Hours Press offered a prize of one thousand francs for the best poem about time, Beckett wrote, in one night, a ninety-eight-line punning poem, *Whoroscope* (1930), which described Descartes's life in an oblique but witty manner that earned for him the prize and his first separate publication.

Whoroscope caused two of Beckett's friends to suggest him to a London publisher for a short study on Marcel Proust. The resulting monograph, *Proust* (1931), anticipates several of the themes Beckett would develop in his mature work: love as painful frustration, friendship as largely an illusion, habit as "the ballast that chains the dog to his vomit," and recognition of "that irremediable solitude to which every human being is condemned." The text is as much a self-diagnosis of Beckett's state of mind and heart as it is of Proust's, stressing the painfulness of life, the unlikelihood of joys, the assuredness of suffering—and turning to art as the only viable consolation.

In December, 1931, Beckett took his M.A. degree from Trinity but became seriously depressed at the prospect of an academic career. He resigned from Trinity in 1932 after only a few months in the classroom, fled to the Continent, and wrote a novel that has remained unpublished, "Dream of Fair to Middling Women." In June, 1933, his father died of a heart attack, leaving him an annuity of two hundred pounds annually. Beckett spent the next three years in London, writing some poetry and more fiction, maintaining an increasingly angry relationship with his taunting mother (who compared him unfavorably to his successful businessman-brother), and undergoing a two-year Jungian psychoanalysis, which he abandoned in 1936.

His collection of ten stories, *More Pricks than Kicks* (1934), focuses on an indolent young Irishman, Belacqua Shuah, who wanders through Ireland though plagued by bad feet. The collection contains one great story, "Dante and the Lobster," which concludes with an extraordinarily powerful passage, full of anguished compassion for all living creatures—even a lobster about to be boiled alive by Belacqua's aunt. Beckett here found his voice and style as a significant writer: language that was precisely controlled, swinging from the colloquial to the cosmic; a tone that altered hilarity with somber despair; and a sad affirmation of pain and injustice as life's leading realities.

LIFE'S WORK
In his late twenties and early thirties, Beckett was a frequently depressed and close-to-impoverished, struggling writer, miserably shuttling between London and Dublin, chafing at the slowness of his analysis, drinking heavily, suffering several breakdowns. Published photographs feature what was to become a famous gaunt, aquiline

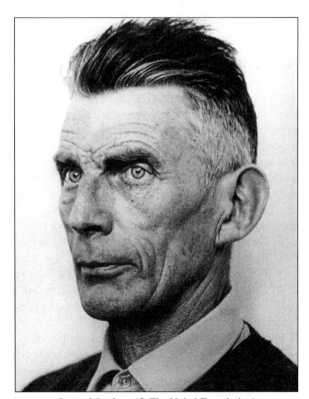

Samuel Beckett. (© The Nobel Foundation)

profile, with a furrowed forehead, sparrowhawk eyes, lined cheeks, and a wide-eyed, anguished stare. What probably saved him from self-destruction was his writing, particularly his first novel, *Murphy*, on which he worked, off and on, between 1934 and the end of 1937; rejected by forty-one publishers, it was first issued by Routledge in 1938 but received almost no critical attention.

The novel is remarkable for its linguistic dexterity, sophisticated humor, and brilliant fusion of philosophical implications with a fluently propelled narrative. Beckett's solipsistic protagonist is a prototype of Watt, Moran, Molloy, and Malone. Murphy is a lazy theological student who—like Beckett—has come to London from Ireland. He lives with a kindhearted whore, Celia, who threatens to return to streetwalking unless he finds work. He becomes a mental hospital attendant but spends most of his energy examining his own mind, regarding it, in Cartesian fashion, as containing everything in the universe. Beckett expressed at length in this text the leading themes of his mature work: loneliness, isolation, physical disintegration, mental alienation, creative failure, and the tragic split between mind and body, self and society, with human reason a ludicrously inadequate instrument for controlling a world of chance and disorder. Murphy's mind and body are united only when both are killed in a gas explosion; his friends soon go on with their own lives: Pity is in short supply.

In October, 1937, Beckett moved back to Paris, largely to escape his domineering mother. He resumed his friendship with Joyce, which had been disrupted after Beckett, in the early 1930's, had rejected the persistent advances of Joyce's schizoid daughter, Lucia. In early 1938, Beckett accepted the advances of the American heiress Peggy Guggenheim; as usual, his part in the brief affair was largely passive; she called him "Oblomov," after the lethargic hero of Ivan Goncharov's novel (1859).

In January, 1938, a pimp accosted Beckett for money on a Parisian street, then stabbed him, barely missing his heart. A piano student, Suzanne Deschevaux-Dumésnil, happened to witness the assault. She became a frequent bedside visitor during his hospital stay and decided to establish herself as his life's companion; again, Beckett simply allowed himself to be mastered.

An excellent seamstress, Deschevaux-Dumésnil sewed for a number of years to augment their income, especially in the late 1940's. She was pleased to devote her life totally to his needs, supplying his routine requirements for food, laundry, and linen, as well as zealously protecting his privacy. Both were intensely shy persons who preferred a reclusive existence with few friendships; Deschevaux-Dumésnil proved even more averse than Beckett to social gatherings. After many years of cohabitation, they married on March 25, 1961, for the same legal reason that Joyce finally married Nora Barnacle: so that the wife would have no difficulty inheriting the husband's estate.

From early 1938 until the outbreak of World War II in September, 1939, Beckett succumbed to spells of lethargy, writing very little. With the coming of war he renounced his previous apolitical views, recognized Adolf Hitler as a demoniac leader capable of "making life hell for my friends," and joined one of the earliest French Resistance units in October, 1940. He served largely as a *boîte aux lettres* (dropping point), translating information gathered by his group into English for further communication to officials in England. When Péron, another group member, was arrested by the Gestapo, his wife warned Samuel and Suzanne in time for them to flee Paris and make their way to unoccupied France, where they passed themselves off as peasants until the war's end. In 1945, Beckett was awarded the Croix de Guerre for his intelligence work.

Beckett spent his evening hours from 1942 to 1944 composing the novel *Watt*, which he could not get published until 1953. It is his most Kafkaesque text, with significant parallels to Franz Kafka's *The Castle* (1926). Watt works as a servant for a Mr. Knott, who is unpredictable and unknowable—an inscrutable God mocking the hearts of all who seek him. Watt's journey to and from Knott's mansion is a characteristically Beckettian journey toward ignorance, incommunicability, and chaos. The book was his last to be written first in English; his decision to make French his original writing language is one Beckett never fully explained.

In 1947, Beckett began the most fertile phase of his

STILL WAITING FOR GODOT

In this opening scene from Samuel Beckett's Waiting for Godot *(pb. 1952), Estragon and Vladimir, tramps who become inseparable in their misery, set up the general mood of the play when one of them says "Nothing to be done," a simple yet profound commentary on the absurdity of life after World War II.*

A country road. A tree. Evening. Estragon, sitting on a low mound, is trying to take off his boot. He pulls at it with both hands, panting. He gives up, exhausted, rests, tries again.

As before. Enter Vladimir.

ESTRAGON: (giving up again). Nothing to be done.

VLADIMIR: (advancing with short, stiff strides, legs wide apart). I'm beginning to come round to that opinion. All my life I've tried to put it from me, saying Vladimir, be reasonable, you haven't yet tried everything. And I resumed the struggle. (He broods, musing on the struggle. Turning to Estragon.) So there you are again.

ESTRAGON: Am I?

VLADIMIR: I'm glad to see you back. I thought you were gone forever.

ESTRAGON: Me too.

VLADIMIR: Together again at last! We'll have to celebrate this. But how? (He reflects.) Get up till I embrace you.

ESTRAGON: (irritably). Not now, not now.

VLADIMIR: (hurt, coldly). May one inquire where His Highness spent the night?

ESTRAGON: In a ditch.

VLADIMIR: (admiringly). A ditch! Where?

ESTRAGON: (without gesture). Over there.

VLADIMIR: And they didn't beat you?

ESTRAGON: Beat me? Certainly they beat me.

VLADIMIR: The same lot as usual?

ESTRAGON: The same? I don't know.

VLADIMIR: When I think of it . . . all these years . . . but for me . . . where would you be . . . (Decisively.) You'd be nothing more than a little heap of bones at the present minute, no doubt about it.

ESTRAGON: And what of it?

VLADIMIR: (gloomily). It's too much for one man. (Pause. Cheerfully.) On the other hand what's the good of losing heart now, that's what I say. We should have thought of it a million years ago, in the nineties.

ESTRAGON: Ah stop blathering and help me off with this bloody thing.

---

career: six years during which he completed a trilogy of novels that are usually regarded as his major fictional texts—*Molloy* (1951; English translation, 1955), *Malone meurt* (1951; *Malone Dies*, 1956), *L'Innommable* (1953; *The Unnamable*, 1958)—and his most famous play, *En attendant Godot* (1952; *Waiting for Godot*, 1954). He decided that he would begin all of his writing from his memories and dreams, no matter how painful, and that in his fiction he would construct first-person monologues, with all speakers variants of the same protagonist/voice.

He resigned himself to being "doomed to spend the rest of my days digging up the detritus of my life and vomiting it out over and over again."

Beckett wrote *Molloy* between September, 1947, and January, 1948. He found himself writing "with élan, in a sort of enthusiasm." The novel consists of two parts: In the first, Molloy tells a disconnected tale of his absurd, compulsive voyage toward his mother; in the second, Moran, a middle-aged Roman Catholic father, writes the story of his quest to seek Molloy. In *Malone Dies*, the paralytic Malone, toothless and dying, writes to relieve his misery and to achieve self-knowledge. In *The Unnamable*, the fable is narrated by an unnamed man who inhabits a jar in a window, lacks features or protuberances, and finds himself compelled to speak in half-incoherent, ominous, intense undertones from what may be an underworld. The only theme seems to be the human need to use language, however dire his condition. The concluding words, "you must go on, I can't go on, I'll go on," have become the bywords of Absurdism.

Waiting for Godot was written by Beckett from October 9, 1948, to January 29, 1949, as a diversion from the relentless pessimism of his trilogy, between the conclusion of *Malone Dies* and inception of *The Unnamable*. The play is static in plot and spare in setting, fiercely concentrating on a quartet of characters who divide into two couples. The more important pair, Vladimir and Estragon, await the coming of the mysterious Godot; the other two, Pozzo and Lucky, are locked into a sadomasochistic master/slave relationship. The drama's meaning has puzzled and fascinated an army of critics. At a minimum, the work conveys the boredom and anguish of the human search for significance in a bleak and cruelly empty world. Beckett's first biographer, Deirdre Bair, has recorded Beckett's view that *Waiting for Godot* is a flawed play, by no means his "outstanding expression of theatrical ability."

The Beckett text that has tantalized readers and critics even more than *Waiting for Godot* is *Fin de partie* (1957; *Endgame*, 1957), perhaps his most complex and surely his most brilliant play. It is an apocalyptic coda to *Waiting for Godot*, reversing the myth of Genesis to indicate the disintegration of the world—possibly after a nuclear holocaust. Beckett maintains the metaphor of life as a play, having a blind, paralyzed Hamm verbally abuse his servant and possible son, Clov, and his dying parents, relegated to what may be the dustbin of Western values. Is Hamm an anti-Prospero announcing the death of humanity? He wearily says, "Old endgame lost of old, play and lose and have done with losing."

From the late 1950's on, both Beckett's fiction and his drama are characterized by increasing experimentation in form with the retention of his basic version of sterile, hopeless desolation. His techniques become increasingly minimal as he evokes the diminishing capacity of his characters. They do less and less as he pares down his literary means to the fewest, barest bones, reducing his texts to the condition nearest silence.

To illustrate: In *Krapp's Last Tape* (1958), a sixty-nine-year-old shuffler contrasts his present shell to his vigorous self when, at thirty-nine, he recorded a tape over which the old man sadly meditates; *Happy Days* (1961) has Winnie prattling cheerfully as she sinks further and further into her sandy grave; *Play* (1963) encases a man, his wife, and his mistress in urns, trapped into repeating the sordid details of their triangle; *Come and Go: Dramaticule* (in German, 1965; in English, 1967) has three dying women review their lives in three minutes; *Breath* (1969) has no actors, no words, only a bit of rubbish onstage, a dim light, two faint cries (birth and death?), then silence; *Not I* (1973) is a twelve-minute monologue for a spotlit female mouth, breathlessly summarizing a wretched life whose import the woman denies.

After having been nominated for the Nobel Prize in Literature from 1957 onward, Beckett received it in 1969. Characteristically, he was absent from the award ceremonies; also characteristically, he distributed the prize money among a number of needy artists, printers, scholars, and old friends. In his old age, he continued to live quietly and work steadily in either a Parisian apartment he bought in the early 1960's or a small country house east of Paris. When not writing, he assisted in productions of his plays on the stages of London, Berlin, and Paris.

SIGNIFICANCE

An austerely self-contained writer more important for his focus than his range, Beckett was a metaphysical pointillist who specialized in rendering humanity's dark-forest moods. The tone of his work is that of a calm and horrible lucidity that regards the storm of humanity's violent strivings as over, with all illusions of progress and stability shattered. For him, agonizing chance and disorder dominate the cosmos, with the entire machinery of existence grinding to a halt. He was beyond any revolt or affirmation, insisting on intoning increasingly sparse and stark odes to despair. Just as Kafka has come to be considered by many the most representative writer of the unhappy first half of the twentieth century, so Beckett is in many ways his appropriate successor, as the most influential laureate of the twentieth century's Holocaust-haunted second half.

—*Gerhard Brand*

FURTHER READING

Bair, Deirdre. *Samuel Beckett: A Biography*. New York: Harcourt Brace Jovanovich, 1978. A huge, 736-page, biography. An indispensable source for Beckett students. Bair was a doctoral candidate in search of a dissertation topic when she spoke to Beckett in November, 1971. He told her that he "would neither help nor hinder" her, leaving her free to conduct three hundred interviews and labor six years over this project.

Coe, Richard N. *Beckett*. New York: Grove Press, 1964. A concisely written study that concentrates on the fiction and demonstrates the relationship between Beckett's work and such intellectual traditions as Cartesianism and existentialism.

Cohn, Ruby. *Samuel Beckett: The Comic Gamut*. New Brunswick, N.J.: Rutgers University Press, 1962. A lucidly written, incisive study of Beckett as a comic writer, in the tradition of Irish humorists and Henri Bergson's philosophy of comedy. Cohn has a particularly valuable chapter on *Endgame*.

Esslin, Martin. *The Theatre of the Absurd*. Rev. ed. Garden City, N.Y.: Doubleday, 1969. A classic text for understanding the contemporary theater. Esslin has a fifty-page chapter on Beckett that puts his work in the context of the tradition of the absurd, in which Esslin also places Eugène Ionesco, Jean Genet, Harold Pinter, and others.

_____, ed. *Samuel Beckett: A Collection of Critical Essays*. Englewood Cliffs, N.J.: Prentice-Hall, 1965. As usual, Esslin's judgment in selecting essays on Beckett is sound, and his introduction is well organized and scholarly. Some of the articles have been translated from foreign languages.

Federman, Raymond. *Journey to Chaos: Samuel Beckett's Early Fiction*. Berkeley: University of California Press, 1965. A learned, philosophically oriented study that not only analyzes the works Beckett wrote prior to *Molloy* but also refers helpfully to the later fiction.

Fletcher, John. *About Beckett: The Playwright and the Work*. New York: Faber & Faber, 2003. An introduction to Beckett, featuring interviews with the playwright, insights about his plays, and observations by people who produced his dramas. Fletcher explains why Beckett's work is enduring and significant.

Fletcher, John, and John Spurling. *Beckett the Playwright*. Rev. ed. New York: Farrar, Straus and Giroux, 1985. A comprehensive interpretation of Beckett's drama, from the earliest, unpublished play "Eleutheria" to *What Where* (1983). The analyses are clear, thorough, and judicious.

Murray, Christopher, ed. *Samuel Beckett: One Hundred Years, Centenary Essays*. Dublin: New Island, 2006. Published in honor of the centenary of Beckett's birth, this collection of essays includes discussions of Beckett and Irish society, his plays, and the philosophy expressed in his work.

Oppenheim, Lois, ed. *Palgrave Advances in Samuel Beckett Studies*. New York: Palgrave Macmillan, 2004. A compilation of essays outlining the history of Beckett studies and explaining how schools of literary and dramatic theory in the twentieth century interpreted Beckett's works.

SEE ALSO: Djuna Barnes; Bertolt Brecht; Albert Camus; Jean Genet; Alberto Giacometti; Eugène Ionesco; James Joyce; Franz Kafka; Eugene O'Neill; Luigi Pirandello; Marcel Proust; Nathalie Sarraute.

RELATED ARTICLES in *Great Events from History: The Twentieth Century*:

1941-1970: 1951-1953: Beckett's Trilogy Expands the Frontiers of Fiction; January 5, 1953: *Waiting for Godot* Expresses the Existential Theme of Absurdity; 1961: Esslin Publishes *The Theatre of the Absurd*; January 24, 1961: *The American Dream* Establishes Albee as the Voice of Pessimism.

1971-2000: February 10, 1971: Guare's *The House of Blue Leaves* Joins Naturalistic and Nonrepresentational Theater; June, 1986: Akalaitis's *Green Card* Confronts Audiences with Harsh Realities.

MENACHEM BEGIN
Prime minister of Israel (1977-1983)

Begin placed pressure on the British Mandate government to withdraw from Palestine, enabling Israel to declare its independence and sovereignty over part of Palestine. He also served as a key opposition leader and eventually as prime minister of Israel.

BORN: August 16, 1913; Brest-Litovsk, Russia (now Belarus)
DIED: March 9, 1992; Tel Aviv, Israel
ALSO KNOWN AS: Menachem Wolfovitch Begin (full name)
AREAS OF ACHIEVEMENT: Government and politics, diplomacy

EARLY LIFE

Menachem Begin (MEH-nah-ghem BAY-gihn) was born on the eve of World War I in the Polish-Jewish city of Brest-Litovsk, occupied by czarist Russia. In 1918, Germany took the area from the Soviet Union in the Treaty of Brest-Litovsk, and, at the Versailles Conference in 1919, it became part of the reestablished nation of Poland. Menachem's father and mother were orthodox Jews who worked for Zionism, the return of Jews to Palestine.

As a child Menachem (whose name means "one who brings comfort") saw a growing anti-Semitism in Brest-Litovsk: Rocks broke windows in Jewish homes; confiscatory, discriminatory taxation on Jews was levied by the Polish government; Jewish students were beaten by their peers. Once he had to watch several leading Jewish citizens receive twenty-five lashes in a public park for alleged "sympathy with Bolsheviks." Begin decided as a youth that Jews should not take such treatment passively and helped organize resistance against unwarranted attacks by fellow students.

Early in life, Begin demonstrated a forceful and effective public speaking personality. He attended a Polish gymnasium and received a good liberal arts education. He studied law in Warsaw and received the degree of *magister juris* from the University of Warsaw. Begin was greatly influenced by Vladimir Jabotinsky, an eloquent Russian journalist who preached Zionist activism and violence if necessary. Begin was a key organizer of the Polish chapter of Betar, Jabotinsky's activist youth organization, and eventually became its commander of seventy thousand.

Meanwhile, in Palestine a splinter group of young Jews broke from the Haganah (the Jewish self-defense organization), which at the time followed a passive self-restraint in trying not to alienate the British as they defended their lands against Arab terrorist attacks. The splinter group eventually adopted the name Irgun Z'vai Leumi, the National Military Organization. The new underground organization received training in sabotage and underground warfare from Polish army officers plus quantities of weapons in exchange for promises to recruit as many Jews as possible from Poland and take them to Palestine.

In the spring of 1939, Begin married Aliza Arnold, after warning her of the exceptionally difficult life she would lead as his wife. Serene and cheerful, she was one of the great strengths of Begin's life. She and Begin escaped Warsaw just ahead of the German Blitzkrieg. They went to the neutral city of Vilna, Lithuania, but Begin was arrested by the Soviet secret police and sentenced to eight years in a labor camp in Siberia. Aliza managed to escape to Palestine. After working fourteen hours a day for nearly a year in extremely cold conditions, Begin and other Polish prisoners were released to join the Polish Liberation Army. Their first assignment was Palestine, in which Begin first set foot in May, 1942.

Begin was already well known to the Irgun as the leader of the Polish Betar, Irgun's best source of recruits. Jabotinsky had recently died; many Irgun members had joined the British army; and a splinter group of the Irgun, the "Stern Gang," Lohamei Herut Yisrael (Fighters for the Freedom of Israel, or Lehi), had taken with them eight hundred Irgun members. Irgun, then, by the end of 1943, numbered scarcely five hundred members. It needed a dedicated, dynamic organizer, and Begin was chosen to lead the decimated Irgun.

LIFE'S WORK

Begin's principal purpose in life was to establish the State of Israel and build it up to survive in strength. He was willing to pay any price to accomplish that objective. "The God of Israel, the Lord of hosts, will help us," Begin declared in 1943. "[T]here will be no retreat. Freedom—or death." Begin's strategy was to demonstrate to the international community Great Britain's inability to govern Palestine—and thus hasten its departure. He did not want to destroy its ability to wage war against Germany and Japan and so did not raid British army bases or installations necessary to the war effort. Instead, Irgun sought to harass nonmilitary targets: disrupt communications; destroy records against illegal Jewish immigration; hamper the collection of taxes; and raid police stations and warehouses for weapons stockpiling. Irgun avoided killing either British or Arab—except when "necessary." Irgun raided a British army payroll train and "confiscated" banknotes amounting to thirty-eight thousand pounds.

Most members of Irgun were part-time saboteurs or propagandists (depending on the division to which they were assigned). Full-time staff of Irgun never numbered more than thirty or forty. Discipline and military training were strict. Irgun had an underground radio station begun in 1944 and the Irgun newspaper, *Herut*. (Haganah's radio station did not begin broadcasting until October, 1945). One of Begin's strong points as a leader was the meticulous and detailed way in which he analyzed problems and planned missions for Irgun. His conduct of meetings was the same way; he even had specific questions detailed for the agenda.

Begin tried to enlist Arabs in an effort to rid Palestine of the British. Irgun leaflets distributed in Arab villages claimed Jewish willingness to see the Arabs as peaceful citizens in the future Jewish state—which was not quite the political arrangement Arabs had in mind.

In response to Irgun raids and bombings, the British in 1944 imposed a curfew on the three major cities, Jerusalem, Haifa, and Tel Aviv, and brought out an old law imposing the death penalty for possessing arms or placing explosive devices. In June, 1946, a British military court condemned to death two Irgun members for stealing weapons from a British military installation. Irgun kidnapped five British officers with the tacit warning that if the Irgun men were hanged, so too would the British die. In July, the high commissioner commuted the death sentences of the two Irgun raiders. Irgun then released the British officers, each with a one-pound note for compensatory damages. On Sabbath, June 29, 1946, the British arrested literally thousands of Jews, including members of the Jewish Agency, and even sought to arrest David Ben-Gurion.

Haganah, Irgun, and Lehi all participated in the planning of the King David Hotel bombing on July 22, 1946. Warnings were telephoned to the hotel and nearby buildings a half hour before the bomb exploded, and some escaped as a result. Nevertheless, one wing of the hotel ignored the warnings, and more than one hundred people were killed in the blast. Haganah immediately and publicly condemned Irgun and disassociated itself from the terrorist act.

Begin detested the humiliation of floggings by British authorities and warned that floggings of Jews must stop or there would be retaliation in kind. When an Irgun suspect was flogged by British police, Irgun captured a British major and three noncommissioned officers and flogged each with eighteen lashes. Then they were set free with an Irgun communiqué showing the emblem of the two banks of the Jordan River and a rifle with the slogan "Only Thus." The British flogged no more Jews or Arabs for the rest of their time in Palestine.

Irgun's (and Begin's) greatest triumph was the successful storming of the impregnable Crusader fortress of Acre, where Jewish prisoners were kept and, in capital cases, executed. In the middle of an Arab city, Begin planned an elaborate operation that blew an enormous hole in the walls and freed 251 prisoners—131 Arabs and 120 Jews. Fifteen Jews were killed and fifteen captured. When three of those captured were executed, Irgun retaliated with the hanging of two innocent British sergeants, one of the most despicable actions ever taken by Irgun in the eyes of its critics. Equally despicable were the murders of five innocent Jews by British soldiers and police

Menachem Begin. (© The Nobel Foundation)

CAMP DAVID ACCORDS

On September 17, 1978, before signing the Camp David Accords, U.S. president Jimmy Carter, Egyptian president Anwar el-Sadat, and Israeli prime minister Menachem Begin spoke to the press at the White House. The following is an excerpt from Begin's speech.

I would like to say a few words about my friend, President Sadat. We met for the first time in our lives last November in Jerusalem. He came to us as a guest, a former enemy, and during our first meeting we became friends.

In the Jewish teachings, there is a tradition that the greatest achievement of a human being is to turn his enemy into a friend, and this we do in reciprocity. Since then, we had some difficult days. [Laughter] I'm not going now to tell you the saga of those days. Everything belongs to the past. Today, I visited President Sadat in his cabin, because in Camp David you don't have houses, you only have cabins. [Laughter] And he then came to visit me. We shook hands. And, thank God, we again could have said to each other, "You are my friend."

And, indeed, we shall go on working in understanding, and in friendship, and with good will. We will still have problems to solve. Camp David proved that any problem can be solved if there is good will and understanding and some, some wisdom . . . .

I express my thanks to all the members of the American delegation, headed by the Secretary of State, a man whom we love and respect. And so, I express my thanks to all the members of the Egyptian delegation who worked so hard together with us, headed by Deputy Prime Minister, Mr. Touhamy, for all they have done to achieve this moment. It is a great moment in the history of our nations and, indeed, of mankind.

I looked for a precedent; I didn't find it. It was a unique conference, perhaps one of the most important since the Vienna Conference in the 19th century, perhaps.

Begin's willingness to cooperate with the new government but not to submit to its authority led to armed conflict between Haganah and Irgun over the disposition of weapons brought in by Irgun on the *Altalena*. Of Irgun's men, fourteen were killed and sixty-nine wounded. The government ended with two killed and six wounded. Much of the desperately needed ammunition had been destroyed. To Ben-Gurion, Israel could not afford to have private armies that were not under the discipline of the government. To Begin's credit, he swallowed his pride and fought the common Arab enemy and did not let the Israeli cause perish in fratricidal conflict. He refused to fight fellow Jews and accepted the authority of the government. On September 20, 1948, Ben-Gurion presented Begin with an ultimatum ordering the immediate disbandment of the Irgun. Begin accepted the order and disbanded his organization.

As the war drew to an end, Begin helped organize the opposition Herut party in Israel. Herut proposed a vigorous capitalist system instead of the labor socialism of the ruling Mapai coalition. Herut also insisted that the Land of Israel included all of biblical Palestine—on both sides of the Jordan River. In the first election to the 120-member Knesset, Israel's parliament, Herut obtained fourteen seats, including one for Begin, a post he held for thirty years.

Though usually a key opposition leader to the government, Begin closed ranks during each of Israel's wars. By 1977, Begin had formed a right-wing coalition called the Likud bloc and controlled sixty-two Knesset seats, a majority. Begin became prime minister of Israel. He was supported partially because of his uncompromising stance on the West Bank captured by Israel in the 1967 war. It was Prime Minister Begin who signed the Camp David agreement in an effort to normalize relations with Egypt (leading to his receiving, with Anwar el-Sadat, the Nobel Peace Prize of 1978), and it was also Begin who ordered the invasion of Lebanon and the war to end the Palestine Liberation Organization's attacks in Israel.

SIGNIFICANCE

No one can doubt Begin's dedication to the cause of Israeli independence and strength. He was a realist. He was

officers in Tel Aviv in retaliation for the hanging of the sergeants. No more Jewish terrorists or British soldiers were executed in the remaining year of British occupation. After Begin became prime minister of Israel, he refused to permit the execution of Arab terrorists.

When the British withdrew from Palestine and the Israeli War of Independence (Arab-Israeli War) began in May, 1948, with the invasion of Palestine by Arab troops from Transjordan, Egypt, Syria, Lebanon, and Iraq, Begin and his Irgun were a thorn in the flesh for the new government of Israel under Prime Minister David Ben-Gurion. The Haganah needed all the help it could get, but neither Irgun nor Lehi was willing to relinquish control of its organization to the new government. They were willing to fight the Arabs. The massacre of Deir Yassin remains the most notorious of uncontrolled Irgun/Lehi actions.

brutal when he thought he needed to be. He suffered much, but he also caused much suffering. He was intensely loyal and a capable commander who tried to protect his subordinates. He brought enormous pressure on the British, who finally were almost too glad to depart Israel, thereby making it possible for Israel to win independence and prevent Arab conquest of part of Palestine. Did the British leave and the Israelis win because of or in spite of Irgun and Begin? Would the British have left anyway, or would they have left in a context more favorable to Arab Palestinians? If the Israelis had refrained from all terrorism and sabotage, would the British have cooperated more or sided with the Arabs more? These are the imponderables of history, to which no more than tentative answers can be given.

The Arabs hated the Israelis for depriving the Palestinian Arabs of the land of their fathers, but many Arabs hated the Jews long before they had such a cause. Begin played a crucial role before 1948, but the Irgun could not win the war for independence. Only the Jewish Agency and the Haganah had the resources to do what seemed impossible at the time. Begin's role as an opposition politician and later as an unpopular prime minister continues to be clouded in controversy and conflict, both of which plagued Begin all of his life.

—William H. Burnside

FURTHER READING

Bauer, Yehuda. *From Diplomacy to Resistance: A History of Jewish Palestine, 1939-1945*. Translated by Alton M. Winters. Philadelphia: Jewish Publication Society of America, 1970. Begin arrived in Israel in 1942, and his most significant historical contributions to Israel were in the years 1942-1948. This book analyzes in detail the historical situation during the critical years for Palestine. Bauer describes the intricate interrelationships and cooperation among Haganah, Irgun, and Lehi. The books examines the ambivalent attitudes of the British government and occupying army in Palestine and their relationship to both Arab and Jew.

Begin, Menachem. *The Revolt*. Translated by Shmuel Katz. New York: Schuman, 1951. In all the controversies surrounding Begin, it is only fair to hear his side of the story. Begin tells of insights and detailed facts that a sweeping narrative cannot. Begin's account, however, ends with 1948 and so is valuable only for the early period.

Bell, J. Bowyer. *Terror Out of Zion: Irgun Zvai Leumi, LEHI, and the Palestine Underground, 1929-1949*.

New York: St. Martin's Press, 1977. A well-written, fascinating insight into the intrigues, mentality, and troublesome times of the Israeli underground groups and their relationships and disagreements. One hundred pages follow Begin's career, especially after his arrival in Palestine. This book was published after Begin became prime minister, giving more historical perspective to the events described.

Cullen, Bob. "Two Weeks at Camp David." *Smithsonian*, September, 2003, 56. Recounts the events that occurred during a 1978 peace conference attended by Begin, Egyptian president Anwar el-Sadat, and U.S. president Jimmy Carter.

Hirschler, Gertrude, and Lester S. Eckman. *Menachem Begin: From Freedom Fighter to Statesman*. New York: Shengold, 1979. A sympathetic biography of Begin with many details of his family and early life. Covers all stages of his life. In the various controversies of his career, Begin is presented in as favorable a light as the authors can persuasively find.

Hirst, David. *The Gun and the Olive Branch: The Roots of Violence in the Middle East*. New York: Harcourt Brace Jovanovich, 1977. A sharply critical analysis of Israeli actions in Palestine, including Begin's role in "Gun Zionism."

O'Brien, Conor Cruise. *The Siege: The Saga of Israel and Zionism*. New York: Simon & Schuster, 1986. A full history of modern Israel written by an Irishman and often placing an unusual interpretation on historical events. O'Brien wrote much about Begin, including his years as prime minister. This is a balanced, scholarly account.

Silver, Eric. *Begin: The Haunted Prophet*. New York: Random House, 1984. A fascinating biography written by an Oxford-educated English journalist who lived in Israel for eleven years as a foreign correspondent. He sees Begin as consistent, who was unswerving in his dedication to Israeli security. He is often critical of Begin but detached in his observations and analysis.

SEE ALSO: David Ben-Gurion; Jimmy Carter; Moshe Dayan; Hussein I; Anwar el-Sadat; Chaim Weizmann.

RELATED ARTICLES in *Great Events from History: The Twentieth Century*:

1941-1970: September 10, 1952: Germany Agrees to Pay Reparations to Israel; September 28, 1970: Sadat Becomes President of Egypt.

1971-2000: November 19-21, 1977: Sadat Becomes

the First Arab Leader to Visit Israel; September 5-17, 1978: Camp David Accords; December 10, 1978: Sadat and Begin Receive the Nobel Peace Prize; June 7, 1981: Israel Destroys Iraqi Nuclear Reactor; September 16-18, 1982: Palestinians Are Massacred in West Beirut; November 21, 1984-January 5, 1985: Evacuation of Ethiopian Jews to Israel.

SAUL BELLOW
Canadian-American writer

In his novels and numerous short stories and articles over several decades, Bellow, as an American writer, achieved international recognition signified only in part by his receiving the Nobel Prize in Literature in 1976.

BORN: June 10, 1915; Lachine, Quebec, Canada
DIED: April 5, 2005; Brookline, Massachusetts
AREA OF ACHIEVEMENT: Literature

EARLY LIFE

Saul Bellow (sawl BEH-loh) was born in Lachine, Canada, the fourth child of religious Jewish parents who had emigrated to Canada two years earlier from Russia. He grew up speaking English, French, Yiddish, and Hebrew. While recovering from a serious respiratory illness at age eight, he acquired a profound love of reading and a sense of self-reliance. A year later, he moved with his family to Chicago, where he spent all of his spare hours in the public libraries. By the time he entered Tuley High School, he had already made his first efforts at writing fiction. His mother's death when he was seventeen was a lasting emotional shock to him.

After graduation from high school in 1933, he enrolled in the University of Chicago, transferring two years later to Northwestern University, where he founded a socialist club and received, in 1937, a bachelor's degree with honors in anthropology and sociology. Thoroughly engaged in the leftist intellectual ferment of the times, Bellow considered himself a follower of the Soviet theorist Leon Trotsky; he even traveled to Mexico City to meet Trotsky in exile but arrived just after Trotsky was assassinated.

Bellow entered graduate school at the University of Wisconsin but soon dropped out. On December 31, 1937, he married Anita Goshkin, a social worker; they would have one child, Gregory, born some years later. Bellow had continued to write since high school, publishing his first story in 1941. He also wrote biographies of American authors for the Works Progress Administra-

tion Writers Project and participated in Mortimer Adler's "Great Books" program for the *Encyclopædia Britannica*. He did some teaching as well. While serving in the merchant marine during World War II, he wrote his first novel, *Dangling Man*. It was published in 1944, and in 1947 his second, *The Victim*, followed. The novels had a mixed critical reception but were highly regarded by antiestablishment intellectuals, especially for their existentialist themes and apparent European influences, notably that of Fyodor Dostoevski.

A Guggenheim Fellowship in 1948, allowing him to begin work on his next novel, launched young Bellow on his brilliant career—a career more successful, perhaps, than that of any other contemporary American writer. Yet as often happens with successful people, Bellow's private life was turbulent: Soon his marriage to Anita failed, and following an unfriendly divorce, he remarried—a pattern he would repeat four times. His dark and beautiful wives, with all of their faults and virtues, would find their way into his novels, as would Bellow himself. The characters representing the author were often larger and stronger than Bellow but not necessarily more handsome. Bellow had deep-set brown eyes, a "theatrically chiseled" nose, and hair that turned to silver somewhat prematurely. He looked physically slight and boyish—he was about five feet, nine inches tall, weighing perhaps 150 pounds in his younger years—but he also had an athletic quality in his build, with a very sturdy chest. Altogether, these physical and psychological aspects of Bellow's life offered an unexpected parallel to those of Ernest Hemingway, a writer whose influence on Bellow was not great.

LIFE'S WORK

Bellow's first important success was *The Adventures of Augie March*, published in 1953—a partly autobiographical bildungsroman, modeled in part on its picaresque predecessor, Mark Twain's *Adventures of Huckleberry Finn* (1884). This exuberant, stylistically innovative novel was both a best seller and a critical success, and after thirty-five years remains a favorite among Bellow's extremely broad and varied readership. For this work, he won the National Book Award for Fiction, the first of three such awards he received. In 1955, he received a second Guggenheim Fellowship, and the following year he married Alexandra Tschacbasov; they had one child, Adam.

Bellow's novella, *Seize the Day*, was published in 1956, together with three stories and a one-act play. The style of *Seize the Day* is beautifully sparse and tight (in marked contrast to the sprawling energy of *The Adventures of Augie March*); Bellow delineates the defeat of middle-aged Tommy Wilhelm, jobless, penniless, his marriage a failure. The concluding paragraphs are as famous as any in contemporary literature. Tommy chances into a funeral parlor, stands by the coffin of a stranger, and begins to weep. "Soon he was past words, past reason, coherence. He could not stop. The source of all tears had suddenly sprung open within him. . . ." The con-

Saul Bellow. (© The Nobel Foundation)

trolled emotional power of this novella places it in contrast to most of Bellow's other works, which tend to be dominated by intellectual argument.

Bellow himself has said his own favorite among his writings is *Henderson the Rain King*, published in 1959. It is a deliberately composed "quest romance" that takes the protagonist (Bellow's first who was not Jewish) to Africa, a place that Bellow had not yet visited. The gigantic, blustering, crazed, and comic Henderson was not universally popular among reviewers and critics, but the novel nevertheless testifies to Bellow's remarkable creative diversity.

After a stay of ten years in the New York City area, Bellow returned permanently to Chicago. Having divorced Alexandra, he married Susan Glassman in December of 1961; their son, Daniel, was born in 1963. From 1960 to 1962 Bellow co-edited the literary magazine *The Noble Savage*, and in 1962 he joined the Committee on Social Thought at the University of Chicago. His novel *Herzog*, a best seller like all of his books from *The Adventures of Augie March* onward, was published in 1964; for it, he won four major prizes, including the National Book Award for Fiction for the second time. More than one critic found this novel "brilliant"—its almost pure realism was the mode in which Bellow worked best.

In 1968 appeared *Mosby's Memoirs, and Other Stories*, the title work proving that Bellow is a master of the realistic short story as well. In that year, Bellow was awarded in France the Croix de Chevalier des Arts et Lettres. By this time, Bellow was separated from Susan; great bitterness would remain between them, as alimony payments would be contested following their divorce, culminating in an open fight in court in 1977. During this same period (from the mid-1960's), Bellow lost the favor of most leftist American intellectuals following his attendance at the same White House dinner in 1965 that Robert Lowell had refused to attend in political protest against United States policy in Vietnam. Bellow's conservatism consisted chiefly in not accepting the ideas and manners of the radicals, but since that time, he has nevertheless come to be identified by many as an establishment figure.

Although *Mr. Sammler's Planet* (1970) was not enthusiastically received by reviewers, it won for its author a third National Book Award for Fiction. The protagonist, an old Polish Jew who is trying to cope with life in a huge metropolis, effectively criticizes the insanity of American culture from the point of view of rational conservatism. What is of most interest here, perhaps, is the dissimilarity of this novel to Bellow's other works.

In *Humboldt's Gift* (1975), Charles Citrine, the protagonist, reminisces about his friend Humboldt, who is based on the poets John Berryman and Delmore Schwartz, whom Bellow had known in his younger years. In this novel, the plot is casual, the style uneven, sometimes careless, but the attention to detail, one of Bellow's strongest points, is superb. The same criticism applies to *The Dean's December* (1982), though now the protagonist, Albert Corde, dramatizes through his own experience the contrast between Eastern (Romanian) communism and Western (American) capitalism. The focus is chiefly on their faults, with those of communism seeming to be most intractable. Bellow's conclusion here is similar to certain implications in his nonfiction work *To Jerusalem and Back: A Personal Account* (1976), in which he suggests that the struggle between Jew and Arab could somehow be dealt with in an orderly way if only each side did not continually act irrationally, against its own interests.

In 1974, he married Alexandra Tulcea, a professor of mathematics at Northwestern University. It seems very likely that Albert Corde's wife, Minna, a professor of astronomy, born in Romania, was based on this new woman in Bellow's life. The last scene in *The Dean's December* places husband and wife together so as to show their mutual love, respect, and concern; perhaps this scene reflects a certain happiness in marriage that Bellow, now in the fullness of his career, had not earlier known.

In 1976, Bellow received the Nobel Prize in Literature. His seventy-minute address at the awards ceremony in Stockholm, Sweden, urged writers worldwide to awaken civilization from a deadening intellectual indolence. His later writing sought to do just that, and although gradually identified with neoconservatives, he showed little interest in adhering to a single political philosophy as he addressed such topics as feminism, post-modernism, Jewish-African American relations, and crime among the impoverished. A collection of short stories, *Him with His Foot in His Mouth*, appeared in 1984, followed by the novel *More Die of Heartbreak*. Its protagonist, Kenneth Trachtenberg, is an intellectual distraught by his inability to reconcile his philosophical leanings with his past and mortality. *The Bellarosa Connection* (1989) is a dialogue in the Fonstein family about the Holocaust, and *A Theft*, published the same year, concerns a woman raised in a traditional midwestern religious environment who must cope with the modern business world as a publishing company executive and who

despairs of achieving romantic love. *The Actual* (1997) tells of an art lover, Harry Trellman, who is reunited with his adolescent ideal woman (his "actual") late in life, and their elderly love affair. Bellow's last novel, *Ravelstein* (2000), considered by many critics to be his finest, is based in part on his friend and colleague at the Committee on Social Thought, Allan Bloom. The story follows the friendship of two university professors and its complications from erotic relations into their old age. His collection of nonfiction, *It All Adds Up* (1994), emphasizes the importance of literature to society.

During his career, Bellow taught at the University of Minnesota, New York University, Princeton University, the University of Puerto Rico, Bard College, and Boston University in addition to the University of Chicago. In 1989 he married Janis Freeman, with whom he had a daughter, Naomi, in 1999. They moved to Brookline, Massachusetts, from Chicago in 1993, because, he said, he was tired of watching old friends there die. Bellow himself died in Brookline on April 5, 2005. He is buried in Brattleboro, Vermont.

SIGNIFICANCE

Bellow's impact on American culture came through his novels, which reflect his sense of himself and his relationship to his society. Bellow partly represents that older sense of America as a haven for European émigrés—first as the son of Russian-Jewish émigrés to Canada, then as a French-Canadian himself, newly arrived in Chicago. He tells of the pain of adjustment in *The Adventures of Augie March*. The pain of being Jewish in a nation that does not really love Jews is a frequent theme in his work, although, ultimately, Bellow accepts casual assimilation as a suitable choice for himself. In this respect, he could be said to symbolize the diversity of the United States without testifying to a false harmony.

Bellow saw himself as an American writer who happened to be Jewish, not as a Jewish writer—though he identified profoundly with Jews, including Israeli Jews. Yet Bellow was not a practicing or religious Jew. He sought religious experience primarily within the realm of ideas. His first loyalty was that of the intellectual to the world of ideas, and it was this special world that is chiefly dramatized in his novels. In so doing, Bellow had an important impact on Americans. In a nation where intellectual novels are uncommon, Bellow made a career writing such works, almost all of them best sellers. He helped Americans examine their role as individuals in relation to society—often in opposition to it—and as individuals in conflict with themselves.

Bellow seldom spoke of patriotism but rather tended to relegate "society" to a sort of naturalistic background. Bellow's vision was clear and honest: His characters are sensitive, aware, and vital. His perceptions were sufficiently compelling that even many of those who have ideologically "rejected" him still read his books faithfully. He always opened up new worlds. Thus he compelled citizens of the whole world, not only Americans, to read his works. His international recognition, in turn, made his impact on Americans all the greater, offering them some hope of attaining the greater sophistication that he felt that they needed. In fact, he is often credited with introducing intellectual modernity into American literature.

—Donald M. Fiene

FURTHER READING

Atlas, James. *Bellow: A Biography*. New York: Random House, 2000. Thorough and balanced biography of the author, placing the events of his life in a larger historical context.

Braham, Jeanne. *A Sort of Columbus: The American Voyages of Saul Bellow's Fiction*. Athens: University of Georgia Press, 1984. Although biography appears only incidentally, this monograph is of interest for its emphasis on the strictly American themes in Bellow's work.

Cronin, Gloria L. *A Room of His Own: In Search of the Feminine in the Novels of Saul Bellow*. Syracuse, N.Y.: Syracuse University Press, 2001. Cronin presents a feminist appreciation of Bellow's work by viewing his texts as a self-ironical search for the "absent mother, lover, sister, female friend, female psyche, and anima" in the lives of his male protagonists.

Fuchs, Daniel. *Saul Bellow: Vision and Revision*. Durham, N.C.: Duke University Press, 1984. Biographical references occur only incidentally in the text, but two chapters are of special interest: "Bellow and the Modern Tradition" and "Bellow and the Example of Dostoevsky." There is also a good final chapter on *The Dean's December*.

Harris, Mark. *Saul Bellow: Drumlin Woodchuck*. Athens: University of Georgia Press, 1980. Anecdotal yet well-documented account of Harris's dealings with Bellow in the 1960's. Shows how certain characters in the novels are based on Bellow and certain women in Bellow's life. Harris admires the writer very much, but not the man.

Turow, Scott. "Missing Bellow." *The Atlantic*, December, 2005. In this profile of Bellow, Turow, himself a novelist, describes his admiration for and personal relationship with Bellow.

Wasserman, Harriet. *Handsome Is: Adventures with Saul Bellow*. New York: Fromm International, 1997. In this memoir, Wasserman, Bellow's literary agent for twenty-five years, presents a close friend's view of Bellow, his literary habits, and his interests.

Wilson, Jonathan. *On Bellow's Planet: Readings from the Dark Side*. London: Associated University Presses, 1985. Original, perceptive discussion of nine of Bellow's novels. Biographical details are given only casually. Good selected bibliography.

SEE ALSO: Margaret Atwood; Joseph Conrad; Mavis Gallant; Erle Stanley Gardner; Jack London; Mary McCarthy; Mordecai Richler; Susan Sontag; H. G. Wells.

RELATED ARTICLES in *Great Events from History: The Twentieth Century:*

1941-1970: 1948: Mailer Publishes *The Naked and the Dead*; 1969: Roth Publishes *Portnoy's Complaint*.

DAVID BEN-GURION
Prime minister of Israel (1948-1953, 1955-1963)

Ben-Gurion dreamed of the state of Israel, then turned that vision into reality. As Israel's first prime minister and defense minister, he laid a solid foundation for the country's survival and prosperity; as its leading statesman, he established the principles that continue to guide it.

BORN: October 16, 1886; Płónsk, Poland, Russian Empire (now in Poland)
DIED: December 1, 1973; Tel Aviv, Israel
ALSO KNOWN AS: David Joseph Gruen (birth name)
AREAS OF ACHIEVEMENT: Government and politics, diplomacy

EARLY LIFE

The son of Avigdor and Sheindel (Friedman) Gruen, David Ben-Gurion (behn-goor-YAWN) was born in Płónsk, Poland. His father was a local leader in Hovevai Zion (lovers of Zion), a forerunner of the Zionist movement, and a product of the Haskalah (Jewish enlightenment), which sought to fuse traditional and modern thought and to revive Hebrew as a living language. At the age of fourteen, he and two friends organized the Ezra Society to teach local children to speak and write Hebrew. Despite opposition from religious leaders who regarded Hebrew as too sacred for daily use, the group attracted 150 students.

Along with his love of Israel, the young Ben-Gurion was imbibing socialist principles. Harriet Beecher Stowe, Leo Tolstoy, and Abraham Mapu shaped his politics, and in 1905 he joined Poalei Zion (workers of Zion), which sought to build a workers' state in Israel. A natural organizer and orator, Ben-Gurion united the seamstresses of Płónsk to strike for a shorter workday, and he repeatedly outdebated non-Zionist opponents who argued for assimilation and socialist revolution in Europe.

Another lifelong belief also revealed itself in Płónsk, then ruled by czarist Russia. The country had witnessed numerous pogroms against the Jews, who rarely fought back against their attackers. Ben-Gurion, whose heroes were the Maccabees and Old Testament warriors, successfully urged his coreligionists to arm themselves for self-defense, as later he would organize the Haganah in Palestine to thwart Arab raids. Never a zealot, he did not want to turn Jews into wolves, but neither did he want his people to be sheep.

In 1906, Ben-Gurion's Zionist dream took him to Petach Tikva in Turkish Palestine, and for the next several years he worked in various settlements, living his idea of creating a Jewish state through labor. He was never physically strong, though, and Poalei Zion recognized that he could make a more significant contribution with his head than with his back. Appointed editor of the organization's newspaper, *Ahdut*, he took as his pseudonym the name of Yosef Ben-Gurion, a moderate leader of the Jewish revolt against the Romans in 66 C.E.

LIFE'S WORK

Believing that Turkey could be persuaded to grant a Jewish state, Ben-Gurion went to Constantinople in 1912 to pursue a law degree, after which he planned to enter the Turkish parliament and work for an independent Israel. The Balkan War interrupted his studies; the outbreak of World War I ended them. He returned to Palestine, where he urged support for Turkey against the entente, fearing that if the Central Powers were defeated, anti-Semitic Russia would be awarded the ancient Jewish homeland. Indifferent to his pro-Ottoman stance, Turkish authorities arrested Ben-Gurion in February, 1915, for his Zionist activities and deported him. Together with Itzhak Ben-Zvi, later to serve as Israel's president, Ben-Gurion went to the United States to encourage Jewish immigration; throughout his life, he believed that a Jewish state would arise and prosper only if Jews settled and worked the land. He made few converts, but one of them was a young girl from Milwaukee, Goldie Mabovitch; as Golda Meir, she would be Israel's prime minister. While in the United States, Ben-Gurion published *Yizkor* (1916) and *Eretz Yisrael* (1918) to promote Jewish settlement in Palestine. These volumes did little to further that cause, but they did enhance Ben-Gurion's reputation. While in the United States, he met and married Paula Munweis (December 5, 1917).

When the United States entered World War I, Ben-Gurion realized that Turkey and the other Central Powers were doomed. His shift of allegiance to the Entente was guaranteed by the Balfour Declaration (November 2, 1917), promising a Jewish homeland in Israel; he could not know that Great Britain was also pledging to give the same territory to the Arabs and to France. Urging the creation of a Jewish Legion to support Great Britain, Ben-Gurion himself enlisted, leaving his pregnant wife. The legion saw little action, but it did return Ben-Gurion to the Middle East, where he immediately resumed his efforts to forge a united labor organization. Crucial to this goal was the Histadrut. Founded in December, 1920, with only 4,433 of the 65,000 Jews of Palestine, it grew throughout the decade, establishing its own bank, newspaper (*Davar*), construction company, and recreational facilities. Under Ben-Gurion's leadership, the various labor factions also joined politically, so that by 1930 his Mapai Party included 80 percent of the region's Jewish workers.

While Ben-Gurion's achievements and reputation grew in Palestine, he could not influence Zionist policy. The Fourteenth and Fifteenth World Zionist Congresses encouraged middle-class rather than worker immigration and favored urban instead of rural development. Ben-Gurion was philosophically opposed to this emphasis on bourgeois capitalism; he also recognized that businessmen, with no tie to the land, were likely to leave the country once prosperity ended, and so they did after 1927. Another disagreement, with Chaim Weizmann, president of the World Zionist Organization, arose over how far to press Great Britain to allow Jewish settlement in Palestine; Weizmann favored conciliation at almost any cost.

Unable to compete within the World Zionist Organization, Ben-Gurion in 1930 created a rival, the World Congress for Labor Palestine, dedicated to "a Jewish state, a laboring society, [and] Jewish-Arab cooperation." Through this new institution, Ben-Gurion hoped to enlist international Jewish support for his views, but Great Britain's efforts to placate the Arabs at Jewish expense were turning mainstream Zionists away from Weizmann. At the Seventeenth World Zionist Congress, the World Congress for Labor Palestine comprised the largest single bloc of votes, and its representatives received two seats on the executive committee. Two years later, when the organization convened again, the World Congress for Labor Palestine held 44.6 percent of the votes, thanks in large measure to Ben-Gurion's vigorous campaigning in Eastern Europe; Ben-Gurion himself was named to the Executive. By 1935, the World Congress for Labor Palestine had gained control, and Ben-Gurion became chair of the Zionist Executive and head of the Jewish Agency.

Although he had refused the presidency of the World Zionist Organization in favor of Weizmann, the two men continued to disagree over unlimited immigration and relations with Great Britain. Realizing that Great Britain never would willingly fulfill the promise of the Balfour Declaration, Ben-Gurion in 1936 began training the Haganah, the underground Jewish army, for future conflicts with the Arabs and British. Throughout World War II, he opposed guerrilla warfare against Great Britain, but as soon as Germany surrendered he went to the United States to secure money for weapons. In October, 1945, he ordered the Haganah to use force if necessary to protect Jews entering Palestine illegally, Great Britain having refused to lift tight restrictions on Jewish immigration, and he supported a number of attacks against British installations. Great Britain responded by arresting Jewish leaders and confiscating weapons, but it also resolved to abandon its mandate, agreeing to a partition plan adopted by the United Nations on November 29, 1947.

After almost two thousand years, after a third of their number had been killed in the Nazi Holocaust, the Jewish people were to have a country of their own—if they could defend it from the armies of five Arab nations poised to invade as soon as the British mandate ended. George C. Marshall, the U.S. secretary of state, urged Ben-Gurion not to declare independence but to wait five or ten years more. Instead, on May 14, 1948, in the Tel Aviv Museum, Ben-Gurion declared "the establishment of the Jewish State in Palestine, to be called the State of Israel."

David Ben-Gurion. (Library of Congress)

Ben-Gurion had been modern Jewry's Moses, leading it to the promised land. Now he would also be its Joshua, as the army he had trained and supplied turned back the invaders. At the same time, he overcame threats from Menachem Begin's Irgun Z'vai Leumi on the right and from the Palmach on the left, each seeking to maintain autonomous military organizations. He thus established the principle of civilian control over the military. Over the next four years (1949-1953), he led the fledgling nation as prime minister and defense minister, doubling the nation's Jewish population and securing international financial support.

At the end of 1953, he temporarily retired—for two years, he said—to Sde Boker, a kibbutz in the Negev desert, fifty miles south of Beersheba. He wanted a rest, a chance to read and write, but he also wanted to foster in others the pioneer spirit that had brought him to Israel almost fifty years earlier. Moreover, he regarded settlement of the Negev as crucial to the country's security against Egypt and hoped others would follow him into this area.

His absence from government actually lasted more than a year. A scandal in the defense ministry led to the resignation of Pinḥas Lavon, and Ben-Gurion replaced him. After the 1955 elections, he also resumed the post of prime minister, leading the country to victory in the 1956 Suez campaign. Although much of the victory was annulled by pressure from the United States to return to prewar borders, Israel had secured freedom of navigation through Elath. Also, France, which had helped Israel during the fighting, agreed to build a nuclear reactor at Dimona.

At the same time that Ben-Gurion was making Israel the strongest military power in the region, he also wanted it to be one of the world's great moral forces. To the newly independent states of Africa and to Burma he sent technicians and scientists, and from these countries came students who would be doctors, nurses, and teachers in their homelands.

Well into his seventies, Ben-Gurion exemplified his definition of a leader: "You must know when to fight your political opponents and when to mark time. . . . And . . . you must constantly reassess chosen policies." In the 1960's, though, he became increasingly inflexible and out of touch with reality. He refused to recognize the evidence that exonerated Pinḥas Lavon, who had been forced to leave the defense ministry in 1955 after perjured testimony and forged documents caused him to be blamed for terrorist acts in Egypt. While Ben-Gurion recruited the next generation of Israel's leaders, among

them Moshe Dayan, Shimon Peres, and Abba Eban, he antagonized many of his older colleagues, such as Moshe Sharett and Golda Meir, by seeming to ignore them in favor of younger protégés. His close ties to Germany brought Israel many benefits, but he failed to gauge the hostility that many of his countryfolk harbored against that country. In 1963, amid growing opposition to his leadership, he resigned from the government; two years later he left the Mapai Party he had done so much to create, challenging it in the 1965 elections. His faction won ten seats, Mapai forty-five. When tension with Egypt increased in 1967, there were calls for Ben-Gurion's return to the prime ministry, but only from those unaware that he was urging peace. It was his disciple, Dayan, who as defense minister led the nation to its swift, overwhelming victory in the Six-Day War.

In 1970, Ben-Gurion left the Knesset, Israel's parliament, for what he thought was the last time, but, on his eighty-fifth birthday, he spoke to a special session called in his honor and received a standing ovation from friends and opponents alike. He then returned to the Negev, and there, after his death on December 1, 1973, he was buried, overlooking the Wilderness of Zin, where Israel's saga had begun three millennia before.

SIGNIFICANCE

Ben-Gurion observed that "history would have been quite different if there had been no Churchill." History also would have been different had there been no Ben-Gurion. As a young pioneer in Turkish Palestine, he had resolved, "I have but a single aim: to serve the Jewish worker in the Land of Israel." He never strayed from that purpose. When others hesitated to pressure Great Britain to declare Israeli independence and to open Israel's borders to unlimited immigration, he pressed boldly on. Though he might have shifted tactics, supporting the Central Powers and then the Entente in World War I, opposing guerrilla warfare against Great Britain and then favoring it, he never altered his goal of building a secure, moral Jewish nation.

Ben-Gurion sacrificed much for his dream. As a young man he was often ill, lonely, and hungry, as he sought work, frequently unsuccessfully, in a malaria-ridden land. Later he would have virtually no family life, traveling around Europe and the United States to cajole and coerce others into sharing his dream. His insistence on principles above politics alienated many former friends. Nor did he accomplish all that he sought, never reconciling Sephardic Jews from Africa and Asia with the European Ashkenazis, certainly not achieving peace with the Arabs. His hope of making Israel a leader among developing world nations remained unrealized.

For what Ben-Gurion did accomplish, though, he will remain, as Charles de Gaulle described him in 1960, the symbol of Zionism and "one of the greatest statesmen of [the twentieth] century." He had built his castles in the air, then had put solid foundations under them. The state of Israel is his legacy; he shaped its history and left a blueprint for its future—to do justly, to love mercy, and to walk humbly with its God.

—Joseph Rosenblum

FURTHER READING

Avi-hai, Avraham. *Ben-Gurion, State-Builder: Principles and Pragmatism, 1948-1963*. New York: John Wiley & Sons, 1974. This work argues that Ben-Gurion was successful in shaping modern Israel, because he could find practical ways to fulfill his ideals. It ends with Ben-Gurion's resignation as prime minister in 1963.

Bar-Zohar, Michael. *Ben-Gurion: A Biography*. New York: Delacorte Press, 1978. Bar-Zohar spent much time with Ben-Gurion and interviewed other Israeli leaders. Presents not only the public figure but also the private man behind the decisions.

Ben-Gurion, David. *David Ben-Gurion in His Own Words*. Edited by Amram Ducovny. New York: Fleet Press, 1968. Ducovny provides a brief biography of the Israeli leader and then arranges Ben-Gurion's statements under such headings as "The Philosopher" (chapter 2) and "The Scholar" (chapter 7). Includes a useful chronology through 1968.

Heller, Joseph. *The Birth of Israel: Ben-Gurion and His Critics*. Gainesville: University Press of Florida, 2000. Chronicles the events that led to the founding of Israel after World War II and the Holocaust, describing how and why Ben-Gurion prevailed in the political struggles to create a Jewish state.

Kurzman, Dan. *Ben-Gurion: Prophet of Fire*. New York: Simon & Schuster, 1983. Based on extensive interviews and archival research as well as published material, this work provides a comprehensive survey of Ben-Gurion's life. Contains fascinating photographs and an extensive bibliography.

Shalom, Zakai. *Ben-Gurion's Political Struggles: A Lion in Winter*. New York: Routledge, 2005. Chronicles Ben-Gurion's career after he resigned from the government in 1963 as well as his political activities during the Six-Day War.

Teveth, Shabtai. *Ben-Gurion and the Palestinian Arabs: From Peace to War*. New York: Oxford University Press, 1985. Maintains that Ben-Gurion determined Israel's attitude toward the Arabs within its borders. Traces the evolution of Ben-Gurion's thoughts on Jewish-Arab relations. Ends with the establishment of the state of Israel.

_____. *Ben-Gurion: The Burning Ground, 1886-1948*. Boston: Houghton Mifflin, 1987. A scholarly companion to Avi-hai's work about Ben-Gurion after 1948. Ben-Gurion's papers are voluminous, and this work draws heavily on them. Ends at 1948 because official documents thereafter were inaccessible at the time of publication and because he sees Ben-Gurion as changing after Israel gained its independence.

SEE ALSO: Konrad Adenauer; Arthur Balfour; Menachem Begin; Moshe Dayan; Abba Eban; Hussein I; George C. Marshall; Golda Meir; Gamal Abdel Nasser; Max Nordau; Chaim Weizmann.

RELATED ARTICLES in *Great Events from History: The Twentieth Century:*

1941-1970: November 29, 1947-July, 1949: Arab-Israeli War Creates Refugee Crisis; May 14, 1948: Israel Is Created as a Homeland for Jews; July 5, 1950: Israel Enacts the Law of Return; September 10, 1952: Germany Agrees to Pay Reparations to Israel; July 26, 1956: Egypt Attempts to Nationalize the Suez Canal; March 17, 1969: Meir Becomes Prime Minister of Israel; November 19-21, 1977: Sadat Becomes the First Arab Leader to Visit Israel.

RUTH BENEDICT
American anthropologist

Depicting culture as an integrated set of traits chosen from the vast range of behavioral possibilities, Benedict directed the focus of American anthropology in the 1930's and 1940's toward the search for describable cultural configurations.

BORN: June 5, 1887; New York, New York
DIED: September 17, 1948; New York, New York
ALSO KNOWN AS: Ruth Fulton (birth name); Anne Singleton (pseudonym)
AREAS OF ACHIEVEMENT: Anthropology, literature, social sciences

EARLY LIFE

Two traumatic events, one physical and one psychological, profoundly affected Ruth Benedict as a child. In 1889, Benedict's father, Frederick Fulton, a gifted homeopathic surgeon, died at the age of thirty-one. His young widow, Beatrice Shattuck Fulton, publicly expressed her immense grief, insisting that twenty-one-month-old Ruth view her father in his coffin, an image that retained potency for Ruth throughout her life. Shortly after her father's death, she began exhibiting signs of emotional trauma, initially with violent tantrums in which members of her family feared for her safety and that of her sister Margery, and later as she became old enough to check her temper, through bouts of depression. Benedict was emotionally withdrawn as a child, preferring solitude and shunning physical contact. She idolized her dead father and disliked her mother, whose frequently recurring expressions of grief Benedict found appalling. Her traumatic response to her father's death was exacerbated by substantial hearing loss sustained as a complication from measles. The condition had occurred when she was an infant but was left undiagnosed until she was five years old. Her partial deafness contributed to her surliness and isolation from her family.

During Benedict's childhood, her mother uprooted her family several times in search of employment before finally settling in Buffalo, New York, where she became head librarian for the Buffalo Public Library. Beatrice Fulton's pay was relatively low, but the job provided security. Although the family settled in the prosperous upper-middle-class area of the then thriving city, the Fultons were poor in contrast to their neighbors. As scholarship students, Benedict and her sister Margery at-

tended the private St. Margaret's Academy where they were distressingly aware of their poverty relative to their socially privileged schoolmates.

After attending Vassar on a full scholarship, Benedict sought to balance the desire for public accomplishment with personal satisfaction. She returned to Buffalo after graduation, and for two years she was employed as a social worker. She then moved with her family to California, where she taught school in a private girls' academy. Both occupations left her unfulfilled and bored. Her marriage in 1914 to Stanley Benedict, a talented young biochemist, and their subsequent move to the New York City suburb of Bedford Hills, left her similarly unsatisfied. Although she wrote poetry, which she published with moderate success under the pseudonym Anne Singleton, and feminist biographies that at the time remained unpublished, she found domestic life and suburban isolation abhorrent. Winter-induced depressions led her to seek external fulfillment, and in 1919, at the age of thirty-one, Benedict enrolled in graduate work at the New School for Social Research in New York City. Later, through the influence of anthropologists Elsie Clews Parsons and Alexander Goldenweiser, she met and convinced Franz Boas of Columbia University to admit her to the doctoral program in anthropology.

LIFE'S WORK

Assisted by Boas's acceptance of her course work from the New School of Social Research, Ruth Benedict earned her Ph.D. in three semesters. As Boas's graduate teaching assistant, personal friend, and aide, and later as a lecturer in anthropology, she assumed a progressively significant role at Columbia.

Her 1923 dissertation, "The Concept of the Guardian Spirit in North America," was the result of library research rather than fieldwork. While narrow in scope, her study contributed to the knowledge of American Indian religion and myth. Although she took several trips into the field, including excursions made between 1922 and 1926 to study the Serrano, Pima, and Zuni, Benedict's partial deafness made the collection of oral myths and folk culture difficult. Because she used lip reading to enhance her limited hearing, it was impractical for her to immerse herself in a foreign linguistic tradition, depending instead on interpreters for interviewing informants. Benedict's forte was interpreting and organizing other anthropologists' data. Her expertise was most evident in her 1934 publication the now-classic *Patterns of Culture*, in which she combined her own fieldwork on the Zuni with Boas's among the Kwakuitl, and Reo Fortune's among the Melanesian Dobus. *Patterns of Culture* was the culmination of more than a decade's ruminations on the definition of culture, including the function of the individual within, and his or her effect on, culture. Furthermore she described the cultural foundations of abnormality.

Benedict's work reflected what was then a preeminent debate among social scientists about the nature of culture and its effect on the individual. In *Patterns of Culture*, she rejected biological determinism, which views immutable biological roles as determining human behavior. She also disdained the British-influenced functionalism of Bronislaw Malinowski and A. R. Radcliffe-Browne in which every aspect of culture had a particular function that needed only to be deciphered by anthropologists. Instead, Benedict adapted a configurationist approach in which individual cultures select attributes from a "great arc" of possible human behavioral traits. Cultures discard some characteristics while emphasizing others, thereby developing their own identifiable cultural configuration or pattern. The pattern is more than the sum of its parts; instead, it is an integrated whole or a gestalt that can be described by anthropologists. Culture was "personality writ large," a describable reflection of the psychological group mind. Unlike functionalism, which defined culture as static and ignored history and diffusion as agents of cultural change, Benedict's patterns were fluid and therefore could be influenced by individuals within cultures.

Within her configurationist approach Benedict also explained deviance, an issue about which she was preoccupied, likely to help her understand her lack of fit in her own culture. While she had always felt herself to be an outsider, Benedict became increasingly aware of her differences as her marriage deteriorated and she attained emotional fulfillment in an intimate and ultimately lesbian relationship with anthropologist Margaret Mead. In *Patterns of Culture* Benedict emphasized the cultural specificity of abnormality; conduct that is defined as normal in one culture was often considered abnormal in another. Because of the malleability of human beings, the vast majority of members of any culture will conform to dictated behavior. A small percentage, however, will discover that their inborn

temperaments or potentialities do not coincide with cultural patterns and will find culture uncongenial, thereby participating in what is culturally defined as abnormal behavior.

Stemming from her belief in the plasticity of human beings, her personal commitment to social reform, and her conviction that anthropologists could be agents of change, Benedict devoted considerable energies to social causes in the form of "applied anthropology." She became a principal spokesperson against racism with her 1940 publication of the popular *Race: Science and Politics*. In addition she developed a resource unit on racism with high school teacher Mildred Ellis in 1942, collabo-

---

ON THE TAKING OF HUMAN LIFE

Ruth Benedict begins the third chapter of her study Patterns of Culture *(1934) with a discussion of the countless meanings associated with the taking of a human life, through murder or suicide, among the world's cultures. Her work was instrumental in legitimizing the study, and significance, of cultural diversity.*

The diversity of cultures can be endlessly documented. A field of human behaviour may be ignored in some societies until it barely exists; it may even be in some cases unimagined. Or it may almost monopolize the whole organized behaviour of the society, and the most alien situations be manipulated only in its terms. Traits having no intrinsic relation one with the other, and historically independent, merge and become inextricable, providing the occasion for behaviour that has no counterpart in regions that do not make these identifications. It is a corollary of this that standards, no matter in what aspect of behaviour, range in different cultures from the positive to the negative pole. We might suppose that in the matter of taking a life all peoples would agree in condemnation. On the contrary, in a matter of homicide, it may be held that one is blameless if diplomatic relations have been severed between neighbouring countries, or that one kills by custom his first two children, or that a husband has right of life and death over his wife, or that it is the duty of the child to kill his parents before they are old. It may be that those are killed who steal a fowl, or who cut their upper teeth first, or who are born on a Wednesday. Among some peoples a person suffers torments at having caused an accidental death; among others it is a matter of no consequence. Suicide also may be a light matter, the recourse of anyone who has suffered some slight rebuff, an act that occurs constantly in a tribe. It may be the highest and noblest act a wise man can perform. The very tale of it, on the other hand, may be a matter for incredulous mirth, and the act itself impossible to conceive as a human possibility. Or it may be a crime punishable by law, or regarded as a sin against the gods.

rated with a Columbia University committee to write a public affairs pamphlet in 1943, and coauthored a children's book on racism with anthropologist Gene Weltfish in 1948.

During World War II, Benedict, along with many of her fellow social scientists, worked for government intelligence agencies. In 1943, she joined the Office of War Information (OWI), where she initiated her pioneering work on national character—the determination of cultural patterns in complex nations. Since fieldwork was infeasible during the war, she perfected techniques for determining "culture at a distance," including analysis of films, fiction, propaganda, and interviews with immigrants. Under the auspices of the OWI, she prepared reports on Thailand, Romania, Finland, Norway, Poland, and Italy. The publication of Benedict's *The Chrysanthemum and the Sword: Patterns of Japanese Culture* (1946) was the pinnacle of national character studies, profoundly influencing public opinion toward Japan by explaining the foreignness of Japanese culture to the American public.

Benedict's final contribution to anthropology involved her directorship of Columbia's ambitious Research in Contemporary Cultures (RCC) project, an interdisciplinary program sponsored by the U.S. Navy and begun in 1947 to study national character. The program's potential was never realized because it ran counter to then-dominant trends in anthropology including movement from interdisciplinary work to specialization; emphasis on quantifiable data in the form of statistics; and distancing from "cultural relativity," which denied ethical absolutes, claiming cultures could only be judged on their own terms (a position many found untenable in the wake of Nazi Germany's concentration and death camps). Benedict, weakened by overwork and a postwar trip to Eastern Europe, died of a heart attack on September 17, 1948.

SIGNIFICANCE

Benedict's work in the field of anthropology, while highly influential in the 1930's, lost prestige in the 1940's as it went against the grain of the then-dominant tradition among American social scientists. Her work was criticized as impressionistic and too similar to the humanities to be properly scientific. Nevertheless, her popular impact continued. *Patterns of Culture* continues to be a standard work in anthropology and other classrooms, popularizing anthropological concepts such as cultural relativity and challenging notions of racial superiority and homophobia.

Benedict's quest for self-fulfillment was a monumental struggle during an era when women's roles were narrowly proscribed by Victorian social convention. Her battle for professional recognition was similarly a tribute to her persistence in the face of blatant academic discrimination. During the early years after she earned her Ph.D., Benedict, because of her age, was ineligible for grants and fellowships. To achieve professional recognition, she was forced to accept a series of yearly renewable appointments as an unpaid lecturer in anthropology at Columbia. She earned a small salary teaching in the Columbia Extension program and with what little money she could spare supported students' fieldwork. By the late 1920's, Benedict was increasingly influential in the anthropology department, but it was not until 1931 that Columbia finally granted her an untenured assistant professorship. Despite these slights and the subsequent decision to choose a less experienced male colleague as chair of the department when Boas retired, Benedict persevered to become one of the most notable women in the field of anthropology.

—*Mary E. Virginia*

FURTHER READING

Banner, Lois W. *Intertwined Lives: Margaret Mead, Ruth Benedict, and Their Circle*. New York: Knopf, 2003. Based on newly acquired letters and other archival materials, Banner examines the two women's relationship within the context of their families, friends, husbands, and others in their social circle.

Caffrey, Margaret M. *Ruth Benedict: Stranger in This Land*. Austin: University of Texas Press, 1989. Caffrey, in this excellent biography, examines Benedict's life from the perspective of her contribution to American intellectual history and as a "case history in cultural feminism." Illustrations, footnotes, bibliography.

Lapsley, Hilary. *Margaret Mead and Ruth Benedict: The Kinship of Women*. Amherst: University of Massachusetts Press, 1999. Explores the unique kinship between women working in a male-dominated field, and gives a biographical account of Benedict and Mead's intimate relationship.

Lavender, Catherine J. *Scientists and Storytellers: Feminist Anthropologists and the Construction of the American Southwest*. Albuquerque: University of New Mexico Press, 2006. Describes how Benedict and three other anthropologists who studied American Indians in the Southwest created a feminist ethnography that emphasized the role of women in Indian culture.

Mead, Margaret. *An Anthropologist at Work: Writings of Ruth Benedict*. Boston: Houghton Mifflin, 1959. A collection of Benedict's writings including journal entries, professional publications, and an autobiographical sketch interspersed with biographical essays written by Mead. Fully footnoted with chronology of achievements and bibliography.

_____. *Ruth Benedict.* New York: Columbia University Press, 1974. Again Mead used Benedict's own writing interspersed with her comments to provide a biographical sketch of Benedict. Included are several publications not found in *An Anthropologist at Work.*

Modell, Judith Schachter. *Ruth Benedict: Patterns of a Life.* Philadelphia: University of Pennsylvania Press, 1983. A detailed biography and analysis of Benedict's work by anthropologist Modell. Contains citations, full bibliography.

Young, Virginia Heyer. *Ruth Benedict: Beyond Relativity, Beyond Pattern.* Lincoln: University of Nebraska

Press, 2005. Young, one of Benedict's graduate students, analyzes her teacher's unpublished and little-known writings, concluding that Benedict was embarking on a new direction in her anthropological studies during the final years of her life.

SEE ALSO: Franz Boas; Henri-Édouard-Prosper Breuil; Sir James George Frazer; Leo Frobenius; Margaret Mead; Max Wertheimer.

RELATED ARTICLES in *Great Events from History: The Twentieth Century:*

1901-1940: 1911: Boas Publishes *The Mind of Primitive Man*; August, 1928: Mead Publishes *Coming of Age in Samoa*; 1934: Benedict Publishes *Patterns of Culture.*

1941-1970: 1950: Boyd Defines Human "Races" by Blood Groups.

EDVARD BENEŠ
President of Czechoslovakia (1935-1938) and president in exile (1940-1945)

Beneš helped undermine Austro-Hungarian rule in the Czech and Slovak region during World War I and became foreign minister of the new republic there in 1918. A brilliant statesman, he negotiated numerous agreements, but as president he was unable to prevent the dismemberment of his country at Munich. During World War II, he headed the Czechoslovakian government in exile and after 1945 endeavored unsuccessfully to maintain Czechoslovakia's political freedom in the face of mounting Communist pressures.

BORN: May 28, 1884; Kožlany, Bohemia, Austro-Hungarian Empire (now in Czech Republic)

DIED: September 3, 1948; Sezimovo Ústí, Czechoslovakia (now in Czech Republic)

AREAS OF ACHIEVEMENT: Government and politics, diplomacy

EARLY LIFE

Edvard Beneš (EHD-vahrt BEH-nehsh) was the youngest of ten children born to a moderately successful farmer who was able to send him to secondary school at Vinohrady. As family funds were too meager to cover the cost of higher education, however, Beneš resorted to tutoring and freelance writing to make ends meet. In 1903, he entered Charles University in Prague to study philology (he did become an accomplished linguist) but

switched to philosophy and came under the influence of Tomáš Masaryk, the leading advocate of Czech nationalism. At Masaryk's urging, Beneš went to France to study at the Sorbonne and at Dijon, and he obtained a doctor of laws degree in political science and sociology from the latter. In Paris he met a Czech student, Hana Vlčkova, whom he married in 1909; she was his lifelong companion and source of constant encouragement.

In 1909, Beneš returned home, completed a Ph.D. at Charles University, and secured a teaching post in political science at the Academy of Commerce in Prague. He also turned away from Marxism, joined Masaryk's Progressive Party, and wrote for its organ. In 1912, he joined the faculty at Charles University as a lecturer in sociology. (After the war, he regularly lectured there on sociology.) In 1913, he also became a lecturer at the Technical College in Prague. By that time, he had become a prolific writer on politics and international affairs and active in the national liberation movement. He had developed a deep hatred for militarism, of both the Austrian and the German varieties, but he was not called up for military service at the outbreak of World War I, because of a leg injury incurred in his youth when he was a star soccer player. In early 1915, he and Masaryk (who was now in exile) formed an underground organization called Maffia, which sought to promote a national uprising and to aid the Allies by supplying secret information

Edvard Beneš. (Library of Congress)

about activities in Austria-Hungary. In September, 1915, Beneš left the country with a forged passport to avoid imminent arrest by the Austrian police and joined Masaryk in Switzerland.

His earlier sojourn in France had imbued Beneš with Western political, economic, and cultural ideas that put him at odds with those Bohemian patriots who looked to Russia for salvation. Beneš and Masaryk became the leading spokespersons for the "Westernist" school in the liberation movement. They represented a "Europeanist" or "realist" stance; that is, they believed the nation must learn how to observe, analyze, and contemplate options carefully, rather than follow the romantic notions of nineteenth century Pan-Slavism. Through their intensive efforts in the three years that followed, Beneš and Masaryk almost single-handedly achieved their goal of an independent Czechoslovak state.

LIFE'S WORK
At their meeting in 1915, Beneš and Masaryk discussed plans for their country's future, arranged to gather funds

to carry on the work, and determined that they would persuade the Allies to support their movement. Beneš functioned essentially as Masaryk's chief of staff. In February, 1916, Beneš became general-secretary of the Czechoslovak National Council, which was seated in Paris, where he had extensive ties. A tireless propagandist, Beneš pounded the Allies with details about how the Czech and Slovak people were working for victory through army desertions and mutinies and civilian riots, sabotage efforts, and demonstrations against the authorities in Austria-Hungary. Their movement contributed materially to the demise of the Habsburg Empire and influenced the Allies to recognize the idea of a Czechoslovak republic. Through his French contacts, Beneš negotiated the specific mention of the liberation of the Czechoslovaks from foreign domination in the entente's note to Woodrow Wilson in January, 1917, which spelled out their war aims, and Wilson included in his Fourteen Points in January, 1918, the demand that the peoples of Austria-Hungary should have the opportunity for autonomous development. Once Masaryk had secured the formation of the Czechoslovak Legion in Russia in 1917, the Czechoslovak National Council in Paris began to function as the government in exile of a state that had hitherto existed only in the minds of its leaders. In May and June, 1918, Beneš obtained French and British recognition of Czechoslovakia as an allied and belligerent nation, and he effectively countered Italian opposition to this recognition. He also was in regular contact with nationalist leaders in Prague, and, when the Habsburg regime collapsed, Beneš was able to secure the establishment of an independent state under the National Council on October 28. Three days later, the Slovaks proclaimed independence and joined with the Czech provinces.

On November 14, a hastily convened parliament approved the émigré committee as the constitutional government, with Masaryk as president and Beneš as foreign minister, and the latter was commissioned to represent the new country at the Paris Peace Conference. After signing in 1919 the Treaty of St. Germain with Austria, which finalized the authority of the Czechoslovak government, Beneš returned home in triumph to take up the duties of foreign minister. He served in this post until 1935 with only a brief interlude from September 26, 1921, to October 7, 1922, as premier.

During his tenure as foreign minister, Beneš gained renown as a European statesman who was devoted to the struggle for international peace and collective security. His major achievement was the formation of the Little Entente with Yugoslavia and Romania in 1920-1921 to check Hungarian ambitions; this Little Entente, linked with the Treaty of Alliance and Friendship with France in 1924, was the foundation of the continental balance of power and the French deterrence system against Germany. Through this tie, Beneš was able to secure French assistance for construction of the Czechoslovak border fortifications, which might have saved the country from German conquest in 1938 if the Sudeten region had not been lost through the ill-fated Munich Agreement. Beneš also concluded one of the first European treaties with Soviet Russia (1922) and treaties of friendship with Poland (1921), Austria (1921), Italy (1924), and Germany (1925). He was an active participant in the Genoa Economics Meeting (1922), the Locarno Conference (1925), disarmament conferences (1927, 1929, 1932), and the Lausanne reparations talks (1932). In 1933, he negotiated the London Convention with the Soviet Union, Yugoslavia, Romania, and Turkey, which defined aggression and thereby applied the 1928 Paris Pact to Eastern Europe, and in 1935 he concluded an alliance (Treaty of Mutual Assistance) with the Soviet Union. He played a leading role in the League of Nations, first as acting vice president in 1920 and then as a member of the council (1923-1927), president of the assembly (1935), and chairs of various committees. In 1924, Beneš and Greek foreign minister Nicholas Politis drafted the celebrated Geneva Protocol, which was designed to prevent aggressive war by requiring that international disputes be submitted to peaceful negotiation and arbitration.

When the aged Masaryk decided to retire, the parliament named his protégé as the new constitutional head of state on December 18, 1935. Beneš tried to check Nazi expansion by means of collective security, but his efforts were torpedoed by France, which allowed Germany to remilitarize the Rhineland, cowered behind the Maginot line, and refused to honor its treaty commitments. After the Austrian Anschluss, Adolf Hitler put pressure on Czechoslovakia to cede the area populated by German-speaking people (the Sudetenland), and when he began to concentrate troops on the border, Beneš ordered a general mobilization on May 21, 1938. By putting the country on a war footing, Beneš forced the führer to back down, but by late summer it appeared certain that Germany would drag Europe into a general conflict over the Sudeten issue. The British and French leaders succeeded in negotiating an agreement at Munich on September 29 that allowed Germany to annex the region. Neither the republic nor its Soviet ally was consulted about the matter, and Czechoslovakia, stripped of its border fortifications, was thrown to the wolves. In response to Hitler's

demands, Beneš resigned on October 5 and went into exile in London.

He traveled to the United States in February, 1939, to teach at the University of Chicago, but when Hitler seized the remainder of Czechoslovakia on March 15, he agreed to assume the leadership of his country's liberation movement. He returned to London in July, established a popular government known as the Czechoslovak National Committee, and a year later converted it into the Provisional Czechoslovak National Government. In July, 1941, the United States, Great Britain, and the Soviet Union accorded recognition to Beneš's government in exile. His wartime strategy was to pay official visits to the two men who would play the decisive roles in shaping the new order, Franklin D. Roosevelt and Joseph Stalin. He went to the United States in May, 1943, and to Moscow in December, 1943. He made it clear that Czechoslovakia would have a new and more cordial relationship with the Soviet Union after the war, and he agreed to the Czechoslovak-Soviet Treaty of Friendship, Mutual Assistance, and Postwar Cooperation that paved the way for the disaster that would befall his country after the liberation. He hoped that voluntary concessions to Stalin would make for goodwill, but his surrender of Ruthenia (Subcarpathian Ukraine), Czechoslovakia's easternmost province, gained nothing.

As the war drew to a close, the Red Army installed native communists in Slovakia. Beneš naïvely thought that he and his government would be able to oust these communists once he appeared on the scene, and he journeyed to Russia and then to Slovakia in March, 1945, where he established provisional headquarters at Košice. He agreed to a coalition government that would include communists, most notably the Czech party leader Klement Gottwald. On May 8, Beneš went to Prague (also liberated by the Soviets), where he was joyously welcomed.

Although Beneš set out to prevent the communists from monopolizing power in Czechoslovakia, his program of strengthening public morale, treating the communists evenhandedly and having them share power responsibility in proportion to their strength, yielding to their demands in social and economic but not political matters, and keeping avenues to the West open while reducing Soviet influence in the country was a failure. His position steadily eroded, and in 1948 the communists carried off a coup. On February 25, Beneš reluctantly signed the death warrant for Czechoslovak freedom by accepting the resignation of the democratic ministers and naming a new government headed by Gottwald. By that time, Beneš was sick. He had already suffered a serious stroke the year before, and he resigned the presidency on June 7 and retired to his country home at Sezimovo Ústí. His physical condition deteriorated rapidly, and he died on September 3, 1948.

SIGNIFICANCE

Beneš was the quintessential European statesman of the interwar years. Unfortunately, the times were not ripe for a person with such a commitment to international peace through collective security. Although he was a Czechoslovak patriot, he had a broader conception of the international order. He was an eternal optimist and an ineffable proponent of democracy on the international scene, and thus he was no match for dictators such as Hitler and Stalin. Although he was a brilliant negotiator and understood the art of compromise, his critics questioned whether he really had the fortitude to stand up to tyranny.

Like that of his country, Beneš's life was a tragic story. A confirmed democrat, he was forced to compromise with antidemocratic forces. His allies never came through when they were needed, and, in the crucial years of 1938 and 1948, he and Czechoslovakia were left alone and ignored as the flame of democracy was extinguished. Whether he was a victim of forces beyond his control or he had contributed to the situation by his own ineptness is a matter for historians to debate. Yet he left his mark as a statesman and fighter for a democratic nation and world.

—*Richard V. Pierard*

FURTHER READING

Beneš, Edvard. *The Fall and Rise of a Nation: Czechoslovakia, 1938-1941.* Edited by Milan Hauner. Boulder, Colo.: Eastern European Monographs, 2001. In newly discovered manuscripts, Beneš described the events of the last two weeks of September, 1938, culminating in the adoption of the Munich Pact. Supplemented with wartime speeches and other documents, the book recounts Germany's campaign to acquire the Sudetenland, the German invasion of Prague in 1939, and Beneš's formation of a government in exile.

_____. *Memoirs: From Munich to New World and New Victory.* Translated by Godfrey Lias. London: Allen & Unwin, 1954. Reprint. New York: Arno Press, 1972. Originally published in Prague in 1947, the Czechoslovak edition was a best seller until its suppression after the Communist coup. It was designed to justify his statesmanship after Munich and the process of undoing the agreement.

_____. *My War Memoirs.* Translated by Paul Selver. Boston: Houghton Mifflin, 1928. A detailed personal account of Beneš's activities in the Czechoslovak national movement, from the beginning of the war to Masaryk's return to preside over the new state.

Bruegel, J. W. *Czechoslovakia Before Munich: The German Minority Problem and British Appeasement Policy.* New York: Cambridge University Press, 1973. Insightful treatment of the Sudeten German question and Beneš's efforts to deal with it. Demonstrates that he failed to grasp the significance of having such a large German minority within his state until it was too late.

Crabitès, Pierre. *Beneš, Statesman of Central Europe.* London: G. Routledge & Sons, 1935. Typical of the popular biographies that were published in the interwar years—laudatory and based on *My War Memoirs* and secondary sources.

Korbel, Josef. *The Communist Subversion of Czechoslovakia, 1938-1948.* Princeton, N.J.: Princeton University Press, 1959. Traces Communist activities in the land from Munich to the coup. Includes the efforts of Beneš to deal with the Communist exile regime and his losing struggle with Gottwald to retain democracy.

_____. *Twentieth Century Czechoslovakia: The Meaning of Its History.* New York: Columbia University Press, 1977. A historical survey that focuses on the key role of Beneš and criticizes his apparent unwillingness to exercise forceful leadership during the Sudeten crisis and the period before the Communist coup.

Mamatey, Victor, and Radomír Luza, eds. *A History of the Czechoslovak Republic, 1918-1948.* Princeton, N.J.: Princeton University Press, 1973. A collection of seventeen detailed scholarly essays on various aspects of the republic's history. The central focus is on Beneš and his leadership.

Taborsky, Edward. *President Edvard Beneš: Between East and West, 1938-1948.* Stanford, Calif.: Hoover Institution Press, 1981. An account by Beneš's personal secretary and legal adviser between 1939 and 1945 who fled to the United States after the coup. He relates the president's deeds during the war years and defends him against his critics.

SEE ALSO: Karel Čapek; Alexander Dubček; Francis Ferdinand; Tomáš Masaryk; Woodrow Wilson.

RELATED ARTICLES in *Great Events from History: The Twentieth Century:*

STEPHEN VINCENT BENÉT
American poet and writer

Benét made his major contribution to literature as a poet and primarily as the author of the book-length poem John Brown's Body. *Benét was a prolific writer in several genres, however, and his canon includes short stories, novels, radio scripts, and nonfiction.*

BORN: July 22, 1898; Bethlehem, Pennsylvania
DIED: March 13, 1943; New York, New York
AREA OF ACHIEVEMENT: Literature

EARLY LIFE

Stephen Vincent Benét (beh-NAY) was born to Frances Neill Rose Benét and James Walker Benét. Benét's father was a captain of ordnance in the U.S. Army, and he also had poetic and literary tastes. Benét was the couple's third child and second son; his sister and brother were Laura Benét and William Rose Benét, who were both active in the literary world. Well-read from his youth and thoroughly educated, Benét began writing early in his life.

During his childhood, his family moved throughout the United States because of his father's position in the Army. Benét and his family were at the Vatervliet, New York, arsenal from 1899 until 1904; the Rock Island, Illinois, arsenal during 1904; the Benicia, California, arsenal from 1905 until 1911; and the Augusta, Georgia, arsenal from 1911 until he was graduated from a coeducational academy and entered Yale College in 1915. There he was with such undergraduates as Archibald MacLeish, Thornton Wilder, Philip Barry, and John Farrar. He left Yale after completing his junior year in 1918 to enlist in the Army, but was honorably discharged because of his bad eyesight. After working briefly for the State Department in Washington, D.C., he reentered Yale. Benét received his B.A. degree in 1919 and his M.A. degree in 1920. At that time, he was given a traveling fellowship by Yale and went to Paris, where he completed his first novel.

Unlike other expatriates in Paris, Benét was not disillusioned or dissatisfied with America; he went to Paris because he could live there cheaply. He was very patriotic and loved his country deeply. While in Paris, he met Rosemary Carr; about a year later, in 1921, they were married in her hometown of Chicago. Their marriage was a happy one, producing three children: Stephanie Jane, born in 1924; Thomas Carr, born in 1925; and Rachel, born in 1931.

LIFE'S WORK

In the nineteenth century, Walt Whitman had called for a national poet for America and sought to be that poet. While he envisioned himself as the poet working in his shirt sleeves among the people and read by the population at large, he was never really a poet of the people, absorbed by the people. Ironically, Benét became the poet that Whitman wanted to be. Although Benét's approach as a poet was a literary, academic one, his poetry was widely read and popular with the public.

Using American legends, tales, songs, and history, he was most effective writing in epic and narrative forms, especially the folk ballad. Benét's primary weakness is related to his strength. He lacks originality; he takes not only his subjects but also his techniques from other sources. In his first published poems, a series of dramatic monologues called *Five Men and Pompey* (1915), the influence of Robert Browning and Edwin Arlington Robinson is evident. As Donald Heiney indicates in *Recent American Literature* (1958), Benét never developed a single stylistic quality that was his own.

His poetry, particularly *John Brown's Body* (1928), which won the Pulitzer Prize, is nevertheless worth reading for its presentation of American folklore and history. As Benét himself indicated in a foreword to *John Brown's Body*, poetry, unlike prose, tells its story through rhyme and meter. By using such a method to tell stories and convey ideas, the poet can cause readers to feel more deeply and to see more clearly; thus, the poet's work will remain in the memory of readers.

John Brown's Body, a book-length narrative poem, became immediately popular with the American public when it was published in 1928; it was the poem that established his position in American literature. Although many critics have complained that a major weakness of the poem is a lack of unity, Parry Stroud points out, in *Stephen Vincent Benét* (1962), several ways in which the epic is unified—through the characters, through the symbolism, and through the consistent and purposeful use of several meters.

First, John Brown himself and the imaginary characters representing the major regional areas of America serve to unify the poem. Jack Ellyat, a Connecticut boy who enlists in the Union Army, is the counterpart of Clay Wingate, a Southerner from Wingate Hall, Georgia. Ellyat eventually marries Melora Vilas, who, with her father, stands for the border states and the West. At the end

Stephen Vincent Benét. (Library of Congress)

gate, the Southerner, to suggest dancing, riding, and other aspects of Southern culture.

In the foreword, Benét indicates that the poem deals with events associated with the Civil War, beginning just before John Brown's raid on Harpers Ferry and ending just after the close of the war and the assassination of Abraham Lincoln. Although he did not intend to write a formal history of the Civil War, he did want the poem to show how the events presented affected different Americans; he was concerned with the Americans of the North and South as well as those of the East and West.

By describing the American landscape and people, Benét gives American historical events a reality greater than mere names and dates can confer. He believed that the people living during the Civil War encountered problems similar to those of his time and that the decisions they made then had a great effect on future generations of Americans.

Growing out of Benét's fondness for his country, *John Brown's Body* will have a permanent place in American literature because it is an epic having uniquely American themes and qualities. He researched the historical details of the war extensively, but he also understood the human complexities involved. Exhibiting a high level of narrative skill, Benét presented five of the most crucial years in American history, poetically interpreting part of the great heritage of America.

Western Star, a fragmentary work, which was to have been another epic like *John Brown's Body*, was published after Benét's death in 1943. He had begun writing it previous to World War II, but on the entry of America into the war, he put it aside, planning to resume work on it when peace was achieved. *Western Star* was to have been Benét's interpretation of the settlement of the United States and of the westward movement of frontier life. He intended to present frontier life in a way similar to that he had used to present the Civil War in *John Brown's Body*—by using actual events and both actual and imaginary persons for his characters. Unfortunately, his early death prevented his completing this work.

Benét earned his living by writing. To support his family, he was often forced to devote less time than he would have liked to his serious writing—rather than concentrating on his poetry, he sometimes had to spend time and energy writing short stories and novels that would bring in money. Although *John Brown's Body* generated substantial sales, he lost most of his capital in the crash of 1929 and never again enjoyed financial security.

Benét achieved mastery of the short fiction form only after laborious and persistent efforts. His preference was

of the war Wingate also marries the woman he loves, the Southern belle Sally Dupre. There are several other minor fictional characters typifying various regions and classes in America: Lucy Weatherby, a Southern coquette; Spade, a slave who runs away; Cudjo, a slave who remains loyal to the Wingates; Jake Diefer, a stolid Pennsylvania farmer for whom Spade works after the war; Luke Breckinridge, an illiterate Tennessee mountaineer who fights for the South; and Shippey, a spy for the North. The war resolves the fates of most of these fictional characters.

Parry Stroud disagrees with the many critics who believe that Benét's style disrupts the unity of the poem. Benét uses three basic meters: traditional blank verse, heroic couplets, and what Benét called his "long rough line." This versatile long line approximates the rhythm of everyday speech more than traditional meters do. Benét also uses rhythmic prose and lyrics. In the foreword that he wrote for the poem in 1941, he states that he intentionally used a variety of meters. For example, he used a light, swift meter for the episodes concerning Clay Win-for poetry and the freedom it offered as opposed to the restrictions of the short story. Perhaps because of this, he never experimented with the short-story form and unflinchingly favored the traditionally structured stories with a definite beginning, middle, and end. He also skillfully employed the traditional device of the narrator to bring about a sense of immediacy and the interesting possibility of self-revelation and concealment that this perspective offered, but he was not an innovator of any new form of the short story.

When World War II broke out, fiercely loyal to democracy, he felt compelled to contribute to the war effort as much as he could. As a result, in the early 1940's he devoted much of his time and energy to writing propagandistic radio scripts and other needed pieces.

During Benét's most creative years, he was handicapped by poor health; from 1930 until his death in 1943, he suffered from arthritis of the spine and other illnesses. He was hospitalized for several weeks in 1939 for a nervous breakdown caused by overwork. On March 13, 1943, when he was forty-four years old, he died in his wife's arms following a heart attack.

SIGNIFICANCE

American history, especially that of the Civil War, is integral to the fiction of Benét. Whether folklore, fantasy, or parable, his writing reverberates with history, not only American but also European, since he lived in France for several years. His characters range from European immigrants to expatriates from America, from slaves to frontiersmen, from the World War I lost generation eccentrics to religionists. His fictional modes include irony, satire, sentimentality, and romanticism. Benét imbues his fiction with themes of national pride, freedom with responsibility, the cardinal virtues, and the fair play of living the good life.

His honors and prizes include a Guggenheim Fellowship (1926), extended for six months (1927); a Pulitzer Prize (1929) for *John Brown's Body*; election to the National Institute of Arts and Letters (1929); an O. Henry Memorial Prize for the short story (1936); an honorary degree by Yale University (1937); election to the American Academy of Arts and Sciences (1938); and a Pulitzer Prize, awarded posthumously, for *Western Star*.

—*Zia Southard and Sherry G. Southard,*
revised by Julia B. Boken Hasan

FURTHER READING

Benét, Stephen Vincent. *Selected Letters of Stephen Vincent Benét*. Edited by Charles A. Fenton. New Haven, Conn.: Yale University Press, 1960. A broad selection of letters reflecting Benét's moods and perceptions about places in the United States and Europe, the people and the literary and social scenes, especially during the 1920's, 1930's, and early 1940's.

Bleiler, Everett Franklin. *The Guide to Supernatural Fiction*. Kent, Ohio: Kent State University Press, 1983. Includes a list and commentary on several stories by Stephen Vincent Benét that deal with themes of fantasy and extrasensory perceptions and hallucinations.

Davenport, Basil. *Introduction to Stephen Vincent Benét: Selected Poetry and Prose*. New York: Rinehart, 1960. Davenport's short essay is a good overview of Benét's life and literature for those unfamiliar with his writing. He stresses how unusual Benét's Americanism seemed during a time when Paris overflowed with expatriates cynical of American idealism. The poet is seen as essentially a romantic, able to show extraordinary feeling for his subjects.

Fenton, Charles A. *Stephen Vincent Benét: The Life and Times of an American Man of Letters*. New Haven, Conn.: Yale University Press, 1958. A definitive biography that presents not only the well-documented life of Benét but also comments on the works. Fenton had the cooperation of Rosemary Carr (Mrs. Benét) and access to Benét's diaries.

Izzo, David Garrett, and Lincoln Konkle, eds. *Stephen Vincent Benét: Essays on His Life and Work*. Jefferson, N.C.: McFarland, 2003. Collection of essays about Benét's life and work, including a reminiscence by his son, a discussion of his relationships with his wife and friends, and an examination of his poetry and short stories.

LaFarge, Christopher. "The Narrative Poetry of Stephen Vincent Benét." *Saturday Review* 27 (1944): 106-108. LaFarge presents a glowing evaluation of Benét, seeing him as an enduring and timely writer who contributed much to the political writing of his day. Benét is lauded for his complex patterns of rhythm, meter, and form and for his rich characterization, but most of all for his clear style that makes his work accessible to general readers.

Stroud, Parry. *Stephen Vincent Benét*. New York: Twayne, 1962. A critique that focuses on Benét's liberalism, reflected in his writings. Stroud places the writer in a historical and cultural frame in an interpretation of Benét's themes. The analysis is clear in its literary perspective and its biographical framework.

Wells, Henry W. "Stephen Vincent Benét." *College English* 5 (1943): 8-13. Written soon after Benét's death, this critical survey of the author's major works, *John Brown's Body* and *Western Star*, strikes an elegiac tone, although a negative one. Wells mostly examines possible reasons for Benét's waning reputation as a poet but also deals briefly with his achievements and skills.

SEE ALSO: Hart Crane; E. E. Cummings; T. S. Eliot; Robert Frost; H. D.; Amy Lowell; Edna St. Vincent Millay; Marianne Moore; Carl Sandburg; Gertrude Stein; Sara Teasdale.

WALTER BENJAMIN
German critic and philosopher

Unappreciated during his own lifetime, Benjamin became a major influence on modern cultural criticism after World War II when former colleagues and friends began publishing his work. Using messianic and Marxist ideas in an idiosyncratic manner, Benjamin criticized all attempts to mask the suffering of humanity with an aesthetic illusion. His work has affected scholars in areas as diverse as literary theory and criticism, cultural studies, urban studies, aesthetics, and architecture.

BORN: July 15, 1892; Berlin, Germany
DIED: September 26, 1940; Port Bou, Spain
AREAS OF ACHIEVEMENT: Philosophy, literature, historiography, scholarship, social sciences

EARLY LIFE

Walter Benjamin (BEHN-jeh-mehn) was born to an upper-middle-class Jewish family living in the West End of Berlin. From his father, a dealer in art and antiquities, he acquired an early interest in culture. While at the prestigious Friedrich-Wilhelm Gymnasium, he was influenced by the antiauthoritarian educational concepts of Gustav Wyneken, eventually taking on a leadership role in the Youth Movement and publishing articles in its journal *Der Anfang*. He separated from the group when members enthusiastically accepted World War I, which Benjamin avoided by feigning sciatica. In Freiburg, Berlin, Munich, and Bern, where he studied philosophy, Benjamin came under the influence of Zionists and leftists, including Martin Buber and Ernst Bloch. His doctoral dissertation, *Der Begriff der Kunstkritik in der deutschen Romantik* (the concept of art criticism in German Romanticism), completed in Bern in 1920, examined Johann Gottlieb Fichte's metaphysics and Friedrich Schlegel's aesthetics.

In 1917, Benjamin had married Dora Pollak, and their only child, Stefan, was born that same year. When the fi-

nancial support of Benjamin's parents became strained by the mounting economic crisis in the Weimar Republic, the couple was compelled to return to Germany so that Benjamin might seek suitable employment.

In 1925, Benjamin submitted his manuscript *Ursprung des deutschen Trauerspiels* (1928; *The Origin of German Tragic Drama*, 1977) as a *Habilitationsschrift* to teach aesthetics and literary history at the University of Frankfurt. Ill suited by temperament for a university career and with a theoretical argument for cultural engagement that was unlikely to be appreciated by apolitical German academics, he was forced to withdraw the application. Freed from domestic responsibilities with the collapse of his marriage after 1924, Benjamin set out to become an unaffiliated intellectual, hoping to support himself with literary journalism. He also soon turned down the possibility of a teaching position in Jerusalem, obtained for him by his lifelong friend Gershom Scholem. Ultimately he would fail in this attempt to become an independent scholar, his genius being recognized only after his death. Benjamin's tragic life has come to represent the twentieth century alienation about which he so perceptively wrote.

LIFE'S WORK

Benjamin launched his career as a literary and cultural critic by publishing several major essays on ethics, violence, and Johann Wolfgang von Goethe, which appeared in journals such as the *Frankfurter Zeitung*, *Die Literarische Welt*, and *Die Gesellschaft*, and by translating works by Charles Baudelaire, Marcel Proust, and Marcel Jouhandeau. In these early essays, as in his thesis on the German drama (*Trauerspiel*), Benjamin attacked the aesthetic delusion, which covered up the tragedies of human experience by mimicking the totality of nature or by evoking a deceptive harmony of language. In one of his first essays, about Goethe's novel *Die Wahlverwandtschaften* (1809; *Elective Affinities*, 1872), Benjamin argued that criticism should reveal the calamity of the human condition by radically demolishing any symbolic representation of nature that would suggest an order to human existence. Behind the allegorical representation of faith in the baroque tragic drama, his thesis uncovered the civilizational trauma of thirty years of war and plague. Allegory showed the importance of apprehending language in a primordial fashion, verbalizing without mediation things in themselves. For Benjamin, only a language free of human intention could reveal such metaphysical truth. The dialectical tension between all literary imagery and historical reality, which should be exposed by the critic to shock readers or viewers, would be a recurrent theme throughout his work. Every "document of civilization" was also in some way a "document of barbarism," as were all "cultural treasures."

The complex philosophy of language by which Benjamin understood the function of words was complemented by a great mastery of his native tongue, German, allowing him to give the highest abstractions a sensuous richness. Embracing Bertolt Brecht's concept of "crude thinking" by which the language of practice is used to articulate theory, Benjamin denied that the dialectician could only explain himself (or herself) through arcane linguistic formulations. Both the argument and style of his writings thus brushed continually against the grain of linguistic or symbolic illusion.

As the critique of modern culture developed, Benjamin saw the fault lying less in language itself and more in the social role of bourgeois intellectuals who turned literature and art into commodities, sold and possessed rather than experienced politically. Culture should articulate the alienating and negative dimensions of human experience, thereby revealing the contradictions of industrial society. For example, the shock of Baudelaire's assaultive use of sacred images in unholy contexts exposed the social truth lying behind the trancelike pretense to normality in bourgeois art.

After 1924, Benjamin's interest in a materialistic analysis of modernity was increasingly enriched by contact with left-wing intellectuals, such as Asja Lacis, a Latvian actress who introduced him to Brecht. He was particularly impressed with the Marxist critique of culture set forth by György Lukács in *Geschichte und Klassenbewusstein* (1923; *History and Class Consciousness*, 1971). In 1926-1927, Benjamin visited Moscow and reported enthusiastically on the wave of artistic experimentation that followed the Russian Revolution, but typically he admitted that he was too much of an "anarchist" to join the Communist Party. Nevertheless, he be-

lieved that "significant literary work" would come only from "a strict alternation between action and writing."

The Nazi takeover of the German state in 1933 forced Benjamin to Paris, where he furthered his interest in French culture, and to Denmark and Ibiza, where he enjoyed extended visits with Brecht. After 1935, there appeared in the *Zeitschrift für Sozialforschung* (journal for social research), published by the exiled Frankfurt Institute for Social Research, a number of important articles by Benjamin on nineteenth century French culture and modern urban life. A stipend from the institute had been secured for him by Theodor Adorno, one of its leading members.

Throughout his later essays, Benjamin defined the task of criticism as the recovery of everyday life, fragmented by the alienating and reifying forces of capitalism. The 1867 World Exhibition in Paris was, for example, a microcosm of the world of commodities wherein the emphasis on individualistic buying and selling prevented realization that production should serve human needs. The discontinuous events of modernity, experienced disjointedly through capitalistic consumerism, technological fetishes, and the crowded metropolis, estranged people from even the integral nature of their own experiences.

Benjamin had hoped to bring these themes together in a masterpiece, the unfinished but later published *Das Passagen-Werk* (1982), which was translated into English and published as *The Arcades Project* (1999). By using the sumptuous commercial galleries of nineteenth century Paris, he wanted to write a modern allegory on the sociotechnological basis of bourgeois culture. The embodiment of modern alienation was the flaneur (dawdler, wanderer, or "man-about-town"), whose stroll past the cafés, brothels, boutiques, dioramas, theaters, newsstands, and baths that jammed the Parisian arcades represented the lonely voyeurism of the urban crowd. The luxuriousness of the shop windows masked any understanding of the oppression required to fill them, just as exchange value obscured the intrinsic use value of capitalist production. Like the bohemian flaneur, bourgeois intellectuals who posed as critics in actuality legitimated the public's consumption of capitalist culture.

Benjamin, however, unlike other critics of the materialism of the modern age, such as the Pre-Raphaelites, sought no return to a simpler culture and life. He applauded, for example, advances in aesthetic techniques that might provide artists with the means of redefining the relationship between themselves and their audience. He was enthusiastic about the revolutionary potential of film. Above all else, he wanted to strip culture of the religious mystification that occurred when it was experienced passively. It was Brecht's blunt interruption of the observer's empathy with the stage that Benjamin found so enticing. As he argued in his famous and influential essay "Das Kunstwerk im Zeitalter seiner technischen Reproduzierbarkeit" (1936; "The Work of Art in the Age of Mechanical Reproduction," 1968), the modern capability exactly to reproduce paintings fortunately destroyed their "aura," that reverential attitude of the cultivated public toward authenticity. The obsession with artistic genuineness deflected public attention away from the fact that life in bourgeois society was itself inauthentic, standardized, and unnatural. In "Der Autor als Produzent" (1966; "The Author as Producer," 1978), Benjamin suggested that literature might be politicized if the traditional ways that writers addressed their readers were overturned.

Feeling that there were "still positions to defend," Benjamin stayed in France well after many of his comrades had fled. Using the ideas of Sigmund Freud, he attacked the fascist glorification of bodily discipline, sexual asceticism, and nationalistic self-sacrifice. With the Stalin-Hitler Pact of 1939, and a short internment with other German refugees at Niève, Benjamin appears to have lost some of his faith in the possibility of meaningful political engagement. Turning back to a melancholic messianism found in his own Jewish heritage, his last work, "Über den Begriff der Geschichte" (1942; "Theses on the Philosophy of History," 1968), would appear to abandon faith in historical progress. Redemption from oppression could be found only in some eschatological interruption of time, a "Now-time" or *Jetzt-zeit*, that allowed for the rediscovery of the dreams of humanity.

After the Nazi invasion of France, Benjamin acquired a visa in Marseilles to enter the United States and, with failing health, tried to escape to Spain. When an official, attempting blackmail, threatened to turn him and his fellow refugees over to the Gestapo, he took his own life with a massive dose of morphine on September 26, 1940, in Port Bou, Spain. Two volumes of his collected writing appeared posthumously only in 1955. From that date, however, his work acquired an immense influence on postmodern criticism.

SIGNIFICANCE

Calling himself the "last of the Europeans," Benjamin wrote incisively about such diverse things as hashish, children's toys, postage stamps, Surrealism, and Kafka. He was, as Hannah Arendt observed, a metaphysician who

thought poetically. Seeing no "hermetic self-sufficiency" to any discipline, his thought allowed him to combine conservative aesthetic sensibilities with structuralist and materialist criticism. The eclectic complexity of his thought, his use of aphorism and the short essay, and the density of his exposition make a unified interpretation of Benjamin extremely difficult. As Jürgen Habermas noted, his thoughts like his friends were not always introduced to one another. His ultimate role was as an essayist: Opinion was like oil to a machine, he wrote; one did not dump a can on a turbine, one applied a little at a time to spindles and joints. In many ways his ideas were like the angels in the Talmudic legend, an innumerable host created to sing their hymn in God's presence and then cease and disappear into the void. Benjamin distrusted any limitation on a dialectical understanding of truth. His fragmentary, eclectic manner, what he called "dialectics at a standstill," well served such an understanding.

—Bland Addison, Jr.

FURTHER READING

Benjamin, Andrew, and Beatrice Hanssen, eds. *Walter Benjamin and Romanticism*. New York: Continuum, 2002. The twelve essays in this volume address Benjamin's writings on Romanticism, especially those dealing with the work of Goethe, Novalis, and Schlegel.

Benjamin, Walter. *The Arcades Project*. Translated by Howard Eiland and Kevin McLaughlin. Cambridge, Mass.: Belknap Press, 1999. Benjamin's great work of cultural criticism and theory, a massive collection of more than one thousand pages. This translation is based on the work in German edited by Rolf Tiedemann. Highly recommended.

_____. *Reflections*. Edited by Peter Demetz. New York: Schocken Books, 1986. Another diverse selection of Benjamin essays, including several autobiographical pieces (notably on his Berlin childhood and visit to Moscow), and an introduction by Demetz focusing on the different currents creating the complexity of his thought.

Buck-Morss, Susan. *Walter Benjamin and the Dialectics of Seeing: A Study of the Arcades Project*. Cambridge, Mass.: MIT Press, 1989. A deep analysis, inspired by a New Left interpretation of Marxism, of what has become Benjamin's masterpiece.

Eagleton, Terry. *Walter Benjamin: Or, Towards a Revolutionary Criticism*. London: Verso and New Left Books, 1981. A difficult but important work showing the influence of Benjamin on neo-Marxist and poststructuralist criticism. Eagleton explores three central themes in Benjamin—the baroque allegory, commodities as cultural objects, and messianic concepts of revolution.

Ferris, David S. *The Cambridge Companion to Walter Benjamin*. New York: Cambridge University Press, 2004. Collection of essays that provide a comprehensive introduction to Benjamin's ideas, investigating various aspects of his work that significantly influenced contemporary historical and critical thinking. Includes discussions of Benjamin's relation to avant-garde movements, his theories on language, and his autobiographical writings.

Hanssen, Beatrice, ed. *Walter Benjamin and the Arcades Project*. New York: Continuum, 2006. A comprehensive introduction to Benjamin's major work. Chapters explore a wide range of topics, including the nature of collecting, the anatomy of melancholy, the flaneur, the physiognomy of ruins, the dialectical image, Benjamin's relation to Baudelaire, the practice of history writing, and modernity and architecture. Highly recommended.

Roberts, Julian. *Walter Benjamin*. London: Macmillan, 1982. A defense of the Marxist interpretation of Benjamin's thought, understood in the context of the culture and history of the early twentieth century.

Scholem, Gershom. *Walter Benjamin: The Story of a Friendship*. Translated by Harry Zohn. Philadelphia: Jewish Publication Society, 1981. An interpretation of Benjamin's romantic messianism by a distinguished scholar of the Kabbala.

Smith, Gary, ed. *On Walter Benjamin: Critical Essays and Recollections*. Cambridge, Mass.: MIT Press, 1988. A useful collection of essays by leading Benjamin scholars and his friends, including Adorno, Scholem, and Habermas. Includes an extensive bibliography.

SEE ALSO: Hannah Arendt; Roland Barthes; Henri Bergson; Bertolt Brecht; Ernst Cassirer; Jacques Derrida; Jürgen Habermas; Martin Heidegger; Edmund Husserl; Franz Kafka; György Lukács; Marcel Proust; Susan Sontag; Thorstein Veblen.

RELATED ARTICLES in *Great Events from History: The Twentieth Century:*

1901-1940: 1913: Husserl Advances Phenomenology; Summer, 1918: Rise of Cultural Relativism Revises Historiography; 1921: Wittgenstein Emerges as an Important Philosopher; October, 1924: Surrealism Is Born; 1927: Heidegger Publishes *Being and Time.*

1941-1970: June 25, 1943: Sartre's *Being and Nothingness* Expresses Existential Philosophy; 1963: Arendt Speculates on the Banality of Evil; 1964-1972: Marcuse Publishes Foundational New Left Works.

ALBAN BERG
Austrian composer

Berg was one of the pioneers in the creation of atonal and twelve-tone music. Though basing his work on the revolutionary system of his teacher Arnold Schoenberg, Berg established a link between the new style and the Romantic past and demonstrated that atonal and twelve-tone music could still be lyrical and emotionally expressive. As a result, his works gained widespread acceptance and thus encouraged a whole generation of innovative and experimental composers.

BORN: February 9, 1885; Vienna, Austro-Hungarian Empire (now in Austria)
DIED: December 24, 1935; Vienna, Austria
AREA OF ACHIEVEMENT: Music

EARLY LIFE

Alban Berg (AHL-bahn behrk) was born in Vienna to a prosperous businessman whose distinguished Bavarian Catholic ancestry included high-ranking military men and public servants. Even so, the Bergs were an artistic family, and Berg's brother and sister both studied music. Berg himself, however, at first seemed more interested in poetry and drama, reading Henrik Ibsen, Oscar Wilde, and the Romantic German literature common at the end of the nineteenth century. Later, as a composer of operas, Berg was to realize his literary ambitions by writing his own librettos.

Despite circumstances that were apparently comfortable, Berg's early life was not without difficulties. As a child, his health was generally frail, and, in 1900, the year his father died, he developed a severe form of asthma that plagued him throughout his life. Perhaps coincidentally, it was also in this year that he first tried his hand at composition, setting three German poems to music. From that point on, composing became his primary interest, and, over the next four years, he created some seventy works, mostly songs and piano duets. Though influenced initially by the Romantic music of Johannes Brahms, Richard Wagner, and Gustav Mahler, Berg had, as yet, no formal musical training. He was, in fact, far too high-strung and moody to be an especially good student: At age eighteen, for example, he failed his general humanities examination and then attempted suicide.

In the following year, 1904, Berg finally completed his schooling and obtained a position working for the government. After a few months at this job, he saw a newspaper advertisement for students placed by Arnold Schoenberg, a thirty-year-old composer and teacher who had already begun to rock the musical world. Berg immediately submitted several of his works to Schoenberg, who recognized Berg's talent and accepted him as a student. Over the next six years, Schoenberg became both mentor and friend to the younger man, and through patient encouragement shaped his whole approach to composition.

LIFE'S WORK

At the time Berg became his pupil, Schoenberg was just beginning to break away from the Wagnerian Romantic tradition and would soon work out an entirely new approach to musical composition. Since the time of Johann Sebastian Bach at least, nearly all Western music had been written from the basis of tonality. Essentially, this means that the construction of a piece of music was centered on a single tone, called the "key." Tension and interest were created by moving away from the key, but, by the end, the tension was resolved by returning to the initial tone. The tools used in the tonal system were the notes of the diatonic scale (do, re, mi, fa, sol, and so on) and chords. A diatonic scale includes any seven tones in order, which are sounded by the white keys on a piano. The notes sounded by the five black keys in between are called "chromatic" tones. The twelve tones together are called a "chromatic scale." Using the chromatic notes increases the emotional energy in a piece of music.

Chords are a combination of tones played simultaneously. In the tonal system, chords are usually built of three notes (triads), each one full tone apart (do-mi-sol, re-fa-la, and so on). A chord can be made out of each note in the diatonic scale. The first chord (do-mi-sol) is called

the tonic and is the chord of rest. Like tones that move away from the key, each of the other chords in the scale, which move away from the tonic, creates tension or activity. The fifth chord (sol-ti-re) is called the dominant, and it represents the most tension. Music theorists say that the dominant chord seeks to be resolved by the tonic. Moving away from the tonic chord is called "dissonance," while coming back to the tonic is "consonance."

Many composers of the Romantic period, such as Ludwig van Beethoven and Hector Berlioz, had sought to express great emotion in their music by increasing the amount of dissonance before finally returning to the tonic. Among their methods was creation of new, more dissonant chords using the chromatic notes. In the last half of the nineteenth century, Wagner had taken this technique to its logical endpoint, employing more and more "chromaticism" and delaying the return to the tonic until a nearly unbearable tension had been created. However, Wagner had still remained within the general system of tonality, ultimately resolving the tension by returning to the fundamental key.

At the beginning of their careers, both Schoenberg and Berg wrote music within this Wagnerian tradition. By 1904, however, Schoenberg had begun to believe that the time had come to do away with consonance and the distinction between the diatonic and chromatic tones. He wished to treat all twelve tones of the scale equally and relate them in music freely to one another, rather than to some central tone. Within a few years, Schoenberg had completely abandoned the tonal system, and his music became increasingly dissonant, always operating at a maximum level of tense, unresolved emotion. His approach became known as atonality.

Soon, however, Schoenberg became dissatisfied with atonality, too: Abandoning the keys and consonant harmonies that were the basis of the tonal system had left nothing but musical anarchy. He now insisted that a whole new set of rules of composition had to be fashioned. Thus, he created the concept of the "tone row," any arbitrary arrangement of twelve tones. The tone row served as the unifying idea of a composition, and its tones were always used in the same order, though each new appearance of the row could start on any note of the scale. The tone row also might be turned upside down (inversion), backward (retrograde), or both (retrograde inversion), but both the melody and the harmony of a piece were always based on the original twelve-tone pattern. This system of composition is known as the twelve-tone system, or the serial technique, and is the foundation for much of the music of the twentieth century.

BERG ON THE OPERA *WOZZECK*

Alban Berg sometimes questioned his achievement in composing Wozzeck *(wr. 1921). Two years after the opera's premiere he wrote an article about it for the journal* Modern Music, *concluding the following.*

What I do consider my particular accomplishment is this. No one in the audience, no matter how aware he may be of the musical forms contained in the framework of the opera, of the precision and logic with which it has been worked out, no one, from the moment the curtain parts until it closes for the last time, pays any attention to the various fugues, inventions, suites, sonata movements, variations, and passacaglias about which so much has been written. No one gives heed to anything but the vast social implications of the work which by far transcend the personal destiny of *Wozzeck*. This, I believe, is my achievement.

The impressionable young Berg enthusiastically embraced Schoenberg's new methods, and the music he wrote under Schoenberg's tutelage followed the creative evolution of his teacher. Berg's first significant atonal work was Five Songs with Orchestra, written in 1912. It was first performed on February 23, 1913, in a concert of music all written by Schoenberg and his pupils. While a few of the music critics present viewed the new works favorably, the audience reacted with such violent hostility that a riot ensued. One woman fainted, and a horn player in the orchestra vowed that he would never again play such trash. While Schoenberg was apparently unaffected by these responses, this first contact with the general public made a deep and lasting impression on Berg. Though throughout his life, Berg wrote many articles praising both Schoenberg's music and the twelve-tone system, his own compositions soon began to develop a distinct style of their own.

In May, 1914, Berg saw a production of Georg Büchner's play *Woyzeck* (1836; English translation, 1927), and he resolved to create an opera out of this tragic story of a poor soldier who jealously murders his love and then commits suicide. Berg began working on the libretto immediately, but his efforts were interrupted by the outbreak of World War I. Despite his fragile health, Berg was drafted into the Austrian army for limited duty at the War Ministry. After the war, he became a teacher and finally completed *Wozzeck* in 1921. It was not until December, 1925, however, that *Wozzeck* was first performed. Scorned in Vienna, Berg arranged for its presentation by the Berlin State Opera. The performance was a tremendous success, and overnight Berg became an international celebrity. *Wozzeck* was repeated several times in Berlin and then moved on to a triumphant world tour. By 1936, it had been performed 166 times in twenty-nine cities, including Philadelphia and New York. For many years, it remained the most popular opera composed in the twentieth century.

Berg's newfound fame seems to have had little effect on him. He continued to teach and write in Vienna, despite the fact that he was largely ignored in his own country. In 1930, he was appointed to membership in the prestigious Prussian Academy of Arts, and, by 1932, he had finally gained enough financial security to purchase a small summer home on the Wörthersee, a lake in Carinthia. He was bitterly disappointed, however, when Adolf Hitler came to power in Germany, in January, 1933. The Nazis immediately branded Berg's works as "anti-German" and banned them. The growing influence of Nazism in Austria also frightened him, and he was especially disturbed when Schoenberg, whose ancestry was Jewish, was forced to emigrate to the United States.

In the last decade of his life, Berg composed a relatively small number of works, but each one was crafted with consummate skill and artistry. Shortly after the premiere of *Wozzeck*, he wrote the Chamber Concerto for piano, violin, and thirteen wind instruments. This work was dedicated to Schoenberg and written almost completely in the serial technique. In 1926, he produced the Lyric Suite, a six-movement work for string quartet that is much more expressive and lyrical and that uses a combination of atonal, twelve-tone, and even tonal methods. So popular did the Lyric Suite become that, in 1928, Berg arranged three of its movements for orchestra.

For most of his last seven years, however, Berg concentrated on the development of one work, an opera called *Lulu*. As with *Wozzeck*, he himself wrote the libretto, using material from two plays by the German writer Frank Wedekind. *Lulu* is a violent story full of murder, blackmail, sexual perversion, imprisonment, and degradation—ideally suited to the social and intellectual ferment of the 1920's and early 1930's.

In the spring of 1935, Berg was commissioned by the American violinist Louis Krasner to write a violin concerto. Absorbed by the effort to finish *Lulu*, the composer procrastinated about the concerto until the death of a young lady friend inspired him to express his grief through music. The Violin Concerto was written with uncharacteristic rapidity and was dedicated "to the memory of an Angel." This was to be Berg's last completed work and perhaps his most beautiful and gentle. In it, he successfully reconciles the twelve-tone method with traditionally tonal harmony by using an Austrian folk tune and the chorale from a Bach cantata as formative elements. Though the piece utilizes a twelve-tone row, the row itself is based on the traditional triad chord structure. The Violin Concerto was first performed in April, 1936, four months after Berg's death, and, ironically, it became his own requiem.

After completing the Violin Concerto, Berg was exhausted and went off to his summer home for a short rest. At some point in the ensuing weeks, he received an insect bite that became infected and abscessed. When he returned to Vienna to work on the *Lulu* score, he was in great pain, and, finally, on December 17, he entered a hospital, where he was diagnosed as suffering from blood poisoning. Despite several transfusions, he weakened and died on December 24, 1935. His final thoughts were given over to the unfinished *Lulu;* as he died, he went through the motions of conducting the music, and his final words instructed the orchestra to play more firmly.

SIGNIFICANCE

Though never completed, *Lulu*, like *Wozzeck*, became a worldwide success. A suite for orchestra and soprano has been adapted from the finished portions of the score and has been performed frequently. The first two acts of the opera were presented in Zurich, Switzerland, in 1937, and the entire completed portions have been staged many times since to great acclaim. Today, Berg is generally regarded as the greatest of the atonal/twelve-tone composers, and his works have influenced those of many other modern composers.

This impact has resulted primarily because Berg became the mediator between the innovative atonal and twelve-tone approaches of Schoenberg and the Romanticism of the nineteenth century. Though almost slavishly loyal to Schoenberg's overall approach, Berg's music retained much of the Romantic outlook, and he proved that atonality can express a variety of moods. His twelve-tone works are gentler and more spontaneous than those of Schoenberg. In *Wozzeck*, tonal and atonal methods are intertwined and dramatically juxtaposed. In *Lulu* and the Violin Concerto, Berg showed that the twelve-tone row could be used flexibly to create both melodic and harmonic materials with a link to the past. In all three of these works, he assimilated folk-tune elements and displayed a highly developed sense of instrumental color often reminiscent of Impressionist composers such as Claude Debussy. The success of *Wozzeck*, the Violin Concerto, and the Lyric Suite have proved that modern serious music does not have to be ugly and can appeal to the average listener. This is, perhaps, Berg's greatest contribution.

—*Thomas C. Schunk*

FURTHER READING

Deri, Otto. *Exploring Twentieth-Century Music*. New York: Holt, Rinehart and Winston, 1968. A well-written text that attempts to aid readers and listeners in understanding and appreciating twentieth century music by explaining how its aesthetic principles and materials evolved. Contains an excellent chapter on the life and works of Berg and offers a detailed analysis of several of Berg's major works. Includes an extensive bibliography and discography.

Hall, Patricia. "Berg's Sketches and the Inception of Wozzeck, 1914-1918." *Musical Times* 146, no. 1892 (Autumn, 2002): 5. Examines the sketches and other documents related to the opera that Berg created from 1914 and 1918, measuring the impact of World War I on Berg's evolution as a composer.

Hansen, Peter S. *An Introduction to Twentieth Century Music*. 4th ed. Boston: Allyn and Bacon, 1978. A standard text on modern music. Presents an appreciative summary of the major movements and musical developments since 1900. Includes a separate chapter on Berg.

Lambert, Constant. *Music Ho! A Study of Music in Decline*. 1934. New ed. London: Hogarth, 1985. Lambert, himself a prominent British composer before his premature death in 1951, offers a challenging view of twentieth century music. He argues that the loss of traditional values in modern society has tended to encourage composers who violate and destroy the traditional rules pretentiously and simply as a pose. He also praises Berg as a composer. Includes a new introduction for this edition.

Machlis, Joseph. *Introduction to Contemporary Music*. 2d ed. London: Dent, 1982. An excellent, extremely well-written text. Introduces modern music through comparison and contrast with earlier periods, creating a painless introduction to music theory. European and American composers are grouped by types; each receives a concise biographical treatment and analysis of important works. Includes an excellent bibliography and discography, and texts and translations of vocal works.

Redlich, Hans F. *Alban Berg: The Man and His Music.* London: J. Calder, 1957. Berg's most important biographer. This work is extremely detailed and informative, but readers unfamiliar with music theory will find Redlich's analyses of Berg's work to be very difficult. In addition, Redlich is opinionated, and many other critics of Berg's works have disagreed with Redlich's highly politicized analyses of *Wozzeck* and *Lulu.*

Reich, Willi. *The Life and Work of Alban Berg.* Translated by Cornelius Cardew. Reprint. New York: Da Capo Press, 1981. Reich is less enlightening than

Redlich about Berg's personal life, but his analyses of Berg's music are both more thorough and more objective. For advanced students, this is a superior work.

SEE ALSO: Samuel Barber; Benjamin Britten; Claude Debussy; Gustav Mahler; Arnold Schoenberg; Ralph Vaughan Williams; Anton von Webern.

RELATED ARTICLES in *Great Events from History: The Twentieth Century:*

1901-1940: 1908-1909: Schoenberg Breaks with Tonality; March 31, 1913: Webern's Six Pieces for Large Orchestra Premieres; 1921-1923: Schoenberg Develops His Twelve-Tone System; December 14, 1925: Berg's *Wozzeck* Premieres in Berlin; June 2, 1937: Berg's *Lulu* opens in Zurich.

FRIEDRICH BERGIUS
German chemist

Bergius discovered how to obtain liquid hydrocarbon fuels by hydrogenation of coal and how to obtain synthetic sugar from wood cellulose. The fuels made by his processes aided Germany during World War II, and Bergius's methods form the basis for the modern synthetic fuels industry.

BORN: October 11, 1884; Goldschmieden, Germany (now Wrocław, Poland)
DIED: March 30, 1949; Buenos Aires, Argentina
AREAS OF ACHIEVEMENT: Chemistry, invention and technology

EARLY LIFE

Friedrich Bergius (FREE-drihk BEHR-gee-ehs) was born to well-educated parents. He gained early experience in chemistry, working first in a small chemical plant owned by his father and later in a larger plant in Mulheim/Ruhr. He studied at the Universities of Breslau and Leipzig. At Leipzig, Bergius worked under the direction of Arthur Hantzsch, who had also influenced the work of Nobel laureate Alfred Werner twenty years earlier. He was granted the Ph.D. in chemistry in 1907 and proceeded to Berlin for a year of postdoctoral work with Walther Hermann Nernst, who was one of the most prominent physical chemists in German academic circles at that time.

Bergius now had his first opportunity to attempt high-pressure reactions in the laboratory. He also participated

in research on the nitrogen/hydrogen/ammonia equilibrium in Nernst's laboratory. After leaving Berlin, Bergius spent a further semester at Karlsruhe in association with the future Nobel laureate Fritz Haber. There, Bergius gained further experience in the application of high-pressure reaction techniques. He was not satisfied with the existing techniques and apparatus, and he saw the need for improvements.

Bergius's first published research was a doctoral dissertation on the use of 100 percent sulfuric acid as a solvent. He began his affiliation with the Hannover Institute of Technology in 1909 and was free to pursue his developing interest in high-pressure reactions. His research was conducted partly at the institute and partly at a private laboratory he established. As his projects reached pilot-plant scale, further facilities were acquired. Early work included a study of the lime/oxygen/calcium peroxide equilibrium, which was undertaken in the hope of finding a better process for manufacturing hydrogen peroxide, but which actually was important mainly because it required the refinement of high-pressure valves, fittings, stirred autoclaves, and other equipment that was of great use later. Bergius and his coworkers also patented a method of using caustic soda to convert chlorobenzene into phenol (needed for the manufacture of plastic). This patent was one of many German patents confiscated by the Allies after World War I and became the basis of the manufacture of phenol by Dow Chemical Company.

As early as 1911, Bergius became interested in the na-

Friedrich Bergius. (© The Nobel Foundation)

ture and origin of coal—one of Germany's most plentiful natural resources. The studies that he made of the coal-forming process (the virtually untranslatable German word is *Inkohlung*) led to the achievements for which he is most famous and for which he was awarded (jointly with Carl Bosch) the 1931 Nobel Prize in Chemistry.

LIFE'S WORK

Bergius, like Bosch and Haber, sought to apply the academic principles of physical chemistry to the solution of industrial chemical problems. His goal was not only to understand chemical reactions in an academic manner but also to develop practical industrial methods for large-scale economical production. His efforts were applied mainly in three areas: the production of pure, inexpensive hydrogen; the liquefaction of coal and peat; and the conversion of cellulose-containing by-products into sugar and starch. Bergius's interests were motivated by a desire to benefit humanity in general and by a desire to help Germany end its dependence on foreign sources for food and fuel. Bergius's success in each of these areas came partly from his energy and persistence in overcom-

ing an array of obstacles and partly from his ability to bring to bear the newest technology, particularly the use of high pressures.

The production of hydrogen from the reaction between steam and coke (the water-gas reaction) produced impure hydrogen. Bergius modified this reaction by performing the process at high pressure and developed purification methods for the hydrogen. He also found it possible to manufacture pure hydrogen by means of a reaction between water and iron. Ultimately, this proved cheaper than the use of the water-gas reaction. Modifications of the water-gas reaction and of the iron-water reaction were explored in which the use of high pressure kept the water liquid at high temperatures.

Coal hydrogenation had been performed in small laboratory experiments as early as 1869 by Marcelin Berthelot in France. Bergius improved on the earlier method by switching to high-pressure conditions instead of the relatively low pressures that were obtained by Berthelot. Using a few grams of powdered coal moistened with petroleum to form a paste and treated with high-pressure hydrogen gas, Bergius was able to obtain promising yields of liquid and gaseous hydrocarbons. Use of a rotating autoclave, which was especially developed for the purpose, permitted successful reactions on the scale of five liters, but problems remained.

The hydrogenation reaction was heat-releasing and thus needed to be conducted in a controlled manner to prevent overheating, which reduced the yield of hydrocarbons and produced useless coke. Attempts to hydrogenate coal in larger batches brought many problems. Overheating became more difficult to control in large reactors, and the batch process was inefficient and needed to be made continuous. As the size and complexity of the apparatus increased, so did the expense of the research, and Bergius sought financial backing from various industrial sources. Eventually, Bergius left his relatively small private laboratory in Hannover and began to assemble a modern high-pressure facility in Essen. By that time, he had conducted many studies on the production of hydrogen and on the hydrogenation of oil and coal and had obtained the first of his many patents. Hundreds of different samples of coal of various kinds were tested to determine which types were most suitable for hydrogenation. Soft coal and lignite (common in Germany) were well suited, but hard anthracite coal was poorly suited for liquefaction.

The coal hydrogenation reaction, when scaled up, involved formidable material-handling problems. The coal was ground to a powder and mixed with oil to form a paste. This paste was preheated and pressed into the reactor by a cylindrical ram. Products were continually removed from the reacting mixture during hydrogenation.

The development site in Rheinau/Mannheim employed about 150 workers and was exceedingly expensive to maintain. It became obvious that better capitalization was needed, which could come only from affiliation with a larger company. Bergius sold his patents to Badische Anilin und Soda Fabrik (BASF), a major corporation, which continued to develop coal hydrogenation at a plant in Leuna. Much further development was needed to create the synthetic fuel industry that existed in Germany by the 1940's (twelve production facilities were eventually brought into operation), but Bergius's direct contributions were over. He turned his attention to another area: the production of synthetic food.

Chemically, starch, cellulose, and glucose (also known as dextrose) are closely related, since starch and cellulose are composed of many glucose units linked together—one pattern of linkage leading to starch and another to cellulose. Although ruminants can digest cellulose as well as starch, humans can digest only starch (or glucose). Strong acids (such as hydrochloric acid, which humans have in their digestive tracts) can eventually break down cellulose into sugar but only at high temperatures. Bergius devoted years of effort to the perfection of the method of converting sawdust, straw, or other agricultural wastes into edible material by hydrochloric acid treatment. Great care and ingenuity were needed to ensure recycling of reactants and the greatest efficiency in the use of heat. An extensive account of this work was published in 1931 as "Die Herstellung von Zucker aus Holz und ähnlichen Naturstoffen" (the preparation of sugar from wood and other natural materials).

Bergius resided in Heidelberg in the late 1920's and was awarded an honorary degree by the university in 1927. In Hannover, a street was named for him, and the university awarded him an honorary degree. Even Harvard University chose to award him an honorary degree in 1936. In Heidelberg, the Bergius household became a meeting place for artists and writers. Among those who came was Gustav Stresemann, a leader in the National Liberal Party and chancellor (1923) who had done much to rejuvenate German industry after World War I by negotiating with the Allies over the question of reparations.

Once again, however, Bergius's research began to suffer from lack of funding. He sold his home, threw all of his personal fortune into the research effort, and even made a personal appeal to President Paul von Hindenburg for support to keep his work going. Ironically, it was only the rise of Adolf Hitler and his preparations for war that finally stimulated meaningful support from the government for the so-called food from wood project. Bergius worked during the war years in Berlin but saw his facilities destroyed by air raids. At the end of the war, the Allies captured numerous documents pertaining to German scientific research. Scholars are still studying these documents, and it may be that additional details of Bergius's research activities may appear. Bergius spent the postwar years until his death in an attempt to find suitable employment and scope for his further plans. He went first to Italy, then to Turkey, Switzerland, and Spain. He left Europe in 1947 to become a scientific adviser to the Argentine government and died in Buenos Aires in 1949.

SIGNIFICANCE

Although his life was rich in achievements, Bergius spent the latter part of his life in circumstances that did not permit him to be as creative as he might have been. The economic chaos in Germany in the 1920's made it so difficult to obtain funding for his research that in 1925 he sold most of his patents to BASF. From that time on, Bergius was excluded from further work on coal liquefaction, the field that he had pioneered.

Turning to cellulose conversion, Bergius again did fundamental work and developed an economically viable process, but only after spending vast sums—including major amounts of his own money. Unfortunately, the commercial interest in his process did not materialize to any great extent. After World War II, having lost his laboratory and sources of funding, he became a sort of scientific refugee and traveled to many countries as a consultant until his death.

—John R. Phillips

FURTHER READING

Bergius, Friedrich. "Chemical Reactions Under High Pressure." In *Chemistry, 1922-1941*. River Edge, N.J.: World Scientific, 1999. Bergius's Nobel lecture is reprinted in this volume, which includes biographies of the laureates.

_____. "An Historical Account of Hydrogenation." In *Proceedings of the World Petroleum Congress* 2. London: Offices of the Congress 1934. Bergius tells what trains of thought led him to develop his coal- and oil-hydrogenation processes. There are nineteen illustrations, mostly showing diagrams of reactors or photographs of process equipment.

Deutch, John M., and Richard K. Lester. *Making Tech-*

nology Work: Applications in Energy and the Environment. New York: Cambridge University Press, 2004. A good introduction to the key technologies in alternative and synthetic fuels, including the use of coal. For advanced students.

Stranges, Anthony N. "Friedrich Bergius and the Rise of the German Synthetic Fuel Industry." *Isis* 75, no. 279 (1984): 643-667. This article traces the growth of the German synthetic fuel industry, concentrating on the period 1910-1925. Includes an extensive list of references to works by and about Bergius.

_____. "Friedrich Bergius and the Transformation of Coal Liquefaction from Empiricism to a Science-Based Technology." *Journal of Chemical Education* 65, no. 9 (1988): 749-751. This article discusses

Bergius's place in the application of the highly theoretical ideas of Nernst and the other founders of chemical thermodynamics.

Szöllösi-Janze, Margit, ed. *Science in the Third Reich.* New York: Berg, 2001. A collection of social science and historical essays examining the scientists and sciences of Nazi Germany.

SEE ALSO: Svante August Arrhenius; Fritz Haber; Paul von Hindenburg; Giulio Natta; Walther Hermann Nernst; Wilhelm Ostwald; Gustav Stresemann.

RELATED ARTICLE in *Great Events from History: The Twentieth Century:*
1901-1940: 1938: Callendar Connects Industry with Increased Atmospheric Carbon Dioxide.

INGMAR BERGMAN
Swedish filmmaker and theater director

Despite fluctuations in the critical appraisal of his many films, Bergman dominated the Scandinavian filmmaking industry from the mid-1940's until the early 1980's, and his films earned international acclaim. His rapport with actors and his innovative stage techniques also earned for him a reputation as one of the world's foremost theatrical directors.

BORN: July 14, 1918; Uppsala, Sweden
DIED: July 30, 2007; Fårö, Sweden
ALSO KNOWN AS: Ernst Ingmar Bergman (full name)
AREAS OF ACHIEVEMENT: Film, theater and entertainment

EARLY LIFE

Ingmar Bergman (BURG-mihn) was born in Uppsala, Sweden, to Erik and Karin Bergman and was reared in the country home of his maternal grandmother. A Lutheran pastor, Erik Bergman believed in strict discipline for his family, which consisted of Ingmar and his brother and sister. Many of Bergman's childhood memories revolve around episodes of punishment by humiliation, such as being made to wear a skirt after wetting his pants; however, not all of his experiences were negative. His grandmother discussed important issues with the boy daily and encouraged his storytelling abilities. Though Bergman's early years were spent in relative poverty, a rich aunt did provide him with inspiration for his future career in filmmaking. She gave his elder brother a magic

lantern film projector, which Bergman so coveted that he traded his collection of toy soldiers for it.

When his father became chaplain to the Royal Hospital, young Bergman was fascinated by the nearby mortuary and cemetery, gaining there a gruesome introduction to death. In 1934, Erik Bergman was appointed parish priest at Hedvig Eleonora Church and the family moved to Stockholm. As an exchange student in Germany, Bergman developed a youthful passion for Nazism. His later disillusionment with Nazi atrocities led him away from politics altogether, although his love for Berlin remained so strong that he tried several times to portray the city in film. Following a brief period of military service, Bergman attended the University of Stockholm but became involved with writing and directing plays and did not complete his degree.

After many successful stage productions for various theaters in Stockholm, Bergman became a screenwriter for Svensk Filmindustri. His first screenplay, *Hets* (1944; *Torment*, 1947), about a young student's battle with his repressive schoolmaster (based on his own experiences at Palmgren's School), was directed by his mentor, veteran director Alf Sjöberg. The best film of his early career is probably *Fängelse* (1949; *The Devil's Wanton*, 1962), which he both wrote and directed for Terrafilm, a company run by independent producer Lorens Marmstedt, to whom Bergman attributed much of his own filmmaking education.

During this early part of his career, Bergman directed

plays for the Helsingborg, Malmö, and Gothenburg city theaters while at the same time working on films for Svensk Filmindustri and Terrafilm. While his professional life flourished, his tumultuous personal life was marked by financial problems, illness, divorces, and romantic affairs with his leading actresses. His marriages were to Else Fischer (1943-1945), Ellen Lundström (1945-1950), Gun Grut (1951-1959), Käbi Laretei (1959-1969), and Ingrid von Rosen (1971-1995).

LIFE'S WORK

Bergman's international reputation was established in the 1950's with a series of dramatic films that explore the complexity of human relationships. The difficulty of establishing and maintaining emotional bonds inside and outside marriage is investigated in *Sommarlek* (1951; *Illicit Interlude*, 1954), *Kvinnors väntan* (1952; *Secrets of Women*, 1961), *Gycklarnas Afton* (1953; *The Naked Night*, 1956), *En lection i kärlek* (1954; *A Lesson in Love*, 1960), and *Sommarnattens leende* (1955; *Smiles of a Summer Night*, 1957), which won the Grand Prix at the Cannes Film Festival and first brought him international attention. Bergman's affair with actress Harriet Andersson, who stars in several of these films, affected his early portrait of Nordic eroticism. Eva Dahlbeck and Gunnar Björnstrand, key members of Bergman's stock film-theater company, played the witty married couple in his lighter films. His repertory of actors who appeared in five or more of his films also included Max von Sydow, Bibi Andersson, Erland Josephson, Ingrid Thulin, and, most famously, Liv Ullmann. Moreover, he came to depend on the skill of cinematographer Sven Nykvist after 1953.

In what Peter Cowie calls his "golden years," Bergman posed philosophical and moral questions about the nature of humankind's existence and the problem of evil. *Det sjunde inseglet* (1957; *The Seventh Seal*, 1958), a medieval allegory set during the Great Plague, contemplates the meaninglessness of life in the face of irrational death. In *Smulltronstället* (1957; *Wild Strawberries*, 1959), Bergman studies one of his favorite character types, the cold intellectual who distances himself from common humanity. Both of these films employ the journey motif favored by Bergman to chart the emotional evolution of his characters, and they feature the sunny presence of Bibi Andersson, the actress/lover with whom Bergman made his most idealistic statements. The battle of rationality and emotion, of science and art, continues in *Ansiktet* (1958; *The Magician*, 1959). One of Bergman's favorite themes during the 1950's was the conflict

Ingmar Bergman. (Library of Congress)

between what Max von Sydow describes as "the very sensitive, highly emotional individual who cannot bear his own feelings" and "the one who is inhibited by his intellect."

After this intensely personal portrait of the artist, Bergman next adapted a fourteenth century legend about a young girl's brutal rape and her father's revenge in *Jungfrukällan* (1960; *The Virgin Spring*, 1960). Though Bergman would later criticize this film as an imitation of Akira Kurosawa's *Rashomon* (1950), *The Virgin Spring* won the Oscar for Best Foreign-Language Film. Returning to very subjective films about faith and doubt, Bergman wrote and directed what he termed his "Chamber Plays": *Såsom i en spegel* (1961; *Through a Glass Darkly*, 1961), *Nattvardsgästerna* (1963; *Winter Light*, 1962), and *Tystnaden* (1963; *The Silence*, 1964). The bleak settings, small cast, and the spare visual/narrative style (what Cowie calls "austere and improvisatory") underscore the themes of alienation and despair that permeate this important trilogy. Though *Through a Glass Darkly* won for Bergman another Academy Award, *The Silence* had to fight censorship boards around the world to preserve its carnal depiction of sexuality.

In 1963, Bergman was appointed as director of the Royal Dramatic Theater in Stockholm, a position he held for only three years, although he continued to direct plays there. His stark production of Henrik Ibsen's *Hedda Gabler* (1890; English translation, 1891) in 1964 was one of his most significant stage contributions. Bergman's next phase of filmmaking featured actress/lover Liv Ullmann, Max von Sydow as his alter ego, and his beloved island of Fårö, a bleak Scandinavian landscape that corresponded to his "innermost imaginings of forms, proportions, colors, horizons, sounds, silences, lights and reflections." One of his most obscure artistic endeavors, *Persona* (1966; English translation, 1967), probes the enigma of human identity through a heavily symbolic style that marks this period. Vivid hallucinations haunt the tortured artist in *Vargtimmen* (1968; *Hour of the Wolf*, 1968), blurring the boundaries between dream and reality. In his most overtly political film, *Skammen* (1968; *Shame*, 1968), war disrupts the lives of two artists who would remain detached from the events of the world. In *En passion* (1969; *The Passion of Anna*, 1970), the characters' inability to break through their essential isolation leads to frustration and violence.

After the failure of his first English-language film, *The Touch* (1971), Bergman staged Ibsen's *Vildanden* (1884; *The Wild Duck*, 1891) and filmed *Viskningar och rop* (1973; *Cries and Whispers*, 1973), two of his finest artistic achievements. Filmed with the startling use of red and white images, *Cries and Whispers* powerfully recounts a family's response to a sister's agonizing death.

After years of independent filmmaking, Bergman began to explore new territory in the 1970's with his lengthy productions for Swedish television. *Scener ur ett äktenskap* (1973; *Scenes from a Marriage*, 1974), Bergman's analysis of a couple's evolution through years of marriage, separation, and divorce, based on Bergman's own relationship with his third wife, appeared in six weekly episodes; *Ansikte mot ansikte* (1976; *Face to Face*, 1976), his psychological dissection of a woman's confrontation with death and madness, was presented in four parts. Bergman's lifelong love of music, inspired in part by his marriage to musician Käbi Laretei and fostered by the success of his lavish stage production of Franz Lehár's operetta *The Merry Widow* (1905) in 1954, culminated in the television production *Trollflöjten* (1975; *The Magic Flute*, 1975), an adaptation of the Mozart opera. The autobiographical study of his childhood, *Fanny och Alexander* (1982; *Fanny and Alexander*, 1983), and his portrait of a theatrical director, *Efter*

repetitionen (1984; *After the Rehearsal*, 1984), both appeared first on Swedish television. All of these productions were later distributed as films, some in edited or condensed versions.

Success was not without its costs for Bergman. Besides the physical toll that filmmaking exacted from him (chronic insomnia and nervous stomach disorders), his financial success in the 1970's led to his arrest and prosecution for tax evasion in 1976. Though he was cleared of the charges in 1979, Bergman endured public humiliation and exile from the landscape that had inspired him after a nervous breakdown caused him to seek refuge in a mental health clinic for more than a month. Despite these personal problems, he continued his career in Germany, producing two German-language films, *Das schlangenei* (1977; *The Serpent's Egg*, 1977), a pessimistic look at Berlin in transition before the rise of Adolf Hitler, and *Herbstsonat* (1978; *Autumn Sonata*, 1978), an exploration of a mother-daughter relationship starring Ingrid Bergman and Ullmann. In *Aus dem leben der marionetten* (1980; *From the Life of the Marionettes*, 1980), a psychiatrist tries to untangle the emotions that led a Munich businessman to murder a prostitute. The film remained one of Bergman's personal favorites, though it failed to receive critical or popular success. While in Germany, Bergman also successfully produced August Strindberg's *Ett drömspel* (1902; *A Dream Play*, 1912) in 1977, a provocative interpretation of Anton Chekhov's *Tri sestry* (1901; *The Three Sisters*, 1920), and his third approach to Ibsen's *Hedda Gabler*. From 1977 until 1984 he served as stage director of the Resienz-Theater in Munich.

During the filming of *The Touch*, Bergman first announced his plans to retire from filmmaking. He reiterated his determination to restrict his creative activity to the stage after the successful production of *Fanny and Alexander*, which won for him four Academy Awards. In this joyous film, he was finally able to confront and exorcise some of the demons of childhood that plagued him over the years; it was a fitting tribute to a lifetime of artistic experimentation and personal exploration. That notwithstanding, he continued to work on films. In 1991 he wrote a screenplay version of his novel *Den goda viljan* (*The Best Intentions*, 1992) about the troubled marriage of his parents before he was born. In 1997, he directed *Lamar och gör sig till* (in the presence of a clown), a made-for-television production set in the 1920's. His last film was *Saraband* (2003; *Saraband*, 2004), a sequel to *Scenes from a Marriage*, again starring Ullmann and Josephson.

Bergman continued to direct theatrical productions, ignoring doctors' warnings to rest from his busy work schedule. He astounded audiences with his imaginative productions of William Shakespeare's classic plays *King Lear* and *Hamlet* in 1984 and 1986, respectively; of Strindberg's *Fröken Julie* (*Miss Julie*) in 1986; of Eugene O'Neill's *Long Day's Journey into Night* in 1988; and of Molière's *The Misanthrope* in 1995. His last dramatic production was *Rosmersholm* in 2004, a radio version of the 1886 Ibsen play. All told, Bergman turned out 54 films, 126 theater productions, and 39 radio plays. He also directed operas and wrote three novels and two volumes of memoirs, *Laterna magica* (1987; *The Magic Lantern*, 1988) and *Tre dagböcker* (three diaries) in 2004 with Maria von Rosen.

Bergman announced his retirement for the final time in 2003. A year later he said in an interview on Swedish television that watching his early films depressed him and that he had pushed the capabilities of cinema beyond the limits. These works, he also said, came from attempts to master the innumerable demons in his own life, which at times drove him to panic and terror.

In October, 2006, Bergman underwent surgery to repair a broken hip. He never fully recovered from it and died in his sleep on July 30, 2007, on Fårö. He was survived by his nine children.

As well as his many Academy Awards and nominations, he also won two British Academy of Film and Television Arts (BAFTA) awards, a Cesar Award from the French Académie des Arts et Techniques du Cinema, and five awards at the Cannes Film Festival. Additionally, he was named to France's Legion of Honor in 1985.

SIGNIFICANCE

Because his films are intensely personal, together forming an emotional autobiography or a cinematic spiritual odyssey, Bergman has been appreciated as one of the true auteurs of the cinema, a poet on film. His influence, however, extends beyond his individual accomplishments. Grounded in the Scandinavian film tradition established by Carl Dreyer, Alf Sjöberg, Victor Sjöström, and others, Bergman dominated the Nordic industry for more than forty years, often to the detriment of younger filmmakers trying to establish careers in his considerable shadow. Enriching that tradition, he earned a reputation as a truly international filmmaker, bringing an artistic respectability to the film medium. The French New Wave filmmakers, though their films differ considerably from his, were inspired by his ability to bring his personal vi-

sion to the screen with almost total control over the writing, shooting, editing, and directing. This new critical interest in film as an art form led to the serious study of film in college programs, particularly in the 1960's and 1970's, influencing a generation of young filmmakers in the United States, especially Woody Allen. Bergman's writings about filmmaking, his published screenplays, his many interviews, and his autobiography have enhanced understanding of the creative process of the contemporary artist.

With a strong background in music, literature, and theater, Bergman tested the boundaries between the different media. His films employ many theatrical conventions, while his stage productions project cinematic style. Relying on familiar ensemble casts, Bergman allowed improvisation from his film actors, encouraging their contributions to the development of the script; while in the theater, however, those same actors, out of respect for his favorite authors, were restricted to the original text. In each medium, Bergman strove to achieve the ideal technical counterpart to the emotional content of the scene or shot. In film he re-created the hallucinatory effect of dreams and extreme psychological states. Through lighting, careful shot composition, and symbolic landscapes, Bergman created the visual equivalent of emotional states or philosophical concepts. His frequent use of the flashback technique complements his belief that confrontation of the past helps one understand the present. Not only did Bergman add to the cinematic language of film, but he also expanded, by way of his religious questionings, existential concerns, and fascination with the psychology of women, the range of appropriate subjects for film. Though his films sparked critical debates about the intellectual interpretation of his images, narratives, and characters, Bergman's primary concern was for an emotional reaction: "I never asked you to understand; I ask only that you feel."

After his death Bergman was hailed as heading the list of great directors, along with Akira Kurosawa and Federico Fellini. Woody Allen said of him that he was probably the greatest film artist since the invention of the motion-picture camera.

—Carol M. Ward

FURTHER READING

Bergman, Ingmar. *Bergman on Bergman: Interviews with Ingmar Bergman by Stig Björkman, Torsten Manns, Jonas Sima*. Translated by Paul Britten Austin. New York: Simon & Schuster, 1973. Transcription of interviews with Bergman from June, 1968, to

April, 1970, discussing his life, filmmaking experiences, and film theory. Includes numerous film stills, a filmography through *Cries and Whispers*, and an index.

_____. *The Magic Lantern: An Autobiography*. Translated by Joan Tate. New York: Viking Press, 1988. Conversational book arranged topically rather than chronologically (though a good chronology is included in the appendix). Includes many interesting anecdotes from Bergman's childhood and much analysis of his parents, especially his poignant discovery of his mother's diary.

Cowie, Peter. *Ingmar Bergman: A Critical Biography*. New York: Charles Scribner's Sons, 1982. An insightful, detailed biography with excellent critical analyses of films through *Fanny and Alexander*; includes film credits, a bibliography, and a list of major theatrical productions.

Kalin, Jesse. *The Films of Ingmar Bergman*. New York: Cambridge University Press, 2003. Kalin defines Bergman's idea of the human condition as the struggle to find meaning in life, and he describes how this concept is expressed in many of the director's films.

Kaminsky, Stuart M., ed. *Ingmar Bergman: Essays in Criticism*. New York: Oxford University Press, 1975. General career essays on Bergman's thematic use of childhood, sex, and religion, as well as essays (sometimes pro and con) about each major film from *The Seventh Seal* to *Scenes from a Marriage*. Excellent choice of writers and topics. Includes a selected filmography.

Marker, Lise-Lone, and Frederick J. Marker. *Ingmar Bergman: Four Decades in the Theater*. New York: Cambridge University Press, 1982. A survey of Bergman's productions of plays by Strindberg, Molière, and Ibsen, including an interview with Bergman about theater. Includes a useful chronology, a selected bibliography, many production stills, and some stage blueprint sketches.

Simon, John. *Ingmar Bergman Directs*. New York: Harcourt Brace Jovanovich, 1972. Includes a short interview with Bergman; a brief overview of his major themes; and detailed analyses of *The Naked Night*, *Smiles of a Summer Night*, *Winter Light*, and *Persona* (with a filmography of these four films). Contains no bibliography or index, but numerous illustrations are included.

Vermilye, Jerry. *Ingmar Bergman: His Life and Films*. Jefferson, N.C.: McFarland, 2002. Overview of Bergman's life and work, including a brief synopsis of each of his films, with information about the cast and crew, and comments by Bergman and film critics.

Wood, Robin. *Ingmar Bergman*. New York: Praeger, 1969. Films grouped thematically to reveal evolution of major concerns through *Shame*. Contains a chronology, a selected filmography, a selected bibliography, and numerous illustrations.

SEE ALSO: Ingrid Bergman; Luis Buñuel; Cecil B. DeMille; Samuel Goldwyn; D. W. Griffith; Alfred Hitchcock; Akira Kurosawa; Fritz Lang; George Lucas; Martin Scorsese; Steven Spielberg; François Truffaut; Orson Welles.

RELATED ARTICLES in *Great Events from History: The Twentieth Century:*

1901-1940: 1937-1939: Renoir's Films Explore Social and Political Themes.

1941-1970: 1956-1960: French New Wave Ushers in a New Era of Cinema; May 17, 1957: Bergman Wins International Fame with *The Seventh Seal*; March 16, 1960: Godard's *Breathless* Revolutionizes Film.

INGRID BERGMAN
Swedish actor

Bergman was an international star of film, theater, and television, acting in fifty films, eleven plays, and five television dramas. Her performances won her three Oscars, two Emmys, a Golden Globe Award, a Tony Award, and other prizes. She reached stardom in the United States and soon became an icon. She is considered one of the greatest actresses from Hollywood's golden era.

BORN: August 29, 1915; Stockholm, Sweden
DIED: August 29, 1982; London, England
AREAS OF ACHIEVEMENT: Film, television, theater and entertainment

EARLY LIFE

Ingrid Bergman (BURG-mihn) was born to Swedish photography-shop owner Justus Bergman and to Friedel Adler Bergman, who was German. The couple had three children. The first two children died shortly after birth. Ingrid was born seven years later. Friedel died when Bergman was just three years old. An aunt came to live with them and offered a hand in raising Ingrid. Aunt Ellen would quickly win the little girl's affection. Ingrid's father, however, was the pillar of love, strength, and acceptance in young Ingrid's life. She adored him. He insisted on exposing his daughter to all art forms. The feelings of serenity and peacefulness she enjoyed while with her father were interrupted every summer when she stayed with her maternal grandparents in Germany. There, Bergman faced discipline and sternness. Despite her resistance to her grandparents, Ingrid learned from them the discipline and perfectionism that she would apply to her acting.

From a young age Bergman enjoyed imitating others: persons, animals, and things. She would alter her voice, imitate motion, maintain posture, and change facial expressions. It was surprising that she could do this because everyone knew her to be shy. However, everything changed when Bergman played out a role. The evening Bergman's father took her to see her first play was the first time when she knew what she wanted to become: an actor.

Tragedy struck the Bergman family again. At the age of twelve, Bergman lost her father to stomach cancer. Six months later, Aunt Ellen died of a heart attack. Orphaned, Bergman had no choice but to live with her Uncle Otto and Aunt Hulda.

LIFE'S WORK

Bergman was accepted to the prestigious Royal Dramatic Theater in Stockholm in the fall of 1933. After completing her first year, she set out to look for a summer job. With the help of a personal connection she met and interviewed with Gustav Molander, a famous Swedish filmmaker. It was Molander who first recognized the rare and original talent in Bergman. She was offered the part of Elsa in a film called *Munkbrogreven* (1934). After this first film, it was clear to all that this young woman had tremendous potential. That autumn, Bergman returned to school to inform them of her decision to leave her formal studies for a career in film.

Bergman continued to make several films a year, including, in 1936, *Intermezzo*, a film written and directed by Molander. Bergman plays a piano teacher who has an affair with a famous violinist. The film caught the eye of Hollywood and American film producer David O. Selznick, who bought the rights to remake the film and invited Bergman to take the leading role.

Intermezzo: A Love Story was released to the American public in 1939. The response was astounding. At five feet, ten inches, Bergman became one of the tallest leading ladies in Hollywood. She possessed an angelic, natural beauty that did not depend on makeup. Her performances were delivered to perfection. Her roles in subsequent films, such as *Adam Had Four Sons* (1941) and *Rage in Heaven* (1941), continued to portray her as a pure and wholesome woman. When *Dr. Jekyll and Mr. Hyde* (1941) was cast, Bergman insisted on switching her part from the "good girl" to the barmaid. She was testing the extent of her own talent. Concurrent with this film, she moved to the stage, with debuts on Broadway in *Liliom* (1940) and *Anna Christie* (1941).

Bergman married Petter Lindström in 1937. Lindström, a Swedish dentist, later became a neurosurgeon in the United States. The couple had a daughter, Pia (who became a journalist), in 1938. Their marriage started out strong. Lindström, who was older and had more business sense than Bergman, made all family and business decisions. He acted as Bergman's agent in negotiating contracts and terms with Hollywood. He overlooked all financial transactions for the family, but his role would eventually evolve to include being Bergman's personal critic. He had insisted, at times, that she had gained too much weight, and he admonished her for having said too much at a press interview. This negativity would eventually chip away at their marriage, and they divorced in 1950.

Casablanca (1942) is the most famous Bergman film, where she played opposite Humphrey Bogart in a wartime romance. Despite the difficulties on the set, this film was a box-office hit and helped Bergman reach superstardom. *Casablanca* remains one of the most-loved romantic classics in the history of American film. Bergman went on to accept the role of Maria in *For Whom the Bell Tolls* (1943), a film based on a novel written by Ernest Hemingway. Her first Oscar for Best Actress came in 1944 for her role as Paula Alquist in the film *Gaslight*. The following year she came out with three films: *Saratoga Trunk*, *Spellbound*, and *The Bells of St. Mary*. The 1946 film *Notorious* is believed by many to be the film in which she gave her finest performance.

In 1949, Bergman wrote a letter to Italian director Roberto Rossellini, offering to loan her famous name to one of his films to help boost his fame. She had seen two of his films and could not understand why his work was

Ingrid Bergman. (AP/Wide World Photos)

not more appreciated. He wrote back, and she left for Italy to star in his film *Stromboli* (1950). During the making of this film, Bergman and Rossellini had an affair, which the press sensationalized and made into a great scandal. In response to this affair, the American public was outraged. Their "wholesome" girl had tragically turned bad. Hollywood producers and their lawyers threatened to drop her from their castings lists and keep her from working if she did not return home.

The scandal escalated when Bergman became pregnant and gave birth to a son, Robertino Rossellini. She knew that she could not return to the United States, so she remained in seclusion in Italy for six years. During that time she made another five films with Rossellini, none of which was internationally acclaimed. In 1952, she gave birth to twin girls, Isabella (who also became a star actor) and Isotta Rossellini (a scholar). The isolation in Italy caused Bergman great misery: Her relationship with her daughter Pia suffered, her career and fame had declined to nothingness, and her marriage to Rossellini was in trouble.

In 1956, French director Jean Renoir cast Bergman as the star of his film *Elena et les hommes*, a role that lifted her fading career. After her performance in *Elena et les hommes*, Hollywood was again interested in her, casting her in the starring role in *Anastasia* (1956). She won her second Oscar for Best Actress for her performance in *Anastasia*.

Bergman divorced Rossellini in 1957. By 1958, she had met and married Lars Schmidt, a theatrical producer from Sweden. Professionally, her career was taking off again. Offers continuously poured in for film, television, and stage. She won an Emmy Award in 1959 for the television miniseries *The Turn of the Screw*, based on Henry James's novel. She made her debut on the London stage in 1965 with *A Month in the Country*. Her third and last Oscar, this time for Best Supporting Actress, recognized her performance in *Murder on the Orient Express* (1974). By 1975, her third marriage ended in a divorce.

Bergman continued to work until the end of her life. Her final role was that of Golda Meir in the television miniseries *A Woman Called Golda* (1982). She won an Emmy Award for her performance. The award was accepted posthumously by her daughter, Pia. On August 29, 1982, in her London apartment, Bergman died in her sleep from complications related to breast cancer.

SIGNIFICANCE

Bergman lived intense dramas on and off the stage. Her roles had elements of love, betrayal, and death. Her personal life was similar. Through it all, she was strong, hardworking, and, most important, true to herself in the face of public outrage and accusations. Bergman will be remembered as an outstanding actor who performed to perfection. Many of her films are classic and timeless, and they will win the hearts and adoration of new and young fans alike.

—*Teresa Iodice-Dadin*

FURTHER READING

Bergman, Ingrid, and Alan Burgess. *Ingrid Bergman, My Story*. New York: Delacorte Press, 1980. An autobiography of Bergman offering stories, memories, events, and personal thoughts.

Chandler, Charlotte. *Ingrid: Ingrid Bergman, A Personal Biography*. New York: Simon & Schuster, 2007. This book tells a very human story of the life of Bergman from her youth and her parents to being an actress. It

presents personal information gathered from interviews.

Spoto, Donald. *Notorious: The Life of Ingrid Bergman*. Cambridge, Mass.: Da Capo Press, 2001. Indexed by years, this work, first published in 1997, recounts much of Bergman's professional and personal life.

SEE ALSO: Humphrey Bogart; Bette Davis; Marlene Dietrich; Clark Gable; Greta Garbo; Lillian Gish; Cary Grant; Rita Hayworth; Katharine Hepburn; Alfred Hitchcock; Gregory Peck; James Stewart; Mae West.

RELATED ARTICLES in *Great Events from History: The Twentieth Century:*

1901-1940: 1934-1935: Hitchcock Becomes Synonymous with Suspense.

1941-1970: November 26, 1942: *Casablanca* Marks the Artistic Apex of 1940's War-Themed Films.

HENRI BERGSON
French philosopher

Bergson rejected the mechanistic view of life held by the noted positivists of his day and instead focused renewed attention on not only the human spirit but also the human creative force, or élan vital. *This energy and its creative potential and inherent freedom opened new intellectual vistas to many creative artists and thinkers.*

BORN: October 18, 1859; Paris, France
DIED: January 4, 1941; Paris, France
ALSO KNOWN AS: Henri-Louis Bergson (full name)
AREA OF ACHIEVEMENT: Philosophy

EARLY LIFE

Henri Bergson (ahn-ree behrg-sohn) was born into a sophisticated, multinational family in the year that Charles Darwin published *On the Origin of Species* (1859), a book that profoundly affected Bergson's thinking and against whose dispassionate view of human existence he reacted significantly. Bergson's father, Michel, studied piano under Frédéric Chopin before leaving his native Warsaw to pursue a career in music elsewhere in Europe and in Great Britain. There he met Katherine Levinson, a beauty of Irish-Jewish lineage. He soon married her and took British citizenship.

Henri, although born in Paris, was taken to London as an infant and remained there until he was eight,

whereupon the family resettled in Paris. There Bergson spent most of his remaining years, taking French citizenship as soon as he turned twenty-one. He attended the Lycée Fontane, later renamed the Lycée Condorcet, from the time he was nine until he was nineteen, the year in which he published his first article, a prizewinning solution to a problem in mathematics, in the *Annales de mathématiques (annals of mathematics)*.

Equally gifted in the sciences and the humanities, Bergson decided on entering the École Normale Supérieure to concentrate on philosophy. Earning his degree and license to teach in 1881, he taught first at the Lycée D'Angers, then at the Lycée Blaise Pascal in Auvergne. His first book, *Essai sur les données immédiates de la conscience* (1889; *Time and Free Will: An Essay on the Immediate Data of Consciousness*, 1910), appeared when he was thirty, at which time he also completed his doctoral dissertation, in Latin, on Aristotle, which won for him a Ph.D. from the University of Paris.

Returning to Paris in 1891, he married a cousin of Marcel Proust, Louise Neuberger. Bergson taught at the Lycée Henri IV until 1900, when he was appointed to the chair in Greek philosophy at the prestigious Collège de France. Before assuming this position, he had published *Matière et mémoire* (1896; *Matter and Memory*, 1911), which was concerned with how the brain's physiology is related to consciousness. He found neurophysiological explanations of consciousness frustratingly limited because they failed to explain satisfactorily the roots of recollection.

LIFE'S WORK

Bergson had gained considerable attention and some celebrity through his early publications, but his *Le Rire: Essai sur la signification du comique* (1900; *Laughter: An Essay on the Meaning of the Comic*, 1911), a short study of the essence of the comic, placed him in the company of the more significant thinkers of his day. Bergson's theory is that people laugh as a result of a mechanistic impediment, physical or mental, to the usual progression of any activity in life. Using such classic writers as Jonathan Swift, Charles Dickens, and Molière to support and illustrate his contentions, Bergson considered laughter a release of tensions caused by a situation in which the flow of life is impeded by the mechanical.

Following this book was *Introduction à la métaphysique* (1903; *An Introduction to Metaphysics*, 1912), in which Bergson defends intuition against the analytical

Henri Bergson. (© The Nobel Foundation)

approach of science, which had been adopted by many humanistic disciplines in an attempt to make them seem more scientific and therefore more credible. Bergson considers analysis, dependent on abstract symbols for its expression, to reside outside humans and outside knowledge, whereas intuition resides within them. It is through intuition, Bergson contends, that humans approach reality in the Platonic sense.

The study for which Bergson is best known is *L'Évolution créatrice* (1907; *Creative Evolution*, 1911), a work that changed the thinking of a whole generation of creative people. Bergson accepts Darwin's evolutionary theory but interjects into it the notion of the *élan vital*, the life energy that Darwin in his mechanistic, analytical approach denies. Perhaps the most influential concept in Bergson's thought at this time was that humans do not exist in time, but rather that time exists in humans, a notion with which William Faulkner experimented in his writing.

This distinction is at the heart of Bergson's departure from that considerable legion of intellectuals that was in his day trying to apply scientific method to all intellectual concerns. Never antiscientific, Bergson insisted, nevertheless, that science must be kept in a proper relation to human intuition and that humans must revere it less than intuition, the quintessential humanizing element in all intellectual processes.

Creative Evolution, widely read by intellectuals, also had considerable appeal to a more general reading public, largely because of Bergson's clarity of expression and overall persuasiveness. Bergson departed from Darwin in postulating that human evolution was not simply a routine, mechanistic alteration of the species but that inherent in it was a creative process that had purpose. Obviously, Bergson was moving away from science toward religion, and he was embraced happily by Roman Catholic and other Christian thinkers of his time.

Immediately before World War I, Bergson was at the peak of his influence, lecturing in Europe and the United States. As war encroached on Europe in 1914, he was inducted into the French Academy. In that year, he was the Gifford Lecturer at Scotland's University of Edinburgh. He gave his first series of lectures, "The Problem of Personality," in the spring, but he could not return to give his final lectures in the fall because war had erupted.

Rather, he wrote two thoughtful essays, "The Meaning of War" and "The Evolution of German Imperialism," in both of which he tried to analyze, according to his own philosophy, the reasons for the conflict. He cast the French as those who represented individual freedom and their opponents as those who venerated the masses rather than the individual. During the war, Bergson served as a French diplomat to Spain and the United States, and, at the war's end, he embraced Woodrow Wilson's League of Nations, becoming president of its Commission on Intellectual Cooperation.

Shortly after the end of the war, Bergson's health began to fail. Badly disabled with arthritis that occasionally caused paralysis of his limbs, he was unable to go to Stockholm in 1928 to receive the 1927 Nobel Prize in Literature that had been reserved and that he was awarded the following year. The award speech in Stockholm stressed Bergson's role in freeing the creative imagination and indicated his profound influence on artists of his day. He was praised for breaking out of the stultifying mold in which he was educated, for forging beyond it to celebrate the greatness of the human spirit, and for realizing its creative potential.

Bergson's last book, *Les Deux Sources de la morale et de la religion* (1932; *The Two Sources of Morality and Religion*, 1935), completed at a time when he was extremely ill and suffered from blinding migraine headaches, discusses his conception of God. This conception was largely Christian, although Bergson remained a Jew. In a will that he executed in 1937, Bergson indicated that he would have become a Catholic at that time had he not felt compelled to support his fellow Jews at a time when their futures and their very lives were being seriously threatened by the Nazi incursions.

Because of Bergson's international celebrity, his age, and his membership in the French Academy, which he once served as president, France's Vichy government excused him from resigning his official offices and registering with the government as Jews were required to do. To show his support for his Jewish compatriots, however, Bergson, then eighty-one years old, resigned his honorary chair in philosophy at the Collège de France. He registered with the government as a Jew, having to stand in line on a bitterly cold, damp day, when he was already ill, until he was served. In consequence he developed a lung inflammation that resulted in his death on January 4, 1941.

HUMAN INSTINCT AND INTELLIGENCE

In the following passage from Creative Evolution *(1907), Henri Bergson explores the functions as well as limitations of human instinct and intelligence.*

If instinct is, above all, the faculty of using an organized natural instrument, it must involve innate knowledge (potential or unconscious, it is true), both of this instrument and of the object to which it is applied. Instinct is therefore innate knowledge of a thing. But intelligence is the faculty of constructing unorganized—that is to say artificial—instruments. If, on its account, nature gives up endowing the living being with the instruments that may serve him, it is in order that the living being may be able to vary his construction according to circumstances. The essential function of intelligence is therefore to see the way out of a difficulty in any circumstances whatever, to find what is most suitable, what answers best the question asked. Hence it bears essentially on the relations between a given situation and the means of utilizing it. What is innate in intellect, therefore, is the tendency to establish relations, and this tendency implies the natural knowledge of certain very general relations, a kind of stuff that the activity of each particular intellect will cut up into more special relations. Where activity is directed toward manufacture, therefore, knowledge necessarily bears on relations. But this entirely formal knowledge of intelligence has an immense advantage over the material knowledge of instinct. A form, just because it is empty, may be filled at will with any number of things in turn, even with those that are of no use. So that a formal knowledge is not limited to what is practically useful, although it is in view of practical utility that it has made its appearance in the world. An intelligent being bears within himself the means to transcend his own nature.

He transcends himself, however, less than he wishes, less also than he imagines himself to do. The purely formal character of intelligence deprives it of the ballast necessary to enable it to settle itself on the objects that are of the most powerful interest to speculation. Instinct, on the contrary, has the desired materiality, but it is incapable of going so far in quest of its object; it does not speculate. Here we reach the point that most concerns our present inquiry. The difference that we shall now proceed to denote between instinct and intelligence is what the whole of this analysis was meant to bring out. We formulate it thus: There are things that intelligence alone is able to seek, but which, by itself, it will never find. These things instinct alone could find; but it will never seek them.

SIGNIFICANCE

Bergson sought to free his fellow intellectuals from the constricted scientific approach to learning that dominated much of the philosophical thinking of his day and that has since continued to dominate intellectual circles. Frequently accused of being antiscientific, Bergson, who understood the sciences well, wanted merely to control the extent to which the scientific method was used in pursuits that were essentially nonscientific.

Bergson's most appreciative audience was found among graphic artists, composers, and writers, many of whom felt constrained by the scientific bias of contemporary society. Thinkers such as Bertrand Russell complained that much of Bergson's work was based on opinion rather than on hard research data; it is hard to deny that such was the case. One cannot ignore, however, the incredible promise that Bergson's writings and his idea of the creative force, the *élan vital*, stirred in a broad range of writers who derived from his writing precisely the kind of justification they required to validate their activities.

Writing about consciousness, Bergson outlined a methodology for many modern writers who were grappling with stream of consciousness as a method. Writers such as Thomas Mann, Marcel Proust, Virginia Woolf, and Paul Valéry, as well as painters such as Claude Monet and Pablo Picasso, imbibed the spirit that emanated from Bergson's writing and translated it into their own media, thereby creating challenging art forms. It is for this kind of contribution that Bergson will be remembered.

—*R. Baird Shuman*

FURTHER READING

Alexander, Ian W. *Bergson: Philosopher of Reflection.* New York: Hillary House, 1957. This book provides an introspective look into Bergson's theories of knowledge and consciousness. It is lucid and direct in presenting the salient parts of Bergson's philosophy and theology, noting the effects of his thinking on creative artists.

Bilsker, Richard. *On Bergson.* Belmont, Calif.: Wadsworth/Thomson Learning, 2002. A concise overview of and introduction to Bergson's philosophy. Part of the Wadsworth Philosophers series.

Čapek, Milič. *Bergson and Modern Physics: A Re-interpretation and Re-evaluation.* Dordrecht, the Netherlands: D. Reidel, 1971. The three portions of this book deal with Bergson's biological theory of knowledge, his notion of "intuition," and his theory of matter and its relationship to modern physics. A good book to read in tandem with Pete A. Y. Gunter's collection below.

Guerlac, Suzanne. *Thinking in Time: An Introduction to Henri Bergson.* Ithaca, N.Y.: Cornell University Press, 2006. Guerlac explains the ideas contained in two of Bergson's texts, *Time and Free Will* and *Matter and Memory*, focusing on his conceptions of duration and memory.

Gunter, Pete A. Y., ed. *Bergson and the Evolution of Physics.* Knoxville: University of Tennessee Press, 1969. Gunter and his contributors try to show that Bergson was not antiscientific and that his emphasis on the *élan vital* and on intuition is positive for science rather than negative, as it has often been portrayed.

Hanna, Thomas, ed. *The Bergsonian Heritage.* New York: Columbia University Press, 1962. The eleven essays in this collection, drawn from a convention held at Hollins College to commemorate the centennial of Bergson's birth, assess Bergson's impact on theology and literature. The book also contains reminiscences by people who knew him at the Sorbonne and the Collège de France.

Mullen, Mary D. *Essence and Operation in the Teaching of St. Thomas in Some Modern Philosophies.* Washington, D.C.: Catholic University Press, 1941. Mullen shows the effect that Bergson had on the developing Thomism of Jacques Maritain, a debt that Maritain acknowledged. The portions of this book that deal with Bergson are chronicles of a spiritual journey that caused Bergson to see the Catholic Church as a creative force.

Pilkington, Anthony Edward. *Bergson and His Influence: A Reassessment.* New York: Cambridge University Press, 1976. This five-chapter book presents an initial overview of Bergsonism, then devotes one chapter each to Bergson's influence on Charles Péguy, Paul Valéry, Marcel Proust, and Julien Benda. The chapter on Benda contains interesting insights into Bergson's theory of mobility.

Russell, Bertrand. *The Philosophy of Bergson.* Cambridge, England: Cambridge University Press, 1914. Russell, more devoted to an undeviating scientific method than Bergson, looks with considerable skepticism on Bergson's theories of knowledge and dependence on intuition in shaping arguments. He particularly questions Bergson's *Creative Evolution*, in which the theory of the *élan vital* is fully expounded.

SEE ALSO: Walter Benjamin; Umberto Boccioni; William Faulkner; Étienne Gilson; Gabriel Marcel; Jacques Maritain; Claude Monet; Pablo Picasso; Marcel Proust; Pierre Teilhard de Chardin; Paul Valéry.

RELATED ARTICLES in *Great Events from History: The Twentieth Century:*

IRVING BERLIN
American songwriter

Berlin, one of the most prolific and recognized American songwriters, had the exceptional ability to make his tunes and rhythms conform to the style and mood of the times in which he lived. He was a prolific songwriter who had a unique ability to bring together words and music to form what many have called musical perfection.

BORN: May 11, 1888; Mogilyov, Russia (now in Belarus)
DIED: September 22, 1989; New York, New York
ALSO KNOWN AS: Israel Baline (birth name)
AREA OF ACHIEVEMENT: Music

EARLY LIFE

In Siberia, at the time when Irving Berlin was born (as Israel Baline), harassment and abuse of Jews was a popular local "entertainment." Hordes of people, often from other villages, would surge through Jewish communities, raping Jewish women, looting homes and businesses, burning synagogues, and beating and murdering Jews while the police stood idly by. Such atrocities fed the anger of some of the czarist system's bitterest foes, who were determined to destroy it and all it represented; others, such as Berlin's father, chose to forsake their homeland for the uncertain future of life in the Lower East Side slums of New York. Moses Baline's decision was particularly understandable: As a cantor in the local synagogue, he was especially targeted for persecution. Therefore, in 1892, a year of increased legal restrictions against the Jews, he took his wife and most of his eight children and headed westward.

The Baline family set up housekeeping in a three-room, windowless apartment on Monroe Street. The father, unable to find work as a cantor, worked in a kosher slaughterhouse and earned extra money by giving Hebrew lessons. After three years, at the time when young Israel entered public school, the family was able to move to slightly better quarters on Cherry Street. In 1896, the elder Baline died, and, shortly afterward, Israel left school to help support the family. His first job was selling newspapers, a task he tried to make less onerous by singing songs on the street corners, songs that he heard played in the local saloons. Sometimes passersby, liking what they heard, would toss him a few pennies.

When he was fourteen, he left home, supporting himself by casual employment as a singing waiter in a beer hall or by making the rounds of various Bowery haunts, belting out songs on his own. He also worked for a time publicizing songs for a sheet-music seller. His first regular job came in 1908, when he was hired as a singing waiter by Pelham's café. At Pelham's, he earned seven dollars a week singing the favorites of George M. Cohan and other popular tunes, which he frequently parodied with his own words. While at Pelham's, he wrote the lyrics to a song, composed by the café's piano player, Nick Nicholson, called "Marie from Sunny Italy," earning seventy-five cents in royalties. His name was listed on the title page as I. Berlin, a result, no doubt of a mistranslation of an incorrect pronunciation, but he liked the

Irving Berlin. (AP/Wide World Photos)

change so much that he decided to keep it, changing his first name as well. Irving sounded more impressive, and less biblical, than Israel.

Berlin continued to work as a singing waiter, now at a bar in Times Square, and continued to write lyrics for other people's songs, but he also started to write his own tunes. None of these early efforts, such as "Queenie, My Own" and "She Was a Dear Little Girl," was particularly memorable. Nor did his background seem to prepare him for his future success in musical comedy. He had only two years of formal schooling, none at all in music, which he could not read. He played the piano a bit, but his skill, such as it was, was restricted to using only the black keys in F sharp. Yet, by 1909, his compositions, which others transcribed, were becoming well known, and he obtained a job as a staff composer at the Seminary Music Company, where he earned twenty-five dollars a week.

His chief assignment there was as lyricist with Ted Snyder, the firm's director, who usually provided the music. Berlin's desire to compose his own music led him, in 1911, to write the song that would establish him as one of the most famous popular composers of his day. When "Alexander's Ragtime Band" first appeared as an instrumental, its success was limited, but then Berlin added words, which he took from another of his unsuccessful songs, and it became a sensation, establishing ragtime as the popular musical idiom of the time. It was one of the first songs of Tin Pan Alley to have its verse and refrain in different keys. Berlin now became a full partner of the firm in which he worked, Waterson, Berlin and Synder Company. The firm's logo was a target with an arrow pinpointing the center, Berlin's name appearing over the bull's-eye.

LIFE'S WORK

In 1912, at the age of twenty-four, Berlin had achieved a degree of success that few musicians attain in a lifetime. His output was enormous. He could write a song a day (although his average was closer to one a week); he had made his stage debut on Broadway in a revue entitled *Up and Down Broadway* (1910), in which he sang many of his own songs; he had written the score for the *Ziegfeld Follies of 1911*; and he was making about $100,000 a year. Berlin's life was marred by a personal tragedy, however, when his bride of five months died of typhoid fever, contracted while on their honeymoon to Cuba; Berlin's first ballad, "When I Lost You," which became a national hit, was a product of this period. Berlin also began working on a revue in which he composed, for the first time, both the words and the music. *Watch Your Step* (1914)

contained the famous contrapuntal song "Play a Simple Melody." The show featured the darlings of the Broadway stage, the dancing Castles, Vernon and Irene, and was featured in London the following year. Berlin was at that time involved with two other stage productions in New York City.

Berlin's theatrical career seemed to come to a temporary halt when he was inducted into the U.S. Army during World War I and sent to Camp Yaphank on Long Island for training. "The U.S. Army Takes Berlin" was how one newspaper headline read. Yet Berlin's commanding officer considered the recruit's talents to be too special for combat. General Franklin Bell wanted to build a base community house for the visiting relatives of the soldiers, and he needed to raise thirty-five thousand dollars. He offered, and Berlin accepted, the proposal to put on an all-soldiers' show as a fund-raiser. Berlin demanded and received an ensemble of three hundred, half in the cast, the remainder comprising the orchestra, the production, and backstage personnel; he conducted the auditions, directed the publicity, and booked the theater. *Yip, Yip, Yaphank* opened in August, 1918, at the Century Theatre in New York City, scheduled for eight performances; it ran for thirty-two. Berlin sang two numbers, "Poor Little Me—I'm on K.P." and the show-stopping "Oh, How I Hate to Get Up in the Morning." The show earned eighty-three thousand dollars for the Camp Yaphank building fund.

When the war ended, Berlin returned to civilian life and Broadway. In 1919, he did the score for the *Ziegfeld Follies*, which contained "A Pretty Girl Is Like a Melody," a song that Berlin dashed off one night because Florenz Ziegfeld needed a number that would make use of the dozens of extra costumes he still had. Impresarios and music publishers were accustomed to ordering songs as one would order a drink in a saloon, and Berlin was very obliging. (Harry Waterston once needed a tune for a musical, and he called Berlin; Berlin sang him one over the telephone.) Berlin was now able to fulfill his two great ambitions: to have his own publishing house, Irving Berlin, Incorporated, and to build his own theater, the Music Box Theatre, which, beginning in 1921, staged Berlin's own revues.

Berlin wisely resisted the temptation to publish every song he wrote; if he had there would have been as many as three thousand in print instead of about a third that number. Nor did all those tunes that were released become hits. Berlin sometimes recycled those that failed, some of them becoming popular in another form, such as, for example, the song "Easter Parade," which began life as a World War I ditty. At times, Berlin might compose a song, think it inappropriate for the occasion, and release it much later. "God Bless America" was not used in *Yip, Yip, Yaphank* because Berlin thought it too much like gilding the patriotic lily; it came out in 1938 instead (Berlin donated the royalties to the Boy Scouts and Girl Scouts of America). Many of Berlin's songs, however, were successes the first time they appeared and continued in popularity, songs such as "Always," "Blue Skies," "Shaking the Blues Away," and "Puttin' on the Ritz," which became a hit for the second time in 1985.

During the 1920's and the 1930's, Berlin did four Music Box revues (1921, 1922, 1923, and 1924); he did the first musical comedy, *The Cocoanuts* (1925), starring the Marx Brothers; and he wrote the film scores for such films as *Top Hat* (1935), *Follow the Fleet* (1936), *On the Avenue* (1937), *Alexander's Ragtime Band* (1938), and *Second Fiddle* (1939). On the stage, with *Face the Music* (1932) and *As Thousands Cheer* (1933), he took the musical revues into a new, socially conscious direction. *Face the Music* was about political corruption and bossism; *As Thousands Cheer* depicted scenes from the daily newspaper. It contained the sentimental but ingratiating "Easter Parade," but it also had a sketch about a lynching, in which a black woman wonders how to tell her children that their father "ain't comin' home no more." "Supper Time" was sung by Ethel Waters, who called it a song that could tell the whole tragic story of a race.

When the United States entered World War II, Berlin returned to more conventional music fare with another all-soldiers' show, *This Is the Army*, written in response to a specific request by the Department of the Army. The revue opened on Broadway on July 4, 1942, and featured Berlin himself dressed in a World War I sergeant's uniform, again singing "Oh, How I Hate to Get Up in the Morning." The musical also contained the popular "I Left My Heart at the Stage Door Canteen" and "This Is the Army, Mr. Jones." The show lasted more than three years. After its Broadway run, it went on the road, playing in all the major American cities, as well as in American bases in Europe, Africa, Australia, and the South Pacific. It was filmed in Hollywood in 1943. Berlin appeared in the film version, which starred Kate Smith, who sang "God Bless America," as well as an assortment of Hollywood stars, including Ronald Reagan. The production earned a total of ten million dollars in royalties for the Army Emergency Relief Fund. Also during the war, Hollywood released *Holiday Inn* (1942), starring Bing Crosby and Fred Astaire, containing one of Berlin's most famous songs: "White Christmas." Few be-

sides Berlin suspected the song's tremendous potential.

After the war, Berlin proved that he was still at the height of his powers with his best musical, *Annie Get Your Gun* (1946), in which the songs, unlike those of the revues of the past, were perfectly integrated with the story, depicting the characters for which they were written and helping to advance the plot. The production, starring Ethel Merman, opened on May 16, 1946, and ran for 1,147 performances. It spawned many road shows and was made into a film in 1950. The story, based loosely on the life of Annie Oakley, contains some of Berlin's finest songs, stunning in their variety: "The Girl That I Marry," "Doin' What Comes Natur'lly," "I Got the Sun in the Morning," "You Can't Get a Man with a Gun," "They Say It's Wonderful," and "There's No Business Like Show Business," the last written as a filler to cover a change of scenery (and almost left out of the final production because Berlin did not believe that his lyricist, Oscar Hammerstein II, really liked it). Probably no other show had as many hits as *Annie Get Your Gun*.

After *Annie Get Your Gun*, Berlin wrote two musicals in rapid succession, both of which enjoyed success. *Miss Liberty* (1949) contained "Let's Take an Old-Fashioned Walk" and a musical version of the poem, by Emma Lazarus, which is on the base of the Statue of Liberty, the lovely "Give Me Your Tired, Your Poor." *Call Me Madam* (1953) was another vehicle for the irrepressible Merman as a fictitious Perle Mesta, the Washington party giver that President Harry S. Truman appointed ambassador to Luxembourg. It contained another of Berlin's famous songs in counterpoint, "You're Just in Love." Berlin's next Broadway production appeared twelve years later. *Mr. President* (1962) lacked the memorable tunes of past productions but did not deserve the panning it received from some critics. In a sense, however, the disappointment felt by the critics serves as a measure of their admiration.

SIGNIFICANCE

The lives of composers are often measured by what is remembered of their music, whether it be opera, symphony, or popular song. If greatness alone were based on this criterion, Berlin would be considered one of the world's best, for he has certainly written more popular music than anyone that comes to mind. Moreover, it is remarkable how many of his tunes have become such permanent fixtures of his own culture and his country's history. It is impossible to remember the words of his songs without thinking of the tunes that went with them: words and music in a perfect marriage.

Berlin's sense of timing and of what the public wanted, or craved, was uncanny, as was his versatility: songs for all occasions. His images, like a picture by Norman Rockwell, reflected what the American people believed themselves, or hoped themselves, to be.

Berlin's music is basic and often mundane; it has sometimes been called corny. Berlin did not care about pleasing everyone. When somebody called *Annie Get Your Gun* "old-fashioned," his retort was, "Yes, an old-fashioned smash." Yet despite his overwhelming success, he continued to be realistic about his talents, realizing that his ability to simplify was in keeping with his lack of musical training. When once told that he should study music seriously, he replied that if he were to do so, he might end up despising his own work. Many would disagree.

—*Wm. Laird Kleine-Ahlbrandt*

FURTHER READING

Ewen, David. *Composers for the American Musical Theater.* New York: Dodd, Mead, 1968. A history of musical theater in the United States from Victor Herbert to Leonard Bernstein. The featured biography of Berlin is thus seen in context with those of the composer's peers.

Freedland, Michael. *Irving Berlin.* New York: Stein and Day, 1974. A very engaging life of the composer, revealed in a succession of anecdotes culled from interviews with his friends and associates. Directed toward the show business aspect of Berlin's life rather than toward his music per se.

Gottfried, Martin. *Broadway Musicals.* New York: Harry N. Abrams, 1979. A lavish picture book with perceptive and knowledgeable commentary regarding this unique American art form and Berlin's contribution to its development.

Jablonski, Edward. "Through History with Irving Berlin." *The Reporter* 27 (October, 1962): 48-50. An incisive commentary on the special contribution that Berlin made to American music in the development of the popular song, a form that he purged of its European harmonic sweetness.

Leopold, David. *Irving Berlin's Show Business: Broadway, Hollywood, America.* New York: Harry N. Abrams, 2005. Berlin's life and music are chronicled through the book's extensive assortment of photographs, drawings, set and costume designs, sheet music, and album covers.

Logan, Joshua. "Irving Berlin." *High Fidelity and Musical America* 28 (May, 1978): 76-81. Logan, a director for three of Berlin's musicals, including *Annie Get Your Gun*, relates how he first met the great man and what it was like to work with him. "There has always been in him a passionate, unquenchable enthusiasm, a powerhouse quality that set every one near him on fire."

Stoddard, Maynard Good. "God Bless America . . . and Irving Berlin." *Saturday Evening Post*, September, 1983, 58-59. Reflections on the occasion of the composer's ninety-fifth birthday, about his place in American music. The conclusion is that Berlin's melodies will last long after rock-and-roll music "has rolled over and died."

Wollcott, Alexander. *Story of Irving Berlin.* New York: G. P. Putnam's Sons, 1925. An impressionistic attempt to understand the composer's gift for melody by conjuring up the atmosphere, themes, and harmonies of the Bowery from where his inspiration sprang. The book reveals almost as much about the author's own sentimentalities and values as it does about its subject's, but it is written with much style, affection, and romance.

SEE ALSO: Fred Astaire; Leonard Bernstein; Judy Garland; George Gershwin; Ira Gershwin; Oscar Hammerstein II; Lorenz Hart; Sir Andrew Lloyd Webber; Dorothy Parker; Cole Porter; Richard Rodgers.

RELATED ARTICLES in *Great Events from History: The Twentieth Century:*

1901-1940: September 6, 1935: *Top Hat* Establishes the Astaire-Rogers Dance Team.

1941-1970: March 15, 1945: *Going My Way* Wins Best Picture.

TIM BERNERS-LEE
English physicist and computer scientist

With colleague Robert Cailliau, Berners-Lee invented the World Wide Web, a global electronic realm of interlinked hypertext documents. The Web uses the Internet, a system of interconnected computer networks, to exchange information and media through hyperlinks, which are reference points within a document that "link" a user to other parts of a site or to other Web sites.

BORN: June 8, 1955; London, England

AREAS OF ACHIEVEMENT: Computer science, physics, mathematics, invention and technology, communications

EARLY LIFE

The son of two mathematicians who worked on the early Manchester University Mark I computer in the early 1950's, Tim Berners-Lee showed an early interest in mathematics. He attended Sheen Mount Primary School in London and subsequently moved on to the Emanuel School from 1969 to 1973, where he earned high recognition in assorted subjects, including mathematics and physics. He entered Queen's College, Oxford University, the following year and pursued his interest in physics. He graduated with an honors B.A. in physics in 1976.

At Oxford he built his first computer from a variety of materials, including an old television. However, his studious side was offset by playing on the Oxford tiddly-winks team against arch rivals Cambridge University, and by hacking Oxford's mainframe computer; upon discovery he was banned from using university computers. He often mulled over earlier conversations with his parents regarding computers and their potential to link otherwise unconnected information.

Upon graduation Berners-Lee started his first job as a programmer with Plessey Telecommunications Ltd. in Poole, County Dorset, England. Plessey was a major telecommunications equipment manufacturer. He married his first wife, Jane, who he knew from his days at Oxford and who also was employed at the Poole facility. Leaving the company after two years, Berners-Lee switched to a programming job at D. G. Nash Ltd. in nearby Ferndown. It was here that he wrote his first multitasking operating-system computer program.

LIFE'S WORK

While in Switzerland on a small consulting job, Berners-Lee learned that CERN (Conseil Européen pour la Re-

cherche Nucléaire; now the European Particle Physics Laboratory, in Geneva) was looking for contract programmers. He was hired as an independent software consultant on a six-month project from June through December of 1980 to work on the proton synchrotron booster.

In his free time at CERN, Berners-Lee created a program for storing information that utilized random associations rather than the fixed associations of bits of data that was the norm at the time. The program, developed with colleague Robert Cailliau, was to help him remember connections among the many different people (more than ten thousand in the CERN phonebook), computers, and projects at CERN. He dubbed this software program Enquire, after *Enquire Within upon Everything*, a book of Victorian advice that he saw in his parents' library.

A principal feature of Enquire was its use of hypertext. "Hypertext" was a term coined in 1965 by Theodor (Ted) Nelson for any medium that includes links that enabled a person to pursue his or her own interests rather than the interests of an author already expressed in a fixed linear sequence. Although Enquire was coded in the common software language of Pascal, it ran on a much more obscure operating system, which few CERN employees knew. He left the floppy disk in the hands of a CERN manager and told him it could help keep track of things; he told his colleague that he could try Enquire if he wished. Few bothered with the disk, however, and it was ultimately lost. This pioneering work would later form the basis for the development of the World Wide Web. Berners-Lee realized that the potential to link and access all the information stored on computers in various places would have incredible possibilities and could lead to a single, global information space. Although Enquire was rudimentary in its capabilities, it tantalized him with possibilities.

Berners-Lee returned to England to lead technical design work at John Poole's Image Computer Systems Ltd., which had been created after Poole's successful development and selling of a product on which Berners-Lee, Poole, and their friend Kevin Rogers had worked some years before. The project explored how to incorporate a microprocessor into a printer so that fancy graphics could be created in lieu of the crude dot-matrix printers of the time.

Somewhat bored by the inability to expand their work beyond printers, Berners-Lee remembered the fellow-

LINKING THE WORLD

In his memoir Weaving the Web *(1999), Tim Berners-Lee describes how he created the World Wide Web. He recounted how Enquire, a software program he wrote while working as a consultant at CERN, the European Particle Physics Laboratory in Geneva, Switzerland, was the genesis for his later invention.*

When I first began tinkering with a software program that eventually gave rise to the idea of the World Wide Web, I named it Enquire, short for *Enquire Within upon Everything*, a musty old book of Victorian advice I noticed as a child in my parents' house outside London. With its title suggestive of magic, the book served as a portal to a world of information, everything from how to remove clothing stains to tips on inventing money. Not a perfect analogy for the Web, but a primitive starting point. . . .

I wrote it [Enquire] in my spare time and for my personal use, and for no loftier reason than to help me remember the connections among the various people, computers, and projects at the lab. Still, a larger vision had taken firm root in my consciousness.

Suppose all the information stored on computers everywhere were linked, I thought. Suppose I could program my program to create a space in which anything could be linked to anything. All the bits of information in every computer at CERN, and on the planet, would be available to me and to anyone else. There would be a single, global information space.

Once a bit of information in that space was labeled with an address, I could tell my computer to get it. By being able to reference anything with equal ease, a computer could represent associations between things that might seem unrelated but somehow did, in fact, share a relationship. A web of information would form.

---

ship program at CERN and applied in 1983. He was granted a fellowship the following year to work on real-time systems for scientific data acquisition and control. He quickly made significant contributions to the FASTBUS system of software and designed a remote procedure call system (an RPC system) to enable myriad computers and networks within CERN to communicate with one another.

Over the next five years his work at CERN allowed him some free time to re-create Enquire on a Compaq computer he had received as a departing gift from his friend and former employer, Poole. Enquire was written to run both on his personal computer and on a VAX minicomputer he used for his work at CERN. He then began to further develop his ideas into a system that functioned the way he wanted it to function. His CERN project supervisor for the RPC project, Ben Segal, had seen in the United States the use of the fledgling Internet, a system that linked universities and labs across the nation. Segal became a lonely voice advocating the Internet's adoption

at CERN. His European colleagues resisted adoption of the American system because several were contributing to the development of an International Standards Organization (ISO) for network protocols (a process of development managed by Europeans but still years away from realization).

Berners-Lee became intrigued by the Internet and realized that it could link computers in a "network of networks." The system of protocols that governed how "packets" of information could be shipped (or transferred) over this network had been dubbed an Internet Protocol (IP) and a Transmission Control Protocol (TCP). Berners-Lee realized that he could incorporate this TCP/IP set of protocols into his RPC system to create an addressing system that identified in a tangible and reliable manner each remote service in the RPC system. His genius was to realize that each person had to be able to retain his or her own software and maintain a way of organizing it on his or her own computer, yet the system had to be able to find the software using Berners-Lee's RPC addressing scheme.

Berners-Lee wrote up his ideas in March of 1989 in a proposal—"Information Management"—to Michael Sendall and Sendall's boss, David Williams, as well as a few other colleagues at CERN. The proposal was ignored. Berners-Lee revised the proposal and tried again more than a year later; still it was ignored. He convinced Sendall to allow him to purchase a new NeXT computer, which was created by Steve Jobs. Sendall gave him the go-ahead to try his hypertext programing on this new machine. Berners-Lee created and coined the acronyms URL (Uniform Resource Locator), HTTP (Hypertext Transfer Protocol), and HTML (Hypertext Markup Language) as the basis for his new information system. He ultimately settled on "World Wide Web" as the name for his invention—a web of information akin to what the human brain itself manages. (He recalled a conversation he had with his father many years earlier on the subject.) The very first Web site was posted to the Internet on August 6, 1991, bringing the global resources of the Internet to everyone with a computer and a modem.

SIGNIFICANCE

The World Wide Web, developed primarily by Berners-Lee and Cailliau, drives the popularity of the Internet. The Web has made it possible for nonspecialists to access and share knowledge and media electronically without knowing a thing about how computers work. The Web has exponentially expanded the reach of the information age, which began—for consumers—in the late 1970's and early 1980's with the introduction of mass-produced PCs and Apple computers. Most significantly, the Web has changed everyday life, impacting business and the economy, interpersonal communications and social relations, research and education, entertainment, knowledge distribution and access, and much more.

In 1994, Berners-Lee founded and became the first director of the World Wide Web Consortium, headquartered at the Massachusetts Institute of Technology. He has been recognized by inductions into the Royal Society, the National Academy of Engineering (U.S.A.), and many other prestigious societies. He was knighted by the queen of England and has received numerous honorary doctorates, hundreds of awards, and acclaim as one of the hundred most distinguished and influential thinkers of the twentieth century.

—Dennis W. Cheek

FURTHER READING

Alesso, H. Peter, and Craig F. Smith. *Thinking in the Web: Berners-Lee, Gödel, and Turing.* Hoboken, N.J.: Wiley-Interscience, 2006. A highly nuanced, informative account of how three key individuals imagined the future and how Berners-Lee and his team at CERN made that vision real.

Berners-Lee, Tim. *Weaving the Web: The Original Design and Ultimate Destiny of the World Wide Web by Its Inventor.* San Francisco, Calif.: HarperSanFrancisco, 1999. Berners-Lee presents in this work exactly what is promised by its title: An authoritative insider's view of how the Web was created, how it has evolved, and where it may be headed.

Berners-Lee, Tim, et al. *A Framework for Web Science.* Hanover, Mass.: Now, 2006. Showcases the continuing work of Berners-Lee and colleagues around the world in advancing the science of decentralized information systems with a particular focus on central engineering questions. This is designed as an advanced undergraduate and graduate school textbook.

Ceruzzi, Paul E. *A History of Modern Computing.* 2d ed. Cambridge, Mass.: MIT Press, 2003. The definitive history of the computer revolution with substantial attention to key players such as Berners-Lee and the impact of their contributions on this dynamically changing field of human invention and endeavor.

Niederst, Jennifer. *Learning Web Design: A Beginner's Guide to HTML, Graphics, and Beyond.* 2d ed. Sebastopol, Calif.: O'Reilly, 2003. A recommended guide for those interested in the design of Web pages. Good for the beginner without any knowledge of Web page design. Includes a CD-ROM, illustrations, and an index.

Yost, Jeffrey R. *The Computer Industry.* Westport, Conn.: Greenwood Press, 2005. An account of how computer use spread from small groups of elite scientists and engineers into widespread application in the United States. Explores the ways in which computers have transformed corporate environments and entire industries, and examines the role of pioneers such as Berners-Lee in a wider social context.

SEE ALSO: Jeff Bezos; Vinton Gray Cerf; Bill Gates; Kurt Gödel; David Hilbert; Grace Murray Hopper; Steve Jobs; John von Neumann.

RELATED ARTICLES in *Great Events from History: The Twentieth Century:*

1971-2000: November-December, 1971: Tomlinson Sends the First E-Mail.; May 11, 1977: First Commercial Test of Fiber-Optic Telecommunications; November 20, 1985: Microsoft Releases the Windows Operating System; September, 1988: Prodigy Introduces Dial-Up Service; 1991-1993: Development of HTML; December 15, 1994: Release of Netscape Navigator 1.0; Mid-1990's: Rise of the Internet and the World Wide Web; May 23, 1995: Sun Microsystems Introduces Java; September 7, 1998: Google Is Founded; 1999: Rise of the Blogosphere.

EDUARD BERNSTEIN
German political theorist and politician

Bernstein was a Marxian political theorist, socialist politician, and historian who originated revisionist socialism. Through revisionist socialism, he tried to modify the traditional Marxian prediction of the imminent collapse of capitalism and the subsequent rule of the proletarian class by proposing a theory according to which social-reformist social change would lead to the realization of socialism.

BORN: January 6, 1850; Berlin, Prussia (now in Germany)
DIED: December 18, 1932; Berlin, Germany
AREAS OF ACHIEVEMENT: Political science, government and politics, economics

EARLY LIFE

Eduard Bernstein was born into a lower-middle-class family of German Jewish ancestry in Berlin. His father was originally a plumber but later became a railroad engineer. Since there were many children in the family—Bernstein was the seventh of fifteen born—his opportunities for a formal education were limited. At age sixteen, he left the gymnasium, an academic secondary school, and became first an apprentice and then a clerk at a bank. After his apprenticeship, his interests began to reach beyond his daily employment. He engaged in working-class political activity and joined the German Social Democratic Party in 1872, devoting occasional evenings and entire weekends to political agitation. He also continued his self-education by developing his public speaking skills and his notable intellectual talents, which brought him to the attention of Socialist Party leaders.

In 1878, Bernstein gave up his secure employment at a bank and moved to Switzerland to become secretary to Karl Höchberg, a wealthy socialist idealist whom he helped edit a socialist periodical and other publications. While engaged in these journalistic pursuits, he read and digested the recently published *Herrn Eugen Dührings Umwälzung der Wissenschaft* (1877-1878; *Herr Eugen Dühring's Revolution in Science*, 1934), by Friedrich Engels. According to Bernstein's recollection, it was this powerful book that converted him to Marxism. The enactment of the antisocialist law under Otto von Bismarck in the same year prompted the German Social Democratic Party to issue its principal newspaper, *Der Sozialdemokrat*, in Zurich for secret distribution in Germany. Bernstein became an early contributor to the party

organ and, having earned the confidence of the party leadership, was appointed its editor late in 1880. During the following decade, he turned this newspaper into an effective instrument of agitation as well as a teaching tool for Marxist orthodoxy. In 1888, pressured by Bismarck, the Swiss government expelled Bernstein, who moved to London. He continued to edit the party newspaper there until the lapse of the antisocialist law in 1890. There Bernstein not only rounded out his own ideological education under the watchful eye of Engels but also was exposed to different socialist groups in England, including the Fabians.

LIFE'S WORK

Although the repeal of the antisocialist legislation restored more normal conditions for political agitation in Germany and permitted socialist exiles to return to their homeland, the imperial government barred Bernstein from returning until 1901. All of his major publications relating to revisionist socialism were thus written abroad but published in Germany. After his work with the party newspaper ended, he edited Ferdinand Lassalle's works, published a historical study of the English Revolution, and contributed to socialist publications in Germany. As he studied Marxian writings more closely, especially the first two volumes of *Das Kapital* (1867, 1885; *Capital*, 1886, 1907, 1909) and the third, issued by Engels in 1894, Bernstein became increasingly disturbed by the gap between Marx's predictions and societal reality as he observed it. Marx had forecast the intensified centralization of capitalism and the advancing impoverishment of the proletariat, whereas British and German economic and social conditions indicated no such trends. The 1890's brought, especially in Germany, increasing prosperity, which improved the condition of the proletariat and moderated the violence of the class struggle. A catastrophic change in the near future appeared to be unlikely. If anything, the British historical developments and the German Social Democratic experience pointed toward a process of evolutionary change.

Bernstein first expounded his new ideas in a series of articles entitled "Probleme des Sozialismus," which appeared between 1896 and 1898 in *Neue Zeit*, the main German socialist periodical, edited by Karl Kautsky. One year later, his book *Die Voraussetzungen des Sozialismus und die Aufgaben de Sozialdemokratie* (1899; *Evolutionary Socialism*, 1909) expanded the theme that he had outlined in the earlier articles. Bernstein rejected Marx's concept of the apocalyptic end of capitalism and the attendant immiseration of the working class. According to Bernstein, Marx had underestimated the economic, social, and political factors that stabilized the capitalist system and led to expanded production that also brought an increase in mass consumption and a rise in the workers' real income. He demonstrated that Marx's prediction that in a capitalist society the rich would become richer and the poor, poorer was not borne out by the facts. Rather, Bernstein found that the class structure under capitalism was becoming more differentiated. Rising income levels improved the condition of many workers, and the traditional middle class, instead of shrinking, as Marx had anticipated, was being expanded by a new middle class of white-collar workers and civil servants. Bernstein also raised serious questions about Marx's theory of historical materialism, or economic determinism. In Bernstein's view, noneconomic factors were often as important in determining historical processes as productive forces and relations of production. Lastly, the most heretical departure from Marxian orthodoxy was Bernstein's contention that the realization of socialism would not come about within the scheme of inexorable determinism that Marx had borrowed from Georg Wilhelm Friedrich Hegel but within a critical intellectual framework informed by the rational principles of Immanuel Kant. In short, he implied that socialism would not be attained as a natural development of history but must be worked for as an ethical goal.

Bernstein's propositions for the revision of Marxian theory created a controversy that lasted for years and resulted in a more rational basis for reformist politics in German social democracy, much of which had been in vogue since the founding of the party in Bismarck's time. In contrast, the 1891 Erfurt Program of the German Social Democratic Party, the theoretical part of which had been drafted by Kautsky and its tactical section by Bernstein, was based on Marxist formulations. Doctrinaire Marxists such as Kautsky, the more eclectic August Bebel, and the radical Rosa Luxemburg all felt threatened by Bernstein's new challenges to party dogma. They wanted to uphold the revolutionary party program in combination with moderate reformist practice, and they strongly objected to broadening reformist politics by collaboration with nonsocialist parties as the theory of revisionist socialism suggested. Bernstein's ideas were hotly debated at party congresses in Germany between 1898 and 1903 as well as at the International Socialist Congress in 1904. Even though revisionist socialist theory was repeatedly rejected by action of the party congresses, it refused to die.

After his return to Germany in 1901, Bernstein was elected to the German Reichstag in the following year and served in the parliamentary body with no interruptions until 1928. His life as a party politician was never as significant as his work as a political theorist and journalist. Moreover, in the political arena he was by no means a consistent supporter of right-wing German social democracy. As a pacifist and internationalist, Bernstein quite often dissented from his reformist party colleagues on issues of foreign policy and militarism. His most notable break with the majority of the German Social Democratic Party came in 1915, during World War I. After reluctantly voting for war credits at the beginning of the war, he joined, late in 1915, a minority of largely leftwing party members, who refused to lend further financial support to the imperial government. First organized as a dissenting group, the defectors formally established the Independent Socialist Party in 1917. At the end of the war, Bernstein, however, returned to the majority German Social Democratic Party and even briefly served in a ministerial position in the government. Yet he always spoke out courageously on controversial issues despite

Eduard Bernstein. (The Granger Collection, New York)

hostility from party and public audiences. He defended many provisions of the Treaty of Versailles and even asserted that imperial Germany was guilty of causing the war. Some of his sharpest attacks were directed at the Russian revolutionary left, the Bolsheviks. He contended that in the Bolsheviks' lust for power they had barbarized Marx's evolutionary teachings, resorted to ruthless violence, and disregarded Marxist economics by leaping into socialism from a lower capitalist base than that of any Western country. These polemical controversies and frequently unpopular stands were not helpful to restoring Bernstein's influence of earlier times. He came to be seen more as a party curiosity than a leader. At the same time, even his enemies granted that he was a man of unimpeachable integrity and intellectual honesty. In the last decade of his life, Bernstein concentrated on writing his memoirs, a party history, and journalistic articles; he also gave lectures before university audiences. He observed with concern the revival of anti-Semitism and the worsening of economic conditions not only in Germany but also throughout the world. His death in December, 1932, spared him the pain of experiencing the advent of a brutal dictatorship.

SIGNIFICANCE

The significance of Bernstein's contribution lay in his sharp criticism of orthodox Marxian theory and the introduction of an eclectic array of doctrines that provided a theoretical foundation for socialist reformist practice. He was not noted for great philosophical originality, and his ideas made only a modest contribution to socialist thought. The basic assumptions of revisionist socialism were not grounded in hard philosophical principles, nor were they, for that matter, always very clear. Common sense and empirical observation of facts were what often informed the philosophy of revisionist socialism and infused it with a rational optimism. Nevertheless, revisionist socialism provided a clear-cut direction for political action that was particularly relevant to the state and society of Germany. Bernstein regarded, above all, the democratization of political and economic institutions as a prerequisite for the realization of a socialist society. In the German Empire, he considered the immediate tasks of the German Social Democratic Party to be the struggle for political rights of the working class and the struggle for all reforms in the state that were likely to improve the conditions of the working class and to transform the state in the direction of democracy. In theory and practice, he reinforced an absolute commitment to a form of socialism that was, above all, democratic. During the Weimar

Republic, the German Social Democratic Party program, adopted at Görlitz in 1921 under his influence, gave recognition to revisionist socialist principles that sharply differentiated this party from the German Communist Party. It was not until after the defeat of Hitler that the German Social Democratic Party threw overboard the remnants of tradition-honored Marxist dogmas and, in the Bad Godesberg program of 1959, declared many revisionist socialist principles to be the prevailing orthodoxy.

—*George P. Blum*

FURTHER READING

Bernstein, Eduard. *Evolutionary Socialism: A Criticism and Affirmation*. Translated by Edith C. Harvey. Reprint. New York: Schocken Books, 1961. This readable exposition is a full statement of Bernstein's critique of Marxism and his formulation of the tasks and possibilities of social democracy.

_____. *My Years of Exile: Reminiscences of a Socialist*. Translated by Bernard Miall. Reprint. Westport, Conn.: Greenwood Press, 1986. This reprint of Bernstein's autobiography, which was first published in English in 1921, covers his years in exile in Switzerland and England. It provides insights into his personality and the milieu of socialist friends and associates, including Engels and Marx.

Fletcher, Roger, ed. *Bernstein to Brandt: A Short History of German Social Democracy*. Baltimore: Edward Arnold, 1987. British and German historians summarize the history of German social democracy from its beginning to the present. Good for a quick overview and a short summary on Bernstein in particular. Contains a very good bibliography.

Gay, Peter. *The Dilemma of Democratic Socialism: Eduard Bernstein's Challenge to Marx*. New York: Columbia University Press, 1952. A classic intellectual biography of Bernstein. Even though it is dated, it remains very useful for an understanding of revisionist socialism and the way stations of its originator.

Hulse, James W. "Bernstein: From Radicalism to Revisionism." In *Revolutionists in London: A Study of Five Unorthodox Socialists*. New York: Oxford University Press, 1970. Secondary material is combined with original research in this biographical chapter on Bernstein, which provides a good introduction to his life and ideas and is particularly suitable for advanced high school students and undergraduates.

Lichtheim, George. *Marxism: An Historical and Critical Study*. New York: Frederick A. Praeger, 1961. An excellent treatment of Marxism as a historical and theoretical body of thought that shows the interconnection between events and ideas. The emergence of revisionist socialism is succinctly analyzed in the broad spectrum of European socialism.

Lidtke, Vernon L. *The Outlawed Party: Social Democracy in Germany, 1878-1890.* Princeton, N.J.: Princeton University Press, 1966. The standard study of the German Social Democratic Party during the "heroic epoch" when Bismarck attempted to suppress it. Bernstein's role as editor of *Sozialdemokrat* and his involvement in party politics before 1890 are well described and judiciously interpreted.

Muravchik, Joshua. "What Is to Be Done: Bernstein Develops Doubts." In *Heaven on Earth: The Rise and Fall of Socialism.* San Francisco, Calif.: Encounter Books, 2002. This book about the development of various socialist movements contains a chapter about Bernstein's life and ideas.

Schorske, Carl E. *German Social Democracy, 1905-1917: The Development of the Great Schism.* Cambridge, Mass.: Harvard University Press, 1955. A classic study of the genesis of the factional split that destroyed the unity of German social democracy. Though it tends to favor the left in the party, Bernstein and revisionist socialism are also placed in their historical context.

Tudor, H., and J. M. Tudor, eds. *Marxism and Social Democracy: The Revisionist Debate, 1896-1898.* New York: Cambridge University Press, 1988. A judicious selection of articles, speeches, and letters illustrates the early debate on revisionist socialism by juxtaposing the orthodox Marxist Bernstein and the revisionist Bernstein as well as his Marxist opponents. An informative introduction by H. Tudor traces the evolution of the revisionist debate. Includes a good bibliography of the primary and secondary publications.

SEE ALSO: Nikolay Ivanovich Bukharin; Bernhard von Bülow; Benedetto Croce; Antonio Gramsci; Adolf Hitler; Vladimir Ilich Lenin; György Lukács; Rosa Luxemburg; Clara Zetkin.

RELATED ARTICLE in *Great Events from History: The Twentieth Century:*

1901-1940: January 15, 1919: Assassination of Rosa Luxemburg.

LEONARD BERNSTEIN
American composer

Combining unusual talent with his appealing stage presence and teaching ability, Bernstein, through his conducting and composing, introduced classical music to a wide general audience.

BORN: August 25, 1918; Lawrence, Massachusetts
DIED: October 14, 1990; New York, New York
AREA OF ACHIEVEMENT: Music

EARLY LIFE

Leonard Bernstein was the son of Samuel Joseph and Jennie Resnick Bernstein, both Russian immigrants. In many ways his early life contains elements often found in the lives of American child prodigies, for his was not a wealthy family, and his natural talent for music came to light almost by accident. The Bernsteins had agreed to store an old upright piano for a relative, and when it arrived, their ten-year-old son would not be parted from it. He composed simple pieces on it almost immediately and begged for lessons. He decided on a professional career even at that early age, but though young Bernstein got his lessons, his practical father knew only too well the vicissitudes inherent in a career in music and steadfastly opposed it.

To ensure that their son received a solid and well-rounded early education, the Bernsteins sent Leonard to the prestigious Boston Latin School. While there, he participated and excelled in athletics as well as traditional academic studies. He was still determined to study music when it came time to graduate and, still against his father's wishes, registered at Harvard University as a music major. Harvard's music faculty was particularly distinguished in the 1930's, and though Bernstein intended a career as a concert pianist, he studied not only piano (with Heinrich Gebhard) but also composition (with Walter Piston and Edward Burlinghame Hill).

Bernstein was graduated from Harvard in 1939 and attended the relatively new Curtis Institute of Music in Philadelphia. Curtis had, at that time, attracted several famous German émigrés to its faculty, among them Fritz Reiner, with whom Bernstein studied conducting. He continued his studies in piano with Isabella Vengerova

Leonard Bernstein. (Hulton Archive/Getty Images)

and orchestration with Randall Thompson while at Curtis, thus laying the foundation for the three avenues his musical career would simultaneously travel. Just as important in his early development, young Bernstein spent summers studying and working with Serge Koussevitzky, conductor of the Boston Symphony, at the Berkshire Music Center in Tanglewood, Massachusetts.

LIFE'S WORK

Bernstein's career was just beginning as the United States entered World War II. The war added to the uncertainties of a young musician trying to establish himself, though uncertainty did not diminish his energies. Indeed, 1941 and 1942 were spent teaching and composing the *Clarinet Sonata*, his first published work. He also produced operas for the Boston Institute of Modern Art during these years, but his first major opportunity came in September, 1942, when Koussevitzky, his former mentor, appointed him assistant conductor at Tanglewood. This position gave Bernstein the base he needed and paved the way for appearances in the 1942-1943 season at New York's Town Hall music forums and the "Serenade Concerts" at New York's Museum of Modern Art.

The New York music world began to take notice of Bernstein's unusual style and verve, and in 1943, he accepted an appointment as assistant conductor of the New York Philharmonic from Arthur Rodzinski, then its conductor. It was, indeed, a combination of talent and good fortune that advanced Bernstein's career to international status late that year. On November 12, 1943, the famous

mezzo-soprano Jennie Tourel performed his song cycle *I Hate Music* at Town Hall. The very next day, he received a call from the New York Philharmonic, asking that he substitute as conductor for the suddenly indisposed Bruno Walter. Bernstein conducted the scheduled program with such skill and enthusiasm that he received not only the acclaim of the audience and his colleagues Rodzinski and Koussevitzky but also a front-page encomium in the next day's *The New York Times*. (This concert has been preserved on a long-playing record distributed by the Philharmonic.) Thus, barely two years out of Curtis, Bernstein found himself at the beginning of an international career with seemingly limitless horizons.

Late in 1943, Bernstein's *Jeremiah* Symphony premiered in Pittsburgh and Boston. It was performed again in New York on February 18, 1944. Though it received a mixed reception, enough of the critics thought it had sufficient merit to award Bernstein the New York City Music Critics Circle Award for the most distinguished new American orchestral work of the 1943-1944 season. The *Jeremiah* Symphony has since become a regularly played work among American orchestras and has won audience acceptance.

Still, broad audience popularity also distinguished Bernstein's career from its earliest years. April 18, 1944, saw the world premiere of *Fancy Free*, a ballet given by Ballet Theatre (now called American Ballet Theatre) at the Metropolitan Opera House in New York. Composer Bernstein also conducted, and his score became the basis for the musical *On the Town* (1944), with choreography by Jerome Robbins and lyrics by Betty Comden and Adolph Green. The musical was a critical success and illustrated the affinity Bernstein always enjoyed with the American musical theater.

In the years after World War II, Bernstein served as guest conductor with numerous orchestras, especially with the newly founded Israel Philharmonic, where he served as musical adviser from 1945 to 1948. He toured in the United States with the Israel Philharmonic in 1951, sharing conducting responsibilities with Koussevitzky. In the summer of that year, he succeeded his mentor as head of the conducting department at Tanglewood and taught music at Brandeis University from 1951 to 1956. He continued his success in the musical theater with a series of perennially popular scores during these years: *Wonderful*

Town (1953), *Candide* (1956), and *West Side Story* (1957). The New York City Opera later placed *Candide* in its regular repertory, and Bernstein himself recorded *West Side Story* with operatic voices, illustrating again the affinity between what are often called "popular" music and "serious" music, a distinction that Bernstein clearly rejected. Earlier Bernstein works are still offered and remain in the record catalogs. These works include *The Age of Anxiety* (1949), a second symphony for piano and orchestra; a short opera, *Trouble in Tahiti* (1952); and incidental music for the Broadway production of *Peter Pan* (1950) and the film *On the Waterfront* (1954), for which he received an Academy Award nomination.

For the 1957-1958 season, just as the New York Philharmonic was about to leave Carnegie Hall for its new house at Lincoln Center, Bernstein was appointed co-conductor of the orchestra with Dimitri Mitropoulos. He was also given directorship of the orchestra's Young People's Concerts. He invigorated the latter with his enthusiasm and energy, even bringing them to national television. Many adult concertgoers owe at least part of their musical knowledge to Bernstein's discussions of the sonata and symphonic forms, the meaning of counterpoint, and Bernstein's musical biographies, one of the most entertaining of which was dedicated to his mentor, teacher, and friend Koussevitzky.

Bernstein introduced similar innovations one year later, when he assumed full directorship of the New York Philharmonic on Mitropoulos's retirement, introducing Thursday "Preview Concerts," in which the conductor spoke to the audience about the music to be performed as well as thematically linked concerts, which established patterns of influence among seemingly unrelated composers. Bernstein thus transformed what might otherwise have been merely evenings of entertainment into instructive, though never patronizing, educational experiences for his adult audiences.

Not content to have taken the New York audiences by storm, Bernstein toured with the New York Philharmonic in Latin America at the close of the 1957-1958 season, and in Europe and Asia the following year, taking the orchestra to twenty-nine cities in seventeen countries, including the Soviet Union, all to great popular acclaim. While in the Soviet Union, Bernstein introduced Russian audiences to a wide variety of compositions rarely presented by Soviet orchestras, including his own compositions as well as those by the Russian-born émigré Igor Stravinsky.

Bernstein's great popularity with New York audiences continued throughout his active tenure with the New York Philharmonic, though after the death of his wife, Chilean-born actor Felicia Montealegre Cohn, as well as with the passing of time, he wanted to direct more of his energies to composing and guest conducting with various orchestras. It was for this reason that Bernstein resigned full-time directorship of the New York Philharmonic after the 1968-1969 season, ceding the baton to Pierre Boulez, the French-born maestro who became music director in the 1971-1972 season. The grateful New York Philharmonic awarded Bernstein the title Conductor Laureate, and he continued to conduct the orchestra for several concerts each season.

From his youth, Bernstein exuded charm. He looked taller than his five feet, eight and one-half inches, and in his later years, his longish, tousled hair turned from gray to silver. His involvement with the music he conducted was genuine, not melodramatic. He was, in truth, a showman, but a showman with real substance, and the enthusiasm that New York audiences displayed whenever he conducted proceeded directly from his unusual rapport with his orchestra and his clear love of music. In the years after he ended active involvement with the Philharmonic, Bernstein conducted all over the world and turned even more to operatic conducting (at Bayreuth and the Metropolitan). His theater piece *Mass* premiered at the Kennedy Center for the Performing Arts in Washington, D.C., in 1971, combining Roman Catholic liturgy with secular and popular tunes. Though it received mixed criticism, it was, like so many Bernstein works, widely acclaimed by audiences.

SIGNIFICANCE

Bernstein, despite his undoubted success, always was a person given to moodiness and, paradoxically, to self-doubt. He was troubled by the world's cruelty and injustice, and this sensitivity led him not only to the themes of many of his works (the *Jeremiah* Symphony, *The Age of Anxiety*, the 1963 work *Kaddish*, *Candide*, *Mass*) and to some of his most expressive conducting (Ludwig van Beethoven, Gustav Mahler), but also to champion such unpopular causes as that of the Black Panthers at their trial in the 1960's and to oppose American involvement in the Vietnam War before it became fashionable to do so.

Regardless of Bernstein's moments of doubt and disillusionment, it remains clear that many owe much of the musical insight they possess to this gifted composer. His compositions are often distinctively American, with rhythms and counterpoint that verge on popular styles, but his love of music was international and universal.

—*Robert J. Forman*

FURTHER READING

Bernstein, Leonard. *Findings*. New York: Simon & Schuster, 1982. Contains a short autobiography, a classified list of compositions by Bernstein, and miscellaneous essays, addresses, and lectures on musical subjects.

_____. *The Joy of Music*. New York: Simon & Schuster, 1959. Bernstein's own introduction to music, designed for adults and incorporating the teaching techniques he used so successfully in both the Thursday evening "Preview Concerts" and the "Young People's Concerts." It is filled with musical illustrations and suggestions for listening.

_____. *The Unanswered Question: Six Talks at Harvard*. Cambridge, Mass.: Harvard University Press, 1976. A technical but interesting work drawn from the undergraduate lectures Bernstein delivered at Harvard as a visiting professor there in 1973.

_____. *Young People's Concerts*. New York: Simon & Schuster, 1970. A companion volume to *The Joy of Music*, based on Bernstein's Emmy Award-winning television series. Discusses what is meant by music, classical music, and melody in terms understandable to both young adults and older listeners.

Briggs, John. *Leonard Bernstein: The Man, His Work, and His World*. Cleveland, Ohio: World, 1961. A biography, particularly good in assessing the reasons for Bernstein's far-ranging popularity and filled with the comments of Bernstein's colleagues and fellow composers, including remarks of the latter on Bernstein's interpretations of their works. Contains a discography to 1960.

Gruen, J., and Ken Heyman. *The Private World of Leonard Bernstein*. New York: Viking Press, 1968. A photo-text study that catches Bernstein in all of his moods. There are also candid photographs of his family and discussions of the philosophy that underlies his complex personality.

Horowitz, Joseph. *Classical Music in America: A History of Its Rise and Fall*. New York: W. W. Norton, 2005. Chapter 7, "Leonard Bernstein and the Classical Music Crisis," is included in this survey of classical music in the United States.

Howard, John Tasker. *Our American Music: A Comprehensive History from 1620 to the Present*. 4th ed. New York: Thomas Y. Crowell, 1965. Sets Bernstein in the tradition of American composers, considering the qualities that make his work "American" in character. Contains a capsule biography and partial list of compositions.

Laird, Paul R. *Leonard Bernstein: A Guide to Research*. New York: Routledge, 2002. An annotated guide that focuses on Bernstein's life and musical works.

SEE ALSO: Benjamin Britten; Aaron Copland; Cheryl Crawford; Claude Debussy; George Gershwin; Vladimir Horowitz; Gustav Mahler; Gian Carlo Menotti; Leontyne Price; Richard Strauss; Arturo Toscanini; Kurt Weill.

RELATED ARTICLES in *Great Events from History: The Twentieth Century:*

1941-1970: April 18, 1944: Robbins's *Fancy Free* Premieres; March 30, 1955: *On the Waterfront* Wins Best Picture; June 18, 1955: Boulez's *Le Marteau sans maître* Premieres; September 26, 1957: Bernstein Joins Symphonic and Jazz Elements in *West Side Story*.

HANS ALBRECHT BETHE
German-born American physicist

Bethe's work in theoretical nuclear physics explained how stars converted mass to energy and broadened the scientific understanding of subatomic events. Long an influential advocate for restraint in the proliferation of nuclear weapons, he laid the theoretical groundwork for the explosion of the first atom bomb.

BORN: July 2, 1906; Strassburg, Germany (now Strasbourg, France)
DIED: March 6, 2005; Ithaca, New York
AREAS OF ACHIEVEMENT: Physics, science

EARLY LIFE
Hans Albrecht Bethe (BAY-tuh) was the only child of Albrecht Theodore Julius Bethe, an eminent German physiologist, and Anna (Kuhn) Bethe, a musician and playwright. Hans came from a long line of university professors; his oldest uncle was a professor of Greek at the University of Leipzig, and his grandmother and mother both had fathers who were professors. The elder Bethe's family was Protestant; his wife's was Jewish. As a child, Hans was frail, lonely, and perhaps overprotected by his mother. Numbers dominated his life. At age five, Hans made a remark to his mother about the properties of zero, and at age seven, he filled a notebook with the powers of two and three. His father was concerned that Hans not progress too far beyond the mathematics appropriate to his grade in school.

The family moved to Frankfurt, Germany, in 1915 in response to an invitation to Albrecht Bethe to start a department of physiology at the University of Frankfurt. Though Hans had earlier received instruction from a private tutor, in Frankfurt he attended the gymnasium, a nine-year school. Hans felt estranged from the other students there since most of his life had been spent in the company of adults. He found some solace in mathematics, especially algebra. In his last few years at the school, the elective physics courses he took convinced him to pursue that field at the University of Frankfurt, which he did beginning in 1924. He discovered that he had little facility for experimental physics, but his interest in mathematics drove him to take up theoretical physics. One of his teachers, a spectroscopist named Karl Meissner, persuaded Bethe to leave Frankfurt to study under Arnold Sommerfeld, professor of theoretical physics at the University of Munich. The year 1926 was Bethe's first in Munich, and under the influential Sommerfeld, Bethe found himself at the center of a great ferment in theoretical physics. Quantum mechanics was replacing the classical model of the atom. The old model pictured tiny particles called electrons orbiting around a hard central core, or nucleus. The quantum theory, however, said that if electrons were represented as if they were waves, heretofore unexplained subatomic phenomena could be understood. In 1926, Sommerfeld shared with his students a new paper by Austrian physicist Erwin Schrödinger, which developed equations for quantum wave mechanics; subsequently, Sommerfeld encouraged Bethe to apply these insights to the effect of electron scattering, which took place when a beam of electrons was directed against a crystal. This study formed the basis of Bethe's doctoral degree in physics, granted in 1928. The next decade would be one of the most productive for Bethe in theoretical physics.

LIFE'S WORK
Bethe spent a short time as an instructor in physics at Frankfurt and at Stuttgart but in 1929 returned to the University of Munich at the request of Sommerfeld to work as a *Privatdozent*, a university lecturer whose fees are paid directly by students. During this time, Bethe wrote a seminal paper that gave mathematical expression to the passage of charged particles through matter. He considered the paper, which appeared in a physics journal in 1930, to be among his best work.

Concurrent with the rise of the Nazi movement in Germany in the early 1930's, Bethe, the recipient of a fellowship from the Rockefeller Foundation International Education Board, studied for a time at Cambridge University in England and at the University of Rome. In Rome, Bethe was profoundly influenced by the personality and theoretical approach of Enrico Fermi, then only thirty years old but already a physicist of international repute. From Fermi, Bethe learned a kind of experimental insight into theoretical problems, and he coauthored a paper with Fermi on electron-electron interaction, which was published in 1932.

Working again with Sommerfeld in Munich in the years 1931 and 1932 brought Bethe in contact with English and American postdoctoral students. One of the Americans, Lloyd Smith from Cornell University in Ithaca, New York, would eventually ask his department chairman to offer Bethe a position. Bethe would go to Cornell highly recommended.

Hans Albrecht Bethe. (© The Nobel Foundation)

the university, Bethe joined the physics department there in February, 1935. (In 1937, he became a full professor, retiring in 1975 to become the John Wendell Anderson Professor Emeritus of Physics.) The department was being reorganized to involve graduate students in basic theoretical research, and Bethe found the students, as well as the professors, eager to learn about nuclear physics but lacking sufficient background. Eventually, Bethe wrote three long articles for *Reviews of Modern Physics* (the first, in collaboration with Robert F. Bacher, was published in 1936, and the remaining two, with M. Stanley Livingston, appeared in 1937). The articles virtually recreated the entire field of nuclear physics; Bethe's Bible, as they came to be known, provided the basic textbook on the subject for a generation of scientists. (Through the years, most of Bethe's major theoretical findings appeared not in books but in hundreds of research articles in a variety of journals.)

At an astrophysics conference in 1938 in Washington, D.C., Bethe met George Gamow and Edward Teller of George Washington University; he was challenged to take up the theoretical problem of how the sun produced the energy it did through thermonuclear reactions. Bethe's answer was first published in 1939; "Energy Production in Stars" won for him a prize of five hundred dollars from the New York Academy of Sciences. (In 1967, Bethe was awarded the Nobel Prize in Physics on the basis of his work in this area.) This and subsequent papers introduced the six-step carbon cycle (in which carbon acts as a catalyst in the production of energy in stars hotter and more massive than the sun), and the P-P reaction (in which protons fuse in a chain reaction that transforms hydrogen into helium, releasing large amounts of energy). The P-P reaction is central to the sun's energy production and may take a million years or more to complete. In presenting the Nobel Prize, Professor O. Klein of the Swedish Academy of Sciences noted that solving the solar energy enigma was only one of many achievements that might have earned Bethe the prize, hailing it as "one of the most important applications of fundamental physics in our days."

In September, 1939, Bethe married Rose Ewald, the daughter of Paul Ewald, one of his Stuttgart professors. Rose had emigrated to the United States in 1936. Their union produced two children, Henry and Monica.

With the advent of World War II, Bethe's life entered a new era. Fearful of the progress of the Nazi regime, he sought to make a contribution to the war effort. From an article in the *Encyclopædia Britannica* on armor penetration, Bethe developed a theory that aided in the pro-

In 1932, Bethe collaborated with Sommerfeld on an article, "Elektronen-theorie der Metalle," published the next year in the *Handbuch der Physik*, which provided the basis for theoretical work on the solid-state basis of metals. On a more personal level, Sommerfeld was a shelter of sorts for Bethe when Adolf Hitler came to power in 1933. Since two of Bethe's grandparents were Jewish, Bethe was forced to resign as assistant professor at the University of Tübingen (a job he had taken the previous year). The Nazis seemed less concerned with the activities of older researchers such as Sommerfeld but demanded doctrinal adherence from younger scientists.

The shelter was only temporary: Increasing political tension and the threat of demonstrations against Bethe if he spoke at a physics colloquium made him eager to accept a lectureship position at the University of Manchester in England and later, in 1934, to become a fellow at the University of Bristol. The next year brought the offer of a permanent position at Cornell. Knowing little about

duction of stronger shields for Allied ships. Ironically, Bethe's article was classified secret, and Bethe himself was not permitted to read it. Yet after becoming a naturalized citizen of the United States in 1941, Bethe received a security clearance and soon afterward began work on radar for the Massachusetts Institute of Technology Radiation Laboratory. In 1943, he received a call from J. Robert Oppenheimer to assist in the production of an atom (fission) bomb. At the urging of Teller, he accepted, even though earlier Bethe had written a theoretical paper doubting the feasibility of fission reactions. From 1943 to 1946, he was chief of the Theoretical Physics Division at Los Alamos Laboratory in New Mexico, charged with developing the theoretical base for a fission explosion. In such a reaction, the nucleus of an atom is split, releasing energy. He later said that there was no alternative to developing the atomic bomb because of fears that German scientists might do it as well, but he insisted that a demonstration explosion should have been used to show off the awesome power of nuclear weapons before bombs were dropped on Japanese cities.

Teller, working under Bethe in the Theoretical Physics Division, insisted on the development of what he called the superbomb, one which would use the power of a fission explosion to trigger a hydrogen-fusion reaction with the subsequent release of vast destructive power. Teller seemed to find little acceptance of the idea, and his friendship with Bethe began to crumble. (It was severed, at least for a time, when in 1954, during loyalty hearings for Oppenheimer, Teller recommended against renewed security clearance for Oppenheimer.) Far from embracing the idea of a superbomb, Bethe became a kind of reluctant midwife to the atom bomb. After the successful test of the first plutonium bomb at Alamogordo, New Mexico, in July of 1945, Bethe began to consider the possibility of some kind of international control of atomic weapons and civilian control of atomic energy in the United States itself.

Nevertheless, in 1952, Bethe returned to Los Alamos for several months of design work on Teller's hydrogen bomb, apparently convinced that revised calculations made such a superbomb a real possibility; if that were true, could the Soviet Union be far behind? The pragmatic Bethe reasoned that since there was no global mechanism of arms control, the United States, in its own defense, ought to develop the hydrogen bomb, if only to maintain the balance of terror when the Soviets developed their own superbomb. Bethe did allow that the American bomb program might well spur the Soviets to mount their own program; in fact, the Soviets tested a hydrogen bomb only three years after the American test in 1952.

At Cornell University after World War II, Bethe developed a world-class physics department, bringing with him from the Manhattan Project Richard Feynman, Philip Morrison, and Robert Wilson, among others. Their research brought fundamental breakthroughs. For example, Bethe first devised crucial calculations that led to the theory of quantum electrodynamics (QED), developed in full by Feynman, Freeman Dyson, and Julian Schwinger.

Bethe's scientific accomplishments ranged from theoretical physics to quantum electrodynamics to nose-cone reentry, but in the 1950's, he became increasingly concerned with public policy regarding nuclear energy. In 1955, Bethe served as a technical adviser to the United States delegation to the International Conference on the Peaceful Uses of Atomic Energy held in Geneva, Switzerland. He was a member of the President's Science Advisory Committee in the late 1950's and played a large part in the negotiations that led to the atmospheric Nuclear Test Ban Treaty in 1963. After the Arab oil embargo in 1974, Bethe concentrated his efforts on advocating the development of a range of energy resources from coal to nuclear power, emphasizing the need for strong nuclear-reactor safety standards. Following the 1986 disaster at the Chernobyl Nuclear Power Plant in the Ukraine, Bethe led a panel of experts who studied whether such an accident could occur in a U.S. reactor. The panel found that U.S. reactors lacked the design flaw that led to the meltdown at Chernobyl.

When, in 1983, President Ronald Reagan called for a Strategic Defense Initiative (dubbed the "space shield" or Star Wars program), Bethe was swift to call the proposal unworkable and destabilizing. The development of weapons that could destroy the very satellites used to monitor atomic testing around the world would defeat a system of checks and balances that Bethe claimed had been effective for decades. In a 1968 *Scientific American* article with Richard Garwin, moreover, he had argued that any such antiballistic missile defense system would be easily thwarted by the use of decoys and therefore largely useless.

Bethe's worry about the misuse of scientific knowledge prompted him twice to make public protests. In 1995 he published an open letter urging fellow scientists to withdraw from all work relating to nuclear weaponry. In 2004, upset with President George W. Bush's attitude toward science, Bethe joined forty-seven other Nobel laureates in signing a letter of endorsement for Senator John Kerry in that year's presidential election.

Into his eighties, Bethe continued to pursue research in theoretical astrophysics, publishing an influential article about the mysterious absence of the predicted flow of neutrinos from the Sun. He also studied the processes producing type II supernova explosions, neutron stars, black holes, and stellar mergers.

Colleagues described Bethe as logical and methodical in his approach to problems, whether in physics or in everyday life. A tall, heavyset man with thinning hair, craggy features, an infectious sense of humor, and a legendary appetite, Bethe enjoyed some mountain climbing and skiing and was an avid stamp collector and amateur historian. However, he drew the most profound pleasures from his intellectual work on the stuff of matter and his insights into the very working of the stars. He died at his home in Ithaca, New York, on March 6, 2005, at the age of ninety-eight, survived by his wife, son, and daughter.

Cornell honored Bethe by naming a new residential college after him. An asteroid was also named for him. Among his many other honors were the Henry Draper Medal (1947), the Max Planck Medal (1955), the Eddington Medal of the Royal Astronomical Society (1961), the Enrico Fermi Award (1961), the Albert Einstein Peace Award (1992, with Joseph Rotblat), and the Bruce Medal (2001).

SIGNIFICANCE

Bethe's grasp of the range of theoretical physics was perhaps as great as that of anyone in history. His ability to select a problem and work out a solution, coolly and pragmatically, resonated with the American tradition of innovation and practical success. In fact, among his peers he was known as the preeminent problem solver. Bethe acknowledged the necessity of military weapons development, but he called on scientists to educate the public on the consequences of certain programs (though without breaking security). Reflecting the spirit of a realist, Bethe believed that the boycotting of weapons research was largely futile; rather, he advocated scientific involvement in such research. The scientific community might aid in designing wise policies, though there must be cooperation with national decisions. Bethe championed the prudent use of atomic energy, though he deplored nuclear arms proliferation. As an influential arms-control advocate, he believed that the mutual superpower reduction of nuclear warheads from tens of thousands down to around two thousand would serve to maintain nuclear deterrence but at a safer level. In sum, the United States should strive for arms control through negotiated

agreements rather than the promulgation of newer, more dangerous "protective" technologies.

For Bethe, the sheer joy of scientific discovery was tempered with the harsh realities of a world teeming with nuclear weapons, realities that he did not hesitate to face. His contributions to the understanding of how stars produce their energy and his more controversial advocacy of atomic energy enriched and challenged the world. As Kurt Gottfried and Edwin E. Salpeter wrote in their obituary to Bethe in the journal *Nature*, "The true extent of his moral strength would only emerge when his role in the birth of the nuclear age posed a host of ethical choices."

—Dan Barnett

FURTHER READING

Bernstein, Jeremy. *Hans Bethe: Prophet of Energy*. New York: Basic Books, 1980. Originally a series of articles for *The New Yorker*, this popular biography is based on interviews with Bethe; a large section is given over to Bethe's views on energy resources for the twenty-first century. Bernstein attempts a semi-popular explanation of the carbon cycle and quantum mechanics. A useful article, although it was not meant as a definitive biography.

Bethe, Hans A. "Countermeasures to ABM Systems." In *ABM: An Evaluation of the Decision to Deploy an Antiballistic Missile System*, edited by Abram Chayes and Jerome B. Wiesner. New York: Harper and Row, 1969. A critique of the proposed anti-ballistic-missile system under Presidents Lyndon B. Johnson and Richard M. Nixon; Bethe's contribution is an expanded reprint of his article on ABMs (coauthored with Richard Garwin) that appeared in the March, 1968, issue of *Scientific American*. In a somewhat technical discussion, Bethe concludes that the ABM is a destabilizing factor and would serve only to increase the race to produce a penetration device for any ABM shield. Though dated, it shows Bethe's logical and systematic thinking.

_____. "Face-Off on Nuclear Defense." *Technology Review* 87 (April, 1984): 38-39. Excerpts from a debate between Bethe and Teller on President Reagan's Star Wars proposal, held at the Kennedy School of Government at Harvard in November of 1983. Bethe calls for small-scale research rather than a vastly expensive weapons program. Useful for the interplay between rival schools of thought represented by Bethe and Teller.

_____. *Selected Works of Hans A. Bethe with Com-*

mentary. River Edge, N.J.: World Scientific, 1997. A collection of Bethe's twenty-eight most important scientific papers, each accompanied by a brief note describing its relation to previous research and its effects on subsequent theory.

_____. "The Technological Imperative." *Bulletin of the Atomic Scientists* 41 (August, 1985): 34-36. Bethe, chair of the magazine's board of sponsors for several years, evaluates modern technological developments in weapons research and concludes that, on balance, they have produced greater world instability. The temptation of ever-new technology need not be what drives U.S. strategic policy.

Brown, Gerald E., and Chang-Hwan Lee, eds. *Hans Bethe and His Physics.* Hackensack, N.J.: World Scientific, 2006. Collection of essays by scientists, friends, and colleagues of Bethe discussing his work in solid state physics, nuclear physics, astrophysics, nuclear energy, and atomic weapons. Includes an appreciation and obituary.

Marshak, Robert E., ed. *Perspectives in Modern Physics: Essays in Honor of Hans A. Bethe on the Occasion of His Sixtieth Birthday, July 1966.* New York: Interscience, 1966. The forty-one essays in this volume contain highly technical articles on quantum mechanics, astrophysics, and nuclear science, but there are also a number of valuable reminiscences (from Oppenheimer and others), as well as a six-page bibliography of Bethe's works.

Schweber, S. S. *In the Shadow of the Bomb: Bethe, Oppenheimer, and the Moral Responsibility of the Scientist.* Princeton, N.J.: Princeton University Press, 2000. A comparison of the lives and careers of Bethe and Oppenheimer, focusing on how the physicists came to terms with the nuclear weapons they helped create.

SEE ALSO: Enrico Fermi; George Gamow; J. Robert Oppenheimer; Erwin Schrödinger; Edward Teller.

RELATED ARTICLES in *Great Events from History: The Twentieth Century:*

1901-1940: July, 1926: Eddington Publishes *The Internal Constitution of the Stars.*

1941-1970: November, 1946: Physicists Develop the First Synchrocyclotron; 1948: Steady-State Theory of the Universe Is Advanced by Bondi, Gold, and Hoyle.

MARY McLEOD BETHUNE
American educator and social reformer

A leading voice and activist for democratic ideals before World War I and up to the early years of the Civil Rights movement, Bethune was instrumental in founding organizations to advance the education and rights of African Americans, inspiring others as she was herself inspired.

BORN: July 10, 1875; Mayesville, South Carolina
DIED: May 18, 1955; Daytona Beach, Florida
ALSO KNOWN AS: Mary Jane McLeod (birth name)
AREAS OF ACHIEVEMENT: Education, social reform, civil rights

EARLY LIFE

Mary McLeod Bethune (meh-CLOWD bay-THYEWN) was born in Mayesville, South Carolina, to Sam and Patsy McLeod, who were former slaves. She was the seventeenth child to be born to the couple and the first to be born free. Her father was a farmer and her mother, Patsy, probably did laundry to supplement the family income in addition to her own work on the family farm. Many of the older McLeod children were either married or on their own, but the younger children assisted with the support of the family by picking cotton. By her own report, Bethune, at nine years of age, could pick 250 pounds of cotton a day.

One incident in particular is reputed to have inspired Bethune's determination to become educated. While she was in a neighboring house being shown around by the white family's young daughters, they happened into a room with books. Bethune picked up one of the books and was examining it when one of the girls spoke sharply to her about putting the book down, reportedly telling her "You can't read, so you shouldn't even handle a book!" Shocked at this response and perhaps vaguely aware of the insult, Bethune became determined to read. As it happened, a young black woman was in the neighborhood to start a school for black children. This teacher approached the McLeods about having Bethune attend. The likelihood of one of the children of this poor family being allowed to go to school seemed remote. Nevertheless, Bethune's desire to go was so strong and apparently so heartfelt that her mother convinced her father to let her go. When she was able to read the Bible to her parents as a result of this schooling, they all, parents and child, came to appreciate the benefits of education.

Bethune did well at the little country school. Her teacher recommended her for further schooling, and her tuition was paid in part by Mary Chrissman, a white dressmaker from Denver, Colorado. The new school, known as Scotia School, was located in Concord, South Carolina. Bethune contributed to her education by doing odd jobs at the school. Having done well in her studies at Scotia, she was again recommended by her teachers for scholarships to continue her studies. She was accepted as a student at the Moody Bible Institute in Chicago, Illinois, and received additional financial support from Chrissman.

At the Moody Institute, Bethune became a member of the Gospel Choir Team that preached and sang throughout Illinois. She had hoped to become a missionary in Africa on completion of her studies, but because she was so young, she was not considered a suitable candidate. Instead, she took a teaching assignment at Haines Normal and Industrial Institute in Augusta, Georgia, where she

Mary McLeod Bethune. (Associated Publishers, Inc.)

met a black woman who was to affect her life in important ways: Lucy Laney, the school's principal and founder and a trailblazer in the education of blacks. Sympathizing with Bethune's compassion for the uneducated black children of the neighborhood around the school, Laney allowed Bethune to teach them on Sunday afternoons. Soon, Bethune had the children singing familiar songs, and she encouraged them to listen to Bible stories later.

The sponsoring Presbyterian Board of Haines Institute sent Bethune to other schools nearby. One of those schools was the Kendall Institute in Sumter, South Carolina. It was here that she met Albertus Bethune, also a teacher, whom she married in May of 1898. Their son, Albert McLeod Bethune, was born a year later. The family soon moved to Palatka, Florida, where Mary Bethune established a Presbyterian mission school. Her husband did not share her enthusiasm for missionary work, however, and the couple was eventually separated.

LIFE'S WORK

Having been born in the South during Reconstruction undoubtedly saddled Bethune with many adversities. She was black, poor, and female, none of which made her more remarkable than other young women alive during the same period. What did distinguish her was her ability to conquer those misfortunes, to share her accomplishments with others, and to choose to devote her life to acts of service to others. From the time she read the Bible to her parents, she seemed to recognize and become inspired by the power of words and their effects on others.

Bethune's lifework began in Daytona Beach when she saw other young black women in need of all varieties of education. Her ambition to provide a place for their schooling took the form of grasping at any possibilities, becoming inventive as the needs arose: discarded, crumpled paper could be smoothed out to write lessons on; burned wooden twigs could become charcoal for pencils; cracked plates or broken chairs—anything that could be salvaged was recycled and returned to useful service. Her crowning achievement in these salvage operations was an area in the city that had been used as a garbage dump, but which she saw could be used for a school. Selflessness and determination proved to be the hallmarks of Bethune's character. She had a dollar and a half as her original budget, but she made do and found creative ways to recruit both students and community assistance for her projects.

The years following the founding of the school with five students on October 3, 1904, led to the rapid growth of her program of education for blacks. By 1906, Bethune had 250 students and employed a few teachers who worked for salaries of fifteen to twenty-five dollars a month. To lessen the drain on the meager finances and to become more independent, she stopped renting and began to buy land for her needs. By 1925, Bethune School merged with the Cookman School for boys to become Bethune-Cookman College. The merged institution included a grade school, high school, and college. Because southern policies of segregation at the time extended to the care of hospital patients, Bethune was led to erect a hospital near the college in 1911 to provide better treatment for the black community. It was named for her father and proved to be another example of her vision.

During the years of the Wilson administration, Bethune became more active in social organizations devoted to protest and social reform. She served on the executive board of the Urban League as well as on committees resisting the discriminatory policies of the Young Women's Christian Association (YWCA). Since many of the positions taken by the YWCA were either condescending or blatantly biased, Bethune became one of several women opposing the racist stance of that association. She was also active in the formation of the National Association of Wage Earners, an organization dedicated to informing women of their rights as workers.

In 1921, Bethune was one of the executive leaders of the International Council of Women of the Darker Races of the World. The intention of this group was to raise the esteem and awareness of darker peoples about themselves and others from what has been called the Third World and what is best called the developing world.

She continued her activities on behalf of black children and women to combat the injustices and inequities they faced. Founding the National Association of Negro Women in 1935 and working with the Franklin D. Roosevelt administration, Bethune directed the Negro branch of the National Youth Administration. She was also founder and president of the National Association of Colored Women's Clubs.

Although she served as president of Bethune-Cookman College from 1904 to 1942 and was one of its trustees until her death in 1955, her influence was not exclusively focused on education. She was a special assistant to the secretary of war during World War II and served on the Committee for National Defense under President Harry S. Truman. She also served as a consultant to the conference that drafted the United Nations charter. These activities and her many honorary degrees and medals never caused her to abandon her main concern: the education of every black child.

Bethune's imagination was not restricted to what she, or anyone, could see immediately. She was known to say "just because you can't see a thing, does not mean that it does not exist." During many of her talks, Bethune would frequently compare the peoples of the world to flowers. Some students would remark that there were no black flowers in the world's gardens. At first, she had only her visionary remark to offer, since there appeared to be no way to rebut the observation. On one of her trips to Europe, however, she was presented with a "black" tulip by one of her hosts in the Netherlands. She later planted the tulips on her campus as proof of her maxim.

Bethune's ability to maintain her lofty vision allowed her to endure in the face of great challenges. The black community was hard hit by the era's wars, economic depressions, riots, and lynchings. For the most part, there was little government intervention on behalf of black victims. Protests by black organizations went unheard, were ignored, or were suppressed. The activities of racist organizations such as the Ku Klux Klan were accepted, permitted, or even encouraged while blacks were denied their civil rights despite their achievements as responsible citizens. Poverty and ignorance, combined with racism, did much to inhibit black people. None of these conditions could dampen Bethune's spirit. Working with Eleanor Roosevelt and some of the nation's top businesspeople, Bethune enhanced her effectiveness as a representative of the black community and as an individual educator. She died of a heart attack in 1955 and was buried on the campus of her beloved college.

SIGNIFICANCE

During times when being an African American often meant being invisible, being disheartened, and being denied chances to achieve intellectually, especially if female, Bethune became a person whose entire life disproved such stereotypes. By white American standards, she possessed little physical beauty, but by any standards her spirit, her energy, and her compassion were evidence of great inner beauty. Bethune's drive to give women access to worlds that had been closed to them, to give all blacks intellectual choices that had been denied them, and to give children an example to follow in providing service to others made her one of the most notable African American leaders of her time. Before her death, she had lived to see Bethune-Cookman become one of the finest of the historically black colleges in the country. She had left her mark on the administrations of two American presidents. Using her keen understanding of human behavior and harnessing her ability to negotiate change in the face of great opposition, Bethune became one of the most influential voices in the struggle for racial equality.

—Maude M. Jennings

FURTHER READING

Bethune, Mary McLeod. *Mary McLeod Bethune: Building a Better World—Essays and Selected Documents*. Edited by Audrey Thomas McCluskey and Elaine M. Smith. Bloomington: Indiana University Press, 1999. Contains seventy of Bethune's writings and other documents dating from 1902 through 1955.

Carruth, Ella Kaiser. *She Wanted to Read: The Story of Mary McLeod Bethune*. New York: Abingdon Press, 1966. A biography written for juveniles that presents a portrait of Bethune's early years. Also includes some coverage of her involvement as a presidential adviser as well as her activities as an organizer and founder of groups concerned with women's rights and labor relations.

Hanson, Joyce A. *Mary McLeod Bethune and Black Women's Political Activism*. Columbia: University of Missouri Press, 2003. Hanson examines Bethune's political activism in the context of the activism of African American women in her time.

Lerner, Gerda, ed. *Black Women in White America: A Documentary History*. New York: Pantheon Books, 1972. Contains excerpts of works and speeches by notable black women including Bethune. Extremely useful for accurate firsthand accounts of her life and her activities in entries such as "A College from a Garbage Dump," "Another Begging Letter," and "A Century of Progress of Negro Women."

McKissack, Patricia, and Fredrick McKissack. *Mary McLeod Bethune: A Great Teacher*. Hillside, N.J.: Enslow, 1991. Another biography directed at juvenile readers that provides an excellent introduction, broadly describing Bethune's life and achievements in fighting bigotry and racial injustice. Focuses much of its attention on Bethune's courage in overcoming adversity. Illustrated.

Salem, Dorothy. *To Better Our World: Black Women in Organized Reform, 1890-1920*. New York: Carlson, 1990. Salem's work is the fourteenth volume in Carlson's Black Women in United States History series. Provides a chronological narrative of the efforts made by black women's organizations to improve the lives of African Americans in the United States. A well-researched historical account that provides insights into the backgrounds of black women reformers, highlighting their resiliency of character in the face of failures as well as successes.

Smith, Elaine M. "Mary McLeod Bethune and the National Youth Association." In *Clio Was a Woman: Studies in the History of American Women*, edited by Mabel E. Deutrich and Virginia C. Purdy. Washington, D.C.: Howard University Press, 1980. An excellent assessment of Bethune's work in supervising the activities of the National Youth Administration with respect to African Americans. Although aimed at a scholarly audience, this essay is accessible to general readers and helps place Bethune's accomplishments within the context of her own time as well as the larger field of women's studies.

SEE ALSO: Jane Addams; W. E. B. Du Bois; Marcus Garvey; Fannie Lou Hamer; Rosa Parks; Jeannette Rankin; Eleanor Roosevelt; Madam C. J. Walker; Ida B. Wells-Barnett; Walter White.

ANEURIN BEVAN
British politician

Bevan was the most eloquent British spokesperson of his time for democratic socialism and also the architect of the National Health Service, one of the most important social reforms of the twentieth century.

BORN: November 15, 1897; Tredegar, Monmouthshire, Wales
DIED: July 6, 1960; Chesham, Buckinghamshire, England
ALSO KNOWN AS: Nye Bevan
AREAS OF ACHIEVEMENT: Government and politics, public health, social reform

EARLY LIFE

Aneurin Bevan (eh-NI-rehn BEHV-ahn) was the son of a coal miner and began work in the mines at the age of thirteen. Bevan overcame a childhood speech impediment and by his late teens was an effective speaker and aspiring leader. In 1919, he won a scholarship from the South Wales Miners to study for two years at the Central London Labour College, a school that specialized in Marxist economics and working-class history. He returned to Tredegar in 1921, held posts in local government and in his miners' lodge, and was elected in 1929 to the House of Commons as the Labour Party candidate for his local constituency, Ebbw Vale. In 1934, he married Jennie Lee, a Labour member of Parliament, who was to be one of his closest political associates.

Bevan was a great platform orator and parliamentary debater, soon recognized as the equal of both David Lloyd George and Winston Churchill. Bevan had been a voracious reader since childhood, and his speaking style was both literate and popular. He soon became a spokesperson for the left wing of his party and was often critical of his own leaders. Bevan wrote frequently for the socialist weekly *Tribune*, which he edited from 1940 to 1945 when he engaged the then little-known George Orwell as literary editor. Bevan was a Marxist, but his Marxism was flexible and imaginative, never sectarian and dogmatic. It was a mode of viewing reality, not a finished philosophical system. Bevan believed in class struggle, but it was class struggle to be waged through election battles. He believed that the greatest weapon the working class had was the vote, but it had yet to learn to use it properly. He often spoke in anger when describing the sufferings of workers and especially the suffering of his own South Wales miners, but he was not the dour, spite-ridden man depicted by his enemies. He was ebullient and zestful,

large in body and in human interests, with friends from many areas of life. He loved good food, clothes, theater, literature, and exhilarating conversation.

LIFE'S WORK

Throughout the 1930's, Bevan attacked the national (predominantly Conservative) governments of Ramsay MacDonald, Stanley Baldwin, and Neville Chamberlain for working much harder to cut payments to the unemployed than they did to end unemployment, the miseries of which Bevan and members of his family had endured during much of the 1920's. Bevan also attacked Baldwin and especially Chamberlain for their appeasement of Adolf Hitler and Benito Mussolini. He criticized his own leaders for failing to rally more support for the Republic in the Spanish Civil War. He joined with Sir Richard Stafford Cripps (who was to become Chancellor of the Exchequer in 1947) and others in a desperate and unrealistic campaign to create a popular or united front of the Labour Party, Communists, Liberals, and even dissident Conservatives to drive Chamberlain from office. The campaign succeeded only in provoking the Labour Party, which had forbidden its members to cooperate with Communists, to expel both Bevan and Cripps in March, 1939. Bevan now had a reputation as an incorrigible party rebel.

In September, 1939, Chamberlain reluctantly led Great Britain into war. In December, Bevan was readmitted into his party. In May, 1940, Churchill replaced the ineffective Chamberlain and invited Labour to enter a new National Coalition Government. Clement Attlee, the leader of the Labour Party, became deputy prime minister; Herbert Morrison became home secretary; and Ernest Bevin, minister of labour. Bevan continued in the role of critic. He called for the early opening of a second front in Europe through a cross-channel invasion. He attacked Churchill for trying to save the monarchies of Italy and Greece and for using troops against the Greek Left. He did not spare his own leaders. He opposed Morrison for censoring newspapers and Bevin for his harsh measures against unofficial strikes. For a time, Bevan was in danger of being expelled again.

In July, 1945, Labour won an overwhelming election victory, and Attlee, now prime minister, made Bevan minister of health and housing. Bevan built more than one million housing units, mainly rental council housing (public housing), but was never given the resources for the more ambitious program he advocated. His main job, however, was to convert the very limited National Health Insurance program, introduced by Lloyd George before World War I, into something more comprehensive, more generous, and more socialist. The old program paid some medical bills for some of the working class; the new National Health Services Bill that Bevan introduced in 1946 covered all medical costs for everyone in Great Britain. The old program was administered in part by private insurance companies; the new program was to be run by a government ministry and to be financed by general taxation. The bill also abolished the purchase of private practices and took over municipal and private hospitals. Private practice, however, was not abolished, and entry into the system was voluntary for both patients and doctors. Bevan hoped to make the service so attractive that few would stay outside it. He did not create, as many doctors feared he might, a full-time state-salaried service but paid doctors through a combination of a small basic salary and capitation fees for every enrolled patient. Despite his many compromises and concessions, the leaders of the British Medical Association assaulted him as a führer who sought to set up a medical dictatorship. They organized a campaign to boycott the service and prevent it from even opening. Bevan, displaying great confidence and dispensing a few additional concessions, outflanked and outmaneuvered the medical opposition and triumphantly opened the service as planned on July 5, 1948. In a few months, 90 percent of the doctors and 97 percent of the population had signed on.

This was one of the last of the Labour victories. The government, which had nationalized many industries and extended the social services, now began a policy of consolidating rather than extending socialist policies. Bevan objected, but he lost. The Conservative opposition and the press depicted him as a raving, embittered proponent of class war; a frustrated Bevan sometimes helped them with angry words, the most notorious being his description of the Tory Party as "lower than vermin." In February, 1950, Labour won reelection but with a very small parliamentary majority. In January, 1951, Bevan became minister of labour. The government, meanwhile, under pressure from the United States, had decided to increase military spending by £4.7 billion over the next three years to counter any possible moves by the Soviet Union in Europe. Bevan argued that the increase was totally unnecessary and would, moreover, because of shortages in raw materials and machine tools, be impossible to carry out. Hugh Gaitskell, the new Chancellor of the Exchequer and a professional economist, assured the cabinet that the program was feasible, provided that cuts

were made in the social services, including the imposition of partial payments for eyeglasses and false teeth. For Bevan, a totally free medical service had become a basic socialist principle. He and two colleagues resigned from the government.

In October, 1951, a divided Labour Party lost a very close election. The conservative Labourites blamed Bevan. Bevan blamed the loss on the economic stringencies introduced to finance the new military spending, much of which the new Conservative government soon canceled as impossible to implement, just as Bevan had predicted. War broke out within the Labour Party. Bevan attacked his leaders for weakening their commitment to nationalization of industry, for ceasing to defend the extension of social welfare, and, above all, for following the United States in a rigid policy of confronting the Soviets everywhere. Bevan, in turn, was blasted as an apologist for the Soviet Union and a hater of the United States. Bevan did not admire the Soviet Union, but he did not believe it posed a military threat to the West. From 1951 to 1956, "Bevanism," a very loosely organized movement of the Left within the Labour Party, challenged the leadership. Bevan and the Bevanites won the solid backing of the constituency sections of the party (the individual membership groups) but were defeated in the parliamentary party and were rejected by the leaders of the largest trade unions, who controlled the bloc vote at the party conferences and provided much of the party money. Bevan had won the party activists but not the party machine. In 1955, he was briefly expelled from the parliamentary party and narrowly missed expulsion from the party itself. Shortly thereafter, Labour lost its second straight election and Gaitskell, by a large margin, defeated Bevan in the election for party leader.

Peace slowly returned to the Labour Party in 1956. Bevan realized that he could not oust Gaitskell as leader, and Gaitskell realized that he could not drive Bevan from the party. The two antagonists cooperated in November, 1956, in opposing Prime Minister Anthony Eden's invasion of the Suez Canal zone. In December, Gaitskell accepted Bevan as the party spokesperson on foreign affairs and shadow foreign minister. At the party conference in October in the following year, Bevan disappointed many of his former followers by delivering a powerful speech opposing unilateral nuclear disarmament. Bevan had often attacked the heavy reliance of NATO on nuclear weapons, but he wanted negotiation. Unilateral disarmament, he argued, would tear up the fabric of international relationships already created. It was "an emotional spasm" that would send a future British foreign secretary "naked into the conference chamber."

In October, 1959, Labour lost its third general election in a row. A few days later, Bevan became deputy leader of the party. He now was in title what he had been in reality for the past two years, the number two man in the party, virtually coleader with Gaitskell. In the same month at a party conference, Bevan gave his last important speech, an exposition of socialist values and a defense of public ownership as necessary to achieve them. A month later, Bevan underwent an operation for cancer and died, on July 6, 1960.

SIGNIFICANCE

The public abuse that Bevan had so often evoked had already died away several years before his death. The Welsh demagogue, once called by Churchill the "minister of disease," had been transformed into a statesman of rare gifts. Perhaps Bevan had mellowed, but, more likely, once the postwar radicalism had ebbed, he was no longer dangerous enough to hate. His death brought forth a tidal wave of eulogy. Bevan had only one important governmental achievement, the building of the National Health Service; that was so soundly built, however, that even Margaret Thatcher, who began in 1979 to demolish most of the works of the 1945 Labour government, was not able to do it much damage. About 90 percent of the British population used the service. Bevan wrote only one book, *In Place of Fear*, published in 1952, a short but eloquent statement of the case for democratic socialism. Bevan had many political disappointments. His life seems incomplete and his vision was never realized, but for British socialists, even in beleaguered times, he remains one of the major prophets.

—*Melvin Shefftz*

FURTHER READING

Beckett, Clare, and Francis Beckett. *Bevan*. London: Haus, 2004. A concise but adequate overview of Bevan's life and career.

Campbell, John. *Nye Bevan and the Mirage of British Socialism*. London: Weidenfeld and Nicolson, 1987. The title proclaims the thesis. A provocative and well-researched book that presents Bevan as a talented individual preaching an outmoded doctrine.

Eckstein, Harry. *The English Health Service: Its Origins, Structure, and Achievements*. Cambridge, Mass.: Harvard University Press, 1958. A standard study of the creation of the National Health Service that depicts Bevan as legislator, administrator, and negotiator.

Foot, Michael. *Aneurin Bevan: A Biography*. Vol. 1. London: Macgibbon and Kee, 1962. Vol. 2. London: Davis-Poynter Limited, 1973. A comprehensive and full-scale biography of more than 1,150 pages, written by a friend and political associate of Bevan who has represented his constituency since his death. The first volume covers the years 1897-1945, the second, 1945-1960. This is an exciting and sometimes moving work, flawed perhaps by its unfair treatment of Bevan's adversaries.

Harris, Kenneth. *Attlee*. London: Weidenfeld and Nicolson, 1982. A good biography of the man who led the Labour Party from 1935 to 1955. It contains much information about Bevan as seen by a colleague who worked with him in some difficult situations.

Jenkins, Mark. *Bevanism: Labour's High Tide*. Nottingham, England: Spokesman, 1979. An excellent study of the rank-and-file rebellion of the Labour left from about 1951 to 1957, of which Bevan was more often the symbol than the leader.

Morgan, Kenneth O. *Labour in Power, 1945-1951*. New York: Oxford University Press, 1984. A carefully researched and well-balanced examination of Labour's most successful government. This presents Bevan in the context of the cabinet and the problems it faced.

Rintala, Marvin. *Creating the National Health Service: Aneurin Bevan and the Medical Lords*. London: Frank Cass, 2003. Recounts Bevan's relationships with two members of Parliament: Lord Moran, a physician who helped Bevan set up the National Health Service (NHS), and Thomas Lord Horder, another physician and the NHS's major medical foe.

Williams, Phillip. *Hugh Gaitskell: A Political Biography*. London: Jonathan Cape, 1979. Almost eight hundred large and well-researched pages on the life of Hugh Gaitskell, who defeated Bevan in the battle for party leadership. Williams is as much a partisan of Gaitskell as Michael Foot is of Bevan, who appears here first as a dangerous enemy and only near the end as a respected political partner.

SEE ALSO: Clement Attlee; Stanley Baldwin; Ernest Bevin; Neville Chamberlain; Sir Winston Churchill; Sir Anthony Eden; David Lloyd George; Ramsay MacDonald; Margaret Thatcher.

RELATED ARTICLES in *Great Events from History: The Twentieth Century*:

1941-1970: July 26, 1945: Labour Party Forms Britain's Majority Government; November 6, 1946: United Kingdom Passes the National Health Service Act.

LORD BEVERIDGE
British economist

As an economist, Beveridge was a pioneer in the study of unemployment and the history of prices. He was the force responsible for building the London School of Economics into one of the world's leading centers of social science scholarship. He is remembered, however, as the intellectual founder of the post-World War II British welfare state.

BORN: March 5, 1879; Rangpur, Bengal, India
DIED: March 16, 1963; Oxford, Oxfordshire, England
ALSO KNOWN AS: William Henry, First Baron Beveridge of Tuggal; William Henry Beveridge, First Baron
AREAS OF ACHIEVEMENT: Economics, social sciences, education

EARLY LIFE

William Henry Beveridge, later known as Lord Beveridge, was born to Henry Beveridge, a judge in the Indian Civil Service, and the former Annette Susannah Ackroyd, the daughter of a self-made Worcestershire businessman. They were mavericks within the Anglo-Indian establishment—he was an outspoken advocate of Indian nationalism and home rule, she a pioneer in the education of Hindu women. Strongly attracted to Indian culture, both became well-known translators of Hindi and Persian texts.

Although he would later pretend otherwise, Beveridge's childhood appears to have been unhappy. While intellectually precocious, he was a sickly and solitary child under the thumb of his mother. In 1892, he won a scholarship to Charterhouse, but he was not good at sports, the school's dominating passion. Worse, he was discouraged from pursuing his interest in the natural sciences—a frustration that would permanently rankle him. In 1897, he went as an exhibitioner to Balliol College, Oxford, and was awarded first-class honors in classics in 1901. Beveridge stayed on at Oxford to study law; won in 1902 a prize fellowship at University College, Oxford; and received a bachelor of civil law degree the following year.

LIFE'S WORK

At this juncture, however, Beveridge abandoned what appeared to be a promising legal or academic career ahead of him to devote himself to the study and solution of social problems. The catalyst for this decision appears to have been his reading of Thomas Henry Huxley, whose vision of applying the inductive methodology of the natural sciences to the discovery of a "science of society" captivated his imagination. His acceptance in 1903 of the position of subwarden at Toynbee Hall, the famous London East End settlement house, brought him into contact with a group of reform-minded activists who were urging stronger government action to deal with poverty and its attendant social pathologies. He was probably most strongly influenced by the Fabian socialist leaders Beatrice Webb and Sidney Webb. Although not embracing their socialism, Beveridge was strongly attracted by their call for a legally guaranteed "national minimum" income—an attraction that was reinforced by a later visit to Germany, where he studied the working of the Bismarckian social-welfare program. Beveridge's major interest was in the problem of unemployment. His book *Unemployment: A Problem of Industry* (1909) was a pioneering study of the functioning of the labor market. He called for the establishment of a nationwide network of labor exchanges to aid job seekers in finding work. What he came to see as the key to solving what contemporaries termed the "social question," however, was the adoption of a comprehensive system of compulsory social insurance covering not simply unemployment but also sickness, disability, and old age. He proposed that the system be financed along the lines of the German model by tripartite contributions from workers, employers, and the state.

In 1905, Beveridge left Toynbee Hall to become a writer on social issues for an influential Conservative daily, the *Morning Post*. In 1908, he accepted the invitation of Winston Churchill, the president of the Board of Trade in the Liberal Party government headed by Prime Minister H. H. Asquith, to join his staff. At that time, Churchill was allied with the "national efficiency" school of social reformers who, alarmed by the large number of men found unfit for military service during the Boer War, thought improvement in the conditions of life for the working class vital for imperial security. Beveridge worked closely with the board's permanent secretary, Sir Hubert Llewellyn Smith, in drafting the Labour Exchanges Act of 1909, which established a countrywide network of labor exchanges, and the provision in the National Insurance Act of 1911 establishing unemployment insurance for two and a quarter million workers in the heavy industries. In 1909, he became a permanent civil servant as administrative head of the new labor exchanges system, and in 1913 he attained the rank of assistant secretary in charge of the Board of Trade's labor exchange and unemployment insurance department. His hope of achieving a full solution to the unemployment problem by the expansion of the unemployment insurance scheme to all workers, however, was stymied by the outbreak of World War I. He himself, in 1915, was temporarily drafted to the new ministry of munitions set up to deal with the crisis in war production.

Like his chief, the former Chancellor of the Exchequer and future prime minister, David Lloyd George, Beveridge was convinced that the war could not be won without a total commitment of the nation's resources—even if that required the use of coercive methods. Long suspicious of what he saw as the trade unions' narrow-minded indifference to any interests except their own, Beveridge played a leading role in drafting the Munitions of War Act of 1915, which sharply limited wartime collective bargaining and imposed quasi-military discipline on workers in the munitions industry. The resulting hostility felt by the trade unions against Beveridge was reinforced when, after his return to the Board of Trade in mid-1916, he pushed for legislation to extend unemployment insurance to all workers engaged in war production. Although his purpose was to protect the workers against the danger of a postwar depression, the unions saw the substitution of a government program of unemployment insurance for union-provided benefits as threatening to undermine the loyalty of their members. Union opposition was largely responsible for keeping Beveridge out of the new ministry of labour, which was established in late 1916 to coordinate labor and employment policies. Instead, he was made second secretary of the new ministry of food, with responsibility for rationing and price control. Because of his success in implementing an effective food-rationing system, he was in early 1919 made a knight commander of the Order of the Bath and was promoted to permanent secretary of the Food Ministry—at the age of thirty-nine, one of the youngest ever to attain that rank.

Beveridge's wartime experiences, however, had undermined his former confidence in state intervention in the economy. All too typically, decisions were made not on the basis of expert knowledge but rather simply on the basis of political expediency. His opposition to continuance of food controls after the end of the war then led him to re-

sign from the civil service in September, 1919, to accept the directorship of the London School of Economics (LSE). Founded by the Webbs in the 1890's as a college of the University of London, the LSE had not made much of a mark and attracted mostly part-time students. Beveridge proved a highly successful fund-raiser and made the LSE one of the favored beneficiaries of Rockefeller Foundation grants for social science research. He expanded the school's physical facilities and built up a distinguished faculty that included economic historians R. H. Tawney (who was also Beveridge's brother-in-law) and Eileen Power, legal historian T. C. Plucknett, political scientist Harold J. Laski, economists Lionel Robbins and F. A. Hayek, sociologist Leonard T. Hobhouse, and anthropologists Bronisław Malinowski and Raymond Firth. Perhaps his most innovative step was his establishment of the Department of Social Biology with Lancelot Hogben as its chair. Hogben brought in an outstanding group of young researchers, and the department

Lord Beveridge. (Library of Congress)

turned out an impressive series of monographs on heredity, population control, statistical method, and human reproduction before Hogben's resignation in 1936 and the department's subsequent dissolution. By the early 1930's, the LSE ranked as one of the world's centers for work in the social sciences.

By mid-decade, however, Beveridge faced worsening difficulties at the LSE. Not only did the Depression reduce the outside funding available, but Beveridge had become the center of bitter intramural controversy. Despite his own continued public activities, Beveridge came strongly to disapprove of political involvements by academics—a position that brought him into recurring conflict with activist-minded members of the staff such as Laski. An even more important source of conflict was his personal commitment to empirical, quantitative-based research and his hostility to the more theoretical and analytical interests of the majority of the school's sociologists and economists. Hogben—who shared Beveridge's view on this methodological issue—became, along with him, a major target of resentment. Beveridge's relations with his staff were further soured by what most saw as his high-handed and dictatorial administrative methods. A faculty revolt in 1936 succeeded in sharply reducing his powers as director. The following year, Beveridge resigned to accept the mastership of University College, Oxford. The public reason he gave was that he wanted more time to continue the research he had begun in 1919 on a history of prices. His hope was that such a history would supply the key to understanding the mechanism responsible for the cyclical ups and downs in economic activity. He succeeded in finishing only the first volume, however, of his planned four-volume *Prices and Wages in England from the Twelfth to Nineteenth Century* (1939), and his scorn for theorizing as "unscientific" made the work a less important contribution than might have otherwise been the case.

At the same time, Beveridge's faith in state planning was undergoing a revival. The confidence in the free market that he had had in the 1920's and early 1930's was undermined by the failure of orthodox economic policies to bring about recovery from the Great Depression. Pushing him in the same direction was his conviction, dating from Adolf Hitler's occupation of the Rhineland in 1936, that another war with Germany was almost inevitable and that, accordingly, Great Britain must prepare. When the war finally did come, Beveridge's ambition was to be placed in charge of directing the mobilization of staff for both industry and the military. In December, 1940, he was brought back into government service as an undersecretary in the ministry of labour. Its head, Ernest Bevin, however—recalling Beveridge's clashes with the trade unions during World War I—shied from allowing him control over wartime staff policy and instead shunted him off to chair an obscure interdepartmental inquiry into the coordination of social insurance programs. Beveridge was at first bitterly disappointed but quickly saw how the new position offered him the opportunity to lay plans for reshaping postwar Great Britain into a more just and equal society. First, he made a detailed investigation of the inadequacies of existing programs. Then, working in close consultation with representatives of the Trades Union Congress, he set forth in his December, 1942, report, *Social Insurance and Allied Services*, a comprehensive program for overcoming the five evils of idleness, ignorance, disease, squalor, and want. His proposed remedies included a free national health service, family allowances, and universal social insurance covering all contingencies from the cradle to the grave. He regarded as the linchpin of the program government policies to maintain full employment—which became the focus of his follow-up recommendations in *Full Employment in a Free Society* (1944).

Beveridge's 1942 recommendations met with a chilly reception from the cabinet, but the report was tremendously popular with the public, with more than 100,000 copies sold within a month of publication. Beveridge himself toured the country making speeches in its support, and a revolt by backbench Labour and Liberal members of the House of Commons in early 1943 forced the government to endorse postwar implementation of the Beveridge proposals. In the hope of positioning himself to take charge of postwar reconstruction, Beveridge ran successfully in a 1944 by-election as the Liberal Party candidate for the seat in the House of Commons from Berwick-upon-Tweed. He was defeated, however, in the 1945 general election. The following year, the new Labour Party prime minister, Clement Attlee, named him the first Baron Beveridge of Tuggal. Although becoming leader of the Liberal Party contingent in the House of Lords, he had to watch from the sidelines as the Attlee government proceeded to erect the postwar British welfare state. Beveridge was not fully satisfied with the results. He regretted the failure because of the cost to adopt subsistence-level old-age pensions and in the 1950's strongly complained about how inflation was further eroding their benefits, which had been inadequate from the start. His major complaint, however—set forth most fully in his book *Voluntary Action: A Report on*

Methods of Social Advance (1948)—was the exclusion of the voluntary "mutual aid" organizations from a share in the administration of the social insurance program.

Beveridge was a complex personality. He could be kindly, generous, even humorous. At other times, however, he was abrasive, domineering, and dogmatically sure of his own views and impatient with opposition. He had a passion for hard work. Although he idealized family life, he himself did not marry until late in his life, on December 15, 1942, when he wed Janet "Jessy" Mair, the widow of a cousin who had been associated with him first as his secretary and aide during World War I and then as academic secretary of the LSE. The couple had no children, although she had one son and three daughters from her first marriage. Over his lifetime, Beveridge accumulated a long list of honorary degrees from universities around the world. Although he resigned his mastership of University College when he ran for the House of Commons, he was an honorary Fellow of Balliol, Nuffield, and University colleges, Oxford. In 1947, he published an affectionate account of his parents titled *India Called Them*. Six years later he published his autobiography, *Power and Influence*. Beveridge and his wife retired to Oxford in 1954. She died five years later; he followed on March 16, 1963.

SIGNIFICANCE

Beveridge denied that his commitment to reform grew out of any sentimental do-goodism. Poverty was a disease threatening the health of the social "organism," while he saw himself as a scientist who would find the cure through empirical research leading to the discovery of objective socioeconomic laws. His larger aim was to heal the class antagonisms that were so pronounced in British society. Nor did he have any illusions about human nature: People worked only because they were compelled to do so. Thus, care must be taken to avoid disincentives to work and the penalization of thrift.

Beveridge was a champion of the contributory principle for social insurance so that beneficiaries would not feel the stigma of receiving charity. Yet he simultaneously had major blind spots. He had no interest in larger philosophical questions about what constituted a good society. He tended to think that all problems were solvable given the proper administrative techniques. He overestimated the disinterestedness of "experts" and thus ignored the possibility that government officialdom could become itself a narrow special interest. In his enthusiasm for governmental planning, he underestimated the danger that expanding the powers of the state could

pose to the personal freedoms that he recognized as central to the British political tradition.

Although his marriage proved a happy one, there was otherwise an almost tragic quality to Beveridge's last years. He never overcame his disappointment at not having a role in the postwar reconstruction of British society. He was depressed about the international situation, seeing in Soviet expansionism a threat to peace. He witnessed how the class lines that he had hoped would be eliminated were paradoxically reinforced by the welfare state. Moreover, he came to lament the stifling of the voluntary sector by the bureaucratized social welfare system that he had done so much to bring about. While reaffirming in his autobiography his faith that the human condition could be improved through the force of "reasonable" ideas, he concluded on a more somber note: "The world is an unhappy place; the picture of yesterday's hopeful collaboration in curing evils of want and disease and ignorance and squalor, as I have tried to draw it here, looks like a dream today."

—John Braeman

FURTHER READING

Beveridge, Janet. *Beveridge and His Plan*. London: Hodder and Stoughton, 1954. A biography written by Beveridge's wife that provides illuminating sidelights drawn from her long association with him prior to their marriage plus information he supplied.

Beveridge, William Henry. *Power and Influence*. 1953. New York: Beechhurst Press, 1955. Beveridge's autobiography is too determinedly cheerful about his life and glosses over the degree of intellectual uncertainty and mind-changing that marked his career.

Chorley, Lord. "Beveridge and the L.S.E." Part 1. *L.S.E.* 44 (November, 1972). Part 2. *L.S.E.* 45 (June, 1973). These articles provide a detailed treatment of Beveridge's eighteen years as director of the London School of Economics.

Harris, José. *William Beveridge: A Biography*. 2d ed. New York: Oxford University Press, 1997. A thoroughly researched, analytically perceptive, and lucidly written work that should remain for the foreseeable future the definitive biography.

Moos, Siegfried. *A Pioneer of Social Advance: William Henry Beveridge, 1879-1963*. Durham, N.C.: Durham University Press, 1963. A brief, eulogistic sketch of Beveridge's life and work.

Walker, Robert, ed. *Ending Child Poverty: Popular Welfare for the Twenty-first Century?* Bristol, England: Policy Press, 1999. Collection of writings examining the work of Beveridge, among others, on the issue of childhood poverty, child welfare, and public welfare in general in the twenty-first century.

SEE ALSO: Clement Attlee; Ernest Bevin; Sir Winston Churchill; Ludwig Erhard; F. A. Hayek; Leonard T.

Hobhouse; John Maynard Keynes; Harold J. Laski; Gunnar Myrdal; Beatrice and Sidney Webb.

RELATED ARTICLE in *Great Events from History: The Twentieth Century:*
   1941-1970: November 6, 1946: United Kingdom Passes the National Health Service Act.

ERNEST BEVIN
British politician

Bevin founded, and for eighteen years led, the Transport and General Workers Union, influenced Labour Party policy during the 1930's, served as minister of labour and national service in World War II, and in the postwar Labour government was foreign secretary and one of the architects of the Cold War.

BORN: March 9, 1881; Winsford, Somerset, England
DIED: April 14, 1951; London, England
AREAS OF ACHIEVEMENT: Labor movement, economics, government and politics, diplomacy

EARLY LIFE

Ernest Bevin (BEHV-ihn) was the last and an illegitimate child of a mother who already had seven children by a husband who had disappeared in 1877. Bevin was orphaned at the age of eight, left school at eleven, worked for two years on farms, and then joined a half brother in Bristol. When eighteen years old, he became a drayman, delivering mineral water with a horse and wagon. After 1900 he attended meetings of the Bristol Socialist Society, in 1910 formed a carmen's branch of the Dockers' Union, and in 1911 became a full-time official of the union. In November, 1918, Bevin ran for the House of Commons as a Labour candidate and lost. In February, 1920, Bevin presented the dockers' case at the hearings of the special Shaw Inquiry with so much vigor and command of the facts that he won a favorable report from the commission and the informal title of the Dockers' K.C. (King's Counsel). In May, he became the assistant general-secretary of the Dockers' Union. In the same month, Bevin supported the London dockers when they refused to load munitions on the *Jolly George*, a ship bound for Poland, then at war with Soviet Russia. In August, Bevin helped found the Council of Action, which threatened to call

strikes should Great Britain enter the war against the Soviet Union, and led the delegation that confronted the prime minister, David Lloyd George. Now a national figure, Bevin merged the Dockers and thirteen other unions in 1922 to form the Transport and General Workers' Union, which began with about 300,000 members and eventually became the largest union in Great Britain, uniting workers in almost every sector of industry and with varying degrees of skill into an effective bargaining machine.

In 1926, Bevin was elected to the General Council of the Trades Union Congress. When the unions called a general strike in May to help the coal miners resist cuts in

Ernest Bevin. (Library of Congress)

wages, Bevin joined the Strike Organization Committee. After nine days, the strike ended in failure, but Bevin had enhanced his reputation as a skillful organizer and shrewd tactician. In 1928 and 1929, he participated actively in the Mond-Turner talks, which brought together Great Britain's leading businessmen and trade union leaders to discuss joint efforts to make industry more productive. Little was accomplished, but again Bevin made an impact as the voice of the broader interests of the British working class.

Bevin was a powerful, if sometimes ungrammatical, speaker. Although he was not tall, his large chest and shoulders gave an impression of bulk and power. He read little but had a retentive memory and quick understanding, and he learned much through conversation. He had, through years of bargaining, accumulated information about the workings of many branches of British industry. He was a declared socialist, but his main concerns were with immediate gains for working men and women. He was a man of strong likes and even stronger dislikes. He had feuds of impressive durability and intensity with a number of his colleagues in the trade unions and in the Labour Party. He did not accept criticism easily, especially when it came from those whom he castigated as "intellectuals," unreliable dilettantes who had entered the Labour Party in search of adventure. Men of intellect whom he liked escaped the label.

LIFE'S WORK

Bevin continued to be an active trade union leader and negotiator, but he moved vigorously into wider spheres. In 1928 and 1929, he worked successfully to save the *Daily Herald*, a commercial newspaper, which was sponsored by the Trades Union Congress and supported the Labour Party. In 1929, he was appointed by the new Labour government to serve, along with four bankers and the great economist John Maynard Keynes, as the only trade unionist on the high-powered Macmillan Committee on Finance and Industry. In the eighteen months of hearings, Bevin learned much about the gold standard and the international banking system. Not intimidated by the prestigious reputations of the other committee members or by the intricacies of monetary theory, Bevin expressed in his usual forceful manner some unorthodox criticisms of the gold standard that have stood the test of time rather well. In August, 1931, the Labour government, headed by Ramsay MacDonald, was reeling from the effects of the Great Depression and its inability to cope with it. MacDonald knew no economics, and his Chancellor of the Exchequer, the strong-willed Philip

Snowden, knew only the economics of the balanced budget and adherence to the gold standard. In August, 1931, MacDonald and Snowden were striving heroically to cut government spending, including unemployment benefits, to balance the budget and impress French and American bankers whom they were asking for a large loan in gold to keep the British pound on the gold standard. They presented their plans to a joint meeting of party and union leaders and ran into a barrage of criticism, led by Bevin, who argued that it was wrong to cut spending and to follow a policy of deflation, thus making the working class pay for the mistakes of British bankers. Bevin convinced several wavering cabinet members to oppose the cuts. MacDonald and Snowden resigned, but they became heads of a new national coalition government, supported by Liberals, Conservatives, and a few Labourites, which made the cuts, balanced the budget, got the loan, and was still forced to go off the gold standard and accept the arrival of managed paper currency. Fortunately, the predicted economic catastrophe did not arrive.

Bevin helped rally the dispirited Labour Party and worked closely with the new leader, Arthur Henderson. He showed his new commitment by running for Parliament in the general election in October and, like most other Labour candidates, lost badly, as the Parliamentary party fell from 289 to 46 seats. Bevin did not run again in the election of 1935, when the party made a modest recovery, but he had determined to ensure that a future Labour government would not betray its supporters, as he believed the MacDonald government had done. Bevin was a director of the *Daily Herald*, and his union contributed amply to party funds and directly sponsored a group of members of Parliament. Bevin influenced policy making at the annual party conferences both by his control of the large union bloc vote and by his effective speeches. He helped develop a program that committed a future Labour government to nationalize some industries and to extend social welfare programs. At the same time, he rejected what he viewed as provocative and posturing "leftism" by Sir Richard Stafford Cripps and Aneurin Bevan. By 1935, Bevin wanted the Labour Party not only to oppose Adolf Hitler and Benito Mussolini verbally but also to support rearmament, a hard policy for many in the party—the semi-Pacifists, such as the leader, George Lansbury, and the leftists, such as Cripps and Bevan (who distrusted the Conservatives almost as much as the fascists)—to accept. In October, 1935, Bevin, in a brutal but effective speech, attacked Lansbury for hawking "your conscience round from body to body to be told what you ought to do with it." Lansbury, old and ailing, resigned a few days later. He had already been considering resignation, but Bevin had probably hastened his departure. Bevin now had helped depose two leaders of his party, MacDonald and Lansbury. Working closely with Hugh Dalton, a former professor of economics who somehow escaped being labeled an "intellectual," Bevin finally succeeded in 1937 in convincing the parliamentary Labour Party to stop voting against rearmament measures.

In September, 1939, Neville Chamberlain took Great Britain into war with Germany. In May, 1940, Winston Churchill replaced the ineffective Chamberlain and invited Labour to serve under him in a national coalition. Clement Attlee became deputy prime minister, and Bevin, even before a parliamentary seat was found for him, became minister of labour and national service. In peacetime, Labour was not an important department, but in war it became essential. Labor was now the scarcest of all scarce commodities, and the competitive market alone could not get the right workers to the right jobs in the right numbers quickly enough. Bevin was given sweeping powers to direct both men and women to essential jobs, but he used them sparingly. By the summer of 1943, he had issued three-quarters of a million individual directives, not a great number for the mobilization that had taken place. Great Britain put a higher percentage of its men and women into the armed forces or into war work than any belligerent except for the Soviet Union. Churchill inspired the British people and Hitler terrified them. Still, Bevin brought to his task several important assets: great negotiating skill, wide knowledge of British workers and British trade unions, and a great fund of credit for past service from which he could draw in asking trade unions to give up, for the duration of the war, some of their most valued safeguards.

In July, 1945, the Labour Party won a sweeping victory and Attlee became prime minister. Attlee initially intended to make Bevin his Chancellor of the Exchequer, the post Bevin himself wanted and was best prepared for. King George VI, however, suggested to Attlee that Bevin be foreign secretary, and Attlee soon came to that decision himself, mainly because he realized that as chancellor, Bevin would have to work closely with the Leader of the House of Commons, Herbert Stanley Morrison, probably the colleague Bevin hated most. Bevin was the last British foreign secretary to represent a world power in charge of a vast empire. Bevin supported Attlee against all plots and cabals, and Attlee gave Bevin a virtually free rein in all areas, except for India, where Attlee himself took direct responsibility. Bevin's foreign policy

had certain clear features. First, he asserted Great Britain's role as a continuing great power, as is well illustrated in his comment on the atomic bomb: "We've got to have the bloody Union Jack flying on top of it." Second, he was ready to oppose all Soviet efforts to extend their empire. Third, he worked in close partnership with the United States in most areas.

The one area where Bevin clearly failed was Palestine, where he often clashed with President Harry S. Truman, who gave occasional support to the Zionists. Labour, out of office, had criticized the 1939 white paper that severely limited Jewish immigration into Palestine. Bevin, however, continued to limit Jewish immigration and sought a settlement that would have Arab support. This provoked a virtual revolt by the Jews of Palestine. After many acts of guerrilla warfare and government reprisals, Great Britain withdrew in May, 1948, leaving Arabs and Jews to fight for the land. Bevin's reputation was somewhat tarnished by the obvious failure of his policy and by the charges that it had been motivated by anti-Semitism. Bevin had made some rather insensitive statements, such as his warning to the Jews in the displaced persons' camps of Europe not to rouse hatred by wanting "to get too much to the head of the queue. . . ." Whatever Bevin's feelings were about Jews, the motive for his Palestine policy was clearly the desire to gain Arab goodwill, which a weakened Great Britain needed to maintain its position in the Middle East. It is hard to imagine any British foreign secretary in this period coming to a significantly different conclusion. Bevin's insensitivity to Jewish feelings, however, probably made a bad situation a little worse.

Bevin's most impressive moment came when he responded quickly and decisively to the very tentative offer of American economic aid to Europe made by General George C. Marshall, then secretary of state, in his commencement address at Harvard on June 5, 1947. Bevin quickly called meetings with officials of the other European nations that eventually led to the Organization for European Economic Co-operation, through which the generous supply of American aid began to flow by April, 1948. Bevin was the effective coauthor of the Marshall Plan. Bevin might also be called the coauthor of another and more controversial American initiative, the Truman Doctrine. Since December, 1944, British troops had been helping a right-wing regime in Greece battle a predominantly communist insurgency. In February, 1947, the British government announced that it could no longer afford the burden and would withdraw its soldiers. Privately, Bevin urged the United States to intervene. The

United States did that and more. The Truman Doctrine of March 11, 1947, pledged not only to defend Greece but also to defend all free nations under attack, from without or within, from communist aggression. This doctrine gave a blank check to any government, however repressive and inept, which could discern the hand of Moscow in the actions of those rebelling against it. The Truman Doctrine went far beyond what the situation in Greece required, and perhaps further than Bevin had expected.

Bevin worked closely with the United States in establishing the new West German Federal Republic, and Great Britain participated in the airlift that broke the Russian blockade of West Berlin. Bevin, too, was perhaps more important than any other European leader in the creation of the North Atlantic Treaty Organization (NATO), set up in April, 1949, which brought the United States and the nations of Western Europe into an alliance for mutual defense. Bevin's most surprising achievement was to carry his party with him against only feeble opposition. Many in the Labour Party disliked both heavy military spending and the alliance with the United States; others harbored warm feelings about the Soviet Union. Bevin, however, overcame these opponents easily. Joseph Stalin, by his brutal rule in Russia and by his imposition of Russian control over Eastern Europe, made Bevin's task easier. Bevin had made his first impact in foreign policy by opposing British efforts to help Poland fight Russia in 1920, but much had happened since then. Bevin in the 1930's had a number of bad encounters with British communists in the Labour Party and within his own union, especially with a rebellious rank-and-file movement among the London busmen. After 1945, he developed an intense hatred for Vyacheslav Mikhailovich Molotov, the Russian foreign secretary, making negotiations very difficult. On March 9, 1951, Bevin, who had been ill for many months, reluctantly left the Foreign Office and took the undemanding post of Lord Privy Seal. He died of a heart attack shortly thereafter, on April 14 in London.

SIGNIFICANCE

Bevin played a large role in twentieth century English history. His importance cannot be contested. He was the most successful trade unionist between the two great wars, helped make Labour Party policy in the 1930's, was the most important minister on the home front during World War II, and made British foreign policy after 1945. The only part of his career that has continued to rouse controversy is his foreign policy.

His faith in the United States and his fierce hostility

to the Soviet Union have been espoused most strongly by the Conservative Party, especially under Margaret Thatcher, and have been under assault by many in the Labour Party. To be sure, it has been possible in later years to call for détente and still support what Bevin did in the postwar years. Europe was economically and militarily much weaker in Bevin's time, and Russia was perceived as more threatening. It may be, however, that Bevin was a bit too fearful of the Soviet Union, a bit too suspicious, and therefore too unwilling to continue negotiating with the hated Molotov. Bevin's policy, and U.S. policy as well, may have become too much one of confrontation. Some of Bevin's greatest triumphs as a trade union leader and as minister of labour had been as a negotiator. It may be one of the tragedies of the twentieth century that in the years after 1945 he did not stay at the bargaining table longer.

—Melvin Shefftz

FURTHER READING

Anderson, Terry. *The United States, Great Britain, and the Cold War.* Columbia: University of Missouri Press, 1981. Useful short study of the beginning of the Cold War.

Barker, Elizabeth. *The British Between the Superpowers, 1945-1950.* London: Macmillan, 1983. A good short study, occasionally critical, of the problems facing Bevin as he tried to carry out ambitious policies with limited resources.

Bullock, Alan. *The Life and Times of Ernest Bevin.* 3 vols. Vols. 1 and 2. London: William Heinemann, 1960-1967. Vol. 3. New York: W. W. Norton, 1983. A massive biography that describes and analyzes Bevin's career. The research is extraordinarily full and the coverage detailed. The judgments are carefully thought out. Perhaps Bullock is too uncritical of Bevin, but this work must be numbered among the outstanding biographies of modern political leaders.

Chaitani, Youssef. *Dissension Among the Allies: Ernest Bevin's Palestine Policy Between Whitehall and the White House.* London: Saqi, 2000. Chronicles the events following World War II that eventually led Bevin to relinquish Britain's control of Palestine.

Donoughe, Bernard, and G. W. Jones. *Herbert Morrison, Portrait of a Politician.* London: Weidenfeld and Nicolson, 1973. Comprehensive study of an important colleague whom Bevin disliked. Had Bevin disliked Morrison a bit less, Bevin would probably have become Chancellor of the Exchequer in 1945 rather than foreign secretary.

Harris, Kenneth. *Attlee*. London: Weidenfeld and Nicolson, 1982. A good biography of the person who led the Labour Party from 1935 to 1955. It contains much information about Bevin in his relations with the leader and prime minister whom he loyally supported.

Hathaway, Robert W. *Ambiguous Partnership: Britain and America, 1944-1947*. New York: Columbia University Press, 1981. An interesting book that shows the incompleteness of American and British cooperation. The interests of the two nations were not always as close as Bevin wished them to be.

Louis, William Roger. *The British Empire in the Middle East, 1945-1951: Arab Nationalism, the United States, and Postwar Imperialism*. New York: Oxford University Press, 1984. A long (747-page), scholarly study of the framework in which Bevin made his Palestine policy. It shows how the aspirations of Zionism collided with British plans for continuing dominance in the Middle East.

Morgan, Kenneth O. *Labour in Power, 1945-1951*. New York: Oxford University Press, 1984. Carefully researched and well-balanced examination of Labour's most successful government. Morgan presents Bevin in the context of the cabinet and the problems it faced, and shows Bevin's strong standing in the cabinet.

Pimlott, Ben. *Hugh Dalton*. London: Jonathan Cape, 1985. A thorough study of the Labour leader who had expected to become foreign secretary in 1945 and became Chancellor of the Exchequer instead. Dalton was one of the colleagues whom Bevin respected, despite his earlier career as a professor of economics.

SEE ALSO: Clement Attlee; Aneurin Bevan; Margaret Bondfield; Neville Chamberlain; George VI; Ramsay MacDonald; Vyacheslav Mikhailovich Molotov; Margaret Thatcher.

RELATED ARTICLES in *Great Events from History: The Twentieth Century:*

1901-1940: May 3-12, 1926: British Workers Launch General Strike.

1941-1970: July 26, 1945: Labour Party Forms Britain's Majority Government; April 3, 1948: Marshall Plan Provides Aid to Europe; July 1, 1950: European Payments Union Is Formed.

JEFF BEZOS
American businessman

Bezos, an Internet innovator and pioneer, revolutionized the way that consumers shop and make purchases using the World Wide Web. His company, Amazon.com, has become one of the largest and most successful Web-based shopping sites.

BORN: January 12, 1964; Albuquerque, New Mexico

ALSO KNOWN AS: Jeffrey Preston Bezos

AREAS OF ACHIEVEMENT: Business and industry, computer science, invention and technology

EARLY LIFE

Jeff Bezos (BAY-zohs) was born in Albuquerque, New Mexico, to Jacklyn, who was still a teenager. Jacklyn's marriage to Jeff's birth father lasted less than a year after Jeff was born. When Bezos was five, his mother married Miguel Bezos, a Cuban refugee, and took his surname.

Bezos spent summers on his grandfather's twenty-five thousand-acre cattle ranch in New Mexico and developed an appreciation for science and hard work. Bezos showed an early interest in science and technology while tinkering in the family's garage in Houston, where his adopted father worked as an executive for Exxon. As a teenager, Bezos wanted to be an astronaut or physicist. His family later moved to Miami, Florida, where Bezos attended high school and graduated at the top of his class. He attended Princeton University and graduated with highest honors in 1986 with a bachelor of science degree in electrical engineering and computer science.

After graduating from college, Bezos accepted a position with Fitel, a high-tech start-up company. At Fitel he created software to track international stock trades. In 1990, he took a position with the Wall Street firm D. E. Shaw, developing a technically sophisticated and successful quantitative hedge fund and becoming the company's youngest senior vice president in 1992. He then married novelist MacKenzie Bezos.

LIFE'S WORK

In 1994, Bezos discovered a Web site that showed the phenomenal growth of the Internet and realized that a unique opportunity was at hand. He envisioned starting the largest store in the world, where people could shop and purchase anything they needed online. He wanted his online store to be easy to use with a focus on excellent selection and customer service. Bezos decided to start this online store with books because traditional bookstores offer only a small sampling of the available in-print titles. His idea was to purchase books on-demand from wholesalers' warehouses as customers placed orders. This would allow him to start with no real estate, little capital, and no inventory. In the summer of 1995, Amazon.com was born in his garage.

Initially, Bezos filled all the orders himself, but business quickly expanded. By the end of 1996 there were more than one hundred Amazon staff members. Bezos periodically updated the site and increased its "user-friendliness." One of his early innovations was to allow customers to sign up for e-mail alerts for new titles of interest. He chose the name "Amazon" after the world's largest river because he wanted to convey a sense of the company's future, endless offerings.

Although Amazon experienced an excellent growth rate, its losses exceeded revenues for nearly eight years. Bezos worked to remedy this situation through innovation, marketing, and good business sense. In 1996 he started the "associates" program, which paid a commission to other Web sites that linked to Amazon.com. In 1997 Amazon.com went public, selling its common shares to investors in the stock market. Bezos used the funds the company earned to enhance the site's distribution functions. He increased the company's name recognition by forging relationships with high-traffic sites such as Yahoo! and America Online, investing in banner ads, and even getting U.S. vice president Al Gore to spend a day answering customer-service calls. In October, 1997, Amazon.com became the first Internet retailer to have one million customers. Bezos also began to focus on international sales, acquiring several European online bookstores and branding them as Amazon sites. These efforts paid off by 2003, when the company posted its first end-of-year profit.

Amazon.com has remained a robust and relevant Web retailer despite increased competition. Bezos has accomplished this by focusing on his core mission of providing customers with great selection, an easy-to-use site, and discount pricing. In 1998, Bezos expanded Amazon .com's offerings to include CDs. By 1999 he announced that "Amazon.com will be a place where you can find anything" and began selling everything from clothing and computers to toys and tools. In 2001, Bezos completed negotiations with Borders Books to take over its online book-selling operation, thereby making a competitor a partner.

Jeff Bezos. (AP/Wide World Photos)

Bezos has always focused on making Amazon more relevant and customer focused. It has included free shipping on orders of $25 or more, e-cards (electronic cards), "1-Click" shopping, wedding and baby registries, forums that allow users to post product reviews, online auctions, "wish lists," and a system that tracks a user's previous purchases and recommends similar items. In 2003, Amazon introduced the controversial "Search Inside" option, a monumental project that allowed customers to keyword search the full text of millions of pages of text. Some publishers were concerned that this feature could inhibit sales of certain types of books. Bezos remained undeterred and chose to focus on long-term goals rather than short-term gain. He believed that what was most important in the competitive world of electronic retailing was building customer loyalty by giving customers the tools they need to make informed purchasing decisions, combined with excellent customer service and fair pricing. This strategy has paid off for Amazon, as the company has had a higher rate of return customers than have most of its online competitors.

In 2002, Bezos started Blue Origin, a company that is developing vehicles and technologies that will allow humans to live in space. His friends say that space exploration has always been his number one interest. The company is working on developing a vertical takeoff and landing vehicle designed to take a small number of astronauts into space.

SIGNIFICANCE

Bezos was an innovator in harnessing the power of the Web for retail sales. His Web start-up company Amazon.com literally changed how Americans shop and led to major changes in the retail world, causing retail giants such as Borders and Barnes & Noble to rethink how they market their products. Many of Bezos's innovations have became standard practice in the world of e-commerce (electronic commerce), practices including e-mail alert services, heavy advertising on popular Web sites, banner ads, e-cards, expedited shipping, and referring customers to products that match their buying patterns.

Bezos demonstrated the incredible possibilities of an Internet start-up company, launching his business without employees, real estate, or inventory, and then growing it into one of the most widely used and recognized Web sites in the world. Furthermore, he has shown that even in the competitive world of e-commerce, a loyal customer base can be built through convenience and a focus on customer service and competitive, if not low, pricing.

—*Robert K. Flatley*

FURTHER READING

"Bezos, Jeff." *Current Biography* 59, no. 6 (June, 1998): 11-14. A biographical account of the life of Bezos, including background information and factors contributing to his success. Also discusses why he was interested in electronic retailing.

Garty, Judy. *Jeff Bezos: Business Genius of Amazon.com.*

A BET ON THE NET

In an interview with the Academy of Achievement on May 4, 2001, Amazon.com founder Jeff Bezos spoke about his parents and their generous contributions to his risky business enterprise.

The first initial start-up capital for Amazon.com came primarily from my parents, and they invested a large fraction of their life savings in what became Amazon.com. And you know, that was a very bold and trusting thing for them to do, because they didn't know. My dad's first question was, "What's the Internet?" Okay. So he wasn't making a bet on this company or this concept. He was making a bet on his son, as was my mother. So I told them that I thought there was a 70 percent chance that they would lose their whole investment, which was a few hundred thousand dollars, and they did it anyway. And, you know, I thought I was giving myself triple the normal odds, because really, if you look at the odds of a start-up company succeeding at all, it's only about ten percent. Here I was, giving myself a 30 percent chance.

Berkley Heights, N.J.: Enslow, 2003. This biography for younger readers covers Bezos's early life and as well as his business career. Includes many quotations from friends and family.

Quittner, Joshua. "An Eye on the Future." *Time*, December 27, 1999. Cover story on Bezos. Includes biographical information, discusses why he started Amazon.com, and explains his vision of the future.

Ressner, Jeffrey. "Ten Questions for Jeff Bezos." *Time*, August 1, 2005. An interview with Bezos, in which he comments on Amazon stock prices, new Amazon acquisitions, the outlook for the company, expansion of items sold on the Amazon site, and the company's plan for video delivery.

Vogelstein, Fred. "Mighty Amazon." *Fortune*, May 26, 2003. A profile of Bezos and reasons for the success of Amazon.com.

SEE ALSO: Bill Gates; Steve Jobs.

RELATED ARTICLES in *Great Events from History: The Twentieth Century:*

BHUMIBOL ADULYADEJ
King of Thailand (r. 1946-   )

Bhumibol used skillful means to rebuild the Thai monarchy, making it into the most stable, powerful, and influential institution in Thailand. He accomplished this through political savvy and by endearing himself to the Thai people through philanthropy and public projects, including those recognized by the United Nations.

BORN: December 5, 1927; Cambridge, Massachusetts

ALSO KNOWN AS: Rama IX of Thailand; Phumiphon Adunlayadet

AREAS OF ACHIEVEMENT: Government and politics, monarchy, agriculture, philanthropy

EARLY LIFE

Bhumibol Adulyadej (BEW-mee-bohl ay-duhl-YAHD-ehj) was born in Cambridge, Massachusetts, to parents who were studying medicine at Harvard University. His father was a Thai prince and son of King Chulalongkorn, fifth king of the Chakri Dynasty of Thailand. His mother was a commoner named Sangwal, but she was known after the birth of her children as the Princess Mother and later was given the title Her Royal Highness Somdej Phra Sri Nakarindra Baromraj Chonni. Bhumibol's family returned to Thailand in 1928, where he studied for a short time at a primary school in Bangkok. In 1933, Bhumibol's family moved to Switzerland, and he continued his secondary education there at the École Nouvelle de la Suisse Romande. He later graduated from Gymnase Classique Cantonal of Lausanne with a *baccalauréat des lettres* in French literature, Latin, and Greek. In 1945 he was admitted to the University of Lausanne to study science.

In 1946, Bhumibol's life changed dramatically. His older brother, Phra Ong Chao Ananda Mahidol, the reigning king of Thailand, was murdered on June 9. Bhumibol was declared king, although his formal coronation did not take place until May 5, 1950. His uncle served as interim king to allow him to complete his education in Switzerland. Because of his new role, Bhumibol decided to study politics and law rather than science; he graduated in 1950. Bhumibol met his future wife, Sirikit Kitiyakara, the daughter of the Thai ambassador to France, while studying in Europe. They were married on April 28, 1950. They eventually had four children, a son and three daughters.

LIFE'S WORK

The Thai monarchy's power and prestige had been in steady decline since 1932, when Thailand became a constitutional monarchy. When the nineteen-year-old Bhumibol Adulyadej (a name that means "strength of the land, incomparable power") came to power in 1946, he began to reverse this trend. His sixty-year-plus reign was so successful and influential that it shaped the monarchy into the most powerful and revered institution in Thailand. Bhumibol's political savvy, dedication to his people, and social and economic development projects in rural areas were decisive factors in this transformation.

In 1957, his support for the ouster of the military dictatorship of Plaek Pibulsonggram in favor of General Sarit Dhanarajata dramatically changed the king's role in Thai politics. Sarit and Bhumibol developed a close working relationship that greatly increased the visibility and influence of the monarchy. Many traditional ceremonies were revived, and Sarit entrusted Bhumibol with the country's political affairs and with developing the economy. Bhumibol directly or indirectly was involved in determining who ruled Thailand, including a series of military dictators, until 1973, when massive protests and the killing of many prodemocratic activists led to the king's appointment of a civilian government. This government, however, lasted only three years because another military dictatorship seized power.

In 1992, Bhumibol helped establish a democratically elected government by opposing a 1991 military coup, leading to general elections and a civilian government. The era of democratically elected governments came to an abrupt end in 2006, when the government of Prime Minister Thaksin Shinawatra was overthrown by the Thai military in a nonaggressive coup. Thaksin's government was frequently accused of corruption, conflicts of interest, and human rights abuses, yet his progressive policies made him a popular politician. It is generally felt that the ouster of Thaksin, a vocal critic of the monarchy, was supported by Bhumibol.

Bhumibol has been actively engaged in social and economic development projects during his reign. He visited every province in Thailand and started many development programs to benefit the populace. His most significant work was in agricultural and rural development. His efforts have directly improved the lives of peasant farmers through road development, electricity, irrigation, and modern farming techniques. The king was acclaimed for his successful effort to get farmers to switch from growing opium poppies to growing vegetables, fruits, and coffee, leading to an 85 percent decline in opium cultivation. Other projects included improvements in livestock, beekeeping, forestry, dairy production, and the development of hybrid seeds. He was awarded the first Human Development Lifetime Achievement Award by the United Nations in 2006.

Bhumibol's personal life has been equally active and wide ranging. As an author, gifted jazz musician, inventor, and sailor, he has written two books, composed music and played with world-renowned musicians such as Benny Goodman and Lionel Hampton, received several patents for agricultural devices, and designed boats. He also is fluent in three European languages.

King Bhumibol is one of wealthiest persons in the world, owning equity in many large Thai companies and owning vast tracts of land and developed properties. His assets include banks, construction companies, and insurance and telecommunications companies.

Although immensely popular in Thailand, Bhumibol is not without his detractors. He has a record of supporting, at times, dictatorships and a corrupt Thai military, instead of democratic movements. In addition, he is protected by *lèse majesté* laws, which make it illegal for anyone to criticize any member of the monarchy or any royal projects. Criticism of the king or monarchy is vigorously suppressed, and government censorship is routine.

SIGNIFICANCE

Bhumibol is the political and emotional pillar of Thailand. He has worked tirelessly to restore people's faith in the monarchy. He is the only Thai king to have visited every province in Thailand. In addition to connecting with the people, he has been very astute politically, breaking the mold of the ceremonial monarch. Instead, Bhumibol has embraced politics by cultivating close working relationships with Thai political leaders and the military. His longevity and political capital have allowed him to develop a base of powerful individuals who regularly seek him out for advice and input regarding the future of Thailand.

His rural and economic development projects transformed the countryside of Thailand. He has modernized Thai farming through the development and funding of major irrigation projects, new livestock breeding techniques, hybrid-seed cultivation, and dairy industry improvements. These projects have raised the standard of living for millions of rural Thai farmers and villagers. He is known for his generosity and has often funded major projects with his own money when government funding was not available. His work received international recognition by the United Nations and continues to serve as a model for other countries. His foundation continues this work.

—Robert K. Flatley

FURTHER READING

Crossette, B. "King Bhumibol's Reign." *The New York Times Magazine*, May 21, 1989. Includes a profile of the king and the Chakri Dynasty in Thailand. Provides an overview of his development projects and his role in government.

Gearing, Julian. "A Very Special Monarch." *Asiaweek*, December 3, 1999, 44-50. Focuses on Bhumibol's role in transforming his country while maintaining stability in changing times. Provides historical background on Bhumibol's ascension to the throne.

Handley, Paul M. *The King Never Smiles: A Biography of Thailand's Bhumibol Adulyadej*. New Haven, Conn.: Yale University Press, 2006. A full-length biography of Bhumibol. Handley provides an extensively researched account of all aspects of the king's life.

Nash, Michael L. "The Thai Monarchy." *Contemporary Review* (August, 1996): 66-70. Discusses the origin of the Thai monarchy and the religious role of the king.

SEE ALSO: Mohammad Hatta; Lee Kuan Yew; Syngman Rhee; Suharto; Sukarno; U Thant.

RELATED ARTICLES in *Great Events from History: The Twentieth Century:*

1941-1970: September 8, 1954: SEATO Is Founded; September 17, 1957: Thai Military Coup; August 8, 1967: Association of Southeast Asian Nations Is Formed.

BENAZIR BHUTTO
Prime minister of Pakistan (1988-1990, 1993-1996)

Prime Minister Bhutto rebuilt the Pakistan Peoples Party, continuing the legacy of her father and leading the party's drive toward democracy and human rights in Pakistan. She introduced measures that benefited women, the poor, and the dispossessed, and was the first woman to lead an elected government of an Islamic nation.

BORN: June 21, 1953; Karachi, Pakistan
DIED: December 27, 2007; Rawalpindi, Pakistan
AREAS OF ACHIEVEMENT: Government and politics, social reform, women's rights

EARLY LIFE

Benazir Bhutto (BEHN-ah-zeer BEW-toh) was born to Nusrat Ispahani and Zulfikar Ali Bhutto, a former prime minister of Pakistan. Her grandfather was Shah Nawaz Bhutto, a wealthy *wadero*, or landowner, and politician. Benazir had a younger brother, Murtaza, born in 1954; a sister, Sanam, born in 1957; and a second brother, Shahnawaz, born in 1958. Bhutto attended the Convent of Jesus and Mary in Karachi and the Rawalpindi Presentation Convent and the Jesus and Mary Convent at Muree. Between 1969 and 1973 she attended Radcliffe College at Harvard University, majoring in political science.

Bhutto, who was shy as a child, was very much her father's daughter, and she adored him. She acted as his assistant in December, 1971, when he spoke at the United Nations, and she accompanied him on trips to India, China, and Europe. She wanted to stay in the United States for graduate studies but her father insisted she study at his alma mater, Oxford University. She followed in her father's footsteps and attended Lady Margaret Hall, Oxford University, from 1973 until 1976. During one year of graduate study (1976-1977) she was elected president of the Oxford Union, a debating society. She returned to Pakistan in 1977 to become an adviser to her father.

Bhutto surprised many people when she chose Asif Ali Zardari, who was more renowned for his social life than for his intellect, as her husband-to-be. They married in December, 1987, and had three children—a son, Bilawal, and two daughters, Bakhtwar and Aseefa. Bhutto chose to use her family name in memory of her father and his legacy.

LIFE'S WORK

Bhutto's father was removed from office by the military under Mohammad Zia-ul-Haq on July 4, 1977, and was arrested, charged with murder, found guilty, and hanged on April 4, 1979. Bhutto inherited the family's political misfortunes, and she would spend nearly six years in prison, under house arrest, or mostly in exile in London. In July, 1984, her younger brother, Shahnawaz, died under mysterious circumstances in Paris. She returned to Lahore, Pakistan, on April 10, 1986, and was greeted by an estimated one million people at the airport. During the following year she spoke at mammoth rallies all over the country. At the end of 1987, after marrying Zardari, her

Benazir Bhutto. (Stephen Hird/Reuters/Landov)

ISLAM AT THE CROSSROADS

On November 7, 1997, Benazir Bhutto, former prime minister of Pakistan, described the growing global importance of Pakistan, Asia, and the Muslim community in general in a speech at Harvard University's John F. Kennedy School of Government.

And, ladies and gentlemen, this is an era where we see an increasing focus on Islam and the West. The entire world community, and specifically the United States, have a fundamental strategic interest in events in the Muslim world. All across the world, in the Middle East, in Southwest Asia and Southeast Asia and Africa, one billion Muslims are at the crossroads. They must choose between progress and extremism. They must choose between education and ignorance. They must choose between the force of new technologies and the forces of old repression. Thus, one billion Muslims must choose between the past and the future.

The United States must do everything within its power to ensure that progressive, pluralistic Muslim countries like Pakistan are in a position to serve as role-models to the entire Islamic world. And, Pakistan is also an important Asian country at the crossroads to the strategic oil reserves of the Gulf and Central Asia and to the markets of South Asia and East Asia. In terms of demographics, in terms of production, in terms of consumption, in terms of markets, in terms of an expanding capital-intensive middle class, the Asian continent will surely set the tone, set the pace, and dominate the economic and geopolitical exigencies of the coming era.

I wonder how many people realize that Pakistan is the second largest Muslim state on earth. A state, as I've said, at the crossroads of the oil-rich Gulf and Central Asia. A state, as I've said, at the crossroads to the markets of South Asia and East Asia. A state that can serve as a model of moderation and modality to one billion Muslims across the planet. As a Pakistani, I wish to explore with you today the West's relationship with the Islamic world and the role that we can play to create a civil, political, economic, and religious dialogue between the East and the West at this critical moment.

---

status changed to that of a "respectable" married woman, which assisted her considerably in a very traditional and conservative Pakistan.

On August 17, 1988, Zia-ul-Haq died in a plane crash, changing the political scene overnight. In the general elections that followed, Bhutto led the Pakistan Peoples Party (PPP) to victory, winning 94 of 207 seats in the assembly and becoming prime minister on December 2. Her immediate goal was to maintain and implement the socialist principles of the party, which included *Roti, Kapra aur Makan* (bread, clothing, and shelter), a slogan coined by her father.

With Bhutto as prime minister, Pakistan enjoyed a remarkable degree of political freedom and freedom of speech. Bhutto soon was hailed as one of the great leaders of the world and was warmly received in the United States and Europe. She dramatically improved relations with India and returned Pakistan to the Commonwealth of Nations. In December, 1988, she hosted the seven-nation South Asian Association for Regional Cooperation meeting in Islamabad.

However, because she was a Bhutto and a woman, opposition was vehement, virulent, poisonous, and unceasing at all levels—political and personal. She was able to get only ten bills of minor significance through the assembly. The opposition was led by the president, Ghulam Ishaq Khan, at the behest of the military, and a willing Nawaz Sharif, leader of the Pakistan Muslim League. Corruption charges dogged her ministry as well. It had been rumored that any contract requiring government approval necessitated a 10 percent fee be paid to her husband. Bhutto also had appointed him to her cabinet.

On August 6, 1990, after serving just twenty months of a five-year term, her government was dismissed by President Ishaq, and her husband was imprisoned. For the next three years she campaigned against the government of Sharif; he was dismissed and Bhutto once again became prime minister (on October 19, 1993). Again, she was besieged by an opposition that staged marches and organized strikes.

Bhutto's 1994 visit to the United States led to the U.S. Senate's passage of the Brown amendment (September 21), which released military equipment to Pakistan. However, controversy was never far behind. In October, 1995, Bhutto purchased a twenty-room mansion in Surrey, England, for $4.35 million. Her troubles increased precipitously on September 20, 1996, when her brother, Mir Murtaza Bhutto, was killed in a police ambush in Karachi. Her husband was accused by many of having ordered the assassination. The murder badly damaged the Bhutto family's reputation and collapsed whatever remained of the legitimacy of her ministry. Charges of corruption persisted, and her government became synonymous with corruption and mismanagement. On November 5, 1996, President Farooq Legari dismissed her government.

In 1997 the Swiss government froze more than $13.7 million found in Bhutto's seven Geneva accounts because of money laundering charges. She and her husband were found guilty of money laundering. Furthermore, it is estimated the family received an estimated $1.5 billion in kickbacks. In April, 1999, in Pakistan, she and her husband were convicted of corruption, sentenced to five years in prison, fined $8.6 million, had their property confiscated, and were disqualified from official politics. Bhutto's husband was imprisoned for murder and corruption (without being formally convicted) and was not released until November, 2004. Bhutto, however, went into self-exile in 1999 and resided in England and then in Dubai, facing corruption charges if she were to return to Pakistan.

On October 18, 2007, Bhutto returned to Pakistan to thousands of supporters, having been granted amnesty by Pakistan's president, Pervez Musharraf. Later that day, on her way to a rally in Karachi, two explosions, set off by suicide bombers, rocked Bhutto's convoy and killed close to 150 people and injured hundreds more. The dead included more than fifty members of her security detail as well as local police officers. Musharraf declared a state of emergency (in effect, martial law) on November 3 and suspended the Pakistani constitution. (The order lasted until December 15.) Bhutto, placed under house arrest by Musharraf in November, announced her candidacy for the presidency. The PPP issued a manifesto in December, one month before Pakistan's national elections to select a new president.

The elections, however, would not be held as planned. Bhutto was assassinated on December 27, following a rally at a park in Rawalpindi. Early reports indicate that she had been shot by a gunman seconds before a suicide bomber exploded a device outside her vehicle. Dozens of others also were killed, and the country—and the world—was stunned. International condemnation was swift, and Musharraf and other Pakistani officials were quick to blame Islamic terrorists for the assassination and bombing. Within days, Bhutto's nineteen-year-old son, Bilawal Bhutto Zardari, a student at Oxford University in England who lacked experience in politics, was named her successor as ceremonial leader of the PPP. Her husband became the party's interim leader of day-to-day operations.

SIGNIFICANCE

In 2007, Bhutto had returned to a military-controlled Pakistan (with a self-declared president since 1999). Her own government, in stark contrast, had returned Pakistan to civilian governing and reintroduced a parliamentary system. In office she had maintained the power of the PPP and, like her father, was later accused of criminal acts and removed from office. However, she evoked the name and memory of her father and used his death as a *shaheed*, or martyr, to mobilize people in support of her party.

Bhutto's 2007 campaign to return to Pakistan and to seek the presidency had led her to Washington, D.C., where she tried to convince U.S. president George W. Bush that she would be a better partner in the war against terrorism than would Musharraf. She hired a lobbying firm, spoke to the American Enterprise Institute, and wrote an opinion piece published in *The Washington Post*. She even met with her bitter rival, Sharif, in Jeddah, Saudi Arabia.

With Bhutto's return to Pakistan in 2007 and with her announcement to run for president, a new chapter in Pakistani—and Middle Eastern—political history began. That chapter, and a return to democracy and the valuing of human rights, ended violently with Bhutto's assassination.

—Roger D. Long

FURTHER READING

Akhund, Iqbal. *Trial and Error: The Advent and Eclipse of Benazir Bhutto*. New York: Oxford University Press, 2000. An attempt to make sense of Bhutto's legacy as the prime mover in Pakistan's turn to democracy in the face of the controversies that have followed her.

Bhutto, Benazir. *Daughter of the East: An Autobiography*. London: Hamilton, 1988. Bhutto's own account of her early life. Essential reading for an understanding of Bhutto and the Bhutto family.

Burns, John F. "Benazir Bhutto, 54, Who Weathered Pakistan's Political Storm for Three Decades, Dies." *The New York Times*, December 28, 2007. A brief but detailed obituary of Bhutto, published one day after her assassination and at a time when circumstances surrounding her death were still uncertain.

Shaikh, Muhammad Ali. *Benazir Bhutto: A Political Biography*. Karachi, Pakistan: Oriental Books, 2000. This is a sympathetic account of Bhutto's life and career based, in part, on a number of interviews with Bhutto and those who knew her well.

Talbot, Ian. *Pakistan: A Modern History*. New York: St. Martin's Press, 1998. Great Britain's leading historian of Pakistan offers a frank description of Bhutto's terms of office in this general history of modern Pakistan.

SEE ALSO: Aung San Suu Kyi; Sir Surendranath Banerjea; Zulfikar Ali Bhutto; Indira Gandhi; Mahatma Gandhi; Le Ly Hayslip; Mohammed Ali Jinnah; Golda Meir; Sarojini Naidu; Vijaya Lakshmi Pandit; Mohammad Zia-ul-Haq.

RELATED ARTICLES in *Great Events from History: The Twentieth Century:*
1971-2000: July 5, 1977: Zia Establishes Martial Law in Pakistan; April 4, 1979: Pakistan Hangs Former Prime Minister Bhutto; November, 1988: Bhutto Becomes the First Woman Elected to Lead a Muslim Country.

ZULFIKAR ALI BHUTTO
President of Pakistan (1971-1973)

Bhutto founded the left-center Pakistan People's Party, concerned with the lives of women, the poor, and the dispossessed peoples of Pakistan. His tenure as president and then prime minister inaugurated a short-lived but still influential political dynasty in Pakistan. His legacy continued with his daughter Benazir Bhutto, who succeeded him as prime minister and as party leader before her exile in 1999.

BORN: January 5, 1928; near Larkana, Sindh, India (now Pakistan)
DIED: April 4, 1979; Rawalpindi, Pakistan
AREAS OF ACHIEVEMENT: Government and politics, social reform

EARLY LIFE
Zulfikar Ali Bhutto (ZEWL-fih-kahr ah-LEE BEW-toh) was born in a tribal society near Larkana in Sindh, India (now Pakistan). He was the son of a wealthy *wadero*, or landowner, and politician named Shah Nawaz Bhutto. Nawaz's second wife, Kakhi Bai, was a Hindu who converted to Islam and changed her name to Khurshid. Their first son died in childhood and the second died at age thirty-nine. Bhutto was the couple's third son.

Bhutto was schooled at the elite Cathedral and John Connon School in Bombay and then at St. Xavier's College. In 1943 he married one of his cousins, Shireen Amir. In September, 1947, he enrolled at the University of Southern California in Los Angeles. In 1949 he transferred to the University of California, Berkeley, majoring in political science. He was fascinated by the life and career of Napoleon Bonaparte, who became his role model, and he amassed a large collection of books on his life.

On a trip home from California, Bhutto met Nusrat Ispahani. On September 8, 1951, they married in Karachi

and then traveled to England, where Bhutto enrolled at Christ Church College, Oxford. He also enrolled at Lincoln's Inn, London, and was called to the bar in 1953. On June 21 of that year his daughter, Benazir, was born in Karachi. She was followed by a son named Murtaza in 1954, a daughter named Sanam in 1957, and a son named Shahnawaz in 1958. Bhutto taught law at Sindh Muslim College and briefly practiced law in Karachi. He quickly abandoned his legal practice for politics but continued to manage his family's business and landed interests after the death of his father.

LIFE'S WORK
In 1957, Bhutto was appointed to Pakistan's delegation to the United Nations and appointed the minister of energy in Ayub Khan's government. He then served as head of the ministries of commerce, information, and industries, helping to negotiate the Indus Waters Treaty with India in 1960 and an oil exploration contract with the Soviet Union in 1961. He was appointed foreign minister in 1963.

Bhutto transformed Pakistan's foreign policy into one that was more pro-Islamic and nonaligned. He also established closer relations with the People's Republic of China by visiting Peking (Beijing) and negotiating military and trade agreements; on March 2, 1963, he signed the Sino-Pakistan Boundary Agreement. He took a belligerent stance toward India and encouraged Ayub Khan to launch operations Gibraltar and Grand Slam in 1965, an invasion of Indian-held territory in Kashmir. In response India attacked Pakistan, leading Bhutto to travel to the United Nations to condemn India. The war lasted two weeks before both sides agreed to a cease-fire and the Tashkent Declaration of January 10, 1966.

The Tashkent Declaration was very unpopular, and Ayub's popularity plummeted as a result. Bhutto opportunistically criticized Ayub for the final treaty, resigned as foreign minister in June, 1967, and founded the Pakistan People's Party (PPP) on November 30. Riots and demonstrations led to the breakdown of law and order, and Bhutto was arrested on November 12, 1968. He was released but continued to demand Ayub's resignation. Finally, Ayub resigned on March 25, 1969, and the army chief Yahya Khan became president. He called for general elections for December 7, 1970.

During the election campaign the charismatic and popular Bhutto campaigned on the slogan *Roti, Kapra aur Makan* (bread, clothing, and shelter). The PPP won a majority of the seats for West Pakistan, but in the more populous East Pakistan the Awami League, led by Sheikh Mujibur Rahman, won an overwhelming victory. Bhutto refused to accept the Bengali Mujibur's victory and his prime ministry of Pakistan. This outraged East Pakistanis, leading them to declare East Pakistan independent on March 26, 1971, as the new state of Bangladesh. A vicious civil war ensued. India invaded East Pakistan, and the Pakistani army surrendered on December 16. Yahya resigned on December 20, handing power to Bhutto as president, commander in chief, and chief martial law administrator of Pakistan.

Bhutto served as president of Pakistan from 1970 until 1973. He appointed a new chief of the army and released Mujibur from prison. (Mujibur returned to Bangladesh to become its prime minister.) On January 2, 1972, Bhutto announced the nationalization of all the major industries of Pakistan and a new industrial policy that favored labor unions. He fired more than two thousand civil servants who had been accused of corruption. In addition, he instituted land reforms limiting the size of landholdings and distributed more than one million acres to landless farmers. He dismissed the heads of the army when they refused to discipline the police, who had gone on strike. These measures were very controversial, and most of them met with failure.

Bhutto was a powerful leader who attracted ardent followers but equally vehement and powerful enemies. On April 14, 1972, he convened the national assembly. One week later, he rescinded martial law and ordered the development of a new constitution. On July 2, he signed the Simla Agreement with Indian prime minister Indira

Zulfikar Ali Bhutto. (Library of Congress)

Gandhi, which secured the release of the ninety-three thousand Pakistani prisoners of war held by India and established the so-called Line of Control between India and Pakistan in Kashmir. On November 28, he inaugurated Pakistan's first atomic reactor.

On April 12, 1973, Bhutto signed the new constitution into law, and he officially recognized Bangladesh in July. In October he gave up the presidency of Pakistan and became its prime minister. Pakistan became an Islamic republic, and between February 22 and 24, he hosted the Second Islamic Summit. Bowing to orthodox pressure, he declared the Ahmadiyya sect to be non-Muslim. He accelerated his economic reform program and built Port Qasim near Karachi. The performance of the economy, however, declined.

As opposition increased, Bhutto turned on his opponents, especially those from the leftist National Awami Party (NAP), founded in 1957 and headed by Abdul Wali Khan. Bhutto soon banned the party. Adding to pressures, Bhutto was accused of ordering the killing of the father of Ahmed Khan Kasuri, a dissident PPP member. On January 11, 1977, the main opposition parties formed the Pakistan National Alliance, although they boycotted the general elections held in March. Bhutto's overwhelming victory led to cries of electoral fraud.

Following increased opposition and the breakdown of law and order, the chief of army staff, Mohammad Zia-ul-Haq, whom Bhutto had appointed in 1976, staged a military coup on July 4, 1977. A few months later Bhutto was charged with the murder of Kasuri's father, found guilty, and sentenced to death. Bhutto was hanged on April 4, 1979.

SIGNIFICANCE

Bhutto, one of Pakistan's most charismatic and colorful leaders, returned Pakistan to civilian rule and reintroduced a parliamentary system of government, which led to a period of democracy. He also created the Pakistan People's Party, which focused on the concerns of women, the poor, and other politically and socially dispossessed peoples. Bhutto's death by hanging affected the country immensely, making his memory one of the most controversial in the nation's history. He was hailed by his supporters as a *shaheed*, a martyr, and his legacy remains long after his death.

—*Roger D. Long*

FURTHER READING

Bhutto, Benazir. *Daughter of the East: An Autobiography.* London: Hamilton, 1988. Although an account of Benazir Bhutto's early life, this work is essential for an understanding of the Bhutto family.

Burki, Shahid Javed. *Pakistan Under Bhutto, 1971-1977.* London: Macmillan, 1988. Burki, a Pakistani economist who served with the World Bank and advised the Pakistan government on the economy, covers all facets of Bhutto's government. His analysis, however, is particularly useful and authoritative on Bhutto's controversial economic policies.

Talbot, Ian. *Pakistan: A Modern History.* New York: St. Martin's Press, 1998. Britain's leading historian of Pakistan places Bhutto's term of office in historical perspective (pages 215-244). A reliable and clearly written guide to "the outstanding political figure of his generation."

Wolpert, Stanley. *Zulfi Bhutto of Pakistan: His Life and Times.* New York: Oxford University Press, 1993. With more than a dozen books to his credit, Wolpert is the most distinguished American historian of India and Pakistan. He is a household name in Pakistan because of his biographies of the country's founders Mohammad Ali Jinnah and Zulfikar Ali Bhutto. Vividly written and based on primary sources and interviews with Benazir Bhutto and with acquaintances. Recommended.

SEE ALSO: Benazir Bhutto; Indira Gandhi; Mahatma Gandhi; Mohammed Ali Jinnah; Sarojini Naidu; Jawaharlal Nehru; Vijaya Lakshmi Pandit; Mohammad Zia-ul-Haq.

RELATED ARTICLES in *Great Events from History: The Twentieth Century:*

1941-1970: November 12, 1970: Bhola Cyclone Devastates East Pakistan.

1971-2000: March 26-December 16, 1971: Bangladesh Secedes from Pakistan; July 5, 1977: Zia Establishes Martial Law in Pakistan; April 4, 1979: Pakistan Hangs Former Prime Minister Bhutto; November, 1988: Bhutto Becomes the First Woman Elected to Lead a Muslim Country; 1989: Amnesty International Exposes the Cruelty of the Death Penalty.

OSAMA BIN LADEN
Saudi Arabian terrorist leader

The leader of the Islamic terrorist organization al-Qaeda, Bin Laden emerged as the spiritual symbol for many anti-Western Islamic fundamentalists in the aftermath of the September 11, 2001, attacks in the United States.

BORN: March 10, 1957; Riyadh, Saudi Arabia
ALSO KNOWN AS: Osama bin Mohammad bin Laden (full name); Usamah Ibn Laden
AREAS OF ACHIEVEMENT: Warfare and conquest, military affairs, crime, government and politics

EARLY LIFE

Osama Bin Laden (oh-SAH-mah bihn LAH-dihn) was born in Riyadh, Saudi Arabia. He was one of a reported fifty-five children of Muhammed bin Awad bin Laden, a Yemeni peasant who became wealthy as a building contractor for the Saudi royal family. Muhammed, who was married twenty-two times, had Bin Laden with his tenth wife, Hamida al-Attas. Bin Laden's parents divorced when he was a child, and his mother then married Muhammad al-Attas and had four more children. Bin Laden was raised by his mother and stepfather, although he received significant financial support from his birth father. After his father's death in 1968, Bin Laden inherited several million dollars.

Bin Laden was an intelligent and diligent student. He attended a prestigious preparatory school, the Al-Thager Model School, from 1968 to 1976. During that time, he became increasingly attracted to the fundamentalist teachings of Sunni Islam. Bin Laden participated in Islamic study groups and supported radical groups such as

Osama Bin Laden. (AP/Wide World Photos)

the Muslim Brotherhood of Egypt. In 1974, he married for the first time, and he eventually had twenty-four children. (Bin Laden married four more women and was once divorced.)

Bin Laden studied economics, civil engineering, and business administration at King Abdulaziz University in Jeddah, Saudi Arabia, but he failed to obtain a degree. While at the university, he was influenced by several professors who espoused a pan-Islamic philosophy that emphasized the importance of jihad, or holy war, to defend Muslim lands from foreign invaders and foreign influences. In addition to a regular curriculum, Bin Laden extensively studied the Islamic holy book, the Qurʾān, as well as Islamic law. The Soviet invasion of Afghanistan in 1979 further radicalized Bin Laden. He supported the Afghan mujahideen (holy warriors) and joined the anti-Soviet insurgency, thereby transitioning from student to Islamic fundamentalist leader.

LIFE'S WORK
In 1979, Bin Laden joined a former professor in organizing support for the mujahideen. They cofounded Maktab al-Khidmat (bureau of services), which recruited foreign fighters and raised money for the insurgency. Bin Laden used his fortune to provide material support for the insurgents and to publicize their cause. He developed close ties with many of the senior anti-Soviet leaders in Afghanistan. Through Maktab al-Khidmat (MAK), Bin Laden developed an extensive network of followers and agents throughout the Middle East. However, MAK provided mostly logistical support for the rebels, and Bin Laden increasingly sought a more radical, military role for MAK. In Peshawar, Pakistan, in 1984, he formed his own company of fighters, who participated in several minor battles against the Soviets.

In 1988, Bin Laden split from MAK and formed al-Qaeda (the base), a multinational Muslim alliance devoted to Islamist jihad. He embraced what many consid-

---

BIN LADEN'S VENGEANCE

In November, 2004, the Middle East news organization Aljazeera posted on its Web site a translation of Osama Bin Laden's message to Americans about the terrorist attacks of September 11, 2001. An excerpt of the transcript follows.

- [W]e fight because we are free men who don't sleep under oppression. We want to restore freedom to our nation, just as you lay waste to our nation. So shall we lay waste to yours.
- No one except a dumb thief plays with the security of others and then makes himself believe he will be secure. Whereas thinking people, when disaster strikes, make it their priority to look for its causes, in order to prevent it happening again . . . .
- So I shall talk to you about the story behind those events and shall tell you truthfully about the moments in which the decision was taken, for you to consider . . . .
- The events that affected my soul in a direct way started in 1982 when America permitted the Israelis to invade Lebanon and the American Sixth Fleet helped them in that. This bombardment began and many were killed and injured and others were terrorised and displaced . . . .
- I couldn't forget those moving scenes, blood and severed limbs, women and children sprawled everywhere. Houses destroyed along with their occupants and high rises demolished over their residents, rockets raining down on our home without mercy.
- In those difficult moments many hard-to-describe ideas bubbled in my soul, but in the end they produced an intense feeling of rejection of tyranny, and gave birth to a strong resolve to punish the oppressors.
- And as I looked at those demolished towers in Lebanon, it entered my mind that we should punish the oppressor in kind and that we should destroy towers in America in order that they taste some of what we tasted and so that they be deterred from killing our women and children.
- So with these images and their like as their background, the events of September 11th came as a reply to those great wrongs. [S]hould a man be blamed for defending his sanctuary?
- Is defending oneself and punishing the aggressor in kind, objectionable terrorism? If it is such, then it is unavoidable for us.

---

ered to be an extremist understanding of the Qurʾān and emphasized jihad against all enemies of Islam, including Muslims who were deficient in their practice of Islam. Not formally trained as a cleric, Bin Laden nevertheless began to issue his own interpretations of the Qurʾān and Islamic holy law. The al-Qaeda leader asserted that any action was justified in the defense of Islam, including attacks on civilians.

After Iraq invaded Kuwait in August, 1990, Bin Laden returned to Saudi Arabia and offered to defend the kingdom against attack with a legion of troops. The Saudi government had earlier asked the United States for military support, fearing Iraq would invade Saudi Arabia as well. Bin Laden's proposal, however, was rejected by the royal family, which angered the al-Qaeda leader. Bin Laden denounced the government and its dependence on Western, particularly U.S., military forces. He was especially critical of the presence of non-Muslim troops in Saudi Arabia. In response, the royal family attempted to arrest Bin Laden, who evaded capture and went into exile. He lived in Sudan from 1991 to 1996. His citizenship was revoked in 1994 and the Saudi government froze his family's assets in 1996, but al-Qaeda continued to enjoy clandestine support from a range of prominent Saudis, who provided the group with funding.

Bin Laden endeavored to create a new base for al-Qaeda in Sudan, but the government forced him to leave under U.S. and Saudi pressure in 1996. He returned to Afghanistan and became involved in the ongoing civil war that broke out after the Soviet withdrawal from that country in 1991. He supported the Taliban, an Afghan fundamentalist Islamic group that grew into the ruling government in Afghanistan, and provided it with money. In addition, al-Qaeda members fought alongside the Taliban. In return, the Taliban allowed Bin Laden to create a series of camps across the country to recruit and train foreign fighters.

In 1998, Bin Laden issued a fatwa, or religious decree, which called upon all Muslims to attack and kill Jews and Westerners, including Americans. The fatwa was controversial in a number of respects. One problem was that Bin Laden was not a cleric, leading many Muslim scholars to assert that his decree lacked legitimacy. Concurrently, al-Qaeda began a series of attacks on Western targets, including bombing the U.S. embassies in Kenya and Tanzania in 1998, which killed 225 people (mainly African civilians). In response, the United States, on the order of President Bill Clinton, launched retaliatory missile strikes on al-Qaeda bases in Afghanistan and Sudan. The raids failed to disrupt al-Qaeda.

Bin Laden expanded his campaign against the United States by providing increased funding for al-Qaeda operations. Bin Laden typically did not plan specific strikes, but he did coordinate attacks and link volunteers with missions, including the failed 2000 millennium attacks and the October, 2000, attack on the USS *Cole* in Aden, Yemen. Bin Laden was likely one of the key planners of the September 11, 2001, attacks on the United States, which killed nearly three thousand people in three different locations. He was indicted by the U.S. government, which promised a $25 million reward for his capture. The United States led an invasion of Afghanistan after the Taliban regime refused to surrender Bin Laden. By December, 2001, the Taliban had been disbanded (al-

though a smaller group remained), while Bin Laden and the remnants of al-Qaeda reportedly fled into the mountains along the Afghanistan-Pakistan border.

Forced into hiding, Bin Laden became less involved in the operations of al-Qaeda, but he continued to issue videotape and audiotape statements to the media, condemning the United States and its allies, especially as the focus of the anti-American effort shifted to Iraq after the 2003 invasion. Individual al-Qaeda cells became increasingly autonomous, and rival organizations emerged. Nevertheless, Bin Laden remained the inspirational leader of the jihad.

SIGNIFICANCE

More than any other figure, Bin Laden was responsible for globalizing Islamic terrorism. Under his leadership, al-Qaeda forged links with other radical Muslim terrorist groups and coordinated strikes against Jewish and Western targets around the world. Al-Qaeda eclipsed existing terrorist groups, such as Hezbollah or Islamic Jihad, as the leading anti-Western radical organization. Whereas other groups had attacked civilian targets, no terrorist organization had attempted attacks of the size or scale of al-Qaeda's. Bin Laden adroitly understood the value of symbolism and purposely escalated the scope of terrorist strikes such as the catastrophic attacks on the World Trade Center in New York and the Pentagon in Virginia.

Bin Laden's tactics forced Western governments to view terrorism as a major, if not *the* major, security threat of the twenty-first century. The strikes on the United States prompted the military actions in Afghanistan late in 2001 and the invasion of Iraq in 2003, which initiated the U.S.-led global war on terror. Bin Laden also emerged as a powerful symbol of Islamic strength for his ability to strike the West and to evade capture or punishment by the United States and its allies.

—*Tom Lansford*

FURTHER READING

Atwan, Abdel Bari. *The Secret History of Al Qaeda.* Berkeley: University of California Press, 2006. Beginning with a short biography of Bin Laden, an examination of the rise of al-Qaeda and Bin Laden's political and religious philosophies as they relate to the concept of jihad.

Bergen, Peter L. *Holy War, Inc.: Inside the Secret World of Osama Bin Laden.* New York: Free Press, 2001. Based on extensive interviews, the book discusses Bin Laden's efforts to develop a global terrorist network and the events that led to his war against the United States and its allies.

Corbin, Jane. *Al Qaeda: In Search of the Terror Network That Shook the World.* New York: Thunder Mouth Press/Nation Books, 2002. An elegant account by a prizewinning BBC reporter.

Lawrence, Bruce, ed. *Messages to the World: The Statements of Osama Bin Laden.* Translated by James Howarth. New York: Verso, 2005. Contains translations of twenty-four public statements made by Bin Laden from 1994 to 2004.

Randal, Jonathan. *Osama: The Making of a Terrorist.* New York: Knopf, 2004. One of the best overviews of Bin Laden's early life, with an excellent analysis of his experiences in Afghanistan during the Soviet occupation.

Rashid, Ahmed. *Taliban: Militant Islam, Oil, and Fundamentalism in Central Asia.* New Haven, Conn.: Yale University Press, 2000. Although focused on the Taliban, this book discusses the links between the Afghan group and Bin Laden, especially in the context of the al-Qaeda leader's support during the Afghan civil wars.

Scheuer, Michael. *Through Our Enemies' Eyes: Osama Bin Laden, Radical Islam, and the Future of America.* 2d ed. Washington, D.C.: Potomac Books, 2006. An examination of Bin Laden's life and how events shaped the al-Qaeda leader's goals and strategies.

SEE ALSO: Yasir Arafat; Saddam Hussein; Ayatollah Khomeini.

RELATED ARTICLES in *Great Events from History: The Twentieth Century:*
  1971-2000: April 4, 1973: Opening of the World Trade Center; 1988: Osama Bin Laden Forms al-Qaeda; 1990's: Algeria and Egypt Crack Down on Islamic Militants; May, 1996: Sudan Expels Osama Bin Laden; February 23, 1998: Osama Bin Laden Declares Jihad Against "Jews and Crusaders"; October 12, 2000: Terrorists Attack USS *Cole.*

VILHELM BJERKNES
Norwegian physicist

Bjerknes made some advances in early radio-wave theory, but he is recognized primarily for his extensive work on the formation and behavior of cyclones, polar fronts, squall lines, and other weather phenomena. Under his direction, the Norwegian Weather Forecasting division at Bergen became the world center for meteorological study between 1918 and 1930.

BORN: March 14, 1862; Christiania (now Oslo), Norway
DIED: April 9, 1951; Oslo, Norway
ALSO KNOWN AS: Vilhelm Frimann Koren Bjerknes (full name)
AREAS OF ACHIEVEMENT: Meteorology, physics, invention and technology

EARLY LIFE
Vilhelm Bjerknes (VIHL-hehlm BYEHRK-nays) was the son of Aletta Koren, a lively and highly practical woman, and the rather absentminded and highly impractical C. A. Bjerknes, a mathematician of some renown who liked to dabble in physics, conducting experiments on the kitchen table. As Vilhelm grew up, he spent much of his time with his father, preferring parental company to that of other children. Bjerknes began his university studies in science at Christiania in 1880, entering the same class as Fridtjof Nansen, who would later become known as an explorer of the polar regions and whose collected data on weather and ocean currents would later be invaluable to Bjerknes in his meteorological investigations. Prior to graduation, Bjerknes collaborated with his father on a number of hydrodynamic projects. At the age of twenty, he published his first minor article. In 1889, he received his degree and determined to go his own way for a time.

Bjerknes's first advanced research was not in the field of meteorology or oceanography but in electrodynamics, under the tutelage of the great German physicist Heinrich Hertz. The young Norwegian's interest in electrodynamics had been prompted, as he notes in *C. A. Bjerknes: Hans liv og arbeide* (1925; *C. A. Bjerknes: His Life and Work,* 1932), by his father's own fascination with the eighteenth century scientist Leonhard Euler. Euler's *Lettres à une princesse d'Allemagne sur divers sujets de physique et de philosophie* (3 vols., 1768-1774; *Letters of Euler to a German Princess, on Different Subjects in Physics and Philosophy,* 1795) contained a nontechnical discussion of corpuscular and wave theories of light as well as the phenomenon of action at a distance, that is, the extension of forces such as gravity through allegedly empty space. Euler's development of the idea of a space-filling medium through which light waves could theoretically propagate themselves—a luminiferous ether—impressed C. A. Bjerknes, and he spent much of his career investigating the similarities between the wave properties of electricity, magnetism, and hydrodynamic phenomena.

This devotion to ether theory and electromagnetic undulation in electrodynamics was, for the younger Bjerknes, both an impetus and a kind of nemesis. Earnest and determined, Bjerknes journeyed to hear the Maxwell lectures of Henri Poincaré in Paris in 1889 after finishing his university degree, then to Bonn to study with Hertz in 1890. His experimental and theoretical collaboration with Hertz was highly productive, especially on subjects such as electric resonance, which made possible the later development of the radio. Yet Albert Einstein's radical new theory of relativity was looming on the scientific horizon, and nothing but obsolescence was in store for the mechanical approach underlying Bjerknes's ideas on electromagnetism and ether, not to mention his father's ambitious attempt to unite the methodologies of hydrodynamics and electrodynamics. Unfortunately, the young Bjerknes would spend many years trying to complete his father's doomed project after taking a position in mechanics at the Högskola in Stockholm in 1893, the year Hertz died. On the other hand, his work in this period had the salutary result of guiding him, by means of his hydrodynamic and thermodynamic investigations, into speculations about the atmosphere and the oceans, on which he published a significant paper as early as 1898. This interest doubtlessly grew and was nourished by Bjerknes's collaboration with Hertz, who had himself written on the origin of the winds. Bjerknes, like his father, saw the central question of both electrodynamics and hydrodynamics as the question of action at a distance, that is, What is the nature of the medium (ether or water, respectively) through which moving bodies execute an effect on one another?

LIFE'S WORK

The originality of Bjerknes's work lay in applying paradigms, metaphors, and analogies from one field to the conceptual apparatuses of another. It was this approach, familiar to him from the work of his father, that led him to impose the models and concepts of thermodynamics, hydrodynamics, and other fields of physics on the data of

meteorology, and to apply ideas on fluid strata and waves to the atmosphere. This syncretizing attitude allowed him to envision such things as fronts (by analogy to military conflict), where warm and cold masses of air clash and converge, tending to create swirling vortices not unlike those of rotating objects and gases in the heavens. Bjerknes's ideas put weather forecasting on scientific ground; indeed, he is best remembered for the fundamental constructs he devised for modern meteorological science.

Bjerknes's first practical contributions were, however, in the field of radio science. He wrote several important articles on electromagnetic wave resonance during and shortly after his time in Bonn, Germany, where he served Hertz as research assistant from 1890 to 1892. On returning to Norway, he completed a doctoral thesis on electrodynamics and began to work on a field of great interest to his father—hydrodynamics. Bjerknes developed two famous circulation theorems for fluids of varying densities in the late 1890's, during his studies of barotropy and vorticity based on earlier work by Hermann von Helmholtz and Lord Kelvin. As a professor of physics at Stockholm (first at the Högskola in 1893, then at the university in 1895-1907), he continued to develop these ideas, including the proposition, independently discovered by another scientist, that movements in the atmosphere are stimulated by heat from the sun while at the same time these motions radiate heat as the result of friction of air masses rubbing against one another. The novelty of Bjerknes's theorems was that they went beyond the immediate description of the physics of circulation, accounting as well for the formation and decay of circulations such as vortices within fluids and—by analogy—within the atmosphere. His notions captured the attention of the Carnegie Foundation during a sojourn in the United States in 1905, and he would receive considerable research support from the foundation for the next several decades.

Bjerknes's theoretical work on hydrodynamics and the application of its principles to meteorology continued after his return to teach at the University of Christiania in 1905, leading to the publication of the two-volume *Dynamic Meteorology and Hydrography* (1910-1911) in collaboration with Johan Wilhelm Sandström and others. In 1912, Bjerknes accepted a chair at the University of Leipzig and took over direction of the newly founded Geophysical Institute. Physical privations caused by World War I, the conscription of most German research assistants, and Nansen's efforts to secure a new position for Bjerknes were developments that finally convinced the aging scientist to return to his own country and pursue his research in Bergen. The stormy Norwegian coast proved an excellent meteorological laboratory, and Bjerknes was spurred on by the need for improved weather prediction for agriculture and the fishing industry in the light of the wartime restriction of imports and communications. It was here that the idea of the weather front emerged.

Beginning in 1919, in a time when studies of the upper atmosphere were limited by the primitive state of aeronautics and the lack of such things as radar images, Bjerknes was able to conceive, on the basis of information collected at hundreds of weather stations in Norway and on the Continent, a comprehensive scheme of atmospheric processes. Assisted by his son Jacob and others, Bjerknes showed once and for all that the atmosphere was no homogeneous or continuous system as such but should be viewed as a composition of distinct masses of air, converging here and there to produce various meteorological effects, depending on conditions. Along with his several collaborators, he proposed the now-familiar idea of perpetual polar fronts, which was soon empirically confirmed. Bjerknes's efforts at a synoptic meteorology, represented in the classic paper *On the Dynamics of the Circular Vortex with Applications to the Atmosphere and Atmospheric Vortex and Wave Motion* (1921), made much use of concepts from electrodynamics as well, describing the genesis of cyclones in terms of wave motion and amplitude disturbances within atmospheric layers of varying density.

Bjerknes spent nine years analyzing data, drawing maps, and synthesizing information into a comprehensive picture of weather dynamics. In 1926, he accepted an extraordinary professorship in mechanics and mathematical physics at the University of Oslo, formerly Christiania, and immersed himself in his lectures and colloquia. While he did publish a book on kinematics and the relatively new field of vector analysis in 1929, his other effort—a theoretical development of his father's ideas on hydrodynamics—did not bear fruit.

SIGNIFICANCE

Bjerknes's lasting achievement lies in establishing modern meteorology as a dependable forecasting tool with a sophisticated theoretical apparatus. While much of his scientific career was devoted to enlarging on his father's already outdated ideas on electrodynamics, he nevertheless managed, through tireless empirical investigation as well as the highly creative manipulation of known concepts, to put dynamic meteorology and physical ocean-ography on firm scientific footing. In this lengthy effort he had the help of many assistants and collaborators and was admired and respected as a collegial leader and an excellent lecturer.

In fact, his cultural sensitivity formed a large part of his scientific motivation, particularly for his later work in weather mapping and prediction. When he left Leipzig during World War I, he returned to Norway to assist his neutral and isolated homeland in surviving the privations of war. His so-called Bergen school of meteorology soon established a comprehensive system of practical weather forecasting in collaboration with Norwegian agriculture and the supremely important national fishing industry. He was no nationalist as such, however, but a cosmopolitan thinker. He envisioned the rise of civil aviation, such as transatlantic flight, and its coming dependence on meteorology. He also insisted on the expansion of the radio communications network for the exchange of meteorological information.

Bjerknes's greatest strides in geophysics began with the formulation of his circulation theorems in 1897, which provided a physicomathematical description of the behavior of real fluids and, by extension, atmospheric phenomena. The vortex was the central dynamic form of his system. Much of his work in the intervening years involved exhaustive empirical description of the state of the atmosphere, calculating humidity, pressure, density, velocity, and temperature. Applying the concept of the wave as well as lines of force from electrodynamics, he developed a global model in which cyclones emerged and traveled a wavelike path along the surface of discontinuity formed by warm and cold fronts. Data amassed by the Bergen school suggested that polar air masses form permanent fronts in conflict with equatorial air masses. The atmospheric struggle conceived and described by Bjerknes and his coworkers forms the basis of all modern meteorology.

—Mark R. McCulloh

FURTHER READING

Devik, Olaf, Carl Ludvig Godske, and Tor Bergeron. "Vilhelm Bjerknes: March 14, 1862-April 9, 1951." *Geofysiske Publikationer* 24 (Spring, 1962): 6-25. A biographical sketch combined with an examination of Bjerknes's contributions, written by colleagues who knew him well. The first article, by Devik, treats Bjerknes's relationship with his father at length, while Bergeron's essays on the Stockholm period and the Bergen school provide a good overview of Bjerknes's most productive period.

Friedman, Robert Marc. "Constituting the Polar Front, 1919-1920." *Isis* 73 (Fall, 1982): 343-362. A thorough bibliography is contained in the footnotes that accompany Friedman's historical essay on a central concept in Bjerknes's dynamic meteorology. The author takes the deconstructionist standpoint that Bjerknes and his followers were motivated largely by a desire for authority within their field.

Harper, Kristine C. *Weather and Climate: Decade by Decade*. New York: Facts On File, 2007. This chronological overview of developments in the field of meteorology includes a separate section about Bjerknes's work in the first decade of the twentieth century, "Meteorologist of the Decade: Vilhelm Bjerknes (1862-1951)."

Jewell, Ralph. "The Meteorological Judgment of Vilhelm Bjerknes." *Social Research* 51 (Autumn, 1984): 783-807. This article traces the evolution of Bjerknes's preoccupation with reforming meteorology. An excellent discussion of his ideas and portrayal of the

physicist in his pursuit of scientific advancement and the common good. The author discusses Bjerknes's connections with the Carnegie Institution of Washington in some detail.

Süsskind, Charles. "Hertz and the Technological Significance of Electromagnetic Waves." *Isis* 56 (Fall, 1965): 342-345. This article gives a brief description of Hertz's thinking on the technical possibilities for wireless telegraphy and telephony during the period when Bjerknes was his assistant.

SEE ALSO: Rudolf Geiger; Fridtjof Nansen; Alfred Wegener; Sir George Hubert Wilkins.

RELATED ARTICLES in *Great Events from History: The Twentieth Century:*

1901-1940: 1919-1921: Bjerknes Discovers Fronts in Atmospheric Circulation.

1941-1970: April, 1950: Meteorologists Make the First Computerized Weather Prediction.

HUGO L. BLACK
Associate justice of the United States (1937-1971)

As a U.S. Supreme Court associate justice, Black sought to define and in some areas extend constitutional protection of civil liberties, while delineating the prerogatives of government; for more than one-third of a century, he propounded the absolute inviolability of the Constitution as the basis of the nation's jurisprudence.

BORN: February 27, 1886; Harlan, Alabama
DIED: September 25, 1971; Bethesda, Maryland
ALSO KNOWN AS: Hugo LaFayette Black (full name)
AREAS OF ACHIEVEMENT: Law, civil rights, political science

EARLY LIFE
Hugo L. Black was the youngest of eight children. His father, William L. Black, was a country storekeeper who surrendered periodically to bouts of secret drinking; his mother, Martha Toland Black, from a well-bred family, was the village postmistress. From the age of six, the young Hugo attended trials at the Clay County courthouse in Ashland. He was educated for a while at Ashland Academy. He attended Birmingham Medical College for one year and, at the age of eighteen, enrolled

at the University of Alabama. By virtue of his excellent academic record, Black was granted early admission to the law school and was graduated with the university's LL.B. degree in 1906.

Black began his practice in Birmingham, where he pleaded labor cases and damage suits. He served briefly as a judge on the city's police court; in 1914, he was elected the county solicitor, or prosecutor. Increasingly, he came to oppose, and sometimes took action against, the summary and forcible extraction of confessions from suspects. During World War I, Black enlisted in the Army and, although he was not called for combat duty, he was discharged as a captain in the field artillery. On his return to civilian life, he resumed his law practice in Alabama; in 1921, he married Josephine Foster, the daughter of a Presbyterian minister, whose lovely dark features had attracted him. During the next twelve years, they became the parents of two sons and one daughter.

Black gave the impression of formidable tenacity and reserve. He was five feet, eight inches tall and wiry; his features were distinguished by his sharp, hooked nose and piercing blue eyes. He spoke in a gentle, melodious drawl that could be sharpened by interrogatory tones or softened with personal warmth. He had a brisk, energetic gait and, for recreation, played a vigorous game of tennis.

LIFE'S WORK

While in private practice, Black occasionally had taken cases of white clients against blacks; as his political ambitions grew, he joined a number of civic organizations. In 1923, he made a decision that later seemed fraught with fateful implications: He became a member of the Ku Klux Klan. It may have been that for a time he was attracted by the Klan's populist appeal, or that he recognized its political strength; he spoke to several meetings of the Klan and then, less than two years later, withdrew abruptly and unceremoniously. Black first emerged into national political prominence in 1926, with a spirited campaign that won for him a seat in the United States Senate. During the early years of the Depression, Black sponsored legislation to promote public works programs and called for a national thirty-hour workweek. In 1932, he won reelection on a platform of broad support for the national Democratic Party and its presidential candidate, Franklin D. Roosevelt. Although he would not risk public disfavor on issues on which his home state was sensitive, such as a proposed antilynching law or the sensa-

Hugo L. Black. (Library of Congress)

tional Scottsboro rape cases, Black became nationally known as the chair of major Senate investigations of public utilities and airmail contracts. Moreover, though he differed with the Roosevelt administration on some economic proposals, he roundly condemned the Supreme Court's rulings against New Deal legislation. Black became an early and staunch proponent of the administration's proposal that would allow the president to appoint additional justices to sit alongside those on the Court who had passed the age of seventy. Much as this measure divided even the Democratic Party, Black's standing in the Senate, and his broad agreement with the administration on economic and judicial matters, were vital considerations when Roosevelt nominated him, in 1937, to succeed retiring Supreme Court Justice Willis Van Devanter. While Black was confirmed easily enough the same year, questions about his Klan affiliation persisted and grew. In response to allegations in newspaper stories, the new justice delivered a brief and compelling statement, which reached millions of radio listeners, disavowing any connection with that organization since his resignation twelve years before.

Expectations that Black would be intellectually unsuited for the Court, or that he would act merely at the administration's behest, were gradually shown to be unfounded. In spite of an education that was limited and exiguous when compared with those of other justices, Black was a fervent autodidact, and even during his years in Washington he had read widely in constitutional law; philosophy; American, British, and ancient history; and the social sciences. During his early years on the Court, Black evinced a basic support for the government on questions of antitrust and held with the administration on controversial economic issues. Questions of civil liberties were enlivened when he wrote the Court's opinion in *Chambers v. Florida* (1940), which invalidated a criminal confession obtained during incommunicado confinement. In *Betts v. Brady* (1942), writing for himself and two colleagues, he contended that indigent defendants should not be convicted without the benefit of counsel. On the other hand, in *Korematsu v. United States* (1944), he held for the Court that wartime circumstances justified the forcible resettlement of Japanese Americans.

Black frequently found with a minority in cases that heralded the onset of the Cold War. In several notable dissents he maintained that communists and other radicals were entitled to the constitutional protection of free speech. In *Dennis v. United States* (1951), he argued in dissent that mere speech, albeit of an admitted communist, could not be proscribed as inciteful or tending to overthrow the government. Elsewhere, Black opposed loyalty oaths or other limitations on the civil liberties of avowed communists. In another celebrated dissent, *Beauharnais v. Illinois* (1952), he contended that the states could not abridge the freedom of speech by attempting to suppress white supremacist literature. On another front, in 1952, Black wrote the Court's opinion in ruling against President Harry S. Truman's use of government force to curtail strikes in the steel industry. Trying times on the bench were made more difficult by the early and unexpected death of Black's wife in 1951. His outlook undoubtedly improved with his remarriage, to Elizabeth De Meritte, six years later.

After Earl Warren became chief justice, in 1953, the Court as a whole took a more expansive view of the civil liberties that Black had defended; other troubling issues also came before it. Justice Black held with the Court in *Brown v. Board of Education* (1954), the landmark decision that struck down racial segregation in public schools. Black's own concern for freedom of expression was further stated in *Konigsberg v. State Bar of California* (1957), in which he held for the majority that political affiliations, such as possible membership in the Communist Party, did not constitute grounds for an applicant's exclusion from the practice of law. Black's objections to other limitations on the freedom of speech were reflected in his opinions in cases of alleged obscenity, such as a New York case of 1959, involving the film version of D. H. Lawrence's novel *Lady Chatterley's Lover* (1928). Black believed that the First Amendment afforded extensive protection against claims of libel, and he found with the majority in the celebrated case of *The New York Times Co. v. Sullivan* (1964); he also did not consider massive adverse publicity grounds for retrial in criminal cases, and thus he dissented when such a case, involving Dr. Sam Sheppard of Ohio, was brought before the Court in 1966.

Black was often regarded as a moving spirit in many of the Court's libertarian decisions, and, to nearly the same extent as Chief Justice Warren, his guidance was provided in controversial decisions. Black wrote for a majority on the Court when he found the sponsorship of

---

IN DEFENSE OF THE FIRST AMENDMENT

In the case of The New York Times Co. v. United States *(1971), Justice Hugo L. Black wrote an opinion expressing his absolutist view of the First Amendment in a case involving the famous Pentagon Papers.*

I adhere to the view that the Government's case against the *Washington Post* should have been dismissed and that the injunction against the *New York Times* should have been vacated without oral argument when the cases were first presented to this Court. I believe that every moment's continuance of the injunctions against these newspapers amounts to a flagrant, indefensible, and continuing violation of the First Amendment. . . . In my view it is unfortunate that some of my Brethren are apparently willing to hold that the publication of news may sometimes be enjoined. Such a holding would make a shambles of the First Amendment. . . .

In the First Amendment the Founding Fathers gave the free press the protection it must have to fulfill its essential role in our democracy. The press was to serve the governed, not the governors. The Government's power to censor the press was abolished so that the press would remain forever free to censure the Government. The press was protected so that it could bare the secrets of government and inform the people. Only a free and unrestrained press can effectively expose deception in government. And paramount among the responsibilities of a free press is the duty to prevent any part of the government from deceiving the people and sending them off to distant lands to die of foreign fevers and foreign shot and shell. In my view, far from deserving condemnation for their courageous reporting, the *New York Times*, the *Washington Post*, and other newspapers should be commended for serving the purpose that the Founding Fathers saw so clearly. In revealing the workings of government that led to the Vietnam war, the newspapers nobly did precisely that which the Founders hoped and trusted they would do. . . .

To find that the President has "inherent power" to halt the publication of news by resort to the courts would wipe out the First Amendment and destroy the fundamental liberty and security of the very people the Government hopes to make "secure." No one can read the history of the adoption of the First Amendment without being convinced beyond any doubt that it was injunctions like those sought here that Madison and his collaborators intended to outlaw in this Nation for all time.

---

prayer in public schools unconstitutional, in *Engel v. Vitale* (1962); in a matter of recurrent concern to him, the right of poor defendants to legal representation, he wrote the Court's opinion in *Gideon v. Wainwright* (1963). Nevertheless, though there and elsewhere Black upheld the rights of criminal defendants, he dissociated himself from other decisions thought to be part of a liberal trend on the Court. He did not believe that public demonstrations or sit-ins, whether to promote racial equality or for other purposes, were speech in the strict sense, and thus he differed from his colleagues in holding that they were not protected by the Constitution. In *Griswold v. Connecticut* (1965), he dissented from the Court's view that a right of privacy extended to married couples using contraceptives. Claims of increasing conservatism, or discomfiture with modern times, were bruited about, but Black persistently maintained that his constitutional faith was unchanged. His last official act on the Court was a separate opinion in the *New York Times v. United States*—or Pentagon Papers—case of 1971, in which he contended that the public had a right to know about the origins of a controversial war; the First Amendment precluded any exercise of prior restraint on the part of the government. For some time failing health had taken its toll, and at the age of eighty-five, Black suffered a sharp decline. On August 27, 1971, he was admitted to Bethesda Naval Hospital; on September 17, his resignation from the Court was formally tendered; and on the next day, he suffered a stroke, from which he died on September 25, 1971.

SIGNIFICANCE

Black served under five chief justices; during his tenure on the bench, vital questions of the New Deal, the Cold War, and the Civil Rights movement came before the Court. Throughout this period, Black formulated and repeatedly maintained his adherence to a specific and distinct view of constitutional law. In his many opinions, presented for the most part in a clear, direct, unvarnished style, Black held that a literal reading of the Constitution bound the nation's highest court to uphold civil liberties even, as arose with claims of libel and obscenity, in unusual and improbable contexts. On the other hand, Black increasingly objected to any legislative function on the part of the Court and rejected any implied doctrines that were not clearly stated in the Constitution itself. From this standpoint, it is useful to note Black's long-standing debate with Justice Felix Frankfurter, who referred to other criteria, such as the balancing of rights and obligations, or the nation's conscience, in deciding difficult cases. Black's libertarian strain led him often to side with Justices Frank Murphy and, particularly, William O. Douglas; yet he maintained that beyond those rights clearly granted in the Constitution there were limitations, and toward the end of his term Black found the views of Chief Justice Warren E. Burger congenial.

It is a measure of Black's importance in American jurisprudence that, though many of the cases and concerns with which he dealt have receded from public attention,

the views he espoused still command respect. There will continue to be some dispute as to whether the resolution of modern dilemmas actually is implicitly stated in the Constitution. Some of Black's opinions decidedly would find more present-day adherents than others, yet his simple but forthright reading of the Constitution must still be reckoned an important force in modern legal thought.

—J. R. Broadus

FURTHER READING

Ball, Howard. *The Vision and the Dream of Justice Hugo L. Black: An Examination of a Judicial Philosophy.* Tuscaloosa: University of Alabama Press, 1975. Topical examination of Black's opinions by an admiring scholar; social relations and the economy are dealt with as well as the justice's better-known positions on civil liberties. Argues that there is a broad consistency to Black's opinions, both in various areas of the law and over the thirty-four years he was on the Court.

Black, Hugo. *A Constitutional Faith.* New York: Alfred A. Knopf, 1969. Succinct statement of Black's judicial philosophy, taken from lectures at Columbia University. His views on the states' obligations under the Bill of Rights and the Fourteenth Amendment, as well as his determination to uphold the First Amendment in applicable cases, are set forth in a clear, trenchant fashion.

Black, Hugo, Jr. *My Father: A Remembrance.* New York: Random House, 1975. Breezy, offhand account of Justice Black's life by his son. The most useful parts of this work concern the elder Black's personal and professional relations with others on the Court, notably Felix Frankfurter and William O. Douglas. The younger Black also depicts vividly the hostility and bitterness with which the Court's decisions on racial issues were received in his father's native state.

Black, Hugo L., and Elizabeth S. Black. *Mr. Justice and Mrs. Black.* New York: Random House, 1986. This book comprises Black's fragmentary memoirs, which discuss his life and career until 1921, an interstitial explanatory passage, and the diaries of Elizabeth Black from 1964 until Hugo's death in 1971. Elizabeth Black's remarks show much about the justice's vitality and commitment to his work on the Court; personal asides indicate his devotion as husband. There is also a touching portrayal of his final illness and last months.

Dunne, Gerald T. *Hugo Black and the Judicial Revolution.* New York: Simon & Schuster, 1977. Thorough and panoramic biography that strikes a judicious balance between the legal and the personal elements in Black's career on the Court. The political and historical context of his most notable opinions is set forth; relations with other justices reveal the extent to which Black shaped, or was affected by, the Court's positions on controversial issues.

Frank, John P. *Inside Justice Hugo L. Black: The Letters.* Austin: Jamail Center for Legal Research, University of Texas, Austin, 2000. Frank, one of Black's former law clerks, provides this portrait of his former boss based on their twenty-five-year correspondence.

Hamilton, Virginia Van Der Veer. *Hugo Black: The Alabama Years.* Baton Rouge: Louisiana State University Press, 1972. Lively, colorful account that traces the offsetting influences of principle and expediency in Black's early legal work and political career. This work provides the most substantial examination of his brief membership in the Ku Klux Klan and provides extensive coverage of his service in the U.S. Senate. Collections of documents and newspapers that are important for the history of Alabama have been used to advantage here.

Magee, James J. *Mr. Justice Black: Absolutist on the Court.* Charlottesville: University Press of Virginia, 1980. A critical assessment of Black's opinions, notably his interpretation of the Bill of Rights, and particularly the First Amendment. This study points out the difficulties of settling intricate modern cases by a literal construction of the Constitution; nevertheless, Black's efforts in this direction have enriched the nation's legal culture.

Strickland, Stephen Parks, ed. *Hugo Black and the Supreme Court: A Symposium.* Indianapolis, Ind.: Bobbs-Merrill, 1967. Studies by nine legal scholars, examining Black's positions on civil liberties, the New Deal, federal taxation, antitrust, and federal civil procedures. The editor concludes that Black may not easily be characterized as liberal or conservative; his extraordinary contribution has been to demonstrate the vitality of the Constitution during the modern age.

Suitts, Steve. *Hugo Black of Alabama: How His Roots and Early Career Shaped the Great Champion of the Constitution.* Montgomery, Ala.: NewSouth Books, 2005. Recounts Black's life and career before he was elected to the U.S. Senate in 1927, focusing on the influences that shaped him. Includes discussion of the politics of his home state, his family, his experiences as a trial lawyer, and his membership in the Ku Klux Klan.

SEE ALSO: Harry A. Blackmun; Warren E. Burger; William O. Douglas; Felix Frankfurter; Franklin D. Roosevelt; Harlan Fiske Stone.

HARRY A. BLACKMUN
Associate justice of the United States (1970-1994)

Blackmun's nomination to the U.S. Supreme Court was almost an afterthought, President Nixon's third choice to fill a vacant seat on the Court. Initially believed to be an unadventurous conservative who could be counted on to vote with his friend, conservative chief justice Warren E. Burger. However, Blackmun came into his own with one of his earliest writings: the majority opinion in the landmark case Roe v. Wade *(1973). Blackmun went on to become a member of the liberal voting bloc that determined the outcome of some of the most important decisions handed down during his tenure on the Court.*

BORN: November 12, 1908; Nashville, Illinois
DIED: March 4, 1999; Arlington, Virginia
ALSO KNOWN AS: Harry Andrew Blackmun (full name)
AREA OF ACHIEVEMENT: Law

EARLY LIFE

Although he was born in Illinois, Harry A. Blackmun was always a Minnesotan. His mother and father, Theo Huegely Reuter Blackmun and Corwin Manning Blackmun, actually lived in St. Paul, but because Corwin traveled extensively for his wholesale produce business, Theo spent the latter part of her pregnancy with her parents in Illinois. Harry and his younger sister, Betty, born in 1917, grew up in a working-class neighborhood of St. Paul, where, in kindergarten, Harry met Warren E. Burger. Blackmun and Burger formed a lifelong friendship, one that would be sorely tested—and undermined—when Blackmun began serving on the Court headed by Burger.

In 1925, Blackmun graduated fourth in his high school class. Expecting to attend the University of Minnesota, he was surprised to win a scholarship to Harvard. Blackmun's undergraduate record as a mathematics major was good, and he gave some thought to a medical career. In 1929, however, he was admitted to Harvard Law School. Blackmun found law school difficult, and his academic performance there was just above average. After graduating in 1932 and passing the Minnesota bar exam, Blackmun began a clerkship with Judge John B. Sanborn of the U.S. Court of Appeals for the Eighth Circuit. Blackmun continued to live at home, helping to support his parents and his sister, even after accepting a position as an associate at the premier law firm June, Driscoll,

Fletcher, Dorsey & Barker in Minneapolis-St. Paul. He did not move out on his own until 1941, when he married Dorothy Clark, with whom he had three daughters: Nancy, born in 1943; Sally, born in 1947; and Susan, born in 1949.

LIFE'S WORK

While he was still in private practice, one of Blackmun's most important legal clients was the Mayo Clinic in Rochester, Minnesota. In 1949, he accepted a position as the clinic's first resident counsel, a job he held for the next nine years. Blackmun later counted this period the happiest of his professional life. He spent his time at the Mayo learning about medicine as well as managing the clinic's legal affairs, and this background would later play a critical role in his handling of the opinion in *Roe v. Wade* (1973).

Burger, long active in Republican politics, had left Minnesota in 1953 to join the administration of President Dwight D. Eisenhower. Once in Washington, he wasted no time trying to find a way for Blackmun to join him there. Blackmun resisted leaving Rochester until 1958, when his former mentor, Judge Sanborn, told him that he was planning to retire, thus leaving a vacant seat on the Eighth Circuit, a seat he would like to see Blackmun fill. Blackmun was agreeable, and in 1959 the campaign managed by Burger and Sanborn succeeded, as Blackmun was nominated to be a federal appellate judge. Confirmed unanimously by the U.S. Senate, Blackmun took his seat on the Eighth Circuit Court of Appeals on November 12, 1959.

Over the next decade, Blackmun would write 217 opinions for the Eighth Circuit. It was a time of enormous upheaval—both social and legal—in the United States. The Civil Rights movement, given impetus by the Supreme Court's momentous *Brown v. Board of Education* decision (1954) outlawing racial segregation, generated numerous cases for lower courts to decide. Blackmun wrote the opinion for one of the most significant of these, *Jones v. Alfred H. Mayer Co.* (1967), which presented the question of whether a property owner could refuse to sell to an African American. The plaintiff brought his case under the Civil Rights Act of 1866, claiming that this law prohibited discrimination both by the government and by private entities. Blackmun personally agreed with this argument, but he felt precedent favored the defendant, for which he decided. When writing the opinion of the circuit court, however, he left the door open for the Supreme Court to reverse this decision, and the following year it did so, ruling that the 1866 law, buttressed by the Fourteenth Amendment, did indeed encompass private discrimination.

If *Jones* affords some indirect insight into Blackmun's attitude toward individual rights, a 1967 case—*Pope v. United States*—concerning the death penalty and the Eighth Amendment's prohibition against cruel and unusual punishment provides stronger evidence of Blackmun's liberal sympathies. Like the six other Eighth Circuit judges who heard the *Pope* appeal, Blackmun voted to uphold the death sentence. Because there was at the time no Supreme Court ruling on the issue, Blackmun felt that capital punishment was a matter for legislatures, rather than courts, to decide. Assigned to write the opinion for a unanimous court, Blackmun took the opportunity in a final paragraph to voice his doubts about capital punishment. Always deferential, he invited his fellow judges to comment on what he had written—and they did. In the end, Blackmun deleted the passage, but he remained convinced of the rightness of his views and profoundly regretted having bowed to criticism.

In June, 1969, Burger succeeded Earl Warren as chief justice of the United States. Not long after, Burger began lobbying President Richard M. Nixon to nominate Blackmun to fill the Court vacancy that opened up when the disgraced Abe Fortas was forced to resign in May, 1969. As things turned out, however, Blackmun would, as he later humorously remarked, play the role of the "third man" in this drama of Court succession. Nixon's first two nominees to fill Fortas's seat, Clement Haynesworth, Jr., and Harrold Carswell, both conservative but controversial southerners, were rejected by the Senate. Blackmun, a midwesterner with a reputation as a conservative—and a close friend of the conservative chief justice—was considered a safe candidate, and on May 12, 1970, the Senate confirmed his nomination unanimously.

Initially, Burger and Blackmun were paired in the popular conscience as the so-called Minnesota twins. It was not long, however, before the two diverged politically, and the division eventually became personal. Burger did, however, vote with Blackmun to uphold a woman's right to abortion in *Roe*, and perhaps owing to Blackmun's special expertise in medical matters, assigned his friend to

write the majority opinion of the Court. Blackmun found this a daunting task, and his first draft, overturning the underlying Texas statute banning abortion on grounds of vagueness, was rejected. The case was re-argued before the Court, after which Blackmun reemerged with a second opinion that based its endorsement of abortion on a constitutional right to privacy.

As Blackmun's ties with Burger disintegrated, the associate justice joined Justices William J. Brennan and Thurgood Marshall to form a liberal voting bloc that frequently prevailed during the years of the Burger Court (1969-1986). Blackmun was also responsible for a trio of breakthrough cases—*Bigelow v. Virginia* (1975), *Virginia State Board of Pharmacy v. Virginia Citizens Consumer Council* (1976), and *Bates v. State Bar of Arizona* (1977)—that afforded First Amendment protection to so-called commercial speech connected with business and advertising. By the time his judicial career was nearing its end, Blackmun gave his personal doubts about capital punishment public voice, announcing in *Collins*

Harry A. Blackmun. (Library of Congress)

v. Collins (1994) that he had concluded that the death penalty was unconstitutional.

Blackmun retired from the Court on June 30, 1994. He died five years later, on March 4, 1999, from complications following a fall.

SIGNIFICANCE

Blackmun played the central role in *Roe v. Wade*, one of the most controversial Supreme Court decisions of the late twentieth century. The 1987 battle over President Ronald Reagan's conservative nominee—Robert Bork—to replace the retiring justice Lewis F. Powell was in many respects a battle over *Roe*. Subsequent Court appointments, as well as state and federal elections, have been colored by the continuing abortion debate. For his part, Blackmun always retained his reserved demeanor, but his judicial temperament evolved in a contrary direction to that of the Court as a whole. During the nearly quarter century he served on the Court, Blackmun became increasingly outspoken about his concern that the nation's highest tribunal was drifting too far to the right politically.

—Lisa Paddock

FURTHER READING

Greenhouse, Linda. *Becoming Justice Blackmun: Harry Blackmun's Supreme Court Journey*. New York: Times Books/Henry Holt, 2005. Greenhouse was the first print reporter to have access to Blackmun's archive, which she used to create an insider's view of Blackmun, his complex relationship with Warren Burger, and his attitude toward the other members of the modern-day Supreme Court.

Schwartz, Bernard. "Watershed Cases: *Roe v. Wade*, 1973." In *A History of the Supreme Court*. New York: Oxford University Press, 1993. This excellent history of the Court gives an in-depth account of the deliberations that went into deciding *Roe* and looks at Blackmun's struggle to craft the majority opinion in the landmark case.

Yarbrough, Tinsley. *The Burger Court: Justices, Rulings, and Legacy*. Santa Barbara, Calif.: ABC-CLIO, 2000. Aimed at general readers, this book includes essays on the justices, major decisions, and legacy of the Burger Court. It also features a number of reference materials, including a chronology and table of cases.

_____. *Harry A. Blackmun: The Outsider Justice*. New York: Oxford University Press, 2007. Supreme Court historian Yarbrough employs details of the justice's biography to connect Blackmun's "outsider" status with his lifelong empathy for vulnerable members of society, such as women facing unwanted pregnancies and death row inmates whose lives have been changed because of Blackmun's judicial pronouncements.

SEE ALSO: Hugo L. Black; William J. Brennan; Stephen G. Breyer; Warren E. Burger; William O. Douglas; Thurgood Marshall; Richard Nixon; Sandra Day O'Connor; Lewis F. Powell; William H. Rehnquist; Earl Warren.

RELATED ARTICLES in *Great Events from History: The Twentieth Century:*

1941-1970: January 16, 1970: Flood Tests Baseball's Reserve Clause.

1971-2000: January 22, 1973: U.S. Supreme Court Expands Women's Reproductive Rights; June 12, 1984: U.S. Supreme Court Upholds Seniority Systems; April 22, 1987: U.S. Supreme Court Upholds the Constitutionality of Capital Punishment; June 29, 1992: U.S. Supreme Court Restricts Abortion Rights.

TONY BLAIR
Prime minister of the United Kingdom (1997-2007)

Blair revitalized the British economy and emerged as a major international figure. His policies and charisma strengthened Great Britain's position in global affairs, yet during his last years in office, he encountered mounting criticism at home for continuing to support the U.S.-led wars in Iraq and Afghanistan.

BORN: May 6, 1953; Edinburgh, Scotland
ALSO KNOWN AS: Anthony Charles Lynton Blair (full name)
AREAS OF ACHIEVEMENT: Diplomacy, government and politics

EARLY LIFE

Tony Blair was born in Edinburgh, Scotland, the son of Leo Charles Lynton Blair, a lawyer and academic, and Hazel Corscadden Blair. He has one brother, William James Lynton Blair, and one sister, Sarah Blair. Blair's childhood in Scotland was interrupted by a three-year stay in Adelaide, Australia, where his father served as a lecturer in law at the University of Adelaide. Before Blair entered school, his family returned to Scotland, and upon his father's appointment to the faculty of Durham University, the Blairs settled in Durham.

Blair attended the Durham Chorister School and then matriculated at Fettes College, Edinburgh. At Fettes, he emerged as a very popular, ambitious, but difficult student. After a year out of school—during which he spent much time with producers of rock music—he entered St. John's College, Oxford, where he joined the Labour Party in 1975. Upon graduation in 1976, he went on to Lincoln's Inn in London as a student barrister. It was there that Blair met Cherie Booth, also a student of law. They were married on March 29, 1980, and had four children: Euan, Nicky, Kathryn, and Leo. Blair was influenced greatly by his wife's Roman Catholic faith.

LIFE'S WORK

Between 1980 and 1983, Blair worked diligently to gain support from the leadership of the Labour Party for a seat in the House of Commons. Clearly identifying himself as a socialist, he was unsuccessful in his attempt to win the Beaconsfield seat. However, he did gain the attention of Michael Foot, the Labour leader. In 1983, Blair was elected to the Commons from Sedgefield on a traditional Labour platform—unilateral disarmament, socialist domestic policies, and withdrawal from the European Economic Community (Common Market). In his first Commons speech (July 6, 1983), Blair focused on the rationalism and morality on which socialism was founded.

During the next eleven years, Blair witnessed repeated electoral defeats for Labour and developed the conceptual base for what was called New Labour. Still focused on reason and morality, Blair wanted to transform the image of the Labour Party and its historic dependence on labor unions. Within five years Blair's mounting influence resulted in his appointment to the shadow cabinet as shadow secretary of state for energy; in 1989 he was named shadow secretary of state for employment. In that capacity, Blair aligned himself with the European movement in support of open shops for employment; many union leaders denounced him, but he was supported by party leadership.

During the tenures of Neil Kinnock and John Smith, Blair continued to transform the image of his party and temper its more radical, traditional policies. While he developed a get-tough policy on crime and its causes, he

Tony Blair. (AP/Wide World Photos)

THE BLAIR DOCTRINE

On April 22, 1999, during the war in Kosovo, British prime minister Tony Blair delivered an address to the Chicago Economic Club. Blair proposed what would later be termed the Blair Doctrine—the need for an international community of nations pursuing common goals.

We live in a world where isolationism has ceased to have a reason to exist. By necessity we have to cooperate with each other across nations.

Many of our domestic problems are caused on the other side of the world. Financial instability in Asia destroys jobs in Chicago and in my own constituency in County Durham. Poverty in the Caribbean means more drugs on the streets in Washington and London. Conflict in the Balkans causes more refugees in Germany and here in the U.S. These problems can only be addressed by international cooperation.

We are all internationalists now, whether we like it or not. We cannot refuse to participate in global markets if we want to prosper. We cannot ignore new political ideas in other counties if we want to innovate. We cannot turn our backs on conflicts and the violation of human rights within other countries if we want still to be secure. . . .

We are witnessing the beginnings of a new doctrine of international community. By this I mean the explicit recognition that today more than ever before we are mutually dependent, that national interest is to a significant extent governed by international collaboration and that we need a clear and coherent debate as to the direction this doctrine takes us in each field of international endeavor. Just as within domestic politics, the notion of community—the belief that partnership and cooperation are essential to advance self-interest—is coming into its own; so it needs to find its own international echo. Global financial markets, the global environment, global security and disarmament issues: none of these can be solved without intense international cooperation.

---

also opposed capital punishment, proposed decriminalization of same-gender sexual acts (homosexuality), and advocated for improvement in the conditions of British prisons.

In 1994, Smith died from heart failure, leaving the Labour Party without leadership. Three candidates vied for the position: Margaret Beckett, John Prescott, and Blair. Blair prevailed and immediately launched a campaign to complete the transformation of his party into New Labour and to position himself nationally as an acceptable alternative to the Conservative prime minister, John Major. Blair abandoned his party's long-standing commitment to nationalization and common ownership, and he focused on a campaign that called for a revolution in education.

In the general elections of May 1, 1997, the Labour Party scored an overwhelming victory over the Conservatives. Blair became prime minister the following day,

and Prescott was appointed his deputy. Through his political acumen, intelligence, wit, and rhetorical skills, Blair achieved victory in two additional general elections and advanced formidable domestic and foreign policy agendas. Domestically, the major issues that confronted Blair's government were education, the state of the economy, Northern Ireland, responding to Scottish and Welsh demands for more authority over local affairs, and crime. Education had been the central theme in Blair's role of opposition leader from 1994 to 1997.

Upon gaining office, Blair's government developed a multiyear approach to the reform of education, from preschool through university. Taxes were raised to support investment in preschool and elementary education, new performance standards were imposed at all levels, and tuition was introduced and increased at Oxford and Cambridge as well as the other universities in Great Britain. The nation embraced Blair's economic agenda, which was focused on new priorities—transportation and capital investments—while striving for a balanced budget.

One major economic challenge that emerged was the collapse of private pension plans and the need for government intervention to provide support for the affected pensioners. In 1998, Blair's government succeeded in bringing about peace in Northern Ireland through direct negotiations with the Irish Republican Army (IRA). The Good Friday Agreement (April 10) ended overt violence in Northern Ireland and brought Catholics and Protestants to the discussion table. In 2007, those who supported the status quo for Northern Ireland as well as those who desired its unification with the Republic of Ireland (officially named Ireland) agreed to serve in the same local Northern Irish assembly. Scotland and Wales developed their own elected assemblies to manage their local affairs; some feared that this would lead to the dismemberment of the United Kingdom.

Blair's government developed extensive public-area video surveillance to minimize crime. In foreign affairs, his support of the war on terror—led by the United States and started after September 11, 2001—and the subsequent wars in Iraq and Afghanistan, was criticized from the outset; the prolonged struggle in Iraq had undermined public support for Blair, leading him to resign as Labour Party leader on June 24, 2007, and as prime minister. His final day in office was June 27, 2007.

SIGNIFICANCE

As prime minister, Blair refocused the Labour Party and brought it into alignment with the new political realities of the day. His domestic priorities included reform in education and health care, as well as full employment. The country's newfound prosperity not only sustained Blair as prime minister for a decade but also improved the standard of living of most British citizens and the position of Britain in world trade.

Also of great significance for Britain under Blair's leadership was the settlement in Northern Ireland and the constitutional evolution of the United Kingdom; Scotland and Wales gained a considerable degree of autonomy with the establishment of their own assemblies. Blair was commended for his call for international cooperation in addressing climate change, for his support for reducing or eliminating debt in African states, and for his significant expansion of aid to combat HIV/AIDS in Africa and elsewhere. He also supported the involvement of North Atlantic Treaty Organization nations in Kosovo and in the U.S.-led wars on terror in Afghanistan and Iraq.

—William T. Walker

FURTHER READING

Blair, Tony. *New Britain: My Vision of a Young Country.* Boulder, Colo.: Westview Press, 2005. Personal insights into Blair's vision of British society, its needs and strengths, and Britain's place in the world in the twenty-first century.

Colebatch, Hal. *Blair's Britain: British Culture Wars and New Labour.* London: Claridge Press, 1999. A thoughtful and provocative study of Blair's transformation of the Labour Party and the party's impact on British economic and social life.

Coughlin, Con. *American Ally: Tony Blair and the War on Terror.* New York: Ecco Press, 2006. A sympathetic treatment of Blair's support of the post-September 11 policies and actions of the United States, including the wars in Afghanistan and Iraq.

Foley, Michael. *The British Presidency: Tony Blair and the Politics of Public Leadership.* New York: Manchester University Press, 2000. A scholarly study of Blair's philosophy of government and his use of power as prime minister.

Rentoul, John. *Tony Blair: Prime Minister.* New York: Warner Books, 2002. A biographical study of Blair intended for general readers. Generally reliable and based in part on interviews with many of Blair's associates.

Riddell, Peter. *The Unfilled Prime Minister: Tony Blair's Quest for a Legacy.* London: Politico's, 2005. A very insightful and penetrating study of Blair's vision of self and government, focused on the impact of his personal imprint on British life.

Seldon, Anthony. *The Blair Effect.* New York: Little, Brown, 2001. A critical but generally sympathetic examination of the initial three years of Blair's ministry.

Stephens, Philip. *Tony Blair: The Making of a World Leader.* New York: Viking Press, 2004. A sympathetic and readable account of Blair's life and his rapid rise to power.

Temple, Michael. *Blair.* London: Haus, 2006. A readable evaluation of Blair's role as prime minister, including his successes and failures.

Williams, Michael. *Crisis and Consensus in British Politics: From Bagehot to Blair.* New York: St. Martin's Press, 2000. Places Blair within the context of nineteenth and twentieth century British leadership. Includes commentary on both domestic and international crises.

SEE ALSO: Osama Bin Laden; Bill Clinton; Saddam Hussein; John Major; Margaret Thatcher; Sir Harold Wilson.

RELATED ARTICLES in *Great Events from History: The Twentieth Century:*

1971-2000: May 1, 1997: Labor Party Wins Majority in British National Elections; May 27, 1997: NATO and Russia Sign Cooperation Pact; August 31, 1997: Princess Diana Dies in a Car Crash; April 10, 1998: Good Friday Agreement; August 15, 1998: Omagh Car Bombing.

LOUIS BLÉRIOT
French aviator

Blériot completed the first overseas flight in a heavier-than-air craft in 1909 and later became a pioneer in the fledgling aeronautics industry. He played a critical role in the French war effort during World War I and the subsequent establishment of commercial aviation.

BORN: July 1, 1872; Cambrai, France
DIED: August 2, 1936; Paris, France
AREAS OF ACHIEVEMENT: Aviation and space exploration, business and industry

EARLY LIFE

The childhood years of Louis Blériot (lwee blay-ree-oh) and the infancy of aviation go together. In other times, Blériot, the son of a local merchant in Cambrai, might have contented himself with a business career. He supplemented a basic education in the French system with a deep practical intuition that earned for him quick success in the business world. By the time Blériot was thirty, he had amassed a modest fortune in manufacturing as a leading producer of headlights and other accessories for the rapidly growing automobile industry. Blériot's first love, however, was always aviation, and once independently wealthy he developed what started as a hobby into a lifelong avocation.

Many governments were slow to realize the possibilities of military and civil aviation; not so the French. Almost from the moment that Wilbur and Orville Wright successfully flew a heavier-than-air craft at Kitty Hawk in December, 1903, French military officers in the diplomatic corps, as well as journalists and amateur aviators, inundated the country with information. Shortly after their epochal achievement, the Wright brothers themselves went to France to demonstrate their technology to an enthralled government and public.

Blériot was among many Europeans for whom Kitty Hawk seized the imagination. As early as 1899, he had experimented with flying machines, including an ungainly—and unsuccessful—device called an ornithopter, which tried to mimic the flapping wings of birds. He corresponded actively with the Wrights and other experimenters.

Blériot's earliest successful flight tests in 1907 were with gliders towed by power boats on the Seine River, near Paris. Their design immediately revealed Blériot's pragmatism and imagination. The gliders imitated the biplane and forward elevator configuration used by the

Wrights but also kept the box-kite-like tail assembly preferred in Europe. The result was an aircraft as maneuverable as the early Wright machines but much more stable. Blériot also exhibited an early preference for aircraft launched from water rather than land, a penchant followed by many other European aviation pioneers.

Blériot's first original aircraft design was a leap into the unknown: a monoplane equipped with large forward wings, an enclosed fuselage, and a tail assembly with rudder, elevators, and ailerons. This formula would become fundamental to virtually all aircraft designs in the twentieth century. It was, however, somewhat ahead of the times. Blériot's monoplane crashed on its fifth test hop. Nevertheless, despite widespread criticism of his radical designs, Blériot persisted. Among the few who encouraged such daring were Gabriel and Charles Voisin, generally recognized as the leading authorities on aviation in France at the time.

LIFE'S WORK

Blériot acquired worldwide fame in 1908 and 1909, when he recorded a pair of spectacular breakthroughs. In the early years of flight, philanthropists and newspaper publishers prodded aviators with trophy cups and cash prizes for specific achievements. On October 31, 1908, Blériot captured a prize of five hundred pounds sterling for the first successful round-trip flight, with landings, between two prearranged points—the French towns of Toury and Artenay—which were a bare fourteen kilometers apart.

In 1909, the London *Daily Mail* offered a prize of one thousand pounds for the first person to pilot a heavier-than-air craft across the English Channel; in other words, to complete the first—and about the shortest possible—overseas flight across open water. Several aviators already had tried the Channel and failed, but Alfred Harmsworth, the visionary patron of the *Daily Mail*'s prize offer, wanted to convince colleagues in the British government that aircraft would soon change the character of European geopolitics.

Blériot made his Channel crossing on July 28, 1909, in Monoplane 11, which he designed and built himself. It was a spidery craft with an engine that produced barely twenty-five horsepower. Taking off from a field outside Calais, Blériot landed in England, near Dover, after about a thirty-minute flight. His aircraft flew a modest eighty meters or so above the water and averaged just over 70 kilometers (43.5 miles) per hour. Perhaps the most breathtaking aspect of the brief flight was that Blériot, relying only on dead reckoning, became the first human being to pilot a heavier-than-air craft out of sight of land: for ten minutes.

Blériot's Channel crossing, modest though it seems in the annals of flight, electrified Europe. It meant that, in the future, England would no longer be insulated from Europe by the Channel. (Legend has it that the British government did not immediately sense this; Blériot contends that he was met at the field in England by a customs officer who merely asked him if he had anything to declare.) The plodding pace of Monoplane 11 cut by half the crossing time of the fastest mailboat; perhaps more ominously, it left its French destroyer escort far behind. The Channel crossing showed that aircraft engines were light and powerful enough, leading to dreams of even more daring ventures.

The broad enthusiasm for aviation symbolized by Blériot's achievement led briefly to the emergence of France as the world leader in the field. The government bestowed on Blériot the Cross of the Legion of Honor. It sponsored the first international air meet at Reims in 1909, where, although Blériot had engine trouble, French aviators reaped awards and set many new speed and distance records.

World War I was the first international conflict in which aircraft played a significant role, and Blériot became deeply involved in the French war effort. When the war began in 1914, lighter-than-air vehicles were still masters of the skies. The first reconnaissance craft designed by Blériot differed little from Monoplane 11. At first, these aircraft were not even armed. The French pilots had instructions to ram German zeppelins headed for the front, but it is doubtful whether they had the speed or power necessary to catch the dirigibles.

During the war, Blériot submitted design after design to the French government, yet technology was moving rapidly beyond the perspective of individual inventors, and his greatest success in military aviation came after joining forces with a team of experts. One result was the famous SPAD fighter, the equal of anything in its class for the duration of the conflict.

After World War I, Blériot's interest returned to commercial aviation. Although large companies increasingly dominated the development and utilization of aircraft in the 1920's and 1930's, Blériot never lost his admiration for individual achievement, even as it reduced his once awe-inspiring flight across the English Channel to relative insignificance. When Charles A. Lindbergh landed at Orly Field outside Paris on May 21, 1927, having completed the world's first solo flight across the Atlantic Ocean, Blériot was there with a French delegation to receive him. Nor did his vision for the future know any bounds. In 1931, Blériot himself offered a cash prize for the first supersonic aircraft, years in advance of any such prototype.

Blériot's own designs also continued to be at the forefront of commercial aviation. In August, 1933, he shipped a giant monoplane to New York to attempt from there a new world distance record. Loaded with some seven thousand liters of fuel, the aircraft, like Lindbergh's much smaller *Spirit of St. Louis*, had such large tanks that there was no forward vision: The pilot had to use mirrors to take off and land. This behemoth of the times completed a record nonstop flight from New York to Rayak, Syria, a distance of more than 6,250 kilometers (3,885 miles). Blériot died in August, 1936, in Paris.

SIGNIFICANCE

Blériot belonged to a generation of daredevils and tinkers who made heavier-than-air aviation a practical real-

Louis Blériot. (Library of Congress)

ity. He flourished at a time when accumulating knowledge about powered flight was in the public domain, and the applications of that knowledge were widely acclaimed. Thus, Blériot and others could innovate quickly, using the work of recent predecessors. The technological challenges of early aviation were amenable to the solutions of pragmatists and often yielded to intuition.

Blériot was a leader, even among these early pioneers who usually were eager to share their knowledge, in disseminating as widely as possible not only the technology of aviation but also the basic knowledge of flying skills accumulated by trial and error. Aviators all over the world, including the United States, got their start in the flying schools he established in more than one dozen countries.

Blériot's early career also demonstrates the level of risk involved in aircraft development. Generally, he and his colleagues flight-tested their own designs. Blériot himself was in more than fifty accidents, including a near-fatal crash in 1907 and one in which his aircraft plunged through the roof of a building during a demonstration in Constantinople (now Istanbul, Turkey). During his epic flight across the English Channel, Blériot was in serious pain from leg burns received in a gasoline explosion only the previous day. Blériot's bravery and imagination, as much as the engines on his aircraft, powered the early development of aviation.

—Ronald W. Davis

FURTHER READING

Collier, Basil. *A History of Air Power*. London: Weidenfeld & Nicolson, 1974. Broad, incisive coverage of aviation technology, especially interrelationships between military and commercial developments.

Elliott, Brian A. *Blériot: Herald of an Age*. Stroud, England: Tempus, 2000. Comprehensive biography, including accounts of Blériot's flight over the English Channel and his airplane manufacturing business.

Gollin, Alfred M. *No Longer an Island: Britain and the Wright Brothers, 1902-1909*. Stanford, Calif.: Stanford University Press, 1984. An important study that places Blériot's Channel crossing in broader historical perspective. Gollin shows that British concern over the potential of aircraft to alter strategic planning began very early, and that Blériot's achievement had a much greater public impact because there was already open debate in Great Britain about the implications of air power.

Josephy, Alvin M., Jr., ed. *The American Heritage History of Flight*. New York: American Heritage, 1962. Typical of many general histories of aviation organized to emphasize the overall development of industry and technology rather than the careers of individuals.

McFarland, Marvin W., ed. *The Papers of Wilbur and Orville Wright*. 2 vols. New York: McGraw-Hill, 1953. Volume 2, covering the period from 1906 to 1948, contains numerous references to Blériot, suggestive of how closely early aviators followed the exploits of their colleagues.

Michaels, Daniel. "Wing and a Prayer: A Ninety-Three-Year-Old Plane Still Flies—Sort Of." *The Wall Street Journal*, August 16, 2002, p. A1. Feature article on *Blériot XI*, the world's oldest plane that still can fly. Includes information on Blériot's construction of the aircraft.

Sunderman, James F., ed. *Early Air Pioneers, 1862-1935*. New York: Franklin Watts, 1961. Deals with the careers of many early aviators, arranged so that the interconnections among these figures are stressed. Particularly useful for its international perspective on technological developments.

Taylor, John W. R., and Kenneth Munson. *History of Aviation*. London: New English Library, 1972. Heavily illustrated and detailed accounts both of major milestones in the history of flight and of contributors to early aviation. One of the best organized sources of biographical accounts.

SEE ALSO: Richard Byrd; Amelia Earhart; Hugo Eckener; Ernst Heinkel; Frederick William Lanchester; Charles A. Lindbergh; Ludwig Prandtl; Charles Stewart Rolls and Sir Frederick Henry Royce; Alberto Santos-Dumont; Andrei Nikolayevich Tupolev; Sir Frank Whittle; Orville and Wilbur Wright; Ferdinand von Zeppelin.

RELATED ARTICLE in *Great Events from History: The Twentieth Century*:

1901-1940: July 25, 1909: First Airplane Flight Across the English Channel.

EUGEN BLEULER
Swiss psychiatrist

Bleuler's major achievements were in the study and treatment of schizophrenia, a term he coined in 1908 to denote the splitting of psychological functions that he observed in many of his patients. He also introduced the related terms "autism" and "ambivalence" into psychiatry. He has been admired as much for his tireless and uncompromising devotion to his psychiatric patients as for his important contributions to psychiatric theory.

BORN: April 30, 1857; Zollikon, Switzerland
DIED: July 15, 1939; Zurich, Switzerland
AREAS OF ACHIEVEMENT: Psychiatry and psychology, medicine

EARLY LIFE

Eugen Bleuler (OY-gehn BLOY-lehr) was born in Zollikon, which was then a farming village and is now a suburb of the city of Zurich, Switzerland. His father was a merchant and local educational administrator, but his ancestral roots reached deeply into the Swiss farming tradition. It is quite significant for Bleuler's personal and professional development that during the 1700's the farmers and their families living in the countryside around Zurich were governed by the aristocrats living in the city. These city authorities restricted the access of the country people to educational opportunities and to certain professions, a state of affairs that caused great resentment among the peasants. Thus, in 1831, they overthrew the aristocracy and established a democratic form of government. The Bleuler family participated in this social and political movement, one of the primary goals of which was to create a university open equally to all citizens. The University of Zurich was founded in 1833 in the hope that the children of the farm families could gain the advanced training necessary to serve the legal, educational, religious, and medical needs of the population, and to do a better job of it than had been done by the officials appointed for this purpose by the aristocracy.

Bleuler was a beneficiary of this democratic revolution in nineteenth century Zurich. One problem with the new educational system, however, was that, since Zurich did not have a strong academic tradition, many of the teaching posts had to be filled by Germans, who did not speak the Swiss dialect. Bleuler was well aware of the long-standing social and interpersonal difficulties brought on by this language gap. During his college years, a young village girl was taken to the university psychiatric clinic with a serious psychological disorder, and the girl's relatives were frustrated by the communication difficulties they encountered with the clinic's German director. The belief among the peasants was that psychiatrists who were attentive to the needs and conversant in the dialect of the Swiss people would be able to provide much more effective treatment. Sentiments such as these influenced Bleuler's decision to devote his life to the practice of psychiatry among his native people. After obtaining his M.D. from the University of Zurich, he served as a resident at Waldau Mental Hospital near Bern and later went to Paris to study briefly with the great French neurologist Jean-Martin Charcot at the Salpêtrière clinic. He also traveled to London and Munich and then returned to Switzerland to begin in earnest his professional psychiatric career.

LIFE'S WORK

In 1886, Bleuler, at age twenty-nine, became medical director of the mental hospital in Rheinau, a secluded town on the Rhine River. This large institution housed 850 patients and was badly in need of rehabilitation and administrative reorganization. Bleuler threw himself into this task and, being a bachelor, lived in the hospital and devoted countless hours to his patients. He participated in all aspects of their treatment and organized a system of occupational or work therapy, which was designed not only to encourage the patients to engage in productive and creative activity but also to provide regular occasions for the patients and the staff to come into close personal contact. It is significant that Bleuler considered work therapy the most essential aspect of psychiatric treatment, for it reveals his firm conviction that, though his mental patients were torn and troubled, they nevertheless remained human beings with hopes, fears, needs, and possibilities. During his years at Rheinau, Bleuler became convinced that, while the neurological aspects of psychiatric disorders and treatment were of great importance, the practice of communicating with patients in a caring and familiar manner in an effort to understand the real meaning of their expressions, symptoms, and behavior was of even greater therapeutic significance. Bleuler thus replaced the microscope, which he had learned to use so well during his medical training and which was still the primary instrument of psychiatric research among his contemporaries, with the human ear and human voice as the most

Eugen Bleuler. (Library of Congress)

essential tools of such research. In addition to being a faithful friend to his patients, Bleuler was also a sympathetic father figure to his staff. He worked alongside them, ate meals with them, arranged for and participated in their social gatherings, and sometimes assisted them in financial matters. The structure and sensitive style of therapy, as well as the democratic manner of dealing with coworkers, that Bleuler developed at Rheinau would characterize all of his subsequent psychiatric work.

In 1898, the Zurich government honored Bleuler by offering him the opportunity of succeeding Auguste Forel as head of the Burghölzli Mental Hospital and professor of psychiatry at the University of Zurich. He accepted the offer, in part to be closer to his aging parents and to his boyhood home, and thus became the first professor of psychiatry in Zurich who spoke the local Swiss dialect. He accepted the teaching aspect of the position with some reluctance, knowing that he would no longer be able to devote his time and attention exclusively to his patients. He came, nevertheless, to view his professional responsibilities as an important opportunity for conveying to his students the insights he had drawn from his wealth of clinical experience.

Bleuler's lectures eventually grew to form the core of

his influential book entitled *Dementia praecox: Oder, Gruppe der Schizophrenien* (1911; *Dementia Praecox: Or, The Group of Schizophrenias*, 1950). He first presented the term "schizophrenia" in a 1908 article in which he said that "dementia praecox," the older and widely accepted term promoted by Emil Kraepelin and meaning "premature dementia," was not accurate, because simple dementia was not universally observed in these patients and because the disorder did not always appear at an early age. Bleuler suggested that "schizophrenia," a coinage derived from Greek words meaning "split mind," was a better term, because he had discovered through extensive clinical observations that the most common characteristic of his schizophrenic patients was the dissociation of different aspects of their personalities—of thoughts from emotions, or of words and intentions from behavior. He distinguished between primary symptoms, those arising directly from the unknown organic process, and secondary symptoms, those involving psychological reactions to the primary symptoms. Bleuler thought that the lack of integration in his patients' personalities caused them to lose contact with reality, a state for which he invented the term "autism." He also noticed that many patients experienced the simultaneous presence of opposite or conflicting thoughts or emotions concerning a particular object, idea, or person, and he described this condition as "ambivalence."

Bleuler's new theory of schizophrenia not only was a terminological and descriptive innovation but also implied new forms of treatment. While most psychiatrists of his day were convinced that hope for those with mental disorders would have to await the discovery of effective physiological treatments, Bleuler was the foremost proponent of the optimistic idea that the symptoms of schizophrenia could be alleviated through psychological forms of therapy. At the Burghölzli Mental Hospital, he continued the therapeutic measures instituted at Rheinau but supplemented them with psychoanalytic techniques being developed by Sigmund Freud and Carl Jung. Bleuler had become acquainted with Freud through discussions of the latter's early neurological research on aphasia, and this relationship formed the basis for years of productive interaction between Freud and several of the Zurich psychiatrists. Jung became a resident at the Burghölzli Mental Hospital in 1900, and he and Bleuler were the first to employ word-association tests in modern psychiatric research.

The first decade of the twentieth century was a critical period in the development of the emerging discipline of psychoanalysis, and Bleuler collaborated with Freud and

Jung, along with other Swiss and Austrian psychiatrists, in various intellectual and organizational endeavors during these early years. They were all present in Salzburg in 1908 for the first international meeting of psychoanalysts, and the first psychoanalytic journal appeared in the same year as a joint venture of the three. By the time of the second congress of the International Psychoanalytic Association in 1910, however, disagreements concerning the structure and purpose of the association had arisen between Bleuler and Freud, and Bleuler decided to resign. Because Bleuler was the most prominent representative of academic psychiatry, his resignation served to weaken the link between psychoanalysis and the larger field of psychiatry. Bleuler continued the teaching and practice of psychiatry at the university and hospital in Zurich for many years and died there in 1939.

SIGNIFICANCE

Bleuler's passion was to understand and to heal the victims of severe mental disorders, particularly schizophrenia. His new theory of schizophrenia recognized the importance of underlying organic factors but is significant in that it was not a purely organic theory but was instead the most successful early twentieth century attempt to recognize and to deal with psychological factors as well. In his efforts to introduce psychological understanding and treatments into the care of psychiatric patients, Bleuler initiated a way of thinking and style of therapy that has come to be known as the existential approach, which emphasizes the importance of finding meaning in life. It is not surprising that Ludwig Binswanger, a major twentieth century exponent of this approach, was a student of Bleuler in Zurich.

Bleuler's selfless and uncompromising search for psychiatric truths motivated every aspect of his professional life. It led him to criticize many of his colleagues for engaging in what he called "the autistic-undisciplined thinking in medicine"—a form of thinking in which the physician or psychiatrist is entrenched in his or her own conceptual system and, therefore, does not make full contact with the reality of the patient. A similar criticism was the basis of Bleuler's disagreements with Freud, for Bleuler believed that both Freud and the International Psychoanalytic Association were becoming overly intent on the simple advancement of psychoanalysis and were sacrificing open-minded evaluation of the theory in the service of this sectarian cause. He also disliked the rigid hierarchical structure the association was assuming and would have preferred a more flexible, democratic organization. Bleuler, it seems, retained the spirit of his Swiss peasant heritage throughout his life and could not rest easy in the face of splits in humanity, neither those between human beings nor those within.

—Gordon L. Miller

FURTHER READING

Alexander, Franz G., and Sheldon T. Selesnick. *The History of Psychiatry*. New York: Harper & Row, 1966. A study of psychiatric theories and therapies from ancient through modern times. Contains several chapters on the emergence and development of psychoanalysis and on the relationship and friction between Bleuler and Freud. Includes references to the Freud-Bleuler correspondence, selections from which have been edited and published by the authors.

Bleuler, Eugen. *Dementia Praecox: Or, The Group of Schizophrenias*. New York: International Universities Press, 1950. Discusses the history of research on schizophrenia and numerous theoretical and therapeutic issues concerning the mental disorder.

_____. *Textbook of Psychiatry*. Translated by A. A. Brill. New York: Dover, 1951. Reprint. Birmingham, Ala.: Classics of Psychiatry & Behavioral Sciences Library, 1988. Contains a biographical sketch of Bleuler by Jacob Shatzky as well as a bibliography of Bleuler's writings.

Bleuler, Manfred. "Some Aspects of the History of Swiss Psychiatry." *American Journal of Psychiatry* 130 (September, 1973): 991-994. This article, written by Bleuler's son (who was also to become a professor of psychiatry at Zurich and director of the Burghölzli Mental Hospital) outlines some of the historical and cultural factors that, in the author's view, have shaped the contributions of Swiss psychiatrists.

Brome, Vincent. *Freud and His Early Circle*. New York: William Morrow, 1968. Discusses the formative years of the psychoanalytic movement and deals with the relationships between the major centers and pioneers, including Bleuler.

Ellenberger, Henri F. *The Discovery of the Unconscious: The History and Evolution of Dynamic Psychiatry*. New York: Basic Books, 1970. A substantial and detailed study of the development of dynamic psychiatry. Deals with Bleuler's life and influence in a number of instances and contains many illustrations of the players in this drama.

Kuhn, Roland. "Eugen Bleuler's Concepts of Psychopathology." *History of Psychiatry* 15, no. 3 (September, 2004): 361-366. Discusses Bleuler's concepts of schizophrenia and other forms of psychopathology.

Zilboorg, Gregory. "Eugen Bleuler and Present-Day Psychiatry." *American Journal of Psychiatry* 114 (October, 1957): 289-298. This article, originally an address delivered to the American Psychiatric Association on the centenary of Bleuler's birth, is an appreciative survey of his personal convictions and professional achievements, along with an appraisal of their enduring relevance.

SEE ALSO: Alfred Adler; Josef Breuer; António Egas Moniz; Sigmund Freud; Erich Fromm; Karen Horney; Pierre Janet; Karl Jaspers; Carl Jung; Harry Stack Sullivan; Wilhelm Wundt.
RELATED ARTICLE in *Great Events from History: The Twentieth Century:*
1901-1940: 1929-1938: Berger Studies the Human Electroencephalogram.

ALEKSANDR BLOK
Russian poet

Blok, one of Russia's greatest poets, was called the last Romantic poet, and his work in literature and drama reflected the profound changes that his country and its people experienced during the era of World War I and the Russian Revolution.

BORN: November 28, 1880; St. Petersburg, Russian Empire (now in Russia)
DIED: August 7, 1921; Petrograd, Russian Soviet Federation of Socialist Republics (now St. Petersburg, Russia)
ALSO KNOWN AS: Aleksandr Aleksandrovich Blok (full name)
AREA OF ACHIEVEMENT: Literature

EARLY LIFE

Aleksandr Blok (blawk) was born into a family of the gentry. His father, Aleksandr L. Blok, was a jurist, a professor of law at Warsaw University, and a talented musician. His mother, the former Aleksandra A. Beketova, was a writer. Blok's parents divorced soon after he was born, and he spent much of his childhood in the family of his maternal grandfather, Andrei Beketov, a botanist and rector of the University of St. Petersburg, in St. Petersburg and at his estate, Shakhmatovo, near Moscow. Blok rarely saw his father. In 1889, Blok's mother married an officer, F. F. Kublitsky-Piottukh, and the family moved back to St. Petersburg. After graduation from the gymnasium, Blok entered the law school at the University of St. Petersburg, but in 1901 he transferred to the historical philology faculty. He was graduated in 1906. Blok had an early interest in drama and in becoming an actor, but by the age of eighteen he had begun to write poetry seriously and was almost immediately successful.

In 1903, Blok married Lyubova D. Mendeleyeva, the daughter of the famous chemist Dimitry Mendeleyev.

She inspired much of his early poetry, but their marriage was always a turbulent one. In his later years, for example, Blok developed strong relationships with actor Natalia Volokhova and singer Lyubov Delmas, who together inspired much of his work at the time.

LIFE'S WORK

Blok's first published poetry appeared in the literary journal *Novyi put'* (new path) in 1903, and his first volume of poetry, *Stikhi o prekrasnoy dame* (verses on a beautiful lady), appeared in 1904. These early works reflected the influence of the philosopher Vladimir Solovyov, his nephew and Blok's cousin Sergei Solovyov, Andrei Bely, and other Symbolists, and they were well received by them. Blok already showed some innovation by giving new meaning to old symbols. It was his second book of poems, *Nechayannaya radost* (inadvertent joy), in 1907 and his lyrical drama *Balaganchik* (*The Puppet Show*, 1963) in 1906 that first gained for Blok real fame.

At this time his poetry was profoundly lyrical and deeply interwoven with mysticism and religious decadence. Blok can thereby also be linked to the tradition of poet Afanasy Fet. Consequently, some literary critics have called him the "last Romantic poet" for his work during this early period, but it is a label that might also be applied to his entire career.

Nechayannaya radost and another volume, *Zemlya v snegu* (1908; land in snow), however, also heralded a change coming about in Blok's worldview, brought on in part by the so-called Revolution of 1905 in Russia and its eventual failure. His classical mystical symbolism was beginning to collapse, and the breakdown of rhyme in these works anticipated Futurism.

Symbolism had its origins in France and had ramifications in several national literatures. It flourished in Russia in the first decade of the twentieth century, contributing significantly to what is known as the "silver age" of Russian poetry (as opposed to the "golden age," presided over by Alexander Pushkin in the nineteenth century). Symbolism exhibited a resurgence of idealism and aestheticism and represented a neo-Romantic reaction against positivism and realism. Most Russian Symbolists were liberal supporters of reform and revolution. In the post-1917 era, the Futurists (who also drew inspiration from their counterparts in Italy) rejected the mysticism of the Symbolists but readily accepted their technical innovations.

In 1909, Blok traveled to Italy, and he also made a rare visit to Warsaw on the occasion of his father's death. Italy and Warsaw both gave impulse to his writing as his fame grew. His later work came more and more to reflect the influence of the post-Romantic poet Apollon Grigoryev. World War I came, and Blok was drafted in 1916. He used his reputation to secure a desk job near Pskov, which he held until March of 1917.

Blok was a member of the left wing of the Socialist Revolutionary Party and in 1917 welcomed the February Revolution. In May, 1917, he took on the job of editing the testimony of former czarist government ministers to the Extraordinary Investigative Commission to the Provisional Government. He also initially welcomed the October Revolution and tried to cooperate with the Bolsheviks after they came to power. As a Left Socialist Revolutionary (Left SR), he was briefly arrested in 1919 as part of the aftermath of the so-called Conspiracy of the Left SRs against the new revolutionary Soviet government. Nevertheless, in 1920 he was elected chair of the officially sponsored new All-Russian Union of Poets.

Blok's two most famous and controversial works were of this later period: the poems *Skify* ("The Scythians") and *Dvenadtsat* (*The Twelve*, 1920), both of which appeared in the crucial year of 1918. In "The Scythians," "Scythian" comes to symbolize both the restless duality of Russian existence between East and West and the artist as eternal nomad. With "The Scythians," Blok also reopened the nineteenth century debate between Slavophiles and Westernizers on Russia's heritage and future. In his own way, Blok came down firmly on the side of the more mystical Slavophiles. *The Twelve* vividly and insightfully tells the story of a platoon of the Red Army during the Russian Civil War. Some Soviet critics have contended that in addition to being the last gasp of Blok's poetic genius, these poems mark his final reconciliation with Bolshevism. In fact, however, during the last two years of his life, Blok was deeply disillusioned with the Bolsheviks and pessimistic about Russia's future. He

Aleksandr Blok. (Library of Congress)

also was not well enough, physically or mentally, to continue to protest. Blok died on August 7, 1921, in Petrograd.

SIGNIFICANCE

In addition to being an important dramatist, essayist, and critic, Blok was the most important Russian Symbolist poet. He was the lord of the silver age of Russian literature, and he epitomized the Symbolist movement in Russia better than any other member. In the process, he drew on, reflected, and drew together much of Russia's rich poetic heritage. A profound mystical Russian nationalist, Blok too was deeply moved by the events of World War I, the Russian Revolution, and the Russian Civil War, and he was intimately involved in them.

Blok's language, themes, and images affected later Russian poetic schools, including some of those to which he was opposed, such as Futurism. He also had a direct influence on some of the most important poets of the Soviet period, such as Vladimir Mayakovsky and Anna Akhmatova. Blok can justly be considered one of Russia's greatest poets.

—Dennis Reinhartz

FURTHER READING

Chukovsky, Kornei. *Alexander Blok as Man and Poet.* Translated and edited by Diana Burgin and Katherine O'Connor. Ann Arbor, Mich.: Ardis, 1982. A very good Soviet monograph, equally divided between biography and critical analysis of Blok's work. Best known as a scholar of children's literature, Chukovsky was a friend of Blok, and his account is enriched by personal reminiscence.

Hackel, Sergei. *The Poet and the Revolution: Aleksandr Blok's "The Twelve."* New York: Oxford University Press, 1975. This book-length study of Blok's most celebrated poem explores his ambivalent responses to the revolution. Includes a bibliography.

Mochulsky, Konstantin. *Aleksandr Blok.* Translated by Doris V. Johnson. Detroit, Mich.: Wayne State University Press, 1983. First published in 1948, this lengthy critical biography is still worth consulting.

Pyman, Avril. *The Life of Aleksandr Blok.* 2 vols. New York: Oxford University Press, 1979-1980. On its completion, this two-volume critical biography was hailed as the definitive study of Blok's life and works. Pyman's narrative combines a novelistic richness of detail with a mastery of the literary and historical background. Illustrated, with extensive notes, a selected bibliography, and an unusually ample index.

Wachtel, Andrew. *Plays of Expectations: Intertextual Relations in Russian Twentieth-Century Drama.* Seattle: Herbert J. Ellison Center for Russian, East European, and Central Asian Studies, University of Washington, 2006. Includes an analysis of Blok's play *The Unknown Woman.*

SEE ALSO: Anna Akhmatova; Vladimir Mayakovsky; Boris Pasternak; Rainer Maria Rilke; Marina Tsvetayeva.

LÉON BLUM
French politician

Blum was responsible for the adoption of landmark social and workers' rights legislation, including the forty-hour workweek, the right to collective bargaining, and the right to paid vacations, that has permanently affected French economic and social life. He was elected prime minister of the first Popular Front government, an electoral coalition formed out of the Communist, Socialist, and Radical Socialist parties in France, and served as head of the French provisional government.

BORN: April 9, 1872; Paris, France
DIED: March 30, 1950; Jouy-en-Josas, France
AREAS OF ACHIEVEMENT: Government and politics, labor movement, social reform, literature

EARLY LIFE

Léon Blum (lay-ohn blewm) enjoyed a happy and healthy middle-class childhood. His father, an Alsatian Jew, was a successful manufacturer of silks and ribbons. The Blum family placed a premium on reading and education, and they expected Léon to become a writer or lawyer. His early education took place at the prestigious Lycée Henri IV, where he studied philosophy under Henri Bergson. He studied for two years at the École Normale Supérieure before being enrolled in law school at the Sorbonne in 1891. He earned his law degree with highest honors in 1894. Shortly thereafter, Blum passed the appropriate examination and became a civil servant for the Conseil d'État; his principal tasks included drafting legislation for the state and settling the claims of private individuals against the state. During a civil service career that lasted twenty-six years, Blum rose to the top rank of *maître de requêtes* (solicitor general).

Blum's intellect, however, drove him well beyond the practice of law. He frequented the literary salons of Paris and by his early twenties he was recognized as a key figure in the literary world. From the age of nineteen, he became involved with the enterprising, durable, and pretentious *La Revue blanche*, a journal in which all forms of art were discussed and analyzed. Blum served as the journal's literary critic from 1894 to 1900, when he was succeeded by André Gide. He then wrote drama criticism for *Comoedia*, *La Petite République*, and *Le Matin* and contributed articles on law and literature to other publications. Blum's best work on literature and society was *Stendhal et le Beylisme*, published in 1914.

While a student at the École Normale Supérieure, Blum was introduced to socialist thought by the school's librarian, Lucien Herr, yet it was only in the wake of the most intense stage of the Dreyfus affair (1898-1899) that Blum became actively interested in politics. Through

Herr, he met Jean Jaurès and quickly became an apostle of the great socialist leader, sharing his vision of a unified socialist movement in France.

The outbreak of World War I and the assassination of Jaurès in July, 1914, persuaded French socialists to end their traditional boycott on governmental participation. Blum accepted an invitation to become chief of staff in the ministry of public works, where he remained until 1917, when he resigned in protest over the government's denial of permission for French socialists to attend an international congress in Stockholm. Shortly thereafter, Blum published *Lettres sur la réforme gouvernementale* (1918), in which he analyzed French governance and expressed the need to give the prime minister executive authority. By the end of World War I, it was clear that Blum would pursue a career in politics. He was drawn, at the age of forty-seven, to active political life at the moment when Jaurès's dream of a unified Socialist Party was about to be shattered by the revolutionary events of 1917-1919.

LIFE'S WORK

Early in 1919, Blum was made chair of the executive board of the Socialist Party and elected to the Chamber of Deputies. At that time, the party was split between those who wanted to emulate the Russian Bolsheviks and join the Third (Communist) International and those who, like Blum, believed in the republican, liberal, reformist socialism of Jaurès. Blum's view was in the minority at the annual Socialist Party congress at Tours in 1920. The majority voted to join the Third International and to expel dissidents such as Blum. They adopted the name of French Communist Party and took over the machinery and treasury of the old Socialist Party.

Blum remained an authentic spokesperson for reformist socialism. To him fell the enormous task of reconstructing the party, financing it, and winning mass support away from the communists. Blum's political philosophy was based on a distinction between the "conquest of power," the "exercise of power," and "participation" in a nonsocialist government. The first was the revolution itself and could occur only when the socialists took over the state and put their programs into place. The exercise of power, however, could occur only if the socialists became the largest party in the chamber and were invited to form a government. This possibility justified working legally within the constitutional framework.

Blum, however, adamantly opposed participation in a nonsocialist government, which he could justify only in a national emergency. He thus declined an invitation to join the government in 1924 and maintained this stance into the mid-1930's. Denounced by some as a doctrinaire theorist, Blum believed that he had to avoid appearing as an opportunist. He was successful. In 1920, the Socialist Party had been left with only 30,000 members as opposed to 130,000 for the Communist Party. By 1932, the socialist strength was more than three times that of the Communists. The rise of Adolf Hitler in Germany and the violent tactics of domestic right-wing organizations during the mid-1930's made it desirable for the left-of-center parties to close ranks. In January, 1936, an electoral coalition known as the Popular Front emerged among the Communist, Socialist, and Radical Socialist parties. Elections in May and June, 1936, produced an overwhelming victory for the Left, and on June 4, Blum became premier of France's first Popular Front government.

The Popular Front was greeted immediately by a wave of demonstrations and strikes among French workers and trade unionists. Blum immediately invited representatives of the unions and employers' organizations to meet together in his official residence, the Matignon Palace. The result was the Matignon Agreements, by which

Léon Blum. (Library of Congress)

workers agreed to end the strikes and return to work. In exchange, they won recognition of their right to be represented by unions and to collective bargaining over wages and working conditions. With the domestic turmoil assuaged, Blum pushed the Popular Front program through the legislature in little more than two months. The major pieces of legislation, destined to have a permanent impact on French national life, provided for the following: a forty-hour workweek, paid holidays, a central marketing organization for grain, a public works program, reform of the Bank of France, nationalization of the armaments industry, and dissolution of armed fascist-style leagues.

It was in foreign policy where the coalition among the leftist parties began to collapse. No issue proved more troubling to Blum than the Spanish Civil War. General Francisco Franco began the military revolt against the Spanish Popular Front government in Madrid in July, 1936, barely a month after the French Popular Front had been installed. The cornerstone of Blum's foreign policy was solidarity with Great Britain. After consulting with the British, Blum decided to follow their lead by observing strict neutrality, or nonintervention, in the Spanish Civil War—even when it became apparent that Germany and Italy were violating their pledges of nonintervention by sending military aid to the Franco rebels. Frequently denounced as typical of Blum's nonactive intellectualism, the policy of nonintervention was not one that Blum desired but rather one forced on him by circumstances. His immediate reaction to the outbreak of the civil war had been to aid the Spanish loyalists with war matériel and money. The Radicals, however, opposed involvement in Spain. In addition, British leaders let it be known that if war erupted between France and Germany over the Spanish issue, England would not feel bound by its earlier guarantees of French security. Blum's only choice, therefore, was nonintervention, since party solidarity was necessary to launch the Popular Front social program.

As the conflict over Spain intensified, the Communists and the left wing of the Socialist Party grew more dissatisfied with the policy of nonintervention. In addition, a serious financial crisis resulted in devaluations of the franc in 1936 and 1937. The crisis forced the prime minister to ask the legislature for emergency powers. When these were denied by the senate in June, 1937, Blum resigned, thus putting an end to the one-year rule of his government. The government fell largely because of weaknesses inherent in the French political system, which Blum had analyzed about twenty years earlier in *Lettres sur la réforme gouvernementale*—the lack of executive authority and the dependence of the government on unstable party coalitions.

In the succeeding Popular Front government headed by the Radical Camille Chautemps, Blum served as vice premier. Chautemps resigned on March 12, 1938, following Adolf Hitler's invasion of Austria. Once again Blum was asked to form a government. Unsuccessful in building a broad-based coalition, his cabinet rested solely on the Socialist/Radical alliance. It was clearly a transition government, and it remained in power for only three weeks. With Blum's second resignation, the Popular Front era came to an end in France.

Although Blum had been unenthusiastic about military expenditures, his first term in office had witnessed the highest level of appropriations for national defense in the peacetime history of France. However, his detractors on the Right accused him of misappropriation. He was subsequently brought to trial by the Vichy regime in 1942 and accused of squandering the nation's military resources, thus leaving France unprepared for war. The trial was blatantly unfair, and Blum used the opportunity to embarrass his accusers with an eloquent defense. The record shows that he became convinced after Germany's absorption of Austria in March, 1938, that war was likely and that France must be prepared. He therefore offered his support, in the interest of national unity, to the more conservative government of Édouard Daladier. When World War II began in September, 1939, Blum supported its vigorous prosecution; after the defeat of France, Blum was among the minority in the National Assembly who voted against turning over all power to Marshal Philippe Pétain. The Vichy regime retaliated by taking Blum into "administrative custody." His trial resulted in imprisonment, first at Bourassol in France and then, from March, 1943, until the liberation, at Buchenwald in Germany. During this period of captivity, Blum wrote one of his most moving books, *À l'Échelle humaine* (1945; *For All Mankind*, 1946), which, despite his personal circumstances, brims with optimism and hope about the future.

Blum's last experience of exercising power came in late 1946 and early 1947. It was a moment of parliamentary crisis. The constitution of the Fourth Republic had been voted but had not yet come into operation. The leaders of the largest parties to emerge from the elections of 1946, the Communists and a Roman Catholic faction, were unsuccessful in forming a government. In this unpromising situation, Blum was asked to take office for one month, until the constitutional framework could be set in motion. His cabinet was composed entirely of socialists. With such a thin base of support, Blum harbored few illusions about what could be accomplished. The last Blum government succeeded in temporarily halting price rises, but Blum's efforts at governing were hamstrung by the same party irresponsibility that had contributed to the collapse of the Third Republic.

Following his final resignation, Blum retired at the age of seventy-five to what he loved best—solitude and books. He died at his home in Jouy-en-Josas on March 30, 1950. The public mourning on the Place de la Concorde in Paris and the flood of condolences from around the world provided eloquent testimony that Blum was indeed one of the preeminent men of twentieth century France.

SIGNIFICANCE

Blum first made his name not as a politician but as a literary critic and man of letters. His subsequent political career can be understood only in relation to the beliefs and standards of this intellectual youth. Through his education, Blum acquired a sense of moral rigor and an appreciation of intellectual honesty and consistency—qualities evident in his published work but which frequently clashed with the compromises necessary in the political world. In 1936, for example, he was forced to abandon his moral inclination to aid the Spanish Republic in its struggle for survival against General Franco to save the political coalition necessary to pass the Popular Front's social and economic reforms through the French legislature. These reforms—including the forty-hour week, the right to collective bargaining, and the right to paid vacations—stand as Blum's most important political achievement. His moral rigor was again challenged in 1946, when he was compelled to abandon his admiration for Charles de Gaulle as a resistance leader in a dramatic confrontation with the general over the nature of postwar French democracy. Blum's career is a classic example of the dilemmas to be faced by an intellectual with his qualities of mind in the compromising and dissembling world of politics.

—William I. Shorrock

FURTHER READING

Alexander, Martin S., and Helen Graham, eds. *The French and Spanish Popular Fronts: Comparative Perspectives*. New York: Cambridge University Press, 1989. This book is a collection of essays, many of which are useful in understanding the Popular Front phase of Blum's life.

Brendon, Piers. *The Dark Valley: A Panorama of the 1930's*. London: Jonathan Cape, 2000. Brendon analyzes historical events in seven countries to provide a better understanding of the causes of World War II. Chapter 14, "Léon Blum and the Popular Front," provides information about Blum and France in the 1930's.

Colton, Joel G. *Léon Blum: Humanist in Politics*. New York: Alfred A. Knopf, 1966. This is a full-scale political biography of Blum that treats the literary years before 1914 only as a prologue to his career in politics. It is especially useful for the period from 1936 through World War II and contains a full bibliography.

Dalby, Louise Elliott. *Léon Blum: Evolution of a Socialist*. New York: Thomas Yoseloff, 1963. This study concentrates on the development of Blum's political thought from anarchism to Marxism to humanist socialism.

Dreifort, John E. *Yvon Delbos at the Quai d'Orsay: French Foreign Policy During the Popular Front, 1936-1938*. Lawrence: University Press of Kansas, 1973. Although the author focuses on the foreign minister of the Popular Front, this book is especially useful for understanding Blum's ideas on the formulation and practice of foreign policy.

Joll, James. *Three Intellectuals in Politics*. New York: Pantheon Books, 1961. This volume contains an interesting short analysis of Blum's career with an emphasis on the travails of an intellectual in political life. Blum's career is compared with those of Walther Rathenau in Germany and Filippo Tommaso Marinetti in Italy.

Judt, Tony. *The Burden of Responsibility: Blum, Camus, Aron, and the French Twentieth Century*. Chicago: University of Chicago Press, 1998. Reprints of three lectures that Judt delivered at the University of Chicago, including "The Prophet Spurned—Léon Blum and the Price of Compromise."

Lacouture, Jean. *Léon Blum*. Translated by George Holoch. New York: Holmes & Meier, 1982. This translation from French concentrates on the political side of Blum's life. Unlike earlier biographies, however, such as those by Colton and Joll, which portray Blum as a nonactive intellectual beset with indecision, Lacouture depicts Blum as a "realist" concerned with the safety of his party and country.

SEE ALSO: Georges Clemenceau; Eugene V. Debs; Francisco Franco; Charles de Gaulle; André Gide; Édouard Herriot; Pierre Mendès-France; Philippe Pétain.

RELATED ARTICLES in *Great Events from History: The Twentieth Century:*
1901-1940: April 18, 1904: *L'Humanité* Gives Voice to French Socialist Politics; December 29, 1920:
Rise of the French Communist Party; February 6, 1934: Stavisky Riots; 1936-1946: France Nationalizes Its Banking and Industrial Sectors.

FRANZ BOAS
German-born American anthropologist

Boas made anthropology a vital discipline in the history of twentieth century social science, and his scholarship, in time, had a significant impact on public policy in the United States. In The Mind of Primitive Man *he argued passionately against the intellectual assumptions of racism.*

BORN: July 9, 1858; Minden, Westphalia, Prussia (now in Germany)
DIED: December 21, 1942; New York, New York
AREAS OF ACHIEVEMENT: Anthropology, social sciences

EARLY LIFE

Franz Boas (BOH-ahs) was the only son of six children (three of whom survived childhood) of Meier Boas and Sophie Meyer Boas, who were Jews. His father was a successful businessman, while his mother was extremely active in political and civic affairs. A spirit of liberalism and freethinking prevailed in the Boas household. It was a family legacy of the ideals of the German Revolution of 1848.

Although a sickly child, Boas had a lively interest in the natural world around him—an interest much encouraged by his mother. His enjoyment of nature, music, and school shaped his early life. After attending primary school and the gymnasium in Minden, Boas began his university studies. For the next four years, he studied at Heidelberg, Bonn, and Kiel. In 1881, at the age of twenty-three, he took his doctorate in physics at Kiel; his dissertation was entitled *Contributions to the Understanding of the Color of Water*. Later, his academic interests moved from physics and mathematics to physical, and, later, cultural geography.

In 1883, after a year in a reserve officer-training program and another year in further study, Boas made his anthropological trip to Baffinland, a territory inhabited by Eskimos. The experience changed his life, for he determined that he would study human phenomena in nature. Following a year in New York City, he became an assistant at the Museum for Volkerbunde in Berlin. As docent in geography at the University of Berlin, he made a field trip to British Columbia to study the Bella Coola Indians.

LIFE'S WORK

The year of 1887 was a critical one in Boas's career: He decided to become an American citizen; he married Marie Krackowizer, who, over the years, was an active supporter of his varied projects; and he became assistant editor at the magazine *Science*. In the summer of 1888, he returned to British Columbia to continue his studies of the northwestern American Indian tribes. Eventually, during his lifetime, he published more than ten thousand pages of material from this area of research.

From 1888 to 1892, he taught at Clark University. He then served as chief assistant in the Department of Anthropology at the World Columbian Exposition. He was also the curator of anthropology at the Field Museum in Chicago and worked for the American Museum of Natural History as curator of ethnology and somatology. From 1899 to 1937, he served as professor of anthropology at Columbia University, where he shaped the disciplinary future of the "science of man" by teaching the leading members of the next generation of anthropologists, including Margaret Mead and Ruth Benedict.

His varied activities continued. Boas took part in the Jesup North Pacific Expedition. As honorary philologist at the Bureau of American Ethnology, he published a three-volume work, *Handbook of American Indian Languages* (1911). Boas founded the International School of American Archaeology and Ethnology in Mexico (1910) and the *International Journal of American Linguistics* (1917). He served from 1908 to 1925 as editor of the *Journal of American Folk-Lore* and chaired a committee on Native American languages for the American Council of Learned Societies.

During all these institutional and educational activities, Boas constantly wrote scholarly and popular books and articles. In 1911, he published *The Mind of Primitive*

Man (rev. ed. 1938), "the Magna Carta of race equality." His book destroyed a claim current among intellectuals that physical type bore an inherent relationship to cultural traits. Other books followed: *Primitive Art* (1927), *Anthropology and Modern Life* (1928), *General Anthropology* (1938), and *Race, Language, and Culture* (1940), a collection of his most important papers. During his lifetime, Boas published more than six hundred articles in both the scholarly and popular press.

Boas's writings, museum work, and teaching contributed to the modern concept of cultural pluralism (or relativism). He moved anthropology away from its nineteenth century origin in armchair theory and speculation and toward its twentieth century development as a science, a careful recording of fact and scholarly monographs grounded in empirical history. Thus, Boas contributed to the development of functionalism. Boas discredited the theory of unilinear evolutionism, with its easy assumption of the innate superiority of Western society. He successfully argued that historical differences were significant because environmental opportunity worked diversely on a basically similar human nature.

During his long and productive career, Boas did not

Franz Boas. (Library of Congress)

neglect his family. He was a strong and loving father; his letters reveal a man committed to his family's welfare and happiness. Unfortunately, two of his six children died suddenly, and his wife was killed in an automobile accident in 1929. Despite these tragic events and a heart attack at seventy-three, Boas continued his scholarly effort. At a Columbia University Faculty Club luncheon, he died suddenly, on December 21, 1942.

SIGNIFICANCE

In his own antiauthoritarian style, Boas created modern anthropology. He disliked authority in all of its cultural forms, which included his own scholarship. Highly critical, he was never satisfied with his work; he never accepted as permanent any single anthropological concept. His scholarly style created a "school," but his personality did not. His life, thought, and significance in American history are of a piece.

Influenced by his freethinking family, Boas never hid his views, such as his dislike of racism and anti-Semitism, from public knowledge. While he was not prepared to accept Germany as the sole villain in World War I, Boas was one of the first of his generation of intellectuals to see the terror behind Adolf Hitler's rise to power. Boas acted accordingly: He publicly denounced Nazism early in its reign. His scholarship, in addition to adding to human knowledge, contributed to human liberation from fear and unreasonable authority.

The spirit of liberalism and the scientific method shaped his work and personality. His belief in cultural relativism was evident not only in his scholarship but also in his kindness to others, whom he met in the academy and in the field. As a result of this attitude, Boas accepted, without judgment, people as he met them—in all of their varied ways.

Boas's work linked him with every major methodological and theoretical doctrine in modern anthropology. Rejecting conventional wisdom, he held a theory only as long as it challenged the current dogma. In that way, he remained in the forefront of anthropological theory.

Boas was not a remote scientist, but a citizen-scholar. His study of the children of the Hebrew Orphan Asylum in New York City, for example, stressed the developmental importance of home environment and resulted in a change in the institution's administration. *The Mind of Primitive Man* was a prime weapon against the intellectual assumptions of racism. With this topic, he was concerned with practical humanitarian consequences for public policy.

In brief, with his personal integrity and varied scientific accomplishments, Boas shaped the course of anthropology in the United States. His precision and scholarly certainty in anthropology were extended to his commitment to the policy consequence of the discipline. In both his life and his thought, Franz Boas made vital contributions to the development and ideals of cultural pluralism in America.

—Donald K. Pickens

FURTHER READING

Boas, Franz. *The Shaping of American Anthropology, 1883-1911: A Franz Boas Reader*. Edited by George W. Stocking, Jr. New York: Basic Books, 1974. A brilliant introduction, this work places Boas in the intellectual context of his time. Organized chronologically, these selections allow the student to follow the evolution of Boas's scholarship.

Glenn, David. "Anthropologists, Few in Number, Revisit a 1919 Debate." *Chronicle of Higher Education* 51, no. 18 (June 7, 2005): A-29. Reports on the American Anthropological Association's decision to rescind its 1919 censure of Boas, explaining the reasons for the original censure and its later revision.

Helm, June, ed. *Pioneers of American Anthropology: The Uses of Biography*. Seattle: University of Washington Press, 1966. Particularly good on Boas's fieldwork among the American Indians of the Pacific Northwest, and a splendid work on how he moved anthropology from an "armchair" or speculative enterprise to a science that was based on empirical data.

Hinsley, Curtis M., Jr. *Savages and Scientists: The Smithsonian Institution and the Development of American Anthropology, 1846-1900*. Washington, D.C.: Smithsonian Institution Press, 1981. This book illustrates the changing intellectual and institutional context for the study of humankind during Boas's early career. In his later career, Boas came to dominate the discipline.

Kardiner, Abram, and Edward Preble. *They Studied Man*. Cleveland, Ohio: World, 1961. Delightfully written, this book is possibly the best introduction to modern anthropology available to students just starting to explore the field.

Lewis, Herbert S. "The Passion of Franz Boas." *American Anthropologist* 103, no. 2 (June, 2001): 445. Discusses Boas's concerns with humans rights and liberty and his desire to eradicate prejudice and discrimination. Examines the political implications of his anthropology.

Penniman, Thomas K. *A Hundred Years of Anthropology*. 3d rev. ed. London: G. Duckworth, 1965. This book is a standard history, particularly strong on the British contributions to the creation of the discipline. The scope includes the related topics of imperialism and colonialism and how they shaped the early concerns of "gentlemen-anthropologists"—a legacy that Boas rejected.

Silverman, Sydel, ed. *Totems and Teachers: Perspectives on the History of Anthropology*. New York: Columbia University Press, 1981. Former students of famous anthropologists tell about their mentors. The essay on Boas is particularly thoughtful and informative because it reveals him as a private person whose ideas about citizenship and contemporary issues influenced his scholarly concerns.

Spencer, Frank, ed. *A History of American Physical Anthropology: 1930-1980*. New York: Academic Press, 1982. A good source for understanding how Boas changed the emphasis in anthropology from one based on racist assumptions to one with a cultural focus.

Stocking, George W., Jr. *Race, Culture, and Evolution: Essays in the History of Anthropology*. 1968. Reprint. Chicago: University of Chicago Press, 1982. Stocking, a leading historian of American anthropology, provides the best intellectual history of anthropology and its place in American thought. The book is richly informative, and it includes a new preface.

SEE ALSO: Ruth Benedict; Émile Durkheim; Sir James George Frazer; Leo Frobenius; Margaret Mead; Ferdinand Julius Tönnies.

RELATED ARTICLES in *Great Events from History: The Twentieth Century*:

1901-1940: 1911: Boas Publishes *The Mind of Primitive Man*; August, 1928: Mead Publishes *Coming of Age in Samoa*; 1934: Benedict Publishes *Patterns of Culture*.

1941-1970: 1965: Anthropologists Claim That Ecuadorian Pottery Shows Transpacific Contact in 3000 B.C.E.

UMBERTO BOCCIONI
Italian painter and sculptor

Boccioni was the foremost painter and sculptor of the Italian Futurist movement, which developed in the years immediately preceding World War I. In addition to being an artist, Boccioni was the leading technical theorist of the movement. His principles of sculpture, in particular, shaped the mixed-media and dynamic productions of the twentieth century.

BORN: October 19, 1882; Reggio di Calabria, Italy
DIED: August 17, 1916; Sorte, near Verona, Italy
AREA OF ACHIEVEMENT: Art

EARLY LIFE

Umberto Boccioni (ewm-BEHR-toh boht-CHYOH-nee) was born in Reggio di Calabria, at the "toe" of Italy's "boot," but his family moved often as his father, Raffaele, a minor civil servant, was transferred. The Boccioni family, including Umberto's mother and his sister, Amelia, moved shortly after his birth to Forli; subsequently, they lived in Genoa, Padua, and Catania, at the latter of which Umberto attended the Technical Institute. Apparently he was interested in art even as a child. While in school, he also contributed critical articles to a local newspaper.

Just before the turn of the century, Boccioni moved to Rome, where he divided his time between commercial work and art study. At the insistence of his father, he studied with a sign maker, and at least part of his income was derived from commercial advertising work. He also studied at the Free School of Nude Painting, but the most significant event of his stay in Rome was his acquaintance with another painting student, Gino Severini, and his introduction through Severini to the older painter Giacomo Balla, who taught the younger men modern painting techniques and with whom Boccioni studied until 1902. The young artist traveled extensively, spending time in Paris, Munich, and St. Petersburg, and studied in Padua and Venice before settling in Milan in 1907 with his mother, who served as a model for his work through most of his short life, and his sister. His earliest paintings show influences as disparate as the medieval artist Albrecht Dürer and the Art Nouveau movement. He seems to have been most significantly affected by the work of the Impressionists and the Symbolists. Although those influences remain in his later works, Boccioni's aims and his methods were dramatically changed by his meeting in 1910 with the writer Filippo Tommaso Marinetti, the originator of Futurism.

LIFE'S WORK

Within a year, Marinetti's ideas for a nationalist art movement that would include disciplines as diverse as music and fashion design had begun to gain adherents, including Boccioni. Marinetti was an avant-garde poet and critic who had spent time in Paris, where he was exposed to the sparks that would ignite the efflorescence of modern art. While publishing a literary magazine, *Poesia*, in Milan, Marinetti wrote the first Futurist Manifesto, published February 20, 1909, in the French newspaper *Le Figaro*, for which he was the Italian literary correspondent. Drawing on such sources as the German writer Friedrich Nietzsche and the French philosopher Henri Bergson, Marinetti constructed a purposely offensive and radical anthem for a new movement that turned its back on the past subjects and techniques of art. In place of homages to the great artists, Marinetti extolled the portrayal of speed, machismo, and violence. Although some of the Futurist rhetoric may have been an Italian nationalist reaction against the European perception of Italy as backward, many critics have found affinities to fascism in some tenets of the Futurist movement.

Boccioni was one of five painters to sign the first manifesto of the Futurist painters on February 11, 1910. On April 11 of the same year, the group issued the *Manifesto tecnico della scultura futurista* (published by Boccioni in 1912; technical manifesto of Futurist painting); as usual with this movement, theory preceded practice. Although five names, including those of Severini and Balla, are affixed to these documents, Boccioni is thought to be largely responsible for them. The first painting manifesto echoes Marinetti's ideas, placing science above nature and arguing for the replacement of traditional static human or natural representations with the symbols of technology, such as ocean liners and automobiles. The technical manifesto is more specific, as Boccioni had begun the work of transforming words into new, or recycled, techniques. The painters vowed to abandon traditional forms and colors, but the Impressionist and Symbolist painters had already begun that task. Most significant for the new Futurist movement was the interest in dynamism: the representation of the multiplication of images caused by the speed of modern life.

A prime example of Futurist dynamism in painting is Boccioni's *Città che sale* (1910-1911; the city rises), which is typical in its urban subject: a construction site. Despite the Futurist celebration of technology in the manifestos, Boccioni chose to depict horses rather than machines at work. The painting's glowing colors and elongated brushstrokes create a violent and vibrant sense of action; in fact, the horses seem to drag their masters into a vortex of movement that may seem as much destructive as constructive. Another major painting by Boccioni, the triptych *Stati d'animo: Gli Addii, Quelli che vanno, Quelli che restano* (states of mind: the farewells, those who go, those who stay), painted and repainted in 1911-1912, also reveals an interest in action unfolding over time. The triptych depicts expressionistically the departure of a train and the feelings of those described in the subtitles. The source of the main title is the work of Bergson; his interest in the relativism of human perspective and perception as well as contemporary experiments with time-lapse photography and film influenced Boccioni's efforts. Also, perhaps surprisingly, there seems to be an affinity between Boccioni's theories of dynamism and Albert Einstein's theory of relativity; for both theorists, matter and energy are related states of being.

The repainted version of *Stati d'animo* includes numerals that reflect the influence of the cubists, particularly Pablo Picasso and Georges Braque. Boccioni's friend and fellow Futurist, Severini, had returned from a stay in Paris to report that the Italians were out of touch with the latest artistic developments. Thanks to financial support from Marinetti, Boccioni visited Paris in 1911 and 1912. Cubist works he saw there supplemented the reading he had done in Italy. After exhibiting several times in Italy, the Futurists finally mounted an exhibition in Paris in 1912 at the Bernheim-Jeune Gallery. This exhibition toured Europe, and only a denial of the Futurists' request for separate gallery space blocked their participation in the historic Armory Show in New York in 1913, the show that introduced European modern art to the United States.

Included in the Bernheim-Jeune catalog for the Futurist show is a discussion of "force-lines," or the idea that objects contain unique and characterizing lines of emotion. Boccioni and other Futurists combined the cool of analysis of the cubists and their dismemberment of subjects into their parts with the Italian movement's expressionistic dynamism, the representation of movement over time. This Futurist interest in all four dimensions as well as the beginnings of cubist sculpture may explain Boccioni's shift to a new field to which he would make his most important contributions: sculpture.

In 1912, Boccioni published his *Manifesto tecnico della scultura futurista*. Perhaps the two most significant elements are a focus on a new relation between the art object and its environment and a call for mixtures of unconventional sculptural materials. His suggestions for materials include glass, cardboard, concrete, and even electric lights. In 1913, Boccioni first exhibited in Paris sculptures intended to illustrate his techniques; the ten pieces and twenty drawings shown survive in photographs, but only four or five pieces of Boccioni's sculptural output still exist (one is of questionable authenticity). Conflicting stories have circulated about the loss or destruction of most of his pieces, after a posthumous exhibition in 1917. They may have been thrown in a stream by a distraught or jealous friend; they may have been exposed accidentally to the elements.

Fortunately, one of the surviving sculptures is the 1913 bronze *Forme uniche della continuatà nello spazio* (unique forms of continuity in space), the last of three striding figures that Boccioni created. Although the energy and sense of a figure caught in time suggest the influence of Rodin, Boccioni's figure is mechanical as well as romantic. It seems to be a form rather than a body, and Boccioni has attempted to break up the form according to the theories most clearly enumerated in the book *Pittura scultura futuriste (dinamismo plastico)* (Futurist painting and sculpture [plastic dynamism]), published in 1914.

Artistic, personal, and political differences soon sundered the Futurist movement. Boccioni joined Marinetti in 1914 in supporting the fascist call for Italian intervention in Eastern Europe. Their opposition to Italian neutrality and their romanticization of war made them ripe for service. Boccioni joined the cycling unit of the Italian army; he eventually landed in the artillery. The horrors and the nuisances of war cured Boccioni of his romanticism, but there was little time or opportunity for producing art. A leave in the summer of 1916 did allow him to produce a few paintings. Although they seem to suggest that he was abandoning Futurist methods in favor of an exploration of Paul Cézanne's geometric techniques, the change may be attributable to the fact that these paintings were commissioned.

In August, after returning to his unit in Sorte, near Verona, Boccioni fell from a horse during military exercises and died the next day, August 17. Despite the loss of most of his sculpture and the relatively short duration of his career, Boccioni's reputation has been enhanced by exhibitions of the remaining sculptures and of his paintings. His theoretical concerns have also proved to be wider than imagined. Besides his manifestos on painting and sculpture, an unpublished manifesto of Futurist architecture was rediscovered in 1971. His fascination with the interplay between object and space might have led him in other directions as well, if not for his early death.

SIGNIFICANCE

Although Boccioni is the best known of the Italian Futurist painters, his influence through the rest of the twentieth century is primarily in sculpture and in the application of his dynamic theories. Despite the loss of most of his sculptural pieces, Boccioni's insistence on merging sculpture and environment can be recognized in works as diverse as Alexander Calder's giant mobiles and Robert Smithson's environmental sculptures, which mold the landscape itself.

Boccioni is open to charges that he never fully succeeded in transforming his theories into art that faithfully represented them. His embrace of fascism has also made him the object of criticism. Yet his work in paint, words, and shapes remains an enduring contribution to the erasure of traditional artistic boundaries and the rise of modern art.

—Helaine Ross

FURTHER READING

Coen, Ester. *Umberto Boccioni.* Translated by Robert Eric Wolf. New York: Metropolitan Museum of Art, 1988. Produced in conjunction with a 1988-1989 exhibition at the Metropolitan Museum of Art, this remains the most updated book-length work in English on the artist. Includes lavish illustrations and supporting materials.

Futurism and Futurisms. New York: Abbeville Press, 1986. A monumental resource on all forms of Futurism, including a dictionary of Futurist terms and personalities and illustrations of the Venice exhibition that the book documents. A catalog organized by Pontus Hultén.

Golding, John. *Boccioni's Unique Forms of Continuity in Space.* Newcastle upon Tyne, England: University of Newcastle upon Tyne, 1972. A transcription of a lecture exploring the evolution of Boccioni's most famous sculpture and his ambivalence about his sources.

Martin, Marianne W. *Futurist Art and Theory, 1909-1915.* Oxford, England: Clarendon Press, 1968. Reprint. New York: Hacker Art Books, 1978. Perhaps the seminal work in English on Futurism, this book documents the rise of the movement and its influences from such French artistic movements as Surrealism and cubism.

Perloff, Marjorie. *The Futurist Moment: Avant-Garde, Avant Guerre, and the Language of Rupture.* New ed. Chicago: University of Chicago Press, 2003. Labeling a whole cavalcade of prewar radical artistic movements Futurist, Perloff insists that they all tore down barriers, both in art and between the art object and the world. New preface by the author.

Rossi, Laura Mattioli, ed. *Boccioni's Materia: A Futurist Masterpiece and the Avant-Garde in Milan and Paris.* New York: Solomon Guggenheim Foundation, 2004. Collection of essays accompanying the exhibition *Materia*—Boccioni's massive painting of his mother—which was mounted at the Guggenheim Museum. The essays explore Boccioni's evolution as an artist, the relationship of his painting to his sculpture, his role in the history of modernism, and other aspects of his work.

Soby, James Thrall, and Alfred H. Barr, Jr. *Twentieth Century Italian Art.* New York: Museum of Modern Art, 1949. Published in conjunction with an exhibition, this books remains valuable for its clear exposition and its early bibliography.

Taylor, Joshua C. *Futurism.* New York: Museum of Modern Art, 1961. A good introduction to the Futurist movement, including translations of four Futurist manifestos, illustrations, and a bibliography.

SEE ALSO: Henri Bergson; Constantin Brancusi; Georges Braque; Alexander Calder; Marcel Duchamp; Albert Einstein; Sir Jacob Epstein; Pablo Picasso.

RELATED ARTICLES in *Great Events from History: The Twentieth Century:*

1901-1940: Summer, 1908: Salon d'Automne Rejects Braque's Cubist Works; February 20, 1909: Marinetti Issues the Futurist Manifesto; 1913: Duchamp's "Readymades" Redefine Art.

HUMPHREY BOGART
American actor

Considered by many the greatest male film star of all time, Bogart portrayed memorable film characters and created a career and a persona that resonated decades after his death.

BORN: December 25, 1899; New York, New York
DIED: January 14, 1957; Hollywood, California
ALSO KNOWN AS: Humphrey DeForest Bogart (full name)
AREAS OF ACHIEVEMENT: Film, theater and entertainment

EARLY LIFE

Humphrey Bogart (BOH-gahrt) was the only son of Manhattan physician Belmont DeForest Bogart and well-respected magazine illustrator Maude Humphrey. The young Bogart had two younger sisters, Frances and Kay. With well-off parents, Bogart was able to attend Delancy School until fifth grade; then, at age fourteen, he went to New York's Trinity School. He had to repeat his third year at Trinity after a bout with scarlet fever.

In 1917, Bogart began attending the Phillips Academy, a preparatory school also attended by his father when he was young, in Andover, Massachusetts. Humphrey, however, did not like the school and failed several courses in his first year. His Phillips education was supposed to prepare him to study medicine at Yale University, but his grades did not improve, so he was sent home. His mother told him he was now on his own financially because he had not taken advantage of the many opportunities given him. Not finding a job after several weeks, he joined the U.S. Navy in 1918, the middle of World War I.

Assigned after training to convoy duty aboard the *Leviathan*, he made more than fifteen Atlantic crossings. Of his time with the Navy, Bogart tells the story of how, during one crossing, a German U-boat shelled the *Leviathan* and Bogart was hit in the mouth with a piece of wood that pierced his upper lip. Tended by the ship's doctor, the resulting wound left nerve damage and a partly paralyzed lip that created his distinctive lisp and snarl. Another version of this story, however, is that Bogart's father, in anger, hit him in the mouth when he was ten years old and damaged a nerve in his upper lip, causing the scar and lisp. Regardless which version is real, Bogart's lisp and tight-set look gave him the distinctive expression that would one day set him apart from other actors.

Out of the Navy after the signing of the November 11,

1918, armistice, Bogart found work and would have several jobs, including tug inspector for the Pennsylvania Railroad, runner for a Wall Street investment firm, and eventually, office boy for an independent film company, World Films. His friendship with the owner of World Films led to a job as stage manager, which in turn led to minor acting roles. These early roles were mostly panned by critics, but he finally got favorable notice for his part in the hit show *Meet the Wife* (1923-1924), a comedy with Mary Boland and Clifton Webb.

Young and handsome, Bogart continued to work as both stage manager and actor, playing mostly romantic juvenile parts he would come to call "Tennis, anyone?" roles. Between 1920 and 1926, he worked regularly in the theater. In 1926, he married his first wife, actress Helen Menken. Incompatible on many levels, the couple stayed together only about eighteen months.

By his thirtieth birthday, Bogart's reputation as a night-clubbing playboy had made him a popular Broadway figure, but he was outgrowing his ability to play the role of a youth. He tried in 1930 for a Hollywood film career, taking a role in a ten-minute short film, *Broadway's Like That*, for Fox Studios, but nothing materialized for Bogart after its appearance. He had married his second wife, actress Mary Philips, in 1928, but the geographical separation caused by his relocation to California and her successful career in New York caused their breakup in 1937. Bogart married actress Mayo Methot in 1938, a union lasting until 1945. Characterized by their drinking bouts and very public spats, they were known as the "Battling Bogarts."

LIFE'S WORK

Bogart's career as a film actor took off after his performance in the Broadway production of Robert E. Sherwood's *The Petrified Forest* (1935). Before this production, he had been under contract with Fox Films and had acted in several films, including *A Devil with Women*, *The Bad Sister*, *A Holy Terror*, *Love Affair*, *Big City Blues*, and *Three on a Match*, in which he played a gangster. No favorable notice came from these film roles. In fact, Fox dropped his contract after sixteen months, believing that his look, the snarl and the lisp, would never appeal to female audiences and that he would consequently never be much of a box-office draw.

However, *The Petrified Forest*, also starring English actor Leslie Howard, changed everything for Bogart. He received great critical reviews for his work as the menacing Duke Mantee. When Warner Bros. bought the screen rights to the play and wanted Howard to reprise his role, Howard refused to sign on unless Bogart was signed to play Mantee. Warner had wanted its contract player, Edward G. Robinson, for the role, but it wanted Howard more, so Bogart got the part. At age thirty-six, Bogart became "Bogie" and a major motion-picture star for his role in the film version of the hit play, which came out in 1936.

The 1930's era of G-men and "public enemies" made gangster films popular. Bogart made twenty-nine of them in the four years between *The Petrified Forest* and *High Sierra* (1941). He played convicts in nine of these films and was executed in eight. Among the best known are *Bullets or Ballots* (1936), *San Quentin* (1937), *Dead End* (1937), *The Roaring Twenties* (1939), and *They Drive by Night* (1940).

A landmark year in Bogart's career was when he made the critically praised *High Sierra* and the iconic *The Maltese Falcon* in 1941, but it was 1942 when he made the film considered by some the best film ever made: *Casablanca*. Bogart won his first Academy Award nomination for his role as nightclub owner Rick Blaine, but he lost the Oscar to Paul Lukas for his role in *Watch on the Rhine*. *Casablanca* won Best Picture, Best Director, and Best Screenplay awards, however.

Bogart's famous Rick Blaine character, a world-weary, urbane, quintessential adventurer, became firmly associated with the actor, defining him in most of his films until his role as a Cockney riverboat captain in *The African Queen* (1951), which won him his first and only Academy Award.

Of Bogart's many different films between 1942 and 1951, *To Have and Have Not* (1944), a dramatization of an Ernest Hemingway novel, is especially significant. During the making of the film he met and worked with Lauren Bacall, the smoldering twenty-year-old actress whom he would marry. The couple had two children: son Stephen and daughter Leslie. The Bogart-Bacall marriage became legendary, and Bogart's life became more domestic. It ended only when Bogart, a longtime smoker, died of throat cancer in 1957.

Bogart and Bacall were among a group of Hollywood actors and directors, including John Huston, Danny Kaye, Gene Kelly, Paul Henried, John Garfield, Marsha Hunt, and Jane Wyatt, who went to Washington, D.C., in 1947 to protest Senator Joseph McCarthy's hearings with the House Committee on Un-American Activities, which were smearing the Hollywood film industry. The couple also actively supported Adlai E. Stevenson in his run for U.S. president in 1952.

Though Bogart's character in *To Have and Have Not* was similar to his role as Rick Blaine, he showed unexpected versatility in *The Treasure of the Sierra Madre* (1948), in the comedy *We're No Angels* (1955), as a sober businessman in *Sabrina* (1954), and as a psychopathic ship's captain in *The Caine Mutiny* (1954). A semblance of Rick came back in *The Barefoot Contessa* (1954), and he played a gangster, once again, in *The Desperate Hours* (1955).

SIGNIFICANCE

Forty-two years after his death, the American Film Institute in 1999 named Bogart the greatest male screen legend of all time. He was the model for every cinematic gangster of much of the 1930's and into the 1950's. His urbane vulnerability was seen in actors from Edward G. Robinson and George Raft to Steve McQueen.

Bogart's name is synonymous with not only classic film but also classic acting. His legacy defines the best of Hollywood.

—Jane L. Ball

Humphrey Bogart. (Hulton Archive/Getty Images)

FURTHER READING

Hyams, Joe. *Bogie: The Biography of Humphrey Bogart*. New York: New American Library, 1966. A look at the very personal side of Bogart's life, with anecdotes about friendships and relationships that begin during his youth and touch on his relationship with his parents. Includes many photographs from his childhood, along with film stills.

Porter, Darwin. *The Secret Life of Humphrey Bogart: The Early Years, 1899-1931*. New York: Georgia Literary Association, 2003. Bogart's Broadway and early Hollywood years are detailed in gossipy tidbits presented in a style that would appeal to Jackie Collins fans. Insights into friendships and romances, with numerous photographs.

Schickel, Richard. *Bogie: A Celebration of the Life and Films of Humphrey Bogart*. New York: Thomas Dunn Books, 2006. An illustrated commemoration of the fiftieth anniversary of Bogart's death in 1957, chronicling his life from childhood through his twenty-plus-year acting career. Reviews of many of his films.

SEE ALSO: Marlon Brando; Bette Davis; Henry Fonda; Cary Grant; Katharine Hepburn; Gene Kelly; Sir Laurence Olivier; Gregory Peck; James Stewart; John Wayne.

RELATED ARTICLES in *Great Events from History: The Twentieth Century*:

1901-1940: September, 1929-January, 1930: *The Maltese Falcon* Introduces the Hard-Boiled Detective Novel.

1941-1970: October 3, 1941: *The Maltese Falcon* Establishes a New Style for Crime Films; November 26, 1942: *Casablanca* Marks the Artistic Apex of 1940's War-Themed Films; June 24, 1954: *The Caine Mutiny* Premieres.

NIELS BOHR
Danish physicist

Bohr discovered the fundamental structure and character of the atom, its components, and how they interact. For this discovery, he won the Nobel Prize in Physics in 1922. He also made significant contributions to the understanding of how quantum and classical physics unify as a single philosophy in his principle of complementarity.

BORN: October 7, 1885; Copenhagen, Denmark
DIED: November 18, 1962; Copenhagen, Denmark
ALSO KNOWN AS: Niels Henrik David Bohr (full name)
AREAS OF ACHIEVEMENT: Physics, mathematics

EARLY LIFE

Niels Bohr (nihls bohr) was born into a family environment that invited genius; his father, Christian Bohr, was a professor of physiology at the University of Copenhagen, and his mother, née Ellen Adler, came from a family of eminent Danish educators. Bohr's younger brother, Harald, would become a professor of mathematics.

Bohr attended Gammelholm Grammar School and entered the University of Copenhagen in 1903. He studied under the tutelage of C. Christiansen, a prominent physicist and an original, creative educator. At the University of Copenhagen, Bohr took his master's degree in physics in 1909 and his Ph.D. in 1911. He published his first scientific work in 1908. The opportunity arose as a result of a prize offered to the individual who solved an investigation of surface tension by means of oscillating fluid jets. He won the gold medal, and his piece appeared in the *Transactions of the Royal Society*.

In the fall of 1911, Bohr studied abroad at the University of Cambridge, pursuing largely theoretical studies under Sir Joseph John Thomson. However, he had not been at Cambridge long before he realized that the true frontier work in theoretical physics was occurring at the laboratories of Nobel laureate (1908) Ernest Rutherford at the nearby University of Manchester. Bohr also was drawn by Rutherford's dynamic personality. Before Bohr arrived at Manchester in the spring of 1912, Rutherford had already deduced the structure of the atom experimentally, although the concept's theoretical foundation still held significant flaws. Bohr, however, was about to uncover an idea that would forever change the face of physics and the very concept of the physical world itself.

LIFE'S WORK

As Bohr pondered the beauty of the emerging picture of the atomic structure, he, like Rutherford, was perplexed by the evident contradictions in theory. Rutherford's atomic model held that the atom was made of a very dense, positively charged central core surrounded by a cloud of negatively charged particles. Yet, based entirely on Newtonian, classical physics, such a structure could not exist, becoming unstable and falling apart. It was no wonder that Rutherford's peers held that the theory was fatally flawed. Yet Bohr had an almost heroic faith in Rutherford's insight and experimental proficiency, so he stubbornly clung to the idea that the experimental evidence had only to be matched with the appropriate theory.

In 1911, the infant science called quantum mechanics had found few applications. Bohr recognized that by linking the statistical methods of quantum mechanics with an invariant number called Planck's constant, for Max Planck, he could theoretically vindicate Rutherford's experimental evidence. Bohr reasoned that energy from the atom, emitted only in well-defined energy levels, was related to electrons falling or rising into stable orbits around the nucleus, a concept somewhat alien to Isaac Newton's classical notions of cause and effect. Using Planck's constant, he was able to derive the calculations necessary to describe the stability and transitions of the electrons, thus defining precisely the nature of the atom itself. The results of his work were ultimately verified by experimental evidence. He published these results in 1913 and for them would win the Nobel Prize in Physics nine years later.

From this work, Bohr reasoned that the model for the atom described in quantum terms must join smoothly with classical physics when the dimensions become larger than atomic size. This logic vindicated Rutherford's physical, experimental evidence as essentially correct. Yet in a larger sense, the idea enabled a philosophical justification of using the quantum set of scientific rules to describe the atomic world and the classical set to describe the larger universe. He called this fusion of ideas the principle of correspondence.

In 1916, Bohr returned to Copenhagen an acclaimed physicist. By 1920, he was named the director of the Institute of Theoretical Physics at Copenhagen. It would later be renamed the Niels Bohr Institute. By this time, Bohr had continued his investigations and uncovered evidence that the active properties, degree of stability, and character of all matter itself were largely dependent on the arrangement of the electron shells of the elements. Yet all the ongoing descriptions of the atomic character were being almost wholly defined in quantum terms, many being derived from a form of statistical probability. Albert Einstein was dissatisfied with this state of affairs, which violated his sense of universal simplicity, and stated, "God does not play dice with the universe."

Niels Bohr. (© The Nobel Foundation)

Bohr recognized that this debate was threatening the very foundation of theoretical physics. He used the example of two experiments to deliver what he called the principle of complementarity. The experiments he referenced were ones that unambiguously showed the electron to be a wave form and another that showed it in equally definitive terms to be a particle. He said that one observation necessarily excluded viewing results that only the other could obtain and vice versa but that one did not necessarily disprove the other. Together, however, the concepts were complementary proofs of each other. It was all a matter of philosophy, as was the foundation of science itself. The principle of complementarity stood as a brilliant turning point in physics. With it, the dominance of classical physics was ended and the new insights of the surreal quantum world were engendered.

Bohr's reputation attracted physicists the world over to Copenhagen to study and discuss the direction of modern physics. Bohr and Einstein frequently debated the consequences of quantum mechanics and the effects of this science on the perception of causality.

Denmark was taken by the Nazi storm troopers in 1940. Bohr was an outspoken anti-Nazi, and his mother was Jewish. Under the threat of imminent arrest, Bohr and his family escaped Copenhagen in 1943 on a fishing boat to Sweden. They eventually traveled to the United States. Bohr worked with the Allies' most influential physicists under the direction of J. Robert Oppenheimer, and they succeeded in building the nuclear bomb that would end the war. Indeed, it was Bohr who first predicted that the isotope uranium 235 would be the element of choice for a nuclear weapon.

After the war, the golden age of physics was irrevocably ended for Bohr. He set about at once to convince both Franklin D. Roosevelt and Winston Churchill of the immediate need to control nuclear weapons. Failing this, he helped establish the First International Conference on the Peaceful Uses of Atomic Energy, eventually winning the first Atoms for Peace Award in the United States (1957). Bohr died in Copenhagen on November 18, 1962.

SIGNIFICANCE

Using the concept of complementarity, Bohr forged the link between quantum mechanics and classical physics. This linkage enabled science to move deliberately ahead into subatomic research using a philosophy that was both unique to the atom's peculiar interior and relative, in a complementary sense, to a larger world. Bohr was a restless scientist who believed that there was an innate unity to many aspects of the physical world, expressed in the abstractions of complementarity, yet he was also practically oriented.

Bohr's creation and forceful leadership of the Institute of Theoretical Physics in Copenhagen served as a wellspring of emerging knowledge about the atom to scientists worldwide. Yet to Bohr it also represented an undisguised empire, directing the pace and direction of atomic science. From Copenhagen, he would personally coordinate and trace the direction of theoretical physics as his institute became the center of world attention to this strange, new science.

His empire would both collapse and race out of his control with the ascension of Adolf Hitler's war machine and his consequent contributions to the development of the atomic bomb by the United States at Alamogordo, New Mexico. He was one of the first scientists to grasp fully the aggregate implications of the bomb to humanity, ex post facto. When Bohr returned to postwar Copenhagen, the impetus of theoretical physics had shifted to the United States. His own energy would be devoted to attempting somehow to repair the damage or at least to slow the proliferation of the nuclear bomb. Yet his influence on modern physics will profoundly overshadow the misfortunes of war and the misapplication of science.

The ability of one person logically to unite the seemingly disparate worlds of quantum and classical physics in a philosophical, mathematical unity called complementarity stands as one of the most important and astonishing intellectual triumphs of science.

—Dennis Chamberland

FURTHER READING

Asimov, Isaac. *Understanding Physics*. Vol. 2, *Light, Magnetism, and Electricity*. New York: Walker, 1966. This book is written for general readers with some acumen in the sciences. Explains Bohr's work through a chronological accounting of modern physics. Written in a historically relevant style, setting Bohr and his peers against the background of a developing science.

Crease, Robert P., and Charles C. Mann. *The Second Creation: Makers of the Revolution in Twentieth Century Physics*. New York: Macmillan, 1985. An altogether exquisite work that tells Bohr's story to general readers like perhaps no other. It gives an easy-to-read, personal, even charming account of Bohr's early professional life, while detailing the science, woven into the fabric of an emerging picture of the bizarre world of the atomic interior.

Folse, Henry J. *The Philosophy of Niels Bohr: The Framework of Complementarity*. New York: North-Holland, 1985. This work details complementarity as a philosophical orientation along with its broad views and many applications. It is written for a college-level audience and superbly details the later, postwar applications of Bohr's work on theories of complementarity.

French, Anthony P., and P. J. Kennedy, eds. *Niels Bohr: A Centenary Volume*. Cambridge, Mass.: Harvard University Press, 1985. A book of essays about Bohr and his ideas, this work varies widely in appeal and depth. Many of the articles are written by those who knew him. The approaches vary from the highly technical to personal treatments.

Lamont, Lansing. *Day of Trinity*. New York: Atheneum, 1965. This is a historical narrative, setting Bohr in the middle of the development of the atomic bomb. He and his son are integrated into the Manhattan Project after escaping from Denmark. It links Bohr with Oppenheimer and Einstein in a completely enthralling and true wartime thriller.

Moore, Ruth. *Niels Bohr: The Man, His Science, and the World They Changed*. New York: Alfred A. Knopf, 1966. If there is a definitive, English-language sketch of Bohr's life, it is probably Moore's sketch of the physicist. Details Bohr's life from birth to his fight for peaceful applications of nuclear power. It is written for all readers, even those without a background in physics.

Ottaviani, Jim. *Suspended in Language: Niels Bohr's Life, Discoveries, and the Century He Shaped.* Ann Arbor, Mich.: G. T. Labs, 2004. A nonfiction graphic novel that recounts Bohr's life, scientific discoveries, and influence. A combination of text and comics. Illustrated by Leland Purvis.

Whitaker, Andrew. *Einstein, Bohr, and the Quantum Dilemma: From Quantum Theory to Quantum Information.* 2d ed. New York: Cambridge University Press, 2006. Chronicles the development of quantum theory, focusing on how Bohr and Albert Einstein debated their views on the subject. This second edition has been updated to include developments in this fast-growing area of twenty-first century science.

SEE ALSO: Albert Einstein; Enrico Fermi; Otto Hahn; Werner Heisenberg; Gustav Hertz; Lise Meitner; J. Robert Oppenheimer; Wolfgang Pauli; Max Planck; Ernest Rutherford; Glenn Theodore Seaborg; Sir Joseph John Thomson.

RELATED ARTICLES in *Great Events from History: The Twentieth Century:*

1901-1940: 1912-1913: Bohr Uses Quantum Theory to Identify Atomic Structure; March 7, 1912: Rutherford Describes the Atomic Nucleus; 1914: Rutherford Discovers the Proton; 1923: De Broglie Explains the Wave-Particle Duality of Light; Spring, 1925: Pauli Formulates the Exclusion Principle; February-March, 1927: Heisenberg Articulates the Uncertainty Principle.

1941-1970: 1947: Lamb and Retherford Discover the Lamb Shift.

HEINRICH BÖLL
German novelist

Böll, who was awarded the Nobel Prize in Literature in 1972, remains one of the greatest German authors of the postwar era. His works evince a keen moral sense and a sincere commitment to social change.

BORN: December 21, 1917; Cologne, Germany
DIED: July 16, 1985; Merten, West Germany (now Germany)
ALSO KNOWN AS: Heinrich Theodor Böll (full name)
AREA OF ACHIEVEMENT: Literature

EARLY LIFE

Heinrich Böll (HIN-rihk bohl) was born in the city of Cologne, a strongly Roman Catholic city located on the banks of the Rhine River in central Germany. This religious heritage is evident in the author's liberal and humanitarian themes. Böll attended elementary and secondary schools in Cologne and was graduated in 1937. He entered an apprenticeship in a bookstore and began to study German literature. During World War II, he served in the German army and was wounded four times. He was finally captured by the Americans near the end of the war. Böll had married Annemarie Cech in 1942, and they eventually had three sons. She often served as his collaborator in the numerous translations of English and American literature that he later published.

After the war, Böll returned to his studies of German literature and began to write his first fictional works. Although still unknown as a writer, he was invited to the 1949 meeting of the Group 47 circle of German writers, who gathered together once a year to read and evaluate one another's texts. Böll's narrative skills earned for him the respect of his peers, and, in 1951, he won the award for the best work read that year. From that point on, he wrote prolifically and won a number of prestigious awards. Throughout his life, he remained in the Cologne area.

LIFE'S WORK

Böll's first works deal with his personal experiences during and in the immediate aftermath of World War II. The major theme of virtually all of his writings—the alienation of the individual at the mercy of vast and impassive social and religious institutions—also becomes evident in these initial texts. The novel *Der Zug war pünktlich* (1949; *The Train Was on Time,* 1956) examines the brutal operations of the Nazi government bureaucracy that utilized the efficient German train system to transport millions to their deaths in concentration camps. He also assails the passivity and lack of compassion of the countless Germans who witnessed these events. His second novel, *Wo warst du, Adam?* (1951; *Adam, Where Art*

Heinrich Böll. (© The Nobel Foundation)

Thou?, 1955), also takes up the strong antiwar themes of his first works. The main character, a soldier named Feinhals, must passively observe the terror of the Nazi era but serves, as do many of Böll's characters, as a kind of moral "witness" figure whose testimony of the horrible events of that time forces the society of postwar Germany to remember a dark past that it would prefer conveniently to forget. This strong sense of social and moral conscience prevails in Böll's writings. These novels also suggest the sharply dualistic moral vision of the world that characterizes many of the figures in his works. Individuals are portrayed as either good or evil, as the helpless victims of persecution or the ruthless executioners of the innocent.

The novel *Und sagte kein einziges Wort* (1953; *Acquainted with the Night*, 1954) was an international success and illustrates Böll's attempts to employ the techniques of modern narration. In alternating first-person accounts, he tells the story of Fred and Käthe Bogner, a married couple who lived in poverty and desperation in

Cologne during the years immediately following World War II. Their marriage is falling apart, and, as a result of the stresses of their impoverished life, Fred has become alienated, unable to keep a job and given to drinking heavily. This novel takes up one of Böll's more controversial themes: the hypocrisy of the Catholic Church. Although it professes the love and compassion of Christ, the established Church—with all its power, wealth, and influence—does nothing to alleviate the very real sufferings of its followers. Böll remains deeply suspicious of social and religious institutions that have come to value their power and authority rather than the individuals whom they are presumably committed to serving.

Das Brot der frühen Jahre (1955; *The Bread of Our Early Years*, 1957) and *Billard um halbzehn* (1959; *Billiards at Half-Past Nine*, 1961) both examine from a critical perspective the postwar years of Germany, its rapid economic recovery, and its new spirit of materialism and prosperity. The latter novel remains one of Böll's most famous texts. It presents the story of the Faehmels, a family of architects in the Cologne area, and chronicles several generations of their involvement in German history in the period from 1907 to the 1950's. Böll is extremely critical of postwar German society and its apparent attempt to forget the Nazi past. As in his other novels, he tends to characterize individuals in this novel in terms of a somewhat dualistic "good/bad" schema. In *Billiards at Half-Past Nine*, he also experiments with more complex modes of narration by having the various family members present their perspectives in different chapters. In 1962, Böll visited the Soviet Union for a brief period.

Böll's next novel, *Ansichten eines Clowns* (1963; *The Clown*, 1965) is one of his most popular and most controversial works. It continues the strong criticism of social and religious institutions found in his earlier texts. Hans Schnier, a satirical pantomime artist now drunk and unemployed, tells in a series of narrative flashbacks the story of his family and his failed marriage to his beloved Marie. Böll assails the hypocrisy of postwar German society in the figure of Schnier's mother, a former racist Nazi who denies her deplorable past and now heads a group promoting intercultural harmony and understanding. Schnier is a typical Böll character who refuses to let postwar Germany forget its participation in the Nazi era. The hypocritical and insensitive stance of the Catholic Church destroys his genuinely innocent but "unlawful" relationship to the woman he truly loves. Schnier is another of those alienated "outsider" figures who provide a critical perspective on society. At the time Böll was working on this text, he and his wife were also translating the well-known American novel *The Catcher in the Rye* (1951), by J. D. Salinger, and the character of the alienated adolescent Holden Caulfield clearly informs that of Hans Schnier. Because of the rather negative view of the Catholic Church presented in this novel, its initial publication generated a rather heated debate in the press. With Böll's increasing prominence, his marked liberal views on social and religious issues began to invoke the wrath of the more conservative elements in German society. Böll also served as a guest professor in the mid-1960's at the University of Frankfurt.

In 1972, Böll was awarded the Nobel Prize in Literature. The novel *Gruppenbild mit Dame* (1971; *Group Portrait with Lady*, 1973) was a decisive factor in the Swedish Academy's selection. The story of a poor woman, Leni Gruyten-Pfeiffer, the novel spans most of twentieth century German history. Leni represents one of the author's "innocent" figures, a generous and deeply spiritual person who dedicates her life to the poor but who is scorned by a materialistic and uncompassionate society. Böll's selection for the Nobel Prize evoked a barrage of negative reactions from the conservative German press, which maintained that the prize was awarded only to liberals and left-wing radicals.

The 1970's were a difficult time for German society. Left-wing terrorism—kidnappings, assassinations, bombings—conducted by the well-known Baader-Meinhof group of radicals polarized public opinion. Many conservatives, especially the right-wing Springer publishing concern, advocated measures that would seemingly compromise democratic rights of civil liberty. Although Böll deplored acts of violence committed by the terrorists, he spoke out for the rights of the individual and as a result was often attacked in the press. His novel *Die verlorene Ehre der Katharina Blum* (1974; *The Lost Honor of Katharina Blum*, 1975) deals with the fate of a young woman who, because of a love affair with a suspected terrorist, is viciously slandered in the popular conservative newspapers. The work is a thinly veiled polemic against the Springer press. This novel was made into a popular film version in 1975 by the German directors Magarethe von Trotta and Volker Schlöndorff.

The novel *Fürsorgliche Belagerung* (1979; *The Safety Net*, 1982) also deals with issues concerning the terrorism of the 1970's and presents the author's criticism of modern Germany's social values. Böll maintained this aggressive stance with regard to human rights in both his literary works and his public speeches throughout his later life. In 1974, he acted as host for the expelled Russian novelist Aleksandr Solzhenitsyn.

One of Böll's last published works recalls the subject matter of his works written at the beginning of his career in 1947. Entitled *Das Vermächtnis* (1982; *A Soldier's Legacy*, 1985), the novel is set during the German occupation of France in 1943. The narrator, a soldier named Wenk, is an alcoholic who drinks to numb the pain he feels at the horror of the violence around him. His superior officer, Schelling, is a moral individual who tries to unmask the black market corruption of the troop. They are the typical Böll characters who represent the "good" people who suffer at the mercy of those who are "evil." Captain Schnecker is one of the latter type, and he eventually has Schelling murdered so that the profiteering can continue.

Although best known for his novels, Böll was also a master of the short-story form, a genre that became popular in Germany after World War II as American literature was more widely read. During his life, he published a number of short-story collections. Böll died on July 16, 1985, in the town of Merten, not far from his beloved city of Cologne. His last work, the novel *Frauen vor Flusslandschaft. Roman in Dialogen und Selbstgesprächen* (*Women in a River Landscape*, 1988), was published in 1985, after his death.

SIGNIFICANCE

In the era after the end of World War II, Böll assumed an important role in the history of German literature, and as winner of the 1972 Nobel Prize in Literature, his place in the canon of world literature has been assured. Although there are some critics who find his technique of stark good-evil characterization simplistic, his talent as a traditional narrative artist established him as a popular author, and his works have been well received throughout the world.

Böll's literary career as well as political pronouncements had often been regarded as controversial, but he remained consistently true to his moral vision of society. Böll's relentless championing of the individual's rights in the face of the impersonal authority of societal institutions and his rigorous efforts to examine the moral guilt of Germany's involvement in the horror of the Nazi period made him a spokesperson for the moral conscience of his wartime generation. His criticisms of the materialistic values of Germany's postindustrial society and his radical espousal of humanitarian and compassionate social values suggest his strongly spiritual and religious vision of the world. In a sense, he can be regarded as a radical Catholic who took the Christian message of love and charity in its purest form and who deplored the seeming inertia and conservatism of the established Church. Throughout his life, Böll remained a committed writer who believed that it was the moral duty of the artist to address the social and political issues of his time.

—*Thomas F. Barry*

FURTHER READING

Burns, Robert A. *The Theme of Non-conformism in the Work of Heinrich Böll*. Coventry, England: University of Warwick, 1973. This volume is a scholarly dissertation that presents a detailed discussion of the "outsider" theme in Böll's major texts up to the early 1970's.

Confino, Alan, and Peter Fritzche, eds. *The Work of Memory: New Direction in the Study of German Society and Culture*. Urbana: University of Illinois Press, 2002. Includes the essay "Awakening from War: History, Trauma, and Testimony in Heinrich Böll," which discusses Böll's postwar fiction.

Conrad, Robert C. *Heinrich Böll*. Boston: Twayne, 1981. This well-written and extensive book offers readers an excellent survey of Böll's works up to *The Lost Honor of Katharina Blum*. It contains a selected bibliography of secondary works (in both German and English) as well as listings of published interviews with the author.

Draugsvold, Ottar G., ed. *Nobel Writers on Writing*. Jefferson, N.C.: McFarland, 2000. Böll's Nobel speech is included in this collection covering more than thirty Nobel Prize-winning authors.

MacPherson, Enid. *A Student's Guide to Böll*. London: Heinemann Educational Books, 1972. This rather slim volume is part of the publisher's Student's Guides to European Literature series and presents a well-written and informative introduction to the author's major themes and works. It should be supplemented with more extensive secondary sources.

Reid, James Henderson. *Heinrich Böll: Withdrawal and Reemergence*. London: Wolff, 1973. A brief but useful introduction to Böll's works for beginning students.

Thomas, R. Hinton, and Wilfried van der Will. *The German Novel and the Affluent Society*. Manchester, England: Manchester University Press, 1968. This volume deals with Böll directly in only one section, but it presents a good portrait of the German literary scene in the 1950's and the 1960's, in which Boll's writing is to be situated.

SEE ALSO: Max Frisch; Günter Grass; Hermann Hesse; Thomas Mann; Erich Maria Remarque; J. D. Salinger; Edith Stein.

RELATED ARTICLE in *Great Events from History: The Twentieth Century*:

1941-1970: September, 1947: German Writers Form Group 47.

MARGARET BONDFIELD
British social reformer and politician

From humble shop assistant, Bondfield became assistant secretary of the Shop Assistants' Union and chair of the Adult Suffrage Society. Elected to the British parliament from Northampton in 1923, she became the first woman chair of the Trades Union Congress in that same year. In 1929 she became the first woman in a British cabinet, serving as minister of labour.

BORN: March 17, 1873; Chard, Somerset, England
DIED: June 16, 1953; Sanderstead, Surrey, England
ALSO KNOWN AS: Margaret Grace Bondfield (full name)
AREAS OF ACHIEVEMENT: Social reform, labor movement, government and politics, women's rights

EARLY LIFE

Margaret Bondfield was the tenth of eleven children in a family that was politically active. Her father, William, a foreman and designer for a lace firm, was a Chartist and a member of the Anti-Corn Law League. Her mother, née Ann Taylor, was the daughter of an energetic Congregationalist minister, George Taylor.

After Margaret attended the local elementary school, she served as a pupil teacher. In 1886, she left for Brighton, where a sister and brother lived with an aunt. As a shop assistant, she lived in a dormitory above her employer's shop and worked a sixty-five-hour week, earning twenty-five pounds a year plus her room and board. In Brighton she was befriended by Hilda Martindale, a Liberal and a women's rights advocate who furthered her education. After managing to save five pounds, in 1894 the young Bondfield moved to London to join her brother Frank, a printer and trade unionist, who introduced her to Amelia Hicks, with whom Bondfield shared living quarters. Hicks was active in the rope and box makers' union; through her, Bondfield met Henry Mayers Hyndman, Harry Quelch, and other members of the Social Democratic Federation but was later repelled by class-war theories. Later, at the Ideal Club, she met Sidney and Beatrice Webb and George Bernard Shaw and became a member of the Fabian Society. Eventually she joined the Independent Labour Party, where she became a friend of Margaret Gladstone, soon to marry Ramsay MacDonald. Through her brother, she also met James McPherson, secretary of the Shop Assistants' Union, and in 1897, at the age of twenty-four, she was elected to its National Executive Council.

LIFE'S WORK

The Shop Assistants' Union was founded in the 1890's and admitted members irrespective of craft or gender as long as they were employed in the industry of distribution. The union was affiliated with the Women's Trade Union League (WTUL), and Bondfield served on its general committee. She became a confidante to its leader, Lady Emilia Dilke, who had just engineered a shift in its policy from opposition to one that favored legislative restrictions on the conditions of labor and so got more male trade-union support.

From 1896 to 1898, Bondfield joined with Edith Hogg in surveying shop assistants' working conditions for the Women's Industrial Council. Its findings led to passage of the Early Closing Act of 1904, supported by Sir John Lubbock (later Lord Avebury), although Bondfield had favored Lord Dilke's bill, which exempted local option. She lobbied for the abolition of the living-in system with the Shop Hours Act of 1906 and the inclusion of maternity benefits in the 1911 Health Insurance Act. Because of her knowledge of shop assistants' grievances and her clear, resonant voice, she was chosen assistant secretary of the Shop Assistants' Union from 1898 to 1908, with a salary of 124 pounds a year. She contributed articles to its journal, the *Shop Assistant* (founded in 1890), under the pseudonym Grace Dare. Membership in the Shop Assistants' Union grew from 2,897 in 1898 to 20,218 in 1907.

In 1899, Bondfield was the only female delegate to the Trades Union Congress (TUC) conference at Plymouth and during this period traveled widely, recruiting members for the Shop Assistants' Union. It was during one of these trips to the Glasgow area that she accomplished the conversion of Mary MacArthur to the cause

Margaret Bondfield. (Library of Congress)

of trade unions. They became inseparable friends, and when the WTUL needed a new secretary, Bondfield recommended MacArthur. In 1906, MacArthur helped found the National Federation of Women Workers (NFWW), the first general union for women. Together with MacArthur and Margaret Llewellyn Davies, and through the Women's Co-operative League, Bondfield lobbied for the passage of the Trade Boards Act of 1909. It fixed minimum wages in four of the most toilsome trades employing women.

As a feminist, Bondfield also became active in the suffrage movement. From 1906 to 1909, she served as president of the Adult Suffrage Society, a group that differed with suffragists who were willing to accept a more limited enfranchisement of both men and women. As an ardent member of both the Independent Labour Party (ILP) and the Labour Party, Bondfield opposed limited suffrage because it might hamper the cause of socialism. In 1907, she debated Teresa Billington-Grieg, a leading member of the Women's Freedom League, which supported limited suffrage. Twice, in 1910 and 1913, Bondfield, as an ILP candidate, unsuccessfully contested a seat on the London County Council from Woolrich. Eventually she supported the Suffrage Act of 1918, even though it granted only heads-of-household suffrage to women over the age of thirty. Later, in 1928, Bondfield and Anne Godwin lobbied to extend the vote to women over twenty-one.

These activities took their toll, and in 1908, exhausted and depressed, she took a holiday in Switzerland. Bondfield loved travel and in 1910 spent five months studying labor and social problems in Lawrence, Massachusetts, and in Chicago. On both trips she was accompanied by Maud Ward, a cooking expert, with whom she shared a home in Hampstead for most of her life. On her return to England she resumed lecturing, and while in Lancashire, she collapsed during a speech. She subsequently resigned her position with the Shop Assistants' Union. After two years' total rest, she returned to social service activities in October, 1912. As a lobbyist for the Women's Industrial Council and aided by Clementina Black, she researched the conditions of work of married women in the Yorkshire woolen industry. Between 1912 and the outbreak of World War I, she became organizing secretary of the Women's Labour League and participated in the campaigns of the Women's Cooperative League for minimum wage, maternity, and child welfare schemes.

In August, 1914, when war threatened, Bondfield opposed British involvement. She arrived at her pacifism through characteristic self-education after reading J. A. Hobson's *Imperialism* (1902), Norman Angell's *Europe's Optical Illusion* (1909), and Henry N. Brailsford's *The War of Steel and Gold* (1915). She also joined E. D. Morrell's Union of Democratic Control. On August 6, 1914, Bondfield, along with MacArthur, Marion Philips, and Susan Lawrence, formed the War Emergency Workers' National Committee to protect working-class interests during hostilities. Bondfield was also a member of the Central Committee on Women's Employment and the Trade Union Advisory Committee of the ministry of munitions. The first provided workshops for approximately nine thousand unemployed women, while the latter, established July 17, 1917, by Winston Churchill, tried to ease friction between the government and the NFWW, the Workers' Union, and the National Union of General Workers. Bondfield's main energies during the war, however, were devoted to the work of organizing secretary of the NFWW.

Shortly after the war began in March of 1915, Bondfield resumed her peace efforts and with Philips attended the Women's International of Socialists and Labour Organizations, in Berne, Switzerland. It called for peace without annexation and self-determination for all minorities. Later, in 1917, as attitudes toward the war hardened, the government refused her permission to travel to the Stockholm peace conference; to an American Federation of Labor conference in the United States; and to the Women's International League for Peace and Freedom Conference at the Hague. This probably resulted from her close association with MacDonald's call for a negotiated peace and opposition to consumption.

After World War I, Bondfield resumed her international travels and attended the initial conference of the International Labour Organization in Washington, D.C. In 1920, she was a member of the joint delegation of the TUC and Labour Party to the Soviet Union. While her experiences led her to oppose British intervention in the civil war there, the trip revealed to her the dictatorial nature of communism, and in 1920 she opposed the application of the British Communist Party for affiliation with the Labour Party. After 1923 she felt ideologically estranged from most of the new leaders of the Independent Labour Party.

Also after the war, the NFWW merged with the National Union of General and Municipal Workers (NUGMW). When MacArthur, her closest friend, died in January, 1921, Bondfield assumed the post of chief women's officer (a post that MacArthur had been slated to fill) and held it until 1938. The amalgamation of the NFWW saw women gradually squeezed out of most leadership positions by men. When confronted by the NUGMW's abolition both of its separate Women's District and its provision for a woman on the General Council (thus reducing her to figurehead status), Bondfield threatened to resign. She was dissuaded only by being given "complete control of all national women's questions."

Ironically, in September, 1923, by the rota system, Bondfield became the first woman chairperson of the TUC General Council, a post she relinquished when, after two previous failures to win a seat in Parliament at Northampton, she succeeded in 1923. She then served as parliamentary secretary to Thomas Shaw, minister of labour for the first Labour government. In the election of October, 1924, she was defeated. Later, as a member of the TUC General Council, she supported the General Strike of 1926 and also Ernest Bevin's decision to call it off. In 1926, at Wallsend, she was returned to Parliament and at that time signed the Blanesburgh Committee's report recommending the lowering of some benefits and abolition of extended benefits, but the extension of the "not genuinely seeking work" clause. This led to her censure by the NUGMW and the Shop Assistants' Union and the greatest battle of her political life. She successfully fought off the attack of a minority of extremists before the TUC, the Labour Party, and her local constituency. In 1929, she was reelected to Parliament by defeating Wal Hannington and a Tory candidate. Ramsay MacDonald appointed her minister of labour, making her the first woman cabinet minister and privy councillor. In the face of the depression in July, 1930, and after March unemployment figures rose to 1.7 million, Bondfield called for an increase in the insurance fund's borrowing power to sixty million pounds. With the help of the Morris Committee, she managed to eliminate the "genuinely seeking work" clause, although the "Anomalies" [Unemployment Insurance No. 3] Bill in 1931 did deprive some married persons of benefits to reduce public expenditures. When MacDonald formed the National government, Bondfield stayed with the Labour Party and lost her seat in 1931; she was defeated again in 1935. She also lost her seat on the TUC General Council and, in 1938, retired as Chief Woman Officer of the NUGMW.

Bondfield continued her interest in women's economic and social problems, and in 1938 she helped found the Women's Group on Public Welfare; she was its chairperson from 1938 to 1945. In 1938, she lectured in the United States, and when World War II began, she made another tour, sponsored by the British Information Services. She also organized voluntary services for civilian evacuation. She died on June 16, 1953, at age eighty.

SIGNIFICANCE

Bondfield's worldview was influenced by her early religious beliefs and later socialist education. Sincere and good-natured, she was a team player and was content to play second fiddle to MacArthur in the WTUL. Bondfield also had the courage of her convictions, as when she differed with the suffragists in support of adult suffrage. She also was a realist, making the best of a hopeless situation when the NFWW was amalgamated with the NUGMW. Her views as a cabinet minister were made in the light of international monetary reality, not narrow sectarian interest or the grandstand play. She received many honors, including an honorary doctor of laws degree from Bristol University in 1929 and the Freedom of Chard, her hometown, in 1930. Few women achieved as many positions of power and accomplished as much social amelioration starting from such humble beginnings.

—*Norbert C. Soldon*

FURTHER READING

Banks, Olive. *Faces of Feminism: A Study of a Social Movement*. New York: St. Martin's Press, 1981. A good, balanced treatment of feminism as a movement for social justice.

Bondfield, Margaret. *A Life's Work*. London: Hutchinson, 1949. A useful autobiography filled with vignettes of early trade-union personalities, but one that is reticent about flaws and silent on some subjects.

Boston, Sarah. *Women Workers and the Trade Union Movement*. London: Davis Poynter, 1980. A consistently sympathetic and uncritical treatment of the topic and particularly valuable for events that followed World War II.

Clegg, H. A. *General Union in a Changing Society: A Short History of the National Union of General and Municipal Workers, 1889-1964*. Oxford, England: Basil Blackwell, 1964. Good on the consolidation of the NFWW with the NUGMW.

Hamilton, Mary Agnes. *Margaret Bondfield*. London: Leonard Parsons, 1924. Written by a friend and contemporary, before Bondfield had to make hard choices.

Howard, Angela, and Sasha Ranaé Adams Tarrant, eds. *Redefining the New Woman, 1920-1963*. New York: Garland, 1997. Includes an essay by Bondfield about women in industry.

Lewenbak, Shiela. *Women and Trade Unions*. London: Ernest Benn, 1977. Excellent history of women's trade unions, but almost entirely omits the textile industry.

Liddington, Jill, and Jill Norris. *One Hand Tied Behind Us: The Rise of the Women's Suffrage Movement*. London: Virago, 1983. A lively, incisive treatment that re-creates the past.

Soldon, Norbert C. *Women in British Trade Unions, 1874-1976*. Dublin: Gill and Macmillan, 1978. A balanced and comprehensive treatment of the role of women in the trade unions of Britain.

SEE ALSO: Nancy Astor; Ernest Bevin; William Morris Hughes; Mother Jones; John L. Lewis; Ramsay MacDonald; Frances Perkins; A. Philip Randolph; George Bernard Shaw; Beatrice and Sidney Webb; Clara Zetkin.

RELATED ARTICLES in *Great Events from History: The Twentieth Century*:

1901-1940: October 10, 1903: Pankhursts Found the Women's Social and Political Union; February 6, 1918: British Women Gain the Vote; July 2, 1928: Great Britain Lowers the Voting Age for Women.

DIETRICH BONHOEFFER
German theologian

Bonhoeffer defined the concept of Christian discipleship, especially as it related to the church in Germany during the 1930's. He provided a unique combination of theology and political ethics that made him a leader in German resistance to Adolf Hitler and also led to his untimely death at the hands of the Nazis in 1945.

BORN: February 4, 1906; Breslau, Germany (now Wrocław, Poland)
DIED: April 9, 1945; Flossenbürg, Germany
AREAS OF ACHIEVEMENT: Religion and theology, philosophy

EARLY LIFE
Dietrich Bonhoeffer (DEE-trik BAHN-hawf-ehr) was born in Breslau, Germany, in an area that is now Wrocław, Poland. His father was Karl Bonhoeffer, a well-known physician and psychiatrist. There were eight children in the family, of whom Dietrich and his twin sister, Sabine, were the sixth and seventh, respectively. The family soon moved to Berlin, where Karl became professor of psychiatry at the University of Berlin. It was there that Dietrich spent his childhood.

The realism that later characterized the philosophy and theology of Bonhoeffer was imparted to him by his father and through the influence of his mother, who was from one of the leading intellectual families in Germany. The family home became a meeting place for friends and neighbors representing some of the most brilliant minds of the day. Included were Adolf von Harnack, an eminent historian of Christian doctrine, and Ernst Troeltsch, a philosopher and theologian. Their influence helped place Bonhoeffer in the liberal spectrum of Christian theology as well as at the forefront of the ecumenical movement.

At the age of sixteen, Bonhoeffer dedicated his life to the study of theology and to service in the Lutheran Church. He entered the University of Tübingen in 1923 and was matriculated at the University of Berlin the following year. He remained in Berlin for the completion of his formal education. During his years at the university, Bonhoeffer became a follower of the post-World War I theology of Karl Barth, soon to become known as neoorthodoxy. These ideas enhanced Bonhoeffer's realism and helped him to accept the tremendous suffering and destruction of the recent conflagration, as well as Germany's lowered status in the community of nations.

When Bonhoeffer was twenty-one, he presented his doctoral dissertation to the faculty at Berlin. It was entitled *Sanctorum Communio: Eine dogmatische Untersuchung zur Soziologie der Kirche*. After it was published in 1930, the work was praised by such scholars as Barth.

Bonhoeffer left Berlin in 1927 to serve two years as an assistant minister to a German-speaking congregation in Barcelona, Spain. He proved to be a tremendous help and encouragement to the church and its elderly pastor. Back in Berlin in 1929, Bonhoeffer soon became a lecturer in systematic theology at the university. Before settling into the routine, however, he went to the United States for a year of additional study at Union Theological Seminary in New York City. Somewhat surprised by the lack of interest in serious theology on the part of American students at the seminary, Bonhoeffer was impressed by their social concern for the poor and needy. Bonhoeffer was well prepared for his life's work when he returned to Berlin in 1931. He was ready to face the challenges to Germany and the world in the person of Hitler.

LIFE'S WORK
By the time Bonhoeffer began his full-time lecturing, he was identified with the ecumenical movement, seeking to unite Christians around the world, and also with the ideas of Barth, whom Bonhoeffer soon met at a seminar in Bonn. At first, the students at the university were skeptical about the youthful professor, but they were soon drawn to him by the depth and relevance of his views. Bonhoeffer's first book, *Schöpfung und Fall* (1937; *Creation and Fall*, 1997), was an outgrowth of these early lectures.

Bonhoeffer's rising popularity in Berlin coincided with the rising popularity of the National Socialist German Workers' (Nazi) Party throughout the country. The Bonhoeffer family had been deeply affected by the defeat of Germany in 1918 and by the humiliation of the nation in the Treaty of Versailles, but they strongly opposed the ultranationalistic philosophy and the superior-race ideology of the Nazi Party. Even while outside the country, Dietrich was kept informed about the growing Nazi influence, particularly as it related to the Jews. His twin sister, Sabine, was married to Gerhard Leibholz, whose father was a Jew, although Gerhard had been baptized as a Lutheran.

Bonhoeffer was soon dismayed by the paralysis of the

German Christians regarding Nazi ideology. His realism, as well as his theology, compelled him to speak out against that ideology. On February 1, 1933, two days after Hitler had become chancellor of Germany, Bonhoeffer addressed the German public on radio and urged them not to adopt an ultranationalistic leader who could easily become a national idol. The broadcast was cut off the air before the speech was completed. In the minds of Nazi leaders, Bonhoeffer was already a marked man.

Most Lutheran leaders succumbed to Nazi pressure and formed the German Christian Movement, a vital part of German nationalism. Bonhoeffer and a minority formed what became known as the Confessing Church, seeking to purify the church through discipline. These leaders were shocked by parallels being drawn between Jesus and Hitler. Unable to accept such ideas, Bonhoeffer went to Great Britain in the fall of 1933, answering the call to pastor two German-speaking congregations in South London. During his eighteen months there, he studied the Sermon on the Mount and the idea of Christian discipleship. The result was his best-known book, *Nachfolge* (1937; *The Cost of Discipleship*, 1948). In this absorbing volume, Bonhoeffer criticized what he called the cheap grace being preached in many churches. He defined cheap grace as "the preaching of forgiveness without requiring repentance." Bonhoeffer then advocated costly grace that "is costly because it costs a man his life, and it is grace because it gives a man the only true life. . . . Above all it is costly because it cost God the life of his Son."

In 1935, Bonhoeffer was called back to Germany by the Confessing Church to lead a clandestine seminary, eventually located in Finkenwalde, Pomerania. This seems to have been a profitable and pleasant time for Bonhoeffer and the small group of students; in 1937, however, the seminary was closed by the Gestapo. Following the closing, Bonhoeffer became active in the resistance movement dedicated to the overthrow of Hitler. From 1937 to his arrest in 1943, Bonhoeffer lived in temporary places of refuge, such as the Benedictine Abbey at Ettal. His spare time during these years was used to write *Ethik* (1949; *Ethics*, 1955). He regarded this work as his greatest contribution as a theologian.

As the clouds of war began gathering over Europe, Bonhoeffer's friends urged him to leave Germany and continue his work abroad. He did return briefly to London and in June, 1939, visited the United States; he soon felt constrained to return to his homeland. Before leaving, Bonhoeffer wrote to Reinhold Niebuhr, an American neoorthodox leader, and declared, "I shall have no right to participate in the reconstruction of Christian life in Germany after the war if I do not share the trials of this time with my people." Taking advantage of one of the last opportunities to do so, Bonhoeffer returned to Berlin on July 27, 1939.

In the spring of 1941, a major conspiracy was organized to assassinate Hitler and overthrow the Nazi government. Bonhoeffer's role in this plot was to use his ecumenical contacts in Great Britain and the United States to convince the allies to stop fighting while the overthrow was in progress. The unsuccessful attempt was made in July, 1944, but by then Bonhoeffer had been in prison for more than a year. He was arrested on April 5, 1943, at his parents' home in Berlin, along with his sister Christel and her husband, for helping smuggle fourteen Jews into Switzerland.

For the next two years, Bonhoeffer wrote and ministered from various German prisons. The writings were later edited and published by his close friend, Eberhard Bethge, under the title *Widerstand und Ergebung* (1951; *Prisoner for God*, 1953; also as *Letters and Papers from Prison*, 1958).

Dietrich Bonhoeffer. (Hulton Archive/Getty Images)

Bonhoeffer's final days were spent in the concentration camp at Flossenbürg. On April 9, 1945, by a special order from Nazi Schutzstaffel (SS) leader Heinrich Himmler, Bonhoeffer was hanged. At about the same time, his brother Klaus and two brothers-in-law were executed elsewhere for resistance activities.

SIGNIFICANCE

Bonhoeffer had a clear understanding of the relationship between church and state. He first clarified the difference between state and government. By state, Bonhoeffer meant an ordered community; by government, he meant the power that creates and maintains order. The Nazi system, therefore, was government representing only the rulers and not the full German state. Bonhoeffer believed that the New Testament teaches that the basis of government is Jesus Christ and that only from Christ does government have authority on earth. By this simple concept, Bonhoeffer destroyed the foundation of Nazi ideology, including the exaltation for the German state and the attempt to use the Church as an instrument of governmental power.

This Christocentric view of government was also used by Bonhoeffer to justify the involvement of the Confessing Church in the Resistance. He declared this involvement to be the responsibility of the church because of "the persecution of lawfulness, truth, humanity and freedom" that permeated the Nazi system. Although he was basically a pacifist, this combination of theology and ethics made Bonhoeffer a leading spokesperson for the Resistance. Behind all that Bonhoeffer preached and practiced was his emphasis on discipline, which he urged all Christians and all Germans to follow.

—Glenn L. Swygart

FURTHER READING

Bethge, Eberhard. *Dietrich Bonhoeffer: Theologian, Christian, Man for His Times: A Biography*. Rev. ed. Translated by Eric Mosbacher et al., edited by Victoria J. Barnett. Minneapolis, Minn.: Fortress Press, 2000. Written by a friend, relative, and associate of Bonhoeffer, this exhaustive biography is a definitive chronicle of Bonhoeffer's life, theological calling, and ideas about Christianity.

Bonhoeffer, Dietrich. *Ethics*. Translated by Reinhard Krauss, Charles C. West, and Douglas W. Stott. Minneapolis, Minn.: Fortress Press, 2005. Edited and first published by Eberhard Bethge in 1949, this book is taken from essays written by Bonhoeffer between 1940 and 1943. It is the best source on why Bonhoeffer became involved in the Resistance.

_____. *Life Together*. Translated by John W. Doberstein. New York: Harper & Row, 1954. This is an outgrowth of Bonhoeffer's life in the close-knit seminary community at Finkenwalde between 1935 and 1937.

_____. *Letters and Papers from Prison*. 1953. Rev. ed. Translated by Reginald H. Fuller, edited by Eberhard Bethge. New York: Macmillan, 1970. This book, originally titled *Prisoner for God*, gives valuable insights into the life of Bonhoeffer during his last two years.

Bosanquet, Mary. *The Life and Death of Dietrich Bonhoeffer*. New York: Harper & Row, 1968. Perhaps the clearest and most objective biography. Much information is from Bonhoeffer's twin sister and from Eberhard Bethge.

Dramm, Sabine. *Dietrich Bonhoeffer: An Introduction to His Thought*. Translated by Thomas Rice. Peabody, Mass.: Hendrickson, 2007. Dramm explains Bonhoeffer's major theoretical ideas, including the nature of God and humanity, his views on Jews, and his concepts of discipleship and ethics.

Ott, Heinrich. *Reality and Faith: The Theological Legacy of Dietrich Bonhoeffer*. Translated by Alex A. Morrison. Philadelphia: Fortress Press, 1972. This is an exhaustive study of Bonhoeffer's theology and its impact.

Rasmussen, Larry. *Dietrich Bonhoeffer: Reality and Resistance*. Nashville, Tenn.: Abingdon Press, 1972. This is a good summary of how Bonhoeffer's theology shaped his political ethics and led him into the Resistance.

Robertson, Edwin. *The Shame and the Sacrifice: The Life and Martyrdom of Dietrich Bonhoeffer*. New York: Macmillan, 1988. An excellent and later evaluation of Bonhoeffer's influence. It includes some interesting insights into the Resistance and those who survived.

SEE ALSO: Karl Barth; Emil Brunner; Rudolf Bultmann; Adolf von Harnack; Heinrich Himmler; Reinhold Niebuhr; Paul Tillich; Ernst Troeltsch; Elie Wiesel; Simon Wiesenthal.

RELATED ARTICLE in *Great Events from History: The Twentieth Century:*

1941-1970: April 9, 1945: Bonhoeffer Is Executed by the Nazis.

PIERRE BONNARD
French painter

One of the most independent of post-Impressionist artists, Bonnard created a style and an artistic vision of art as an enchanting celebration of life. This style and vision, at one and the same time, freed him from his Impressionist predecessors and carried on their tradition of art as a loving record of human and natural beauty.

BORN: October 3, 1867; Fontenay-aux-Roses, France
DIED: January 23, 1947; Le Cannet, France
AREA OF ACHIEVEMENT: Art

EARLY LIFE

Pierre Bonnard (pyehr baw-nahr) was born in an exclusive suburb of Paris at the home of his father, who was an important official in the French war ministry. He was sent to expensive private schools and began his senior studies in the classics and philosophy. He was not a particularly good student, but his father had ambitions for him to enter the civil service. He studied law, as his father wished him to do, but he was interested in art and registered as well in a private art school, the Académie Julian. He also studied for a time at the École des Beaux-Arts, but he proved too undisciplined and spent much of his time sketching in the Paris museums with another young artist, Édouard Vuillard, whose career was to be closely tied to that of Bonnard. In 1899, he failed his oral law exams, but his father helped him by arranging employment for him in an office. Only his sale of a poster for a champagne advertisement persuaded his reluctant father that he should have a chance to become a professional artist. He continued to work at the Académie Julian, where he developed associations with other young artists, including Vuillard, and the group were to form themselves, somewhat informally and very loosely, into an association that came to be known as the Nabis (a lighthearted word meaning "prophets"), who discussed and began to experiment with new ways of painting and drawing. In 1890, Bonnard took his turn, as was the law of the day, in the French army, but he returned to Paris to begin his career as an artist in earnest, sharing a studio with Vuillard and other Nabis at 28 rue Pigalle.

LIFE'S WORK

The Nabis believed that the Impressionist revolution in French art, which had been in force through the 1860's, 1870's, and 1880's, was inadequate for their needs as young artists. The Impressionists had felt the same about their predecessors, repudiating the high finish and restricted subject matter of early nineteenth century painting for a loose, vivacious, improvisatory recording of day-to-day life. Their battle for recognition was still going on in the early 1890's, but Bonnard's associates were strongly influenced by Paul Gauguin, who had turned away from his Impressionist contemporaries to painting in which the message became important, in which works carried spiritual or social symbols, and in which the spontaneous recording of minute-to-minute reality, rapidly painted with deliberately loose draftsmanship and visible brush marks (the common marks of Impressionism), were rejected for a deliberate patterning, a determination to flatten the canvas in ways that were strongly influenced by Japanese drawing and painting. The more serious members of the group followed Gauguin zealously into what he called "Symbolist" painting.

Bonnard, however, stubbornly hung back from total commitment to Gauguin's preaching of the new faith. A tall, slender, wispy man, who was to look very much the same until his death, Bonnard seemed anything but the wild romantic figure of the artist, and he was noted for his whimsical sense of humor and good nature. He was not, however, easy to convince, and he never gave way on his own ideas about how he wanted to paint. He picked up the enthusiasm for Japanese art, and it began to show up immediately in his work; yet he never seemed interested in using his painting for the purpose of portentous symbolic comments on life.

Always modest about his talents, Bonnard accepted the Nabis' idea that the painter was not to record the minute details of reality but to represent on canvas his personal, imaginative response to that reality. The message that came through in Bonnard's case was a tender celebration of ordinary, mundane life, which linked him to the Impressionists, even if his style was clearly much more rigorously patterned than was the Impressionist inclination. He was, in that sense, the most Impressionist of the post-Impressionists. He was not reluctant to use his gift in minor ways; he continued to do posters and design covers for sheet music, and he became particularly successful as a book illustrator. Tiffany's of New York asked him to design a stained-glass window. He knew Henri de Toulouse-Lautrec, who was doing similar work, and there is often a similarity in their posters, although Bonnard's rendering of Paris nightlife is less intimate and less melancholy. He had his first one-man show in 1896; during this time, his color range was rather narrow, strongly leaning toward low-keyed blacks and blues. The double influence of Gauguin and the Japanese was very strong, particularly in his lack of bright, natural colors and in the flatness of his design, but his own charmingly innocent humor pervades his work.

By the late 1890's, he was established, and he entered a loose contractual arrangement with the dealer Bernheim-Jeunes, which provided him with a steady income. At the turn of the century an obvious change occurred in his work: There was an explosion of color, in the tradition of the Impressionists, and a similar flooding of incident and detail into his paintings of common life. The Japanese habit of "layering" their works, putting one subject over another with little concern for the European habit of connecting the subject lines with careful perspectival gradation, was particularly attractive to Bonnard. His paintings are often difficult on first viewing to understand, since background, middle ground, and foreground subjects seem to be equally important and often on the same plane.

Without much theorizing, Bonnard continued to break the rules of painting in several ways. He often deliberately broke perspectival obligations, distorted, and used a kind of flicking painterly shorthand to suggest objects in his works. He rejected the Impressionist insistence on working from real life; even his landscapes, seemingly so immediate and improvisatory, were painted in the studio, an act of supreme Impressionist heresy. He was to say that the presence of a subject intimidated him and prevented him from expressing himself freely.

In the first decade of the century, Bonnard began to spend more time in the country, in the first instance in a group of villages outside Paris. In 1910, he went to the south of France and was deeply moved by its brash, lush fecundity, a perfect mirror image of the rich density of his paintings. From that time forward, he moved on a regular basis between Paris, a house outside Paris on the Seine very near Claude Monet's studio at Giverny, and a small house in the south, near Cannes.

He was always inclined to pick at his work, never entirely confident of his technique. There was a period in which he concentrated on drawing, bringing a linearity back into his work, but by the 1920's his softening of the line, his natural inclination to blur outlines, and a new spurt of ebullient color took over and established his final stylistic position.

There was about Bonnard's work, particularly in the later years, a kind of shambling tenderness and sweet-

natured charm that worked even in his long series of intimate paintings of nudes, which are often compared to those of Edgar Degas. Like Degas, Bonnard catches his subjects at intimate moments and at odd angles, but his nudes seem less sexually vibrant, less erotically charged with voyeurism. There is a gentleness about his work, a modesty even in his wittiness, which is all of a piece with his peculiar habit of being able to paint anywhere. Often in hotel rooms, he would simply pin a canvas on the wall and set to work.

Bonnard was admired from early in his career but not considered a major figure, and his international reputation began substantially only in the 1920's. He lived a quiet life, working steadily through the 1930's, moving back and forth between the north and the south of France. He avoided Paris during World War II and produced a considerable number of watercolors and gouaches during that period, since oils were hard to obtain during the war. In 1925, he had married Maria Boursin, who had been his companion since their youth and was often a subject of his paintings; in 1940, she died. He continued to work steadily, with the work becoming, when possible, more richly colorful than ever. He died in his house at Le Cannet, near Cannes, on January 23, 1947.

SIGNIFICANCE

Bonnard began his career with a group of young rebels determined to free themselves from the powerful influence of Impressionism, and that impetus was to explode into several different ways of painting in the twentieth century, many of serious consequence to the history of painting. Bonnard, however, made his own way, not through any group or any particular theoretical structure but through a fastidious picking and choosing of those aspects of the new ideas and the old that were consistent with his own character as an artist. He, in a sense, invented himself as an artist by developing a private style quite unlike that of anyone else, which included touches of Gauguin's Symbolist theory, large swatches of Japanese design, the Impressionist love for the mingling of nature at its most beautiful and human beings at their moments of quiet innocence, and his own very subtly sophisticated amusement at life. Bonnard was not a member of any school or the leader of any group but was a kind of odd man out who developed a personal style that is immediately recognizable as beholden to many but peculiarly his own. He proved that the single artist could resist the power of movements and make his own way in the face of enthusiasms that demanded attention if he had talent and an idea of what art was meant to be, however individual. In the practice of his singularity, he produced some of the best paintings of the twentieth century.

—*Charles Pullen*

FURTHER READING

Callen, Anthea. *Techniques of the Impressionists.* London: New Burlington Books, 1987. The best introduction to Bonnard is through an understanding of technique, particularly that of the Impressionists, since he is so like them in the way he uses paint. This book has an excellent introduction to the subject.

Farr, Dennis, and John House. *Impressionist and Post-Impressionist Masterpieces from the Courtauld Collection.* New Haven, Conn.: Yale University Press, 1987. An exhibition catalog that contains an interesting discussion of three works by Bonnard.

Rewald, John. *Pierre Bonnard.* New York: Museum of Modern Art, 1948. Prepared for a Bonnard exhibition, this work contains an excellent, short critical biography of the painter and generous illustrations of Bonnard's drawings, paintings, and lithographs, and photographs of Bonnard and his surroundings.

_____. *Post-Impressionism from Van Gogh to Gauguin.* New York: Museum of Modern Art, 1962. Bonnard is only a minor figure in this work, but it is an intensive study of how the major painters of the late nineteenth century resisted the Impressionists and established themselves as something else, often of equal importance. Helps to show Bonnard's individuality.

Soby, James Thrall, et al. *Bonnard and His Environment.* New York: Doubleday, 1964. Another good, short critical biography and a rich full-color selection of his paintings.

Terrasse, Antoine. *Bonnard: Shimmering Color.* Translated by Laurel Hirsch. New York: Harry N. Abrams, 2000. Bonnard's grandnephew describes the artist's work. Contains 173 illustrations, 112 of them in full color.

Turner, Elizabeth Hutton. *Pierre Bonnard: Early and Late.* Washington, D.C.: Philip Watson and the Phillips Collection, 2002. Examines both the early Nabi or Symbolist period of Bonnard's career and his later Impressionist or color period to chart his artistic development and vision. Includes illustrations of 130 of his works.

Zutter, Jörg, ed. *Pierre Bonnard: Observing Nature.* Seattle: University of Washington Press, 2003. This book, which accompanied an exhibition of Bonnard's work, contains 110 illustrations to chart the evolution of his art.

SEE ALSO: Marc Chagall; Maurice Denis; Marcel Duchamp; Pablo Picasso; Édouard Vuillard.

SIR ROBERT LAIRD BORDEN
Prime minister of Canada (1911-1920)

As prime minister of Canada during the years of World War I and the Peace at Versailles, Borden played a crucial role in transforming the status of Canada from that of a dominion to that of a nation.

BORN: June 26, 1854; Grand Pré, Nova Scotia, Canada
DIED: June 10, 1937; Ottawa, Ontario, Canada
AREAS OF ACHIEVEMENT: Government and politics, diplomacy

EARLY LIFE

Robert Laird Borden was born in the small village of Grand Pré, Nova Scotia. His mother, Eunice, a woman of strong character and high energy, exercised a dominant influence on his life. His father, Andrew, owned a farm but chiefly was occupied in business affairs, in which he was only moderately successful. At age fifteen, Borden cut short his formal education to accept the post of assistant master at the private school he attended. At age nineteen, Borden accepted the position of assistant master at Glenwood Institute at Matawan, New Jersey. Remaining in teaching offered very little in the way of future prospects. He therefore turned to the study of law at a Halifax law firm and was admitted to the bar in 1878. After his marriage to Laura Bond in 1898, Borden, strikingly handsome, founded a law firm in Halifax that later became one of the largest and most successful in the Maritime Provinces. In 1896, he accepted the Conservative nomination for Halifax, largely as a result of his friendship with Sir Charles Tupper, one of the original "fathers of confederation."

Borden was for the most part an obscure back-bench member of the opposition in his first term in the Canadian parliament. He was, however, invited by the Con-

Sir Robert Laird Borden. (Library of Congress)

servative Party caucus in 1900 to assume the temporary leadership of the party. He remained in that position, despite some dissatisfaction within his party, until 1911, when Sir Wilfrid Laurier and the Liberals lost the election to the Conservatives. In Parliament, Borden had gained a reputation as a very hardworking person who had an extraordinary mastery over detail, but who lacked eloquence in debates in the House of Commons.

LIFE'S WORK

As prime minister of Canada for nine years, Borden's major concern was Anglo-Canadian relations, and within those relations the changing structure of the British Empire. During the early years of his ministry as leader of the Conservative Party, Borden was considered to be a strong supporter of the Empire and the imperial connection in general. By the end of his ministry, and mainly as a consequence of the events of World War I and Canada's participation in those events, he would be the most instrumental of all dominion statesmen in having changed the structure of the Empire into what is now known as the British Commonwealth of Nations. His role in promoting greater dominion autonomy within the

Empire during the later stages of World War I was absolutely crucial.

In the first years of his ministry, Borden's devotion to a close imperial tie was manifested in attempting to persuade the Canadian parliament to contribute to the cost of the construction of three new British dreadnoughts for the Royal Navy. A bill for this purpose was put forward at the behest of Winston Churchill, who was then Great Britain's First Lord of the Admiralty. Churchill's plea came as a result of Germany's spectacular rise in naval armaments. Borden's naval bill appropriating the money for these ships was defeated by the Canadian Senate in 1913, and with the bill's defeat, Borden's first attempt to maintain and strengthen Canada's imperial connection failed somewhat ignominiously.

With the outbreak of World War I, Borden's view of the imperial connection would undergo an astounding change. Sometimes in advance of Canadian nationalism, sometimes carried along by it, Borden, more than any other imperial statesman, was responsible for what ultimately amounted to a revolution within the British Empire. As a result of a trip to Great Britain in 1915 and the treatment he received at the hands of the government in London, his views of Canada's relationship to the Empire changed markedly and initiated on his part an ever-increasing tendency to emphasize Canadian national interests over imperial interests. Canada had placed a large number of men in the field and was, in addition, making enormous economic sacrifices in a military effort over which it had little or no control. This lack of consultation, both in principle and in fact, led Borden to assert Canadian interests with increasing frequency as the war progressed.

As a consequence of dramatic increases in Canadian casualties in the field, Borden traveled to London again in 1917, expressly to press David Lloyd George for a greater Canadian voice in the direction of the war. Indeed, Borden at one point in their conversations threatened to withdraw Canada from the Empire unless Britain saw fit to give Canada a larger voice in the direction of the war. This threat was instrumental in Lloyd George's ultimate decision to create a novel governmental body known as the Imperial War Cabinet, which included the prime minister of Britain and all the other prime ministers of the dominions, creating a body through which the dominions would receive a greater voice in the direction of the war. Borden had established once and for all the principle of shared authority in imperial military policy.

Having set this precedent, Borden soon began to carry this principle into all phases of imperial relations. When the armistice was announced in November, 1918, Borden hastily sailed to Britain with the intent that Canada be consulted as to the terms of peace, a demand that came as a complete surprise to the British government. He demanded of Lloyd George that Canada, as well as the other dominions, be given representation at the Peace Conference at Versailles, which in effect meant a demand for international recognition for Canada and the other dominions as autonomous nations. He also demanded that when the peace treaty was signed that it be submitted to the Canadian parliament for ratification. Moreover, Borden in 1920 asked for and secured from the British government separate Canadian diplomatic representation at Washington, thus giving Canada an international status it did not possess prior to that date (inasmuch as its interests in the United States had previously been represented through the British embassy). Therefore, as a consequence of Borden's efforts and demands, Canada had entered World War I as a dominion; by 1920 it was for all practical purposes a sovereign nation-state.

SIGNIFICANCE

When Borden became the Conservative prime minister of Canada in 1911, he was considered by most political experts in that country to be an uninspiring but careful administrator and a devout adherent to the cause of British imperialism. When he resigned his office in 1920 because of ill health, he had become a strong Canadian nationalist and one of the most important architects of what was to become the British Commonwealth of Nations.

The rather remarkable transformation of Borden's views from imperialist to nationalist can be accounted for primarily in terms of the rising tide of dominion nationalism in general, and Canadian nationalism in particular. Had World War I not occurred, there is sufficient evidence to suggest that Borden would have remained the "old" imperialist he had been during his earlier years in Canadian politics. As a statesman of the senior dominion, however, he took an unprecedented lead in pressuring British officialdom to make dramatic concessions to Canadian autonomy as well as the autonomy of the other dominions within the Empire.

Beginning his political career as a true believer in the old imperialist system, he ended that career by taking the lead in asserting boldly and aggressively the rights of the dominions, and in the process, unconsciously perhaps, found himself revolutionizing the entire nature and structure of the Empire. In the realm of important Cana-

dian domestic legislation, there is little of significance to which Borden could point. Indeed, there is little to indicate that he made any progress in the age-old problem of the relation of English-speaking Canada to Quebec, or French-speaking Canada. In fact, he only heightened those historical tensions by unsuccessfully attempting to force conscription on Quebec in 1917. Nevertheless, it is clear that Borden put his unique and lasting stamp on British imperial policy and therefore on the long history of the British Empire.

—Harold A. Wilson

FURTHER READING

Borden, Robert L. *Canada in the Commonwealth: From Conflict to Co-operation*. Oxford, England: Clarendon Press, 1929. Treats the historical development of Canada's relationship to the British Commonwealth and the part that Borden played within the context of that development.

_____. *Robert Laird Borden: His Memoirs*. Edited by Henry Borden. 2 vols. Toronto, Ont.: Macmillan, 1938. Contains the significant correspondence of Borden during his years in office. Also represents Borden's personal views and interpretations of domestic and imperial events in which he played an important role.

Brown, Robert C. *Robert Laird Borden*. Vol. 1. Toronto, Ont.: Macmillan, 1975. A highly informative biography, especially in terms of Borden's early years and those forces that helped shape his political career and attitudes. It possesses much interesting and useful information on events that had an important bearing on his official life.

Dawson, Robert M., ed. *The Development of Dominion Status, 1900-1936*. Hamden, Conn.: Archon Books, 1965. A historical overview of the nature of the changing status of the dominions within the Empire in the latter part of the nineteenth century and the crucial years of the twentieth century. By far the best documentary history of the period. Dawson's very full commentary is exceedingly valuable.

Glazebrook, George P. de T. *A History of Canadian External Relations*. Rev. ed. Toronto, Ont.: McClelland & Stewart, 1966. An excellent survey of Canadian dealings with Great Britain as well as with the other dominions and the United States.

Lloyd George, David. *War Memoirs*. Boston: Little, Brown, 1934. A splendid source on the British effort in World War I as well as the British prime minister's views of and insights into the problems connected with the dominions' participation in that war effort.

Lower, Arthur. *Colony to Nation*. 4th ed. Don Mills, Ont.: Longmans Canada, 1964. This work is an excellent interpretive history of Canada, representing as it does an impartial attack on imperialist methods.

Wilson, Harold A. *The Imperial Policy of Sir Robert Borden*. Gainesville: University of Florida Press, 1966. A detailed account of Borden's imperial policy as prime minister, with an emphasis on the effect that policy had on the changing nature and structure of the British Empire.

SEE ALSO: William Lyon Mackenzie King; Sir Wilfrid Laurier; Bonar Law; David Lloyd George; Jeanne Sauvé; Pierre Trudeau.
RELATED ARTICLES in *Great Events from History: The Twentieth Century:*
1901-1940: October, 1909: Canada Cement Affair Prompts Legislative Reform; 1911-1920: Borden Leads Canada Through World War I; July 10, 1920-September, 1926: Meighen Era in Canada; 1921-1948: King Era in Canada; August, 1930-1935: Bennett Era in Canada.

BJÖRN BORG
Swedish tennis player

Borg became the first male tennis player to win five consecutive Wimbledon championships. He also captured a host of other honors, including six French Open championships.

BORN: June 5, 1956; Södertälje, Sweden
ALSO KNOWN AS: Björn Rune Borg (full name)
AREA OF ACHIEVEMENT: Sports

EARLY LIFE

Björn Borg (byawrn bohrg) was the only child of Rune and Margaretha Borg. He spent his childhood in a Stockholm suburb (Södertälje) noted for producing automobile parts and hockey stars. In fact, Borg's first love was ice hockey. At the age of nine, he was the starting center for Södertälje's junior team, with visions of one day playing for the Swedish national team. Borg's father, however, was one of the country's leading table-tennis players. In 1966, after winning the city championship, the elder Borg selected a tennis racket as his prize and gave it to his son.

Björn was elated at his father's choice. Even though he continued to play hockey, it was immediately obvious that tennis would become his sport. Unable to be enrolled in the beginners' program at the Södertälje Tennis Club because it was overcrowded, Borg spent the next six weeks batting tennis balls against the family garage door. Finally, a vacancy opened in the junior program, and Borg was able to practice in more formal surroundings.

In 1967, a nationally known tennis coach (Percy Rosburg) came to Södertälje to scout another player for Sweden's Davis Cup team. Rosburg was amazed by the ability of the young Borg, especially by his uncanny facility to return almost any ball hit to him. Borg was, therefore, asked to train with Rosburg at the Salk Tennis Club in Stockholm. The invitation meant a ninety-minute train ride each way, but Borg seized the opportunity.

From the beginning, Borg was an unorthodox player in that he used a two-handed grip at all times. This resulted from the fact that his first racket was simply too heavy. As his strength developed, he began to hit his forehand shots with one hand, but he retained, despite substantial criticism, a two-handed backhand. The consensus in the tennis world was that no male tournament player could succeed with a two-handed backhand. Borg was convinced he knew better. Indeed, despite his apparent handicap, he won his first tournament at the age of eleven and followed that the next year with a victory in his age division in the Swedish National School matches. At the age of thirteen, he was triumphant in both the thirteen-year-old and fourteen-year-old age divisions in the Swedish National Junior Championships.

While it was obvious the young Borg was a tournament contender, a substantial obstacle loomed in his path: school. It was not that Borg was a bad student, but the time required for effective tournament play had a deleterious effect on his academic standing. In fact, several of his teachers suggested that he should complete his education before undertaking a career in tennis. Borg's reaction was to suggest to his parents that the most sensible course was to leave school instead. Borg's decision was heartily supported by the Swedish Tennis Association. Faced with such pressure, the school system capitulated.

Borg promptly competed in the Madrid Grand Prix (March, 1972), where his victory over Jan Erik Lundquist allowed him, at the age of fifteen, to qualify for the

Swedish Davis Cup team. In addition, Borg captured the junior crowns at Berlin, Barcelona, Milan, Wimbledon, and Miami. He was, as a consequence, considered the junior world's champion.

Borg's debut in Davis Cup competition was quite spectacular. He won both his singles matches against New Zealand and became a national hero. Borg's participation in Davis Cup competition brought him into contact with Lennart Bergelin, the leader of the Swedish Davis Cup team. It was Bergelin, after Rosburg, who was most responsible for Borg's development as a tournament player. Bergelin insisted not only that his players should develop a considerable degree of mental toughness but also that intensive daily practice was essential. In Borg, he found an individual who was more than willing to subordinate everything to the game of tennis. In 1972, Borg turned professional. His career was under way, and his childhood, such as it was, came to an end.

LIFE'S WORK

Turning professional involves more than a simple act of will and a public announcement. Most important, the individual competitor must secure financial resources sufficient to meet considerable expenses. Fortunately for Borg, the Swedish Tennis Association was so desirous of keeping him available for Davis Cup competition that it arranged for him to be employed by Scandinavian Airlines as a public relations officer. Borg was thereupon obligated to play in all major Swedish tournaments and the Davis Cup for a salary of $400,000 a year, plus free air travel anywhere. With his immediate financial needs satisfied, Borg could concentrate on becoming the best tennis player in the world.

Borg's performance on the tennis circuit in his first years was somewhat erratic. Nevertheless, he acquired an increasing confidence in his game and refined his already impassive on-court demeanor. Indeed, reporters and fans alike were astonished at his ability to ignore distractions that elicited vitriolic displays from other players. He was often called "Ice Borg."

Borg was particularly fortunate in that his appearance at the 1973 Wimbledon tournament coincided with a boycott of the competition by the Association of Tennis Professionals. In consequence, the appearance of the young, blond, teenage Borg provided the tennis media, in the absence of other possible stories, with an opportunity to create an overnight sensation. Borg soon found himself surrounded by adoring, vocal, youthful fans whenever he ventured beyond the confines of the tennis pavilion.

Although Borg had yet to win a major tournament, he was successful in defeating several of the reigning luminaries of the game, such as Roscoe Tanner and Arthur Ashe. On June 3, 1974, Borg disposed of Ilie Nastase in the Italian Open, becoming the youngest player to win a major international tournament. Borg followed that impressive performance within two weeks in Paris, becoming the youngest player ever to win the French Open. Unfortunately for Borg, his efforts in the French and Italian tournaments exhausted his physical and mental resources, so much so that he was destroyed in the third round of the 1974 Wimbledon competition.

Borg quickly rallied, however, to win a tournament in Sweden as well as the U.S. Professional Tennis Championship. As a result, his commercial endorsements became so numerous that Borg found it necessary to employ an agent to supervise his burgeoning financial empire. Borg undertook so many endorsements, in fact, that he became the object of numerous humorous asides. In this, as in so many instances, Borg went his own way—even to the extent of moving his mother and father to Monaco when he determined it was necessary to avoid the exactions of the infamous Swedish tax collector.

Borg continued to play on the international circuit, winning the French Open again (1975) as well as the U.S. Professional Tennis Championship (1975). He helped Sweden beat Czechoslovakia for its first Davis Cup the same year. (By the end of his career Borg had won thirty-three consecutive Davis Cup matches, a record.) In addition to his tournament play, Borg undertook a series of exhibitions that afforded him publicity and substantial revenues. Nevertheless, despite considerable improvement in his game, he failed to advance to the Wimbledon final round.

The year 1976 opened auspiciously for Borg with a financially rewarding victory over Guillermo Villas in the World Championship of Tennis. Unfortunately, this triumph was followed by a devastating loss during the opening rounds of the French Open. This defeat proved a blessing in disguise, however, as Borg gained an unexpected respite before Wimbledon. He used the occasion to develop a powerful, accurate first serve, a deficiency that had proved his undoing in the past. Borg then proceeded to astonish the tennis world by defeating the heavily favored Nastase for the Wimbledon championship. Borg, at twenty, was the youngest Wimbledon champion in forty-five years and the first in twenty-three years to survive the tournament without the loss of a single set. Still, Borg followed his victory at Wimbledon with yet another loss in the U.S. Open. Despite Borg's

Björn Borg. (AP/Wide World Photos)

truly impressive effort, including one of the most spectacular tiebreakers in history, Jimmy Connors frustrated Borg's attempt to win the only major tournament to escape his grasp.

Indeed, such was to be the pattern for the remainder of Borg's career. He won the Wimbledon championship on an unprecedented five occasions in a row, a feat not equaled until 2007 (by Roger Federer). Because of his victory over Connors in 1977, the Association of Tennis Professionals ranked him first in the world in August. However, the most celebrated of his victories came at Wimbledon in 1980, when he defeated John McEnroe. The five-set duel, pitting the stolid Borg against the mercurial McEnroe, is considered among the best singles matches ever played. After a grueling fourth set, during which they exchanged leads in a thirty-four-point tiebreaker, McEnroe won. Borg responded by taking the next nineteen points, winning the nearly four-hour match. The next year, after a come-from-behind victory over Connors, Borg was defeated by McEnroe in four sets. He said later, "Of all the Wimbledon finals I played, that is

the one I should have won, yet it didn't bother me when I lost. So I decided it was time to go."

Borg won the French Open a record six times (four in succession)—in fact, the 1981 victory brought him his last major title—and a host of exhibition matches and invitational tournaments. Yet he never captured the U.S. Open—a prerequisite for the coveted Grand Slam of tennis. His last entry into a Grand Slam final, in fact, was in the U.S. Open in 1981, when McEnroe again prevailed in four sets. By then, however, he had won enough Grand Slam victories, eleven, to make him third on the all-time list of champions, and he had defeated more players in singles finals (nine) than any other player.

Borg's approach to tennis required not only an awesome mental commitment but also rigorous and lengthy daily practice to keep his mind and body in near-perfect union. As the 1981 season ended, he was physically exhausted and mentally drained. He entered only one tournament in 1982, losing in the quarterfinals. Not surprisingly, therefore, in 1983, after fifteen years of competition, Borg announced his retirement at the age of twenty-seven. The all-consuming demands of the game had taken their toll, and what was fun became a chore, a duty, and an obligation that had to be abandoned if he were to avoid collapse in the face of the mental and physical stress that his playing style demanded. His career finished with 576 match victories and 124 losses, an 82 percent game win rate, and a total of 62 singles titles. These successes earned him more than $3.6 million in prize money.

In the early 1990's Borg, playing with an old-style wooden racket, attempted a comeback. He retired two years later after losing all his matches. Borg did, however, join the over-thirty-five Nuveen Tour along with Jimmy Connors, John McEnroe, and other "grand old men" of tennis later in the 1990's.

In 1979 Borg won the Sports Personality of the Year Overseas Personality Award from the British Broadcasting Association, and in 2006 it gave him a Lifetime Achievement Award. He was inducted into the International Tennis Hall of Fame in 1987. In 1999 a Swedish jury voted him the best Swedish sportsman of all time. Various sports publications have named him among the greatest tennis players of the twentieth century.

Borg's life after professional tennis was sometimes troubled with controversy. His personal life was turbulent—two marriages and an affair with a teenager. In 1989 an accidental excessive dose of sleeping pills taken after he was left weak from food poisoning was announced in the media as a drug overdose. His clothing line ran into financial difficulties in 1990 and had to be liquidated; it was revived a year later. When in 2006 he announced that he was going to auction away his Wimbledon trophies and two of his rackets, he caused an uproar among fans and fellow professionals. Only an outraged call from McEnroe prompted him to change his mind.

Borg lives on the outskirts of Stockholm and has been married to Patricia Oestfeld, his third wife, since 2002. He has two children. In addition to overseeing his clothing and accessories brand marketed by the Björn Borg Group, he coaches Sweden's top junior tennis players.

SIGNIFICANCE

Borg was not, by conventional standards, a great tennis player. He was not tall enough, at five feet, eleven inches, to give himself a natural advantage while serving or executing overhead smashes. His famous two-handed backhand and his consummate mastery of the topspin forehand never found favor with other professionals. Still, he was a superb athlete whose absolute concentration, agility, and swiftness allowed him to tire his opponents. His most impressive victories were the result of exhaustive campaigns of attrition, in which Borg systematically blunted his opponent's offensive with a consistent counterattack that made a virtue of monotony.

Aside from his many accomplishments, Borg's impact on the game of tennis was quite profound. He dramatically affected recreational tennis in that his use of heavy topspin on ground strokes spawned millions of amateur imitators. Moreover, he was the first legitimate international tennis superstar. The attention lavished on the young phenomenon by fans and the sports media was largely responsible for catapulting the game into the big business it has become. Equally important, Borg's performance on the international circuit galvanized the Swedish Tennis Association's program of junior education, so much so that in 1985, Sweden had as many players among the top sixteen seeds at the U.S. Open as did the United States—despite the enormous disparity in terms of population. Borg never joined the select company of Don Budge or Rod Laver insofar as the Grand Slam of tennis was concerned, but his impact on the game was quite exceptional, if not unequaled.

—*J. K. Sweeney*

FURTHER READING

Amdur, Neil. "A Breakdown." *World Tennis*, April, 1984. Written after Borg's retirement, this article discusses the tennis star's life and mental-emotional state.

Borg, Björn. *The Björn Borg Story*. Translated by Joan Tate. Chicago: Henry Regnery, 1975. This slim volume (ninety-six pages) was supposedly written without benefit of a ghostwriter. It contains little in the way of personal biography beyond what appeared in the press but has much information concerning the matches played to that point.

Borg, Björn, as told to Eugene L. Scott. *My Life and Game*. New York: Simon & Schuster, 1980. Only half of this work involves Borg's autobiographical comments—none of which disputes the picture painted by the media, except his assertion that he did indeed have emotions. Of particular interest are assessments of Borg by various rivals, and his rebuttal.

Borg, Mariana. *Love Match: My Life with Björn*. London: Sidgwick & Jackson, 1981. This work provides candid photographs of Borg interspersed with anecdotes by his first wife designed to demonstrate the human side of her husband. The couple divorced shortly after Borg's retirement.

Fein, Paul. *Tennis Confidential: Today's Greatest Players, Matches, and Controversies*. Washington, D.C.: Brassey's, 2002. This collection of previously published essays, features, and interviews by Fein, a tennis journalist, includes a chapter on Borg and other information about his playing style, winning games, and reign at Wimbledon.

Phillips, B. J. "The Tennis Machine." *Time*, June 30, 1980. Provides a good overview of Borg's life and career, from childhood to his fifth Wimbledon championship.

Robson, Douglas. "The Fall." *Tennis*, September, 2006. Recounts Borg's enigmatic retirement from the game of tennis.

Wertheim, L. Jon. "Björn Borg." *Sports Illustrated*, July 11, 2005. Discusses Borg's tennis career, his disinterest in the trappings of success, and his life after retiring from the game of tennis.

SEE ALSO: Chris Evert; Billie Jean King; Rod Laver; Martina Navratilova; Fred Perry; Pete Sampras; Hazel Wightman.

JORGE LUIS BORGES
Argentine writer and critic

Author of an important body of short stories, poems, and essays, Borges embraced metaphor and the fantastic and rejected the realism that was predominant in Latin American literature of the time. His work has influenced modern fiction and criticism around the world.

BORN: August 24, 1899; Buenos Aires, Argentina
DIED: June 14, 1986; Geneva, Switzerland
ALSO KNOWN AS: B. Suárez Lynch (pseudonym);
　　H. Bustos Domecq (pseudonym); F. Bustos
　　(pseudonym)
AREA OF ACHIEVEMENT: Literature

EARLY LIFE

The son of Jorge Guillermo and Leonor Alcevedo de Borges, Jorge Luis Borges (HOHR-hay lew-EES BOHR-hays) was born in Buenos Aires. His ancestors had been involved in Argentina's history, having fought for the country's independence and later against various dictators; these ancestors would serve as subjects for some of Borges's poems. So, too, would his childhood home in Palermo (a working-class neighborhood on the north side of Buenos Aires), with its windmill to draw water, its garden, and its trees and birds. A frail child who did not enter school until he was nine, Borges spent much time in his father's extensive library, an activity that he later called "the chief event of my life." There he read many of the works that would inform his writing, by authors such as Mark Twain, Charles Dickens, Lewis Carroll, Miguel de Cervantes, Percy Bysshe Shelley, John Keats, and Algernon Charles Swinburne. He read their works in English because his paternal grandmother, Frances Haslam, had come from Great Britain and "Georgie," as he was called at home, learned her language before he knew Spanish. Even *Don Quixote de la Mancha* (1605) he first encountered in English. When he later read the original, he felt that he was reading a translation. From Haslam, he also heard stories about the Argentine frontier of the 1870's; one of these stories, about an Englishwoman abducted by Indians, provided the basis of "Historia del guerrero y la cautiva" (1949; "Story of the Warrior and the Captive," 1962).

Borges's literary vocation, along with his weak eyes, he inherited from his father, a lawyer and man of letters who had published some poetry and a novel. Borges claimed that his father taught him that language could be magical and musical, and from his youth Borges was destined to fulfill the literary dream that failing sight denied his father. Certainly he came to writing early: At age six, he produced a short summary of various Greek myths, anticipating his lifelong interest in minotaurs, labyrinths, and the fantastic. About three years later, *El País*, a Buenos Aires daily, published his Spanish translation of Oscar Wilde's "The Happy Prince"; the translation was so mature in style that the work was attributed to Borges's father.

In 1914, the family went to Europe so that the elder Borges could be treated for increasing blindness. Borges enrolled at the College of Geneva; unable to return to Argentina because of World War I, he spent the next several years in this Swiss city. There he learned French, Latin, and German, and he read voraciously. When travel was again possible, the Borgeses moved to Lugano and Majorca before settling temporarily in Spain. In Seville, Borges published his first poem (in *Grecia*, December 31, 1919), a Whitmanesque hymn to the sea, and joined a group of avant-garde writers who called themselves *ultraístas* (radicals). Their emphasis on metaphor and rejection of the psychological, realistic novel would influence Borges's views of literary composition.

LIFE'S WORK

On returning to Argentina, Borges organized a number of young poets under the banner of *ultraísmo* and published the short-lived *Prisma* (December, 1921, and May, 1922), dedicated to their vision of literature. He would edit two other magazines, both called *Proa*, in the 1920's, and he contributed to almost a dozen others. In addition, he published seven books during this decade, four volumes of poetry and three of essays. In many ways, these are apprentice pieces—Borges said that later he sought out copies and burned them—but they reveal a number of interests that underlie his mature work. Commenting on his first collection of poetry, *Fervor de Buenos Aires* (1923; translated in *Selected Poems, 1923-1967*, 1973), he stated, "I think I have never strayed beyond that book. I feel that all my subsequent writing has only developed themes taken up there. I feel that all during my lifetime I have been rewriting that one book." Much of the volume, like his others of this period, is devoted to Argentina. Although much of his later work is less regional in flavor, Borges remained a literary nationalist. In 1950, he published an essay on the literature of the Argentine frontier (*Aspectos de la literatura gauchesca*) and ten years later another on gaucho poetry, having coedited an anthology of such works in 1955 (*Poesía gauchesca*).

More characteristic of Borges's best-known writing are the discussions of time and space. In "El Truco," which describes a Latin American card game, Borges notes that, because the number of possible combinations of cards is finite, players must repeat hands that others held in the past. Not only are the hands the same, though; the players, too, according to Borges, become their predecessors. "Caminata" (stroll) claims that, if the viewer stops looking at the street, the scene vanishes. Borges is herein playing with George Berkeley's idealism and challenging the conventional notion of reality. If what seems real may be obliterated with a blink, that which is "False and dense/ like a garden traced on a mirror" can become real ("Benarés"). Already, too, one finds the learned allusions, the depth of reading so typical of Borges.

Although Borges is best known as a writer of short stories, he came to this genre slowly, hesitantly. According to Borges, he began writing short stories after an accident in 1938 left him uncertain of his mental abilities. Fearing that failure with a poem or essay would be too devastating, he turned instead to a new form and produced "Pierre Menard, autor del *Quijote*" (1942; "Pierre Menard, Author of the *Quixote*," 1962). Actually, he had been thinking about, even writing, prose fiction well before this. In *Discusión* (1932), he had included an essay that anticipated his practice, commenting in "El arte narrativo y la magia" (narrative art and magic) that the novel should resemble "a precise game of staying on the alert, of echoes, and of affinities." Rejecting supposedly realistic, psychological narratives, he praises the work of Edgar Allan Poe, Herman Melville, and William Morris, for whom plot rather than character is primary. In addition to theorizing, he began publishing a number of short stories, thinly disguised as essays; many of his later pieces, including "Pierre Menard, Author of the *Quixote*" wear a similar mask.

In August, 1933, he accepted the editorship of *Revista Multicolor de los Sábados*, a Saturday supplement published by *Crítica*, Argentina's most popular newspaper. Borges contributed about thirty original pieces and a number of translations. Among the former was "Hombre de las orillas" (September 16, 1933; "Streetcorner Man," 1970), a short story camouflaged as reporting and published under the pseudonym F. Bustos, indicating Borges's reluctance to be associated with the work. Here,

too, he presented a series of six fictionalized biographies of malefactors; these were later collected as *Historia universal de la infamia* (1935; *A Universal History of Infamy*, 1972). In 1936, "El acercamiento a Almontásism" ("The Approach to al Mu'tasism," 1970) appeared in a collection of essays, *Historia de la eternidad*; this short story was disguised as a book review. Frequently Borges subsequently assumed the role of a reader of extant works rather than the creator of new ones. While "Pierre Menard, Author of the *Quixote*" was thus not Borges's first short story, it did signal a willingness to admit to himself and others that he was turning his attention to another genre. His production of poems was already diminishing: Between 1929 and 1943 he published only six.

His life was changing in another way also. Until 1937, he had refused regular employment, living off the irregular income he earned by writing and allowances from his father. In that year, he took the post of first assistant at the Miguel Cané Library. Seemingly, such a job would have been ideal for the bookish Borges, but he despised his nonliterary colleagues (whose interests were gambling

Jorge Luis Borges. (© Washington Post; reprinted by permission of the D.C. Public Library)

"NOTHING BUT DETAILS"

Jorge Luis Borges's Ficciones, 1935-1944 *is detailed and exacting in focus yet "magical" in effect. He used details to make meaning, as in the following example of Magical Realism that is realized through his protagonist's imagination.*

To sleep is to be abstracted from the world; [local boy Ireneo] Funes, on his back in his cot, in the shadows, imagined every crevice and every molding of the various houses which surrounded him. (I repeat, the least important of his recollections was more minutely precise and more lively than our perception of a physical pleasure or a physical torment.) Toward the east, in a section which was not yet cut into blocks of homes, there were some new unknown houses. Funes imagined them black, compact, made of a single obscurity; he would turn his face in this direction in order to sleep. He would also imagine himself at the bottom of the river, being rocked and annihilated by the current.

Without effort, he had learned English, French, Portuguese, Latin. I suspect, nevertheless, that he was not very capable of thought. To think is to forget a difference, to generalize, to abstract. In the overly replete world of Funes there was nothing but details, almost contiguous details.

---

and women), the pay was poor, and fifty people had been hired to do the work of fifteen. "La biblioteca de Babel" (1942; "The Library of Babel," 1962) reflects the boredom, even horror, that Borges felt. Because there was little to do and he could not converse with his coworkers, he spent five or six hours daily reading and writing, producing a stream of translations and stories, among them the first Spanish version of Franz Kafka's *Die Verwandlung* (1915; *The Metamorphosis*, 1936) in 1938, an anthology of fantastic literature (edited with his close friend Adolfo Bioy Casares), and two volumes of fiction that shun the realism prevalent in Latin American literature of the period. Young authors such as Octavio Paz and Julio Cortázar were deeply influenced by this new approach that Borges was advocating in his essays and demonstrating in his books.

Borges's politics were as atypical as his writing style in the 1940's, for he supported democracy and the Allies when Argentina was ruled by a military regime friendly to the Nazis and fascists. When Juan Perón came to power in 1946, Borges was "promoted" from librarian to inspector of chickens and rabbits. In choosing this post for Borges, the dictator was demonstrating his dim view of intellectuals. Borges resigned immediately, but he needed to replace the salary on which, limited as it was, he had come to depend. Despite an almost pathological

fear of speaking in public, he began lecturing on British and American literature at various private schools in Argentina and Uruguay. At first he wrote out what he wanted to say, then sat silently while another read the lecture; but soon he overcame his phobia and delivered his learned talks himself. He also continued to write, publishing one of his best collections of short stories, *El Aleph* (1949, 1952; translated in *The Aleph, and Other Stories, 1933-1969*, 1970). If Perón had meant by his appointment that Borges was as timid as a chicken or a rabbit, he was mistaken, for, as president of the Argentine Society of Writers, he repeatedly spoke out against the regime.

With the fall of Perón, Borges's fortunes improved. In 1955, he was named director of the Argentine National Library, where he initiated a series of lectures and revived its defunct journal, *La Biblioteca*. The following year, he received the first of what would prove to be a number of honorary doctorates when the University of Cuyo (Argentina) presented him with the degree on April 29, 1956. In 1956, he also received the National Prize for Literature and was appointed professor of English and American literature at the University of Buenos Aires.

Borges's sight had been failing for a long time: He had had the first of eight eye operations in 1927. Immediately after he became head of the Argentine National Library, he lost his vision. In "Poema de los dones" (1960; "Poem About Gifts," 1964), he comments on the irony of gaining so many books just when he could no longer read them. While his blindness did not prevent him from writing, it did return him to poetry, and, because he found formal verse to be easier to compose mentally than free verse, he became especially fond of the sonnet. He also abandoned fiction for a time, writing no short stories between 1953 and 1970.

As early as 1928, Borges had won a literary award for *El idioma de los argentinos* (1928; the language of the Argentines), and by the 1940's many of his countryfolk recognized him as Argentina's leading writer. International appreciation came slowly, though. Not until 1961, when he shared the first Fomentor Prize with Samuel Beckett, did he become known widely in Europe and North America. *Ficciones, 1935-1944* (1944; English translation, 1962) appeared simultaneously in six languages, and he made the first of several visits to the United States as a visiting professor and guest lecturer.

Further honors came to him, among them the Jerusalem Prize (1971), the Gold Medal from the Académie Française (1979), the Miguel de Cervantes Award (Spain, 1980), and the Balzan Prize (Italy, 1980).

Borges, who had opposed military dictatorships throughout his life, in his last years came to support the junta ruling Argentina. When it collapsed after the Falklands war with Great Britain, Borges left his native land for Geneva, where he died of cancer on June 14, 1986. He was buried at Plainpalais, Switzerland, close to John Calvin.

SIGNIFICANCE

Borges's labyrinthine body of work traces the image of his mind—learned, profound, philosophical, questioning, and often laughing. As recondite as he could be, he nevertheless did much to shape contemporary literature. Indeed, Carlos Fuentes has said that without Borges, modern Latin American literature could not exist, for he made possible its flight from nineteenth century realism. In the United States, Robert Coover, Donald Barthelme, John Gardner, and John Barth are among his disciples, and Vladimir Nabokov's *Pale Fire* (1962) reveals a Borgesian influence. Borges's view that each author alters the reading not only of works that come after him but also of his predecessors' writings has affected Harold Bloom's literary criticism.

Borges was especially fond of the detective story and wrote a number of orthodox works in this genre. In a larger sense, everything he wrote seeks to resolve a mystery, the mystery of existence. Language and things are metaphors, vehicles for that unknown tenor, reality, that Borges continually sought. In his quest, he commented on the library of Babel that is the world, at the same time that he was creating an ordered, alternate universe of literature more enduring than its vexed double.

—Joseph Rosenblum

FURTHER READING

Bloom, Harold, ed. *Jorge Luis Borges*. Philadelphia: Chelsea House, 2004. An analysis of five of Borges's short stories, providing plot summaries, lists of characters, and extracts from critical essays. Includes an introductory essay by Bloom and a bibliography.

Borges, Jorge Luis. "Autobiographical Essay." In *The Aleph, and Other Stories*. New York: E. P. Dutton, 1970. A modest but essentially accurate chronological account, particularly useful for understanding the early influences on the writer and for his assessment of his various works.

Cheselka, Paul. *The Poetry and Poetics of Jorge Luis Borges*. New York: P. Lang, 1987. Concentrating on the poetry that Borges wrote before 1964, Cheselka undertakes a chronological survey of the verse, examining its themes and the way that Borges presents them.

Christ, Ronald J. *The Narrow Act: Borges' Art of Illusion*. New York: New York University Press, 1969. Among the first book-length studies of Borges in English and one of the best. Looks at Borges's use of British and American authors to understand how and why he chooses these sources.

Cortinez, Carlos, ed. *Borges, the Poet*. Fayetteville: University of Arkansas Press, 1986. Begins with three conversations with Borges—on Emily Dickinson, Hispanic literature, and North American writing—followed by twenty-four essays that explore such matters as Asian influences on Borges's poetry, his use of imagery, and the relationship between the poetry and various nineteenth and twentieth century works.

DiGiovanni, Norman Thomas. *The Lesson of the Master: On Borges and His Work*. New York: Continuum, 2003. DiGiovanni first met Borges in 1967 and worked with the author to translate his prose and poetry into English. He provides a memoir of his experiences, describing his friendship and collaboration with Borges and analyzing some of Borges's work.

Strathern, Paul. *Borges in Ninety Minutes*. Chicago: I. R. Dee, 2006. A brief but incisive introduction to Borges, providing information about his life and ideas.

Sturrock, John. *Paper Tigers: The Ideal Fiction of Jorge Luis Borges*. Oxford, England: Clarendon Press, 1977. Concentrates on the stories in *Ficciones, 1935-1944* and *Aleph, and Other Stories* because they are the most enigmatic and hence most fascinating of Borges's prose fiction. Sturrock maintains that these works are reflexive critiques of how stories should be told, and he sets the fiction in its cultural and philosophical context and offers close readings of themes, images, and techniques.

Updike, John. "Books: The Author as Librarian." *New Yorker*, October 30, 1965. A key article in the development of Borges's reputation in the United States and an incisive analysis of his work. Discusses Borges's economy of language, imagery, and use of the imagination. Updike suggests that Borges's approach to literature may provide an escape from the dead end that the novel seemed to have reached. The essay includes a careful analysis of "The Waiting" and "The Library of Babel." Available in book form in Updike's collection *Picked-Up Pieces* (New York: Alfred A. Knopf, 1976).

Williamson, Edwin. *Borges: A Life*. New York: Viking, 2004. Drawing on interviews and extensive research, this is the most comprehensive and well-reviewed Borges biography to date.

SEE ALSO: Samuel Beckett; Federico García Lorca; Gabriel García Márquez; Vladimir Nabokov; Pablo Neruda; Octavio Paz; Juan Perón.

RELATED ARTICLES in *Great Events from History: The Twentieth Century:*

  1941-1970: 1944: Borges's *Ficciones* Transcends Traditional Realism; 1955-1970: Latin American Fiction "Boom."

NORMAN BORLAUG
American plant pathologist

A humanitarian and scientist, Borlaug received the 1970 Nobel Peace Prize for his genetic modifications of wheat and other crops, which produced large yields in the world's developing countries. His biotechnological work adapting plants to resist diseases and survive in varied climates enabled the Green Revolution, providing practical ways to ease hunger and malnutrition by consistently growing substantial quantities of nutritious food quickly to feed expanding populations.

BORN: March 25, 1914; Saude, Iowa
ALSO KNOWN AS: Norman Ernest Borlaug (full name)
AREAS OF ACHIEVEMENT: Agriculture, genetics, horticulture, science

EARLY LIFE

Norman Borlaug (BOR-lawg) was born in Saude, Iowa, a town named for his ancestors' community in Norway. Both his parents, Henry O. Borlaug and Clara Vaala Borlaug, were descendants of Norwegian immigrants who had left Norway because of famine. Borlaug and his family lived near his paternal grandparents, who settled near the northeastern Iowa town Protivin, southeast of Cresco. Borlaug and his two younger sisters tended livestock, wheat, and corn on their family's farm. He helped his father build a barn and learned about the technological and scientific applications that can improve agriculture.

Borlaug attended a rural school for eight grades before enrolling in Cresco High School. Fascinated by plants and soils, he took agricultural science courses. After graduation in 1932, Borlaug moved to St. Paul, Minnesota, taking general classes at the University of Minnesota before focusing on forestry. Through his studies Borlaug came to realize the great impact of the Depression, seeing hungry people begging for food. While em-

ployed in forestry work, he encountered Civilian Conservation Corps workers suffering malnutrition. Borlaug completed a bachelor of science degree in forestry by 1937. On September 24, 1937, Borlaug married Margaret G. Gibson; they had two children.

When the U.S. Forest Service delayed hiring Borlaug as a full-time employee, he enrolled in classes at his alma mater. He heard a lecture by Plant Pathology Department chair Elvin Charles Stakman, an expert on stem rust. Stakman urged Borlaug to pursue advanced degrees in plant pathology. Borlaug benefited from the university's global reputation for wheat breeding research, gaining knowledge of agricultural endeavors worldwide. He worked as a research assistant and then as an instructor for the department. In 1941, Borlaug completed a master of science degree, and in 1942 he earned his Ph.D. under the guidance of Jonas Jergon Christensen. Borlaug's dissertation was published as a bulletin by the Minnesota Agricultural Experiment Station.

LIFE'S WORK

Borlaug accepted a position as a microbiologist with Du Pont in Wilmington, Delaware, to oversee research of herbicides and pesticides until 1944. That same year the Rockefeller Foundation and Mexican ministry of agriculture created a research project to assist Mexican farmers with scientific agriculture. Jacob George Harrar, the project's head agricultural scientist, requested that Borlaug join the group as a research scientist for the International Wheat Research and Production Program. Borlaug moved to Mexico and focused on transforming Mexican wheat from tall, fragile strains to dwarf, sturdy plant types. By 1960, he began serving as associate director for the Inter-American Food Crop Program, sponsored by the Rockefeller Foundation, breeding dwarf wheat hybrids.

Starting in 1964, Borlaug conducted research for the International Maize and Wheat Improvement Center (CIMMYT) based in El Batán, Mexico. The center was supported by its founders, the Ford and Rockefeller Foundations and the Mexican government. Borlaug directed the CIMMYT's wheat research and production program until 1979. Using genetic engineering, Borlaug and his colleagues created cereal crops that matured quickly and produced large yields, were not labor-intensive, and did not detrimentally affect the environment. They were interested in growing plants that provided nutrients, minerals, and vitamins crucial for health. Borlaug thought high-yield crops could have prevented the ravaging effects of the Dust Bowl of the 1930's, so he focused on breeding high-yield plants throughout his career.

During the 1960's, Borlaug represented the CIMMYT on a trip to Pakistan and India because the war between the two nations had intensified famine in that region. He tried to share his ideas but initially confronted a resistant bureaucracy and people who would not accept different agricultural methods. Borlaug stressed the benefits of planting dwarf wheat seeds to produce plants with sufficient nutrients and calories to combat malnutrition. Eventually governments aided his work, and Borlaug considered how to create dwarf versions of other crops, including protein-rich maize. His work in Asia led to the production of ample food to feed populations and often resulted in a surplus. Borlaug educated farmers in the Middle East and Eastern Europe regarding high-yield agriculture methods. He adapted plants to thrive in diverse climates and resist foreign pests and diseases.

On October 21, 1970, the Norwegian Nobel Institute named Borlaug as the recipient of the 1970 Nobel Peace Prize. He was selected because of his efforts to provide sufficient crops and food in developing countries threatened by famine and malnutrition, and for enabling the success of the Green Revolution. Borlaug traveled to Norway to accept his prize on December 10 at the University of Oslo. Borlaug, who said in his acceptance speech that his colleagues deserved winning the prize too, discussed how nineteenth century famines had killed millions of Europeans and noted how hunger and strife often coexist. Plentiful food, he said, encourages peace.

Governments and colleges sought Borlaug's expertise as a consultant and visiting lecturer. By 1984, he accepted a position at the Texas Agricultural & Mechanical University (Texas A&M) as an international agriculture professor in that school's Department of Soil and Crop Science. In 1986, he created the World Food Prize Foundation to reward and inspire innovative food-related

projects to stop hunger. The foundation also sponsored youth institutes to educate students regarding agriculture, and it provided internships at agricultural research centers worldwide for students seeking better farming conditions internationally.

During the 1980's, Borlaug became president of the Sasakawa Africa Association (SAA), which aided sub-Saharan African populations affected by famine and drought. Nippon Foundation chair Ryoichi Sasakawa asked Borlaug to show farmers in Africa the scientific agricultural methods suitable for their lands, and the SAA was formed. In 1986, the SAA joined with the Carter Center's Global 2000 Programme (the center founded by former U.S. president Jimmy Carter). As its first director, Borlaug was asked to establish demonstration plots, teach farmers practical techniques, and provide high-yield seeds and chemical fertilizers. Successful farmers reimbursed the project after harvests and taught other African agriculturists.

In 2000, Borlaug returned to Oslo to present a talk commemorating the thirtieth anniversary of his Nobel Prize. Discussing the Green Revolution, Borlaug spoke about his continuing work to mitigate hunger, but he warned that famines could occur as populations exceeded available food yields. Norman Borlaug University, a virtual institution, began offering agribusiness certificates to students in 2000. Classes featured agricultural topics, including food science and biotechnology. In 2007, the multinational agricultural corporation Monsanto gave $2.5 million to the university to establish the Borlaug-Monsanto Chair for Plant Breeding and International Crop Improvement at Texas A&M.

Interested in preserving agricultural history, Borlaug gave his papers to Iowa State University's archives of American agriculture, and he provided land from his childhood farm to the Norman Borlaug Heritage Foundation for educational purposes. Borlaug defended agricultural research and biotechnology for effectively feeding hungry people, writing articles denouncing critics who he asserted had unrealistic perceptions and expectations.

SIGNIFICANCE

Historians estimate that Borlaug's work alone saved the lives of approximately one billion starving people during the 1960's. He was the first agricultural scientist to receive the Nobel Peace Prize. Researchers and agriculturists appropriated Borlaug's methods to produce high-yield crops, which appealed culturally to consumers in specific countries. In addition to mitigating malnutrition,

Borlaug's work enabled countries to earn money for improvements by exporting agricultural surpluses. Indian wheat production grew from 17 million tons in 1968 to 73.5 million tons in 1999. Because Borlaug emphasized the constant need for sufficient food in impoverished countries, the U.S. Department of Agriculture's Foreign Agricultural Service oversees the Norman E. Borlaug International Agricultural Science and Technology Fellows Program, arranging exchanges of agriculturists and scientists to work in developing nations.

Humanitarian groups and governments worldwide honored Borlaug with awards, and universities presented him with honorary degrees. In 1977, Borlaug received the U.S. Presidential Medal of Freedom. He was awarded the National Medal of Science in 2005 and a Congressional Gold Medal, the highest civilian award issued by the U.S. government, in 2007. Peers and colleagues, too, have recognized Borlaug's accomplishments. In 1982, the Council for Agricultural Science and Technology presented Borlaug its initial Distinguished Achievement Award in Food and Agricultural Science. The National Academy of Science awarded Borlaug its Public Welfare Medal.

—Elizabeth D. Schafer

FURTHER READING

Bickel, Lennard. *Facing Starvation: Norman Borlaug and the Fight Against Hunger*. Pleasantville, N.Y.: Reader's Digest Press, 1974. Illustrated account written by an Australian science journalist, emphasizing Borlaug's humanitarian motivations and achievements.

Dil, Anwar S., ed. *Norman Borlaug on World Hunger*. Foreword by Edwin J. Wellhausen. San Diego, Calif.: Intercultural Forum/Bookservice International, 1997. Collection of Borlaug's essays, speeches, and other writings prepared by a renowned Pakistani linguist to honor anniversaries of CIMMYT and the World Food Prize. Includes a foreword by a former CIMMYT director general.

Easterbrook, Gregg. "Forgotten Benefactor of Humanity." *Atlantic Monthly*, January, 1997, 75-82. Provides an overview of Borlaug's career, describing the impact of the Dust Bowl and Depression on his agricultural views, commitment to high-yield agriculture, and responses to criticisms of biotechnology.

Hesser, Leon F. *The Man Who Fed the World: Nobel Prize Laureate Norman Borlaug and His Battle to End World Hunger*. Foreword by Jimmy Carter. Dallas, Tex.: Durban House, 2006. Laudatory biography penned by a U.S. government agriculturist and friend who worked worldwide with Borlaug, who authorized this account.

Paarlberg, Don. *Norman Borlaug: Hunger Fighter*. Washington, D.C.: Foreign Economic Service, U.S. Department of Agriculture, 1970. Chronicle of Borlaug's early high-yield wheat research and applications written by a Purdue University agricultural economics professor who held several federal agricultural positions, including overseeing Food for Peace famine relief efforts.

Pence, Gregory E. "Norman Borlaug: He Fed a Billion People, but You Don't Know His Name." In *Brave New Bioethics*. Lanham, Md.: Rowman & Littlefield, 2002. Discusses Borlaug's monumental but little-known work feeding the world's hungry. Recommended in conjunction with Pence's 2002 edited collection.

_____, ed. *The Ethics of Food: A Reader for the Twenty-First Century*. Lanham, Md.: Rowman & Littlefield, 2002. A collection of writings on the ethics of food, food production, agriculture, genetically modified foods, and other related topics, with the essay "Are We Going Mad?" by Norman Borlaug.

Perkins, John H. *Geopolitics and the Green Revolution: Wheat, Genes, and the Cold War*. New York: Oxford University Press, 1997. Describes Borlaug's professional relationship with Stakman and the University of Minnesota's international importance in wheat breeding research. Includes a chapter discussing the Rockefeller Foundation's work.

Webb, Patrick. *Food as Aid: Trends, Needs, and Challenges in the Twenty-first Century*. Rome: World Food Programme, 2003. A report on global food aid in the twenty-first century. Available at http://www.wfp.org.

SEE ALSO: Rachel Carson; George Washington Carver; Fritz Haber; Barbara McClintock; Thomas Hunt Morgan; Nikolai Ivanovich Vavilov.

RELATED ARTICLES in *Great Events from History: The Twentieth Century:*

1941-1970: September, 1944: Borlaug Begins Work on High-Yield Wheat; 1964: Green Revolution; December 10, 1970: Borlaug Receives the Nobel Prize for His Work on World Hunger.

1971-2000: 1972-1973: Worldwide Droughts Bring Famine; November 16, 1974: U.N. Declaration on Hunger and Malnutrition; September, 1976: Land Institute Is Founded to Develop Alternative Grains.

MAX BORN
German physicist

Born made fundamental contributions to the emerging theory of quantum mechanics. He also wrote extensively on relativity and atomic physics for popular readers. As professor of physics at Göttingen, he served as mentor to emerging physicists, including J. Robert Oppenheimer and Werner Heisenberg. He was honored with a Nobel Prize in Physics in 1954.

BORN: December 11, 1882; Breslau, Germany (now Wrocław, Poland)
DIED: January 5, 1970; Göttingen, West Germany (now in Germany)
AREAS OF ACHIEVEMENT: Physics, mathematics

EARLY LIFE

Max Born was the son of Gustav Born, a physician and embryologist, and Margarethe Kauffmann, daughter of a wealthy industrialist. Born's mother gave birth to a sister, Käthe, about eighteen months later but died during her third pregnancy, when Born was only four years old. The Borns were nonreligious Jews but nonetheless experienced anti-Semitism. Born's father remarried in 1892, providing him with a stepmother, but his father died in 1900, before Born's eighteenth birthday.

Born began his education at the Kaiser Wilhelm Gymnasium, a school that stressed Latin and Greek but did offer solid mathematics education. He was a satisfactory but not exceptional student. His family was relieved when he passed the exam that permitted his entry to a university. Initially, Born had difficulty deciding what and where to study. He first attended the University of Breslau as a student in the philosophy faculty, which included the sciences and mathematics. In 1902 he moved on to Heidelberg and returned to Breslau. In the summer of 1904, he entered the University of Göttingen.

Göttingen at the time was a center for mathematics study, featuring three world-class intellects: department chair Felix Klein, David Hilbert, and the young Hermann Minkowski, brought in by Hilbert and one of only two professors of Jewish background. Born at first sought to concentrate in pure mathematics but incurred the displeasure of Klein. Born then chose Carl Runge, an applied mathematician, to be his dissertation adviser. He completed a thesis on the mathematical theory of elasticity and passed his Ph.D. oral examination on July 11, 1906.

Before Born could begin a university teaching career, he had to habilitate, that is, present a research paper beyond his Ph.D. work and pass a further oral examination. Unwilling to present himself as a candidate in pure mathematics, he decided to qualify as a physicist, traveling first to Cambridge University in England and then back to the University of Breslau. Ultimately, he returned to Göttingen, where he was able to habilitate in 1909. Habilitation made Born a Privatdocent, one who could lecture to paying students but did not receive a salary from the university.

On August 2, 1913, Born and Hedwig Ehrenberg were married in the Berlin suburb of Granau. Hedwig's father had converted from Judaism to the Lutheran Church in order to marry her mother; he expected Born to do likewise. At first Born resisted, although he agreed to complete some religious instruction. Months after the ceremony, Born relented and allowed himself to be baptized, although he never attempted to distance himself from his Jewish origins.

A daughter, Irene, was born the following year, and was christened in the Lutheran Church. The Borns would have two other children, daughter Margarethe and a son, Gustav.

LIFE'S WORK

In 1912, Born and Hungarian physicist Theodore von Kármán, who had been a student at Göttingen, published an analysis of lattice vibrations in crystalline solids in an attempt to explain anomalies in the heat capacities of solids. A simpler treatment by Dutch physical chemist Peter Debye appeared in the same year, diverting attention from Born and Kármán's work. The dynamics of crystals would remain an interest for Born throughout his career.

In 1915, the young Born family moved to Berlin, where Born had been named an *extraordinarius*, or associate professor. Berlin was then the center of German physics, with both Max Planck and Albert Einstein in residence. However, World War I had begun in August of 1914, and the conflict rapidly devolved into prolonged trench warfare. Born had to face the possibility of doing war research as well as being called to military service. Fritz Haber, an eminent German physical chemist, was in charge of the physical chemistry institute in Berlin and an advocate of gas warfare. He sought Born's assistance in the development of protective masks, but Born resisted, believing the use of poison gas to be immoral. Instead, Born was attached as a sergeant to the army unit

Max Born. (AP/Wide World Photos)

charged with artillery research. This provided an environment in which he could devote some time to fundamental physical issues, including the nature of ionic crystals. Born and Haber would together develop the Born-Haber cycle, by which chemically important quantities could be calculated from physical data.

In 1919, Born was called to Frankfurt as *ordinarius*, or full professor. Postwar conditions in Frankfurt were rather dismal, however, and the Borns accepted an invitation to return to Göttingen in 1921.

As head of the physical institute at Göttingen, Born had the opportunity to hire some of the best physicists of his day as assistants. These included Wolfgang Pauli and Werner Heisenberg, both of whom would win Nobel Prizes. With Heisenberg, Born worked out the matrix formulation of quantum mechanics and, later, the famous uncertainty principle, which asserts that it is not possible to simultaneously determine the position and velocity of a subatomic particle. Born's strong command of mathematics supplemented Heisenberg's more intuitive insight.

It was Born and Heisenberg's uncertainty principle

that Einstein objected to in his famous statement that "God does not play dice." At scientific conferences and through numerous letters and publications, Einstein maintained that the quantum mechanics being developed by Born, Heisenberg, and others could not be an adequate description of nature. Einstein would propose experiments to circumvent the work of Born and Heisenberg. Danish physicist Niels Bohr would, in turn, point out the problems in Einstein's proposals. Austrian physicist Erwin Schrödinger complicated matters by introducing a wave formulation of quantum mechanics, which gave the same predictions as the matrix mechanics of Heisenberg. Born first suggested the generally accepted interpretation of Schrödinger's wave function as specifying the probability for finding the particle of interest at a given point in space.

Born made contributions to many areas of physics and served as doctoral mentor to a number of students who would gain eminence in their own right. In 1933, with the rise of the political power of the Nazis in Germany, Born and other professors of Jewish ancestry were suspended from their teaching positions and then dismissed. The Born family made its way to Cambridge University in England, where Born was named Stokes lecturer. In 1936 he assumed the Tait Chair in Natural Philosophy at the University of Edinburgh, becoming a British subject in 1939. Long after the war, in 1953, he retired to Göttingen, where he could enjoy the salary that was due him as a professor under the German restitution laws. In 1954 he shared the Nobel Prize in Physics with Walther Bothe of Germany.

SIGNIFICANCE

Born's contributions to physics began with the emergence of Einstein's relativity theory and continued through the development of quantum mechanics in its early twenty-first century form. Born's effectiveness as a collaborator and mentor may have overshadowed his own contributions. His work was not recognized with a Nobel Prize until 1954. His many contributions include his work on the dynamics of crystal lattices, relativity theory, and the uncertainty principle. He served as doctoral adviser to a number of eminent physicists, including J. Robert Oppenheimer, who became prominent in the American physics community and became director of the Manhattan Project. The Born-Oppenheimer approximation remains the starting point for most molecular quantum mechanical calculations. Perhaps ironically, Heisenberg, generally credited as the discoverer of the uncertainty principle and head of the German atomic bomb program, was Born's doctoral student as well.

Born wrote extensively, for both general and professional audiences. He is the author of a monograph on the dynamics of crystal lattices, updated with Chinese physicist Huang Kun, that is still considered a standard work in the field. Likewise, a monograph on optics, coauthored with Czech-born American physicist Emil Wolf, is a standard reference in that field. Born also wrote on relativity and atomic physics for general audiences.

—Donald R. Franceschetti

FURTHER READING

Born, Max. *My Life: Recollections of a Nobel Laureate*. New York: Charles Scribner's Sons, 1975. Born began this autobiography in 1940 and completed it near the end of his life. A richly detailed recounting of his early life. His treatment of his later years is somewhat abbreviated.

_____, ed. *The Born-Einstein Letters, 1916-1955: Friendship, Politics, and Physics in Uncertain Times.* New York: Macmillan, 2005. Born and Einstein maintained an extensive correspondence over a period of forty years on topics ranging from politics to the quantum theory, a portion of which is presented here and edited by Born.

Greenspan, Nancy Thorndike. *The End of the Certain World: The Life and Science of Max Born, the Nobel Physicist Who Ignited the Quantum Revolution.* New York: Basic Books, 2005. A full-length biography written by a friend of the Born family.

SEE ALSO: Niels Bohr; Walther Bothe; Sir James Chadwick; Arthur Holly Compton; Albert Einstein; Hans Geiger; Fritz Haber; Werner Heisenberg; Gustav Hertz; David Hilbert; J. Robert Oppenheimer; Wolfgang Pauli; Max Planck.

RELATED ARTICLES in *Great Events from History: The Twentieth Century:*

1901-1940: February-March, 1927: Heisenberg Articulates the Uncertainty Principle; Summer, 1928: Gamow Explains Radioactive Alpha Decay with Quantum Tunneling; November, 1934: Yukawa Proposes the Existence of Mesons.

LOUIS BOTHA
Prime minister of the Union of South Africa (1910-1919)

During the Boer War, Botha fought valiantly to preserve the independence of the Transvaal. When the war was lost, he worked successfully for a united South Africa under the British crown and became the first prime minister of the Union of South Africa.

BORN: September 27, 1862; near Greytown, Natal (now in South Africa)
DIED: August 27, 1919; Pretoria, Transvaal, Union of South Africa (now in South Africa)
AREAS OF ACHIEVEMENT: Government and politics, diplomacy, warfare and conquest

EARLY LIFE

Louis Botha (lew-EE BOH-tah) was born in the territory that was later to become the Union of South Africa, which consisted of four distinct entities: two British possessions, Cape Colony and Natal, and two independent Boer republics, the Orange Free State and the Transvaal. Botha was born in Natal but grew up in the Orange Free State and was associated during his public life with the Transvaal. Reared on an isolated farm in a typically large Boer family, he received little formal schooling but learned much about human nature, white and black. When only eighteen, he was entrusted with the sheep and cattle that the family pastured on the borders of Zululand. After his father's death, he joined a party of Boers who were taking part in a civil war among the Zulus and was rewarded with a farm in the district of Vryheid; he took part in the government of the small republic that was organized there, and, when Vryheid was merged with the Transvaal, he became active in this larger sphere. Farming remained his chief interest, however, and he rapidly expanded his holdings in land and livestock. In 1888, he married Annie Emmett, a relative of the Irish patriot Robert Emmett, and lived happily with her until his death.

In the meantime, tension between the Boer republics and the British Empire was growing. The discovery of gold on the Rand had brought a stream of immigrants, chiefly British, into the Transvaal; The Boers called them "Uitlanders," and, although they brought prosperity with them, the government of President Paul Kruger was careless of their rights, taxing them heavily and denying them the franchise. They in turn were supported by Sir Alfred Milner, the governor of Cape Colony, who pressed the Boers to recognize British suzerainty. Botha, now a member of the Volksraad, or legislature, favored concessions to the Uitlanders, as did Jan Christian Smuts, who later became Botha's loyal ally in peace and war. Both Kruger and Milner were stubborn, however, and Kruger precipitated a war on October 11, 1899.

LIFE'S WORK

The war began with a Boer invasion of Natal, intended to overwhelm the British troops there before reinforcements could arrive. Initially the invasion was a success; the British were cut off at Ladysmith, while the commandos—mounted infantry organized into regional units—swept around them and far into Natal, at one point capturing Winston Churchill, who was covering the war as a journalist. Botha at first served as a simple field cornet—a local commander—under Petrus Joubert, but his natural aggressiveness and the illness of his superiors made him practically second in command on the Natal front;

Louis Botha. (Library of Congress)

later he became commander, and finally, after the death of Joubert, commandant general of the Transvaal. As British reinforcements poured in, the Boers found it expedient to retreat to the Tugela River, where they could block any British advance into the Transvaal while still keeping the Ladysmith garrison under siege. Botha fortified the line with a series of nearly invisible trenches, hoping to lure the British into a trap. Sir Redvers Buller was repulsed at the Battle of Colenso but evaded the trap. On his second try, at Spion Kop, he was foiled only by a heroic counterattack organized by Botha himself. At Pieter's Hill (February 27, 1900), Buller finally broke through and relieved Ladysmith. On the same day, Boer resistance on their other front in the west collapsed. Botha, now in supreme command, could only fight delaying actions before Johannesburg and Pretoria were occupied and the Transvaal government fled eastward toward the Mozambique border.

Some thought the war had ended, but Botha simply shifted to a guerrilla campaign, in which the Boers won many small victories and even penetrated the Cape Colony. Lord Kitchener, now the British commander, responded ruthlessly, devastating Boer farms and herding women and children into concentration camps. By May, 1902, Botha and Smuts were ready to make peace and to dissuade those among the Boers who wished to fight to the death. The Boer republics became British colonies, but otherwise the terms were mild.

Following the peace, Botha and two other generals went to Europe to try to raise money for the relief of Boers impoverished by the war. They got little from private sources but did get an appropriation of eight million pounds from Parliament after Botha had argued the case in a magazine article. Back in Africa, Botha, having skillfully repaired his own shattered fortunes, returned to politics. His main objects were to effect a reconciliation between Boers and Britons (and also between the "bitter-enders" and the "hand-suppers," the patriots and the quislings among the Boers) and to obtain self-government within the Empire for the former republics, perhaps eventually as part of a unified South Africa. He began by founding Het Volk (the people), an association through which the Boers could assert themselves and recover their self-confidence. The Transvaal attained self-government in 1907, and Botha became its first prime minister. Among other problems with which he had to deal were the related problems of language and education. The peace treaty had guaranteed equality for English and Afrikaans, the Boers' Dutch dialect. Many English speakers expected Dutch to die out, while some

Boers expected the English to learn Dutch; Botha and Smuts simply wished children to be instructed in the language they already knew. Botha naturally was very interested in farming; he established a land bank, and he hoped to make the Boers' somewhat primitive farming methods more scientific, even if it meant keeping on English-speaking experts originally appointed by Milner. Already popular in England, he reaffirmed that popularity by presenting King Edward with a typical South African product, the largest diamond in the world, for the crown jewels.

Meanwhile sentiment had been growing for a union, or at least a federation, of the four South African colonies under the Crown, and in 1908 a national convention was called. Botha and Smuts had little difficulty in persuading the other delegates to support a close union rather than a loose federation and to accept English and Afrikaans as equally official languages. More difficult was the question of a capital. In the end, Botha's compromise was accepted: Pretoria was to be the seat of the executive, Cape Town the meeting place of the Parliament, and Bloemfontein the seat of the supreme court. The constitution was ratified by the British parliament, and Botha was invited to become the first prime minister; he held this post until his death.

The last period of Botha's life brought for him a whole series of triumphs in peace and war, but it was also a period of almost intolerable emotional strain, caused by the opposition of the bitter-enders, some of whom had been his comrades in the war. Somewhat reluctantly he had taken General Jan Hertzog into his cabinet, but Hertzog was so violently opposed to Botha's policy of reconciliation and so vocal in expressing his hatred of the British that he had to be maneuvered out again. The outbreak of war in 1914 produced an inevitable crisis. Botha thought that both duty and self-interest obliged South Africa to support Great Britain, but the bitter-enders wished to stay neutral or even to seize the opportunity to restore the republics. An armed rebellion erupted, which Botha put down easily and mercifully. Botha could then answer Great Britain's request that he occupy German Southwest Africa with South African troops. Like the Boers in 1899, the Germans were vastly outnumbered but had geography on their side. Botha himself led the invasion, moving swiftly and efficiently, and giving the Germans no time to organize a guerrilla campaign. He was also merciful, even letting the German reservists keep their rifles for defense against the natives. Later he sent South African troops under Smuts to fight in German East Africa. At the end of the war, Botha and Smuts participated in the Versailles Conference, where both enjoyed considerable prestige and influence; they were unsuccessful, however, in moderating the terms that were to be imposed on the Germans. Botha, moreover, was in ill health and died on August 27, 1919, soon after his return to South Africa.

SIGNIFICANCE

In contemplating Botha's career, one is struck by the number of fields in which he achieved success without any formal training and sometimes without a meaningful apprenticeship: farming, stock breeding, business speculation, war (regular and guerrilla, including fortification), statecraft, and diplomacy. Smuts spoke of Botha's intuition, which may be a fair term, for Botha often reached appropriate conclusions in a short time and without communicating the thought processes that led to them. Smuts also spoke of Botha's sympathy, his ability to place himself in the position of another, whether to win his friendship or defeat him in battle. The great theme that ran through his life was the theme of reconciliation: of Botha with Kitchener, of bitter-enders with hand-suppers, of Boer with Briton, of Germany with the allies. One would like to add "of black with white," but Botha, though he spoke several African languages and was fair enough in specific dealings, was never willing to share power with the native South Africans.

Basil Williams called Botha "a simple, God-fearing man, not clever, but with the immense wisdom of the patient and loving." Smuts called him "the greatest, sweetest, cleanest soul of all my days." These pronouncements may seem extravagant, but they find confirmation in the facts of his life.

—John C. Sherwood

FURTHER READING

Davenport, T. R. H., and Christopher Saunders. *South Africa: A Modern History.* 5th ed. New York: St. Martin's Press, 2000. A highly condensed and detailed history written from a liberal, African point of view. One can trace the events and policies of Botha's career back to their sources in the past and forward to their often disastrous consequences in the future. Includes a foreword by Desmond Tutu.

Engelenburg, Franz V. *General Louis Botha.* Introduction by J. C. Smuts. London: George G. Harrap, 1929. Originally written in Afrikaans by a journalist who knew Botha well, the book has much interesting detail. It is better on the politics than on the military aspects.

Garson, Noel G. *Louis Botha or John X. Merriman: The Choice of South Africa's First Prime Minister.* London: Athlone Press, 1969. A brief but thorough piece of research. Perhaps the choice of Botha was inevitable, for Merriman's support came chiefly from the bitter-enders.

Pakenham, Thomas. *The Boer War.* New York: Random House, 1979. Thoroughly researched, massively annotated and detailed, equally good on the political and military aspects. Pakenham goes beyond previous histories in his coverage of civilian sufferings and of the part played by blacks. Includes a bibliography and illustrations.

Scholtz, Leopold. *Why the Boers Lost the War.* New York: Palgrave Macmillan, 2005. Scholtz, a South African journalist and historian, analyzes the most important strategic decisions and military theories of both the Boers and the British to determine why Britain emerged victorious.

Warwick, Peter, ed. *The South African War.* London: Longman, 1980. A well-edited anthology of essays on all aspects of the war: "Women in the War," "The Poetry of War," and so forth. Especially relevant to Botha's career are "Military Aspects of the War" and "Reconstruction in the Transvaal." The book has extensive bibliographies and lavish illustrations.

Williams, Basil. *Botha, Smuts, and South Africa.* London: Hodder & Stoughton, 1946. Written by a distinguished British scholar, this book covers a large body of material in a compact and readable form. Includes maps and a brief bibliography.

SEE ALSO: H. H. Asquith; Sir Winston Churchill; John Maynard Keynes; Lord Kitchener; David Lloyd George; Albert Lutuli; Nelson Mandela; Alan Paton; Jan Christian Smuts; Desmond Tutu.

RELATED ARTICLES in *Great Events from History: The Twentieth Century:*

1901-1940: May 31, 1902: Treaty of Vereeniging Ends the Boer War; May 31, 1910: Formation of the Union of South Africa.

WALTHER BOTHE
German physicist

Bothe was awarded the Nobel Prize in Physics for his invention of the coincidence counting technique and for discoveries made using it, including the nature of cosmic rays and the fashion in which X rays interact with electrons. He was one of Germany's leading atomic scientists and constructed its first cyclotron.

BORN: January 8, 1891; Oranienburg, Germany
DIED: February 8, 1957; Heidelberg, West Germany (now in Germany)
ALSO KNOWN AS: Walther Wilhelm Georg Bothe (full name)
AREAS OF ACHIEVEMENT: Physics, invention and technology

EARLY LIFE

Walther Bothe (VAHL-tehr BOH-tah) was born to Fritz Bothe, a merchant, and Charlotte Bothe. Walther studied physics, chemistry, and mathematics at the University of Berlin. As a graduate student, he became one of the few ever to study under the famous Max Planck. After obtaining his doctorate in 1914, he began to work for Hans Geiger in the radioactivity laboratory of the Physika-lische-Technische Reichsanstalt (physical-technical institute).

World War I soon intervened, and Bothe became a machine gunner in the German army. Captured by the Russians in 1915, he spent the next five years as a prisoner of war in Siberia. While there, he was able to continue his studies in mathematics and physics as well as learn Russian. He married a Russian woman, Barbara Below, in 1920 and returned to the Reichsanstalt in Berlin. He and his wife had two daughters.

While performing research at the Reichsanstalt, Bothe began a simultaneous teaching career at the University of Berlin. It was an exciting, if somewhat confusing, time for anyone in the field of physics. The nature of radioactivity and the structure of the atom were two topics that defied understanding within the confines of the familiar (classical) rules of physics.

Among the most accurate measurements of the day were those of the spectroscopists, those who measured the various colors of light emitted by atoms. Niels Bohr had proposed a very curious model of the atom to explain these measurements. In Bohr's model, electrons orbited a nucleus of protons (neutrons were yet to be discovered). Strangely, the electrons could have only certain specific values (quanta) of energy or angular momentum. For unknown reasons, other values were not allowed. Bohr's conjectures were accepted only because they worked, not because they made sense in terms of known physics.

To extend the theory, Bohr and others calculated how an X ray and an electron would interact. It was supposed that since X rays are electromagnetic waves, the energy and the momentum of the wave would be spread out all along the wave. It was at this point that Bothe and his coworker, Geiger, entered the picture.

LIFE'S WORK

Bothe and Geiger decided to test Bohr's new theory. They wanted to compare it with a theory of Arthur Holly Compton. In the Compton effect, an X ray (treated as a particle) strikes an electron with the result that the electron recoils in one direction while the X ray scatters in a different direction and also has less energy.

According to Compton, the total energy of the electron and incident X ray (before the collision) should be the same as that of the recoil electron and scattered X ray (after the collision). This is called conservation of energy and momentum and is believed to be fundamental in nature. Yet according to Bohr, the energy and momentum of the X ray are spread all along the wave and are not localized at the site of the electron. Bohr predicted energy and momentum would be conserved only on the average and for a large number of collisions. A recoil electron might have absorbed some energy from many X-ray waves and would therefore not be related to any specific incident X ray.

In the experiment of Bothe and Geiger, X rays struck gas atoms inside a Geiger counter tube. The tube was connected to a pointer that moved when a recoil electron was detected. A second counter tube was placed beside the first, with the hope that it would detect the scattered X ray. If it did, its pointer also moved. Both pointers were continuously photographed on film moving through a camera at about ten meters per minute. Many hundreds of meters of film had to be developed, hung from the ceiling to dry, and then painstakingly inspected.

Bothe and Geiger were able to show that the tubes did indeed record coincident events, two events occurring at essentially the same time. The conclusion was that the recoil electron and the scattered X ray were produced simultaneously, and, hence, Bohr's latest theory was wrong. In fact, energy and momentum were conserved in individual collisions.

Walther Bothe. (© The Nobel Foundation)

In 1926, Bothe joined many other physicists in studying radioactivity. Heavy elements such as radium and uranium were known to emit alpha particles. These particles were allowed to strike targets of carbon, boron, or some other light element. Bothe was keenly interested in any radiation that the target might now emit, hoping that it would give him some insight into the structure of the atomic nucleus.

Some of these reactions emitted protons, and Bothe was among the first to use electronic counters to detect them. In 1930, Bothe and Hans Becker studied the radiation from a beryllium target. They found it to be surprisingly penetrating and assumed that it consisted of high-energy gamma rays. They missed another major discovery, for not long after James Chadwick showed that this radiation must consist of neutral particles, which he named neutrons.

At about the same time as his work with beryllium, Bothe worked with Werner Kolhörster in analyzing cosmic rays. Using Bothe's coincidence method, they placed one counter tube above a second counter tube and placed absorbing material between the tubes. If both tubes signaled a count at the same time, it was assumed that a single cosmic ray had gone through both tubes and had not been trapped in the absorber. Somewhat to their surprise, their results were not those expected from high-energy gamma rays. Instead, their experiments implied that cosmic rays are charged particles. Bothe pointed out that to penetrate the earth's atmosphere, these particles would need to have an energy equivalent to being accelerated through a thousand million volts. Since this was a thousand times more energy than any process known then could produce, it was a very radical suggestion. History, however, has shown it to be correct.

During the 1930's, Bothe continued his studies of multiple scattering of electrons and began similar studies with neutrons. An article by him on both the experimental and theoretical aspects of scattering appeared in the 1933 edition of the *Handbuch der Physick* (handbook of physics).

When the Nazis came to power, they urged that the scientific theories of Jews, such as Albert Einstein, no longer be taught. Bothe could not agree with the restriction, and in 1932 he moved his work to the politically more tolerant Heidelberg, eventually becoming a professor at the university and simultaneously the director of the Physics Institute of the Max Planck Institute for Medical Research.

Bothe's reputation for excellence was such that in 1939 he was called to be one of the chief scientists in the German atomic bomb project. One road to the bomb was to construct a nuclear reactor in which to make the element plutonium. Bothe was called on to decide the key issue of whether carbon could be used to slow neutrons in the nuclear reactor. According to Bothe's measurements, carbon would absorb too many neutrons and was unsuitable. This result was in error, and it is very curious that someone of Bothe's ability would have made this mistake. Bothe had no liking for Adolf Hitler, and it may be that he purposely reported the wrong results, for this became one of the key reasons for Hitler's failure to develop the bomb.

To better study nuclear reactions, Bothe needed a cyclotron, a machine that can accelerate particles, such as protons, and cause them to collide with target nuclei. Bothe supervised the construction of the first cyclotron in Germany, completing it in 1944. After the war, Bothe used the cyclotron he had constructed at Heidelberg to produce radioactive isotopes for medical studies. He continued his work with cosmic rays and was senior author of *Nuclear Physics and Cosmic Rays* (1948) as well as of many scientific articles.

Bothe devoted the same intensity to his hobbies that he gave to his scientific studies. He was an excellent pianist and took special pleasure in playing the works of Johann Sebastian Bach and Ludwig van Beethoven. On holidays he liked to go to the mountains and paint. His oil and watercolor paintings were quite professional looking. Bothe is described as being a strict taskmaster in the laboratory but hospitable and relaxed at home. He was awarded the Nobel Prize in Physics in 1954 and died on February 8, 1957.

SIGNIFICANCE

Bothe was a physicist's physicist. Other physicists consulted his works for definitive statements of a problem, its current status, and experimental techniques for studying it. As such, his influence among physicists was great, although he was little known to the public. Perhaps it was the growing awareness and acknowledgment of this influence that led to his somewhat belated award of the Nobel Prize. When it came, Bothe was in failing health and unable to attend the ceremony, but at least he had the satisfaction of living to see his work widely recognized.

The coincidence method pioneered by Bothe is now a common and widely used technique in nuclear physics. Electronic counters are used instead of film to record the results, and it was Bothe who pioneered the use of these electronic counting circuits. Among his other achievements, he was the first to show that high-energy cosmic rays are particles and the first to introduce a widely used notation for nuclear reactions. In addition to the Nobel Prize, Bothe was decorated a Knight of the Order of Merit for Science and Arts (1952), awarded the Max Planck Medal (1953), and awarded the Grand Cross of the Order for Federal Services of Germany (1954).

—Charles W. Rogers

FURTHER READING

Beyerchen, Alan D. *Scientists Under Hitler: Politics and the Physics Community in the Third Reich*. New Haven, Conn.: Yale University Press, 1977. This excellent work describes the political involvement (or noninvolvement) of many of Germany's top scientists. Nobel laureates become public figures and are often pressured into some kind of political action.

Dardo, Mauro. *Nobel Laureates and Twentieth-Century Physics*. New York: Cambridge University Press, 2004. Chronicles major developments in physics since 1901, the year the first Nobel Prize in Physics was awarded. Includes information about the work of Bothe and other prize winners.

Goudsmit, Samuel A. *Alsos*. New York: Henry Schuman, 1947. Reprint. Los Angeles: Tomash, 1983. Alsos was the code name for the intelligence mission to discover the status of the German atomic bomb project. Includes Goudsmit's interview and appraisal of Bothe at the war's end. Readers should be cautioned that Werner Heisenberg believed that Goudsmit undervalued the German achievements. Keeping this in mind, the book is quite useful.

Irving, David. *The German Atomic Bomb: A History of Nuclear Research in Nazi Germany*. Reprint. New York: Da Capo Press, 1983. A fascinating and easy-to-read account. Details Bothe's work on the project from start to finish. Gives an exciting account of how the Allies sabotaged German efforts to procure heavy water and explores other reasons for the lack of success of the German project. Highly recommended.

Nobel Foundation. *1942-1962*. Vol. 3 in *Physics*. New York: Elsevier, 1964. This work is among the very few that describe Bothe's Nobel work in an accessible manner for general readers.

Rhodes, Richard. *The Making of the Atomic Bomb*. New York: Simon & Schuster, 1986. One of the most comprehensive books on the subject that is readily accessible to general readers. Includes references to Bothe from his production of neutrons in 1930 to his completion of Germany's first cyclotron in 1944.

Weart, Spencer R. *Scientists in Power*. Cambridge, Mass.: Harvard University Press, 1979. Weart describes the French World War II atomic bomb project and follows its postwar development to the first plutonium production in 1949. He discusses Bothe's use of the French cyclotron as well as Bothe's error in measuring the absorption of neutrons by carbon.

SEE ALSO: Niels Bohr; Max Born; Sir James Chadwick; Arthur Holly Compton; Hans Geiger; Werner Heisenberg; Gustav Hertz; Adolf Hitler; Frédéric Joliot and Irène Joliot-Curie; Max Planck; Sir Joseph John Thomson.

RELATED ARTICLES in *Great Events from History: The Twentieth Century:*
1901-1940: 1920-1930: Millikan Investigates Cosmic Rays; February, 1932: Chadwick Discovers the Neutron.

HORATIO W. BOTTOMLEY
British journalist and businessman

Born into poverty, Bottomley acquired and squandered up to four fortunes. As editor of the popular newspaper John Bull, *he became the self-appointed tribune of the British "person in the street" before and during World War I. His exploits as a superpatriot made him a popular idol until his fraud conviction in 1922.*

BORN: March 23, 1860; Bethnal Green, London, England

DIED: May 26, 1933; London, England

ALSO KNOWN AS: Horatio William Bottomley (full name)

AREAS OF ACHIEVEMENT: Journalism, business and industry

EARLY LIFE

Horatio W. Bottomley was born to Elizabeth (née Holyoake) Bottomley, the daughter of engineer George Holyoake and sister of George Jacob Holyoake, secularist and founder of the modern British cooperative movement. Bottomley's father was William King Bottomley, a tailor who died after a fit of mania. By the time he was five years old, Horatio had lost both parents and was sent to an orphanage founded by Sir Josiah Mason at Erdington, near Birmingham. He ran away from the orphanage at age fourteen and spent his early years doing a series of odd jobs: office boy in a solicitor's office, worker in a jeweler's shop, and reader for George Jacob Holyoake's *The Secularist* and for Charles Bradlaugh's famous free-thinking magazine, *National Reformer*.

While working for the solicitor, Bottomley learned shorthand and was admitted to the exclusive Institute of Shorthand Writers. He then served for three years as a reporter in the Supreme Court of Judicature, where he added to the legal skills that some say made him Great Britain's finest lay lawyer. By 1883, he was a partner in the firm of Walpole and Bottomley, law reporters, and also wrote for the *National Reformer*. For many years, Bottomley believed that Bradlaugh was his real father. Facially he resembled Bradlaugh, with a large upper lip, massive head, and piercing eyes. He had a stocky figure with an obstinate John Bullish appearance.

In 1880, though a secularist, Bottomley married Eliza Norton at St. John's Church. Eliza was the daughter of a vinegar salesman from Battersea. Throughout his life, Bottomley professed religious belief only when it was advantageous. He had one daughter, Florence, who married an American millionaire, Jefferson Cohn.

LIFE'S WORK

In 1884, Bottomley founded the *Hackney Hansard,* which recorded the proceedings of local debating clubs and municipal bodies. He soon expanded his publishing interests to include a weekly journal, *The Debater, Youth* (a boy's paper whose subeditor was Alfred Harmsworth), *Baby* (a mother's magazine), the *Financial Times* (as a competitor to the *Financial News*), and *Draper's Record.*

In 1889, Bottomley, with the help of the financier Osborne O'Hagan, floated a company, the Hansard Union, with £500,000 capital. Its board of directors included Sir Henry Isaacs, the lord mayor of London, the publisher C. Kegan Paul, and Coleridge Kennard of the *Evening News.* On April 13, the Hansard Union bought

Horatio W. Bottomley. (Library of Congress)

five companies for £325,000 (one of which printed the parliamentary Hansards, while the other four were also in the publishing trade). In May, Bottomley's brother-in-law offered the Hansard Union two other companies for £105,000. To ensure continued dividends Bottomley persuaded the board to increase capital to a million by issuing debentures of £250,000 and later £50,000 to continue to pay dividends. By summer, however, only £1,120 was left in Hansard's bank account: Some £600,000 had "disappeared" and the company declared bankruptcy. Hansard Union shareholders charged Bottomley with conspiracy to defraud. Inspired by Bradlaugh's example, Bottomley successfully defended himself in a trial through the use of banter and facetious logic.

Though the trial judge, Justice Sir Henry Hawkins, urged him to become a barrister, Bottomley moved from Fleet Street to the City (London's financial district), encouraged no doubt by his easy manipulation of the legal system. Bottomley launched his financial career with the Joint Stock Trust and Institute and a number of Australian gold mining companies. He constantly merged, reconstructed, and amalgamated them to keep investors pacified. By 1897, the *Financial Times* featured him as one of its "Men of Millions," claiming that he had made three million pounds promoting companies. On the negative side, between 1901 and 1905, sixty-seven bankruptcy petitions and writs were filed against him.

Bottomley lived well and spent his money freely. He was an incorrigible womanizer, and he spent considerable sums on mistresses. He was addicted to Pommery champagne and drank it morning, noon, and night. Bottomley built a fine country home, the Dicker, at Hailsham in Sussex near Eastbourne, maintained a luxurious flat in Pall Mall, and kept a villa for his wife near Roquebrune on the French Riviera. In 1898, Bottomley started his own racing stable, on which he claimed he broke even. He won £80,000 when Wargrave won the Cesarewitch, and £70,000 with Northern Farmer's victory at the Steward's Cup. In 1914, he promoted the Ahearn-Carpentier boxing match, which was canceled because of World War I.

Bottomley was aided in his political and financial enterprises by a "stable" of bodyguards, friends, and a professional claque that included Tommy Cox, H. J. Houston, John Harrison (known as "the People's Perkins"), and Willie Lotinga. They were useful at law courts and political or company shareholders' meetings to quiet hecklers or cheer their champion. Bottomley's reputation was also furthered by his newspaper enterprises. In

1898, he bought the *Sun* newspaper from Harry Marks and used it to secure justice for two brothers wrongfully imprisoned for murder and also to start a fund for Ruby Bennett, orphan of a soon-to-be-executed murderer. The end of the Western Australian mining boom led Bottomley to sell the paper.

In 1906, two months after he had entered Parliament, Bottomley again felt the need to control a newspaper. The result was *John Bull*, a newspaper Bottomley launched ostensibly to expose the injustices of the day. Bottomley left the management of the paper to Julius Elias (later Lord Southwood), and by 1912, circulation had increased from fifteen thousand to 1.5 million. The paper's style was fearless, dogmatic, and lively; politicians, business and labor leaders, and judges were frequent targets. Well-known journalists such as Frank Harris, Herbert Vivian, A. G. Hales, Charles Palmer, and Charles Pilley served on the paper's staff, often ghost-writing articles signed by Bottomley.

One of the newspaper's features was the John Bull Exposure Bureau, which employed a team of retired police officers and reporters to investigate organizations or individuals targeted by readers. In 1910, the headmaster of the reformatory training shop, the Akbar, wrote concerning abuses to prisoners. The Liberal under secretary of state for the Home Department, C. F. G. Masterman, investigated and recommended that the two men involved in brutality be removed but gratuitously called *John Bull*'s charges random and reckless. Bottomley accused Masterman of a whitewash, setting off a vendetta that eventually ruined Masterman's political career.

Bottomley frequently used his journalistic enterprises to aid his financial fortunes. His paper, the *Joint Stock Circular*, advised readers to buy shares in companies he controlled, and some of his exposés culminated in extortion, as when an attack on the Waring and Gillow Company ceased after they agreed to carpet his offices. On another occasion, Bottomley paid a printer to libel him so that he could sue him and win to try to tar all of his critics as liars. Bottomley's bête noire was Edward Bell, an incorruptible solicitor with a fanatical dislike for fraudulent financiers; Bell succeeded in forcing Bottomley to refund £20,000 to James Platt, a retired woolen merchant, and repay John Murray £2,000 because of Bottomley's intentional misrepresentation of the facts. Bell also succeeded in reclaiming £100,000 invested in various bogus companies for the executrix of the estate of Robert Master, an elderly retired Indian civil servant, in spite of Bottomley's burglaries of Master's diaries and other pertinent documents.

Bottomley's downfall began when he chose the Prudential Assurance Company as a target and detailed how more than one hundred of its agents had committed suicide, implying that this resulted from guilt at having victimized poor policyholders or from despair at their low salaries as compared with the directors' fortunes. Prudential retaliated by accusing Bottomley of systematic fraud and blackmail. Eventually, he was found guilty of contempt of court and fined one hundred pounds. Justice Darling believed that this was a better punishment than sending him to prison, where he would be unable to repay his creditors, but the revelations ruined his political career.

Bottomley's political career had officially begun in 1906 after unsuccessful attempts to win a seat in Parliament from Hornsey in 1887, when he was only twenty-seven years old. In 1900, he ran as a Liberal from South Hackney and, though unsuccessful, won one thousand pounds in damages from his opponent, who called him a fraudulent company promoter. By 1906, Bottomley turned a negative 280-vote margin into a majority of 3,479.

In Parliament, Bottomley took an individualist stand. He opposed the government's Licensing Bill and Sunday Closing legislation. He advocated a five-shilling-a-week old-age pension paid for by an employer's tax of a penny on the pound on all wages, a supertax on share certificates, a tax on betting stakes, and state appropriation of all dormant bank accounts and securities. In some form, all eventually became law. His shady financial reputation, however, and the maverick radicalism of *John Bull*, which attacked all parties indiscriminately, ruined his political career.

In 1907, stockholders of the Joint Stock Trust petitioned for its liquidation and in 1909 charged him with fraud. Only by making pertinent ledgers and evidence disappear and through evasion, good-natured badinage, and half-truths did he manage once again to survive. By 1911, a cash-flow problem forced him to declare bankruptcy after he had placed most of his property in the hands of relatives, and he was forced to resign his seat in Parliament in 1912.

Undaunted, he turned to promoting lotteries and sweepstakes as a way to recoup his fortune. He usually cleverly rigged these sweepstakes, and one based in Lucerne, Switzerland, called the Patrick O'Brien Sweepstakes, netted him £150,000.

World War I presented Bottomley with new opportunities for both fame and fortune. *John Bull*'s radical headline "To Hell with Serbia" within a fortnight was replaced by articles attacking "The Potty Potentate of

Potsdam" and calling for the use of poison gas (before the Germans had used it) and a policy of taking no prisoners. Bottomley fueled the anti-German war hysteria, proposing that naturalized Germans should have to wear a distinctive badge. He traveled the length and breadth of the British Isles making patriotic recruiting speeches. Most were modeled on his Prince of Peace speech made at the September 14 rally at the London Opera House. Five thousand attended while another fifteen thousand waited outside. An even larger rally was held at Albert Hall on January 14, 1915, with members of the Irish Guards and men of the newly formed Sportsmen's and Footballers' Battalions. In Hull, a thousand men joined the colors after hearing him speak. He gave 340 lectures in three years and took between 65 percent and 85 percent of the gross. In 1915, the Northcliffe Press founded an illustrated paper called the *Sunday Pictorial* and paid Bottomley one hundred pounds for a series of weekly articles that continued until 1921. The series made him the most famous journalist in Great Britain.

In September, 1917, Bottomley visited General Sir William Robertson on the Somme and in December, the Grand Fleet at Scapa Flow. *John Bull* was particularly harsh on that section of the Labour Party that opposed the war, calling them traitors and demanding their court-martial. Bottomley also got a chance to even a score with Ramsay MacDonald, who had attacked him in 1911 as "a man of doubtful parentage who has lived all his life on the threshold of jail" by publishing a facsimile of MacDonald's birth certificate showing that the Labour leader was illegitimate.

Bottomley was unable to contain his greed and soon dressed up his prewar lotteries with patriotic hype, calling them successively the Victory Bond Club, the War Stock Combination, the Thrift Prize Bond Club, and the Victory Club Sweepstakes. By 1918, he had paid off his debtors and was returned to his South Hackney seat by eight thousand votes. When, through sloppy or deliberate mismanagement, his lottery schemes led to demands for repayment that he was unable to satisfy, Chancery Court appointed a receiver to examine them. Odhams Press, publisher of *John Bull*, decided to retire Bottomley and purchased his shares for £25,000. Meanwhile, Bottomley had incurred large racing debts, which were then covered by loans from an admirer, Reuben Bigland. When Bottomley reneged on a £1,000 loan and refused to back Bigland's support for a £60,000 scheme to turn water into gasoline, he won Bigland's enmity. Bigland proceeded to ruin him both politically and financially by airing some fifty-seven of his past frauds. Bottomley un-

wisely sued for libel because he was in the middle of organizing an Independent Parliamentary Group (including Charles Palmer, Christopher Lowther, and General Townshend) with the hope of someday becoming prime minister. The trial revealed Bottomley's sordid financial practices, and the jury ruled in Bigland's favor. Forty-eight hours later, in March, 1922, Bottomley was charged with fraudulently converting money belonging to shareholders of the Victory Bonds Club. He was convicted in May and sentenced to seven years in jail.

On his early release after five years in prison, Bottomley, ever the optimist, founded in 1928 a new weekly, *John Blunt*, but it failed. For a time he made a living through journalism and lecturing, but following the death of his wife in February, 1930, he suffered another bankruptcy; thereafter, until his death in 1933, he was supported mainly by his old-age pension and by his mistress Peggy Primrose. She had visited him at prison and after his death scattered his ashes on the Sussex Down.

SIGNIFICANCE

Horatio W. Bottomley's story is the story of a talent without a moral anchor. He always looked for the quick and easy scheme. Bottomley never learned the meaning of moderation. An incurable gambler, he was intoxicated with his own talents. Though greedy and hedonistic, he could show sympathy for those outside the orbit of his fraudulent financial schemes. Surrounding himself with an aura of success, he led those impressed by bluff and show to trust him in spite of evidence to the contrary.

Indeed, before his fall in 1921, he was one of the most popular figures in Great Britain. Few could equal his gift for capturing the mood of the bluff, beer-drinking, race-going British "man in the street."

—*Norbert C. Soldon*

FURTHER READING

Bigland, Reuben. *Horatio Bottomley*. London: Forwood, 1922. By the Birmingham printer, racetrack tout, and former friend whose vendetta against Bottomley sent him to jail.

Blathways, Raymond H. B. *The Man as He Is Today*. London: Odhams, 1916. Written during the period when Bottomley's star was ascending.

Bottomley, Horatio. *Bottomley's Book*. London: Odhams, 1909. Bottomley's defense of his practices.

Felsted, Theodore. *Horatio Bottomley: A Biography of an Outstanding Personality*. London: John Murray, 1936. Good biography, weak on war years.

Green, Jonathon. *Directory of Infamy*. London: Mills and

Boon, 1980. Another biographical account of Bottomley's life.

Houston, Henry. *The Real Horatio Bottomley.* London: Hurst and Blackett, 1923. By one of his closest advisers and main traveling companion.

Hyman, Alan. *The Rise and Fall of Horatio Bottomley: The Biography of a Swindler.* London: Cassell, 1972. Excellent biography. Good on Bottomley's activities during World War I.

Minney, R. J. *Viscount Southwood.* London: Odhams, 1954. A biography of Julius Elias, editor of *John Bull.*

Parris, Matthew. "He Was a Shameless Liar and Thief. He Went to Wormwood Scrubbs. He Was a Lovable Scallywag." *Spectator* 287, no. 9027 (August 11, 2001). Recounts Bottomley's life and crimes.

Symons, Julian. *Horatio Bottomley.* London: Cressett Press, 1955. Probably the best balanced biography of Bottomley.

Tenax [Edward Bell]. *The Gentle Art of Exploiting Gullibility.* London: David Weir, 1923. Written by the shareholder and Bottomley's bête noire.

SEE ALSO: Lord Beaverbrook; Alfred and Harold Harmsworth; William Randolph Hearst; Clare Boothe Luce; Henry R. Luce; Ramsay MacDonald.

RELATED ARTICLE in *Great Events from History: The Twentieth Century:*

1971-2000: December, 1976: Murdoch Extends His Media Empire to the United States.

NADIA BOULANGER
French composer and educator

Boulanger forged a musical career spanning more than eighty years, teaching generations of students the arts of performance, composition, and thinking. At a time when very few women were in prominent musical positions, Boulanger steadfastly pursued her goals. She is one of the most revered music teachers—female or male—of the twentieth century.

BORN: September 16, 1887; Paris, France
DIED: October 22, 1979; Paris, France
ALSO KNOWN AS: Nadia Juliette Boulanger (full name); Mademoiselle
AREAS OF ACHIEVEMENT: Music, education

EARLY LIFE

Nadia Boulanger (bew-lahn-jehr) was born in the Montmartre neighborhood of Paris. Her father, Ernest, was a conductor, composer, and professor at the Paris Conservatory, where he met her mother, Raïssa Myschetsky Shuvalov. Russian-born Shuvalov studied voice with Ernest and, although forty-three years younger, married him in 1919. Nadia was the second of four children born to the Boulangers. Two of the girls died in infancy, but Nadia and younger sister Marie Julliet, affectionately called Lili, survived.

Although initially indifferent to music, Boulanger began studying sight-reading, singing, and solfeggio at the conservatory as well as organ and composition. In 1897 she was awarded a first prize in solfeggio. Her father's death in 1900 strengthened her resolve to study music. By age sixteen, she had already accumulated significant honors: a second prize in harmony at the conservatory, an appointment as Gabriel Fauré's substitute organist, a first prize in harmony, and a first prize in organ, accompaniment, fugue, and composition.

Boulanger's association with highly regarded piano virtuoso Raoul Pugno led to the creation of her piano lesson studio in 1905. She also collaborated with Pugno in composition and in piano performance. Her first major disappointment, though, was her inability to win first prize at the Prix de Rome competition, a prize awarded only to men at the time. It was Boulanger's sister Lili, considered by critics to be a genius and more talented than her older sister, who became the first woman to win the first prize in 1913.

Boulanger toured with Pugno, traveling to Berlin and Moscow. While in Russia, Pugno fell ill on the tour and died in 1914. This unexpected and devastating event led Boulanger to temporarily cease her activities. In 1918, Lili also died, profoundly affecting Boulanger. Her grief never subsided as she dedicated the rest of her life to honoring Lili's memory.

LIFE'S WORK

In 1920, Boulanger was a professor at the École Normale de Musique in Paris. In her harmony, counterpoint, accompaniment, and music history classes, she methodically stimulated students' curiosity and then challenged them to satisfy that curiosity. Established the following year was an American conservatory, the École de Fontainebleau. Her new students there included a virtual Who's Who of twentieth century composers such as Aaron Copland, Virgil Thomson, Elliott Carter, Roy Harris, Walter Piston, and Roger Sessions.

Boulanger's long-anticipated first trip to the United States was arranged by friend Walter Damrosch, conductor of the New York Symphony Orchestra. In two months during 1925 she presented twenty-six concerts and several lectures that were enormously successful, leading to job offers. However, Boulanger declined the offers because of her mother's failing health from Parkinson's disease. Relying on a wheelchair, Raïssa was unable to care for herself. Boulanger, who was physically and emotionally exhausted by this time, provided for her mother until she died in 1935. The lingering deterioration was dreadfully reminiscent of Lili's illness years before. Boulanger was now the only surviving member of her immediate family.

Boulanger's reputation as a teacher continued to spread. She advised composer Astor Piazzolla to stop writing symphonic music and devote his time to the Argentine tango. She did not accept Maurice Ravel and George Gershwin as her students because she concluded they were already proficient composers. She categorized her students in three groups: talented with no money, wealthy with no talent, and wealthy with talent. She often remarked that she never had enough students from the third group.

Ever the benefactor, Boulanger would recruit aristocratic patrons to support the talented but impoverished students. She cultivated a friendship with one patron in particular, Princess de Polignac, who had ties to composer Igor Stravinsky. The friendship was timely because the 1929 stock market crash in the United States had reduced the enrollment at Fontainebleau and forced Boulanger to find new opportunities. The princess asked Boulanger in 1936 to be the first woman to conduct London's Royal Philharmonic Orchestra. This milestone was repeated a few years later when she was also the first woman conductor of the Boston Symphony and the Philadelphia Orchestra.

BOULANGER'S FAMOUS STUDENTS

Given that neither Nadia Boulanger nor her assistant, Annette Dieudonné, kept records of their students, it is impossible to form a complete list of musicians who studied with Boulanger. Nonetheless, the names below, which are some of the most famous in music, provide some sense of Boulanger's influence.

- Burt Bacharach (b. 1928), pianist, composer
- Daniel Barenboim (b. 1942), pianist, conductor
- Robert Russell Bennett (1894-1981), composer, arranger
- Lennox Berkeley (1903-1969), composer
- Leonard Bernstein (1918-1990), pianist, composer, conductor
- Idil Biret (b. 1941), concert pianist
- Marc Blitzstein (1905-1964), composer
- Elliott Carter (b. 1908), composer
- Paul Chihara (b. 1938), composer
- Aaron Copland (1900-1990), composer
- Clifford Curzon (1907-1982), pianist
- David Diamond (1915-2005), composer
- Jean Françaix (1912-1997), composer, pianist, orchestrator
- Sir John Eliot Gardiner (b. 1943), conductor
- Philip Glass (b. 1937), composer
- Roy Harris (1898-1979), composer
- Quincy Jones (b. 1933), music arranger, record producer
- Wojciech Kilar (b. 1932), film music composer
- Ralph Kirkpatrick (1911-1984), musicologist, harpsichordist
- Gail Kubik (1974-1984), composer, film scorist, violinist, teacher
- Robert D. Levin (b. 1942), pianist, composer
- Dinu Lipatti (1917-1950), pianist
- Gian Carlo Menotti (b. 1911), composer, librettist
- Astor Piazzolla (1921-1992), tango composer
- Walter Piston (1894-1976), composer, music theorist
- Ned Rorem (b. 1923), composer, diarist
- Harold Shapero (b. 1920), composer
- Robert Sherlaw Johnson (1932-2000), composer, pianist, teacher, liturgist
- Charles Strouse (b. 1928), composer
- Henryk Szeryng (1918-1988), violinist
- Virgil Thomson (1896-1989), composer
- David Ward-Steinman (b. 1936), composer, professor
- David Wilde (b. 1935), pianist, composer

Two more American tours in 1938 and 1939 included more than one hundred combined performances and lectures. In 1939, France had surrendered to Hitler's Nazi Germany, prompting Boulanger to move to the United States in 1940 and remain there until 1946. During this period she taught at such prestigious schools as Wellesley, Juilliard, and Radcliffe, while continuing to perform. Returning to France after World War II, she was appointed to the faculty of the École de Fontainebleau without even applying. Fontainebleau was closed during the war and reopened on a smaller scale, with Boulanger teaching private lessons and hosting a Wednesday class. During the lessons she incorporated references to ethics, art, and literature. The training and assignments were custom designed for individuals but were lengthy and demanding. New students were mixed with older students in the Wednesday sessions, and the work was equally difficult. Boulanger often ridiculed students in front of others, believing it would encourage them to improve next time. This method had worked for years but was losing favor with the new students.

In 1950, Boulanger was appointed director at Fontainebleau, a position she retained until her death. Her elevated status allowed her to continue discovering talented new students. By now she was acquainted with Leonard Bernstein, Pierre Boulez, and Stravinsky, among many others. While her teaching was legendary, her public piano and organ performances ended because of her arthritis, but she continued lecturing and conducting. In 1962, at the invitation of Bernstein, Boulanger conducted the New York Philharmonic in a sold-out concert.

The remaining years of Boulanger's life were spent teaching in England at American violinist and conductor Yehudi Menuhin's school in Surrey, at the Royal Academy of Music, and at the Royal College of Music, while also continuing at Fontainebleau. Poor health restricted her travels beginning in 1976, and she was forced to stay at Fontainebleau. Eventually she became too frail to teach, and her time was spent visiting with friends and colleagues. Students often comforted her by singing music by Wolfgang Amadeus Mozart or Robert Schumann. In 1932 she had received the Legion of Honor. In 1977, French president Valéry Giscard d'Estaing appointed her Grand Officer of the Legion of Honor.

SIGNIFICANCE

Boulanger was referred to as a master teacher by friends, colleagues, historians, critics, and students. For decades she taught students to assimilate ideas, facts, history, and the concepts of music and convert them into individual compositional processes and styles. She inspired admiration and devotion, but also fear, in her students. Besides teaching she also excelled in performance, composition, and conducting.

There were notable firsts in Boulanger's career: She was the first woman to conduct major symphonies, the first person to revive the music of Claudio Monteverdi and then record it, and the first teacher to educate more

than six hundred individual composers. Her teaching methods are as valid and influential today as they were at the beginning of the twentieth century. Boulanger's passion embraced all music, from antiquity to modern times, with the only requirement being quality.

—Douglas D. Skinner

FURTHER READING

Campbell, Don G. *Master Teacher Nadia Boulanger*. Washington, D.C.: Pastoral Press, 1984. The focus of this book is on articles written early in her career. Divided into four sections: reflections on the master teacher by students and colleagues, her life, notable quotations from Boulanger, and essays on musical styles and composers.

Hamm, Charles. *Music in the New World*. New York: W. W. Norton, 1983. This book of 700-plus pages is an in-depth music history, written in a narrative style and including numerous pictures, musical examples, and several references to Boulanger. *Recorded Anthology of American Music*, by New World Records, serves as a compatible musical example source.

Kendall, Alan. *The Tender Tyrant: A Life Devoted to Music*. Wilton, Conn.: Lyceum Books, 1977. The first half is biographical in nature, presented chronologically. The second half probes the foundations of her teaching, her musical philosophy, and what made her unique.

Monsaingeon, Bruno, trans. *Mademoiselle: Conversations with Nadia Boulanger*. Manchester, England: Carcanet Press, 1985. This work brings together research, analyses of a film on Boulanger, and radio interviews with her. The author organized the text into fabricated interviews with questions and answers. The concluding material contains a series of tributes from notable musical personalities such as Leonard Bernstein and Yehudi Menuhin.

Perlis, Vivian, and Libby Van Cleve. *Composers' Voices from Ives to Ellington*. New Haven, Conn.: Yale University Press, 2005. An oral history of composers who shaped American music. Also included are transcripts, commentary, and two compact discs of recorded interviews with musical examples (part 6, "From the Boulangerie").

Rosenstiel, Leonie. *Nadia Boulanger: A Life in Music*. New York: W. W. Norton, 1982. Boulanger provided personal papers, records, and numerous interviews to the author for this portrait of the renowned composer and educator. A comprehensive biography with more than four hundred pages.

SEE ALSO: Leonard Bernstein; Pierre Boulez; Maria Callas; Aaron Copland; George Gershwin; Maurice Ravel; Igor Stravinsky; Shinichi Suzuki.
RELATED ARTICLES in *Great Events from History: The Twentieth Century:*
1901-1940: 1921: Boulanger Takes Copland as a Student; October 18, 1923: Stravinsky Completes His Wind Octet.
1971-2000: July 25, 1976: *Einstein on the Beach* Introduces Minimalist Music to Mainstream Audiences.

PIERRE BOULEZ
French composer and conductor

Boulez's compositions, essays, and lectures changed the direction of Western music. Though he emerged from the French tradition of Claude Debussy, Maurice Ravel, and Olivier Messiaen, he rejected his roots and redirected his spiritual allegiance to the Austro-German tradition as embodied by Arnold Schoenberg, Alban Berg, and Anton von Webern. He also became one of the most influential conductors of modern music in both Europe and the United States.

BORN: March 26, 1925; Montbrison, France
AREA OF ACHIEVEMENT: Music

EARLY LIFE

Pierre Boulez (bew-lehz) was born in Montbrison, in the Loire section of the southeastern part of France. He came from a respectable middle-class, Roman Catholic family. His father was an engineer and technical director of a local steel company, while his mother, who tended to be freethinking, was a homemaker. He was introduced to orchestral music on a radio that his father had brought back from the United States. An elder brother of the same name, Pierre, had died in infancy, and the death of that brother confirmed Boulez's Darwinian and therefore deterministic view of existence. As he himself has stated, "I believe I survived because I was the stronger. He was the sketch, I the drawing." These two modern strains, Darwinism and electronic technology, provide the backdrop for Boulez's spiritual evolution.

Because Montbrison had no *lycée*, the young Pierre attended the best school in the area, the Roman Catholic Seminary Institut Victor de la Prade. Extremely devout, he remained there until he was fifteen, taking first honors in chemistry and physics. He also sang in the choir and took piano lessons privately in the larger nearby town of Saint-Étienne. By the time he was sixteen, he was unalterably dedicated to music, a fact that disturbed his father greatly, because it was assumed that young Pierre was to pursue an engineering career, as he had. He deferred to his father's wishes and studied mathematics at the University of Lyon with the hope of entering the École Polytechnic in Paris, but he spent most of the year practicing the piano and studying musical theory. In direct conflict with his father's wishes, he entered in 1943 not the École Polytechnic in Paris but rather the famous Paris Conservatoire, where he excelled in all of his courses, taking the premier prize in harmony. He received excellent instruction from Olivier Messiaen, the deeply religious visionary composer and organist. Messiaen was a maverick professor and performer and introduced his students to the exotic sources of his own music: Gregorian chants, Asiatic rhythms and techniques, and the actual songs of hundreds of birds. It was during Messiaen's class that Boulez discovered the genius of Claude Debussy, Igor Stravinsky's *The Rite of Spring*, and the early works of Arnold Schoenberg. He also took private lessons from Andrée Vaurabourg, the wife of Arthur Honegger.

In 1945 Boulez heard a performance of Schoenberg's Woodwind Quintet under René Leibowitz's direction, and the performance became a revelation to him of a whole new set of musical possibilities. He asked Leibowitz to teach him the rules of this new musical aesthetic. Boulez found in twelve-tone music a completely new musical language, a language that freed him from the past clichés and exhausted formulas of a long dead but unburied Romanticism. He adopted Leibowitz as his new mentor and began an allegiance to the Austro-German tradition, a much more stringently intellectual and analytical approach to music. The composers who grew out of this tradition were the classic moderns of twentieth century music: Schoenberg, Alban Berg, and, most important, Anton von Webern.

By 1948, after working as the musical director of the new Compagnie Renaud-Barrault under his only conducting teacher, the distinguished composer-conductor Roger Désormière, Boulez produced two pieces of music that gradually drew the interest of the French musical establishment: his Second Piano Sonata and his cantata, *Le Soleil des eaux*. It was, however, the stunning performance by Yvonne Loriod (Messiaen's wife) of the Second Piano Sonata at the Darmstadt Festival in 1952 that propelled the young Boulez into the international musical spotlight.

LIFE'S WORK

Boulez's career began in 1948 with his Second Sonata; therefore, many critics saw him as the composer of a French expression of the Austro-German school of compositional style, a style called serialism. In keeping with his pattern of rejecting the fatherly influences in his life, Boulez did not ground his first works in a French tradition that started with Jean-Philippe Rameau and flowered with Debussy and Messiaen but rather used them to pay homage to his native country's avowed enemies, Germany and Austria. He even attributed the German presence in France during the occupation as the occasion that brought high culture to his homeland.

In the serial or twelve-tone system of composition introduced by Schoenberg, Boulez found the possibility of breaking away from what he viewed as the exhausted forms of a late and decadent Romanticism as found, for example, in composers such as Johannes Brahms or Peter Ilich Tchaikovsky. He wished to move away from the concept of tonality (that is, music written in a certain key or tonal center that remains the same throughout the piece) to atonality, in which there is no tonal center dictating the rules of composition. Schoenberg had invented a system that not only eradicated the musical habits of the past but also enlarged the parameters of musical expression by extending the range of musical possibilities from the standard seven tones to all twelve tones of the chromatic scale. For Boulez, these radical new forms meant that he had found a musical grammar that successfully replaced tonality by expanding the limits of musical expression but remained rooted in a mathematical system that kept it from collapsing into mere emotional declamation. The new musical aesthetic could save music from the pathos of old Vienna and its counterpart, the cult of personal stylistic evolution.

After receiving this revelation, Boulez rigidly adhered to any and all ramifications of it. He promoted the composers who had engendered his own stylistic developments: Schoenberg, Berg, and Webern. These composers were responsible for purifying the language that moved music into new possibilities. To remain consistent, Boulez also promoted those earlier composers who influenced these three classic moderns, such as Richard Wagner, Gustav Mahler, and Ludwig van Beethoven. Boulez himself summed up the significance of serial or twelve-tone music: "With it, music moved out of the world of Newton and into the world of Einstein. The tonal idea was based on a universe defined by gravity and attraction. The serial idea is based on a universe that finds itself in perpetual expansion."

Out of Boulez's newfound dogma came what has come to be regarded as his masterpiece. Indeed, some scholars find *Le Marteau sans maître* (1954, revised 1957) worthy of comparison to Stravinsky's *The Rite of Spring* or Schoenberg's *Pierrot Lunaire*, two benchmarks of the modernist movement of the twentieth century. As he did with his earlier *Le Soleil des eaux*, Boulez used sections of René Char's brilliant but complex poems. He attempted to follow the accents and meters of Char's poetry with the rhythms and dynamics of his own music. The piece is scored for seven instruments: alto voice, viola, guitar, vibraphone, xylophone, flute, and percussion. There are nine movements, but only four contain parts of Char's poems. Over the years, numerous imitations of the exotic instrumentation have been at-

Pierre Boulez. (Library of Congress)

tempted by many composers. The music embodies the tonal equivalent of the message of Char's apocalyptic poem, that civilization is mechanistically moving toward its own doom. It has no master to guide it, and Boulez used his music to call the attention of the world to its condition.

Because of the quickly spreading fame of Boulez as a composer, he came into considerable demand as a teacher and conductor all over Europe but particularly in Germany and Paris. With the support of Suzanne Tezenas, the wealthy widow of the French fascist author Pierre Drieu la Rochelle, and of the Compagnie Renaud-Barrault, he founded the Domaine Musical series of concerts at which he lectured on and presented the works of contemporary composers and the neglected works of the past he considered to be especially relevant to modern sensibilities. The concerts became an important part of the musical life of Paris from 1954 until 1967. He also began to accept academic positions in universities in both Europe and the United States. He lectured at the University of Darmstadt for twelve years, was professor of composition at the University of Basel from 1960 to 1963, and served as a visiting lecturer at Harvard University in 1963. He delivered his now famous lectures at Darmstadt, which were subsequently published as *Penser de musique aujourd'hui* (1964; *Boulez on Music Today*, 1971).

Boulez produced fewer compositions in the 1960's and 1970's, probably because of the time spent working as a conductor and lecturer. His compositional style changed dramatically because of the influence of the American composer John Cage. Boulez had met Cage years before in Paris, had become fast friends, and then, consistent with his rejection of father figures, had had a falling out. Yet Cage's experiments with aleatory (chance) music and open form became major influences on Boulez's work. With Boulez's *Deux Improvisations sur Mallarmé* (1953), *Strophes* (1957), and Third Piano Sonata (1958), he moved into an exploration of the possibilities of open form, which meant that the work is, theoretically, never finished. All works become works in progress and, therefore, are open; they are treated as if they possess an organic life of their own and are permitted to join themselves with larger entities as later works emerge. All during the late 1950's and 1960's, Boulez followed this aleatory model, believing that the composition of a particular piece was primarily a process. Both *Deux Improvisations sur Mallarmé* and *Strophes* eventually became part of his next great work, *Pli selon pli* (1962). In his Third Piano Sonata, which remains unfin-

ished, the pianist has the choice of arranging the order of the piece's five movements and also may choose among movements to play or may omit certain sections. The performer is given alternative paths or options.

In his later work, Boulez focused on spatial explorations. In *Domaines for Clarinet Alone or with Twenty-one Other Instruments* (1968), he experimented with the physical distribution of the players themselves by having the clarinetist actually move within the various instrumental groups. In . . . *explosante-fixe* . . . (1971), a thirty-minute work for three flutes, chamber orchestra, and live electronic music, the musicians involved have a wide range of forms on which to decide as well as the task of determining how many and specifically what instruments will be used. He returned to his longest-standing work in progress, *Livre pour quatuor* (1958), and arranged it for full string orchestra, changing the title, appropriately, to *Livre pour cordes* (1968).

Boulez moved in the same direction in which many modern poets and novelists, such as James Joyce, Marcel Proust, and his beloved Stéphane Mallarmé, had moved. Just as they viewed the subject of poetry as the making of poetry, Boulez saw the subject of music as the making of music. In Boulez's view, authentic contemporary aesthetics always produces some version of a portrait of the artist. Modern art is always about itself, and the only operation that saves it from becoming an empty act of solipsism is the act itself. The imaginative energy of the creative artist is, therefore, the sole creator of meaning in a deterministic and violent universe.

Boulez's later career, although he has never stopped composing music, has been spent in becoming one of the most influential and controversial conductors both in Europe and in the United States. In 1963 he returned to Paris after a long and bitter hiatus to conduct triumphantly the first French performance of Berg's *Wozzeck* at the Paris Opéra, an accomplishment that garnered for him numerous invitations for conducting engagements. His performance of his own piece, *Pli selon pli*, at the Edinburgh Festival became an international musical event. It was his invitation to conduct Wagner's *Parsifal* at Germany's most sacred musical shrine, Bayreuth, that catapulted him into the front rank of major conductors. His brilliant performances, characterized by lucidity and coherence, captured the attention of the conductor of the Cleveland Orchestra, George Szell, who subsequently engaged him for a number of performances with his orchestra during the late 1960's. Boulez's recordings with the Cleveland Orchestra, particularly his stunning interpretation of Stravinsky's *The Rite of Spring*, won for him worldwide recognition as one of Western music's most accomplished conductors. His association with Szell also brought him into proximity with the New York Philharmonic Orchestra, since Szell had been a musical adviser and frequent conductor of the Philharmonic for many years.

The climax of Boulez's conducting career came in 1970-1971, when he became the musical director of both the British Broadcasting Company Symphony in London and America's most renowned orchestra, the New York Philharmonic. His tenure at the Philharmonic was marked by controversy and innovation, because he considered the primary mission of a major orchestra to be the education of the public. Unfortunately, the board of directors lost its nerve after ticket sales plummeted as a result of Boulez's intellectually stimulating but unpopular programming. Boulez also inaugurated a series of informal "Rug Concerts," which were similar to his highly successful Domaine Musical concerts in Paris during the late 1950's. These concerts were widely attended by young people who wished to hear and understand the latest in contemporary music. He was determined to teach the younger generation the language of twentieth century music by connecting it to its sources and inspirations in both the eighteenth and nineteenth centuries.

In 1974, Boulez relinquished his position at the Philharmonic and moved back to Paris, where he became the director of France's most sophisticated musical research facility, the Institut de Recherche et de Coordination Acoustique/Musique, or IRCAM. Music critic Peter Heyworth, of the London *Observer*, calls IRCAM a "milestone in the history of Western music as crucial as the advent of the airplane has been in the field of transport." Only someone like Boulez, with his international reputation as a great composer, conductor, and writer, could have marshaled the financial support for such an enormous enterprise. At the institute, Boulez resumed his experiments with music produced through electronic media. In the 1950's he had tried using tape recordings for sound manipulation but found them too constraining and awkward. IRCAM acquired the most advanced computer and recording technologies, and with these he could coordinate recorded and live music in accordance with his wishes. Among the fruits of these experiments was *Répons* (1984), for chamber orchestra and six instrumental groups, whose sounds could be electronically processed by a computer in real time.

Boulez held the professorship in "invention, technique et langage en musique" at the Collège de France from 1976 to 1995. During the late 1970's and 1980's re-

visions of older works occupied much of his creative energy. These included new versions of *Notations, Pli selon pli*, and *Le Visage nuptial*. In 1995 he was named principal guest conductor for the Chicago Symphony Orchestra and went on a world tour to celebrate his seventieth birthday. In 2007 he finished an immense project, recording the entire cycle of eight symphonies by Gustav Mahler for Deutsche Grammophon, and that same year he conducted his last opera, Leoš Janáček's *From the House of the Dead* (1930). In addition to being a composer and conductor, Boulez was a provocative, insightful writer, turning out articles and books that both championed modern music and analyzed contemporary productions, often incisively. He once dismissed as useless some of the music of Arnold Schoenberg and criticized Stravinsky as an epigone of various historical styles.

Boulez received many of the most prestigious awards available to modern conductors and composers. In 1985 he won the Sonning Award, Denmark's highest musical honor. In 1996 he was awarded Sweden's Polar Prize—the "Nobel Prize of Music"—by King Gustav of Sweden. Israel's Wolf Foundation presented him with the Wolf Prize in 2000, a prize that honors achievement in the interest of humankind and friendly relations among peoples. *Répons* won a Grammy Award in 2000, and *Sur Incises* (1996/1998), a work for three pianos, three harps, and three mallet percussion instruments, garnered the Grawemeyer Award in 2001 from the University of Louisville in Kentucky. In 2002 he received the Glenn Gould Prize from Canada in recognition of his contribution to music. He also holds an honorary doctorate from the University of Frankfurt (1996).

Iconoclastic, outspoken, and polemical, Boulez was famous for his biting pronouncements. He once remarked that "the most elegant solution for the problem of opera is to blow up the opera houses." This bit of bluntness, well known among art musicians, caused him surprising trouble in 2001. Three months after the terrorist attacks on New York's World Trade Center towers, while sleeping in a Basel hotel after conducting at a festival, Boulez was arrested in an antiterrorist raid by the Swiss police. The authorities took his remark about the opera houses seriously, even though it had been made four decades in the past. His passport was confiscated for three hours before he was released.

SIGNIFICANCE

Boulez is regarded as one of the twentieth century's most brilliant and controversial musical figures. Considered an "angry young man" in art music of the 1950's and 1960's, he set out to divert Western music from what he saw as decadence and decline. In the process he became one of the most influential composers of the modern era; *Le Marteau sans maître* probably has as many imitators as Schoenberg's *Pierrot Lunaire*, and Boulez's Second Piano Sonata has become a staple in the repertoire of pianists who are seriously devoted to contemporary music.

No major composer of the twentieth century is so consistently literary both in his texts and in his role as possibly the most compelling writer on music in the second half of the century. By choosing the complicated texts of René Char, Henri Michaux, and Stéphane Mallarmé, Boulez demonstrates not only his authenticity as a genuine modernist but also that, in music as well as poetry, form is never more than an extension or revelation of content. He characterized his own style as "organized delirium," which would certainly apply to the poets whose texts he favored and places him firmly in the tradition of French dramatist Antonin Artaud. His project as a composer has been, however, to externalize his interior conflict and embody it in forms appropriate to its expression. When that expression and attention change, it is incumbent on him to generate new forms. Yet those forms must come out of only musical materials, a lesson he learned well from the composer he most admired and imitated, Anton von Webern. Few composers, conductors, and writers in the second half of the twentieth century were as influential as Boulez. Moreover, Boulez was widely hailed for the precision and creativity of his conducting. He raised the standard for both performances and recordings of modernist classics.

—Patrick Meanor

FURTHER READING

Boulez, Pierre. *Notes of an Apprenticeship.* Translated by Herbert Weinstock. New York: Alfred A. Knopf, 1968. A collection of eighteen essays on music in the twentieth century. Boulez lays out quite clearly the major musical developments and schools of the modern era. The profundity of his insights combined with the security of his rhetoric seems, at times, to constitute a final statement on whatever he may be discussing. Unrelentingly provocative and bursting with insights.

Gilly, Cécile. *Boulet on Conducting: Conversations with Cécile Gilly.* Translated by Richard Stokes. London: Faber & Faber, 2003. Boulez expresses his views on the art of conducting, the work of other composer-conductors, such as Hector Berlioz and Richard Wag-

ner, and how the role of the conductor has changed during his career.

Machlis, Joseph. *Introduction to Contemporary Music.* New York: Norton, 1961. Machlis, the author of the clearest and most intelligent introductory text on music, *The Enjoyment of Music*, makes even the complexities of modern music understandable. His lengthy chapter on Boulez and a highly readable analysis of *Le Marteau sans maître* serve as an excellent introduction to the difficulties of Boulez's musical ideas and procedures.

Peyser, Joan. *Boulez.* New York: Schirmer, 1976. The definitive work on Boulez as a composer, conductor, and human being. Peyser writes with great honesty and insight on the personal coldness of Boulez and his inability or unwillingness to participate in even the most common forms of social intercourse. Highly readable and a required book for a full understanding of this composer.

_____. *Twentieth Century Music: The Sense Behind the Sound.* New York: Schirmer, 1970. The most accessible book on the complexities of modern music. Peyser's short chapter on Boulez places him squarely within the Austro-German tradition of Schoenberg and Webern, but the author also shows how Boulez's roots were originally those of Debussy and Messiaen. Highly informative.

Thomson, Virgil. *A Virgil Thomson Reader.* New York: Houghton Mifflin, 1981. There are many references to Boulez throughout this witty and brilliantly written collection of essays and reviews that cover a fifty-year span in music. Thomson's review of both of Boulez's books constitutes the single most intelligent short piece written in English on the composer. Thomson's honest admiration for Boulez vivify his comments and honor his subject.

Whittall, Arnold. "Boulez at Eighty: The Path from the New Music." *Tempo* 59 (July, 2005): 3-15. Whittall analyzes Boulez's compositions in the 1950's and 1960's to differentiate the modernism and classicism in his work. He also comments on Boulez' personality.

SEE ALSO: Alban Berg; Claude Debussy; Gustav Mahler; Olivier Messiaen; Arnold Schoenberg; Igor Stravinsky; Anton von Webern.

RELATED ARTICLES in *Great Events from History: The Twentieth Century:*